VOLUME 4

MUTUAL & FEDERAL SOUTH AFRICAN CRICKET ANNUAL 2001

Edited by COLIN BRYDEN
Statistics by Andrew Samson
Scorecards formatted by Ros Brodie

Published with the cooperation of the United Cricket Board of South Africa

Publishers: Mutual & Federal Insurance Company Ltd, PO Box 1120, Johannesburg
2000

Name of publication:	Mutual & Federal South African Cricket Annual 2001
Publishers:	Mutual & Federal, 75 President Street, Johannesburg www.mf.co.za
Editor:	Colin Bryden
Production Editor:	Alison Ward, MWP Media
Typeface:	Times New Roman
Repro:	Colin Bryden Communications, MWP Media, Creda Communications
Printing:	Creda Communications

Contents

Section A: Editorial

EDITOR'S NOTES

Another year of stirring deeds on the field; another year of controversy off it. It seems to be a pattern in South African cricket. For as long as the national team keeps winning, the game will remain healthy and with the World Cup to be staged in South Africa next summer the immediate outlook is bright. Administrators, though, cannot afford to overlook the problem areas surrounding the game.

The focus of this publication should be largely on the triumphs of the players, notably the exceptional achievement in the West Indies, where South Africa became only the second touring team in 19 years to win a Test series and the first in history to win both a Test and one-day series in the Caribbean.

Even in triumph, though, there was a cloud, in this case of marijuana smoke. The foolish actions of six members of the touring party were in the privacy of a hotel room but illegal nonetheless. Disciplinary action was instituted, with the players being fined R10 000 each, but the impractical decision was then taken to keep the incident secret. Inevitably, it leaked out and the controversy was greater than would have been the case if it had been handled more professionally.

The cricket year started with the shadow of the Hansie Cronje scandal hanging over the game. At the time of writing, the book was not yet closed, with Cronje due to mount a challenge in the Supreme Court to the life ban imposed on him by the United Cricket Board of South Africa.

Judge Edwin King, meanwhile, completed his inquiry into match-fixing and related issues. What started with the promise of being a no-holds-barred investigation petered out, with many questions remaining unanswered. After several postponements, the King Commission never did resume after the sensational first hearings in June 2000. The Judge cited, as one of the main reasons for halting proceedings, the challenge by Cronje's legal team to the constitutionality of his position as commissioner.

Another factor was the refusal of the Indian authorities to cooperate with South African investigators led by public prosecutor Shamila Batohi. The Indian police, who appeared to offer no substantial assistance to the South Africans, meanwhile blamed South Africa for their own stalled investigation because they were unable to obtain authenticated voice samples of Cronje.

Judge King's final report, which followed two interim reports, contained no sensational insights or findings, although there was a jolt for Cronje and his lawyers when the judge said he could not form an opinion on whether the former captain had told the whole truth and therefore could not recommend to the Director of Public Prosecutions whether or not an offer of provisional amnesty should be confirmed. It was thus not certain whether any criminal charges might be laid against him.

Despite the high-profile, expensive setting up of an anti-corruption unit, headed by Sir Paul Condon, the supposed war on corruption declared by the International Cricket Council was stifled by the inertia of most Test-playing countries. Sir Paul's report to the ICC annual meeting in May was no more than an intelligent overview of the situation.

EDITOR'S NOTES

After the initial flurry of sensational allegations and investigations which followed the Cronje confessions, no notable progress was made. What was depressingly clear was that a stumbling block to proper investigation was the labyrinth of official control of cricket in countries with greatly differing cultures, not only of lifestyle but of attitudes towards corruption.

In essence, it is probably fair to assume there is less corruption in cricket than there was when Cronje was taking payments from the likes of MK Gupta. There is greater awareness and stricter policing. Most countries, however, no matter how committed they are to the game being clean, would prefer to draw a discreet veil over the past.

Players named by Gupta, an international who's who, had their names cleared by sympathetic home boards and Gupta himself refused to give sworn testimony to Condon. Sanjeev Chawla, the man whose cellphone conversations with Cronje were the undoing of the South African captain, was briefly taken into custody in London, where he runs a clothing import business, but was released because there was "insufficient evidence to provide a realistic prospect of conviction".

There were other issues of concern in the administration of the game. The umpires association was temporarily disbanded, amid allegations that transformation was not being pursued with sufficient eagerness, and a split between the organisation of professional umpiring and the amateur game seemed imminent.

Percy Sonn, after a single full term, was challenged as president of the UCB by Dr Mtutuzeli Nyoka, the recently-elected chairman of the Gauteng board, who made some trenchant personal criticisms of the incumbent. Dr Nyoka also made some outspoken comments on the implementation of an empowerment policy for the awarding of contracts for the 2003 World Cup.

On the positive side of the administration front, the transition from Ali Bacher to Gerald Majola as chief executive of the board was made smoothly, with Dr Bacher taking his considerable administrative skills a short journey across northern Johannesburg to the offices of the World Cup 2003 organising committee, where he took command as executive director.

Majola, who is the subject of a profile in one of the feature articles in these pages, wasted little time in showing he was well-equipped for the job, putting his own stamp on affairs. His speech at the end of a transformation conference in the Pilanesberg at the end of June rightly earned him a standing ovation after an outstanding analysis of the state of the game and an inspiring vision of the future, in which the standard of play on the field was of prime consideration.

One of Majola's many challenges will be to keep some of the elected officials on an even keel.

THE NATIONAL TEAM

Under the captaincy of Shaun Pollock, the national team had an outstanding year, winning six successive series, beating New Zealand and Sri Lanka in both versions of the game at home before doing the same in the West Indies.

For a man thrust into the leadership role in the most unexpected circumstances, Pollock did a magnificent job, justifiably being named as one of the finalists by his contemporaries in a player of the year poll of current international cricketers. The input and sheer hard work of Graham Ford and Corrie van Zyl, coach and assistant coach, was crucial.

The merit of the series win in the West Indies was best appreciated by those fortunate enough to be on the tour. The demands were considerable but Pollock led his men cheerfully and they were able to remain positive and focused on their task, slipping up only in the fifth Test, when the series was won and immediately after the would-be secret action against the dagga smokers. This was followed by defeat in the first one-day international but the side then bounced back in the most resilient fashion to win the next five matches by convincing margins.

There were numerous excellent performances during the season, with Pollock himself showing that the captaincy had if anything inspired him to even greater deeds, especially with the bat.

Virtually all the regular players made important contributions and there was an especially exciting debut by Mfuneko Ngam, who showed the potential to become a match-winning fast bowler provided he is able to overcome injuries.

Both Neil McKenzie and Boeta Dippenaar made maiden Test centuries to emphasise that there is increasing depth in the Test squad. One positive outcome of the Cronje scandal has been that there has been an opportunity for the likes of McKenzie to become established at Test level, filling a batting position in which Cronje was not always convincing.

The coming season will provide Pollock and his players to what is now the supreme challenge in cricket, that of taking on Australia in their own backyard before returning to South Africa for a second series of three Test matches.

WORLD TEST CHAMPIONSHIP

For the first time in history, an official world championship will be at stake when South Africa play against Australia in the coming season.

It is not a perfect system but it is a positive step in providing Test cricket with a context. An obvious disadvantage is that the championship itself is not often likely to be on the line and supporters of teams in the lower reaches of the perpetual log table are unlikely to be greatly thrilled by the prospect of their side contesting seventh or eighth place.

For South Africa, though, it would be a huge boost to be presented with the championship trophy. An advantage for South Africa is that Australia won both the most recent series between the two countries, so that the current champions will be defending points and cannot improve, while South Africa can only go upwards.

ATTENDANCES AND REVENUE

Crowd figures for Test matches during the season were disappointing and John Blair, the treasurer, singled out the Wanderers in his report at the annual meeting. Only 17 000 attended the rain-affected Test at the country's biggest ground, although in fairness the play was effectively reduced to two days. Coming after the previous season, however, when the returns for the Wanderers Test against England were considerably below the figures for Kingsmead and Newlands, it seemed to indicate that an effort was needed to boost attendances at Test matches in Johannesburg. That said, crowds of 22 000 in Durban and 21 000 at Centurion for the matches against Sri Lanka were hardly inspiring.

Provinces seemed to be having increasing difficulty in balancing their books and the UCB had to advance loans to affiliates, which Blair attributed to poor financial management in some cases.

2003 WORLD CUP

Not surprisingly, there have been one or two rumbles about aspects of the organisation of the World Cup. It is such a big event that there is an eagerness to be involved in the decision making and to share in the glory and the profits. The mere fact that a separate organisation was set up to run the tournament was always likely to cause some uncertainties about areas of control.

The overall impression, however, is that Dr Ali Bacher will supervise an excellent World Cup. Characteristically he has been tireless in trying to take care of every detail. The fixtures will be announced soon after the publication of this Annual and a ticketing policy will be made public.

The involvement of a World Cup policy committee under the chairmanship of Professor Jakes Gerwel was a necessary move in order to engage opinion makers and leaders from a cross section of society.

The World Cup is expected to provide a financial bonanza for cricket in South Africa but it is to be hoped that provinces will not have run up such debts before the tournament that the cash flow will merely cancel out liabilities. It will be another generation before the next World Cup comes around.

CRICKET IN AFRICA

The UCB could be justly proud of the fruits of the efforts of the likes of Hoosain Ayob in developing cricket in Africa. Namibia's surprise qualification for the 2003 World Cup meant that four African teams would be competing at the tournament, as many as there are from Asia and more than from any other region of the world. Uganda also did well at the ICC Trophy tournament in Toronto.

TRANSFORMATION AND THE QUOTA SYSTEM

Transformation remains a key item on the South African cricket agenda and Professor Andre Odendaal, chairman of the transformation monitoring committee, was able to report good progress towards the objective of people of colour filling 50 percent of senior administrative and management roles.

Fifty players of colour played provincial cricket last season, which is almost 25 percent of the total, of whom no fewer than 37 were classified as regulars, who played in five or more matches. A statistical report on these players showed that a significant number performed at a consistently high level. Provinces will be expected to field a minimum of three players of colour in the coming season.

One of the complaints about the quota system is that black players are demeaned by being labelled "quota players" but Odendaal's report makes it clear there are a large group of players who are worthy choices on merit.

The most obvious comment is that a quota is no longer a quota when it is exceeded. At this stage, the only provinces which regularly go beyond the minimum are Boland, Eastern Province and Western Province, with the latter at one stage having five players of colour in their first-choice eleven.

The flow of players through a previously almost exclusively white schools system will surely be seen at first-class level within a few years. Cricket will then truly be a sport deserving of the unstinting support of all South Africans.

HIGH PERFORMANCE . . . Nicky Boje established himself as South Africa's number one slow bowler in Tests and one-day games *Picture: Tertius Pickard, TOUCHLINE PHOTO*

FIVE CRICKETERS OF THE YEAR

NICKY BOJE

Perhaps the most fortuitous moment of recent South African cricket was Paul Adams' despairing dive at Centurion Park when, in trying to stop an England boundary during the one-innings Test in January 2000, he suffered a fractured finger.

Adams' misfortune opened the door for Nicky Boje, who stepped boldly through to become without question the country's number one spin bowler and providing the bonus of excellent batting and fielding.

Boje was not selected for the tour of India soon after that Centurion Test, with Clive Eksteen chosen as the back-up to Adams. When Adams' injury did not recover in time, Boje received his call-up. He has not looked back.

He made his long-awaited Test debut during the tense victory in Mumbai but bowled only five overs in a match dominated by the pace bowlers. Eksteen bowled 13 overs, also without success, and it was a mild surprise when Boje was preferred for the second Test in Bangalore, when South Africa opted to play only one spinner.

Boje produced an heroic performance as South Africa clinched the series with an innings victory. A more than useful bowling return of 15-7-10-2 in the first innings was followed by a superb nightwatchman innings of 85 before he took the first three Indian wickets in the second innings, bowling with supreme confidence and getting his pace and loop just right. He finished with 5-83 and was named man of the match.

He went on to be a key player in a drawn series in Sri Lanka, man of the indoor series against Australia and man of the match in the final of the Singapore Challenge tournament.

He was on an irresistible roll and started the 2000/01 series by batting spectacularly in the one-day series against New Zealand. Given his opportunity to bat high in the order, he hit two centuries and a fifty as he hammered 355 runs, at close to a run a ball, at an average of 88.75. Yet another man of the series award was in the bag.

There was no longer a question about who would be South Africa's spin bowler in the home Tests against New Zealand and Sri Lanka, nor on the tour of the West Indies. So far had Boje advanced that he remained the number one choice despite being less than fully fit throughout the Caribbean tour. Even a 75 percent fit Boje, it was reckoned, was crucial to the South African cause.

Only when the series was won, with one match to be played, was Boje sent home for an operation on his left shoulder and to rest his right knee. It was not a spectacular series for Boje but he made some crucial contributions. His tumbling catch of Ramnaresh Sarwan in Port of Spain was a killer blow to the West Indies in a tense second Test victory. In the series-clinching match at St John's he took the first three wickets in the second innings and would have had five wickets at reasonable cost if a straightforward catch off Brian Lara had been held at deep square leg.

NICO BOJE was born in Bloemfontein on 20 March 1973 to a sporting family. His father and brother Louis were outstanding rugby players and Nicky was good enough to emerge through the tough ranks of Grey College to play at Craven Week level before concentrating on cricket. Louis also played cricket for Free State B.

Boje played for Free State Schools for four years and SA Schools for three years, the first as twelfthman and the third, in 1991, as captain. He made his debut for Free State in 1990/91

ON HIS TOES . . . more runs for Neil McKenzie during a season in which he showed skill and an excellent temperament *Picture: Tertius Pickard, TOUCHLINE PHOTO*

and won national one-day colours in 1995/96. He attributes a winter at the Plascon Academy to the huge improvement in his batting.

His temperament was seldom in doubt, especially after he and Alan Dawson took their side to an unlikely victory in the Commonwealth Games semifinal in 1998 by putting on an unbeaten 35 for the last wicket in a low-scoring game.

His first Test cap was elusive, however, and he had to endure disappointments on tours of India in 1996/97 and New Zealand in 1998/99 when he might reasonably have expected a call on slow pitches. Boje, though, never gave up, taking the attitude that selection was out of his hands. "All I can do is to perform whenever I get an opportunity to play," he said in an interview during 2000.

When opportunity finally knocked, Boje took full advantage.

Colin Bryden

NEIL McKENZIE

In a game in which professionalism and technology often sit uneasily with tradition, Neil McKenzie represents a happy blend of the best of the old and the new. Already something of a byword in South African cricket for the superstitions which so fascinate television commentators, McKenzie is proof that a mild eccentricity need not preclude success at the highest level.

Chosen initially as a Test player during South African cricket's *annus horribilis* in 2000, McKenzie made his Test debut in Sri Lanka under difficult circumstances. With the South African team still shaken from the Hansiegate scandal, McKenzie was chosen to open the batting ahead of Boeta Dippenaar, a more obvious candidate. It is fair to say that he was not an outstanding success as South Africa turned around a drubbing in the first Test match to draw the series.

If nothing else, however, McKenzie slowly displayed a characteristic that will stand him in good stead throughout his career: the ability to learn and absorb and adjust his game. As the South African winter tour wound through Australia and back to Singapore, he began to look more comfortable at the crease and there were signs of increasing confidence.

At home for the tours by New Zealand and Sri Lanka, McKenzie started to repay the faith of the selectors. A 55 in the first Test against New Zealand in Bloemfontein was followed by a maiden Test century against the Kiwis at St George's Park. It was an innings that mixed common sense with a variety of well-executed attacking shots as he and Nicky Boje added 136 for the eighth wicket to repair a South African first innings that had creaked ominously at 209 for seven.

McKenzie's contribution was 120 and he followed this in a matter of weeks with another 120, this time unbeaten, in the second one-day international against Sri Lanka in East London.

There was a third international century for McKenzie before the home season was up, 103 in the third Test against Sri Lanka at SuperSport Park. His efforts were overshadowed by the pyrotechnics of Shaun Pollock's maiden Test hundred, but again McKenzie produced an innings of maturity. The home side had been 204 for seven before he and Pollock put on 150 for the eighth wicket and McKenzie provided the perfect foil to Pollock's uninhibited hitting.

His knack of adjusting to different conditions and circumstances was again evident in the Caribbean. He made a slow start to the Test series in the Caribbean but after making 72 in the first innings in Barbados once again settled down.

TRUE PACE . . . Mfuneko Ngam lets go with another thunderbolt during an impressive Test debut against New Zealand at the Wanderers Picture: Duif du Toit, TOUCHLINE PHOTO

It is no criticism to suggest that McKenzie is by no means the finished article. Despite playing 14 successive Test matches since his debut in Sri Lanka, he may have awaited one or two team announcements with some anxiety. Gradually, however, he has established himself, looking most at home a five, but filling in adequately at three whenever Jacques Kallis was required to carry a disproportionate share of the bowling.

McKenzie's technique is simple, neat and demonstrates an admirable economy of movement and effort. He stands still at the crease and waits on the ball and although he is probably more comfortable on the back foot, he is a fine driver of the ball.

Most notably, though, he is particularly strong off his legs with an especial liking for the pull and the hook. This part of his game, quite obviously, has been inherited from his father Kevin who played for Transvaal and South Africa during isolation.

In another respect, too, the younger McKenzie is a chip off the old block. The unassuming Kevin was one of the most popular players in South Africa and Neil is equally well-liked, both by teammates and opponents. Like his father, Neil always seems slightly embarrassed by acclaim and his conduct on and off the field has never been anything less than exemplary.

Which is not to suggest an indifferent approach to competition or practice. Always a natural ball player, McKenzie's fielding at times approached the sublime in the Caribbean. He may lack the lightning pace along the ground of a Jonty Rhodes or Herschelle Gibbs, but his catching, stopping and throwing in the West Indies matched anything produced by his illustrious colleagues.

NEIL DUNCAN McKENZIE was born in Johannesburg in 1975 and educated at KES, one of the country's best-established cricketing nurseries, and RAU. He played for SA Schools in 1993 and 1994, captaining the side in 1994 as well as leading the SA under 19 team to England in 1995.

He followed his father to the Wanderers, falling under the influence of Ken Rutherford as the former New Zealand captain preached his gospel of adventurous cricket. But with Gauteng riven by internal strife McKenzie moved across the Jukskei River in the 1999/2000 season.

Why Gauteng allowed McKenzie to escape is anyone's guess but the Northerns Titans had no doubts about his quality, almost immediately appointing him to the captaincy. His subsequent international commitments have since forced him to relinquish the position but the shift of province enabled McKenzie to earn a Standard Bank Cup winner's medal in the summer of 2000/01.

Peter Robinson

MFUNEKO NGAM

The decision by the United Cricket Board to offer Mfuneko Ngam a contract even before he'd completed his first Test is the strongest evidence of the exciting potential the rookie paceman revealed in his international debut.

After only a handful of first-class games, the 21-year-old was called up for the third Test against New Zealand at the Wanderers in place of the injured Allan Donald and had it not been for a rare catching lapse by Daryll Cullinan, his first over in Test cricket would have been nothing short of sensational. The normally reliable slip fielder dropped Adam Parore off Ngam's fourth ball.

Later, however, the new cap picked up his first Test wicket, Mark Richardson, and finished the innings with two for 34.

The UCB's decision to offer him a contract might have been seen by the cynics as another piece of affirmative selection. But any fair observer would agree that Ngam had emerged as one of the country's most promising young bowlers entirely on merit. A speed gun which hovered near the 150kmh mark and nine wickets in a further two Tests against the Sri Lankans were undeniable signals that South Africa's development programme had unearthed another fast bowling jewel.

Having made his senior debut towards the end of the 1999/2000 season, Ngam made rapid strides to become an automatic choice at the start of the next season.

His fluent action and ability to generate pace without any apparent effort made him a player to watch and he quickly made his mark in Eastern Province's opening SuperSport Series game against Western Province, taking seven wickets in the match. His incisiveness placed him a level ahead of more experienced colleagues as he confirmed a reputation which had spread through club cricket in Port Elizabeth that the Aberdare express was far too sharp for the average league player.

He announced himself on the national stage in a televised one-day fixture over Free State at St George's Park, impressing all those who saw him as he whipped out Boeta Dippenaar and Kosie Venter in a blistering opening spell.

From there it was a quick step into the national side and although, as a promising black player, Ngam probably had the inside track as the most likely replacement for the injured Donald, subsequent performances were to show that his elevation to national stardom had nothing to do with affirmative selection.

Injuries, though, were to catch up with the man dubbed "Black Thunder" by television commentator Mike Haysman. He'd already suffered a shoulder injury early in the season and he was finally sidelined for the summer by a stress fracture in his right femur.

Ngam's eagerness and an uncomplaining personality may have contributed to his injuries. A teammate said you never knew if he was suffering because he always insisted he was okay. But the medical authorities realised something serious was up after he spoke of a sore hip following the second Test against Sri Lanka in Cape Town.

There was speculation that Ngam's comparatively slight frame had been put under too much stress given the rigours of his particular discipline and that a poor diet when he was growing up had contributed to a relatively weak skeletal system.

The injury highlighted the fact that Ngam was not as strong as he should be and he was put on a rehabilitation and strengthening programme under the supervision of PE sports physiotherapist Sophie Chandler.

Growing up in the remote Eastern Cape town of Middledrift, MFUNEKO NGAM, born on 29 January 1979, had sport in his blood from a young age and as a boy he remembers being enthralled by the sight on television of Allan Donald hurling down his express deliveries.

Even with the sport's development programme trying to spread the game to all corners of the country, there didn't seem much prospect for a young boy stuck away in the Eastern Cape's poor and vast interior. But, and this theme is a common thread running through his life, Ngam was prepared to do the hard work himself because "I wanted to be just like Allan Donald".

A family move to Port Elizabeth in the early nineties opened up other avenues but Ngam still used to practice a great deal by himself after school – he joined the Motherwell Cricket Club but now plays for Aberdare – before being noticed in a trials match to be selected for an EP under 18 team for a tournament in Saldanha.

He came to the attention of current EP coach Adrian Birrell, then heading the province's youth coaching programme, who quickly noticed that here was someone special.

Never one to take the accolades, Birrell says Ngam was so easy to handle because he'd done most of the hard work himself and it was merely a matter of guiding him in the right direction. That route took him through the normal schools channels to his EP B debut in 1998 and ultimately the national side.

His career may have been put on temporary hold but the sight of Ngam and fellow Eastern Cape development product Makhaya Ntini operating in tandem holds all sorts of exciting possibilities for South African cricket. Their success should serve as a huge inspiration for generations to come.

Neale Emslie

MAKHAYA NTINI

Border right-arm fast bowler MAKHAYA NTINI has had to overcome more than the usual setbacks to get to the top in his chosen sport. Born in the tiny village of Mdingi near King William's Town, on 6 July 1977, he was discovered by the Border cricket development programme at the age of 14 bowling with flapping tackie and ripped shirt, plucked out of obscurity and educated at Dale College in King William's Town.

He advanced through the ranks to international status as a fiery fast bowler, becoming the first black African to be capped at Test cricket by South Africa in 1997/98. But during 1999 his career plunged to the depths of despair after his arrest on a rape charge, followed by a very public trial, conviction and sentence.

He lost his place in the South African squad selected for the World Cup in England and was banned from all cricket until his appeal was heard later that year.

The United Cricket Board of South Africa supported him throughout and their decision to pay him his monthly salary as a contracted player led to some criticism. But in October the appeal was upheld and the charge against the young bowler dropped.

A match against North West B for Border B in early November 1999 proved his fitness, and he immediately regained his place in the Border senior team. A month later he took a hat-trick against Free State at Bloemfontein. But he was not selected for his country during that season.

Some good bowling performances in early 2000 kept his name in the selectors' notebook and on 22 March 2000 Ntini made his return to international cricket in a limited-overs match against India in Sharjah. It was the first time he had worn the green and gold since the 1998 tour of England. His 3-36 helped materially in South Africa's victory by 10 wickets, South Africa's first ODI win by that margin. Since then he has been a regular in the one-day and Test teams.

As first-change bowler after Shaun Pollock and Allan Donald have bowled 10 or 12 overs with the new ball, he has made the most of his opportunities. In the six home Test matches last season he captured 23 wickets (avg 19.21), second only to Shaun Pollock. For good measure he added 11 one-day wickets (avg 19.81) in seven home internationals.

His ability to bowl long spells at top pace with the old ball is testament to his superb fitness and stamina. Even at the end of a long, hot day he can be seen jogging energetically back to his bowling mark.

"Makhaya has been the find of the season," said South African skipper, Shaun Pollock. "He's very, very fit and able to bowl lots of overs at a time."

ALL-OUT EFFORT . . . Makhaya Ntini showed pace, skill, commitment and fitness in a season of consistent performances *Picture: Duif du Toit, TOUCHLINE PHOTO*

Border coach Richard Pybus feels that Ntini will develop further and will become a better bowler as his career progresses. "He must still add some variety to his bowling, and no doubt other skills will be added. But remember he's only 24, and most fast bowlers peak at about 28."

Last summer Ntini recorded his career-best figures in both Tests (6-66 v New Zealand, first Test, Bloemfontein), and limited-overs matches (5-37 v Sri Lanka at Newlands), and was named as man of the series against New Zealand.

Ntini was an integral part of the attack on tour in the West Indies where he had early success against West Indies's champion bat, Brian Lara.

As a young man his ambitions were to earn plenty of money, drive a smart car and play cricket. That he has achieved all three at such a young age, says much for him. He has become a role model for the black youth of South Africa, and accepted that position with aplomb.

At Buffalo Park, he can often be seen talking to the youth, encouraging them in their play, and his autograph is prized. During play he is kept busy signing autographs from the fine-leg position.

Ntini's two heroes were South African all-rounder Brian McMillan and former West Indian fast bowler, the late Malcolm Marshall, upon whom he modelled his bowling style.

Pybus is convinced that what Ntini went through two years ago would have broken lesser men than the Border bowler. "There were many people having a go at Makhaya," Pybus said, "and it says a lot for Makkie that he managed to overcome the turmoil. He kept his focus, persevered and worked hard at his game and is a true inspiration to all cricketers."

These days, with his hectic playing schedule, Ntini savours all the spare time he can enjoy with his partner, Thandeka, and the newest member of the Ntini clan, his 14-month old son, Thando, at their home in Gonubie just outside East London.

Peter Martin

SHAUN POLLOCK

It is more than a theory that the performances of cricketers suffer when they have to bear the responsibility of captaincy. In Shaun Pollock's case, however, leadership has seemed only to inspire him to greater deeds.

Having taken over as captain in the most challenging circumstances on the day before a limited overs match against Australia, after his predecessor admitted taking money from a bookmaker, Pollock promptly led his side to a series victory over the world champions, something neither Kepler Wessels nor Hansie Cronje had been able to achieve.

He had never captained a side at first-class level and suffered a harsh learning experience when South Africa were beaten by an innings by Sri Lanka at Galle in his first Test in charge. Since then, however, his record has been outstanding.

A shared indoor series in Australia and victory in a one-day tournament in Singapore were followed by elimination at the semifinal stage in the ICC Trophy in Kenya before a glorious run of success was resumed.

Thumping Test and one-day series wins at home against New Zealand and Sri Lanka were followed by arguably the most impressive achievement in the new age of South African cricket, a Test and one-day series double in the West Indies.

STAR QUALITY . . . there were two centuries for Shaun Pollock as he joined the elite Test all-rounders with 2000 runs and 200 wickets *Picture: Duif du Toit, TOUCHLINE PHOTO*

Through it all, Pollock's cricketing performances were outstanding and he was man of the series in the Tests against Sri Lanka and player of the summer in the West Indies.

His bowling has become almost impeccable. He seldom bowls a bad ball and he probes relentlessly on a nagging length around the off stump. Because he is able to move the ball both ways, batsmen allow the ball to go by at their peril.

In recent years, Pollock's batting had receded and although he climbed to the top of the world Test bowling rankings, his status as an outstanding all-rounder slipped. That was put to rights in spectacular fashion at Centurion when a succession of blazing strokes took him to a maiden Test century off just 95 deliveries.

With that breakthrough out of the way, Pollock batted superbly throughout the series in the Caribbean, looking composed, confident and utterly reliable. A second century followed in Bridgetown, Barbados, where a few days earlier he had paid homage at the graveside of Malcolm Marshall, his mentor.

Bowling was hard work on the slow West Indian pitches but he finished the series as South Africa's joint leading wicket-taker with Jacques Kallis, taking nine wickets in the fifth Test at Kingston. During that match, he became only the eighth player and the first South African in Test history to complete the double of 2000 runs and 200 wickets.

As captain, Pollock showed a refreshingly relaxed attitude. There was no shortage of passion and intensity on the field but once the day's play was over, Pollock quickly put any cares behind him. This ability to switch on and switch off was undoubtedly a factor in South Africa, for the first time since unity, being able to finish a long tour as strongly as they began it.

As a tactician, Pollock was usually prepared to take the attacking option but he could play the game of attrition as well, notably in one of the slowest days of recent Test cricket when he was content for the batsmen to grind out a winning lead on a brute of a pitch in St John's, Antigua.

A hallmark had been modesty and a stock phrase at Pollock victory press conferences has become: "All credit to the guys, they played really well." He extends the plaudits to the backroom men, the team management and coaches. However much is due to the "guys", it still takes a strong leader to pull the elements together.

SHAUN MACLEAN POLLOCK, born in Port Elizabeth on 16 July 1973, could hardly have had better sporting genes and seemed to have inherited the batting skills of his uncle, Graeme, as well as the fast bowling ability of his father, Peter.

Having to compete against older boys when he joined his elder brother, Gavin, in backyard cricket games meant his competitive spirit was honed early but his father did not push him to become a cricketer. As a youngster at Northwood high school in Durban he participated enthusiastically in all sports.

He played for South African Schools in 1991 and was an almost immediate success when he started playing senior provincial cricket in 1991/92. Since making his Test debut against England in 1995/96 he has become an automatic choice for his country.

Tough challenges lie ahead, notably in Australia, but captain Pollock has shown he has what it takes. It is a notoriously taxing job, however, and one of the difficulties may be to maintain the balance and equanimity he has shown in his first year.

Colin Bryden

FIVE CRICKETERS OF THE YEAR

NICO BOJE (Born Bloemfontein 20/3/1973)
Teams: Free State and South Africa

Season	Teams	M	Inns	NO	Runs	HS	Avg	100	50	Ct	St	Balls	Runs	Wkts	Avg	BB	5I	10M
1990/91	OFS/OFSB	3	5	3	163	77	81.50	0	1	2	0	622	292	13	22.46	6-100	1	0
1991/92	OFSB	3	3	1	42	22*	21.00	0	0	2	0	324	189	3	63.00	1-12	0	0
1992/93	OFS	1	2	1	25	19*	25.00	0	0	0	0	252	136	1	136.00	1-17	0	0
1993/94	OFS	9	11	4	134	36	19.14	0	0	3	0	2865	1115	35	31.85	6-101	1	0
1994/95	SAA in Zim	2	2	0	159	102	79.50	1	1	0	0	564	238	8	29.75	4-65	0	0
1994/95	OFS	9	16	2	291	66	20.78	0	1	3	0	2145	958	25	38.32	5-38	2	0
1995/96	SA U24 in SL	4	2	0	53	53	26.50	0	1	0	0	419	172	10	17.20	4-31	0	0
1995/96	FS/SAA/SA Stud	9	12	1	282	69	25.63	0	2	4	0	2441	973	27	36.03	4-39	0	0
1996	SAA in Eng	7	9	2	289	89	41.28	0	3	5	0	964	562	12	46.83	5-58	1	0
1996/97	SA in Ind	3	4	0	58	33	14.50	0	0	2	0	204	110	1	110.00	1-16	0	0
1996/97	FS	6	11	0	189	34	17.18	0	0	10	0	1128	532	11	48.36	3-60	0	0
1997/98	FS/SA Acad	11	16	4	683	105*	56.91	2	4	9	0	2645	913	35	26.08	6-34	2	1
1998/99	SAA in SL	3	2	0	25	25	12.50	0	0	1	0	594	181	8	22.62	3-46	0	0
1998/99	FS	5	10	2	500	116	62.50	1	5	2	0	881	415	8	51.87	3-42	0	0
1998/99	SA in NZ	1	1	1	18	18*	-	0	0	0	0	144	45	1	45.00	1-25	0	0
1999/00	FS/FGN	9	18	4	536	76*	38.28	0	4	8	0	1929	667	21	31.76	5-38	1	0
1999/00	SA in Ind	2	2	0	99	85	49.50	0	1	0	0	348	110	7	15.71	5-83	1	0
2000	SA in SL	3	6	1	124	35	24.80	0	0	2	0	607	273	10	27.30	5-62	1	0
2000/01	FS/SA	7	9	1	375	105	46.87	1	2	2	0	1321	448	19	23.57	5-67	1	0
2000/01	SA in WI	6	10	2	158	36	19.75	0	0	4	0	1271	534	20	26.70	4-17	0	0
Totals																		
Tests		15	22	3	522	85	27.47	0	2	8	0	2958	1159	44	26.34	5-62	2	0
SuperSport Series		49	81	17	2336	116	36.50	3	14	34	0	11996	4626	149	31.04	6-34	7	1
All First-Class		103	151	29	4203	116	34.45	5	25	59	0	21668	8863	275	32.22	6-34	11	1
Limited Overs Internationals		56	34	8	780	129	30.00	2	2	16	0	2111	1552	43	36.09	4-25	0	
All Limited Overs		139	93	27	1775	129	26.89	2	5	39	0	5892	4068	128	31.78	4-16	0	

NEIL DOUGLAS McKENZIE (Born Johannesburg 24/11/1975)
Teams: Gauteng, Northerns and South Africa

Season	Teams	M	Inns	NO	Runs	HS	Avg	100	50	Ct	St	Balls	Runs	Wkts	Avg	BB	5I	10M
1994/95	TvlB	1	2	0	57	53	28.50	0	1	2	0	6	0	0	-	-	0	0
1995/96	Tvl	9	15	1	559	150*	39.92	2	3	7	0	54	18	1	18.00	1-11	0	0
1996/97	Tvl	9	17	2	511	139	34.06	1	3	4	0	18	14	0	-	-	0	0
1997/98	Gau/Gau XI/SAA	9	15	0	450	135	30.00	1	2	9	0	12	18	0	-	-	0	0
1998/99	Gau	6	11	2	311	99	34.55	0	3	2	0	36	27	1	27.00	1-6	0	0
1999/00	Nor/GN/SAA/SA Inv	12	19	1	861	175	47.83	2	4	7	0	90	35	1	35.00	1-16	0	0
2000	SA in SL	3	6	0	54	25	9.00	0	0	2	0	0	0	0	-	-	0	0
2000/01	Nor/SA	9	14	3	672	123	61.09	3	3	8	0	0	0	0	-	-	0	0
2000/01	SA in WI	7	13	1	403	72	33.58	0	3	7	0	0	0	0	-	-	0	0
Totals																		
Tests		14	23	2	722	120	34.38	2	3	13	0	0	0	0	-	-	0	0
SuperSport Series		39	67	7	2229	175	37.15	4	13	26	0	120	67	1	67.00	1-6	0	0
All First-Class		65	112	10	3878	175	38.01	9	22	48	0	216	112	3	37.33	1-6	0	0
Limited Overs Internationals		26	23	1	625	120*	28.40	1	2	7	0	22	11	0	-	-	0	
All Limited Overs		87	78	9	2193	120*	31.78	4	10	25	0	184	175	4	43.75	2-19	0	

MFUNEKO NGAM (Born Middledrift 29/1/1979)
Teams: Eastern Province and South Africa

Season	Teams	M	Inns	NO	Runs	HS	Avg	100	50	Ct	St	Balls	Runs	Wkts	Avg	BB	5I	10M
1997/98	EPB	1	2	0	2	2	1.00	0	0	0	0	18	21	0	-	-	0	0
1998/99	EPB	4	6	0	41	16	6.83	0	0	2	0	522	220	8	27.50	4-25	0	0
1999/00	EP/UCB XI	3	4	1	12	6	4.00	0	0	2	0	578	251	8	31.37	3-52	0	0
2000/01	SAA in WI	4	5	0	8	3	1.60	0	0	3	0	586	256	13	19.69	3-21	0	0
2000/01	EP/SA	6	6	2	34	18*	8.50	0	0	2	0	1136	552	21	26.28	4-78	0	0
Totals																		
Tests		3	1	1	0	0*	-	0	0	1	0	392	189	11	17.18	3-26	0	0
SuperSport Series		5	8	1	45	18*	6.42	0	0	2	0	1166	525	16	32.81	4-78	0	0
All First-Class		18	23	3	97	18*	4.85	0	0	9	0	2840	1300	50	26.00	4-25	0	0
All Limited Overs		14	1	1	0	0*	-	0	0	4	0	602	404	24	16.83	4-20	0	

MAKHAYA NTINI (Born Mdingi 6/7/1977)
Teams: Border and South Africa

Season	Teams	M	Inns	NO	Runs	HS	Avg	100	50	Ct	St	Balls	Runs	Wkts	Avg	BB	5I	10M
1995/96	Bdr	8	13	2	69	19*	6.27	0	0	0	0	1140	630	17	37.05	3-49	0	0
1996/97	Bdr	9	9	2	16	5	2.28	0	0	0	0	1333	847	25	33.88	6-49	1	0
1997/98	Bdr/SA	6	7	5	46	22	23.00	0	0	0	0	854	528	16	33.00	3-45	0	0
1997/98	SA in Aus	1	0	0	0	0	-	0	0	0	0	162	108	2	54.00	2-24	0	0
1998	SA in Eng	7	2	1	4	4*	4.00	0	0	2	0	1107	578	19	30.42	4-72	0	0
1998/99	Bdr/SAA	8	11	5	19	9	3.16	0	0	6	0	1031	630	18	35.00	3-51	0	0
1999/00	Bdr/BE	8	13	6	89	34*	12.71	0	0	1	0	1120	582	22	26.45	4-55	0	0
2000	SA in SL	1	2	0	8	8	4.00	0	0	0	0	114	73	1	73.00	1-73	0	0
2000/01	Bdr/SA	8	5	3	27	10	13.50	0	0	3	0	1610	688	36	19.11	6-59	2	0
2000/01	SA in WI	5	6	2	47	24*	11.75	0	0	2	0	671	372	11	33.81	4-31	0	0
Totals																		
Tests		15	15	6	58	11	6.44	0	0	4	0	2505	1169	41	28.51	6-66	1	0
SuperSport Series		33	43	17	223	34*	8.57	0	0	7	0	5086	2830	91	31.09	6-49	2	0
All First-Class		61	68	26	325	34*	7.73	0	0	14	0	9142	5036	167	30.15	6-49	3	0
Limited Overs Internationals		23	4	2	5	3*	2.50	0	0	10	0	1063	743	32	23.21	5-37	1	
All Limited Overs		64	17	6	32	8	2.90	0	0	15	0	2754	1998	80	24.97	5-37	2	

SHAUN MACLEAN POLLOCK (Born Port Elizabeth 16/7/1973)
Teams: KwaZulu-Natal, Warwickshire and South Africa

Season	Teams	M	Inns	NO	Runs	HS	Avg	100	50	Ct	St	Balls	Runs	Wkts	Avg	BB	5I	10M
1991/92	NtlB	1	2	1	39	26	39.00	0	0	0	0	126	40	3	13.33	2-22	0	0
1992/93	Ntl	1	2	0	25	23	12.50	0	0	1	0	208	90	4	22.50	3-28	0	0
1993/94	Ntl	6	8	1	166	56	23.71	0	1	2	0	1010	382	11	34.72	3-33	0	0
1994/95	Ntl	8	10	3	155	44	22.14	0	0	4	0	1487	591	31	19.06	4-24	0	0
1995/96	SAU24 in SL	3	2	0	65	37	32.50	0	0	0	0	504	243	4	60.75	3-55	0	0
1995/96	Ntl/SA/SAA	10	11	3	348	74*	43.50	0	2	4	0	2041	798	51	15.64	7-33	5	1
1996	Warwicks	13	21	1	606	150*	30.30	2	1	5	0	2680	1183	42	28.16	6-56	1	0
1996/97	Ntl/SA	9	17	3	471	79	33.64	0	3	4	0	1614	660	36	18.33	5-48	1	0
1997/98	SA in Pak	4	6	3	277	82	92.33	0	2	2	0	642	333	11	30.27	5-37	1	0

Season	Teams	M	Inns	NO	Runs	HS	Avg	100	50	Ct	St	Balls	Runs	Wkts	Avg	BB	5I	10M
1997/98	SA in Aus	5	8	1	224	100	32.00	1	0	4	0	1294	497	22	22.59	7-87	1	0
1997/98	Ntl/SA	6	9	1	319	92	39.87	0	3	3	0	1091	449	22	20.40	6-50	1	0
1998	SA in Eng	6	8	2	187	50	31.16	0	1	3	0	1601	594	24	24.75	5-53	1	0
1998/99	KZN/SA	7	13	1	269	92	22.41	0	1	6	0	1698	616	35	17.60	5-43	3	0
1998/99	SA in NZ	4	4	2	152	69*	76.00	0	1	4	0	903	324	17	19.05	5-33	1	0
1999/00	KZN/SA	9	11	1	286	64	28.60	0	3	12	0	2139	757	32	23.65	5-39	1	0
1999/00	SA in Zim	1	1	0	61	61	61.00	0	1	2	0	198	55	7	7.85	4-32	0	0
1999/00	SA in Ind	2	3	0	6	5	2.00	0	0	3	0	439	133	9	14.77	4-24	0	0
2000	SA in SL	3	6	0	87	33	14.50	0	0	1	0	564	247	11	22.45	3-40	0	0
2000/01	KZN/SA	7	6	0	182	111	30.33	1	0	8	0	1520	515	27	19.07	6-30	1	0
2000/01	SA in WI	7	12	6	389	106*	64.83	1	1	5	0	1537	547	21	26.04	5-28	1	0
Totals																		
Tests		56	81	17	2015	111	31.48	2	8	36	0	12428	4694	231	20.32	7-87	12	0
SuperSport Series		28	39	5	1041	92	30.61	0	8	27	0	5788	2038	107	19.04	7-33	4	1
All First-Class		112	160	29	4314	150*	32.93	5	20	73	0	23296	9054	420	21.55	7-33	18	1
Limited Overs Internationals		132	87	30	1411	75	24.75	0	5	46	0	6936	4380	190	23.05	6-35	3	
All Limited Overs		228	149	44	2391	87	22.77	0	10	76	0	11212	7039	319	22.06	6-21	5	

MUTUAL & FEDERAL CRICKET ANNUAL CRICKETERS OF THE YEAR

The tradition of honouring five South African Cricketers of the Year was established in the first edition of the South African Cricket Annual in 1952 by the first Editor, Geoffrey A Chettle, who marked the occasion by naming five "stalwarts who have recently left the international field", Eric and Athol Rowan, Dudley Nourse, Norman "Tufty" Mann and Geoff Chubb. Initially the honour was bestowed once only, as remains the case with the Wisden Cricketers' Almanack, but Special Tributes were introduced to recognise long-serving and exceptional performers Graeme Pollock and Mike Procter in 1977 before a system evolved whereby the five outstanding players of the season were chosen, whether or not they had received the award previously.

Ackerman HM (WP)	1971
Adcock NAT (Tvl)	1954
Alabaster JC (New Zealand)	1962
Armitage RLS (EP)	1982
Azharuddin M (India)	1997
Bacher A (Tvl)	1961
Barlow EJ (Tvl)	1962
and Special Tribute (WP)	1981
Barnard LJ (N Tvl)	
Special Tribute	1990
Barrington KF (England)	1965
Bath BF (Tvl)	1974
Benaud R (Australia)	1958
Benkenstein DM (Ntl)	1997
Bestall D (Ntl)	1975
Bezuidenhout SJ (EP)	1973
Biggs AL (EP)	1969
Bland KC (Rhodesia)	1962
Boje N (Free State)	2001
Bosch T (N Tvl)	1991
Botten JT (NE Tvl)	1959
Boucher MV (Border)	1998/00
Brickett DJ (EP)	1980
Bruyns A (WP)	1972
Burke JW (Australia)	1958
Burke SF (NE Tvl)	1964
Callaghan DJ (EP)	1988
Carlstein PR (Tvl)	1963
Cheetham JE (WP)	1953
Chevalier GA (WP)	1970
Chubb GWA (Tvl)	1952
Clarke ST (W Indians/Tvl)	1984/85
Clift PB (Rhodesia)	1979
Close DB (D Robins)	1974
Cole JM (Ntl)	1961
Compton DCS (England)	1957
Connolly AN (Australia)	1970
Cook SJ (Tvl)	1981/83
Cooper KR (Ntl)	1981
Craig ID (Australia)	1958
Cronje WJ (OFS)	1992/95/98
Cullinan DJ (WP/Border/Gau)	1989/96/99
Davidson AK (Australia)	1958
Davison BF (Rhodesia)	1973
Day NT (Tvl/N Tvl)	1981/85
De Vaal PD (Tvl)	1971
De Villiers PS (N Tvl)	1989/95
Dick AE (New Zealand)	1962
Dodds PM (Ntl)	1963
Doherty MJD (GW)	1972
Donald AA (OFS)	1993/96/97/98
Drakes VC (Border)	2000
Dumbrill R (Ntl)	1965
Du Preez JH (Rhodesia)	1967
Du Preez VF (N Tvl)	1982
Dyer DD (Ntl)	1974
Endean WR (Tvl)	1953
Estwick RO (Tvl)	1988
Farrer WS (Border)	1961
Fellows-Smith JP (Tvl)	1960
Ferrandi JH (WP)	1959
Ferreira AM (N Tvl)	1978
Fletcher DAG (Rhodesia)	1975
Fotheringham HR (Ntl/Tvl)	1977/83
and Special Tribute (Ntl)	1990
Foulkes I (Border)	1978
Fuller ERH (WP)	1956
Funston KJ (Tvl)	1957
Gamsy D (Ntl)	1969
Gatting MW (English XI)	1990
Gibbs HH (WP)	1999
Gibson OD (Border)	1993

MUTUAL & FEDERAL CRICKET ANNUAL CRICKETERS OF THE YEAR

Gleeson JW (Australia)	1970
Goddard TL (Ntl)	1955
Greig AW (EP)	1972
Greve VS (Tvl)	1973
Griffin GM (Ntl)	1960
Gripper RA (Rhodesia)	1968
Hanley RW (EP/Tvl)	1975/84
Haysman MD (Australians)	1987
Hayward M (EP)	2000
Heine PS (Tvl)	1955
Henry O (OFS)	1993
and Special Tribute (Boland)	1986
Henwood PP (Ntl)	1974
Heron JG (Rhodesia)	1976
Hobson DL (WP)	1975
Hudson AC (Ntl)	1992
Innes GAS (WP)	1959
Irvine BL (Ntl)	1968
Jack SD (Tvl)	1991
Jackman RD (Rhodesia)	1973
Jefferies ST (WP)	1982
Jennings RV (Tvl)	1980
and Special Tribute	1985
Kallicharran AI (W Indians/Tvl)	1983
Kallis JH (WP)	1999/00
Kaschula RH (Rhodesia)	1972
Keith HJ (Ntl)	1955
Kirsten G (WP)	1994/95/96
Kirsten PN (WP)	1977/84
Klusener L (Ntl)	1997/99
Kourie AJ (Tvl)	1980
and Special Tribute	1987
Kuiper AP (WP)	1982/84/90
Lamb AJ (WP/OFS)	1980/88
and Special Tribute (WP)	1982
Lance HR (Tvl)	1965
Lara BC (West Indies)	1993
Lawrence GB (Rhodesia)	1960
Le Roux FJ (N Tvl)	1979
Le Roux GS (WP)	1978/86/87
Le Roux RA (OFS)	1979
Lewis DJ (Rhodesia)	1956
Liddle JR (WP)	1956
Lillee DK (Int Wanderers)	1976
Lindsay DT (NE Tvl)	1964
Macaulay MJ (OFS)	1964
and Special Tribute (EP)	1978
Mackay KD (Australia)	1958
Mackay-Coghill D (Tvl)	1969
Maguire JN (EP)	1990
Maile JBR (WP)	1960
Mann NBF (EP)	1952
Mansell PNF (Rhodesia)	1955
Marshall MD (Ntl)	1994/95
Matthews CR (WP)	1991
May PBH (England)	1957
McCurdy RJ (EP)	1990
McEwan KS (WP/EP)	1983/86/87/89
and Special Tribute (EP)	1990
McGlew DJ (Ntl)	1953
McKenzie GD (Australia)	1967
McKenzie KA (Tvl)	1974/86
McKenzie ND (Nor)	2001
McKinnon AH (EP)	1959
McLean RA (Ntl)	1955
McMillan BM (WP)	1991/96
Morby-Smith L (WP)	1964
Morris RET (WP)	1978
Motz RC (New Zealand)	1962
Murray ARA (EP)	1956
Muzzell PJ (Border)	1969
Muzzell RK (WP)	1968
Neilson DR (Tvl)	1977
and Special Tribute	1981
Ngam M (EP)	2001
Nourse AD (Ntl)	1952
Ntini M (Border)	2001
O'Linn S (Tvl)	1960
Ontong RC (N Tvl)	
Special Tribute	1990
Page HA (Tvl)	1985
Partridge JT (Rhodesia)	1963
Pfuhl GP (WP)	1971
and Special Tribute	1980
Pienaar RF (WP/Tvl)	1983/90
Pithey AJ (Rhodesia)	1959
Pollock PM (EP)	1963
Pollock RG (EP/Tvl)	1961/84
and Special Tribute (EP/Tvl)	1977/87
Pollock SM (Ntl)	1996/98/01
Pressdee JS (NE Tvl)	1966
Pringle MW (WP)	1992

MUTUAL & FEDERAL CRICKET ANNUAL CRICKETERS OF THE YEAR

Procter MJ (Ntl)	1967
and Special Tribute	1977
Rabone GO (New Zealand)	1954
Rackemann CG (Australians)	1986
Reid JR (New Zealand)	1954
Rhodes JN (Ntl)	1992/99
Rice CEB (Tvl)	1971/85/86/88
Richards BA (Ntl)	1968
and Special Tribute	1984
Richardson C (OFS)	1961
Richardson DJ (EP)	1995
Rindel MJR (N Tvl)	1989
Roberts B (Tvl)	1988
Robertson SD (Rhodesia)	1972
Rosendorff N (OFS)	1969
Rowan AMB (Tvl)	1952
Rowan EAB (Tvl)	1952
Rowe LG (W Indians)	1984
Rushmere MW (EP)	1988
Rutherford KR (Gauteng)	2000
Schonegevel DJ (GW)	1968
Seeff L (WP)	1981
Shaw TG (EP)	1994
Short AM (Ntl)	1970
Simons EO (N Tvl/WP)	1985/89
Simpson RB (Australia)	1967
Smith AJS (Ntl)	1976
Smith MJK (England)	1965
Smith SB (Australians)	1987
Smith VI (Ntl)	1956
Statham JB (England)	1957
Strydom S (OFS)	1966
Strydom WT (OFS)	1977
Swart PD (WP)	1975
Symcox PL (Ntl)	1998
Tayfield HJ (Ntl)	1953
Taylor MD (Australians)	1986
Titmus FJ (England)	1965
Trimborn PHJ (Ntl)	1967
Trotman EN (Border)	1989
Ullyett RB (Rhodesia)	1964
Van der Bijl VAP (Ntl)	1971
and Special Tribute	1979
Van der Merwe PL (WP)	1963
Van Ryneveld CB (WP)	1964
Versfeld BJ (Ntl)	1966
Waddington JE (GW)	1953
Waite JHB (Tvl)	1954
Waqar Younis (Pakistan)	1993
Wardle JH (England)	1957
Warne SK (Australia)	1994
Watson GLG (Tvl)	1970
Watson WK (EP)	1979
Waugh SR (Australia)	1994/97
Wessels KC (Australians/EP)	1987/92
White RC (Tvl)	1966
Whitfield BJ (Ntl)	1987
Wilkins CP (Border)	1966
Wilmot AL (EP)	1973
and Special Tribute	1980
Yachad M (N Tvl)	1985/91

SOUTH AFRICANS HONOURED BY WISDEN CRICKETERS' ALMANACK

Thirty six South Africans have been named as Cricketer of the Year by Wisden. Those honoured since 1966 are:

Bland KC	1966
Cook SJ	1990
D'Oliveira BL	1967
Donald AA	1992
Greig AW	1975
Klusener L	2000
Lamb AJ	1981
McEwan KS	1978
Pollock PM	1966
Pollock RG	1966
Procter MJ	1970
Radford NV	1986
Rhodes JN	1999
Rice CEB	1981
Richards BA	1969
Smith CL	1984
Smith RA	1990
Van der Bijl VAP	1981
Wessels KC	1995

SA GEARS UP FOR WORLD CUP

Rodney Hartman

The eighth World Cup is the only major global sports event that South Africa will host this decade. It is a huge opportunity for the country and will come at a time that will be important for the morale of South Africa and for international cricket.

In a cricket context, it forms part of a seven-year deal that the International Cricket Council has concluded with the World Sports Group and The News Corporation. The latter two have together acquired the commercial rights for all global cricket tournaments (World Cups, mini-World Cups, under-19 World Cups etc) staged from 2000 to the ninth World Cup in the West Indies in 2007. The WSG/Newscorp partnership in turn guarantees the ICC a return of $550million for their seven-year association.

Dr Ali Bacher, executive director of 2003 CWC, has signed a 30-page host's agreement in which the ICC sets out exactly who does what in building what is essentially a huge jigsaw puzzle. In the realm of major sporting events, the Olympic Games, say, is done and dusted in a fortnight. The 2003 World Cup will run for 42 days during which 54 cricket matches will be played on 34 days of actual cricket. On 20 of those days, two matches will be staged.

We are expecting 750 000 ticket-holders, tens of thousands from abroad, and a media contingent of some 2000. There will be VIPs of note.

The prize money is in keeping with the nature of so important an event, showing a five-fold increase from the $1million on offer in 1999 to the $5million allotted to 2003. The international captains are being asked to propose a formula as to its actual breakdown.

The opening ceremony will be held in Cape Town on Wednesday, February 5, followed by the opening match under floodlights at Newlands the next day. The final will be at the Wanderers in Johannesburg on Wednesday, March 19. There will be 42 pool/group matches played on 22 consecutive days. On 20 of those days there will be two matches played per day. The nine Super Six matches will be played over nine consecutive days.

The first semifinal will be played in Port Elizabeth as a day game on Thursday, March 13, and the second semifinal will be played in Durban as a day/night game on Saturday, March 15.

All games will be day games, except in Cape Town and Durban, the only two centres where day/night games are scheduled. A reserve day will be set aside for each match, but the final will have two reserve days.

At the time of writing the World Cup pools had not yet been finalised but they should not differ much from the following:

GROUP A	GROUP B
Australia	South Africa
Pakistan	Sri Lanka
India	New Zealand
England	West Indies
Zimbabwe	Bangladesh
Netherlands	Kenya
Namibia	Canada

HEADING SOUTH . . . Canadian captain Joe Harris receives an official invitation to the 2003 World Cup from Dr Ali Bacher after Canada won the ICC Trophy third-place match against Scotland in Toronto. Looking on is Dr Geoff Edwards, president of the Canadian Cricket Association.

Picture: CRICINFO

SA GEARS UP FOR WORLD CUP

It is clear from the above that one pool looks considerably tougher than the other. This is not a cunning ploy by us to ensure that South Africa has an easy passage. The pools are compiled according to a seedings system devised by the executive board of the International Cricket Council. The seedings are based on an international rankings list calculated according to the results of all limited overs internationals between the end of the last World Cup in June 1999 until the cutoff date of September 30, 2001.

Games in South Africa will be staged in Johannesburg, Cape Town, Durban, Port Elizabeth, Centurion, Bloemfontein, Paarl, Potchefstroom, East London, Benoni, Kimberley and Pietermaritzburg. The United Cricket Board of South Africa has allocated R35-million to the affiliates for the upgrading of their grounds for the tournament. The affiliates in turn will contribute an additional R25-million.

In terms of South Africa's commitment to developing cricket in Africa, six games will be staged in Zimbabwe and SA's proposal was that Kenya host two games as well.

Tickets will go on sale on July 1, 2002, on a unique, computerised system, costing R36-million, that has been devised by Dimension Data and the UCB. At every World Cup venue, access at the turnstiles will be controlled. Only bar-coded tickets will allow a spectator access into the ground.

All security will fall under a high-powered Security Directorate encompassing the expertise of top legal, security and trade union representatives.

The coins used for the toss will be 1oz pure gold supplied by the Chamber of Mines. There will be a separate coin for each game, 54 in all. The face of President Thabo Mbeki will appear on one side of the coin, with the 2003 Cricket World Cup logo, the names of the two competing teams, the date and venue of the match on the other side.

All World Cup affairs are governed by the 2003 Cricket World Cup Policy Committee, headed by Professor Jakes Gerwel, who was director general in the President's Office of former President Nelson Mandela. The other committee members are: John Blair (treasurer), Mrs Coco Cachalia, Peter Chingoka, Colin Hall, Richard Harrison, Prof Denver Hendricks, Prof Michael Katz, Rob Kurz, Dr Mtutuzeli Nyoka, Khaya Ngqula, Adv Percy Sonn, Dr Ali Bacher (executive director) and Ian Smith (commercial director).

At the heart of our endeavours at 2003 CWC stands our mission statement. It reads:

1. We aim to unite all the peoples of the country behind the event, by following it, supporting it and participating in it.
2. We will use the opportunity to raise the profile of cricket in South Africa and throughout Africa and to develop the sport on the continent like never before.
3. We will make the most of a unique opportunity to make money for South African cricket to ensure the sport's financial viability and security in the future.
4. It is our intention to have the support and involvement of the Government at all levels-local, provincial and national.
5. We aim to give added value to the global sponsors and suppliers and local suppliers and ensure they have a good commercial return on their investment.
6. The management team that organises the competition must reflect the demographics of South Africa.
7. South African companies that are given commercial opportunities through the World Cup must have a satisfactory black empowerment element.

8. All grounds must host an acceptable number of black spectators.
9. We intend to contribute significantly to the lasting enhancement of the image of South Africa abroad as a commercial, sporting and tourism destination.
10. We will fulfil the objectives of the International Cricket Council in awarding the 2003 World Cup to South Africa.
11. The 2003 Cricket World Cup is also about: Developing people, spreading ownership of the World Cup, the transfer of skills, broadening the cricket market (blacks, youth, women and girls), facilitating a mentoring process for black South Africans, eg. mentoring black cricket writers.
12. We want all South Africans to be proud of the event.

I am sometimes asked to explain some of the above points. No 8, for example, inspires us to take at least 50 000 tickets out of the system and donate them to cricket folk in the previously disadvantaged areas. No 7 is self-explanatory. It is happening. In respect of Nos 1, 2 and 11, we have developed a close relationship with Sowetan, South Africa's biggest daily newspaper, and Sowetan Sunday World, South Africa's fastest growing newspaper. They fall under the Nail group, a byword for black empowerment, which is a member of our official publications consortium along with Touchline Media, Mail and Guardian, and Penguin Books.

In addition, there is the promised legacy. This will take the form of 50 turf cricket ovals that are promised to previously disadvantaged areas as a monument, if you like, of the 2003 endeavours.

In respect of all our goals, we are getting there. Our commitment is to make this World Cup the most successful of its kind to date with a distinctly African flavour.

Rodney Hartman is Communications Co-Director of 2003 CWC and part of the senior management team. He was previously sports editor of the Sunday Times newspaper.

2003 Cricket World Cup contact details:
Address: Summer Place, 69 Melville Road, Hyde Park, Johannesburg, 2196, PO Box 782, Northlands, 2116. Telephone: (011) 446 3600, Facsimile: (011) 446 3622. e-mail: 2003CWC@cricket.co.za.

HIGHS AND LOWS OF A TEAM PHYSIO

Craig Smith

They were real tears that Meyrick Pringle cried the night we were knocked out of the 1992 World Cup in the semifinal against England in Sydney. Yet we weren't really supposed to have made the final, let alone harbour any thoughts of winning it, were we?

But under Kepler Wessels, the newcomers to international cricket had a roller-coaster ride of a tournament. The fairytale dream was drowned on a rainy Sydney evening, with a giant electronic scoreboard reading "South Africa to win need 22 runs off 1 ball". Actually, it was "only" 21. There was no chance of the dream having a happy ending, with Chris Lewis bowling 15 no-balls and Brian McMillan sweeping the next one for six!

The next time I witnessed grown cricketers cry just happened to be another World Cup semifinal. This time it was Birmingham '99, against the old rival, Australia. You remember that one? Never before in 10 years of cricket have I been in such a depressing and quiet dressing room after a game of cricket. It was as though the players' destiny had been ripped out of their hearts.

But I suppose that's the cruelty of sport! One winner and one loser.

There are many memories from ten years of touring with the SA cricket team that I'd like to share with you.

If we start by looking at the stats, 68 cricketers have played for SA since our re-introduction in 1991. Of those, 44 have played in Test matches and 65 in one-dayers. We've played in every Test-playing country, most more times than once, including ten trips to the Indian sub-continent. Since November 1991, the SA side have been involved in more than 60 series or tournaments at home and abroad and have played 84 Tests and 229 one-day internationals. It amounts to about 1450 days of cricket (Tests, one-dayers, warm-up matches and practice days), which is close to four years.

If I were to cast my eye around the world of international cricket, there would be a few areas where I would like to wave my magic wand and initiate some changes.

For example, the facilities!

To go from the wonderful grounds and dressing rooms of Australia and South Africa to the poorly-developed facilities in some parts of the sub-continent is like sunning yourself on Camps Bay beach and then laying down your towel down in northern Scotland in mid-winter.

The 1996 World Cup in India, Pakistan and Sri Lanka made a profit of millions of pounds. Yet the last time we toured India and Sri Lanka in 2000, the facilities for the players in both countries had not changed much. It's ironic that the richest cricket board in the world has some of the worst facilities. When we were in India in 1996, playing the first Test match in Ahmedabad, our lunch was prepared on concrete slabs and the plates were washed in filthy dish-water. The players resorted to eating peanut butter toast for five days.

It would make me happy to see some of the millions of dollars that are made from TV rights, sponsorships and ticket sales, spent by the administrators on providing facilities befitting the occasion for the cricketers, who provide the thrilling fireworks.

I am convinced that the future of the game should also involve the development of more scientific input by the ICC and the national boards, which should consider the benefits of research into medicine and science, embarking on structured research programmes that can assist areas such as improving a cricketer's resistance to injury as well as improving cricket performance and training methods.

PAIN IN THE NECK . . . South African team physiotherapist Craig Smith provides treatment for Test batsman Neil McKenzie *Picture: Duif du Toit, TOUCHLINE PHOTO*

HIGHS AND LOWS OF A TEAM PHYSIO

There are other developmental issues that I feel should be standard for all Test venues around the world. For example, the boundary ropes should be a specific safe distance away from the advertising hoardings to allow players to dive to stop the ball without the fear of injury from colliding with the boards. Ask Allan Donald or Ricky Ponting their views on this issue.

Each Test venue should have at least three practice pitches (nets) off the field to allow professional cricketers the opportunity to practice and prepare properly. Only one of the five Test venues in the West Indies had adequate practice facilities.

Each ground should have a separate medical/physio room attached to the dressing room with a modern physio table and equipment to treat the players. Dressing rooms around the world, especially for visiting teams, should be a standard size to accommodate the extra players and baggage that touring teams have in their squads.

Being a team physio to the South African or any international cricket side is a rewarding and satisfying position. But it involves many different things.

The physio is considered the "doc" for the team and any medical situation from a common cold to a dislocated shoulder, an infected grass burn, a sprained ankle or a severed tendon is initially managed by the physio. This is commonly referred to as multi-skilling, with most physios also helping out the coaching staff, doing the warm-ups and stretches and assisting the manager wherever possible. Sometimes, the physio has to take over when the manager goes down ill or is detained elsewhere.

In cases where a doctor or orthopaedic specialist is required, one is called in. The physio needs to have a good support team of GPs and specialists at home and around the world to assist in any situation when the need arises. It's not uncommon to work until 11pm on busy nights, or for 77 days in a row on a 10-week tour. When the breaks come your way and you have an afternoon off by the pool or a round of golf with the boys, you take it.

Over the years, we've managed some interesting injuries and in most cases, one thing has shone through. South African cricketers have big hearts. Broken fingers or toes, swollen and damaged tendons, ruptured ligaments or deep gashes could not keep some of our players off the field.

There are some memorable examples worth mentioning, including Fanie de Villiers playing through an entire season with a broken and swollen toe. Fanie refused to go for an x-ray as he felt that knowing the toe was broken would weaken his resolve to complete the remaining tests.

Throughout last season and on the tour of the West Indies, Nicky Boje played with patella tendinitis, requiring treatment and supportive strapping every day. Added to this was a torn tendon in his left shoulder that eventually required an operation. This tough cricketer often displayed the heart of a lion.

Kepler Wessels was not someone to let an injury keep him off the field. On the 1994 tour of England he awoke one morning to find his troublesome knee swollen and puffy. A doctor drained a large syringe full of blood out of his knee and he went on to complete the match.

As a fast bowler, Allan Donald has had his share of bowling injuries. Fast bowlers' legs and arms are their prized possessions and AD's ankles have borne the brunt of thousands of overs bowled. He has had ankle impingement problems, an acutely painful bruised heel and a broken foot bone, which required surgery. He has had to bite the bullet on many occasions.

One of the toughest customers is Mark Boucher. When he sliced his index finger tendon in Melbourne in August 2000 it was not until just before the start of play that he decided not to play. His finger didn't completely heal through the season but he kept playing, even in the Caribbean when the ball was bouncing unevenly.

UNITED CRICKET BOARD SOUTH AFRICA
Official Sports Drink of the SA Cricket Team.
It's what you put in.
Energade
FCB JHB BRO17550

HIGHS AND LOWS OF A TEAM PHYSIO

There are very few players that you can't get onto the field but thankfully there are more of those who you can't get off. Jonty Rhodes, Shaun Pollock, Lance Klusener and Jacques Kallis spring to mind as players who have spent much of their careers on the physio's table but who are always out in the middle giving their all.

The most freakish injury I've encountered was in 1992 when Fanie de Villiers and Kepler Wessels collided head-to-head in going for a high catch at practice before a one-day match at Newlands. Both had the deepest gashes around the left eye that I have seen. Twelve stitches each later, both of them played against India.

LOWEST POINT

Looking back over the years, I would think that the lowest ebb the SA team sunk to was probably the losing streak of ten one-dayers in 1994, six of them in a row in Pakistan. And this was Bob Woolmer's first tour of duty!

Also low were the 1996 World Cup quarterfinal loss to the West Indies in Karachi and the 1999 semifinal tie in Birmingham which resulted in Australia going through to the final.

GREATEST ACHIEVEMENT

Our greatest achievement to date has probably been the Test series win in the West Indies at the end of last season. Added to this was winning the ICC trophy in Bangladesh in 1998. We had lost Polly to a back injury, Gary Kirsten had a broken finger and AD was still in the UK with Warwickshire yet we still beat the Windies in the final.

The win over Australia in Melbourne's indoor stadium, enabling South Africa to shade the Aussies 3-2 over two series, was also right up there. The 1994 Sydney Test, the 2000 Kandy Test and the Trinidad victory last season go down as great wins etched into my mind.

All of the above will be topped by defeating Australia away and home in the coming season and capping it all off by winning the World Cup on home soil in 2003.

PERSONALITIES

If I were to mull over the characters who have come in and out of the squad over the years, then there are a few who come to mind.

Pat Symcox was always in the thick of things be it on or off the field. Symmo roomed with Fanie de Villiers and their hotel room was always the meeting place for the players after a day's play to sink a few castles and reflect on the match. Symmo has a great cricketing brain and I was a bit sad when he announced his retirement just before the '99 World Cup as I believe the team would have been more competitive had he been involved.

On the field, Hansie Cronje was a superb leader and an inspirational captain. He gave 110 percent, he pushed himself and his players very hard, always led from the front and he had a great desire to win. Off the field he was a gentleman. He is currently trying to put his life back together. I suppose we might never know the full story.

In the current team, "roomies" Mark Boucher and Jacques Kallis are known as the Mark and Jacques show, always in the thick of things going on around the team.

Neil McKenzie is one of the funniest cricketers you'll ever find, magnetizing his mates towards himself. He is a shrewd card player too. But he'll be remembered more in my mind for his quirky, superstitious nature when preparing for a match or an innings.

Craig Smith, a qualified physiotherapist with an honours degree in sports science, has been involved with South African cricket since 1990 and has been present at every match played by the national team since the comeback tour of India in 1991.

NEW MAN IN CHARGE . . . Gerald Majola gets his bearings in front of the United Cricket Board logo, which itself was to change during the year

Picture: Duif du Toit, TOUCHLINE PHOTO

MAJOLA'S VISION FOR SUCCESS

Michael Doman

Gerald Majola is part of a sporting dynasty that rivals another Eastern Cape family of greats, the Pollocks. Majola's late father Eric is a sporting legend in his home region and Mongezi Gerald and his late brother Khaya have been synonymous with Eastern Province cricket from the late 1970s.

Gerald's teenaged son, Allister, already has provincial representative colours, so the genes appear to have been passed on.

Now, settled in after his first few months in the job of chief executive of the United Cricket Board (he replaced 2003 Cricket World Cup executive director Dr Ali Bacher), Majola believes that even though some people in sporting circles may still not have bought into the post-apartheid unified dispensation, there is a new willingness for formerly opposing parties to throw in their lot together.

Black administrators have earned trust and respect. "You can see a change. People believe in what you say, that we're not here to do cricket down; we're also here to foster cricket," Majola says. "Yes, we played in different organisations, but it is accepted that we played national cricket. I don't think you'll ever have a 100 percent acceptance (of the new unified set-up) from both sides of the political divide but I think we are winning."

Majola's top priorities are transformation, the national team and devising plans to rejuvenate ailing domestic cricket.

Describing himself as a pragmatist, he says he propounds an open-door policy with the national team, with manager Goolam Rajah as intermediary. The team has done well in recent years, and there is a glint in Majola's eyes when he contemplates South Africa winning the World Cup in 2003 and, with a world Test championship in place, Australian captain Steve Waugh handing over the trophy for the leading five-day side to Shaun Pollock in the not-too-distant future.

Majola predicts that the 2003 World Cup in South Africa will be the best ever. Winning on the field is one thing but there is another level on which the World Cup could deliver victory.

"As with the Rugby World Cup in 1995, it should be a vehicle to help unify the country. It should enhance the government's vision of nation-building and reconciliation," he says. South Africa should strive to make the eighth staging of the tournament the best yet, something along the lines of Sydney's "best ever" Olympic Games. "The world should be seeing that we can live together here and that cricket can be a sport for all," he adds.

South Africa's glut of quality all-rounders equips the country well for the one-day world championship. "Lance Klusener, Shaun Pollock, Jacques Kallis, Nicky Boje and Mark Boucher - I don't think any other country is blessed with these resources. The only team threat talent-wise is Australia, the champions."

Transformation in the national team is happening at a satisfying pace, according to Majola, who says the quota system will become unnecessary in a couple of years' time if the current improvement is maintained. "I think by the World Cup we should have at least three young (black) players in the squad on merit. Of the new generation Mfuneko Ngam is doing tremendously well. Justin Ontong from Boland is magic but just not scoring runs. If Jonty Rhodes goes, that's his replacement."

Ontong, sent on the senior tour of the West Indies, did well enough but may need to be given sufficient opportunities, like a young Daryll Cullinan, according to Majola.

His promise to the national team is that he will hear them out. "They shouldn't have that much power maybe. People will have power if you let them run with it. We should be close to them and they should understand where we are coming from. I have strong views but I would listen to them too, to what they want, to find out what their obstacles, problems and views are. You cannot just take decisions for them. It's not fair, they won't perform. They must stay positive. Cricket is our product and our national team is what we sell to the public."

Transformation has progressed but Majola believes the pace must be kept up. "It is a process and we must make sure that we don't lose the impetus of setting the trend for other codes of sport. We must transform, but not at the expense of standards."

Describing himself as results-orientated, the 41-year-old Majola believes careful assessment of what different regions need is paramount. "It's not just a case of spreading mini-cricket all over and then finding we are still struggling to get two (black) players in some provincial teams. We have to understand the dynamics of each province."

"Development" to Majola means developing the game in all areas. "For example, I would term Nantie Hayward a development player, because he came through the ranks and was developed by Eastern Province. He comes from a disadvantaged background and also didn't go to the Greys of this world. You can still develop youngsters at Grey too. But the major emphasis is previously disadvantaged individuals and schools."

Proper marketing is seen as a vital ingredient in improving the lot of four-day cricket in South Africa. Officials and sponsors are well aware that as an entertainment "brand", cricket will have to be innovative. "We have to go the provincial CEOs and find out what the problems are, why no people are coming. We need to know so we can help them. If international cricket is the emphasis now it does not mean we should fold our arms."

Of vital importance to the rejuvenation of the domestic competitions is the participation of the top players. "Whatever recipe we devise, we must have the national players participating to put more bums on seats."

In his playing days, Majola represented Kwazakhele Rugby Union from 1980 to 1991, playing one season for the Tygerberg union as well.

His cricketing pedigree is impressive. Although he rates his leading of the SA Schools side of 1978-79 to victory in the South African Cricket Board's Booley Bowl (B Section) competition as a significant achievement, he represented Eastern Province at senior provincial level from 1974 to 1991. In that period he was selected for the SA A team (1987) and earned South African Council on Sport (Sacos) colours in 1988.

Majola entered unified cricket's administrative structures in the late 1990s, first at Eastern Province, where he was also the professional unit chairman. He became a UCB council member in 1998 and a national selector in 1999.

Before taking on cricket's top job Majola built up wide experience in the automotive field, insurance and property.

He overcame his trepidation at taking on one of the biggest jobs in South African sport after positive telephone conversations with his late brother Khaya, head of the UCB's amateur cricket and development portfolio until his death last year, and former president Nelson Mandela. Just as when waiting to go out to bat, he was experiencing definite nerves.

Mandela, he said, told him: "Just go out there and do it for us."

Michael Doman is cricket correspondent of the Cape Argus. He played first-class cricket for the Western Province Cricket Board team as a top-order batsman in the early 1980s.

WORLD TEST CHAMPIONSHIP

Michael Owen-Smith

The inaugural world test championship was never going to be perfect. But it represents a start and the system can be modified and improved without straying from the basic principle during its course of evolution. The intention of the championship is to add "interest, context and excitement to the highest form of the game," to quote from the International Cricket Council's press release.

That it certainly does although one personally feels that the ICC could have come up with a better points system without straying from the prime virtue of simplicity. At the moment teams are awarded two points for a series win (assuming they play a minimum of two matches) and one each for a drawn series.

There is no maximum number of matches for any particular series. In other words South Africa can continue to play five-Test series against the West Indies and England as can the latter against Australia. So far, so good. The major change one would like to see would be for teams to be rewarded for excellence. If, for example, a team manages to win 3-0 or 5-0, there should be at least one bonus point. There should also be some sort of reward for a team that wins an individual match by an innings, more than 200 runs or by seven or more wickets. The aim of the game must always be to reward excellence and to encourage the participants to be as attacking in their outlook as is humanly possible.

There also needs to be consistency in the board room. It is simply not fair to give South Africa two points for winning a home series against Zimbabwe when they, in fact, played two one-match series, the first at home and the second away. How must Sri Lanka feel about being done out of an away win against England in 1998 when they played only one Test and Zimbabwe about their similar home series against India?

There is one other very important point that needs to be addressed and that is a direct outcome of the report of Sir Paul Condon's Anti-Corruption Unit. If cricket is to become a "clean" game again, there is no room for matches that do not count, the so-called "dead rubber" in either Tests or one-day internationals. There is enough evidence to suggest that corruption is not restricted to the one-day form of the game but also raised its ugly head during certain Test matches, especially on the Asian sub-continent.

South Africa's final Test match in the West Indies last April was a case in point as were the last two matches of Australia's home series against the same opposition. Nobody has suggested that anything untoward happened in either case but the temptation is there. That is why one would like to see bonus points at stake in every single Test match that is played. It is a similar principle to the one used to decide the seedings for the 2003 World Cup. Make every game count.

It might well have persuaded England to take on Pakistan with very much more aggressive intent in the final game of their two-match series at Old Trafford this year. England needed only a draw to clinch the series and it showed in their outlook. How much better it would have been for the whole concept of Test cricket if they had gone for the jugular from the start.

So much for the mechanics of the system. There is little doubt that it has been a success in terms of context and interest. There may not have been too many spectators at the Test series between India and Zimbabwe on the African continent but you can rest assured that the whole cricketing world was following it closely. This was one of the series in which two points

WORLD CHAMPIONS . . . Australia's Shane Warne, Steve Waugh and Adam Gilchrist get their hands on the world championship trophy
Picture: ALLSPORT

were going to have quite an impact on the log because the two countries had never played more than a one-off Test in Zimbabwe before. The same applied to the series between Zimbabwe and the West Indies that followed.

There is one other very important reason for introducing a Test match championship. It was, in fact, the driving force that made former New Zealand chief executive Chris Doig pursue the concept with such zeal during his time in office. With every side due to play every other side both home and away over a five-year period, it ensures that the powerhouses of Australia, South Africa and elsewhere will be seen in action in every full member country on a regular basis.

Zimbabwe played its first test match in 1992 against India, yet had to wait until 1999 to host Australia in a Test match for the first time. There was a time when it looked as though the game was going to develop into separate A and B sections, albeit on an unofficial basis. That can now no longer happen.

The first championship log was backdated to June 1996. The intention is to have a five-year cut-off period but it would be unfair for a team to lose points because of fixture scheduling, so series will replace each other as they are played. That will inevitably lead to some series hanging on longer than the historic five-year date.

When all the teams have played each other, a straightforward points system will replace the current points average, which decides the placing.

ICC TEST CHAMPIONSHIP TABLE, AUGUST 2001

Team	Played	Won	Lost	Drawn	Points	Average
Australia	13	10	2	1	21	1.62
South Africa	15	10	3	2	22	1.47
England	14	7	5	2	16	1.14
Sri Lanka	13	5	5	3	13	1.00
West Indies	13	6	6	1	13	1.00
New Zealand	15	6	7	2	14	0.93
India	13	3	6	4	10	0.77
Pakistan	15	3	7	5	11	0.73
Zimbabwe	14	2	10	2	6	0.43
Bangladesh	1	0	1	0	0	-

2001/02 FIXTURES

(home teams first):
September: Pakistan v New Zealand, Zimbabwe v South Africa.
October: Bangladesh v Zimbabwe, South Africa v India.
November: Australia v New Zealand.
December: Australia v South Africa, India v England, Zimbabwe v Bangladesh, Sri Lanka v Zimbabwe.
January: Bangladesh v Pakistan.
February: New Zealand v England, India v Zimbabwe, Pakistan v West Indies, South Africa v Australia.
March: West Indies v New Zealand April: South Africa v Bangladesh, West Indies v India, Zimbabwe v Australia.
May: England v Sri Lanka.
July: England v India, Sri Lanka v Bangladesh.

Michael Owen-Smith, the son of a Test cricketer, is cricket correspondent of the Cape Times.

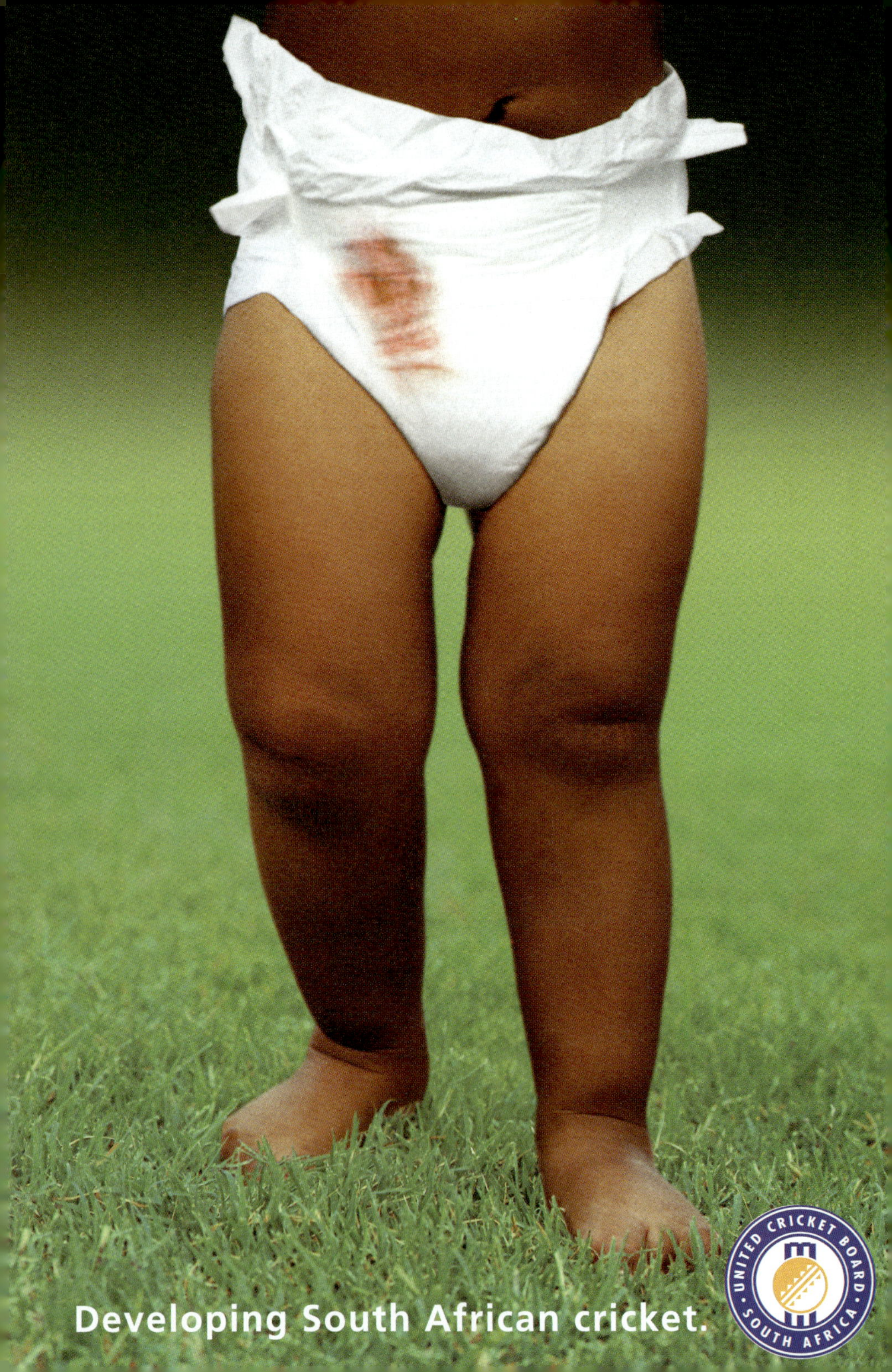
Developing South African cricket.
UNITED CRICKET BOARD SOUTH AFRICA

ICC TEST CHAMPIONSHIP RESULTS GRID

A W A Y

HOME		Aus	Bdesh	Eng	Ind	NZ	Pak	RSA	SL	WI	Zim
H	Australia	-	3-1 (5) 98/99	3-0 (3) 99/00	2-0 (3) 97/98	3-0 (3) 99/00	1-0 (3) 97/98	-	5-0 (5) 00/01	-	
O	Bangladesh	-		-	-	-	-	-	-	-	-
M	England	2-3 (6) 1997	-		1-0 (3) 1996	1-2 (4) 1999	1-1 (2) 2001	2-1 (5) 1998	-	3-1 (5) 2000	1-0 (2) 2000
E	India	2-1 (3) 00/01	-	-		1-0 (3) 99/00	1-1 (2) 98/99	0-2 (2) 99/00	0-0 (3) 97/98	-	1-0 (2) 00/01
	New Zealand	0-3 (3) 99/00	-	0-2 (3) 96/97	1-0 (2) 98/99		1-1 (3) 00/01	0-1 (3) 98/99	2-0 (2) 96/97	2-0 (2) 99/00	2-0 (2) 97/98
	Pakistan	0-1 (3) 98/99	-	0-1 (3) 00/01	-	1-1 (2) 96/97		0-1 (3) 97/98	1-2 (3) 99/00	3-0 (3) 97/98	0-1 (2) 98/99
	South Africa	1-2 (3) 96/97	-	2-1 (5) 99/00	2-0 (3) 96/97	2-0 (3) 00/01	1-1 (3) 97/98		2-0 (3) 00/01	5-0 (5) 98/99	2-0 (2) 99/00
	Sri Lanka	1-0 (3) 99/00	-	1-2 (3) 00/01	0-0 (2) 97/98	2-1 (3) 97/98	0-2 (3) 99/00	1-1 (3) 00/01		-	2-0 (2) 97/98
	West Indies	2-2 (4) 98/99	-	3-1 (6) 97/98	1-0 (5) 96/97	-	1-0 (3) 99/00	1-2 (5) 00/01	1-0 (2) 96/97		2-0 (2) 99/00
	Zimbabwe	- 00/01	2-0 (2) 96/97	0-0 (2) 2001	1-1 (2) 00/01	0-2 (2) 97/98	0-1 (2)	- 99/00	0-1 (3) 2001	0-1 (2)	

SAME SCHOOLS, DIFFERENT SHADES

John Young

In the two decades before cricket unity, traditional English-speaking boys' schools provided 73% of the players for the South African Schools team. The SA under-15 and SA Schools teams chosen in 2000 had 77% representation from the same schools which suggests that not much has changed. Closer examination reveals that South African youth cricket has changed a great deal.

The statistics for 2000 actually represent a shift back to English-speaking boys' schools, reversing a trend towards other schools and clubs that provided increasing numbers of SA Schools players after unity. The chief difference is in the number of players of colour (reflected below in brackets as a percentage of the overall total of players selected):

The table below shows the percentage of SA Schools players provided by English-speaking boys' schools (ESBS), Afrikaans schools and other schools and clubs. The figures for 2000 include players selected for the South African under 15 team.

Period	**ESBS**	**AFRIKAANS**	**OTHER**
1962-71	88	3	9
1972-81	73	14	13
1982-91	74 (3)	16	10 (2)
Post-Unity:			
1992-99	60 (12)	26	14 (11)
2000	77 (38)	15	8 (4)

Representation of players of colour has grown from 5% before unity to 23% in the post-unity years to 1999 and 42% in South Africa's two youth teams last year.

Between 1982 and 1991, 122 boys earned SA Schools caps. Ninety of these were educated at English-speaking boys' schools, of whom only three were not white: Craig Marais and Herschelle Gibbs from Bishops (1984 and 1991) and Morgan Mfobo from SACS (1991). Twenty-six players earned national youth colours in 2000. Of these, 20 were ESBS boys and exactly half of these were players of colour.

The role of South African cricket's traditional nurseries has been preserved and a far broader range of young talent now has access to good facilities and coaching. Some players of colour received UCB, provincial or school bursaries, others simply enrolled.

There have been some unusual years. In 1990, captain Nicky Boje was joined by a number of Afrikaans speakers from Boland. In that year, the ESBS provided just five of the 13 selected (38%). More typical selections took place in 1983 (83%) and 1985 (75%). In the modern era, ESBS provided 'only' 50% of the SA Schools team in 1998 and 1999 but in 2000 the figure was back to 75%, more in line with the percentages at the beginning of the post-unity period: 1992 (77%) and 1993 (70%).

Some English-speaking boys' schools have been identified as nurseries by the UCB and this has had an effect on the make-up of the national schools selection. One of the first Xhosa-speakers to earn SA Schools selection, Eastern Province's Lulama Masikazana, would almost certainly have earned those colours out of Grey High School if he were playing today. In 1992 he represented the United Cavaliers.

SAME SCHOOLS, DIFFERENT SHADES

Conrad Jantjes (CBC Boksburg) and Robin Peterson (Alexander Road), both capped in 1996, are other examples of players who in the present environment would be encouraged to attend one of the 'bigger' cricket schools. Which is not to suggest that all talented cricketers should attend such schools but there is a trend towards such 'transfers'. Alexander Road has produced many fine cricketers and when Thami Tsolekile (SA Schools captain 1998-99) played for Pinelands High School they expected to beat the traditional boys' schools.

The percentage of players selected for SA Schools from outside the ESBS grew from 26% in the pre-unity decade to 40% in the period 1992-1999. In the year 2000, that figure fell again to 25%.

Afrikaans-speaking representation in the SA Schools team has grown steadily. In another of post-apartheid South Africa's little ironies, the best period of representation for white Afrikaners has been since the advent of democracy and majority rule. From 3% in the 1960s, through 14% and 16% in the next two decades, the post-unity period saw Afrikaans schools provide 26% of the national schools team. Afrikaans representation has also spread beyond its traditional power base of Grey College in Bloemfontein.

Between 1972 and 1991, Grey boys made up nearly half of Afrikaans speakers in the Schools XI. Since unity, Grey's contribution has slipped to 14% as schools like Daniel Pienaar and Afrikaans Seuns Hoër have grown in cricketing stature.

A significant change has occurred in the background of the players selected from clubs and co-ed schools. The overall percentage of players from these schools and clubs has not changed much (10% pre-unity to 14% post-unity) but the percentage of players of colour has changed radically. Salieg Nackerdien (1983), Shukri Conrad (1984) and Masikazana were the only persons of colour in this category to make the select XI before unity (2% of the total).

Between 1992 and 1999 these clubs and schools had 14 players selected, of whom 11 were players of colour (11% of the total). The SA under 15 team selected to participate in the World Youth Challenge last year was the first in which the majority of the players were not white. Denis Lindsay's selection panel included players from every group of people who have a history of playing cricket: Xhosa speakers from the Eastern Cape, a Muslim from the Western Cape, a South African of Indian descent from KwaZulu-Natal, white Afrikaans speakers from Bloemfontein and Pretoria and English speakers from Pietermaritzburg and Johannesburg.

The original selection of 14 included 11 players attending traditional English-speaking boys' schools. According to one selector, they only became aware of the 'representivity' issue once the team was announced and the historic implications were pointed out by Dr Ali Bacher. Taken as a whole, the period after unity has shown a shift away from the traditional English-speaking boys' schools in the selection of the SA Schools team. However, if the 2000 figures are an indication then schools like Grey High, Durban HS, SACS, King Edward VII, St Andrew's and Selborne will continue to be the training grounds for the majority of the country's best cricketers. Those best cricketers are now more likely to be drawn from the majority of the population.

At one level, the number of players of colour at traditional schools represents a feather in the cap for the development programme but it also reveals a major challenge for the next phase. The challenge is to upgrade cricket coaching and facilities in black, coloured and Indian schools so that players from those schools can compete on an equal footing.

John Young, a freelance writer, is a former schoolteacher who continues to spend many hours coaching young cricketers as well as maintaining a keen interest in trends in schools cricket.

Section B: International Cricket

ICC KNOCKOUT TROPHY 2000/01

South Africa went to the ICC Knockout tournament in Nairobi, Kenya, as defending champions, having won the inaugural tournament in Dhaka, Bangladesh, in 1998/99. On this occasion, however, the campaign ended at the semifinal stage when a magnificent innings by Sourav Ganguly, the Indian captain, put the game beyond South Africa's reach. New Zealand were surprise winners, beating India in an exciting final.

South Africa sent 14 players to the tournament, including the uncapped Eastern Province off-spinner Shafiek Abrahams, who at the age of 32 was likely to be the last player to win national recognition after starting his provincial career in pre-unity days under the former SA Cricket Board. Abrahams, however, together with Neil McKenzie and Makhaya Ntini, did not get a game in Kenya.

The squad was: Shaun Pollock (captain), Mark Boucher (vice-captain), Shafiek Abrahams, Nicky Boje, Boeta Dippenaar, Allan Donald, Andrew Hall, Jacques Kallis, Gary Kirsten, Lance Klusener, Neil McKenzie, Makhaya Ntini, Jonty Rhodes, Roger Telemachus. Manager, Goolam Rajah; coach, Graham Ford; assistant coach, Corrie van Zyl; physiotherapist, Craig Smith.

All matches were played at the Nairobi Gymkhana club which had improved its facilities for the occasion. A disappointing aspect was the poor attendances, with high prices blamed for the lack of support by the local population. Mainly through television and advertising income, the tournament generated a profit of US$13-million for international cricket development.

ENGLAND v SOUTH AFRICA — ICC Knockout Trophy Quarterfinal

Played at Nairobi Gymkhana, Nairobi on 10 October 2000 — Toss: England
Umpires: DB Hair & S Venkataraghavan (TV: SA Bucknor)
Debuts: Eng: AP Grayson. SA: None
Result: South Africa won by 8 wickets
Man of Match: Jacques Kallis

Magnificent bowling by Pollock and Telemachus, who between them conceded only five runs in the first eight overs, put England under pressure from the start. The left-handed Trescothick edged Pollock between wicketkeeper and slip for four in the ninth over, then slashed another boundary and pulled a six in the same over before giving a sharp return chance. His aggressive burst was cut short in Pollock's next over when he hit a slower ball to mid-on. Thereafter only Hick had the better of a disciplined bowling attack.

On a small ground, England's total of 182 was never likely to be enough. Hall went cheaply but Kirsten and Kallis batted positively before Dippenaar played a delightful innings, notching his first international half-century and finishing the match by hitting White over long-off for six.

ENGLAND	Runs	Mins	Balls	4	6
ME Trescothick c Donald b Pollock	26	42	36	3	1
†AJ Stewart c Dippenaar b Donald	18	70	47	3	-
*N Hussain c Boucher b Donald	5	18	11	-	-
GA Hick c Hall b Kallis	65	108	68	9	-
GP Thorpe c Hall b Boje	14	39	31	1	-
A Flintoff c Klusener b Pollock	25	41	37	2	-
C White run out (Rhodes)	3	5	2	-	-
MA Ealham c Boucher b Pollock	10	30	26	1	-
AP Grayson c Pollock b Kallis	0	1	1	-	-
AR Caddick run out (Boje)	0	9	4	-	-
D Gough not out	6	9	5	1	-
Extras (lb 2, w 5, nb 3)	10				
TOTAL (44.1 overs)	**182**				

SOUTH AFRICA	Runs	Mins	Balls	4	6
AJ Hall c Hick b Gough	1	15	11	11	-
G Kirsten c Hick b White	32	48	34	7	-
JH Kallis not out	78	146	110	10	-
HH Dippenaar not out	65	113	86	9	2
JN Rhodes					
L Klusener					
†MV Boucher					
*SM Pollock					
N Boje					
R Telemachus					
AA Donald					
Extras (w 2, nb 6)	8				
TOTAL (for 2 wkts) (39.1 overs)	**184**				

SA	O	M	R	W
Pollock	9.1	2	27	3
Telemachus	9	2	45	0
Donald	8	1	25	2
Kallis	8	0	26	2
Boje	5	0	24	1
Klusener	5	0	33	0

Eng	O	M	R	W
Caddick	7	1	40	0
Gough	9	2	43	1
White	8.1	0	40	1
Ealham	10	1	41	0
Grayson	5	0	20	0

Fall of Wickets	Eng	SA
1st	33 (1)	19 (1)
2nd	50 (3)	52 (2)
3rd	55 (2)	-
4th	89 (5)	-
5th	154 (6)	-
6th	160 (7)	-
7th	167 (4)	-
8th	168 (9)	-
9th	174 (10)	-
10th	182 (8)	-

INDIA v SOUTH AFRICA

ICC Knockout Trophy Semifinal

Played at Nairobi Gymkhana, Nairobi on 13 October 2000

Toss: India

Umpires: SA Bucknor & P Willey (TV: DR Shepherd)

Debuts: Ind: None. SA: None

Result: India won by 95 runs

Man of Match: Sourav Ganguly

India made a flying start, in stark contrast to England three days earlier. Ganguly and Tendulkar posted 43 off the first eight overs, 38 more than England at the same stage. Tendulkar was dropped by Klusener at midwicket off Telemachus when he had 35 but was out soon afterwards, caught at slip.

Ganguly had been relatively quiet while Tendulkar went for his shots but the Indian captain went on to flay the South African bowling. Boje, South Africa's only spinner, was hit for three sixes in the two overs he bowled. The left-hander was caught by Rhodes off Klusener when he had 75 but it was a no-ball. Ganguly and Dravid put on 145 at almost a run a ball. Klusener dismissed Dravid in the 40th over and Yuvraj Singh was missed by Boje at midwicket in the same over before he too joined in the run feast. Ganguly hit two sixes off successive balls from Kallis in the 47th over, the first a mistimed pull which sailed over the short leg-side boundary.

South Africa lost three wickets in the first five overs and despite a valiant effort from Boucher were unable to get back into the game.

Telemachus was called before the match referee, Cammie Smith of the West Indies, and banned for one international match for "conduct unbecoming" after he barged into Dravid while he was bowling during the Indian innings.

INDIA	Runs	Mins	Balls	4	6
*SC Ganguly not out	141	216	142	12	6
SR Tendulkar c Klusener b Kallis	39	61	50	4	-
RS Dravid c Boucher b Klusener	58	106	71	8	-
Yuvraj Singh c Rhodes b Kallis	41	39	35	6	-
RR Singh run out (Donald)	0	1	1	-	-
VG Kambli lbw b Donald	0	1	1	-	-
†V Dahiya c Hall b Donald	1	3	3	-	-
AB Agarkar					
A Kumble					
Z Khan					
BK Venkatesh Prasad					
Extras (b 1, lb 6, w 5, nb 3)	15				
TOTAL (for 6 wkts) (50 overs)	**295**				

SOUTH AFRICA	Runs	Mins	Balls	4	6
G Kirsten run out (Ganguly)	12	19	13	2	-
AJ Hall b Khan	1	10	4	-	-
JH Kallis c Ganguly b Venkatesh Prasad	15	29	18	3	-
HH Dippenaar c Dahiya b Khan	5	4	6	1	-
JN Rhodes c Venkatesh Prasad b Yuvraj Singh	32	73	55	2	1
†MV Boucher c Tendulkar b Ganguly	60	98	77	9	-
L Klusener c Dahiya b Kumble	29	67	37	2	-
*SM Pollock st Dahiya b Kumble	4	17	10	-	-
N Boje b Tendulkar	10	24	16	-	-
R Telemachus c Venkatesh Prasad b Tendulkar	13	13	13	2	-
AA Donald not out	1	1	1	-	-
Extras (b 3, lb 4, w 7, nb 4)	18				
TOTAL (41 overs)	**200**				

SA	O	M	R	W
Pollock	10	1	43	0
Telemachus	9	0	62	0
Donald	10	1	34	2
Kallis	10	0	71	2
Klusener	6	0	29	1
Boje	2	0	26	0
Hall	3	0	23	0

Ind	O	M	R	W
Khan	5	0	27	2
Venkatesh Prasad	8	0	54	1
Kumble	9	1	28	2
Agarkar	7	1	21	0
Yuvraj Singh	4	1	15	1
Tendulkar	5	0	32	2
Singh	2	0	11	0
Ganguly	1	0	5	1

Fall of Wickets	Ind	SA
1st	66 (2)	13 (2)
2nd	211 (3)	23 (1)
3rd	293 (4)	28 (4)
4th	293 (5)	50 (3)
5th	293 (6)	106 (5)
6th	295 (7)	161 (6)
7th	-	171 (8)
8th	-	179 (7)
9th	-	199 (10)
10th	-	200 (9)

OTHER RESULTS

FIRST ROUND

Kenya v India, 3 October 2000. Toss: India. **Kenya** 208/9 in 50 overs (RD Shah 60, MO Odumbe 51, Zaheer Khan 3/48). **India** 209/2 in 42.3 overs (SC Ganguly 66, RS Dravid 68*). **India won by 8 wickets.**

Sri Lanka v West Indies, 4 October 2000. Toss: West Indies. **Sri Lanka** 287/6 in 50 overs (DA Gunawardene 132, DPMD Jayawardene 72, RP Arnold 41). **West Indies** 179 in 46.4 overs (LR Williams 41, DNT Zoysa 3/34). **Sri Lanka won by 108 runs.**

Bangladesh v England, 5 October 2000. Toss: Bangladesh. **Bangladesh** 232/8 in 50 overs (Javed Omar 63*, Naimur Rahman 46, MA Ealham 3/48). **England** 236/2 in 43.5 overs (AJ Stewart 87*, N Hussain 95). **England won by 8 wickets.**

QUARTERFINALS

Australia v India, 7 October 2000. Toss: Australia. **India** 265/9 in 50 overs (Yuvraj Singh 84). **Australia** 245 in 46.4 overs (RT Ponting 46, MG Bevan 42). **India won by 20 runs.**

Pakistan v Sri Lanka, 8 October 2000. Toss: Sri Lanka. **Sri Lanka** 194 in 45.3 overs (Azhar Mahmood 3/52). **Pakistan** 195/1 in 43.1 overs (Saeed Anwar 105*, Imran Nazir 40, Yousuf Youhana 42*). **Pakistan won by 9 wickets.**

New Zealand v Zimbabwe, 9 October 2000. Toss: Zimbabwe. **New Zealand** 265/7 in 50 overs (RG Twose 85, CD McMillan 52, HK Olonga 3/58). **Zimbabwe** 201 in 42.2 overs (ADR Campbell 47, SV Carlisle 67, PJ Wiseman 4/45). **New Zealand won by 64 runs.**

SEMIFINALS

New Zealand v Pakistan, 11 October 2000. Toss: Pakistan. **Pakistan** 252 in 49.2 overs (Saeed Anwar 104, Abdur Razzaq 48, SB O'Connor 5/46). **New Zealand** 255/8 in 49 overs (NJ Astle 49, RG Twose 87, CD McMillan 51*). **New Zealand won by 2 wickets.**

FINAL

India v New Zealand, 15 October 2000. Toss: New Zealand. **India** 264/6 in 50 overs (SC Ganguly 117, SR Tendulkar 69). **New Zealand** 265/6 in 49.4 overs (CL Cairns 102*, CZ Harris 46, BK Venkatesh Prasad 3/27). **New Zealand won by 4 wickets.**

SOUTH AFRICA: ICC KNOCKOUT TROPHY IN KENYA 2000/01 AVERAGES

Name	M	Inns	NO	Runs	HS	Avg	BF	SR	100	50	Ct	St	O	M	Runs	Wkts	Avg	RpO	BB	4I
N Boje	2	1	0	10	10	10.00	16	62.50	0	0	0	0	7	0	50	1	50.00	7.14	1-24	0
MV Boucher	2	1	0	60	60	60.00	77	77.92	0	1	3	0	0	0	0	0	-	-	-	0
HH Dippenaar	2	2	1	70	65*	70.00	92	76.08	0	1	1	0	0	0	0	0	-	-	-	0
AA Donald	2	1	1	1	1*	-	1	100.00	0	0	1	0	18	2	59	4	14.75	3.27	2-25	0
AJ Hall	2	2	0	2	1	1.00	15	13.33	0	0	3	0	3	0	23	0	-	7.66	-	0
JH Kallis	2	2	1	93	78*	93.00	128	72.65	0	1	0	0	18	0	97	4	24.25	5.38	2-26	0
G Kirsten	2	2	0	44	32	22.00	47	93.61	0	0	0	0	0	0	0	0	-	-	-	0
L Klusener	2	1	0	29	29	29.00	37	78.37	0	0	2	0	11	0	62	1	62.00	5.63	1-29	0
SM Pollock	2	1	0	4	4	4.00	10	40.00	0	0	1	0	19.1	3	70	3	23.33	3.65	3-27	0
JN Rhodes	2	1	0	32	32	32.00	55	58.18	0	0	1	0	0	0	0	0	-	-	-	0
R Telemachus	2	1	0	13	13	13.00	13	100.00	0	0	0	0	18	2	107	0	-	5.94	-	0
Totals	22	15	3	358	78*		491	72.91	0	3	12	0	94.1	7	468	13			3-27	0
			Extras	26						subs	0			b & lb	9	3 run outs				
			Total	384		32.00					12			Total	477	16	29.81	5.06		

PULLING AWAY . . . Nicky Boje on the way to a thrilling limited overs century against New Zealand at Centurion Park *Picture: Tertius Pickard, TOUCHLINE PHOTO*

NEW ZEALAND IN SOUTH AFRICA 2000/01

Colin Bryden

The New Zealand team arrived in South Africa immediately after one of the most significant triumphs in their country's cricket history, having won the ICC Knockout Trophy in Nairobi, Kenya.

If they had high hopes of a successful tour they were to be quickly dashed, with South Africa dominating the limited overs series which started the tour before going on to win the Test series in similarly convincing fashion.

While South Africa played much outstanding cricket, the tourists were unusually unlucky in suffering a freakishly high number of injuries, mainly to their fast bowlers, although the capable opening batsman, Matt Horne, and the world-class left-arm slow bowler Daniel Vettori were also ruled out.

Chris Cairns, the match winner in Nairobi, struggled through the limited overs games but was clearly suffering from a right knee injury and went home before the Test matches. Simon Doull and Dion Nash did not get to South Africa at all. Geoff Allott played only in alternate limited overs games because of a back injury and also did not stay for the Tests.

All-rounder Scott Styris and off-spinner Paul Wiseman were injured too and in a bizarre twist, Andrew Penn, who had been selected originally but could not travel because he was injured in a club game, arrived as a replacement, took five wickets in an innings against Border and promptly broke down again.

Such setbacks would have tested the best of teams and New Zealand simply did not have the resources to mount a real challenge to a solid South African batting order, although Chris Martin, who owed his appearances in the Tests to the misfortunes of others, established himself as a spirited and capable fast-medium bowler.

One of the few New Zealanders who lit up the South African summer was Roger Twose, the combative left-handed batsman, who played superbly in the one-day games but was not available for the Test matches, having retired from the longer version of the game.

Mark Richardson, a left-handed opening batsman, performed solidly while Mathew Sinclair made 150, the highest score by a New Zealand batsman in South Africa, in the Port Elizabeth Test. Stephen Fleming, the captain, battled manfully and conducted himself with dignity but it was an unequal struggle.

From a South African point of view, the misfortunes of their opponents should not detract from a consistently high level of professionalism. It was Shaun Pollock's first home Test series and the team did all that could have been expected of them.

Neil McKenzie established himself as a Test player and Makhaya Ntini made a major advance to be the leading wicket taker in the Test series, while Mfuneko Ngam made an exciting debut in the rain-ruined third Test. A highlight of the series was Allan Donald's achievement in becoming the first South African to take 300 Test wickets, reaching the landmark in the first Test in Bloemfontein, his home town.

GAUTENG v NEW ZEALANDERS — Limited Overs Match

Played at Soweto Cricket Oval, Soweto on 18 October 2000 — Toss: New Zealanders
Umpires: ST Jivan & SB Lambson (TV: KH Hurter)
Debuts: Gau: None. NZ: None
Result: New Zealanders won by 79 runs
Man of Match: Nathan Astle

NEW ZEALAND IN SOUTH AFRICA 2000/01

New Zealand made a confident start to the tour, with Nathan Astle hammering a century and Fleming, the captain, ending a lean spell as he shared a second wicket stand of 185 with the opening batsman. Leg-spinner Brooke Walker, who had not been part of the ICC trophy-winning squad, took four wickets as the tourists gained a convincing win, despite a fine 98-run opening stand between international players Adam Bacher and Andrew Hall.

NEW ZEALANDERS	Runs	Mins	Balls	4	6
†CJ Nevin c Seymore b Hall	6	11	9	1	-
NJ Astle b de Bruyn	137	223	168	10	2
*SP Fleming c Ndima b de Bruyn	82	139	104	8	-
RG Twose b Mataboge	24	24	17	1	2
CD McMillan c Street b de Bruyn	10	24	12	-	-
AC Parore not out	1	3	1	-	-
CM Spearman not out	0	1	1	-	-
BGK Walker					
PJ Wiseman					
DR Tuffey					
SB O'Connor					
Extras (b 1, lb 6, w 19, nb 10)	36				
TOTAL (for 5 wkts) (50 overs)	**296**				

GAUTENG	Runs	Mins	Balls	4	6
AM Bacher c Nevin b Walker	54	81	73	6	-
AJ Hall c and b Wiseman	44	93	71	4	-
SG Koenig c Fleming b Walker	10	21	20	1	-
AJ Seymore not out	48	83	59	4	-
Z de Bruyn c Nevin b Walker	17	26	32	-	-
G Toyana c sub (SB Styris) b Walker	11	24	21	-	-
SS Ndima c McMillan b Fleming	22	17	18	2	1
†MR Street not out	5	5	6	-	-
*CE Eksteen					
TK Mataboge					
JT Mafa					
Extras (lb 3, w 3)	6				
TOTAL (for 6 wkts) (50 overs)	**217**				

Gau	O	M	R	W
Hall	10	0	48	1
Mafa	8	0	53	0
Mataboge	10	0	54	1
de Bruyn	8	0	63	3
Eksteen	9	0	38	0
Bacher	5	0	33	0

NZ	O	M	R	W
O'Connor	5	1	17	0
Tuffey	10	0	46	0
McMillan	8	0	54	0
Astle	6	0	29	0
Wiseman	10	0	33	1
Walker	10	1	32	4
Fleming	1	0	3	1

Fall of Wickets	NZ	Gau
1st	14 (1)	98 (1)
2nd	199 (3)	104 (2)
3rd	245 (4)	116 (3)
4th	295 (2)	156 (5)
5th	296 (5)	176 (6)
6th	-	205 (7)

SOUTH AFRICA v NEW ZEALAND — 1st Limited Overs International

Played at North West Stadium, Potchefstroom on 20 October 2000 — Toss: New Zealand
Umpires: RE Koertzen & DL Orchard (TV: DF Becker)
Debuts: SA: None. NZ: None
Result: No Result

Daryll Cullinan was recalled to the South African limited overs squad in place of Neil McKenzie in the only change from the party that went to Kenya for the ICC Knockout tournament.

It was the first international match staged in Potchefstroom and a capacity crowd of 10 000, packed into a well-prepared ground, saw some thrilling batting on an ideal one-day pitch before a huge thunderstorm washed out play. An earlier stoppage came with Boje on 84 but five further overs were possible during which the left-hander completed a superb maiden international century off 89 balls. He was well supported by Dippenaar.

SOUTH AFRICA	Runs	Mins	Balls	4	6
HH Dippenaar c O'Connor b Harris	57	119	104	6	-
G Kirsten c Cairns b O'Connor	13	32	18	1	-
N Boje not out	105	111	93	12	-
JH Kallis not out	8	27	16	-	-
DJ Cullinan					
JN Rhodes					
L Klusener					
†MV Boucher					
*SM Pollock					
AA Donald					
M Ntini					
Extras (lb 3, w 2, nb 3)	8				
TOTAL (for 2 wkts) (38 overs)	**191**				

NEW ZEALAND
NJ Astle
CJ Nevin
*SP Fleming
RG Twose
CL Cairns
CD McMillan
CZ Harris
†AC Parore
SB Styris
SB O'Connor
GI Allott

NZ	O	M	R	W
Allott	7	1	33	0
O'Connor	8	0	41	1
Cairns	8	1	34	0
Styris	3	0	21	0
Harris	7	1	32	1
Astle	5	0	27	0

Fall of Wickets	SA
1st	33 (2)
2nd	162 (1)

SOUTH AFRICA v NEW ZEALAND — 2nd Limited Overs International

Played at Willowmoore Park, Benoni on 22 October 2000 — Toss: New Zealand
Umpires: DF Becker & RE Koertzen (TV: SB Lambson)
Debuts: SA: None. NZ: None
Result: South Africa won by 6 wickets
Man of Match: Nicky Boje

Boje played his second sparkling pinch-hitting innings in three days and was rewarded with both a victory for his team and the man of the match award. The start was delayed by an hour after overnight rain and New Zealand struggled on a slow pitch, with low and uneven bounce, which Fleming expected to become more difficult for batting in the second innings. His theory could not be put to the test because his batsmen did not score enough runs.

Telemachus bowled superbly after serving a one-match suspension for barging into an opponent in Kenya while Donald picked up wickets with the first deliveries of his first two spells.

Kirsten and Boje took South Africa a long way towards victory in a second wicket stand of 111 off 140 balls, with Boje again striking the ball cleanly.

NEW ZEALAND	Runs	Mins	Balls	4	6
CJ Nevin lbw b Telemachus	5	21	16	-	-
NJ Astle b Donald	58	162	105	7	-
*SP Fleming b Donald	5	28	22	1	-
RG Twose b Kallis	16	34	32	1	-
CL Cairns b Klusener	26	52	44	1	1
CZ Harris c Kallis b Pollock	19	53	38	3	-
CD McMillan lbw b Pollock	13	22	18	2	-
†AC Parore c Rhodes b Kallis	11	19	11	2	-
SB Styris not out	10	19	9	1	-
BGK Walker not out	5	8	7	-	-
PJ Wiseman					
Extras (b 1, lb 10, w 13, nb 2)	26				
TOTAL (for 8 wkts) (50 overs)	**194**				

SOUTH AFRICA	Runs	Mins	Balls	4	6
G Kirsten b Styris	57	106	93	3	-
HH Dippenaar c Styris b Cairns	9	28	22	2	-
N Boje c Twose b Harris	64	97	83	6	1
JH Kallis not out	39	56	52	7	-
DJ Cullinan c Cairns b Harris	0	17	14	-	-
JN Rhodes not out	17	20	17	3	-
L Klusener					
†MV Boucher					
*SM Pollock					
R Telemachus					
AA Donald					
Extras (lb 3, w 7, nb 1)	11				
TOTAL (for 4 wkts) (46.4 overs)	**197**				

SA	O	M	R	W
Pollock	10	1	32	2
Telemachus	10	5	16	1
Kallis	7	1	34	2
Donald	10	1	51	2
Klusener	8	0	32	1
Boje	5	1	18	0

NZ	O	M	R	W
Cairns	8	0	38	1
Styris	10	1	24	1
Astle	3	0	19	0
McMillan	3	0	20	0
Harris	10	0	39	2
Wiseman	4.4	0	24	0
Walker	8	2	30	0

Fall of Wickets	NZ	SA
1st	10 (1)	25 (2)
2nd	38 (3)	136 (1)
3rd	65 (4)	158 (3)
4th	118 (5)	159 (5)
5th	134 (2)	-
6th	162 (7)	-
7th	165 (6)	-
8th	183 (8)	-

SOUTH AFRICA v NEW ZEALAND — 3rd Limited Overs International

Played at SuperSport Park, Centurion on 25 October 2000 — Toss: New Zealand
Umpires: SB Lambson & DL Orchard (TV: BG Jerling)
Debuts: SA: None. NZ: None
Result: South Africa won by 115 runs (D/L method), target revised to 305 in 43 overs
Man of Match: Nicky Boje

Boje hammered his second century in three matches. He made a career-best 129 then had a hand in three of New Zealand's first six wickets as South Africa won a rain-interrupted match.

Boje shared a South African second wicket record stand of 160 with Kirsten as South Africa piled up their highest total against a Test nation, after being sent in on an excellent batting pitch. It was only four short of their highest against all-comers, against Holland in the 1996 World Cup.

An already difficult task for New Zealand became near-impossible after a rain interruption early in their innings which left them with a revised target of 305 from 43 overs.

Astle shared stands of 56 off 46 balls with Fleming and 72 off 74 balls with Twose as New Zealand stayed on target for a while. Then Roger Telemachus bowled Twose and Cairns with successive deliveries to start a collapse.

Boje was in sparkling form and South Africa raced to 95 for one in the first 15 overs. Aftera period of consolidation, the scoring rate accelerated again in the last 20 overs. Boje reached his fifty off 47 balls with six fours and his century off 101 deliveries with nine boundaries before cutting loose. He was caught on the straight boundary off the penultimate ball of the innings.

SOUTH AFRICA	Runs	Mins	Balls	4	6
DJ Cullinan b Cairns	22	34	28	2	1
G Kirsten c Parore b Cairns	94	135	113	8	-
N Boje c Cairns b Allott	129	164	114	13	1
JH Kallis c Twose b Styris	45	47	38	2	2
L Klusener not out	17	17	11	2	-
JN Rhodes not out	0	1	0	-	-
HH Dippenaar					
†MV Boucher					
*SM Pollock					
R Telemachus					
AA Donald					
Extras (lb 5, w 4, nb 8)	17				
TOTAL (for 4 wkts) (50 overs)	**324**				

NEW ZEALAND	Runs	Mins	Balls	4	6
CJ Nevin c Boje b Telemachus	7	4	7	1	-
NJ Astle c Dippenaar b Boje	46	121	64	3	2
*SP Fleming c Kirsten b Pollock	35	34	26	7	-
RG Twose b Telemachus	40	60	37	7	-
CL Cairns b Telemachus	0	1	1	-	-
CD McMillan run out (Boje/Boucher)	13	11	11	1	1
CZ Harris c Cullinan b Donald	17	36	26	2	-
†AC Parore not out	17	43	23	-	1
SB Styris c Boucher b Donald	1	3	2	-	-
SB O'Connor c Boucher b Pollock	1	5	3	-	-
GI Allott c Boucher b Pollock	0	3	3	-	-
Extras (b 5, lb 5, w 1, nb 1)	12				
TOTAL (33.4 overs)	**189**				

NZ	O	M	R	W
O'Connor	6	0	46	0
Allott	10	0	69	1
Cairns	8	0	62	2
Styris	10	0	56	1
Harris	10	0	55	0
Astle	6	0	31	0

SA	O	M	R	W
Pollock	7.4	1	37	3
Telemachus	6	1	45	3
Donald	7	1	27	2
Kallis	7	0	39	0
Klusener	5	0	29	0
Boje	1	0	2	1

Fall of Wickets	SA	NZ
1st	44 (1)	7 (1)
2nd	204 (2)	63 (3)
3rd	283 (4)	135 (4)
4th	322 (3)	135 (5)
5th	-	149 (6)
6th	-	151 (2)
7th	-	185 (7)
8th	-	187 (9)
9th	-	189 (10)
10th	-	189 (11)

SOUTH AFRICA v NEW ZEALAND — 4th Limited Overs International

Played at De Beers Diamond Oval, Kimberley on 28 October 2000 — Toss: South Africa
Umpires: BG Jerling & RE Koertzen (TV: WA Diedricks)
Debuts: SA: None. NZ: None
Result: South Africa won by 5 wickets
Man of Match: Gary Kirsten

South Africa clinched the series when they had the better of a run feast on a true batting pitch and fast outfield. New Zealand set a formidable target after being sent in but Kirsten and Kallis batted superbly, putting on 172 for the second wicket, beating the record of 160 set by Kirsten and Boje in the previous match.

Twose had a lucky let-off before he had scored when the South Africans celebrated what they thought was a run-out after quick fielding by Rhodes, who flicked the ball into the stumps as Twose strayed from the non-striker's end. Although fixed cameras were operating in line with the creases, a power failure affected the television van and television umpire Diedricks had no conclusive picture.

The English-born left-hander went on to play aggressively, sharing a third wicket stand of 110 with Fleming. The pattern of the innings was set by Nevin, who hooked and drove impressively.

South Africa batted aggressively from the start with Cullinan and Kirsten putting on 43 in 6.3 overs before Kallis joined Kirsten, who reached a South African record tenth one-day century off 104 balls. Boucher and Boje both hit sixes off Cairns in the 49th over to enable South Africa to win.

NEW ZEALAND	Runs	Mins	Balls	4	6
CJ Nevin b Boje	68	86	69	8	1
NJ Astle c Boucher b Telemachus	5	19	14	1	-
*SP Fleming run out (Dippenaar/Boucher)	85	139	103	5	-
RG Twose c Pollock b Kallis	89	109	91	9	1
CL Cairns c Pollock b Kallis	21	25	16	1	1
CD McMillan c Kirsten b Pollock	1	4	3	-	-
CZ Harris not out	11	7	5	2	-
†AC Parore not out	0	1	0	-	-
SB Styris					
BGK Walker					
SB O'Connor					
Extras (b 2, lb 2, w 2, nb 1)	7				
TOTAL (for 6 wkts) (50 overs)	**287**				

SOUTH AFRICA	Runs	Mins	Balls	4	6
DJ Cullinan c Astle b Cairns	17	23	22	3	-
G Kirsten c Parore b Cairns	101	144	107	10	-
JH Kallis c Walker b Styris	93	112	111	7	2
JN Rhodes b Harris	25	30	23	2	-
L Klusener c Fleming b Styris	9	16	9	-	-
N Boje not out	20	19	11	1	1
†MV Boucher not out	18	13	11	2	1
HH Dippenaar					
*SM Pollock					
R Telemachus					
AA Donald					
Extras (lb 2, w 3, nb 1)	6				
TOTAL (for 5 wkts) (48.5 overs)	**289**				

SA	O	M	R	W
Pollock	10	0	40	1
Telemachus	9	0	60	1
Donald	5	0	46	0
Kallis	8	0	46	2
Boje	10	0	42	1
Klusener	8	0	49	0

NZ	O	M	R	W
Cairns	9.5	2	67	2
O'Connor	8	0	46	0
Styris	10	0	56	2
Harris	10	0	58	1
Walker	7	0	41	0
Astle	4	0	19	0

Fall of Wickets	NZ	SA
1st	20 (2)	43 (1)
2nd	113 (1)	215 (3)
3rd	223 (3)	221 (2)
4th	272 (5)	247 (5)
5th	275 (6)	255 (4)
6th	283 (4)	-

SOUTH AFRICA v NEW ZEALAND — 5th Limited Overs International

Played at Kingsmead, Durban on 1 November 2000 — Toss: South Africa
Umpires: WA Diedricks & DL Orchard (TV: IL Howell)
Debuts: SA: None. NZ: None
Result: South Africa won by 6 wickets (D/L method), target revised to 153 in 32 overs
Man of Match: Jacques Kallis

Klusener hit two successive sixes in an unbeaten 41 off 18 balls as South Africa won with nine balls to spare after being set a stiff target under the Duckworth-Lewis scoring method.

New Zealand struggled in their innings, which was twice interrupted by rain and South Africa's task looked difficult on a pitch which helped seam bowlers until Klusener joined Kallis and cut loose. Klusener hit three fours in an over from Geoff Allott, then finished the match with successive sixes off O'Connor. Kallis played a crucial innings, held two slip catches and took his 100th limited overs international wicket in his 113th match.

There was an interruption of more than an hour when New Zealand were on 81 for five after 27.3 overs. Cairns hammered Klusener for three fours in an over when play resumed and then hit a straight six in Klusener's next over as he and Harris added 33 off 5.1 overs before the second stoppage.

NEW ZEALAND	Runs	Mins	Balls	4	6
CJ Nevin c Kallis b Pollock	0	2	2	-	-
NJ Astle c Kallis b Donald	3	17	14	-	-
*SP Fleming lbw b Ntini	21	96	64	3	-
RG Twose b Kallis	38	76	52	5	1
CL Cairns not out	25	50	30	3	1
CD McMillan c Boucher b Ntini	3	16	17	-	-
CZ Harris not out	9	28	17	-	-
†AC Parore					
SB Styris					
SB O'Connor					
GI Allott					
Extras (lb 14, w 1)	15				
TOTAL (for 5 wkts) (32.4 overs)	**114**				

SOUTH AFRICA	Runs	Mins	Balls	4	6
DJ Cullinan lbw b Allott	7	10	8	-	1
G Kirsten c Parore b Cairns	3	8	5	-	-
JH Kallis not out	50	136	81	4	-
N Boje c Harris b Astle	29	77	51	4	-
JN Rhodes b Astle	19	23	21	1	-
L Klusener not out	41	31	18	3	3
AJ Hall					
†MV Boucher					
*SM Pollock					
AA Donald					
M Ntini					
Extras (lb 1, w 7, nb 1)	9				
TOTAL (for 4 wkts) (30.3 overs)	**158**				

SA	O	M	R	W
Pollock	6	2	22	1
Donald	6	3	11	1
Ntini	8	2	21	2
Kallis	6	1	14	1
Klusener	4	0	26	0
Hall	2.4	1	6	0

NZ	O	M	R	W
Allott	6	1	38	1
Cairns	7	0	29	1
O'Connor	5.3	1	22	0
Styris	6	0	27	0
Astle	5	0	32	2
McMillan	1	0	9	0

Fall of Wickets	NZ	SA
1st	2 (1)	11 (2)
2nd	8 (2)	11 (1)
3rd	71 (4)	76 (4)
4th	73 (3)	100 (5)
5th	81 (6)	-

ANXIOUS MOMENT . . . Roger Twose of New Zealand looks skyward after top-edging a pull against Roger Telemachus during the one-day international at Newlands
Picture: Carl Fourie, TOUCHLINE PHOTO

SOUTH AFRICA v NEW ZEALAND — 6th Limited Overs International

Played at Newlands, Cape Town on 4 November 2000 — Toss: South Africa
Umpires: IL Howell & RE Koertzen (TV: WA Diedricks)
Debuts: SA: S Abrahams. NZ: None
Result: South Africa won by 3 wickets
Man of Match: Lance Klusener. Man of Series: Nicky Boje

Klusener pounded fours off the last two balls bowled by O'Connor as South Africa snatched a dramatic win in the final match of the series. Before Klusener's onslaught it seemed New Zealand would win on the back of a maiden international century by Twose, who shared a record 150-run fourth wicket stand with Cairns.

Twose, 32, had previous highest scores in the 90s in both Tests and one-day internationals. He had made 20 half-centuries before breaking through in his 75th one-day international. He was dropped on the boundary by debutant Abrahams off left-arm spinner Boje when he was on 97.

The stand between Twose and Cairns was the highest for any wicket for New Zealand against South Africa. The pair enabled New Zealand to recover from a poor start in which they lost their first three wickets for 39 runs after being sent in on an overcast day on a good batting pitch. Cairns hit two successive straight sixes off Kallis and two sixes in an over from Pollock.

Left-arm fast bowler O'Connor took three wickets in his opening spell but Rhodes and Boucher gave South Africa hope of overhauling the highest one-day international total at Newlands with a fifth wicket stand of 106. Both men were out in successive overs and the odds swung New Zealand's way but Klusener found a calm ally in Abrahams as the pair put on an unbeaten 69 off the last 53 balls.

NEW ZEALAND	Runs	Mins	Balls	4	6
CJ Nevin c Abrahams b Telemachus	12	32	20	1	-
NJ Astle c Boje b Pollock	8	27	18	1	-
*SP Fleming c Rhodes b Donald	8	31	23	1	-
RG Twose c Kallis b Boje	103	160	115	10	2
CL Cairns c Pollock b Telemachus	84	92	72	7	4
CD McMillan lbw b Pollock	7	20	14	-	-
CZ Harris c Pollock b Telemachus	6	37	18	-	-
†AC Parore run out (Cullinan)	1	5	2	-	-
SB Styris run out (Pollock)	8	16	9	-	-
BGK Walker not out	2	12	7	-	-
SB O'Connor not out	1	5	4	-	-
Extras (lb 7, w 7, nb 2)	16				
TOTAL (for 9 wkts) (50 overs)	**256**				

SOUTH AFRICA	Runs	Mins	Balls	4	6
DJ Cullinan b O'Connor	10	13	15	2	-
G Kirsten c and b Harris	25	58	43	1	-
JH Kallis lbw b O'Connor	0	1	1	-	-
N Boje c Parore b O'Connor	8	14	13	1	-
JN Rhodes st Parore b Walker	69	99	80	5	1
†MV Boucher b Harris	46	75	66	2	-
L Klusener not out	59	65	42	2	4
*SM Pollock c sub (DR Tuffey) b Walker	8	18	17	-	-
S Abrahams not out	16	42	26	2	-
R Telemachus					
AA Donald					
Extras (lb 9, w 5, nb 3)	17				
TOTAL (for 7 wkts) (50 overs)	**258**				

SA	O	M	R	W
Pollock	10	1	44	2
Telemachus	10	1	30	3
Donald	10	0	47	1
Kallis	5	0	52	0
Abrahams	10	0	40	0
Klusener	2	0	27	0
Boje	3	0	9	1

NZ	O	M	R	W
Cairns	10	0	45	0
O'Connor	9	1	55	3
Styris	9	0	47	0
Harris	10	0	45	2
Walker	9	1	43	2
Astle	3	0	14	0

Fall of Wickets	NZ	SA
1st	23 (2)	16 (1)
2nd	24 (1)	16 (3)
3rd	39 (3)	30 (4)
4th	189 (5)	65 (2)
5th	218 (6)	171 (5)
6th	238 (4)	173 (6)
7th	239 (8)	189 (8)
8th	249 (7)	-
9th	253 (9)	-

BOLAND v NEW ZEALANDERS — First-class 3-day match

Played at Boland PKS Park, Paarl on 7,8,9 November 2000 — Toss: New Zealanders
Umpires: WA Diedricks & IL Howell
Debuts: Bol: H Davids (FC). NZ: HJH Marshall, CS Martin & SB Styris (all FC for NZ)
Close of Play: Day 1: NZ (1) 273-5 (Richardson 118*, Styris 5*, 104 overs). Day 2: Bol (1) 189-9 (Carter 7*, Williams 4*, 70 overs).
Result: Match drawn

Richardson ground out a patient century as New Zealand started the first-class section of their tour. It was the left-handed opening batsman's first innings in South Africa after arriving four days earlier. Sinclair, another tour debutant, played more attackingly and dominated a second wicket stand of 113 with Richardson.

Richardson, a retreaded spin bowler who was a late developer as a batsman, made a double century against Sussex while touring England with New Zealand A in June 2000 and hit a career-best 306 against Zimbabwe A at Kwekwe in September.

Off-spinner Paul Wiseman sprained his left ankle while warming up before the match and did not play again on the tour. Styris, who replaced him in the match, staked a Test claim with an impressive all-round performance but he too was to fall victim to the injury bogey.

NEW ZEALANDERS

FIRST INNINGS	*Runs*	*Mins*	*Balls*	*4*	*6*	*SECOND INNINGS*	*Runs*	*Mins*	*Balls*	*4*	*6*
MH Richardson not out	173	525	403	14	1						
CM Spearman c Palframan b Carter	7	50	33	1	-	(1) c Davids b Koch	27	87	59	4	-
MS Sinclair c de Lange b Henderson	86	133	120	13	1	run out (Carter/Palframan)	51	139	101	6	1
*CD McMillan c Trott b Henderson	0	9	7	-	-	not out	52	157	152	4	-
HJH Marshall c Henderson b Carter	38	141	127	4	-						
†AC Parore c Davids b van Wyk	3	37	23	-	-	(2) b Williams	5	48	35	1	-
SB Styris not out	73	150	126	5	1						
BGK Walker						(5) not out	5	57	49	-	-
DR Tuffey											
KP Walmsley											
CS Martin											
Extras (b 3, lb 5, w 4, nb 11)	23					Extras (lb 2)	2				
TOTAL (for 5 wkts dec) (138 overs)	**403**					**TOTAL (for 3 wkts dec) (66 overs)**	**142**				

BOLAND

	Runs	*Mins*	*Balls*	*4*	*6*		*Runs*	*Mins*	*Balls*	*4*	*6*
IJL Trott c Parore b Martin	11	31	22	2	-	c and b Walker	30	98	73	4	-
JM Henderson c Tuffey b Walmsley	61	190	129	11	-						
H Davids b Martin	6	20	20	-	-	(2) c Tuffey b Martin	16	40	26	1	-
KC Jackson b Styris	4	33	20	1	-	(3) not out	3	57	30	-	-
*JL Ontong b Styris	56	141	108	4	-						
†SJ Palframan lbw b Styris	2	29	24	-	-						
CdeW de Lange c Styris b Martin	20	66	46	2	-						
DM Koch c Walmsley b Walker	7	25	23	-	-						
JM van Wyk lbw b Walker	0	9	11	-	-						
NM Carter not out	7	28	19	1	-						
HS Williams c Parore b McMillan	4	7	4	1	-						
Extras (b 4, lb 2, w 1, nb 4)	11					Extras (b 4)	4				
TOTAL (70.2 overs)	**189**					**TOTAL (for 2 wkts) (21.3 overs)**	**53**				

Bowling	*O*	*M*	*R*	*W*		*O*	*M*	*R*	*W*
BOLAND									
Williams	22	3	70	0		9	4	18	1
Carter	27	4	61	2		7	2	26	0
van Wyk	13	2	38	1		4	0	13	0
Koch	18	6	36	0		14	8	13	1
de Lange	27	9	82	0		19	6	51	0
Henderson	21	4	65	2		10	2	14	0
Ontong	10	0	43	0		3	1	5	0
NEW ZEALANDERS									
Tuffey	12	1	31	0		7	4	13	0
Martin	16	6	45	3		6	1	16	1
Walmsley	11	1	33	1		7	3	19	0
Styris	10	1	25	3					
McMillan	4.2	2	11	1					
Walker	17	6	38	2	(4)	1.3	0	1	1

Fall of Wickets	**NZ**	**Bol**	**NZ**	**Bol**
	1st	1st	2nd	2nd
1st	39 (2)	23 (1)	15 (2)	32 (2)
2nd	152 (3)	33 (3)	52 (1)	53 (1)
3rd	153 (4)	45 (4)	103 (3)	-
4th	247 (5)	138 (2)	-	-
5th	264 (6)	148 (6)	-	-
6th	-	151 (5)	-	-
7th	-	168 (8)	-	-
8th	-	170 (9)	-	-
9th	-	185 (7)	-	-
10th	-	189 (11)	-	-

NORTH WEST v NEW ZEALANDERS — First-class 3-day match

Played at North West Stadium, Potchefstroom on 11,12,13 November 2000 — Toss: New Zealanders

Umpires: SB Lambson & AG O'Connor

Debuts: NW: None. NZ: None

Close of Play: Day 1: NW (1) 0-2 (de Vos 0*, Thomas 0*, 4.5 overs). Day 2: NW (2) 37-2 (de Vos 8*, Hewitt 12*, 9 overs).

Result: New Zealanders won by 265 runs

NEW ZEALAND IN SOUTH AFRICA 2000/01

Opening batsman Craig Spearman hit a century in each innings as the tourists gained an easy win - too easy, according to coach David Trist, who said he would have preferred his team to have had a tougher work-out before the first Test. Spearman was in fluent form, especially in the second innings when he raced to his century off 124 balls.

O'Connor took two wickets for no runs before bad light stopped play on the first day and Tuffey continued the destruction on day two.

North West's bowling was seriously affected in the second innings by an injury to Thomas, who was hit on the gloves while batting, and the absence through illness of Francois van der Merwe.

NEW ZEALANDERS

FIRST INNINGS	*Runs*	*Mins*	*Balls*	*4*	*6*	*SECOND INNINGS*	*Runs*	*Mins*	*Balls*	*4*	*6*
MH Richardson c Hewitt b van der Merwe	11	23	15	2	-	c Jacobs b Light	39	104	81	5	-
CM Spearman c Poole b Light	100	241	196	14	1	retired out	115	149	131	16	2
MS Sinclair c Venter b Jacobs	37	67	61	5	-	(4) not out	22	41	39	1	-
*SP Fleming c Venter b Dreyer	16	50	41	3	-	(3) not out	52	85	91	7	1
NJ Astle b van der Merwe	63	140	140	9	-						
†AC Parore not out	32	78	78	5	-						
SB Styris c Jacobs b van der Merwe	9	15	11	2	-						
BGK Walker not out	4	18	15	1	-						
DR Tuffey											
SB O'Connor											
CS Martin											
Extras (b 1, lb 2, nb 5)	8					Extras (b 2, lb 8, w 4)	14				
TOTAL (for 6 wkts dec) (92 overs)	**280**					**TOTAL (for 2 wkts dec) (57 overs)**	**242**				

NORTH WEST

AG Lawson c Fleming b O'Connor	0	2	4	-	-	(2) c Spearman b O'Connor	0	5	1	-	-
HM de Vos lbw b O'Connor	7	63	43	1	-	(1) lbw b Styris	13	112	84	1	-
A Jacobs c Fleming b O'Connor	0	16	11	-	-	b Tuffey	13	15	16	3	-
AC Thomas c Fleming b Tuffey	16	67	59	2	-	(9) c Parore b O'Connor	3	8	7	-	-
GM Hewitt b Tuffey	8	40	17	2	-	(4) b O'Connor	15	27	21	3	-
*MC Venter c Fleming b Tuffey	5	23	18	-	-	(5) b Tuffey	4	29	25	1	-
C Light st Parore b Walker	8	20	20	-	1	(6) c Astle b Martin	23	54	34	4	-
M Strydom b Martin	9	36	30	2	-	(7) c Parore b O'Connor	39	70	48	6	-
†EG Poole b Martin	35	57	39	6	1	(8) b Tuffey	27	71	42	5	-
JN Dreyer c Astle b Martin	6	17	15	1	-	(11) not out	2	6	4	-	-
F van der Merwe not out	2	17	14	-	-	(10) c Parore b O'Connor	7	19	16	1	-
Extras (lb 1, w 1, nb 2)	4					Extras (lb 11)	11				
TOTAL (44.4 overs)	**100**					**TOTAL (49.4 overs)**	**157**				

Bowling	*O*	*M*	*R*	*W*		*O*	*M*	*R*	*W*
NORTH WEST									
Dreyer	20	2	75	1		15	3	49	0
van der Merwe	22	6	74	3					
Thomas	15	6	39	0	(2)	2	0	9	0
Jacobs	6	1	17	1	(3)	2	0	15	0
Light	18	2	43	1	(4)	24	2	94	1
Strydom	11	2	29	0	(5)	14	2	65	0
NEW ZEALANDERS									
O'Connor	12	6	14	3	(2)	17.4	7	51	5
Tuffey	13	6	23	3	(1)	19	3	58	3
Martin	10.4	4	27	3	(4)	6	1	18	1
Walker	9	1	35	1	(5)	1	0	1	0
Styris					(3)	6	1	18	1

Fall of Wickets	**NZ** 1st	**NW** 1st	**NZ** 2nd	**NW** 2nd
1st	13 (1)	0 (1)	101 (1)	6 (2)
2nd	86 (3)	0 (3)	171 (2)	23 (3)
3rd	124 (4)	16 (2)	-	42 (4)
4th	214 (2)	27 (4)	-	51 (5)
5th	257 (5)	40 (5)	-	64 (1)
6th	267 (7)	47 (6)	-	84 (6)
7th	-	49 (7)	-	139 (7)
8th	-	75 (8)	-	143 (9)
9th	-	93 (10)	-	155 (8)
10th	-	100 (9)	-	157 (10)

SOUTH AFRICA v NEW ZEALAND — 1st Test

Played at Goodyear Park, Bloemfontein on 17,18,19,20,21 November 2000 — Toss: South Africa

Umpires: AV Jayaprakash & DL Orchard (TV: RE Koertzen)

Debuts: SA: None. NZ: CS Martin & BGK Walker

Close of Play: Day 1: SA (1) 270-3 (Kallis 153*, McKenzie 42*, 83.4 overs). Day 2: NZ (1) 54-2 (Spearman 14*, Fleming 10*, 20.2 overs). Day 3: NZ (2) 82-1 (Richardson 50*, Sinclair 11*, 31.2 overs). Day 4: NZ (2) 260-5 (McMillan 25*, Walker 5*, 116 overs)

Result: South Africa won by 5 wickets

Man of Match: Jacques Kallis & Makhaya Ntini

TARGET ACHIEVED . . . Allan Donald is congratulated by his teammates after becoming the first South African to take 300 Test wickets *Picture: Duif du Toit, TOUCHLINE PHOTO*

With Gibbs suspended and Rhodes having retired from Test matches, there was room for both Dippenaar and McKenzie, with the latter able to bat in the middle order after struggling in the unaccustomed role of opener in Sri Lanka. New Zealand gave new caps to leg-spinner Walker and pace bowler Martin, with Wiseman (ankle) and Styris (knee) ruled out by injuries.

Kallis hit his highest Test score, batting skilfully on a pitch with early life after Dippenaar was caught at second slip off the second ball of the match. There was controversy, however, when the New Zealanders felt he had been run out when he had 76. For the second time on the tour, there were no adequate pictures when the television umpire was consulted. On this occasion, a drive by Cullinan was deflected into the stumps by O'Connor, the bowler, and it appeared Kallis, backing up, might have been out of his ground.

With the television rights having been granted to the independent e-tv company, who employed their own production team, only two cameras instead of four were available square of the wickets and according to a spokesman the key frame could not be located immediately because of a technical fault. The right picture was found after the close of play and showed, ironically, that Kallis was safely in.

Kallis was in cracking form, reaching his fifty off 77 balls and his century off 174. He played shots to all parts of the ground. McKenzie made his first Test half-century, showing determination and a willingness to wait for the right balls to hit.

The New Zealand pace bowlers brought their side back into the match on the second morning when they took three wickets and slowed down the scoring rate before Boucher and Boje came together in an attacking partnership.

Needing three wickets to reach 300 in Tests, Donald struck in his first spell when Richardson was bowled, playing a loose shot against a ball which cut back. Sinclair fell to Pollock soon afterwards and New Zealand were condemned to a long struggle to avoid the follow on. Sinclair was caught at first slip but the batsman was only given out after a referral to television umpire Koertzen. Sinclair edged the ball low to Cullinan who dived and threw the ball up almost as soon as he caught it. Umpire Orchard wanted Koertzen to judge whether the fielder had the ball fully under control.

Fleming and Astle had a lively partnership but Boje bowled Fleming with his fifth ball of the match and Astle was out three balls later, slashing at Ntini to be well caught by Kallis at second slip.

Donald reached 299 when McMillan was caught behind but Pollock took the next two wickets and there was a stubborn stand of 28 in 81 minutes between Walker and O'Connor before the second new ball finally brought the 300th wicket for the Bloemfontein hero, with O'Connor missing a full length ball and being trapped lbw. A cannon placed on the boundary edge fired three shots to acclaim Donald's achievement in his 63rd Test. He became the first South African and the 15th player worldwide to reach the landmark.

New Zealand put up a determined fight in the second innings with Richardson, Fleming and McMillan all batting for more than four hours. With conditions favouring batsmen, it was a great effort by Ntini, who kept charging in, to claim his first five-wicket haul in Tests. Donald took three key wickets, including that of Fleming, who fell one short of what would have been only his third century in 54 Tests, during which he had hit 26 half-centuries. He was out to a vicious lifting delivery which he could only fend to gully.

South Africa survived a scare on the final afternoon, losing five wickets before clinching what should have been an easy win. O'Connor and Martin both took early wickets before Tuffey had a three-wicket burst. Boucher finished the match in style with three successive swept fours off Walker.

SOUTH AFRICA

FIRST INNINGS	*Runs*	*Mins*	*Balls*	*4*	*6*	*SECOND INNINGS*	*Runs*	*Mins*	*Balls*	*4*	*6*
HH Dippenaar c Astle b O'Connor	0	2	2	-	-	c Parore b Tuffey	27	58	48	5	-
G Kirsten c Astle b Martin	31	115	75	2	-	lbw b O'Connor	1	8	6	-	-
JH Kallis c Parore b O'Connor	160	345	289	26	-	lbw b Martin	13	22	18	2	-
DJ Cullinan b Walker	29	80	71	3	-	lbw b Tuffey	22	56	35	4	-
ND McKenzie c Parore b Martin	55	184	135	11	-	not out	13	52	37	1	-
†MV Boucher lbw b Walker	76	172	121	7	-	(7) not out	22	13	11	4	-
L Klusener b O'Connor	9	51	37	-	-	(6) c McMillan b Tuffey	4	13	5	1	-
N Boje c Tuffey b Astle	43	68	57	6	1						
*SM Pollock c Sinclair b Martin	25	61	42	4	-						
AA Donald not out	21	42	35	4	-						
M Ntini											
Extras (b 5, lb 7, nb 10)	22					Extras (nb 1)	1				
TOTAL (for 9 wkts dec) (142.1 overs)	**471**					**TOTAL (for 5 wkts) (26.3 overs)**	**103**				

NEW ZEALAND

	Runs	*Mins*	*Balls*	*4*	*6*		*Runs*	*Mins*	*Balls*	*4*	*6*
MH Richardson b Donald	23	28	22	4	-	lbw b Donald	77	256	186	8	-
CM Spearman c Klusener b Pollock	23	125	84	2	-	c McKenzie b Ntini	15	56	43	2	-
MS Sinclair c Cullinan b Pollock	1	12	6	-	-	c Klusener b Donald	20	103	72	2	-
*SP Fleming b Boje	57	155	103	8	-	c Kirsten b Donald	99	274	210	12	-
NJ Astle c Kallis b Ntini	37	77	51	6	-	b Ntini	8	57	39	1	-
CD McMillan c Boucher b Donald	16	40	32	1	-	c Kirsten b Kallis	78	276	187	12	-
†AC Parore lbw b Pollock	11	46	35	-	-	(8) c Kallis b Ntini	12	88	75	2	-
BGK Walker not out	27	136	111	-	-	(7) c Boucher b Ntini	10	108	96	1	-
DR Tuffey b Pollock	0	9	11	-	-	b Ntini	6	29	22	-	-
SB O'Connor lbw b Donald	15	81	58	2	-	b Ntini	0	19	15	-	-
CS Martin c Boucher b Kallis	7	33	23	1	-	not out	0	9	6	-	-
Extras (b 1, lb 7, w 2, nb 2)	12					Extras (b 2, lb 10, w 1, nb 4)	17				
TOTAL (89 overs)	**229**					**TOTAL (157.4 overs)**	**342**				

Bowling	*O*	*M*	*R*	*W*		*O*	*M*	*R*	*W*
NEW ZEALAND									
O'Connor	30	4	87	3		7	0	28	1
Tuffey	26	6	96	0	(3)	8	1	38	3
Martin	22.1	4	89	3	(2)	5	3	18	1
Walker	27	4	92	2		6.3	2	19	0
Astle	24	5	57	1					
McMillan	13	2	38	0					
SOUTH AFRICA									
Donald	21	4	69	3		28	14	43	3
Pollock	22	10	37	4		25	11	47	0
Ntini	14	4	48	1		31.4	12	66	6
Kallis	13	5	30	1		23	4	88	1
Boje	16	4	35	1		40	14	61	0
Klusener	3	2	2	0		10	3	25	0

Fall of Wickets	**SA**	**NZ**	**NZ**	**SA**
	1st	1st	2nd	2nd
1st	0 (1)	28 (1)	33 (2)	3 (2)
2nd	97 (2)	29 (3)	93 (3)	16 (3)
3rd	164 (4)	72 (2)	145 (1)	55 (1)
4th	279 (3)	151 (4)	175 (5)	69 (4)
5th	304 (5)	153 (5)	247 (4)	75 (6)
6th	330 (7)	176 (6)	285 (7)	-
7th	409 (8)	183 (7)	325 (6)	-
8th	429 (6)	185 (9)	340 (9)	-
9th	471 (9)	213 (10)	341 (8)	-
10th	-	229 (11)	342 (10)	-

BORDER v NEW ZEALANDERS

Limited Overs Match

Played at Ntselamanzi Cricket Ground, Alice on 24 November 2000

Toss: New Zealanders

Umpires: L King & NS Majiza (TV: RE Koertzen)

Debuts: Bdr: None. NZ: None

Result: New Zealanders won by 2 wickets

Man of Match: Laden Gamiet

The touring team were handed a victory in poor light. A blazing innings of 84 by Border opening batsman Laden Gamiet was the outstanding performance of the day and enabled Border to set a target which looked likely to prove beyond New Zealand on a deteriorating pitch.

In cold weather and gathering gloom, both teams showed a sporting willingness to complete the fixture in front of about 1000 spectators. Border captain Pieter Strydom brought on wicketkeeper Ian Mitchell to bowl the 48th over despite having Test bowler Ntini with four overs unbowled. "The light was too bad to bring on the quick bowlers like Makhaya," said Strydom.

Astle, bowling gentle-paced seamers, was New Zealand's most successful bowler. Due to a mistake by McMillan and the umpires he was allowed to bowl 11 overs, one more than the limit.

BORDER	Runs	Mins	Balls	4	6
LL Gamiet b Astle	84	111	103	12	2
†I Mitchell lbw b O'Connor	2	34	21	-	-
SC Pope c Sinclair b Walmsley	10	40	14	2	-
*PC Strydom run out (Penn)	2	10	10	-	-
CB Sugden lbw b Astle	36	58	55	3	2
W Wiblin lbw b Astle	3	12	8	-	-
DL Makalima c Sulzberger b Walmsley	28	66	49	1	-
GT Love lbw b Astle	0	1	1	-	-
L Graham not out	24	44	40	1	-
M Ntini not out	0	3	1	-	-
M Matomela					
Extras (b 5, lb 16, w 14, nb 2)	37				
TOTAL (for 8 wkts) (50 overs)	**226**				

NEW ZEALANDERS	Runs	Mins	Balls	4	6
MH Richardson lbw b Pope	43	113	83	3	1
CM Spearman b Graham	31	63	51	3	1
†MS Sinclair st Mitchell b Strydom	7	30	22	-	-
NJ Astle c Mitchell b Pope	13	25	29	2	-
CD McMillan c Graham b Strydom	55	57	44	6	3
GP Sulzberger b Love	6	16	10	-	-
AJ Penn lbw b Pope	0	4	5	-	-
*SP Fleming lbw b Pope	4	7	7	-	-
DR Tuffey not out	38	37	32	3	1
SB O'Connor not out	7	20	11	-	-
KP Walmsley					
Extras (b 5, lb 9, w 9)	23				
TOTAL (for 8 wkts) (49 overs)	**227**				

NZ	O	M	R	W
O'Connor	9	1	42	1
Tuffey	6	1	35	0
Walmsley	7	0	42	2
Sulzberger	10	2	43	0
Penn	5	1	13	0
Astle	11	2	25	4
McMillan	2	0	5	0

Bdr	O	M	R	W
Ntini	6	2	13	0
Matomela	7	0	22	0
Graham	5	0	19	1
Love	10	1	60	1
Strydom	10	0	49	2
Pope	10	0	38	4
Mitchell	1	0	12	0

Fall of Wickets	Bdr	NZ
1st	32 (2)	58 (2)
2nd	95 (3)	86 (3)
3rd	105 (4)	105 (1)
4th	129 (1)	116 (4)
5th	153 (6)	140 (6)
6th	166 (5)	141 (7)
7th	166 (8)	157 (8)
8th	218 (7)	186 (5)

BORDER v NEW ZEALANDERS — First-class 3-day match

Played at Buffalo Park, East London on 25,26,27 November 2000 — Toss: New Zealanders
Umpires: IL Howell & CM Schoof (TV: RE Koertzen)
Debuts: Bdr: M Matomela & M Zondeki (both FC). NZ: None
Close of Play: Day 1: Bdr (1) 34-3 (Mitchell 22*, Strydom 2*, 12 overs). Day 2: Bdr (2) 36-2 (Pope 10*, Wiblin 0*, 13 overs).
Result: New Zealanders won by 211 runs
Notes: Spearman retired hurt with his score on 57 and the total on 119-0 in New Zealand's 2nd innings.

McMillan and Astle hammered the Border bowling, putting on an unbeaten 141 in 102 minutes as New Zealand turned in a sparkling batting performance. This was followed up by impressive bowling from Andrew Penn, who had arrived as a replacement for Scott Styris.

With star bowlers Ntini and Vasbert Drakes being rested, Border called up Monde Zondeki, an 18-year-old fast bowler from Dale College, Ntini's old school. Zondeki captured his first wicket in first class cricket when he bowled Sinclair for 28.

Adam Parore, the only New Zealand batsman who had not made a good score on tour, opened the batting in the second innings and hit an unbeaten century as New Zealand set Border an impossible victory target of 424. Tuffey took five wickets as Border's batting failed again but New Zealand suffered another injury blow when Penn had to leave the field with a side strain, a recurrence of the injury which prevented him from starting the tour after he was first selected.

NEW ZEALANDERS

FIRST INNINGS	*Runs*	*Mins*	*Balls*	*4*	*6*	*SECOND INNINGS*	*Runs*	*Mins*	*Balls*	*4*	*6*
MH Richardson run out (Graham)	45	144	134	5	-						
CM Spearman c Strydom b Graham	56	152	107	8	-	retired hurt	57	117	86	10	1
MS Sinclair b Zondeki	28	53	44	6	-	not out	25	56	50	2	-
*SP Fleming c Love b Strydom	29	79	63	5	-						
NJ Astle not out	69	136	123	11	-						
CD McMillan not out	76	102	70	9	3						
†AC Parore						(1) not out	101	174	147	15	-
BGK Walker											
AJ Penn											
DR Tuffey											
KP Walmsley											
Extras (b 6, lb 1, nb 1)	8					Extras (lb 1, nb 1)	2				
TOTAL (for 4 wkts dec) (90 overs)	**311**					**TOTAL (for 0 wkts dec) (47 overs)**	**185**				

BORDER

CB Sugden c Sinclair b Penn	1	9	9	-	-	b Tuffey	15	33	33	2	-
†I Mitchell c Parore b Tuffey	22	69	51	4	-	c Spearman b Walmsley	11	52	26	1	-
GT Love c Sinclair b Penn	0	14	8	-	-	(8) c sub (GP Sulzberger) b Tuffey	5	24	22	1	-
SC Pope c Spearman b Walker	9	21	11	1	-	(3) b Walmsley	33	78	54	6	-
W Wiblin c Spearman b Penn	13	49	29	2	-	(4) b Walker	46	96	67	7	1
*PC Strydom lbw b Walker	18	29	17	3	-	(5) c Astle b Tuffey	32	126	100	6	-
LL Gamiet c Astle b Penn	0	11	6	-	-	(6) c Walker b McMillan	18	37	30	4	-
DL Makalima b Penn	2	14	5	-	-	(7) c Parore b Tuffey	18	71	62	2	-
L Graham b Walmsley	6	27	15	1	-	not out	14	49	36	2	-
M Matomela lbw b Walker	0	15	11	-	-	c Fleming b Tuffey	0	13	10	-	-
M Zondeki not out	0	4	3	-	-	st Parore b Walker	12	25	24	2	-
Extras (nb 2)	2					Extras (lb 4, nb 4)	8				
TOTAL (27.1 overs)	**73**					**TOTAL (76.4 overs)**	**212**				

Bowling	*O*	*M*	*R*	*W*		*O*	*M*	*R*	*W*
BORDER									
Zondeki	16	5	42	1		10	1	46	0
Graham	18	4	85	1		12	4	21	0
Matomela	13	3	72	0		6	0	33	0
Strydom	16	4	37	1	(5)	7	1	24	0
Pope	8	4	17	0					
Love	19	5	51	0	(4)	12	0	60	0
NEW ZEALANDERS									
Tuffey	9	1	22	1		21	5	69	5
Penn	12	3	38	5		9	3	30	0
Walker	5	1	13	3	(4)	23.4	7	58	2
Walmsley	1.1	1	0	1	(3)	13	7	24	2
Astle						4	2	8	0
McMillan						6	1	19	1

Fall of Wickets

	NZ	Bdr	NZ	Bdr
	1st	1st	2nd	2nd
1st	98 (1)	1 (1)	-	24 (1)
2nd	106 (2)	3 (3)	-	32 (2)
3rd	149 (3)	24 (4)	-	91 (3)
4th	170 (4)	38 (2)	-	108 (4)
5th	-	61 (5)	-	135 (6)
6th	-	65 (6)	-	173 (5)
7th	-	67 (7)	-	183 (7)
8th	-	68 (8)	-	184 (8)
9th	-	73 (10)	-	188 (10)
10th	-	73 (9)	-	212 (11)

SOUTH AFRICA v NEW ZEALAND — 2nd Test

Played at St George's Park, Port Elizabeth on 30 November, 1,2,3,4 December 2000 — Toss: South Africa
Umpires: RE Koertzen & ID Robinson (TV: DL Orchard)
Debuts: SA: None. NZ: None
Close of Play: Day 1: NZ (1) 206-7 (Sinclair 88*, O'Connor 3*, 91 overs). Day 2: SA (1) 123-3 (Cullinan 13*, Pollock 5*, 52 overs). Day 3: SA (1) 361-8 (Boje 51*, Donald 9*, 142 overs). Day 4: SA (2) 29-1 (Kirsten 22*, Kallis 6*, 13 overs)
Result: South Africa won by 7 wickets
Man of Match: Neil McKenzie

Sinclair defied South Africa's fast bowling attack after New Zealand were sent in to bat on a well-grassed but true pitch in hot, windless weather. Sinclair, who made 214 against the West Indies in Wellington on debut 11 months earlier, had not reached 50 in six subsequent Test matches. Powerful off-side drives, particularly off the back foot, were the hallmark of Sinclair's batting against a pace-dominated attack.

South Africa were hampered when Donald could not bowl between lunch and tea because of what was described as a bruised right heel. Donald came back and finished with four wickets.

Sinclair made the highest score by a New Zealander in a Test against South Africa, surpassing the 142 made by John Reid in Johannesburg in 1961/62. He became the first New Zealander to score a century in nine Tests against South Africa since the end of isolation. The previous hundred for New Zealand was by Barry Sinclair in Auckland in 1963/64 when Peter Pollock, father of the current captain Shaun, was a fast bowler for South Africa. The two Sinclairs are unrelated.

Kirsten and Dippenaar put on 81 for South Africa's first wicket but steady bowling brought the tourists back into the game, with Astle's nagging medium pace proving especially frustrating for the batsmen.

A stylish maiden Test century by McKenzie enabled South Africa to regain the ascendancy and he shared an eighth wicket stand of 136 with Boje, a record for South Africa against New

Zealand. They came together when South Africa were still 89 behind. McKenzie drove and pulled powerfully and reached his century off 164 balls with 17 fours.

A lead of 63 proved to be an important asset. Donald took an early wicket but bowled only seven overs in the innings because of a stomach muscle injury. Richardson batted solidly and New Zealand seemed to have made a fair recovery despite Boje taking the important wickets of Sinclair and Fleming on either side of lunch on the fourth day.

Pollock sparked a collapse in which the last seven wickets fell for 37 runs. Richardson was caught behind cutting at the South African captain and McMillan padded up to the next ball, an inswinger, and was out lbw. Five balls later Astle flashed at Ntini and was caught behind. Parore drove Ntini to cover soon afterwards and the contest was as good as over.

As in the first Test, New Zealand showed spirit in defending a small target but Kirsten shepherded South Africa to a series-clinching win.

NEW ZEALAND

FIRST INNINGS	*Runs*	*Mins*	*Balls*	*4*	*6*	*SECOND INNINGS*	*Runs*	*Mins*	*Balls*	*4*	*6*
MH Richardson b Ntini	26	106	76	3	-	c Boucher b Pollock	60	172	150	8	-
CM Spearman c Kirsten b Donald	16	90	72	3	-	lbw b Donald	0	12	7	-	-
MS Sinclair c Kirsten b Donald	150	399	321	23	1	lbw b Boje	17	80	44	3	-
*SP Fleming c and b Pollock	14	49	34	3	-	c Cullinan b Boje	8	6	5	2	-
NJ Astle lbw b Pollock	2	8	5	-	-	c Boucher b Ntini	18	78	46	3	-
CD McMillan c Ntini b Pollock	39	104	81	5	-	lbw b Pollock	0	2	1	-	-
†AC Parore c Boucher b Donald	2	41	38	-	-	c Kirsten b Ntini	5	26	17	1	-
BGK Walker c Cullinan b Pollock	3	33	22	-	-	lbw b Klusener	19	111	80	2	-
SB O'Connor b Kallis	20	119	92	1	-	b Klusener	8	74	63	-	-
KP Walmsley c Cullinan b Donald	5	28	14	1	-	lbw b Klusener	0	7	6	-	-
CS Martin not out	5	8	9	-	-	not out	0	4	2	-	-
Extras (b 4, lb 5, w 2, nb 5)	16					Extras (b 6, lb 3, nb 4)	13				
TOTAL (126.3 overs)	**298**					**TOTAL (69.3 overs)**	**148**				

SOUTH AFRICA

	Runs	*Mins*	*Balls*	*4*	*6*		*Runs*	*Mins*	*Balls*	*4*	*6*
HH Dippenaar lbw b Martin	35	127	114	4	-	lbw b O'Connor	0	19	15	-	-
G Kirsten c Parore b Walmsley	49	184	118	9	-	not out	47	131	104	5	-
JH Kallis c Parore b Astle	12	20	22	2	-	c O'Connor b Martin	23	64	49	5	-
DJ Cullinan b Walker	33	95	75	5	1	b Walmsley	11	22	20	2	-
*SM Pollock c Spearman b Martin	33	120	110	5	-						
ND McKenzie c Spearman b McMillan	120	277	207	20	-	(5) not out	7	21	17	-	1
†MV Boucher b O'Connor	0	5	5	-	-						
L Klusener c Parore b Martin	6	20	12	1	-						
N Boje c Parore b O'Connor	51	235	168	8	-						
AA Donald lbw b Martin	9	41	32	1	-						
M Ntini not out	0	5	5	-	-						
Extras (b 7, lb 4, w 2)	13					Extras (lb 1)	1				
TOTAL (144.4 overs)	**361**					**TOTAL (for 3 wkts) (34.1 overs)**	**89**				

Bowling	*O*	*M*	*R*	*W*		*O*	*M*	*R*	*W*
SOUTH AFRICA									
Donald	26.3	2	69	4		7	1	16	1
Pollock	32	15	64	4		15	4	44	2
Kallis	21	8	44	1	(5)	7	2	17	0
Ntini	22	7	59	1	(3)	16	6	24	2
Klusener	6	2	8	0	(6)	9.3	5	8	3
Boje	19	5	45	0	(4)	15	2	30	2
NEW ZEALAND									
O'Connor	26.4	8	68	2		8	4	9	1
Martin	29	8	104	4		12	3	32	1
Walmsley	13	2	40	1	(5)	5	2	7	1
Walker	23	5	61	1		7.1	1	32	0
Astle	36	18	46	1	(3)	2	0	8	0
McMillan	17	6	31	1					

Fall of Wickets	**NZ**	**SA**	**NZ**	**SA**
	1st	1st	2nd	2nd
1st	43 (2)	81 (1)	4 (2)	4 (1)
2nd	55 (1)	96 (3)	54 (3)	53 (3)
3rd	95 (4)	114 (2)	64 (4)	71 (4)
4th	101 (5)	151 (4)	111 (1)	-
5th	172 (6)	181 (5)	111 (6)	-
6th	194 (7)	184 (7)	115 (5)	-
7th	203 (8)	209 (8)	122 (7)	-
8th	276 (9)	345 (6)	147 (9)	-
9th	291 (3)	361 (10)	147 (10)	-
10th	298 (10)	361 (9)	148 (8)	-

PG BISON
6
PG BISON
6
PG BISON
6
PG BISON
6
PG BIS
6
PG BISON
6

NEW ZEALAND IN SOUTH AFRICA 2000/01

SOUTH AFRICA v NEW ZEALAND — 3rd Test

Played at Wanderers Stadium, Johannesburg on 8,9,10,11,12 December 2000 — Toss: South Africa
Umpires: DL Orchard & G Sharp (TV: RE Koertzen)
Debuts: SA: M Ngam. NZ: HJH Marshall
Close of Play: Day 1: No play. Day 2: SA (1) 18-1 (Dippenaar 5*, Boje 0*, 5.4 overs). Day 3: No play. Day 4: No play.
Result: Match drawn
Man of Match: C Scott (Groundsman) and Ground Staff. Man of Series: Makhaya Ntini

With Donald ruled out by a stomach muscle injury, Mfuneko Ngam, 21, made his Test debut in his 16th first-class game. Rain prevented play on the first day but Ngam gave an electrifying display of fast bowling when the match did get under way. He should have had a wicket with his fourth ball in Test cricket but Cullinan at first slip dropped a sharp chance at shoulder height to his right off Parore. Ngam was unlucky again in his third over when Parore, on eight, offered a more straightforward opportunity to Cullinan.

Ntini finally dismissed Parore but Ngam struck in his second spell when Richardson edged a lifting ball for a catch behind. It was a proud day for the development programme as Ntini and Ngam bowled splendidly to put South Africa in a strong position if there had been three more days of play. Ngam's fastest delivery was timed at 146 kmh and Ntini was consistently better than 140kmh.

Hamish Marshall, 20, one of identical twin brothers, spent an anxious 60 minutes on both sides of tea without a run to his name before pushing the 38th ball he received, from Pollock, into the covers and scurrying through for his first Test run.

Not a ball was bowled on the third and fourth days. When the rain finally stopped, there was no prospect of a result. Dippenaar batted superbly, however, to reward the handful of spectators who turned up on the final day of the series, playing a series of stunning strokes to reach his first Test century.

The series ended on a farcical note when the adjudicator, former umpire Ted Wood, named the ground staff as man of the match.

NEW ZEALAND

FIRST INNINGS	*Runs*	*Mins*	*Balls*	*4*	*6*
MH Richardson c Boucher b Ngam	46	146	119	6	-
†AC Parore c McKenzie b Ntini	10	86	60	1	-
MS Sinclair c Klusener b Pollock	24	63	39	5	-
*SP Fleming b Ntini	14	67	45	1	-
NJ Astle c Kallis b Ntini	12	72	54	-	-
CD McMillan c Klusener b Kallis	4	31	21	-	-
HJH Marshall not out	40	173	121	7	-
BGK Walker lbw b Klusener	17	70	58	2	-
DR Tuffey c Boucher b Ngam	8	36	21	1	-
SB O'Connor c Kallis b Pollock	9	36	24	1	-
CS Martin b Kallis	0	4	5	-	-
Extras (b 2, lb 9, w 1, nb 4)	16				
TOTAL (93.5 overs)	**200**				

SOUTH AFRICA

HH Dippenaar b O'Connor	100	238	192	21	-
G Kirsten c Richardson b Martin	10	21	17	2	-
N Boje c Sinclair b Martin	22	71	50	3	-
JH Kallis not out	79	271	211	12	-
DJ Cullinan not out	31	126	112	4	-
ND McKenzie					
†MV Boucher					
L Klusener					
*SM Pollock					
M Ntini					
M Ngam					
Extras (lb 17, w 2)	19				
TOTAL (for 3 wkts dec) (97 overs)	**261**				

NEW ZEALAND IN SOUTH AFRICA 2000/01

Bowling	*O*	*M*	*R*	*W*	*O*	*M*	*R*	*W*
SOUTH AFRICA								
Pollock	26	9	41	2				
Ngam	19	8	34	2				
Kallis	15.5	4	26	2				
Ntini	18	9	29	3				
Klusener	12	2	43	1				
Boje	3	0	16	0				
NEW ZEALAND								
O'Connor	15	5	52	1				
Martin	15	4	43	2				
Tuffey	19	4	60	0				
Astle	26	15	31	0				
McMillan	17	5	41	0				
Marshall	1	0	4	0				
Sinclair	4	0	13	0				

Fall of Wickets	NZ	SA
	1st	1st
1st	37 (2)	18 (2)
2nd	83 (1)	87 (3)
3rd	83 (3)	187 (1)
4th	112 (4)	-
5th	113 (5)	-
6th	117 (6)	-
7th	148 (8)	-
8th	174 (9)	-
9th	199 (10)	-
10th	200 (11)	-

SOUTH AFRICA v NEW ZEALAND 2000/01 TEST AVERAGES

SOUTH AFRICA

Batting & Fielding

Name	M	Inns	NO	Runs	HS	Avg	100	50	Ct	St
ND McKenzie	3	4	2	195	120	97.5	1	1	2	0
JH Kallis	3	5	1	287	160	71.75	1	1	4	0
MV Boucher	3	3	1	98	76	49	0	1	8	0
N Boje	3	3	0	116	51	38.66	0	1	0	0
G Kirsten	3	5	1	138	49	34.5	0	0	5	0
HH Dippenaar	3	5	0	162	100	32.4	1	0	0	0
DJ Cullinan	3	5	1	126	33	31.5	0	0	4	0
AA Donald	2	2	1	30	21*	30	0	0	0	0
SM Pollock	3	2	0	58	33	29	0	0	1	0
L Klusener	3	3	0	19	9	6.33	0	0	4	0
M Ntini	3	1	1	0	0*	-	0	0	1	0
M Ngam	1	0	0	0	0	-	0	0	0	0
Totals	33	38	8	1229	160		3	4	29	0
				Extras	56				subs	0
				Total	1285		42.83			29

Bowling

Name	Overs	Mdns	Runs	Wkts	Avg	BB	5I	10M
M Ngam	19	8	34	2	17.00	2-34	0	0
M Ntini	101.4	38	226	13	17.38	6-66	1	0
AA Donald	82.3	21	197	11	17.90	4-69	0	0
SM Pollock	120	49	233	12	19.41	4-37	0	0
L Klusener	40.3	14	86	4	21.50	3-8	0	0
JH Kallis	79.5	23	205	5	41.00	2-26	0	0
N Boje	93	25	187	3	62.33	2-30	0	0
Totals	536.3	178	1168	50		6-66	1	0
		b & lb	49	0	run outs			
		Total	1217	50	24.34			

NEW ZEALAND IN SOUTH AFRICA 2000/01

NEW ZEALAND

Batting & Fielding

Name	M	Inns	NO	Runs	HS	Avg	100	50	Ct	St
MH Richardson	3	5	0	232	77	46.40	0	2	1	0
MS Sinclair	3	5	0	212	150	42.40	1	0	2	0
SP Fleming	3	5	0	192	99	38.40	0	2	0	0
CD McMillan	3	5	0	137	78	27.40	0	1	1	0
BGK Walker	3	5	1	76	27*	19.00	0	0	0	0
NJ Astle	3	5	0	77	37	15.40	0	0	2	0
CM Spearman	2	4	0	54	23	13.50	0	0	2	0
SB O'Connor	3	5	0	52	20	10.40	0	0	1	0
AC Parore	3	5	0	40	12	8.00	0	0	7	
CS Martin	3	5	3	12	7	6.00	0	0	0	0
DR Tuffey	2	3	0	14	8	4.66	0	0	1	0
KP Walmsley	1	2	0	5	5	2.50	0	0	0	0
HJH Marshall	1	1	1	40	40*	-	0	0	0	0
Totals	33	55	5	1143	150		1	5	17	0
				Extras	74				subs	0
				Total	1217		24.34			17

Bowling

Name	Overs	Mdns	Runs	Wkts	Avg	BB	5I	10M
KP Walmsley	18	4	47	2	23.50	1-7	0	0
CS Martin	83.1	22	286	11	26.00	4-104	0	0
SB O'Connor	86.4	21	244	8	30.50	3-87	0	0
DR Tuffey	53	11	194	3	64.66	3-38	0	0
BGK Walker	63.4	12	204	3	68.00	2-92	0	0
NJ Astle	88	38	142	2	71.00	1-46	0	0
CD McMillan	47	13	110	1	110.00	1-31	0	0
HJH Marshall	1	0	4	0	-	-	0	0
MS Sinclair	4	0	13	0	-	-	0	0
Totals	444.3	121	1244	30		4-104	0	0
		b & lb	41	0	run outs			
		Total	1285	30	42.83			

NEW ZEALAND IN SOUTH AFRICA 2000/01 FIRST-CLASS AVERAGES

Batting & Fielding

Name	M	Inns	NO	Runs	HS	Avg	100	50	Ct	St
SB Styris	2	2	1	82	73*	82.00	0	1	1	0
HJH Marshall	2	2	1	78	40*	78.00	0	0	0	0
MH Richardson	6	9	1	500	173*	62.50	1	2	1	0
MS Sinclair	6	11	2	461	150	51.22	1	2	4	0
CM Spearman	5	10	1	416	115	46.22	2	2	6	0
CD McMillan	5	8	2	265	78	44.16	0	3	1	0
SP Fleming	5	8	1	289	99	41.28	0	3	5	0
NJ Astle	5	7	1	209	69*	34.83	0	2	6	0
AC Parore	6	9	2	181	101*	25.85	1	0	14	2
BGK Walker	6	7	3	85	27*	21.25	0	0	2	0
SB O'Connor	4	5	0	52	20	10.40	0	0	1	0
CS Martin	5	5	3	12	7	6.00	0	0	0	0
DR Tuffey	53	0	14	8	4.66	0	0	3	0	
KP Walmsley	3	2	0	5	5	2.50	0	0	1	0
AJ Penn	1	0	0	0	0	-	0	0	0	0
Totals	66	88	18	2649	173*		5	15	45	2
				Extras	131				subs	1
				Total	2780		39.71			46

Bowling

Name	Overs	Mdns	Runs	Wkts	Avg	BB	5I	10M
SB Styris	16	2	43	4	10.75	3-25	0	0
AJ Penn	21	6	68	5	13.60	5-38	1	0
SB O'Connor	116.2	34	309	16	19.31	5-51	1	0
KP Walmsley	50.1	16	123	6	20.50	2-24	0	0
CS Martin	121.5	34	392	19	20.63	4-104	0	0
DR Tuffey	134	31	410	15	27.33	5-69	1	0
BGK Walker	120.5	27	350	12	29.16	3-13	0	0
CD McMillan	57.2	16	140	3	46.66	1-11	0	0
NJ Astle	92	40	150	2	75.00	1-46	0	0
HJH Marshall	1	0	4	0	-	-	0	0
MS Sinclair	4	0	13	0	-	-	0	0
Totals	734.3	206	2002	82		5-38	3	0
		b & lb	67	0	run outs			
		Total	2069	82	25.23			

SOUTH AFRICA v NEW ZEALAND 2000/01: LIMITED OVERS INTERNATIONAL AVERAGES

Name	M	Inns	NO	Runs	HS	Avg	BF	SR	100	50	Ct	St	O	M	Runs	Wkts	Avg	RpO	BB	4I
S Abrahams	1	1	1	16	16*	-	26	61.53	0	0	1	0	10	0	40	0	-	4.00	-	0
N Boje	6	6	2	355	129	88.75	365	97.26	2	1	2	0	19	1	71	3	23.66	3.73	1-2	0
MV Boucher	6	2	1	64	46	64.00	77	83.11	0	0	5	0	0	0	0	0	-	-	-	0
DJ Cullinan	6	5	0	56	22	11.20	87	64.36	0	0	1	0	0	0	0	0	-	-	-	0
HH Dippenaar	4	2	0	66	57	33.00	126	52.38	0	1	1	0	0	0	0	0	-	-	-	0
AA Donald	6	0	0	0	0	-	0	-	0	0	0	0	38	5	182	6	30.33	4.78	2-27	0
AJ Hall	1	0	0	0	0	-	0	-	0	0	0	0	2.4	1	6	0	-	2.25	-	0
JH Kallis	6	6	3	235	93	78.33	299	78.59	0	2	4	0	33	2	185	5	37.00	5.60	2-34	0
G Kirsten	6	6	0	293	101	48.83	379	77.30	1	2	2	0	0	0	0	0	-	-	-	0
L Klusener	6	4	3	126	59*	126.00	80	157.50	0	1	0	0	27	0	163	1	163.00	6.03	1-32	0
M Ntini	2	0	0	0	0	-	0	-	0	0	0	0	8	2	21	2	10.50	2.62	2-21	0
SM Pollock	6	1	0	8	8	8.00	17	47.05	0	0	4	0	43.4	5	175	9	19.44	4.00	3-37	0
JN Rhodes	6	5	2	130	69	43.33	141	92.19	0	1	2	0	0	0	0	0	-	-	-	0
R Telemachus	4	0	0	0	0	-	0	-	0	0	0	0	35	7	151	8	18.87	4.31	3-30	0
Totals	66	38	12	1349	129		1597	84.47	3	8	22	0	216.2	23	994	34			3-30	0
				Extras	68						subs	0			b & lb	46	4 run outs			
				Total	1417		54.50					22			Total	1040	38	27.36	4.80	

NEW ZEALAND v SOUTH AFRICA 2000/01: LIMITED OVERS INTERNATIONAL AVERAGES

Name	M	Inns	NO	Runs	HS	Avg	BF	SR	100	50	Ct	St	O	M	Runs	Wkts	Avg	RpO	BB	4I
GI Allott	3	1	0	0	0	0.00	3	0.00	0	0	0	0	23	2	140	2	70.00	6.08	1-38	0
NJ Astle	6	5	0	120	58	24.00	215	55.81	0	1	1	0	26	0	142	2	71.00	5.46	2-32	0
CL Cairns	6	5	1	156	84	39.00	163	95.70	0	1	3	0	50.5	3	275	6	45.83	5.40	2-62	0
SP Fleming	6	5	0	154	85	30.80	238	64.70	0	1	1	0	0	0	0	0	-	-	-	0
CZ Harris	6	5	2	62	19	20.66	104	59.61	0	0	2	0	47	1	229	6	38.16	4.87	2-39	0
CD McMillan	6	5	0	37	13	7.40	63	58.73	0	0	0	0	4	0	29	0	-	7.25	-	0
CJ Nevin	6	5	0	92	68	18.40	114	80.70	0	1	0	0	0	0	0	0	-	-	-	0
SB O'Connor	5	2	1	2	1*	2.00	7	28.57	0	0	1	0	36.3	2	210	4	52.50	5.75	3-55	0
AC Parore	6	4	2	29	17*	14.50	36	80.55	0	0	4	1	0	0	0	0	-	-	-	0
Name	M	Inns	NO	Runs	HS	Avg	BF	SR	100	50	Ct	St	O	M	Runs	Wkts	Avg	RpO	BB	4I
SB Styris	6	3	1	19	10*	9.50	20	95.00	0	0	1	0	48	1	231	4	57.75	4.81	2-56	0
RG Twose	6	5	0	286	103	57.20	327	87.46	1	1	2	0	0	0	0	0	-	-	-	0
BGK Walker	3	2	2	7	5*	-	14	50.00	0	0	1	0	24	3	114	2	57.00	4.75	2-43	0
PJ Wiseman	1	0	0	0	0	-	0	-	0	0	0	0	4.4	0	24	0	-	5.14	-	0
Totals	66	47	9	964	103		1304	73.92	1	5	16	1	264	12	1394	26			3-55	0
				Extras	76						subs	1			b & lb	23	0 run outs			
				Total	1040		27.36					17			Total	1417	26	54.50	5.36	

SRI LANKA IN SOUTH AFRICA 2000/01

Colin Bryden

Sanath Jayasuriya led a Sri Lankan team which prepared for an encounter with South Africa's fast bowlers by simulating, before departure, some of the difficulties they would face on bouncy pitches, including facing tennis balls hurled down from close range.

It was a team which did not include Sri Lanka's two premier batsman of the previous decade and a half, with Arjuna Ranatunga retired and Aravinda de Silva not picked. The touring party included several young players with a view to them gaining experience in South Africa ahead of the 2003 World Cup. When the side was struggling with injuries, however, it was the veteran De Silva who was called up as a replacement and rushed into action.

South Africa were convincing winners of both the Test and the limited overs series and it is likely they would have won all three Test matches had rain not intervened in the first Test at Kingsmead. The next two matches were won by South Africa within three days, with the match at Newlands being decided by a South African Test record margin of an innings and 229 runs.

An unbalanced itinerary did not help the Sri Lankan cause and the tourists had only themselves to blame. The original fixture list separated the Test and one-day series but they requested changes in order to accommodate a commitment to a one-day series in New Zealand at the end of January. With Test dates at Kingsmead over the Christmas period and Newlands at New Year being sacrosanct, the only solution was to split the limited overs games into two segments. This did not help the tourists to make adequate preparations for either form of the game.

The left-handed Kumar Sangakkara provided the tourists with some cheer, confirming the promise he had shown when South Africa toured Sri Lanka earlier in the year. He topped the Test run scorers and the averages for his country. Mahela Jayawardene was in sparkling form at the start of the tour and made 98 in his first innings of the Test series before falling away under pressure from the South African fast bowlers.

The form of the opening batsmen, Jayasuriya and Marvan Atapattu, was a major disappointment for the tourists, with the side unable to make solid starts.

The bowling relied as usual on Muttiah Muralitharan, the great off-spin bowler, who was outstanding in Durban, where he took 11 wickets and became the 17th player in history to take 300 Test wickets, achieving the feat in 58 matches, the second-fastest behind Dennis Lillee of Australia (56). South Africa restricted Muralitharan to a single wicket in Cape Town and injury kept him out of the final Test as South Africa dominated both matches. Dilhara Fernando, a tall fast bowler, bowled with genuine pace.

The South African batsmen, led by Gary Kirsten, feasted on the Sri Lankan bowling, although the batting highlight was provided by Shaun Pollock, who made a thrilling maiden Test century at Centurion. Pollock was the leading wicket taker in the series and was named man of the series.

NFO XI v SRI LANKANS — One-day Match

Played at NFO Ground, Randjesfontein on 7 December 2000 — Toss: None, SL batted first by mutual consent
Umpires: CJ Mitchley & S Wadvalla
Result: Match drawn

The tourists used the pipe-opener for batting practice in ideal conditions and there was no chance of a result even before rain stopped play. Hall played some blazing strokes.

BEATEN BY PACE . . . Tillekeratne Dilshan has his leg stump uprooted by Mfuneko Ngam during the first Test at Kingsmead *Picture: Duif du Toit, TOUCHLINE PHOTO*

SRI LANKANS	Runs	Mins	Balls	4	6
MS Atapattu c Pothas b Kemp	52	95	85	9	-
*ST Jayasuriya c Ontong b de Bruyn	66	99	71	10	2
†K Sangakkara b Langeveldt	18	37	30	3	-
DPMD Jayawardene c Bruyns b de Bruyn	70	113	88	12	-
RP Arnold retired out	54	111	75	9	-
TM Dilshan not out	16	42	33	2	-
RS Kaluwitharana c Oppenheimer b Koortzen	4	11	15	-	-
WPUJC Vaas					
GP Wickramasinghe					
M Muralitharan					
CRD Fernando					
Extras (lb 4, w 3, nb 9)	16				
TOTAL (for 6 wkts dec) (64.5 overs)	**296**				

NFO XI	Runs	Mins	Balls	4	6
ML Bruyns not out	11	45	29	1	-
AJ Hall not out	61	45	41	9	1
JDC Bryant					
JM Kemp					
PPJ Koortzen					
Z de Bruyn					
†N Pothas					
JL Ontong					
*JME Oppenheimer					
CK Langeveldt					
PV Mpitsang					
Extras (b 1, lb 1, nb 6)	8				
TOTAL (for 0 wkts) (10.4 overs)	**80**				

NFO	O	M	R	W
Mpitsang	11	3	24	0
Langeveldt	10	1	44	1
Kemp	15	3	50	1
Hall	7	0	37	0
Ontong	11	0	64	0
de Bruyn	10	1	73	2
Koortzen	0.5	0	0	1

SL	O	M	R	W
Vaas	5	0	41	0
Fernando	2	0	26	0
Muralitharan	3	0	10	0
Wickramasinghe	0.4	0	1	0

Fall of Wickets	SL	NFO
1st	123 (1)	-
2nd	127 (2)	-
3rd	164 (3)	-
4th	250 (4)	-
5th	286 (5)	-
6th	296 (7)	-

EASTERN PROVINCE v SRI LANKANS — First-class 3-day match

Played at St George's Park, Port Elizabeth on 9,10 December 2000 Toss: Sri Lankans
Umpires: WA Diedricks & KH Hurter
Debuts: EP: None. SL: None
Close of Play: Day 1: SL (1) 253-9 (Zoysa 19*, Muralitharan 2*, 72 overs).
Result: Sri Lankans won by 8 wickets
Notes: GJ-P Kruger took a hat-trick in Sri Lankans 1st innings. His victims were Sangakkara, Arnold and Dilshan.

Fernando showed plenty of pace and promise as Eastern Province collapsed on an under-prepared pitch. Sri Lanka batted soundly in reply before a hat-trick by Kruger ripped out their middle order, although Jayawardene went on to a well-played 87. A second mediocre batting performance by the host meant the match was over in two days and further reduced Sri Lanka's already limited preparation for the international matches.

EASTERN PROVINCE

FIRST INNINGS	Runs	Mins	Balls	4	6	*SECOND INNINGS*	Runs	Mins	Balls	4	6
MR Benfield c Muralitharan b Zoysa	0	11	8	-	-	(2) c Kaluwitharana b Fernando	22	34	15	4	1
*CC Bradfield b Fernando	4	6	4	1	-	(1) lbw b Wickramasinghe	30	88	75	3	-
JDC Bryant c Jayawardene b Zoysa	37	70	53	3	2	c Dilshan b Fernando	50	116	95	8	-
DJ Callaghan b Fernando	9	18	14	1	-	c Dilshan b Wickramasinghe	0	6	3	-	-
JM Kemp run out (Zoysa)	0	18	9	-	-	c Kaluwitharana b Zoysa	1	29	30	-	-
MW Creed b Muralitharan	6	31	20	1	-	not out	40	142	74	4	-
RJ Peterson run out (Arnold/Muralitharan)	1	13	4	-	-	c Jayasuriya b Fernando	23	33	39	4	-
S Abrahams lbw b Muralitharan	9	36	38	1	-	lbw b Muralitharan	5	14	14	1	-
†DW Murray not out	8	34	23	1	-	c Dilshan b Muralitharan	32	63	63	2	1
M Hayward b Fernando	1	5	4	-	-	b Muralitharan	0	7	6	-	-
GJ-P Kruger c Kaluwitharana b Fernando	0	2	3	-	-	st Kaluwitharana b Muralitharan	0	2	3	-	-
Extras (lb 12, w 5)	17					Extras (b 2, lb 6, nb 3)	11				
TOTAL (30 overs)	**92**					**TOTAL (69 overs)**	**214**				

SRI LANKANS

	Runs	Mins	Balls	4	6		Runs	Mins	Balls	4	6
MS Atapattu c Murray b Kruger	42	82	68	6	-	not out	19	30	19	2	-
*ST Jayasuriya c Callaghan b Hayward	38	78	57	7	-	c Bradfield b Kemp	0	9	6	-	-
K Sangakkara c Peterson b Kruger	37	105	80	5	1	c Peterson b Kemp	6	10	8	1	-
DPMD Jayawardene lbw b Kemp	87	184	145	11	2	not out	14	9	7	3	-
RP Arnold lbw b Kruger	0	1	1	-	-						
TM Dilshan c Kemp b Kruger	0	1	1	-	-						
†RS Kaluwitharana c Murray b Creed	15	56	30	2	-						
DNT Zoysa not out	27	57	34	5	-						
GP Wickramasinghe b Kemp	0	1	1	-	-						
CRD Fernando c Murray b Kemp	4	9	13	-	-						
M Muralitharan c Belfield b Kemp	7	21	14	1	-						
Extras (b 2, lb 1, w 2, nb 4)	9					Extras (b 1, lb 1)	2				
TOTAL (73.2 overs)	**266**					**TOTAL (for 2 wkts) (6.4 overs)**	**41**				

Bowling	*O*	*M*	*R*	*W*		*O*	*M*	*R*	*W*
SRI LANKANS									
Zoysa	8	2	16	2		14	3	55	1
Fernando	11	6	27	4		16	2	76	3
Wickramasinghe	5	1	28	0	(4)	11	4	34	2
Muralitharan	6	2	9	2	(3)	28	11	41	4
EASTERN PROVINCE									
Hayward	11	0	60	1					
Kemp	21.2	4	59	4	(1)	3.4	1	15	2
Kruger	20	5	76	4	(2)	3	0	24	0
Creed	10	2	26	1					
Peterson	7	1	24	0					
Abrahams	4	1	18	0					

Fall of Wickets	EP 1st	SL 1st	EP 2nd	SL 2nd
1st	9 (2)	85 (2)	47 (2)	11 (2)
2nd	13 (1)	85 (1)	81 (1)	23 (3)
3rd	22 (4)	176 (3)	85 (4)	-
4th	28 (5)	176 (5)	103 (5)	-
5th	69 (3)	176 (6)	114 (3)	-
6th	69 (6)	224 (7)	147 (7)	-
7th	71 (7)	232 (4)	164 (8)	-
8th	91 (8)	232 (9)	214 (9)	-
9th	92 (10)	236 (10)	214 (10)	-
10th	92 (11)	266 (11)	214 (11)	-

EASTERN PROVINCE v SRI LANKANS — Limited Overs Match

Played at PPC Oval, Port Elizabeth on 13 December 2000

Toss: Eastern Province

Umpires: GB Cuddembey & WA Diedricks (TV: KH Hurter)

Debuts: EP: None. SL: None

Result: Match tied

Man of Match: Justin Kemp

What had looked likely to be an easy win for the tourists turned into a desperate scramble. Five runs were needed off the last over, bowled by South Africa A seamer Kruger, but three wickets fell, including two run-outs, with Wickramasinghe out off the last ball when he hit the ball straight to Eastern Province captain Bradfield at mid-off.

Kemp played a thrilling innings for Eastern Province after Vaas and Wickramasinghe had the home side floundering on a slow pitch.

EASTERN PROVINCE	*Runs*	*Mins*	*Balls*	*4*	*6*
MR Benfield lbw b Vaas	0	1	1	-	-
*CC Bradfield b Vaas	82	169	136	3	2
RJ Peterson b Wickramasinghe	4	30	25	-	-
JDC Bryant c Jayasuriya b Vaas	9	12	10	2	-
JM Kemp b Muralitharan	93	129	109	9	2
MW Creed b Jayasuriya	2	11	9	-	-
U Abrahams lbw b Vaas	5	6	10	-	-
†DW Murray not out	3	7	3	-	-
S Abrahams not out	4	2	3	-	-
MW Pringle					
GJ-P Kruger					
Extras (b 5, lb 7, w 4, nb 2)	18				
TOTAL (for 7 wkts) (50 overs)	**220**				

SRI LANKANS	*Runs*	*Mins*	*Balls*	*4*	*6*
*ST Jayasuriya c Benfield b S Abrahams	69	118	87	5	1
†RS Kaluwitharana lbw b Kruger	1	7	5	-	-
MS Atapattu st Murray b Peterson	27	82	58	2	-
DPMD Jayawardene c Kemp b Kruger	21	41	34	2	-
K Sangakkara c Pringle b Creed	34	66	45	2	-
RP Arnold c Kruger b Kemp	14	38	31	1	-
TM Dilshan b Kruger	20	34	27	1	-
WPUJC Vaas b Pringle	7	9	7	-	-
K Weeraratne run out (Murray)	3	12	4	-	-
M Muralitharan not out	2	8	2	-	-
GP Wickramasinghe run out (Bradfield)	1	3	1	-	-
Extras (b 2, lb 11, w 7, nb 1)	21				
TOTAL (50 overs)	**220**				

SL	*O*	*M*	*R*	*W*
Vaas	10	1	27	4
Wickramasinghe	10	3	31	1
Weeraratne	6	0	37	0
Muralitharan	10	2	31	1
Jayasuriya	6	0	37	1
Arnold	5	0	29	0
Dilshan	3	0	16	0

EP	*O*	*M*	*R*	*W*
Pringle	8	0	59	1
Kruger	10	2	23	3
Creed	9	0	36	1
Kemp	7	0	29	1
S Abrahams	10	0	43	1
Peterson	6	1	17	1

Fall of Wickets	*EP*	*SL*
1st	0 (1)	10 (2)
2nd	11 (3)	96 (3)
3rd	26 (4)	120 (1)
4th	201 (2)	144 (4)
5th	206 (5)	181 (6)
6th	212 (6)	195 (5)
7th	216 (7)	208 (8)
8th	-	216 (7)
9th	-	219 (9)
10th	-	220 (11)

SOUTH AFRICA v SRI LANKA — 1st Limited Overs International

Played at St George's Park, Port Elizabeth on 15 December 2000

Toss: Sri Lanka

Umpires: WA Diedricks & RE Koertzen (TV: IL Howell)

Debuts: SA: None. SL: None

Result: South Africa won by 4 wickets

Man of Match: Jonty Rhodes

McKenzie returned to the South African squad for the first two limited overs games following the retirement of Daryll Cullinan from one-day international cricket. Allan Donald, recovering from a stomach muscle injury, was also included but did not play in either match

Rhodes, having had a break from international cricket after deciding to retire from Test matches, played a crucial innings as he and Klusener steered South Africa to victory. South Africa had been in trouble after good bowling by the tall left-armer Zoysa and two direct-hit run-outs.

Sri Lanka included both their wicketkeepers, Kaluwitharana and Sangakkara, and they were mainly responsible for Sri Lanka's total. Pollock was the most successful bowler but Klusener bowled a tight spell at a crucial stage.

SRI LANKA	*Runs*	*Mins*	*Balls*	*4*	*6*	SOUTH AFRICA	*Runs*	*Mins*	*Balls*	*4*	*6*
*ST Jayasuriya b Pollock	3	13	11	-	-	G Kirsten st Kaluwitharana b Muralitharan	58	116	70	6	-
†RS Kaluwitharana b Kallis	55	96	69	7	-	AJ Hall c Kaluwitharana b Zoysa	18	37	24	3	-
MS Atapattu c and b Telemachus	2	11	13	-	-	N Boje run out (Jayawardene)	6	8	10	1	-
DPMD Jayawardene c Boucher b Ntini	13	42	28	2	-	JH Kallis c and b Zoysa	0	4	4	-	-
K Sangakkara b Pollock	84	135	114	8	-	HH Dippenaar c Kaluwitharana b Vaas	19	29	24	2	-
RP Arnold c Boucher b Klusener	5	20	12	1	-	JN Rhodes not out	61	123	80	3	-
TM Dilshan run out (Kallis/Rhodes/Boucher)	18	35	22	2	-	†MV Boucher run out (Arnold)	9	20	19	-	-
WPUJC Vaas b Pollock	18	39	28	1	-	L Klusener not out	39	66	54	4	-
DNT Zoysa c Pollock b Kallis	1	4	4	-	-	*SM Pollock					
M Muralitharan not out	2	8	2	-	-	R Telemachus					
GP Wickramasinghe b Pollock	1	4	3	-	-	M Ntini					
Extras (lb 5, w 7, nb 7)	19					Extras (lb 8, w 4, nb 1)	13				
TOTAL (49.5 overs)	**221**					**TOTAL (for 6 wkts) (47.2 overs)**	**223**				

SA	*O*	*M*	*R*	*W*	SL	*O*	*M*	*R*	*W*	Fall of Wickets	*SL*	*SA*
Pollock	9.5	1	36	4	Vaas	9	1	50	1	1st	16 (1)	49 (2)
Telemachus	10	1	46	1	Zoysa	9	0	35	2	2nd	21 (3)	56 (3)
Kallis	9	1	34	2	Wickramasinghe	7.2	0	44	0	3rd	63 (4)	57 (4)
Ntini	5	0	44	1	Muralitharan	10	1	39	1	4th	91 (2)	91 (5)
Klusener	10	0	26	1	Jayasuriya	7	0	31	0	5th	112 (6)	126 (1)
Boje	6	0	30	0	Arnold	5	1	16	0	6th	159 (7)	143 (7)
										7th	211 (8)	-
										8th	214 (9)	-
										9th	219 (5)	-
										10th	221 (11)	-

SOUTH AFRICA v SRI LANKA — 2nd Limited Overs International

Played at Buffalo Park, East London on 17 December 2000
Toss: South Africa
Umpires: IL Howell & DL Orchard (TV: WA Diedricks)
Debuts: SA: None. SL: None
Result: South Africa won by 95 runs
Man of Match: Neil McKenzie

Included in South Africa's starting line-up for the first time in ten matches, McKenzie hit a maiden limited overs international century as South Africa hammered Sri Lanka. McKenzie enabled his team to overcome a poor start and take advantage of ideal batting conditions. South Africa's total of 302 for seven was the highest in an international match at Buffalo Park.

McKenzie was dropped on 35 when he swept Muralitharan to Chandana at square leg. It proved a costly error as he and Rhodes put on 88 for the fourth wicket, with Rhodes racing to his second successive half-century, playing in his 189th one-day international, a record for South Africa.

It was an ideal one-day innings, with McKenzie batting fluently in the anchor role while first Rhodes then Boucher went for their shots.

Sri Lanka were never on target after Kaluwitharana and Jayasuriya were dismissed in the first five overs by Pollock. With the match effectively decided, Arnold and Vaas shared a face-saving unbeaten seventh wicket stand of 60, evidently opting for batting practice ahead of the Test matches.

SOUTH AFRICA	Runs	Mins	Balls	4	6
G Kirsten c Jayawardene b Zoysa	6	29	13	-	-
AJ Hall lbw b Vaas	0	2	1	-	-
JH Kallis c Arnold b Wickramasinghe	35	68	48	4	1
ND McKenzie not out	120	183	135	13	1
JN Rhodes c Muralitharan b Jayasuriya	50	67	51	3	1
†MV Boucher c Wickramasinghe b Muralitharan	55	53	48	5	1
L Klusener c Chandana b Zoysa	6	13	6	1	-
N Boje run out (Atapattu)	7	9	4	1	-
*SM Pollock					
R Telemachus					
M Ntini					
Extras (lb 12, w 5, nb 6)	23				
TOTAL (for 7 wkts) (50 overs)	**302**				

SRI LANKA	Runs	Mins	Balls	4	6
*ST Jayasuriya b Pollock	7	20	9	-	-
†RS Kaluwitharana lbw b Pollock	2	12	9	-	-
MS Atapattu c Boucher b Ntini	36	81	57	4	-
DPMD Jayawardene c and b Boje	59	129	84	5	-
K Sangakkara c Hall b Ntini	11	27	21	1	-
RP Arnold not out	39	94	56	3	-
UDU Chandana lbw b Klusener	2	5	3	-	-
WPUJC Vaas not out	34	59	68	2	-
DNT Zoysa					
M Muralitharan					
GP Wickramasinghe					
Extras (lb 3, w 7, nb 7)	17				
TOTAL (for 6 wkts) (50 overs)	**207**				

SL	O	M	R	W
Vaas	10	0	54	1
Zoysa	10	0	68	2
Wickramasinghe	7	0	39	1
Muralitharan	10	0	47	1
Chandana	7	0	43	0
Arnold	1	0	10	0
Jayasuriya	5	0	29	1

SA	O	M	R	W
Pollock	10	0	34	2
Telemachus	9	1	44	0
Ntini	10	0	38	2
Kallis	8	0	30	0
Klusener	9	2	32	1
Boje	3	0	21	1
McKenzie	1	0	5	0

Fall of Wickets	SA	SL
1st	1 (2)	8 (2)
2nd	24 (1)	17 (1)
3rd	69 (3)	80 (3)
4th	157 (5)	106 (5)
5th	257 (6)	141 (4)
6th	279 (7)	147 (7)
7th	302 (8)	-

KWAZULU-NATAL v SRI LANKANS — Limited Overs Match

Played at Chatsworth Stadium, Chatsworth on 19 December 2000 Toss: KwaZulu-Natal
Umpires: IL Howell & WA Diedricks (TV: M Gajjar)
Debuts: KZN: None. SL: None
Result: Sri Lankans won by 55 runs
Man of Match: Mahela Jayawardene

Having committed to a match in Chatsworth, Sri Lanka's imperfect preparation for the Test series continued with Jayawardene again proving the best of their batsmen against an attack in which the left-armer Gilder and off-spinner Bender impressed. Bodi played a sparkling innings for the Natalians.

SRI LANKANS	Runs	Mins	Balls	4	6
DA Gunawardene lbw b Gilder	3	28	18	-	-
†RS Kaluwitharana c Brown b Gilder	13	12	9	3	-
*MS Atapattu c and b Kent	14	40	35	1	-
DPMD Jayawardene b Bender	85	124	88	7	1
K Sangakkara c Watson b Bender	28	53	46	3	-
RP Arnold run out (Watson/Bender/Brown)	23	48	45	-	-
WPUJC Vaas not out	52	48	41	1	3
TM Dilshan b Gilder	13	27	19	-	-
M Pushpakumara b Gilder	1	8	4	-	-
K Weeraratne not out	4	8	2	-	-
CRD Fernando					
Extras (b 4, lb 10, w 10, nb 6)	30				
TOTAL (for 8 wkts) (50 overs)	**266**				

KWAZULU-NATAL	Runs	Mins	Balls	4	6
*DJ Watson c Sangakkara b Vaas	42	110	74	1	-
A Mall b Fernando	14	21	20	1	-
R Gobind c Pushpakumara b Fernando	14	24	28	2	-
JC Kent c Pushpakumara b Weeraratne	23	26	29	3	-
AM Amla c Atapattu b Pushpakumara	4	17	19	-	-
†DL Brown c Gunawardene b Pushpakumara	14	12	13	2	-
GH Bodi c Dilshan b Weeraratne	53	64	54	6	1
KS Bender run out (Atapattu/Pushpakumara)	0	4	2	-	-
GM Gilder c Atapattu b Vaas	28	38	25	2	2
SM Adam lbw b Weeraratne	5	16	10	-	-
BBN Hlongwane not out	0	1	0	-	-
Extras (b 4, lb 1, w 3, nb 6)	14				
TOTAL (44.4 overs)	**211**				

KZN	O	M	R	W
Gilder	10	0	43	4
Adam	8	0	49	0
Kent	10	1	56	1
Hlongwane	5	0	30	0
Bodi	7	0	40	0
Bender	10	0	34	2

SL	O	M	R	W
Vaas	8	0	35	2
Fernando	8	0	39	2
Weeraratne	7.4	0	37	3
Arnold	10	0	35	0
Pushpakumara	9	0	52	2
Jayawardene	2	0	8	0

Fall of Wickets	SL	KZN
1st	19 (2)	22 (2)
2nd	31 (1)	43 (3)
3rd	56 (3)	76 (4)
4th	121 (5)	95 (5)
5th	192 (4)	115 (6)
6th	192 (6)	120 (1)
7th	234 (8)	120 (8)
8th	248 (9)	192 (9)
9th	-	211 (7)
10th	-	211 (10)

KWAZULU-NATAL v SRI LANKANS — First-class 3-day match

Played at The Oval, Pietermaritzburg on 21 (no play),22,23 December 2000 — Toss: Sri Lankans
Umpires: M Gajjar & DL Orchard (TV: WA Diedricks)
Debuts: KZN: L Dladla (FC). SL: None
Close of Play: Day 1: No play. Day 2: SL (1) 257-8*.
Result: Match drawn

Sri Lanka, already short of quality preparation for the Test series, suffered a blow when the first day was abandoned because of a saturated outfield. Further rain and bad light cut 39.4 overs from the second day's play during which Jayawardene continued his good form. Another failure by Jayasuriya in a shaky top order was a concern for the tourists. Gilder troubled the early batsmen with his pace and bounce before Jayawardene and Dilshan put on 134 for the fifth wicket at a run a minute.

It was Jayawardene's third score in the 80s on tour and the fifth time in seven matches he had top-scored for a team which collectively had yet to notch a century in South Africa.

Bruyns and Watson put on 168 for the first wicket as the home side carried out a vow by skipper Stewart to "do a job for our country" ahead of the first Test. Kent was the victim of a poor decision when he was given out by television umpire Diedricks. Kent drove Chandana and the ball bounced a metre short of the shin pads of Dilshan at silly point before rebounding into the gloves of Kaluwitharana.

SRI LANKANS

FIRST INNINGS	*Runs*	*Mins*	*Balls*	*4*	*6*
*ST Jayasuriya c Kent b Gilder	14	26	14	3	-
MS Atapattu c Mall b Gilder	8	8	13	2	-
K Sangakkara c Stewart b Adam	3	17	10	-	-
DPMD Jayawardene b Bodi	87	158	119	15	-
RP Arnold c Amla b Gilder	5	15	11	1	-
TM Dilshan c Bruyns b Kent	54	167	116	9	-
†RS Kaluwitharana c Wingfield b Bodi	40	59	50	8	-
UDU Chandana c Stewart b Wingfield	2	19	14	-	-
DNT Zoysa not out	24	36	39	3	-
GP Wickramasinghe not out	4	25	15	-	-
CRD Fernando					
Extras (w 2, nb 14)	16				
TOTAL (for 8 wkts dec) (64.2 overs)	**257**				

KWAZULU-NATAL

	Runs	Mins	Balls	4	6
ML Bruyns b Wickramasinghe	89	181	156	13	-
DJ Watson c Jayawardene b Chandana	81	222	158	11	-
A Mall c Kaluwitharana b Jayawardene	34	72	67	5	-
JC Kent c Kaluwitharana b Chandana	1	8	9	-	-
AM Amla c Dilshan b Jayawardene	0	19	16	-	-
*†ELR Stewart not out	39	61	62	4	1
WR Wingfield not out	39	58	48	4	1
GH Bodi					
GM Gilder					
SM Adam					
L Dladla					
Extras (b 7, lb 2, nb 7)	16				
TOTAL (for 5 wkts) (84.3 overs)	**299**				

Bowling	*O*	*M*	*R*	*W*
KWAZULU-NATAL				
Gilder	13.2	1	55	3
Adam	8	1	49	1
Dladla	9	1	26	0
Kent	13	3	48	1
Wingfield	7	2	26	1
Bodi	14	1	53	2
SRI LANKANS				
Zoysa	7.3	3	20	0
Fernando	14	2	55	0
Wickramasinghe	11	4	33	1
Dilshan	3	1	13	0
Chandana	28	4	109	2
Arnold	9	3	22	0
Jayasuriya	4	1	11	0
Jayawardene	8	1	27	2

Fall of Wickets	**SL**	**KZN**
	1st	1st
1st	15 (2)	168 (1)
2nd	27 (1)	197 (2)
3rd	27 (3)	203 (4)
4th	46 (5)	217 (5)
5th	180 (4)	218 (3)
6th	210 (6)	-
7th	228 (8)	-
8th	230 (7)	-
9th	-	-
10th	-	-

SOUTH AFRICA v SRI LANKA — 1st Test

Played at Kingsmead, Durban on 26,27,28,29,30 December 2000 — Toss: South Africa
Umpires: DL Orchard & Riazuddin (TV: IL Howell)
Debuts: SA: None. SL: None
Close of Play: Day 1: SA (1) 230-3 (Kirsten 112*, McKenzie 5*, 79.2 overs). Day 2: SL (1) 62-2 (Sangakkara 25*, Jayawardene 31*, 23 overs). Day 3: SA (2) 47-1 (Kirsten 20*, Kallis 1*, 12.3 overs). Day 4: No play.
Result: Match drawn
Man of Match: Gary Kirsten

Ngam kept his place in the team with Donald still not recovered from his muscle injury.

Kirsten hit his 11th Test century, equalling Cullinan's South African record and set a record by scoring a century against a seventh Test opponent as South Africa built a strong position on the first day. After heavy rain during the previous week, including the day before the match, the pitch was slow.

Kirsten was seldom troubled as he made his second successive Test century at Kingsmead, following his match-saving 275 against England a year before. Cullinan was in superb form in a stand of 108 with Kirsten before going down the pitch to Muralitharan and hitting the ball on the full to mid-wicket.

The 21-year-old Fernando bowled impressively for Sri Lanka, taking a wicket in his first over and producing some fiery deliveries before going on to take his first five-wicket haul in his second Test.

Although the new ball was due soon after the start of the second day, it was not taken until the 100th over, by which time Muralitharan had dismissed McKenzie and Boucher. Kirsten and Klusener batted solidly, although both found scoring difficult against accurate bowling and defensive fields. Kirsten seemed set for a second successive double century at Kingsmead before he was caught behind when the ball brushed his bat as he tried to avoid a bouncer from Fernando.

A direct hit by Ntini from cover ran out Atapattu and Jayasuriya cut Ngam to deep point as both Sri Lankan openers were out for nought. Sangakkara and Jayawardene fought back strongly, however, putting on a record 168 for the third wicket. Remarkably, the other nine wickets cost a mere 48 runs as the rest of the batting folded.

Sangakkara's dismissal, when he drove a low catch to extra cover off left-arm spinner Nicky Boje, sparked a dramatic slump. Jayawardene advanced to within two runs of his fifth Test century before Klusener was able to generate extra bounce from an otherwise placid pitch to brush the batsman's glove.

Pollock, with the second new ball, took the last three wickets in five deliveries. His second victim was Zoysa, who top-edged a pull to Ngam. It was Pollock's 200th wicket in his 49th Test.

Prompted no doubt by the prospect of having to face Muralitharan on a wearing pitch in the final innings, South Africa did not enforce the follow-on but they were thwarted by the loss of the fourth day to rain. Trying to push along the scoring rate, they struggled against Muralitharan. Pollock, promoting himself to number four, was the off-spinner's 300th Test victim when he was caught off his pad at silly point. Muralitharan went on to complete his 24th five-wicket haul and to take ten in a match for the fifth time.

Set to make 345 in 82 overs, Sri Lanka held on for a draw despite being put under pressure by Boje's left-arm spin. Bad light stopped play eight overs early.

Lakshman Kiriella, the Sri Lankan minister of tourism and sport, made a presentation to Muralitharan during the tea break. The spin bowler said he aimed to go on to take 500 Test wickets.

SOUTH AFRICA

FIRST INNINGS	*Runs*	*Mins*	*Balls*	*4*	*6*	*SECOND INNINGS*	*Runs*	*Mins*	*Balls*	*4*	*6*
HH Dippenaar c Kaluwitharana b Fernando	11	39	27	1	-	lbw b Muralitharan	22	49	36	3	-
G Kirsten c Kaluwitharana b Fernando	180	574	461	20	-	c Arnold b Muralitharan	34	115	71	2	-
JH Kallis c Muralitharan b Fernando	21	87	56	2	-	b Muralitharan	15	47	41	1	-
DJ Cullinan c Atapattu b Muralitharan	59	139	116	7	1	(9) not out	2	5	4	-	-
ND McKenzie c Dilshan b Muralitharan	9	65	48	1	-	(7) lbw b Muralitharan	13	19	16	1	1
†MV Boucher c Arnold b Muralitharan	17	32	24	1	-	c Vaas b Muralitharan	10	7	7	2	-
L Klusener c Sangakkara b Muralitharan	50	157	121	5	-	(8) not out	11	19	10	2	-
N Boje b Muralitharan	32	71	51	3	-	(5) c Sangakkara b Fernando	8	19	8	1	-
*SM Pollock c Kaluwitharana b Fernando	2	13	13	-	-	(4) c Dilshan b Muralitharan	11	20	17	1	-
M Ntini b Fernando	8	9	12	2	-						
M Ngam not out	0	3	1	-	-						
Extras (b 5, lb 10, w 1, nb 15)	31					Extras (b 4, lb 3, nb 7)	14				
TOTAL (152.3 overs)	**420**					**TOTAL (for 7 wkts dec) (34 overs)**	**140**				

SRI LANKA

	Runs	*Mins*	*Balls*	*4*	*6*		*Runs*	*Mins*	*Balls*	*4*	*6*
MS Atapattu run out (Ntini)	0	6	6	-	-	c Boucher b Boje	20	132	98	1	-
*ST Jayasuriya c McKenzie b Ngam	0	16	8	-	-	c Cullinan b Ngam	26	60	44	5	-
K Sangakkara c Kirsten b Boje	74	269	213	8	1	st Boucher b Boje	17	55	37	1	-
DPMD Jayawardene c Boucher b Klusener	98	270	195	13	-	c Boucher b Ntini	7	27	18	-	-
RP Arnold b Boje	3	17	9	-	-	c Dippenaar b Pollock	30	124	100	3	-
TM Dilshan b Ngam	6	59	45	1	-	not out	28	150	119	3	-
†RS Kaluwitharana c Boucher b Ntini	16	31	27	2	-	c Boje b Pollock	1	9	9	-	-
WPUJC Vaas c Boucher b Pollock	2	24	19	-	-	not out	3	27	25	-	-
DNT Zoysa c Ngam b Pollock	3	12	7	-	-						
CRD Fernando not out	5	9	3	1	-						
M Muralitharan c Boucher b Pollock	0	1	1	-	-						
Extras (nb 9)	9					Extras (b 4, lb 7, nb 6)	17				
TOTAL (87.4 overs)	**216**					**TOTAL (for 6 wkts) (74 overs)**	**149**				

Bowling	*O*	*M*	*R*	*W*	*O*	*M*	*R*	*W*
SRI LANKA								
Vaas	26	1	84	0	9	1	25	0
Zoysa	20	3	62	0	5	0	21	0
Fernando	34	4	98	5	10	0	48	1
Muralitharan	58.3	16	122	5	10	1	39	6
Arnold	14	3	39	0				
SOUTH AFRICA								
Pollock	20.4	7	40	3	16	5	35	2
Ngam	12	0	59	2	13	3	34	1
Ntini	16	5	36	1	10	4	18	1
Kallis	9	3	17	0	6	1	14	0
Boje	19	4	44	2	24	12	30	2
Klusener	11	5	20	1	5	1	7	0

Fall of Wickets	**SA** 1st	**SL** 1st	**SA** 2nd	**SL** 2nd
1st	31 (1)	0 (1)	46 (1)	41 (2)
2nd	86 (3)	2 (2)	75 (3)	69 (3)
3rd	194 (4)	170 (3)	91 (2)	80 (1)
4th	238 (5)	184 (4)	92 (4)	80 (4)
5th	269 (6)	184 (5)	108 (6)	132 (5)
6th	358 (7)	201 (7)	114 (5)	140 (7)
7th	401 (2)	208 (6)	132 (7)	-
8th	410 (9)	208 (8)	-	-
9th	420 (10)	215 (9)	-	-
10th	420 (8)	216 (11)	-	-

SOUTH AFRICA v SRI LANKA — 2nd Test

Played at Newlands, Cape Town on 2,3,4 January 2001 — Toss: Sri Lanka
Umpires: IL Howell & EA Nicholls (TV: WA Diedricks)
Debuts: SA: None. SL: None
Close of Play: Day 1: SA (1) 130-2 (Kallis 49*, Cullinan 17*, 49 overs). Day 2: SA (1) 426-6 (Klusener 44*, Boje 7*, 139 overs).
Result: South Africa won by an innings and 229 runs
Man of Match: Shaun Pollock

SOMETHING TO REMEMBER . . . Shaun Pollock receives a special presentation after taking his 200th Test wicket at Kingsmead
Picture: Duif du Toit, TOUCHLINE PHOTO

SRI LANKA IN SOUTH AFRICA 2000/01

Herschelle Gibbs, banned from international cricket until December 31 for agreeing to accept a bribe from his former captain Hansie Cronje, was not included in the squad originally named for the first two Tests, although convenor Rushdi Magiet said the selectors reserved the right to make changes. No sooner had Gibbs' ban expired than he was back in the team at the expense of Dippenaar.

Donald was again unable to take his place because of a stomach muscle injury.

Pollock was in irresistible form as South Africa took command from the moment Atapattu was caught at second slip in the fifth over. Pollock took four for nine in his first spell of eight overs, taking the wickets in the space of 13 balls for no runs.

The Sri Lankans were virtually defenceless against a bombardment of short-pitched bowling. Ngam took three wickets as he and Pollock exploited a pitch with good bounce and some lateral movement. All ten Sri Lankans were caught, seven in the cordon between wicketkeeper and gully.

South Africa were batting before tea and Gibbs was the only failure, staying on the back foot and pushing at the second ball he received to be caught behind.

Kallis edged a drive to first slip off the second ball of the second day but Cullinan hit his 12th Test century and his fourth in successive Tests at Newlands. It was a commanding innings although he had some anxious moments against Muralitharan before again moving ahead of Kirsten on the all-time century list.

Sri Lanka's tactics were puzzling. The second new ball was due immediately after lunch when South Africa's total was 214 for three off 80 overs. But Jayasuriya started the post-lunch period by giving Arnold his first over of the match.

Arnold had an early success when he held a return catch from McKenzie in his third over but no further wickets fell during 28 overs in which Arnold and Muralitharan bowled in tandem. The total had advanced to 305 and Cullinan had passed his century when the new ball was eventually taken. Muralitharan beat Cullinan with a top-spinner on 87 and had him dropped by Dilshan at silly mid-off on 89.

Boucher took over as the senior batsman after Cullinan's dismissal as he and Klusener added 94 in 96 minutes for the sixth wicket. Boucher holed out to deep backward square leg off Arnold six overs from the close and Klusener also fell to the part-timer just short of his century, pulling to mid-wicket the following morning after hitting the previous ball for a straight six.

Sri Lanka's batting was again ineffective against pace, with Ngam taking the first two wickets in an opening spell during which he was timed at 147kmh. There was some defiance from Jayawardene and Arnold but Boje, with his second delivery of the match, won an lbw verdict when Jayawardene missed a sweep.

It was the biggest winning margin in South Africa's Test history and Sri Lanka's heaviest defeat.

SRI LANKA

FIRST INNINGS	*Runs*	*Mins*	*Balls*	*4*	*6*	*SECOND INNINGS*	*Runs*	*Mins*	*Balls*	*4*	*6*
MS Atapattu c Kallis b Pollock	5	18	19	-	-	lbw b Pollock	13	59	39	3	-
*ST Jayasuriya c Boucher b Pollock	8	28	12	1	-	c Pollock b Ngam	0	7	2	-	-
†K Sangakkara c Cullinan b Ngam	32	105	76	5	-	c Boucher b Ngam	11	23	18	2	-
DPMD Jayawardene c Kallis b Pollock	0	3	3	-	-	lbw b Boje	45	90	65	8	-
RP Arnold c Kirsten b Pollock	0	7	3	-	-	c Gibbs b Boje	26	78	42	3	-
TM Dilshan c Pollock b Kallis	5	41	24	-	-	c Boucher b Boje	17	31	32	3	-
DA Gunawardene c Kallis b Ngam	24	69	54	4	-	b Ntini	13	21	17	2	-
WPUJC Vaas c Pollock b Ngam	7	46	29	1	-	c and b Boje	38	34	26	6	2
DNT Zoysa c and b Pollock	10	22	11	-	1	c Klusener b Ntini	0	7	5	-	-
CRD Fernando not out	0	6	1	-	-	c Boucher b Ngam	5	31	23	-	-
M Muralitharan c Ntini b Pollock	0	2	3	-	-	not out	1	10	7	-	-
Extras (w 1, nb 3)	4					Extras (lb 6, w 1, nb 4)	11				
TOTAL (38.4 overs)	**95**					**TOTAL (45.2 overs)**	**180**				

SOUTH AFRICA					
G Kirsten c Dilshan b Muralitharan	52	156	114	7	-
HH Gibbs c Sangakkara b Vaas	0	3	2	-	-
JH Kallis c Jayawardene b Fernando	49	206	150	6	-
DJ Cullinan run out (Vaas)	112	289	232	12	3
ND McKenzie c and b Arnold	47	131	109	5	1
†MV Boucher c Jayawardene b Arnold	92	200	143	10	-
L Klusener c Jayasuriya b Arnold	97	210	143	13	1
N Boje not out	31	108	75	3	-
*SM Pollock					
M Ntini					
M Ngam					
Extras (lb 5, w 1, nb 18)	24				
TOTAL (for 7 wkts dec) (158.2 overs)	**504**				

Bowling	*O*	*M*	*R*	*W*	*O*	*M*	*R*	*W*
SOUTH AFRICA								
Pollock	13.4	6	30	6	9	3	29	1
Ngam	13	3	26	3	8.2	1	36	3
Kallis	6	2	19	1	7	1	29	0
Ntini	6	2	20	0	11	2	52	2
Boje					10	3	28	4
SRI LANKA								
Vaas	32	6	109	1				
Zoysa	26	6	80	0				
Fernando	25	2	105	1				
Muralitharan	43	11	99	1				
Jayasuriya	7	1	28	0				
Arnold	24.2	4	76	3				
Jayawardene	1	0	2	0				

Fall of Wickets	SL 1st	SA 1st	SL 2nd
1st	12 (1)	1 (2)	4 (2)
2nd	13 (2)	97 (1)	18 (3)
3rd	13 (4)	130 (3)	53 (1)
4th	13 (5)	231 (5)	99 (4)
5th	33 (6)	317 (4)	112 (5)
6th	66 (3)	411 (6)	119 (6)
7th	84 (7)	504 (7)	131 (7)
8th	95 (8)	-	135 (9)
9th	95 (9)	-	172 (8)
10th	95 (11)	-	180 (10)

SOUTH AFRICA v SRI LANKA — 3rd Limited Overs International

Played at Boland PKS Park, Paarl on 9 January 2001 — Toss: Sri Lanka
Umpires: WA Diedricks & DL Orchard (TV: SB Lambson)
Debuts: SA: None. SL: None
Result: South Africa won by 8 wickets
Man of Match: Jacques Kallis

Donald's return was again delayed. Having recovered from a stomach muscle injury he was kept out by an abscess on his right elbow. With Telemachus suffering a neck spasm, Alan Dawson came in as an emergency replacement. Kirsten suffered a cracked metacarpal when he was hit on the left hand during a net practice on the morning of the match. He was to miss the rest of the international season.

Sri Lankan all-rounder Upul Chandana went home because of a broken finger, suffered during a net practice.

Jayasuriya returned to form after scoring only ten runs in the first two one-day internationals and 34 in four innings in the first two Tests. He struck the ball crisply as he and Kaluwitharana gave the side a rare good start. Kaluwitharana was dropped four times, including difficult caught and bowled chances to Pollock on 11 and Kallis on 30. He was dropped twice off Boje on 81, by Gibbs at mid-wicket and Dawson at wide long-on.

It was a challenging target for South Africa but Dippenaar and Kallis batted superbly and Rhodes was in dazzling form.

Kallis received treatment for a bruised right hand after dropping Kaluwitharana. He took his right hand off his bat several times early in his innings but batted more comfortably as his anchor innings progressed. It took him 88 balls to reach 50 with only one four but he accelerated towards the end.

SRI LANKA	Runs	Mins	Balls	4	6
*ST Jayasuriya lbw b Boje	66	112	83	7	1
†RS Kaluwitharana b Pollock	83	164	117	8	-
MS Atapattu not out	51	93	71	1	-
DPMD Jayawardene b Boje	22	20	16	3	-
WPUJC Vaas c Gibbs b Kallis	3	8	4	-	-
K Sangakkara not out	16	10	9	2	-
RP Arnold					
K Weeraratne					
DNT Zoysa					
CRD Fernando					
M Muralitharan					
Extras (b 1, lb 4, w 1)	6				
TOTAL (for 4 wkts) (50 overs)	**247**				

SOUTH AFRICA	Runs	Mins	Balls	4	6
HH Dippenaar c Muralitharan b Weeraratne	65	121	100	5	-
HH Gibbs lbw b Vaas	1	9	2	-	-
JH Kallis not out	100	202	139	3	1
JN Rhodes not out	75	89	59	5	-
ND McKenzie					
†MV Boucher					
L Klusener					
N Boje					
*SM Pollock					
AC Dawson					
M Ntini					
Extras (w 2, nb 7)	9				
TOTAL (for 2 wkts) (48.5 overs)	**250**				

SA	O	M	R	W
Pollock	10	0	33	1
Dawson	9	0	58	0
Ntini	8	0	40	0
Kallis	8	0	40	1
Klusener	5	0	32	0
Boje	10	0	39	2

SL	O	M	R	W
Vaas	9.5	1	37	1
Zoysa	10	0	48	0
Fernando	7	0	54	0
Muralitharan	10	0	39	0
Weeraratne	6	0	30	1
Jayasuriya	5	0	31	0
Arnold	1	0	11	0

Fall of Wickets	SL	SA
1st	110 (1)	5 (2)
2nd	184 (2)	116 (1)
3rd	217 (4)	-
4th	225 (5)	-

SOUTH AFRICA v SRI LANKA — 4th Limited Overs International

Played at Newlands, Cape Town on 11 January 2001 — Toss: South Africa
Umpires: RE Koertzen & SB Lambson (TV: BG Jerling)
Debuts: SA: None. SL: None
Result: South Africa won by 99 runs
Man of Match: Makhaya Ntini

South Africa gained a crushing win to clinch the series with two matches to spare. A big total set it up with Dippenaar showing fluent form as he dominated stands of 53 for the first wicket with Gibbs and 67 for the second wicket with Boje.

Kallis and Rhodes both hit half-centuries in the second half of the innings with Rhodes racing to a South African record fifth successive one-day international fifty off 45 balls. Kallis needed 64 balls to reach 50 with his first boundary, a six, and hit three further sixes off the next 15 balls before being caught at long-on in the final over.

Klusener limped off with an injured right knee after bowling only three balls but Ntini bowled with fire to claim his first five-wicket haul in one-day internationals. He also held a catch and made a run-out from deep cover.

SOUTH AFRICA	Runs	Mins	Balls	4	6
HH Dippenaar c Sangakkara b Muralitharan	77	102	86	12	1
HH Gibbs c Weeraratne b Vaas	13	45	21	1	-
N Boje b Jayasuriya	32	69	38	2	-
JH Kallis c Muralitharan b Zoysa	82	109	79	-	4
JN Rhodes c Kaluwitharana b Vaas	53	55	52	5	-
L Klusener c Jayasuriya b Vaas	2	2	2	-	-
ND McKenzie c Wickramasinghe b Zoysa	18	34	21	-	-
†MV Boucher not out	5	5	3	1	-
*SM Pollock not out	1	2	1	-	-
R Telemachus					
M Ntini					
Extras (lb 3, w 1, nb 3)	7				
TOTAL (for 7 wkts) (50 overs)	**290**				

SRI LANKA	Runs	Mins	Balls	4	6
*ST Jayasuriya c Gibbs b Telemachus	12	25	21	1	-
†RS Kaluwitharana b Ntini	74	151	107	5	-
K Weeraratne b Ntini	13	34	16	2	-
MS Atapattu c Pollock b Kallis	10	42	26	-	-
K Sangakkara c Boucher b Ntini	1	4	2	-	-
DPMD Jayawardene c Pollock b Telemachus	37	61	47	-	-
RP Arnold c Ntini b Kallis	21	31	19	3	-
WPUJC Vaas run out (Ntini/Boje)	1	6	3	2	-
DNT Zoysa not out	3	14	8	-	-
GP Wickramasinghe c Boucher b Ntini	2	6	5	-	-
M Muralitharan c Boucher b Ntini	0	1	1	-	-
Extras (lb 6, w 10, nb 1)	17				
TOTAL (42.2 overs)	**191**				

SL	O	M	R	W
Vaas	10	0	44	3
Zoysa	7	0	52	2
Wickramasinghe	5	0	31	0
Weeraratne	2	0	24	0
Muralitharan	10	0	53	1
Jayasuriya	10	0	50	1
Arnold	6	0	33	0

SA	O	M	R	W
Pollock	8	0	29	0
Telemachus	8	0	44	2
Kallis	8	0	31	2
Ntini	8.2	0	37	5
Klusener	0.3	0	0	0
McKenzie	2.3	0	6	0
Boje	7	0	38	0

Fall of Wickets	SA	SL
1st	53 (2)	25 (1)
2nd	120 (1)	63 (3)
3rd	133 (3)	98 (4)
4th	217 (5)	101 (5)
5th	219 (6)	150 (2)
6th	283 (7)	174 (6)
7th	284 (4)	178 (8)
8th	-	187 (7)
9th	-	191 (10)
10th	-	191 (11)

MAJESTIC . . . Daryll Cullinan hits a coverdrive. He scored his fourth century in successive Newlands Test matches and his fifth against Sri Lanka

Picture: Duif du Toit/TOUCHLINE PHOTO

SOUTH AFRICA v SRI LANKA — 5th Limited Overs International

Played at Goodyear Park, Bloemfontein on 14 January 2001 — Toss: South Africa
Umpires: BG Jerling & RE Koertzen (TV: DF Becker)
Debuts: SA: JM Kemp. SL: None
Result: South Africa won by 5 wickets
Man of Match: Herschelle Gibbs

Gibbs made his first substantial contribution since returning from suspension to guide South Africa to their tenth consecutive one-day win with eight overs to spare. It took South Africa to within one of the world record of 11 successive wins set by the West Indies in 1984/85.

Gibbs was the junior partner in stands of 51 with Dippenaar and 61 with Boje. After reaching his half-century off 79 balls, Gibbs became more adventurous in his strokeplay and hit off-spinner Arnold for four and six off successive balls.

Sri Lanka were racing along at six runs an over in the early stages of their innings but none of their batsmen was able to play a major innings. Sangakkara was the top scorer with 33 and it took some determined batting by the tail to enable the tourists to get beyond 200.

Pollock made the best use of early cloud cover and a pitch with good bounce after Donald, in his first match for more than a month, was hammered for 35 in a four-over opening spell.

Aravinda de Silva, playing in his first match of the tour after arriving as a replacement, looked in good form before spooning a return catch to Kallis.

SRI LANKA	Runs	Mins	Balls	4	6
*ST Jayasuriya c Boucher b Pollock	23	32	17	3	1
†RS Kaluwitharana c Boje b Pollock	9	21	15	1	-
MS Atapattu b Ntini	20	56	28	2	-
PA de Silva c and b Kallis	20	21	24	3	-
DPMD Jayawardene c Boucher b Kallis	1	11	7	-	-
RP Arnold c Pollock b Boje	32	71	53	4	-
K Sangakkara c Dippenaar b Pollock	33	72	52	3	-
WPUJC Vaas c Kallis b Donald	7	27	27	1	-
GP Wickramasinghe c Boucher b Boje	32	49	40	2	-
CRD Fernando not out	12	43	29	-	-
M Muralitharan run out (Kemp)	6	9	5	-	-
Extras (lb 1, w 9, nb 1)	11				
TOTAL (49.2 overs)	**206**				

SOUTH AFRICA	Runs	Mins	Balls	4	6
HH Dippenaar c Arnold b Wickramasinghe	28	46	42	5	-
HH Gibbs run out (Atapattu)	79	163	112	7	1
N Boje lbw b Muralitharan	40	40	31	5	-
JH Kallis lbw b Vaas	31	55	48	1	1
ND McKenzie c sub (TM Dilshan) b de Silva	0	5	5	-	-
JN Rhodes not out	11	22	14	-	-
†MV Boucher not out	8	9	7	1	-
JM Kemp					
*SM Pollock					
AA Donald					
M Ntini					
Extras (lb 1, w 2, nb 7)	10				
TOTAL (for 5 wkts) (42 overs)	**207**				

SA	O	M	R	W
Pollock	10	2	44	3
Donald	7	0	42	1
Kallis	8	0	33	2
Ntini	10	1	38	1
Kemp	5	0	15	0
Boje	9.2	0	33	2

SL	O	M	R	W
Vaas	8	2	30	1
Fernando	4	0	38	0
de Silva	6	0	32	1
Wickramasinghe	3	0	23	1
Muralitharan	10	1	31	1
Jayasuriya	9	1	34	0
Arnold	2	0	18	0

Fall of Wickets	SL	SA
1st	24 (2)	51 (1)
2nd	35 (1)	112 (3)
3rd	67 (4)	177 (4)
4th	78 (5)	180 (5)
5th	80 (3)	192 (2)
6th	142 (6)	-
7th	152 (7)	-
8th	160 (8)	-
9th	194 (9)	-
10th	206 (11)	-

SOUTH AFRICA v SRI LANKA — 6th Limited Overs International

Played at Wanderers Stadium, Johannesburg on 17 January 2001 — Toss: South Africa
Umpires: DF Becker & DL Orchard (TV: WA Diedricks)
Debuts: SA: None. SL: None
Result: Sri Lanka won by 4 runs (D/L method), target revised to 209 in 42 overs
Man of Match: Russel Arnold. Man of Series: Jacques Kallis

Sri Lanka's spin bowlers ended South Africa's 10-match winning streak. Faced with a modest target of 209 in 42 overs, five less than Sri Lanka's total in a rain-reduced match, South Africa were on target for victory when they reached 169 for four with eight overs remaining.

Rhodes missed a reverse sweep against Muralitharan to start a slide in which the last six wickets fell for 35 runs. Off-spinner De Silva dismissed Boucher and Kemp in the space of three balls and top-scorer McKenzie was bowled for 47 by the first ball of the next over from Sri Lankan captain and left-arm spinner Jayasuriya.

With 27 needed and one wicket left, Pollock hit sixes off Jayasuriya and Muralitharan. Thirteen were needed off the last over but Pollock could manage only a single off Jayasuriya's third ball. Donald hit a single and Pollock hit the penultimate ball for a straight six. He went for a big hit off the last ball but the ball went back to Jayasuriya who ran out Donald.

It was a remarkable comeback by Sri Lanka who were on 21 for three, after being sent in, when a violent thunderstorm stopped play for two hours. All the wickets fell to Telemachus. When the players returned Atapattu and Arnold made half-centuries as Sri Lanka made a strong recovery.

Sri Lanka suffered a blow when Vaas collapsed with a groin injury after bowling the fifth ball of his fifth over, one delivery after bowling Jacques Kallis.

SRI LANKA	*Runs*	*Mins*	*Balls*	*4*	*6*
*ST Jayasuriya c Boucher b Telemachus	6	8	6	1	-
†RS Kaluwitharana lbw b Telemachus	4	17	16	-	-
MS Atapattu c Kallis b Kemp	55	118	83	6	-
PA de Silva c Dippenaar b Telemachus	7	18	18	1	-
DPMD Jayawardene c Boucher b Kemp	25	68	36	1	-
RP Arnold not out	65	78	56	7	-
K Sangakkara run out (Rhodes)	22	30	17	3	-
WPUJC Vaas not out	13	24	20	-	-
DNT Zoysa					
CRD Fernando					
M Muralitharan					
Extras (lb 6, w 11)	17				
TOTAL (for 6 wkts) (42 overs)	**214**				

SOUTH AFRICA	*Runs*	*Mins*	*Balls*	*4*	*6*
HH Dippenaar lbw b Fernando	18	58	41	2	-
HH Gibbs c Sangakkara b Vaas	3	12	8	-	-
JH Kallis b Vaas	18	27	14	4	-
N Boje c Kaluwitharana b Jayasuriya	46	90	50	4	-
ND McKenzie b Jayasuriya	47	127	74	4	-
JN Rhodes b Muralitharan	23	37	27	1	-
†MV Boucher c and b de Silva	7	9	7	1	-
JM Kemp c Arnold b de Silva	0	2	2	-	-
*SM Pollock not out	21	26	15	-	3
R Telemachus b Muralitharan	1	4	7	-	-
AA Donald run out (Jayasuriya)	1	17	9	-	-
Extras (lb 3, w 14, nb 2)	19				
TOTAL (42 overs)	**204**				

SA	*O*	*M*	*R*	*W*
Pollock	9	1	37	0
Telemachus	8	1	25	3
Donald	6	0	31	0
Kallis	9	0	53	0
Kemp	7	0	34	2
Boje	3	0	28	0

SL	*O*	*M*	*R*	*W*
Vaas	4.5	0	27	2
Zoysa	7	0	19	0
Jayawardene	0.1	0	4	0
Fernando	7	0	56	1
Muralitharan	9	2	25	2
de Silva	6	0	31	2
Jayasuriya	8	0	39	2

Fall of Wickets	*SL*	*SA*
1st	7 (1)	7 (2)
2nd	12 (2)	38 (3)
3rd	20 (4)	55 (1)
4th	85 (5)	131 (4)
5th	124 (3)	169 (6)
6th	174 (7)	179 (7)
7th	-	179 (8)
8th	-	181 (5)
9th	-	182 (10)
10th	-	204 (11)

SOUTH AFRICA v SRI LANKA — 3rd Test

Played at SuperSport Park, Centurion on 20,21,22 January 2001 — Toss: Sri Lanka
Umpires: RE Koertzen & P Willey (TV: DL Orchard)
Debuts: SA: JM Kemp. SL: None
Close of Play: Day 1: SA (1) 375-9 (Donald 10*, Ntini 8*, 90 overs). Day 2: SL (2) 184-3 (Sangakkara 64*, de Silva 21*, 47 overs).
Result: South Africa won by an innings and 7 runs
Man of Match: Shaun Pollock. Man of Series: Pollock

Kemp won his first Test cap when Klusener failed a fitness test and was sent for microscopic surgery on his right knee to repair damaged cartilage before the tour of the West Indies. Kirsten failed to recover from a broken bone in his left hand, while Donald returned in place of Ngam, who had a stress fracture of the right thigh.

Sri Lanka were hit even harder, however, with both Muralitharan and Vaas, their two most effective Test bowlers in recent years, unable to play because of groin injuries. Fast bowler Ruchira Perera was called up from Kenya where he had been on tour with Sri Lanka A, arriving the evening before the match.

Sri Lanka's depleted attack did well on a lively pitch in humid conditions, however, until they were taken apart by an inspired Pollock, who slammed a maiden Test century between tea and the close. South Africa had been struggling at 204 for seven before he and fellow centurion McKenzie put on 150 in 105 minutes in a record eighth wicket stand.

Pollock, playing in his 51st Test, had a previous highest score of 92 but had not made a half-century in his previous 16 Test innings. He treated all the bowlers with almost dismissive ease as he reached 50 off 35 balls with ten fours. His century included 14 fours and three sixes off 95 balls as he equalled the record for the fastest Test century by a South African, set on the same ground by Jonty Rhodes against the West Indies in 1998/99. He was caught on the deep cover boundary off a no-ball by Fernando when he was on 90.

McKenzie played a fine innings, although overshadowed by Pollock, before hooking a catch to fine leg.

Sri Lanka made yet another disastrous start, with Atapattu falling to the speed of Gibbs at cover and being run out after being sent back. Jayasuriya fell into a trap when he slashed Donald to a wide third man and Sangakkara was bowled off an inside edge two balls later. Gibbs held a sensational diving catch at backward point when De Silva could reasonably have expected four runs for a square cut off Kallis.

Ntini then took four wickets in 25 balls as Sri Lanka slid to another depressingly low total. Atapattu failed again, edging Pollock to first slip, but with Jayasuriya dropping down the order, Sangakkara led a spirited fightback against a team affected by what physiotherapist Craig Smith described as a "low-grade viral flu" that affected Donald, Boucher, Dippenaar and Cullinan as well as team manager Goolam Rajah and coach Graham Ford.

Sangakkara and Arnold went on the attack in a third wicket stand of 113 in 102 minutes. Both left-handers went for their shots, taking advantage of attacking field placings, with many boundaries being scored in the third man area.

Sri Lanka went into the third day needing only 75 runs to avoid an innings defeat with seven wickets in hand but they failed to achieve even this modest target. The slide started with the 11th ball of the day. when De Silva was caught low down at third slip by Pollock off Kallis.

Jayasuriya was bowled by Donald and Kemp, bowling impressively on his Test debut, took three wickets as Sri Lanka slid to their second successive innings defeat inside three days.

Sangakkara was last man out two short of a maiden Test century and was unlucky to be given out lbw by English umpire Peter Willey when he played across the line to a ball which pitched outside leg stump.

Pollock was named man of the series and said he was pleased with the way the team had played throughout the season. "We played really good cricket all the way through. At the beginning of the season we talked about the need for consistency and we achieved it. We dominated all six Tests we played."

SOUTH AFRICA

FIRST INNINGS	*Runs*	*Mins*	*Balls*	*4*	*6*
HH Dippenaar c Kaluwitharana b Perera	20	29	25	4	-
HH Gibbs c Kaluwitharana b Zoysa	1	20	11	-	-
JH Kallis c Arnold b Fernando	7	53	35	1	-
DJ Cullinan c Kaluwitharana b Wickramasinghe	48	105	64	7	1
ND McKenzie c Wickramasinghe b Zoysa	103	266	191	11	1
†MV Boucher c Kaluwitharana b Zoysa	38	64	45	6	1
N Boje c Jayasuriya b Arnold	6	16	15	1	-
JM Kemp run out (Sangakkara/Kaluwitharana)	2	18	14	-	-
*SM Pollock c Sangakkara b Zoysa	111	123	106	16	3
AA Donald not out	10	49	34	-	-
M Ntini c Kaluwitharana b Wickramasinghe	10	32	24	1	-
Extras (b 4, lb 2, w 1, nb 15)	22				
TOTAL (91.3 overs)	**378**				

NEW NAME IN THE BOOK . . . Justin Kemp is congratulated after taking a wicket during his Test debut against Sri Lanka at Centurion Park

Picture: Duif du Toit, TOUCHLINE PHOTO

SRI LANKA IN SOUTH AFRICA 2000/01

SRI LANKA											
MS Atapattu run out (Gibbs/Dippenaar)	3	21	25	-	-	c Cullinan b Pollock	0	18	16	-	-
*ST Jayasuriya c McKenzie b Donald	16	39	18	3	-	(6) b Donald	16	46	36	1	-
K Sangakkara b Donald	3	21	9	-	-	(2) lbw b Ntini	98	346	215	14	-
PA de Silva c Gibbs b Kallis	5	27	21	1	-	(5) c Pollock b Kallis	22	33	36	5	-
DPMD Jayawardene c Boucher b Ntini	17	55	40	3	-	(3) c Dippenaar b Kallis	23	38	35	5	-
RP Arnold b Ntini	13	48	29	1	-	(4) c Pollock b Boje	71	102	82	13	-
†RS Kaluwitharana c Boucher b Ntini	32	41	30	4	1	c Boucher b Kemp	10	54	41	1	-
DNT Zoysa c Kallis b Ntini	1	13	6	-	-	c and b Kemp	2	15	16	-	-
GP Wickramasinghe c Gibbs b Kemp	21	45	25	4	-	c Boucher b Ntini	1	6	5	-	-
CRD Fernando lbw b Kemp	0	5	2	-	-	c Kallis b Kemp	1	13	10	-	-
PDRL Perera not out	1	28	17	-	-	not out	0	4	1	-	-
Extras (lb 3, w 3, nb 1)	7					Extras (lb 2, w 2, nb 4)	8				
TOTAL (36.5 overs)	**119**					**TOTAL (81.3 overs)**	**252**				

Bowling	*O*	*M*	*R*	*W*		*O*	*M*	*R*	*W*
SRI LANKA									
Zoysa	22	8	76	4					
Perera	19	3	73	1					
Fernando	16	1	107	1					
Wickramasinghe	12.3	3	51	2					
Arnold	14	2	50	1					
de Silva	2	1	5	0					
Jayasuriya	6	3	10	0					
SOUTH AFRICA									
Donald	9	2	28	2	(3)	7	0	39	1
Pollock	7	3	15	0	(1)	17	5	43	1
Kallis	5	1	15	1	(2)	14	1	39	2
Ntini	11	5	39	4	(5)	19.3	5	51	2
Kemp	4.5	1 1	9	2	(4)	13	2	33	3
Boje						11	2	45	1

Fall of Wickets	**SA**	**SL**	**SL**
	1st	1st	2nd
1st	17 (2)	6 (1)	9 (1)
2nd	31 (1)	24 (2)	43 (3)
3rd	54 (3)	25 (3)	156 (4)
4th	115 (4)	40 (4)	187 (5)
5th	168 (6)	54 (5)	212 (6)
6th	185 (7)	71 (6)	234 (7)
7th	204 (8)	76 (8)	242 (8)
8th	354 (5)	97 (7)	243 (9)
9th	359 (9)	98 (10)	248 (10)
10th	378 (11)	119 (9)	252 (2)

SOUTH AFRICA v SRI LANKA 2000/01 TEST AVERAGES

SOUTH AFRICA

Batting & Fielding

Name	M	Inns	NO	Runs	HS	Avg	100	50	Ct	St
G Kirsten	2	3	0	266	180	88.66	1	1	2	0
L Klusener	2	3	1	158	97	79	0	2	1	0
DJ Cullinan	3	4	1	221	112	73.66	1	1	3	0
ND McKenzie	3	4	0	172	103	43	1	0	2	0
SM Pollock	3	3	0	124	111	41.33	1	0	6	0
MV Boucher	3	4	0	157	92	39.25	0	1	14	1
N Boje	3	4	1	77	32	25.66	0	0	2	0
JH Kallis	3	4	0	92	49	23	0	0	5	0
HH Dippenaar	2	3	0	53	22	17.66	0	0	2	0
M Ntini	3	2	0	18	10	9	0	0	1	0
JM Kemp	1	1	0	2	2	2	0	0	1	0
HH Gibbs	2	2	0	1	1	0.5	0	0	3	0
AA Donald	1	1	1	10	10*	-	0	0	0	0
M Ngam	2	1	1	0	0*	-	0	0	1	0
Totals	33	39	5	1351	180		4	5	43	1
				Extras	91				subs	0
				Total	1442		42.41			43

SRI LANKA IN SOUTH AFRICA 2000/01

Bowling

Name	Overs	Mdns	Runs	Wkts	Avg	BB	5I	10M
JM Kemp	17.5	3	52	5	10.40	3-33	0	0
SM Pollock	83.2	29	192	13	14.76	6-30	1	0
N Boje	64	21	147	9	16.33	4-28	0	0
M Ngam	46.2	7	155	9	17.22	3-26	0	0
M Ntini	73.3	23	216	10	21.60	4-39	0	0
AA Donald	16	2	67	3	22.33	2-28	0	0
L Klusener	16	6	27	1	27.00	1-20	0	0
JH Kallis	47	9	133	4	33.25	2-39	0	0
Totals	364	100	989	54		6-30	1	0
		b & lb	22	2	run outs			
		Total	1011	56	18.05			

SRI LANKA

Batting & Fielding

Name	M	Inns	NO	Runs	HS	Avg	100	50	Ct	St
K Sangakkara	3	6	0	235	98	39.16	0	2	4	0
DPMD Jayawardene	3	6	0	190	98	31.66	0	1	2	0
RP Arnold	3	6	0	143	71	23.83	0	1	4	0
TM Dilshan	2	4	1	56	28*	18.66	0	0	3	0
DA Gunawardene	1	2	0	37	24	18.50	0	0	0	0
WPUJC Vaas	2	4	1	50	38	16.66	0	0	1	0
RS Kaluwitharana	2	4	0	59	32	14.75	0	0	8	0
PA de Silva	1	2	0	27	22	13.50	0	0	0	0
ST Jayasuriya	3	6	0	66	26	11.00	0	0	2	0
GP Wickramasinghe	1	2	0	22	21	11.00	0	0	1	0
MS Atapattu	3	6	0	41	20	6.83	0	0	1	0
CRD Fernando	3	5	2	11	5*	3.66	0	0	0	0
DNT Zoysa	3	5	0	16	10	3.20	0	0	0	0
M Muralitharan	2	3	1	1	1*	0.50	0	0	1	0
PDRL Perera	1	2	2	1	1*	-	0	0	0	0
Totals	33	63	7	955	98		0	4	27	0
			Extras	56				subs	0	
			Total	1011		18.05			27	

Bowling

Name	Overs	Mdns	Runs	Wkts	Avg	BB	5I	10M
M Muralitharan	111.3	28	260	12	21.66	6-39	2	1
GP Wickramasinghe	12.3	3	51	2	25.50	2-51	0	0
RP Arnold	52.2	9	165	4	41.25	3-76	0	0
CRD Fernando	85	7	358	8	44.75	5-98	1	0
DNT Zoysa	73	17	239	4	59.75	4-76	0	0
PDRL Perera	19	3	73	1	73.00	1-73	0	0
WPUJC Vaas	67	8	218	1	218.00	1-109	0	0
DPMD Jayawardene	1	0	2	0	-	-	0	0
PA de Silva	2	1	5	0	-	-	0	0
ST Jayasuriya	13	4	38	0	-	-	0	0
Totals	436.2	80	1409	32		6-39	3	1
		b & lb	33	2	run outs			
		Total	1442	34	42.41			

SRI LANKA IN SOUTH AFRICA 2000/01 FIRST-CLASS AVERAGES

Batting & Fielding

Name	M	Inns	NO	Runs	HS	Avg	100	50	Ct	St
DPMD Jayawardene	5	9	1	378	98	47.25	0	3	4	0
K Sangakkara	5	9	0	281	98	31.22	0	2	4	0
TM Dilshan	4	6	1	110	54	22.00	0	1	7	0
RS Kaluwitharana	4	6	0	114	40	19.00	0	0	13	1
RP Arnold	5	8	0	148	71	18.50	0	1	4	0
DA Gunawardene	1	2	0	37	24	18.50	0	0	0	0
WPUJC Vaas	2	4	1	50	38	16.66	0	0	1	0
MS Atapattu	5	9	1	110	42	13.75	0	0	1	0
PA de Silva	1	2	0	27	22	13.50	0	0	0	0
DNT Zoysa	5	7	2	67	27*	13.40	0	0	0	0
ST Jayasuriya	5	9	0	118	38	13.11	0	0	3	0
GP Wickramasinghe	3	4	1	26	21	8.66	0	0	1	0
CRD Fernando	5	6	2	15	5*	3.75	0	0	0	0
M Muralitharan	3	4	1	8	7	2.66	0	0	2	0
UDU Chandana	1	1	0	2	2	2.00	0	0	0	0
PDRL Perera	1	2	2	1	1*	-	0	0	0	0
Totals	55	88	12	1492	98		0	7	40	1
			Extras	83				subs	0	
			Total	1575		20.72			40	

Bowling

Name	Overs	Mdns	Runs	Wkts	Avg	BB	5I	10M
DPMD Jayawardene	9	1	29	2	14.50	2-27	0	0
M Muralitharan	145.3	41	310	18	17.22	6-39	2	1
GP Wickramasinghe	39.3	12	146	5	29.20	2-34	0	0
CRD Fernando	126	17	516	15	34.40	5-98	1	0
RP Arnold	61.2	12	187	4	46.75	3-76	0	0
DNT Zoysa	102.3	25	330	7	47.14	4-76	0	0
UDU Chandana	28	4	109	2	54.50	2-109	0	0
PDRL Perera	19	3	73	1	73.00	1-73	0	0
WPUJC Vaas	67	8	218	1	218.00	1-109	0	0
PA de Silva	2	1	5	0	-	-	0	0
TM Dilshan	3	1	13	0	-	-	0	0
ST Jayasuriya	17	5	49	0	-	-	0	0
Totals	619.5	130	1985	55		6-39	3	1
		b & lb	62	4	run outs			
		Total	2047	59	34.69			

SOUTH AFRICA v SRI LANKA 2000/01: LIMITED OVERS INTERNATIONAL AVERAGES

Name	M	Inns	NO	Runs	HS	Avg	BF	SR	100	50	Ct	St	O	M	Runs	Wkts	Avg	RpO	BB	4I
N Boje	6	5	0	131	46	26.20	133	98.49	0	0	2	0	38.2	0	189	5	37.80	4.93	2-33	0
MV Boucher	6	5	2	84	55	28.00	84	100.00	0	1	11	0	0	0	0	0	-	-	-	0
AC Dawson	1	0	0	0	0	-	0	-	0	0	0	0	9	0	58	0	-	6.44	-	0
HH Dippenaar	5	5	0	207	77	41.40	293	70.64	0	2	2	0	0	0	0	0	-	-	-	0
AA Donald	2	1	0	1	1	1.00	9	11.11	0	0	0	0	13	0	73	1	73.00	5.61	1-42	0
HH Gibbs	4	4	0	96	79	24.00	143	67.13	0	1	2	0	0	0	0	0	-	-	-	0
AJ Hall	2	2	0	18	18	9.00	25	72.00	0	0	1	0	0	0	0	0	-	-	-	0
JH Kallis	6	6	1	266	100*	53.20	332	80.12	1	1	3	0	50	1	221	7	31.57	4.42	2-31	0
JM Kemp	2	1	0	0	0	0.00	2	0.00	0	0	0	0	12	0	49	2	24.50	4.08	2-34	0
G Kirsten	2	2	0	64	58	32.00	83	77.10	0	1	0	0	0	0	0	0	-	-	-	0
L Klusener	4	3	1	47	39*	23.50	62	75.80	0	0	0	0	24.3	2	90	2	45.00	3.67	1-26	0
ND McKenzie	5	4	1	185	120*	61.66	235	78.72	1	0	0	0	3.3	0	11	0	-	3.14	-	0
M Ntini	5	0	0	0	0	-	0	-	0	0	1	0	41.2	1	197	9	21.88	4.76	5-37	1
SM Pollock	6	2	2	22	21*	-	16	137.50	0	0	4	0	56.5	4	213	10	21.30	3.74	4-36	1
JN Rhodes	6	6	3	273	75*	91.00	283	96.46	0	4	0	0	0	0	0	0	-	-	-	0
R Telemachus	4	1	0	1	1	1.00	7	14.28	0	0	1	0	35	3	159	6	26.50	4.54	3-25	0
Totals	66	47	10	1395	120*		1707	81.72	2	10	27	0	283.3	11	1260	42			5-37	2
			Extras	81						subs	0			b & lb	26	4 run outs				
			Total	1476		39.89					27			Total	1286	46	27.95	4.53		

SRI LANKA v SOUTH AFRICA 2000/01: LIMITED OVERS INTERNATIONAL AVERAGES

Name	M	Inns	NO	Runs	HS	Avg	BF	SR	100	50	Ct	St	O	M	Runs	Wkts	Avg	RpO	BB	4I
RP Arnold	6	5	2	162	65*	54.00	196	82.65	0	1	3	0	15	1	88	0	-	5.86	-	0
MS Atapattu	6	6	1	174	55	34.80	278	62.58	0	2	0	0	0	0	0	0	-	-	-	0
UDU Chandana	1	1	0	2	2	2.00	3	66.66	0	0	1	0	7	0	43	0	-	6.14	-	0
PA de Silva	2	2	0	27	20	13.50	42	64.28	0	0	1	0	12	0	63	3	21.00	5.25	2-31	0
TM Dilshan	1	1	0	18	18	18.00	22	81.81	0	0	0	0	0	0	0	0	-	-	-	0
CRD Fernando	3	1	1	12	12*	-	29	41.37	0	0	0	0	18	0	148	1	148.00	8.22	1-56	0
ST Jayasuriya	6	6	0	117	66	19.50	147	79.59	0	1	1	0	44	1	214	4	53.50	4.86	2-39	0
Name	M	Inns	NO	Runs	HS	Avg	BF	SR	100	50	Ct	St	O	M	Runs	Wkts	Avg	RpO	BB	4I
DPMD Jayawardene	6	6	0	157	59	26.16	218	72.01	0	1	1	0	0.1	0	4	0	-	24.00	-	0
RS Kaluwitharana	6	6	0	227	83	37.83	333	68.16	0	3	4	1	0	0	0	0	-	-	-	0
M Muralitharan	6	3	1	8	6	4.00	8	100.00	0	0	3	0	59	4	234	6	39.00	3.96	2-25	0
K Sangakkara	6	6	1	167	84	33.40	215	77.67	0	1	2	0	0	0	0	0	-	-	-	0
WPUJC Vaas	6	6	2	76	34*	19.00	150	50.66	0	0	0	0	51.4	4	242	9	26.88	4.68	3-44	0
K Weeraratne	2	1	0	13	13	13.00	16	81.25	0	0	1	0	8	0	54	1	54.00	6.75	1-30	0
GP Wickramasinghe	4	3	0	35	32	11.66	48	72.91	0	0	2	0	22.2	0	137	2	68.50	6.13	1-23	0
DNT Zoysa	5	2	1	4	3*	4.00	12	33.33	0	0	1	0	43	0	222	6	37.00	5.16	2-35	0
Totals	66	55	9	1199	84		1717	69.83	0	9	20	1	280.1	10	1449	32			3-44	0
			Extras	87						subs	1			b & lb	27	5 run outs				
			Total	1286		27.95					21			Total	1476	37	39.89	5.26		

SOUTH AFRICA IN WEST INDIES 2000/01

Back, from left: Corrie van Zyl (assistant coach), Nicky Boje, Lance Klusener, Herschelle Gibbs, Boeta Dippenaar, Makhaya Ntini, Roger Telemachus, Justin Kemp, Andre Nel, Jacques Kallis, Neil McKenzie, Justin Ontong, Paul Adams, Craig Smith (physiotherapist). Front: Gary Kirsten, Allan Donald, Mark Boucher, Graham Ford (coach), Shaun Pollock (captain), Goolam Rajah (manager), Jonty Rhodes, Daryll Cullinan.

SOUTH AFRICA IN WEST INDIES 2000/01

Colin Bryden

The record books provided a graphic illustration of the difficulty faced by teams touring the West Indies. Despite poor form on overseas tours, West Indies had not been beaten in a home Test series since 1994/95 when Australia, led by Mark Taylor, won a four-match series 2-1. That setback had ended an unbeaten home series streak going back to 1972/73 when Ian Chappell led Australia to a 2-0 victory.

The home record was in dramatic contrast to their away form, which showed 18 defeats in 20 away Test matches, including two 5-0 clean sweeps, by South Africa in 1998/99 and Australia in the current season. Significantly, though, after the humiliation in South Africa, the West Indies had shared a series with Steve Waugh's powerful Australians.

A side issue was that since the advent of one-day internationals, the West Indies had not suffered a double reverse by losing at home in both a Test and a limited overs series.

That South Africa were able to win in both forms of the game was one of the most outstanding achievements in the country's cricket history.

It was a tribute to the leadership of Shaun Pollock, the dedication and determination of the players, intelligent planning, which included a pre-tour reconnaissance by manager Goolam Rajah and physiotherapist Craig Smith, and sheer hard work, especially by the coaches, Graham Ford and Corrie van Zyl.

Only two of the players who had toured the West Indies with South Africa A six months earlier, Justin Kemp and Justin Ontong, featured in the senior tour but the fact that Hylton Ackerman, a national selector, was coach of the A team undoubtedly helped in planning for the major tour.

No-one who was in the West Indies could fail to be impressed by the effort that was required to win in difficult conditions. The crowds were passionate in their support for the home team and the pitches were slow and awkward. Under new leadership, with Carl Hooper having been recalled as captain after almost two years away from the international scene, the West Indies were doughty opponents for much of the tour, although they appeared to lose heart as South Africa produced one outstanding performance after another in the one-day series.

That it was the home side that seemed dispirited at the end of a tour which lasted more than two-and-a-half months was a telling commentary on the unity and sense of purpose in the team, notwithstanding a controversy when six members of the party were fined R10 000 for smoking marijuana while celebrating the Test series win after the victory in the fourth Test in St John's, Antigua and the disciplinary action was kept secret, inevitably leaking out several weeks after the event.

Pollock's personal contribution was immense. He must take credit for the team spirit which sustained the side for such a long time, in contrast to the dip in performances which had been seen on several previous long tours. As a player he was in supreme form. He was arguably the outstanding batsman in the Test series, despite batting as low as number nine, while he never lost heart as a bowler on cruelly unhelpful pitches. He would have been man of the series for his contributions in the Tests but with only one award for the whole summer he had to wait until the end of the one-day games to be honoured.

SOUTH AFRICA IN WEST INDIES 2000/01

Most of the players made a worthwhile contribution to a 2-1 Test series win and a 5-2 triumph in the one-day games but there were consistently outstanding efforts from Herschelle Gibbs, Daryll Cullinan and Jacques Kallis, with the latter starring as a bowler in the Test series.

The West Indies unveiled some exciting young talent but over the course of the series they were subjected to a rigorous examination as they came under the scrutiny of a team brains trust, aided by video technology, that must be among the best in the world at pinpointing weaknesses in opposition players.

In the end it was the more experienced players who did best, with the wicketkeeper Ridley Jacobs becoming the first and so far only West Indian to score a Test century against South Africa in 11 encounters. Brian Lara and Hooper made seven half-centuries between them but such was the steady pressure exerted by the South African bowlers and fielders that neither was able to go on to make a three-figure score.

Courtney Walsh, at the age of 38, bowled superbly in what he finally confirmed would be his last Test series. He was the leading wicket-taker on either side, finishing with 25 at under 20 runs apiece. There were presentations to the great warrior throughout the series, with the most significant being in Port of Spain after he became the first bowler in history to take 500 Test wickets, with Kallis being an unwilling and unlucky participant in the historic moment. When Walsh walked off the Test arena for the last time in his home town of Kingston, he had taken his world record haul to 519 wickets.

Andre Nel of Easterns was the only uncapped player in the 15-man party selected for the Test series, while Ontong of Boland was a newcomer in a 16-player one-day squad.

The squads selected were:

Test matches: Shaun Pollock (captain), Mark Boucher (vice-captain), Paul Adams, Nicky Boje, Daryll Cullinan, Boeta Dippenaar, Allan Donald, Herschelle Gibbs, Jacques Kallis, Justin Kemp, Gary Kirsten, Lance Klusener, Neil McKenzie, Andre Nel, Makhaya Ntini with Roger Telemachus joining the tour before the third Test at the conclusion of the SuperSport Series in South Africa.

One-day matches: Pollock, Boucher, Boje, Dippenaar, Donald, Gibbs, Kallis, Kemp, Kirsten, Klusener, McKenzie, Nel, Ntini, Justin Ontong, Jonty Rhodes, Telemachus.

Manager, Goolam Rajah; coach, Graham Ford; assistant coach, Corrie van Zyl; physiotherapist, Craig Smith.

Boje returned home after the fourth Test for treatment to an injured shoulder and was due to be replaced by the uncapped Goolam Bodi of KwaZulu-Natal, who suffered a broken finger while playing for Leyland and Farington in a Northern Premier league match in England on the day he was due to depart for the West Indies. Adams then stayed on for the one-day games instead of departing after the Test series.

BUSTA CUP XI v SOUTH AFRICANS — First-class 3-day match

Played at Everest Cricket Club, Georgetown on 4,5,6 March 2001 — Toss: South Africans

Umpires: CR Duncan & JH Hampshire

Debuts: BC: None. SA: None

Close of Play: Day 1: SA (1) 271-9*. Day 2: SA (2) 124-3 (Cullinan 24*, McKenzie 0*, 39 overs).

Result: Match drawn

Notes: SL Campbell kept wicket in South Africans' 2nd innings.

The Busta XI included promising young West Indian players other than those involved in the Busta International Shield final between Jamaica and Guyana being played over the same weekend.

SOUTH AFRICA IN WEST INDIES 2000/01

Most of the South African batsmen were able to spend a reasonable time at the crease adjusting to the slow pitch conditions, although without going on to play a dominating innings. Boucher was in good form. For the West Indian team, Dillon bowled well to show he was fully recovered from an injury which cut short his tour of Australia.

Donald had a poor first spell for South Africa as the Busta XI made a flying start, with Ganga in particularly good form, but came back strongly after lunch to take two quick wickets, while Ntini took three wickets for no runs in six balls to finish off the innings.

SOUTH AFRICANS

FIRST INNINGS	*Runs*	*Mins*	*Balls*	*4*	*6*	*SECOND INNINGS*	*Runs*	*Mins*	*Balls*	*4*	*6*
G Kirsten c Willett b Jeremy	21	102	67	2	-	c Campbell b Benn	55	111	95	4	1
HH Gibbs c Hinds b Benn	36	82	74	5	-	c Campbell b Jeremy	28	72	44	6	-
JH Kallis c Wilkinson b Hinds	45	196	139	3	-	c and b Hinds	4	26	31	-	-
DJ Cullinan c Joseph b Benn	20	76	54	2	-	c Willett b Benn	24	57	50	2	1
ND McKenzie lbw b Christopher	13	17	9	3	-	c Willett b Christopher	16	75	54	-	-
†MV Boucher b Dillon	56	110	99	6	1	c sub (D Mohammed) b Benn	48	65	51	7	1
L Klusener c Dillon b Christopher	27	74	43	4	-	c Joseph b Benn	60	75	69	6	4
N Boje c Browne b Hinds	1	7	6	-	-	not out	30	74	48	3	-
*SM Pollock c Willett b Hinds	6	25	14	-	-	not out	2	14	11	-	-
AA Donald not out	1	22	16	-	-						
M Ntini not out	24	17	13	2	1						
Extras (b 6, lb 9, w 1, nb 5)	21					Extras (b 8, lb 4, w 2, nb 8)	22				
TOTAL (for 9 wkts dec) (90 overs)	**271**					**TOTAL (for 7 wkts dec) (77 overs)**	**289**				

BUSTA CUP XI

	Runs	Mins	Balls	4	6		Runs	Mins	Balls	4	6
D Ganga st Boucher b Boje	80	165	112	11	-	c Boucher b Klusener	35	88	61	2	-
*SL Campbell b Ntini	55	100	70	9	-	c Kallis b Klusener	86	132	96	17	-
SC Joseph lbw b Donald	6	20	13	-	-	run out (Pollock)	8	36	32	1	-
TA Willett c Cullinan b Donald	1	8	10	-	-	not out	7	42	41	-	-
RO Hinds not out	27	87	67	3	-						
SJ Benn b Boje	6	13	9	-	1						
M Dillon b Pollock	2	10	6	-	-	(5) c Ntini b Cullinan	2	14	13	-	-
KCB Jeremy c Boucher b Ntini	9	20	9	2	-	(6) not out	8	20	23	1	-
KJ Wilkinson c Boucher b Ntini	0	1	1	-	-						
RJ Christopher b Ntini	0	4	4	-	-						
†CO Browne absent hurt											
Extras (b 4, nb 6)	10					Extras (b 1, lb 6, nb 2)	9				
TOTAL (50.5 overs)	**196**					**TOTAL (for 4 wkts) (44 overs)**	**155**				

Bowling	*O*	*M*	*R*	*W*		*O*	*M*	*R*	*W*
BUSTA CUP XI									
Dillon	18	9	31	1		11	2	27	0
Christopher	16	3	60	2		9	2	39	1
Jeremy	15	3	40	1	(4)	9	2	43	1
Benn	22	0	77	2	(5)	25	4	111	4
Hinds	19	2	48	3	(3)	17	4	38	1
Ganga						1	0	1	0
Joseph						5	1	18	0
SOUTH AFRICANS									
Donald	12	3	51	2		6	1	36	0
Pollock	11	2	48	1		5	1	14	0
Ntini	7.5	1	31	4	(4)	6	0	45	0
Kallis	5	1	8	0	(3)	4	1	10	0
Boje	14	0	51	2	(6)	9	2	30	0
Cullinan	1	0	3	0	(7)	6	3	8	1
Klusener					(5)	8	4	5	2

Fall of Wickets	**SA**	**BC**	**SA**	**BC**
	1st	1st	2nd	2nd
1st	50 (2)	106 (2)	61 (2)	95 (1)
2nd	61 (1)	124 (3)	78 (3)	130 (3)
3rd	119 (4)	126 (4)	114 (1)	139 (2)
4th	135 (5)	160 (1)	125 (4)	141 (5)
5th	187 (3)	170 (6)	181 (5)	-
6th	220 (6)	175 (7)	191 (6)	-
7th	221 (8)	196 (8)	282 (7)	-
8th	243 (7)	196 (9)	-	-
9th	243 (9)	196 (10)	-	-
10th	-	-	-	-

WEST INDIES v SOUTH AFRICA — 1st Test

Played at Bourda, Georgetown on 9,10,11,12,13 March 2001 — Toss: West Indies
Umpires: JH Hampshire & EA Nicholls (TV: C Alfred)
Debuts: WI: None. SA: None
Close of Play: Day 1: WI (1) 232-7 (Hooper 12*, Ramnarine 4*, 90 overs). Day 2: SA (1) 130-1 (Kirsten 80*, Kallis 39*, 54 overs). Day 3: WI (2) 50-0 (Hinds 13*, Gayle 26*, 15 overs). Day 4: WI (2) 286-4 (Sarwan 71*, Hooper 31*, 105 overs)
Result: Match drawn
Man of Match: Gary Kirsten

SWEEPING CHANGE . . . Carl Hooper goes on the sweep against South Africa during the first Test in his home town, Georgetown, Guyana, after being made captain of the West Indies to end a two-year break from Test cricket

Picture: Duif du Toit, TOUCHLINE PHOTO

Hooper captained the West Indies for the first time in his home town. He had been out of international cricket since announcing his retirement shortly before the 1999 World Cup. Although he entered the first Test after setting a West Indian domestic run scoring record, by making 954 runs at an average of 95.40, his selection was not met with universal acclaim, with the renowned commentator and former fast bowling star Michael Holding announcing that he would refuse to commentate on the series, while Sir Garfield Sobers was among the critics. Another great West Indian player, Sir Vivian Richards, who allowed his name to be inscribed on the trophy for which the teams would play, announced his support for the new captain, however.

Hooper was not given much time to prepare his new charges, with the team only able to get together for the first time on the day before the match because of the scheduling of the Busta Shield final in Jamaica.

The new captain made the best possible start by winning the toss and deciding to bat on a hard-rolled, bare pitch. The tall, left-handed Chris Gayle, whose highest score in four previous Tests was 33, hit the ball with great power although with limited footwork as West Indies hurried to 101 for one at lunch. Another youngster, Marlon Samuels, also batted well before Klusener, bowling off-cutters, effectively put a brake on the scoring. Klusener conceded only 17 runs off 17 overs before Lara took him on and hammered a boundary to long-on before hitting a catch off the next ball to mid-off. Donald struck twice in successive balls in the 81st over, although the new ball was not claimed, as South Africa fought back well.

A disciplined innings by Hooper, well supported by a resolute Dillon, enabled West Indies to top 300.

Kirsten and Kallis shared a century stand as South Africa moved into a strong position on the second day. Kirsten, playing in his 69th Test, a record for South Africa, reached his half-century off 109 balls with eight fours. He added three more fours and hit a rare six when he swept Ramnarine over the mid-wicket boundary as he went to his century off 224 balls. Kallis was content to play the supporting role in a record second wicket stand against the West Indies. Neither batsman looked in difficulty before Kallis was the victim of a poor decision when he edged the ball into his pads and was given out by umpire Hampshire.

South Africa lost two wickets quickly to the leg-spin of Ramnarine before Boucher shared a good stand with Kirsten before Kirsten cut at Walsh, edging a catch behind, to start a slide in which the last six wickets fell for 58 runs.

The small lead was quickly wiped out as Gayle hit five offside boundaries in two overs from Pollock. The scoring slowed down on the fourth day, however, with disciplined bowling and fielding keeping a tight clamp on the West Indians until Hooper and Sarwan broke loose late in the day, hitting 62 runs off the last 11 overs.

Sarwan fell nine runs short of a maiden Test century when he was sent back after turning Boje to fine leg and Hooper declared when McLean was out to the next ball. A target of 306 in 76 overs was unrealistic on a slow pitch and Gibbs, dropped by Hooper at second slip off Dillon when he had two, batted soundly to ensure that South Africa safely played out time.

WEST INDIES

FIRST INNINGS	*Runs*	*Mins*	*Balls*	*4*	*6*	*SECOND INNINGS*	*Runs*	*Mins*	*Balls*	*4*	*6*
WW Hinds c Boje b Pollock	13	55	37	1	-	c Boucher b Donald	14	75	51	3	-
CH Gayle c Boucher b Kallis	81	217	159	14	-	c Boucher b Boje	44	161	112	8	-
MN Samuels b Boje	40	109	87	6	-	b Kallis	51	276	202	5	-
BC Lara c Donald b Klusener	47	129	106	5	-	c Pollock b Ntini	45	109	82	5	-
RR Sarwan b Donald	7	104	83	-	-	run out (Gibbs)	91	212	181	10	-
*CL Hooper c Klusener b Boje	69	206	156	7	-	c Cullinan b Boje	35	95	65	2	1
†RD Jacobs lbw b Donald	0	1	1	-	-	not out	18	31	15	3	-
NAM McLean b Klusener	6	28	15	1	-	lbw b Boje	0	1	1	-	-
D Ramnarine run out (Gibbs)	5	19	13	1	-						
M Dillon c Cullinan b Ntini	9	115	88	1	-						
CA Walsh not out	2	12	9	-	-						
Extras (b 2, lb 12, w 2, nb 9)	25					Extras (b 10, lb 10, w 2, nb 8, pen 5)	35				
TOTAL (124.1 overs)	**304**					**TOTAL (for 7 wkts dec) (117 overs)**	**333**				

SOUTH AFRICA

	Runs	*Mins*	*Balls*	*4*	*6*		*Runs*	*Mins*	*Balls*	*4*	*6*
G Kirsten c Jacobs b Walsh	150	447	338	13	1	c Hinds b Ramnarine	24	130	101	4	-
HH Gibbs b Dillon	8	51	24	1	-	not out	83	254	215	10	-
JH Kallis lbw b McLean	50	241	181	4	-	lbw b McLean	30	97	90	5	-
DJ Cullinan c Jacobs b Ramnarine	7	18	11	1	-	not out	4	25	11	-	-
ND McKenzie b Ramnarine	4	26	19	-	-						
†MV Boucher lbw b Walsh	52	133	94	5	-						
L Klusener lbw b McLean	5	16	10	1	-						
N Boje c Hinds b Dillon	15	41	33	3	-						
*SM Pollock not out	17	65	33	1	-						
AA Donald c Lara b Ramnarine	2	14	9	-	-						
M Ntini c Jacobs b Dillon	11	16	12	2	-						
Extras (b 4, lb 5, nb 2)	11					Extras (b 1)	1				
TOTAL (127 overs)	**332**					**TOTAL (for 2 wkts) (69.3 overs)**	**142**				

Bowling	*O*	*M*	*R*	*W*		*O*	*M*	*R*	*W*
SOUTH AFRICA									
Donald	23	9	43	2		20	8	51	1
Pollock	18	2	54	1		17	4	51	0
Ntini	12	2	48	1	(5)	20	5	50	1
Kallis	17	2	33	1	(3)	15	2	36	1
Klusener	35	14	56	2	(6)	8	1	27	0
Boje	19.1	6	56	2	(4)	37	13	93	3
WEST INDIES									
Walsh	28	7	56	2		10	3	19	0
Dillon	27	5	64	3		5	1	21	0
McLean	22	0	75	2	(4)	10	3	25	1
Ramnarine	41	9	105	3	(3)	27.3	14	46	1
Hooper	8	0	21	0		14	8	23	0
Samuels	1	0	2	0	(7)	2	0	3	0
Sarwan					(6)	1	0	4	0

Fall of Wickets

	WI	**SA**	**WI**	**SA**
	1st	1st	2nd	2nd
1st	43 (1)	25 (2)	51 (1)	66 (1)
2nd	131 (3)	171 (3)	78 (2)	134 (3)
3rd	165 (2)	186 (4)	147 (4)	-
4th	206 (4)	198 (5)	210 (3)	-
5th	221 (5)	274 (1)	299 (6)	-
6th	221 (7)	285 (7)	333 (5)	-
7th	228 (8)	287 (6)	333 (8)	-
8th	238 (9)	310 (8)	-	-
9th	300 (10)	315 (10)	-	-
10th	304 (6)	332 (11)	-	-

WEST INDIES v SOUTH AFRICA — 2nd Test

Played at Queens Park Oval, Port-of-Spain on 17,18,19,20,21 March 2001 — Toss: South Africa
Umpires: BR Doctrove & DB Hair (TV: CE Cumberbatch)
Debuts: WI: None. SA: None
Close of Play: Day 1: WI (1) 2-0 (Hinds 0*, Gayle 0*, 1 over). Day 2: WI (1) 250-7 (Jacobs 26*, Ramnarine 2*, 91 overs). Day 3: SA (2) 130-2 (Gibbs 57*, Cullinan 41*, 54 overs). Day 4: WI (2) 32-1 (Gayle 18*, Ramnarine 11*, 11 overs)
Result: South Africa won by 69 runs
Man of Match: Daryll Cullinan

The Queen's Park Oval became the first ground outside of England or Australia to stage 50 Test matches and it provided a stage for an enthralling match.

For the second time in successive Tests, South Africa built a strong first innings position but were unable to capitalise as the lower order batting subsided.

Pollock opted to make first use of a pitch with a reputation for uneven bounce in the later stages of matches. The surface had a fair covering of grass and there was both bounce and movement for the West Indian fast bowlers on the first morning. Kirsten and Gibbs batted well to remain together until the lunch break but both were out within 13 balls of the resumption.

The packed crowd of about 20 000, backed by the loud sound system in the "Trini Posse" stand, were in a frenzy but Kallis and Cullinan put on a thrilling display of high-quality batting as they added 99 runs at better than a run a minute. Kallis was in dominant form, hitting seven fours as well as two sixes over long-off against leg-spinner Dinanath Ramnarine, as he raced to a half-century off 77 balls. It seemed a desperation move when Hinds was brought on to bowl his gentle seamers for the first time in 16 Tests but with his third ball Hinds induced a return catch from Kallis.

Cullinan, in superb touch, went on to his 13th Test century, reclaiming the South African record from Kirsten, before top-edging a sweep against Ramnarine. Wickets had fallen steadily at the other end, however, and the last eight wickets added only 125 runs, with the last five falling for 30.

Hinds ended a promising stand between Cullinan and Boucher when Boucher chipped a catch to mid-wicket, while Ramnarine, who was hit for 32 runs in four overs while Kallis and Cullinan were together, took three wickets in ten balls.

There were times on the second day when the West Indies threatened to take control but Donald struck four crucial blows, each time dismissing a batsman who was set, to keep the tourists in contention. He had Samuels caught at third slip, playing a loose drive, then Hinds was caught behind. It was a record 153rd dismissal for Boucher, who earlier had dropped Samuels before he had scored off a low edge from Pollock. Ntini picked up the vital wicket of Lara, who edged a drive to second slip. Donald broke a good stand between Sarwan and Hooper when Sarwan slashed a catch to first slip and later trapped Hooper lbw with the second new ball.

Jacobs survived a confident appeal for lbw against Donald and went on to play a spirited innings. Pollock claimed two wickets early on the third day but Dillon again made an important contribution in a ninth wicket stand of 71 with Jacobs which tilted the balance back to the West Indies.

Amid emotional scenes, the odds swung sharply in favour of the West Indies as Courtney Walsh took two wickets in three balls, including his 500th in Tests, before the deficit of 56 had been wiped out. Kirsten edged a cut to be victim number 499 and Kallis was lbw second ball to a delivery which cut back, although once again Kallis was unlucky with umpire Hair playing his part in the historic moment by awarding Walsh the verdict despite an apparent inside edge.

With the match barely halfway through its allotted time, it was a moment of crisis for South Africa. Gibbs and Cullinan, under tremendous pressure from both the West Indian bowlers and an exuberant crowd, weathered the immediate storm and batted out the third day, although Gibbs was dropped on 32 when Sarwan dived but could not hold a scorching cover drive off McLean.

With the pitch becoming slower, neither batsman could play his normal attacking game and they showed rare discipline and control as they continued their partnership on the fourth morning, taking their third wicket stand to 149 before Cullinan went for a big hit against Ramnarine and skied a catch to Brian Lara at backward point.

It turned out to be a vital breakthrough. McKenzie was dropped by Lara at slip off Ramnarine before he had scored but was then almost completely tied down by Ramnarine, Dillon and Walsh. The new ball was due shortly before lunch but was not taken. Only ten runs were scored in 15 overs in the hour after lunch against Walsh and Ramnarine, with South Africa losing two wickets. Walsh bowled a spell of six overs, taking one for one, with Gibbs pulling a catch to mid-wicket after scoring a painstaking 87 in almost six hours off 275 balls.

McKenzie and Boucher had a useful stand before the new ball was finally taken, with Walsh and Dillon mowing down the remaining five batsmen for just 47 more runs. An honours

BREAKING BARRIERS . . . joy for the West Indies as Courtney Walsh becomes the first bowler to take 500 Test wickets *Picture: Duif du Toit, TOUCHLINE PHOTO*

board had been erected at the ground and, after taking his 500th wicket the previous day, Walsh said it was one of his remaining ambitions to take five in an innings at Queen's Park for the first time to get his name on the board. He duly achieved it when Donald was lbw.

West Indies were left with 232 to win. They started the last day needing exactly 200 with nine wickets standing after Hinds was lbw to Kallis, who came on to bowl after only six overs.

The final morning at last provided the decisive turning points of what Pollock said afterwards was "the most intense Test match I have played in" as the West Indies quickly lost four wickets for 19 runs to crash to 51 for five.

Ramnarine, the nightwatchman, was quickly caught at second slip off Donald. Samuels and Gayle fell to edges as they played off the back foot to Donald and Pollock before Ntini, with his first delivery, dismissed Lara for the third time in succession when the left-hander went back and was trapped in front of his stumps. There was no doubt that the ball would have hit the stumps but the ball clearly pitched outside leg stump so umpire Doctrove erred.

Such a good start to the day was a bonus, admitted Pollock, but he said his players showed their worth during a 92-run stand between Ramnaresh Sarwan and West Indian captain Carl Hooper. "It was a waiting game and a patience game," said Pollock. "We discussed the fact that every now and then partnerships would develop and that when it happened we had to hang in. We knew that when a break came we could go through."

So effectively did South Africa hang in that Sarwan and Hooper could add only 57 runs during the afternoon session before Sarwan succumbed to the pressure and a planned trap when he hooked Kallis and was caught spectacularly by a leaping Boje at square leg. The last five wickets fell for 19 runs, with Jacobs brilliantly run out by a direct hit by Gibbs at the bowler's end after Hooper called him through for a leg bye as the ball trickled towards backward point. Kallis ripped through the tail.

SOUTH AFRICA

FIRST INNINGS	*Runs*	*Mins*	*Balls*	*4*	*6*	*SECOND INNINGS*	*Runs*	*Mins*	*Balls*	*4*	*6*
HH Gibbs b Walsh	34	133	85	3	-	c sub (S Chanderpaul) b Walsh	87	351	275	11	-
G Kirsten c Hooper b McLean	23	126	91	1	-	c Jacobs b Walsh	22	58	39	3	-
JH Kallis c and b Hinds	53	98	80	7	2	lbw b Walsh	0	2	2	-	-
DJ Cullinan c Dillon b Ramnarine	103	216	155	14	-	c Lara b Ramnarine	73	241	178	6	-
ND McKenzie c Gayle b Walsh	9	31	22	2	-	c Jacobs b Dillon	25	173	134	1	-
†MV Boucher c Hooper b Hinds	16	46	37	2	-	(7) b Dillon	38	37	25	-	-
L Klusener c Jacobs b Ramnarine	15	27	23	3	-	(6) c Gayle b Dillon	5	110	78	5	-
N Boje c Jacobs b Ramnarine	3	7	7	-	-	c Jacobs b Walsh	9	31	18	2	-
*SM Pollock not out	15	26	12	1	-	b Walsh	8	50	26	-	-
AA Donald c Jacobs b McLean	0	3	1	-	-	lbw b Walsh	1	12	8	-	-
M Ntini c and b McLean	7	17	17	1	-	not out	5	19	10	1	-
Extras (nb 8)	8					Extras (b 1, lb 4, nb 9)	14				
TOTAL (86.5 overs)	**286**					**TOTAL (130.4 overs)**	**287**				

WEST INDIES

WW Hinds c Boucher b Donald	56	165	114	12	-	lbw b Kallis	2	25	21	-	-
CH Gayle lbw b Pollock	10	34	27	1	-	c Boucher b Pollock	23	102	65	2	-
MN Samuels c Klusener b Donald	35	101	66	4	-	(4) c Kallis b Donald	9	33	29	2	-
BC Lara c Kallis b Ntini	12	57	39	1	-	(5) lbw b Ntini	0	20	11	-	-
RR Sarwan c Cullinan b Donald	34	129	90	4	-	(6) c Boje b Kallis	39	175	114	6	-
*CL Hooper lbw b Donald	53	165	126	5	-	(7) not out	54	226	172	5	-
†RD Jacobs not out	93	233	177	12	-	(8) run out (Gibbs)	4	22	19	-	-
NAM McLean c Ntini b Pollock	3	13	10	-	-	(9) c Boucher b Kallis	2	23	21	-	-
D Ramnarine b Pollock	2	17	17	-	-	(3) c Kallis b Donald	11	33	28	2	-
M Dillon b Ntini	21	118	87	4	-	lbw b Kallis	0	3	2	-	-
CA Walsh run out (Ntini/Pollock)	0	20	5	-	-	b Pollock	0	11	6	-	-
Extras (b 9, lb 4, w 3, nb 7)	23					Extras (b 7, lb 4, nb 7)	18				
TOTAL (125 overs)	**342**					**TOTAL (80.1 overs)**	**162**				

Bowling	*O*	*M*	*R*	*W*		*O*	*M*	*R*	*W*
WEST INDIES									
Walsh	21	5	47	2		36.4	13	61	6
Dillon	17	2	74	0	(3)	28	8	58	3
McLean	16.5	2	60	3	(2)	18	1	76	0
Ramnarine	18	6	57	3		35	8	64	1
Hooper	9	1	25	0		13	3	23	0
Hinds	5	0	23	2					
SOUTH AFRICA									
Donald	30	6	91	4		15	4	32	2
Pollock	28	11	55	3		23.1	8	35	2
Ntini	16	4	56	2	(4)	16	4	22	1
Kallis	21	10	44	0	(3)	16	6	40	4
Boje	19	2	65	0					
Klusener	11	5	18	0	(5)	10	5	22	0

Fall of Wickets	SA 1st	WI 1st	SA 2nd	WI 2nd
1st	62 (2)	24 (2)	38 (2)	20 (1)
2nd	62 (1)	94 (3)	38 (3)	35 (3)
3rd	161 (3)	118 (1)	187 (4)	50 (4)
4th	189 (5)	123 (4)	198 (1)	50 (2)
5th	221 (6)	198 (5)	204 (6)	51 (5)
6th	256 (7)	235 (6)	253 (5)	143 (6)
7th	264 (8)	242 (8)	264 (7)	150 (8)
8th	265 (4)	250 (9)	276 (8)	159 (9)
9th	266 (10)	321 (10)	278 (10)	159 (10)
10th	286 (11)	342 (11)	287 (9)	162 (11)

WEST INDIES PRESIDENT'S XI v SOUTH AFRICANS First-class 3-day match

Played at Kensington Oval, Bridgetown on 24,25,26 March 2001 Toss: South Africans
Umpires: V Bullen & D Holder
Debuts: Pre: None. SA: A Nel
Close of Play: Day 1: Pre (1) 17-0 (Ganga 10*, Garrick 5*, 4 overs). Day 2: SA (2) 29-0 (Kirsten 18*, Gibbs 11*, 14 overs).
Result: Match drawn

McKenzie, who had not impressed in the first two Tests, spent valuable time at the crease, although seldom achieving fluency, while Dippenaar, who might have challenged for his place, was out cheaply in his first innings of the tour. Pollock was in excellent form.

For the President's XI, Cameron Cuffy, a tall and powerfully-built 31-year-old fast bowler from the Windward Islands, bowled himself into contention for a Test call-up. The pitch, two strips away from the Test surface, had more pace and bounce than those used for the first two Tests.

Ganga and Powell played useful innings for the President's XI before Boje started a collapse when Powell swung across the line and was bowled.

Gibbs played a patient, composed innings as South Africa used most of the final day for batting practice. Boje, struggling with a shoulder injury, did not field in the second innings.

SOUTH AFRICANS

FIRST INNINGS	*Runs*	*Balls*	*4*	*6*	*SECOND INNINGS*	*Runs*	*Balls*	*4*	*6*
HH Gibbs b Stuart	15	45	2	-	(2) c Garrick b Mohammed	55	133	7	-
G Kirsten b Cuffy	16	25	2	-	(1) c Chanderpaul b Mohammed	26	88	4	-
HH Dippenaar lbw b King	1	4	-	-	not out	38	105	5	-
ND McKenzie b Stuart	58	140	-	1	not out	15	69	1	-
L Klusener c Mohammed b Stuart	22	28	3	-					
JM Kemp c Stuart b Mohammed	13	33	2	-					
†MV Boucher c Ganga b Cuffy	8	33	-	-					
*SM Pollock b Stuart	79	117	11	-					
N Boje c Hibbert b Cuffy	21	50	4	-					
PR Adams lbw b Hinds	1	18	-	-					
A Nel not out	2	21	-	-					
Extras (b 7, lb 11, w 3, nb 13)	34				Extras (b 4, lb 2, nb 3)	9			
TOTAL (83.3 overs)	**270**				**TOTAL (for 2 wkts dec) (66 overs)**	**143**			

WEST INDIES PRESIDENTS' XI

	Runs	*Balls*	*4*	*6*		*Runs*	*Balls*	*4*	*6*
D Ganga c Adams b Kemp	43	83	4	-	not out	33	90	4	-
LV Garrick c Boucher b Nel	5	19	1	-	c Kirsten b Nel	28	72	2	-
RO Hinds c Kemp b Klusener	23	59	2	-					
*S Chanderpaul c Boucher b Kemp	12	61	1	-	(3) not out	20	46	3	-
RL Powell b Boje	47	105	7	1					
TM Dowlin c Pollock b Boje	16	64	2	-					
†KH Hibbert b Klusener	2	24	-	-					
D Mohammed c Gibbs b Boje	0	3	-	-					
CEL Stuart c Gibbs b Nel	11	38	1	-					
RD King b Nel	6	21	1	-					
CE Cuffy not out	0	0	-	-					
Extras (b 4, lb 3, w 2, nb 12)	21				Extras (lb 2, nb 1)	3			
TOTAL (77.5 overs)	**186**				**TOTAL (for 1 wkt) (34 overs)**	**84**			

Bowling	*O*	*M*	*R*	*W*		*O*	*M*	*R*	*W*
WEST INDIES PRESIDENT'S XI									
King	17	4	51	1		15	3	36	0
Cuffy	17	3	38	3		18	6	30	0
Stuart	16.3	2	57	4		11	0	29	0
Mohammed	20	2	57	1		16	5	35	2
Hinds	8	2	27	1		6	2	7	0
Powell	5	0	22	0					
SOUTH AFRICANS									
Nel	17.5	3	53	3	(2)	9	2	27	1
Kemp	16	3	50	2	(3)	5	0	16	0
Pollock	6	2	9	0	(1)	6	2	12	0
Klusener	12	5	14	2	(5)	4	4	0	0
Adams	13	5	38	0	(4)	9	3	25	0
Kirsten	1	0	4	0		1	0	2	0
Boje	12	7	11	3					

Fall of Wickets	**SA**	**Pre**	**SA**	**Pre**
	1st	1st	2nd	2nd
1st	26 (1)	25 (2)	60 (1)	55 (2)
2nd	31 (3)	77 (3)	109 (2)	-
3rd	53 (2)	82 (1)	-	-
4th	85 (5)	134 (4)	-	-
5th	107 (6)	166 (5)	-	-
6th	132 (7)	167 (6)	-	-
7th	173 (4)	169 (8)	-	-
8th	225 (9)	169 (7)	-	-
9th	250 (10)	181 (10)	-	-
10th	270 (8)	186 (9)	-	-

WEST INDIES v SOUTH AFRICA — 3rd Test

Played at Kensington Oval, Bridgetown on 29,30,31 March, 1,2 April 2001 — Toss: West Indies
Umpires: SA Bucknor & DB Hair (TV: H Moore)
Debuts: WI: None. SA: None
Close of Play: Day 1: SA (1) 244-5 (Cullinan 108*, Boje 3*, 90 overs). Day 2: WI (1) 7-0 (Hinds 0*, Gayle 5*, 4 overs). Day 3: WI (1) 252-5 (Hooper 74*, Jacobs 14*, 94 overs). Day 4: SA (2) 52-3 (Cullinan 12*, Kallis 5*, 36 overs)
Result: Match drawn
Man of Match: Daryll Cullinan

Cullinan hit his second century in successive Tests as South Africa recovered from early setbacks after being sent in. There was steep bounce and sharp sideways movement early on and Kirsten received an almost unplayable delivery, which kicked off a length, resulting in a gloved catch to third slip. Gibbs and Kallis did well to dampen the early fire but conditions remained difficult when Cullinan started his innings.

Dillon bowled more loose deliveries than the other two fast bowlers, with Cuffy having replaced McLean, but it was Dillon who picked up the wickets of both Gibbs and Kallis.

Cullinan and McKenzie wrested the initiative away from the West Indies in a record fourth wicket stand of 149. Cullinan was again in top form while McKenzie showed the benefit of having batted for a long time in the game against the President's XI, with his timing and judgment intact again. McKenzie played some sizzling off-side drives off both the front and back foot and was strong on the hook and pull. His six came when he pulled a short ball from Dillon over midwicket.

Hooper was disappointed that his players put down hard-hit chances from Gibbs, on 17, and McKenzie, on 43. Both were dropped in the covers off Cuffy, with Samuels and Hinds the culprits. Lara put down a simple chance when Cullinan, on 122, lofted Hooper to mid-wicket the next morning after Cullinan and Boje had repulsed the second new ball. It proved not to be an expensive miss, unlike the chance Pollock gave to Gayle at slip off Walsh when he had scored 45. Pollock went on to play almost flawlessly and received stoic support from Donald in a record ninth wicket stand of 132. After making a Test-best score, Donald was out when Pollock was on 99 but the captain went on to make his second Test century as the total became the highest in matches between South Africa and the West Indies.

After their batting feats, neither Donald nor Pollock could make a breakthrough at the start of the West Indian innings and it was the back-up fast bowlers, Kallis and Ntini, who plunged the home side into trouble. Both generated plenty of pace and Kallis made the ball swing.

A century partnership between Lara and Hooper took West Indies out of immediate danger and finally gave the spectators something to cheer. Lara again fell short of a Test century against South Africa despite getting the benefit of the doubt from the television umpire when he

edged Shaun Pollock low to wicketkeeper Mark Boucher on 21. It seemed the ball had carried but there was enough doubt for the green light to be shown.

Donald left the field with a strained right hamstring, ironically sustained when he ducked to avoid a bouncer while batting and the West Indies were looking good until late on the third day when Lara pulled Kallis to mid-on. Jacobs, though, did even better than his fellow left-hander. Like Pollock on the second day, he made the bulk of his runs after the last of the remaining recognised batsmen had been dismissed. Jacobs had made only 14 when his captain, Carl Hooper, fell victim to the last ball of a freakishly long first over of the day. Play was suspended for 56 minutes after just two deliveries while bowlers' footmarks were repaired.

Jacobs turned the tide again, first with sheer aggression and then with sensible batting. He was dropped by Cullinan at first slip off Ntini on 25 and missed by the same fielder off Boje on 56. He had twice narrowly missed scoring a maiden Test century and he could have fallen short again because on 97 he edged Ntini to Boucher. Astonishingly there was no appeal because it was such a fine edge that it took the television stump microphone to pick it up. Jacobs took advantage of the reprieve by hooking the next ball powerfully for six onto the roof of the Hall/Griffith stand at long leg to become the first West Indian to score a Test century against South Africa in nine matches.

Kallis, who bowled superbly on what had become a good batting pitch, finished with his best figures in Test cricket.

With Kirsten completing his first "pair" in 71 Test matches when he fended a catch to third slip off Cuffy, South Africa made a shaky start. Cullinan and Kallis, who dropped down the order for what proved an all-too-brief rest after his bowling efforts, batted out the last 19 overs on the fourth day but three wickets fell quickly to the spinners on the final morning and South Africa were in danger of defeat before Cullinan and Pollock added 70 for the seventh wicket.

What seemed a token declaration, with the West Indies left to bat for a minimum of 28 overs, heralded a dramatic collapse in which the West Indies lost seven wickets for 48 runs, with South Africa managing to send down 38.4 overs before conceding the draw.

With Boje and Klusener rushing through their overs, Ramnarine indulged in some quite disgraceful time-wasting when the minimum 15 overs were completed with 15 minutes of the last hour remaining, going down with "cramp" and getting treatment and several times holding up play as a bowler was ready to start running in. Dillon sent for new boots but was not allowed to put them on. Astonishingly the match referee, former England captain Mike Denness, did no more than call in the two batsmen and the West Indian team management to issue a warning that time-wasting would not be tolerated - although it already had been, to the extent that only 16 balls could be bowled in the last 15 minutes.

SOUTH AFRICA

FIRST INNINGS	*Runs*	*Mins*	*Balls*	*4*	*6*	*SECOND INNINGS*	*Runs*	*Mins*	*Balls*	*4*	*6*
G Kirsten c Gayle b Walsh	0	2	3	-	-	(2) c Samuels b Cuffy	0	7	4	-	-
HH Gibbs c Hooper b Dillon	34	96	72	4	-	(1) c Sarwan b Hooper	19	58	48	3	-
JH Kallis c Jacobs b Dillon	11	107	66	-	-	(5) c Sarwan b Hooper	20	73	93	3	-
DJ Cullinan c and b Dillon	134	367	272	14	-	c Lara b Ramnarine	82	266	238	8	2
ND McKenzie c Dillon b Hinds	72	186	152	9	1	(3) c Jacobs b Ramnarine	12	65	46	1	-
†MV Boucher c Jacobs b Cuffy	3	39	32	-	-	(7) c Jacobs b Ramnarine	0	5	6	-	-
N Boje c Ramnarine b Dillon	34	142	105	3	-	(9) not out	9	49	34	1	-
L Klusener b Walsh	1	26	19	-	-	(6) c Cuffy b Ramnarine	4	21	16	-	-
*SM Pollock not out	106	241	195	13	-	(8) c Hooper b Walsh	40	106	97	6	-
AA Donald c Hooper b Walsh	37	215	123	4	-	lbw b Ramnarine	0	2	1	-	-
M Ntini c and b Ramnarine	0	18	10	-	-						
Extras (b 6, lb 4, w 2, nb 10)	22					Extras (lb 3, nb 8)	11				
TOTAL (173.1 overs)	**454**					**TOTAL (for 9 wkts dec) (95.5 overs)**	**197**				

WEST INDIES

WW Hinds c Boucher b Kallis	2	69	46	-	-	(2) c Cullinan b Boje	8	29	33	1	-
CH Gayle c Cullinan b Ntini	40	95	71	8	-	(1) c Boucher b Kallis	48	56	39	11	-
MN Samuels c McKenzie b Kallis	6	46	33	1	-	c Cullinan b Boje	3	22	20	-	-
BC Lara c Boje b Kallis	83	287	186	13	-	b Klusener	8	66	59	-	-
RR Sarwan c Gibbs b Ntini	16	107	67	3	-	b Kallis	0	7	5	-	-
*CL Hooper c Boucher b Kallis	74	195	148	11	-	c Boucher b Boje	5	23	17	1	-
†RD Jacobs not out	113	257	215	11	4	c McKenzie b Boje	1	22	27	-	-
M Dillon b Boje	14	85	65	1	-	not out	2	33	22	-	-
D Ramnarine lbw b Boje	6	68	41	1	-	not out	0	24	14	-	-
CE Cuffy lbw b Kallis	4	57	39	1	-						
CA Walsh b Kallis	4	8	6	1	-						
Extras (b 4, lb 9, nb 12)	25					Extras (b 8, lb 1, nb 4)	13				
TOTAL (151 overs)	**387**					**TOTAL (for 7 wkts) (38.4 overs)**	**88**				

Bowling	*O*	*M*	*R*	*W*		*O*	*M*	*R*	*W*
WEST INDIES									
Walsh	45	15	87	3		14	3	28	1
Dillon	34	1	147	4	(4)	4	2	7	0
Cuffy	30	7	71	1	(2)	10	4	28	1
Ramnarine	33.1	6	86	1	(5)	31.5	10	78	5
Hooper	18	5	31	0	(3)	34	12	49	2
Hinds	10	5	13	1					
Samuels	2	0	6	0	(6)	2	1	4	0
Gayle	1	0	3	0					
SOUTH AFRICA									
Donald	14	7	30	0					
Pollock	35	11	84	0	(1)	5	0	25	0
Kallis	36	17	67	6	(2)	8	1	34	2
Ntini	28	7	93	2					
Boje	28	7	67	2	(3)	16.4	10	17	4
Klusener	10	3	33	0	(4)	9	7	3	1

Fall of Wickets

	SA 1st	WI 1st	SA 2nd	WI 2nd
1st	0 (1)	37 (1)	2 (2)	34 (2)
2nd	53 (2)	49 (2)	31 (1)	59 (3)
3rd	58 (3)	57 (3)	36 (3)	64 (1)
4th	207 (5)	102 (5)	80 (5)	64 (5)
5th	230 (6)	218 (4)	95 (6)	72 (6)
6th	306 (4)	252 (6)	97 (7)	82 (7)
7th	307 (7)	316 (8)	167 (8)	82 (4)
8th	315 (8)	353 (9)	197 (4)	-
9th	447 (10)	381 (10)	197 (10)	-
10th	454 (11)	387 (11)	-	-

WEST INDIES v SOUTH AFRICA — 4th Test

Played at Recreation Ground, St John's on 6,7,8,9,10 April 2001 — Toss: West Indies
Umpires: EA Nicholls & S Venkataraghavan (TV: PC Whyte)
Debuts: WI: NC McGarrell. SA: None
Close of Play: Day 1: SA (1) 210-7 (Pollock 36*, Boje 28*, 98 overs). Day 2: WI (1) 130-6 (Hooper 16*, Jacobs 1*, 63 overs). Day 3: SA (2) 122-3 (McKenzie 44*, Cullinan 17*, 76 overs). Day 4: WI (2) 101-4 (Lara 5*, Sarwan 4*, 45 overs)
Result: South Africa won by 82 runs
Man of Match: Shaun Pollock

West Indies took a most remarkable gamble when they decided they might be able to beat South Africa with spin rather than pace. During the later stages of the third Test word came to the television production team that the pitch for the Test match in St John's would not be the one originally earmarked but an adjacent strip.

It proved to be seriously under-prepared and as the match proceeded it became ever more difficult to score runs with humps, hollows and large patches of rough visible to the least agronomically-qualified eye.

For the first time since the late 1970s, when Kerry Packer enticed the best West Indian fast bowlers to play World Series Cricket, West Indies went into the match with only two fast bowlers, with McGarrell, a left-armer, reinforcing the spin of Ramnarine and Hooper at the expense of the unlucky Cuffy. The experienced Chanderpaul returned in place of Samuels to bolster the batting. For South Africa, Donald could not play because of his injured hamstring and Kemp came in.

Surprisingly, in view of the near certainty that the pitch would deteriorate, Hooper chose to send South Africa in, seeing some dampness that he thought the South African bowlers might have been able to exploit. His bowlers nearly did the job for him, with McGarrell taking four key wickets while only Gibbs and McKenzie of the top order batsmen played with any confidence. Gibbs was in superb form in reaching the 80s for the third time in the series before sweeping at Hooper and being caught behind as the ball looped off the back of his bat.

Pollock and Boje batted through the first afternoon and Kemp offered further support to the captain on the second morning.

In trying to justify his decision to bat second, Hooper said that the West Indian batsmen had the opportunity to take advantage of the best of the pitch on the second and third days. It was an opportunity squandered, however, as South Africa took a decisive lead. It was a pitch on which batsmen required patience and it was not an attribute shown in abundance by the West Indian batsmen. The first five wickets fell to ill-judged attacking strokes as the batsmen tried to release the pressure applied by accurate bowling. Sarwan fell again to an obvious hook trap.

The match had moved forward rapidly but the third day was a virtual stalemate after the West Indies lost their last four wickets quickly. Dillon could bowl only three balls because of a sprained right thumb but South Africa batted cautiously against a negative line from the leg-spinner, Ramnarine. The scoring rate almost ground to a halt as only 72 runs were scored in 61 overs between lunch and the close. Ramnarine, bowling outside leg stump, conceded only nine runs in 23 overs before a flurry of boundaries by Cullinan.

Pollock defended the slow scoring. "They bowled well and it was difficult to score. There is still a lot of time to go and it looked as though the pitch was quite difficult for batting." This proved an accurate assessment and when Pollock declared, after again batting well, it was based on the number of overs available (131) rather than the runs needed (323).

Boje took three of the first four wickets to fall and South Africa seemed headed for an easy win. Lara, though, showed his exceptional ability and played a thrilling innings on a pitch which made strokeplay almost impossible for most of his teammates.

South Africa's victory was delayed and Boje's figures suffered after Lara, on 64, swept the left-armer to deep square leg where Ntini dropped the chance. Lara continued to attack the spin bowler and eventually Pollock called for the new ball, with Kallis finally finishing off an outstanding match and series victory for South Africa. Lara was ninth out when, as happened several times, his bottom hand came off the bat as he drove, on this occasion resulting in a simple catch to cover.

The South African players were joined by their reserves and team management in a huddle in the middle of the field after completing the most significant triumph since Pollock took over the captaincy.

SOUTH AFRICA

FIRST INNINGS	*Runs*	*Mins*	*Balls*	*4*	*6*	*SECOND INNINGS*	*Runs*	*Mins*	*Balls*	*4*	*6*
G Kirsten c Dillon b McGarrell	8	67	54	-	-	(2) c Sarwan b Walsh	9	22	16	2	-
HH Gibbs c Jacobs b Hooper	85	236	188	12	2	(1) c Gayle b Ramnarine	45	226	195	6	-
JH Kallis b Dillon	5	4	6	1	-	(6) not out	30	178	138	3	-
DJ Cullinan c Lara b Ramnarine	4	38	34	-	-	(5) c Gayle b McGarrell	28	107	86	5	-
ND McKenzie c Jacobs b McGarrell	35	77	78	4	1	(3) b Walsh	44	285	186	3	-
L Klusener lbw b McGarrell	0	10	7	-	-	(7) c Hinds b Walsh	1	23	15	-	-
†MV Boucher c Gayle b McGarrell	1	11	14	-	-	(8) c Jacobs b Walsh	3	13	9	-	-
*SM Pollock not out	48	242	194	1	-	(9) not out	41	108	92	5	1
N Boje lbw b Walsh	36	176	122	5	1	(4) c sub (SC Joseph) b Hooper	0	2	2	-	-
JM Kemp b Dillon	16	54	38	1	-						
M Ntini b Dillon	0	2	1	-	-						
Extras (b 2, lb 5, nb 2)	9					Extras (b 6, lb 3, w 4, nb 1)	14				
TOTAL (122.2 overs)	**247**					**TOTAL (for 7 wkts dec) (123 overs)**	**215**				

VICTORY ACHIEVED . . . the whole South African touring party linked arms in a huddle in the middle of the field in St John's, Antigua, after completing a series victory in the West Indies

Picture: Duif du Toit, TOUCHLINE PHOTO

WEST INDIES

CH Gayle c Pollock b Kallis	11	36	34	1	-	c McKenzie b Boje	12	57	47	2	-
WW Hinds c Boucher b Pollock	9	56	42	1	-	c Kirsten b Boje	29	93	85	4	-
S Chanderpaul c Cullinan b Kemp	40	206	122	5	-	lbw b Boje	16	84	46	1	-
BC Lara c McKenzie b Kemp	19	50	42	2	1	(5) c McKenzie b Kallis	91	221	199	8	4
RR Sarwan c Boje b Kallis	25	72	73	3	-	(6) c Boucher b Pollock	26	91	93	4	-
*CL Hooper c Kirsten b Klusener	17	94	78	1	-	(4) c McKenzie b Klusener	21	42	49	3	-
M Dillon b Klusener	0	6	6	-	-	(9) c Cullinan b Boje	1	17	9	-	-
†RD Jacobs not out	3	56	40	-	-	(7) c Kirsten b Pollock	0	2	3	-	-
NC McGarrell lbw b Klusener	0	20	17	-	-	(8) c Kemp b Pollock	6	45	40	-	-
D Ramnarine run out (McKenzie)	2	4	4	-	-	c Kirsten b Kallis	9	64	27	1	-
CA Walsh lbw b Pollock	4	5	3	1	-	not out	4	8	4	1	-
Extras (b 3, lb 3, nb 4)	10					Extras (b 18, lb 3, nb 4)	25				
TOTAL (76.1 overs)	**140**					**TOTAL (99.4 overs)**	**240**				

Bowling	*O*	*M*	*R*	*W*		*O*	*M*	*R*	*W*
WEST INDIES									
Walsh	31	14	45	1		38	13	56	4
Dillon	18.2	4	47	3		0.3	0	3	0
McGarrell	43	19	72	4	(4)	15	3	41	1
Ramnarine	20	6	45	1	(6)	42	24	55	1
Hooper	10	2	31	1		24	7	37	1
Hinds					(3)	3.3	0	14	0
SOUTH AFRICA									
Pollock	22.1	11	25	2		19	5	41	3
Kallis	17	8	24	2		15.4	6	23	2
Ntini	6	2	27	0					
Kemp	8	2	17	2		6	3	7	0
Boje	12	4	26	0	(3)	45	9	118	4
Klusener	11	4	15	3	(5)	14	6	30	1

Fall of Wickets	**SA**	**WI**	**SA**	**WI**
	1st	1st	2nd	2nd
1st	29 (1)	13 (1)	17 (2)	36 (1)
2nd	35 (3)	21 (2)	95 (1)	56 (2)
3rd	53 (4)	50 (4)	96 (4)	86 (4)
4th	120 (5)	88 (5)	123 (3)	89 (3)
5th	126 (6)	126 (3)	135 (5)	138 (6)
6th	136 (7)	127 (7)	146 (7)	138 (7)
7th	148 (2)	132 (6)	156 (8)	155 (8)
8th	223 (9)	134 (9)	-	176 (9)
9th	247 (10)	136 (10)	-	229 (5)
10th	247 (11)	140 (11)	-	240 (10)

VICE CHANCELLOR'S XI v SOUTH AFRICANS — Limited Overs Match

Played at Salem Oval, Montserrat on 12 April 2001 — Toss: South Africans

Umpires: E Hinds & BEW Morgan

Result: South Africans won by 4 wickets

The South Africans took a short ferry trip from Antigua to play on the volcano-ravaged island of Montserrat, the first big match played there since the Chances Peak volcano erupted in 1995, causing the capital, Plymouth, to be evacuated. A further eruption in 1997 killed 19 people and destroyed Plymouth. The southern part of the island remained out of bounds because of the still-active volcano which formed a dramatic background to the small Salem Park ground.

Curtly Ambrose, the former great West Indian fast bowler who retired after the 2000 tour of England, was the "honouree" in a match which South Africa won reasonably comfortably despite a fine innings by Chanderpaul. Dippenaar kept wicket capably as Boucher took a rest and then batted well, while Klusener played his best innings of the tour. Donald bowled off a full run to show he was well on the way to recovery from injury.

VICE CHANCELLOR'S XI	***Runs***
*D Ganga c Donald b Adams	45
LV Garrick c Dippenaar b Kemp	29
S Chanderpaul c Dippenaar b Donald	70
DA Williams lbw b Klusener	9
SC Joseph run out	1
RO Hinds c Dippenaar b Kemp	7
IDR Bradshaw c Dippenaar b Kemp	0
MV Nagamootoo lbw b Donald	0
T Greenaway c Pollock b Nel	6
†V Nagamootoo not out	3
CEL Ambrose c Kirsten b Adams	10
Extras (b 12, lb 7, w 15, nb 4)	38
TOTAL (47.5 overs)	**218**

SOUTH AFRICANS	***Runs***
G Kirsten c Garrick b Hinds	39
HH Gibbs b Bradshaw	9
†HH Dippenaar run out	52
ND McKenzie b Hinds	2
L Klusener c Ganga b Bradshaw	41
JM Kemp lbw b MV Nagamootoo	4
*SM Pollock not out	37
R Telemachus not out	20
PR Adams	
AA Donald	
A Nel	
Extras (b 2, w 10, nb 6)	18
TOTAL (for 6 wkts) (48 overs)	**222**

SA	O	M	R	W
Telemachus	8	0	31	0
Nel	10	2	39	1
Donald	8	1	36	2
Kemp	8	0	35	3
Adams	8.5	1	42	2
Klusener	5	2	16	1

VC	O	M	R	W
Ambrose	6	1	17	0
Bradshaw	9	0	36	2
Greenaway	10	0	64	0
Hinds	10	1	48	2
MV Nagamootoo	10	1	29	1
Williams	2	0	15	0
Ganga	1	0	11	0

Fall of Wickets	VC	SA
1st	51 (2)	16 (2)
2nd	99 (1)	92 (1)
3rd	108 (4)	96 (4)
4th	128 (5)	117 (3)
5th	178 (6)	140 (6)
6th	178 (7)	183 (5)
7th	181 (3)	-
8th	186 (9)	-
9th	198 (8)	-
10th	218 (11)	-

JAMAICA v SOUTH AFRICANS

Two-day Match

Played at Jarrett Park, Montego Bay on 15,16 April 2001

Toss: South Africans

Umpires: C Fletcher & M Noble

Debuts: Jam: None. SA: None

Close of Play: Day 1: Jam (1) 60-2 (Garrick 28*, MN Samuels 20*, 14 overs).

Result: Match drawn

What had originally been planned as a three-day match was reduced to two days because of the late inclusion of the fixture in Montserrat. South Africa gave a shaky batting display against an attack in which the former West Indian fast bowler Franklyn Rose was impressive, together with new ball partner Audley Sanson. Klusener again showed a return to form.

Donald, told to prove his fitness for the fifth Test by bowling at full pace, dismissed both Jamaica's Test opening batsmen in an impressive spell but the diminutive Garrick, who regularly opened for Jamaica ahead of Hinds, survived, somewhat fortunately, and went on to dominate the second day.

After another fine spell by Donald, Garrick, hooking and cutting strongly, put on 161 for the third wicket with Samuels in a performance which was to earn both men selection for the final Test. The match ended farcically with Jamaica declining to take the option of an early finish and South Africa bringing on a variety of bowlers and part-time fielders, including both coaches and the physiotherapist, Craig Smith.

SOUTH AFRICANS	Runs	Mins	Balls	4	6
HH Dippenaar c Garrick b Breese	13	54	39	3	-
G Kirsten c Hibbert b Rose	21	111	79	1	-
JH Kallis c Sanson b Perry	30	90	74	4	-
DJ Cullinan c Hibbert b Sanson	21	58	37	2	1
ND McKenzie lbw b Sanson	17	45	26	2	1
L Klusener c and b MN Samuels	41	125	85	2	1
*†MV Boucher lbw b Sanson	0	6	8	-	-
PR Adams c and b Gayle	15	31	32	2	-
AA Donald b MN Samuels	12	56	47	1	-
M Ntini not out	4	6	3	1	-
A Nel					
Extras (b 8, lb 5, nb 12)	25				
TOTAL (for 9 wkts dec) (71.2 overs)	**199**				

JAMAICA	Runs	Mins	Balls	4	6
LV Garrick not out	174	393	279	23	-
CH Gayle b Donald	8	9	7	2	-
WW Hinds lbw b Donald	2	11	9	-	-
MN Samuels lbw b Klusener	84	198	146	9	-
RL Powell c Kirsten b Ntini	12	18	15	2	-
*RG Samuels c Nel b Ntini	0	12	9	-	-
GR Breese c Kirsten b Nel	15	41	27	2	-
NO Perry not out	66	98	84	10	-
†KH Hibbert					
FA Rose					
AA Sanson					
Extras (b 7, lb 5, w 1, nb 6)	19				
TOTAL (for 6 wkts) (96 overs)	**380**				

Jam	O	M	R	W
Rose	11	2	27	1
Sanson	16.2	4	28	3
Breese	13	1	51	1
Perry	7	1	24	1
Gayle	13	5	34	1
Hinds	8.4	3	17	0
MN Samuels	2.2	0	5	2

SA	O	M	R	W
Donald	12	3	42	2
Nel	19	1	88	1
Adams	24	4	81	0
Ntini	14	2	42	2
Kallis	5	1	19	0
Klusener	10	1	23	1
Kirsten	8	0	42	0
McKenzie	4	0	31	0

Fall of Wickets	SA	Jam
1st	23 (1)	9 (2)
2nd	63 (2)	13 (3)
3rd	95 (3)	174 (4)
4th	119 (4)	187 (5)
5th	126 (5)	189 (6)
6th	128 (7)	219 (7)
7th	152 (8)	-
8th	191 (9)	-
9th	199 (6)	-

WEST INDIES v SOUTH AFRICA — 5th Test

Played at Sabina Park, Kingston on 19,20,21,22,23 April 2001 Toss: West Indies
Umpires: SA Bucknor & S Venkataraghavan (TV: T Wilson)
Debuts: WI: LV Garrick. SA: None
Close of Play: Day 1: WI (1) 214-9 (Ramnarine 28*, Walsh 0*, 90 overs). Day 2: WI (2) 34-0 (Garrick 21*, Gayle 10*, 17 overs). Day 3: WI (2) 255-7 (Jacobs 67*, Ramnarine 9*, 107 overs). Day 4: SA (2) 140-3 (McKenzie 40*, Kallis 5*, 64 overs)
Result: West Indies won by 130 runs
Man of Match: Ridley Jacobs

With the Test series won, Boje had returned home for an operation on his left shoulder and to rest his right knee after struggling through the first four Test matches. It meant a recall for Adams. Donald returned after injury but Kemp kept his place at the expense of Ntini.

There was confusion about the selection of the West Indian team. It was first announced that the 13-man squad picked for the Antigua Test would be retained but on the day before the game Garrick was called up. He won his first Test cap at the expense of Hinds, while Samuels and Cuffy replaced Sarwan and McGarrell. After much speculation, Walsh confirmed that he would retire from Test cricket at the end of the match.

There was a sensational start when Garrick cut the first ball from Donald tamely to Pollock at gully, joining Jimmy Cook as the only men to be out to the first ball of a match on their debut. Cook suffered the same fate against India in Durban in 1992/93.

Lara found himself in familiar territory as he played virtually a lone hand against South Africa's fast bowlers on the first day. While Donald and Pollock bowled superbly on a pitch with good bounce, Lara was almost flawless before top-edging a hook and being caught at slip off a slower ball from Pollock. Lara shared a stand of 53 for the fifth wicket with Hooper and 54 for the seventh wicket with Dillon, who was dropped three times in making 24, twice early on by Boucher off Pollock and Kemp, and later when he hit Adams to a diving Klusener at mid-on.

If South Africa thought they were on their way to their third win of the series they were in for a rude shock as Walsh, in front of his home supporters, inspired the West Indies to a commanding position. Walsh started the West Indian fightback when he had Kirsten caught at third slip for the opening batsman's third nought in five innings and he later bowled Klusener and had Boucher caught at mid-wicket.

Fellow fast bowler Cuffy took two key wickets soon after lunch on the second day when he had Gibbs caught behind and Cullinan taken at first slip. Dillon dismissed the solid Kallis and hastened the destruction of South Africa's lower order when he took three wickets in nine balls at the end of the innings.

McKenzie batted soundly while Pollock became only the eighth player in history, and the first South African, to achieve the Test double of 2000 runs and 200 wickets, reaching the milestone in style when he pulled Cuffy for six over mid-wicket. He joined Richie Benaud (Australia), Garfield Sobers (West Indies), Ian Botham (England), Imran Khan (Pakistan), Kapil Dev (India), Richard Hadlee (New Zealand) and Wasim Akram (Pakistan). South Africa's total was their lowest in Tests against the West Indies.

Garrick and Gayle stretched the lead to 118 by the end of the second day but South Africa came back strongly on the third day. Runs were reduced to a trickle and wickets fell steadily until Hooper was caught at third slip when he gloved a bouncer from Kallis. At that stage, the overall lead was 210 with five wickets down.

Once again, however, Jacobs came to the rescue with an attacking half-century. The West Indian vice-captain went for his shots from the start. He had some luck early on but hit some crunching shots. Samuels, 20, the youngest player in the team, blossomed during a crucial sixth wicket stand of 58.

GREAT OPINIONS . . . Sir Vivian Richards, after whom the series was named, in the commentary box with former South African great Mike Procter in Richards' home island of Antigua

Picture: Duif du Toit, TOUCHLINE PHOTO

The South Africans, having bowled and fielded with superb discipline, wilted under a hot sun and the effects of Jacobs' assault. Having conceded only 104 runs before tea, they gave up another 107 in 32 overs until the close.

South Africa were eventually set an improbable 386 to win. Kirsten reached double figures for the first time in six Test innings but was then caught off a bottom edge trying to withdraw his bat against a Dillon lifter. South African hopes remained reasonably high while Gibbs and McKenzie were batting during a confident 65-run second-wicket partnership. Gibbs was out for a superbly-crafted 51 when he swung across the line against Hooper. It opened the door for Walsh to capture the key wicket of Cullinan.

South Africa lost only one wicket before lunch on the final day as McKenzie and Kallis batted through most of the morning before Ramnarine had McKenzie caught at silly mid-off. At that stage, on 209 for four with 59 overs remaining, South Africa still had a chance of earning a draw, or even pushing for an improbable victory.

Ramnarine struck with his second delivery after lunch when Kallis went for a pull shot and was bowled off a bottom edge. Two balls later Mark Boucher was caught behind for nought and South Africa were doomed.

Hooper, who had delayed taking the second new ball, enabling Ramnarine to take his crucial wickets, then called up Walsh for his final spell in Test cricket, just a few kilometres from where he was born. Walsh had the crowd in ecstasy when he trapped Kemp leg before for his second nought of the match, then knocked Donald's middle stump out of the ground.

Dillon claimed the last wicket when Adams sliced a catch to backward point. Walsh was cheered off the field as he completed his Test career with a world record haul of 519 wickets in 132 matches. It was the first win by the West Indies in 14 Tests.

WEST INDIES

FIRST INNINGS	*Runs*	*Mins*	*Balls*	*4*	*6*	*SECOND INNINGS*	*Runs*	*Mins*	*Balls*	*4*	*6*
LV Garrick c Pollock b Donald	0	1	1	-	-	c Boucher b Donald	27	98	75	2	-
CH Gayle c Kemp b Donald	25	115	79	3	-	b Pollock	32	255	180	3	-
S Chanderpaul c Boucher b Kallis	7	65	50	-	-	c Cullinan b Kemp	7	45	31	-	-
BC Lara c Kallis b Pollock	81	222	156	12	-	b Adams	14	66	50	2	-
MN Samuels c Boucher b Donald	3	9	12	-	-	b Pollock	59	145	97	9	-
*CL Hooper c Kirsten b Pollock	25	83	71	4	-	c Pollock b Kallis	5	31	21	-	-
†RD Jacobs c Boucher b Pollock	0	9	6	-	-	c McKenzie b Klusener	85	186	191	7	-
M Dillon c Boucher b Donald	24	119	77	1	1	c Gibbs b Pollock	13	54	40	2	-
D Ramnarine not out	35	116	86	4	-	c Cullinan b Pollock	9	49	40	1	-
CE Cuffy c Boucher b Pollock	3	31	21	-	-	not out	13	52	43	1	-
CA Walsh c Adams b Pollock	4	39	22	-	-	c Kirsten b Adams	3	14	14	-	-
Extras (b 4, lb 12, w 2)	18					Extras (b 14, lb 13, w 4, nb 3)	34				
TOTAL (96.5 overs)	**225**					**TOTAL (129.5 overs)**	**301**				

SOUTH AFRICA

	Runs	*Mins*	*Balls*	*4*	*6*		*Runs*	*Mins*	*Balls*	*4*	*6*
HH Gibbs c Jacobs b Cuffy	18	83	67	1	-	(2) b Hooper	51	162	120	5	-
G Kirsten c Gayle b Walsh	0	29	15	-	-	(1) c Jacobs b Dillon	14	66	45	1	-
JH Kallis c and b Dillon	17	89	54	2	-	(5) b Ramnarine	51	159	129	5	-
DJ Cullinan c Lara b Cuffy	6	17	11	1	-	lbw b Walsh	18	45	46	-	-
ND McKenzie lbw b Ramnarine	45	170	99	4	-	(3) c Garrick b Ramnarine	55	281	216	1	-
L Klusener b Walsh	13	58	42	-	1	not out	31	92	64	4	-
†MV Boucher c Garrick b Walsh	13	33	32	-	-	c Jacobs b Ramnarine	0	1	2	-	-
*SM Pollock c Jacobs b Dillon	24	56	29	3	1	c Jacobs b Dillon	3	38	26	-	-
JM Kemp c Walsh b Dillon	0	8	2	-	-	lbw b Walsh	0	4	1	-	-
AA Donald not out	1	14	5	-	-	b Walsh	10	10	7	2	-
PR Adams c Hooper b Dillon	3	9	11	-	-	c Samuels b Dillon	4	9	5	1	-
Extras (w 1)	1					Extras (b 4, lb 13, nb 1)	18				
TOTAL (61.1 overs)	**141**					**TOTAL (110 overs)**	**255**				

Bowling	*O*	*M*	*R*	*W*		*O*	*M*	*R*	*W*
SOUTH AFRICA									
Donald	25	5	54	4		20	8	54	1
Pollock	26.5	17	28	5		34	8	66	4
Kallis	16	5	38	1		28	10	56	1
Kemp	16	3	45	0	(5)	18	9	30	1
Adams	11	1	43	0	(4)	21.5	7	54	2
Klusener	2	1	1	0		8	3	14	1
WEST INDIES									
Walsh	18	8	31	3		22	6	62	3
Cuffy	17	6	58	2		10	3	13	0
Dillon	15.1	5	32	4		19	3	59	3
Ramnarine	11	4	20	1		31	6	61	3
Hooper						28	8	43	1

Fall of Wickets	WI	SA	WI	SA
	1st	1st	2nd	2nd
1st	0 (1)	9 (2)	47 (1)	37 (1)
2nd	21 (3)	24 (1)	55 (3)	102 (2)
3rd	50 (2)	35 (4)	77 (4)	124 (4)
4th	54 (5)	51 (3)	103 (2)	190 (3)
5th	107 (6)	77 (6)	126 (6)	209 (5)
6th	113 (7)	97 (7)	184 (5)	209 (7)
7th	167 (4)	137 (8)	229 (8)	235 (8)
8th	188 (8)	137 (5)	255 (9)	236 (9)
9th	203 (10)	137 (9)	287 (7)	250 (10)
10th	225 (11)	141 (11)	301 (11)	255 (11)

JAMAICA v SOUTH AFRICANS

Limited Overs Match

Played at Sabina Park, Kingston on 25 April 2001
Toss: South Africans
Umpires: N Malcolm & T Wilson
Result: South Africans won by 6 wickets

Klusener bounced back from a disappointing Test series to get his team's one-day campaign off to a good start. He took five wickets, bowling at fast-medium pace after sending down mainly slow cutters during the Tests. On a breezy day, he made the ball swing sharply. Then he made his highest score of the tour. Ricardo Powell slammed three huge leg-side sixes off Adams before being last man out. Ontong bowled a tidy mixture of leg-spin and off-spin in his first outing in a South African shirt, then hit the winning runs with a straight six.

JAMAICA	*Runs*	*Mins*	*Balls*	*4*	*6*
LV Garrick c Gibbs b Ntini	20	58	41	3	-
DE Bernard lbw b Klusener	59	119	89	8	-
WW Hinds c Ontong b Klusener	4	29	19	1	-
RL Powell run out (Rhodes)	52	110	60	1	3
WE Cuff c Gibbs b Ontong	7	21	21	-	-
*RG Samuels c Rhodes b Ontong	9	17	19	1	-
LR Williams b Klusener	9	19	14	1	-
FA Rose b Klusener	3	6	7	-	-
†MG Sinclair b Klusener	0	4	3	-	-
DS McKenzie c Pollock b Adams	0	3	3	-	-
RO Cunningham not out	0	3	1	-	-
Extras (b 6, lb 7, w 7, nb 2)	22				
TOTAL (46.4 overs)	**185**				

SOUTH AFRICANS	*Runs*	*Mins*	*Balls*	*4*	*6*
HH Gibbs c Cunningham b Bernard	54	103	72	6	-
G Kirsten b Rose	9	13	10	2	-
†HH Dippenaar c Powell b Cunningham	13	49	26	1	-
JN Rhodes lbw b Hinds	49	102	72	3	-
L Klusener not out	42	77	64	4	-
JL Ontong not out	12	20	13	-	1
*SM Pollock					
R Telemachus					
A Nel					
M Ntini					
PR Adams					
Extras (lb 1, w 7, nb 2)	10				
TOTAL (for 4 wkts) (45.4 overs)	**189**				

SA	*O*	*M*	*R*	*W*
Telemachus	6.4	3	9	0
Nel	6	0	23	0
Ntini	7	1	38	1
Klusener	10	1	23	5
Ontong	10	0	38	2
Adams	7	0	41	1

Jam	*O*	*M*	*R*	*W*
Rose	8	1	20	1
McKenzie	5	0	24	0
Williams	6	0	26	0
Cunningham	10	1	49	1
Bernard	5	0	27	1
Powell	8	0	22	0
Hinds	3	0	14	1
Garrick	0.4	0	6	0

Fall of Wickets	*Jam*	*SA*
1st	35 (1)	16 (2)
2nd	58 (3)	45 (3)
3rd	102 (2)	106 (1)
4th	121 (5)	167 (4)
5th	141 (6)	-
6th	176 (7)	-
7th	180 (8)	-
8th	182 (9)	-
9th	183 (10)	-
10th	185 (4)	-

WEST INDIES v SOUTH AFRICA

1st Limited Overs International

Played at Sabina Park, Kingston on 28 April 2001
Toss: West Indies
Umpires: SA Bucknor & BEW Morgan (TV: JR Gayle)
Debuts: WI: LV Garrick. SA: JL Ontong
Result: West Indies won by 3 wickets
Man of Match: Neil McGarrell

Jacobs hammered a four off the last ball as the West Indies gained a narrow win. Lara and Hooper put on 89 for the fourth wicket but then superb South African fielding pegged back the home side. Fortunes swung wildly in the closing overs after Lara was sensationally caught by a diving Rhodes at backward point off Donald. It was Rhodes' second remarkable catch after he dived full length to hold a flying drive by Gayle off Donald.

South Africa struck a crucial blow when a limping Hooper, who batted with a runner towards the end of his innings, skied a catch to long-on. Jacobs and Ricardo Powell had difficulty in pushing the score along and Powell was run out after a mix-up with Jacobs. McGarrell hit Kallis for a straight six but then fell to a return catch by Kallis, who had to turn, twist and dive as McGarrell scooped the ball over the bowler.

Eight were needed off the last over, bowled by Donald. It came down to five off the last two balls. Jacobs had a wild swing and got two to square leg. The last ball was a low full toss which Jacobs pounded past backward point for four.

McGarrell's left-arm spin bowling was mainly responsible for pegging back South Africa. He bowled an unbroken spell. Fellow spinners Hooper and Samuels took two wickets each as South Africa were unable to mount any substantial partnerships after McGarrell broke a second wicket stand of 64 between Kirsten and Kallis.

SOUTH AFRICA	*Runs*	*Mins*	*Balls*	*4*	*6*
G Kirsten b Hooper	38	91	63	5	-
HH Gibbs run out (Lara)	8	12	7	2	-
JH Kallis c Cuffy b McGarrell	23	57	39	3	-
JN Rhodes lbw b McGarrell	36	65	53	1	-
ND McKenzie c Jacobs b Cuffy	21	32	26	1	-
†MV Boucher c and b Samuels	14	33	27	1	-
L Klusener b McGarrell	0	1	1	-	-
*SM Pollock not out	26	49	37	3	-
JL Ontong c Powell b Hooper	11	14	12	1	-
R Telemachus c and b Samuels	3	9	17	-	-
AA Donald b Dillon	3	14	6	-	-
Extras (b 1, lb 4, w 9, nb 3)	17				
TOTAL (47.4 overs)	**200**				

WEST INDIES	*Runs*	*Mins*	*Balls*	*4*	*6*
LV Garrick c Boucher b Pollock	7	27	24	-	-
CH Gayle c Rhodes b Donald	27	68	34	4	-
MN Samuels c Boucher b Kallis	17	27	21	3	-
BC Lara c Rhodes b Donald	54	104	97	4	-
*CL Hooper c Kirsten b Telemachus	43	117	68	4	-
RL Powell run out (Ontong/Boucher)	6	43	23	-	-
†RD Jacobs not out	17	37	23	1	-
NC McGarrell c and b Kallis	14	10	10	-	1
M Dillon not out	2	8	3	-	-
KCB Jeremy					
CE Cuffy					
Extras (b 1, lb 5, w 6, nb 3)	15				
TOTAL (for 7 wkts) (50 overs)	**202**				

WI	*O*	*M*	*R*	*W*
Dillon	6.4	1	33	1
Cuffy	10	2	37	1
Jeremy	5	0	30	0
Hooper	10	1	45	2
McGarrell	10	0	32	3
Samuels	6	0	18	2

SA	*O*	*M*	*R*	*W*
Pollock	10	1	31	1
Telemachus	9	0	38	1
Donald	10	0	40	2
Kallis	10	1	34	2
Klusener	6	1	30	0
Ontong	5	0	23	0

Fall of Wickets	*SA*	*WI*
1st	11 (2)	14 (1)
2nd	75 (3)	51 (3)
3rd	87 (1)	60 (2)
4th	131 (5)	149 (4)
5th	149 (4)	162 (5)
6th	149 (7)	177 (6)
7th	159 (6)	193 (8)
8th	179 (9)	-
9th	184 (10)	-
10th	200 (11)	-

WEST INDIES v SOUTH AFRICA — 2nd Limited Overs International

Played at Recreation Ground, St John's on 2 May 2001

Toss: South Africa

Umpires: CE Mack & BEW Morgan (TV: PC Whyte)

Debuts: WI: None. SA: None

Result: South Africa won by 8 wickets

Man of Match: Herschelle Gibbs

Gibbs and Kallis shared a record second wicket partnership of 179 as South Africa cruised to an easy win to level the series. It was a masterly exhibition of batting by the pair, whose stand was the highest for any wicket for South Africa against the West Indies and the highest recorded at the Recreation Ground. Both men hit sixes which cleared the stands and sailed into the streets surrounding the small ground. It was the first time West Indies had been beaten in five one-day internationals in Antigua.

Chasing a moderate total of 220, Gibbs and Kallis saw off the threat of fast bowler Cuffy, who bowled a lively opening spell which claimed the wicket of Kirsten. The rest of the West Indian bowling seldom posed a threat.

Stung by their defeat in Kingston, South Africa produced a top-class display of bowling and fielding. Gayle hit some crunching boundaries early on but lost momentum when fielding

TAKE THAT . . . Herschelle Gibbs hooks a six during a match-winning innings in the one-day match in Antigua *Picture: Tertius Pickard, TOUCHLINE PHOTO*

restrictions were lifted at the end of 15 overs. Chanderpaul, in his first one-day international in more than a year, helped Hooper lift a flagging scoring rate. They put on 86 for the fourth wicket in just 13 overs. Chanderpaul's dismissal, when he was run out after a misunderstanding with Hooper, started a collapse in which five wickets fell while only 30 runs were scored off the last 39 balls of the innings.

WEST INDIES	Runs	Mins	Balls	4	6
LV Garrick run out (Kallis/Telemachus)	16	79	61	1	-
CH Gayle c Pollock b Klusener	50	109	72	7	-
BC Lara c Pollock b Klusener	13	45	38	-	-
S Chanderpaul run out (Dippenaar/Boucher)	60	73	54	2	3
*CL Hooper c Ontong b Pollock	48	72	46	4	1
†RD Jacobs not out	13	32	16	-	-
MN Samuels run out (Rhodes)	3	3	4	-	-
NC McGarrell b Kallis	3	5	7	-	-
NAM McLean c Gibbs b Kallis	0	2	1	-	-
M Dillon not out	1	3	3	-	-
CE Cuffy					
Extras (b 1, lb 4, w 5, nb 3)	13				
TOTAL (for 8 wkts) (50 overs)	**220**				

SOUTH AFRICA	Runs	Mins	Balls	4	6
HH Gibbs st Jacobs b McGarrell	104	155	141	8	3
G Kirsten b Cuffy	5	15	8	1	-
JH Kallis not out	78	163	112	5	2
JN Rhodes not out	21	25	23	2	-
HH Dippenaar					
†MV Boucher					
L Klusener					
*SM Pollock					
JL Ontong					
R Telemachus					
AA Donald					
Extras (lb 2, w 2, nb 9)	13				
TOTAL (for 2 wkts) (45.5 overs)	**221**				

SA	O	M	R	W
Pollock	10	1	34	1
Telemachus	9	0	50	0
Donald	10	1	40	0
Kallis	10	1	38	2
Klusener	5	0	28	2
Ontong	6	0	25	0

WI	O	M	R	W
Dillon	6.5	0	39	0
Cuffy	10	1	27	1
McLean	4	0	40	0
McGarrell	10	0	34	1
Hooper	10	1	42	0
Samuels	3	0	22	0
Gayle	2	0	15	0

Fall of Wickets	WI	SA
1st	63 (1)	11 (2)
2nd	80 (2)	190 (1)
3rd	104 (3)	-
4th	190 (4)	-
5th	208 (5)	-
6th	214 (7)	-
7th	218 (8)	-
8th	218 (9)	-

WEST INDIES v SOUTH AFRICA — 3rd Limited Overs International

Played at Queens Park, St George's on 5 May 2001 — Toss: West Indies
Umpires: BEW Morgan & EA Nicholls (TV: E Jones)
Debuts: WI: None. SA: None
Result: South Africa won by 132 runs
Man of Match: Jacques Kallis

Kallis hit his seventh one-day international century as South Africa piled on the runs after being sent in on a good batting pitch.

West Indies gambled by strengthening their batting at the expense of their pace bowling. Gibbs played a cavalier innings, which included drives for six off both Cuffy and Dillon, while Kirsten returned to form with a fluent performance.

It meant Kallis only started batting in the 15th over but he played a measured innings, placing the ball skilfully and hitting only four fours before he had a lucky escape when he was on 86. Kallis thrashed Gayle to mid-wicket. Both Cuffy and Dillon went for the ball before Cuffy pulled away. Dillon held it but stepped on the boundary before tossing it infield to Cuffy.

Pollock took three wickets in his first spell, including that of the big-hitting Powell, who went in as an opener. Powell hit a six over mid-wicket off Pollock but in trying to repeat the shot in the same over top-edged a catch to mid-wicket. The West Indies' last real hopes went when Lara had his leg stump knocked out of the ground by Ntini.

SOUTH AFRICA	Runs	Mins	Balls	4	6
G Kirsten run out (Gayle)	50	105	65	7	-
HH Gibbs c Powell b McGarrell	46	70	48	4	2
JH Kallis c and b Gayle	107	125	108	4	2
JN Rhodes b Hooper	47	56	51	5	-
L Klusener not out	25	35	29	-	1
*SM Pollock not out	1	1	1	-	-
HH Dippenaar					
†MV Boucher					
JL Ontong					
AA Donald					
M Ntini					
Extras (lb 5, w 4, nb 2)	11				
TOTAL (for 4 wkts) (50 overs)	**287**				

WEST INDIES	Runs	Mins	Balls	4	6
CH Gayle c Kirsten b Pollock	1	5	3	-	-
RL Powell c Ntini b Pollock	15	28	14	1	1
S Chanderpaul c Dippenaar b Pollock	16	44	32	2	-
BC Lara b Ntini	31	64	39	4	-
*CL Hooper run out (Ntini/Boucher)	29	69	45	4	-
MN Samuels lbw b Klusener	20	35	21	3	-
†RD Jacobs run out (Ontong/Boucher)	10	19	15	1	-
WW Hinds c Ntini b Ontong	11	27	22	1	-
NC McGarrell c and b Ontong	8	30	21	-	-
M Dillon b Ntini	4	22	21	-	-
CE Cuffy not out	1	8	3	-	-
Extras (lb 2, w 5, nb 2)	9				
TOTAL (39 overs)	**155**				

WI	O	M	R	W
Dillon	6	0	43	0
Cuffy	10	0	54	0
McGarrell	10	0	60	1
Hooper	10	1	32	1
Samuels	9	0	61	0
Gayle	5	0	32	1

SA	O	M	R	W
Pollock	6	0	23	3
Kallis	6	0	35	0
Donald	6	0	26	0
Ntini	7	1	27	2
Klusener	7	0	30	1
Ontong	7	1	12	2

Fall of Wickets	SA	WI
1st	88 (2)	2 (1)
2nd	129 (1)	24 (2)
3rd	219 (4)	48 (3)
4th	286 (3)	87 (4)
5th	-	119 (5)
6th	-	126 (6)
7th	-	133 (7)
8th	-	146 (8)
9th	-	153 (9)
10th	-	155 (10)

WEST INDIES v SOUTH AFRICA

4th Limited Overs International

Played at Queens Park, St George's on 6 May 2001

Toss: South Africa

Umpires: GT Johnson & EA Nicholls (TV: E Jones)

Debuts: WI: None. SA: None

Result: South Africa won by 8 wickets

Man of Match: Allan Donald

Kallis did not play because of a hamstring injury but the West Indies suffered their third successive crushing defeat and completed a miserable weekend in Grenada. Having taken a pounding when South Africa batted first the previous day, the West Indians could not score enough runs after being sent in.

A thrilling contest between Lara and Donald was the main competitive highlight of the match. Lara pulled, drove and cut the first three balls by the fast bowler for fours. Donald switched to bowling around the wicket and, although he was cut for another boundary by Lara, he got his man when Lara charged down the wicket but edged a catch behind. Donald went on to take three more wickets in a fiery performance. Samuels took 26 balls to make his first ten runs but then hit some powerful drives, especially straight down the ground.

Klusener limped off with a groin injury after bowling one ball of his seventh over and was unable to play again on the tour.

Gibbs and Kirsten gave South Africa a quickfire start, putting on 58 for the first wicket in 10.4 overs. Dippenaar, playing his third match since replacing McKenzie, who had a hamstring injury, made full use of his first opportunity to bat at international level on the tour.

WEST INDIES	Runs	Mins	Balls	4	6
CH Gayle c Rhodes b Kemp	9	33	27	-	1
RL Powell c Ntini b Kemp	7	18	9	1	-
S Chanderpaul c Kemp b Ntini	10	40	27	2	-
BC Lara c Boucher b Donald	25	61	42	4	-
*CL Hooper c Kemp b Donald	46	95	78	4	1
MN Samuels lbw b Pollock	65	109	71	8	-
†RD Jacobs c Pollock b Ntini	8	31	14	1	-
NC McGarrell c Donald b Kemp	2	7	6	-	-
NAM McLean c Gibbs b Donald	7	15	10	1	-
KCB Jeremy not out	8	15	11	1	-
CE Cuffy c Boucher b Donald	3	9	4	-	-
Extras (lb 3, w 6, nb 1)	10				
TOTAL (49.3 overs)	**200**				

SOUTH AFRICA	Runs	Mins	Balls	4	6
HH Gibbs c Chanderpaul b Jeremy	27	51	30	5	-
G Kirsten c Powell b Hooper	72	137	104	7	-
HH Dippenaar not out	62	122	109	5	-
JN Rhodes not out	30	36	38	2	1
L Klusener					
†MV Boucher					
*SM Pollock					
JM Kemp					
JL Ontong					
AA Donald					
M Ntini					
Extras (lb 4, w 2, nb 4)	10				
TOTAL (for 2 wkts) (46.1 overs)	**201**				

SA	O	M	R	W
Pollock	10	3	16	1
Kemp	8.5	0	54	3
Donald	9.3	1	38	4
Ntini	10	1	26	2
Klusener	6.1	0	32	0
Ontong	5	0	31	0

WI	O	M	R	W
Cuffy	8	2	36	0
McLean	6	0	34	0
Jeremy	4	1	18	1
McGarrell	4.1	0	21	0
Hooper	10	1	29	1
Gayle	10	0	38	0
Samuels	4	0	21	0

Fall of Wickets	WI	SA
1st	11 (2)	58 (1)
2nd	22 (1)	154 (2)
3rd	49 (3)	-
4th	61 (4)	-
5th	128 (5)	-
6th	174 (7)	-
7th	177 (8)	-
8th	185 (6)	-
9th	189 (9)	-
10th	200 (11)	-

WEST INDIES v SOUTH AFRICA — 5th Limited Overs International

Played at Kensington Oval, Bridgetown on 9 May 2001

Toss: South Africa

Umpires: BR Doctrove & EA Nicholls (TV: H Moore)

Debuts: WI: None. SA: None

Result: South Africa won by 7 wickets

Man of Match: Herschelle Gibbs

Gibbs hit his second century of the series and the fifth of his one-day international career as South Africa clinched the series with another comprehensive victory, becoming the first touring team to the West Indies to win both a Test and one-day series.

West Indies were seldom in the game despite a fine innings by Lara, who lacked support as the West Indies were bowled out for 199 after being sent in on a good batting pitch. South Africa's bowling and fielding was again too good for the rest of the West Indian batsmen.

Two outstanding pieces of fielding by Gibbs stopped two promising partnerships. A direct hit from mid-wicket ran out Chanderpaul and he held a sensational diving catch at full stretch to his right off a scorching drive by Jacobs. Thirty-five runs were scored off 23 balls before Jacobs's dismissal, which came in the same over that he pulled a six off Ntini.

Gibbs then thrashed the West Indian bowling, although he was dropped by Jacobs off Cuffy when he had 11 and was lucky to survive an appeal for a catch behind off Hooper when he had 72.

WEST INDIES	Runs	Mins	Balls	4	6
D Ganga c and b Kallis	15	37	37	2	-
CH Gayle c Boucher b Kallis	6	21	15	-	-
BC Lara b Kallis	92	182	125	9	-
*CL Hooper b Ntini	21	49	33	4	-
MN Samuels c Boucher b Donald	1	12	7	-	-
S Chanderpaul run out (Gibbs)	24	30	33	2	-
†RD Jacobs c Gibbs b Ntini	21	40	27	-	1
M Dillon c Boucher b Donald	0	4	3	-	-
D Ramnarine c Rhodes b Donald	2	10	5	-	-
KCB Jeremy c Ntini b Kallis	5	13	13	1	-
CE Cuffy not out	0	1	0	-	-
Extras (lb 4, w 6, nb 2)	12				
TOTAL (49.2 overs)	**199**				

SOUTH AFRICA	Runs	Mins	Balls	4	6
G Kirsten c Lara b Samuels	18	49	31	3	-
HH Gibbs c Hooper b Ramnarine	107	138	132	12	3
JH Kallis run out (Jeremy/Samuels)	18	40	34	1	-
HH Dippenaar not out	42	62	47	5	-
JN Rhodes not out	10	14	8	1	-
†MV Boucher					
*SM Pollock					
JM Kemp					
JL Ontong					
AA Donald					
M Ntini					
Extras (lb 1, w 4, nb 2)	7				
TOTAL (for 3 wkts) (41.4 overs)	**202**				

SA	O	M	R	W
Pollock	10	2	23	0
Kallis	6.2	1	22	4
Ntini	10	1	47	2
Donald	10	0	41	3
Ontong	8	0	38	0
Kemp	5	0	24	0

WI	O	M	R	W
Cuffy	7.4	1	44	0
Dillon	3	0	18	0
Hooper	8	0	35	0
Samuels	10	1	37	1
Ramnarine	10	0	48	1
Gayle	3	0	19	0

Fall of Wickets	WI	SA
1st	20 (2)	54 (1)
2nd	24 (1)	103 (3)
3rd	68 (4)	182 (2)
4th	73 (5)	-
5th	116 (6)	-
6th	177 (7)	-
7th	180 (8)	-
8th	187 (9)	-
9th	199 (10)	-
10th	199 (3)	-

TAKING HIS CHANCE . . . Boeta Dippenaar plays a square drive in Barbados as he makes the most of an opportunity to get into action

Picture: Tertius Pickard, TOUCHLINE PHOTO

WEST INDIES v SOUTH AFRICA — 6th Limited Overs International

Played at Queens Park Oval, Port-of-Spain on 12 May 2001 — Toss: West Indies
Umpires: SA Bucknor & CR Duncan (TV: CE Cumberbatch)
Debuts: WI: None. SA: A Nel
Result: South Africa won by 53 runs
Man of Match: Neil McKenzie

Nel made an outstanding debut as a re-jigged South African team won again. Sent in on a pitch which had early life as well as uneven bounce, South Africa struggled. But Nel bowled with pace and accuracy before limping off with a hamstring injury in his ninth over, as the West Indies were bowled out for 137.

South Africa rested four of their leading players after taking a winning 4-1 lead in the series and they were in trouble before a third wicket stand of 92 between McKenzie and Kemp. South Africa changed their batting order, with McKenzie batting at number three in his first match since injuring a hamstring in the first one-day international, and Kemp promoted to number four. Cuffy bowled superbly in an unbroken spell and received good support from a new opening partner, Corey Collymore.

Pollock and Nel put an immediate clamp on the West Indian scoring rate, with Nel taking his first international wicket when he had Ganga caught at first slip. Chanderpaul and Lara built what seemed a potential winning position for the West Indies before Lara was run out by a direct hit from Rhodes at extra cover. Adams had Chanderpaul stumped and Nel dismissed Hooper and Powell with successive balls in the second over of his second spell.

The South African team included all five players named the previous day, with physiotherapist Craig Smith, when it was revealed they had been fined R10 000 each by an internal disciplinary committee, more than a month earlier, for smoking marijuana in a hotel room in Antigua while celebrating South Africa's Test series win. The players named were Gibbs, Kemp, Telemachus, Adams and Nel.

Pollock said before the game he was not worried about the controversy. "It's something that happened four weeks ago. We have dealt with it and put it behind us."

SOUTH AFRICA	Runs	Mins	Balls	4	6
HH Dippenaar lbw b Cuffy	7	52	37	-	-
HH Gibbs b Cuffy	1	8	4	1	-
ND McKenzie c Jacobs b Collymore	73	163	117	8	-
JM Kemp lbw b Hooper	46	83	70	3	1
JH Kallis b Hooper	3	6	8	-	-
JN Rhodes c Lara b Collymore	25	55	28	2	-
*SM Pollock c and b Samuels	5	4	6	-	-
†MV Boucher b Jeremy	3	10	12	-	-
R Telemachus b Jeremy	2	6	7	-	-
PR Adams b Samuels	6	5	8	-	-
A Nel not out	3	4	3	-	-
Extras (b 2, lb 9, w 4, nb 1)	16				
TOTAL (49.5 overs)	**190**				

WEST INDIES	Runs	Mins	Balls	4	6
D Ganga c Kemp b Nel	11	41	36	1	-
S Chanderpaul st Boucher b Adams	27	131	84	-	-
BC Lara run out (Rhodes)	41	66	63	5	-
MN Samuels b Telemachus	29	68	42	4	-
*CL Hooper c Boucher b Nel	8	19	17	-	-
RL Powell c Boucher b Nel	0	1	1	-	-
†RD Jacobs c Adams b Kallis	7	17	16	-	-
D Ramnarine c Boucher b Kemp	1	14	6	-	-
KCB Jeremy b Telemachus	0	5	4	-	-
CE Cuffy not out	3	13	8	-	-
CD Collymore lbw b Pollock	1	7	10	-	-
Extras (w 4, nb 5)	9				
TOTAL (47 overs)	**137**				

WI	O	M	R	W
Cuffy	10	2	26	2
Collymore	8.5	1	29	2
Jeremy	9	0	42	2
Hooper	10	0	27	2
Ramnarine	7	0	41	0
Samuels	5	1	14	2

SA	O	M	R	W
Pollock	9	3	15	1
Nel	8.1	2	20	3
Telemachus	9	0	26	2
Kallis	8	0	25	1
Adams	6	0	24	1
Kemp	6.5	0	27	1

Fall of Wickets	SA	WI
1st	2 (2)	18 (1)
2nd	31 (1)	71 (3)
3rd	123 (4)	97 (2)
4th	131 (5)	108 (5)
5th	152 (3)	108 (6)
6th	157 (7)	126 (7)
7th	170 (8)	131 (4)
8th	177 (9)	132 (8)
9th	184 (10)	135 (9)
10th	190 (6)	137 (11)

WEST INDIES v SOUTH AFRICA — 7th Limited Overs International

Played at Arnos Vale, Kingstown on 16 May 2001 — Toss: South Africa
Umpires: SA Bucknor & BR Doctrove (TV: GT Browne)
Debuts: WI: None. SA: None
Result: West Indies won by 6 wickets
Man of Match: Cameron Cuffy

Fast bowler Cuffy, playing on his home island, set up a consolation win for the West Indies in the final one-day international. South Africa never recovered from Cuffy's early strikes which reduced them to 40 for four after they won the toss and batted. Cuffy bowled all his overs in one spell. For virtually the first time in the series, the West Indies kept the pressure on the South Africans, with consistent performances from all their bowlers, who were backed up by good fielding.

Kallis batted patiently to prevent a total collapse by the tourists before being caught at mid-wicket in the penultimate over when he went for a big hit against off-spinner Samuels.

The West Indies found run-scoring on a dry, slow pitch much easier than the South Africans, with Samuels hitting seven fours. Only eight fours were hit in the whole South African innings.

Rhodes became the first South African to play in 200 one-day internationals.

Pollock was named man of the series, an award for both the Test and one-day contests.

SOUTH AFRICA	Runs	Mins	Balls	4	6
HH Gibbs c Collymore b Cuffy	1	10	12	-	-
G Kirsten c Ganga b Collymore	6	26	14	1	-
ND McKenzie c Ganga b Cuffy	13	47	24	2	-
JL Ontong c Gayle b Cuffy	2	5	3	-	-
JH Kallis c Lara b Samuels	69	144	147	3	-
JN Rhodes b McGarrell	16	55	34	1	-
†MV Boucher c McGarrell b Samuels	25	48	48	1	-
JM Kemp not out	12	21	14	-	-
*SM Pollock not out	7	7	7	-	-
R Telemachus					
M Ntini					
Extras (lb 6, w 3, nb 3)	12				
TOTAL (for 7 wkts) (50 overs)	**163**				

WEST INDIES	Runs	Mins	Balls	4	6
D Ganga run out (Pollock/Boucher)	15	55	45	2	-
CH Gayle b Kallis	28	68	39	5	-
BC Lara c Gibbs b Kemp	18	51	33	2	-
MN Samuels not out	54	112	91	7	-
*CL Hooper c Gibbs b Kemp	5	19	14	-	-
S Chanderpaul not out	31	51	49	4	-
†RD Jacobs					
NC McGarrell					
KCB Jeremy					
CE Cuffy					
CD Collymore					
Extras (lb 5, w 4, nb 4)	13				
TOTAL (for 4 wkts) (44.2 overs)	**164**				

WI	O	M	R	W
Cuffy	10	3	24	3
Collymore	9	0	37	1
Jeremy	6	0	19	0
McGarrell	10	0	26	1
Hooper	10	0	37	0
Samuels	5	0	14	2

SA	O	M	R	W
Pollock	8	3	17	0
Telemachus	7	0	35	0
Ntini	6	0	29	0
Kallis	8	0	29	1
Kemp	6	1	16	2
Ontong	8	0	30	0
Rhodes	1.2	0	3	0

Fall of Wickets	SA	WI
1st	2 (1)	40 (1)
2nd	9 (2)	56 (2)
3rd	14 (4)	92 (3)
4th	40 (3)	102 (5)
5th	79 (6)	-
6th	132 (7)	-
7th	150 (5)	-

WEST INDIES v SOUTH AFRICA 2000/01 TEST AVERAGES

WEST INDIES

Batting & Fielding

Name	M	Inns	NO	Runs	HS	Avg	100	50	Ct	St
RD Jacobs	5	10	4	317	113*	52.83	1	2	21	0
BC Lara	5	10	0	400	91	40.00	0	3	5	0
CL Hooper	5	10	1	358	74	39.77	0	4	6	0
CH Gayle	5	10	0	326	81	32.60	0	1	7	0
RR Sarwan	4	8	0	238	91	29.75	0	1	3	0
MN Samuels	4	8	0	206	59	25.75	0	2	2	0
S Chanderpaul	2	4	0	70	40	17.50	0	0	0	0
WW Hinds	4	8	0	133	56	16.62	0	1	4	0

LV Garrick	1	2	0	27	27	13.50	0	0	2	0
D Ramnarine	5	9	2	79	35*	11.28	0	0	2	0
M Dillon	5	9	1	84	24	10.50	0	0	5	0
CE Cuffy	2	3	1	20	13*	10.00	0	0	1	0
CA Walsh	5	8	2	21	4*	3.50	0	0	1	0
NC McGarrell	1	2	0	6	6	3.00	0	0	0	0
NAM McLean	2	4	0	11	6	2.75	0	0	1	0
Totals	55	105	11	2296	113*		1	14	60	0
			Extras	226				subs	2	
			Total	2522		26.82			62	

Bowling

Name	Overs	Mdns	Runs	Wkts	Avg	BB	5I	10M
WW Hinds	18.3	5	50	3	16.66	2-23	0	0
CA Walsh	263.4	87	492	25	19.68	6-61	1	0
NC McGarrell	58	22	113	5	22.60	4-72	0	0
M Dillon	168	31	512	20	25.60	4-32	0	0
D Ramnarine	290.3	93	617	20	30.85	5-78	1	0
NAM McLean	66.5	6	236	6	39.33	3-60	0	0
CE Cuffy	67	20	170	4	42.50	2-58	0	0
CL Hooper	158	46	283	5	56.60	2-49	0	0
CH Gayle	1	0	3	0	-	-	0	0
RR Sarwan	1	0	4	0	-	-	0	0
MN Samuels	7	1	15	0	-	-	0	0
Totals	1099.3	311	2495	88		6-61	2	0
		b & lb	61	0	run outs			
		Total	2556	88	29.04			

SOUTH AFRICA

Batting & Fielding

Name	M	Inns	NO	Runs	HS	Avg	100	50	Ct	St
SM Pollock	5	9	5	302	106*	75.50	1	0	4	0
HH Gibbs	5	10	1	464	87	51.55	0	4	2	0
DJ Cullinan	5	10	1	459	134	51.00	2	2	10	0
ND McKenzie	5	9	0	301	72	33.44	0	2	7	0
JH Kallis	5	10	1	267	53	29.66	0	3	4	0
G Kirsten	5	10	0	250	150	25.00	1	0	6	0
N Boje	4	7	1	106	36	17.66	0	0	4	0
MV Boucher	5	9	0	126	52	14.00	0	1	18	0
L Klusener	5	9	1	75	31*	9.37	0	0	2	0
AA Donald	4	7	1	51	37	8.50	0	0	1	0
M Ntini	4	5	1	23	11	5.75	0	0	1	0
JM Kemp	2	3	0	16	16	5.33	0	0	2	0
PR Adams	1	2	0	7	4	3.50	0	0	1	0
Totals	55	100	12	2447	150		4	12	62	0
			Extras	109				subs	0	
			Total	2556		29.04			62	

LG
OFFICIAL SUPPLIER AND SUPPORTER OF THE SA CRICKET TEAM
UNITED CRICKET BOARD
World's Quietest
MAGICWAVE

SOUTH AFRICA IN WEST INDIES 2000/01

Bowling

Name	Overs	Mdns	Runs	Wkts	Avg	BB	5I	10M
JH Kallis	189.4	67	395	20	19.75	6-67	1	0
SM Pollock	228.1	77	464	20	23.20	5-28	1	0
AA Donald	147	47	355	14	25.35	4-54	0	0
L Klusener	118	49	219	8	27.37	3-15	0	0
N Boje	176.5	51	442	15	29.46	4-17	0	0
JM Kemp	48	17	99	3	33.00	2-17	0	0
M Ntini	98	24	296	7	42.28	2-56	0	0
PR Adams	32.5	8	97	2	48.50	2-54	0	0
Totals	1038.3	340	2367	89		6-67	2	0
		b & lb	155	5	run outs			
		Total	2522	94	26.82			

SOUTH AFRICA IN WEST INDIES 2000/01 FIRST-CLASS AVERAGES

Batting & Fielding

Name	M	Inns	NO	Runs	HS	Avg	100	50	Ct	St
SM Pollock	7	12	6	389	106*	64.83	1	1	5	0
HH Gibbs	7	14	1	598	87	46.00	0	5	4	0
DJ Cullinan	6	12	1	503	134	45.72	2	2	11	0
HH Dippenaar	1	2	1	39	38*	39.00	0	0	0	0
ND McKenzie	7	13	1	403	72	33.58	0	3	7	0
JH Kallis	6	12	1	316	53	28.72	0	3	5	0
G Kirsten	7	14	0	368	150	26.28	1	1	7	0
MV Boucher	7	12	0	238	56	19.83	0	2	23	1
N Boje	6	10	2	158	36	19.75	0	0	4	0
L Klusener	7	12	1	184	60	16.72	0	1	2	0
M Ntini	5	6	2	47	24*	11.75	0	0	2	0
AA Donald	5	8	2	52	37	8.66	0	0	1	0
JM Kemp	3	4	0	29	16	7.25	0	0	3	0
PR Adams	2	3	0	8	4	2.66	0	0	2	0
A Nel	1	1	1	2	2*	-	0	0	0	0
Totals	77	135	19	3334	150		4	18	76	1
			Extras	195				subs		
			Total	3529		30.42			76	

Bowling

Name	Overs	Mdns	Runs	Wkts	Avg	BB	5I	10M
DJ Cullinan	7	3	11	1	11.00	1-8	0	0
L Klusener	142	62	238	12	19.83	3-15	0	0
A Nel	26.5	5	80	4	20.00	3-53	0	0
JH Kallis	198.4	69	413	20	20.65	6-67	1	0
SM Pollock	256.1	84	547	21	26.04	5-28	1	0
N Boje	211.5	60	534	20	26.70	4-17	0	0
AA Donald	165	51	442	16	27.62	4-54	0	0
JM Kemp	69	20	165	5	33.00	2-17	0	0
M Ntini	111.5	25	372	11	33.81	4-31	0	0
PR Adams	54.5	16	160	2	80.00	2-54	0	0
G Kirsten	2	0	6	0	-	-	0	0
Totals	1245.1	395	2968	112		6-67	2	0
		b & lb	175	6	run outs			
		Total	3143	118	26.63			

WEST INDIES v SOUTH AFRICA 2000/01: LIMITED OVERS INTERNATIONAL AVERAGES

Name	M	Inns	NO	Runs	HS	Avg	BF	SR	100	50	Ct	St	O	M	Runs	Wkts	Avg	RpO	BB	4I
S Chanderpaul	6	6	1	168	60	33.60	279	60.21	0	1	1	0	0	0	0	0	-	-	-	0
CD Collymore	2	1	0	1	1	1.00	10	10.00	0	0	1	0	17.5	1	66	3	22.00	3.70	2-29	0
CE Cuffy	7	4	3	7	3*	7.00	15	46.66	0	0	1	0	65.4	11	248	7	35.42	3.77	3-24	0
M Dillon	4	4	2	7	4	3.50	30	23.33	0	0	0	0	22.3	1	133	1	133.00	5.91	1-33	0
D Ganga	3	3	0	41	15	13.66	118	34.74	0	0	2	0	0	0	0	0	-	-	-	0
LV Garrick	2	2	0	23	16	11.50	85	27.05	0	0	0	0	0	0	0	0	-	-	-	0
CH Gayle	6	6	0	121	50	20.16	190	63.68	0	1	2	0	20	0	104	1	104.00	5.20	1-32	0
WW Hinds	1	1	0	11	11	11.00	22	50.00	0	0	0	0	0	0	0	0	-	-	-	0
CL Hooper	7	7	0	200	48	28.57	301	66.44	0	0	1	0	68	4	247	6	41.16	3.63	2-27	0
RD Jacobs	7	6	2	76	21	19.00	111	68.46	0	0	2	1	0	0	0	0	-	-	-	0
KCB Jeremy	5	3	1	13	8*	6.50	28	46.42	0	0	0	0	24	1	109	3	36.33	4.54	2-42	0
BC Lara	7	7	0	274	92	39.14	437	62.70	0	2	3	0	0	0	0	0	-	-	-	0
NC McGarrell	5	4	0	27	14	6.75	44	61.36	0	0	1	0	44.1	0	173	6	28.83	3.91	3-32	0
NAM McLean	2	2	0	7	7	3.50	11	63.63	0	0	0	0	10	0	74	0	-	7.40	-	0
RL Powell	4	4	0	28	15	7.00	47	59.57	0	0	3	0	0	0	0	0	-	-	-	0
D Ramnarine	2	2	0	3	2	1.50	11	27.27	0	0	0	0	17	0	89	1	89.00	5.23	1-48	0
MN Samuels	7	7	1	189	65	31.50	257	73.54	0	2	3	0	42	2	187	7	26.71	4.45	2-14	0
Totals	77	69	10	1196	92		1996	59.91	0	6	20	1	331.1	20	1430	35			3-24	0
			Extras	81						subs	0			b & lb	34	3 run outs				
			Total	1277		21.64					20			Total	1464	38	38.52	4.42		

SOUTH AFRICA v WEST INDIES 2000/01: LIMITED OVERS INTERNATIONAL AVERAGES

Name	M	Inns	NO	Runs	HS	Avg	BF	SR	100	50	Ct	St	O	M	Runs	Wkts	Avg	RpO	BB	4I
PR Adams	1	1	0	6	6	6.00	8	75.00	0	0	1	0	6	0	24	1	24.00	4.00	1-24	0
MV Boucher	7	3	0	42	25	14.00	87	48.27	0	0	10	1	0	0	0	0	-	-	-	0
HH Dippenaar	5	3	2	111	62*	111.00	193	57.51	0	1	1	0	0	0	0	0	-	-	-	0
AA Donald	5	1	0	3	3	3.00	6	50.00	0	0	1	0	45.3	2	185	9	20.55	4.06	4-38	1
HH Gibbs	7	7	0	294	107	42.00	374	78.60	2	0	5	0	0	0	0	0	-	-	-	0
JH Kallis	6	6	1	298	107	59.60	448	66.51	1	2	2	0	48.2	3	183	10	18.30	3.78	4-22	1
JM Kemp	4	2	1	58	46	58.00	84	69.04	0	0	3	0	26.4	1	121	6	20.16	4.53	3-54	0
G Kirsten	6	6	0	189	72	31.50	285	66.31	0	2	2	0	0	0	0	0	-	-	-	0
Name	M	Inns	NO	Runs	HS	Avg	BF	SR	100	50	Ct	St	O	M	Runs	Wkts	Avg	RpO	BB	4I
L Klusener	4	2	1	25	25*	25.00	30	83.33	0	0	0	0	24.1	1	120	3	40.00	4.96	2-28	0
ND McKenzie	3	3	0	107	73	35.66	167	64.07	0	1	0	0	0	0	0	0	-	-	-	0
A Nel	1	1	1	3	3*	-	3	100.00	0	0	0	0	8.1	2	20	3	6.66	2.44	3-20	0
M Ntini	4	0	0	0	0	-	0	-	0	0	4	0	33	3	129	6	21.50	3.90	2-26	0
JL Ontong	6	2	0	13	11	6.50	15	86.66	0	0	2	0	39	1	159	2	79.50	4.07	2-12	0
SM Pollock	7	4	3	39	26*	39.00	51	76.47	0	0	3	0	63	13	159	7	22.71	2.52	3-23	0
JN Rhodes	7	7	3	185	47	46.25	235	78.72	0	0	4	0	1.2	0	3	0	-	2.25	-	0
R Telemachus	4	2	0	5	3	2.50	24	20.83	0	0	0	0	34	0	149	3	49.66	4.38	2-26	0
Totals	77	50	12	1378	107		2010	68.55	3	6	38	1	329.1	26	1252	50			4-22	2
			Extras	86						subs	0			b & lb	25	9	run outs			
			Total	1464		38.52					38			Total	1277	59	21.64	3.87		

Get ready to be bowled over
by Shaun and the boys.
Coverage of all
International matches
played in South Africa.
SABC
topsport
INSPIRATION FOR THE NATION

SOUTH AFRICAN INTERNATIONAL CRICKETERS

The following list contains the names of all those who have represented South Africa in Test cricket. Those who have also played in official limited overs internationals are denoted +. Unofficial Test matches were played against the Australian Imperial Forces 1919/20, SB Joel's XI 1924/25, SAB England XI 1981/82, Arosa Sri Lanka and the West Indian XI 1982/83, West Indian XI 1983/84, Australian XI 1985/86 and 1986/87 and English XI 1989/90 (marked *). Appearances in these unofficial Test matches are shown in brackets.

A total of 279 players have appeared in official Test matches.

TEST CRICKETERS

ACKERMAN Hylton Deon (HD), B Cape Town 14.2.1973.
4-2 v P in SA 1997/98; 2 v SL in SA 1997/98.

+ADAMS Paul Regan, B Cape Town 20.1.1977.
34-2 v E in SA 1995/96; 3 v I in I 1996/97; 2 v I in SA 1996/97; 2 v A in SA 1996/97; 2 v P in P 1997/98; 1 v A in A 1997/98; 1 v P in SA 1997/98; 2 v SL in SA 1997/98; 4 v E in E 1998; 2 v WI in SA 1998/99; 3 v NZ in NZ 1998/99; 1 v Z in SA 1999/00; 1 v Z in Z 1999/00; 4 v E in SA 1999/00; 3 v SL in SL 2000; 1 v WI in WI 2000/01.

ADCOCK Neil Amwin Treharne, B Sea Point, Cape Town 8.3.1931.
26-5 v NZ in SA 1953/54; 4 v E in E 1955; 5 v E in SA 1956/57; 5 v A in SA 1957/58;5 v E in E 1960; 2 v NZ in SA 1961/62.

ANDERSON James Henry (Biddy), B Kimberley 26.4.1874. D Melkamer Farm, Bredasdorp, CP 11.3.1926.
1-v A in SA 1902/03.

ASHLEY William Hare (Gobo), B Mowbray, Cape Town 10.2.1862. D Plumtree, Rhodesia 14.7.1930.
1-v E in SA 1888/89.

BACHER Aron (Ali), B Johannesburg 24.5.1942.
12-3 v E in E 1965; 5 v A in SA 1966/67; 4 v A in SA 1969/70.

+BACHER Adam Marc, B Johannesburg 29.10.1973.
19-3 v I in SA 1996/97; 2 v A in SA 1996/97; 3 v P in P 1997/98; 3 v A in A 1997/98; 3 v P in SA 1997/98; 1 v SL in SA 1997/98; 1 v E in E 1998; 1 v WI in SA 1998/99; 1 v Z in SA 1999/00; 1 v Z in Z 1999/00.

BALASKAS Xenophon Constantine, B Kimberley 15.10.1910. D Hyde Park, Sandton, Gauteng 12.5.1994.
9-2 v E in SA 1930/31; (To A 1931/32); 2 v NZ in NZ 1931/32; 1 v E in E 1935;3 v A in SA 1935/36; 1 v E in SA 1938/39.

BARLOW Edgar John, B Pretoria 12.8.1940.
30-5 v NZ in SA 1961/62; 5 v A in A 1963/64; 3 v NZ in NZ 1963/64;5 v E in SA 1964/65; 3 v E in E 1965; 5 v A in SA 1966/67; 4 v A in SA 1969/70.

BAUMGARTNER Harold Vane, B Henley-on-Thames, Oxfordshire, England 17.11.1883. D Accra, Gold Coast 8.4.1938.
1-v E in SA 1913/14.

BEAUMONT Rolland, B Newcastle, Natal 4.2.1884. D Berea Nursing Home, Durban 25.5.1958.
5-2 v A in E 1912; 1 v E in E 1912; 2 v E in SA 1913/14.

BEGBIE Denis Warburton, B Middelburg, Transvaal 12.12.1914.
5-(To E 1947); 3 v E in SA 1948/49; 2 v A in SA 1949/50.

BELL Alexander John (Sandy), B East London 15.4.1906. D Mowbray, Cape Town 1.8.1985.
16-3 v E in E 1929; 3 v E in SA 1930/31; 5 v A in A 1931/32; 2 v NZ in NZ 1931/32;3 v E in E 1935.

BISSET Murray, B Port Elizabeth 14.4.1876. D Salisbury, Rhodesia 24.10.1931.
3-2 v E in SA 1898/99; (To E 1901); 1 v E in SA 1909/10.

BISSETT George Finlay, B Kimberley 5.11.1905. D Botha's Hill, Natal 14.11.1965.
4-(To E 1924); 4 v E in SA 1927/28.

BLANCKENBERG James Manuel, B Claremont, Cape Town 31.12.1892. Presumed dead.
18(+2)-5 v E in SA 1913/14; (*2 v AIF 1919/20); 3 v A in SA 1921/22; 5 v E in SA 1922/23; 5 v E in E 1924.

BLAND Kenneth Colin, B Bulawayo, Rhodesia 5.4.1938.
21-5 v NZ in SA 1961/62; 4 v A in A 1963/64; 3 v NZ in NZ 1963/64; 5 v E in SA 1964/65; 3 v E in E 1965; 1 v A in SA 1966/67.

BOCK Ernest George, B Kimberley 17.9.1908. D Springs Nursing Home, Springs, Transvaal 5.9.1961.
1-v A in SA 1935/36.

+BOJE Nico (Nicky), B Bloemfontein 20.3.1973.
15-(To I 1996/97); (To NZ 1998/99); 2 v I in I 1999/00; 3 v SL in SL 2000; 3 v NZ in SA 2000/01; 3 v SL in SA 2000/01; 4 v WI in WI 2000/01.

BOND Gerald Edward (Boysie), B Cape Town 5.4.1909. D Cape Town 27.8.1965.
1-v E in SA 1938/39.

+BOSCH Tertius, B Vereeniging, Transvaal 14.3.1966. D Westville Hospital, Westville, Durban 14.2.2000.
1-v WI in WI 1991/92.

BOTTEN James Thomas (Jackie), B Pretoria 21.6.1938.
3-v E in E 1965.

+BOUCHER Mark Verdon, B East London 3.12.1976.
42-1 v P in P 1997/98; (To A 1997/98); 3 v P in SA 1997/98; 2 v SL in SA 1997/98; 5 v E in E 1998; 5 v WI in SA 1998/99; 3 v NZ in NZ 1998/99; 1 v Z in SA 1999/00; 1 v Z in Z 1999/00; 5 v E in SA 1999/00; 2 v I in I 1999/00; 3 v SL in SL 2000; 3 v NZ in SA 2000/01; 3 v SL in SA 2000/01; 5 v WI in WI 2000/01.

BRANN William Henry, B Port Elizabeth 4.4.1899. D Port Elizabeth 22.9.1953.
3-v E in SA 1922/23.

BRISCOE Arthur Wellesley (Dooley), B Johannesburg 6.2.1911. D Kombolcha, Ethiopia (War) 22.4.1941.
2-1 v A in SA 1935/36; 1 v E in SA 1938/39.

BROMFIELD Harry Dudley (Brom), B Mossel Bay, CP 26.6.1932.
9-5 v NZ in SA 1961/62; 3 v E in SA 1964/65; 1 v E in E 1965.

BROWN Lennox Sidney, B Randfontein, Transvaal 24.11.1910. D Durban 1.9.1983.
2-1 v A in A 1931/32; 1 v NZ in NZ 1931/32.

BURGER Christopher George de Villiers, B Randfontein, Transvaal 12.7.1935.
2-v A in SA 1957/58.

BURKE Sydney Frank, B Pretoria 11.3.1934.
2-1 v NZ in SA 1961/62; 1 v E in SA 1964/65.

BUYS Isaac Daniel, B Somerset East, CP 4.2.1895. Presumed dead.
1(+1)-1 v E in SA 1922/23; (*1 v SBJ 1924/25).

CAMERON Horace Brakenridge (Jock), B Port Elizabeth 5.7.1905. D Joubert Park Hospital, Johannesburg 2.11.1935.
26-5 v E in SA 1927/28; 4 v E in E 1929; 5 v E in SA 1930/31; 5 v A in A 1931/32;2 v NZ in NZ 1931/32; 5 v E in E 1935.

CAMPBELL Thomas, B Edinburgh, Scotland 9.2.1882. D Milnedale Railway Siding, Natal 5.10.1924.
5-4 v E in SA 1909/10; (To A 1910/11); 1 v E in E 1912.

CARLSTEIN Peter Rudolph, B Klerksdorp, Transvaal 28.10.1938.
8-1 v A in SA 1957/58; 5 v E in E 1960; 2 v A in A 1963/64.

CARTER Claude Pagdett, B Durban 23.4.1881. D Addington Hospital, Durban 8.11.1952.
10-2 v E in E 1912; 2 v E in SA 1913/14; 3 v A in SA 1921/22; 3 v E in E 1924.

CATTERALL Robert Hector, B Port Elizabeth 10.7.1900. D Springkell Sanatorium, Kempton Park, Transvaal 3.1.1961.
24(+5)-5 v E in SA 1922/23; 5 v E in E 1924; (*5 v SBJ 1924/25); 5 v E in SA 1927/28;5 v E in E 1929; 4 v E in SA 1930/31.

CHAPMAN Horace William, B Durban 30.6.1890. D Durban 1.12.1941.
2-1 v E in SA 1913/14; 1 v A in SA 1921/22.

CHEETHAM John Erskine (Jack), B Mowbray, Cape Town 26.5.1920. D Parktown, Johannesburg 21.8.1980.
24-1 v E in SA 1948/49; 3 v A in SA 1949/50; 5 v E in E 1951; 5 v A in A 1952/53;2 v NZ in NZ 1952/53; 5 v NZ in SA 1953/54; 3 v E in E 1955.

CHEVALIER Grahame Anton, B Cape Town 9.3.1937.
1-v A in SA 1969/70.

CHRISTY James Alexander Joseph, B Pretoria 12.12.1904. D Addington Hospital, Durban 1.2.1971.
10-2 v E in E 1929; 1 v E in SA 1930/31; 5 v A in A 1931/32; 2 v NZ in NZ 1931/32.

CHUBB Geoffrey Walter Ashton, B East London 12.4.1911. D East London 28.8.1982.
5-v E in E 1951.

COCHRAN John Alexander Kennedy, B Johannesburg 15.7.1909. D Johannesburg 15.6.1987.
1-v E in SA 1930/31.

COEN Stanley Keppel (Shunter), B Heilbron, OFS 14.10.1902. D Entabeni Hospital, Westridge, Durban 29.1.1967.
2-v E in SA 1927/28.

COMMAILLE John McIllwaine Moore (Mick), B Cape Town 21.2.1883. D Sea Point, Cape Town 28.7.1956.
12-5 v E in SA 1909/10; (To A 1910/11); 5 v E in E 1924; 2 v E in SA 1927/28.

COMMINS John Brian, B East London 19.2.1965.
3-2 v NZ in SA 1994/95; 1 v P in SA 1994/95; (To I 1996/97).

CONYNGHAM Dalton Parry (Conky), B Durban 10.5.1897. D Durban 7.7.1979.
1(+2)-1 v E in SA 1922/23; (*2 v SBJ 1924/25).

COOK Frederick James, B Java, Dutch East Indies 1870. D near Helles, Gallipoli, Turkey (War) 30.11.1915.
1-v E in SA 1895/96.

+COOK Stephen James, B Johannesburg 31.7.1953.
3(+19)-(*3 v E XI 1981/82; *2 v SL 1982/83; *2 v WI 1982/83; *4 v WI 1983/84;*3 v A 1985/86; *4 v A 1986/87; *1 v E XI 1989/90); 2 v I in SA 1992/93;1 v SL in SL 1993/94.

COOPER Alfred Henry Cecil, B Johannesburg 2.9.1893. D Johannesburg 18.7.1963.
1(+1)-1 v E in SA 1913/14; (*1 v AIF 1919/20).

COX Joseph Lovell, B Pietermaritzburg 28.6.1886. D Bulawayo, Rhodesia 4.7.1971.
3(+1)-(To E 1912); 3 v E in SA 1913/14; (*1 v AIF 1919/20).

CRIPPS Godfrey, B Mussoorie, India 19.10.1865. D near Adelaide, Australia 27.7.1943.
1-v E in SA 1891/92; (To E 1894).

CRISP Robert James (Bob), B Calcutta, India 28.5.1911. D Colchester, Essex, England 2.3.1994.
9-5 v E in E 1935; 4 v A in SA 1935/36.

+CRONJE Wessel Johannes (Hansie), B Bloemfontein 25.9.1969.
68-1 v WI in WI 1991/92; 3 v I in SA 1992/93; 3 v SL in SL 1993/94; 3 v A in A 1993/94; 3 v A in SA 1993/94; 3 v E in E 1994; 3 v NZ in SA 1994/95; 1 v P in SA 1994/95;1 v NZ in NZ 1994/95; 1 v Z in Z 1995/96; 5 v E in SA 1995/96; 3 v I in I 1996/97; 3 v I in SA 1996/97; 3 v A in SA 1996/97; 3 v P in P 1997/98; 3 v A in A 1997/98; 2 v P in SA 1997/98; 2 v SL in SA 1997/98; 5 v E in E 1998; 5 v WI in SA 1998/99; 3 v NZ in NZ 1998/99; 1 v Z in SA 1999/00; 1 v Z in Z 1999/00; 5 v E in SA 1999/00; 2 v I in I 1999/00.

+CULLINAN Daryll John, B Kimberley 4.3.1967.
70-1 v I in SA 1992/93; 3 v SL in SL 1993/94; 3 v A in A 1993/94; 1 v E in E 1994;3 v NZ in SA 1994/95; 1 v P in SA 1994/95; 1 v NZ in NZ 1994/95; 1 v Z in Z 1995/96; 5 v E in SA 1995/96; 3 v I in I 1996/97; 3 v I in SA 1996/97; 3 v A in SA 1996/97; 3 v P in P 1997/98; 1 v A in A 1997/98; 1 v P in SA 1997/98; 2 v SL in SA 1997/98; 5 v E in E 1998; 5 v WI in SA 1998/99; 3 v NZ in NZ 1998/99; 1 v Z in SA 1999/00; 1 v Z in Z 1999/00; 5 v E in SA 1999/00; 1 v I in I 1999/00; 3 v SL in SL 2000; 3 v NZ in SA 2000/01; 3 v SL in SA 2000/01; 5 v WI in WI 2000/01.

CURNOW Sydney Harry, B Benoni, Transvaal 16.12.1907. D Perth, Australia 28.7.1986.
7-3 v E in SA 1930/31; 4 v A in A 1931/32.

DALTON Eric Londesbrough, B Durban 2.12.1906. D Entabeni Hospital, Westridge, Durban 3.6.1981.
15-1 v E in E 1929; 1 v E in SA 1930/31; 2 v A in A 1931/32; 2 v NZ in NZ 1931/32;4 v E in E 1935; 1 v A in SA 1935/36; 4 v E in SA 1938/39.

DAVIES Eric Quail, B King William's Town, CP 26.8.1909. D Port Alfred, CP 11.11.1976.
5-2 v A in SA 1935/36; 3 v E in SA 1938/39.

DAWSON Oswald Charles, B Rossburgh, Durban 1.9.1919.
9-5 v E in E 1947; 4 v E in SA 1948/49.

DEANE Hubert Gouvaine (Nummy), B Eshowe, Natal (Zululand) 21.7.1895. D Lower Houghton, Johannesburg 21.10.1939.
17(+4)-5 v E in E 1924; (*4 v SBJ 1924/25); 5 v E in SA 1927/28; 5 v E in E 1929;2 v E in SA 1930/31.

+DE VILLIERS Petrus Stephanus (Fanie), B Vereeniging, Transvaal 13.10.1964.
18-(To SL 1993/94); 3 v A in A 1993/94; 3 v A in SA 1993/94; 3 v E in E 1994;3 v NZ in SA 1994/95; 1 v P in SA 1994/95; 1 v NZ in NZ 1994/95; (To Z 1995/96); 2 v I in I 1996/97; 2 v P in SA 1997/98.

+DIPPENAAR Hendrik Human (Boeta), B Kimberley 14.6.1977.
7-1 v Z in SA 1999/00; 1 v Z in Z 1999/00; (To I 1999/00); (To SL 2000); 3 v NZ in SA 2000/01; 2 v SL in SA 2000/01; (To WI 2000/01).

DIXON Cecil Donovan (Dickie), B Potchefstroom, Transvaal 12.2.1891. D Illovo, Johannesburg 9.9.1969.
1(+1)-1 v E in SA 1913/14; (*1 v AIF 1919/20); (To E 1924).

+DONALD Allan Anthony, B Bloemfontein 20.10.1966.
69(+2)-(*1 v A 1986/87; *1 v E XI 1989/90); 1 v WI in WI 1991/92; 4 v I in SA 1992/93; 3 v SL in SL 1993/94; 3 v A in A 1993/94; 3 v A in SA 1993/94; 3 v E in E 1994; 1 v P in SA 1994/95; 1 v NZ in NZ 1994/95; 1 v Z in Z 1995/96; 5 v E in SA 1995/96; 2 v I in I 1996/97; 3 v I in SA 1996/97; 3 v A in SA 1996/97; 2 v P in P 1997/98; 2 v A in A 1997/98; 3 v P in SA 1997/98; 2 v SL in SA 1997/98; 5 v E in E 1998; 5 v WI in SA 1998/99; 2 v NZ in NZ 1998/99; 1 v Z in SA 1999/00; 1 v Z in Z 1999/00; 4 v E in SA 1999/00; 2 v I in I 1999/00; 2 v NZ in SA 2000/01; 1 v SL in SA 2000/01; 4 v WI in WI 2000/01.

DOWER Robert Reid, B Kokstad, CP 4.6.1876. D Cape Town 15.9.1964.
1-v E in SA 1898/99.

DRAPER Ronald George, B Oudtshoorn, CP 24.12.1926.
2-v A in SA 1949/50.

DUCKWORTH Christopher Anthony Russell, B Que Que, Rhodesia 22.3.1933.
2-(To E 1955); 2 v E in SA 1956/57; (To E 1960).

DUMBRILL Richard, B Wandsworth, London, England 19.11.1938.
5-3 v E in E 1965; 2 v A in SA 1966/67.

DUMINY Jacobus Petrus (Koos), B Bellville, CP 16.12.1897. D Groote Schuur Hospital, Cape Town 31.1.1980.
3-2 v E in SA 1927/28; 1 v E in E 1929.

DUNELL Owen Robert, B Port Elizabeth 15.7.1856. D Lyons, France 21.10.1929.
2-v E in SA 1888/89.

DU PREEZ John Harcourt (Jackie), B Salisbury, Rhodesia 14.11.1942.
2-v A in SA 1966/67.

DU TOIT Jacobus Francois (Vlooi), B Jacobsdal, OFS 2.4.1869. D Lindley, OFS 10.7.1909.
1-v E in SA 1891/92.

DYER Dennis Victor, B Berea, Durban 2.5.1914. D Durban 16.6.1990.
3-v E in E 1947.

+EKSTEEN Clive Edward, B Johannesburg 2.12.1966.
7-1 v SL in SL 1993/94; 2 v NZ in SA 1994/95; 1 v P in SA 1994/95;1 v NZ in NZ 1994/95; 1 v E in SA 1995/96; 1 v I in I 1999/00.

ELGIE Michael Kelsey (Kim), B Berea, Durban 6.3.1933.
3-v NZ in SA 1961/62.

+ELWORTHY Steven, B Bulawayo, Rhodesia 23.2.1965.
2-1 v E in E 1998; 1 v NZ in NZ 1998/99.

ENDEAN William Russell, B Parkview, Johannesburg 31.5.1924.
28-1 v E in E 1951; 5 v A in A 1952/53; 2 v NZ in NZ 1952/53; 5 v NZ in SA 1953/54;5 v E in E 1955; 5 v E in SA 1956/57; 5 v A in SA 1957/58.

FARRER William Stephen (Buster), B King William's Town, CP 8.12.1936.
6-3 v NZ in SA 1961/62; (To A 1963/64); 3 v NZ in NZ 1963/64.

FAULKNER George Aubrey, B Port Elizabeth 17.12.1881. D Walham Green, London, England 10.9.1930.
25-5 v E in SA 1905/06; 3 v E in E 1907; 5 v E in SA 1909/10; 5 v A in A 1910/11;3 v E in E 1912; 3 v A in E 1912; 1 v E in E 1924.

FELLOWS-SMITH Jonathan Payn (Pom-Pom) B Berea, Durban 3.2.1932.
4-v E in E 1960.

FICHARDT Charles Gustav, B Bloemfontein 20.3.1870. D Rhodes Nursing Home, Cape Town 30.5.1923.
2-1 v E in SA 1891/92; 1 v E in SA 1895/96.

FINLASON Charles Edward, B Camberwell, London, England 19.2.1860. D Surbiton, Surrey, England 31.7.1917.
1-v E in SA 1888/89.

FLOQUET Claude Eugene, B Aliwal North, CP 3.11.1884. D Port Elizabeth 22.11.1963.
1-v E in SA 1909/10.

FRANCIS Howard Henry, B Westbury, Clifton, Bristol, Gloucestershire, England 26.5.1868. D Sea Point, Cape Town 7.1.1936.
2-v E in SA 1898/99.

FRANCOIS Cyril Matthew (Froggy), B Lewisham, London, England 20.6.1897. D near Pretoria 26.5.1944.
5(+1)-5 v E in SA 1922/23; (*1 v SBJ 1924/25).

FRANK Charles Newton, B Jagersfontein, OFS 27.1.1891. D Bryanston, Johannesburg 25.12.1961.
3(+1)-(*1 v AIF 1919/20); 3 v A in SA 1921/22.

FRANK William Hughes Bowker, B King William's Town, CP 23.11.1872. D Durban 16.2.1945.
1-v E in SA 1895/96.

FULLER Edward Russell Henry, B Worcester, CP 2.8.1931.
7-2 v A in A 1952/53; 2 v NZ in NZ 1952/53; 2 v E in E 1955; 1 v A in SA 1957/58.

FULLERTON George Murray, B Kensington, Johannesburg 8.12.1922.
7-2 v E in E 1947; 2 v A in SA 1949/50; 3 v E in E 1951.

FUNSTON Kenneth James, B Pretoria 3.12.1925.
18-5 v A in A 1952/53; 2 v NZ in NZ 1952/53; 3 v NZ in SA 1953/54;3 v E in SA 1956/57; 5 v A in SA 1957/58.

GAMSY Dennis, B Glenwood, Durban 17.2.1940.
2-(To E 1965); 2 v A in SA 1969/70.

+GIBBS Herschelle Herman, B Green Point, Cape Town 23.2.1974.
28-2 v I in I 1996/97; 1 v I in SA 1996/97; 1 v A in SA 1996/97; 2 v A in A 1997/98; 1 v P in SA 1997/98; 4 v WI in SA 1998/99; 3 v NZ in NZ 1998/99; 5 v E in SA 1999/00; 2 v I in I 1999/00; 2 v SL in SA 2000/01; 5 v WI in WI 2000/01.

GLEESON Robert Anthony, B Port Elizabeth 6.12.1873. D Port Elizabeth 27.9.1919.
1-v E in SA 1895/96.

GLOVER George Keyworth, B Wakefield, Yorkshire, England 13.5.1870. D Kimberley 15.11.1938.
1-(To E 1894); 1 v E in SA 1895/96.

GODDARD Trevor Leslie, B Durban 1.8.1931.
41-5 v E in E 1955; 5 v E in SA 1956/57; 5 v A in SA 1957/58; 5 v E in E 1960;5 v A in A 1963/64; 3 v NZ in NZ 1963/64; 5 v E in SA 1964/65; 5 v A in SA 1966/67; 3 v A in SA 1969/70.

GORDON Norman (Mobil), B Boksburg, Transvaal 6.8.1911.
5-v E in SA 1938/39.

GRAHAM Robert, B Grahamstown, CP 16.9.1877. D Upperton, Eastbourne, Sussex, England 21.4.1946.
2-v E in SA 1898/99; (To E 1901).

GRIEVESON Ronald Eustace, B Johannesburg 24.8.1909. D Waverley Gardens Nursing Home, Waverley, Johannesburg 24.7.1998.
2-v E in SA 1938/39.

GRIFFIN Geoffrey Merton, B Greytown, Natal 12.6.1939.
2-v E in E 1960.

HALL Alfred Ewart, B Bolton, Lancashire, England 23.1.1896. D South Rand Hospital, The Hill, Johannesburg 1.1.1964.
7(+5)-4 v E in SA 1922/23; (*5 v SBJ 1924/25); 2 v E in SA 1927/28; 1 v E in SA 1930/31.

HALL Glen Gordon, B Pretoria 24.5.1938. D Ramsgate, Natal 26.6.1987.
1-v E in SA 1964/65.

HALLIWELL Ernest Austin (Barberton), B Drayton Green, Ealing, Middlesex, England 7.9.1864. D Hillbrow Nursing Home, Johannesburg 2.10.1919.
8-1 v E in SA 1891/92; (To E 1894); 3 v E in SA 1895/96; 1 v E in SA 1898/99; (To E 1901); 3 v A in SA 1902/03; (To E 1904).

HALSE Clive Gray, B Empangeni, Natal (Zululand) 28.2.1935.
3-v A in A 1963/64.

HANDS Philip Albert Myburgh (Pam), B Claremont, Cape Town 18.3.1890. D Parys, OFS 27.4.1951.
7(+2)-5 v E in SA 1913/14; (*2 v AIF 1919/20); 1 v A in SA 1921/22; 1 v E in E 1924.

HANDS Reginald Harry Myburgh, B Claremont, Cape Town 26.7.1888. D near Bruay, Bethune, France (War) 20.4.1918.
1-v E in SA 1913/14.

HANLEY Martin Andrew, B Aliwal North, CP 10.11.1918. D Bishopscourt, Cape Town 2.6.2000.
1-v E in SA 1948/49.

HARRIS Terence Anthony (Tony), B Kimberley 27.8.1916. D Plettenberg Bay, CP 7.3.1993.
3-2 v E in E 1947; 1 v E in SA 1948/49.

HARTIGAN Gerald Patrick Desmond, B King William's Town, CP 30.12.1884. D Addington Hospital, Durban 7.1.1955.
5-1 v A in E 1912; 1 v E in E 1912; 3 v E in SA 1913/14.

HARVEY Robert Lyon, B Swinburne, OFS 14.9.1911. D Kloof, KZN 20.7.2000.
2-v A in SA 1935/36.

HATHORN Christopher Maitland Howard (Tottie), B Pietermaritzburg 7.4.1878. D Parktown West, Johannesburg 17.5.1920.
12-(To E 1901); 3 v A in SA 1902/03; (To E 1904); 5 v E in SA 1905/06;3 v E in E 1907; 1 v A in A 1910/11.

+HAYWARD Mornantau (Nantie), B Uitenhage, CP 6.3.1977.
6-(To E 1998); 3 v E in SA 1999/00; 1 v I in I 1999/00; 2 v SL in SL 2000.

HEARNE Frank, B Ealing, Middlesex, England 23.11.1858. D Mowbray, Cape Town 14.7.1949.
4-1 v E in SA 1891/92; (To E 1894); 3 v E in SA 1895/96. (Note: Also 2-E v SA in SA 1888/89).

HEARNE George Alfred Lawrence, B Catford, London, England 27.3.1888. D Barberton, Transvaal 13.11.1978.
3(+1)-(*1 v AIF 1919/20); 2 v E in SA 1922/23; 1 v E in E 1924.

HEINE Peter Samuel, B Winterton, Natal 28.6.1928.
14-4 v E in E 1955; 5 v E in SA 1956/57; 4 v A in SA 1957/58; 1 v NZ in SA 1961/62.

+HENRY Omar, B Stellenbosch, CP 23.1.1952.
3(+2)-(*2 v A 1986/87); (To WI 1991/92); 3 v I in SA 1992/93.

HIME Charles Frederick William, B Bermuda 24.10.1869. D Pietermaritzburg 6.12.1940.
1-v E in SA 1895/96.

+HUDSON Andrew Charles, B Eshowe, Natal (Zululand) 17.3.1965.
35-1 v WI in WI 1991/92; 4 v I in SA 1992/93; 3 v SL in SL 1993/94; 3 v A in A 1993/94; 3 v A in SA 1993/94; 2 v E in E 1994; 2 v NZ in SA 1994/95; 1 v NZ in NZ 1994/95; 1 v Z in Z 1995/96; 5 v E in SA 1995/96; 3 v I in I 1996/97; 3 v I in SA 1996/97; 1 v A in SA 1996/97; (To P 1997/98); 3 v P in SA 1997/98.

HUTCHINSON Philip, B West Dean, Sussex, England 25.1.1862. D Durban 30.9.1925.
2-v E in SA 1888/89.

IRONSIDE David Ernest James, B Lourenco Marques, Mozambique 2.5.1925.
3-v NZ in SA 1953/54.

IRVINE Brian Lee, B Durban 9.3.1944.
4-v A in SA 1969/70.

+**JACK** Steven Douglas, B Durban 4.8.1970.
2-v NZ in SA 1994/95; (To NZ 1994/95).

JOHNSON Clement Lecky (Boy), B Carbury, County Kildare, Ireland 31.3.1871. D Maraisburg, Roodepoort, Transvaal 31.5.1908.
1-(To E 1894); 1 v E in SA 1895/96.

+**KALLIS** Jacques Henry, B Pinelands, CP 16.10.1975.
50-2 v E in SA 1995/96; 3 v A in SA 1996/97; 1 v P in P 1997/98; 3 v A in A 1997/98; 3 v P in SA 1997/98; 2 v SL in SA 1997/98; 5 v E in E 1998; 5 v WI in SA 1998/99; 3 v NZ in NZ 1998/99; 1 v Z in SA 1999/00; 1 v Z in Z 1999/00; 5 v E in SA 1999/00; 2 v I in I 1999/00; 3 v SL in SL 2000; 3 v NZ in SA 2000/01; 3 v SL in SA 2000/01; 5 v WI in WI 2000/01.

KEITH Headley James, B Dundee, Natal 25.10.1927. D Pennington, KZN 17.11.1997.
8-1 v A in A 1952/53; 4 v E in E 1955; 3 v E in SA 1956/57.

+**KEMP** Justin Miles, B Queenstown, CP 2.10.1977.
3-1 v SL in SA 2000/01; 2 v WI in WI 2000/01.

KEMPIS Gustav Adolph, B Port Elizabeth 4.8.1865. D Chiloane Island, Mozambique 19.5.1890.
1-v E in SA 1888/89.

+**KIRSTEN** Gary, B Cape Town 23.11.1967.
73-3 v A in A 1993/94; 3 v A in SA 1993/94; 3 v E in E 1994; 3 v NZ in SA 1994/95; 1 v P in SA 1994/95; 1 v NZ in NZ 1994/95; 1 v Z in Z 1995/96; 5 v E in SA 1995/96; 3 v I in I 1996/97; 3 v I in SA 1996/97; 3 v A in SA 1996/97; 3 v P in P 1997/98; 3 v A in A 1997/98; 3 v P in SA 1997/98; 2 v SL in SA 1997/98; 5 v E in E 1998; 5 v WI in SA 1998/99; 3 v NZ in NZ 1998/99; 5 v E in SA 1999/00; 2 v I in I 1999/00; 3 v SL in SL 2000; 3 v NZ in SA 2000/01; 2 v SL in SA 2000/01; 5 v WI in WI 2000/01.

+**KIRSTEN** Peter Noel, B Pietermaritzburg 14.5.1955.
12(+19)-(*3 v E XI 1981/82; *2 v SL 1982/83; *2 v WI 1982/83; *4 v WI 1983/84;*3 v A 1985/86; *4 v A 1986/87; *1 v E XI 1989/90); 1 v WI in WI 1991/92;4 v I in SA 1992/93; 1 v A in A 1993/94;3 v A in SA 1993/94; 3 v E in E 1994.

+**KLUSENER** Lance, B Durban 4.9.1971.
42-2 v I in I 1996/97; 3 v I in SA 1996/97; 2 v A in SA 1996/97; 2 v P in P 1997/98; 2 v A in A 1997/98; 2 v P in SA 1997/98; 3 v E in E 1998; 1 v WI in SA 1998/99; 3 v NZ in NZ 1998/99; 1 v Z in SA 1999/00; 1 v Z in Z 1999/00; 5 v E in SA 1999/00; 2 v I in I 1999/00; 3 v SL in SL 2000; 3 v NZ in SA 2000/01; 2 v SL in SA 2000/01; 5 v WI in WI 2000/01.

KOTZE Johannes Jacobus (Kodgee) (Boerjong), B Hopefield, CP 7.8.1879. D Rondebosch, Cape Town 7.7.1931.
3-(To E 1901); 2 v A in SA 1902/03; (To E 1904); 1 v E in E 1907.

+**KUIPER** Adrian Paul, B Johannesburg 24.8.1959.
1(+7)-(*2 v E XI 1981/82; *2 v SL 1982/83; *2 v WI 1983/84; *1 v E XI 1989/90); 1 v WI in WI 1991/92.

KUYS Frederick, B George, CP 21.3.1870. D Oudtshoorn, CP 12.9.1953.
1-v E in SA 1898/99.

LANCE Herbert Roy (Tiger), B Pretoria 6.6.1940.
13-2 v NZ in SA 1961/62; 3 v E in E 1965; 5 v A in SA 1966/67; 3 v A in SA 1969/70.

LANGTON Arthur Chudleigh Beaumont (Chud), B Pietermaritzburg 2.3.1912. D near Maiduguri, Nigeria (War) 27.11.1942.
15-5 v E in E 1935; 5 v A in SA 1935/36; 5 v E in SA 1938/39.

LAWRENCE Godfrey Bernard (Goofy), B Salisbury, Rhodesia 31.3.1932.
5-v NZ in SA 1961/62.

LE ROUX Frederick Louis, B Durban 5.2.1882. D Durban 22.9.1963.
1-v E in SA 1913/14.

LEWIS Percy Tyson (Plum), B Cape Town 2.10.1884. D Durban 30.1.1976.
1-v E in SA 1913/14.

+LIEBENBERG Gerhardus Frederick Johannes, B Upington, CP 7.4.1972.
5-(To E 1994); 1 v SL in SA 1997/98; 4 v E in E 1998.

LINDSAY Denis Thomson, B Benoni, Transvaal 4.9.1939.
19-3 v A in A 1963/64; 3 v NZ in NZ 1963/64; 3 v E in SA 1964/65; 3 v E in E 1965;5 v A in SA 1966/67; 2 v A in SA 1969/70.

LINDSAY John Dixon, B Barkly East, CP 8.9.1908. D Benoni, Transvaal 31.8.1990.
3-v E in E 1947.

LINDSAY Nevil Vernon, B Harrismith, OFS 30.7.1886. D Pietermaritzburg 2.2.1976.
1(+1)-1 v A in SA 1921/22; (*1 v SBJ 1924/25).

LING William Victor Stone, B Kimberley 3.10.1891. D State Mines, Brakpan, Transvaal 26.9.1960.
6(+3)-3 v A in SA 1921/22; 3 v E in SA 1922/23; (*3 v SBJ 1924/25).

LLEWELLYN Charles Bennett (Buck), B Pietermaritzburg 26.9.1876. D Chertsey, Surrey, England 7.6.1964.
15-1 v E in SA 1895/96; 1 v E in SA 1898/99; (To E 1901); 3 v A in SA 1902/03;(To E 1904); 5 v A in A 1910/11; 2 v A in E 1912; 3 v E in E 1912.

LUNDIE Eric Balfour (Bill), B Willowvale, CP (Transkei) 15.3.1888. D near Passchendaele, Belgium (War) 12.9.1917.
1-v E in SA 1913/14.

MACAULAY Michael John, B Durban 19.4.1939.
1-v E in SA 1964/65; (To E 1965).

MANN Norman Bertram Fleetwood (Tufty), B Benoni, Transvaal 28.12.1920. D Princess Nursing Home, Hillbrow, Johannesburg 31.7.1952.
19-5 v E in E 1947; 5 v E in SA 1948/49; 5 v A in SA 1949/50; 4 v E in E 1951.

MANSELL Percy Neville Frank, B St George's, Shropshire, England 16.3.1920. D Somerset West, WC 9.5.1995.
13-2 v E in E 1951; 5 v A in A 1952/53; 2 v NZ in NZ 1952/53; 4 v E in E 1955.

MARKHAM Lawrence Anderson (Fish), B Mbabane, Swaziland 12.9.1924. D Pietermaritzburg 5.8.2000.
1-v E in SA 1948/49.

MARX Waldemar Frederick Eric, B Johannesburg 4.7.1895. D Durban 2.6.1974.
3-v A in SA 1921/22.

+MATTHEWS Craig Russell, B Cape Town 15.2.1965.
18-3 v I in SA 1992/93; 2 v A in A 1993/94; 3 v A in SA 1993/94; 3 v E in E 1994;2 v NZ in SA 1994/95; 1 v NZ in NZ 1994/95; 1 v Z in Z 1995/96; 3 v E in SA 1995/96.

McCARTHY Cuan Neil, B Pietermaritzburg 24.3.1929. D Johannesburg 14.8.2000.
15-5 v E in SA 1948/49; 5 v A in SA 1949/50; 5 v E in E 1951.

McGLEW Derrick John (Jackie), B Pietermaritzburg 11.3.1929. D Craighall Park, Johannesburg 9.6.1998.
34-2 v E in E 1951; 4 v A in A 1952/53; 2 v NZ in NZ 1952/53; 5 v NZ in SA 1953/54;5 v E in E 1955; 1 v E in SA 1956/57; 5 v A in SA 1957/58; 5 v E in E 1960; 5 v NZ in SA 1961/62.

+McKENZIE Neil Douglas, B Johannesburg 24.11.1975.
14-3 v SL in SL 2000; 3 v NZ in SA 2000/01; 3 v SL in SA 2000/01; 5 v WI in WI 2000/01.

McKINNON Atholl Henry, B Port Elizabeth 20.8.1932. D Durban 2.12.1983.
8-1 v E in E 1960; 1 v NZ in SA 1961/62; 2 v E in SA 1964/65; 2 v E in E 1965;2 v A in SA 1966/67.

McLEAN Roy Alastair, B Pietermaritzburg 9.7.1930.
40-3 v E in E 1951; 5 v A in A 1952/53; 2 v NZ in NZ 1952/53; 4 v NZ in SA 1953/54;5 v E in E 1955; 5 v E in SA 1956/57; 4 v A in SA 1957/58; 5 v E in E 1960; 5 v NZ in SA 1961/62; 2 v E in SA 1964/65.

+**McMILLAN** Brian Mervin, B Welkom, OFS 22.12.1963.
38(+4)-(*3 v A 1986/87; *1 v E XI 1989/90); 4 v I in SA 1992/93; 2 v SL in SL 1993/94;1 v A in A 1993/94; 3 v A in SA 1993/94; 3 v E in E 1994; 3 v NZ in SA 1994/95;1 v P in SA 1994/95; 1 v Z in Z 1995/96; 5 v E in SA 1995/96; 3 v I in I 1996/97; 3 v I in SA 1996/97; 2 v A in SA 1996/97; 3 v P in P 1997/98; 3 v A in A 1997/98; 1 v E in E 1998.

McMILLAN Quintin, B Germiston, Transvaal 23.6.1904. D Robinson Hospital, Randfontein, Transvaal 3.7.1948.
13-2 v E in E 1929; 5 v E in SA 1930/31; 4 v A in A 1931/32; 2 v NZ in NZ 1931/32.

MEINTJES Douglas James, B Pretoria 9.6.1890. D Johannesburg 17.7.1979.
2(+3)-(*2 v AIF 1919/20); 2 v E in SA 1922/23; (To E 1924); (*1 v SBJ 1924/25).

MELLE Michael George, B Forest Town, Johannesburg 3.6.1930.
7-2 v A in SA 1949/50; 1 v E in E 1951; 4 v A in A 1952/53; (To NZ 1952/53).

MELVILLE Alan, B Carnarvon, CP 19.5.1910. D Sabie, Transvaal 18.4.1983.
11-5 v E in SA 1938/39; 5 v E in E 1947; 1 v E in SA 1948/49.

MIDDLETON James (Bonnor), B Chester-le-Street, County Durham, England 30.9.1865. D Newlands, Cape Town 23.12.1913.
6-(To E 1894); 2 v E in SA 1895/96; 2 v E in SA 1898/99; 2 v A in SA 1902/03;(To E 1904).

MILLS Charles Henry, B Peckham, London, England 26.11.1867. D Southwark, London, England 26.7.1948.
1-v E in SA 1891/92; (To E 1894).

MILTON William Henry, B Little Marlow, Buckinghamshire, England 3.12.1854. D Cannes, France 6.3.1930.
3-2 v E in SA 1888/89; 1 v E in SA 1891/92.

MITCHELL Bruce, B Ferreira Deep Gold Mine, Johannesburg 8.1.1909. D Abbotsford, Johannesburg 2.7.1995.
42-5 v E in E 1929; 5 v E in SA 1930/31; 5 v A in A 1931/32; 2 v NZ in NZ 1931/32;5 v E in E 1935; 5 v A in SA 1935/36; 5 v E in SA 1938/39; 5 v E in E 1947;5 v E in SA 1948/49.

MITCHELL Frank, B Market Weighton, Yorkshire, England 13.8.1872. D Blackheath, Kent, England 11.10.1935.
3-(To E 1904); 2 v A in E 1912; 1 v E in E 1912. (Note: Also 2-E v SA in SA 1898/99).

MORKEL Denijs Paul Beck, B Plumstead, Cape Town 25.1.1906. D Nottingham, England 6.10.1980.
16-5 v E in SA 1927/28; 5 v E in E 1929; 5 v A in A 1931/32; 1 v NZ in NZ 1931/32.

MURRAY Anton Ronald Andrew, B Grahamstown, CP 30.4.1922. D Cape Town 17.4.1995.
10-4 v A in A 1952/53; 2 v NZ in NZ 1952/53; 4 v NZ in SA 1953/54; (To E 1955).

NEL John Desmond (Jack), B Cape Town 10.7.1928.
6-5 v A in SA 1949/50; 1 v A in SA 1957/58.

NEWBERRY Claude, B Port Elizabeth 1889. D France (War) aged 27, 1.8.1916.
4-v E in SA 1913/14.

NEWSON Edward Serrurier (Bob), B Sea Point, Cape Town 2.12.1910. D Durban 24.4.1988.
3-1 v E in SA 1930/31; 2 v E in SA 1938/39.

NGAM Mfuneko, B Middledrift, CP 29.1.1979.
3-1 v NZ in SA 2000/01; 2 v SL in SA 2000/01.

NICHOLSON Frank (Nipper), B Millom, Cumberland, England 17.9.1909. D Port Elizabeth 30.7.1982.
4-v A in SA 1935/36.

NICOLSON John Fairless William, B Durban 19.7.1899. D Kilkeel Hospital, County Down, Northern Ireland 13.12.1935.
3-v E in SA 1927/28.

NORTON Norman Ogilvie (Pompey), B Grahamstown, CP 11.5.1881. D Mater Dei Nursing Home, Southernwood, East London 27.6.1968.
1-v E in SA 1909/10.

NOURSE Arthur Dudley, B Durban 12.11.1910. D Durban 14.8.1981.
34-4 v E in E 1935; 5 v A in SA 1935/36; 5 v E in SA 1938/39; 5 v E in E 1947;5 v E in SA 1948/49; 5 v A in SA 1949/50; 5 v E in E 1951.

NOURSE Arthur William (Dave), B South Norwood, Surrey, England 25.1.1879. D Provincial Hospital, Glendinningvale, Port Elizabeth 8.7.1948.
45(+7)-3 v A in SA 1902/03; 5 v E in SA 1905/06; 3 v E in E 1907; 5 v E in SA 1909/10;5 v A in A 1910/11; 3 v A in E 1912; 3 v E in E 1912; 5 v E in SA 1913/14; (*2 v AIF 1919/20); 3 v A in SA 1921/22; 5 v E in SA 1922/23; 5 v E in E 1924;(*5 v SBJ 1924/25).

+NTINI Makhaya, B Mdingi, near King William's Town, CP 6.7.1977.
15-(To A 1997/98); 2 v SL in SA 1997/98; 2 v E in E 1998; 1 v SL in SL 2000; 3 v NZ in SA 2000/01; 3 v SL in SA 2000/01; 4 v WI in WI 2000/01.

NUPEN Eiulf Peter (Buster), B Johannesburg 1.1.1902. D Lady Dudley Nursing Home, Johannesburg 29.1.1977.
17(+4)-2 v A in SA 1921/22; 4 v E in SA 1922/23; 2 v E in E 1924; (*4 v SBJ 1924/25);5 v E in SA 1927/28; 3 v E in SA 1930/31; 1 v A in SA 1935/36.

OCHSE Arthur Edward (Okey), B Graaff-Reinet, CP 11.3.1870. D Middle Farm, Petit Puits, Messines Ridge, France (War) 11.4.1918.
2-v E in SA 1888/89.

OCHSE Arthur Lennox, B Graaff-Reinet, CP 11.10.1898. D Eldorado Farm, near Middelburg, CP 5.5.1949.
3-1 v E in SA 1927/28; 2 v E in E 1929.

O'LINN Sidney (Micky), B Oudtshoorn, CP 5.5.1927.
7-5 v E in E 1960; 2 v NZ in SA 1961/62.

OWEN-SMITH Harold Geoffrey Owen (Tuppy), B Rondebosch, Cape Town 18.2.1909. D Rosebank, CapeTown 28.2.1990.
5-v E in E 1929.

PALM Archibald William, B Rondebosch, Cape Town 8.6.1901. D Somerset West, CP 17.8.1966.
1-v E in SA 1927/28.

PARKER George Macdonald, B Cape Town 27.5.1899. D Thredbo, New South Wales, Australia 1.5.1969.
2-v E in E 1924.

PARKIN Durant Clifford (Dante), B Port Elizabeth 20.2.1873. D Sangster's Farm (Eagle's Crag), Albany, CP 20.3.1936.
1-v E in SA 1891/92; (To E 1894).

PARTRIDGE Joseph Titus, B Bulawayo, Rhodesia 9.12.1932. D Harare, Zimbabwe 6.6.1988.
11-5 v A in A 1963/64; 3 v NZ in NZ 1963/64; 3 v E in SA 1964/65.

PEARSE Charles Ormerod Cato (Ormy), B Pietermaritzburg 10.10.1884. D Durban 7.5.1953.
3-v A in A 1910/11.

PEGLER Sidney James, B Durban 28.7.1888. D Harewood Nursing Home, Plumstead, Cape Town 10.9.1972.
16-1 v E in SA 1909/10; 4 v A in A 1910/11; 3 v A in E 1912; 3 v E in E 1912;5 v E in E 1924.

PITHEY Anthony John, B Umtali, Rhodesia 17.7.1933.
17-3 v E in SA 1956/57; 2 v E in E 1960; 4 v A in A 1963/64; 3 v NZ in NZ 1963/64;5 v E in SA 1964/65.

PITHEY David Bartlett, B Salisbury, Rhodesia 4.10.1936.
8-3 v A in A 1963/64; 3 v NZ in NZ 1963/64; 2 v A in SA 1966/67.

PLIMSOLL Jack Bruce, B Kalk Bay, Cape Town 27.10.1917. D Cape Town 11.11.1999.
1-v E in E 1947.

POLLOCK Peter Maclean, B Pietermaritzburg 30.6.1941.
28-3 v NZ in SA 1961/62; 5 v A in A 1963/64; 3 v NZ in NZ 1963/64;5 v E in SA 1964/65; 3 v E in E 1965; 5 v A in SA 1966/67; 4 v A in SA 1969/70.

POLLOCK Robert Graeme, B Durban 27.2.1944.
23(+16)-5 v A in A 1963/64; 1 v NZ in NZ 1963/64; 5 v E in SA 1964/65;3 v E in E 1965; 5 v A in SA 1966/67; 4 v A in SA 1969/70; (*3 v E XI 1981/82; *2 v SL 1982/83; *2 v WI 1982/83; *4 v WI 1983/84; *3 v A 1985/86; *2 v A 1986/87).

+POLLOCK Shaun Maclean, B Port Elizabeth 16.7.1973.
56-5 v E in SA 1995/96; 3 v I in SA 1996/97; 2 v A in SA 1996/97; 3 v P in P 1997/98; 3 v A in

A 1997/98; 3 v P in SA 1997/98; 2 v SL in SA 1997/98; 4 v E in E 1998; 5 v WI in SA 1998/99; 3 v NZ in NZ 1998/99; 1 v Z in SA 1999/00; 1 v Z in Z 1999/00; 5 v E in SA 1999/00; 2 v I in I 1999/00; 3 v SL in SL 2000; 3 v NZ in SA 2000/01; 3 v SL in SA 2000/01; 5 v WI in WI 2000/01.

POORE Robert Montagu, B Carysfort House, Dublin, Ireland 20.3.1866. D Boscombe, Hampshire, England 14.7.1938.
3-v E in SA 1895/96.

POTHECARY James Edward, B Cape Town 6.12.1933.
3-v E in E 1960.

POWELL Albert William (Bertie), B Kimberley 18.7.1873. D Cape Town 11.9.1948.
1-v E in SA 1898/99.

PRINCE Charles Frederick Henry, B Boshof, OFS 11.9.1874. D Wynberg, Cape Town 2.2.1949.
1-v E in SA 1898/99; (To E 1901).

+PRINGLE Meyrick Wayne, B Adelaide, CP 22.6.1966.
4-1 v WI in WI 1991/92; 2 v I in SA 1992/93; 1 v E in SA 1995/96.

PROCTER Michael John, B Durban 15.9.1946.
7(+1)-3 v A in SA 1966/67; 4 v A in SA 1969/70; (*1 v E XI 1981/82).

PROMNITZ Henry Louis Ernest, B near King William's Town, CP 23.2.1904. D East London 7.9.1983.
2-v E in SA 1927/28.

QUINN Neville Anthony, B Tweefontein, OFS 21.2.1908. D Kenilworth, Kimberley 5.8.1934.
12-4 v E in E 1929; 1 v E in SA 1930/31; 5 v A in A 1931/32; 2 v NZ in NZ 1931/32.

REID Norman, B Newlands, Cape Town 26.12.1890. D Newlands, Cape Town 6.6.1947.
1-v A in SA 1921/22.

+RHODES Jonathan Neil (Jonty), B Pietermaritzburg 27.7.1969.
52-(To WI 1991/92); 4 v I in SA 1992/93; 3 v SL in SL 1993/94; 3 v A in A 1993/94; 3 v A in SA 1993/94; 3 v E in E 1994; 3 v NZ in SA 1994/95; 1 v P in SA 1994/95;1 v NZ in NZ 1994/95; 1 v Z in Z 1995/96; 5 v E in SA 1995/96; 1 v I in I 1996/97; 1 v A in SA 1996/97; 1 v P in P 1997/98; 1 v A in A 1997/98; 5 v E in E 1998; 5 v WI in SA 1998/99; 3 v NZ in NZ 1998/99; 1 v Z in SA 1999/00; 1 v Z in Z 1999/00; 3 v E in SA 1999/00; 3 v SL in SL 2000.

RICHARDS Alfred Renfrew, B Grahamstown, CP 14.12.1867. D Salisbury Hospital, Salisbury, Rhodesia 9.1.1904.
1-v E in SA 1895/96.

RICHARDS Barry Anderson, B Morningside, Durban 21.7.1945.
4(+6)-4 v A in SA 1969/70; (*3 v E XI 1981/82; *1 v SL 1982/83, *2 v WI 1982/83).

RICHARDS William Henry Matthews (Dicky), B Grahamstown, CP 26.3.1862. D Wynberg, Cape Town 4.1.1903.
1-v E in SA 1888/89.

+RICHARDSON David John, B Johannesburg 16.9.1959.
42(+5)-(*1 v WI 1983/84; *4 v A 1986/87); 1 v WI in WI 1991/92; 4 v I in SA 1992/93; 3 v SL in SL 1993/94; 3 v A in A 1993/94; 3 v A in SA 1993/94; 3 v E in E 1994; 3 v NZ in SA 1994/95; 1 v P in SA 1994/95; 1 v NZ in NZ 1994/95; 1 v Z in Z 1995/96; 5 v E in SA 1995/96; 3 v I in I 1996/97; 3 v I in SA 1996/97; 3 v A in SA 1996/97; 2 v P in P 1997/98; 3 v A in A 1997/98.

ROBERTSON John Benjamin, B Wynberg, Cape Town 5.6.1906. D Cape Town 5.7.1985.
3-v A in SA 1935/36.

ROSE-INNES Albert, B Port Elizabeth 16.2.1868. D East London 22.11.1946.
2-v E in SA 1888/89.

ROUTLEDGE Thomas William, B Liverpool, Lancashire, England 18.4.1867. D Billingham, County Durham, England 9.5.1927.
4-1 v E in SA 1891/92; (To E 1894); 3 v E in SA 1895/96.

ROWAN Athol Matthew Burchell, B Kensington, Johannesburg 7.2.1921. D Hermanus, WC 22.2.1998.
15-5 v E in E 1947; 5 v E in SA 1948/49; 5 v E in E 1951.

ROWAN Eric Alfred Burchell, B Johannesburg 20.7.1909. D Edenvale Hospital, Transvaal 30.4.1993.
26-5 v E in E 1935; 3 v A in SA 1935/36; 4 v E in SA 1938/39; 4 v E in SA 1948/49; 5 v A in SA 1949/50; 5 v E in E 1951.

ROWE George Alexander, B Grahamstown, CP 15.6.1874. D Pinelands, CP 8.1.1950.
5-(To E 1894); 2 v E in SA 1895/96; 2 v E in SA 1898/99; (To E 1901);1 v A in SA 1902/03.

+RUSHMERE Mark Weir, B Port Elizabeth 7.1.1965.
1-v WI in WI 1991/92.

SAMUELSON Sivert Vause, B York, Natal 21.11.1883. D Durban 18.11.1958.
1-v E in SA 1909/10.

+SCHULTZ Brett Nolan, B East London 26.8.1970.
9-2 v I in SA 1992/93; 3 v SL in SL 1993/94; 1 v Z in Z 1995/96; 1 v E in SA 1995/96; 1 v A in SA 1996/97; 1 v P in P 1997/98.

SCHWARZ Reginald Oscar, B Lee, London, England 4.5.1875. D Etaples, France (War) 18.11.1918.
20-(To E 1904); 5 v E in SA 1905/06; 3 v E in E 1907; 4 v E in SA 1909/10; 5 v A in A 1910/11; 2 v A in E 1912; 1 v E in E 1912.

SECCULL Arthur William, B King William's Town, CP 14.9.1868. D Johannesburg 20.7.1945.
1-(To E 1894); 1 v E in SA 1895/96.

SEYMOUR Michael Arthur (Kelly) B Kokstad, CP 5.6.1936.
7-4 v A in A 1963/64; 2 v E in SA 1964/65; 1 v A in SA 1969/70.

SHALDERS William Alfred, B Kimberley 12.2.1880. D Cradock, CP 18.3.1917.
12-1 v E in SA 1898/99; (To E 1901); 3 v A in SA 1902/03; (To E 1904); 5 v E in SA 1905/06; 3 v E in E 1907.

SHEPSTONE George Harold, B Pietermaritzburg 9.4.1876. D Springkell Sanatorium, Germiston, Transvaal 3.7.1940.
2-1 v E in SA 1895/96; 1 v E in SA 1898/99; (To E 1904).

SHERWELL Percy William, B Isipingo, Natal 17.8.1880. D Bulawayo, Rhodesia 17.4.1948.
13-5 v E in SA 1905/06; 3 v E in E 1907; 5 v A in A 1910/11.

SIEDLE Ivan Julian (Jack), B Berea, Durban 11.1.1903. D St. Augustine's Hospital, Bulwer, Durban 24.8.1982.
18(+3)-(*3 v SBJ 1924/25); 1 v E in SA 1927/28; 3 v E in E 1929; 5 v E in SA 1930/31; 4 v E in E 1935; 5 v A in SA 1935/36.

SINCLAIR James Hugh, B Swellendam, CP 16.10.1876. D Yeoville, Johannesburg 23.2.1913.
25-3 v E in SA 1895/96; 2 v E in SA 1898/99; (To E 1901); 3 v A in SA 1902/03;(To E 1904); 5 v E in SA 1905/06; 3 v E in E 1907; 4 v E in SA 1909/10; 5 v A in A 1910/11.

SMITH Charles James Edward, B Gamtoos River, CP 25.12.1872. D Norman Nursing Home, Joubert Park, Johannesburg 27.3.1947.
3-v A in SA 1902/03.

SMITH Frederick William, B Uitenhage, CP 31.3.1861. D Johannesburg Hospital, Parktown, Johannesburg 17.4.1914.
3-2 v E in SA 1888/89; 1 v E in SA 1895/96.

SMITH Vivian Ian, B Durban 23.2.1925.
9-4 v E in E 1947; 3 v A in SA 1949/50; 1 v E in E 1955; 1 v A in SA 1957/58.

+SNELL Richard Peter, B Durban 12.9.1968.
5(+1)-(*1 v E XI 1989/90); 1 v WI in WI 1991/92; 2 v SL in SL 1993/94;1 v A in A 1993/94; (To E 1994); 1 v NZ in SA 1994/95.

SNOOKE Stanley de la Courtte, B St Mark's, CP (Tembuland) (Transkei) 11.11.1878. D Wynberg, Cape Town 6.4.1959.
1-v E in E 1907.

SNOOKE Sibley John (Tip), B St Mark's, CP (Tembuland) (Transkei) 1.2.1881. D Humewood, Port Elizabeth 14.8.1966.
26-(To E 1904); 5 v E in SA 1905/06; 3 v E in E 1907; 5 v E in SA 1909/10; 5 v A in A 1910/11; 2 v A in E 1912; 3 v E in E 1912; 3 v E in SA 1922/23.

SOLOMON William Rodger Thomson, B Fort Beaufort, CP 23.4.1872. D Cradock, CP 13.7.1964.
1-v E in SA 1898/99.

STEWART Robert Burnard, B Azumgurh, India 3.9.1856. D Cala, CP 12.9.1913.
1-v E in SA 1888/89.

+**STEYN** Philippus Jeremia Rudolf, B Kimberley 30.6.1967.
3-1 v NZ in SA 1994/95; 1 v P in SA 1994/95; 1 v NZ in NZ 1994/95; (To Z 1995/96).

STRICKER Louis Anthony, B Beaconsfield, Kimberley 26.5.1884. D Rondebosch, Cape Town 5.2.1960.
13-4 v E in SA 1909/10; 5 v A in A 1910/11; 2 v A in E 1912; 2 v E in E 1912.

+**STRYDOM** Pieter Coenraad, B Somerset East, CP 10.6.1969.
2-1 v E in SA 1999/00; 1 v I in I 1999/00.

SUSSKIND Manfred John (Fred), B Johannesburg 8.6.1891. D Johannesburg Stock Exchange, Johannesburg 9.7.1957.
5(+3)-5 v E in E 1924; (*3 v SBJ 1924/25).

+**SYMCOX** Patrick Leonard, B Kimberley 14.4.1960.
20-3 v SL in SL 1993/94; 2 v A in A 1993/94; (To E 1994); (To NZ 1994/95); 1 v Z in Z 1995/96; 3 v I in I 1996/97; 1 v A in SA 1996/97; 3 v P in P 1997/98; 3 v A in A 1997/98; 1 v P in SA 1997/98; (To E 1998); 3 v WI in SA 1998/99.

TABERER Henry Melville, B Keiskammahoek, CP 7.10.1870. D Stormfontein Farm, Colesberg, CP 5.6.1932.
1-v A in SA 1902/03.

TANCRED Augustus Bernard, B Port Elizabeth 20.8.1865. D Monte Rosa Hospital, Cape Town 23.11.1911.
2-v E in SA 1888/89.

TANCRED Louis Joseph, B Port Elizabeth 7.10.1876. D Park Lane Nursing Home, Parktown, Johannesburg 28.7.1934.
14(+1)-(To E 1901); 3 v A in SA 1902/03; (To E 1904); 5 v E in SA 1905/06; 1 v E in E 1907; 2 v A in E 1912; 2 v E in E 1912; 1 v E in SA 1913/14; (*1 v AIF 1919/20).

TANCRED Vincent Maximillian, B Port Elizabeth 7.7.1875. D Florida, Roodepoort, Transvaal 3.6.1904.
1-v E in SA 1898/99.

TAPSCOTT George Lancelot (Dusty), B Barkly West, CP 7.11.1889. D Kimberley 13.12.1940.
1-v E in SA 1913/14.

TAPSCOTT Lionel Eric (Doodles), B Kimberley 18.3.1894. D Kenilworth, Cape Town 7.7.1934.
2-v E in SA 1922/23.

TAYFIELD Hugh Joseph (Toey), B Durban 30.1.1929. D Hillcrest, Natal 24.2.1994.
37-5 v A in SA 1949/50; (To E 1951); 5 v A in A 1952/53; 2 v NZ in NZ 1952/53; 5 v NZ in SA 1953/54; 5 v E in E 1955; 5 v E in SA 1956/57; 5 v A in SA 1957/58; 5 v E in E 1960.

TAYLOR Alistair Innes (Scotch), B Johannesburg 25.7.1925.
1-v E in SA 1956/57.

TAYLOR Daniel, B Durban 9.1.1887. D Durban 24.1.1957.
2-v E in SA 1913/14.

TAYLOR Herbert Wilfred, B Durban 5.5.1889. D Newlands, Cape Town 8.2.1973.
42(+5)-3 v A in E 1912; 3 v E in E 1912; 5 v E in SA 1913/14; 3 v A in SA 1921/22; 5 v E in SA 1922/23; 5 v E in E 1924; (*5 v SBJ 1924/25); 5 v E in SA 1927/28;3 v E in E 1929; 4 v E in SA 1930/31; 5 v A in A 1931/32; 1 v NZ in NZ 1931/32.

+**TERBRUGGE** David John, B Ladysmith, Natal 31.1.1977.
4-v WI in SA 1998/99; (To SL 2000).

THEUNISSEN Nicolaas Hendrik Christiaan de Jong, B Colesberg, CP 4.5.1867. D Willemsdal, Transvaal 9.11.1929.
1-v E in SA 1888/89.

THORNTON George, B Skipton, Yorkshire, England 24.12.1867. D Kensington, London, England 31.1.1939.
1-v A in SA 1902/03.

TOMLINSON Denis Stanley, B Umtali, Rhodesia 4.9.1910. D Durban 11.7.1993.
1-v E in E 1935.

TRAICOS Athanasios John, B Zagazig, Egypt 17.5.1947.
3-v A in SA 1969/70.
(Note: Also 1-Z v I in Z 1992/93; 2-Z v NZ in Z 1992/93; 1-Z v I in I 1992/93).

TRIMBORN Patrick Henry Joseph, B Glenwood, Durban 18.5.1940.
4-3 v A in SA 1966/67; 1 v A in SA 1969/70.
TUCKETT Lindsay, B Durban 6.2.1919.
9-5 v E in E 1947; 4 v E in SA 1948/49.
TUCKETT Lindsay Richard (Len), B Durban 19.4.1885. D Bloemfontein 8.4.1963.
1-v E in SA 1913/14.
TWENTYMAN JONES Percy Sydney, B Beaufort West, CP 13.9.1876. D Cape Town 8.3.1954.
1-v A in SA 1902/03.
VAN DER BIJL Pieter Gerhard Vintcent, B Kenilworth, Cape Town 21.10.1907. D Kalk Bay, Cape Town 16.2.1973.
5-v E in SA 1938/39.
VAN DER MERWE Edward Alexander, B Rustenburg, Transvaal 9.11.1903. D JG Strijdom Hospital, Auckland Park, Johannesburg 26.2.1971.
2-1 v E in E 1929; (To A 1931/32); 1 v A in SA 1935/36.
VAN DER MERWE Peter Laurence, B Paarl, CP 14.3.1937.
15-3 v A in A 1963/64; 2 v NZ in NZ 1963/64; 2 v E in SA 1964/65; 3 v E in E 1965; 5 v A in SA 1966/67.
VAN RYNEVELD Clive Berrange, B St James, Cape Town 19.3.1928.
19-5 v E in E 1951; 5 v NZ in SA 1953/54; 5 v E in SA 1956/57; 4 v A in SA 1957/58.
VARNALS George Derek, B Durban 24.7.1935.
3-v E in SA 1964/65.
VILJOEN Kenneth George, B Windsorton, CP 14.5.1910. D Krugersdorp, Transvaal 21.1.1974.
27-3 v E in SA 1930/31; 4 v A in A 1931/32; 1 v NZ in NZ 1931/32; 4 v E in E 1935; 4 v A in SA 1935/36; 4 v E in SA 1938/39; 5 v E in E 1947; 2 v E in SA 1948/49.
VINCENT Cyril Leverton, B Johannesburg 16.2.1902. D St. Augustine's Hospital, Bulwer, Durban 24.8.1968.
25-5 v E in SA 1927/28; 4 v E in E 1929; 5 v E in SA 1930/31; 5 v A in A 1931/32; 2 v NZ in NZ 1931/32; 4 v E in E 1935.
VINTCENT Charles Henry, B Mossel Bay, CP 2.9.1866. D George, CP 28.9.1943.
3-2 v E in SA 1888/89; 1 v E in SA 1891/92.
VOGLER Albert Edward Ernest, B Swartwater, near Queenstown, CP 28.11.1876. D Fort Napier Hospital, Pietermaritzburg 9.8.1946.
15-5 v E in SA 1905/06; 3 v E in E 1907; 5 v E in SA 1909/10; 2 v A in A 1910/11.
WADE Herbert Frederick, B Durban 14.9.1905. D Inanda, Sandton, Transvaal 23.11.1980.
10-5 v E in E 1935; 5 v A in SA 1935/36.
WADE Walter Wareham (Billy), B Durban 18.6.1914.
11-3 v E in SA 1938/39; 5 v E in SA 1948/49; 3 v A in SA 1949/50.
WAITE John Henry Bickford, B Johannesburg 19.1.1930.
50-4 v E in E 1951; 5 v A in A 1952/53; 2 v NZ in NZ 1952/53; 5 v NZ in SA 1953/54; 5 v E in E 1955; 5 v E in SA 1956/57; 5 v A in SA 1957/58; 5 v E in E 1960; 5 v NZ in SA 1961/62; 4 v A in A 1963/64; 3 v NZ in NZ 1963/64; 2 v E in SA 1964/65.
WALTER Kenneth Alexander, B Johannesburg 5.11.1939.
2-v NZ in SA 1961/62.
WARD Thomas Alfred, B Rawalpindi, India 2.8.1887. D East Springs Gold Mine, Transvaal 16.2.1936.
23(+2)-3 v A in E 1912; 2 v E in E 1912; 5 v E in SA 1913/14; (*2 v AIF 1919/20); 3 v A in SA 1921/22; 5 v E in SA 1922/23; 5 v E in E 1924.
WATKINS John Cecil, B Durban 10.4.1923.
15-3 v A in SA 1949/50; 5 v A in A 1952/53; 2 v NZ in NZ 1952/53; 3 v NZ in SA 1953/54; 2 v E in SA 1956/57.
WESLEY Colin (Tich), B Durban 5.9.1937.
3-v E in E 1960.

+WESSELS Kepler Christoffel, B Bloemfontein 14.9.1957.
16(+1)-(*1 v E XI 1989/90); 1 v WI in WI 1991/92; 4 v I in SA 1992/93;3 v SL in SL 1993/94; 2 v A in A 1993/94; 3 v A in SA 1993/94; 3 v E in E 1994. (Note: Also 4-A v E in A 1982/83; 1-A v SL in SL 1982/83; 5-A v P in A 1983/84; 2-A v WI in WI 1983/84; 5-A v WI in A 1984/85; 6-A v E in E 1985; 1-A v NZ in NZ 1985/86; *4-A XI v SA in SA 1986/87).

WESTCOTT Richard John, B Lisbon, Portugal 19.9.1927.
5-3 v NZ in SA 1953/54; 2 v A in SA 1957/58.

WHITE Gordon Charles, B Port St Johns, CP (Transkei) 5.2.1882. D Gaza, Palestine (War) 17.10.1918.
17-(To E 1904); 5 v E in SA 1905/06; 3 v E in E 1907; 4 v E in SA 1909/10; 3 v A in E 1912; 2 v E in E 1912.

WILLOUGHBY Joseph Thomas, B Aldershot, Hampshire, England 7.11.1874. D Plumstead, Cape Town 11.3.1952.
2-v E in SA 1895/96.

WIMBLE Clarence Skelton, B Graaff-Reinet, CP 22.4.1861. D Johannesburg 28.1.1930.
1-v E in SA 1891/92.

WINSLOW Paul Lyndhurst, B Johannesburg 21.5.1929.
5-2 v A in SA 1949/50; 3 v E in E 1955.

WYNNE Owen Edgar, B Johannesburg 1.6.1919. D at sea, False Bay, CP 13.7.1975.
6-3 v E in SA 1948/49; 3 v A in SA 1949/50.

ZULCH Johan Wilhelm (Billy), B Lydenburg, Transvaal 2.1.1886. D Umkomaas, Natal 19.5.1924.
16(+2)-5 v E in SA 1909/10; 5 v A in A 1910/11; 3 v E in SA 1913/14;(*2 v AIF 1919/20); 3 v A in SA 1921/22.

S.A. INTERNATIONAL CRICKETERS WHO HAVE APPEARED ONLY IN UNOFFICIAL TESTS

BILLING McGregor Edward (Max), B Port Elizabeth 12.1.1887. D Morningside, Durban 3.11.1965.
(1 v SBJ 1924/25).

BOLTON James Lardner, B Cape Town 30.1.1895. D Cape Town 1.11.1969.
(1 v SBJ 1924/25).

BUDGEN Edward Albert (Hookie), B Heidelberg, Transvaal 9.12.1884. D Port Elizabeth 6.10.1962.
(1 v AIF 1919/20).

DAVIES Marchant Starr, B Balfour, CP 31.5.1896. D Port Elizabeth 22.2.1973.
(2 v AIF 1919/20).

DUFF William Dick, B Pietermaritzburg 19.9.1890. D Johannesburg 7.10.1953.
(2 v SBJ 1924/25).

ELWORTHY Francis William, B Cambridge, Cambridgeshire, England 11.6.1893. D Johannesburg 15.3.1978.
(1 v AIF 1919/20).

FOTHERINGHAM Henry Richard, B Empangeni, Natal (Zululand) 4.4.1953.
(7-3 v WI 1983/84; 3 v A 1985/86; 1 v E XI 1989/90).

HANDS Kenneth Charles Myburgh, B Stellenbosch, CP 22.3.1892. D Paris, France 18.11.1954.
(1 v SBJ 1924/25).

HANLEY Rupert William (Spook), B Port Elizabeth 29.1.1952.
(2 v WI 1983/84).

HOBSON Denys Laurence, B Port Elizabeth 3.9.1951.
(4-1 v E XI 1981/82; 1 v SL 1982/83; 2 v WI 1983/84).

JEFFERIES Stephen Thomas, B Cape Town 8.12.1959.
(11-2 v E XI 1981/82; 2 v SL 1982/83; 2 v WI 1982/83; 2 v WI 1983/84; 2 v A 1985/86; 1 v A 1986/87).

JENNINGS Raymond Vernon, B Vanderbijlpark, Transvaal 9.8.1954.
(14-3 v E XI 1981/82; 2 v SL 1982/83; 2 v WI 1982/83; 3 v WI 1983/84; 3 v A 1985/86; 1 v E XI 1989/90).

SOUTH AFRICAN INTERNATIONAL CRICKETERS

KOURIE Alan John, B Johannesburg 30.7.1951.
(16-3 v E XI 1981/82; 2 v SL 1982/83; 2 v WI 1982/83; 4 v WI 1983/84; 3 v A 1985/86; 2 v A 1986/87).

LE ROUX Garth Stirling, B Kenilworth, Cape Town 4.9.1955.
(15-2 v E XI 1981/82; 2 v SL 1982/83; 2 v WI 1982/83; 2 v WI 1983/84; 3 v A 1985/86; 4 v A 1986/87).

McEWAN Kenneth Scott, B Bedford, CP 16.7.1952.
(7-4 v WI 1983/84; 1 v A 1985/86; 2 v A 1986/87).

McKENZIE Kevin Alexander, B Pretoria 16.7.1948.
(7-2 v WI 1982/83; 2 v A 1985/86; 3 v A 1986/87).

MUNRO Campbell, B Alicedale, CP 22.7.1899.
(1 v SBJ 1924/25).

NESER Vivian Herbert (Boet), B Klerksdorp, Transvaal 16.6.1894. D Pretoria 22.12.1956.
(5 v SBJ 1924/25).

PAGE Hugh Ashton, B Salisbury, Rhodesia 3.7.1962.
(7-3 v A 1985/86; 4 v A 1986/87).

PIENAAR Roy Francois, B Johannesburg 17.7.1961.
(1 v E XI 1989/90).

+**RICE** Clive Edward Butler, B Johannesburg 23.7.1949.
(18-3 v E XI 1981/82; 2 v SL 1982/83; 2 v WI 1982/83; 4 v WI 1983/84; 3 v A 1985/86; 4 v A 1986/87).

ROBBINS Victor Clark, B Umhlali, Natal 9.1.1891. D Durban 16.6.1947.
(1 v SBJ 1924/25).

+**RUNDLE** David Bryan, B Cape Town 25.9.1965.
(1 v E XI 1989/90); (To A 1993/94).

SEEFF Lawrence, B Kensington, Johannesburg 1.5.1959.
(1 v SL 1982/83).

VAN DER BIJL Vintcent Adriaan Pieter, B Rondebosch, Cape Town 19.3.1948.
(6-3 v E XI 1981/82; 1 v SL 1982/83; 2 v WI 1982/83).

+**VAN ZYL** Cornelius Johannes Petrus Gerthardus, B Bloemfontein 1.10.1961.
(1 v A 1985/86); (To WI 1991/92).

WATSON William Kenneth, B Port Elizabeth 21.5.1955.
(3-1 v E XI 1981/82; 2 v WI 1983/84).

WHITFIELD Brian Jonathan, B Durban 14.3.1959.
(4 v A 1986/87).

+**YACHAD** Mandy, B Johannesburg 17.11.1960.
(1 v WI 1983/84).

S.A. INTERNATIONAL CRICKETERS WHO HAVE BEEN ON FIRST-CLASS OVERSEAS TOURS WITHOUT PLAYING IN OFFICIAL OR UNOFFICIAL TESTS

+**BENKENSTEIN** Dale Martin, B Salisbury, Rhodesia 9.6.1974.
(To NZ 1998/99).

BISSET Arthur Vintcent Crossley (Artie), B Kenilworth, Cape Town 15.1.1879. D Wynberg, Cape Town 8.3.1955.
(To E 1901).

+**CALLAGHAN** David John, B Queenstown, CP 1.2.1965.
(To A 1993/94); (To NZ 1994/95).

CASTENS Herbert Hayton, B Pearston, CP 23.11.1864. D Fulham, London, England 18.10.1929.
(To E 1894).

COOLEY Bertram Clifford (Bib), B Durban 1874. D Durban 17.8.1935.
(To E 1901).

+**CROOKES** Derek Norman, B Mariannhill, near Pinetown, Natal 5.3.1969.
(To I 1996/97).

SOUTH AFRICAN INTERNATIONAL CRICKETERS

CROOKES Norman Samuel, B Renishaw, Natal 15.11.1935.
(To E 1965).
DAVEY Darnton Charles (Don), B Mansfield, Nottinghamshire, England 7.7.1856. D Durban 7.10.1911.
(To E 1894).
+**HALL** Andrew James, B Johannesburg 31.7.1975.
(To SL 2000).
HORWOOD Stanley Ebden, B Port Elizabeth 22.7.1877. D Plumstead, Cape Town 15.8.1959.
(To E 1904).
INNES Gerald Alfred Skerten, B Wynberg, Cape Town 16.11.1931. D Cape Town 11.7.1982.
(To A and NZ 1952/53).
KEMPIS George Stephen, B Port Elizabeth 25.11.1871. D Scottburgh, Natal 17.3.1948.
(To E 1894).
LOGAN James Douglas, B Cape Town 24.6.1880. D Matjiesfontein, CP 3.1.1960.
(To E 1901).
+**MPITSANG** Phenyo Victor, B Kimberley 28.3.1980.
(To NZ 1998/99).
+**NEL** Andre, B Germiston, Transvaal 15.7.1977.
(To WI 2000/01).
NORTON Eric Bertram (Pop), B Grahamstown, CP 5.12.1919.
(To A and NZ 1952/53).
OVENSTONE Douglas MacPherson, B Sea Point, Cape Town 31.7.1921.
(To E 1947).
+**PALFRAMAN** Steven John, B East London 12.5.1970.
(To SL 1993/94).
PAYN Leslie William, B Umzinto, Natal 6.5.1915. D Scottburgh, Natal 2.5.1992.
(To E 1947).
REID Allan (Jupp), B Observatory, Cape Town 1.10.1877. D Wyncarrol Rest Home, Rosebank, Cape Town 31.10.1948.
(To E 1901).
+**RINDEL** Michael John Raymond, B Durban 9.2.1963.
(To NZ 1994/95); (To E 1998).
ROBINSON Cyril Deason, B Durban 18.7.1873. D Kearsney, Natal 26.8.1948.
(To E 1907).
SEWELL Cyril Otto Hudson (Skilly), B Pietermaritzburg 19.12.1874. D Bexhill-on-Sea, Sussex, England 19.8.1951.
(To E 1894).
+**SHAW** Timothy Gower, B Empangeni, Natal (Zululand) 5.7.1959.
(To E 1994).
+**SIMONS** Eric Owen, B Cape Town 9.3.1962.
(To NZ 1994/95).
SMITH Harry Ernest (Blackie), B Cradock, CP 21.4.1884. D Boksburg, Transvaal 25.4.1935.
(To E 1907).
+**STEWART** Errol Leslie Rae, B Durban 30.7.1969.
(To A 1993/94).
STEYN Stephen Sebastian Louis (Stodgy), B Cape Town 11.3.1905. D Cape Town 14.10.1993.
(To A 1931/32).
+**TELEMACHUS** Roger, B Stellenbosch, CP 27.3.1973.
(To SL 2000); (To WI 2000/01).
WALLACH Benjamin, B Queenstown, CP 18.9.1873. D Troyeville, Johannesburg 25.5.1935.
(To E 1904).
WILLIAMS Robert James (Bob), B Viljoensdrift, OFS 12.4.1912. D Durban 14.5.1984.
(To E 1935).

SOUTH AFRICAN INTERNATIONAL CRICKETERS

S.A. LIMITED OVERS INTERNATIONAL CRICKETERS WHO HAVE NOT APPEARED IN TEST MATCHES OR BEEN ON FIRST-CLASS OVERSEAS TOURS

ABRAHAMS Shafiek, B Port Elizabeth 4.3.1968.
BRYSON Rudi Edwin, B Springs, Transvaal 25.7.1968.
DAWSON Alan Charles, B Cape Town 27.11.1969.
KOEN Louis Johannes, B Paarl, CP 28.3.1967.
ONTONG Justin Lee, B Paarl, CP 4.1.1980.
POTHAS Nic, B Johannesburg 18.11.1973.
WILLIAMS Henry Smith, B Pniel, CP 11.6.1967.
WILLOUGHBY Charl Myles, B Cape Town 3.12.1974.

SOUTH AFRICAN UNOFFICIAL LIMITED OVERS INTERNATIONAL CRICKETERS

ARMITAGE Robert Lawrence Sugden, B Grahamstown, CP 9.7.1955. D Grahamstown, EC 9.12.2000.
BARNARD Llewellyn Jamieson (Lee), B Johannesburg 5.1.1956.
BENTLEY Robert Mulock, B Bindura, Southern Rhodesia 3.11.1958.
FERREIRA Anthonie Michal (Yogi), B Pretoria 13.4.1955.
MADSEN Trevor Roy, B Durban 22.12.1957.
MATTHEWS Brett Anthony, B Cape Town 5.7.1962.

PLAYERS WHO REPRESENTED SOUTH AFRICA IN INTERNATIONAL MATCHES UNDER THE SOUTH AFRICAN CRICKET BOARD OF CONTROL (SACBOC)

In 1956/57 Kenyan Asians (KA) toured South Africa and played three "Test" matches against representative teams chosen by SACBOC. In 1958/59 a South African team toured East Africa and Rhodesia and played two "Test" matches against Kenya (K) and one against East Africa (EA). BL D'Oliveira captained South Africa in five of the six international matches. A Variawa captained the side in the third "Test" against Kenyan Asians when D'Oliveira was injured. The following players represented South Africa:

ABED Gesant (Tiny) (Western Province), B Durban 9.5.1931.
5 - 2 v KA in SA 1956/57, 2 v K in K 1958/59, 1 v EA in K 1958/59.
ABED Salie (Lobo) (Western Province), B Durban 17.11.1929.
6 - 3 v KA in SA 1956/57, 2 v K in K 1958/59, 1 v EA in K 1958/59.
ABRAHAMS Cecil (Western Province), B Athlone, Cape Town 8.3.1932.
6 - 3 v KA in SA 1956/57, 2 v K in K 1958/59, 1 v EA in K 1958/59.
ABRAHAMS Hassim (Kitel) (Transvaal), B Vrededorp, Transvaal 24.5.1938.
3 - 3 v KA in SA 1956/57.
ASMAL Dawood Ahmed (Natal), B Stanger, Natal 10.6.1937. D Durban 29.3.1991.
Toured East Africa and Rhodesia in 1958/59 - no "Tests".
BELL Alexander J (Western Province), emigrated to Zimbabwe - no biographical details available.
3 - 3 v KA in SA 1956/57.
BULBULIA Abdul Samad (Sam) (Transvaal), B Johannesburg 22.2.1933.
1 - 1 v KA in SA 1956/57.
BULBULIA Mohamed (Koeka) (Transvaal), B Johannesburg 5.7.1935
1 - 1 v K in K 1958/59.
DEEDAT Ahmed Ismail (Natal), B Pietermaritzburg 6.11.1934. D Durban 15.8.1998.
4 - 1 v KA in SA 1956/57, 2 v K in K 1958/59, 1 v EA in K 1958/59.
DINATH Abbas (Transvaal), B Krugersdorp, Transvaal 25.11.1925, D Krugersdorp, Transvaal 14.4.1994.
1 - 1 v KA in SA 1956/57.

D'OLIVEIRA Basil Lewis (Western Province), B Signal Hill, Cape Town 4.10.1931.
5 - 2 v KA in SA 1956/57, 2 v K in K 1958/59, 1 v EA in K 1958/59.
GARDA Mohamed (Transvaal), B Johannesburg 15.7.1931. D Johannesburg 28.9.1997.
1 - 1 v KA in SA 1956/57.
GEORGE Amien (Western Province), B on board ship Seedebonde, Cape Town 17.9.1927. D Durban 22.6.1983.
1 - 1 v KA in SA 1956/57.
JEEWA Essop Ismail (Natal), B Durban 17.2.1928. D Durban 27.6.1995.
2 - 2 v KA in SA 1956/57, toured East Africa and Rhodesia in 1958/59 - no "Tests".
LANGA George (Transvaal), B Johannesburg 24.5.1925. D Johannesburg 19.10.1997.
3 - 2 v K in K 1958/59, 1 v EA in K 1958/59.
MALAMBA Ben Ndzima (Western Province), B Ndabeni, Cape Town 16.4.1931. D Cape Town 13.9.1999.
3 - 3 v KA in SA 1956/57, toured East Africa and Rhodesia in 1958/59 - no "Tests".
MEYER Cecil Andrew (Chong) (Transvaal), B Mafeking, CP 23.12.1920.
1 - 1 v KA in SA 1956/57.
NEETHLING John James (Coetie) (Western Province), B Goodwood, Cape Town 20.7.1932.
3 - 2 v K in K 1958/59, 1 v EA in K 1958/59.
PETERSEN Eric (Western Province), B Mowbray, Cape Town 6.9.1931.
3 - 2 v K in K 1958/59, 1 v EA in K 1958/59.
RAZIET Salamodien (Western Province), B Stellenbosch, CP 21.3.1932.
6 - 3 v KA in SA 1956/57, 2 v K in K 1958/59, 1 v EA in K 1958/59.
SOLOMON Sydney Norman (Western Province), emigrated to Canada - no biographical details available.
3 - 2 v K in K 1958/59, 1 v EA in K 1958/59.
VARIAWA Mohamed Amien (Transvaal), B Cape Town 23.4.1927. D Potchefstroom, Transvaal 31.12.1985.
3 - 3 v KA in SA 1956/57.
WILLIAMS Owen Leslie (Western Province), B Claremont, Cape Town 8.4.1932.
2 - 1 v K in K 1958/59, 1 v EA in K 1958/59.

CONTRACTED PLAYERS 2001/02

The following players were offered contracts by the United Cricket Board of South Africa until 30 April 2002: Shaun Pollock, Mark Boucher, Paul Adams, Nicky Boje, Allan Donald, Boeta Dippenaar, Herschelle Gibbs, Mornantau Hayward, Justin Kemp, Jacques Kallis, Gary Kirsten, Lance Klusener, Neil McKenzie, Andre Nel, Mfuneko Ngam, Makhaya Ntini, Justin Ontong, Jonty Rhodes, Roger Telemachus.

Both Allan Donald and Jonty Rhodes indicated their preference to play only one-day internationals. Although this preference was accepted by the UCBSA and the national selectors, both players agreed that they would be available for Test selection if needed. Daryll Cullinan was not offered a contract because he indicated he was available only for Test selection and, due to commitments with his English county, Kent, would only be available to play for South Africa in some Tests in the 2001/02 season. This did not mean he could not be selected for those Tests.

The UCBSA decided not to disclose the salaries or categories of contracted players. These would be regarded as a private matter between employer and employee.

SOUTH AFRICAN TEST MATCH RECORDS

Opponents	First Match	Won by SA	Won by Opponents	Drawn	Total
England	1888/89	23	50	47	120
Australia	1902/03	14	34	17	65
New Zealand	1931/32	15	3	9	27
West Indies	1991/92	7	2	2	11
India	1992/93	6	2	4	12
Sri Lanka	1993/94	6	1	4	11
Pakistan	1994/95	3	1	3	7
Zimbabwe	1995/96	3	0	0	3
	Total	77	93	86	256

GROUNDS (9)

Port Elizabeth	St George's Park	1888/89 to date	19 Tests
Cape Town	Newlands	1888/89 to date	33 Tests
Johannesburg	(1) The Wanderers	1895/96 to 1938/39	22 Tests
	(2) Ellis Park	1948/49 to 1953/54	6 Tests
	(3) Wanderers Stadium	1956/57 to date	22 Tests
Durban	(1) Lord's	1909/10 to 1921/22	4 Tests
	(2) Kingsmead	1922/23 to date	28 Tests
Centurion	Centurion Park (SuperSport Park)	1995/96 to date	6 Tests
Bloemfontein	Springbok Park (Goodyear Park)	1999/00 to date	2 Tests

HIGHEST INNINGS TOTAL FOR EACH CENTRE

Port Elizabeth	For:	502	v England	1964/65
	Against:	549-7*	by Australia	1949/50
Cape Town	For:	529-7*	v India	1996/97
	Against:	559-9*	by England	1938/39
Johannesburg	For:	620	v Australia	1966/67
	Against:	628-8*	by Australia	1996/97
Durban	For:	622-9*	v Australia	1969/70
	Against:	654-5	by England	1938/39
Centurion	For:	399-5*	v West Indies	1998/99
	Against:	381-9*	by England	1995/96
Bloemfontein	For:	471-9*	v New Zealand	2000/01
	Against:	342	by New Zealand	2000/01

LOWEST INNINGS TOTAL FOR EACH CENTRE

Port Elizabeth	For:	30	v England	1895/96
	Against:	106	by Pakistan	1997/98
Cape Town	For:	35	v England	1898/99
	Against:	92	by England	1898/99
Johannesburg	For:	72	v England	1956/57
	Against:	79	by New Zealand (Ellis Park)	1953/54
	Against (at Wanderers Stadium):	122	by England	1999/00
Durban	For:	99	v Australia	1949/50
	Against:	66	by India	1996/97
Centurion	For:	200	v Sri Lanka	1997/98
	Against:	119	by Sri Lanka	2000/01
Bloemfontein	For:	417	v Zimbabwe	1999/00
	Against:	192	by Zimbabwe	1999/00

SOUTH AFRICAN TEST MATCH RECORDS

HIGHEST INDIVIDUAL SCORE FOR EACH CENTRE

Port Elizabeth	For:	174	L Klusener v England	1999/00
	Against:	167	AL Hassett (Australia)	1949/50
Cape Town	For:	209	RG Pollock v Australia	1966/67
	Against:	189	JW Burke (Australia)	1957/58
Johannesburg	For:	231	AD Nourse v Australia (The Wanderers)	1935/36
	For (at Wanderers Stadium):	182	DT Lindsay v Australia	1966/67
	Against:	214	GS Blewett (Australia)	1996/97
Durban	For:	275	G Kirsten v England	1999/00
	Against:	243	E Paynter (England)	1938/39
Centurion	For:	134	G Kirsten v West Indies	1998/99
	Against:	141	GA Hick (England)	1995/96
Bloemfontein	For:	160	JH Kallis v New Zealand	2000/01
	Against:	99	SP Fleming (New Zealand)	2000/01

BEST BOWLING ANALYSIS FOR EACH CENTRE

Port Elizabeth	For:	7-84	AA Donald v India	1992/93
	Against:	8-7	GA Lohmann (England)	1895/96
Cape Town	For:	7-63	AE Hall v England	1922/23
	Against:	8-11	J Briggs (England)	1888/89
Johannesburg	For:	9-113	HJ Tayfield v England	1956/57
	Against:	9-28	GA Lohmann (England) (The Wanderers)	1895/96
	Against (at Wanderers Stadium):	6-34	AK Davidson (Australia)	1957/58
Durban	For:	8-69	HJ Tayfield v England	1956/57
	Against:	7-46	AR Caddick (England)	1999/00
Centurion	For:	5-36	AA Donald v Australia	1996/97
	Against:	6-80	CA Walsh (West Indies)	1998/99
Bloemfontein	For:	6-66	M Ntini v New Zealand	2000/01
	Against:	4-93	HK Olonga (Zimbabwe)	1999/00

HIGHEST INNINGS TOTALS

For:	622-9*	v Australia at Kingsmead	1969/70
	621-5*	v New Zealand at Auckland	1998/99
	620	v Australia at Wanderers Stadium	1966/67
	595	v Australia at Adelaide	1963/64
	572-7	v England at Kingsmead	1999/00
	552-5*	v England at Manchester	1998
	538	v England at Leeds	1951
	533	v England at Nottingham	1947
	530	v England at Kingsmead	1938/39
	529-7*	v India at Newlands	1996/97
Against:	654-5	by England at Kingsmead	1938/39
	628-8*	by Australia at Wanderers Stadium	1996/97
	608	by England at Ellis Park	1948/49
	578	by Australia at Melbourne	1910/11
	559-9*	by England at Newlands	1938/39
	554-8*	by England at Lord's	1947
	554	by Australia at Melbourne	1931/32
	551	by England at Nottingham	1947
	549-7*	by Australia at St George's Park	1949/50
	542	by Australia at Newlands	1966/67

LOWEST INNINGS TOTALS

For:	30	v England at St George's Park	1895/96
	30	v England at Birmingham	1924
Against:	66	by India at Kingsmead	1996/97

SOUTH AFRICAN TEST MATCH RECORDS

HIGHEST FOURTH INNINGS TOTALS

For:	To win: 297-4 v Australia at Melbourne (Set 295 to win)	1952/53
	To draw: 423-7 v England at The Oval (Set 451 to win)	1947
	To lose: 335 v New Zealand at Newlands (Set 408 to win)	1961/62
Against:	To win: 336-5 by Australia at Kingsmead (Set 336 to win)	1949/50
	To draw: 654-5 by England at Kingsmead (Set 696 to win)	1938/39
	To lose: 339 by Australia at Adelaide (Set 378 to win)	1910/11

HIGHEST MATCH AGGREGATE

1981 runs for 35 wickets v England at Kingsmead 1938/39
(The match, originally scheduled as a "timeless" Test, lasted 10 days but there was no play on one day. It was abandoned as a draw because the English team had to catch a ship home)

LOWEST MATCH AGGREGATE (Completed match)

234 runs for 29 wickets v Australia at Melbourne 1931/32
(The lowest aggregate for any Test match)

LARGEST MARGINS OF VICTORY

By an innings:

For:	South Africa beat Sri Lanka at Newlands by an innings and 229 runs	2000/01
Against:	Australia beat South Africa at St George's Park by an innings and 259 runs	1949/50

By a margin of runs:

For:	South Africa beat England at Lord's by 356 runs	1994
Against:	Australia beat South Africa at Melbourne by 530 runs	1910/11

NARROWEST MARGINS OF VICTORY

By one wicket:

For:	South Africa beat England at The Wanderers	1905/06
Against:	England beat South Africa at Newlands	1922/23

By a margin of runs:

For:	South Africa beat Australia at Sydney by 5 runs	1993/94
Against:	England beat South Africa at Leeds by 23 runs	1998

MOST CENTURIES IN A MATCH (BOTH TEAMS)

6	South Africa (3) v England (3) at Kingsmead	1938/39

MOST CENTURIES IN A MATCH (ONE TEAM)

4	Australia v South Africa at Ellis Park	1949/50
4	South Africa v India at Calcutta	1996/97

MOST CONSECUTIVE VICTORIES BY SOUTH AFRICA

5 v Australia (1, 1966/67), Australia (4, 1969/70)
5 v New Zealand (2, 1994/95), Pakistan (1, 1994/95), New Zealand (1, 1994/95), Zimbabwe (1, 1995/96)
5 v West Indies (5, 1998/99)

MOST CONSECUTIVE VICTORIES IN HOME MATCHES BY SOUTH AFRICA

10 v Pakistan (1, 1997/98), Sri Lanka (2, 1997/98), West Indies (5, 1998/99), Zimbabwe (1, 1999/00), England (1, 1999/00)

Note: This equalled the world record established by India between 1988/89 and 1994/95

MOST CONSECUTIVE MATCHES WITHOUT A DEFEAT BY SOUTH AFRICA

14 v West Indies (5, 1998/99), New Zealand (3, 1998/99), Zimbabwe (1, 1999/00), Zimbabwe (1, 1999/00), England (4, 1999/00)

MOST CONSECUTIVE DEFEATS BY SOUTH AFRICA

8 v England (2, 1888/89), England (1, 1891/92), England (3, 1895/96), England (2, 1898/99)

MOST CONSECUTIVE MATCHES WITHOUT A VICTORY BY SOUTH AFRICA

28 v England (3, 1935), Australia (5, 1935/36), England (5, 1938/39), England (5, 1947), England (5, 1948/49), Australia (5, 1949/50)

BATTING

MOST CENTURIES FOR SOUTH AFRICA

14	DJ Cullinan
12	G Kirsten
9	AD Nourse
8	B Mitchell
7	JH Kallis, DJ McGlew, RG Pollock, HW Taylor
6	EJ Barlow, WJ Cronje
5	RA McLean

HIGHEST AGGREGATE IN A SERIES

Five-match series:			
732	(avg 73.20)	GA Faulkner v Australia in Australia	1910/11
621	(avg 69.00)	AD Nourse v England in England	1947
606	(avg 86.57)	DT Lindsay v Australia in South Africa	1966/67
603	(avg 75.37)	EJ Barlow v Australia in Australia	1963/64
Four-match series:			
517	(avg 73.85)	RG Pollock v Australia in South Africa	1969/70
Three-match series:			
427	(avg 427.00)	DJ Cullinan v New Zealand in New Zealand	1998/99
Two-match series:			
323	(avg 161.50)	DJ McGlew v New Zealand in New Zealand	1952/53

HIGHEST INDIVIDUAL INNINGS

275*	DJ Cullinan	v New Zealand at Auckland	1998/99
275	G Kirsten	v England at Kingsmead	1999/00
274	RG Pollock	v Australia at Kingsmead	1969/70
255*	DJ McGlew	v New Zealand at Wellington	1952/53
236	EAB Rowan	v England at Leeds	1951
231	AD Nourse	v Australia at The Wanderers	1935/36
211*	HH Gibbs	v New Zealand at Christchurch	1998/99
210	G Kirsten	v England at Manchester	1998
209	RG Pollock	v Australia at Newlands	1966/67
208	AD Nourse	v England at Nottingham	1951
204	GA Faulkner	v Australia at Melbourne	1910/11
201	EJ Barlow	v Australia at Adelaide	1963/64

1000 RUNS IN TESTS

				Opponents							
	Matches	Innings	Runs	Eng	Aus	NZ	WI	Ind	SL	Pak	Zim
G Kirsten	73	129	4806	1146	697	701	586	608	562	492	14
DJ Cullinan	70	115	4554	1081	153	823	737	688	917	117	38
WJ Cronje	68	111	3714	706	788	471	291	524	452	299	183
B Mitchell	42	80	3471	2732	573	166	-	-	-	-	-
AD Nourse	34	62	2960	2037	923	-	-	-	-	-	-
JH Kallis	50	81	2952	599	256	463	752	136	347	220	179
HW Taylor	42	76	2936	2287	640	9	-	-	-	-	-
JN Rhodes	52	80	2532	809	372	150	378	289	340	99	95
TL Goddard	41	78	2516	1193	1090	233	-	-	-	-	-
EJ Barlow	30	57	2516	742	1149	625	-	-	-	-	-
DJ McGlew	34	64	2440	736	604	1100	-	-	-	-	-
JHB Waite	50	86	2405	923	839	643	-	-	-	-	-
RG Pollock	23	41	2256	750	1453	53	-	-	-	-	-
AW Nourse	45	83	2234	1415	819	-	-	-	-	-	-
RA McLean	40	73	2120	1068	480	572	-	-	-	-	-
SM Pollock	56	81	2015	393	150	170	450	151	310	322	69

AC Hudson	35	63	2007	154	481	91	163	690	202	87	139
BM McMillan	38	62	1968	549	478	82	-	551	2	183	123
EAB Rowan	26	50	1965	1364	601	-	-	-	-	-	-
GA Faulkner	25	47	1754	874	880	-	-	-	-	-	-
L Klusener	42	59	1676	478	94	38	87	374	433	128	44
KC Bland	21	39	1669	858	399	412	-	-	-	-	-
WR Endean	28	52	1630	442	691	497	-	-	-	-	-
HH Gibbs	28	47	1563	203	132	365	674	184	1	4	-
RH Catterall	24	43	1555	1555	-	-	-	-	-	-	-
MV Boucher	42	57	1439	296	-	106	294	45	324	194	180
KG Viljoen	27	50	1365	953	315	97	-	-	-	-	-
DJ Richardson	42	64	1359	306	376	273	10	249	79	53	13
HB Cameron	26	45	1239	971	155	113	-	-	-	-	-
DT Lindsay	19	31	1130	206	838	86	-	-	-	-	-
JH Sinclair	25	47	1069	634	435	-	-	-	-	-	-
KC Wessels	16	29	1027	238	173	-	133	295	188	-	-
SJ Snooke	26	46	1008	713	295	-	-	-	-	-	-

Note: KC Wessels is the only player to have scored 1000 Test runs for two different countries.

KC Wessels (for Aust)	24	42	1761	754	-	73	537	-	141	256	-

BEST BATTING AVERAGES FOR SOUTH AFRICA

(Qualification - 500 runs, Average 40.00)

	Matches	Innings	NO	Runs	HS	Avg	100s	50s
BA Richards	4	7	0	508	140	72.57	2	2
RG Pollock	23	41	4	2256	274	60.97	7	11
AD Nourse	34	62	7	2960	231	53.81	9	14
A Melville	11	19	2	894	189	52.58	4	3
KC Bland	21	39	5	1669	144*	49.08	3	9
B Mitchell	42	80	9	3471	189*	48.88	8	21
EJ Barlow	30	57	2	2516	201	45.74	6	15
DJ Cullinan	70	115	12	4554	275*	44.21	14	20
EAB Rowan	26	50	5	1965	236	43.66	3	12
DJ McGlew	34	64	6	2440	255*	42.06	7	10
JH Kallis	50	81	9	2952	160	41.00	7	16
GA Faulkner	25	47	4	1754	204	40.79	4	8
HW Taylor	42	76	4	2936	176	40.77	7	17
G Kirsten	73	129	10	4806	275	40.38	12	23

A CENTURY ON DEBUT

163	AC Hudson v West Indies at Bridgetown	1991/92

The following made centuries on debut against a specific country:

103	JAJ Christy v New Zealand at Christchurch	1931/32
113	B Mitchell v New Zealand at Christchurch	1931/32
255*	DJ McGlew v New Zealand at Wellington	1952/53
109	ARA Murray v New Zealand at Wellington	1952/53
114	EJ Barlow v Australia at Brisbane	1963/64
118	KC Wessels v India at Kingsmead	1992/93
101*	JN Rhodes v Sri Lanka at Moratuwa	1993/94
105	KC Wessels v England at Lord's	1994
113	BM McMillan v Pakistan at Wanderers Stadium	1994/95
135	AC Hudson v Zimbabwe at Harare	1995/96

A CENTURY IN EACH INNINGS

189 and 104*	A Melville v England at Nottingham	1947
120 and 189*	B Mitchell v England at The Oval	1947
102 and 133	G Kirsten v India at Calcutta	1996/97

SOUTH AFRICAN TEST MATCH RECORDS

FOUR CENTURIES IN SUCCESSIVE INNINGS

A Melville	103 v England at Kingsmead	1938/39
	189 and 104* v England at Nottingham	1947
	117 v England at Lord's	1947

A CENTURY BEFORE LUNCH

HGO Owen-Smith	v England at Leeds (third day)	1929

Note: BA Richards was 94* on the first day of the match v Australia at Kingsmead 1969/70

FASTEST CENTURIES

80 minutes	JH Sinclair (104)	v Australia at Newlands	1902/03
95 minutes	PW Sherwell (115)	v England at Lord's	107

Note: The fastest recorded for South Africa in terms of balls faced:

95 balls	JN Rhodes (103*)	v West Indies at Centurion Park	1998/99
95 balls	SM Pollock (111)	v Sri Lanka at Centurion Park	2000/01
100 balls	L Klusener (102*)	v India at Newlands	1996/97

SLOWEST CENTURY

545 minutes	DJ McGlew (105)	v Australia at Kingsmead	1957/58

YOUNGEST PLAYER TO SCORE A CENTURY

19 years 318 days	RG Pollock	122 v Australia at Sydney	1963/64

OLDEST PLAYER TO SCORE A CENTURY

42 years 295 days	AW Nourse	111 v Australia at The Wanderers	1921/22

CENTURIES AGAINST FOUR OR MORE OPPONENTS

7	G Kirsten	Against Australia, England, India, New Zealand, Pakistan, Sri Lanka and West Indies.
5	WJ Cronje	Against Australia, England, India, New Zealand and Sri Lanka.
	DJ Cullinan	Against England, India, New Zealand, Sri Lanka and West Indies.
	JH Kallis	Against Australia, England, New Zealand, West Indies and Zimbabwe.
4	AC Hudson	Against Australia, India, West Indies and Zimbabwe.

Note: WR Endean, DJ McGlew and JHB Waite all scored centuries against Australia, England and New Zealand, the only opponents of South Africa during the times of their careers.

CARRYING BAT THROUGH A COMPLETED INNINGS

AB Tancred	26*	(47)	v England at Newlands	1888/89
JW Zulch	43*	(103)	v England at Newlands	1909/10
TL Goddard	56*	(99)	v Australia at Newlands	1957/58
DJ McGlew	127*	(292)	v New Zealand at Kingsmead	1961/62
G Kirsten	100*	(239)	v Pakistan at Faisalabad	1997/98

RECORD PARTNERSHIP FOR EACH WICKET

1st	260	B Mitchell and IJ Siedle	v England at Newlands	1930/31
2nd	315*	HH Gibbs and JH Kallis	v New Zealand at Christchurch	1998/99
3rd	341	EJ Barlow and RG Pollock	v Australia at Adelaide	1963/64
4th	214	HW Taylor and HG Deane	v England at The Oval	1929
5th	192	G Kirsten and MV Boucher	v England at Kingsmead	1999/00
6th	200	RG Pollock and HR Lance	v Australia at Kingsmead	1969/70
7th	246	DJ McGlew and ARA Murray	v New Zealand at Wellington	1952/53
8th	150	ND McKenzie and SM Pollock	v Sri Lanka at Centurion Park	2000/01
9th	195	MV Boucher and PL Symcox	v Pakistan at Wanderers Stadium (The world Test record for this wicket)	1997/98
10th	103	HGO Owen-Smith and AJ Bell	v England at Leeds	1929

BOWLING

50 WICKETS IN TESTS

			Opponents								Wickets/
	M	Wkts	Eng	Aus	NZ	WI	Ind	SL	Pak	Zim	match
AA Donald	69	325	86	48	21	43	57	29	27	14	4.71
SM Pollock	56	231	53	20	25	49	19	30	21	14	4.12
HJ Tayfield	37	170	75	64	31	-	-	-	-	-	4.59
TL Goddard	41	123	63	53	7	-	-	-	-	-	3.00
PM Pollock	28	116	32	52	32	-	-	-	-	-	4.14
NAT Adcock	26	104	57	14	33	-	-	-	-	-	4.00
PR Adams	34	96	28	5	10	9	23	9	5	7	2.82
JH Kallis	50	94	16	7	8	37	5	10	4	7	1.88
PS de Villiers	18	85	12	22	26	-	5	-	20	-	4.72
CL Vincent	25	84	72	10	2		-	-	-	-	3.36
GA Faulkner	25	82	68	14	-	-	-	-	-	-	3.28
BM McMillan	38	75	17	15	13	-	23	2	4	1	1.97
L Klusener	42	73	11	10	7	11	17	4	9	4	1.73
AEE Vogler	15	64	60	4	-	-	-	-	-	-	4.26
JH Sinclair	25	63	46	17	-	-	-	-	-	-	2.52
JM Blanckenberg	18	60	48	12	-	-	-	-	-	-	3.33
NBF Mann	19	58	42	16	-	-	-	-	-	-	3.05
PS Heine	14	58	39	17	2	-	-	-	-	-	4.14
RO Schwarz	20	55	27	28	-	-	-	-	-	-	2.75
AMB Rowan	15	54	54	-	-	-	-	-	-	-	3.60
CR Matthews	18	52	12	16	13	-	9	-	-	2	2.88
EP Nupen	17	50	47	3	-	-	-	-	-	-	2.94

BEST AVERAGES (Qualification - 40 wickets)

	Matches	Runs	Wickets	Avg	BB	5WI	10WM
MJ Procter	7	616	41	15.02	6-73	1	-
SM Pollock	56	4694	231	20.32	7-87	12	-
NAT Adcock	26	2195	104	21.10	6-43	5	-
AA Donald	69	7034	325	21.64	8-71	20	3
AE Hall	7	886	40	22.15	7-63	3	1
AEE Vogler	15	1455	64	22.73	7-94	5	1
PM Pollock	28	2806	116	24.18	6-38	9	1
PS de Villiers	18	2063	85	24.27	6-23	5	2

MOST WICKETS IN A SERIES

Five-match series:

37 (avg 17.18)	HJ Tayfield v England in South Africa	1956/57
36 (avg 21.75)	AEE Vogler v England in South Africa	1909/10
33 (avg 19.78)	AA Donald v England in England	1998
30 (avg 28.10)	HJ Tayfield v Australia in Australia	1952/53

Four-match series:

26 (avg 13.57)	MJ Procter v Australia in South Africa	1969/70

Three-match series:

25 (avg 17.92)	CB Llewellyn v Australia in South Africa	1902/03

Two-match series:

16 (avg 20.18)	Q McMillan v New Zealand in New Zealand	1931/32

10 WICKETS IN A MATCH

13-165	HJ Tayfield	v Australia at Melbourne	1952/53
13-192	HJ Tayfield	v England at Wanderers Stadium	1956/57
12-127	SJ Snooke	v England at The Wanderers	1905/06
12-139	AA Donald	v India at St George's Park	1992/93
12-181	AEE Vogler	v England at The Wanderers	1909/10
11-112	AE Hall	v England at Newlands (on Test debut)	1922/23

11-113	AA Donald	v Zimbabwe at Harare	1995/96
11-127	AA Donald	v England at Wanderers Stadium	1999/00
11-150	EP Nupen	v England at The Wanderers	1930/31
11-196	SF Burke	v New Zealand at Newlands (on Test debut)	1961/62
10-87	PM Pollock	v England at Nottingham	1965
10-108	PS de Villiers	v Pakistan at Wanderers Stadium	1994/95
10-116	CB Llewellyn	v Australia at The Wanderers	1902/03
10-123	PS de Villiers	v Australia at Sydney	1993/94

SEVEN WICKETS IN AN INNINGS

9-113	HJ Tayfield	v England at Wanderers Stadium	1956/57
8-53	GB Lawrence	v New Zealand at Wanderers Stadium	1961/62
8-64	L Klusener	v India at Calcutta (on Test debut)	1996/97
8-69	HJ Tayfield	v England at Kingsmead	1956/57
8-70	SJ Snooke	v England at The Wanderers	1905/06
8-71	AA Donald	v Zimbabwe at Harare	1995/96
7-23	HJ Tayfield	v Australia at Kingsmead	1949/50
7-29	GF Bissett	v England at Kingsmead	1927/28
7-63	AE Hall	v England at Newlands (on Test debut)	1922/23
7-65	SJ Pegler	v England at Lord's	1912
7-81	HJ Tayfield	v Australia at Melbourne	1952/53
7-84	GA Faulkner	v England at The Oval	1912
7-84	AA Donald	v India at St George's Park	1992/93
7-87	SM Pollock	v Australia at Adelaide	1997/98
7-91	JT Partridge	v Australia at Sydney	1963/64
7-94	AEE Vogler	v England at The Wanderers	1909/10
7-95	WH Ashley	v England at Newlands (on first class debut)	1888/89
7-128	AEE Vogler	v England at Lord's	1907

HAT-TRICK

GM Griffin	v England at Lord's	1960

Note: EJ Barlow took a hat-trick and went on to take four wickets in five balls for the Rest of the World v England at Leeds, 1970, but the Test match status of this match was later revoked.

ALL-ROUND PLAY

2000 RUNS AND 200 WICKETS

SM Pollock	2015 runs (Avg 31.48) and 231 wickets (Avg 20.32)

2000 RUNS AND 100 WICKETS

TL Goddard	2516 runs (Avg 34.46) and 123 wickets (Avg 26.22)

1000 RUNS AND 50 WICKETS

GA Faulkner	1754 runs (Avg 40.79) and 82 wickets (Avg 26.58)
JH Kallis	2952 runs (Avg 41.00) and 94 wickets (Avg 27.44)
L Klusener	1676 runs (Avg 34.20) and 73 wickets (Avg 35.86)
BM McMillan	1968 runs (Avg 39.36) and 75 wickets (Avg 33.82)
JH Sinclair	1069 runs (Avg 23.23) and 63 wickets (Avg 31.68)

200 RUNS AND 20 WICKETS IN A SERIES

GA Faulkner	545 runs (Avg 60.55) and 29 wickets (Avg 21.89) v England	1909/10
TL Goddard	235 runs (Avg 23.50) and 25 wickets (Avg 21.12) v England	1955
TL Goddard	294 runs (Avg 32.66) and 26 wickets (Avg 16.23) v Australia	1966/67

MJ Procter	209 runs (Avg 34.83) and 26 wickets (Avg 13.57) v Australia	1969/70
JH Kallis	267 runs (Avg 29.66) and 20 wickets (Avg 19.75) v West Indies	2000/01
SM Pollock	302 runs (Avg 75.50) and 20 wickets (Avg 23.20) v West Indies	2000/01

BEST PERFORMANCES IN A MATCH

JH Sinclair	110 runs (106-4) and 9 wickets (6-26,3-63) v England at Newlands	1898/99
CB Llewellyn	94 runs (90-4*) and 9 wickets (6-92,3-124) v Australia at The Wanderers	1902/03
GA Faulkner	201 runs (78-123) and 8 wickets (5-120,3-40) v England at The Wanderers	1909/10
PS de Villiers	66 runs (66*) and 10 wickets (6-81, 4-27) v Pakistan at Wanderers Stadium	1994/95
SM Pollock	100 runs (70*-30) and 8 wickets (2-55, 6-50) v Pakistan at Kingsmead	1997/98
JH Kallis	198 runs (110-88*) and 7 wickets (2-34,5-90) v West Indies at Newlands	1998/99

WICKETKEEPING

MOST DISMISSALS IN A CAREER

			Matches	Avg/Match
167	(ct 163,st 4)	MV Boucher	42	3.97
152	(ct 150,st 2)	DJ Richardson	42	3.61
141 *	(ct 124,st 17)	JHB Waite	50	2.82
59 *	(ct 57,st 2)	DT Lindsay	19	3.10
51	(ct 39,st 12)	HB Cameron	26	1.96

Note: * Waite did not keep wicket in one of his 50 matches. He did not take a catch on that occasion. Lindsay was in the field for four of his 19 matches and took three catches there.

MOST DISMISSALS IN A SERIES

Five-match series:

26	(ct 23,st 3)	JHB Waite	v New Zealand in South Africa	1961/62
26	(ct 25, st 1)	MV Boucher	v England in England	1998
24	(ct 24)	DT Lindsay	v Australia in South Africa	1966/67
23	(ct 16,st 7)	JHB Waite	v New Zealand in South Africa	1953/54

Four-match series:

16	(ct 16)	DJ Richardson	v India in South Africa	1992/93

Three-match series:

18	(ct 17,st 1)	MV Boucher	v Pakistan in South Africa	1997/98
17	(ct 17)	DJ Richardson	v Sri Lanka in Sri Lanka	1993/94
16	(ct 16)	DJ Richardson	v New Zealand in South Africa	1994/95

MOST DISMISSALS IN A MATCH

9	(ct 9)	DJ Richardson	v India at St George's Park	1992/93
9	(ct 8,st 1)	MV Boucher	v Pakistan at St George's Park	1997/98
8	(ct 8)	DT Lindsay	v Australia at Wanderers Stadium	1966/67
8	(ct 8)	DJ Richardson	v Sri Lanka at Colombo-SSC	1993/94
7	(ct 5,st 2)	JHB Waite	v New Zealand at St George's Park	1953/54
7	(ct 4,st 3)	JHB Waite	v New Zealand at Newlands	1961/62
7	(ct 7)	DT Lindsay	v Australia at St George's Park	1969/70
7	(ct 7)	DJ Richardson	v Pakistan at Wanderers Stadium	1994/95
7	(ct 7)	DJ Richardson	v New Zealand at Auckland	1994/95
7	(ct 7)	MV Boucher	v Sri Lanka at Newlands	1997/98
7	(ct 7)	MV Boucher	v England at Lord's	1998
7	(ct 7)	MV Boucher	v England at Wanderers Stadium	1999/00
7	(ct 7)	MV Boucher	v India at Mumbai	1999/00
7	(ct 6,st 1)	MV Boucher	v Sri Lanka at Kingsmead	2000/01

MOST DISMISSALS IN AN INNINGS

6	(ct 6)	DT Lindsay	v Australia at Wanderers Stadium	1966/67
6	(ct 6)	MV Boucher	v Pakistan at St George's Park	1997/98
6	(ct 6)	MV Boucher	v Sri Lanka at Newlands	1997/98

SOUTH AFRICAN TEST MATCH RECORDS

1000 RUNS AND 100 DISMISSALS

MV Boucher	1439 runs (Avg 28.21) and 167 dismissals	(ct 163,st 4)
DJ Richardson	1359 runs (Avg 24.26) and 152 dismissals	(ct 150,st 2)
JHB Waite	2405 runs (Avg 30.44) and 141 dismissals	(ct 124,st 17)

1000 RUNS AND 50 DISMISSALS

HB Cameron	1239 runs (Avg 30.21) and 51 dismissals	(ct 39,st 12)
DT Lindsay	1130 runs (Avg 37.66) and 59 dismissals	(ct 57,st 2)

A CENTURY AND SIX DISMISSALS IN AN INNINGS

DT Lindsay	182 and ct 6	v Australia at Wanderers Stadium	1966/67

NO BYES CONCEDED IN A TOTAL OF OVER 500

559-9*	WW Wade	v England at Newlands	1938/39
531	DT Lindsay	v England at Wanderers Stadium	1964/65
520	JHB Waite	v Australia at Melbourne	1952/53

Note: DJ Richardson conceded one bye, the 545th run of the innings,when Australia scored 628-8* at Wanderers Stadium, 1996/97.

NO BYES CONCEDED IN A FIVE-TEST SERIES

MV Boucher	v West Indies in South Africa (the first such instance in Test cricket)	1998/99

Note: 2431 runs were scored without a bye being conceded by Boucher, a world record, between the second innings against England at Leeds in 1998 and the second innings against New Zealand at Auckland in 1998/99

FIELDING

MOST CATCHES IN A CAREER

	Matches	Catches
DJ Cullinan	70	67
G Kirsten	73	62
B Mitchell	42	56
BM McMillan	38	49
TL Goddard	41	48
AW Nourse	45	43
JH Kallis	50	43
WR Endean *	28	41
AC Hudson	35	36
SM Pollock	56	36
EJ Barlow	30	35
JN Rhodes	52	34
WJ Cronje	68	33
L Klusener	42	28
CL Vincent	25	27
HJ Tayfield	37	26

Note: * Endean's catches include three when he kept wicket.

MOST CATCHES IN A SERIES

12	AEE Vogler	v England in South Africa	1909/10
12	B Mitchell	v England in South Africa	1930/31
12	TL Goddard	v England in South Africa	1956/57

MOST CATCHES IN A MATCH

6	AEE Vogler	v England at Lord's, Durban	1909/10
6	B Mitchell	v Australia at Melbourne	1931/32

MOST CATCHES IN AN INNINGS

4	AEE Vogler	v England at Lord's, Durban	1909/10
4	AW Nourse	v England at Kingsmead	1922/23
4	B Mitchell	v Australia at Melbourne	1931/32

4	TL Goddard	v Australia at Sydney	1963/64
4	AJ Traicos	v Australia at Kingsmead (on Test debut)	1969/70
4	AC Hudson	v India at Newlands	1992/93
4	HH Gibbs	v West Indies at Kingsmead	1998/99
4	G Kirsten	v England at Newlands	1999/00

MISCELLANEOUS

MOST APPEARANCES

73	G Kirsten *	50	JHB Waite	42	L Klusener
70	DJ Cullinan	50	JH Kallis	42	MV Boucher
69	AA Donald	45	AW Nourse	41	TL Goddard
68	WJ Cronje	42	HW Taylor	40	RA McLean
56	SM Pollock	42	B Mitchell		
52	JN Rhodes	42	DJ Richardson		

* G Kirsten made 53 successive appearances.

MOST CAPTAINCIES

Matches			Won	Drawn	Lost	% wins
53	WJ Cronje	1993/94-1999/00	27	15	11	50.94
18	HW Taylor	1913/14-1924	1	7	10	5.55
16	KC Wessels	1991/92-1994	5	8	3	31.25
15	AD Nourse	1948/49-1951	1	5	9	6.66
15	JE Cheetham	1952/53-1955	7	3	5	46.66
14	DJ McGlew	1955-1961/62	4	4	6	28.57
14	SM Pollock	2000-2000/01	7	5	2	50.00
13	PW Sherwell	1905/06-1910/11	5	2	6	38.46
13	TL Goddard	1963/64-1964/65	1	10	2	7.69
12	HG Deane	1927/28-1930/31	2	6	4	16.66
10	HF Wade	1935-1935/36	1	5	4	10.00
10	A Melville	1938/39-1947	0	6	4	0.00
Other captains with three or more Test wins:						
5	SJ Snooke	1909/10	3	0	2	60.00
8	PL van der Merwe	1965-1966/67	4	3	1	50.00
4	A Bacher	1969/70	4	0	0	100.00

PLAYERS WHO HAVE APPEARED FOR TWO COUNTRIES

F Hearne	E v SA in SA 1888/89(2); SA v E in SA 1891/92(1), 1895/96(3).
F Mitchell	E v SA in SA 1898/99(2); SA v E in E 1912(1), SA v A in E 1912(2).
AJ Traicos	SA v A in SA 1969/70 (3); Z v I in Z 1992/93(1), Z v NZ in Z 1992/93(2),Z v I in I 1992/93(1).
KC Wessels	A v E in A 1982/83(4), A v SL in SL 1982/83(1), A v P in A 1983/84(5), A v WI in WI 1983/84(2), A v WI in A 1984/85(5), A v E in E 1985(6), A v NZ in NZ 1985/86(1); SA v WI in WI 1991/92(1), SA v I in SA 1992/93(4), SA v SL in SL 1993/94(3), SA v A in A 1993/94(2), SA v A in SA 1993/94(3), SA v E in E 1994(3).

YOUNGEST TEST PLAYERS ON DEBUT

Y	Days	Player	Debut Match	Date	Born
18	340	PR Adams	v England at St George's Park	26/12/1995	20/1/1977
19	1	AE Ochse	v England at St George's Park	12/3/1889	11/3/1870
19	50	WA Shalders	v England at Newlands	1/4/1899	10/2/1880
19	120	JH Sinclair	v England at St George's Park	13/2/1896	16/10/1876
19	123	PR Carlstein	v Australia at St George's Park	28/2/1958	28/10/1938
19	158	CB Llewellyn	v England at The Wanderers	2/3/1896	26/9/1876
19	252	MG Melle	v Australia at Ellis Park	10/2/1950	3/6/1930
19	267	CN McCarthy	v England at Kingsmead	16/12/1948	24/3/1929
19	282	RG Pollock	v Australia at Brisbane	6/12/1963	27/2/1944
19	308	EP Nupen	v Australia at Lord's, Durban	5/11/1921	1/1/1902
19	329	GH Shepstone	v England at The Wanderers	2/3/1896	8/4/1876
19	347	JM Blanckenberg	v England at The Wanderers	13/12/1913	31/12/1893

SOUTH AFRICAN TEST MATCH RECORDS

OLDEST TEST PLAYERS ON DEBUT

Y	Days	Player	Debut Match	Date	Born
40	295	O Henry	v India at Kingsmead	13/11/1992	23/1/1952
40	56	GWA Chubb	v England at Nottingham	7/6/1951	12/4/1911
39	105	SJ Cook	v India at Kingsmead	13/11/1992	31/7/1953
38	272	JD Lindsay	v England at Nottingham	7/6/1947	8/9/1908

FATHERS AND SONS WHO WERE BOTH TEST PLAYERS

F Hearne and GAL Hearne
AW Nourse and AD Nourse
LR Tuckett and L Tuckett
JD Lindsay and DT Lindsay
PM Pollock and SM Pollock

BROTHERS WHO WERE BOTH TEST PLAYERS

3 - AB, LJ and VM Tancred

2 - PAM and RHM Hands (A third brother, KCM Hands, appeared for "South Africa" in the unofficial Tests in 1924/25)
G and PN Kirsten
AR and WHM Richards
GL and LE Tapscott
AJ and DB Pithey
AMB and EAB Rowan
D and HW Taylor
PM and RG Pollock
S de la C and SJ Snooke
HF and WW Wade

ON THE FIELD THROUGHOUT AN ENTIRE MATCH

DJ McGlew v New Zealand at Wellington 1952/53
HH Gibbs v New Zealand at Christchurch 1998/99

SOUTH AFRICA versus AUSTRALIA

Season	Venue	SA captain	Aus captain	Won by SA	Won by Aus	Drawn	Total
1902/03	South Africa	HM Taberer (a)	J Darling	0	2	1	3
1910/11	Australia	PW Sherwell	C Hill	1	4	0	5
1912	England	F Mitchell (b)	SE Gregory	0	2	1	3
1921/22	South Africa	HW Taylor	HL Collins	0	1	2	3
1931/32	Australia	HB Cameron	WM Woodfull	0	5	0	5
1935/36	South Africa	HF Wade	VY Richardson	0	4	1	5
1949/50	South Africa	AD Nourse	AL Hassett	0	4	1	5
1952/53	Australia	JE Cheetham	AL Hassett	2	2	1	5
1957/58	South Africa	DJ McGlew (c)	ID Craig	0	3	2	5
1963/64	Australia	TL Goddard	R Benaud (d)	1	1	3	5
1966/67	South Africa	PL van der Merwe	RB Simpson	3	1	1	5
1969/70	South Africa	A Bacher	WM Lawry	4	0	0	4
1993/94	Australia	KC Wessels (e)	AR Border	1	1	1	3
1993/94	South Africa	KC Wessels	AR Border	1	1	1	3
1996/97	South Africa	WJ Cronje	MA Taylor	1	2	0	3
1997/98	Australia	WJ Cronje	MA Taylor	0	1	2	3
	Tests in South Africa			9	18	9	36
	Tests in Australia			5	14	7	26
	Tests in England			0	2	1	3
	Total			14	34	17	65

Notes:
(a) JH Anderson (2nd) and EA Halliwell (3rd) also captained South Africa
(b) LJ Tancred (3rd) also captained South Africa
(c) CB van Ryneveld (2nd,3rd,4th,5th) also captained South Africa
(d) RB Simpson (2nd,3rd,4th,5th) also captained Australia
(e) WJ Cronje (3rd) also captained South Africa

HIGHEST INNINGS TOTALS

For South Africa:
622-9* at Kingsmead (2nd Test) 1969/70

For Australia:
628-8* at Wanderers Stadium (1st Test) 1996/97

SOUTH AFRICAN TEST MATCH RECORDS

LOWEST INNINGS TOTALS

For South Africa:

36 and 45	at Melbourne (5th Test) +	1931/32

+ The aggregate of 81 (12 extras) for two innings is the lowest in Test cricket.

For Australia:

75	at Kingsmead (3rd Test)	1949/50

LARGEST MARGINS OF VICTORY

Australia beat South Africa at St George's Park by an innings and 259 runs	1949/50
Australia beat South Africa at Melbourne by 530 runs	1910/11
South Africa beat Australia at St George's Park by 323 runs	1969/70
South Africa beat Australia at Wanderers Stadium by 307 runs	1969/70

NARROWEST MARGINS OF VICTORY

Australia beat South Africa at St George's Park by 2 wickets	1996/97
South Africa beat Australia at Sydney by 5 runs	1993/94
South Africa beat Australia at Adelaide by 38 runs	1910/11

BATTING

INDIVIDUAL CENTURIES

For South Africa (40):

114	EJ Barlow (5)	at Brisbane	1963/64
109		at Melbourne	1963/64
201		at Adelaide	1963/64
127		at Newlands	1969/70
110		at Wanderers Stadium	1969/70
126	KC Bland	at Sydney	1963/64
122	WJ Cronje	at Wanderers Stadium	1993/94
162*	WR Endean	at Melbourne	1952/53
204	GA Faulkner (3)	at Melbourne	1910/11
115		at Adelaide	1910/11
122*		at Manchester	1912
152	CN Frank	at The Wanderers	1921/22
102	AC Hudson	at Newlands	1993/94
102	BL Irvine	at St George's Park	1969/70
101	JH Kallis	at Melbourne	1997/98
108*	G Kirsten	at Adelaide	1997/98
182	DT Lindsay (3)	at Wanderers Stadium	1966/67
137		at Kingsmead	1966/67
131		at Wanderers Stadium	1966/67
108	DJ McGlew (2)	at Wanderers Stadium	1957/58
105		at Kingsmead	1957/58
231	AD Nourse (2)	at The Wanderers	1935/36
114		at Newlands	1949/50
111	AW Nourse	at The Wanderers	1921/22
122	RG Pollock (5)	at Sydney	1963/64
175		at Adelaide	1963/64
209		at Newlands	1966/67
105		at St George's Park	1966/67
274		at Kingsmead	1969/70
140	BA Richards (2)	at Kingsmead	1969/70
126		at St George's Park	1969/70
143	EAB Rowan	at Kingsmead	1949/50
101	JH Sinclair (2)	at The Wanderers	1902/03
104		at Newlands	1902/03

103	SJ Snooke	at Adelaide	1910/11
111	KG Viljoen	at Melbourne	1931/32
115	JHB Waite (2)	at Wanderers Stadium	1957/58
134		at Kingsmead	1957/58
105	JW Zulch (2)	at Adelaide	1910/11
150		at Sydney	1910/11

For Australia (65):

159*	WW Armstrong (2)	at The Wanderers	1902/03
132		at Melbourne	1910/11
132	W Bardsley (3)	at Sydney	1910/11
121		at Manchester	
1912			
164		at Lord's	1912
122	R Benaud (2)	at Wanderers Stadium	1957/58
100		at Wanderers Stadium	1957/58
214	GS Blewett	at Wanderers Stadium	1996/97
169	BC Booth (2)	at Brisbane	1963/64
102*		at Sydney	1963/64
226	DG Bradman (4)	at Brisbane	1931/32
112		at Sydney	1931/32
167		at Melbourne	1931/32
299*		at Adelaide	1931/32
121	WA Brown	at Newlands	1935/36
189	JW Burke	at Newlands	1957/58
109	AG Chipperfield	at Kingsmead	1935/36
203	HL Collins	at The Wanderers	1921/22
112	JHW Fingleton (3)	at Newlands	1935/36
108		at The Wanderers	1935/36
118		at Kingsmead	1935/36
119	JM Gregory	at The Wanderers	1921/22
178	RN Harvey (8)	at Newlands	1949/50
151*		at Kingsmead	1949/50
100		at Ellis Park	1949/50
116		at St George's Park	1949/50
109		at Brisbane	1952/53
190		at Sydney	1952/53
116		at Adelaide	1952/53
205		at Melbourne	1952/53
112	AL Hassett (3)	at Ellis Park	1949/50
167		at St George's Park	1949/50
163		at Adelaide	1952/53
142	C Hill (3)	at The Wanderers	1902/03
191		at Sydney	1910/11
100		at Melbourne	1910/11
114	C Kelleway (2)	at Manchester	1912
102		at Lord's	1912
157	WM Lawry	at Melbourne	1963/64
101	SJE Loxton	at Ellis Park	1949/50
137	CG Macartney (2)	at Sydney	1910/11
116		at Lord's, Durban	1921/22
149	SJ McCabe (2)	at Kingsmead	1935/36
189*		at The Wanderers	1935/36
154	CC McDonald	at Adelaide	1952/53
118 & 101*	J Moroney (2)	at Ellis Park	1949/50
111	AR Morris (2)	at Ellis Park	1949/50
157		at St George's Park	1949/50
105	RT Ponting	at Melbourne	1997/98
127	KE Rigg	at Sydney	1931/32
142	J Ryder	at Newlands	1921/22
153	RB Simpson	at Newlands	1966/67

134	KR Stackpole	at Newlands	1966/67
170	MA Taylor (2)	at Melbourne	1993/94
169*		at Adelaide	1997/98
159	VT Trumper (2)	at Melbourne	1910/11
214*		at Adelaide	1910/11
113*	ME Waugh (4)	at Kingsmead	1993/94
116		at St George's Park	1996/97
100		at Sydney	1997/98
115*		at Adelaide	1997/98
164	SR Waugh (2)	at Adelaide	1993/94
160		at Wanderers Stadium	1996/97
161	WM Woodfull	at Melbourne	1931/32

Note: DG Bradman made centuries in the four matches in which he batted in the 1931/32 series. He was injured and did not bat in the 5th Test.

HIGHEST AGGREGATE IN A SERIES

		Runs	Matches		
For South Africa:	In South Africa:	606	5	DT Lindsay (Avg 86.57)	1966/67
	In Australia:	732	5	GA Faulkner (Avg 73.20)	1910/11
For Australia:	In South Africa:	660	5	RN Harvey (Avg 132.00)	1949/50
	In Australia:	834	5	RN Harvey (Avg 92.66)	1952/53

HIGHEST INDIVIDUAL INNINGS

For South Africa:	In South Africa:	274	RG Pollock at Kingsmead	1969/70
	In Australia:	204	GA Faulkner at Melbourne	1910/11
For Australia:	In South Africa:	214	GS Blewett at Wanderers Stadium	1996/97
	In Australia:	299*	DG Bradman at Adelaide	1931/32

A CENTURY ON DEBUT IN THE SERIES

For South Africa:

114	EJ Barlow at Brisbane	1963/64

For Australia:

142	C Hill at The Wanderers	1902/03
132	W Bardsley at Sydney	1910/11
226	DG Bradman at Brisbane	1931/32
127	KE Rigg at Sydney	1931/32
109	AG Chipperfield at Kingsmead	1935/36
112	AL Hassett at Ellis Park	1949/50
101	SJE Loxton at Ellis Park	1949/50
169	BC Booth at Brisbane	1963/64
170	MA Taylor at Melbourne	1993/94
164	SR Waugh at Adelaide	1993/94
214	GS Blewett at Wanderers Stadium	1996/97
105	RT Ponting at Melbourne	1997/98

CARRYING BAT THROUGH A COMPLETED INNINGS

For South Africa:	TL Goddard	56* (99) at Newlands	1957/58
For Australia:	WW Armstrong	159* (309) at The Wanderers	1902/03
	MA Taylor	169* (350) at Adelaide	1997/98

SOUTH AFRICAN TEST MATCH RECORDS

RECORD PARTNERSHIP FOR EACH WICKET

For South Africa:

1st	176	DJ McGlew and TL Goddard at Wanderers Stadium	1957/58
2nd	173	LJ Tancred and CB Llewellyn at The Wanderers	1902/03
3rd	341	EJ Barlow and RG Pollock at Adelaide	1963/64
4th	206	CN Frank and AW Nourse at The Wanderers	1921/22
5th	129	JHB Waite and WR Endean at Wanderers Stadium	1957/58
6th	200	RG Pollock and HR Lance at Kingsmead	1969/70
7th	221	DT Lindsay and PL van der Merwe at Wanderers Stadium	1966/67
8th	124	AW Nourse and EA Halliwell at The Wanderers	1902/03
9th	85	RG Pollock and PM Pollock at Newlands	1966/67
10th	74	BM McMillan and PL Symcox at Adelaide	1997/98

For Australia:

1st	233	JHW Fingleton and WA Brown at Newlands	1935/36
2nd	275	CC McDonald and AL Hassett at Adelaide	1952/53
3rd	242	C Kelleway and W Bardsley at Lord's	1912
4th	169	MA Taylor and ME Waugh at Melbourne	1993/94
5th	385	SR Waugh and GS Blewett at Wanderers Stadium	1996/97
6th	108	SR Waugh and IA Healy at Newlands	1993/94
7th	160	R Benaud and GD McKenzie at Sydney	1963/64
8th	83	AG Chipperfield and CV Grimmett at Kingsmead	1935/36
9th	78	DG Bradman and WJ O'Reilly at Adelaide	1931/32
	78	KD Mackay and I Meckiff at Wanderers Stadium	1957/58
10th	82	VS Ransford and WJ Whitty at Melbourne	1910/11

BOWLING

MOST WICKETS IN A SERIES

		Wickets	Matches		
For South Africa:	In South Africa:	26	5	TL Goddard (Avg 16.23)	1966/67
		26	4	MJ Procter (Avg 13.57)	1969/70
	In Australia:	30	5	HJ Tayfield (Avg 28.10)	1952/53
For Australia:	In South Africa:	44	5	CV Grimmett (Avg 14.59)	1935/36
	In Australia:	37	5	WJ Whitty (Avg 17.08)	1910/11

10 WICKETS IN A MATCH

For South Africa:			
13-165	HJ Tayfield	at Melbourne	1952/53
10-116	CB Llewellyn	at The Wanderers	1902/03
10-123	PS de Villiers	at Sydney	1993/94
For Australia:			
14-199	CV Grimmett	at Adelaide	1931/32
13-173	CV Grimmett	at Kingsmead	1935/36
12-128	SK Warne	at Sydney	1993/94
11-24	H Ironmonger	at Melbourne	1931/32
11-109	SK Warne	at Sydney	1997/98
10-88	CV Grimmett	at Newlands	1935/36
10-110	CV Grimmett	at The Wanderers	1935/36

SEVEN WICKETS IN AN INNINGS

For South Africa:			
7-23	HJ Tayfield	at Kingsmead	1949/50
7-81	HJ Tayfield	at Melbourne	1952/53
7-87	SM Pollock	at Adelaide	1997/98
7-91	JT Partridge	at Sydney	1963/64
For Australia:			
7-34	JV Saunders	at The Wanderers	1902/03
7-40	CV Grimmett	at The Wanderers	1935/36

7-56	SK Warne	at Sydney	1993/94
7-83 & 7-116	CV Grimmett	at Adelaide	1931/32
7-100	CV Grimmett	at Kingsmead	1935/36

HAT-TRICK

For South Africa: No instance.

For Australia: TJ Matthews (2) at Manchester 1912
(He achieved the hat-trick in each innings on the second afternoon)
LF Kline at Newlands 1957/58

WICKETKEEPING

MOST DISMISSALS IN A SERIES

For South Africa:
24 (ct 24) DT Lindsay in South Africa 1966/67

For Australia:
21 (ct 13,st 8) RA Saggers in South Africa 1949/50

MOST DISMISSALS IN A MATCH

For South Africa:
8 (ct 8) DT Lindsay at Wanderers Stadium 1966/67

For Australia:
8 (ct 7,st 1) HB Taber at Wanderers Stadium (on Test debut) 1966/67

MOST DISMISSALS IN AN INNINGS

For South Africa: 6 (ct 6) DT Lindsay at Wanderers Stadium 1966/67

For Australia: 6 (ct 6) ATW Grout at Wanderers Stadium (on Test debut) 1957/58

FIELDING

MOST CATCHES IN A SERIES

For South Africa: 9 WR Endean in Australia 1952/53

For Australia: 13 RB Simpson in South Africa 1957/58

MOST CATCHES IN A MATCH

For South Africa: 6 B Mitchell at Melbourne 1931/32

For Australia: 6 VY Richardson at Kingsmead 1935/36

MOST CATCHES IN AN INNINGS

For South Africa: 4 B Mitchell (Melbourne, 1931/32), TL Goddard (Sydney, 1963/64), AJ Traicos (Kingsmead, 1969/70) (on Test debut)

For Australia: 5 VY Richardson at Kingsmead (a Test match record) 1935/36

SOUTH AFRICA versus ENGLAND

Season	Venue	SA captain	England captain	Won by SA	Won by Eng	Drawn	Total
1888/89	South Africa	OR Dunnell (a)	CA Smith (b)	0	2	0	2
1891/92	South Africa	WH Milton	WW Read	0	1	0	1
1895/96	South Africa	EA Halliwell (c)	TC O'Brien (d)	0	3	0	3
1898/99	South Africa	M Bisset	Lord Hawke	0	2	0	2
1905/06	South Africa	PW Sherwell	PF Warner	4	1	0	5
1907	England	PW Sherwell	RE Foster	0	1	2	3
1909/10	South Africa	SJ Snooke	HDG Leveson Gower (e)	3	2	0	5
1912	England	F Mitchell (f)	CB Fry	0	3	0	3
1913/14	South Africa	HW Taylor	JWHT Douglas	0	4	1	5
1922/23	South Africa	HW Taylor	FT Mann	1	2	2	5
1924	England	HW Taylor	AER Gilligan (g)	0	3	2	5
1927/28	South Africa	HG Deane	RT Stanyforth (h)	2	2	1	5

1929	England	HG Deane	JC White (i)	0	2	3	5
1930/31	South Africa	EP Nupen (j)	APF Chapman	1	0	4	5
1935	England	HF Wade	RES Wyatt	1	0	4	5
1938/39	South Africa	A Melville	WR Hammond	0	1	4	5
1947	England	A Melville	NWD Yardley	0	3	2	5
1948/49	South Africa	AD Nourse	FG Mann	0	2	3	5
1951	England	AD Nourse	FR Brown	1	3	1	5
1955	England	JE Cheetham (k)	PBH May	2	3	0	5
1956/57	South Africa	CB van Ryneveld (l)	PBH May	2	2	1	5
1960	England	DJ McGlew	MC Cowdrey	0	3	2	5
1964/65	South Africa	TL Goddard	MJK Smith	0	1	4	5
1965	England	PL van der Merwe	MJK Smith	1	0	2	3
1994	England	KC Wessels	MA Atherton	1	1	1	3
1995/96	South Africa	WJ Cronje	MA Atherton	1	0	4	5
1998	England	WJ Cronje	AJ Stewart	1	2	2	5
1999/00	South Africa	WJ Cronje	N Hussain	2	1	2	5
	Tests in South Africa			16	26	26	68
	Tests in England			7	24	21	52
	Total			23	50	47	120

Notes:
(a) WH Milton (2nd) also captained South Africa
(b) MP Bowden (2nd) also captained England
(c) AR Richards (3rd) also captained South Africa
(d) Lord Hawke (2nd,3rd) also captained England
(e) FL Fane (4th,5th) also captained England
(f) LJ Tancred (2nd,3rd) also captained South Africa
(g) JWHT Douglas (4th) also captained England
(h) GTS Stevens (5th) also captained England
(i) AW Carr (4th,5th) also captained England
(j) HG Deane (2nd,3rd) and HB Cameron (4th,5th) also captained South Africa
(k) DJ McGlew (3rd,4th) also captained South Africa
(l) DJ McGlew (2nd) also captained South Africa

HIGHEST INNINGS TOTALS

For South Africa:	572-7	at Kingsmead (3rd Test)	1999/00
For England:	654-5	at Kingsmead (5th Test)	1938/39

LOWEST INNINGS TOTALS

For South Africa:	30	at St George's Park (1st Test)	1895/96
	30	at Birmingham (1st Test)	1924
For England:	76	at Leeds (2nd Test)	1907

LARGEST MARGINS OF VICTORY

England beat South Africa at Newlands by an innings and 202 runs 1888/89
South Africa beat England at Newlands by an innings and 37 runs 1999/00
South Africa beat England at Wanderers Stadium by an innings and 21 runs 1999/00
South Africa beat England at Lord's by 356 runs 1994
England beat South Africa at Newlands by 312 runs 1956/57

NARROWEST MARGINS OF VICTORY

South Africa beat England at The Wanderers by one wicket 1905/06
England beat South Africa at Newlands by one wicket 1922/23
England beat South Africa at Kingsmead by two wickets 1948/49
(The winning run, a leg bye, was scored off the last possible ball of the match)
England beat South Africa at Centurion Park by two wickets 1999/00
(England declared their first innings at 0-0 and South Africa forfeited their second innings, the only occasion an innings has been forfeited in Test cricket)
South Africa beat England at Wanderers Stadium by 17 runs 1956/57

BATTING

INDIVIDUAL CENTURIES

For South Africa (72):

138	EJ Barlow	at Newlands	1964/65
144*	KC Bland (2)	at Wanderers Stadium	1964/65
127		at The Oval	1965
108	MV Boucher	at Kingsmead	1999/00
120	RH Catterall (3)	at Birmingham	1924
120		at Lord's	1924
119		at Kingsmead	1927/28
126	WJ Cronje	at Nottingham	1998
108	DJ Cullinan (2)	at Wanderers Stadium	1999/00
120		at Newlands	1999/00
117	EL Dalton (2)	at The Oval	1935
102		at The Wanderers	1938/39
116*	WR Endean	at Leeds	1955
123	GA Faulkner	at The Wanderers	1909/10
112	TL Goddard	at Wanderers Stadium	1964/65
102	CMH Hathorn	at The Wanderers	1905/06
132	JH Kallis (2)	at Manchester	1998
105		at Newlands	1999/00
110	G Kirsten (3)	at Wanderers Stadium	1995/96
210		at Manchester	1998
275		at Kingsmead	1999/00
104	PN Kirsten	at Leeds	1994
174	L Klusener	at St George's Park	1999/00
104*	DJ McGlew (2)	at Manchester	1955
133		at Leeds	1955
142	RA McLean (3)	at Lord's	1955
100		at Kingsmead	1956/57
109		at Manchester	1960
100*	BM McMillan	at Wanderers Stadium	1995/96
103	A Melville (4)	at Kingsmead	1938/39
189 & 104*		at Nottingham	1947
117		at Lord's	1947
123	B Mitchell (7)	at Newlands	1930/31
164*		at Lord's	1935
128		at The Oval	1935
109		at Kingsmead	1938/39
120 & 189*		at The Oval	1947
120		at Newlands	1948/49
120	AD Nourse (7)	at Newlands	1938/39
103		at Kingsmead	1938/39
149		at Nottingham	1947
115		at Manchester	1947
112		at Newlands	1948/49
129*		at Ellis Park	1948/49
208		at Nottingham	1951
129	HGO Owen-Smith	at Leeds +	1929
154	AJ Pithey	at Newlands	1964/65
137	RG Pollock (2)	at St George's Park	1964/65
125		at Nottingham	1965
117	JN Rhodes	at Lord's	1998
156*	EAB Rowan (2)	at Ellis Park	1948/49
236		at Leeds	1951
115	PW Sherwell	at Lord's +	1907
141	IJ Siedle	at Newlands	1930/31
106	JH Sinclair	at Newlands +	1898/99

109	HW Taylor (7)	at Lord's, Durban	1913/14
176		at The Wanderers	1922/23
101		at The Wanderers	1922/23
102		at Kingsmead	1922/23
101		at The Wanderers	1927/28
121		at The Oval	1929
117		at Newlands	1930/31
125	PGV van der Bijl	at Kingsmead	1938/39
124	KG Viljoen	at Manchester	1935
125	WW Wade	at St George's Park	1948/49
113	JHB Waite	at Manchester	1955
105	KC Wessels	at Lord's	1994
147	GC White (2)	at The Wanderers	1905/06
118		at Lord's, Durban	1909/10
108	PL Winslow	at Manchester +	1955

Notes: (a) + His maiden century was scored in a Test Match.
(b) A Melville scored centuries in three successive innings in 1947 and had made a century in his previous Test innings in 1938/39.

For England (96):

120	R Abel	at Newlands	1888/89
148*	LEG Ames (2)	at The Oval	1935
115		at Newlands	1938/39
185*	MA Atherton (3)	at Wanderers Stadium	1995/96
103		at Birmingham	1998
108		at St George's Park	1999/00
148*	KF Barrington (2)	at Kingsmead	1964/65
121		at Wanderers Stadium	1964/65
117	G Boycott	at St George's Park	1964/65
104	LC Braund	at Lord's	1907
116	MA Butcher	at Leeds	1998
163	DCS Compton (7)	at Nottingham	1947
208		at Lord's	1947
115		at Manchester	1947
113		at The Oval	1947
114		at Ellis Park	1948/49
112		at Nottingham	1951
158		at Manchester	1955
101	MC Cowdrey (3)	at Newlands	1956/57
155		at The Oval	1960
105		at Nottingham	1965
104	D Denton	at The Wanderers	1909/10
172	ER Dexter	at Wanderers Stadium	1964/65
119	JWHT Douglas	at Lord's, Durban	1913/14
219	WJ Edrich (3)	at Kingsmead	1938/39
189		at Lord's	1947
191		at Manchester	1947
143	FL Fane	at The Wanderers	1905/06
129	CB Fry	at The Oval	1907
106	PA Gibb (2)	at The Wanderers	1938/39
120		at Kingsmead	1938/39
138*	WR Hammond (6)	at Birmingham	1929
101*		at The Oval	1929
136*		at Kingsmead	1930/31
181		at Newlands	1938/39
120		at Kingsmead	1938/39
140		at Kingsmead	1938/39
122	TW Hayward	at The Wanderers	1895/96
132	EH Hendren (2)	at Leeds	1924
142		at The Oval	1924
110	GA Hick (2)	at Leeds	1994

141		at Centurion Park	1995/96
124	AJL Hill	at Newlands +	1895/96
187	JB Hobbs (2)	at Newlands	1909/10
211		at Lord's	1924
105	N Hussain (2)	at Lord's	1998
146*		at Kingsmead	1999/00
100	L Hutton (4)	at Leeds	1947
158		at Ellis Park	1948/49
123		at Ellis Park	1948/49
100		at Leeds	1951
110*	DJ Insole	at Kingsmead	1956/57
102	M Leyland (2)	at Lord's	1929
161		at The Oval	1935
136*	FG Mann	at St George's Park	1948/49
138	PBH May (3)	at Leeds	1951
112		at Lord's	1955
117		at Manchester	1955
102	CP Mead (3)	at The Wanderers	1913/14
117		at St George's Park	1913/14
181		at Kingsmead	1922/23
122*	PH Parfitt	at Wanderers Stadium	1964/65
108*	JM Parks	at Kingsmead	1964/65
117 & 100	E Paynter (3)	at The Wanderers	1938/39
243		at Kingsmead	1938/39
175	G Pullar	at The Oval	1960
152	W Rhodes	at The Wanderers	1913/14
117	PE Richardson	at Wanderers Stadium	1956/57
108	RWV Robins	at Manchester	1935
140 & 111	CAG Russell (2)	at Kingsmead	1922/23
137	RT Simpson	at Nottingham	1951
121	MJK Smith	at Newlands	1964/65
119	RH Spooner	at Lord's	1912
164	AJ Stewart	at Manchester	1998
122	H Sutcliffe (6)	at Lord's	1924
102		at The Wanderers	1927/28
114		at Birmingham	1929
100		at Lord's	1929
104 & 109*		at The Oval	1929
100*	MW Tate	at Lord's	1929
122	GE Tyldesley (2)	at The Wanderers	1927/28
100		at Kingsmead	1927/28
112	JT Tyldesley	at Newlands	1898/99
112	BH Valentine	at Newlands	1938/39
132*	PF Warner	at The Wanderers	1898/99
195	C Washbrook	at Ellis Park	1948/49
111	AJ Watkins	at Ellis Park	1948/49
134*	H Wood	at Newlands +	1891/92
115*	FE Woolley (3)	at The Wanderers	1922/23
134*		at Lord's	1924
154		at Manchester	1929
113	RES Wyatt (2)	at Manchester	1929
149		at Nottingham	1935

Note: + His maiden century was scored in a Test Match.

HIGHEST AGGREGATE IN A SERIES

		Runs	Matches		
For South Africa:	In South Africa:	582	5	HW Taylor (Avg 64.66)	1922/23
	In England:	621	5	AD Nourse (Avg 69.00)	1947
For England:	In South Africa:	653	5	E Paynter (Avg 81.62)	1938/39
	In England:	753	5	DCS Compton (Avg 94.12)	1947

SOUTH AFRICAN TEST MATCH RECORDS

HIGHEST INDIVIDUAL INNINGS

For South Africa:	In South Africa:	275	G Kirsten at Kingsmead	1999/00
	In England:	236	EAB Rowan at Leeds	1951
For England:	In South Africa:	243	E Paynter at Kingsmead	1938/39
	In England:	211	JB Hobbs at Lord's	1924

A CENTURY ON DEBUT IN THE SERIES

For South Africa:			
105	KC Wessels	at Lord's	1994
For England:			
132*	PF Warner	at The Wanderers (on Test debut)	1898/99
104	LC Braund	at Lord's	1907
119	RH Spooner	at Lord's	1912
119	JWHT Douglas	at Lord's, Durban	1913/14
117 & 100	E Paynter	at The Wanderers	1938/39
106	PA Gibb	at The Wanderers (on Test debut)	1938/39
163	DCS Compton	at Nottingham	1947
138	PBH May	at Leeds (on Test debut)	1951
117	PE Richardson	at Wanderers Stadium	1956/57

CARRYING BAT THROUGH A COMPLETED INNINGS

For South Africa:			
AB Tancred	26* (47)	at Newlands	1888/89
JW Zulch	43* (103)	at Newlands	1909/10
For England:			
PF Warner	132* (237)	at The Wanderers (on Test debut)	1898/99

RECORD PARTNERSHIP FOR EACH WICKET

For South Africa:			
1st	260	B Mitchell and IJ Siedle at Newlands	1930/31
2nd	238	G Kirsten and JH Kallis at Manchester	1998
3rd	319	A Melville and AD Nourse at Nottingham	1947
4th	214	HW Taylor and HG Deane at The Oval	1929
5th	192	G Kirsten and MV Boucher at Kingsmead	1999/00
6th	171	JHB Waite and PL Winslow at Manchester	1955
7th	123	HG Deane and EP Nupen at Kingsmead	1927/28
8th	119	L Klusener and MV Boucher at St George's Park	1999/00
9th	137	EL Dalton and ACB Langton at The Oval	1935
10th	103	HGO Owen-Smith and AJ Bell at Leeds	1929
For England:			
1st	359	L Hutton and C Washbrook at Ellis Park	1948/49
2nd	280	PA Gibb and WJ Edrich at Kingsmead	1938/39
3rd	370	WJ Edrich and DCS Compton at Lord's	1947
4th	197	WR Hammond and LEG Ames at Newlands	1938/39
5th	237	DCS Compton and NWD Yardley at Nottingham	1947
6th	206*	KF Barrington and JM Parks at Kingsmead	1964/65
7th	115	JWHT Douglas and MC Bird at Lord's, Durban	1913/14
8th	154	CW Wright and HR Bromley-Davenport at The Wanderers	1895/96
9th	71	H Wood and JT Hearne at Newlands	1891/92
10th	92	CAG Russell and AER Gilligan at Kingsmead	1922/23

BOWLING

MOST WICKETS IN A SERIES

		Wickets	Matches		
For South Africa:	In South Africa:	37	5	HJ Tayfield (Avg 17.18)	1956/57
	In England:	33	5	AA Donald (Avg 19.78)	1998

For England:	In South Africa:	49	4	SF Barnes (Avg 10.93)	1913/14
	In England:	34	3	SF Barnes (Avg 8.29)	1912

10 WICKETS IN A MATCH

For South Africa:			
13-192	HJ Tayfield	at Wanderers Stadium	1956/57
12-127	SJ Snooke	at The Wanderers	1905/06
12-181	AEE Vogler	at The Wanderers	1909/10
11-112	AE Hall	at Newlands (on Test debut)	1922/23
11-127	AA Donald	at Wanderers Stadium	1999/00
11-150	EP Nupen	at The Wanderers	1930/31
10-87	PM Pollock	at Nottingham	1965
For England:			
17-159	SF Barnes	at The Wanderers	1913/14
15-28	J Briggs	at Newlands	1888/89
15-45	GA Lohmann	at St George's Park	1895/96
15-99	C Blythe	at Leeds	1907
14-144	SF Barnes	at Lord's, Durban	1913/14
13-57	SF Barnes	at The Oval	1912
13-91	JJ Ferris	at Newlands	1891/92
12-71	GA Lohmann	at The Wanderers	1895/96
12-89	JH Wardle	at Newlands	1956/57
12-101	R Tattersall	at Lord's	1951
12-112	AV Bedser	at Manchester	1951
12-130	G Geary	at The Wanderers	1927/28
12-171	AP Freeman	at Manchester	1929
11-90	AER Gilligan	at Birmingham	1924
11-97	JB Statham	at Lord's	1960
11-110	SF Barnes	at Lord's	1912
11-118	C Blythe	at Newlands	1905/06
10-104	C Blythe	at Newlands	1909/10
10-105	SF Barnes	at Lord's, Durban	1913/14
10-115	SF Barnes	at Leeds	1912
10-119	JC Laker	at The Oval	1951
10-122	ARC Fraser	at Nottingham	1998
10-138	DE Malcolm	at The Oval	1994
10-175	DVP Wright	at Lord's	1947
10-207	AP Freeman	at Leeds	1929

EIGHT WICKETS IN AN INNINGS

For South Africa:			
9-113	HJ Tayfield	at Wanderers Stadium	1956/57
8-69	HJ Tayfield	at Kingsmead	1956/57
8-70	SJ Snooke	at The Wanderers	1905/06

(The best in England is 7-65 by SJ Pegler, at Lord's, 1912)

For England:			
9-28	GA Lohmann	at The Wanderers	1895/96
9-57	DE Malcolm	at The Oval	1994
9-103	SF Barnes (b)	at The Wanderers	1913/14
8-7	GA Lohmann	at St George's Park	1895/96
8-11	J Briggs	at Newlands	1888/89
8-29	SF Barnes	at The Oval	1912
8-56	SF Barnes (a)	at The Wanderers	1913/14
8-59	C Blythe	at Leeds	1907

Note: (a) in the first innings (b) in the second innings of the same match.

HAT-TRICK

For South Africa:

GM Griffin	at Lord's	1960

For England:

GA Lohmann	at St George's Park	1895/96
TWJ Goddard	at The Wanderers	1938/39

WICKETKEEPING

MOST DISMISSALS IN A SERIES

For South Africa:

26	(ct 25,st 1)	MV Boucher in England	1998

For England:

27	(ct 25,st 2)	RC Russell in South Africa	1995/96

MOST DISMISSALS IN A MATCH

For South Africa:

7	(ct 7)	MV Boucher at Lord's	1998
7	(ct 7)	MV Boucher at Wanderers Stadium	1999/00

For England:

11	(ct 11)	RC Russell at Wanderers Stadium	1995/96

MOST DISMISSALS IN AN INNINGS

For South Africa:

5	(ct 5)	MV Boucher at Lord's	1998
5	(ct 5)	MV Boucher at Wanderers Stadium	1999/00

For England:

6	(ct 6)	RC Russell at Wanderers Stadium	1995/96

FIELDING

MOST CATCHES IN A SERIES

For South Africa:

12	AEE Vogler	in South Africa	1909/10
12	B Mitchell	in South Africa	1930/31
12	TL Goddard	in South Africa	1956/57

For England:

12	JT Ikin	in England	1951

MOST CATCHES IN A MATCH

For South Africa:

6	AEE Vogler	at Lord's, Durban	1909/10

For England:

5	WR Hammond	at Kingsmead	1938/39
5	JT Ikin	at Manchester	1951

MOST CATCHES IN AN INNINGS

For South Africa:

4	AEE Vogler	at Lord's, Durban	1909/10
4	AW Nourse	at Kingsmead	1922/23
4	G Kirsten	at Newlands	1999/00

For England: No comparable performance.

SOUTH AFRICA versus INDIA

Season	Venue	SA captain	India captain	Won by SA	Won by Ind	Drawn	Total
1992/93	South Africa	KC Wessels	M Azharuddin	1	0	3	4
1996/97	India	WJ Cronje	SR Tendulkar	1	2	0	3
1996/97	South Africa	WJ Cronje	SR Tendulkar	2	0	1	3
1999/00	India	WJ Cronje	SR Tendulkar	2	0	0	2
	Tests in South Africa			3	0	4	7
	Tests in India			3	2	0	5
	Total			6	2	4	12

SOUTH AFRICAN TEST MATCH RECORDS

HIGHEST INNINGS TOTALS

For South Africa:	529-7*	at Newlands (2nd Test)	1996/97
For India:	410	at Wanderers Stadium (3rd Test)	1996/97

LOWEST INNINGS TOTALS

For South Africa:	105	at Ahmedabad (1st Test)	1996/97
For India:	66	at Kingsmead (1st Test)	1996/97

LARGEST MARGINS OF VICTORY

South Africa beat India at Bangalore by an innings and 71 runs	1999/00
South Africa beat India at Calcutta by 329 runs	1996/97
South Africa beat India at Kingsmead by 328 runs	1996/97
South Africa beat India at Newlands by 282 runs	1996/97
India beat South Africa at Kanpur by 280 runs	1996/97
South Africa beat India at St George's Park by 9 wickets	1992/93

NARROWEST MARGINS OF VICTORY

South Africa beat India at Mumbai by 4 wickets	1999/00
India beat South Africa at Ahmedabad by 64 runs	1996/97

BATTING

INDIVIDUAL CENTURIES

For South Africa (10):

135	WJ Cronje	at St George's Park	1992/93
153*	DJ Cullinan (2)	at Calcutta	1996/97
122*		at Wanderers Stadium	1996/97
146	AC Hudson	at Calcutta	1996/97
102 & 133	G Kirsten (3)	at Calcutta	1996/97
103		at Newlands	1996/97
102*	L Klusener	at Newlands	1996/97
103*	BM McMillan	at Newlands	1996/97
118	KC Wessels	at Kingsmead	1992/93

For India (9):

103	PK Amre	at Kingsmead	1992/93
109	M Azharuddin (4)	at Calcutta	1996/97
163*		at Kanpur	1996/97
115		at Newlands	1996/97
102		at Bangalore	1999/00
148	RS Dravid	at Wanderers Stadium	1996/97
129	Kapil Dev	at St George's Park	1992/93
111	SR Tendulkar (2)	at Wanderers Stadium	1992/93
169		at Newlands	1996/97

HIGHEST AGGREGATE IN A SERIES

		Runs	Matches		
For South Africa:	In South Africa:	296	3	BM McMillan (Avg 98.66)	1996/97
	In India	322	3	G Kirsten (Avg 53.66)	1996/97
For India:	In South Africa:	277	3	RS Dravid (Avg 55.40)	1996/97
	In India:	388	3	M Azharuddin (Avg 77.60)	1996/97

A CENTURY ON DEBUT IN THE SERIES

For South Africa:	118	KC Wessels at Kingsmead	1992/93
For India:	103	PK Amre at Kingsmead (on Test debut)	1992/9

SOUTH AFRICAN TEST MATCH RECORDS

RECORD PARTNERSHIP FOR EACH WICKET

For South Africa:			
1st	236	AC Hudson and G Kirsten at Calcutta	1996/97
2nd	212	G Kirsten and DJ Cullinan at Calcutta	1996/97
3rd	114	G Kirsten and DJ Cullinan at Newlands	1996/97
4th	94	AC Hudson and DJ Cullinan at Newlands	1996/97
5th	164	JH Kallis and L Klusener at Bangalore	1999/00
6th	112	BM McMillan and SM Pollock at Wanderers Stadium	1996/97
7th	101*	BM McMillan and SM Pollock at Newlands	1996/97
8th	147*	BM McMillan and L Klusener at Newlands	1996/97
9th	60	PS de Villiers and AA Donald at Ahmedabad	1996/97
10th	74	BM McMillan and AA Donald at Kingsmead	1996/97
For India:			
1st	90	V Rathore and NR Mongia at Wanderers Stadium	1996/97
2nd	85	M Prabhakar and SV Manjrekar at Newlands	1992/93
3rd	54	RS Dravid and SR Tendulkar at Wanderers Stadium	1996/97
4th	145	RS Dravid and SC Ganguly at Wanderers Stadium	1996/97
5th	87	M Azharuddin and PK Amre at Kingsmead	1992/93
6th	222	SR Tendulkar and M Azharuddin at Newlands	1996/97
7th	76	RS Dravid and J Srinath at Wanderers Stadium	1996/97
8th	161	M Azharuddin and A Kumble at Calcutta	1996/97
9th	77	Kapil Dev and A Kumble at St George's Park	1992/93
10th	52	AB Agarkar and M Kartik at Mumbai	1999/00

BOWLING

MOST WICKETS IN A SERIES

		Wickets	Matches		
For South Africa:	In South Africa:	20	4	AA Donald (Avg 19.70)	1992/93
		20	3	AA Donald (Avg 15.95)	1996/97
	In India:	14	3	PR Adams (Avg 20.28)	1996/97
For India:	In South Africa:	18	4	A Kumble (Avg 25.94)	1992/93
		18	3	J Srinath (Avg 28.72)	1996/97
	In India:	17	3	J Srinath (Avg 20.94)	1996/97

10 WICKETS IN A MATCH

For South Africa:	12-139	AA Donald	at St George's Park	1992/93
For India:	10-153	BK Venkatesh Prasad	at Kingsmead	1996/97

SEVEN WICKETS IN AN INNINGS

For South Africa:	8-64	L Klusener	at Calcutta	1996/97
	7-84	AA Donald	at St George's Park	1992/93
For India:	No instance. The best performance is 6-21 by J Srinath at Ahmedabad			1996/97

WICKETKEEPING

MOST DISMISSALS IN A SERIES

For South Africa:	16 (ct 16)	DJ Richardson in South Africa	1992/93
For India:	14 (ct 14)	NR Mongia in South Africa	1996/97

MOST DISMISSALS IN A MATCH

For South Africa:	9 (ct 9)	DJ Richardson at St George's Park	1992/93
For India:	8 (ct 8)	NR Mongia at Kingsmead	1996/97

MOST DISMISSALS IN AN INNINGS

For South Africa:	5 (ct 5)	DJ Richardson at St George's Park	1992/93
	5 (ct 5)	MV Boucher at Mumbai	1999/00
For India:	5 (ct 5)	NR Mongia at Kingsmead	1996/97

FIELDING

MOST CATCHES IN A SERIES

For South Africa:	8	BM McMillan in South Africa	1992/93
	8	BM McMillan in India	1996/97
For India:	6	M Azharuddin in South Africa	1992/93
	6	RS Dravid in South Africa	1996/97

MOST CATCHES IN A MATCH

For South Africa:	4	BM McMillan at St George's Park	1992/93
	4	AC Hudson at Newlands	1992/93
For India:	3	J Srinath at Newlands	1992/93
	3	V Rathore at Kingsmead	1996/97
	3	RS Dravid at Newlands	1996/97
	3	M Azharuddin at Wanderers Stadium	1996/97
	3	VVS Laxman at Mumbai	1999/00
	3	W Jaffer at Bangalore	1999/00

Note: VVS Laxman took 3 catches as a substitute at Kanpur 1996/97

MOST CATCHES IN AN INNINGS

For South Africa:	4	AC Hudson at Newlands	1992/93
For India:	3	VVS Laxman at Mumbai	1999/00
	3	W Jaffer at Bangalore	1999/00

SOUTH AFRICA versus NEW ZEALAND

Season	Venue	SA captain	NZ captain	Won by SA	Won by NZ	Drawn	Total
1931/32	New Zealand	HB Cameron	ML Page	2	0	0	2
1952/53	New Zealand	JE Cheetham	WM Wallace	1	0	1	2
1953/54	South Africa	JE Cheetham	GO Rabone (a)	4	0	1	5
1961/62	South Africa	DJ McGlew	JR Reid	2	2	1	5
1963/64	New Zealand	TL Goddard	JR Reid	0	0	3	3
1994/95	South Africa	WJ Cronje	KR Rutherford	2	1	0	3
1994/95	New Zealand	WJ Cronje	KR Rutherford	1	0	0	1
1998/99	New Zealand	WJ Cronje	DJ Nash	1	0	2	3
2000/01	South Africa	SM Pollock	SP Fleming	2	0	1	3
	Tests in South Africa			10	3	3	16
	Tests in New Zealand			5	0	6	11
	Total			15	3	9	27

Note: (a) B Sutcliffe (4th,5th) also captained New Zealand

HIGHEST INNINGS TOTALS

For South Africa:	621-5*	at Auckland (1st Test)	1998/99
For New Zealand:	505	at Newlands (3rd Test)	1953/54

LOWEST INNINGS TOTALS

For South Africa:	148	at Ellis Park (2nd Test)	1953/54
For New Zealand:	79	at Ellis Park (4th Test)	1953/54

LARGEST MARGINS OF VICTORY

South Africa beat New Zealand at Wellington by an innings and 180 runs	1952/53
South Africa beat New Zealand at Kingsmead by an innings and 58 runs	1953/54
South Africa beat New Zealand at Wanderers Stadium by an innings and 51 runs	1961/62
New Zealand beat South Africa at Wanderers Stadium by 137 runs	1994/95

NARROWEST MARGINS OF VICTORY

South Africa beat New Zealand at Kingsmead by 30 runs	1961/62
New Zealand beat South Africa at St George's Park by 40 runs	1961/62

SOUTH AFRICAN TEST MATCH RECORDS

BATTING

INDIVIDUAL CENTURIES

For South Africa (23):

122*	XC Balaskas	at Wellington	1931/32
103	JAJ Christy	at Christchurch	1931/32
112	WJ Cronje (2)	at Newlands	1994/95
101		at Auckland	1994/95
275*	DJ Cullinan (2)	at Auckland	1998/99
152		at Wellington	1998/99
100	HH Dippenaar	at Wanderers Stadium	2000/01
116	WR Endean	at Auckland	1952/53
211*	HH Gibbs (2)	at Christchurch	1998/99
120		at Wellington	1998/99
148*	JH Kallis (2)	at Christchurch	1998/99
160		at Springbok Park	2000/01
128	G Kirsten	at Auckland	1998/99
255*	DJ McGlew (3)	at Wellington	1952/53
127*		at Kingsmead	1961/62
120		at Wanderers Stadium	1961/62
120	ND McKenzie	at St George's Park	2000/01
101	RA McLean (2)	at Kingsmead	1953/54
113		at Newlands	1961/62
113	B Mitchell	at Christchurch	1931/32
109	ARA Murray	at Wellington	1952/53
109	DJ Richardson	at Newlands	1994/95
101	JHB Waite	at Wanderers Stadium	1961/62

For New Zealand (8):

109	PT Barton	at St George's Park	1961/62
101	PGZ Harris	at Newlands	1961/62
107	GO Rabone	at Kingsmead	1953/54
135	JR Reid (2)	at Newlands	1953/54
142		at Wanderers Stadium	1961/62
138	BW Sinclair	at Auckland	1963/64
150	MS Sinclair	at St George's Park	2000/01
100	HG Vivian	at Wellington	1931/32

HIGHEST AGGREGATE IN A SERIES

		Runs	Matches		
For South Africa:	In South Africa:	426	5	DJ McGlew (Avg 60.85)	1961/62
	In New Zealand:	427	3	DJ Cullinan (Avg 427.00)	1998/99
For New Zealand:	In South Africa:	546	5	JR Reid (Avg 60.66)	1961/62
	In New Zealand:	274	3	MJ Horne (Avg 45.66)	1998/99

HIGHEST INDIVIDUAL INNINGS

For South Africa:	In South Africa:	160	JH Kallis at Springbok Park	2000/01
	In New Zealand:	275*	DJ Cullinan at Auckland	1998/99
For New Zealand:	In South Africa:	150	MS Sinclair at St George's Park	2000/01
	In New Zealand:	138	BW Sinclair at Auckland	1963/64

A CENTURY ON DEBUT IN THE SERIES

For South Africa:

103	JAJ Christy at Christchurch	1931/32
113	B Mitchell at Christchurch	1931/32
255*	DJ McGlew at Wellington	1952/53
109	ARA Murray at Wellington	1952/53

For New Zealand:

100	HG Vivian at Wellington	1931/32

CARRYING BAT THROUGH A COMPLETED INNINGS

For South Africa:		
DJ McGlew	127* (292) at Kingsmead	1961/62
For New Zealand:	No instance	

RECORD PARTNERSHIP FOR EACH WICKET

For South Africa:

1st	196	JAJ Christy and B Mitchell at Christchurch	1931/32
2nd	315*	HH Gibbs and JH Kallis at Christchurch	1998/99
3rd	183	G Kirsten and DJ Cullinan at Auckland	1998/99
4th	145	DJ Cullinan and WJ Cronje at Wellington	1998/99
5th	141	DJ Cullinan and JN Rhodes at Auckland	1998/99
6th	126*	DJ Cullinan and SM Pollock at Auckland	1998/99
7th	246	DJ McGlew and ARA Murray at Wellington	1952/53
8th	136	ND McKenzie and N Boje at St George's Park	2000/01
9th	60	PM Pollock and NAT Adcock at St George's Park	1961/62
10th	47	DJ McGlew and HD Bromfield at St George's Park	1961/62

For New Zealand:

1st	126	GO Rabone and ME Chapple at Newlands	1953/54
2nd	90	MJ Horne and NJ Astle at Auckland	1998/99
3rd	94	MB Poore and B Sutcliffe at Newlands	1953/54
4th	171	BW Sinclair and SN McGregor at Auckland	1963/64
5th	174	JR Reid and JEF Beck at Newlands	1953/54
6th	100	HG Vivian and FT Badcock at Wellington	1931/32
7th	84	JR Reid and GA Bartlett at Wanderers Stadium	1961/62
8th	74	SA Thomson and DJ Nash at Wanderers Stadium	1994/95
9th	69	CFW Allcott and IB Cromb at Wellington	1931/32
10th	57	SB Doull and RP de Groen at Wanderers Stadium	1994/95

BOWLING

MOST WICKETS IN A SERIES

		Wickets	Matches		
For South Africa:	In South Africa:	28	5	GB Lawrence (Avg 18.28)	1961/62
	In New Zealand:	16	2	Q McMillan (Avg 20.18)	1931/32
For New Zealand:	In South Africa:	22	5	AR MacGibbon (Avg 20.63)	1953/54
		22	5	JC Alabaster (Avg 28.04)	1961/62
	In New Zealand:	12	3	JR Reid (Avg 23.16)	1963/64
		12	3	RW Blair (Avg 27.25)	1963/64

10 WICKETS IN A MATCH

For South Africa:	11-196	SF Burke at Newlands (on Test debut)	1961/62
For New Zealand:	No instance. The best performance is 8-134 by MN Hart at Wanderers Stadium		1994/95

SEVEN WICKETS IN AN INNINGS

For South Africa:	8-53	GB Lawrence at Wanderers Stadium	1961/62
For New Zealand:	No instance. The best performance is 6-60 by JR Reid at Dunedin		1963/64

WICKETKEEPING

MOST DISMISSALS IN A SERIES

For South Africa:	26 (ct 23,st 3)	JHB Waite in South Africa	1961/62
For New Zealand:	23 (ct 21,st 2)	AE Dick in South Africa	1961/62

SOUTH AFRICAN TEST MATCH RECORDS

MOST DISMISSALS IN A MATCH

For South Africa:	7 (ct 5,st 2)	JHB Waite at St George's Park	1953/54
	7 (ct 4,st 3)	JHB Waite at Newlands	1961/62
	7 (ct 7)	DJ Richardson at Auckland	1994/95
For New Zealand:	7 (ct 6,st 1)	AE Dick at Kingsmead	1961/62

MOST DISMISSALS IN AN INNINGS

For South Africa:	4 (8 instances)	JHB Waite 4, DJ Richardson 3, MV Boucher 1
For New Zealand:	4 (5 instances)	AE Dick 3, AC Parore 2

SOUTH AFRICA versus PAKISTAN

Season	Venue	SA captain	Pakistan captain	Won by SA	Won by Pak	Drawn	Total
1994/95	South Africa	WJ Cronje	Salim Malik	1	0	0	1
1997/98	Pakistan	WJ Cronje	Saeed Anwar	1	0	2	3
1997/98	South Africa	WJ Cronje (a)	Rashid Latif (b)	1	1	1	3
	Tests in South Africa			2	1	1	4
	Tests in Pakistan			1	0	2	3
	Total			3	1	3	7

Notes: (a) G Kirsten (1st) also captained South Africa
(b) Aamir Sohail (1st, 2nd) also captained Pakistan

HIGHEST INNINGS TOTALS

For South Africa:	460	at Wanderers Stadium (Only Test)	1994/95
For Pakistan:	456	at Rawalpindi (1st Test)	1997/98

LOWEST INNINGS TOTALS

For South Africa:	214	at Faisalabad (3rd Test)	1997/98
For Pakistan:	92	at Faisalabad (3rd Test)	1997/98

LARGEST MARGINS OF VICTORY

South Africa beat Pakistan at Wanderers Stadium by 324 runs 1994/95

NARROWEST MARGINS OF VICTORY

Pakistan beat South Africa at Kingsmead by 29 runs 1997/98
South Africa beat Pakistan at Faisalabad by 53 runs 1997/98

BATTING

INDIVIDUAL CENTURIES

For South Africa (3):

100*	G Kirsten	at Faisalabad	1997/98
113	BM McMillan	at Wanderers Stadium	1994/95
108	PL Symcox	at Wanderers Stadium	1997/98

For Pakistan (5):

115	Ali Naqvi	at Rawalpindi *	1997/98
128*	Azhar Mahmood (3)	at Rawalpindi + *	1997/98
136		at Wanderers Stadium	1997/98
132		at Kingsmead	1997/98
118	Saeed Anwar	at Kingsmead	1997/98

Notes: (a) + His maiden century was scored in a Test match.
(b) * Ali Naqvi and Azhar Mahmood provided the first instance of two players scoring centuries on their Test debuts in the same innings.

RECORD PARTNERSHIP FOR EACH WICKET

For South Africa:

1st	135	G Kirsten and AM Bacher at Sheikhupura	1997/98
2nd	114	G Kirsten and JH Kallis at Rawalpindi	1997/98
3rd	83	JH Kallis and HD Ackerman at Kingsmead	1997/98

4th	79	G Kirsten and WJ Cronje at Wanderers Stadium	1994/95
5th	43	PL Symcox and WJ Cronje at Faisalabad	1997/98
6th	157	JN Rhodes and BM McMillan at Wanderers Stadium	1994/95
7th	106	SM Pollock and DJ Richardson at Rawalpindi	1997/98
8th	124	G Kirsten and PL Symcox at Faisalabad	1997/98
9th	195	MV Boucher and PL Symcox at Wanderers Stadium	1997/98
10th	71	PS de Villiers and AA Donald at Wanderers Stadium	1994/95
For Pakistan:			
1st	101	Saeed Anwar and Aamir Sohail at Kingsmead	1997/98
2nd	69	Ali Naqvi and Mohammad Ramzan at Rawalpindi	1997/98
3rd	72	Ijaz Ahmed and Mohammad Wasim at Wanderers Stadium	1997/98
4th	93	Asif Mujtaba and Inzamam-ul-Haq at Wanderers Stadium	1994/95
5th	44	Ali Naqvi and Mohammad Wasim at Rawalpindi	1997/98
6th	144	Inzamam-ul-Haq and Moin Khan at Faisalabad	1997/98
7th	35	Salim Malik and Wasim Akram at Wanderers Stadium	1994/95
8th	40	Inzamam-ul-Haq and Kabir Khan at Wanderers Stadium	1994/95
9th	80	Azhar Mahmood and Shoaib Akhtar at Kingsmead	1997/98
10th	151	Azhar Mahmood and Mushtaq Ahmed at Rawalpindi	1997/98

BOWLING

10 WICKETS IN A MATCH

For South Africa:

10-108	PS de Villiers	at Wanderers Stadium	1994/95

For Pakistan:

10-133	Waqar Younis	at St George's Park	1997/98

BEST BOWLING IN AN INNINGS

For South Africa:

6-23	PS de Villiers	at St George's Park	1997/98

For Pakistan:

6-78	Mushtaq Ahmed	at Kingsmead	1997/98
6-78	Waqar Younis	at St George's Park	1997/98

SOUTH AFRICA versus SRI LANKA

Season	Venue	SA captain	SL captain	Won by SA	Won by SL	Drawn	Total
1993/94	Sri Lanka	KC Wessels	A Ranatunga	1	0	2	3
1997/98	South Africa	WJ Cronje	A Ranatunga	2	0	0	2
2000	Sri Lanka	SM Pollock	ST Jayasuriya	1	1	1	3
2000/01	South Africa	SM Pollock	ST Jayasuriya	2	0	1	3
	Total			6	1	4	11

HIGHEST INNINGS TOTALS

For South Africa:	504-7*	at Newlands (2nd Test)	2000/01
For Sri Lanka:	522	at Galle (1st Test)	2000

LOWEST INNINGS TOTALS

For South Africa:	200	at Centurion Park (2nd Test)	1997/98
For Sri Lanka:	95	at Newlands (2nd Test)	2000/01

LARGEST MARGINS OF VICTORY

South Africa beat Sri Lanka at Newlands by an innings and 229 runs	2000/01
South Africa beat Sri Lanka at Colombo-SSC by an innings and 208 runs	1993/94
Sri Lanka beat South Africa at Galle by an innings and 15 runs	2000

NARROWEST MARGINS OF VICTORY

South Africa beat Sri Lanka at Kandy by 7 runs	2000

SOUTH AFRICAN TEST MATCH RECORDS

BATTING

INDIVIDUAL CENTURIES

For South Africa (11):			
122	WJ Cronje	at Colombo-SSC	1993/94
102	DJ Cullinan (5)	at Colombo-PSS	1993/94
113		at Newlands	1997/98
103		at Centurion Park	1997/98
114*		at Galle	2000
112		at Newlands	2000/01
180	G Kirsten	at Kingsmead	2000/01
118*	L Klusener	at Kandy	2000
103	ND McKenzie	at Centurion Park	2000/01
111	SM Pollock	at Centurion Park	2000/01
101*	JN Rhodes	at Moratuwa	1993/94
For Sri Lanka (5):			
120	MS Atapattu	at Kandy	2000
148	ST Jayasuriya	at Galle	2000
167	DPMD Jayawardene (2)	at Galle	2000
101*		at Colombo-SSC	2000
131	A Ranatunga	at Moratuwa	1993/94

Note: SSC - Sinhalese Sports Club, PSS - P Saravanamuttu Stadium

HIGHEST AGGREGATE IN A SERIES

		Runs	Matches		
For South Africa:	In South Africa:	284	2	DJ Cullinan (Avg 71.00)	1997/98
	In Sri Lanka:	275	3	L Klusener (Avg 68.75)	2000
For Sri Lanka:	In South Africa:	235	3	K Sangakkara (Avg 39.16)	2000/01
	In Sri Lanka:	321	3	DPMP Jayawardene (Avg 80.25)	2000

RECORD PARTNERSHIP FOR EACH WICKET

For South Africa:			
1st	137	KC Wessels and AC Hudson at Colombo-SSC	1993/94
2nd	96	G Kirsten and JH Kallis at Newlands	2000/01
3rd	116	JH Kallis and DJ Cullinan at Newlands	1997/98
4th	116	G Kirsten and WJ Cronje at Centurion Park	1997/98
5th	86	DJ Cullinan and MV Boucher at Newlands	2000/01
6th	124	L Klusener and MV Boucher at Kandy	2000
7th	95	SM Pollock and MV Boucher at Newlands	1997/98
8th	150	ND McKenzie and SM Pollock at Centurion Park	2000/01
9th	45	N Boje and PR Adams at Kandy	2000
10th	43	L Klusener and M Hayward at Kandy	2000
For Sri Lanka:			
1st	193	MS Atapattu and ST Jayasuriya at Galle	2000
2nd	103	ST Jayasuriya and RP Arnold at Colombo-SSC	2000
3rd	168	K Sangakkara and DPMD Jayawardene at Kingsmead	2000/01
4th	118	RS Mahanama and A Ranatunga at Centurion Park	1997/98
5th	121	PA de Silva and A Ranatunga at Moratuwa	1993/94
6th	103	A Ranatunga and HP Tillakaratne at Moratuwa	1993/94
7th	43	PA de Silva and GP Wickramasinghe at Centurion Park	1997/98
8th	117	DPMD Jayawardene and WPUJC Vaas at Galle	2000
9th	48	GP Wickramasinghe and M Muralitharan at Newlands	1997/98
10th	22	WPUJC Vaas and M Muralitharan at Galle	2000

BOWLING

MOST WICKETS IN A SERIES

		Wickets	Matches		
For South Africa:	In South Africa:	14	2	AA Donald (Avg 18.35)	1997/98
	In Sri Lanka:	20	3	BN Schultz (Avg 16.30)	1993/94

For Sri Lanka:	In South Africa:	16	2	M Muralitharan (Avg 25.00)	1997/98
	In Sri Lanka:	26	3	M Muralitharan (Avg 18.46)	2000

BEST BOWLING IN A MATCH

For South Africa:

9-106	BN Schultz	at Colombo-SSC	1993/94

For Sri Lanka:

13-171	M Muralitharan	at Galle	2000

BEST BOWLING IN AN INNINGS

For South Africa:

6-30	SM Pollock	at Newlands	2000/01

For Sri Lanka:

7-84	M Muralitharan	at Galle	2000

SOUTH AFRICA versus WEST INDIES

Season	Venue	SA captain	WI captain	Won by SA	Won by WI	Drawn	Total
1991/92	West Indies	KC Wessels	RB Richardson	0	1	0	1
1998/99	South Africa	WJ Cronje	BC Lara	5	0	0	5
2000/01	West Indies	SM Pollock	CL Hooper	2	1	2	5
	Total			7	2	2	11

HIGHEST INNINGS TOTALS

For South Africa:	454	at Bridgetown (3rd Test)	2000/01
For West Indies:	387	at Bridgetown (3rd Test)	2000/01

LOWEST INNINGS TOTALS

For South Africa:	141	at Kingston (5th Test)	2000/01
For West Indies:	121	at St George's Park (2nd Test)	1998/99

LARGEST MARGINS OF VICTORY

South Africa beat West Indies at Centurion Park by 351 runs	1998/99
South Africa beat West Indies at St George's Park by 178 runs	1998/99
South Africa beat West Indies at Newlands by 149 runs	1998/99
West Indies beat South Africa at Kingston by 130 runs	2000/01
South Africa beat West Indies at Kingsmead by 9 wickets	1998/99

NARROWEST MARGINS OF VICTORY

South Africa beat West Indies at Wanderers Stadium by 4 wickets	1998/99
West Indies beat South Africa at Bridgetown by 52 runs	1991/92
South Africa beat West Indies at Port of Spain by 69 runs	2000/01

BATTING

INDIVIDUAL CENTURIES

For South Africa (10):

100	MV Boucher	at Centurion Park	1998/99
168	DJ Cullinan (3)	at Newlands	1998/99
103		at Port of Spain	2000/01
134		at Bridgetown	2000/01
163	AC Hudson	at Bridgetown	1991/92
110	JH Kallis	at Newlands	1998/99
134	G Kirsten (2)	at Centurion Park	1998/99
150		at Georgetown	2000/01
106*	SM Pollock	at Bridgetown	2000/01
103*	JN Rhodes	at Centurion Park	1998/99

For West Indies (1):

113*	RD Jacobs	at Bridgetown	2000/01

HIGHEST AGGREGATE IN A SERIES

		Runs	Matches		
For South Africa:	In South Africa:	485	5	JH Kallis (Avg 69.28)	1998/99
	In West Indies:	464	5	HH Gibbs (Avg 51.55)	2000/01
For West Indies:	In South Africa:	317	5	RD Jacobs (Avg 45.28)	1998/99
	In West Indies:	400	5	BC Lara (Avg 40.00)	2000/01

HIGHEST INDIVIDUAL INNINGS

For South Africa:	In South Africa:	168	DJ Cullinan at Newlands	1988/99
	In West Indies:	163	AC Hudson at Bridgetown	1991/92
For West Indies:	In South Africa:	86	CL Hooper at Newlands	1998/99
	In West Indies:	113*	RD Jacobs at Bridgetown	2000/01

RECORD PARTNERSHIP FOR EACH WICKET

For South Africa:

1st	97	G Kirsten and HH Gibbs at Kingsmead	1998/99
2nd	146	G Kirsten and JH Kallis at Georgetown	2000/01
3rd	235	JH Kallis and DJ Cullinan at Newlands	1998/99
4th	149	DJ Cullinan and ND McKenzie at Bridgetown	2000/01
5th	115	G Kirsten and JN Rhodes at Centurion Park	1998/99
6th	92	JN Rhodes and SM Pollock at St George's Park	1998/99
7th	92	JH Kallis and MV Boucher at Centurion Park	1998/99
8th	75	SM Pollock and N Boje at St John's	2000/01
9th	132	SM Pollock and AA Donald at Bridgetown	2000/01
10th	25	PL Symcox and DJ Terbrugge at Wanderers Stadium	1998/99

For West Indies:

1st	99	DL Haynes and PV Simmons at Bridgetown	1991/92
2nd	88	CH Gayle and MN Samuels at Georgetown	2000/01
3rd	160	S Chanderpaul and BC Lara at Kingsmead	1998/99
4th	91	S Chanderpaul and CL Hooper at Wanderers Stadium	1998/99
5th	116	BC Lara and CL Hooper at Bridgetown	2000/01
6th	92	RR Sarwan and CL Hooper at Port of Spain	2000/01
7th	81	RD Jacobs and NAM McLean at Centurion Park	1998/99
8th	65	RD Jacobs and NAM McLean at Newlands	1998/99
9th	71	RD Jacobs and M Dillon at Port of Spain	2000/01
10th	64	RD Jacobs and M Dillon at Newlands	1998/99

BOWLING

MOST WICKETS IN A SERIES

		Wickets	Matches		
For South Africa:	In South Africa:	29	5	SM Pollock (Avg 16.65)	1998/99
	In West Indies:	20	5	JH Kallis (Avg 19.75)	2000/01
		20	5	SM Pollock (Avg 23.20)	2000/01
For West Indies:	In South Africa:	22	4	CA Walsh (Avg 18.90)	1998/99
	In West Indies:	25	5	CA Walsh (Avg 19.68)	2000/01

BEST BOWLING IN A MATCH

For South Africa:

9-94	SM Pollock	at Kingston	2000/01

For West Indies:

8-79	CEL Ambrose	at St George's Park	1998/99

BEST BOWLING IN AN INNINGS

For South Africa:

6-67	JH Kallis	at Bridgetown	2000/01

For West Indies:

7-84	FA Rose	at Kingsmead	1998/99

WICKETKEEPING

MOST DISMISSALS IN A SERIES

For South Africa:

18	(ct 18)	MV Boucher in West Indies	2000/01

For West Indies:

21	(ct 21)	RD Jacobs in West Indies	2000/01

FIELDING

MOST CATCHES IN A SERIES

For South Africa:	10	WJ Cronje in South Africa	1998/99
	10	DJ Cullinan in West Indies	2000/01
For West Indies:	8	CL Hooper in South Africa	1998/99
	7	CH Gayle in West Indies	2000/01

MOST CATCHES IN AN INNINGS

For South Africa:	4	HH Gibbs at Kingsmead	1998/99
For West Indies:	4	CL Hooper at St George's Park	1998/99

SOUTH AFRICA versus ZIMBABWE

Season	Venue	SA captain	Zimbabwe captain	Won by SA	Won by Zim	Drawn	Total
1995/96	Zimbabwe	WJ Cronje	A Flower	1	0	0	1
1999/00	South Africa	WJ Cronje	ADR Campbell	1	0	0	1
1999/00	Zimbabwe	WJ Cronje	A Flower	1	0	0	1
	Total			3	0	0	3

HIGHEST INNINGS TOTALS

For South Africa:	462-9*	at Harare (Only Test)	1999/00
For Zimbabwe:	283	at Harare (Only Test)	1995/96

LOWEST INNINGS TOTALS

For South Africa:	346	at Harare (Only Test)	1995/96
For Zimbabwe:	102	at Harare (Only Test)	1999/00

LARGEST MARGINS OF VICTORY

South Africa beat Zimbabwe at Harare by an innings and 219 runs 1999/00

BATTING

INDIVIDUAL CENTURIES

For South Africa (3):

125	MV Boucher	at Harare	1999/00
135	AC Hudson	at Harare	1995/96
115	JH Kallis	at Harare	1999/00

HIGHEST INDIVIDUAL INNINGS

For South Africa:	In South Africa:	70	JN Rhodes at Springbok Park	1999/00
	In Zimbabwe:	135	AC Hudson at Harare	1995/96
For Zimbabwe:	In South Africa:	85	GJ Whittall at Springbok Park	1999/00
	In Zimbabwe:	63	A Flower at Harare	1995/96

SOUTH AFRICAN TEST MATCH RECORDS

RECORD PARTNERSHIP FOR EACH WICKET

For South Africa:

1st	43	HH Dippenaar and AM Bacher at Springbok Park	1999/00
2nd	76	HH Dippenaar and JH Kallis at Harare	1999/00
3rd	56	JH Kallis and DJ Cullinan at Springbok Park	1999/00
4th	100	JH Kallis and WJ Cronje at Harare	1999/00
5th	60	AC Hudson and JN Rhodes at Harare	1995/96
6th	101	AC Hudson and BM McMillan at Harare	1995/96
7th	44	MV Boucher and L Klusener at Harare	1999/00
8th	148	MV Boucher and SM Pollock at Harare	1999/00
9th	79	BM McMillan and AA Donald at Harare	1995/96
10th	54	MV Boucher and PR Adams at Springbok Park	1999/00

For Zimbabwe:

1st	13	MH Dekker and GW Flower at Harare	1995/96
2nd	51	MH Dekker and ADR Campbell at Harare	1995/96
3rd	29	MW Goodwin and NC Johnson at Harare	1999/00
4th	53	ADR Campbell and A Flower at Springbok Park	1999/00
5th	97	A Flower and GJ Whittall at Harare	1995/96
6th	15	ADR Campbell and GJ Rennie at Harare	1999/00
7th	45	GJ Rennie and GJ Whittall at Harare	1999/00
8th	43	CB Wishart and HH Streak at Harare	1995/96
9th	48	PA Strang and BC Strang at Harare	1995/96
10th	42	HH Streak and ACI Lock at Harare	1995/96

BOWLING

10 WICKETS IN A MATCH

For South Africa:	11-113	AA Donald	at Harare	1995/96
For Zimbabwe:	No instance. The best performance is 5-105 by ACI Lock at Harare			1995/96

SEVEN WICKETS IN AN INNINGS

For South Africa:	8-71	AA Donald	at Harare	1995/96
For Zimbabwe:	No instance. The best performance is 5-101 by BC Strang at Harare			1995/96

SOUTH AFRICA TEST CAREER RECORDS

As at 1 September 2001

Name	M	Inns	NO	Runs	HS	Avg	100	50	Ct	St	Balls	Runs	Wkts	Avg	BB	5I	10M
HD Ackerman	4	8	0	161	57	20.12	0	1	1	0	0	0	0	-	-	0	0
PR Adams	34	41	11	197	29	6.56	0	0	21	0	6606	3063	96	31.90	6-55	1	0
NAT Adcock	26	39	12	146	24	5.40	0	0	4	0	6391	2195	104	21.10	6-43	5	0
JH Anderson	1	2	0	43	32	21.50	0	0	1	0	0	0	0	-	-	0	0
WH Ashley	1	2	0	1	1	0.50	0	0	0	0	173	95	7	13.57	7-95	1	0
A Bacher	12	22	1	679	73	32.33	0	6	10	0	0	0	0	-	-	0	0
AM Bacher	19	33	1	833	96	26.03	0	5	11	0	6	4	0	-	-	0	0
XC Balaskas	9	13	1	174	122*	14.50	1	0	5	0	1572	806	22	36.63	5-49	1	0
EJ Barlow	30	57	2	2516	201	45.74	6	15	35	0	3021	1362	40	34.05	5-85	1	0
HV Baumgartner	1	2	0	19	16	9.50	0	0	1	0	166	99	2	49.50	2-99	0	0
R Beaumont	5	9	0	70	31	7.77	0	0	2	0	6	0	0	-	-	0	0
DW Begbie	5	7	0	138	48	19.71	0	0	2	0	160	130	1	130.00	1-38	0	0
AJ Bell	16	23	12	69	26*	6.27	0	0	6	0	3342	1567	48	32.64	6-99	4	0
M Bisset	3	6	2	103	35	25.75	0	0	2	1	0	0	0	-	-	0	0
GF Bissett	4	4	2	38	23	19.00	0	0	0	0	989	469	25	18.76	7-29	2	0
JM Blanckenberg	18	30	7	455	59	19.78	0	2	9	0	3888	1817	60	30.28	6-76	4	0
KC Bland	21	39	5	1669	144*	49.08	3	9	10	0	394	125	2	62.50	2-16	0	0
EG Bock	1	2	2	11	9*	-	0	0	0	0	138	91	0	-	-	0	0
N Boje	15	22	3	522	85	27.47	0	2	8	0	2958	1159	44	26.34	5-62	2	0
GE Bond	1	1	0	0	0	0.00	0	0	0	0	16	16	0	-	-	0	0
T Bosch	1	2	2	5	5*	-	0	0	0	0	237	104	3	34.66	2-61	0	0
JT Botten	3	6	0	65	33	10.83	0	0	1	0	828	337	8	42.12	2-56	0	0
MV Boucher	42	57	6	1439	125	28.21	3	8	163	4	0	0	0	-	-	0	0
WH Brann	3	5	0	71	50	14.20	0	1	2	0	0	0	0	-	-	0	0
AW Briscoe	2	3	0	33	16	11.00	0	0	1	0	0	0	0	-	-	0	0
HD Bromfield	9	12	7	59	21	11.80	0	0	13	0	1810	599	17	35.23	5-88	1	0
LS Brown	2	3	0	17	8	5.66	0	0	0	0	318	189	3	63.00	1-30	0	0
CGdeV Burger	2	4	1	62	37*	20.66	0	0	1	0	0	0	0	-	-	0	0
SF Burke	2	4	1	42	20	14.00	0	0	0	0	660	257	11	23.36	6-128	2	1
ID Buys	1	2	1	4	4*	4.00	0	0	0	0	144	52	0	-	-	0	0

SOUTH AFRICA TEST CAREER RECORDS

Name	M	Inns	NO	Runs	HS	Avg	100	50	Ct	St	Balls	Runs	Wkts	Avg	BB	5I	10M
HB Cameron	26	45	4	1239	90	30.21	0	10	39	12	0	0	0	-	-	0	0
T Campbell	5	9	3	90	48	15.00	0	0	7	1	0	0	0	-	-	0	0
PR Carlstein	8	14	1	190	42	14.61	0	0	3	0	0	0	0	-	-	0	0
CP Carter	10	15	5	181	45	18.10	0	0	2	0	1475	694	28	24.78	6-50	2	0
RH Catterall	24	43	2	1555	120	37.92	3	11	12	0	342	162	7	23.14	3-15	0	0
HW Chapman	2	4	1	39	17	13.00	0	0	1	0	126	104	1	104.00	1-51	0	0
JE Cheetham	24	43	6	883	89	23.86	0	5	13	0	6	2	0	-	-	0	0
GA Chevalier	1	2	1	0	0*	0.00	0	0	1	0	253	100	5	20.00	3-68	0	0
JAJ Christy	10	18	0	618	103	34.33	1	5	3	0	138	92	2	46.00	1-15	0	0
GWA Chubb	5	9	3	63	15*	10.50	0	0	0	0	1425	577	21	27.47	6-51	2	0
JAK Cochran	1	1	0	4	4	4.00	0	0	0	0	138	47	0	-	-	0	0
SK Coen	2	4	2	101	41*	50.50	0	0	1	0	12	7	0	-	-	0	0
JMM Commaille	12	22	1	355	47	16.90	0	0	1	0	0	0	0	-	-	0	0
JB Commins	3	6	1	125	45	25.00	0	0	2	0	0	0	0	-	-	0	0
DP Conyngham	1	2	2	6	3*	-	0	0	1	0	366	103	2	51.50	1-40	0	0
FJ Cook	1	2	0	7	7	3.50	0	0	0	0	0	0	0	-	-	0	0
SJ Cook	3	6	0	107	43	17.83	0	0	0	0	0	0	0	-	-	0	0
AHC Cooper	1	2	0	6	6	3.00	0	0	1	0	0	0	0	-	-	0	0
JL Cox	3	6	1	17	12*	3.40	0	0	1	0	576	245	4	61.25	2-74	0	0
G Cripps	1	2	0	21	18	10.50	0	0	0	0	15	23	0	-	-	0	0
RJ Crisp	9	13	1	123	35	10.25	0	0	3	0	1428	747	20	37.35	5-99	1	0
WJ Cronje	68	111	9	3714	135	36.41	6	23	33	0	3800	1288	43	29.95	3-14	0	0
DJ Cullinan	70	115	12	4554	275*	44.21	14	20	67	0	120	71	2	35.50	1-10	0	0
SH Curnow	7	14	0	168	47	12.00	0	0	5	0	0	0	0	-	-	0	0
EL Dalton	15	24	2	698	117	31.72	2	3	5	0	864	490	12	40.83	4-59	0	0
EQ Davies	5	8	3	9	3	1.80	0	0	0	0	768	481	7	68.71	4-75	0	0
OC Dawson	9	15	1	293	55	20.92	0	1	10	0	1294	578	10	57.80	2-57	0	0
PS de Villiers	18	26	7	359	67*	18.89	0	2	11	0	4805	2063	85	24.27	6-23	5	2
HG Deane	17	27	2	628	93	25.12	0	3	8	0	0	0	0	-	-	0	0
HH Dippenaar	7	10	0	268	100	26.80	1	0	3	0	0	0	0	-	-	0	0
CD Dixon	1	2	0	0	0	0.00	0	0	1	0	240	118	3	39.33	2-62	0	0
AA Donald	69	88	31	638	37	11.19	0	0	17	0	15037	7034	325	21.64	8-71	20	3
RR Dower	1	2	0	9	9	4.50	0	0	2	0	0	0	0	-	-	0	0
RG Draper	2	3	0	25	15	8.33	0	0	0	0	0	0	0	-	-	0	0
JH du Preez	2	2	0	0	0	0.00	0	0	2	0	144	51	3	17.00	2-22	0	0
JF du Toit	1	2	2	2	2*	-	0	0	1	0	85	47	1	47.00	1-47	0	0

SOUTH AFRICA TEST CAREER RECORDS

Name	M	Inns	NO	Runs	HS	Avg	100	50	Ct	St	Balls	Runs	Wkts	Avg	BB	5I	10M
CAR Duckworth	2	4	0	28	13	7.00	0	0	3	0	0	0	0	-	-	0	0
R Dumbrill	5	10	0	153	36	15.30	0	0	3	0	816	336	9	37.33	4-30	0	0
JP Duminy	3	6	0	30	12	5.00	0	0	2	0	60	39	1	39.00	1-17	0	0
OR Dunell	2	4	1	42	26*	14.00	0	0	1	0	0	0	0	-	-	0	0
DV Dyer	3	6	0	96	62	16.00	0	1	0	0	0	0	0	-	-	0	0
CE Eksteen	7	11	2	91	22	10.11	0	0	5	0	1536	494	8	61.75	3-12	0	0
MK Elgie	3	6	0	75	56	12.50	0	1	4	0	66	46	0	-	-	0	0
S Elworthy	2	3	1	61	48	30.50	0	0	0	0	516	238	9	26.44	4-66	0	0
WR Endean	28	52	4	1630	162*	33.95	3	8	41	0	0	0	0	-	-	0	0
WS Farrer	6	10	2	221	40	27.62	0	0	2	0	0	0	0	-	-	0	0
GA Faulkner	25	47	4	1754	204	40.79	4	8	20	0	4227	2180	82	26.58	7-84	4	0
JP Fellows-Smith	4	8	2	166	35	27.66	0	0	2	0	114	61	0	-	-	0	0
CG Fichardt	2	4	0	15	10	3.75	0	0	2	0	0	0	0	-	-	0	0
CE Finlason	1	2	0	6	6	3.00	0	0	0	0	12	7	0	-	-	0	0
CE Floquet	1	2	1	12	11*	12.00	0	0	0	0	48	24	0	-	-	0	0
HH Francis	2	4	0	39	29	9.75	0	0	1	0	0	0	0	-	-	0	0
CM Francois	5	9	1	252	72	31.50	0	1	5	0	684	225	6	37.50	3-23	0	0
CN Frank	3	6	0	236	152	39.33	1	0	0	0	0	0	0	-	-	0	0
WHB Frank	1	2	0	7	5	3.50	0	0	0	0	58	52	1	52.00	1-52	0	0
ERH Fuller	7	9	1	64	17	8.00	0	0	3	0	1898	668	22	30.36	5-66	1	0
GM Fullerton	7	13	0	325	88	25.00	0	3	10	2	0	0	0	-	-	0	0
KJ Funston	18	33	1	824	92	25.75	0	5	7	0	0	0	0	-	-	0	0
D Gamsy	2	3	1	39	30*	19.50	0	0	5	0	0	0	0	-	-	0	0
HH Gibbs	28	47	2	1563	211*	34.73	2	7	19	0	0	0	0	-	-	0	0
RA Gleeson	1	2	1	4	3	4.00	0	0	2	0	0	0	0	-	-	0	0
GK Glover	1	2	1	21	18*	21.00	0	0	0	0	65	28	1	28.00	1-28	0	0
TL Goddard	41	78	5	2516	112	34.46	1	18	48	0	11736	3226	123	26.22	6-53	5	0
N Gordon	5	6	2	8	7*	2.00	0	0	1	0	1966	807	20	40.35	5-103	2	0
R Graham	2	4	0	6	4	1.50	0	0	2	0	240	127	3	42.33	2-22	0	0
RE Grieveson	2	2	0	114	75	57.00	0	1	7	3	0	0	0	-	-	0	0
GM Griffin	2	4	0	25	14	6.25	0	0	0	0	432	192	8	24.00	4-87	0	0
AE Hall	7	8	2	11	5	1.83	0	0	4	0	2361	886	40	22.15	7-63	3	1
GG Hall	1	1	0	0	0	0.00	0	0	0	0	186	94	1	94.00	1-94	0	0
EA Halliwell	8	15	0	188	57	12.53	0	1	9	2	0	0	0	-	-	0	0
CG Halse	3	3	3	30	19*	-	0	0	1	0	587	260	6	43.33	3-50	0	0
PAM Hands	7	12	0	300	83	25.00	0	2	3	0	37	18	0	-	-	0	0

SOUTH AFRICA TEST CAREER RECORDS

Name	M	Inns	NO	Runs	HS	Avg	100	50	Ct	St	Balls	Runs	Wkts	Avg	BB	5I	10M
RHM Hands	1	2	0	7	7	3.50	0	0	0	0	0	0	0	-	-	0	0
MA Hanley	1	1	0	0	0	0.00	0	0	0	0	232	88	1	88.00	1-57	0	0
TA Harris	3	5	1	100	60	25.00	0	1	1	0	0	0	0	-	-	0	0
GPD Hartigan	5	10	0	114	51	11.40	0	1	0	0	252	141	1	141.00	1-72	0	0
RL Harvey	2	4	0	51	28	12.75	0	0	0	0	0	0	0	-	-	0	0
CMH Hathorn	12	20	1	325	102	17.10	1	0	5	0	0	0	0	-	-	0	0
M Hayward	6	7	4	26	13	8.66	0	0	1	0	1034	507	19	26.68	4-75	0	0
F Hearne	4	8	0	121	30	15.12	0	0	2	0	62	40	2	20.00	2-40	0	0
GAL Hearne	3	5	0	59	28	11.80	0	0	3	0	0	0	0	-	-	0	0
PS Heine	14	24	3	209	31	9.95	0	0	8	0	3890	1455	58	25.08	6-58	4	0
O Henry	3	3	0	53	34	17.66	0	0	2	0	427	189	3	63.00	2-56	0	0
CFW Hime	1	2	0	8	8	4.00	0	0	0	0	55	31	1	31.00	1-20	0	0
AC Hudson	35	63	3	2007	163	33.45	4	13	36	0	0	0	0	-	-	0	0
P Hutchinson	2	4	0	14	11	3.50	0	0	3	0	0	0	0	-	-	0	0
DEJ Ironside	3	4	2	37	13	18.50	0	0	1	0	986	275	15	18.33	5-51	1	0
BL Irvine	4	7	0	353	102	50.42	1	2	2	0	0	0	0	-	-	0	0
SD Jack	2	2	0	7	7	3.50	0	0	1	0	462	196	8	24.50	4-69	0	0
CL Johnson	1	2	0	10	7	5.00	0	0	1	0	140	57	0	-	-	0	0
JH Kallis	50	81	9	2952	160	41.00	7	16	43	0	6489	2580	94	27.44	6-67	2	0
HJ Keith	8	16	1	318	73	21.20	0	2	9	0	108	63	0	-	-	0	0
JM Kemp	3	4	0	18	16	4.50	0	0	3	0	395	151	8	18.87	3-33	0	0
GA Kempis	1	2	1	0	0*	0.00	0	0	0	0	168	76	4	19.00	3-53	0	0
G Kirsten	73	129	10	4806	275	40.38	12	23	62	0	325	135	2	67.50	1-0	0	0
PN Kirsten	12	22	2	626	104	31.30	1	4	8	0	54	30	0	-	-	0	0
L Klusener	42	59	10	1676	174	34.20	3	8	28	0	5969	2618	73	35.86	8-64	1	0
JJ Kotze	3	5	0	2	2	0.40	0	0	3	0	413	243	6	40.50	3-64	0	0
AP Kuiper	1	2	0	34	34	17.00	0	0	1	0	0	0	0	-	-	0	0
F Kuys	1	2	0	26	26	13.00	0	0	0	0	60	31	2	15.50	2-31	0	0
HR Lance	13	22	1	591	70	28.14	0	5	7	0	948	479	12	39.91	3-30	0	0
ACB Langton	15	23	4	298	73*	15.68	0	2	8	0	4199	1827	40	45.67	5-58	1	0
GB Lawrence	5	8	0	141	43	17.62	0	0	2	0	1334	512	28	18.28	8-53	2	0
FL le Roux	1	2	0	1	1	0.50	0	0	0	0	54	24	0	-	-	0	0
PT Lewis	1	2	0	0	0	0.00	0	0	0	0	0	0	0	-	-	0	0
GFJ Liebenberg	5	8	0	104	45	13.00	0	0	1	0	0	0	0	-	-	0	0
DT Lindsay	19	31	1	1130	182	37.66	3	5	57	2	0	0	0	-	-	0	0
JD Lindsay	3	5	2	21	9*	7.00	0	0	4	1	0	0	0	-	-	0	0

SOUTH AFRICA TEST CAREER RECORDS

Name	M	Inns	NO	Runs	HS	Avg	100	50	Ct	St	Balls	Runs	Wkts	Avg	BB	5I	10M
NV Lindsay	1	2	0	35	29	17.50	0	0	1	0	0	0	0	-	-	0	0
WVS Ling	6	10	0	168	38	16.80	0	0	1	0	18	20	0	-	-	0	0
CB Llewellyn	15	28	1	544	90	20.14	0	4	7	0	2292	1421	48	29.60	6-92	4	1
EB Lundie	1	2	1	1	1	1.00	0	0	0	0	286	107	4	26.75	4-101	0	0
MJ Macaulay	1	2	0	33	21	16.50	0	0	0	0	276	73	2	36.50	1-10	0	0
NBF Mann	19	31	1	400	52	13.33	0	1	3	0	5796	1920	58	33.10	6-59	1	0
PNF Mansell	13	22	2	355	90	17.75	0	2	15	0	1506	736	11	66.90	3-58	0	0
LA Markham	1	1	0	20	20	20.00	0	0	0	0	104	72	1	72.00	1-34	0	0
WFE Marx	3	6	0	125	36	20.83	0	0	0	0	228	144	4	36.00	3-85	0	0
CR Matthews	18	25	6	348	62*	18.31	0	1	4	0	3980	1502	52	28.88	5-42	2	0
CN McCarthy	15	24	15	28	5	3.11	0	0	6	0	3499	1510	36	41.94	6-43	2	0
DJ McGlew	34	64	6	2440	255*	42.06	7	10	18	0	32	23	0	-	-	0	0
ND McKenzie	14	23	2	722	120	34.38	2	3	13	0	0	0	0	-	-	0	0
AH McKinnon	8	13	7	107	27	17.83	0	0	1	0	2546	925	26	35.57	4-128	0	0
RA McLean	40	73	3	2120	142	30.28	5	10	23	0	4	1	0	-	-	0	0
BM McMillan	38	62	12	1968	113	39.36	3	13	49	0	6048	2537	75	33.82	4-65	0	0
Q McMillan	13	21	4	306	50*	18.00	0	1	8	0	2021	1243	36	34.52	5-66	2	0
DJ Meintjes	2	3	0	43	21	14.33	0	0	3	0	246	115	6	19.16	3-38	0	0
MG Melle	7	12	4	68	17	8.50	0	0	4	0	1667	851	26	32.73	6-71	2	0
A Melville	11	19	2	894	189	52.58	4	3	8	0	0	0	0	-	-	0	0
J Middleton	6	12	5	52	22	7.42	0	0	1	0	1064	442	24	18.41	5-51	2	0
CH Mills	1	2	0	25	21	12.50	0	0	2	0	140	83	2	41.50	2-83	0	0
WH Milton	3	6	0	68	21	11.33	0	0	1	0	79	48	2	24.00	1-5	0	0
B Mitchell	42	80	9	3471	189*	48.88	8	21	56	0	2519	1380	27	51.11	5-87	1	0
F Mitchell	3	6	0	28	12	4.66	0	0	0	0	0	0	0	-	-	0	0
DPB Morkel	16	28	1	663	88	24.55	0	4	13	0	1704	821	18	45.61	4-93	0	0
ARA Murray	10	14	1	289	109	22.23	1	1	3	0	2374	710	18	39.44	4-169	0	0
JD Nel	6	11	0	150	38	13.63	0	0	1	0	0	0	0	-	-	0	0
C Newberry	4	8	0	62	16	7.75	0	0	3	0	558	268	11	24.36	4-72	0	0
ES Newson	3	5	1	30	16	7.50	0	0	3	0	874	265	4	66.25	2-58	0	0
M Ngam	3	1	1	0	0*	-	0	0	1	0	392	189	11	17.18	3-26	0	0
F Nicholson	4	8	1	76	29	10.85	0	0	3	0	0	0	0	-	-	0	0
JFW Nicolson	3	5	0	179	78	35.80	0	1	0	0	24	17	0	-	-	0	0
NO Norton	1	2	0	9	7	4.50	0	0	0	0	90	47	4	11.75	4-47	0	0
AD Nourse	34	62	7	2960	231	53.81	9	14	12	0	20	9	0	-	-	0	0
AW Nourse	45	83	8	2234	111	29.78	1	15	43	0	3234	1553	41	37.87	4-25	0	0

SOUTH AFRICA TEST CAREER RECORDS

Name	M	Inns	NO	Runs	HS	Avg	100	50	Ct	St	Balls	Runs	Wkts	Avg	BB	5I	10M
M Ntini	15	15	6	58	11	6.44	0	0	4	0	2505	1169	41	28.51	6-66	1	0
EP Nupen	17	31	7	348	69	14.50	0	2	9	0	4159	1788	50	35.76	6-46	5	1
S O'Linn	7	12	1	297	98	27.00	0	2	4	0	0	0	0	-	-	0	0
AE Ochse	2	4	0	16	8	4.00	0	0	0	0	0	0	0	-	-	0	0
AL Ochse	3	4	1	11	4*	3.66	0	0	1	0	649	362	10	36.20	4-79	0	0
HGO Owen-Smith	5	8	2	252	129	42.00	1	1	4	0	156	113	0	-	-	0	0
AW Palm	1	2	0	15	13	7.50	0	0	1	0	0	0	0	-	-	0	0
GM Parker	2	4	2	3	2*	1.50	0	0	0	0	366	273	8	34.12	6-152	1	0
DC Parkin	1	2	0	6	6	3.00	0	0	1	0	130	82	3	27.33	3-82	0	0
JT Partridge	11	12	5	73	13*	10.42	0	0	6	0	3684	1373	44	31.20	7-91	3	0
COC Pearse	3	6	0	55	31	9.16	0	0	1	0	144	106	3	35.33	3-56	0	0
SJ Pegler	16	28	5	356	35*	15.47	0	0	5	0	2989	1572	47	33.44	7-65	2	0
AJ Pithey	17	27	1	819	154	31.50	1	4	3	0	12	5	0	-	-	0	0
DB Pithey	8	12	1	138	55	12.54	0	1	6	0	1424	577	12	48.08	6-58	1	0
JB Plimsoll	1	2	1	16	8*	16.00	0	0	0	0	237	143	3	47.66	3-128	0	0
PM Pollock	28	41	13	607	75*	21.67	0	2	9	0	6522	2806	116	24.18	6-38	9	1
RG Pollock	23	41	4	2256	274	60.97	7	11	17	0	414	204	4	51.00	2-50	0	0
SM Pollock	56	81	17	2015	111	31.48	2	8	36	0	12428	4694	231	20.32	7-87	12	0
RM Poore	3	6	0	76	20	12.66	0	0	3	0	9	4	1	4.00	1-4	0	0
JE Pothecary	3	4	0	26	12	6.50	0	0	2	0	828	354	9	39.33	4-58	0	0
AW Powell	1	2	0	16	11	8.00	0	0	2	0	20	10	1	10.00	1-10	0	0
CFH Prince	1	2	0	6	5	3.00	0	0	0	0	0	0	0	-	-	0	0
MW Pringle	4	6	2	67	33	16.75	0	0	0	0	652	270	5	54.00	2-62	0	0
MJ Procter	7	10	1	226	48	25.11	0	0	4	0	1514	616	41	15.02	6-73	1	0
HLE Promnitz	2	4	0	14	5	3.50	0	0	2	0	528	161	8	20.12	5-58	1	0
NA Quinn	12	18	3	90	28	6.00	0	0	1	0	2922	1145	35	32.71	6-92	1	0
N Reid	1	2	0	17	11	8.50	0	0	0	0	126	63	2	31.50	2-63	0	0
JN Rhodes	52	80	9	2532	117	35.66	3	17	34	0	12	5	0	-	-	0	0
AR Richards	1	2	0	6	6	3.00	0	0	0	0	0	0	0	-	-	0	0
BA Richards	4	7	0	508	140	72.57	2	2	3	0	72	26	1	26.00	1-12	0	0
WHM Richards	1	2	0	4	4	2.00	0	0	0	0	0	0	0	-	-	0	0
DJ Richardson	42	64	8	1359	109	24.26	1	8	150	2	0	0	0	-	-	0	0
JB Robertson	3	6	1	51	17	10.20	0	0	2	0	738	321	6	53.50	3-143	0	0
A Rose-Innes	2	4	0	14	13	3.50	0	0	2	0	128	89	5	17.80	5-43	1	0
TW Routledge	4	8	0	72	24	9.00	0	0	2	0	0	0	0	-	-	0	0
AMB Rowan	15	23	6	290	41	17.05	0	0	7	0	5193	2084	54	38.59	5-68	4	0

SOUTH AFRICA TEST CAREER RECORDS

Name	M	Inns	NO	Runs	HS	Avg	100	50	Ct	St	Balls	Runs	Wkts	Avg	BB	5I	10M
EAB Rowan	26	50	5	1965	236	43.66	3	12	14	0	19	7	0	-	-	0	0
GA Rowe	5	9	3	26	13*	4.33	0	0	4	0	998	456	15	30.40	5-115	1	0
MW Rushmere	1	2	0	6	3	3.00	0	0	0	0	0	0	0	-	-	0	0
SV Samuelson	1	2	0	22	15	11.00	0	0	1	0	108	64	0	-	-	0	0
BN Schultz	9	8	2	9	6	1.50	0	0	2	0	1733	749	37	20.24	5-48	2	0
RO Schwarz	20	35	8	374	61	13.85	0	1	18	0	2639	1417	55	25.76	6-47	2	0
AW Seccull	1	2	1	23	17*	23.00	0	0	1	0	60	37	2	18.50	2-37	0	0
MA Seymour	7	10	3	84	36	12.00	0	0	2	0	1458	588	9	65.33	3-80	0	0
WA Shalders	12	23	1	355	42	16.13	0	0	3	0	48	6	1	6.00	1-6	0	0
GH Shepstone	2	4	0	38	21	9.50	0	0	2	0	115	47	0	-	-	0	0
PW Sherwell	13	22	4	427	115	23.72	1	1	20	16	0	0	0	-	-	0	0
IJ Siedle	18	34	0	977	141	28.73	1	5	7	0	19	7	1	7.00	1-7	0	0
JH Sinclair	25	47	1	1069	106	23.23	3	3	9	0	3598	1996	63	31.68	6-26	1	0
CJE Smith	3	6	1	106	45	21.20	0	0	2	0	0	0	0	-	-	0	0
FW Smith	3	6	1	45	12	9.00	0	0	2	0	0	0	0	-	-	0	0
VI Smith	9	16	6	39	11*	3.90	0	0	3	0	1655	769	12	64.08	4-143	0	0
RP Snell	5	8	1	95	48	13.57	0	0	1	0	1025	538	19	28.31	4-74	0	0
S de la C Snooke	1	1	0	0	0	0.00	0	0	2	0	0	0	0	-	-	0	0
SJ Snooke	26	46	1	1008	103	22.40	1	5	24	0	1620	702	35	20.05	8-70	1	1
WRT Solomon	1	2	0	4	2	2.00	0	0	1	0	0	0	0	-	-	0	0
RB Stewart	1	2	0	13	9	6.50	0	0	2	0	0	0	0	-	-	0	0
PJR Steyn	3	6	0	127	46	21.16	0	0	0	0	0	0	0	-	-	0	0
LA Stricker	13	24	0	342	48	14.25	0	0	3	0	174	105	1	105.00	1-36	0	0
PC Strydom	2	3	0	35	30	11.66	0	0	1	0	36	27	0	-	-	0	0
MJ Susskind	5	8	0	268	65	33.50	0	4	1	0	0	0	0	-	-	0	0
PL Symcox	20	27	1	741	108	28.50	1	4	5	0	3561	1603	37	43.32	4-69	0	0
HM Taberer	1	1	0	2	2	2.00	0	0	0	0	60	48	1	48.00	1-25	0	0
AB Tancred	2	4	1	87	29	29.00	0	0	2	0	0	0	0	-	-	0	0
LJ Tancred	14	26	1	530	97	21.20	0	2	3	0	0	0	0	-	-	0	0
VM Tancred	1	2	0	25	18	12.50	0	0	0	0	0	0	0	-	-	0	0
GL Tapscott	1	2	0	5	4	2.50	0	0	1	0	0	0	0	-	-	0	0
LE Tapscott	2	3	1	58	50*	29.00	0	1	0	0	12	2	0	-	-	0	0
HJ Tayfield	37	60	9	862	75	16.90	0	2	26	0	13568	4405	170	25.91	9-113	14	2
AI Taylor	1	2	0	18	12	9.00	0	0	0	0	0	0	0	-	-	0	0
D Taylor	2	4	0	85	36	21.25	0	0	0	0	0	0	0	-	-	0	0

SOUTH AFRICA TEST CAREER RECORDS

Name	M	Inns	NO	Runs	HS	Avg	100	50	Ct	St	Balls	Runs	Wkts	Avg	BB	5I	10M
HW Taylor	42	76	4	2936	176	40.77	7	17	19	0	342	156	5	31.20	3-15	0	0
DJ Terbrugge	4	5	5	14	4*	-	0	0	2	0	600	253	9	28.11	3-27	0	0
NHCdeJ Theunissen	1	2	1	2	2*	2.00	0	0	0	0	80	51	0	-	-	0	0
G Thornton	1	1	1	1	1*	-	0	0	1	0	24	20	1	20.00	1-20	0	0
DS Tomlinson	1	1	0	9	9	9.00	0	0	0	0	60	38	0	-	-	0	0
AJ Traicos	3	4	2	8	5*	4.00	0	0	4	0	470	207	4	51.75	2-70	0	0
PHJ Trimborn	4	4	2	13	11*	6.50	0	0	7	0	747	257	11	23.36	3-12	0	0
L Tuckett	9	14	3	131	40*	11.90	0	0	9	0	2104	980	19	51.57	5-68	2	0
LR Tuckett	1	2	1	0	0*	0.00	0	0	2	0	120	69	0	-	-	0	0
PS Twentyman Jones	1	2	0	0	0	0.00	0	0	0	0	0	0	0	-	-	0	0
PGV van der Bijl	5	9	0	460	125	51.11	1	2	1	0	0	0	0	-	-	0	0
EA van der Merwe	2	4	1	27	19	9.00	0	0	3	0	0	0	0	-	-	0	0
PL van der Merwe	15	23	2	533	76	25.38	0	3	11	0	79	22	1	22.00	1-6	0	0
CB van Ryneveld	19	33	6	724	83	26.81	0	3	14	0	1554	671	17	39.47	4-67	0	0
GD Varnals	3	6	0	97	23	16.16	0	0	0	0	12	2	0	-	-	0	0
KG Viljoen	27	50	2	1365	124	28.43	2	9	5	0	48	23	0	-	-	0	0
CL Vincent	25	38	12	526	60	20.23	0	2	27	0	5851	2631	84	31.32	6-51	3	0
CH Vintcent	3	6	0	26	9	4.33	0	0	1	0	369	193	4	48.25	3-88	0	0
AEE Vogler	15	26	6	340	65	17.00	0	2	20	0	2764	1455	64	22.73	7-94	5	1
HF Wade	10	18	2	327	40*	20.43	0	0	4	0	0	0	0	-	-	0	0
WW Wade	11	19	1	511	125	28.38	1	3	15	2	0	0	0	-	-	0	0
JHB Waite	50	86	7	2405	134	30.44	4	16	124	17	0	0	0	-	-	0	0
KA Walter	2	3	0	11	10	3.66	0	0	3	0	495	197	6	32.83	4-63	0	0
TA Ward	23	42	9	459	64	13.90	0	2	19	13	0	0	0	-	-	0	0
JC Watkins	15	27	1	612	92	23.53	0	3	12	0	2805	816	29	28.13	4-22	0	0
C Wesley	3	5	0	49	35	9.80	0	0	1	0	0	0	0	-	-	0	0
KC Wessels	16	29	2	1027	118	38.03	2	6	12	0	0	0	0	-	-	0	0
RJ Westcott	5	9	0	166	62	18.44	0	1	0	0	32	22	0	-	-	0	0
GC White	17	31	2	872	147	30.06	2	4	10	0	498	301	9	33.44	4-47	0	0
JT Willoughby	2	4	0	8	5	2.00	0	0	0	0	275	159	6	26.50	2-37	0	0
CS Wimble	1	2	0	0	0	0.00	0	0	0	0	0	0	0	-	-	0	0
PL Winslow	5	9	0	186	108	20.66	1	0	1	0	0	0	0	-	-	0	0
OE Wynne	6	12	0	219	50	18.25	0	1	3	0	0	0	0	-	-	0	0
JW Zulch	16	32	2	985	150	32.83	2	4	4	0	24	28	0	-	-	0	0

LIMITED OVERS INTERNATIONAL RECORDS

As at 31 August 2001

SUMMARY OF RESULTS

	Played	Won	Lost	Tied	No Result
v Australia	45	22	21	2	0
v England	23	16	7	0	0
v Holland	1	1	0	0	0
v India	38	24	13	0	1
v Kenya	3	3	0	0	0
v New Zealand (a)	27	17	7	0	3
v Pakistan	29	19	10	0	0
v Sri Lanka	25	14	10	0	1
v United Arab Emirates	1	1	0	0	0
v West Indies	25	17	8	0	0
v Zimbabwe	12	9	2	0	1
Total:	229	143	78	2	6

Note (a): Excludes one match abandoned without a ball bowled.

ONE-DAY INTERNATIONAL CAPTAINS

		Results					Toss	
		Played	Won	Lost	Tied	No Result	Won	Lost
CEB Rice	1991/92	3	1	2	0	0	1	2
KC Wessels	1991-94	52	20	30	0	2	24	28
WJ Cronje	1993-99	138	99	35	1	3	72	66
SM Pollock	1999-	36	23	11	1	1	19	17

SUMMARY OF RESULTS WHEN BATTING FIRST OR SECOND

	Played	Won	Lost	Tied	No Result
Batting first	115	73	38	1	3
Batting second	114	70	40	1	3

HIGHEST INNINGS TOTALS

FOR

328-3	(50)	v Holland (WC)	Rawalpindi	1995/96
324-4	(50)	v New Zealand	Centurion	2000/01
321-2	(50)	v United Arab Emirates (WC)	Rawalpindi	1995/96
321-8	(50)	v Pakistan	Nairobi	1996/97
320-7	(50)	v India	Nagpur	1999/00
314-7	(50)	v New Zealand	Verwoerdburg	1994/95
314-3	(50)	v Pakistan	Sharjah	1995/96
311-9	(50)	v Sri Lanka	Lahore	1997/98
310-6	(50)	v Australia	Bloemfontein	1996/97
305-8	(50)	v Kenya	Nairobi	1996/97
303-5	(50)	v Zimbabwe	Harare	1995/96
302-7	(50)	v Sri Lanka	East London	2000/01
301-3	(50)	v India	Kochi	1999/00
300-6	(50)	v New Zealand	Brisbane	1997/98

LIMITED OVERS INTERNATIONAL RECORDS

AGAINST

310	(48.5)	by India	Nagpur	1999/00
302-7	(49.4)	by India	Kochi	1999/00
298-9	(50)	by New Zealand	Brisbane	1997/98
295-5	(50)	by Australia	Melbourne-Colonial	2000
295-6	(50)	by India	Nairobi	2000/01
294-7	(50)	by Sri Lanka	Colombo-RPS	2000
293-8	(50)	by West Indies	Lahore	1997/98
292-9	(50)	by West Indies	East London	1998/99
287-4	(50)	by India	New Delhi	1991/92
287-6	(50)	by West Indies	Kingston	1991/92
287-5	(49)	by Australia	Centurion	1996/97
287-6	(50)	by New Zealand	Kimberley	2000/01

LOWEST INNINGS TOTALS

(Excludes reduced overs matches)

FOR

69	(28)	v Australia	Sydney	1993/94
101	(26.5)	v Pakistan	Sharjah	1999/00
117	(48)	v India	Nairobi	1999/00
123	(46.2)	v Australia	Wellington	1994/95
129	(41.4)	v England	East London	1995/96
140-9	(50)	v West Indies	Cape Town	1992/93
144-9	(50)	v Australia	Cape Town	1999/00
147-7	(50)	v New Zealand	Hobart	1993/94
149	(45)	v England	Johannesburg	1999/00
152	(43.4)	v West Indies	Port of Spain	1991/92

AGAINST

98	(34)	by Sri Lanka	Colombo-RPS	1993/94
103	(25.1)	by Kenya	Nairobi	1996/97
103	(41)	by England (WC)	The Oval	1999
105	(36)	by Sri Lanka	Bloemfontein	1997/98
109	(32.3)	by Pakistan	Johannesburg	1994/95
110	(35.2)	by Sri Lanka (WC)	Northampton	1999
111	(38)	by England	Johannesburg	1999/00
114	(37.1)	by Pakistan	Cape Town	1997/98
115	(43.4)	by England	East London	1995/96
121	(28.1)	by Pakistan	Singapore	2000

Note: The lowest in South Africa is:

43	(19.5)	Pakistan v West Indies	Cape Town	1992/93

This is the lowest total in Limited Overs Internationals

HIGHEST TOTALS BATTING SECOND BY SOUTH AFRICA

297-5	(48.1)	v West Indies (won)	Lahore	1997/98
289-5	(48.5)	v New Zealand (won)	Kimberley	2000/01
288-2	(46.4)	v India (won)	New Delhi	1991/92
283-4	(46.4)	v England (won)	Dhaka	1998/99
276-3	(48)	v England (won)	Centurion	1995/96
264-9	(50)	v Sri Lanka (lost)	Colombo-RPS	2000
259-6	(48.3)	v Zimbabwe (won)	Johannesburg	1996/97

Note: The highest in South Africa is:

300-6	(48)	Pakistan v Sri Lanka (won)	Kimberley	1997/98

LIMITED OVERS INTERNATIONAL RECORDS

HIGHEST TOTALS BATTING SECOND AGAINST SOUTH AFRICA

310	(48.5)	by India (lost)	Nagpur	1999/00
302-7	(49.4)	by India (won)	Kochi	1999/00
298-9	(50)	by New Zealand (lost)	Brisbane	1997/98
287-5	(49)	by Australia (won)	Centurion	1996/97
283-6	(49.5)	by India (won)	Vadodara	1999/00
272-5	(49.4)	by Australia (WC) (won)	Leeds	1999
265-5	(48.2)	by England (won)	Bloemfontein	1995/96
262-9	(50)	by Pakistan (lost)	Lahore	1997/98

HIGHEST MATCH AGGREGATES

630-17	(98.5)	India v South Africa	Nagpur	1999/00
603-10	(99.4)	India v South Africa	Kochi	1999/00
598-15	(100)	South Africa v New Zealand	Brisbane	1997/98
590-13	(98.1)	South Africa v West Indies	Lahore	1997/98
580-18	(92.3)	South Africa v Pakistan	Nairobi	1996/97
576-11	(98.5)	South Africa v New Zealand	Kimberley	2000/01

Note: The highest in South Africa is:

595-13	(98)	Pakistan v Sri Lanka	Kimberley	1997/98

LOWEST TOTAL BATTING FIRST AND WINNING BY SOUTH AFRICA

129	(41.4)	v England (won by 14 runs)	East London	1995/96

LOWEST MATCH AGGREGATES

(Excludes reduced overs matches)

211-15	(62.3)	South Africa v Sri Lanka	Bloemfontein	1997/98
229-11	(64.5)	South Africa v Pakistan	Cape Town	1997/98
237-12	(70.4)	South Africa v India	Nairobi	1999/00
241-19	(78)	Australia v South Africa	Sydney	1993/94
244-20	(85.2)	South Africa v England	East London	1995/96

Note: The lowest in South Africa is:

88-13	(32.2)	Pakistan v West Indies	Cape Town	1992/93

This is the lowest match aggregate in Limited Overs Internationals

LARGEST MARGINS OF VICTORY

By runs	202	v Kenya	Nairobi	1996/97
	169	v United Arab Emirates (WC)	Rawalpindi	1995/96
	160	v Holland (WC)	Rawalpindi	1995/96
	157	v Pakistan	Johannesburg	1994/95
By wickets	10	v India	Sharjah	1999/00
	9	v Australia (WC)	Sydney	1991/92
	9	v Pakistan	Cape Town	1997/98
	9	v Zimbabwe	Nairobi	1999/00

NARROWEST MARGINS OF VICTORY

By runs	1	v New Zealand	Hobart	1997/98
	1	v England	Cape Town	1999/00
	2	v New Zealand	Brisbane	1997/98
By wickets	2	v Australia	Faridabad	1996/97
	2	v New Zealand	Napier	1998/99
	2	v England	East London	1999/00
	2	v India	Faridabad	1999/00

LIMITED OVERS INTERNATIONAL RECORDS

LARGEST MARGINS OF DEFEAT

By runs	107	by West Indies	Kingston	1991/92
	103	by Australia	Sydney	1993/94
By wickets	10	by West Indies	Port of Spain	1991/92
	9	by West Indies	Bloemfontein	1992/93
	9	by England	Bloemfontein	1999/00

NARROWEST MARGINS OF DEFEAT

By runs	1	by Australia	Bloemfontein	1993/94
	2	by India	Calcutta	1993/94
By wickets	2	by Sri Lanka	Nairobi	1996/97
	2	by Zimbabwe	Durban	1999/00

TIED MATCHES

v Australia (WC)	Birmingham	1999
v Australia	Melbourne-Colonial	2000

MOST SUCCESSIVE VICTORIES

10	England (5), United Arab Emirates, New Zealand, England, Pakistan, Holland	1995/96
10	New Zealand (5), Sri Lanka (5)	2000/01

MOST SUCCESSIVE DEFEATS

10	Australia (2), England (2), Australia and Pakistan (3 each)	1993/94-1994/95

BATTING

HIGHEST INDIVIDUAL INNINGS

FOR

188*	G Kirsten	v United Arab Emirates (WC)	Rawalpindi	1995/96

AGAINST

150	S Chanderpaul	for West Indies	East London	1998/99

CENTURIES

FOR (38)

105*	N Boje (2)	v New Zealand	Potchefstroom	2000/01
129		v New Zealand	Centurion	2000/01
169*	DJ Callaghan	v New Zealand	Verwoerdburg	1994/95
112	WJ Cronje (2)	v Australia	Johannesburg	1993/94
100*		v Australia	Peshawar	1994/95
110*	DJ Cullinan (3)	v Pakistan	Sharjah	1995/96
124		v Pakistan	Nairobi	1996/97
106		v India	Jaipur	1996/97
125	HH Gibbs (5)	v West Indies	Port Elizabeth	1998/99
101		v Australia (WC)	Leeds	1999
111		v India	Kochi	1999/00
104		v West Indies	St John's	2000/01
107		v West Indies	Bridgetown	2000/01
108	AC Hudson (2)	v India	Bloemfontein	1992/93
161		v Holland (WC)	Rawalpindi	1995/96
111	JH Kallis (7)	v New Zealand	Perth	1997/98
109*		v Pakistan	Durban	1997/98
113*		v Sri Lanka	Dhaka	1998/99

100		v New Zealand	Dunedin	1998/99
100		v New Zealand	Auckland	1998/99
100*		v Sri Lanka	Paarl	2000/01
107		v West Indies	St George's	2000/01
112*	G Kirsten (10)	v Australia	Melbourne	1993/94
116		v England	Centurion	1995/96
188*		v United Arab Emirates (WC)	Rawalpindi	1995/96
106		v India	Sharjah	1995/96
115*		v India	Sharjah	1995/96
118*		v Pakistan	Nairobi	1996/97
105*		v Australia	Indore	1996/97
103		v New Zealand	Brisbane	1997/98
115		v India	Kochi	1999/00
101		v New Zealand	Kimberley	2000/01
103*	L Klusener (2)	v New Zealand	Auckland	1998/99
101*		v Zimbabwe	Nairobi	1999/00
120*	ND McKenzie	v Sri Lanka	East London	2000/01
127	BM McMillan	v Zimbabwe	Harare	1995/96
121	JN Rhodes	v Pakistan	Nairobi	1996/97
106	MJR Rindel	v Pakistan	Johannesburg	1994/95

AGAINST (29)

111	Aamir Sohail	for Pakistan (WC)	Karachi	1995/96
100*	NJ Astle	for New Zealand	Auckland	1998/99
103	MG Bevan (2)	for Australia	Centurion	1996/97
106		for Australia	Melbourne-Colonial	2000
150	S Chanderpaul	for West Indies	East London	1998/99
105*	SC Ganguly (2)	for India	Jamshedpur	1999/00
141*		for India	Nairobi	2000/01
100	AC Gilchrist	for Australia	Sydney	1997/98
105	CL Hooper (2)	for West Indies	Lahore	1997/98
108		for West Indies	East London	1998/99
110	Ijaz Ahmed (2)	for Pakistan	Rawalpindi	1994/95
114*		for Pakistan	Durban	1994/95
107	Javed Miandad	for Pakistan	East London	1992/93
111*	BC Lara (2)	for West Indies	Bloemfontein	1992/93
111		for West Indies (WC)	Karachi	1995/96
105	SV Manjrekar	for India	New Delhi	1991/92
108	AC Parore	for New Zealand	Verwoerdburg	1994/95
114	WV Raman	for India	Verwoerdburg	1992/93
109	RJ Shastri	for India	New Delhi	1991/92
122	PV Simmons (2)	for West Indies	Kingston	1991/92
104		for West Indies	Port of Spain	1991/92
114	SR Tendulkar (2)	for India	Mumbai	1996/97
122		for India	Vadodara	1999/00
103	RG Twose	for New Zealand	Cape Town	2000/01
103	PA Wallace	for West Indies	Dhaka	1998/99
107	ME Waugh (2)	for Australia	Sydney	1993/94
115*		for Australia	Port Elizabeth	1996/97
120*	SR Waugh (2)	for Australia (WC)	Leeds	1999
114*		for Australia	Melbourne-Colonial	2000

LIMITED OVERS INTERNATIONAL RECORDS

SUCCESSIVE FIFTIES

JN Rhodes (5)	69 v New Zealand; 61*, 50, 75* and 53 v Sri Lanka	2000/01
KC Wessels (4)	50, 71 and 90 v India; 81* v Australia (WC)	1991/92
G Kirsten (4)	66 v Kenya; 118* v Pakistan; 84 v India; 105* v Australia	1996/97
DJ Cullinan (4)	53, 89 and 57* v Australia; 51 v Pakistan	1996/97-1997/98
G Kirsten (4)	51 v India; 89 v Pakistan; 64 v West Indies; 50 v Sri Lanka	1996/97-1997/98

MOST RUNS

	Runs	Avg
G Kirsten	5700	40.71
WJ Cronje	5565	38.64
JN Rhodes	4677	32.93

BEST BATTING AVERAGES

(Qualification 1000 runs)

	Runs	Avg
JH Kallis	4379	43.79
L Klusener	2562	42.00
G Kirsten	5700	40.71

BEST BATTING STRIKE RATES

(Qualification 1000 runs)

	Runs	Balls	Runs/100 balls
L Klusener	2562	2856	89.70
SM Pollock	1411	1765	79.94
JN Rhodes	4677	5924	78.95

RECORD PARTNERSHIPS

FOR			
1st	235	G Kirsten and HH Gibbs v India (Kochi)	1999/00
2nd	179	HH Gibbs and JH Kallis v West Indies (St John's)	2000/01
3rd	162	HH Gibbs and WJ Cronje v West Indies (Port Elizabeth)	1998/99
4th	232	DJ Cullinan and JN Rhodes v Pakistan (Nairobi)	1996/97
5th	183*	JH Kallis and JN Rhodes v Pakistan (Durban)	1997/98
6th	137	WJ Cronje and SM Pollock v Zimbabwe (Johannesburg)	1996/97
7th	114	MV Boucher and L Klusener v India (Nagpur)	1999/00
8th	91	DM Benkenstein and L Klusener v West Indies (Cape Town)	1998/99
9th	44	L Klusener and S Elworthy v Sri Lanka (WC) (Northampton)	1999
10th	51	RP Snell and PS de Villiers v Sri Lanka (Colombo-RPS)	1993/94
AGAINST			
1st	165	N Hussain and NV Knight for England (Bloemfontein)	1999/00
2nd	180	SR Tendulkar and RS Dravid for India (Nagpur)	1999/00
3rd	175	DM Jones and ME Waugh for Australia (Sydney)	1993/94
4th	226	S Chanderpaul and CL Hooper for West Indies (East London)	1998/99
5th	148*	Ijaz Ahmed and Basit Ali for Pakistan (Faisalabad)	1994/95
6th	124	CD McMillan and CZ Harris for New Zealand (Adelaide)	1997/98
7th	93	SKL de Silva and HDPK Dharmasena for Sri Lanka (Lahore)	1997/98
8th	119	PR Reiffel and SK Warne for Australia (Port Elizabeth)	1993/94
9th	80*	Arshad Laiq and S Dukanwala for United Arab Emirates (WC)(Rawalpindi)	1995/96
10th	72	Abdur Razzaq and Waqar Younis for Pakistan (Durban)	1997/98

BOWLING

BEST BOWLING

FOR

9-0-23-6	AA Donald	v Kenya	Nairobi	1996/97

AGAINST

10-6-6-5	SB Joshi	for India	Nairobi	1999/00

FIVE WICKETS IN AN INNINGS

FOR (15)

10-0-32-5	WJ Cronje	v India	Cape Town	1992/93
8.4-0-29-5	AA Donald (2)	v India	Calcutta	1991/92
9-0-23-6		v Kenya	Nairobi	1996/97
7.3-0-30-5	JH Kallis	v West Indies	Dhaka	1998/99
8.4-0-42-5	L Klusener (6)	v India	Bloemfontein	1996/97
10-0-49-6		v Sri Lanka	Lahore	1997/98
7.1-0-24-5		v Australia	Melbourne	1997/98
7.1-1-25-5		v Pakistan	Cape Town	1997/98
8.3-3-21-5		v Kenya (WC)	Amstelveen	1999
10-0-47-5		v Pakistan	Sharjah	1999/00
8.2-0-37-5	M Ntini	v Sri Lanka	Cape Town	2000/01
10-2-35-6	SM Pollock (3)	v West Indies	East London	1998/99
9.2-1-36-5		v Australia (WC)	Birmingham	1999
9-1-20-5		v England	Johannesburg	1999/00
9.5-0-40-5	RP Snell	v Australia	Melbourne	1993/94

AGAINST (4)

10-6-6-5	SB Joshi	for India	Nairobi	1999/00
10-0-44-5	M Muralitharan	for Sri Lanka	Colombo-RPS	2000
10-0-25-5	Waqar Younis	for Pakistan	Durban	1992/93
6.1-0-16-5	Wasim Akram	for Pakistan	East London	1992/93

Note: The best in South Africa is 8.2-3-19-6 HK Olonga for Zimbabwe v England, Cape Town 1999/00

ECONOMICAL BOWLING

(5 overs or more)

FOR

Runs per over					
0.87	SM Pollock	8-4-7-3	v Zimbabwe	Port Elizabeth	1999/00
1.00	PS de Villiers	5-2-5-0	v West Indies	Bombay	1993/94
1.11	WJ Cronje	9-2-10-3	v West Indies	Cape Town	1998/99
1.20	MW Pringle	5-3-6-1	v West Indies	Port of Spain	1991/92
1.22	SM Pollock	8.1-3-10-3	v Kenya	Nairobi	1999/00
1.25	CR Matthews	8-5-10-4	v Australia	Durban	1993/94
1.25	PS de Villiers	8-1-10-2	v England	East London	1995/96
1.25	SM Pollock	8-3-10-2	v Sri Lanka (WC)	Northampton	1999
1.37	MW Pringle	8-4-11-4	v West Indies (WC)	Christchurch	1991/92
1.37	BM McMillan	8-1-11-3	v United Arab Emirates (WC)	Rawalpindi	1995/96

AGAINST

0.60	SB Joshi	10-6-6-5	for India	Nairobi	1999/00
1.09	PAJ DeFreitas	11-4-12-1	for England	Manchester	1994
1.20	GR Larson	10-5-12-2	for New Zealand	Hobart	1993/94
1.25	TM Moody	8-3-10-1	for Australia	Melbourne	1997/98
1.30	GD McGrath	10-1-13-2	for Australia	Cape Town	1999/00
1.33	CJ McDermott	6-2-8-1	for Australia	Sydney	1993/94

LIMITED OVERS INTERNATIONAL RECORDS

EXPENSIVE BOWLING

(5 overs or more)

FOR

Runs per over					
10.40	JH Kallis	5-0-52-0	v New Zealand	Cape Town	2000/01
10.00	JH Kallis	5-0-50-0	v Pakistan	Durban	1997/98
9.40	M Hayward	5-0-47-1	v Sri Lanka	Galle	2000
9.20	AA Donald	5-0-46-0	v New Zealand	Kimberley	2000/01
8.93	PL Symcox	7.1-0-64-0	v New Zealand	Auckland	1998/99
8.80	M Ntini	5-0-44-1	v Sri Lanka	Port Elizabeth	2000/01
8.60	S Elworthy	5-0-43-0	v Sri Lanka	Nottingham	1998
8.50	JH Kallis	6-0-51-0	v West Indies	East London	1998/99
8.00	RP Snell	7-0-56-1	v New Zealand (WC)	Auckland	1991/92
8.00	WJ Cronje	5-0-40-0	v Australia	Cape Town	1993/94
8.00	AA Donald	9-0-72-3	v England	Centurion	1995/96

AGAINST

10.83	J Srinath	6-0-65-0	for India	Nagpur	1999/00
8.75	AC Dale	8-1-70-0	for Australia	Bloemfontein	1996/97
8.66	Arshad Laiq	6-0-52-0	for United Arab Emirates (WC)	Rawalpindi	1995/96
8.60	NC McGarrell	5-0-43-2	for West Indies	Johannesburg	1998/99
8.40	NJ Astle	5-0-42-0	for New Zealand	Brisbane	1997/98
8.33	SB O'Connor	6-0-50-0	for New Zealand	Brisbane	1997/98
8.20	GS Blewett	5-0-41-0	for Australia	Centurion	1996/97
8.20	NC McGarrell	5-0-41-0	for West Indies	Durban	1998/99
8.20	DL Vettori	5-0-41-0	for New Zealand	Christchurch	1998/99
8.20	T Kumaran	5-0-41-0	for India	Kochi	1999/00

MOST WICKETS

	Wkts	Avg
AA Donald	226	21.39
SM Pollock	190	23.05
L Klusener	137	28.18

BEST BOWLING AVERAGES

(Qualification 50 wickets)

	Runs	Wkts	Avg
AA Donald	4835	226	21.39
SM Pollock	4380	190	23.05
CR Matthews	1975	79	25.00

MOST ECONOMICAL BOWLING

(Qualification 600 balls)

	Balls Bowled	Runs Conceded	Runs/over
PS de Villiers	4422	2636	3.57
SM Pollock	6936	4380	3.78
CR Matthews	3003	1975	3.94

WICKETKEEPING

MOST DISMISSALS IN A MATCH

FOR

5 (ct 5)	DJ Richardson	v Pakistan	Johannesburg	1994/95
5 (ct 5)	DJ Richardson	v Zimbabwe	Harare	1995/96
5 (ct 5)	MV Boucher	v England	Johannesburg	1999/00
5 (ct 5)	MV Boucher	v Australia	Durban	1999/00
5 (ct 5)	MV Boucher	v Pakistan	Colombo-SSC	2000

AGAINST

6 (ct 6)	AC Gilchrist	for Australia	Cape Town	1999/00
5 (ct 5)	A Flower	for Zimbabwe	Harare	1995/96

MOST DISMISSALS

	Ct	St	Total
DJ Richardson	148	17	165
MV Boucher	132	5	137

FIELDING

MOST CATCHES IN A MATCH

FOR

5	JN Rhodes	v West Indies	Bombay	1993/94
4	KC Wessels	v West Indies	Kingston	1991/92

AGAINST

Three catches have been taken against South Africa on six occasions.

Note: The best in South Africa is 4 CL Hooper West Indies v Pakistan, Durban 1992/93

MOST CATCHES

JN Rhodes	91
WJ Cronje	73
DJ Cullinan	62

RECORD PARTNERSHIPS AGAINST INDIVIDUAL COUNTRIES

(partnerships of 20 or more only)

SOUTH AFRICA v AUSTRALIA

South Africa

1st	118	AC Hudson and G Kirsten (Indore)	1996/97
2nd	140	KC Wessels and WJ Cronje (Melbourne)	1993/94
3rd	149	WJ Cronje and DJ Cullinan (Centurion)	1996/97
4th	122	JH Kallis and DJ Cullinan (East London)	1996/97
5th	134	WJ Cronje and JN Rhodes (Sydney)	1997/98
6th	70	JN Rhodes and DN Crookes (Cape Town)	1996/97
7th	87*	MV Boucher and L Klusener (Johannesburg)	1999/00
8th	56*	SM Pollock and N Boje (Melbourne-Colonial)	2000
9th	31	SM Pollock and DJ Richardson (Melbourne)	1997/98
10th	40	PL Symcox and AA Donald (Sydney)	1997/98

Australia

1st	105	MA Taylor and MJ Slater (Melbourne)	1993/94
2nd	126	AC Gilchrist and RT Ponting (Sydney)	1997/98
3rd	175	DM Jones and ME Waugh (Sydney)	1993/94

4th	222	MG Bevan and SR Waugh (Melbourne-Colonial)	2000
5th	124	MG Bevan and MJ Slater (Gauhati)	1996/97
6th	62	AR Border and IA Healy (Cape Town)	1993/94
7th	68	IA Healy and PR Reiffel (Sydney)	1993/94
8th	119	PR Reiffel and SK Warne (Port Elizabeth)	1993/94
9th	57	IJ Harvey and AJ Bichel (Perth)	1997/98
10th	45*	MG Bevan and AC Dale (East London)	1996/97

SOUTH AFRICA v ENGLAND

South Africa			
1st	156	AC Hudson and G Kirsten (Centurion)	1995/96
2nd	72	GFJ Liebenberg and JH Kallis (The Oval)	1998
3rd	132*	JH Kallis and HH Dippenaar (Nairobi)	2000/01
4th	117	WJ Cronje and JN Rhodes (Dhaka)	1998/99
5th	71	DJ Cullinan and WJ Cronje (Birmingham)	1994
6th	74	WJ Cronje and MV Boucher (Johannesburg)	1999/00
7th	69	SM Pollock and PL Symcox (Birmingham)	1998
8th	59	SM Pollock and CR Matthews (Cape Town)	1995/96
9th	30	BM McMillan and PS de Villiers (East London)	1995/96
10th	26*	L Klusener and AA Donald (Manchester)	1998
England			
1st	165	N Hussain and NV Knight (Bloemfontein)	1999/00
2nd	71	MA Atherton and GA Hick (Bloemfontein)	1995/96
3rd	113	NV Knight and GA Hick (Birmingham)	1998
4th	73	GA Hick and NH Fairbrother (WC) (Sydney)	1991/92
5th	70	GP Thorpe and SJ Rhodes (Manchester)	1994
6th	112	NH Fairbrother and AJ Hollioake (Dhaka)	1998/99
7th	49	AJ Hollioake and RC Russell (Dhaka)	1998/99
8th	42	DG Cork and PAJ DeFreitas (WC) (Rawalpindi)	1995/96
10th	24	CMW Read and AD Mullally (Johannesburg)	1999/00

SOUTH AFRICA v INDIA

South Africa			
1st	235	G Kirsten and HH Gibbs (Kochi)	1999/00
2nd	120	G Kirsten and DJ Cullinan (Hamilton)	1994/95
3rd	113	DJ Cullinan and WJ Cronje (Jaipur)	1996/97
4th	154	G Kirsten and WJ Cronje (Sharjah)	1995/96
5th	102*	JN Rhodes and WJ Cronje (Bloemfontein)	1996/97
6th	60*	G Kirsten and BM McMillan (Sharjah)	1995/96
7th	114	MV Boucher and L Klusener (Nagpur)	1999/00
8th	88	DJ Richardson and PL Symcox (Mumbai)	1996/97
9th	20	N Boje and R Telemachus (Nairobi)	2000/01
10th	21*	DJ Richardson and AA Donald (Mohali)	1993/94
India			
1st	153	SC Ganguly and SR Tendulkar (Vadodara)	1999/00
2nd	180	SR Tendulkar and RS Dravid (Nagpur)	1999/00
3rd	88	SC Ganguly and RS Dravid (Jamshedpur)	1999/00
4th	105	RS Dravid and M Azharuddin (Port Elizabeth)	1996/97
5th	95	M Azharuddin and PK Amre (Calcutta)	1993/94
6th	92	AD Jadeja and RR Singh (Kochi)	1999/00
7th	51	AD Jadeja and NR Mongia (Mumbai)	1996/97
8th	34	PK Amre and KS More (Port Elizabeth)	1992/93
	34	J Srinath and NR Mongia (Sharjah)	1995/96

9th	28	SS Karim and A Kumble (Bloemfontein)	1996/97
10th	62	AD Jadeja and J Srinath (Sharjah)	1999/00

SOUTH AFRICA v NEW ZEALAND

South Africa			
1st	176	G Kirsten and HH Gibbs (WC) (Birmingham)	1999
2nd	172	G Kirsten and JH Kallis (Kimberley)	2000/01
3rd	112	G Kirsten and JH Kallis (Auckland)	1998/99
4th	145	JH Kallis and DJ Cullinan (Auckland)	1998/99
5th	106	JN Rhodes and MV Boucher (Cape Town)	2000/01
6th	47	L Klusener and JN Rhodes (Auckland)	1998/99
7th	54	JH Kallis and SM Pollock (Hobart)	1997/98
8th	69*	L Klusener and S Abrahams (Cape Town)	2000/01
9th	20	SM Pollock and DJ Richardson (Adelaide)	1997/98
New Zealand			
1st	114	MJ Greatbatch and RT Latham (WC) (Auckland)	1991/92
2nd	98	MJ Greatbatch and KR Rutherford (Christchurch)	1994/95
3rd	110	SP Fleming and RG Twose (Kimberley)	2000/01
4th	150	RG Twose and CL Cairns (Cape Town)	2000/01
5th	106	AC Parore and SA Thomson (Verwoerdburg)	1994/95
6th	124	CD McMillan and CZ Harris (Adelaide)	1997/98
7th	73	CL Cairns and AC Parore (Brisbane)	1997/98
8th	69	AC Parore and DJ Nash (Brisbane)	1997/98
9th	32	DJ Nash and DL Vettori (Brisbane)	1997/98

SOUTH AFRICA v PAKISTAN

South Africa			
1st	190	G Kirsten and MJR Rindel (Johannesburg)	1994/95
2nd	145	AC Hudson and WJ Cronje (Johannesburg)	1994/95
3rd	105	ND McKenzie and WJ Cronje (Sharjah)	1999/00
4th	232	DJ Cullinan and JN Rhodes (Nairobi)	1996/97
5th	183*	JH Kallis and JN Rhodes (Durban)	1997/98
6th	88	JN Rhodes and DJ Richardson (Durban)	1994/95
7th	42	DJ Richardson and EO Simons (Durban)	1994/95
8th	45*	L Klusener and MV Boucher (WC) (Nottingham)	1999
9th	28*	RP Snell and CR Matthews (Durban)	1994/95
Pakistan			
1st	123	Imran Nazir and Shahid Afridi (Sharjah)	1999/00
2nd	115	Imran Nazir and Younis Khan (Sharjah)	1999/00
3rd	136*	Ijaz Ahmed and Salim Malik (Durban)	1994/95
4th	165	Javed Miandad and Asif Mujtaba (East London)	1992/93
5th	148*	Ijaz Ahmed and Basit Ali (Faisalabad)	1994/95
6th	47	Inzamam-ul-Haq and Abdur Razzaq (Sharjah)	1999/00
7th	55	Asif Mujtaba and Wasim Akram (Johannesburg)	1994/95
	55	Moin Khan and Azhar Mahmood (WC) (Nottingham)	1999
8th	81*	Salim Malik and Aaqib Javed (Sharjah)	1995/96
9th	41	Azhar Mahmood and Saqlain Mushtaq (Lahore)	1997/98
10th	72	Abdur Razzaq and Waqar Younis (Durban)	1997/98

LIMITED OVERS INTERNATIONAL RECORDS

SOUTH AFRICA v SRI LANKA

South Africa

Wkt	Runs	Partners	Season
1st	150	G Kirsten and AJ Hall (Galle)	2000
2nd	111	HH Dippenaar and JH Kallis (Paarl)	2000/01
3rd	134*	JH Kallis and JN Rhodes (Paarl)	2000/01
4th	88	ND McKenzie and JN Rhodes (East London)	2000/01
5th	100	ND McKenzie and MV Boucher (East London)	2000/01
6th	100	PL Symcox and JN Rhodes (Nottingham)	1998
7th	80*	JN Rhodes and L Klusener (Port Elizabeth)	2000/01
8th	44*	JH Kallis and DM Benkenstein (Dhaka)	1998/99
9th	44	L Klusener and S Elworthy (WC) (Northampton)	1999
10th	51	RP Snell and PS de Villiers (Colombo-RPS)	1993/94

Sri Lanka

Wkt	Runs	Partners	Season
1st	110	RS Mahanama and UC Hathurusingha (Kandy)	1993/94
	110	ST Jayasuriya and RS Kaluwitharana (Paarl)	2000/01
2nd	129	DA Gunawardene and MS Atapattu (Colombo-SSC)	2000
3rd	65	ST Jayasuriya and PA de Silva (Johannesburg)	1997/98
4th	108	MS Atapattu and A Ranatunga (Port Elizabeth)	1997/98
5th	120	K Sangakkara and RP Arnold (Galle)	2000
6th	62	RP Arnold and K Sangakkara (Bloemfontein)	2000/01
7th	93	SKL de Silva and HDPK Dharmasena (Lahore)	1997/98
8th	36*	HDPK Dharmasena and WPUJC Vaas (Lahore)	1997/98
9th	55	HDPK Dharmasena and DK Liyanage (Lahore)	1997/98
10th	27	UDU Chandana and M Muralitharan (Johannesburg)	1997/98

SOUTH AFRICA v WEST INDIES

South Africa

Wkt	Runs	Partners	Season
1st	88	G Kirsten and HH Gibbs (St George's)	2000/01
2nd	179	HH Gibbs and JH Kallis (St John's)	2000/01
3rd	162	HH Gibbs and WJ Cronje (Port Elizabeth)	1998/99
4th	112	G Kirsten and WJ Cronje (Lahore)	1997/98
5th	98	JH Kallis and JN Rhodes (Centurion)	1998/99
6th	94	WJ Cronje and DM Benkenstein (Bloemfontein)	1998/99
7th	62	DM Benkenstein and MV Boucher (Cape Town)	1998/99
8th	91	DM Benkenstein and L Klusener (Cape Town)	1998/99
9th	36*	L Klusener and PL Symcox (Centurion)	1998/99

West Indies

Wkt	Runs	Partners	Season
1st	154*	DL Haynes and BC Lara (Port of Spain)	1991/92
2nd	138	S Chanderpaul and BC Lara (WC) (Karachi)	1995/96
3rd	105	PV Simmons and RB Richardson (Kingston)	1991/92
4th	226	S Chanderpaul and CL Hooper (East London)	1998/99
5th	67	CL Hooper and MN Samuels (St George's)	2000/01
6th	61	BC Lara and RD Jacobs (Bridgetown)	2000/01
7th	46	AL Logie and DL Haynes (WC) (Christchurch)	1991/92
8th	24	JC Adams and IR Bishop (WC) (Karachi)	1995/96
	24	KF Semple and RN Lewis (Centurion)	1998/99
9th	30	RN Lewis and CEL Ambrose (Bloemfontein)	1998/99
10th	47	RN Lewis and RD King (Bloemfontein)	1998/99

SOUTH AFRICA v ZIMBABWE

South Africa

Wkt	Runs	Partners	Season
1st	125*	HH Gibbs and L Klusener (Nairobi)	1999/00
2nd	112	KC Wessels and PN Kirsten (WC) (Canberra)	1991/92

3rd	86	BM McMillan and WJ Cronje (Harare)	1995/96
4th	104	HH Gibbs and WJ Cronje (Johannesburg)	1999/00
5th	123	DJ Cullinan and WJ Cronje (Centurion)	1996/97
6th	137	WJ Cronje and SM Pollock (Johannesburg)	1996/97
7th	82	JH Kallis and L Klusener (Durban)	1999/00
8th	43	SM Pollock and L Klusener (WC) (Chelmsford)	1999
10th	35	L Klusener and AA Donald (WC) (Chelmsford)	1999
Zimbabwe			
1st	99	NC Johnson and GW Flower (Nairobi)	1999/00
2nd	66	NC Johnson and MW Goodwin (WC) (Chelmsford)	1999
3rd	46	GW Flower and MW Goodwin (Nairobi)	1999/00
4th	27	NC Johnson and MW Goodwin (Port Elizabeth)	1999/00
5th	93	GW Flower and DL Houghton (Johannesburg)	1996/97
6th	51	ADR Campbell and DL Houghton (Cape Town)	1996/97
7th	91	A Flower and GJ Whittall (Durban)	1999/00
8th	50*	ADR Campbell and HH Streak (Harare)	1995/96
9th	28	AJ Traicos and MP Jarvis (WC) (Canberra)	1991/92

SOUTH AFRICA LIMITED OVERS INTERNATIONAL CAREER RECORDS

As at 1 September 2001

Name	M	InnS	NO	Runs	HS	Avg	BF	SR	100	50	Ct	St	Balls	Runs	Wkts	Avg	RpO	BB	4I
S Abrahams	1	1	1	16	16*	-	26	61.53	0	0	1	0	60	40	0	-	4.00	-	0
PR Adams	16	8	4	33	15*	8.25	53	62.26	0	0	4	0	749	554	23	24.08	4.43	3-26	0
AM Bacher	8	8	0	168	45	21.00	294	57.14	0	0	3	0	0	0	0	-	-	-	0
DM Benkenstein	20	18	3	296	69	19.73	451	65.63	0	1	1	0	18	22	0	-	7.33	-	0
N Boje	56	34	8	780	129	30.00	864	90.27	2	2	16	0	2111	1552	43	36.09	4.41	4-25	1
T Bosch	2	0	0	0	0	-	0	-	0	0	0	0	51	66	0	-	7.76	-	0
MV Boucher	91	63	16	969	68	20.61	1364	71.04	0	7	132	5	0	0	0	-	-	-	0
RE Bryson	7	4	3	32	17*	32.00	26	123.07	0	0	1	0	378	323	7	46.14	5.12	2-34	0
DJ Callaghan	29	25	6	493	169*	25.94	725	68.00	1	0	6	0	444	365	10	36.50	4.93	3-32	0
SJ Cook	4	4	0	67	35	16.75	118	56.77	0	0	1	0	0	0	0	-	-	-	0
WJ Cronje	188	175	31	5565	112	38.64	7273	76.51	2	39	73	0	5354	3966	114	34.78	4.44	5-32	2
DN Crookes	32	23	3	296	54	14.80	412	71.84	0	1	20	0	1221	1011	25	40.44	4.96	3-30	0
DJ Cullinan	138	133	16	3860	124	32.99	5483	70.39	3	23	62	0	174	124	5	24.80	4.27	2-30	0
AC Dawson	4	1	0	6	6	6.00	3	200.00	0	0	0	0	222	188	5	37.60	5.08	3-36	0
PS de Villiers	83	36	15	170	20*	8.09	215	79.06	0	0	15	0	4422	2636	95	27.74	3.57	4-27	2
HH Dippenaar	21	16	3	535	77	41.15	865	61.84	0	5	5	0	0	0	0	-	-	-	0
AA Donald	136	33	14	89	13	4.68	238	37.39	0	0	18	0	7125	4835	226	21.39	4.07	6-23	12
CE Eksteen	6	2	2	6	6*	-	25	24.00	0	0	3	0	222	181	2	90.50	4.89	1-26	0
S Elworthy	35	13	7	71	23	11.83	113	62.83	0	0	9	0	1534	1110	39	28.46	4.34	3-17	0
HH Gibbs	70	70	4	2063	125	31.25	2772	74.42	5	9	26	0	0	0	0	-	-	-	0
AJ Hall	18	17	1	391	81	24.43	553	70.70	0	1	8	0	230	173	5	34.60	4.51	2-8	0
M Hayward	17	5	1	12	4	3.00	28	42.85	0	0	3	0	801	691	17	40.64	5.17	4-31	1
O Henry	3	3	1	20	11	10.00	26	76.92	0	0	1	0	149	125	2	62.50	5.03	1-31	0
AC Hudson	89	88	1	2559	161	29.41	3969	64.47	2	18	18	0	6	3	0	-	3.00	-	0
SD Jack	2	2	0	7	6	3.50	8	87.50	0	0	3	0	108	86	3	28.66	4.77	2-41	0
JH Kallis	126	123	23	4379	113*	43.79	6413	68.28	7	30	49	0	4428	3402	117	29.07	4.60	5-30	2
JM Kemp	6	3	1	58	46	29.00	86	67.44	0	0	3	0	232	170	8	21.25	4.39	3-54	0
G Kirsten	154	154	14	5700	188*	40.71	8042	70.87	10	38	50	1	30	23	0	-	4.60	-	0
PN Kirsten	40	40	6	1293	97	38.02	2307	56.04	0	9	11	0	183	152	6	25.33	4.98	3-31	0
L Klusener	113	94	33	2562	103*	42.00	2856	89.70	2	14	20	0	4916	3862	137	28.18	4.71	6-49	6

SOUTH AFRICA LIMITED OVERS INTERNATIONAL CAREER RECORDS

Name	M	InnS	NO	Runs	HS	Avg	BF	SR	100	50	Ct	St	Balls	Runs	Wkts	Avg	RpO	BB	4I
LJ Koen	5	5	0	82	28	16.40	169	48.52	0	0	3	0	0	0	0	-	-	-	0
AP Kuiper	25	23	7	539	63*	33.68	662	81.41	0	3	3	0	588	518	18	28.77	5.28	3-33	0
GFJ Liebenberg	4	4	0	94	39	23.50	199	47.23	0	0	0	0	0	0	0	-	-	-	0
CR Matthews	56	22	9	141	26	10.84	202	69.80	0	0	10	0	3003	1975	79	25.00	3.94	4-10	3
ND McKenzie	26	23	1	625	120*	28.40	989	63.19	1	2	7	0	22	11	0	-	3.00	-	0
BM McMillan	78	52	16	841	127	23.36	1151	73.06	1	0	42	0	3623	2589	70	36.98	4.28	4-32	1
PV Mpitsang	2	1	1	1	1*	-	1	100.00	0	0	0	0	60	63	2	31.50	6.30	2-49	0
A Nel	1	1	1	3	3*	-	3	100.00	0	0	0	0	49	20	3	6.66	2.44	3-20	0
M Ntini	23	4	2	5	3*	2.50	30	16.66	0	0	10	0	1063	743	32	23.21	4.19	5-37	2
JL Ontong	6	2	0	13	11	6.50	15	86.66	0	0	2	0	234	159	2	79.50	4.07	2-12	0
SJ Palframan	7	4	0	55	28	13.75	80	68.75	0	0	9	0	0	0	0	-	-	-	0
SM Pollock	132	87	30	1411	75	24.75	1765	79.94	0	5	46	0	6936	4380	190	23.05	3.78	6-35	9
N Pothas	3	1	0	24	24	24.00	41	58.53	0	0	4	1	0	0	0	-	-	-	0
MW Pringle	17	8	3	48	13*	9.60	56	85.71	0	0	2	0	870	604	22	27.45	4.16	4-11	1
JN Rhodes	200	182	40	4677	121	32.93	5924	78.95	1	22	91	0	8	3	0	-	2.25	-	0
CEB Rice	3	2	0	26	14	13.00	37	70.27	0	0	0	0	138	114	2	57.00	4.95	1-46	0
DJ Richardson	122	77	33	868	53	19.72	1300	66.76	0	1	148	17	0	0	0	-	-	-	0
MJR Rindel	22	22	1	575	106	27.38	861	66.78	1	2	8	0	270	242	6	40.33	5.37	2-15	0
DB Rundle	2	2	0	6	6	3.00	11	54.54	0	0	3	0	96	95	5	19.00	5.93	4-42	1
MW Rushmere	4	4	0	78	35	19.50	174	44.82	0	0	1	0	0	0	0	-	-	-	0
BN Schultz	1	0	0	0	0	-	0	-	0	0	0	0	54	35	1	35.00	3.88	1-35	0
TG Shaw	9	6	4	26	17*	13.00	35	74.28	0	0	2	0	504	298	9	33.11	3.54	2-19	0
EO Simons	23	18	4	217	24	15.50	295	73.55	0	0	6	0	1212	810	33	24.54	4.00	4-42	1
RP Snell	42	28	8	322	63	16.10	330	97.57	0	2	7	0	2095	1574	44	35.77	4.50	5-40	3
ELR Stewart	5	5	1	57	23*	14.25	111	51.35	0	0	3	0	0	0	0	-	-	-	0
PJR Steyn	1	1	0	4	4	4.00	14	28.57	0	0	0	0	0	0	0	-	-	-	0
PC Strydom	10	8	3	48	34	9.60	94	51.06	0	0	3	0	252	206	2	103.00	4.90	1-18	0
PL Symcox	80	54	13	694	61	16.92	827	83.91	0	3	23	0	3991	2762	72	38.36	4.15	4-28	1
R Telemachus	25	7	2	27	13	5.40	54	50.00	0	0	1	0	1324	976	37	26.37	4.42	4-43	1
DJ Terbrugge	4	2	1	5	5	5.00	14	35.71	0	0	0	0	126	105	4	26.25	5.00	4-20	1
CJPG van Zyl	2	2	1	3	3*	3.00	11	27.27	0	0	0	0	108	93	0	-	5.16	-	0
KC Wessels	55	54	4	1627	90	32.54	3149	51.66	0	12	30	0	12	11	0	-	5.50	-	0
HS Williams	7	2	1	8	7	8.00	11	72.72	0	0	2	0	329	228	9	25.33	4.15	3-38	0
CM Willoughby	1	1	0	0	0	0.00	2	0.00	0	0	0	0	60	39	2	19.50	3.90	2-39	0
M Yachad	1	1	0	31	31	31.00	77	40.25	0	0	1	0	0	0	0	-	-	-	0

SOUTH AFRICA A IN WEST INDIES 2000/01

South Africa A had a successful tour of the West Indies at the start of a season which was to end with the full national team touring the Caribbean. The A team, led by Dale Benkenstein, drew all five of their first class matches, including two against West Indies A, with weather playing a role. In the first "Test" the tourists were in deep trouble when rain stopped play but in the second encounter it was South Africa A who were on top when rain intervened.

South Africa A won all four of the limited overs matches they played, thus returning home unbeaten. The wins included two against West Indies A, with a scheduled third match rained out.

The tour provided valuable information for the South African selectors, with Hylton Ackerman, one of the panel, joining Shukri Conrad as one of two coaches after the withdrawal for business reasons of Hugh Page.

Conrad said the tour had been well worthwhile and he had been particularly pleased with the performances of some of the younger players. "We were surprised that most of the wickets were low and slow and we battled with that in the beginning. For instance, the batters were not getting forward enough at first but it certainly improved once we got used to the conditions. Some of the outstanding performers were Charl Willoughby, Graeme Smith and Mfuneko Ngam, with some good batting from Gerald Dros and Mark Bruyns."

The touring party was: Dale Benkenstein (KZN, captain), Nic Pothas (Gau, vice-captain), Mark Bruyns (KZN), James Bryant (EP), Gerald Dros (Nor), Justin Kemp (EP), Garnett Kruger (EP), Charl Langeveldt (Bol), Victor Mpitsang (FS), Mfuneko Ngam (EP), Justin Ontong (Bol), Robin Peterson (EP), Ashwell Prince (WP), Graeme Smith (WP), Doug Watson (KZN), Charl Willoughby (WP). Manager, Henry Paulse; coaches, Shukri Conrad and Hylton Ackerman.

Kruger was included after Dewald Pretorius (FS) withdrew because of injury, while Watson replaced Boeta Dippenaar (FS), who was selected for the senior national team.

BARBADOS v SOUTH AFRICA A — First-class 4-day match

Played at Windward Club, Lucas Street, St Philip, on 22,23,24,25 August 2000 — Toss: Barbados
Umpires: D Holder & M Jones
Debuts: Bar: SM Clarke, CA Glasgow, CF Lopez, DT Mason, DM Richards, KJ Wilkinson & RA Yearwood (all FC).
SAA: None
Close of Play: Day 1: SAA (1) 240-7 (Prince 51*, Langeveldt 7*, 77 overs). Day 2: Bar (1) 218-7 (Glasgow 12*, Bradshaw 20*, 72 overs). Day 3: SAA (2) 113-3 (Bruyns 50*, Benkenstein 10*, 42 overs).
Result: Match drawn

Ontong, Benkenstein and Prince all batted impressively and South Africa A were well placed before Benkenstein was run out by a direct hit from mid-on, starting a slide in which the last six wickets fell for 69 runs.

Ngam impressed with his pace but Barbados took a narrow first innings lead after a maiden first class half-century by the left-handed Ian Bradshaw, batting at number nine. Bruyns batted solidly in the second innings and Barbados, left with 42 overs to bat, were given a scare by the South African fast bowlers, losing five wickets in the first 18 overs.

SOUTH AFRICA A

FIRST INNINGS	*Runs*	*Mins*	*Balls*	*4*	*6*	*SECOND INNINGS*	*Runs*	*Mins*	*Balls*	*4*	*6*
†ML Bruyns b Bradshaw	3	39	24	-	-	c Bradshaw b Hinds	85	276	209	10	-
DJ Watson b Hinds	30	95	64	7	-	lbw b Lopez	10	26	16	1	-
GC Smith c Glasgow b Graham	8	23	19	1	-	c Wallace b Hinds	30	129	70	4	-
JL Ontong b Bradshaw	57	112	69	8	-	c Glasgow b Hinds	0	9	4	-	-
*DM Benkenstein run out (Clarke)	57	186	141	7	-	b Lopez	57	206	146	2	2
AG Prince c Clarke b Bradshaw	69	195	146	7	-	lbw b Lopez	13	39	32	2	-
JM Kemp lbw b Graham	5	33	18	-	-	not out	7	54		-	-
RJ Peterson b Graham	0	7	3	-	-	c Glasgow b Lopez	0	2	2	-	-
CK Langeveldt not out	28		34	3	-	c Wallace b Lopez	6	16		-	-
M Ngam c Mason b Bradshaw	0	20	12	-	-						
CM Willoughby not out	1	4	1	-	-						
Extras (b 8, lb 3, w 1, nb 12)	24					Extras (lb 1, w 1, nb 18)	20				
TOTAL (for 9 wkts dec) (89 overs)	**282**					**TOTAL (for 8 wkts dec) (87.4 overs)**	**228**				

BARBADOS

	Runs	Mins	Balls	4	6		Runs	Mins	Balls	4	6
*PA Wallace c Langeveldt b Ngam	15	61	43	2	-	b Willoughby	0	3	4	-	-
SM Clarke c Kemp b Peterson	21	118	79	2	-	c Bruyns b Ngam	5	31	17	-	-
RA Yearwood c Peterson b Ngam	2	10	6	-	-	c Bruyns b Willoughby	17	26	25	3	-
DM Richards b Langeveldt	53	123	92	11	-						
RO Hinds c Ngam b Kemp	54	123	93	9	-	(4) c Bruyns b Ngam	0	1	1	-	-
KJ Wilkinson b Langeveldt	0	11	6	-	-	(5) not out	48	150	111	8	-
DT Mason c Ontong b Peterson	0	4	1	-	-	(6) c Ngam b Langeveldt	13	39	33	2	-
†CA Glasgow c Kemp b Willoughby	24	159	110	1	-	(7) c Bruyns b Langeveldt	31	77	68	5	-
IDR Bradshaw c Kemp b Ngam	62	150	129	9	-	(8) not out	0	25	13	-	-
HRO Graham lbw b Willoughby	1	3	2	-	-						
CF Lopez not out	7	6	10	1	-						
Extras (b 8, lb 6, w 1, nb 33)	48					Extras (b 14, nb 12)	26				
TOTAL (89.4 overs)	**287**					**TOTAL (for 6 wkts) (42 overs)**	**140**				

Bowling	*O*	*M*	*R*	*W*		*O*	*M*	*R*	*W*
BARBADOS									
Bradshaw	23	7	61	4		17	5	47	0
Lopez	17	1	64	0		18.4	4	61	5
Graham	19	3	74	3	(4)	13	5	30	0
Hinds	19	2	50	1	(3)	34	5	73	3
Clarke	11	3	22	0		1	0	1	0
Mason						4	1	15	0
SOUTH AFRICA A									
Willoughby	22	8	60	2		12	2	46	2
Ngam	18.4	2	56	3		8	0	35	2
Peterson	20	4	47	2	(4)	7	3	16	0
Langeveldt	14	0	68	2	(3)	8	3	9	2
Kemp	10	2	36	1		3	0	15	0
Ontong	5	1	6	0		4	2	5	0

Fall of Wickets	SAA 1st	Bar 1st	SAA 2nd	Bar 2nd
1st	26 (1)	33 (1)	26 (2)	0 (1)
2nd	51 (3)	39 (3)	90 (3)	22 (2)
3rd	77 (2)	67 (2)	90 (4)	22 (4)
4th	146 (4)	147 (4)	177 (1)	34 (3)
5th	213 (5)	154 (6)	197 (6)	67 (6)
6th	229 (7)	159 (7)	213 (5)	127 (7)
7th	229 (8)	185 (5)	214 (8)	-
8th	273 (6)	264 (8)	228 (9)	-
9th	281 (10)	270 (10)	-	-
10th	-	287 (9)	-	-

BARBADOS v SOUTH AFRICA A — Limited Overs match

Played at Kensington Oval, Bridgetown on 27 August 2000 — Toss: South Africa A

Umpires: D Holder & M Jones

Debuts: Bar: None. SAA: None

Result: South Africa A won by 7 wickets (D/L method), target revised to 76 in 37 overs

The left-armed Willoughby took full advantage of a helpful pitch and heavy cloud cover as the Barbados batting was decimated, with four wickets falling in the first five overs. Because of rain interruptions South Africa A's target was reduced.

BARBADOS	***Runs***	***Mins***	***Balls***	***4***	***6***	**SOUTH AFRICA A**	***Runs***	***Mins***	***Balls***	***4***	***6***
*PA Wallace c Bruyns b Willoughby	0	1	2	-	-	†ML Bruyns not out	28	120	77	3	-
MR Maynard c Dros b Willoughby	1	11	4	-	-	AG Prince lbw b Bradshaw	16	36	26	2	-
CCG Humphrey lbw b Mpitsang	3	17	12	-	-	G Dros b Bradshaw	0	17	10	-	-
RO Hinds c and b Willoughby	1	13	16	-	-	JL Ontong lbw b Humphrey	19	53	41	1	-
SA Graham lbw b Willoughby	3	22	12	-	-	JDC Bryant not out	1	11	8	-	-
A Braithwaite c Kemp b Willoughby	14	84	45	1	-	*DM Benkenstein					
†CO Browne c Ontong b Langeveldt	22	28	24	3	-	JM Kemp					
RO Hurley c Benkenstein b Kemp	7	20	14	-	-	RJ Peterson					
IDR Bradshaw not out	17	46	33	3	-	CK Langeveldt					
HRO Graham c Benkenstein b Willoughby	1	9	9	-	-	PV Mpitsang					
CF Lopez c Ontong b Peterson	0	12	5	-	-	CM Willoughby					
Extras (lb 4, w 5, nb 11)	20					Extras (lb 3, w 5, nb 4)	12				
TOTAL (27.3 overs)	**89**					**TOTAL (for 3 wkts) (25.5 overs)**	**76**				

SAA	O	M	R	W
Willoughby	9	1	24	6
Mpitsang	6	1	17	1
Langeveldt	5	0	21	1
Kemp	6	0	22	1
Peterson	1.3	0	1	1

Bar	O	M	R	W
Bradshaw	8	3	20	2
Lopez	3	0	16	0
HRO Graham	4	1	14	0
Braithwaite	3	0	7	0
Hurley	5	2	9	0
Humphrey	2.5	0	7	1

Fall of Wickets	Bar	SAA
1st	0 (1)	26 (2)
2nd	3 (2)	32 (3)
3rd	6 (3)	74 (4)
4th	6 (4)	-
5th	14 (5)	-
6th	43 (7)	-
7th	63 (8)	-
8th	73 (6)	-
9th	84 (10)	-
10th	89 (11)	-

WINDWARD ISLANDS v SOUTH AFRICA A — First-class 3-day match

Played at Arnos Vale, Kingstown on 1,2,3 September 2000 — Toss: South Africa A
Umpires: C Sutherland & K Whyttle
Debuts: WI: RK Currency, IO Jackson, K Peters & F Thomas. SAA: None
Close of Play: Day 1: SAA (1) 9-1 (Watson 5*, Bryant 4*, 6 overs). Day 2: WI (1) 64-2 (Eugene 5*, Harris 2*).
Result: Match drawn

Preparations for the first four-day match against West Indies A were severely hampered by the weather, with most of the first day being washed out. South Africa A were in danger of being humiliated before Dros and Kruger more than doubled the total in a last wicket stand.

SOUTH AFRICA A

FIRST INNINGS	Runs	Mins	Balls	4	6	*SECOND INNINGS*	Runs	Mins	Balls	4	6
DJ Watson c Pope b Butler	7	38	26	1	-	not out	35	-	-	3	-
GC Smith c Currency b Butler	1	12	8	-	-	not out	32	-	-	3	-
JDC Bryant c Eugene b Thomas	7	44	18	1	-						
*G Dros not out	67	283	187	4	-						
AG Prince c Currency b Butler	13	23	19	-	-						
JL Ontong c and b Marshall	9	51	35	-	-						
†ML Bruyns c Pope b Peters	1	10	11	-	-						
RJ Peterson c Pope b Peters	0	2	1	-	-						
CK Langeveldt c Pope b Butler	5	41	41	-	-						
PV Mpitsang lbw b Marshall	11	48	54	1	-						
GJ-P Kruger b Peters	58	80	72	8	-						
Extras (b 3, lb 3, nb 10)	16					Extras (lb 1, w 1, nb 1)	3				
TOTAL (77.5 overs)	**195**					**TOTAL (for 0 wkts) (20 overs)**	**70**				

WINDWARD ISLANDS

	Runs	Mins	Balls	4	6
DS Smith c Peterson b Kruger	31	64	52	2	-
RK Currency c Bryant b Kruger	16	71	35	1	-
J Eugene not out	130	293	205	11	1
D Harris c Bryant b Peterson	2	23	18	-	-
RA Marshall c Mpitsang b Peterson	0	6	3	-	-
†U Pope c and b Peterson	31	107	106	3	-
DC Butler b Peterson	1	24	19	-	-
CC Alexander lbw b Langeveldt	10	52	43	1	-
IO Jackson lbw b Langeveldt	5	63	30	-	-
K Peters c Dros b Peterson	11	29	25	1	-
F Thomas lbw b Dros	0	3	2	-	-
Extras (b 5, lb 3, w 5, nb 26)	39				
TOTAL (85.2 overs)	**276**				

Bowling	O	M	R	W		O	M	R	W
WINDWARD ISLANDS									
Butler	19	6	51	4		5	1	12	0
Thomas	11	0	42	1		2	0	21	0
Peters	18.5	7	25	3		3	0	7	0
Marshall	18	12	10	2	(6)	1	0	1	0
Alexander	8	0	46	0	(4)	4	0	15	0
Jackson	3	0	15	0	(5)	5	1	13	0
SOUTH AFRICA A									
Mpitsang	18	4	54	0					
Langeveldt	13	0	81	2					
Kruger	14	3	52	2					
Peterson	33	10	68	5					
Ontong	5	2	8	0					
Dros	2.2	0	5	1					

Fall of Wickets	SAA 1st	WI 1st	SAA 2nd
1st	1 (2)	57 (1)	-
2nd	16 (1)	62 (2)	-
3rd	21 (3)	65 (4)	-
4th	38 (5)	67 (5)	-
5th	54 (6)	175 (6)	-
6th	57 (7)	181 (7)	-
7th	57 (8)	223 (8)	-
8th	71 (9)	245 (9)	-
9th	93 (10)	275 (10)	-
10th	195 (11)	276 (11)	-

WEST INDIES A v SOUTH AFRICA A — 1st 'Test'

Played at Arnos Vale, Kingstown on 6,7,8,9 September 2000 — Toss: South Africa A
Umpires: BR Doctrove & G Greaves
Debuts: WIA: None. SAA: None
Close of Play: Day 1: WIA (1) 17-0 (Ganga 8*, Haniff 4*, 8 overs). Day 2: SAA (2) 50-3 (Smith 10*, Dros 4*, 17 overs). Day 3: SAA (2) 188-7 (Pothas 39*, Kruger 3*).
Result: Match drawn

The South African batsmen struggled against a good-quality attack in which the Test bowler Dillon and the capable Stuart did well, while the leg-spinner Ramnarine was difficult to score off. Willoughby and Ngam struck back for the tourists before Ramnarine and Dillon provided sturdy lower order resistance. Extras were responsible for much of the difference between the two sides on the first innings.

Smith and Pothas both played long defensive innings but West Indies A were set a modest target of 137 to win. They were within nine runs of victory when rain started to fall five minutes before tea on the final day, the match eventually being abandoned.

SOUTH AFRICA A

FIRST INNINGS	*Runs*	*Mins*	*Balls*	*4*	*6*	*SECOND INNINGS*	*Runs*	*Mins*	*Balls*	*4*	*6*
ML Bruyns lbw b Stuart	16	60	44	1	-	(2) b Black	3	45	20	-	-
DJ Watson c Ganga b Stuart	5	42	26	1	-	(1) lbw b Dillon	4	20	10	1	-
GC Smith c Browne b Dillon	34	255	130	4	-	c Joseph b Black	47	216	141	2	-
*DM Benkenstein c Morton b Dillon	5	28	13	-	-	lbw b Morton	25	35	26	4	-
G Dros b Stuart	15	162	77	1	-	c Browne b Dillon	12	21	15	2	-
JL Ontong c Ramnarine b Dillon	10	52	42	1	-	st Browne b Ramnarine	22	141	86	-	-
†N Pothas c Haniff b Stuart	8	40	31	-	-	not out	42	151	128	2	1
RJ Peterson c and b Ramnarine	11	38	26	2	-	c Browne b Stuart	10	75	29	-	-
GJ-P Kruger not out	28	68	57	3	-	c Ganga b Stuart	4	46	31	-	-
M Ngam c Powell b Samuels	3	34	32	-	-	lbw b Stuart	2	29	15	-	-
CM Willoughby c Stuart b Ramnarine	0	5	10	-	-	b Stuart	0	1	1	-	-
Extras (w 1, nb 8)	9					Extras (b 4, nb 19)	23				
TOTAL (79.3 overs)	**144**					**TOTAL (81.5 overs)**	**194**				

WEST INDIES A

	Runs	*Mins*	*Balls*	*4*	*6*		*Runs*	*Mins*	*Balls*	*4*	*6*
D Ganga c Pothas b Willoughby	8	63	43	1	-	c Bruyns b Ontong	24	113	80	2	-
A Haniff b Ngam	5	78	52	-	-	c Willoughby b Ontong	50			3	-
RS Morton lbw b Willoughby	6	19	7	1	-	not out	36	160	88	4	-
SC Joseph lbw b Willoughby	19	78	55	2	1	not out	10			2	-
RL Powell c Pothas b Ngam	1	5	4	-	-						
MN Samuels c Pothas b Kruger	18	60	45	3	-						
*†CO Browne c Pothas b Kruger	5	31	18	1	-						
D Ramnarine c Ontong b Kruger	38	148	99	2	-						
M Dillon c Smith b Peterson	52			5	1						
MI Black b Kruger	0	3	2	-	-						
CEL Stuart not out	0			-	-						
Extras (b 14, lb 4, w 9, nb 23)	50					Extras (b 6, lb 1, w 1)	8				
TOTAL (73.5 overs)	**202**					**TOTAL (for 2 wkts) (40 overs)**	**128**				

Bowling	*O*	*M*	*R*	*W*		*O*	*M*	*R*	*W*
WEST INDIES A									
Dillon	22	11	32	3		22	6	43	2
Black	10	3	27	0		19	5	38	2
Stuart	14	2	42	4		19.5	5	50	4
Ramnarine	29.3	12	39	2	(5)	13	1	34	1
Samuels	4	2	4	1	(6)	6	3	10	0
Morton					(4)	2	0	15	1
SOUTH AFRICA A									
Willoughby	21	8	38	3		11	3	33	0
Ngam	17	6	46	2		9	2	18	0
Peterson	7.5	2	34	1	(4)	4	0	22	0
Kruger	16	3	39	4	(3)	3	0	10	0
Ontong	7	1	20	0	(6)	9	2	24	2
Dros	5	1	7	0	(5)	4	0	14	0

Fall of Wickets	**SAA**	**WIA**	**SAA**	**WIA**
	1st	1st	2nd	2nd
1st	17 (2)	28 (1)	12 (1)	73 (1)
2nd	26 (1)	39 (2)	16 (2)	112 (2)
3rd	32 (4)	41 (3)	46 (4)	-
4th	76 (5)	42 (5)	61 (5)	-
5th	92 (3)	93 (6)	125 (3)	-
6th	93 (6)	93 (4)	130 (6)	-
7th	110 (8)	100 (7)	174 (8)	-
8th	124 (7)	168 (8)	190 (9)	-
9th	139 (10)	168 (10)	194 (10)	-
10th	144 (11)	202 (9)	194 (11)	-

GUYANA v SOUTH AFRICA A — First-class 3-day match

Played at Uitvlugt Community Centre, Uitvlugt on 12,13,14 September 2000 — Toss: Guyana
Umpires: D Balgobin & D Anandjit
Debuts: Guy: KF Bazil, S Chattergoon, H Garbarran, R Griffith, E Katchay & SE Thompson (all FC). SAA: None
Close of Play: Day 1: SAA (1) 2-0 (Bruyns 1*, Watson 1*, 1 over). Day 2: SAA (1) 166-5 (Kemp 24*, Pothas 7*, 77 overs).
Result: Match drawn

On a slow pitch, runs were difficult to come by in an undistinguished match. Watson batted doggedly for the tourists.

GUYANA

FIRST INNINGS	*Runs*	*Mins*	*Balls*	*4*	*6*	*SECOND INNINGS*	*Runs*	*Mins*	*Balls*	*4*	*6*
*NA de Groot c Pothas b Ngam	7	39	28	1	-	b Kemp	11	108	72	2	-
S Chattergoon b Langeveldt	7	53	30	1	-	c and b Kemp	17	83	54	1	1
H Garbarran c Bryant b Ngam	2	10	10	-	-	b Benkenstein	10	63	46	2	-
N Deonarine c Benkenstein b Bruyns	19	161	115	1	-	not out	24	114	87	4	-
TM Dowlin b Kemp	46	208	160	4	-	lbw b Ontong	3	37	32	-	-
H Pooran lbw b Kemp	13	29	26	3	-	not out	8	37	34	-	-
†V Nagamootoo c Bryant b Mpitsang	32	70	60	6	-						
SE Thompson c Bruyns b Ontong	6	33	25	1	-						
E Katchay c Langeveldt b Ontong	28	57	50	3	1						
KF Bazil run out	6	21	17	1	-						
R Griffith not out	5	20	14	-	-						
Extras (b 9, lb 5, w 1, nb 3)	18					Extras (b 4, lb 1, w 1, nb 2)	8				
TOTAL (87 overs)	**189**					**TOTAL (for 4 wkts) (54 overs)**	**81**				

SOUTH AFRICA A

	Runs	*Mins*	*Balls*	*4*	*6*
ML Bruyns b Griffith	8	34	25	-	-
DJ Watson c Dowlin b Thompson	69	236	204	7	-
JDC Bryant lbw b Griffith	0	1	1	-	-
*DM Benkenstein c and b Katchay	26	82	72	3	1
AG Prince b Thompson	29	75	69	3	1
JM Kemp lbw b Dowlin	24	80	79	2	1
†N Pothas c de Groot b Bazil	10	45	38	1	-
JL Ontong b Griffith	35	84	72	2	1
CK Langeveldt not out	10	90	70	1	-
PV Mpitsang b Katchay	0	5	3	-	-
M Ngam lbw b Katchay	0	9	6	-	-
Extras (b 1, lb 3)	4				
TOTAL (104 overs)	**215**				

Bowling	*O*	*M*	*R*	*W*		*O*	*M*	*R*	*W*
SOUTH AFRICA A									
Ngam	15	6	27	2		6	1	17	0
Mpitsang	12	6	27	1		11	6	7	0
Langeveldt	15	3	43	1		9	5	6	0
Kemp	15	4	25	2		7	1	13	2
Ontong	25	10	49	2		12	3	22	1
Bruyns	5	2	4	1	(7)	4	3	1	0
Benkenstein					(6)	5	1	10	1
GUYANA									
Griffith	18	6	41	3					
Katchay	20	5	46	3					
Bazil	38	13	54	1					
Chattergoon	1	1	0	0					
Thompson	23	6	61	2					
Dowlin	4	1	9	1					

Fall of Wickets	**Guy**	**SAA**	**Guy**
	1st	1st	2nd
1st	18 (1)	22 (1)	34 (2)
2nd	22 (3)	22 (3)	44 (1)
3rd	22 (2)	76 (4)	57 (3)
4th	87 (4)	127 (5)	66 (5)
5th	105 (6)	152 (2)	-
6th	116 (5)	167 (6)	-
7th	137 (8)	169 (7)	-
8th	155 (7)	210 (8)	-
9th	177 (10)	215 (10)	-
10th	189 (9)	215 (11)	-

WEST INDIES A v SOUTH AFRICA A — 2nd 'Test'

Played at Bourda, Georgetown on 16,17,18,19 September 2000 — Toss: South Africa A
Umpires: CR Duncan & D Somwaru
Debuts: WIA: None. SAA: None
Close of Play: Day 1: SAA (1) 109-1 (Bruyns 50*, Smith 15*, 48 overs). Day 2: SAA (1) 254-7 (Kemp 5*, Langeveldt 0*, 138 overs). Day 3: WIA (2) 37-1 (Smith 18*, 15.4 overs).
Result: Match drawn

Benkenstein made the right decision when he sent West Indies A in, with Willoughby, Ngam and Langeveldt taking full advantage of helpful conditions early on, routing the home batsmen. South Africa A were already in the lead with nine first wickets in hand at the end of the first day.

It was a slow pitch which required patience and Bruyns provided it in a marathon innings spanning nine hours. South Africa A seemed set for victory but rain severely reduced the amount of play possible on the last two days and the series ended in stalemate.

WEST INDIES A

FIRST INNINGS	*Runs*	*Mins*	*Balls*	*4*	*6*	*SECOND INNINGS*	*Runs*	*Mins*	*Balls*	*4*	*6*
A Haniff c Prince b Ngam	9	25	21	1	-	c Pothas b Ngam	18	73	53	3	-
DS Smith c Benkenstein b Willoughby	14	32	18	2	-	b Langeveldt	23	122	69	3	-
RS Morton c Bruyns b Willoughby	8	47	24	2	-	not out	60	144	96	9	-
SC Joseph c Ngam b Langeveldt	9	20	17	1	-	c Bruyns b Ontong	1	22	17	-	-
MN Samuels lbw b Langeveldt	0	14	10	-	-	not out	19	70	56	3	-
RO Hinds b Ngam	1	30	20	-	-						
*†CO Browne c Benkenstein b Ngam	19	93	47	3	-						
D Ramnarine b Willoughby	3	27	17	-	-						
MI Black lbw b Kemp	1	13	11	-	-						
CEL Stuart b Langeveldt	13	52	38	1	-						
KCB Jeremy not out	6	27	16	1	-						
Extras (b 5, lb 2, w 2, nb 3)	12					Extras (b 1, lb 1, nb 2)	4				
TOTAL (40 overs)	**95**					**TOTAL (for 3 wkts) (48.4 overs)**	**125**				

SOUTH AFRICA A

	Runs	Mins	Balls	4	6
ML Bruyns lbw b Stuart	126	540	409	11	-
DJ Watson lbw b Ramnarine	33	150	132	4	-
GC Smith c Joseph b Stuart	28	89	84	3	-
*DM Benkenstein c Morton b Stuart	15	115	65	-	-
AG Prince b Stuart	5	46	31	-	-
JL Ontong lbw b Hinds	20	93	80	3	-
†N Pothas b Black	3	58	33	-	-
JM Kemp c Jeremy b Ramnarine	20	89	59	2	-
CK Langeveldt c and b Black	0	16	13	-	-
M Ngam c sub (N Deonarine) b Ramnarine	3	41	21	-	-
CM Willoughby not out	6	20	7	1	-
Extras (b 1, lb 3, w 1, nb 21)	26				
TOTAL (153.3 overs)	**285**				

Bowling	*O*	*M*	*R*	*W*		*O*	*M*	*R*	*W*
SOUTH AFRICA A									
Willoughby	14	3	35	3		14	3	31	0
Ngam	10	3	21	3		14	4	36	1
Langeveldt	10	6	15	3	(4)	6	4	13	1
Kemp	6	1	17	1	(5)	4.4	1	14	0
Ontong					(3)	9	3	25	1
Bruyns						1	0	4	0
WEST INDIES A									
Black	37	7	87	2					
Stuart	30	9	60	4					
Jeremy	19	6	42	0					
Ramnarine	44.3	14	66	3					
Samuels	14	10	10	0					
Hinds	9	3	16	1					

Fall of Wickets

	WIA	SAA	WIA
	1st	1st	2nd
1st	23 (1)	80 (2)	37 (1)
2nd	27 (2)	130 (3)	63 (2)
3rd	44 (4)	169 (4)	73 (4)
4th	48 (5)	186 (5)	-
5th	48 (3)	239 (6)	-
6th	51 (6)	249 (1)	-
7th	63 (8)	253 (7)	-
8th	72 (9)	257 (9)	-
9th	83 (7)	273 (10)	-
10th	95 (10)	285 (8)	-

JAMAICA v SOUTH AFRICA A — Limited Overs match

Played at Kensington Cricket Club, East Kingston on 21 September 2000 — Toss: South Africa A
Umpires: C Fletcher & M Noble
Result: South Africa A won by 79 runs

Dros played a fine innings to give South Africa a comfortable win in a warm-up match before the one- day series against West Indies A.

SOUTH AFRICA A	Runs	Mins	Balls	4	6
DJ Watson c Samuels b Stewart	43	96	85	2	2
AG Prince c Breese b Mais	11	13	10	2	-
G Dros not out	92	188	121	4	2
JDC Bryant c Samuels b McKenzie	34	64	52	2	-
*DM Benkenstein c Garrick b Lambert	19	26	32	1	-
JM Kemp not out	14	18	9	1	1
†N Pothas					
RJ Peterson					
GJ-P Kruger					
PV Mpitsang					
M Ngam					
Extras (lb 4, w 10, nb 11)	25				
TOTAL (for 4 wkts) (50 overs)	**238**				

JAMAICA	Runs	Mins	Balls	4	6
LV Garrick c Kemp b Ngam	16	54	38	1	-
BA Parchment c Kemp b Peterson	39	138	69	4	-
†KH Hibbert c Prince b Kruger	20	55	45	1	-
DE Bernard run out (Prince)	14	42	30	1	-
*RG Samuels b Kemp	16	37	25	1	1
TL Lambert c Bryant b Peterson	7	17	10	-	-
GR Breese c Pothas b Peterson	13	13	17	1	-
RO Stewart c sub (JL Ontong) b Kruger	2	11	5	-	-
DS McKenzie not out	8	18	13	1	-
SK Dennis c Ngam b Kemp	5	5	4	1	-
DH Mais lbw b Kemp	0	9	3	-	-
Extras (lb 5, w 9, nb 5)	19				
TOTAL (45.1 overs)	**159**				

Jam	O	M	R	W
Mais	10	1	64	1
McKenzie	9	1	36	1
Stewart	7	2	21	1
Breese	8	0	32	0
Dennis	6	0	30	0
Bernard	5	0	24	0
Lambert	5	0	27	1

SAA	O	M	R	W
Ngam	8	0	21	1
Mpitsang	8	1	34	0
Kruger	9	0	30	2
Kemp	8.1	1	32	3
Peterson	10	0	28	3
Benkenstein	2	1	9	0

Fall of Wickets	SAA	Jam
1st	19 (2)	37 (1)
2nd	80 (1)	77 (3)
3rd	159 (4)	104 (2)
4th	200 (5)	115 (4)
5th	-	129 (6)
6th	-	131 (5)
7th	-	144 (7)
8th	-	144 (8)
9th	-	149 (10)
10th	-	159 (11)

WEST INDIES A v SOUTH AFRICA A — 1st 'Limited Overs International'

Played at Sabina Park, Kingston on 23 September 2000 — Toss: West Indies A

Umpires: N Malcolm & T Wilson

Debuts: WIA: None. SAA: None

Result: South Africa A won by 83 runs

Notes: Match reduced to 41 overs per side after rain interruption with SAA 69-1 in 21 overs

Despite having to re-set their sights after rain interrupted their innings, South Africa A gained a comfortable win, with Bryant playing a sparkling innings. South Africa's pace bowlers continued their good form, with Langeveldt proving the most successful on the day.

SOUTH AFRICA A	Runs	Mins	Balls	4	6
ML Bruyns c Dillon b Williams	42	106	62	5	-
DJ Watson c Joseph b Jeremy	10	53	34	1	-
G Dros c Joseph b Williams	54	86	77	7	-
JDC Bryant lbw b Stuart	50	49	40	4	1
*DM Benkenstein b Dillon	8	22	10	-	-
JM Kemp b Stuart	5	15	6	-	-
JL Ontong c Joseph b Stuart	4	4	4	-	-
†N Pothas not out	1	4	1	-	-
CK Langeveldt					
M Ngam					
CM Willoughby					
Extras (b 1, lb 3, w 6, nb 2)	12				
TOTAL (for 7 wkts) (41 overs)	**186**				

WEST INDIES A	Runs	Mins	Balls	4	6
A Haniff c Pothas b Willoughby	9	27	24	-	-
*†CO Browne c Bruyns b Langeveldt	30	54	31	5	-
RS Morton c Pothas b Langeveldt	14	49	22	1	-
SC Joseph lbw b Kemp	0	4	1	-	-
MN Samuels c Kemp b Langeveldt	12	32	26	1	-
RO Hinds c Pothas b Langeveldt	2	16	12	-	-
LR Williams not out	19	52	39	2	-
M Dillon lbw b Dros	2	12	7	-	-
D Ramnarine c Pothas b Dros	0	6	5	-	-
KCB Jeremy b Benkenstein	4	18	9	-	-
CEL Stuart c Pothas b Ngam	6	11	9	-	-
Extras (b 1, w 4)	5				
TOTAL (31.2 overs)	**103**				

WIA	O	M	R	W
Dillon	8	2	27	1
Stuart	8	0	33	3
Jeremy	8	1	36	1
Williams	8	0	50	2
Ramnarine	9	0	36	0

SAA	O	M	R	W
Willoughby	7	1	23	1
Ngam	4.2	0	21	1
Langeveldt	9	2	23	4
Kemp	6	1	22	1
Dros	3	1	7	2
Benkenstein	2	0	6	1

Fall of Wickets	SAA	WIA
1st	28 (2)	24 (1)
2nd	87 (1)	50 (2)
3rd	142 (3)	55 (4)
4th	173 (4)	63 (3)
5th	179 (5)	71 (5)
6th	184 (7)	72 (6)
7th	186 (6)	79 (8)
8th	-	79 (9)
9th	-	89 (10)
10th	-	103 (11)

WEST INDIES A v SOUTH AFRICA A 2nd 'Limited Overs International'

Played at Sabina Park, Kingston on 24 September 2000 Toss: West Indies A
Umpires: SA Bucknor & C Fletcher
Debuts: WIA: None. SAA: None
Result: South Africa A won by 4 wickets

After another good bowling performance, with Kemp leading the way, South Africa A clinched the series, with Smith and Benkenstein putting on 98 for the fourth wicket.

WEST INDIES A	Runs	Mins	Balls	4	6
A Haniff lbw b Kruger	5	20	15	-	-
*†CO Browne c Benkenstein b Kemp	30	98	64	1	1
RS Morton run out	15	79	46	2	-
SC Joseph c Willoughby b Benkenstein	19	47	33	2	-
MN Samuels lbw b Kemp	31	71	58	3	-
RO Hinds c Pothas b Benkenstein	2	10	4	-	-
LR Williams c Ontong b Kemp	11	37	24	-	-
M Dillon c Bryant b Kemp	8	25	20	-	-
D Ramnarine b Langeveldt	13	27	22	1	-
MI Black run out	2	7	3	-	-
KCB Jeremy not out	1	7	3	-	-
Extras (b 2, lb 14, w 22, nb 2)	40				
TOTAL (50 overs)	**177**				

SOUTH AFRICA A	Runs	Mins	Balls	4	6
GC Smith c Browne b Black	59	156	98	6	-
ML Bruyns b Black	3	20	17	-	-
G Dros c Morton b Black	11	18	18	2	-
JDC Bryant c Joseph b Black	0	1	1	-	-
*DM Benkenstein not out	68	168	99	4	1
JL Ontong c Hinds b Ramnarine	13	27	20	-	-
†N Pothas c Joseph b Ramnarine	6	12	13	-	-
JM Kemp not out	3	12	10	-	-
CK Langeveldt					
GJ-P Kruger					
CM Willoughby					
Extras (b 2, w 9, nb 6)	17				
TOTAL (for 6 wkts) (46.1 overs)	**180**				

SAA	O	M	R	W
Willoughby	10	3	16	0
Kruger	9	0	29	1
Langeveldt	10	1	30	1
Kemp	10	0	43	4
Dros	3	0	16	0
Benkenstein	6	0	20	2
Ontong	2	0	7	0

WIA	O	M	R	W
Dillon	8	1	20	0
Black	8	4	17	4
Jeremy	5	0	29	0
Williams	5	0	17	0
Ramnarine	10	1	39	2
Samuels	1.1	0	11	0
Hinds	9	1	45	0

Fall of Wickets	WIA	SAA
1st	17 (1)	12 (2)
2nd	62 (2)	27 (3)
3rd	78 (3)	27 (4)
4th	111 (4)	125 (1)
5th	116 (6)	148 (6)
6th	142 (5)	163 (7)
7th	153 (7)	-
8th	161 (8)	-
9th	171 (10)	-
10th	177 (9)	-

SOUTH AFRICA A IN WEST INDIES 2000/01 FIRST-CLASS AVERAGES

Batting & Fielding

Name	M	Inns	NO	Runs	HS	Avg	100	50	Ct	St
G Dros	2	3	1	94	67*	47.00	0	1	1	0
GJ-P Kruger	2	3	1	90	58	45.00	0	1	0	0
ML Bruyns	5	7	0	242	126	34.57	1	1	8	0
DM Benkenstein	4	6	0	185	57	30.83	0	2	3	0
GC Smith	4	7	1	180	47	30.00	0	0	1	0
DJ Watson	5	8	1	193	69	27.57	0	1	0	0
AG Prince	4	5	0	129	69	25.80	0	1	1	0
JL Ontong	5	7	0	153	57	21.85	0	1	2	0
N Pothas	3	4	1	63	42*	21.00	0	0	6	0
JM Kemp	3	4	1	56	24	18.66	0	0	4	0
CK Langeveldt	4	5	2	49	28*	16.33	0	0	2	0
PV Mpitsang	2	2	0	11	11	5.50	0	0	1	0
RJ Peterson	3	5	0	21	11	4.20	0	0	3	0
CM Willoughby	3	4	2	7	6*	3.50	0	0	1	0
JDC Bryant	2	2	0	7	7	3.50	0	0	4	0
M Ngam	4	5	0	8	3	1.60	0	0	3	0
Totals	55	77	10	1488	126		1	8	40	0
			Extras	125				subs	0	
			Total	1613		24.07			40	

SOUTH AFRICA A IN WEST INDIES 2000/01

Bowling

Name	Overs	Mdns	Runs	Wkts	Avg	BB	5I	10M
ML Bruyns	10	5	9	1	9.00	1-4	0	0
DM Benkenstein	5	1	10	1	10.00	1-10	0	0
GJ-P Kruger	33	6	101	6	16.83	4-39	0	0
M Ngam	97.4	24	256	13	19.69	3-21	0	0
JM Kemp	45.4	9	120	6	20.00	2-13	0	0
CK Langeveldt	75	21	235	11	21.36	3-15	0	0
RJ Peterson	71.5	19	187	8	23.37	5-68	1	0
CM Willoughby	94	27	243	10	24.30	3-35	0	0
G Dros	11.2	1	26	1	26.00	1-5	0	0
JL Ontong	76	24	159	6	26.50	2-24	0	0
PV Mpitsang	41	16	88	1	88.00	1-27	0	0
Totals	560.3	153	1434	64		5-68	1	0
		b & lb	89	1 run outs				
		Total	1523	65	23.43			

BANGLADESH IN SOUTH AFRICA 2000/01

Having recently acquired Test-playing status, Bangladesh made a short tour of South Africa during October 2000. It was an appropriate choice of venue because their South African coach, Eddie Barlow, had played a substantial role in raising the standard of the team to the level required by the International Cricket Council. Sadly, Barlow had suffered a stroke and his illness eventually led to him having to resign from the job.

The tour showed just how far the tourists had to go before becoming a force in world cricket, especially on pitches outside the Asian sub-continent. They were beaten by Griqualand West in their only first-class match and were outplayed in three limited overs matches. Originally due to play against South Africa A, they played against a wider spread of South Africa's fringe players in the form of Board President's teams.

GRIQUALAND WEST v BANGLADESHIS — First-class 4-day match

Played at De Beers Diamond Oval, Kimberley on 12,13,14,15 October 2000 — Toss: Griqualand West
Umpires: ST Jivan & AE Williams
Debuts: GW: AK Kruger (FC). Ban: Mohammad Rafiq (FC)
Close of Play: Day 1: GW (1) 285-8 (Koortzen 102*, Kidwell 2*, 110 overs). Day 2: Ban (1) 275-9 (Akram Khan 97*, Hasibul Hussain 0*, 82 overs). Day 3: GW (2) 263-6 (Bossenger 25*, Kruis 9*, 96 overs).
Result: Griqualand West won by 82 runs

A final afternoon batting collapse saw the new ICC full members lose their short-tour opener. Set a victory target of 331 off a minimum of 79 overs, the visitors were given a brisk 112-run start by Javed Omar and Al-Sahariar, then found little-known Griqua leg-spinner, Craig Copeland, too much to handle.

Bowling splendidly and receiving good support from the fielders, Copeland took the first seven Bangladesh wickets to fall, before returning to finish off the visitors' innings in the last hour. The 23- year-old's career-best figures of 8/101 in 30.3 overs gave him a remarkable 12/213 match-return.

Earlier Griqua match highlights were maiden first-class centuries for Pieter Koortzen (first innings) and Grant Elliott (second innings). Fast bowler Deon Kruis took five wickets in the Bangladeshi first innings. The visitors were enthusiastic but inexperienced. Akram Khan's unbeaten 129 and 51 and skipper and offspinner Naimur Rahman's six wickets in the match were encouraging.

GRIQUALAND WEST

FIRST INNINGS	*Runs*	*Mins*	*Balls*	*4*	*6*	*SECOND INNINGS*	*Runs*	*Mins*	*Balls*	*4*	*6*
JM Arthur b Mohammad Rafiq	47	117	123	7	-	run out (Al-Sahariar Rokon)	3	13	15	-	-
*MI Gidley b Naimur Rahman	21	112	87	2	-	b Naimur Rahman	19	79	80	1	-
GD Elliott c sub (Ranjan Das) b Naimur Rahman	44	98	86	4	1	b Mushfiqur Rahman	125	291	239	10	-
WM Dry c Khaled Mashud b Naimur Rahman	0	4	6	-	-	c Javed Omar b Enamul Hoque	41	72	60	5	-
PPJ Koortzen c Aminul Islam b Hasibul Hussain	127	279	243	18	-	lbw b Mohammad Rafiq	10	37	31	1	-
LL Bosman run out (Javed Omar/Khaled Mashud)	12	35	28	2	-	lbw b Mohammad Rafiq	21	58	62	4	-
†W Bossenger c and b Mohammad Rafiq	1	31	13	-	-	hit wicket b Naimur Rahman	36	114	100	3	-
GJ Kruis lbw b Mohammad Rafiq	0	4	1	-	-	c Javed Omar b Naimur Rahman	59	110	103	8	1
AK Kruger b Mushfiqur Rahman	48	96	89	6	-	not out	15	33	26	3	-
EW Kidwell not out	15	63	46	2	-						
CA Copeland c Khaled Mashud b Mushfiqur Rahman	0	16	9	-	-						
Extras (b 1, lb 7, nb 1)	9					Extras (b 4, lb 3, nb 3)	10				
TOTAL (121.5 overs)	**324**					**TOTAL (for 8 wkts dec) (118.5 overs)**	**339**				

BANGLADESHIS

Javed Omar c Gidley b Kruis	10	30	29	2	-	c Bossenger b Copeland	41	122	96	7	-
Al-Sahariar Rokon c Elliott b Kruis	47	132	115	5	-	c Kidwell b Copeland	70	104	80	13	-
Habibul Bashar c Bossenger b Kruis	10	13	8	2	-	c Elliott b Copeland	20	49	34	2	-
Aminul Islam c Arthur b Copeland	27	134	107	4	-	b Copeland	0	1	1	-	-
Akram Khan not out	129	241	202	13	4	not out	51	146	122	6	-
Mushfiqur Rahman c Kruis b Copeland	6	42	30	1	-	(8) c Bossenger b Copeland	15	53	45	1	-
*Naimur Rahman c Bosman b Copeland	0	1	1	-	-	(6) c Dry b Copeland	10	14	14	1	-
†Khaled Mashud b Kruis	0	7	8	-	-	(7) c Kruis b Copeland	0	2	2	-	-
Enamul Hoque c Arthur b Kruis	1	9	7	-	-	c Bosman b Gidley	4	18	15	-	-
Mohammad Rafiq c Bosman b Gidley	51	57	51	5	4	b Kruis	7	18	16	1	-
Hasibul Hussain lbw b Copeland	19	71	36	4	-	lbw b Copeland	1	5	4	-	-
Extras (lb 5, w 5, nb 23)	33					Extras (b 7, lb 8, w 2, nb 12)	29				
TOTAL (95.1 overs)	**333**					**TOTAL (69.3 overs)**	**248**				

Bowling	*O*	*M*	*R*	*W*		*O*	*M*	*R*	*W*
BANGLADESH									
Hasibul Hussain	22	4	92	1		13	1	48	0
Mushfiqur Rahman	15.5	4	39	2		11	4	16	1
Enamul Hoque	24	4	59	0	(5)	16	1	54	1
Naimur Rahman	31	11	60	3		37.5	7	116	3
Mohammad Rafiq	24	5	46	3	(3)	38	10	80	2
Habibul Bashar	3	0	14	0					
Javed Omar	2	0	6	0	(6)	3	0	18	0
GRIQUALAND WEST									
Kruis	29	5	80	5		13	3	41	1
Kidwell	17	2	78	0		10	0	39	0
Copeland	34.1	6	112	4		30.3	1	101	8
Kruger	8	0	36	0		4	0	26	0
Gidley	7	2	22	1		12	2	26	1

Fall of Wickets	**GW**	**Ban**	**GW**	**Ban**
	1st	1st	2nd	2nd
1st	72 (2)	26 (1)	5 (1)	112 (2)
2nd	72 (1)	44 (3)	50 (2)	136 (1)
3rd	73 (4)	102 (2)	129 (4)	136 (4)
4th	164 (3)	133 (4)	157 (5)	158 (3)
5th	197 (6)	172 (6)	201 (6)	172 (6)
6th	199 (7)	172 (7)	238 (3)	172 (7)
7th	199 (8)	173 (8)	304 (7)	218 (8)
8th	279 (9)	176 (9)	339 (8)	231 (9)
9th	321 (5)	261 (10)	-	246 (10)
10th	324 (11)	333 (11)	-	248 (11)

SA PRESIDENT'S XI v BANGLADESHIS — 1st Limited Overs match

Played at Goodyear Park, Bloemfontein on 18 October 2000 — Toss: Bangladeshis
Umpires: WA Diedricks & S Wadvalla
Result: South African President's XI won by 7 wickets
Man of Match: Andre Nel

On a good batting pitch, the Bangladeshi batsmen were unable to come to terms with a lively pace attack in which Andre Nel, Dewald Pretorius and Charl Langeveldt all bowled impressively. Only fighting innings by Al-Saharian and the captain, Naimur Rahman, gave them respectability.

A century opening partnership between Mark Bruyns and Doug Watson made a South African victory a formality and Dale Benkenstein chipped in with an aggressive unbeaten 44.

BANGLADESHIS	*Runs*	*Mins*	*Balls*	*4*	*6*
Javed Omar c Amla b Pretorius	6	12	13	-	-
Al-Sahariar Rokon c Nel b Morkel	38	85	53	3	-
Habibul Bashar c Pothas b Nel	0	3	3	-	-
Aminul Islam c Pretorius b Langeveldt	23	66	52	2	-
Akram Khan lbw b Nel	12	51	38	-	-
Mushfiqur Rahman lbw b Langeveldt	0	8	3	-	-
*Naimur Rahman run out (Ontong)	52	74	61	3	-
†Khaled Mashud c Amla b Pretorius	11	28	25	-	-
Mohammad Rafiq not out	12	21	17	-	1
Enamul Hoque c Ontong b Morkel	5	13	9	-	-
Ranjan Das c and b Nel	0	2	3	-	-
Extras (lb 5, w 11, nb 3)	19				
TOTAL (45.4 overs)	**178**				

SA PRESIDENT'S XI	*Runs*	*Mins*	*Balls*	*4*	*6*
ML Bruyns st Khaled Mashud b Enamul Hoque	55	107	77	6	-
DJ Watson c and b Enamul Hoque	39	103	94	3	-
IJL Trott b Habibul Bashar	10	25	19	1	-
JL Ontong not out	23	68	60	-	-
*DM Benkenstein not out	44	47	45	4	1
AM Amla					
†N Pothas					
JA Morkel					
CK Langeveldt					
A Nel					
D Pretorius					
Extras (lb 5, w 5)	10				
TOTAL (for 3 wkts) (49.1 overs)	**181**				

SAP	***O***	***M***	***R***	***W***
Pretorius	8	2	24	2
Nel	9.4	0	36	3
Morkel	10	2	40	2
Langeveldt	8	0	27	2
Benkenstein	5	0	21	0
Ontong	5	0	25	0

Ban	***O***	***M***	***R***	***W***
Ranjan Das	10	0	29	0
Mushfiqur Rahman	7	2	23	0
Mohammad Rafiq	9.1	0	41	0
Naimur Rahman	10	1	32	0
Enamul Hoque	10	0	32	2
Habibul Bashar	3	0	19	1

Fall of Wickets	***Ban***	***SAP***
1st	13 (1)	104 (2)
2nd	14 (3)	105 (1)
3rd	82 (4)	127 (3)
4th	82 (2)	-
5th	83 (6)	-
6th	125 (5)	-
7th	156 (8)	-
8th	159 (7)	-
9th	177 (10)	-
10th	178 (11)	-

SA PRESIDENT'S XI v BANGLADESHIS — 2nd Limited Overs match

Played at The Oval, Pietermaritzburg on 22 October 2000 — Toss: SA President's XI
Umpires: AE Williams & S Wadvalla
Result: South African President's XI won by 10 wickets
Man of Match: Charl Langeveldt

The Bangladeshis' problems against quality pace bowling were ruthlessly exposed by a pace attack in which only Langeveldt remained from the team that played in Bloemfontein. It was Langeveldt, though, who did the most damage after Willoughby and Ngam made the early breakthroughs.

BANGLADESHIS	Runs	Mins	Balls	4	6
Javed Omar c Tsolekile b Ngam	0	25	16	-	-
Al-Sahariar Rokon c Langeveldt b Willoughby	7	18	14	1	-
Habibul Bashar b Willoughby	11	17	19	1	-
Aminul Islam c van Jaarsveld b Langeveldt	6	38	16	1	-
Akram Khan c Tsolekile b Langeveldt	9	18	19	-	-
*Naimur Rahman c van Jaarsveld b Langeveldt	5	15	8	1	-
†Khaled Mashud c Amla b Langeveldt	1	21	11	-	-
Mohammad Rafiq lbw b Langeveldt	0	3	2	-	-
Mushfiqur Rahman c Tsolekile b Kemp	0	13	6	-	-
Hasibul Hussain not out	0	4	1	-	-
Ranjan Das c Tsolekile b Kemp	0	1	1	-	-
Extras (lb 2, w 8, nb 2)	12				
TOTAL (18.3 overs)	**51**				

SA PRESIDENT'S XI	Runs	Mins	Balls	4	6
ML Bruyns not out	18	62	50	2	-
GC Smith not out	28	62	35	4	-
AM Amla					
M van Jaarsveld					
*DM Benkenstein					
JL Ontong					
JM Kemp					
†TL Tsolekile					
CK Langeveldt					
M Ngam					
CM Willoughby					
Extras (lb 3, w 4)	7				
TOTAL (for 0 wkts) (14.1 overs)	**53**				

SAP	O	M	R	W
Willoughby	8	1	22	2
Ngam	5	0	19	1
Langeveldt	4	1	7	5
Kemp	1.3	0	1	2

Ban	O	M	R	W
Hasibul Hussain	5	1	12	0
Ranjan Das	4	0	10	0
Naimur Rahman	2	0	15	0
Mushfiqur Rahman	2	1	4	0
Mohammad Rafiq	1	0	5	0
Javed Omar	0.1	0	4	0

Fall of Wickets	Ban	SAP
1st	11 (2)	-
2nd	14 (1)	-
3rd	24 (3)	-
4th	38 (5)	-
5th	48 (4)	-
6th	49 (6)	-
7th	49 (8)	-
8th	51 (7)	-
9th	51 (9)	-
10th	51 (11)	-

SA PRESIDENT'S XI v BANGLADESHIS — 3rd Limited Overs match

Played at Kingsmead, Durban on 23 October 2000 — Toss: Bangladeshis
Umpires: S Wadvalla & AE Williams
Result: South African President's XI won by 202 runs
Man of Match: Mfuneko Ngam

After their humiliating batting collapse the previous day, the tourists opted to field first, enabling the President's XI to produce a solid batting performance during which they scored at better than five runs an over. Batting second did not make any difference to the Bangladeshis' performance and they were again swept aside by the South African pace attack, being reduced to 23 for seven by Ngam and Willoughby before recovering slightly to exceed their Pietermaritzburg total by six runs.

SA PRESIDENT'S XI	Runs	Mins	Balls	4	6
GC Smith b Naimur Rahman	56	100	69	6	-
AM Amla c Aminul Islam b Naimur Rahman	68	114	90	5	1
JA Rudolph c Khaled Mashud b Hasibul Hussain	48	70	65	2	-
M van Jaarsveld c Aminul Islam b Naimur Rahman	62	71	63	5	-
*DM Benkenstein not out	14	23	12	-	-
JL Ontong c Mushfiqur Rahman b Hasibul Hussain	2	4	3	-	-
JM Kemp not out	1	3	1	-	-
†TL Tsolekile					
CK Langeveldt					
M Ngam					
CM Willoughby					
Extras (lb 1, w 4, nb 3)	8				
TOTAL (for 5 wkts) (50 overs)	**259**				

BANGLADESHIS	Runs	Mins	Balls	4	6
Al-Sahariar Rokon c van Jaarsveld b Willoughby	4	27	21	1	-
Habibul Bashar lbw b Willoughby	1	11	6	-	-
†Khaled Mashud lbw b Willoughby	1	20	13	-	-
Aminul Islam c Tsolekile b Ngam	1	20	8	-	-
Akram Khan not out	10	93	61	-	-
*Naimur Rahman b Ngam	1	7	5	-	-
Mushfiqur Rahman c Tsolekile b Ngam	0	6	3	-	-
Mohammad Rafiq b Ngam	4	4	4	1	-
Enamul Hoque c Rudolph b Langeveldt	10	24	25	1	-
Hasibul Hussain c Ontong b Kemp	4	20	13	-	-
Monjurul Islam run out (Ngam/Tsolekile)	6	10	9	1	-
Extras (lb 1, w 10, nb 4)	15				
TOTAL (27.2 overs)	**57**				

BANGLADESH IN SOUTH AFRICA 2000/01

Ban	*O*	*M*	*R*	*W*
Hasibul Hussain	8	0	33	2
Monjurul Islam	6	0	28	0
Mushfiqur Rahman	5	0	28	0
Mohammad Rafiq	9	0	54	0
Naimur Rahman	9	0	45	3
Enamul Hoque	10	0	51	0
Habibul Bashar	3	0	19	0

SAP	*O*	*M*	*R*	*W*
Willoughby	8	3	9	3
Ngam	8	0	20	4
Kemp	6	0	14	1
Langeveldt	5.2	1	13	1

Fall of Wickets	*SAP*	*Ban*
1st	118 (1)	4 (2)
2nd	133 (2)	12 (1)
3rd	232 (3)	14 (3)
4th	248 (4)	19 (4)
5th	256 (6)	23 (6)
6th	-	23 (7)
7th	-	27 (8)
8th	-	42 (9)
9th	-	50 (10)
10th	-	57 (11)

SOUTH AFRICA UNDER 19 IN NEW ZEALAND

Back, from left: Chad Baxter, Craig Thysen, Imraan Khan, Stephen Cook, Monde Zondeki, Christo Karemaker, Michael Price, Gerhard de Bruin, Hashim Amla, Warren Hauptfleisch, Ian Postman, James Schorn. Front: Zwelibanzi Homani, Hylton Ackerman (coach), Rivash Gobind (captain), Peter Habberton (manager), Johan Botha (vice-captain), Lawrence Mahatlane (assistant coach), Shane Jabaar (physiotherapist).

SOUTH AFRICA UNDER 19 IN NEW ZEALAND

On the face of it, the South African under 19 team had a disappointing tour of New Zealand. They were convincingly beaten in the first two of three four-day matches against their New Zealand counterparts, drew a rain-affected third match and shared a limited overs series 1-1 with one match washed out.

The results don't tell the story, according to Hylton Ackerman, the Test selector who coached the youngsters. "We had a marvellous time," enthused Ackerman, "we spent a month learning about cricket."

Ackerman said the players would benefit from the experience, especially because many of the squad will still be eligible for selection for the 2002 Under 19 World Cup in Christchurch, where they were based for much of the recent tour.

Ackerman was concerned, though, that there are flaws in the current under-age system which he planned to report on in detail to the United Cricket Board.

"Our young cricketers only play limited overs cricket, which means the batsmen don't get into the habit of scoring centuries, while the bowlers don't know how to bowl long spells." He said the side was under-prepared at the start of their tour in mid-January.

"They were picked on their performances of one week of one-day cricket in December, then they went off on their school holidays and only got together again in time to fly to New Zealand. Our opponents had been together for a month and quite a few of them have played at senior level. We went almost straight into the first four-day game, which was the first time any of our players had played in a long match."

Ackerman singled out several individuals who he said had the potential to make an impact at senior level. Hashim Amla made half-centuries in each of the three four-day games. "He's only 17 but he was our best batsman," said Ackerman. Johan Botha was an all-rounder who showed plenty of determination, bowling brisk away swingers and batting soundly. "He was injured in a warm-up game. It was another example of inexperience. He bowled superbly then went to field at silly point where he got his ankle smashed so that he missed the first international. He should never have fielded there."

Monde Zondeki bowled with genuine pace, Imraan Khan was just 16 but showed ability as an off-spinner and batsman, and opening batsman James Schorn was reminiscent of the former Border and Natal batsman Chris Wilkins. "He's a wonderful striker of the ball but his defence is poor," said Ackerman.

A consistent thorn in the flesh of the South Africans was Brendon McCullum, of Otago, the Kiwi captain and wicketkeeper, who hit centuries in each of the three 'Tests'.

The South African Under 19 squad was: Rivash Gobind (captain), Johan Botha, Hashim Amla, Chad Baxter, Stephen Cook, Gerhard de Bruin, Warren Hauptfleisch, Zwelibanzi Homani, Christo Karemaker, Imraan Khan, Ian Postman, Michael Price, James Schorn, Craig Thysen, Monde Zondeki. Manager, Peter Habberton; coach, Hylton Ackerman; assistant coach, Lawrence Mahatlane; physiotherapist, Shane Jabaar.

TOUR RESULTS

Oamaru, 24-26 January 2001. South Africa Under 19 280-9* (JR Schorn 94, R Gobind 33, C Baxter 75, J Hodson 4-63) and 177-2* (JR Schorn 73*, R Gobind 73). Otago Under 19 157 (M Joyce 60, J Botha 6-10) and 216 (A Wilkinson 34, B Ryan 56*, G de Bruin 4-38, I Khan 4-91). South Africa Under 19 won by 84 runs.

SOUTH AFRICA UNDER 19 IN NEW ZEALAND

NEW ZEALAND U-19 v SOUTH AFRICA U-19 — 1st Youth Test

Played at Molyneux Park, Alexandra on 29,30,31 January 2001 — Toss: South Africa U-19
Umpires: RS Dunne & G Wilkinson
Close of Play: Day 1: NZ (1) 167-3 (Todd 66*, Taylor 54*, 53 overs). Day 2: SA (2) 72-2 (Gobind 9*, Amla 33*, 30 overs).
Result: New Zealand U-19 won by an innings and 67 runs

SOUTH AFRICA UNDER 19

FIRST INNINGS	*Runs*	*Mins*	*Balls*	*4*	*6*	*SECOND INNINGS*	*Runs*	*Mins*	*Balls*	*4*	*6*
SC Cook lbw b Butler	23	60	52	1	-	c McCullum b Butler	4	28	15	-	-
JR Schorn c McCullum b Robin	3	20	16	-	-	lbw b Butler	26	37	35	3	-
*R Gobind run out (Ellis)	68	174	106	10	-	c Todd b Robin	13	87	71	2	-
HM Amla c Taylor b Butler	4	29	21	-	-	c Taylor b Robertson	69	159	135	9	-
C Baxter c McCullum b Robin	8	9	10	2	-	b Woodcock	7	58	54	1	-
W Hauptfleisch c Lynch b Todd	3	9	12	-	-	c Robertson b Ellis	37	136	130	2	1
I Khan run out (Butler)	9	21	17	1	-	b Woodcock	4	16	19	-	-
†Z Homani c McCullum b Robin	2	12	14	-	-	lbw b Woodcock	7	50	54	-	-
C Karemaker lbw b Robin	5	32	28	-	-	c Nicol b Robin	13	42	40	1	-
G de Bruin c McCullum b Robertson	3	14	7	-	-	not out	0	6	3	-	-
I Postman not out	1	1	1	-	-	lbw b Ellis	0	2	3	-	-
Extras (b 6, lb 10, nb 5)	21					Extras (lb 2, nb 1)	3				
TOTAL (46.3 overs)	**150**					**TOTAL (93 overs)**	**183**				

NEW ZEALAND UNDER 19

	Runs	Mins	Balls	4	6
R Nicol b de Bruin	4	16	17	-	-
RK Lynch lbw b Hauptfleisch	18	56	42	2	-
GR Todd c Amla b Hauptfleisch	71	210	173	7	-
SL Stewart c Homani b de Bruin	3	26	30	-	-
R Taylor run out (Baxter/Hauptfleisch)	59	117	95	6	1
*†BB McCullum c Homani b de Bruin	123	223	141	16	1
L Woodcock run out (de Bruin)	22	53	58	-	-
A Ellis c Cook b Karemaker	63	190	165	9	-
I Robertson c Homani b Khan	6	34	22	1	-
IG Butler c Gobind b Karemaker	0	6	4	-	-
TP Robin not out	0	4	1	-	-
Extras (lb 11, w 9, nb 11)	31				
TOTAL (122.5 overs)	**400**				

Bowling	*O*	*M*	*R*	*W*		*O*	*M*	*R*	*W*
NEW ZEALAND UNDER 19									
Robin	18	5	65	4		20	7	67	2
Butler	14	4	32	2		9	2	25	2
Ellis	9	3	25	0	(5)	11	8	6	2
Todd	5	3	11	1					
Robertson	0.3	0	1	1	(3)	26	11	46	1
Woodcock					(4)	25	11	29	3
Nicol					(6)	2	0	8	0
SOUTH AFRICA UNDER 19									
Karemaker	24.5	4	120	2					
de Bruin	25	9	54	3					
Hauptfleisch	29	9	71	2					
Khan	20	5	45	1					
Postman	23	4	90	0					
Amla	1	0	9	0					

Fall of Wickets

	SA	NZ	SA
	1st	1st	2nd
1st	15 (2)	10 (1)	29 (1)
2nd	35 (1)	33 (2)	30 (2)
3rd	50 (4)	51 (4)	76 (3)
4th	63 (5)	174 (5)	117 (5)
5th	67 (6)	205 (3)	124 (4)
6th	86 (7)	253 (7)	131 (7)
7th	99 (8)	371 (6)	146 (8)
8th	125 (9)	393 (9)	183 (9)
9th	149 (10)	393 (10)	183 (6)
10th	150 (3)	400 (8)	183 (11)

NEW ZEALAND U-19 v SOUTH AFRICA U-19 — 2nd Youth Test

Played at Bert Sutcliffe Oval, Lincoln on 4,5,6,7 February 2001 — Toss: South Africa U-19
Umpires: JM Busby & PR Williams
Close of Play: Day 1: SA (1) 294-8 (Khan 20*, de Bruin 38*, 100 overs). Day 2: SA (2) 9-0 (Baxter 6*, Schorn 3*, 4 overs). Day 3: NZ (2) 11-0 (Todd 2*, Lynch 6*, 11 overs).
Result: New Zealand U-19 won by 6 wickets
Notes: R Nicol retired hurt with his score on 87 and the total on 234-4 in New Zealand Under 19's 2nd innings.

SOUTH AFRICA UNDER 19

FIRST INNINGS	*Runs*	*Mins*	*Balls*	*4*	*6*	*SECOND INNINGS*	*Runs*	*Mins*	*Balls*	*4*	*6*
C Baxter lbw b Butler	7	32	24	-	-	c Woodcock b Whiteman	51	182	136	8	-
†JR Schorn c McCullum b Butler	0	2	1	-	-	c McCullum b Woodcock	8	58	46	1	-
*R Gobind c Taylor b Butler	18	90	66	2	-	c Lynch b Woodcock	2	15	11	-	-
HM Amla c Nicol b Todd	37	81	51	5	-	c Lynch b Whiteman	58	124	104	5	1
M Price lbw b Todd	6	37	35	1	-	c Todd b Woodcock	64	136	102	7	2
J Botha c Taylor b Whiteman	101	234	173	15	-	c Lynch b Robin	32	71	61	3	-
W Hauptfleisch c Lynch b Robin	9	46	30	1	-	run out (Stewart)	2	16	9	-	-
C Thysen c Taylor b Nicol	32	143	110	4	-	b Woodcock	1	8	10	-	-
I Khan c Robin b Nicol	28	143	98	3	-	not out	15	64	47	-	-
G de Bruin c Whiteman b Nicol	42	75	57	7	-	c and b Robin	0	13	6	-	-
M Zondeki not out	1	15	10	-	-	b Whiteman	19	32	24	4	-
Extras (b 8, lb 8, w 2, nb 9)	27					Extras (b 1, lb 4, w 1, nb 1)	7				
TOTAL (107.3 overs)	**308**					**TOTAL (92.3 overs)**	**259**				

NEW ZEALAND UNDER 19

	Runs	*Mins*	*Balls*	*4*	*6*		*Runs*	*Mins*	*Balls*	*4*	*6*
GR Todd c Schorn b Zondeki	12	16	14	3	-	c Price b Zondeki	3	49	38	-	-
RK Lynch lbw b Botha	20	65	34	3	-	c Schorn b de Bruin	12	89	66	-	-
SL Stewart c Schorn b Thysen	23	42	43	3	-	c Schorn b Thysen	17	73	51	1	-
R Nicol b Botha	1	8	4	-	-	retired hurt	87	231	156	9	-
R Taylor lbw b Thysen	1	7	4	-	-	run out (Botha)	72	150	117	7	-
*†BB McCullum c Thysen b Botha	186	243	172	22	3	not out	46	68	42	3	1
L Woodcock c Schorn b Botha	3	15	15	-	-	not out	8	21	13	1	-
S Whiteman c Gobind b Thysen	5	31	23	-	-						
I Robertson b de Bruin	28	95	63	2	-						
IG Butler c Schorn b Thysen	3	42	28	-	-						
TP Robin not out	13	51	25	-	1						
Extras (b 2, lb 9, w 2, nb 3)	16					Extras (lb 8, w 2, nb 2)	12				
TOTAL (70.2 overs)	**311**					**TOTAL (for 4 wkts) (80.1 overs)**	**257**				

Bowling	*O*	*M*	*R*	*W*		*O*	*M*	*R*	*W*
NEW ZEALAND UNDER 19									
Butler	22	3	69	3	(4)	6	2	15	0
Robin	20	6	48	1	(1)	22	3	68	2
Whiteman	18	6	41	1	(2)	16.3	6	37	3
Woodcock	16	3	37	0	(3)	27	10	52	4
Todd	14	4	50	2	(7)	6	1	17	0
Robertson	6	2	24	0	(5)	5	0	29	0
Nicol	11.3	4	23	3	(6)	10	1	36	0
SOUTH AFRICA UNDER 19									
Zondeki	15	3	79	1		20	7	42	1
de Bruin	13	2	68	1		14	4	33	1
Hauptfleisch	11	0	26	0	(6)	8	2	25	0
Thysen	18	2	79	4	(5)	13	0	49	1
Khan	7	1	30	0	(3)	11	2	48	0
Botha	6.2	0	18	4	(4)	13.1	1	41	0
Amla						1	0	11	0

Fall of Wickets

	SA	NZ	SA	NZ
	1st	1st	2nd	2nd
1st	2 (2)	26 (1)	30 (2)	12 (1)
2nd	26 (1)	61 (3)	36 (3)	25 (2)
3rd	62 (3)	63 (2)	123 (1)	47 (3)
4th	73 (4)	64 (4)	128 (4)	181 (5)
5th	80 (5)	64 (5)	208 (6)	-
6th	106 (7)	71 (7)	216 (7)	-
7th	222 (8)	106 (8)	217 (8)	-
8th	237 (6)	209 (9)	228 (5)	-
9th	298 (10)	238 (10)	233 (10)	-
10th	308 (9)	311 (6)	259 (11)	-

NEW ZEALAND U-19 v SOUTH AFRICA U-19 — 3rd Youth Test

Played at Pukekura Park, New Plymouth on 10,11 (no play),12 (no play),13 February 2001 — Toss: New Zealand U-19

Umpires: GA Baxter & T Parlane

Close of Play: Day 1: NZ (1) 267-7 (Ellis 24*, Whiteman 10*, 100 overs). Day 2: no play. Day 3: no play.

Result: Match drawn

NEW ZEALAND UNDER 19

FIRST INNINGS	*Runs*	*Mins*	*Balls*	*4*	*6*
RK Lynch c Homani b Karemaker	16	56	41	2	-
GR Todd b Botha	11	35	23	1	-
SL Stewart c Karemaker b Postman	34	69	52	6	-
R Nicol c Botha b Thysen	13	77	59	1	-
R Taylor c Zondeki b Postman	6	16	11	-	-
*†BB McCullum c Homani b Karemaker	100	153	121	14	1
L Woodcock run out (Price)	38	223	159	2	-
A Ellis c Price b Zondeki	66	226	180	9	-
S Whiteman b Karemaker	14	67	50	3	-
I Robertson lbw b Zondeki	15	84	65	1	-
TP Robin not out	1	8	8	-	-
Extras (lb 12, w 5, nb 5)	22				
TOTAL (127.2 overs)	**336**				

SOUTH AFRICA UNDER 19					
SC Cook b Woodcock	19	58	54	2	-
JR Schorn c Ellis b Robin	20	48	28	2	1
*R Gobind c Whiteman b Woodcock	9	38	35	-	-
HM Amla not out	76	150	122	11	-
J Botha run out (Robin)	28	56	42	3	1
M Price not out	20	66	62	4	-
C Thysen					
†Z Homani					
C Karemaker					
M Zondeki					
I Postman					
Extras (b 6, lb 2, nb 1)	9				
TOTAL (for 4 wkts) (57 overs)	**181**				

Bowling	*O*	*M*	*R*	*W*
SOUTH AFRICA UNDER 19				
Zondeki	21.4	8	43	2
Botha	31.4	6	56	1
Karemaker	25	7	68	3
Postman	19	1	85	2
Thysen	27	9	59	1
Price	3	0	13	0
NEW ZEALAND UNDER 19				
Robin	8	2	26	1
Whiteman	10	1	38	0
Woodcock	15	5	36	2
Ellis	7	1	27	0
Robertson	11	3	29	0
Todd	4	0	13	0
Nicol	2	0	4	0

Fall of Wickets	NZ	SA
	1st	1st
1st	28 (2)	43 (2)
2nd	39 (1)	48 (1)
3rd	77 (3)	63 (3)
4th	85 (5)	142 (5)
5th	93 (4)	-
6th	210 (6)	-
7th	243 (7)	-
8th	277 (9)	-
9th	331 (8)	-
10th	336 (10)	-

NEW ZEALAND U-19 v SOUTH AFRICA U-19 — 1st Youth Limited Overs International

Played at Owen Delany Park, Taupo on 16,17 (no play) February 2001 — Toss: South Africa U-19

Umpires: T Parlane & IW Shine

Result: No Result

Notes: Close of Play: Day 1: SA 76-1 (Schorn 24*, Baxter 13*, 15 overs)

NEW ZEALAND UNDER 19	*Runs*	*Mins*	*Balls*	*4*	*6*
GR Todd c Homani b Zondeki	46	122	76	5	-
J Ryder c Baxter b de Bruin	10	29	21	1	-
SL Stewart c Botha b Thysen	42	62	55	7	1
*†BB McCullum run out (Botha/Zondeki)	12	19	12	1	-
R Taylor lbw b de Bruin	11	37	32	-	1
R Nicol st Homani b de Bruin	44	77	53	2	-
A Ellis not out	48	62	47	3	1
S Whiteman run out (Amla)	7	4	6	-	-
L Woodcock not out	1	7	2	-	-
IG Butler					
TP Robin					
Extras (b 1, lb 12, w 16, nb 4)	33				
TOTAL (for 7 wkts) (50 overs)	**254**				

SOUTH AFRICA UNDER 19	*Runs*	*Mins*	*Balls*	*4*	*6*
SC Cook run out (Woodcock)	28	41	32	4	-
JR Schorn not out	24	63	45	4	-
C Baxter not out	13	21	16	1	-
HM Amla					
*J Botha					
M Price					
C Thysen					
I Khan					
†Z Homani					
G de Bruin					
M Zondeki					
Extras (lb 4, w 4, nb 3)	11				
TOTAL (for 1 wkt) (15 overs)	**76**				

SA	*O*	*M*	*R*	*W*
Zondeki	10	0	52	1
de Bruin	10	1	52	3
Thysen	10	0	48	1
Botha	10	0	51	0
Khan	10	0	38	0

NZ	*O*	*M*	*R*	*W*
Robin	4	0	25	0
Butler	4	0	18	0
Ellis	4	0	17	0
Whiteman	3	0	12	0

Fall of Wickets	*NZ*	*SA*
1st	34 (2)	50 (1)
2nd	111 (3)	-
3rd	131 (4)	-
4th	134 (1)	-
5th	156 (5)	-
6th	221 (6)	-
7th	231 (8)	-

NEW ZEALAND U-19 v SOUTH AFRICA U-19 — 2nd Youth Limited Overs International

Played at Owen Delany Park, Taupo on 18 February 2001 — Toss: South Africa U-19

Umpires: T Parlane & IW Shine

Result: South Africa U-19 won by 7 wickets

NEW ZEALAND UNDER 19	Runs	Mins	Balls	4	6
GR Todd c Amla b Karemaker	2	12	14	-	-
RK Lynch run out (Price)	14	52	31	1	-
SL Stewart c de Bruin b Hauptfleisch	38	96	67	3	-
*†BB McCullum st Homani b Hauptfleisch	22	42	36	2	-
R Taylor c Karemaker b Price	20	53	48	1	1
R Nicol c and b Price	1	5	4	-	-
A Ellis b de Bruin	18	81	55	-	-
S Whiteman b de Bruin	12	19	11	-	-
L Woodcock not out	21	36	30	1	-
IG Butler not out	8	8	6	-	-
I Robertson					
Extras (lb 7, w 20, nb 2)	29				
TOTAL (for 8 wkts) (50 overs)	**185**				

SOUTH AFRICA UNDER 19	Runs	Mins	Balls	4	6
*R Gobind lbw b Ellis	25	65	48	-	-
JR Schorn c and b Nicol	44	42	4	6	2
C Baxter lbw b Ellis	41	67	51	-	1
HM Amla not out	47	80	59	3	1
J Botha not out	26	35	37	3	-
M Price					
W Hauptfleisch					
†Z Homani					
C Karemaker					
G de Bruin					
I Postman					
Extras (lb 1, w 3)	4				
TOTAL (for 3 wkts) (37.5 overs)	**187**				

SA	O	M	R	W
de Bruin	10	2	25	2
Karemaker	10	1	41	1
Botha	10	0	39	0
Hauptfleisch	6	1	14	2
Postman	3	0	23	0
Price	10	1	27	2
Amla	1	0	9	0

NZ	O	M	R	W
Butler	6	0	30	0
Woodcock	4	1	32	0
Nicol	10	0	33	1
Whiteman	4	0	26	0
Ellis	7.5	0	33	2
Robertson	6	1	32	0

Fall of Wickets	NZ	SA
1st	10 (1)	62 (2)
2nd	45 (2)	88 (1)
3rd	88 (4)	149 (3)
4th	93 (3)	-
5th	97 (6)	-
6th	123 (5)	-
7th	142 (8)	-
8th	175 (7)	-

NEW ZEALAND U-19 v SOUTH AFRICA U-19 — 3rd Youth Limited Overs International

Played at Eden Park Outer Oval, Auckland on 20 February 2001 — Toss: South Africa U-19

Umpires: KC Manley & MH Spencer-Smith

Result: New Zealand U-19 won by 19 runs

NEW ZEALAND UNDER 19	Runs	Mins	Balls	4	6
GR Todd b Khan	50	115	64	7	-
J Ryder run out (Cook)	4	6	4	1	-
SL Stewart c Amla b Zondeki	1	6	8	-	-
*†BB McCullum c Zondeki b Botha	44	32	23	6	2
R Taylor c Baxter b Botha	1	17	11	-	-
R Nicol run out (Baxter)	45	118	90	1	-
A Ellis c and b Price	16	50	52	1	-
S Whiteman not out	32	39	29	3	1
TP Robin b de Bruin	20	12	10	2	1
L Woodcock b de Bruin	3	6	4	-	-
IG Butler b de Bruin	1	2	3	-	-
Extras (b 1, lb 7, w 14)	22				
TOTAL (50 overs)	**239**				

SOUTH AFRICA UNDER 19	Runs	Mins	Balls	4	6
SC Cook c Ellis b Whiteman	16	35	21	2	1
JR Schorn c Ryder b Todd	93	175	106	8	4
C Baxter c McCullum b Ellis	0	16	6	-	-
HM Amla c Ryder b Ellis	0	9	6	-	-
*J Botha c McCullum b Ellis	42	57	55	6	-
M Price b Woodcock	15	23	21	1	1
I Khan c Nicol b Todd	9	39	22	-	-
G de Bruin st McCullum b Woodcock	0	5	5	-	-
†Z Homani not out	14	24	15	1	-
C Karemaker b Woodcock	9	16	18	1	-
M Zondeki lbw b Woodcock	0	1	2	-	-
Extras (b 2, lb 5, w 12, nb 3)	22				
TOTAL (45.5 overs)	**220**				

SA	O	M	R	W
de Bruin	10	0	64	3
Zondeki	7	1	35	1
Botha	8	0	47	2
Karemaker	10	1	38	0
Khan	10	2	31	1
Price	5	0	16	1

NZ	O	M	R	W
Robin	3	0	23	0
Butler	5	0	36	0
Whiteman	6	1	21	1
Ellis	10	1	23	3
Nicol	9	0	56	0
Woodcock	7.5	0	35	4
Todd	5	0	19	2

Fall of Wickets	NZ	SA
1st	6 (2)	39 (1)
2nd	7 (3)	54 (3)
3rd	73 (4)	55 (4)
4th	88 (5)	117 (5)
5th	129 (1)	141 (6)
6th	174 (7)	194 (2)
7th	196 (6)	195 (8)
8th	225 (9)	197 (7)
9th	235 (10)	220 (10)
10th	239 (11)	220 (11)

NEW ZEALAND UNDER 19 v SOUTH AFRICA UNDER 19 2000/01 'TEST' AVERAGES

NEW ZEALAND

Batting & Fielding

Name	M	Inns	NO	Runs	HS	Avg	100	50	Ct	St
BB McCullum	3	4	1	455	186	151.66	3	0	7	0
A Ellis	2	2	0	129	66	64.50	0	2	1	0
R Nicol	3	4	1	105	87*	35.00	0	1	2	0
R Taylor	3	4	0	138	72	34.50	0	2	5	0
GR Todd	3	4	0	97	71	24.25	0	1	2	0
L Woodcock	3	4	1	71	38	23.66	0	0	1	0
SL Stewart	3	4	0	77	34	19.25	0	0	0	0
RK Lynch	3	4	0	66	20	16.50	0	0	5	0
I Robertson	3	3	0	49	28	16.33	0	0	1	0
S Whiteman	2	2	0	19	14	9.50	0	0	2	0
IG Butler	2	2	0	3	3	1.50	0	0	0	0
TP Robin	3	3	3	14	13*	-	0	0	2	0
Totals	33	40	6	1223	186		3	6	28	0
			Extras	81				subs	0	
			Total	1304		38.35			28	

Bowling

Name	Overs	Mdns	Runs	Wkts	Avg	BB	5I	10M
L Woodcock	83	29	154	9	17.11	4-52	0	0
IG Butler	51	11	141	7	20.14	3-69	0	0
R Nicol	25.3	5	71	3	23.66	3-23	0	0
TP Robin	88	23	274	10	27.40	4-65	0	0
A Ellis	27	12	58	2	29.00	2-6	0	0
S Whiteman	44.3	13	116	4	29.00	3-37	0	0
GR Todd	29	8	91	3	30.33	2-50	0	0
I Robertson	48.3	16	129	2	64.50	1-1	0	0
Totals	396.3	117	1034	40		4-52	0	0
		b & lb	47	4 run outs				
		Total	1081	44	24.56			

SOUTH AFRICA

Batting & Fielding

Name	M	Inns	NO	Runs	HS	Avg	100	50	Ct	St
HM Amla	3	5	1	244	76*	61.00	0	3	1	0
J Botha	2	3	0	161	101	53.66	1	0	1	0
M Price	2	3	1	90	64	45.00	0	1	2	0
R Gobind	3	5	0	110	68	22.00	0	1	2	0
M Zondeki	2	2	1	20	19	20.00	0	0	1	0
I Khan	2	4	1	56	28	18.66	0	0	0	0
C Baxter	2	4	0	73	51	18.25	0	1	0	0
C Thysen	2	2	0	33	32	16.50	0	0	1	0
SC Cook	2	3	0	46	23	15.33	0	0	1	0
G de Bruin	2	4	1	45	42	15.00	0	0	0	0
W Hauptfleisch	2	4	0	51	37	12.75	0	0	0	0
JR Schorn	3	5	0	57	26	11.40	0	0	6	0
C Karemaker	2	2	0	18	13	9.00	0	0	1	0
Z Homani	2	2	0	9	7	4.50	0	0	5	0
I Postman	2	2	1	1	1*	1.00	0	0	0	0
Totals	33	50	6	1014	101		1	6	21	0
			Extras	67				subs	0	
			Total	1081		24.56			21	

SOUTH AFRICA UNDER 19 IN NEW ZEALAND

Bowling

Name	Overs	Mdns	Runs	Wkts	Avg	BB	5I	10M
J Botha	51.1	7	115	5	23.00	4-18	0	0
G de Bruin	52	15	155	5	31.00	3-54	0	0
C Thysen	58	11	187	6	31.16	4-79	0	0
C Karemaker	49.5	11	188	5	37.60	3-68	0	0
M Zondeki	56.4	18	164	4	41.00	2-43	0	0
W Hauptfleisch	48	11	122	2	61.00	2-71	0	0
I Postman	42	5	175	2	87.50	2-85	0	0
I Khan	38	8	123	1	123.00	1-45	0	0
M Price	3	0	13	0	-	-	0	0
HM Amla	2	0	20	0	-	-	0	0
Totals	400.4	86	1262	30		4-18	0	0
		b & lb	42	4 run outs				
		Total	1304	34	38.35			

CHAMPIONS CUP 2000/01

As Standard Bank Cup champions, KwaZulu-Natal were invited to play in a four-team tournament in Perth, Western Australia, contested by the limited overs champions of four countries. Although Western Australia, the hosts, were convincing winners, KwaZulu-Natal did well to reach the final, beating the champions from New Zealand and India, while Wade Wingfield was named man of the series.

CENTRAL DISTRICTS v KWAZULU-NATAL

Champions Cup

Played at WACA Ground, Perth on 29 March 2001

Toss: KwaZulu-Natal

Umpires: RL Parry & RJ Woolridge (TV: PD Parker)

Debuts: CD: None. KZN: None

Result: KwaZulu-Natal won by 7 wickets

Man of Match: Wade Wingfield

CENTRAL DISTRICTS	*Runs*	*Mins*	*Balls*	*4*	*6*
DP Kelly c Watson b Gilder	6	5	8	1	-
*CM Spearman c Benkenstein b Kent	15	27	13	-	2
BF Smith c Watson b Wingfield	75	150	123	6	-
GP Sulzberger c Bruyns b Baptiste	5	27	19	1	-
MW Douglas c Stewart b Wingfield	2	13	8	-	-
JDP Oram c Watson b Bodi	30	51	38	4	-
JMH How c Bruyns b Gilder	50	69	62	5	-
†BBJ Griggs run out (Benkenstein)	20	41	22	1	-
AM Schwass run out (Benkenstein)	3	6	3	-	-
EP Thompson not out	6	6	7	-	-
BE Hefford not out	1	3	1	-	-
Extras (lb 2, w 4, nb 3)	9				
TOTAL (for 9 wkts) (50 overs)	**222**				

KWAZULU-NATAL	*Runs*	*Mins*	*Balls*	*4*	*6*
DJ Watson not out	76	172	117	4	2
A Mall c Spearman b Thompson	12	11	10	3	-
WR Wingfield c Douglas b Oram	61	107	83	6	-
ML Bruyns c Griggs b Sulzberger	29	29	30	3	-
*DM Benkenstein not out	36	19	17	8	-
JC Kent					
†ELR Stewart					
GH Bodi					
EAE Baptiste					
ANW Tweedie					
GM Gilder					
Extras (lb 4, w 7)	11				
TOTAL (for 3 wkts) (43 overs)	**225**				

KZN	*O*	*M*	*R*	*W*
Kent	10	2	43	1
Gilder	10	3	51	2
Wingfield	8	1	30	2
Baptiste	6	0	18	1
Tweedie	9	0	44	0
Bodi	7	0	34	1

CD	*O*	*M*	*R*	*W*
Thompson	9	0	60	1
Hefford	8	2	35	0
Oram	8	1	21	1
Schwass	8	1	38	0
Sulzberger	10	0	67	1

Fall of Wickets	*CD*	*KZN*
1st	7 (1)	16 (2)
2nd	28 (2)	136 (3)
3rd	45 (4)	177 (4)
4th	65 (5)	-
5th	124 (6)	-
6th	157 (3)	-
7th	211 (7)	-
8th	215 (8)	-
9th	216 (9)	-

Perth, 30 March 2001: Mumbai 231-8 in 50 overs (RF Morris 32, W Jaffer 82, SV Bahutule 32*, KM Harvey 3-40). **Western Australia** 234-3 in 46.5 overs (JL Langer 119*, SM Katich 30, MW Goodwin 30, ME Hussey 32*). Western Australia won by 7 wickets.

WESTERN AUSTRALIA v KWAZULU-NATAL

Champions Cup

Played at WACA Ground, Perth on 31 March 2001

Toss: KwaZulu-Natal

Umpires: PD Parker & RL Parry (TV: IH Lock)

Debuts: WA: None. KZN: None

Result: Western Australia won by 81 runs

Man of Match: Michael Hussey

WESTERN AUSTRALIA	*Runs*	*Mins*	*Balls*	*4*	*6*
†RJ Campbell c Kent b Wingfield	42	55	47	6	-
*JL Langer c Mall b Gilder	0	5	2	-	-
SM Katich run out (Bodi/Bender)	68	147	110	7	-
MW Goodwin c Gilder b Wingfield	69	122	89	5	-
ME Hussey not out	62	44	44	4	2
MJ Nicholson not out	8	19	11	1	-
MJ North					
KM Harvey					
GB Hogg					
DJ Wates					
J Angel					
Extras (b 1, lb 8, w 9, nb 3)	21				
TOTAL (for 4 wkts) (50 overs)	**270**				

KWAZULU-NATAL	*Runs*	*Mins*	*Balls*	*4*	*6*
DJ Watson c Langer b Nicholson	12	41	37	-	-
A Mall c Hussey b Wates	44	53	45	8	-
WR Wingfield c Campbell b Wates	11	41	28	2	-
ML Bruyns lbw b Harvey	2	25	14	-	-
*DM Benkenstein c Langer b Angel	1	25	18	-	-
GH Bodi c Campbell b Wates	0	6	4	-	-
JC Kent c Hogg b Hussey	3	8	6	-	-
†ELR Stewart c Campbell b Hussey	3	13	15	-	-
KS Bender b Hogg	19	64	44	2	-
ANW Tweedie not out	70	62	68	10	-
GM Gilder c North b Hogg	1	6	5	-	-
Extras (lb 5, w 17, nb 1)	23				
TOTAL (47 overs)	**189**				

KZN	O	M	R	W
Kent	9	0	61	0
Gilder	9	0	43	1
Wingfield	9	1	42	2
Tweedie	6	1	25	0
Bodi	9	0	49	0
Bender	8	0	41	0

WA	O	M	R	W
Angel	10	3	38	1
Wates	8.3	1	27	3
Nicholson	8	2	34	1
Harvey	6	1	16	1
Hussey	6.3	2	19	2
Hogg	6	0	35	2
Katich	2	0	15	0

Fall of Wickets	WA	KZN
1st	4 (2)	57 (1)
2nd	60 (1)	65 (2)
3rd	180 (3)	79 (4)
4th	216 (4)	83 (3)
5th	-	83 (6)
6th	-	87 (7)
7th	-	89 (5)
8th	-	93 (8)
9th	-	164 (9)
10th	-	189 (11)

KWAZULU-NATAL v MUMBAI — Champions Cup

Played at WACA Ground, Perth on 1 April 2001 — Toss: Mumbai
Umpires: IH Lock & RJ Woolridge (TV: RL Parry)
Debuts: KZN: None. Mum: None
Result: KwaZulu-Natal won by 6 wickets
Man of Match: Wade Wingfield

MUMBAI	Runs	Mins	Balls	4	6
RF Morris c Stewart b Kent	30	62	39	4	-
W Jaffer c Stewart b Tweedie	5	7	5	1	-
VG Kambli c Amla b Gilder	16	21	16	3	-
JV Paranjpe c Amla b Baptiste	34	84	55	4	-
SV Bahutule run out (Kent)	15	46	38	1	-
AP Dani c Watson b Benkenstein	16	44	37	-	1
*†SS Dighe c Kent b Benkenstein	3	23	22	-	-
PL Mhambrey b Kent	31	54	45	3	-
RR Powar c Benkenstein b Tweedie	19	18	19	2	-
NM Kulkarni not out	2	22	10	-	-
SR Saxena b Kent	0	1	2	-	-
Extras (b 4, lb 2, w 6, nb 3)	15				
TOTAL (47.3 overs)	**186**				

KWAZULU-NATAL	Runs	Mins	Balls	4	6
DJ Watson run out (Jaffer)	30	61	43	4	-
A Mall run out (Dani)	23	33	25	4	-
JC Kent c Dighe b Mhambrey	6	29	16	-	-
ML Bruyns not out	54	118	75	5	-
AM Amla c Dighe b Saxena	15	33	31	1	1
WR Wingfield not out	51	80	82	5	1
*DM Benkenstein					
†ELR Stewart					
EAE Baptiste					
ANW Tweedie					
GM Gilder					
Extras (lb 4, w 5, nb 2)	11				
TOTAL (for 4 wkts) (45 overs)	**190**				

KZN	O	M	R	W
Gilder	8	0	26	1
Tweedie	9	1	53	2
Kent	8.3	1	25	3
Baptiste	8	1	20	1
Wingfield	9	1	29	0
Benkenstein	5	0	27	2

Mum	O	M	R	W
Mhambrey	10	1	24	1
Saxena	10	0	57	1
Bahutule	10	1	41	0
Kulkarni	7	1	24	0
Dani	7	0	33	0
Morris	1	0	7	0

Fall of Wickets	Mum	KZN
1st	7 (2)	45 (2)
2nd	34 (3)	67 (1)
3rd	66 (1)	67 (3)
4th	110 (5)	90 (5)
5th	110 (4)	-
6th	120 (7)	-
7th	136 (6)	-
8th	164 (9)	-
9th	186 (8)	-
10th	186 (11)	-

Perth, 2 April 2001: Central Districts 268-9 in 50 overs (JMH How 40, JDP Oram 74, GP Sulzberger 57, SR Saxena 3-39, NM Kulkarni 3-38). **Mumbai** 162 in 38.3 overs (VR Mane 53, SV Bahutule 38, AM Schwass 3-41). Central Districts won by 106 runs.
Perth, 3 April 2001: Western Australia 257-8 in 50 overs (MJ North 56, PC Worthington 54, JL Langer 60). **Central Districts** 149 in 32.2 overs (JMH How 39). Western Australia won by 108 runs.

WESTERN AUSTRALIA v KWAZULU-NATAL — Champions Cup Final

Played at WACA Ground, Perth on 4 April 2001 — Toss: KwaZulu-Natal
Umpires: PD Parker & RL Parry (TV: RJ Woolridge)
Debuts: WA: None. KZN: None
Result: Western Australia won by 6 wickets
Man of Series: Wade Wingfield

CHAMPIONS CUP 2000/01

KWAZULU-NATAL	Runs	Mins	Balls	4	6
DJ Watson c Campbell b Angel	13	40	34	2	-
A Mall c Campbell b Nicholson	21	45	33	4	-
WR Wingfield run out (Langer/Campbell)	28	64	51	2	-
GH Bodi c Angel b Nicholson	4	8	10	-	-
ML Bruyns c and b Hogg	33	86	40	1	-
*DM Benkenstein c Campbell b Angel	7	8	10	1	-
JC Kent not out	81	86	82	7	-
†ELR Stewart b Harvey	46	51	42	3	-
KS Bender lbw b Harvey	0	1	1	-	-
ANW Tweedie not out	0	4	0	-	-
EAE Baptiste					
Extras (b 1, lb 2, w 4, nb 3)	10				
TOTAL (for 8 wkts) (50 overs)	**243**				

WESTERN AUSTRALIA	Runs	Mins	Balls	4	6
†RJ Campbell c and b Wingfield	29	39	27	3	-
MJ North c Benkenstein b Baptiste	55	121	89	2	-
*JL Langer c Bender b Baptiste	34	58	54	2	-
SM Katich not out	67	105	65	4	-
MW Goodwin c Kent b Tweedie	21	51	47	-	-
ME Hussey not out	16	30	15	-	-
GB Hogg					
KM Harvey					
MJ Nicholson					
BA Williams					
J Angel					
Extras (lb 3, w 18, nb 1)	22				
TOTAL (for 4 wkts) (49.1 overs)	**244**				

WA	O	M	R	W
Angel	10	2	39	2
Williams	10	1	63	0
Nicholson	10	0	50	2
Harvey	10	0	44	2
North	2	0	12	0
Hogg	8	0	32	1

KZN	O	M	R	W
Wingfield	8.1	0	46	1
Tweedie	6	0	37	1
Bender	10	0	38	0
Kent	10	0	53	0
Baptiste	10	0	40	2
Bodi	5	0	27	0

Fall of Wickets	KZN	WA
1st	34 (1)	60 (1)
2nd	34 (2)	122 (3)
3rd	41 (4)	142 (2)
4th	96 (3)	189 (5)
5th	106 (6)	-
6th	133 (5)	-
7th	228 (8)	-
8th	228 (9)	-

Section C: Senior domestic cricket

UNITED CRICKET BOARD OF SOUTH AFRICA

Officers 2001/02

President: Advocate Percy Sonn
Vice-President: Robbie Kurz
Treasurer: John Blair
General Council: Henry Paulse (Boland), Ray Mali (Border), Cassim Suliman (Easterns), Ronnie Pillay Potgieter (EP), Charlie Robinson (Free State), Dr Mtutuzeli Nyoka (Gauteng), Ahmed Jinnah (Griqualand West), Dr Logan Naidoo (KwaZulu-Natal), Brandon Foot (Northerns), Mickey Gordon (North West), Arnold Bloch (WP). Three black African representatives: Tim Khumalo, Peter Bacela, Gabriel Nkagisang.
Chief Executive: Gerald Majola, PO Box 55009, Northlands 2116. Tel (011) 880 2810. Fax (011) 880 6578.
Directors: Finance and Administration: Diteko Modise. **Amateur Cricket:** Maxwell Jordaan. **Cricket Operations:** Brian Basson. **Coaching:** Anton Ferreira. **Communications:** Bronwyn Wilkinson. **Marketing:** Ros Goldin.
National team manager: Goolam Rajah. **Deputy director, Coaching and Amateur Cricket:** Neels Momberg.

COMMITTEES

Executive: PHF Sonn (president), R Kurz (vice-president), JH Blair (treasurer), MG Majola (chief executive), R Mali, T Khumalo, A Bloch, C Robinson.
National selection committee: Rushdi Magiet (convenor), Peter Bacela, Morris Garda, Haroon Lorgat, Graeme Pollock, Mike Procter.
Finance: John Blair (convenor), Haroon Lorgat, Rob Kurz, Gerald Majola (CEO), one provincial CEO to be elected from the CEOs forum.
Remuneration: Mervyn King, Joe Pamensky, John Blair, Dr Logan Naidoo.
Remaining committees were due to be announced following the adoption of a strategic business plan.

UNITED CRICKET BOARD PRESIDENTS

1991-92	GF Dakin
1992-98	K Mackerdhuj
1998-2000	RC White
2000-	PHF Sonn

Honorary Life Members: GF Dakin, B Leendertz, K Mackerdhuj, JL Pamensky

FEATURES OF THE SEASON 2000/01

HIGHEST TOTALS

525-7*	Free State v Gauteng	Bloemfontein
504-7*	South Africa v Sri Lanka	Cape Town
471-9*	South Africa v New Zealand	Bloemfontein
469	Western Province v Border	Cape Town
463	Western Province v North West	Potchefstroom
451-9*	Northerns v Eastern Province	Port Elizabeth
448	Eastern Province v North West	Port Elizabeth
427-4*	Griqualand West v Gauteng	Johannesburg
421	Eastern Province v KwaZulu-Natal	Durban
420	South Africa v Sri Lanka	Durban

LOWEST TOTALS

65	Northerns v Western Province	Centurion
73	Border v New Zealanders	East London
92	Eastern Province v Sri Lankans	Port Elizabeth
95	Sri Lanka v South Africa	Cape Town
100	North West v New Zealanders	Potchefstroom
102	Free State v Boland	Paarl
106	Easterns v North West	Benoni
108	Eastern Province v Northerns	Port Elizabeth
110	Free State v Eastern Province	Bloemfontein
119	Sri Lanka v South Africa	Centurion

BATTING

LEADING FIRST-CLASS AVERAGES

	Name	M	Inns	NO	Runs	HS	Avg	100	50
1	LD Ferreira (WP)	4	6	0	397	201	66.16	1	2
2	MH Richardson (NZ)	6	9	1	500	173*	62.50	1	2
3	ND McKenzie (Nor/SA)	9	14	3	672	123	61.09	3	3
4	SG Koenig (Gau)	7	13	0	789	155	60.69	3	4
5	JH Kallis (WP/SA)	8	13	1	671	160	55.91	1	4
6	G Kirsten (WP/SA)	6	10	1	496	180	55.11	1	2
7	AG Prince (WP)	8	14	4	539	120*	53.90	1	2
8	MS Sinclair (NZ)	6	11	2	461	150	51.22	1	2
9	DPMD Jayawardene (SL)	5	9	1	378	98	47.25	0	3
10	N Boje (FS/SA)	7	9	1	375	105	46.87	1	2
11	HD Ackerman (WP)	9	16	3	606	128	46.61	3	2
12	CM Spearman (NZ)	5	10	1	416	115	46.22	2	2
13	GFJ Liebenberg (FS)	8	13	0	595	202	45.76	1	4
14	DN Crookes (Eas)	8	16	1	671	117	44.73	1	5
15	CD McMillan (NZ)	5	8	2	265	78	44.16	0	3
16	JC Kent (KZN)	7	13	3	435	178*	43.50	1	2
17	LJ Wilkinson (FS)	9	15	0	642	169	42.80	1	3
18	MV Boucher (Bdr/SA)	8	11	3	341	92	42.62	0	2
19	GC Smith (WP)	9	16	0	676	183	42.25	2	3
20	JL Ontong (Bol)	9	15	2	546	131*	42.00	1	4

(Qualification: 6 completed innings)

FEATURES OF THE SEASON 2000/01

LEADING RUN-SCORERS

1	SG Koenig (Gau)	789
2	PC Strydom (Bdr)	693
3	GC Smith (WP)	676
4	ND McKenzie (Nor/SA)	672
5	DN Crookes (Eas)	671
	JH Kallis (WP/SA)	671
7	SC Pope (Bdr)	647
8	LJ Wilkinson (FS)	642
9	JA Rudolph (Nor)	638
10	MI Gidley (GW)	636

HIGHEST INDIVIDUAL INNINGS

GFJ Liebenberg	202	Free State v Northerns	Centurion
LD Ferreira	201	Western Province v North West	Potchefstroom
AM Bacher	190	Gauteng v KwaZulu-Natal	Johannesburg
PJR Steyn	188*	Northerns v Griqualand West	Centurion
JM Kemp	188	Eastern Province v North West	Port Elizabeth
GC Smith	183	Western Province v Border	Cape Town
G Kirsten	180	South Africa v Sri Lanka	Durban
JC Kent	178*	KwaZulu-Natal v Eastern Province	Durban
AJ Seymore	174	Easterns v Northerns	Centurion
MH Richardson	173*	New Zealanders v Boland	Paarl

CENTURY IN EACH INNINGS

CM Spearman	100 & 115	New Zealanders v North West	Potchefstroom

CENTURY ON FIRST-CLASS DEBUT

No instances

CENTURY ON FIRST-CLASS DEBUT IN SOUTH AFRICA

(Having previously played first-class cricket elsewhere)

Akram Khan	129*	Bangladeshis v Griqualand West	Kimberley
MH Richardson	173*	New Zealanders v Boland	Paarl

CARRYING BAT THROUGH A COMPLETED INNINGS

MI Gidley	73*	Griqualand West v Gauteng	Johannesburg
CC Bradfield	64*	Eastern Province v Northerns	Port Elizabeth

WICKET PARTNERSHIPS OF 200 OR MORE

Runs	Wkt			
261	2nd	JA Rudolph (141) & M van Jaarsveld (132)	Northerns v Boland	Centurion
254	1st	JM Arthur (165) & MI Gidley (86)	Griqualand West v Gauteng	Johannesburg
227*	4th	HD Ackerman (109*) & AG Prince (120*)	Western Province v Northerns	Centurion
206*	3rd	PJR Steyn (188*) & ND McKenzie (75*)	Northerns v Griqualand West	Centurion
204	8th	M Strydom (124) & AC Thomas (95*)	North West v Western Province	Potchefstroom

OTHER NOTABLE PARTNERSHIPS

(Over 150 for 7th or 8th wicket, over 100 for 9th or 10th wicket)

Runs	Wkt			
174	10th	AC Thomas (106*) & GA Roe (66)	North West v Griqualand West	Kimberley

Equals South African first-class record

150	8th	ND McKenzie (103) & SM Pollock (111)	South Africa v Sri Lanka	Centurion

South African Test record.

FEATURES OF THE SEASON 2000/01

CENTURIES

There were 59 first-class centuries scored during the season:

HD Ackerman	(3)	128	Western Province v Eastern Province	Port Elizabeth
		100*	Western Province v Free State	Cape Town
		109*	Western Province v Northerns	Centurion
Akram Khan		129*	Bangladeshis v Griqualand West	Kimberley
JM Arthur		165	Griqualand West v Gauteng	Johannesburg
AM Bacher		190	Gauteng v KwaZulu-Natal	Johannesburg
PH Barnard		120	Boland v Free State	Paarl
GH Bodi		104	KwaZulu-Natal v Easterns	Benoni
N Boje		105	Free State v Griqualand West	Kimberley
LL Bosman		115*	Griqualand West v North West	Kimberley
ML Bruyns		102*	KwaZulu-Natal v Gauteng	Durban
DJ Callaghan		129	Eastern Province v Western Province	Port Elizabeth
DN Crookes		117	Easterns v Eastern Province	Benoni
DJ Cullinan		112	South Africa v Sri Lanka	Cape Town
H Davids		124	Boland v Northerns	Centurion
HH Dippenaar		100	South Africa v New Zealand	Johannesburg
G Dros		100*	Northerns v Gauteng	Johannesburg
GD Elliott		125	Griqualand West v Bangladeshis	Kimberley
LD Ferreira		201	Western Province v North West	Potchefstroom
AI Gait		112	Free State v Border	Bloemfontein
MI Gidley		151	Griqualand West v Gauteng	Kimberley
JH Kallis		160	South Africa v New Zealand	Bloemfontein
JM Kemp		188	Eastern Province v North West	Port Elizabeth
JC Kent		178*	KwaZulu-Natal v Eastern Province	Durban
G Kirsten		180	South Africa v Sri Lanka	Durban
SG Koenig	(3)	108	Gauteng v Griqualand West	Johannesburg
		116	Gauteng v Free State	Bloemfontein
		155	Gauteng v Griqualand West	Kimberley
PPJ Koortzen	(2)	127	Griqualand West v Bangladeshis	Kimberley
		102	Griqualand West v Gauteng	Kimberley
MJ Lavine		113	North West v Border	Potchefstroom
GFJ Liebenberg		202	Free State v Northerns	Centurion
C Light		101	North West v Boland	Paarl
ND McKenzie	(3)	123	Northerns v Gauteng	Johannesburg
		120	South Africa v New Zealand	Port Elizabeth
		103	South Africa v Sri Lanka	Centurion
JA Morkel		117	Easterns v North West	Benoni
JL Ontong		131*	Boland v Eastern Province	Paarl
AC Parore		101*	New Zealanders v Border	East London
SM Pollock		111	South Africa v Sri Lanka	Centurion
SC Pope	(2)	125	Border v Boland	East London
		100	Border v North West	Potchefstroom
AG Prince		120*	Western Province v Northerns	Centurion
AG Puttick		153*	Western Province v Easterns	Cape Town
MH Richardson		173*	New Zealanders v Boland	Paarl
JA Rudolph	(2)	141	Northerns v Boland	Centurion
		144	Northerns v Easterns	Centurion
AJ Seymore		174	Easterns v Northerns	Centurion
MS Sinclair		150	New Zealand v South Africa	Port Elizabeth
GC Smith	(2)	126	Western Province v Boland	Cape Town
		183	Western Province v Border	Cape Town

FEATURES OF THE SEASON 2000/01

CM Spearman	(2)	100	New Zealanders v North West	Potchefstroom
	&	115	New Zealanders v North West	Potchefstroom
PJR Steyn		188*	Northerns v Griqualand West	Centurion
M Strydom		124	North West v Western Province	Potchefstroom
AC Thomas		106*	North West v Griqualand West	Kimberley
M van Jaarsveld		132	Northerns v Boland	Centurion
JF Venter		112*	Free State v Gauteng	Bloemfontein
LJ Wilkinson		169	Free State v Griqualand West	Kimberley

BOWLING

LEADING FIRST-CLASS AVERAGES

	Name	M	Overs	Mdns	Runs	Wkts	Avg	BB	5I	10M
1	GA Roe (NW)	8	291.1	92	631	40	15.77	7-47	3	0
2	CK Langeveldt (Bol)	5	125.4	33	359	21	17.09	5-19	1	0
3	M Muralitharan (SL)	3	145.3	41	310	18	17.22	6-39	2	1
4	PJ Botha (Bdr)	6	152.3	54	375	21	17.85	4-48	0	0
5	KCG Benjamin (Eas)	5	190.4	45	549	29	18.93	6-73	1	0
6	JM Kemp (EP/SA)	7	241.3	69	552	29	19.03	6-56	2	0
7	SM Pollock (KZN/SA)	7	253.2	98	515	27	19.07	6-30	1	0
8	M Ntini (Bdr/SA)	8	268.2	89	688	36	19.11	6-59	2	0
9	SB O'Connor (NZ)	4	116.2	34	309	16	19.31	5-51	1	0
10	DJ Callaghan (EP)	9	156	51	356	18	19.77	5-24	3	1
11	AA Donald (FS/SA)	4	127.4	32	341	17	20.05	4-69	0	0
12	CS Martin (NZ)	5	121.5	34	392	19	20.63	4-104	0	0
13	A Nel (Eas)	4	154	38	361	17	21.23	5-43	2	0
14	AC Dawson (WP)	7	238.2	74	583	27	21.59	5-51	1	0
15	HS Williams (Bol)	6	245.2	70	629	29	21.68	6-40	4	0
16	CM Willoughby (WP)	8	298.5	107	683	31	22.03	5-26	1	0
17	PV Mpitsang (FS)	9	268.1	62	733	33	22.21	5-24	3	0
18	CW Henderson (WP)	7	400.3	138	801	36	22.25	5-6	3	0
19	GJ Kruis (GW)	10	433	118	1083	46	23.54	5-50	2	0
20	N Boje (FS/SA)	7	220.1	70	448	19	23.57	5-67	1	0

(Qualification: 15 wickets)

LEADING WICKET-TAKERS

1	GJ Kruis (GW)	46
2	VC Drakes (Bdr)	41
3	GA Roe (NW)	40
4	D Pretorius (FS)	37
5	CW Henderson (WP)	36
	M Ntini (Bdr/SA)	36
7	PV Mpitsang (FS)	33
8	JF Venter (FS)	31
	CM Willoughby (WP)	31
10	S Elworthy (Nor)	30
	MJ Lavine (NW)	30
	GJ Smith (Nor)	30

FEATURES OF THE SEASON 2000/01

TEN WICKETS IN A MATCH

CA Copeland	12-213	Griqualand West v Bangladeshis	Kimberley
M Muralitharan	11-161	Sri Lanka v South Africa	Durban
DJ Callaghan	10-111	Eastern Province v Free State	Bloemfontein
MJ Lavine	10-124	North West v Boland	Paarl

SEVEN WICKETS IN AN INNINGS

CA Copeland	8-101	Griqualand West v Bangladeshis	Kimberley
GA Roe	7-47	North West v Free State	Bloemfontein
WJ du Toit	7-82	Boland v Easterns	Paarl
GT Love	7-116	Border v Western Province	Cape Town

HAT-TRICKS

GJ-P Kruger	Eastern Province v Sri Lankans	Port Elizabeth
GJ Kruis	Griqualand West v KwaZulu-Natal	Durban

FIVE WICKETS IN AN INNINGS

There were 76 cases of 5 wickets in an innings in first-class cricket during the season:

S Abrahams		5-37	Eastern Province v North West	Port Elizabeth
ZA Abrahim		5-22	Griqualand West v Gauteng	Johannesburg
HC Bakkes		6-108	Free State v Gauteng	Bloemfontein
KCG Benjamin		6-73	Easterns v Border	East London
GH Bodi		6-63	KwaZulu-Natal v Gauteng	Durban
N Boje		5-67	Free State v Griqualand West	Kimberley
AG Botha		6-106	Easterns v Boland	Paarl
RE Bryson		5-33	Northerns v Eastern Province	Port Elizabeth
DJ Callaghan	(3)	5-24	Eastern Province v Easterns	Benoni
		5-31	Eastern Province v Free State	Bloemfontein
	&	5-80	Eastern Province v Free State	Bloemfontein
NM Carter	(2)	6-63	Boland v Griqualand West	Kimberley
		6-122	Boland v Western Province	Cape Town
CA Copeland	(2)	8-101	Griqualand West v Bangladeshis	Kimberley
		5-52	Griqualand West v Gauteng	Johannesburg
AC Dawson		5-51	Western Province v Easterns	Cape Town
VC Drakes		5-80	Border v Eastern Province	Port Elizabeth
WJ du Toit		7-82	Boland v Easterns	Paarl
S Elworthy	(2)	5-81	Northerns v Gauteng	Johannesburg
		5-41	Northerns v Boland	Centurion
CRD Fernando		5-98	Sri Lanka v South Africa	Durban
GE Flusk		5-55	Easterns v Border	East London
NA Fusedale		5-170	Gauteng v Griqualand West	Kimberley
OD Gibson		6-53	Gauteng v KwaZulu-Natal	Johannesburg
AJ Hall		5-93	Gauteng v Northerns	Johannesburg
CW Henderson	(3)	5-40	Western Province v Eastern Province	Port Elizabeth
		5-6	Western Province v Northerns	Centurion
		5-62	Western Province v Border	Cape Town
T Henderson		6-56	Border v Free State	Bloemfontein
P Joubert		5-10	Northerns v Eastern Province	Port Elizabeth
JM Kemp	(2)	6-56	Eastern Province v Border	Port Elizabeth
		5-69	Eastern Province v KwaZulu-Natal	Durban
JC Kent		6-77	KwaZulu-Natal v Easterns	Benoni
GJ Kruis	(2)	5-80	Griqualand West v Bangladeshis	Kimberley
		5-50	Griqualand West v KwaZulu-Natal	Kimberley

FEATURES OF THE SEASON 2000/01

CK Langeveldt		5-19	Boland v Free State	Paarl
MJ Lavine	(3)	6-55	North West v Gauteng	Potchefstroom
		5-97	North West v Griqualand West	Kimberley
		6-53	North West v Boland	Paarl
GT Love		7-116	Border v Western Province	Cape Town
JT Mafa		6-62	Gauteng v Griqualand West	Johannesburg
PV Mpitsang	(3)	5-64	Free State v Northerns	Centurion
		5-24	Free State v North West	Bloemfontein
		5-70	Free State v Eastern Province	Bloemfontein
M Muralitharan	(2)	5-122	Sri Lanka v South Africa	Durban
	&	6-39	Sri Lanka v South Africa	Durban
A Nel	(2)	5-64	Easterns v KwaZulu-Natal	Benoni
		5-43	Easterns v Free State	Benoni
M Ntini	(2)	6-59	Border v Eastern Province	Port Elizabeth
		6-66	South Africa v New Zealand	Bloemfontein
SB O'Connor		5-51	New Zealanders v North West	Potchefstroom
AJ Penn		5-38	New Zealanders v Border	East London
RJ Peterson		5-87	Eastern Province v Border	Port Elizabeth
BT Player		5-26	Boland v Free State	Paarl
SM Pollock		6-30	South Africa v Sri Lanka	Cape Town
GA Roe	(3)	7-47	North West v Free State	Bloemfontein
		5-79	North West v Western Province	Potchefstroom
		6-31	North West v Easterns	Benoni
GJ Smith		5-25	Northerns v Eastern Province	Port Elizabeth
M Strydom		6-23	North West v Griqualand West	Kimberley
CR Tatton		5-80	Griqualand West v North West	Kimberley
R Telemachus		6-54	Western Province v Boland	Cape Town
DJ Terbrugge		5-39	Gauteng v North West	Potchefstroom
AC Thomas		6-26	North West v Easterns	Benoni
DH Townsend		5-49	Northerns v Border	East London
DR Tuffey		5-69	New Zealanders v Border	East London
F van der Merwe	(2)	5-62	North West v Eastern Province	Port Elizabeth
		5-84	North West v Border	Potchefstroom
JJ van der Wath		5-59	Free State v Eastern Province	Bloemfontein
JF Venter	(2)	6-90	Free State v Boland	Paarl
		5-103	Free State v Western Province	Cape Town
HS Williams	(4)	5-43	Boland v Northerns	Centurion
		6-40	Boland v Griqualand West	Kimberley
		5-38	Boland v Border	East London
		5-66	Boland v Easterns	Paarl
CM Willoughby		5-26	Western Province v Free State	Cape Town

ALL-ROUNDERS

CENTURY AND FIVE WICKETS IN AN INNINGS

N Boje	77 & 105, 5-67	Free State v Griqualand West	Kimberley

FEATURES OF THE SEASON 2000/01

400 RUNS AND 20 WICKETS IN THE SEASON

Name	M	Runs	Avg	Wkts	Avg
JM Kemp (EP/SA)	7	455	41.36	29	19.03
JC Kent (KZN)	7	435	43.50	22	25.22
MJ Lavine (NW)	9	477	29.81	30	33.16
PC Strydom (Bdr)	10	693	38.50	23	25.17
AC Thomas (NW)	10	531	40.84	28	28.14
JF Venter (FS)	9	494	38.00	31	27.67

WICKETKEEPING AND FIELDING

LEADING WICKETKEEPERS

	Name	M	Ct	St	Total
1	W Bossenger (GW)	10	38	1	39
	D Jennings (Eas)	8	37	2	39
3	DW Murray (EP)	9	38	0	38
4	EG Poole (NW)	10	37	0	37
	CFK van Wyk (Nor)	9	35	2	37
6	MV Boucher (Bdr/SA)	8	32	2	34
	I Mitchell (Bdr)	9	32	2	34
8	TL Tsolekile (WP)	9	30	1	31
9	GL Brophy (FS)	8	27	2	29
10	ELR Stewart (KZN)	9	26	1	27

Some of the above dismissals may have been taken in the field

MOST DISMISSALS IN A MATCH

MN van Wyk	10 (all ct)	Free State v Border	Bloemfontein
EG Poole	9 (all ct)	North West v Easterns	Benoni
D Jennings	8 (all ct)	Easterns v KwaZulu-Natal	Benoni
EG Poole	8 (all ct)	North West v Gauteng	Potchefstroom
DW Murray	8 (all ct)	Eastern Province v KwaZulu-Natal	Durban
ELR Stewart	8 (all ct)	KwaZulu-Natal v Griqualand West	Durban
MV Boucher	8 (all ct)	Border v Northerns	East London
I Mitchell	8 (all ct)	Border v Boland	East London
MS de Kock	8 (7 ct, 1 st)	Boland v Easterns	Paarl

MOST DISMISSALS IN AN INNINGS

D Jennings	6 (all ct)	Easterns v KwaZulu-Natal	Benoni
EG Poole	5 (all ct)	North West v Gauteng	Potchefstroom
D Jennings	5 (4 ct, 1 st)	Easterns v Eastern Province	Benoni
ELR Stewart	5 (all ct)	KwaZulu-Natal v Griqualand West	Durban
RS Kaluwitharana	5 (all ct)	Sri Lanka v South Africa	Centurion
MN van Wyk	5 (all ct)	Free State v Border	Bloemfontein
MN van Wyk	5 (all ct)	Free State v Border	Bloemfontein
I Mitchell	5 (all ct)	Border v Boland	East London
EG Poole	5 (all ct)	North West v Easterns	Benoni
MS de Kock	5 (all ct)	Boland v Easterns	Paarl
CFK van Wyk	5 (all ct)	Northerns v Western Province	Centurion
I Mitchell	5 (all ct)	Border v North West	Potchefstroom

FEATURES OF THE SEASON 2000/01

LEADING FIELDERS

	Name	M	Ct
1	NC Johnson (WP)	9	24
2	LJ Koen (Bol)	8	17
3	JL Ontong (Bol)	9	16
	GC Smith (WP)	9	16
	M van Jaarsveld (Nor)	9	16
6	GD Elliott (GW)	10	15
7	W Wiblin (Bdr)	10	13
8	CC Bradfield (EP)	8	11
	DN Crookes (Eas)	8	11
	HH Gibbs (WP/SA)	7	11
	A Jacobs (NW)	7	11
	JH Kallis (WP/SA)	8	11

MOST CATCHES IN A MATCH (FIELDERS)

GFJ Liebenberg	5	Free State v North West	Bloemfontein
M van Jaarsveld	5	Northerns v Boland	Centurion
JL Ontong	5	Boland v Border	East London

FIRST-CLASS AVERAGES 2000/01

Name	M	Inns	NO	Runs	HS	Avg	100	50	Ct	St	Balls	Runs	Wkts	Avg	BB	5I	10M
S Abrahams (EP)	7	11	0	204	85	18.54	0	1	6	0	919	343	8	42.87	5-37	1	0
U Abrahams (EP)	4	8	0	150	51	18.75	0	1	0	0	0	0	0	-	-	0	0
ZA Abrahim (GW)	9	14	4	267	57	26.70	0	1	4	0	1639	790	28	28.21	5-22	1	0
HD Ackerman (WP)	9	16	3	606	128	46.61	3	2	10	0	0	0	0	-	-	0	0
SM Adam (KZN)	1	0	0	0	0	-	0	0	0	0	48	49	1	49.00	1-49	0	0
PR Adams (WP)	5	7	4	159	61*	53.00	0	1	4	0	1221	582	18	32.33	3-33	0	0
Akram Khan (Ban)	1	2	2	180	129*	-	1	1	0	0	0	0	0	-	-	0	0
Al Sahariar Rokon (Ban)	1	2	0	117	70	58.50	0	1	0	0	0	0	0	-	-	0	0
Aminul Islam (Ban)	1	2	0	27	27	13.50	0	0	1	0	0	0	0	-	-	0	0
AM Amla (KZN)	4	7	0	161	69	23.00	0	2	2	0	0	0	0	-	-	0	0
RP Arnold (SL)	5	8	0	148	71	18.50	0	1	4	0	368	187	4	46.75	3-76	0	0
JM Arthur (GW)	4	7	0	272	165	38.85	1	0	7	0	0	0	0	-	-	0	0
NJ Astle (NZ)	5	7	1	209	69*	34.83	0	2	6	0	552	150	2	75.00	1-46	0	0
MS Atapattu (SL)	5	9	1	110	42	13.75	0	0	1	0	0	0	0	-	-	0	0
AM Bacher (Gau)	8	15	1	552	190	39.42	1	3	3	0	60	29	0	-	-	0	0
HC Bakkes (FS)	7	9	1	154	54*	19.25	0	1	4	0	1329	625	20	31.25	6-108	1	0
EAE Baptiste (KZN)	6	8	2	157	57	26.16	0	1	6	0	702	241	6	40.16	1-23	0	0
PH Barnard (Bol)	4	6	0	184	120	30.66	1	0	5	0	0	0	0	-	-	0	0
JE Bastow (KZN)	5	6	2	19	6	4.75	0	0	2	0	871	364	14	26.00	4-46	0	0
MR Benfield (EP)	8	16	1	329	93	21.93	0	2	5	0	0	0	0	-	-	0	0
KCG Benjamin (Eas)	5	9	3	110	48*	18.33	0	0	3	0	1144	549	29	18.93	6-73	1	0
DM Benkenstein (KZN)	8	15	2	399	86	30.69	0	2	4	0	252	104	3	34.66	1-19	0	0
JA Beukes (FS)	3	6	0	86	64	14.33	0	1	4	0	6	0	0	-	-	0	0
GH Bodi (KZN)	9	12	2	332	104	33.20	1	2	2	0	1437	750	29	25.86	6-63	1	0
N Boje (FS/SA)	7	9	1	375	105	46.87	1	2	2	0	1321	448	19	23.57	5-67	1	0
LL Bosman (GW)	7	12	2	371	115*	37.10	1	2	6	0	90	36	0	-	-	0	0
W Bossenger (GW)	10	17	2	439	74*	29.26	0	3	38	1	0	0	0	-	-	0	0
AG Botha (Eas)	7	14	4	259	59	25.90	0	1	9	0	1466	614	24	25.58	6-106	1	0
J Botha (EP)	2	4	0	88	43	22.00	0	0	0	0	96	45	2	22.50	1-4	0	0
PJ Botha (Bdr)	6	11	0	229	50	20.81	0	1	3	0	915	375	21	17.85	4-48	0	0
MV Boucher (Bdr/SA)	8	11	3	341	92	42.62	0	2	32	2	0	0	0	-	-	0	0

FIRST-CLASS AVERAGES 2000/01

Name	M	Inns	NO	Runs	HS	Avg	100	50	Ct	St	Balls	Runs	Wkts	Avg	BB	5I	10M
CC Bradfield (EP)	8	16	1	558	91	37.20	0	3	11	0	0	0	0	-	-	0	0
D Brand (Eas)	3	6	0	125	39	20.83	0	0	5	0	222	83	3	27.66	1-5	0	0
FC Brooker (Nor)	6	10	1	135	31	15.00	0	0	2	0	0	0	0	-	-	0	0
J Brooker (GW)	5	8	0	216	77	27.00	0	2	2	0	66	43	0	-	-	0	0
GL Brophy (FS)	8	12	2	241	40	24.10	0	0	27	2	0	0	0	-	-	0	0
NG Brouwers (Nor)	6	8	2	127	59	21.16	0	1	2	0	516	247	6	41.16	3-43	0	0
ML Bruyns (KZN)	9	17	1	548	102*	34.25	1	3	10	0	132	83	1	83.00	1-47	0	0
JDC Bryant (EP)	9	18	2	363	70	22.68	0	2	7	0	0	0	0	-	-	0	0
RE Bryson (Nor)	2	2	2	11	11*	-	0	0	0	0	306	193	10	19.30	5-33	1	0
DJ Callaghan (EP)	9	16	1	347	129	23.13	1	0	7	0	936	356	18	19.77	5-24	3	1
NM Carter (Bol)	7	11	2	74	21	8.22	0	0	1	0	1534	839	28	29.96	6-63	2	0
UDU Chandana (SL)	1	1	0	2	2	2.00	0	0	0	0	168	109	2	54.50	2-109	0	0
SC Cook (Gau)	2	4	1	132	55	44.00	0	1	0	0	0	0	0	-	-	0	0
CA Copeland (GW)	4	5	1	15	10	3.75	0	0	2	0	874	515	21	24.52	8-101	2	1
MW Creed (EP)	8	14	1	351	47	27.00	0	0	3	0	369	203	4	50.75	1-24	0	0
DN Crookes (Eas)	8	16	1	671	117	44.73	1	5	11	0	521	254	3	84.66	2-49	0	0
DJ Cullinan (Gau/SA)	7	11	2	359	112	39.88	1	1	9	0	0	0	0	-	-	0	0
AW Cyster (Bol)	1	2	0	24	21	12.00	0	0	0	0	0	0	0	-	-	0	0
H Davids (Bol)	6	12	1	336	124	30.54	1	1	4	0	0	0	0	-	-	0	0
AC Dawson (WP)	7	9	4	111	53*	22.20	0	1	1	0	1430	583	27	21.59	5-51	1	0
P de Bruyn (Eas)	8	16	2	447	83	31.92	0	4	6	0	634	306	12	25.50	4-34	0	0
Z de Bruyn (Gau)	8	14	1	404	66	31.07	0	3	5	0	720	434	7	62.00	2-34	0	0
MS de Kock (Bol)	2	4	1	20	17*	6.66	0	0	10	1	0	0	0	-	-	0	0
CdeW de Lange (Bol)	5	8	0	71	25	8.87	0	0	3	0	1104	496	7	70.85	2-44	0	0
PA de Silva (SL)	1	2	0	27	22	13.50	0	0	0	0	12	5	0	-	-	0	0
DJJ de Vos (Nor)	3	6	1	233	97	46.60	0	2	2	0	414	234	1	234.00	1-70	0	0
HM de Vos (NW)	6	11	0	130	35	11.81	0	0	2	0	9	8	0	-	-	0	0
BC de Wett (NW)	1	2	0	36	30	18.00	0	0	0	0	0	0	0	-	-	0	0
TM Dilshan (SL)	4	6	1	110	54	22.00	0	1	7	0	18	13	0	-	-	0	0
HH Dippenaar (FS/SA)	6	10	0	243	100	24.30	1	0	2	0	0	0	0	-	-	0	0
L Dladla (KZN)	1	0	0	0	0	-	0	0	0	0	54	26	0	-	-	0	0
AA Donald (FS/SA)	4	5	3	53	21*	26.50	0	0	1	0	766	341	17	20.05	4-69	0	0
VC Drakes (Bdr)	9	16	1	360	53	24.00	0	1	3	0	2208	975	41	23.78	5-80	1	0
JN Dreyer (NW)	5	9	2	66	40	9.42	0	0	1	0	768	529	8	66.12	2-57	0	0
G Dros (Nor)	6	10	2	308	100*	38.50	1	0	7	0	699	332	14	23.71	3-32	0	0

FIRST-CLASS AVERAGES 2000/01

Name	M	Inns	NO	Runs	HS	Avg	100	50	Ct	St	Balls	Runs	Wkts	Avg	BB	5I	10M
WM Dry (GW)	6	11	0	176	80	16.00	0	1	2	0	0	0	0	-	-	0	0
WJ du Toit (Bol)	1	2	0	38	32	19.00	0	0	0	0	336	154	8	19.25	7-82	1	0
CE Eksteen (Gau)	4	7	0	89	50	12.71	0	1	1	0	1102	429	9	47.66	2-62	0	0
GD Elliott (GW)	10	17	0	577	125	33.94	1	3	15	0	876	390	10	39.00	2-18	0	0
S Elworthy (Nor)	7	11	3	224	75*	28.00	0	1	0	0	1460	711	30	23.70	5-41	2	0
Enamul Hoque (Ban)	1	2	0	5	4	2.50	0	0	0	0	240	113	1	113.00	1-54	0	0
CRD Fernando (SL)	5	6	2	15	5*	3.75	0	0	0	0	756	516	15	34.40	5-98	1	0
LD Ferreira (WP)	4	6	0	397	201	66.16	1	2	4	0	0	0	0	-	-	0	0
SP Fleming (NZ)	5	8	1	289	99	41.28	0	3	5	0	0	0	0	-	-	0	0
GE Flusk (Eas)	8	13	2	126	31*	11.45	0	0	4	0	1170	618	24	25.75	5-55	1	0
NA Fusedale (Gau)	3	4	2	26	20*	13.00	0	0	0	0	859	438	15	29.20	5-170	1	0
AI Gait (FS)	8	13	0	374	112	28.76	1	2	7	0	0	0	0	-	-	0	0
LL Gamiet (Bdr)	10	18	0	383	80	21.27	0	1	8	0	0	0	0	-	-	0	0
MF George (Gau)	6	9	4	178	58	35.60	0	1	1	0	714	420	7	60.00	2-43	0	0
HH Gibbs (WP/SA)	7	12	0	316	91	26.33	0	2	11	0	0	0	0	-	-	0	0
OD Gibson (Gau)	5	8	1	143	52	20.42	0	1	2	0	975	444	16	27.75	6-53	1	0
MI Gidley (GW)	10	17	1	636	151	39.75	1	4	6	0	619	284	6	47.33	2-22	0	0
GM Gilder (KZN)	7	7	2	39	14	7.80	0	0	2	0	932	527	13	40.53	3-55	0	0
GV Grace (EP)	2	4	0	30	13	7.50	0	0	0	0	0	0	0	-	-	0	0
L Graham (Bdr)	4	6	2	46	19	11.50	0	0	2	0	684	319	7	45.57	3-69	0	0
DA Gunawardene (SL)	1	2	0	37	24	18.50	0	0	0	0	0	0	0	-	-	0	0
Habibul Bashar (Ban)	1	2	0	30	20	15.00	0	0	0	0	18	14	0	-	-	0	0
AJ Hall (Gau)	3	5	1	157	92	39.25	0	1	4	0	564	277	8	34.62	5-93	1	0
PL Harris (WP)	1	2	1	10	8	10.00	0	0	0	0	332	145	4	36.25	3-56	0	0
Hasibul Hussain (Ban)	1	2	0	20	19	10.00	0	0	0	0	210	140	1	140.00	1-92	0	0
M Hayward (EP)	7	11	5	115	26	19.16	0	0	1	0	1287	774	19	40.73	3-69	0	0
CW Henderson (WP)	7	9	2	113	28*	16.14	0	0	4	0	2403	801	36	22.25	5-6	3	0
JM Henderson (Bol)	8	15	1	584	98	41.71	0	5	2	0	474	247	5	49.40	2-39	0	0
T Henderson (Bdr)	7	13	2	108	22*	9.81	0	0	1	0	1177	525	18	29.16	6-56	1	0
F Herbst (Gau)	2	3	2	45	35*	45.00	0	0	1	0	90	46	0	-	-	0	0
GM Hewitt (NW)	8	14	0	357	62	25.50	0	1	10	0	0	0	0	-	-	0	0
BP Horan (Gau)	2	3	0	43	23	14.33	0	0	2	0	264	109	2	54.50	2-17	0	0
AC Hudson (KZN)	2	4	0	97	38	24.25	0	0	2	0	0	0	0	-	-	0	0
KC Jackson (Bol)	3	5	1	41	25	10.25	0	0	2	0	0	0	0	-	-	0	0
A Jacobs (NW)	7	13	0	193	33	14.84	0	0	11	0	120	67	2	33.50	1-17	0	0

Name	M	Inns	NO	Runs	HS	Avg	100	50	Ct	St	Balls	Runs	Wkts	Avg	BB	5I	10M
Javed Omar (Ban)	1	2	0	51	41	25.50	0	0	2	0	30	24	0	-	-	0	0
ST Jayasuriya (SL)	5	9	0	118	38	13.11	0	0	3	0	102	49	0	-	-	0	0
DPMD Jayawardene (SL)	5	9	1	378	98	47.25	0	3	4	0	54	29	2	14.50	2-27	0	0
D Jennings (Eas)	8	16	2	188	53	13.42	0	1	37	2	0	0	0	-	-	0	0
NC Johnson (WP)	9	15	2	490	84	37.69	0	5	24	0	690	322	12	26.83	2-5	0	0
D Jordaan (Eas)	5	10	0	206	75	20.60	0	1	5	0	6	13	0	-	-	0	0
LCR Jordaan (NW)	1	2	1	25	20*	25.00	0	0	0	0	42	34	0	-	-	0	0
P Joubert (Nor)	3	5	3	137	72*	68.50	0	1	2	0	534	221	9	24.55	5-10	1	0
JH Kallis (WP/SA)	8	13	1	671	160	55.91	1	4	11	0	1205	528	17	31.05	3-77	0	0
RS Kaluwitharana (SL)	4	6	0	114	40	19.00	0	0	13	1	0	0	0	-	-	0	0
JM Kemp (EP/SA)	7	11	0	455	188	41.36	1	2	3	0	1449	552	29	19.03	6-56	2	0
JC Kent (KZN)	7	13	3	435	178*	43.50	1	2	10	0	1044	555	22	25.22	6-77	1	0
Khaled Mashud (Ban)	1	2	0	0	0	0.00	0	0	2	0	0	0	0	-	-	0	0
EW Kidwell (GW)	7	11	5	68	15*	11.33	0	0	3	0	1005	603	17	35.47	4-71	0	0
G Kirsten (WP/SA)	6	10	1	496	180	55.11	1	2	8	0	0	0	0	-	-	0	0
JWF Klopper (Bdr)	1	1	0	0	0	0.00	0	0	0	0	24	23	0	-	-	0	0
L Klusener (KZN/SA)	6	7	1	193	97	32.16	0	2	5	0	643	269	10	26.90	4-111	0	0
DM Koch (Bol)	1	1	0	7	7	7.00	0	0	0	0	192	49	1	49.00	1-13	0	0
LJ Koen (Bol)	8	14	0	546	97	39.00	0	5	17	0	6	5	0	-	-	0	0
SG Koenig (Gau)	7	13	0	789	155	60.69	3	4	4	0	6	5	0	-	-	0	0
PPJ Koortzen (GW)	10	17	1	578	127	36.12	2	2	2	0	325	152	4	38.00	1-12	0	0
AK Kruger (GW)	1	2	1	63	48	63.00	0	0	0	0	72	62	0	-	-	0	0
GJ-P Kruger (EP)	4	6	1	18	13*	3.60	0	0	0	0	1001	491	19	25.84	4-49	0	0
GJ Kruis (GW)	10	16	1	212	59	14.13	0	1	6	0	2598	1083	46	23.54	5-50	2	0
CK Langeveldt (Bol)	5	8	1	72	20	10.28	0	0	2	0	754	359	21	17.09	5-19	1	0
MJ Lavine (NW)	9	16	0	477	113	29.81	1	1	10	0	1938	995	30	33.16	6-53	3	1
AG Lawson (NW)	9	18	1	289	64	17.00	0	3	6	0	12	12	0	-	-	0	0
MR Lewis (FS)	8	11	4	176	49*	25.14	0	0	9	0	606	341	8	42.62	2-44	0	0
GFJ Liebenberg (FS)	8	13	0	595	202	45.76	1	4	10	0	12	5	0	-	-	0	0
C Light (NW)	9	16	0	299	101	18.68	1	0	2	0	793	333	6	55.50	2-48	0	0
J Louw (GW)	5	8	0	132	50	16.50	0	1	9	0	730	414	12	34.50	3-25	0	0
GT Love (Bdr)	10	17	7	187	30	18.70	0	0	6	0	2232	979	28	34.96	7-116	1	0
EF Mabhena (Eas)	1	2	0	4	2	2.00	0	0	0	0	0	0	0	-	-	0	0
RB MacQueen (KZN)	2	3	0	77	42	25.66	0	0	1	0	222	125	1	125.00	1-80	0	0
JT Mafa (Gau)	3	5	0	0	0	0.00	0	0	1	0	515	352	11	32.00	6-62	1	0

FIRST-CLASS AVERAGES 2000/01

Name	M	Inns	NO	Runs	HS	Avg	100	50	Ct	St	Balls	Runs	Wkts	Avg	BB	5I	10M
DL Makalima (Bdr)	8	15	1	167	42*	11.92	0	0	4	0	0	0	0	-	-	0	0
A Mall (KZN)	6	10	0	270	64	27.00	0	1	4	0	0	0	0	-	-	0	0
HA Manack (Gau)	2	3	0	19	12	6.33	0	0	0	0	30	16	1	16.00	1-16	0	0
HJH Marshall (NZ)	2	2	1	78	40*	78.00	0	0	0	0	6	4	0	-	-	0	0
CS Martin (NZ)	5	5	3	12	7	6.00	0	0	0	0	731	392	19	20.63	4-104	0	0
WB Masimula (Gau)	3	5	2	41	22	13.66	0	0	1	0	340	175	7	25.00	3-44	0	0
TK Mataboge (Gau)	2	1	0	2	2	2.00	0	0	1	0	264	144	1	144.00	1-48	0	0
M Matomela (Bdr)	1	2	0	0	0	0.00	0	0	0	0	114	105	0	-	-	0	0
ND McKenzie (Nor/SA)	9	14	3	672	123	61.09	3	3	8	0	0	0	0	-	-	0	0
AP McLaren (GW)	1	1	0	27	27	27.00	0	0	0	0	0	0	0	-	-	0	0
CD McMillan (NZ)	5	8	2	265	78	44.16	0	3	1	0	344	140	3	46.66	1-11	0	0
I Mitchell (Bdr)	9	17	1	446	83	27.87	0	3	32	2	25	10	2	5.00	2-0	0	0
Mohammad Rafiq (Ban)	1	2	0	58	51	29.00	0	1	1	0	372	126	5	25.20	3-46	0	0
ET Mokoenanyana (Eas)	3	6	0	76	28	12.66	0	0	7	0	0	0	0	-	-	0	0
TJ Mokoenanyana (FS)	1	2	2	0	0*	-	0	0	1	0	42	24	0	-	-	0	0
JA Morkel (Eas)	7	12	0	241	117	20.08	1	0	1	0	1196	621	19	32.68	4-36	0	0
PV Mpitsang (FS)	9	11	2	56	23	6.22	0	0	1	0	1609	733	33	22.21	5-24	3	0
R Munnik (WP)	2	3	0	80	45	26.66	0	0	1	0	223	109	5	21.80	4-58	0	0
M Muralitharan (SL)	3	4	1	8	7	2.66	0	0	2	0	873	310	18	17.22	6-39	2	1
DW Murray (EP)	9	15	2	289	58*	22.23	0	1	38	0	0	0	0	-	-	0	0
Mushfiqur Rahman (Ban)	1	2	0	21	15	10.50	0	0	0	0	161	55	3	18.33	2-39	0	0
JG Myburgh (Nor)	3	6	0	138	68	23.00	0	1	2	0	24	7	0	-	-	0	0
Naimur Rahman (Ban)	1	2	0	10	10	5.00	0	0	0	0	413	176	6	29.33	3-60	0	0
SS Ndima (Gau)	1	2	0	38	38	19.00	0	0	0	0	0	0	0	-	-	0	0
A Nel (Eas)	4	6	2	84	44	21.00	0	0	1	0	924	361	17	21.23	5-43	2	0
M Ngam (EP/SA)	6	6	2	34	18*	8.50	0	0	2	0	1136	552	21	26.28	4-78	0	0
R Niewoudt (NW)	5	9	1	287	98	35.87	0	1	6	0	24	12	0	-	-	0	0
M Ntini (Bdr/SA)	8	5	3	27	10	13.50	0	0	3	0	1610	688	36	19.11	6-59	2	0
SB O'Connor (NZ)	4	5	0	52	20	10.40	0	0	1	0	698	309	16	19.31	5-51	1	0
JL Ontong (Bol)	9	15	2	546	131*	42.00	1	4	16	0	1207	658	17	38.70	4-120	0	0
JM Otto (Gau)	4	6	0	149	88	24.83	0	2	2	0	6	3	0	-	-	0	0
G Outram (NW)	1	1	0	14	14	14.00	0	0	0	0	0	0	0	-	-	0	0
A Paleker (Nor)	4	6	2	127	38*	31.75	0	0	3	0	0	0	0	-	-	0	0
SJ Palframan (Bol)	7	11	0	174	46	15.81	0	0	23	3	0	0	0	-	-	0	0
AC Parore (NZ)	6	9	2	181	101*	25.85	1	0	14	2	0	0	0	-	-	0	0
AJ Penn (NZ)	1	0	0	0	0	-	0	0	0	0	126	68	5	13.60	5-38	1	0

Name	M	Inns	NO	Runs	HS	Avg	100	50	Ct	St	Balls	Runs	Wkts	Avg	BB	5I	10M
PDRL Perera (SL)	1	2	2	1	1*	-	0	0	0	0	114	73	1	73.00	1-73	0	0
AN Petersen (Nor)	1	2	0	32	30	16.00	0	0	1	0	0	0	0	-	-	0	0
RJ Peterson (EP)	8	15	2	289	96*	22.23	0	1	2	0	1979	919	24	38.29	5-87	1	0
BT Player (Bol)	7	12	2	172	73	17.20	0	1	10	0	1138	431	12	35.91	5-26	1	0
SM Pollock (KZN/SA)	7	6	0	182	111	30.33	1	0	8	0	1520	515	27	19.07	6-30	1	0
EG Poole (NW)	10	18	0	284	50	15.77	0	1	37	0	0	0	0	-	-	0	0
SC Pope (Bdr)	10	19	0	647	125	34.05	2	3	2	0	210	82	1	82.00	1-18	0	0
N Pothas (Gau)	8	14	1	418	93	32.15	0	4	16	0	0	0	0	-	-	0	0
D Pretorius (FS)	8	11	4	50	14*	7.14	0	0	4	0	1659	881	37	23.81	4-51	0	0
AG Prince (WP)	8	14	4	539	120*	53.90	1	2	7	0	0	0	0	-	-	0	0
AAW Pringle (Bol)	5	8	1	47	27	6.71	0	0	3	0	1023	486	13	37.38	4-49	0	0
MW Pringle (EP)	3	4	1	64	25	21.33	0	0	1	0	655	234	10	23.40	4-32	0	0
AG Puttick (WP)	7	12	1	441	153*	40.09	1	2	5	0	0	0	0	-	-	0	0
BL Reddy (Eas)	3	5	1	69	28	17.25	0	0	1	0	498	242	4	60.50	3-39	0	0
JN Rhodes (KZN)	3	5	0	159	76	31.80	0	1	1	0	0	0	0	-	-	0	0
MH Richardson (NZ)	6	9	1	500	173*	62.50	1	2	1	0	0	0	0	-	-	0	0
MJR Rindel (Eas)	7	14	0	504	91	36.00	0	4	0	0	12	8	0	-	-	0	0
GA Roe (NW)	8	14	5	175	66	19.44	0	1	3	0	1747	631	40	15.77	7-47	3	0
JA Rudolph (Nor)	9	17	0	638	144	37.52	2	2	7	0	407	214	5	42.80	2-13	0	0
K Sangakkara (SL)	5	9	0	281	98	31.22	0	2	4	0	0	0	0	-	-	0	0
JR Schorn (FS)	2	4	0	28	11	7.00	0	0	2	0	0	0	0	-	-	0	0
DM Senekal (EP)	2	4	2	31	15	15.50	0	0	1	0	366	174	5	34.80	3-42	0	0
AJ Seymore (Eas/Gau)	7	14	0	543	174	38.78	1	4	8	0	0	0	0	-	-	0	0
MS Sinclair (NZ)	6	11	2	461	150	51.22	1	2	4	0	24	13	0	-	-	0	0
WJ Smit (FS)	5	7	0	247	94	35.28	0	2	2	0	0	0	0	-	-	0	0
GC Smith (WP)	9	16	0	676	183	42.25	2	3	16	0	24	17	0	-	-	0	0
GJ Smith (Nor)	9	11	3	45	15	5.62	0	0	3	0	1984	869	30	28.96	5-25	1	0
CM Spearman (NZ)	5	10	1	416	115	46.22	2	2	6	0	0	0	0	-	-	0	0
ELR Stewart (KZN)	9	15	4	398	79	36.18	0	2	26	1	0	0	0	-	-	0	0
PJR Steyn (Nor)	8	15	1	527	188*	37.64	1	2	3	0	0	0	0	-	-	0	0
QR Still (Nor)	3	5	1	81	34	20.25	0	0	1	0	102	53	2	26.50	1-4	0	0
JG Strydom (Bol)	4	8	0	216	73	27.00	0	1	4	0	6	1	0	-	-	0	0
M Strydom (NW)	9	16	2	454	124	32.42	1	1	5	0	734	411	8	51.37	6-23	1	0
PC Strydom (Bdr)	10	18	0	693	86	38.50	0	7	7	0	1403	579	23	25.17	3-29	0	0
SB Styris (NZ)	2	2	1	82	73*	82.00	0	1	1	0	96	43	4	10.75	3-25	0	0
CB Sugden (Bdr)	10	19	0	367	54	19.31	0	2	9	0	0	0	0	-	-	0	0

FIRST-CLASS AVERAGES 2000/01

Name	M	Inns	NO	Runs	HS	Avg	100	50	Ct	St	Balls	Runs	Wkts	Avg	BB	5I	10M
CR Tatton (GW)	7	11	1	42	14*	4.20	0	0	3	0	1416	651	15	43.40	5-80	1	0
R Telemachus (WP)	6	7	1	65	24	10.83	0	0	1	0	1013	552	22	25.09	6-54	1	0
DJ Terbrugge (Gau)	5	7	4	47	12*	15.66	0	0	0	0	1001	363	11	33.00	5-39	1	0
AC Thomas (NW)	10	18	5	531	106*	40.84	1	2	3	0	1752	788	28	28.14	6-26	1	0
DH Townsend (Nor)	8	10	0	89	45	8.90	0	0	1	0	1436	761	29	26.24	5-49	1	0
G Toyana (Gau)	5	9	0	114	42	12.66	0	0	2	0	48	31	0	-	-	0	0
IJL Trott (Bol)	9	18	2	385	93	24.06	0	3	5	0	115	65	0	-	-	0	0
TL Tsolekile (WP)	9	12	0	382	95	31.83	0	3	30	1	0	0	0	-	-	0	0
BH Tucker (GW)	4	6	0	135	47	22.50	0	0	0	0	0	0	0	-	-	0	0
DR Tuffey (NZ)	5	3	0	14	8	4.66	0	0	3	0	804	410	15	27.33	5-69	1	0
ANW Tweedie (KZN)	2	3	1	20	20*	10.00	0	0	1	0	180	109	5	21.80	4-65	0	0
J Uys (Eas)	1	2	1	43	26	43.00	0	0	0	0	6	4	0	-	-	0	0
WPUJC Vaas (SL)	2	4	1	50	38	16.66	0	0	1	0	402	218	1	218.00	1-109	0	0
AM van den Berg (Eas)	3	6	0	116	59	19.33	0	1	0	0	24	18	0	-	-	0	0
F van der Merwe (NW)	5	9	3	61	24*	10.16	0	0	2	0	943	522	20	26.10	5-62	2	0
JJ van der Wath (FS)	4	8	1	92	49	13.14	0	0	7	0	765	411	15	27.40	5-59	1	0
M van Jaarsveld (Nor)	9	17	0	630	132	37.05	1	5	16	0	12	5	0	-	-	0	0
CFK van Wyk (Nor)	9	15	2	256	59	19.69	0	1	35	2	0	0	0	-	-	0	0
JM van Wyk (Bol)	1	1	0	0	0	0.00	0	0	0	0	102	51	1	51.00	1-38	0	0
MN van Wyk (FS)	7	11	0	179	49	16.27	0	0	15	0	78	36	2	18.00	2-25	0	0
RE Veenstra (KZN)	1	2	0	60	38	30.00	0	0	0	0	240	92	1	92.00	1-55	0	0
JF Venter (FS)	9	15	2	494	112*	38.00	1	3	4	0	1736	858	31	27.67	6-90	2	0
MC Venter (NW)	7	12	1	116	44*	10.54	0	0	8	0	0	0	0	-	-	0	0
BGK Walker (NZ)	6	7	3	85	27*	21.25	0	0	2	0	725	350	12	29.16	3-13	0	0
KP Walmsley (NZ)	3	2	0	5	5	2.50	0	0	1	0	301	123	6	20.50	2-24	0	0
DJ Watson (KZN)	9	17	2	532	81	35.46	0	5	6	0	0	0	0	-	-	0	0
BM White (Eas)	3	6	0	99	33	16.50	0	0	2	0	0	0	0	-	-	0	0
W Wiblin (Bdr)	10	19	2	470	88	27.64	0	3	13	0	36	19	0	-	-	0	0
GP Wickramasinghe (SL)	3	4	1	26	21	8.66	0	0	1	0	237	146	5	29.20	2-34	0	0
LJ Wilkinson (FS)	9	15	0	642	169	42.80	1	3	9	0	0	0	0	-	-	0	0
HS Williams (Bol)	6	10	7	57	33	19.00	0	0	2	0	1472	629	29	21.68	6-40	4	0
JW Williams (Eas)	1	2	2	0	0*	-	0	0	0	0	0	0	0	-	-	0	0
CM Willoughby (WP)	8	6	3	29	17	9.66	0	0	2	0	1793	683	31	22.03	5-26	1	0
WR Wingfield (KZN)	6	10	4	192	89*	32.00	0	1	2	0	416	214	7	30.57	2-36	0	0
M Zondeki (Bdr)	1	2	1	12	12	12.00	0	0	0	0	156	88	1	88.00	1-42	0	0
DNT Zoysa (SL)	5	7	2	67	27*	13.40	0	0	0	0	615	330	7	47.14	4-76	0	0

SOUTH AFRICAN FIRST-CLASS RECORDS

(a) The symbol * denotes an innings declared, an unbroken partnership, or a not out innings, as appropriate.
(b) The Currie Cup was superseded by the Castle Cup in 1991/92. Both are denoted by '(CC)'. Castle Cup also includes Currie Cup where applicable. In 1996/97 the competition became the SuperSport Series (SS). The Castle Bowl is denoted by (CB), the President's Competition by (PC) and the UCB Bowl by (UB).
(c) Matches denoted (SACB) are three-day matches played between 1971/72 and 1990/91 under the auspices of the South African Cricket Board of Control and its successor, the South African Cricket Board. These matches were granted first-class status retrospectively following the formation of the United Cricket Board of South Africa in 1991.
(d) Figures are correct to 1 April 2001.

TEAM RECORDS

INNINGS TOTALS

Highest (600 or more) in South Africa:

676	MCC v Griqualand West at Kimberley	1938/39
664-6*	Natal v Western Province (CC) at Durban	1936/37
663-6*	South Africa v Arosa Sri Lanka at Cape Town	1982/83
654-5	England v South Africa (5th Test) at Durban	1938/39
640-5*	Gauteng v Griqualand West (SS) at Kimberley	1999/00
628-8*	Australia v South Africa (1st Test) at Johannesburg	1996/97
622-9*	South Africa v Australia (2nd Test) at Durban	1969/70
620	South Africa v Australia (1st Test) at Johannesburg	1966/67
620	Australians v Griqualand West at Kimberley	1966/67
618-4*	South Africa v Rest of South Africa at Johannesburg	1964/65
609	Transvaal v Orange Free State (CC) at Johannesburg	1934/35
608-6*	Transvaal v Natal at Johannesburg	1939/40
608	England v South Africa (2nd Test) at Johannesburg	1948/49
603	Griqualand West v Western Province (CC) at Kimberley	1929/30
602-9*	Transvaal v Northern Transvaal (CC) at Johannesburg	1993/94
602	Griqualand West v Rhodesia (CC) at Kimberley	1929/30
601	Western Province v Border (CC) at Cape Town	1929/30

Overseas:

692	South Africans v Cambridge University at Cambridge	1901
621-5*	South Africa v New Zealand (1st Test) at Auckland	1998/99
613-8*	South Africans v Sussex at Hove	1994
611	South Africans v Nottinghamshire at Nottingham	1904

Lowest (40 or less) in South Africa:

16 and 18	Border v Natal (CC) at East London	1959/60 (a)
23	Border v Natal (CC) at East London	1920/21
29	Griqualand West v Transvaal (CC) at Johannesburg	1950/51
30	South Africa v England (1st Test) at Port Elizabeth	1895/96
31	Griqualand West v Natal (CC) at Johannesburg	1906/07
34	Griqualand West v Transvaal (CC) at Port Elizabeth	1902/03
34	Border v Eastern Province (CC) at East London	1946/47 (b)
34	Eastern Province v Natal (CC) at Port Elizabeth	1980/81
35	South Africa v England (2nd Test) at Cape Town	1898/99
36	Eastern Province v Transvaal (CC) at Port Elizabeth	1937/38
37	Eastern Province v Western Province (CC) at Port Elizabeth	1933/34
37	Orange Free State v Transvaal (CC) at Bloemfontein	1936/37
38	Transvaal v Western Province (SACB) at Cape Town	1981/82
39	Natal v Western Province (SACB) at Cape Town	1981/82
40	Eastern Province v Orange Free State (CC) at Durban	1910/11
40	Orange Free State v Transvaal B (CC) at Johannesburg	1960/61

Note: (a) Border's 1959/60 aggregate established a world record.
(b) Border were set only 42 to win. This is the lowest target in first-class cricket for a losing team to be set.

SOUTH AFRICAN FIRST-CLASS RECORDS

Overseas:

30	South Africa v England (1st Test) at Birmingham	1924
32	Derbyshire v South Africans at Derby	1947
36	Scotland v South Africans at Glasgow	1924
36	South Africa v Australia (5th Test) at Melbourne	1931/32
	(First innings. They were dismissed for 45 in the second innings.)	
40	Gloucestershire v South Africans at Clifton	1901

MATCH AGGREGATES

Highest:

In South Africa:	1981 for 35 wickets	South Africa v England (5th Test) at Durban	1938/39
In SuperSport Series:	1456 for 38 wickets	Griqualand West v Natal at Kimberley	1925/26
SA teams abroad:	1744 for 40 wickets	New South Wales v South Africans at Sydney	1910/11

Lowest (for completed matches):

In South Africa:	198 for 22 wickets	Eastern Province v Transvaal (CC) at Port Elizabeth	1937/38
SA teams abroad:	234 for 29 wickets	Australia v South Africa (5th Test) at Melbourne	1931/32

DURATION OF MATCHES

Longest:

10 days (no play on 8th)	South Africa v England (5th Test) at Durban	1938/39
7 days (play each day)	Transvaal v Kimberley (CC) at Johannesburg	1890/91

Shortest:

Two matches have begun and been completed on the same day:

Transvaal v Orange Free State (CC) at Johannesburg	1906/07
Eastern Province v Orange Free State (CC) at Port Elizabeth	1912/13

MOST RUNS SCORED IN A SINGLE DAY

By one side:

618 for 4 wickets - South Africa v Rest of South Africa at Johannesburg 1964/65

By both sides:

616 for 16 wickets - Transvaal v Orange Free State (CC) at Johannesburg 1929/30

FEWEST RUNS SCORED IN A SINGLE DAY

By one side:

138 for 5 wickets - South Africa v England (5th Test) at Port Elizabeth (1st day) 1956/57

By both sides:

122 for 8 wickets - South Africa v England (5th Test) at Port Elizabeth (3rd day) 1956/57

LARGE MARGINS OF VICTORY

By a margin of runs:

530 runs	Australia beat South Africa (4th Test) at Melbourne	1910/11
411 runs	Rhodesia beat International Wanderers at Salisbury	1972/73
386 runs	Transvaal beat Griqualand West (CC) at Johannesburg	1929/30

An innings and:

374 runs	MCC beat Orange Free State at Bloemfontein	1913/14
(a) 359 runs	Western Province beat Griqualand West (CC) at Johannesburg	1906/07
357 runs	Transvaal beat Orange Free State (CC) at Johannesburg	1929/30

Note: (a) In 1906/07 Griqualand West were beaten three times in 10 days by an innings and more than 300 runs.

HIGHST FOURTH INNINGS TOTALS

654-5 (set 696)	England v South Africa (5th Test) at Durban	1938/39
529-9 (set 579)	Combined XI v South Africans at Perth	1963/64
500-7 (and won)	SA Universities v Western Province at Stellenbosch	1978/79
447 (lost by 111)	Orange Free State v Transvaal (CC) at Bloemfontein	1926/27
443-4 (and won)	Free State v KwaZulu-Natal (SS) at Durban	1999/00
442 (lost by 44)	South Africans v New South Wales at Sydney	1910/11
438-8 (and won)	Free State v West Indians at Bloemfontein	1998/99

SOUTH AFRICAN FIRST-CLASS RECORDS

VICTORY LOSING ONLY ONE WICKET

Rhodesia (549-1*) beat Orange Free State (252-235) (CC) at Bloemfontein	1967/68
Transvaal (325-1*) beat Northern Transvaal (97-173) (CC) at Pretoria	1980/81
Transvaal (362-1*) beat Arosa Sri Lanka (122-200) at Johannesburg	1982/83

VICTORY AFTER FOLLOWING ON

Transvaal (122-288) beat Natal (254-79) (CC) by 77 runs at Cape Town	1897/98
South Africans (95-281) beat Kent (273-101) by two runs at Catford	1907
Orange Free State (163-298) beat Western Province (393-44) (CC) by 24 runs at Cape Town	1926/27
Natal (115-458) beat Transvaal (370-190) by 13 runs at Durban	1932/33
Transvaal B (293-362) beat North-Eastern Transvaal (468-87) (CC) by 100 runs at Johannesburg	1962/63
Natal B (121-413) beat Orange Free State (319-196) (CC) by 19 runs at Bloemfontein	1975/76
Natal B (205-456-8*) beat Border (403-6*-222) (CB) by 36 runs at East London	1988/89

CLOSE FINISHES

Two matches played by South African touring teams overseas ended in a tie, v Worcestershire in 1901 and v Middlesex in 1904. Two matches were tied in 1985/86. Both ties involved Eastern Province B, the matches against Boland at Grahamstown and Natal B at Pietermaritzburg being played consecutively. On 34 occasions in which South African teams have been involved, the margin of victory has been one wicket and on another 34 occasions the margin has been 10 runs or less.

LOWEST INNINGS TOTAL TO INCLUDE A CENTURY

172 (G Boycott 107)	Northern Transvaal v Rhodesia at Pretoria	1971/72
177 (JH Sinclair 106)	South Africa v England (2nd Test) at Cape Town	1898/99
Currie Cup/Castle Cup/SuperSport Series:		
190 (HD Freakes 122*)	Eastern Province v Natal at Johannesburg	1931/32
190 (KS McEwan 102)	Western Province v Eastern Province at Port Elizabeth	1986/87
World record:		
143 (CEB Rice 105*)	Nottinghamshire v Hampshire at Bournemouth	1981

HIGHEST INNINGS TOTAL NOT INCLUDING A CENTURY

517	South Africa v Australia at Adelaide (highest score 87)	1997/98
512	South Africans v South Australia at Adelaide (highest score 97)	1931/32
503	Transvaal v Orange Free State (CC) at Bloemfontein (highest score 91)	1903/04

BATTING

HIGHEST INDIVIDUAL INNINGS

337*	DJ Cullinan	Transvaal v Northern Transvaal (CC) at Johannesburg	1993/94
307*	TN Lazard	Boland v Western Province at Worcester	1993/94
306*	EAB Rowan	Transvaal v Natal at Johannesburg	1939/40
304*	AW Nourse	Natal v Transvaal at Johannesburg	1919/20
300	DCS Compton	MCC v North-Eastern Transvaal at Benoni	1948/49

Note: The highest score by a South African is 356 by BA Richards, for South Australia v Western Australia at Perth, 1970/71 (he scored 325 runs in a day).

HIGHEST MAIDEN CENTURIES

261*	SSL Steyn	Western Province v Border (CC) at Cape Town	1929/30
240	WFE Marx	Transvaal v Griqualand West (CC) at Johannesburg (On debut in first-class cricket - a world record until 1993/94)	1920/21

DOUBLE CENTURIES

Players who have scored most double centuries:

7 AW Nourse 6 G Kirsten, AD Nourse 5 EJ Barlow, RG Pollock, EAB Rowan

Note: BA Richards scored six double centuries in all first-class cricket, only one of them in South Africa.

EJ Barlow scored six double centuries in all first-class cricket, including five for South African teams, three of them in South Africa and two in Australia. PN Kirsten scored eight double centuries in all first-class cricket, two of them in South Africa.

SOUTH AFRICAN FIRST-CLASS RECORDS

Two double centuries in the same innings:

AD Nourse 240, IJ Siedle 207	Natal v Western Province (CC) at Durban (This was Siedle's last innings in first-class cricket)	1936/37
TL Goddard 222, HM Ackerman 200*	North-Eastern Transvaal v Western Province (CC) at Cape Town	1966/67

A CENTURY ON FIRST-CLASS DEBUT

(Notable instances, current players and since 1989/90)

240	WFE Marx	Tvl v GW (CC) at Johannesburg	1920/21
183*	R Watson-Smith	Bdr v OFS (CC) at Bloemfontein	1969/70
	(Watson-Smith scored 125* in his next innings for Bdr v GW (CC) at East London and thus scored 308 runs in his first two innings without being dismissed - a world record)		
108	JN Rhodes	Ntl v WP (CC) at Durban	1988/89
150	KA Forde	Ntl B v EP B (CB) at Port Elizabeth	1989/90
100	PAH Upton	WP B v N Tvl B (CB) at Cape Town [Constantia]	1990/91
117*	AG Lawson	Bdr v OFS (CC) at Bloemfontein	1991/92
129*	BA Nash	Ntl B v OFS B (PC) at Durban	1991/92
119	JPB Mulder	W Tvl v GW (UB) at Kimberley	1991/92
104	JD Nel	W Tvl v E Tvl (UB) at Springs	1992/93
103	CC Wait	EP B v WP B (UB) at Cape Town [Goodwood]	1993/94
+122*	JM Henderson	Bol B v OFS B (UB) at Bloemfontein	1994/95
+101	CR Wilson	Bdr B v E Tvl (UB) at Springs	1994/95
105	D Moffat	EP B v Ntl B (UB) at Port Elizabeth	1997/98
112	A Jacobs	NW v WP B (UB) at Potchefstroom	1997/98
+118	MA Alexander	GW B v Nor B (UB) at Centurion	1998/99
187	GC Smith	UCB Inv XI v GW at Kimberley	1999/00

+ Second innings.

A CENTURY ON DEBUT IN OTHER COUNTRIES

In Australia:		
146	LA Stricker, SA v S Australia at Adelaide	1910/11
201*	AW Nourse, SA v S Australia at Adelaide	1910/11
102	JAJ Christy, SA v W Australia at Perth	1931/32
182	DJ McGlew, SA v W Australia at Perth	1952/53
104	DT Lindsay, SA v S Australia at Adelaide	1963/64
113	DJ Cullinan, SA v Queensland at Brisbane	1993/94
105	AC Hudson, SA v Queensland at Brisbane	1993/94
186*	JH Kallis, WP v Queensland at Brisbane	1995/96
120	JB Commins, WP v Queensland at Brisbane	1995/96
100	SM Pollock, SA v W Australia at Perth	1997/98
In England:		
103	CMH Hathorn, SA v Hampshire at Southampton	1901
102	HB Cameron, SA v Worcestershire at Worcester	1929
103	IR Fullerton, Fezelas v Combined Services at Portsmouth	1961
In Ireland:		
107	AM Amla, SA Acad v Ireland at Dublin	1999
In New Zealand:		
123	B Mitchell, SA v Auckland at Auckland	1931/32
113	HW Taylor, SA v Auckland at Auckland	1931/32
100*	ARA Murray, SA v Canterbury at Christchurch	1952/53
255*	DJ McGlew, SA v NZ at Wellington	1952/53
In Sri Lanka:		
123	GFJ Liebenberg, SA Under 24 v SL Board Pres XI at Colombo	1995/96
105*	DM Benkenstein, SA Under 24 v SL Board Pres XI at Colombo	1995/96
In West Indies:		
163	AC Hudson, SA v WI at Bridgetown	1991/92
131	GFJ Liebenberg, FS v Barbados at Bridgetown	1996/97
111	HH Dippenaar, FS v Barbados at Bridgetown	1996/97
In Zimbabwe (1993/94 onwards):		
152	CF Craven, OFS B v ZB XI (UB) at Harare	1993/94
104	DJ Callaghan, SA A v Mashonaland at Harare	1994/95

164	JB Commins, SA A v Mashonaland at Harare	1994/95
102	N Boje, SA A v Mashonaland at Harare	1994/95
109	DN Crookes, Ntl B v ZB XI (UB) at Harare	1994/95
135	AC Hudson, SA v Zim at Harare	1995/96
105	MI Gidley, GW v ZB XI (UB) at Harare	1995/96
100	GC Victor, EP B v ZB XI (UB) at Harare	1995/96
185	GL Brophy, SA Acad v Zim Pres XI at Harare	1998/99
115	JH Kallis, SA v Zim at Harare	1999/00
125	MV Boucher, SA v Zim at Harare	1999/00

A DOUBLE CENTURY AND A CENTURY IN THE SAME MATCH

210	112*	AM Bacher, Tvl v GW (SS) at Kimberley	1996/97
200*	171	HH Gibbs, SA v Ind A at Nagpur	1996/97

CENTURIES IN EACH INNINGS

(Current players and recent instances)

115	147*	KC Wessels, EP v OFS (CC) at Port Elizabeth	1991/92
138	121*	FJC Cronje, GW v W Tvl (UB) at Potchefstroom	1992/93
106	111	MJR Rindel, N Tvl v Ntl (CC) at Durban	1992/93
150	107	WJ Cronje, OFS v Ntl (CC) at Bloemfontein	1993/94
107	127	WR James, Matabeleland Select XI v SA A at Bulawayo	1994/95
101	104*	PB du Plessis, Bdr B v WP B (UB) at East London	1995/96
102	133	G Kirsten, SA v Ind at Calcutta	1996/97
177	119*	W Wiblin, Bdr v WP (SS) at East London	1997/98
125	131*	G Kirsten, SA v Gloucestershire at Bristol	1998
105	102*	HH Dippenaar, FS v KZ-Ntl (SS) at Durban	1998/99
101*	106*	JN Rhodes, SA v NZ A at Christchurch	1998/99
131	129	JDC Bryant, EP v WP (SS) at Cape Town	1999/00
100	115	CM Spearman, NZ v NW at Potchefstroom	2000/01

THREE OR MORE CENTURIES IN SUCCESSIVE INNINGS

Six centuries:

MJ Procter (Rhodesia 1970/71) equalled the world record held jointly by CB Fry (1901) and DG Bradman (1938/39). 119 v Natal B (CC) at Bulawayo; 129 v Transvaal B (CC) at Salisbury; 107 v Orange Free State (CC) at Bloemfontein; 174 v North-Eastern Transvaal (CC) at Pretoria; 106 v Griqualand West (CC) at Kimberley and 254 v Western Province at Salisbury.

Four centuries:

DG Bradman (New South Wales and Australia, all v South Africa)	1931/32
PBH May (MCC)	1956/57
PN Kirsten (WP and SA Universities) (he scored six centuries in seven innings)	1976/77

Note: KS McEwan for Essex in 1977, SJ Cook for Somerset in 1989

Three centuries:

D Denton (MCC/England)	1909/10	J Moroney (Australians)	1949/50
CG Macartney (NSW/Australia)	1910/11	AR Morris (Australians)	1949/50
JW Zulch (Transvaal)	1920/21	AD Nourse (Natal)	1950/51
JAJ Christy (Transvaal)	1927/28/29	EAB Rowan (Transvaal)	1952/53
EL Dalton (South Africans) (a)	1929	JR Reid (New Zealanders)	1961/62
XC Balaskas (Griqualand West)	1929/30	RC White (Transvaal B/Transvaal)	1965/66/67
HB Cameron (Transvaal)	1933/34/35	R Kent (Border)	1977/78/79
AD Nourse (South Africans)	1935	KC Wessels (Australian XI/EP)	1986/87
IJ Siedle (Natal) (b)	1936/37	MI Gidley (Griqualand West)	1994/95/96
A Melville (South Africa)	1947	JN Rhodes (Natal)	1996/97
B Mitchell (South Africans)	1947	Azhar Mahmood (Pakistanis)	1997/98
DCS Compton (MCC)	1948/49		

Note: (a) Dalton's first centuries in first-class cricket. (b) Siedle's last three innings in first-class cricket.

YOUNGEST SOUTH AFRICAN CENTURY-MAKER

16 years 304 days - DJ Cullinan	Border v Natal B (CB) at East London	1983/84

SOUTH AFRICAN FIRST-CLASS RECORDS

YOUNGEST SOUTH AFRICAN DOUBLE CENTURY-MAKER

17 years 122 days - JG Myburgh Northerns B v Easterns (UB) at Pretoria 1997/98

MOST CENTURIES IN A SEASON

6 - BA Richards (Natal/SA) 1969/70, MJ Procter (Rhodesia) 1970/71 and PN Kirsten (WP/SA Universities) 1976/77

MOST CENTURIES IN A CAREER

RG Pollock	61	G Kirsten	34
AD Nourse	41	BA Richards	33
AW Nourse	38	DJ Cullinan	33
EJ Barlow	37	B Mitchell	30
PN Kirsten	37	EAB Rowan	30
SJ Cook	36	HW Taylor	30

Note: In all first-class cricket, AJ Lamb 89 centuries, BA Richards 80, KS McEwan 74, KC Wessels 66, SJ Cook 64, RG Pollock 64, PN Kirsten 57, RA Smith 56, BF Davison 53, MJ Procter 48, CEB Rice 48, CL Smith 47, EJ Barlow 43.

CARRYING BAT THROUGH A COMPLETED INNINGS

(Current players and recent instances)

MW Rushmere	136*	(277)	EP v N Tvl (CC) at Port Elizabeth	1987/88
PJR Steyn	57*	(98)	OFS v EP (CC) at Port Elizabeth	1988/89
AG Lawson	117*	(250)	Bdr v OFS (CC) at Bloemfontein	1991/92
TN Lazard	108*	(220)	WP v N Tvl (CC) at Verwoerdburg	1991/92
MH Dekker	162*	(312)	Zim A v Tvl at Johannesburg	1995/96
DJ Watson	103*	(246)	Ntl B v FS B (UB) at Durban	1995/96
BM White	159*	(365)	Tvl v Bol (CC) at Johannesburg	1995/96
G Kirsten	100*	(239)	SA v Pak at Faisalabad	1997/98
MA Taylor	169*	(350)	Aus v SA at Adelaide	1997/98
JM Henderson	117*	(235)	Bol v FS (SS) at Stellenbosch	1998/99
MI Gidley	73*	(160)	GW v Gau (SS) at Johannesburg	2000/01
CC Bradfield	64*	(149)	EP v Nor (SS) at Port Elizabeth	2000/01

Note: DJ McGlew carried his bat four times, EW Warner three times, TL Goddard, E Mall and JH van den Berg twice each.

HIGHEST AGGREGATE IN A SEASON BY A HOME PLAYER

	M	I	NO	Runs	HS	Avg	100	50	Season
HD Ackerman (WP)	16	29	2	1373	202*	50.85	5	6	1997/98
BA Richards (Ntl)	12	18	2	1285	186*	80.31	4	8	1973/74
BA Richards (Ntl)	10	19	1	1247	197	69.27	5	5	1972/73
BA Richards (Ntl)	10	18	2	1172	169	73.25	6	3	1969/70
SJ Cook (Tvl)	13	21	2	1142	201*	60.10	4	5	1982/83
RG Pollock (EP)	10	19	5	1097	167*	78.35	5	4	1974/75
BA Richards (Ntl)	8	15	1	1089	219	77.78	4	4	1971/72
PN Kirsten (WP)	9	15	1	1074	173*	76.71	6	1	1976/77
HH Dippenaar (FS)	11	21	3	1070	147	59.44	4	6	1998/99
BA Richards (Ntl)	11	21	4	1051	159	61.82	3	5	1975/76
KC Bland (Rho)	10	18	3	1048	151*	69.86	3	7	1964/65
RG Pollock (EP)	8	14	2	1043	196	86.91	3	5	1968/69
SJ Cook (Tvl)	11	21	3	1016	166	56.44	2	6	1983/84
DT Lindsay (NE Tvl)	10	14	0	1014	216	72.42	4	4	1966/67
RG Pollock (EP)	10	19	4	1013	194	67.53	3	5	1975/76
AM Bacher (Tvl)	10	19	2	1012	210	59.52	4	3	1996/97
RF Pienaar (Tvl)	11	20	4	1010	152*	63.12	3	6	1989/90
RG Pollock (EP)	9	16	0	1005	274	62.81	4	4	1969/70
Note also:									
RG Pollock (Tvl)	8	11	1	961	233	96.10	5	3	1978/79
MJ Procter (Rho)	8	8	0	956	254	119.50	6	-	1970/71
AD Nourse (Ntl)	5	6	1	846	260*	169.20	4	-	1936/37

BA Richards played domestic cricket in Australia in 1970/71, returning to South Africa for one match at the end of the season. In all, he played the same number of innings as in 1973/74, but had an even better record:

	M	I	NO	Runs	HS	Avg	100	50
In Australia (South Australia)	10	16	2	1538	356	109.85	6	3
In SA (Transvaal Inv XI)	1	2	0	207	140	103.50	1	1
	11	18	2	1745	356	109.06	7	4

SOUTH AFRICAN FIRST-CLASS RECORDS

FOR A TOURING TEAM

	M	I	NO	Runs	HS	Avg	100	50	Season
JR Reid (New Zealand)	17	30	2	1915	203	68.39	7	9	1961/62

FOR SOUTH AFRICAN TEAMS ABROAD

In England:	M	I	NO	Runs	HS	Avg	100	50	Season
B Mitchell	23	37	4	2014	189*	61.03	8	8	1947
In Australia and New Zealand:									
EJ Barlow	18	32	2	1900	209	63.33	6	8	1963/64

FAST SCORING

The figures in brackets indicate the time, when known, taken to reach 100. MG Francis holds the record for the fastest century in South Africa.

Score	Mins			
300	181	(66)	DCS Compton, MCC v NE Tvl at Benoni	1948/49
250*	225		HW Taylor, Ntl v Tvl (CC) at Johannesburg	1912/13
202	165	(80)	L Hutton, MCC v EP at Port Elizabeth	1938/39
115*	66	(53)	MG Francis, OFS v GW at Bloemfontein	1927/28

MJ Procter increased his score from 100 to 150 in 12 minutes, Western Province v Australians at Cape Town 1969/70

IR Redpath increased his score from 101 to 152 in 12 minutes, Australians v Orange Free State at Bloemfontein 1969/70

FB Touzel increased his score from 50 to 100 in 9 minutes, off 14 balls, Western Province B v Griqualand West (UB) at Kimberley (6x6, 2x4, 1x3, 1x2, 1x1), 1993/94 (Scored in contrived circumstances to expedite a declaration)

CENTURY BEFORE LUNCH

(Recent instances only)

MW Rushmere	(151*)	SA Inv XI v Eng XI at Pietermaritzburg (Score increased from 41* to 151* on third morning)	1989/90
LJ Koen	(177*)	Bol v GW (CB) at Stellenbosch (Innings started on third morning, 126* at lunch)	1990/91
HH Gibbs	(163*)	WP v Ntl (SS) at Cape Town (Score increased from 47* to 163* on second morning)	1996/97

Note: BA Richards hit a century before lunch on nine occasions during his career. RG Draper (GW) hit centuries before lunch in three successive Currie Cup matches 1951/52-1952/53

MOST SIXES IN AN INNINGS

13	FB Touzel	(128*)	Western Province B v Griqualand West (UB) at Kimberley (Scored in contrived circumstances to expedite a declaration)	1993/94
10	HR Lance	(122)	Transvaal v Eastern Province (CC) at Johannesburg	1966/67
10	EA Brandes	(165*)	Zimbabwe Board XI v Griqualand West (UB) at Kimberley	1994/95
9	PJ Heather	(109*)	Transvaal v Border (CC) at Durban	1910/11
9	MJ Procter	(155)	Western Province v Australians at Cape Town	1969/70
9	SM Skeete	(119)	Eastern Transvaal v Border B (UB) at Springs	1994/95
9	AP Kuiper	(117*)	Boland v Free State (SS) at Paarl	1996/97
9	H Pangarker	(128*)	Western Province B v Natal B (UB) at Cape Town	1997/98
9	JM Kemp	(188)	Eastern Province v North West (SS) at Port Elizabeth	2000/01

HITS FOR SIX OFF CONSECUTIVE BALLS

5	DT Lindsay	off WT Greensmith	Fezelas v Essex at Chelmsford	1961
5	MJ Procter	off AA Mallett	Western Province v Australians at Cape Town	1969/70
5	JM Kemp	off M Strydom	Eastern Province v North West (SS) at Port Elizabeth	2000/01

MOST RUNS OFF AN OVER

34 (646666)	FB Touzel off FJJ Viljoen (Scored in contrived circumstances to expedite a declaration)	Western Province B v Griqualand West (UB) at Kimberley	1993/94
32 (666644)	IR Redpath off N Rosendorff	Australians v Orange Free State at Bloemfontein	1969/70
31 (1) MH Bowditch and (66666)	MJ Procter off AA Mallett	Western Province v Australians at Cape Town	1969/70
31 (666661)	JM Kemp off M Strydom	Eastern Province v North West (SS) at Port Elizabeth	2000/01
30 (444666)	HB Cameron off H Verity	South Africans v Yorkshire at Sheffield	1935
30 (446646)	PL Winslow off JT Ikin	South Africans v Lancashire at Manchester	1955
30 (066666)	DT Lindsay off WT Greensmith	Fezelas v Essex at Chelmsford	1961

30 (246666) JD du Toit off CE Eksteen Boland v Transvaal at Vereeniging 1989/90
29 (1) HB Jordaan and (446644) PGV van der Bijl off JM Buchanan, Western Province v Eastern Province (CC) at Cape Town (this was the last possible over and Western Province won with one ball of the eight-ball over still remaining) 1937/38
Note: For South Africa v Australia (3rd Test) at CapeTown, JH Sinclair hit 34 (44624464) off eight successive balls 1902/03

MOST BOUNDARIES IN AN INNINGS

Sixes	Fours		
-	53	AW Nourse (304*) Ntl v Tvl at Johannesburg	1919/20

SLOW SCORING

The slowest 100s on record are:

100 in 545 mins	DJ McGlew, South Africa v Australia (3rd Test) at Durban	1957/58
100 in 488 mins	PE Richardson, England v South Africa (1st Test) at Johannesburg	1956/57
100 in 484 mins	DJ Schonegevel, Griqualand West v Northern Transvaal (CC) at Kimberley	1972/73

The slowest 50s on record are:

50 in 333 mins	BA Young, New Zealand v South Africa (2nd Test) at Durban	1994/95
50 in 313 mins	DJ McGlew, South Africa v Australia (4th Test) at Johannesburg	1957/58
50 in 296 mins	BM White, Border v Northerns (SS) at Centurion	1999/00

Longest period before opening score:

101 mins	GI Allott, New Zealand v South Africa (1st Test) at Auckland (He was out for 0. The longest known instance in first class cricket of a player scoring 0)	1998/99
87 mins	VR Hogg, Zimbabwe-Rhodesia B v Natal B (CB) at Pietermaritzburg (He was out for 0. The longest known instance in first class cricket of a player scoring 0 until the innings by GI Allott, above)	1979/80
73 mins	BJ Versfeld, Natal v Transvaal (CC) at Durban (He went on to make 100 in 350 minutes and 201* in 559 minutes)	1965/66

Note: B Mitchell (58) for South Africa v Australia (1st Test) at Brisbane did not add to his score for 90 minutes 1931/32

WICKET PARTNERSHIP RECORDS

In South Africa:

1st	424	IJ Siedle (174) and JFW Nicolson (252*) Natal v OFS (CC) at Bloemfontein	1926/27
2nd	415	AD Jadeja (254*) and SV Manjrekar (186) Indians v Combined Bowl XI at Springs	1992/93
	338	PG Amm (157) and LJ Koen (202*) Eastern Province v Boland (CC) at Port Elizabeth	1995/96
3rd	399	RT Simpson (130*) and DCS Compton (300) MCC v NE Transvaal at Benoni	1948/49
	360	TN Lazard (307*) and JB Commins (165) Boland v Western Province at Worcester	1993/94
	337	PG Amm (214) and KS McEwan (191) Eastern Province v Transvaal (CC) at Port Elizabeth	1988/89
4th	342	EAB Rowan (195) and PJM Gibb (203) Transvaal v NE Transvaal (CC) at Johannesburg	1952/53
5th	385	SR Waugh (160) and GS Blewett (214) Australia v South Africa at Johannesburg	1996/97
	355	AJ Lamb (294) and JJ Strydom (107) OFS v Eastern Province (CC) at Bloemfontein	1987/88
6th	259	SA Jones (209*) and O Henry (125) Boland v Border (CB) at East London	1987/88
7th	299	B Mitchell (159) and A Melville (153) Transvaal v Griqualand West (CC) at Kimberley	1946/47
8th	222	SSL Steyn (261*) and DPB Morkel (114) Western Province v Border (CC) at Cape Town	1929/30
9th	221	NV Lindsay (160*) and GR McCubbin (97) Transvaal v Rhodesia at Bulawayo	1922/23
	217	AW Nourse (112*) and BC Cooley (113) Natal v Western Province (CC) at Johannesburg	1906/07
10th	174	HR Lance (168) and D Mackay-Coghill (58*) Transvaal v Natal (CC) at Johannesburg	1965/66
	174	AC Thomas (106*) and GA Roe (66) North West v Griqualand West (SS) at Kimberley	2000/01

For South African teams abroad:

1st	330	B Mitchell (195) and EAB Rowan (171) SA v Surrey at The Oval	1935
2nd	315*	HH Gibbs (211*) and JH Kallis (148*) SA v New Zealand at Christchurch	1998/99
3rd	341	EJ Barlow (201) and RG Pollock (175) SA v Australia at Adelaide	1963/64
4th	242	WJ Cronje (145) and DJ Cullinan (113) SA v Queensland at Brisbane	1993/94
5th	262	KG Viljoen (152) and HB Cameron (132) SA v Derbyshire at Ilkeston	1935
6th	187	EL Dalton (157) and Q McMillan (86) SA v Kent at Canterbury	1929
7th	246	DJ McGlew (255*) and ARA Murray (109) SA v New Zealand at Wellington	1952/53
8th	156	GC White (162*) and RO Schwarz (71) SA v Gloucestershire at Bristol	1907
9th	268	JB Commins (164) and N Boje (102) SA A v Mashonaland at Harare	1994/95
10th	103	HGO Owen-Smith (129) and AJ Bell (26*) SA v England at Leeds	1929

SOUTH AFRICAN FIRST-CLASS RECORDS

BATSMEN WHO HAVE SCORED 7000 RUNS IN A CAREER

+ Denotes current player

	Career	M	I	NO	Runs	HS	Avg	100	50
AJ Lamb	1972-95	467	772	108	32502	294	48.94	89	166
BA Richards	1964-82	339	576	58	28358	356	54.74	80	152
BF Davison	1967-87	467	766	79	27453	189	39.96	53	148
KS McEwan	1972-91	428	705	67	26628	218	41.73	74	122
CEB Rice	1969-93	482	766	123	26331	246	40.95	48	137
KC Wessels	1973-99	316	539	50	24738	254	50.58	66	132
+RA Smith	1980-	386	653	83	24325	209*	42.67	57	122
PN Kirsten	1973-96	327	568	59	22635	271	44.46	57	107
MJ Procter	1965-88	401	667	58	21936	254	36.01	48	109
SJ Cook	1972-94	270	475	57	21143	313*	50.58	64	87
RG Pollock	1960-86	262	437	54	20940	274	54.67	64	99
EJ Barlow	1959-82	283	493	28	18212	217	39.16	43	86
CL Smith	1977-91	269	466	60	18028	217	44.40	47	88
PM Walker	1956-72	469	788	110	17650	152*	26.03	13	92
AW Greig	1965-78	350	579	45	16660	226	31.19	26	97
RC Ontong	1972-94	367	604	87	15234	204*	29.46	20	78
AW Nourse	1896-1935	228	371	39	14216	304*	42.81	38	60
+DJ Cullinan	1983-	216	370	53	13988	337*	44.12	38	65
NG Featherstone	1967-81	329	528	54	13922	147	29.37	12	88
HW Taylor	1909-35	206	339	26	13105	250*	41.86	30	64
+G Kirsten	1987-	178	316	34	12781	275	45.32	34	60
AD Nourse	1931-52	175	269	27	12472	260*	51.53	41	54
HM Ackerman	1963-81	234	409	33	12219	208	32.49	20	60
DJ McGlew	1947-66	190	299	34	12170	255*	45.92	27	68
WJ Cronje	1987-99	184	310	33	12103	251	43.69	32	57
EAB Rowan	1929-53	157	258	17	11710	306*	48.58	30	54
SH Martin	1925-49	267	457	31	11511	191*	27.02	13	68
CB Llewellyn	1894-1912	267	461	34	11425	216	26.75	18	52
B Mitchell	1925-49	173	281	30	11395	195	45.39	30	55
TL Goddard	1952-69	179	297	19	11279	222	40.57	26	54
RA McLean	1949-65	200	318	19	10969	207	36.68	22	65
CP Wilkins	1962-82	198	357	21	10966	156	32.63	18	61
RF Pienaar	1977-98	199	346	27	10896	153	34.15	18	62
A Melville	1928-48	190	295	15	10598	189	37.85	25	53
BL Irvine	1962-76	157	271	26	9919	193	40.48	21	46
JHB Waite	1948-65	199	314	34	9812	219	35.04	23	45
B Roberts	1982-91	205	333	34	9182	184	30.70	13	40
+AC Hudson	1984-	151	270	20	9156	206	36.62	20	47
AM Ferreira	1974-91	245	386	70	9064	133	28.68	5	43
HR Fotheringham	1971-89	147	247	27	8814	184	40.06	21	48
MW Rushmere	1983-99	144	253	37	8494	188	39.32	20	41
PB Clift	1971-87	319	446	91	8383	106	23.61	2	31
IA Greig	1974-91	253	339	50	8301	291	28.72	8	40
+JH Kallis	1993-	126	200	22	8107	186*	45.54	19	49
KG Viljoen	1926-48	133	209	25	7964	215	43.28	23	30
AP Kuiper	1977-97	165	276	31	7899	161*	32.24	9	46
BM McMillan	1984-99	155	245	41	7898	140	38.71	14	46
A Bacher	1959-73	120	212	10	7894	235	39.07	18	45
+GFJ Liebenberg	1989-	135	237	11	7816	229	34.58	17	38
WR Endean	1945-64	134	230	25	7757	247	37.83	15	34
IJ Siedle	1922-36	123	204	11	7730	265*	40.05	17	32
AL Wilmot	1960-88	147	266	26	7687	222*	32.02	12	31

+JN Rhodes	1988-	143	226	26	7668	156*	38.34	15	43
PR Carlstein	1954-79	148	255	16	7554	229	31.60	9	46
KC Bland	1956-73	131	219	28	7249	197	37.95	13	34
DJ Callaghan	1983-	135	222	26	7145	171	36.45	17	34
DT Lindsay	1958-73	124	214	15	7074	216	35.54	12	36
AJ Pithey	1950-68	124	213	16	7073	170	35.90	13	41

BOWLING

OUTSTANDING ANALYSIS IN AN INNINGS

10 WICKETS

O	M	R	W		
12	2	26	10	AEE Vogler, EP v GW (CC) at Johannesburg	1906/07
23.5	7	59	10	ST Jefferies, WP v OFS (CC) at Cape Town	1987/88

NINE WICKETS (outstanding instances)

9	19	AMB Rowan, Tvl v Aus at Johannesburg	1949/50
9	22	MG Melle, SA v Tasmania at Launceston	1952/53
9	23	WP Howell, Aus v WP at Cape Town	1902/03
9	23	JT Botten, NE Tvl v GW (CC) at Pretoria	1958/59
9	28	GA Lohmann, Eng v SA (2nd Test) at Johannesburg	1895/96
9	29	JT Botten, NE Tvl v Rho (CC) at Pretoria	1963/64
9	32	JM Gregory, AIF v Ntl at Durban	1919/20
9	32	AF Hagemann, Bdr v GW (CC) at Kimberley	1960/61
9	46	VA Barnes, WP v Ntl (SACB) at Ladysmith	1983/84
9	48	EP Nupen, Tvl v GW (CC) at Johannesburg	1931/32
9	52	MH Bowditch, WP v Ntl (CC) at Cape Town	1965/66
	(The first occasion Bowditch had bowled in first class cricket. He had played in one match previously)		
9	53	Q McMillan, SA v S Australia at Adelaide	1931/32
9	54	K McLaren, GW v Ntl B (CC) at Umzinto	1973/74
9	56	MJ Horton, Worcestershire v SA at Worcester	1955
9	57	N Edwards, Tvl v Ntl (SACB) at Tongaat	1984/85
9	57	DE Malcolm, Eng v SA (3rd Test) at The Oval	1994
9	64	RJ Crisp, WP v Ntl (CC) at Durban	1933/34
9	64	DL Hobson, WP v EP (CC) at Cape Town	1978/79
9	71	MJ Procter, Rho v Tvl (CC) at Bulawayo	1972/73
9	72	GJ Parsons, Bol v Tvl B (CB) at Johannesburg	1984/85

EIGHT WICKETS (outstanding instances)

8	7	GA Lohmann, Eng v SA (1st Test) at Port Elizabeth	1895/96
8	8	MG Melle, Tvl v GW (CC) at Johannesburg	1950/51
8	11	J Briggs, Eng v SA (2nd Test) at Cape Town	1888/89
8	12	RW Norden, Tvl v Rho (CC) at Johannesburg	1904/05
8	13	DPB Morkel, SA v W Australia at Perth	1931/32
8	18	JJ Kotze, Tvl v GW (CC) at Port Elizabeth	1902/03
8	20	JL Cox, Ntl v Tvl (CC) at Durban	1910/11
8	22	GM Gilder, SA A v Worcestershire at Worcester	1996
8	24	AEE Vogler, EP v OFS (CC) at Johannesburg	1906/07
8	25	GA Rowe, WP v SWD (CC) at Mossel Bay	1904/05
8	28	FTM Drummer, WP v Bdr (CC) at East London	1966/67
8	29	SF Barnes, Eng v SA (3rd Test) at The Oval	1912
8	29	VA Barnes, WP v Ntl (SACB) at Durban	1982/83
8	29	VA Barnes, Tvl v WP (SACB) at Johannesburg	1985/86
8	31	WP Howell, Aus v WP at Cape Town	1902/03
		(Howell took 9-23 in the second innings)	
8	31	RJ Crisp, WP v GW (CC) at Johannesburg	1931/32
		(The other two batsmen were absent)	
8	32	L Tuckett, OFS v GW (CC) at Kimberley	1951/52
8	34	S Haigh, Lord Hawke's XI v Cape Colony at Cape Town	1898/99
8	34	AJ Bell, WP v EP (CC) at Cape Town	1929/30

8	34	L Klusener, Ntl v WP (CC) at Durban	1995/96
8	35	GK Glover, GW v EP (CC) at Cape Town	1893/94
8	35	JT Botten, Fezelas v Gloucestershire at Bristol	1961
8	35	VAP van der Bijl, Ntl v WP (CC) at Pietermaritzburg	1971/72
8	35	M Rampersad, Ntl v Tvl (SACB) at Johannesburg	1984/85
SEVEN WICKETS (outstanding instances)			
7	4	WA Henderson, NE Tvl v OFS (CC) at Bloemfontein	1937/38
7	9	JT Partridge, Rho v Bdr (CC) at Bulawayo	1959/60
7	10	AC King, Ntl v GW (CC) at Johannesburg	1906/07
7	11	SF Burke, OFS v EP (CC) at Port Elizabeth	1958/59
7	11	GM Griffin, Ntl v Bdr (CC) at East London	1959/60
SIX WICKETS (outstanding instances)			
6	1	VI Smith, SA v Derbyshire at Derby	1947
6	3	TL Goddard, Ntl v Bdr (CC) at East London	1959/60
6	7	AER Gilligan, Eng v SA (1st Test) at Birmingham	1924
6	8	JP McNally, GW v EP (CC) at Kimberley	1934/35
FIVE WICKETS (outstanding instances)			
5	2	S Elworthy, Nor v GW (SS) at Centurion	1997/98
5	5	AJ Kourie, Tvl v EP (CC) at Johannesburg	1986/87
5	6	JJ Kotze, WP v GW (CC) at Johannesburg	1906/07
5	6	H Ironmonger, Aus v SA (5th Test) at Melbourne	1931/32
5	6	CW Henderson, WP v Nor (SS) at Centurion	2000/01
5	7	AS Kennedy, MCC v Bdr at East London	1922/23

BEST BOWLING IN A MATCH

17 WICKETS			
17	54	WP Howell, Aus v WP at Cape Town	1902/03
17	159	SF Barnes, Eng v SA (2nd Test) at Johannesburg	1913/14
16 WICKETS			
16	38	AEE Vogler, EP v GW (CC) at Johannesburg	1906/07
16	136	EP Nupen, Tvl v GW (CC) at Johannesburg	1931/32
15 WICKETS			
15	28	J Briggs, Eng v SA (2nd Test) at Cape Town	1888/89
15	45	GA Lohmann, Eng v SA (1st Test) at Port Elizabeth	1895/96
15	49	JT Botten, NE Tvl v GW (CC) at Pretoria	1958/59
15	68	GK Glover, GW v EP (CC) at Cape Town	1893/94
15	68	AMB Rowan, Tvl v Aus at Johannesburg	1949/50
15	99	C Blythe, Eng v SA (2nd Test) at Leeds	1907
14 WICKETS			
14	58	AEE Vogler, EP v OFS (CC) at Johannesburg	1906/07
14	59	AF Hagemann, Bdr v GW (CC) at Kimberley	1960/61
14	79	DW McCosh, N Tvl B v EP B (CB) at Port Elizabeth	1988/89
14	86	JM Gregory, AIF v Ntl at Durban	1919/20
14	96	JH Wardle, MCC v OFS at Bloemfontein	1956/57
14	101	JT Partridge, Rho v Ntl at Salisbury	1961/62
14	111	VAP van der Bijl, Ntl v N Tvl (CC) at Pretoria	1981/82
14	113	DL Hobson, WP v Ntl (CC) at Cape Town	1975/76
14	115	AE Hall, Tvl v Ntl (CC) at Johannesburg	1926/27
14	119	J Mercer, Glamorgan v SA at Pontypridd	1929
14	126	HJ Tayfield, SA v Hampshire at Southampton	1955
14	144	SF Barnes, Eng v SA (4th Test) at Durban	1913/14
14	153	VI Smith, Ntl v EP (CC) at Durban	1955/56
14	154	DLC McCay, WP v Ntl B (CC) at Cape Town	1966/67
14	199	CV Grimmett, Aus v SA (4th Test) at Adelaide	1931/32
13 WICKETS (outstanding instances)			
13	53	VAP van der Bijl, Ntl v WP (CC) at Pietermaritzburg	1971/72
13	57	SF Barnes, Eng v SA (3rd Test) at The Oval	1912
13	59	JE Waddington, GW v Bdr (CC) at Kimberley	1947/48

13	61	AJ Bell, WP v EP (CC) at Cape Town (All 13 were bowled)	1929/30
13	65	NAT Adcock, Tvl v OFS at Johannesburg	1953/54
13	66	VI Smith, SA v Derbyshire at Derby	1947
13	66	L Tuckett, OFS v GW (CC) at Kimberley	1951/52
13	73	JH Sinclair, SA v Gloucestershire at Clifton	1901
13	79	AT Lyons, EP v GW (CC) at Port Elizabeth	1902/03
13	79	SF Barnes, MCC v OFS at Bloemfontein	1913/14
12 WICKETS (outstanding instances)			
12	33	RW Norden, Tvl v Rho (CC) at Johannesburg	1904/05
12	53	RW Hanley, Tvl v EP (CC) at Johannesburg	1983/84
12	56	MG Melle, SA v Tasmania at Launceston	1952/53
12	58	GV Wienand, Bdr v EP (CC) at East London	1946/47
12	59	SF Burke, NE Tvl v Tvl B (CC) at Johannesburg	1963/64
12	64	JC Kerby, Tvl B v GW (CC) at Kimberley	1960/61
12	64	MJ Macaulay, OFS v GW (CC) at Bloemfontein	1963/64
12	66	AP Igglesden, Bol v GW (UB) at Kimberley	1992/93
12	71	GA Lohmann, Eng v SA (2nd Test) at Johannesburg	1895/96
12	78	RK Tyldesley, Lancashire v SA at Manchester	1924
12	82	VA Barnes, WP v Ntl (SACB) at Ladysmith	1983/84
12	83	HJ Tayfield, SA XI v MCC at Pretoria	1956/57
12	83	S Gabriels, WP v Ntl (SACB) at Cape Town	1983/84
12	84	MJG Davis, N Tvl B v W Tvl (UB) at Potchefstroom	1994/95
12	85	LE de Villiers, OFS v Bdr (CC) at Johannesburg	1931/32
12	85	VAP van der Bijl, Ntl v WP (CC) at Cape Town	1973/74
12	88	EW Kidwell, Tvl B v Bol B (UB) at Randjesfontein	1995/96
12	89	JH Wardle, Eng v SA (2nd Test) at Cape Town	1956/57
11 WICKETS (outstanding instances)			
11	24	H Ironmonger, Aus v SA (5th Test) at Melbourne	1931/32
11	33	VAP van der Bijl, Ntl v SAU at Durban	1975/76
11	37	JJ Kotze, Tvl v GW (CC) at Port Elizabeth	1902/03
11	45	S de la C Snooke, WP v Bdr (CC) at Durban	1910/11
11	45	AA Jones, N Tvl v OFS (CC) at Pretoria	1972/73
11	45	A Jabaar, WP v Ntl (SACB) at Cape Town	1977/78
11	50	GA Rowe, WP v SWD (CC) at Mossel Bay	1904/05
11	51	HWH Bergins, WP v Tvl (SACB) at Johannesburg	1975/76
11	52	VA Barnes, WP v Ntl (SACB) at Durban	1982/83
11	55	AE Hall, Tvl v EP (CC) at Port Elizabeth	1925/26
11	56	EA Budgen, WP v GW (CC) at Durban	1910/11
11	57	XC Balaskas, WP v EP (CC) at Cape Town	1934/35
11	58	GM Griffin, Ntl v WP (CC) at Durban	1959/60
11	58	A Jabaar, WP v EP (SACB) at Cape Town	1983/84
11	59	GA Faulkner, SA v Leicestershire at Leicester	1912
11	59	SF Burke, NE Tvl v GW (CC) at Benoni	1963/64
10 WICKETS (outstanding instances)			
10	15	AL Adams, WP v EP (SACB) at Cape Town	1979/80
10	30	MG Melle, Tvl v GW (CC) at Johannesburg	1950/51
10	31	PS Hubbard, Bdr v EP (CC) at East London	1936/37
10	33	VA Barnes, WP v Ntl (SACB) at Cape Town	1988/89
10	34	D Govindjee, EP v Tvl (SACB) at Port Elizabeth	1981/82
10	35	S Draai, EP v Tvl (SACB) at Johannesburg	1979/80
10	39	GH Shepstone, Tvl v Bdr (CC) at Port Elizabeth	1902/03
10	40	RO Schwarz, SA v Northamptonshire at Northampton	1907
10	41	S Draai, EP v Ntl (SACB) at Tongaat	1983/84
10	43	AW Greig, EP v WP (CC) at Port Elizabeth	1971/72
10	44	SF Barnes, MCC v GW at Kimberley	1913/14
10	44	FJ Wickham, Tvl v EP (CC) at Port Elizabeth	1937/38
10	44	LJ Coldwell, Worcestershire v Rho at Bulawayo	1964/65
10	46	HB Fawcus, OFS v EP (CC) at Durban	1910/11
10	46	GG Arnold, OFS v GW (CC) at Bloemfontein	1976/77
10	48	GA Rowe, WP v GW (CC) at Johannesburg	1896/97

10	48	JM Cole, Ntl v NE Tvl (CC) at Pretoria	1960/61
10	48	PM Pollock, EP v WP (CC) at Port Elizabeth	1962/63
10	49	PJ Marneweck, N Tvl B v Bdr (CB) at East London	1981/82

MOST WICKETS IN A DAY

16	38	AEE Vogler, EP v GW (CC) at Johannesburg	1906/07
15	28	J Briggs, Eng v SA (2nd Test) at Cape Town	1888/89
14	96	JH Wardle, MCC v OFS at Bloemfontein	1956/57
14	113	DL Hobson, WP v Ntl (CC) at Cape Town	1975/76

FOUR WICKETS WITH CONSECUTIVE BALLS

S Haigh	MCC v The Army at Roberts Heights	1905/06
AF Borland	Ntl v GW (CC) at Kimberley	1926/27
RJ Crisp	WP v GW (CC) at Johannesburg	1931/32
RJ Crisp	WP v Ntl (CC) at Durban	1933/34
WA Henderson	NE Tvl v OFS (CC) at Bloemfontein (He went on to take five wickets in six balls)	1937/38

A HAT-TRICK IN BOTH INNINGS OF A MATCH

TJ Matthews Aus v SA (1st Test) at Manchester 1912

HAT-TRICKS

(Recent instances)

TG Shaw, EP v Bol at Robertson 1990/91
CJ van Heerden, OFS v Ntl (CC) at Bloemfontein 1990/91
RP Snell, Tvl v WP (CC) at Johannesburg 1992/93
CZ Harris, NZ v OFS at Bloemfontein 1994/95
RE Veenstra, Ntl v Tvl (CC) at Johannesburg 1994/95
(He took the last wicket in the first innings and took wickets with his first two balls in the second innings)
F Davids, WP B v ZB XI (UB) at Cape Town 1994/95
(He took the last wicket in the first innings and took wickets with his first two balls opening the bowling in the second innings)
CW Henderson, Bol v Warwickshire at Paarl 1994/95
MW Pringle, SA Inv XI v Eng XI at Soweto 1995/96
D Taljard, Bdr v Pak at East London 1997/98
M Ntini, Bdr v FS (SS) at Bloemfontein 1999/00
GJ-P Kruger, EP v SL at Port Elizabeth 2000/01
GJ Kruis, GW v KZN (SS) at Durban 2000/01

Note: RJ Crisp performed this feat three times. Those who have done it twice are AF Borland, GA Faulkner, TL Goddard, TWJ Goddard, S Haigh, JJ Kotze, TJ Matthews (in the same match), VI Smith, HJ Tayfield and CJ van Heerden.

MOST WICKETS IN A SEASON

By home players (55 or more):

	M	Runs	Wkts	Avg	Season
VAP van der Bijl (Natal)	11	1119	75	14.92	1981/82
VAP van der Bijl (Natal)	13	1084	65	16.67	1975/76
JT Partridge (Rhodesia)	11	1064	64	16.62	1962/63
VAP van der Bijl (Natal)	12	1037	64	16.20	1973/74
JT Botten (NE Tvl)	7	664	63	10.53	1958/59
AJ Kourie (Tvl)	13	1501	63	23.82	1982/83
MJ Procter (Rhodesia)	11	1049	60	17.48	1972/73
JN Maguire (EP)	10	903	60	15.05	1989/90
VC Drakes (Bdr)	10	979	60	16.31	1999/00
MJ Procter (Natal)	8	936	59	15.86	1976/77
ST Jefferies (WP)	12	1386	58	23.89	1982/83
ST Clarke (Tvl)	10	738	58	12.72	1984/85
HJ Tayfield (Natal/Tvl)	9	1036	56	18.50	1956/57
VC Drakes (Bdr)	9	820	56	14.64	1998/99
AEE Vogler (EP/Tvl)	9	580	55	10.54	1906/07

By overseas players (100 or more):

R Benaud (Australia)	18	2056	106	19.39	1957/58
SF Barnes (England)	12	1117	104	10.74	1913/14

SOUTH AFRICAN TEAMS ABROAD

In Australia and New Zealand:					
HJ Tayfield	17	2196	84	26.14	1952/53
In England:					
SJ Pegler	34	2885	189	15.26	1912

OUTSTANDING BOWLING ON DEBUT

12 wickets in a match:

13-146	(4-24/9-122)	GG Hall, SAU v WP at Cape Town	1960/61
13-204	(7-82/6-122)	JHD Piton, Tvl v Kimberley (CC) at Johannesburg	1890/91
		(His second match. He did not bowl in his first match)	
12-120	(9-52/3-68)	MH Bowditch, WP v Ntl (CC) at Cape Town	1965/66
		(His second match. He did not bowl in his first match)	

Eight or more wickets in an innings:

9-52	MH Bowditch, WP v Ntl (CC) at Cape Town	1965/66
9-122	GG Hall, SAU v WP at Cape Town	1960/61
8-64	WB Gadsden, Ntl v Tvl at Durban	1928/29
8-89	LW Payn, Ntl v OFS (CC) at Bloemfontein	1936/37

BOWLERS WHO HAVE TAKEN 300 WICKETS IN A CAREER

	Career	M	Runs	Wkts	Avg	Best	5WI	10WM
MJ Procter	1965-88	401	27679	1417	19.53	9-71	70	15
+AA Donald	1985-	299	26177	1169	22.39	8-37	65	9
CB Llewellyn	1894-1912	267	23715	1013	23.41	9-55	82	20
NV Radford	1978-95	296	26707	994	26.86	9-70	48	7
CEB Rice	1969-93	482	20922	930	22.49	7-62	23	1
PB Clift	1971-87	319	21610	876	24.66	8-17	26	2
HJ Tayfield	1945-62	187	18890	864	21.86	9-113	67	16
AW Greig	1965-78	350	24702	856	28.85	8-25	33	8
RC Ontong	1972-94	367	26487	845	31.34	8-67	33	4
GS le Roux	1975-88	239	17800	838	21.24	8-107	35	3
PM Walker	1956-72	469	23881	834	28.63	7-58	25	2
VAP van der Bijl	1967-82	156	12692	767	16.54	8-35	46	12
AM Ferreira	1974-91	245	17708	583	30.37	8-38	18	2
EJ Barlow	1959-82	283	13785	571	24.14	7-24	16	2
TL Goddard	1952-69	179	11563	534	21.65	6-3	24	1
SH Martin	1925-49	267	15063	532	28.31	8-24	21	6
JH Sinclair	1892-1911	129	10527	491	21.43	8-32	33	10
PM Pollock	1958-71	127	10620	485	21.89	7-19	27	2
ST Jefferies	1978-93	142	13204	478	27.62	10-59	19	4
AH McKinnon	1952-68	111	9937	470	21.14	7-37	38	9
GA Faulkner	1902-24	118	7826	449	17.42	7-26	33	8
WK Watson	1974-91	143	11034	446	24.73	7-50	16	-
O Henry	1977-93	123	10841	434	24.97	7-22	22	3
+MW Pringle	1985-	119	10876	429	25.35	7-60	15	3
PS de Villiers	1985-97	102	9553	427	22.37	7-80	23	3
SJ Pegler	1908-30	103	8324	425	19.58	8-54	32	5
AJ Kourie	1970-88	127	9869	421	23.44	8-113	24	3
+SM Pollock	1991-	112	9054	420	21.55	7-33	18	1
IA Greig	1974-91	253	13023	419	31.08	7-43	10	2
+CE Eksteen	1985-	124	11992	418	28.68	7-29	17	1
TG Shaw	1980-96	138	12118	417	29.05	7-79	15	2
RW Hanley	1970-86	113	8491	408	20.81	7-31	23	3
NAT Adcock	1952-62	99	6989	405	17.25	8-39	19	4
+S Elworthy	1987-	118	11395	401	28.41	7-65	14	3
JT Botten	1957-71	98	8125	399	20.36	9-23	24	5

RO Schwarz	1901-14	125	7000	398	17.58	8-55	25	3
AEE Vogler	1903-12	83	7182	393	18.27	10-26	31	7
SJ Base	1981-99	134	11397	388	29.37	7-60	16	1
JT Partridge	1951-66	77	7812	376	20.77	8-69	24	3
JE Waddington	1934-58	83	9185	375	24.49	9-105	35	8
DL Hobson	1970-84	105	10296	374	27.52	9-64	22	6
PD Swart	1965-84	167	9365	370	25.31	6-85	5	1
CP Carter	1897-1924	107	6796	366	18.56	7-37	23	2
VI Smith	1945-57	97	8233	365	22.55	9-88	26	8
CJPG van Zyl	1981-93	104	8160	349	23.38	8-84	12	2
JJ Kotze	1901-10	72	6217	348	17.86	8-18	30	9
GB Lawrence	1952-66	77	6146	342	17.97	8-42	15	1
EP Nupen	1920-36	74	6077	334	18.19	9-48	33	12
EO Simons	1982-98	123	8511	330	25.79	6-26	9	1
HGO Owen-Smith	1927-49	101	7410	319	23.22	7-153	20	3
PHJ Trimborn	1961-75	94	7102	314	22.61	6-36	12	1
+CW Henderson	1990-	86	8877	312	28.45	7-57	10	-
BM McMillan	1984-99	155	9074	310	29.27	5-35	4	-
AW Nourse	1896-1935	228	7125	305	23.36	6-33	13	1

ALL-ROUND PLAY

100 RUNS AND 10 WICKETS IN A MATCH

AE Trott	101*	7-74 /4-66	Lord Hawke's XI v Tvl at Johannesburg	1898/99
GA Faulkner	42 -68*	6-72 /4-94	Tvl v WP (CC) at Cape Town	1908/09
GA Faulkner	54 -73	5-32 /5-106	SA v Queensland at Brisbane	1910/11
XC Balaskas	132	5-87 /6-43	GW v EP (CC) at Kimberley	1929/30
XC Balaskas	101	6-142/6-93	GW v WP (CC) at Kimberley	1929/30
	(In successive matches)			
LS Brown	63 -37	6-89 /4-54	NE Tvl v Tvl (CC) at Springs	1937/38
JR Liddle	31 -77	7-97 /5-115	OFS v Rho (CC) at Bulawayo	1951/52
PNF Mansell	94*-13*	7-71 /3-79	Rho v NE Tvl (CC) at Pretoria	1951/52
ARA Murray	78 -44*	5-77 /5-54	EP v Bdr at East London	1953/54
JPD Flanagan	98 -17	8-113/2-86	Tvl B v Ntl B (CC) at Johannesburg	1968/69
CEB Rice	90 -11	7-62 /4-50	Tvl v WP (CC) at Johannesburg	1975/76
AL Barnes	107	6-50 /4-47	Tvl v EP (SACB) at Johannesburg	1975/76
I Foulkes	130	3-62 /7-54	Bdr v EP B (CB) at East London	1977/78
PD de Vaal	100*	3-32 /7-94	E Tvl v W Tvl (UB) at Potchefstroom	1991/92
MJG Davis	60 -46	8-37 /4-47	N Tvl B v W Tvl (UB) at Potchefstroom	1994/95
N Boje	104* -9*	5-84 /6-34	FS v Nor (SS) at Bloemfontein	1997/98

Note: MJ Procter scored 108 and took 7-35/6-38 for Gloucestershire v Worcestershire at Cheltenham, 1977 and scored 73 and 35 and took 7-16/7-60 for Gloucestershire v Worcestershire at Cheltenham, 1980.
RC Ontong scored 130 and took 5-39/8-67 for Glamorgan v Nottinghamshire at Nottingham, 1985.

500 RUNS AND 50 WICKETS IN A SEASON

South African players:	Runs	Avg	Wkts	Avg	Season
AEE Vogler	505	36.07	55	10.54	1906/07
PNF Mansell	571	43.92	52	17.63	1951/52
MJ Procter	695	40.88	52	16.01	1971/72
MJ Procter	870	48.33	60	17.48	1972/73
Overseas players:					
JR Reid	1012	37.48	51	19.54	1953/54
R Benaud	817	51.06	106	19.39	1957/58
AK Davidson	813	54.20	72	15.13	1957/58

SOUTH AFRICAN FIRST-CLASS RECORDS

4000 RUNS AND 200 WICKETS IN A CAREER

The following list, which is alphabetical, covers those who have made 4000 runs and taken 200 wickets in South African domestic cricket or for South African teams overseas. Some of the players have also played in overseas domestic cricket and these are marked *. Those who are current cricketers are marked + .

	Runs	Wickets		Runs	Wickets
EJ Barlow *	14406	444	BM McMillan *	6899	293
+N Boje	4203	275	B Mitchell	11395	249
+PJ Botha	4903	215	AW Nourse	14216	305
PD de Vaal	4208	240	RC Ontong *	4281	311
GA Faulkner *	5525	402	MJ Procter *	7203	569
AM Ferreira *	4976	248	CEB Rice *	9009	451
TL Goddard *	11154	522	EO Simons	4264	330
O Henry *	4342	418	JH Sinclair *	4262	467
AJ Kourie	4470	421	PD Swart *	4068	299
PNF Mansell	4598	299	PL Symcox	4206	264

WICKETKEEPING

MOST DISMISSALS IN AN INNINGS

7 (ct 7,st 0)	MS Smith, Ntl v Bdr (CC) at East London	1959/60
7 (ct 6,st 1)	N Kirsten, Bdr v Rho (CC) at East London	1959/60
7 (ct 6,st 1)	RJ East, OFS v WP B (CB) at Cape Town	1984/85
7 (ct 4,st 3)	F Abrahams, EP v Ntl (SACB) at Durban	1986/87
7 (ct 6,st 1)	A Coetzee, EP v Tvl (SACB) at Port Elizabeth	1987/88
7 (ct 7,st 0)	DJ Richardson, EP v OFS (CC) at Bloemfontein	1988/89
7 (ct 5,st 2)	N White, WP v Ntl (SACB) at Cape Town	1989/90
7 (ct 7,st 0)	PJL Radley, OFS v WP (CC) at Cape Town	1990/91
7 (ct 7,st 0)	P Kirsten, GW v W Tvl (UB) at Potchefstroom	1993/94
7 (ct 7,st 0)	HM de Vos, W Tvl v E Tvl (UB) at Potchefstroom	1993/94

MOST DISMISSALS IN A MATCH

11 (ct 10,st 1)	IA Healy, Aus v N Tvl at Verwoerdburg	1993/94
11 (ct 11,st 0)	RC Russell, Eng v SA (2nd Test) at Johannesburg (The world Test record)	1995/96
10 (ct 10,st 0)	RV Jennings, Tvl v Arosa Sri Lanka at Johannesburg	1982/83
10 (ct 10,st 0)	DA Murray, WI XI v SA at Port Elizabeth	1983/84
10 (ct 8,st 2)	RJ Ryall, WP v Tvl (CC) at Cape Town	1984/85
10 (ct 10,st 0)	SJ Rixon, Aus XI v SA at Johannesburg	1985/86
10 (ct 10,st 0)	RV Jennings, Tvl v N Tvl (CC) at Verwoerdburg	1986/87
10 (ct 10,st 0)	SJ Rixon, Aus XI v SA at Johannesburg	1986/87
10 (ct 10,st 0)	RV Jennings, Tvl v OFS (CC) at Johannesburg	1986/87
10 (ct 10,st 0)	DJ Richardson, EP v OFS (CC) at Bloemfontein	1988/89
10 (ct 9,st 1)	DJ Richardson, EP v N Tvl (CC) at Verwoerdburg	1989/90
10 (ct 10,st 0)	HM de Vos, W Tvl v E Tvl (UB) at Potchefstroom	1993/94
10 (ct 10,st 0)	MO Johnston, Tvl B v Bol B (UB) at Randjesfontein	1995/96
10 (ct 10,st 0)	J Burger, GW v N Tvl B (UB) at Kimberley	1995/96
10 (ct10,st 0)	MN van Wyk, FS v Bdr (SS) at Bloemfontein	2000/01

MOST DISMISSALS IN A SEASON

65 (ct 57,st 8)	RV Jennings	1982/83
55 (ct 49,st 6)	RV Jennings	1984/85
47 (ct 45,st 2)	RJ Ryall	1990/91
46 (ct 45,st 1)	DT Lindsay 1966/67	
46 (ct 45,st 1)	NT Day	1984/85
45 (ct 43,st 2)	AJS Smith	1975/76
45 (ct 42,st 3)	MV Boucher	1997/98

SOUTH AFRICAN FIRST-CLASS RECORDS

WICKETKEEPERS WHO HAVE DISMISSED 200 BATSMEN IN A CAREER

+ Denotes current player. Some of the catches may have been taken while the player was not keeping wicket.

	Career	Caught	Stumped	Total
RV Jennings	1973-92	567	54	621
DJ Richardson	1977-97	579	40	619
JHB Waite	1948-65	427	84	511
RJ Ryall	1980-94	384	38	422
NT Day	1975-91	312	29	341
DT Lindsay	1958-73	284	38	322
AJS Smith	1971-83	308	11	319
GP Pfuhl	1967-79	280	34	314
D Gamsy	1958-72	278	33	311
B McBride	1980-94	280	30	310
RJ East	1973-89	288	8	296
+MV Boucher	1995-	283	13	296
+SJ Palframan	1990-	263	24	287
+N Pothas	1993-	237	22	259
HB Cameron	1924-35	155	69	224
BL Irvine	1962-76	200	7	207
PJL Radley	1989-98	190	17	207

LARGEST INNINGS WITHOUT BYES

589	DP Marais, Ntl v Aus at Pietermaritzburg	1957/58

FIELDING

MOST CATCHES IN A MATCH

7	SP de Vigne	NE Tvl v OFS (CC) at Benoni	1950/51
7	A Barrow	Tvl B v N Tvl B (CB) at Pietersburg	1982/83
7	CB Lambert	N Tvl v Bol (CC) at Paarl	1994/95

MOST CATCHES IN AN INNINGS

6	J Seymour	Kent v SA at Canterbury	1904

MOST CATCHES IN A SEASON

24	NC Johnson	2000/01
21	MJ Procter 1972/73, AJ Kourie 1984/85, LJ Koen 1999/00, GFJ Liebenberg 1999/00	

FIELDERS WHO HAVE HELD 150 CATCHES IN A CAREER

237	EJ Barlow (1959-82)	171	AW Nourse (1896-1935)
237	RG Pollock (1960-86)	156	KC Wessels (1973-99)
228	B Mitchell (1925-49)	156	PNF Mansell (1936-61)
201	DJ Cullinan (1983-)	155	BM McMillan (1984-99)
172	TL Goddard (1952-69)		

FIRST-CLASS CAREER RECORDS

As at 1 April 2001

Name	M	Inns	NO	Runs	HS	Avg	100	50	Ct	St	Balls	Runs	Wkts	Avg	BB	5I	10M
S Abrahams	55	75	14	1408	85	23.08	0	7	43	0	10658	4145	143	28.98	6-39	7	2
U Abrahams	6	11	0	204	51	18.54	0	1	0	0	6	0	0	-	-	0	0
ZA Abrahim	24	38	10	488	67	17.42	0	2	10	0	3955	1981	69	28.71	6-53	2	0
HD Ackerman	92	150	13	5663	202*	41.33	16	29	72	0	90	46	0	-	-	0	0
SM Adam	9	8	1	56	23	8.00	0	0	5	0	1458	610	28	21.78	5-57	1	0
PR Adams	75	79	34	638	61*	14.17	0	1	41	0	16371	7676	248	30.95	7-69	10	0
AM Amla	22	37	4	937	107	28.39	2	6	10	0	246	172	3	57.33	2-53	0	0
JM Arthur	110	207	8	6657	165	33.45	13	34	74	0	6	0	0	-	-	0	0
AM Bacher	79	142	9	4909	210	36.90	10	24	79	0	243	127	1	127.00	1-25	0	0
R Bailey	1	2	1	25	25*	25.00	0	0	0	0	0	0	0	-	-	0	0
HC Bakkes	68	98	20	1807	101	23.16	1	7	28	0	10915	4792	178	26.92	6-28	8	0
EAE Baptiste	245	341	50	8070	136*	27.73	3	47	120	0	41533	17823	723	24.65	8-76	32	4
PH Barnard	70	132	10	4226	250	34.63	9	22	33	0	6	2	0	-	-	0	0
JE Bastow	17	17	6	128	35*	11.63	0	0	5	0	2676	1281	49	26.14	6-37	1	0
KS Bender	3	5	0	101	34	20.20	0	0	2	0	273	108	4	27.00	2-7	0	0
MR Benfield	37	72	4	1792	122	26.35	1	12	25	0	36	22	0	-	-	0	0
KCG Benjamin	108	136	33	1199	52*	11.64	0	1	24	0	19409	9556	403	23.71	7-51	18	2
DM Benkenstein	83	118	13	4258	203*	40.55	8	27	55	0	2140	960	25	38.40	2-24	0	0
JA Beukes	15	28	1	511	97	18.92	0	3	11	0	18	7	0	-	-	0	0
GH Bodi	17	21	5	447	104	27.93	1	2	5	0	2212	1321	41	32.21	6-63	2	0
N Boje	103	151	29	4203	116	34.45	5	25	59	0	21668	8863	275	32.22	6-34	11	1
LL Bosman	33	57	4	1377	115*	25.98	1	8	21	0	486	295	8	36.87	3-25	0	0
W Bossenger	47	80	11	1837	124*	26.62	2	9	152	9	0	0	0	-	-	0	0
AG Botha	37	61	10	1092	94	21.41	0	5	31	0	6756	3014	99	30.44	8-53	2	1
J Botha	2	4	0	88	43	22.00	0	0	0	0	96	45	2	22.50	1-4	0	0
PJ Botha	115	203	13	4903	136	25.80	5	24	59	0	13521	5845	215	27.18	6-32	5	0
MV Boucher	81	118	18	3428	125	34.28	5	20	284	13	18	20	0	-	-	0	0
CC Bradfield	49	91	9	2704	163	32.97	5	10	41	0	43	13	0	-	-	0	0
D Brand	10	19	1	398	61	22.11	0	1	18	3	420	157	5	31.40	2-42	0	0
FC Brooker	55	96	8	2374	111	26.97	1	13	35	0	54	74	0	-	-	0	0

FIRST-CLASS CAREER RECORDS

Name	M	Inns	NO	Runs	HS	Avg	100	50	Ct	St	Balls	Runs	Wkts	Avg	BB	5I	10M
J Brooker	8	14	0	284	77	20.28	0	2	4	0	78	63	0	-	-	0	0
GL Brophy	23	38	3	1030	185	29.42	1	5	73	5	0	0	0	-	-	0	0
NG Brouwers	11	17	2	297	59	19.80	0	2	11	0	1516	583	20	29.15	6-57	1	0
DL Brown	4	6	0	50	20	8.33	0	0	3	2	0	0	0	-	-	0	0
ML Bruyns	83	128	6	4294	144	35.19	11	22	123	4	606	247	5	49.40	2-3	0	0
JDC Bryant	37	67	10	2160	149	37.89	5	11	33	0	32	29	1	29.00	1-22	0	0
RE Bryson	90	118	23	1632	100	17.17	1	5	20	0	14910	7841	293	26.76	7-68	16	3
DJ Callaghan	135	222	26	7145	171	36.45	17	34	105	0	8183	3434	120	28.61	5-24	3	1
NM Carter	9	15	2	134	37	10.30	0	0	2	0	1822	950	35	27.14	6-63	2	0
SC Cook	2	4	1	132	55	44.00	0	1	0	0	0	0	0	-	-	0	0
CA Copeland	8	10	1	29	10	3.22	0	0	4	0	1670	967	39	24.79	8-101	4	1
MW Creed	22	36	7	728	72	25.10	0	3	9	0	1634	889	18	49.38	4-30	0	0
DN Crookes	92	142	13	4920	155*	38.13	10	29	97	0	13945	6437	189	34.05	7-114	8	0
DJ Cullinan	216	370	53	13988	337*	44.12	38	65	209	0	548	300	6	50.00	2-27	0	0
AW Cyster	1	2	0	24	21	12.00	0	0	0	0	0	0	0	-	-	0	0
H Davids	6	12	1	336	124	30.54	1	1	4	0	0	0	0	-	-	0	0
AC Dawson	66	93	22	1607	143	22.63	1	9	38	0	11654	4864	191	25.46	6-18	9	0
P de Bruyn	32	54	5	1354	202	27.63	2	6	27	0	3509	1778	65	27.35	6-38	3	0
Z de Bruyn	31	57	8	1451	126*	29.61	1	9	13	0	1876	1163	26	44.73	6-120	1	0
MS de Kock	2	4	1	20	17*	6.66	0	0	10	1	0	0	0	-	-	0	0
CdeW de Lange	7	11	0	87	25	7.90	0	0	5	0	1350	645	7	92.14	2-44	0	0
DJJ de Vos	43	70	11	1455	105*	24.66	1	8	30	0	3856	1867	50	37.34	6-32	3	1
HM de Vos	47	86	7	2073	115	26.24	2	9	42	2	9	8	0	-	-	0	0
BC de Wett	1	2	0	36	30	18.00	0	0	0	0	0	0	0	-	-	0	0
HH Dippenaar	52	90	7	3384	200*	40.77	10	13	39	0	7	12	0	-	-	0	0
L Dladla	1	0	0	0	0	-	0	0	0	0	54	26	0	-	-	0	0
AA Donald	299	347	129	2612	55*	11.98	0	1	110	0	55897	26177	1169	22.39	8-37	65	9
VC Drakes	117	192	21	3817	180*	22.32	4	15	39	0	21811	11311	466	24.27	8-59	22	3
JN Dreyer	22	32	12	236	40	11.80	0	0	5	0	3939	2350	60	39.16	5-81	2	0
G Dros	52	89	12	2148	100*	27.89	1	8	51	0	1361	664	21	31.61	3-21	0	0
WM Dry	48	85	9	2083	99	27.40	0	15	25	0	666	415	8	51.87	2-39	0	0
WJ du Toit	2	4	0	39	32	9.75	0	0	0	0	462	226	8	28.25	7-82	1	0
CE Eksteen	124	163	40	1707	58	13.87	0	2	92	0	31176	11992	418	28.68	7-29	17	1
GD Elliott	15	25	0	743	125	29.72	1	5	16	0	1128	526	11	47.81	2-18	0	0
S Elworthy	118	175	26	3056	89	20.51	0	9	39	0	21448	11395	401	28.41	7-65	14	3

Name	M	Inns	NO	Runs	HS	Avg	100	50	Ct	St	Balls	Runs	Wkts	Avg	BB	5I	10M
CT Enslin	16	19	2	252	51	14.82	0	1	8	0	1752	950	30	31.66	4-46	0	0
EJ Ferreira	18	34	0	601	63	17.67	0	4	12	0	0	0	0	-	-	0	0
LD Ferreira	55	100	2	2466	201	25.16	4	11	30	0	102	68	1	68.00	1-25	0	0
GE Flusk	11	15	2	150	31*	11.53	0	0	4	0	1356	715	26	27.50	5-55	1	0
NA Fusedale	15	17	4	226	44*	17.38	0	0	13	0	3262	1546	41	37.70	5-170	1	0
AI Gait	19	35	0	937	112	26.77	2	5	19	0	0	0	0	-	-	0	0
LL Gamiet	27	46	1	889	80	19.75	0	1	20	0	0	0	0	-	-	0	0
MF George	16	20	9	259	58	23.54	0	1	5	0	2386	1386	39	35.53	6-61	1	0
HH Gibbs	104	178	8	6982	211*	41.07	15	33	74	0	132	74	3	24.66	2-14	0	0
OD Gibson	119	179	23	3571	101*	22.89	1	17	50	0	21654	12074	425	28.40	7-55	17	3
MI Gidley	83	146	14	4816	160	36.48	10	24	43	0	9382	4424	77	57.45	5-48	1	0
GM Gilder	47	46	9	387	39	10.45	0	0	16	0	7975	3811	149	25.57	8-22	6	2
GV Grace	21	39	1	721	112*	18.97	2	0	10	0	186	131	1	131.00	1-30	0	0
L Graham	4	6	2	46	19	11.50	0	0	2	0	684	319	7	45.57	3-69	0	0
AJ Hall	36	52	10	1384	119	32.95	1	12	20	0	5882	2696	103	26.17	5-20	4	0
PL Harris	2	4	2	15	8	7.50	0	0	0	0	560	240	4	60.00	3-56	0	0
GS Hayward	1	2	1	59	56*	59.00	0	1	1	0	150	84	3	28.00	2-36	0	0
M Hayward	53	51	21	505	55*	16.83	0	1	19	0	9704	5128	183	28.02	6-31	6	2
CW Henderson	86	124	38	1312	53*	15.25	0	1	33	0	22261	8877	312	28.45	7-57	10	0
JM Henderson	40	74	5	1891	135	27.40	3	9	20	0	1805	899	22	40.86	3-13	0	0
T Henderson	30	46	8	606	81	15.94	0	1	12	0	4808	2027	84	24.13	6-56	3	0
F Herbst	2	3	2	45	35*	45.00	0	0	1	0	90	46	0	-	-	0	0
GM Hewitt	28	50	3	1198	151	25.48	1	6	25	0	78	81	0	-	-	0	0
BP Horan	11	12	5	114	28	16.28	0	0	3	0	1343	698	20	34.90	4-43	0	0
AC Hudson	151	270	20	9156	206	36.62	20	47	140	0	24	5	0	-	-	0	0
KC Jackson	82	151	8	4041	150	28.25	6	24	68	0	687	404	8	50.50	2-18	0	0
A Jacobs	24	41	7	921	112	27.08	1	4	27	0	246	133	3	44.33	1-2	0	0
D Jennings	11	20	5	274	53	18.26	0	1	52	2	0	0	0	-	-	0	0
NC Johnson	108	166	20	4671	150	31.99	6	32	129	0	10824	5388	174	30.96	5-79	2	0
D Jordaan	80	148	11	4636	123	33.83	8	26	86	0	1519	708	16	44.25	3-9	0	0
LCR Jordaan	48	50	24	221	20*	8.50	0	0	9	0	10336	4162	173	24.05	6-30	11	1
P Joubert	22	33	12	371	72*	17.66	0	1	14	0	3455	1490	50	29.80	5-10	1	0
JH Kallis	126	200	22	8107	186*	45.54	19	49	94	0	13875	6010	215	27.95	6-60	5	0
JM Kemp	37	57	7	1783	188	35.66	3	8	31	0	4567	1993	86	23.17	6-56	2	0
JC Kent	22	35	7	1230	178*	43.92	3	6	19	0	2184	1100	36	30.55	6-77	1	0

FIRST-CLASS CAREER RECORDS

Name	M	Inns	NO	Runs	HS	Avg	100	50	Ct	St	Balls	Runs	Wkts	Avg	BB	5I	10M
EW Kidwell	41	50	23	349	27*	12.92	0	0	11	0	6514	3690	121	30.49	7-58	4	1
G Kirsten	178	316	34	12781	275	45.32	34	60	141	0	1673	810	20	40.50	6-68	1	0
JWF Klopper	1	1	0	0	0	0.00	0	0	0	0	24	23	0	-	-	0	0
L Klusener	96	130	30	3525	174	35.25	5	17	57	0	14992	7177	268	26.77	8-34	9	2
DM Koch	18	29	6	360	54	15.65	0	1	9	0	3244	1438	41	35.07	5-128	1	0
LJ Koen	94	163	14	6014	202*	40.36	10	35	145	0	12	6	0	-	-	0	0
SG Koenig	75	131	5	4642	155	36.84	7	25	45	0	122	67	1	67.00	1-0	0	0
PPJ Koortzen	19	35	2	1037	127	31.42	2	5	6	0	1087	630	13	48.46	3-60	0	0
AK Kruger	1	2	1	63	48	63.00	0	0	0	0	72	62	0	-	-	0	0
GJ-P Kruger	26	33	12	205	58	9.76	0	1	5	0	4141	2058	82	25.09	7-64	1	1
GJ Kruis	49	74	15	800	59	13.55	0	2	20	0	10025	4642	160	29.01	7-58	6	0
DR Laing	62	101	10	2358	128	25.91	3	14	26	0	6106	2770	69	40.14	3-18	0	0
CK Langeveldt	20	28	9	293	56	15.42	0	1	7	0	3005	1454	56	25.96	5-19	1	0
MJ Lavine	33	53	1	1522	113	29.26	2	6	31	0	5728	2861	100	28.61	6-53	4	1
AG Lawson	62	114	9	2714	117*	25.84	4	14	29	0	24	14	0	-	-	0	0
MR Lewis	9	13	5	185	49*	23.12	0	0	9	0	642	363	9	40.33	2-44	0	0
GFJ Liebenberg	135	237	11	7816	229	34.58	17	38	139	4	72	28	1	28.00	1-10	0	0
C Light	42	71	2	2078	121	30.11	5	8	26	0	1663	826	18	45.88	4-42	0	0
J Louw	5	8	0	132	50	16.50	0	1	9	0	730	414	12	34.50	3-25	0	0
GT Love	44	55	18	708	85*	19.13	0	2	13	0	8303	3677	102	36.04	7-116	3	0
EF Mabhena	1	2	0	4	2	2.00	0	0	0	0	0	0	0	-	-	0	0
RB MacQueen	20	24	5	346	42	18.21	0	0	16	0	4228	2114	50	42.28	5-125	1	0
JT Mafa	5	5	0	0	0	0.00	0	0	1	0	695	459	17	27.00	6-62	1	0
DL Makalima	11	21	1	319	78	15.95	0	1	7	0	0	0	0	-	-	0	0
A Mall	15	26	0	768	86	29.53	0	6	8	0	0	0	0	-	-	0	0
HA Manack	33	58	5	1400	173	26.41	3	5	15	0	138	78	2	39.00	1-16	0	0
WB Masimula	15	22	11	75	22	6.81	0	0	5	0	1426	698	26	26.84	4-35	0	0
TK Mataboge	2	1	0	2	2	2.00	0	0	1	0	264	144	1	144.00	1-48	0	0
M Matomela	1	2	0	0	0	0.00	0	0	0	0	114	105	0	-	-	0	0
ND McKenzie	65	112	10	3878	175	38.01	9	22	48	0	216	112	3	37.33	1-6	0	0
AP McLaren	8	14	0	277	67	19.78	0	1	15	1	0	0	0	-	-	0	0
I Mitchell	29	51	6	1153	96	25.62	0	6	93	4	25	10	2	5.00	2-0	0	0
ET Mokoenanyana	7	12	1	137	28	12.45	0	0	8	0	18	25	0	-	-	0	0
TJ Mokoenanyana	1	2	2	0	0*	-	0	0	1	0	42	24	0	-	-	0	0
JA Morkel	10	16	2	274	117	19.57	1	0	3	0	1830	899	30	29.96	6-36	1	0

FIRST-CLASS CAREER RECORDS

Name	M	Inns	NO	Runs	HS	Avg	100	50	Ct	St	Balls	Runs	Wkts	Avg	BB	5I	10M
PV Mpitsang	28	30	8	119	23	5.40	0	0	4	0	4627	2207	73	30.23	5-24	3	0
R Munnik	20	33	0	780	138	23.63	1	3	15	0	2494	1433	46	31.15	4-58	0	0
DW Murray	28	47	7	736	103*	18.40	1	1	80	5	0	0	0	-	-	0	0
JG Myburgh	20	35	5	978	203	32.60	1	4	13	0	123	59	2	29.50	1-4	0	0
SS Ndima	2	3	0	56	38	18.66	0	0	2	0	0	0	0	-	-	0	0
A Nel	24	31	13	164	44	9.11	0	0	11	0	4190	1663	78	21.32	5-43	4	0
M Ngam	18	23	3	97	18*	4.85	0	0	9	0	2840	1300	50	26.00	4-25	0	0
R Niewoudt	5	9	1	287	98	35.87	0	1	6	0	24	12	0	-	-	0	0
M Ntini	61	68	26	325	34*	7.73	0	0	14	0	9142	5036	167	30.15	6-49	3	0
JL Ontong	35	58	3	1506	131*	27.38	1	9	31	0	3086	1545	38	40.65	4-120	0	0
JM Otto	4	6	0	149	88	24.83	0	2	2	0	6	3	0	-	-	0	0
G Outram	1	1	0	14	14	14.00	0	0	0	0	0	0	0	-	-	0	0
A Paleker	6	10	2	228	46	28.50	0	0	5	0	66	41	0	-	-	0	0
SJ Palframan	88	141	12	3049	147	23.63	3	11	263	24	0	0	0	-	-	0	0
AN Petersen	1	2	0	32	30	16.00	0	0	1	0	0	0	0	-	-	0	0
RJ Peterson	24	38	4	595	96*	17.50	0	1	12	0	4838	2372	72	32.94	6-67	4	0
BT Player	93	141	26	2417	133*	21.01	4	6	47	0	14318	6536	212	30.83	6-43	4	0
GA Pollock	33	58	5	1531	115	28.88	3	7	18	0	125	76	3	25.33	3-21	0	0
SM Pollock	112	160	29	4314	150*	32.93	5	20	73	0	23296	9054	420	21.55	7-33	18	1
EG Poole	32	49	7	733	50	17.45	0	1	103	10	0	0	0	-	-	0	0
SC Pope	71	127	12	3330	125	28.95	4	16	57	2	1498	941	31	30.35	7-62	2	0
N Pothas	86	133	25	3889	165	36.00	7	17	237	22	6	5	0	-	-	0	0
D Pretorius	25	29	7	214	43	9.72	0	0	6	0	4699	2301	97	23.72	5-50	2	0
AG Prince	53	83	7	2794	133	36.76	5	16	33	0	6	3	0	-	-	0	0
AAW Pringle	5	8	1	47	27	6.71	0	0	3	0	1023	486	13	37.38	4-49	0	0
MW Pringle	119	152	26	2189	105	17.37	1	7	42	0	23557	10876	429	25.35	7-60	15	3
AG Puttick	7	12	1	441	153*	40.09	1	2	5	0	0	0	0	-	-	0	0
BL Reddy	3	5	1	69	28	17.25	0	0	1	0	498	242	4	60.50	3-39	0	0
JN Rhodes	143	226	26	7668	156*	38.34	15	43	112	0	138	65	1	65.00	1-13	0	0
MJR Rindel	111	204	17	6863	174	36.70	13	37	60	0	3211	1653	44	37.56	4-17	0	0
GA Roe	54	78	27	518	66	10.15	0	1	16	0	10388	4195	147	28.53	7-47	3	0
JA Rudolph	18	34	1	1043	144	31.60	3	4	13	0	1578	838	32	26.18	5-87	2	0
JR Schorn	2	4	0	28	11	7.00	0	0	2	0	0	0	0	-	-	0	0
BN Schultz	60	57	16	309	36*	7.53	0	0	10	0	12062	5687	233	24.40	8-36	12	0
DM Senekal	3	5	2	39	15	13.00	0	0	1	0	516	242	7	34.57	3-42	0	0

Name	M	Inns	NO	Runs	HS	Avg	100	50	Ct	St	Balls	Runs	Wkts	Avg	BB	5I	10M
AJ Seymore	44	85	0	2465	174	29.00	4	14	46	0	0	0	0	-	-	0	0
WJ Smit	17	28	0	574	94	20.50	0	4	10	0	68	42	0	-	-	0	0
GC Smith	14	25	1	1058	187	44.08	3	3	19	0	24	17	0	-	-	0	0
GJ Smith	67	83	30	625	68	11.79	0	2	12	0	11729	5696	201	28.33	6-35	6	0
ELR Stewart	87	144	19	4773	207*	38.18	10	21	189	8	138	64	1	64.00	1-19	0	0
PJR Steyn	129	235	15	6858	188*	31.17	11	30	64	1	54	24	1	24.00	1-22	0	0
QR Still	39	67	10	1699	129*	29.80	2	11	25	0	3939	1920	52	36.92	5-53	2	0
MR Street	5	8	3	153	47	30.60	0	0	23	3	0	0	0	-	-	0	0
JG Strydom	4	8	0	216	73	27.00	0	1	4	0	6	1	0	-	-	0	0
M Strydom	42	75	6	1845	129	26.73	2	8	27	0	4683	2512	69	36.40	6-23	2	0
PC Strydom	89	152	12	4893	127	34.95	7	34	60	0	5310	2285	83	27.53	4-12	0	0
CB Sugden	44	74	4	2023	106	28.90	1	12	44	0	120	59	2	29.50	2-24	0	0
AJ Swanepoel	41	53	23	290	39	9.66	0	0	14	0	6748	3094	80	38.67	5-29	2	1
CR Tatton	17	23	7	82	14*	5.12	0	0	8	0	4299	1925	48	40.10	5-80	2	0
R Telemachus	48	66	14	746	59	14.34	0	2	10	0	7572	3877	153	25.33	6-21	6	0
DJ Terbrugge	34	39	18	202	20	9.61	0	0	11	0	6819	2652	116	22.86	5-32	3	0
AC Thomas	13	23	5	645	106*	35.83	1	2	6	0	2047	895	30	29.83	6-26	1	0
DH Townsend	32	41	14	261	45	9.66	0	0	6	0	5517	2756	116	23.75	6-36	7	1
G Toyana	24	39	3	683	63	18.97	0	2	16	0	54	40	0	-	-	0	0
IJL Trott	9	18	2	385	93	24.06	0	3	5	0	115	65	0	-	-	0	0
TL Tsolekile	16	21	1	487	95	24.35	0	3	50	6	0	0	0	-	-	0	0
BH Tucker	7	12	0	224	47	18.66	0	0	1	0	0	0	0	-	-	0	0
ANW Tweedie	6	11	1	113	29	11.30	0	0	2	0	785	501	15	33.40	4-65	0	0
J Uys	9	18	3	289	57	19.26	0	1	1	0	644	408	10	40.80	5-87	1	0
AM van den Berg	12	20	0	352	94	17.60	0	2	2	0	241	134	2	67.00	2-44	0	0
F van der Merwe	6	10	3	76	24*	10.85	0	0	3	0	1177	660	20	33.00	5-62	2	0
JJ van der Wath	14	24	7	314	57*	18.47	0	1	9	0	2184	1147	40	28.67	5-26	3	0
M van Jaarsveld	61	102	9	3573	238*	38.41	8	16	68	0	398	224	5	44.80	1-1	0	0
CFK van Wyk	9	15	2	256	59	19.69	0	1	35	2	0	0	0	-	-	0	0
JM van Wyk	3	4	0	35	19	8.75	0	0	0	0	354	186	2	93.00	1-34	0	0
MN van Wyk	29	51	6	1150	121	25.55	1	3	42	0	78	36	2	18.00	2-25	0	0
RE Veenstra	69	85	11	1521	135*	20.55	1	2	22	0	11615	5171	194	26.65	6-38	4	0
JF Venter	90	153	14	4256	193	30.61	4	28	53	0	12508	6318	192	32.90	6-78	7	1
MC Venter	73	126	8	2819	129	23.88	6	9	45	0	102	94	1	94.00	1-42	0	0
DJ Watson	71	115	9	3830	220	36.13	5	23	43	0	183	73	4	18.25	2-7	0	0

Name	M	Inns	NO	Runs	HS	Avg	100	50	Ct	St	Balls	Runs	Wkts	Avg	BB	5I	10M
BM White	78	149	7	4000	180*	28.16	7	17	76	0	1922	870	25	34.80	3-23	0	0
W Wiblin	43	78	7	2464	177	34.70	5	12	46	0	60	27	0	-	-	0	0
LJ Wilkinson	110	190	10	5709	226*	31.71	8	28	110	0	888	513	6	85.50	1-13	0	0
HS Williams	69	97	28	582	33	8.43	0	0	20	0	13079	5158	219	23.55	6-27	10	0
JW Williams	1	2	2	0	0*	-	0	0	0	0	0	0	0	-	-	0	0
CM Willoughby	53	73	30	182	17*	4.23	0	0	10	0	10445	4350	173	25.14	5-26	3	0
JGH Wilson	1	0	0	0	0	-	0	0	2	0	132	69	0	-	-	0	0
WR Wingfield	21	36	6	716	89*	23.86	0	3	9	0	1590	801	19	42.15	2-18	0	0
M Zondeki	1	2	1	12	12	12.00	0	0	0	0	156	88	1	88.00	1-42	0	0

WHO'S WHO 2000/01

This section includes all players who appeared in domestic first-class cricket, Limited Overs Internationals, Standard Bank Cup matches, or on tours for South African teams during the 2000/01 season. Some players, who did not appear in 2000/01, but may re-appear in 2001/02 or are contracted to provinces for 2001/02 are also included. All details are as at 17 May 2001.

ABBREVIATIONS

B	Born	Ed	Education
RHB	Right-hand batsman	LHB	Left-hand batsman
RF	Right-arm fast bowler	LF	Left-arm fast bowler
RFM	Right-arm fast-medium bowler	LFM	Left-arm fast-medium bowler
RMF	Right-arm medium-fast bowler	LMF	Left-arm medium-fast bowler
RM	Right-arm medium bowler	LM	Left-arm medium bowler
OB	Off-break bowler	LB	Leg-break bowler
LBG	Leg-break/googly bowler	SLA	Slow left-arm bowler
SLC	Slow left-arm chinaman bowler	WK	Wicket-keeper
FC	First-Class	SS	SuperSport Series
LOI	Limited Overs International	*	not out
HSTest	Highest Test score	BBTest	Best Test bowling
HSLOI	Highest Limited Overs International score	BBLOI	Best Limited Overs International bowling
HSFC	Highest First-class score	BBFC	Best First-class bowling
HSSA	Highest First-class score in SA	BBSA	Best First-class bowling in SA
HSSS	Highest SuperSport Series score	BBSS	Best SuperSport Series bowling
HSLO	Highest Limited Overs score	BBLO	Best Limited Overs bowling
HSDLO	Highest Domestic Limited Overs score	BBDLO	Best Domestic Limited Overs bowling
COY	SA Annual's Cricketer of the Year	Wisden	Wisden Cricketer of the Year

Notes:

Nicknames are only given where they are not a normal contraction of a first name.

Details of highest scores are given where the player has made 10 or more, and best bowling figures where he has taken 2 or more wickets.

Highest scores and best bowling in South Africa are only given where they are inferior to overall best performances.

Highest scores and best bowling in the SuperSport Series are only given where they are inferior to best performances overall and in South Africa. They refer only to matches in the SuperSport Series (and Castle Cup and Currie Cup A Section), and do *not* include performances in the UCB Bowl.

Highest scores and best bowling in Limited Overs include performances in all matches in List A as produced by the Association of Cricket Statisticians and Historians.

Highest scores and best bowling in Domestic Limited Overs include performances in the Gillette Cup, Datsun Shield, Nissan Shield, Total Power Series, Benson & Hedges Series, as well as the Standard Bank League and Cup, and are only given where they are inferior to overall best Limited Overs performances.

ABRAHAMS Shafiek (EP/SA). B 4/3/68 Port Elizabeth. RHB OB. Ed Bethelsdorp HS, UPE. EP SACOS Schools XI 1986-87, SASSSA 1987. FC debut SA Students XI v Ind (EL) 1992/93, EP debut 1993/94. LOIs: 1 (2000/01). HSLOI 16* v NZ (CT) 2000/01. HSFC 85 EP v Bol (Paarl) 2000/01. BBFC 6-39 EPB v NorB (PE) 1997/98. BBSS 5-37 EP v NW (PE) 2000/01. HSLO 40 EP v Nor (Cent) 1998/99. BBLO 4-15 EP v FS (PE) 1998/99. Tours: SA to Ken 2000/01; SAA to Zim 1994/95.

ABRAHAMS Umar (EP). B 7/2/81 Port Elizabeth. LHB RM. Ed Grey HS (PE). EP Schools 1996-99. SA Schools 1998-99. FC debut EPB v KZNB (Dbn) 1998/99, EP debut 2000/01. HSFC 51 EP v Bol (Paarl) 2000/01. Tours: SA U-19 to Pak 1998/99; World Cup 2000.

ABRAHIM Zahir Ahmed (GW). B 5/6/72 Robertson. LHB RFM. Ed Langenberg Senior Secondary School, UWC. FC debut BolB v TvlB (Randjesfontein) 1995/96, GW debut 1997/98. HSFC 67 GWB v NorB (Cent) 1998/99. BBFC 6-53 GW v UCB Inv (Kby) 1999/00. HSSS 57 GW v NW (Kby) 2000/01. BBSS 5-22 GW v Gau (Jhb) 2000/01. HSLO 10* GW v Bol (Paarl) 2000/01. BBLO 2-23 GW v FS (Bfn) 1998/99.

WHO'S WHO 2000/01

ACKERMAN Hylton Deon (HD) (WP). B 14/2/73 Cape Town. RHB RM. Ed Rondebosch BHS. WP Schools 1990. Son of HM Ackerman (Bdr/NE Tvl/Ntl/Northants/WP/WPB 1963-1981). FC debut WPB v ET (Spr) 1993/94, WP same season. Tests: 4 (1997/98). HSTest 57 v Pak (Dbn) 1997/98. HSFC 202* WP v Nor (Cent) 1997/98. HSLO 92 WP v Nor (Cent) 2000/01. Tours: SAA to Eng 1996; SL 1998/99; SA U-24 to SL 1995/96.
ADAM Shaun Michael (KZN). B 13/9/79 Durban. RHB LF. Ed Durban HS. Ntl Schools 1996-97. FC debut Ntl v WP (Dbn) 1997/98. HSFC 23 Ntl v Gau (Dbn) 1997/98. BBFC 5-57 Ntl v Gau (Dbn) 1997/98. BBLO 3-29 KZN v GW (Kby) 1998/99. Tours: SA U-19 to Pak 1998/99. Athletics (Ntl 1992).
ADAMS Paul Regan (Gogga) (WP/SA). B 20/1/77 Cape Town. RHB SLC. Ed Plumstead High School. WPB Schools 1994. FC debut WPB v Eas (Spr) 1995/96, WP same season. Tests: 34 (1995/96-2000/01). LOIs: 16 (1995/96-2000/01). HSTest 29 v Eng (CT) 1995/96. BBTest 6-55 v Ind (Kanpur) 1996/97. HSLOI 15* v Aus (Sydney) 1997/98. BBLOI 3-26 v Eng (EL) 1995/96. HSFC 61* WP v Bol (CT) 2000/01. BBFC 7-69 WP v GW (CT) 1997/98. HSLO 15* SA v Aus (Sydney) 1997/98. BBLO 3-12 WP v KZN (Dbn) 1998/99. Tours: SA to Aus 1997/98; Eng 1998; Ind 1996/97; NZ 1998/99; Pak 1997/98; SL 2000; Zim 1999/00; WI 2000/01; Ken 1999/00; Shar 1995/96; World Cup 1996; SAA to Eng 1996.
AMLA Ahmed Mahomed (KZN/Pres). B 15/9/79 Durban. RHB LB. Ed Tongaat Secondary School, Univ of Natal. Ntl Schools 1996-97. Brother of HM Amla (KZN 1999/00). FC debut NtlB v WPB (CT) 1997/98, KZN debut 1999/00. HSFC 107 SAAc v Ire (Dublin) 1999. HSSA 104 KZN v Bdr (EL) 1999/00. BBFC 2-53 KZN v Eng (Dbn) 1999/00. HSLO 68 SA Pres v Ban (Dbn) 2000/01. HSDLO 21 KZN v FS (Dbn) 1999/00. Tours: SA U-19 to Pak 1998/99.
AMLA Hashim Mahomed (KZN). B 31/3/1983 Durban. RHB RM. Ed Durban HS. KZN Schools 1999-2000. SA Schools 2000. Brother of AM Amla (KZN/KZNB 1997/98-2000/01). FC debut KZN v Eng (Dbn) 1999/00. Tours: SA U-19 to NZ 2000/01. Table Tennis (KZN U14 1996).
ARTHUR John Michael (Mickey) (GW). B 17/5/68 Johannesburg. RHB. Ed Westville BHS. Ntl Schools 1984-86. FC debut GW v NtlB (Kby) 1986/87. OFS 1990/91-1994/95, GW 1986/87-1989/90 and 1995/96-2000/01. HSFC 165 GW v Gau (Jhb) 2000/01. HSLO 126* OFS v WP (Bfn) 1991/92. Tours: SAA to Zim 1994/95.
BACHER Adam Marc (Gau). B 29/10/73 Johannesburg. RHB RM. Ed King Edward VII, UNISA. Tvl Schools 1990-91. Nephew of A Bacher (Tvl/TvlB/SA 1959-1973, Former UCBSA MD) and brother of M Bacher (TvlB/NTB 1983-1984). FC debut TvlB v NtlB (Dbn) 1993/94, Tvl debut 1994/95. Tests: 19 (1996/97-1999/00). LOIs: 8 (1996/97). HSTest 96 v Aus (Cent) 1996/97 and 96 v Pak (Sheikhupura) 1997/98. HSLOI 45 v Aus (Dbn) 1996/97 and 45 v Aus (Sydney) 1997/98. HSFC 210 Tvl v GW (Kby) 1996/97. HSLO 140 Tvl v NW (Foch) 1996/97. Tours: SA to Aus 1997/98; Eng 1998; Pak 1997/98; Zim 1999/00; SA U-24 to SL 1995/96.
BAILEY Rupert (Nor). B 20/2/80 Paarl. LHB LBG. Ed Paarl BHS. Bol Schools 1997-98. FC debut Bol v WI (Paarl) 1998/99, LO debut for Northerns 2000/01. HSFC 25* Bol v WI (Paarl) 1998/99. HSLO 14 Nor v GW (Kby) 2000/01.
BAKKES Herman Charles (FS). B 24/12/69 Port Elizabeth. RHB RFM. Ed Kroonstad HS, Potch Univ. SACD Schools 1986-87. FC debut OFS v Tvl (Vga) 1991/92. HSFC 101 FS v Bol (Bfn) 1997/98. BBFC 6-28 OFSB v EPB (Bfn) 1991/92. BBSS 6-43 FS v Bdr (Bfn) 1996/97. HSLO 82 FS v NW (Bfn) 1997/98. BBLO 5-7 FS v WP (CT) 1997/98. Tours: SAA to SL 1998/99. Tennis (NOFS Schools 1984-1985).
BAPTISTE Eldine Ashworth Elderfield (KZN). B 12/3/60 Liberta, Antigua. RHB RFM. Ed All Saints SS, Liberta. FC debut Kent v Oxf U (Oxford) 1981, KZN debut 1999/00. Kent 1981-1987, Leeward Islands 1981/82-1990/91, Northamptonshire 1991, EP 1991/92-1998/99. Tests: 10 for WI (1983/84-1989/90). LOIs: 43 for WI (1983/84-1989/90). HSTest 87* v Eng (Birmingham) 1984. BBTest 3-31 v Eng (Manchester) 1984. HSLOI 31 v Ind (Ahmedabad) 1987/88. BBLOI 2-10 v Aus (Sydney) 1983/84. HSFC 136* Kent v Yorks (Sheffield) 1983. BBFC 8-76 Kent v Warwicks (Birmingham) 1987. HSSA 97 EP v Bdr (PE) 1993/94. BBSA 5-30 EP v WP (PE) 1991/92. HSLO 65 EP v Bol (Paarl) 1997/98. BBLO 6-13 EP v NTCD (Pietersburg) 1992/93. Tours: WI to Aus 1983/84, 1984/85; Eng 1984; Ind 1983/84, 1987/88; World Cup 1987; Young WI to Zim 1986/87.
BARNARD Pieter Hendrik (Bol). B 8/5/70 Nelspruit. RHB occ WK. Ed Nelspruit HS, Pretoria Univ. NT Schools 1988-89. FC debut NTB v OFSB (Vbg) 1990/91, Bol debut 2000/01. NT 1991/92-1994/95, NTB 1990/91-1994/95, GW 1995/96-1999/00. HSFC 250 GW v Gau (Kby) 1998/99. HSLO 85 NT v OFSCD (Vga) 1992/93. Provincial tennis (NT).
BASTOW Jonathan Edward (KZN). B 12/2/74 Pietermaritzburg. RHB RFM. Ed Howick HS, Ntl Univ (Pmb). FC debut NtlB v WPB (Dbn) 1996/97, Ntl debut 1997/98. HSFC 35* KZNB v NW (Foch) 1998/99. BBFC 6-37 NtlB v Eas (Dbn) 1997/98. BBSS 4-46 KZN v GW (Dbn) 2000/01. HSLO 10 KZN v EP (Dbn) 2000/01. BBLO 6-26 KZN v FS (Bfn) 2000/01. Athletics (Ntl 1988).
BENDER Kyle Saxon (KZN). B 23/6/74 Durban. RHB OB. Ed Durban HS, Ntl Tech. NtlB Schools 1991. FC debut KZNB v NW (Foch) 1998/99, LO debut for KZN 1998/99. HSFC 34 KZNB v WPB (Dbn) 1998/99. BBFC 2-7 KZNB v WPB (Dbn) 1998/99. HSLO 19 KZN v WA (Perth) 2000/01. BBLO 2-34 KZN v SL (Chat) 2000/01. HSDLO 14* KZN v Eas (Ben) 2000/01.
BENFIELD Mark Rowland (EP). B 3/12/76 Potgietersrus. RHB RM. Ed St Stithian's College, RAU. TvlB Schools 1992, Tvl Schools 1993-94, SA Schools 1993-94(T). FC debut TvlB v NTB (Jhb) 1995/96, EP debut 1999/00. Gau 1996/97-1997/98, TvlB 1995/96-1996/97. HSFC 122 TvlB v EPB (Jhb) 1996/97. HSSS 93 EP v KZN (Dbn) 2000/01. HSLO 72 EP v Nor (PE) 2000/01. Tours: SA U-19 to Ind 1995/96.
BENJAMIN Kenneth Charlie Griffith (Eas). B 8/4/67 St John's, Antigua. RHB RFM. Ed All Saints SS. FC debut Leeward Islands v Windward Islands (Castries) 1988/89, Eas debut 2000/01. Leeward Islands 1988/89-1998/99, Worcestershire 1993, Gau 1999/2000. Tests: 26 for WI (1991/92-1997/98). LOIs: 26 for WI (1992/93-1996/97). HSTest 43* v Eng

(Bridgetown) 1993/94. BBTest 6-66 v Eng (Kingston) 1993/94. HSLOI 17 v Aus (Brisbane) 1992/93. BBLOI 3-34 v SL (Sharjah) 1993/94. HSFC 52* Leeward Islands v Trinidad & Tobago (Basseterre) 1991/92. BBFC 7-51 Leeward Islands v Jamaica (Basseterre) 1990/91. HSSA 48* Eas v KZN (Ben) 2000/01. BBSA 6-48 Gau v Bdr (Jhb) 1999/00. HSLO 22 Eas v Gau (Jhb) 2000/01. BBLO 4-33 Leeward Islands v Jamaica (Kingston) 1996/97. BBDLO 3-17 Gau v NW (Jhb) 1999/00. Tours: WI to Aus 1992/93, 1996/97; Eng 1995; Ind 1993/94, 1994/95; NZ 1994/95; SL 1993/94; Shar 1993/94.

BENKENSTEIN Dale Martin (KZN/Pres). B 9/6/74 Salisbury, Rhodesia. RHB RM/OB. Ed Michaelhouse. Ntl Schools 1990- 92(C), SA Schools 1992(C). Son of MM Benkenstein (Rhod/Z-RB/NtlB 1970-1980), brother of BR Benkenstein (NtlB 1993/94) and BN Benkenstein (NtlB/GW 1994-1996). FC debut Ntl v EP (Dbn) 1993/94. LOIs: 20 (1998/99-1999/00). HSLOI 69 v WI (CT) 1998/99. HSFC 203* NtlB v NTB (Dbn) 1994/95. BBFC 2-24 SAA v SLA (Cent) 1999/00. HSSS 129 Ntl v Bdr (Dbn) 1996/97. BBSS 2-38 Ntl v Bdr (Dbn) 1996/97. HSLO 107* Ntl v NW (Foch) 1997/98. BBLO 4-23 Ntl v Bdr (EL) 1996/97. Tours: SA to Ind 1999/00; NZ 1998/99; Ban 1998/99; Ken 1999/00; Shar 1999/00; World Cup 1999 (did not play); SAA to SL 1998/99 (capt); WI 2000/01 (capt); SA U-24 to SL 1995/96 (capt). COY 1997.

BEUKES Jonathan Alan (FS). B 15/3/79 Kimberley. LHB OB. Ed Grey College (Bfn). FS Schools 1994-97. Nephew of AP Beukes (GW/OFS 1970-1986). FC debut FS v Ntl (Bfn) 1997/98. HSFC 97 FS v Gau (Jhb) 1999/00. HSLO 35 FS v WP (CT) 1998/99. Hockey (FS/SA Schools 1996-97).

BODI Goolam Hussain (KZN). B 4/1/79 Hathuran, India. LHB SLC. Ed Azaadville Secondary. TvlB Schools 1995, Gau Schools 1996-97. SA Schools 1997. FC debut TvlB v WPB (CT) 1996/97, KZN debut 1999/00. Tvl/TvlB 1996/97. HSFC 104 KZN v Eas (Ben) 2000/01. BBFC 6-63 KZN v Gau (Dbn) 2000/01. HSLO 106* KZN v v EP (Dbn) 2000/01. BBLO 5-46 KZN v EP (Dbn) 2000/01. SA U-19 v Eng U-19 1997/98; World Cup 1998.

BOJE Nico (Nicky) (FS/SA). B 20/3/73 Bloemfontein. LHB SLA. Ed Grey College (Bfn). OFS Schools 1987-90, SA Schools 1989(T)-90-91(C). Brother of EHL Boje (OFSB 1989-1990). FC debut OFSB v NtlB (Pmb) 1990/91, OFS same season. Tests: 15 (1999/00-2000/01). LOIs: 56 (1995/96-2000/01). HSTest 85 v Ind (Bangalore) 1999/00. BBTest 5-62 v SL (Colombo-SSC) 2000. HSLOI 129 v NZ (Centurion) 2000/01. BBLOI 4-25 v Pak (Colombo-RPS) 2000. HSFC 116 FS v WP (Bfn) 1998/99. BBFC 6-34 FS v Nor (Bfn) 1997/98. HSLO 129 SA v NZ (Centurion) 2000/01. BBLO 4-16 SA v SL (Kuala Lumpur) 1998/99. HSDLO 79* OFS v NT (Bfn) 1994/95. BBDLO 4-18 OFS v EP (Bfn) 1993/94. Tours: SA to Aus 2000; Ind 1996/97, 1999/00; NZ 1998/99; SL 2000; WI 2000/01; Zim 1995/96; Ban 1998/99; Ken 1996/97, 2000/01; Shar 1999/00; Sing 2000; World Cup 1999; SAA to Zim 1994/95; Eng 1996; SL 1998/99; SA U-24 to SL 1995/96. COY 2001. Rugby (OFS Craven Week).

BOSMAN Lungile Loots (GW). B 14/4/77 Kimberley. RHB RM. Ed Tshireleco High. GW Schools 1995-96. FC debut GW v FS (Bfn) 1997/98. HSFC 115* GW v NW (Kby) 2000/01. BBFC 3-25 GW v Pak (Kby) 1997/98. BBSS 2-69 GW v Gau (Kby) 1999/00. HSLO 89 GW v Gau (Kby) 2000/01. Tours: SAA to SL 1998/99.

BOSSENGER Wendell (GW). B 23/10/76 Cape Town. RHB WK. Ed Wynberg Boys High. WP Schools 1994. FC debut GW v Bol (Paarl) 1996/97. HSFC 124* GW v Ntl (Kby) 1997/98. HSLO 48* GW v Eas (Ben) 2000/01.

BOTHA Anthony Greyvensteyn (Eas). B 17/11/76 Pretoria. LHB SLA. Ed Maritzburg College, Maritzburg Technikon. Ntl Schools 1993-95, SA Schools 1995. FC debut NtlB v FSB (Dbn) 1995/96, Eas debut 1999/00. KZN 1996/97-1998/99, KZNB 1995/96-1998/99. HSFC 94 NtlB v EPB (PE) 1997/98. BBFC 8-53 NtlB v NorB (Cent) 1997/98. HSSS 79 Eas v GW (Kby) 1999/00. BBSS 6-106 Eas v Bol (Paarl) 2000/01. HSLO 36 Eas v Bol (Paarl) 1999/00. BBLO 3-16 SAAc v NZAc (Cent) 1997/98. BBDLO 3-38 Ntl v Gau (Jhb) 1997/98. Tours: SA U-19 to Ind 1995/96. Hockey (Midlands U-21 1995).

BOTHA Johan (EP). B 2/5/82 Johannesburg. RHB RM. Ed Grey HS (PE). EP Schools 1997-2000, SA Schools 1999-2000(C). FC debut EP v Bdr (PE) 2000/01. HSFC 43 EP v FS (Bfn) 2000/01. Tours: SA U-19 to NZ 2000/01; World Cup 2000.

BOTHA Peterus Johannes (Piet) (Bdr). B 28/9/66 Vereeniging. RHB RFM. Ed Dr Malan HS (Meyerton), RAU. FC debut TvlB v NtlB (Dbn) 1987/88, Bdr debut 1992/93. Tvl 1989/90-1991/92, TvlB 1987/88-1991/92. HSFC 136 Bdr v FS (Bfn) 1996/97. BBFC 6-32 Bdr v Bol (Paarl) 1997/98. HSLO 105 Tvl v NTCD (Pietersburg) 1990/91. BBLO 4-37 Bdr v Eas (EL) 1997/98.

BOUCHER Mark Verdon (Bdr/SA). B 3/12/76 East London. RHB WK. Ed Selborne College. Bdr Schools 1994-95, SA Schools 1994. FC debut BdrB v NtlB (Dbn) 1995/96, Bdr same season. Tests: 42 (1997/98-2000/01). LOIs: 91 (1997/98-2000/01). HSTest 125 v Zim (Harare) 1999/00. HSLOI 68 v Ind (Nagpur) 1999/00. HSFC 125 SA v Zim (Harare) 1999/00. HSSA 112 Bdr v Gau (Jhb) 1999/00. HSLO 70 Bdr v Nor (EL) 2000/01. Tours: SA to Aus 1997/98, 2000; Eng 1998; Ind 1999/00; NZ 1998/99; Pak 1997/98; SL 2000; Zim 1999/00; WI 2000/01; Ban 1998/99; Ken 1999/00, 2000/01; Shar 1999/00; World Cup 1999. SA U-19 to Eng 1995; Ind 1995/96. COY 1998, 2000. Squash (UPE, Bdr, SA U-19 1989-1994).

BRADFIELD Carl Crispin (EP). B 18/1/75 Grahamstown. LHB RM. Ed Grey HS (PE), Kingswood College, UPE. EP Schools 1992-93, SA Schools 1993. FC debut EPB v GW (Kby) 1993/94, EP debut 1996/97. HSFC 163 EPB v Eas (PE) 1996/97. HSSS 154* EP v KZN (Dbn) 1999/00. HSLO 96* EP v Gau (PE) 1999/00. Rugby (EP Craven Week).

BRAND Derek (Eas). B 29/5/75 Bellville. RHB RM WK. Ed Tygerberg High. WP Schools 1992-93. FC debut Eas v KZNB (Ben) 1998/99. HSFC 61 Eas v KZNB (Ben) 1998/99. BBFC 2-42 Eas v GW (Ben) 1999/00. HSSS 45 Eas v GW (Kby) 1999/00. HSLO 131 Eas v NW (Ben) 1999/00. BBLO 2-8 Eas v NW (Foch) 1998/99. Action Cricket (WP/SA 1995-98).

BROOKER Finley Clint (Nor). B 26/12/72 Kimberley. RHB RM. Ed Floors SSHS. GW Schools 1990. Brother of J Brooker (GW/GWB 1998-2000). FC debut GW v EP (Kby) 1992/93, Nor debut 2000/01. GW 1992/93-1999/00, GWB

1998/99. HSFC 111 GW v WI (Kby) 1998/99. HSSS 78 GW v WP (Kby) 1998/99. HSLO 40 GW v WP (Kby) 1998/99. Tours: SA U-24 to SL 1995/96. Hockey (GW).

BROOKER Jason (GW). B 16/1/77 Kimberley. RHB RMF. Ed Floors SSHS. GW Schools 1993-95. Brother of FC Brooker (GW/GWB/Nor 1992-2000). FC debut GWB v NorB (Cent) 1998/99, GW debut 2000/01. HSFC 77 GW v FS (Kby) 2000/01. HSLO 23 GW v Eas (Ben) 2000/01. Hockey (GW 1996-98).

BROPHY Gerard Louis (FS). B 26/11/75 Welkom. RHB WK. Ed CBC Welkom, CBC Boksburg, Wits Technikon. ET Schools 1992-93. FC debut TvlB v EPB (Jhb) 1996/97, FS debut 1999/00. Gau 1998/99, TvlB 1996/97. HSFC 185 SAAc v Zim Pres (Har) 1998/99. HSSA 73 FS v Bdr (Bfn) 1999/00. HSLO 50* FS v Gau (Jhb) 1999/00. Hockey (ET 1991).

BROUWERS Nigel Grant (Nor). B 4/9/76 Port Elizabeth. LHB SLA. EP Schools 1994-95. FC debut EPB v KZNB (Dbn) 1998/99, Nor debut 2000/01. EPB 1998/99. HSFC 59 Nor v FS (Cent) 2000/01. BBFC 6-57 EPB v GWB (PE) 1998/99. BBSS 3-43 Nor v GW (Cent) 2000/01. BBLO 2-38 Nor v EP (PE) 2000/01.

BROWN Duncan Loudon (KZN). B 23/6/79 Durban. RHB WK. Ed Westville BHS, UNISA. Ntl Schools 1996-97. FC debut KZNB v NW (Foch) 1998/99, KZN debut 1999/00. HSFC 20 KZNB v NorB (Dbn) 1998/99. HSLO 14 KZN v SL (Chat) 2000/01.

BRUYNS Mark Lloyd (KZN/Pres). B 8/11/73 Pietermaritzburg. RHB RM WK. Ed Maritzburg College. Ntl Schools 1990-91. Nephew of A Bruyns (WP/Ntl 1965-1976). FC debut NtlB v BdrB (EL) 1993/94, Ntl same season. HSFC 144 SAA v SLA (Cent) 1999/00. HSSS 142 KZN v NW (Potch) 1999/00. BBFC 2-3 KZN v EP (PE) 1998/99. HSLO 111 Ntl v Gau (Jhb) 1997/98. Tours: SAA to SL 1998/99; WI 2000/01; SA U-24 to SL 1995/96.

BRYANT James Douglas Campbell (EP). B 4/2/76 Durban. RHB. Ed Maritzburg College, UPE. Ntl Schools 1993. FC debut EPB v Eas (PE) 1996/97, EP debut 1998/99. HSFC 149 EP v Nor (PE) 1999/00. HSLO 105* EP v WP (CT) 2000/01. Tours: SAA to WI 2000/01.

BRYSON Rudi Edwin (Nor). B 25/7/68 Springs. RHB RFM. Ed Springs BHS. NT Schools 1985-86. FC debut NTB v TvlB (Vbg) 1987/88, NT debut 1993/94. EP 1989/90-1992/93, EPB 1988/89-1989/90, Surrey 1992. LOIs: 7 (1996/97). HSLOI 17* v Aus (CT) 1996/97. BBLOI 2-34 v Aus (CT) 1996/97. HSFC 100 EP v Bol (Worc) 1991/92. BBFC 7-68 EPB v GW (Kby) 1988/89. HSSS 62 NT v Bdr (Vbg) 1994/95. BBSS 6-48 EP v Bdr (PE) 1991/92. HSLO 44* NT v Ntl (Dbn) 1995/96. BBLO 4-17 NT v GW (Kby) 1996/97. Hockey (Tvl and SA Schools 1985-1986).

CALLAGHAN David John (EP). B 1/2/65 Queenstown. RHB RM. Ed Dale, Selborne College and Grey HS (PE), UPE. EP Schools 1981-83, SA Schools 1983-83(E). Cousin of JM Kemp (EP/EPB/SA 1996-2000), nephew of RTdeV Kemp (Bdr 1967-1976). FC debut EPB v GW (Kby) 1983/84, EP debut 1984/85. GW 1985/86, Nottinghamshire 1988. LOIs: 29 (1992/93-1999/00). HSLOI 169* v NZ (Vbg) 1994/95. BBLOI 3-32 v NZ (Vbg) 1994/95. HSFC 171 EP v SADF (PE) 1984/85. BBFC 5-24 EP v Eas (Ben) 2000/01. HSSS 148 EP v Ntl (Pmb) 1987/88. HSLO 169* SA v NZ (Vbg) 1994/95. HSDLO 107* EP v Gau (Jhb) 1999/00. BBLO 4-31 EP v Gau (Jhb) 1999/00. Tours: SA to Aus 1993/94; Ind 1993/94; NZ 1994/95; SAA to Zim 1994/95. COY 1988. Rugby (EP). Missed much of 1991/92 season due to cancer.

CARTER Neil Miller (Bol). B 29/1/75 Cape Town. LHB LMF. Ed Hottentots Holland HS, Cape Tech. FC debut Bol v Gau (Paarl) 1999/00. HSFC 37 Bol v EP (PE) 1999/00. BBFC 6-63 Bol v GW (Kby) 2000/01. HSLO 27 Bol v WP (CT) 2000/01. BBLO 4-31 Bol v Eas (Ben) 1999/00. Hockey (Bol 1991), Cross Country (Bol 1992).

COOK Stephen Craig (Gau). B 29/11/82 Johannesburg. RHB RM. Ed King Edward VII. Gau Schools 1999-2000, SA Schools 2000. Son of SJ Cook (Tvl/TvlB/Som/SA 1972-1994). FC debut Gau v GW (Jhb) 2000/01. HSFC 55 Gau v KZN (Dbn) 2000/01. Tours: SA U-19 to NZ 2000/01.

COPELAND Craig Anthony (GW). B 2/1/77 Cape Town. RHB LBG. Ed Pinelands HS, Cape Tech. WP Schools 1995. FC debut WPB v Eas (CT) 1998/99, GW debut 1999/00. HSFC 10 GW v Nor (Cent) 2000/01. BBFC 8-101 GW v Ban (Kby) 2000/01. BBSS 5-52 GW v Gau (Jhb) 2000/01.

CREED Murray Wayne (EP). B 5/3/79 Port Elizabeth. RHB RFM. Ed Grey HS (PE) & UPE. EP Schools 1995-97, SA Schools 1997. FC debut EPB v NW (PE) 1997/98, EP debut 1998/99. HSFC 72 EP v Nor (PE) 1998/99. BBFC 4-30 EP v Nor (PE) 1998/99. HSLO 47 EP v Gau (Jhb) 1999/00. BBLO 2-22 EP v WP (CT) 1998/99. SA U-19 v Eng U-19 1997/98; World Cup 1998. Athletics (EP, 1995).

CROOKES Derek Norman (Eas). B 5/3/69 Mariannhill. RHB OB. Ed Hilton College, Natal Technikon. Ntl Schools 1986-88(C), SA Schools 1988(C). Son of NS Crookes (Ntl/SA 1962-1969). FC debut NtlB v EPB (PE) 1989/90, Eas debut 2000/01. Ntl 1990/91-1996/97, NtlB 1989/90-1994/95, Gau 1997/98-1999/00. LOIs: 32 (1994/95-1999/00). HSLOI 54 v Ind (Sharjah) 1995/96. BBLOI 3-30 v Pak (Nairobi) 1996/97. HSFC 155* SAA v Som (Taunton) 1996. BBFC 7-114 Ntl v FS (Dbn) 1996/97. HSSA 128* Ntl v GW (Dbn) 1996/97. HSLO 114 Gau v NW (Jhb) 1997/98. BBLO 4-29 Gau v Bdr (Jhb) 1998/99. Tours: SA to Ind 1996/97, 1999/00; Pak 1994/95; Ban 1998/99; Ken 1996/97, 1999/00; Shar 1995/96, 1999/00; World Cup 1999 (did not play); SAA to Eng 1996; SL 1998/99.

CULLINAN Daryll John (Gau/SA). B 4/3/67 Kimberley. RHB OB. Ed Queens College, Stell Univ. Bdr Schools 1981-84, SA Schools 1983-83(E)-84(C). Brother of RE Cullinan (Bdr/OFSB 1984-1990). FC debut Bdr v SAU (EL) 1983/84. Bdr 1983/84-1984/85 and 1994/95-1995/96, WP 1985/86-1990/91, Gau 1991/92-1993/94 and 1996/97-2000/01, Derbyshire 1995, Kent 2001. Tests: 70 (1992/93-2000/01). LOIs: 138 (1992/93-2000/01). HSTest 275* v NZ (Auckland) 1998/99, joint SA Test record. HSLOI 124 v Pak (Nairobi) 1996/97. BBLOI 2-30 v Eng (Manchester) 1998. HSFC 337* Tvl v NT (Jhb) 1993/94, SA FC record. BBFC 2-27 Bdr v NtlB (EL) 1983/84. HSLO 124 SA v Pak (Nairobi) 1996/97. BBLO 2-30 SA v Eng (Manchester) 1998. HSDLO 111* Tvl v Imp (Jhb) 1993/94. Tours: SA to Aus 1993/94, 1997/98, 2000; Eng 1994, 1998;

Ind 1993/94, 1996/97, 1999/00; NZ 1994/95, 1998/99; Pak 1994/95, 1997/98; SL 1993/94, 2000; WI 2000/01; Zim 1995/96, 1999/00; Ban 1998/99; Ken 1996/97; Shar 1995/96; Sing 2000; World Cup 1996, 1999. COY 1989, 1996, 1999.

CYSTER Andrew William (Bol). B 31/3/79 Stellenbosch. LHB. Ed Stellenbosch HS, Stell Univ. Bol Schools 1996. FC debut Bol v Eas (Paarl) 2000/01. HSFC 21 Bol v Eas (Paarl) 2000/01.

DAVIDS Henry (Bol). B 19/1/80 Stellenbosch. RHB RMF. Ed Stellenbosch HS. Bol Schools 1996-98. FC debut Bol v NZ (Paarl) 2000/01. HSFC 124 Bol v Nor (Cent) 2000/01. HSLO 26 Bol v KZN (Dbn) 2000/01. Athletics (Bol 1995-98).

DAWSON Alan Charles (WP/SA). B 27/11/69 Cape Town. RHB RMF. Ed SACS. FC debut WP v EP (CT) 1992/93. LOIs: 4 (1998/99-2000/01). BBLOI 3-36 v Zim (Nairobi) 1999/00. HSFC 143 WP v Bdr (EL) 1998/99. BBFC 6-18 WPB v FSB (CT) 1995/96. BBSS 6-51 WP v Bdr (EL) 1999/00. HSLO 44* WP v EP (CT) 1993/94. BBLO 5-13 WP v GW (Kby) 2000/01. Tours: SA to Ban 1998/99; Ken 1999/00; World Cup 1999 (did not play); SAA to SL 1998/99.

DEACON Wycliffe Andrew (FS). B 23/6/80 Kroonstad. LHB LFM. Ed Steynsrus Hoerskool, Grey College (Bfn), UOFS. FS Schools 1996-1998. No FC, LO debut for FS 2000/01. Tennis (Eastern FS 1995-96).

DE BRUYN Pierre (Eas). B 31/3/77 Pretoria. RHB RFM. Ed Zwartkop Hoerskool, Pretoria Technikon. NT Schools 1993-95. Twin brother of E de Bruyn (NorB 1997/98).FC debut NTB v TvlB (Jhb) 1995/96, Eas debut 1999/00. Nor/NorB 1995/96-1998/99. HSFC 202 NorB v GWB (Cent) 1998/99. BBFC 6-38 NTB v BolB (Paarl) 1995/96. HSSS 83 Eas v KZN (Ben) 2000/01. BBSS 4-34 Eas v Bol (Paarl) 2000/01. HSLO 68 Eas v NW (Potch) 2000/01. BBLO 4-28 Eas v NW (Ben) 1999/00.

DE BRUYN Zander (Gau). B 5/7/75 Johannesburg. RHB RFM. Ed Hoerskool Helpmekaar, Hoerskool Randburg. Tvl Schools 1991-94, SA Schools 1994. FC debut TvlB v NTB (Jhb) 1995/96, Tvl debut 1996/97. HSFC 126* TvlB v GW (Kby) 1995/96. BBFC 6-120 TvlB v WPB (CT) 1996/97. HSSS 71 Gau v KZN (Jhb) 1998/99. BBSS 2-14 Gau v WP (CT) 1999/00. HSLO 104* Tvl v Eas (Ben) 1997/98. BBLO 3-24 Gau v Eas (Ben) 1999/00. Rugby (TvlB Craven Week 1993), Athletics (Javelin, Tvl Champs 1994).

DE KOCK Manfred Stephen (Bol). B 3/2/75 Paarl. RHB WK. Ed Klein Nederburg Secondary. Bol Schools 1993-94. FC debut Bol v Bdr (EL) 2000/01. HSFC 17* Bol v Bdr (EL) 2000/01. Hockey (Bol Schools 1993).

DE LANGE Con de Wet (Bol). B 11/2/81 Bellville. RHB SLA. Ed Worcester Gymnasium. Bol Schools 1996-99. SA Schools 1999. Nephew of CPL de Lange (NT/NTB 1981-1986). FC debut Bol v SL (Paarl) 1997/98. HSFC 25 Bol v WP (CT) 2000/01. BBFC 2-44 Bol v Eas (Paarl) 2000/01. HSLO 30* Bol v KZN (Dbn) 2000/01. BBLO 3-17 Bol v Eas (Paarl) 1999/00. Tours: SA U-19 to Pak 1998/99.

DE STADLER Mark (WP). B 6/7/75 Cape Town. RHB RM. Ed Crestway SS, South Peninsula Tech. No FC, LO debut for WP 2000/01. Volleyball (WP U-21, 1993-94).

DE VOS Dirk Johannes Jacobus (Nor). B 15/6/75 Pretoria. RHB OB. Ed Potch Gym. WT Schools 1991-93, SA Schools 1992-93. Brother of HM de Vos (NW 1991-2000). FC debut WT v ET (Spr) 1992/93, NTB debut 1993/94, NT debut 1995/96. WT 1992/93. HSFC 105* NorB v EPB (Pta) 1998/99. BBFC 6-32 Nor v FS (Bfn) 1999/00. HSSS 97 Nor v Eas (Cent) 2000/01. HSLO 84 Nor v KZN (Dbn) 1998/99. BBLO 6-26 Nor v Eas (Ben) 1998/99. Rugby (WT Schools).

DE VOS Hendrik Moller (NW). B 5/10/69 Klerksdorp. RHB WK. Ed Hoervolkskool Potch, Potch Univ. Brother of DJJ de Vos (WT/Nor/NorB 1992-2000). FC debut WT v Bol (Bfel) 1991/92. HSFC 115 WT v FSB (Potch) 1995/96. HSSS 61* NW v KZN (Potch) 1999/00. HSLO 91 WT v Tvl (Potch) 1994/95.

DE WETT Burton Christopher (NW). B 25/12/80 East London. LHB LBG. Ed Selborne College, Bdr Tech. Bdr Schools 1996-98. FC debut NW v WP (Potch) 2000/01. HSFC 30 NW v WP (Potch) 2000/01. HSLO 35 NW v KZN (Dbn) 2000/01.

DIPPENAAR Hendrik Human (Boeta) (FS/SA). B 14/6/77 Kimberley. RHB OB. Ed Grey College (Bfn). OFS Schools 1992-1994, SA Schools 1995(T). FC debut FS v Eng (Bfn) 1995/96. Tests: 7 (1999/00-2000/01). LOIs: 21 (1999/00-2000/01). HSTest 100 v NZ (Jhb) 2000/01. HSLOI 77 v SL (CT) 2000/01. HSFC 200* FS v Bol (Bfn) 1999/00. HSLO 77 SA v SL (CT) 2000/01. HSDLO 75 FS v GW (Bfn) 1998/99. Tours: SA to Aus 2000; Ind 1999/00; SL 2000; WI 2000/01; Zim 1999/00; Ken 1999/00, 2000/01; Sing 2000; SA U-19 to Eng 1995; Ind 1995/96. Golf (OFS U-15).

DLADLA Lucky (KZN). B 9/8/80 Pietermaritzburg. RHB RFM. Ed Maritzburg College, Varsity College. KZN Schools 1997-98. FC debut KZN v SL (Pmb) 2000/01.

DONALD Allan Anthony (FS/SA). B 20/10/66 Bloemfontein. RHB RF. Ed Hoer Tegniese Bloemfontein. OFS Schools 1984-85, SA Schools 1984(T)-85. FC debut OFS v Tvl (Jhb) 1985/86. Warwickshire 1987-2000. Tests: 69 (1991/92-2000/01). LOIs: 136 (1991/92-2000/01). HSTest 37 v WI (Bridgetown) 2000/01. BBTest 8-71 v Zim (Harare) 1995/96. HSLOI 13 v SL (Nottingham) 1998. BBLOI 6-23 v Ken (Nairobi) 1996/97. HSFC 55* SA v Tasmania (Devonport) 1997/98. BBFC 8-37 OFS v Tvl (Jhb) 1986/87. HSSA 46* OFS v WP (CT) 1990/91. HSLO 23* Warw v Leics (Leicester) 1989. BBLO 6-15 Warw v York (Birmingham) 1995. HSDLO 19* OFS v Tvl (Jhb) 1988/89. BBDLO 5-25 OFS v NTCD (Pietersburg) 1991/92. Tours: SA to Aus 1993/94, 1997/98; Eng 1994, 1998; Ind 1991/92, 1993/94, 1996/97, 1999/00; NZ 1994/95, 1998/99; Pak 1997/98; SL 1993/94; WI 1991/92, 2000/01; Zim 1995/96, 1999/00; Ken 1996/97, 2000/01; World Cup 1992, 1996, 1999. COY 1993, 1996, 1997, 1998. Wisden 1992.

DRAKES Vasbert Conniel (Bdr). B 5/8/69 Springhead, St Andrew, Barbados. RHB RF. Ed St Lucy SS. FC debut Barbados v Leeward Islands (Bridgetown) 1991/92, Bdr debut 1996/97. Barbados 1991/92-1997/98, Sussex 1996-1997, Nottinghamshire 1999, Warwickshire 2001. LOIs: 5 for WI (1994/95). HSLOI 16 v Aus (Port-of-Spain) 1994/95. HSFC 180* Bar v Leew Is (Anguilla) 1994/95. BBFC 8-59 Bdr v Ntl (Dbn) 1996/97. HSSA 100 Bar v NT (Vbg) 1993/94. HSSS 98 Bdr v GW (Kby) 1997/98. HSLO 104 Bdr v Bol (Paarl) 1996/97. BBLO 5-19 Sussex v Ireland (Hove) 1996. BBDLO 4-16 Bdr v Nor (Cent) 1997/98. COY 2000.

DREYER Jan Nicolaas (NW). B 9/9/76 Amanzimtoti. RHB RM. Ed Gimnasium High. WT Schools 1993-95. FC debut NW v TvlB (Jhb) 1996/97. KZN/KZNB 1998/99, NW 1996/97-1997/98 and 1999/00-2000/01. HSFC 40 NW v EP (PE) 2000/01. BBFC 5-81 FS/GW/NW XI v SLA (Potch) 1999/00. BBSS 5-97 NW v WP (CT) 1999/00. HSLO 45* NW v WP (CT) 1997/98. BBLO 3-38 KZN v Nor (Dbn) 1998/99. Rugby (WT Schools 1994-95, WT U-21 1996).

DROS Gerald (Nor). B 2/4/73 Pretoria. RHB RM. Ed St Albans, Pretoria Univ. NT Schools 1990-92, SA Schools 1992. FC debut NTB v TvlB (Jhb) 1993/94, NT same season. HSFC 100* Nor v Gau (Jhb) 2000/01. BBFC 3-21 Nor v EP (PE) 1999/00. HSLO 105* Nor v GW (Cent) 1999/00. BBLO 3-21 Nor v Bdr (EL) 2000/01. Tours: SAA to WI 2000/01.

DRY Willem Moolman (GW). B 9/1/71 Vryburg. RHB RM. Ed Hoer Landbou Skool Noord Kaapland, Pretoria Technikon. GW Schools 1988-89. FC debut NTB v TvlB (Jhb) 1993/94, GW debut 1995/96. NTB 1993/94-1994/95. HSFC 99 GW v EPB (PE) 1995/96. HSSS 80 GW v FS (Kby) 2000/01. BBFC 2-39 NTB v TvlB (Jhb) 1993/94. HSLO 150* GW v Bdr (Kby) 1999/00.

DU TOIT Willem Johannes (Bol). B 18/3/81 Cape Town. RHB RF. Ed Paul Roos Gymnasium. Bol Schools 1996-99, SA Schools 1998. FC debut Bol v EP (Paarl) 1998/99. HSFC 32 Bol v Eas (Paarl) 2000/01. BBFC 7-82 Bol v Eas (Paarl) 2000/01. Tours: SA U-19 to Pak 1998/99.

EKSTEEN Clive Edward (Gau). B 2/12/66 Johannesburg. RHB SLA. Ed Northcliff BHS. SA Schools 1984. FC debut SADF v Bol (Stb) 1985/86, Tvl debut 1988/89. NTB 1985/86-1986/87, TvlB 1987/88-1990/91. Tests: 7 (1993/94-1999/00). LOIs: 6 (1991/92-1994/95). HSTest 22 v NZ (CT) 1994/95. BBTest 3-12 v Eng (Jhb) 1995/96. HSFC 58 Tvl v ZimA (Jhb) 1995/96. BBFC 7-29 Tvl v WP (CT) 1993/94. HSSS 50 Gau v NW (Potch) 2000/01. HSLO 55* Gau v GW (Jhb) 1998/99. BBLO 5-13 Tvl v Bol (Paarl) 1995/96. Tours: SA to Ind 1991/92, 1999/00; NZ 1994/95; Pak 1994/95; SL 1993/94.

ELLIOTT Grant David (GW). B 21/3/79 Johannesburg. RHB RFM. Ed St Stithians. Gau Schools 1995-97. SA Schools 1997. FC debut TvlB v NtlB (Dbn) 1996/97, GW debut 1999/00. HSFC 125 GW v Ban (Kby) 2000/01. BBFC 2-18 GW v Gau (Kby) 2000/01. HSSS 83 GW v KZN (Kby) 2000/01. HSLO 94 GW v KZN (Kby) 2000/01. BBLO 3-32 GW v Bol (Paarl) 2000/01. SA U-19 v Pak U-19 1996/97; v Eng U-19 1997/98; World Cup 1998.

ELWORTHY Steven (Nor). B 23/2/65 Bulawayo, Rhodesia. RHB RFM. Ed Chaplin HS (Gwelo), Sandown HS, Wits Univ. Tvl Schools 1983-84. FC debut TvlB v NtlB (Jhb) 1987/88, NT debut 1989/90. NTB 1988/89-1989/90, Lancashire 1995/96-1996. Tests 2 (1998-1998/99). LOIs: 35 (1997/98-1999/00). HSTest 48 v Eng (Nottingham) 1998. BBTest 4-66 v NZ (Wellington) 1998/99. HSLOI 23 v SL (Northampton) 1999. BBLOI 3-17 v Ind (Sharjah) 1999/00. HSFC 89 Nor v Bol (Cent) 1997/98. BBFC 7-65 NT v Ntl (Dbn) 1994/95. HSLO 116* NT v GW (Vbg) 1994/95. BBLO 4-14 Lanc v Glos (Manchester) 1996. BBDLO 4-23 NT v FS (Bfn) 1996/97. Tours: SA to Eng 1998; Ind 1999/00; NZ 1998/99; Ban 1998/99; Ken 1999/00; Shar 1999/00; World Cup 1999; SAA to Zim 1994/95.

ENSLIN Christian Thinus (NW). B 16/9/75 Klerksdorp. RHB RM. Ed Klerksdorp HS, Potch Univ. FC debut WT v BdrB (Qtn) 1995/96. HSFC 51 NW v NorB (Foch) 1997/98. BBFC 4-46 WT v Eas (Potch) 1995/96. HSSS 36 NW v WP (CT) 1999/00. BBSS 3-58 NW v GW (Potch) 1999/00. HSLO 52 NW v Nor (Cent) 2000/01. BBLO 4-39 NW v EP (Foch) 1998/99. Rugby (WT U-18 1994).

FERREIRA Evert Johann (Bdr). B 29/4/76 Pretoria. RHB. Ed Vereeniging High. NT Schools 1993-94. FC debut Bol v Bdr (Paarl) 1997/98, LO debut for Bdr 2000/01. Bol 1997/98-1998/99. HSFC 63 Bol v Gau (Jhb) 1998/99. HSLO 123 Bol v Bdr (EL) 1997/98.

FERREIRA Lloyd Douglas (WP). B 6/5/74 Parktown, Johannesburg. RHB LM. Ed Michaelhouse, Stell Univ. Ntl Schools 1992. FC debut Bol v Aus (Stb) 1993/94, WP debut 1997/98. Bol 1993/94-1996/97. HSFC 201 WP v NW (Potch) 2000/01. HSLO 125* Bol v Bdr (Paarl) 1996/97.

FERREIRA Quentin (Nor). B 28/12/72 East London. RHB RFM. Ed Sandringham HS, RAU. Tvl Schools 1991. Brother of D Ferreira (OFSB 1989-1993). FC debut EP v Bdr (EL) 1996/97, Nor debut 1998/99. EP/EPB 1996/97-1997/98. HSFC 63* Nor v FS (Cent) 1998/99. BBFC 4-17 EPB v Eas (Ben) 1997/98. BBSS 3-19 Nor v WP (CT) 1998/99. HSLO 34* Nor v Bdr (EL) 1998/99. BBLO 3-40 EP v Bdr (PE) 1996/97. Hockey (ST Schools 1990-91, ST U-21 1992-93).

FLUSK Gareth Edward (Eas). B 8/11/74 Johannesburg. LHB LM. Ed St Barnabas College, Wits Univ. FC debut TvlB v Zim Brd (Byo) 1995/96, Eas debut 1999/00. TvlB 1995/96. HSFC 31* Eas v KZN (Ben) 2000/01. BBFC 5-55 Eas v Bdr (EL) 2000/01. HSLO 20 Eas v Bol (Ben) 1999/00. BBLO 2-14 Eas v GW (Kby) 1999/00.

FUSEDALE Neil Andrew (Gau). B 11/11/67 Hendon, England. RHB SLA. Ed St Martins, Sandown High. Tvl Schools 1986. FC debut TvlB v ET (Spr) 1994/95, Gau debut 2000/01. TvlB 1994/95-1996/97, Eas 1997/98-1998/99. Gau LO 1994/95-1996/97 and 1999/00–2000/01. HSFC 44* TvlB v WPB (CT) 1996/97 and 44 TvlB v NtlB (Dbn) 1996/97. BBFC 5-170 Gau v GW (Kby) 2000/01. HSSS 20* Gau v GW (Jhb) 2000/01. HSLO 32* Berkshire v Kent (Finchampstead) 1994. BBLO 3-26 Eas v Bdr (EL) 1997/98. HSDLO 14 Tvl v Bol (Paarl) 1994/95. Tennis coach, Golf (3 handicap).

GAIT Andrew Ian (FS). B 19/12/78 Bulawayo, Rhodesia. RHB. Ed Kearsney College, UNISA. Ntl Schools 1996. FC debut FS v EP (Bfn) 1998/99. HSFC 112 FS v Bdr (Bfn) 2000/01. HSLO 138* FS v GW (Bfn) 2000/01. SA U-19 v Eng U-19 1997/98; World Cup 1998.

GAMIET Laden Liep (Bdr). B 23/1/78 East London. RHB RM. Ed Selborne College. Bdr Schools 1994-95. FC debut BdrB v WPB (EL) 1995/96, Bdr debut 1999/00. BdrB 1995/96-1996/97, NorB 1997/98. HSFC 80 Bdr v WP (CT) 2000/01. HSLO 87 Bdr v Nor (Cent) 2000/01. SA U-19 v Pak U-19 1996/97. Hockey (Bdr Schools 1994-95).

GEORGE Mulligan Frank (Gau). B 10/9/76 Cape Town. RHB RFM. Ed Mondale Senior Secondary, Cape Technikon. WP Schools 1994-1995, SA Schools 1995 (13th man). FC debut WPB v NtlB (CT) 1997/98, Gau debut 2000/01. WP 1997/98-

1998/99, WPB 1997/98. HSFC 58 Gau v NW (Potch) 2000/01. BBFC 6-61 WP v GW (CT) 1997/98. HSLO 10* WP v FS (CT) 1997/98. BBLO 2-34 WP v Nor (CT) 1997/98.

GIBBS Herschelle Herman (WP/SA). B 23/2/74 Green Point, Cape Town. RHB RFM/LB. Ed Diocesan College. WP Schools 1989-92, SA Schools 1991-92. FC debut WPB v TvlB (CT) 1990/91, WP same season. Tests: 28 (1996/97-2000/01). LOIs: 70 (1996/97-2000/01). HSTest 211* v NZ (Christchurch) 1998/99. HSLOI 125 v WI (PE) 1998/99. HSFC 211* SA v NZ (Christchurch) 1998/99. HSSA 163* WP v Ntl (CT) 1996/97. BBFC 2-14 SAA v Som (Taunton) 1996. HSLO 125 SA v WI (PE) 1998/99. HSDLO 110* WP v FS (Bfn) 1997/98. Tours: SA to Aus 1997/98; Ind 1996/97, 1999/00; NZ 1998/99; WI 2000/01; Ken 1996/97, 1999/00; Shar 1999/00; World Cup 1999; SAA to Eng 1996; SL 1998/99. COY 1999. Rugby (SA Schools 1992).

GIBSON Ottis Delroy (Gau). B 16/3/69 Sion Hill, St James, Barbados. RHB RF. Ed Ellerslie Secondary. FC debut Barbados v Windward Islands (Bridgetown) 1990/91, Gau debut 2000/01. Bdr 1992/93-1994/95, GW 1998/99-1999/00, Barbados 1990/91-1997/98, Glamorgan 1994-1996. Tests: 2 for WI (1995-1998/99). LOIs: 15 for WI (1995-1996/97). HSTest 37 v SA (CT) 1998/99. BBTest 2-81 v Eng (Lord's) 1995. HSLOI 52 v Aus (Brisbane) 1995/96. BBLOI 5-40 v SL (Perth) 1995/96. HSFC 101* WI v Somerset (Taunton) 1995. BBFC 7-55 Bdr v Ntl (Dbn) 1994/95. HSSA 83* Bdr v Tvl (Jhb) 1992/93. HSLO 76 GW v Gau (Kby) 1998/99. BBLO 5-40 WI v SL (Perth) 1995/96. BBDLO 5-19 Bdr v GW (Kby) 1992/93. Tours: WI to Aus 1995/96; Eng 1995; Ind 1996/97; SA 1998/99; Shar 1995/96. COY 1993.

GIDLEY Martyn Ian (GW). B 30/9/68 Leicester, England. LHB OB. Ed Loughborough GS. FC debut Leics v Notts (Nottingham) 1989, GW debut 1994/95. Leicestershire 1989-1992, OFS 1993/94, OFSB 1990/91-1993/94. HSFC 160 GW v NtlB (Dbn) 1995/96. BBFC 5-48 OFS v NT (Bfn) 1993/94. HSSS 151 GW v Gau (Kby) 2000/01. HSLO 108* GW v FS (Bfn) 1996/97. BBLO 4-11 GW v Eas (Ben) 1996/97.

GILDER Gary Michael (KZN). B 6/7/74 Salisbury, Rhodesia. RHB LFM. Ed Northwood, Natal Technikon. Ntl Schools 1991-92, SA Schools 1992. FC debut NtlB v WT (Potch) 1994/95, Ntl debut 1996/97. HSFC 39 KZN v Gau (Jhb) 1998/99. BBFC 8-22 SAA v Worc (Worc) 1996. BBSA 6-61 KZN v WP (CT) 1999/00. HSLO 36 KZN v Eas (Ben) 2000/01. BBLO 6-25 Ntl v NW (Foch) 1997/98. Tours: SAA to Eng 1996; SL 1998/99. Soccer (Ntl Schools, Ntl U-19).

GOBIND Rivash (KZN). B 20/4/82 Durban. LHB RMF. Ed Effingham Secondary. KZN Schools 1998-99, SA Schools 1999. No FC, LO debut for KZN 2000/01. HSLO 14 KZN v SL (Chats) 2000/01. Tours: SA U-19 to NZ 2000/01 (capt), World Cup 2000.

GRACE Graham Vernon (EP). B 16/8/75 Salisbury, Rhodesia. LHB. Ed St Andrew's College (Gtn), PE Tech. EP Schools 1993- 94(C). FC debut EPB v NW (Potch) 1996/97, EP debut 1997/98. HSFC 112* EPB v NW (PE) 1997/98. HSSS 44 EP v Nor (PE) 1998/99. HSLO 62 EP v WP (CT) 1998/99. Hockey (EP U-19 1993).

GRAHAM Liam (Bdr). B 16/3/76 Johannesburg. RHB LFM. Ed St Stithians College. FC debut Bdr v WP (EL) 2000/01. HSFC 19 Bdr v WP (EL) 2000/01. BBFC 3-69 Bdr v WP (EL) 2000/01. HSLO 24* Bdr v NZ (Alice) 2000/01. BBLO 3-18 Bdr v Nor (Cent) 2000/01. HSDLO 10* Bdr v Nor (EL) 2000/01.

HALL Andrew James (Gau/SA). B 31/7/75 Johannesburg. RHB RFM. Ed Hoerskool Alberton. Tvl Schools 1993. FC debut Tvl v ZimA (Jhb) 1995/96. LOIs: 18 (1998/99-2000/01). HSLOI 81 v SL (Galle) 2000/01. BBLOI 2-8 v Aus (Melbourne-CS) 2000. HSFC 119 Gau v KZN (Jhb) 1998/99. BBFC 5-20 Gau v EP (Jhb) 1999/00. HSLO 129* Gau v Bdr (EL) 1999/00. BBLO 4-58 Gau v Nor (Jhb) 1999/00. Tours: SA to Aus 2000; SL 2000; Ken 2000/01; Sing 2000. Action Cricket (SA 1994).

HARRIS Paul Lee (WP). B 2/11/78 Salisbury, Rhodesia. RHB SLA. Ed Fish Hoek HS, CT College of Education. WP Schools 1996-97. FC debut WPB v EPB (PE) 1998/99, WP debut 2000/01. BBFC 3-56 WP v FS (CT) 2000/01.

HAYWARD Graham Sydney (EP). B 28/4/77 Uitenhage. RHB RM. FC debut EPB v KZNB (Dbn) 1998/99, LO debut for EP 2000/01. HSFC 56* EPB v KZNB (Dbn) 1998/99. BBFC 2-36 EPB v KZNB (Dbn) 1998/99. HSLO 10 EP v FS (PE) 2000/01.

HAYWARD Mornantau (Nantie) (EP). B 6/3/77 Uitenhage. RHB RF. Ed Daniel Pienaar Technical High. EP Schools 1994-95. SA Schools 1995. FC debut EPB v Zim Brd (Harare) 1995/96, EP debut 1996/97. Tests: 6 (1999/00-2000). LOIs: 17 (1998-2000). HSTest 13 v SL (Kandy) 2000. BBTest 4-75 v Eng (PE) 1999/00. BBLOI 4-31 v Ind (Sharjah) 1999/00. HSFC 55* EP v Bol (PE) 1997/98. BBFC 6-31 EP v Eas (PE) 1999/00. HSLO 19* EP v WP (CT) 1996/97. BBLO 5-37 EP v KZN (Dbn) 1998/99. Tours: SA to Aus 2000; Eng 1998; Ind 1999/00; SL 2000; Shar 1999/00; Sing 2000; SA U-19 to Ind 1995/96. COY 2000. Baseball (EP 1995).

HENDERSON Claude William (WP). B 14/6/72 Worcester. RHB SLA. Ed Worcester HS. Bol Schools 1988-90, SA Schools 1990. Brother of JM Henderson (Bol/BolB/TvlB 1994-2000). FC debut Bol v EP (Robertson) 1990/91, WP debut 1998/99. Bol 1990/91-1997/98. HSFC 53* Bol v Ntl (Stb) 1993/94. BBFC 7-57 Bol v EP (Paarl) 1994/95. HSLO 32 Worc CB v Kent CB (Kidderminster) 2000. BBLO 6-29 Bol v Eas (Paarl) 1997/98. HSDLO 27* WP v Gau (Jhb) 2000/01. Tours: SAA to SL 1998/99. Tennis, rugby, athletics, squash, golf.

HENDERSON James Michael (Bol). B 6/8/75 Worcester. LHB OB. Ed Worcester Gymnasium, Cape Technikon. Bol Schools 1991-93(C). Brother of CW Henderson (Bol/WP/WPB 1990-2000). FC debut BolB v OFSB (Bfn) 1994/95, scoring 122*, Bol debut same season. Bol 1994/95 and 1997/98-2000/01, BolB 1994/95-1995/96, TvlB 1996/97. HSFC 135 SAAc v NZAc (Krugersdorp) 1997/98. BBFC 3-13 Bol v FS (Stb) 1998/99. HSSS 117* Bol v FS (Stb) 1998/99. HSLO 83 Bol v Eas (Ben) 1998/99. BBLO 2-40 Bol v GW (Kby) 1998/99.

HENDERSON Tyron (Bdr). B 1/8/74 Durban. RHB RFM. Ed Durban HS, Univ Dbn Westville. Ntl Schools 1992. Grandson of JK Henderson (NET 1950/51), great nephew of WA Henderson (NET 1937-1946). FC debut Bdr v Bol (EL)

1998/99. HSFC 81 Bdr v Gau (Jhb) 1999/00. BBFC 6-56 Bdr v FS (Bfn) 2000/01. HSLO 59* Bdr v NW (Potch) 1999/00. BBLO 5-5 Bdr v WP (EL) 1998/99.

HERBST Francois (Gau). B 17/7/77 Boksburg. RHB RM. Ed Hoerskool Oosterlig, RAU. Eas Schools 1995. FC debut Gau v GW (Jhb) 2000/01. HSFC 35* Gau v KZN (Dbn) 2000/01. Rugby (Falcons U-21 1998-1999).

HEWITT Glen Michael (NW). B 16/4/73 Johannesburg. RHB OB. Ed Jeppe HS, Wits Univ. TvlB Schools 1990. FC debut TvlB v BdrB (EL) 1993/94, NW debut 1996/97. HSFC 151 NW v KZN (Potch) 1999/00. HSLO 108 NW v FS (Foch) 1996/97.

HLONGWANE Bongwa Benjamin Nduduzu (KZN). B 8/7/81 Pietermaritzburg. RHB RFM. Glenwood HS, Varsity College. KZN Schools 1999. No FC, LO debut for KZN 2000/01.

HORAN Brendan Patrick (Gau) B 17/9/74 Cape Town. RHB RMF. Ed Grey HS (PE), Rhodes Univ. EP Schools 1991-92, SA Schools 1992. FC debut Bdr v Ntl (EL) 1995/96, Gau debut 2000/01. Bdr 1995/96-1996/97, BdrB 1995/96. HSFC 28 BdrB v Eas (Spr) 1995/96. BBFC 4-43 Bdr v WP (CT) 1995/96. HSSS 23 Gau v KZN (Dbn) 2000/01. HSLO 10 Bdr v WP (CT) 1995/96 and 10 Bdr v Tvl (Jhb) 1996/97. BBLO 3-40 Bdr v FS (Bfn) 1995/96. Hockey (EP Settlers 1992).

HUDSON Andrew Charles (KZN). B 17/3/65 Eshowe. RHB RM. Ed Kearsney College. Ntl Schools 1982. FC debut NtlB v GW (Kby) 1984/85, Ntl debut 1986/87. Tests: 35 (1991/92-1997/98). LOIs: 89 (1991/92-1997/98). HSTest 163 v WI (Bridgetown) 1991/92, on debut. HSLOI 161 v Holl (Rawalpindi) 1995/96. HSFC 206 Ntl v Gau (Dbn) 1997/98. HSLO 161 SA v Holl (Rawalpindi) 1995/96. HSDLO 109 Ntl v WT (Foch) 1995/96. Tours: SA to Aus 1993/94; Eng 1994; Ind 1991/92, 1993/94, 1996/97; NZ 1994/95; Pak 1994/95, 1997/98; SL 1993/94; WI 1991/92; Zim 1995/96; Ken 1996/97; Shar 1995/96; World Cup 1992, 1996. COY 1992.

JACKSON Kenneth Conrad (Bol). B 16/8/64 Kitwe, N Rhodesia. RHB RM. Ed Rondebosch BHS. WP Schools 1987-88. Half brother of IJL Trott (Bol 1999-2000). FC debut WPB v Bdr (EL) 1988/89, Bol debut 1993/94. WP 1990/91-1993/94, WPB 1988/89-1991/92. HSFC 150 WPB v NtlB (Dbn) 1990/91. BBFC 2-18 WP v Bdr (CT) 1991/92. HSSS 120 Bol v EP (Paarl) 1996/97. HSLO 105* Bol v GW (Kby) 1995/96. BBLO 3-24 Holland v Lanc CB (Liverpool) 1999. BBDLO 2-9 Bol v EP (PE) 1998/99.

JACOBS Arno (NW). B 13/3/77 Potchefstroom. LHB WK. Ed Hoer Volkskool (Potch), Potch Univ. WT Schools 1993-95. Brother of S Jacobs (Gau/TvlB 1987-1999). FC debut NW v WPB (Potch) 1997/98, scoring 112. HSFC 112 NW v WPB (Potch) 1997/98. HSSS 66 NW v KZN (Potch) 1999/00. HSLO 116* NW v KZN (Potch) 1999/00.

JENNINGS Dylan (Eas). B 14/9/79 Johannesburg. LHB WK. Ed King Edward VII. Gau Schools 1996-97. Son of RV Jennings (Tvl/TvlB/NT/SA 1973-1992). FC debut SAAc v Ire (Lurgan) 1999, Eas debut 2000/01. Gau 1999/2000. HSFC 53 Eas v WP (CT) 2000/01. HSLO 27 Eas v Bol (Ben) 2000/01.

JOHNSON Neil Clarkson (WP) B 24/1/70 Salisbury, Rhodesia. LHB RFM. Ed Howick HS, Kingswood College, UPE. EP Schools 1988, SA Schools 1988. FC debut EPB v NtlB (PE) 1989/90, WP debut 2000/01. EPB 1989/90-1991/92, KZN 1992/93-1997/98, Leicestershire 1997, Hampshire 2001. Tests: 13 for Zim (1998/99-2000). LOIs: 48 for Zim (1998/99-2000). HSTest 107 v Pak (Peshawar) 1998/99. BBTest 4-77 v WI (Kingston) 1999/00. HSLOI 132* v Aus (Lord's) 1999. BBLOI 4-42 v Ken (Taunton) 1999. HSFC 150 Leic v Lanc (Leicester) 1997. BBFC 5-79 Ntl v Bol (Stb) 1993/94. HSSA 136 Ntl v Bdr (EL) 1993/94. HSLO 146* Ntl v GW (Kby) 1996/97. BBLO 4-19 Ntl v Ken (Dbn) 1996/97. Tours: Zim to Eng 2000; Pak 1998/99; SA 1999/00; WI 1999/00; Ban 1998/99 (x 2); Ken 1999/00; Shar 1998/99; Sing 1999; World Cup 1999; SAA to Zim 1994/95.

JORDAAN Deon (Eas). B 3/12/70 Bloemfontein. LHB RM. Ed Grey College (Bfn), UOFS. FC debut OFSB v WPB (CT) 1991/92, Eas debut 1999/00. OFSB 1991/92, GW 1992/93, WP/WPB 1993/94-1994/95, FS 1995/96-1996/97, Nor/NorB 1997/98-1998/99. HSFC 123 GW v EP (Kby) 1992/93. BBFC 3-9 Eas v Gau (Jhb) 1999/00. HSSS 117 FS v Bdr (Bfn) 1996/97. HSLO 116 WP v Imp (CT) 1993/94.

JORDAAN Lucas Cornelius Rudolph (Corrie) (NW). B 20/7/63 Johannesburg. RHB SLA. Ed Roodepoort HS. FC debut TvlB v WPB (CT) 1990/91, NW debut 1996/97. Tvl 1991/92, TvlB 1990/91-1991/92, Eas 1991/92-1995/96. HSFC 20* NW v Gau (Potch) 2000/01. BBFC 6-30 NW v WPB (CT) 1998/99. BBSS 2-69 NW v WP (CT) 1999/00. BBLO 3-25 NW v Nor (Foch) 1997/98.

JOUBERT Pierre (Nor). B 2/5/78 Pretoria. RHB RFM. Ed Eldoraigne High School. NT Schools 1993-96, SA Schools 1995-96. FC debut NTB v TvlB (Jhb) 1995/96, NT debut 1996/97. HSFC 72* Nor v EP (PE) 2000/01. BBFC 5-10 Nor v EP (PE) 2000/01. HSLO 50* Nor v Gau (Jhb) 1999/00. BBLO 3-23 Nor v Gau (Jhb) 1998/99. Tours: SA U-19 to Eng 1995; Ind 1995/96. SA U-19 v Pak U-19 1996/97.

KALLIS Jacques Henry (WP/SA). B 16/10/75 Pinelands, Cape Town. RHB RFM. Ed Wynberg BHS. WP Schools 1991-93, SA Schools 1993. FC debut WPB v WT (Potch) 1993/94, WP debut 1994/95. Middlesex 1997. Glamorgan 1999. Tests: 50 (1995/96-2000/01). LOIs: 126 (1995/96-2000/01). HSTest 160 v NZ (Bfn) 2000/01. BBTest 6-67 v WI (Bridgetown) 2000/01. HSLOI 113* v SL (Dhaka) 1998/99. BBLOI 5-30 v WI (Dhaka) 1998/99. HSFC 186* WP v Qld (Brisbane) 1995/96. BBFC 6-60 WP v Bol (Paarl) 1999/00. HSSA 160 SA v NZ (Bfn) 2000/01. HSSS 146 WP v Tvl (CT) 1995/96. HSLO 155* Glam v Sur (Pontypridd) 1999. BBLO 5-30 SA v WI (Dhaka) 1998/99. HSDLO 116* WP v EP (PE) 1994/95. BBDLO 5-47 WP v EP (CT) 2000/01. Tours: SA to Aus 1997/98, 2000; Eng 1998; Ind 1999/00; NZ 1998/99; Pak 1997/98; SL 2000; WI 2000/01; Zim 1999/00; Ban 1998/99; Ken 1999/00, 2000/01; Shar 1995/96, 1999/00; Sing 2000; World Cup 1996, 1999; SAA to Eng 1996; SA U-24 to SL 1995/96. COY 1999, 2000.

KEMP Justin Miles (EP/SA/Pres). B 2/10/77 Queenstown. RHB RFM. Ed Queens College, UPE. Bdr Schools 1995. Son of JW Kemp (Bdr 1975-1976), grandson of JM Kemp (Bdr 1947/48), cousin of DJ Callaghan (EP/EPB/GW/Notts 1983-

2000). FC debut EPB v NW (Potch) 1996/97, EP debut 1997/98. Tests: 3 (2000/01). LOIs: 6 (2000/01). HSTest 16 v WI (St John's) 2000/01. BBTest 3-33 v SL (Cent) 2000/01. HSLOI 46 v WI (Port-of-Spain) 2000/01. BBLOI 3-54 v WI (St George's) 2000/01. HSFC 188 EP v NW (PE) 2000/01. BBFC 6-56 EP v Bdr (PE) 2000/01. HSLO 95* EP v Bol (PE) 2000/01. BBLO 6-20 EP v FS (PE) 2000/01. Tours: SA to WI 2000/01; SAA to WI 2000/01; SA U-19 to Ind 1995/96.

KENT John Carter (KZN). B 7/5/79 Cape Town. RHB RMF. Ed Durban HS & UNISA. Ntl Schools 1996-97, SA Schools 1997. FC debut NtlB v NorB (Cent) 1997/98, KZN debut 1998/99. HSFC 178* KZN v EP (Dbn) 2000/01. BBFC 6-77 KZN v Eas (Ben) 2000/01. HSLO 81* KZN v WA (Perth) 2000/01. BBLO 4-29 KZN v EP (Dbn) 2000/01. HSDLO 71 KZN v Bdr (Dbn) 1999/00. SA U-19 v Eng U-19 1997/98; World Cup 1998. Hockey (Ntl U18, 1996/97).

KIDWELL Errol Wayne (GW). B 6/6/75 Vereeniging. RHB RF. Ed Riverside High, Technikon SA. Tvl Schools 1993. FC debut TvlB v NTB (Jhb) 1995/96, GW debut 1999/00. Gau 1995/96-1998/99, TvlB 1995/96-1996/97. HSFC 27* TvlB v EPB (Jhb) 1996/97. BBFC 7-58 Gau v Nor (Jhb) 1997/98. HSSS 25 GW v NW (Potch) 1999/00. HSLO 37* Gau v GW (Jhb) 1998/99. BBLO 5-36 Tvl v Eas (Jhb) 1996/97.

KIRSTEN Gary (WP/SA). B 23/11/67 Cape Town. LHB OB. Ed Rondebosch BHS, UCT. WP Schools 1983-85, SA Schools 1985(C). Son of N Kirsten (Bdr 1946-1960), brother of PN Kirsten (WP/Bdr/Sus/Derbs/SA 1973-1996), AM Kirsten (WPB 1986-1989) and P Kirsten (GW/WP/WPB 1992-1999). FC debut WPB v Bol (Stb) 1987/88, WP debut 1988/89. Tests: 73 (1993/94-2000/01, 1 as captain). LOIs: 154 (1993/94-2000/01). HSTest 275 v Eng (Durban) 1999/00, joint SA Test record. HSLOI 188* v UAE (Rawalpindi) 1995/96. HSFC 275 SA v Eng (Dbn) 1999/00. BBFC 6-68 WP v NT (Vbg) 1993/94. HSSS 244 WP v Bdr (EL) 1995/96. HSLO 188* SA v UAE (Rawalpindi) 1995/96. HSDLO 104* WP v EP (PE) 1995/96. Tours: SA to Aus 1993/94, 1997/98, 2000; Eng 1994, 1998; Ind 1996/97, 1999/00; NZ 1994/95, 1998/99; Pak 1994/95, 1997/98; SL 2000; WI 2000/01; Zim 1995/96; Ken 1996/97, 2000/01; Shar 1995/96, 1999/00; Sing 2000; World Cup 1996, 1999. COY 1994, 1995, 1996. Rugby (WP Craven Week).

KLOPPER Johan Wilhelm Francois (Bdr). B 4/10/72 Grahamstown. RHB RM. Ed Port Alfred HS. FC debut Bdr v Eas (EL) 2000/01. LO debut for Bdr 1997/98. BBLO 2-39 Bdr v Gau (Jhb) 2000/01.

KLUSENER Lance (KZN/SA). B 4/9/71 Durban. LHB RFM. Ed Durban HS. FC debut NtlB v BdrB (EL) 1993/94, Ntl same season. Tests: 42 (1996/97-2000/01). LOIs: 113 (1995/96-2000/01). HSTest 174 v Eng (PE) 1999/00. BBTest 8-64 v Ind (Calcutta) 1996/97, on debut. HSLOI 103* v NZ (Auckland) 1998/99. BBLOI 6-49 v SL (Lahore) 1997/98. HSFC 174 SA v Eng (PE) 1999/00. BBFC 8-34 Ntl v WP (Dbn) 1995/96. HSSS 75 Ntl v EP (PE) 1994/95. HSLO 142* SA v Northants (Northampton) 1998. BBLO 6-49 SA v SL (Lahore) 1997/98. HSDLO 91 Ntl v WT (Foch) 1995/96. BBDLO 4-19 Ntl v OFS (Bfn) 1994/95. Tours: SA to Aus 1997/98, 2000; Eng 1998; Ind 1996/97, 1999/00; NZ 1998/99; Pak 1997/98; SL 2000; WI 2000/01; Zim 1999/00; Ken 1999/00, 2000/01; Shar 1999/00; Sing 2000; World Cup 1999; SAA to Eng 1996; SA U-24 to SL 1995/96. COY 1997, 1999. Wisden 2000.

KOCH Donovan Marius (Bol). B 11/10/76 Somerset West. RHB RMF. Ed Hottentots Holland HS. WP Schools 1994. FC debut WPB v NtlB (CT) 1997/98, Bol debut 1998/99. HSFC 54 WPB v EPB (Bellville) 1997/98. BBFC 5-128 Bol v GW (Paarl) 1998/99. HSSS 28 Bol v GW (Paarl) 1998/99. HSLO 26* Bol v WP (CT) 1998/99 and 26 Bol v KZN (Paarl) 1999/00. BBLO 3-25 Bol v WP (CT) 1998/99. Action Cricket (SA U23, 1994).

KOEN Louis Johannes (Bol). B 28/3/67 Paarl. RHB. Ed Paarl Gymnasium. Bol Schools 1984-85, SA Schools 1985. Brother of PA Koen (WPB/Bol 1984-1990). FC debut WPB v EPB (PE) 1987/88, Bol debut 1990/91. WPB 1987/88-1989/90, EP 1991/92-1998/99. EPB 1993/94, Bol 1990/91-1991/92 and 1999/00-2000/01. LOIs: 5 (1996/97-1999/00). HSLOI 28 v Eng (EL) 1999/00. HSFC 202* EP v Bol (PE) 1995/96. HSLO 151 EP v GW (Kby) 1998/99.

KOENIG Sven Gaetan (Gau). B 9/12/73 Durban. LHB OB. Ed Hilton College, UCT. Ntl Schools 1989-91, SA Schools 1991. FC debut WPB v ET (Spr) 1993/94, Gau debut 1997/98. WP/WPB 1993/94-1996/97. HSFC 155 Gau v GW (Kby) 2000/01. HSLO 109 Gau v Bdr (Jhb) 2000/01. Tours: SAA to Eng 1996.

KOORTZEN Pieter Petrus Johannes (GW). B 24/9/79 Kimberley. RHB OB. Ed Diamantveld HS. SACD Schools 1993, GW Schools 1994-1996. FC debut GW v WP (Kby) 1996/97. HSFC 127 GW v Ban (Kby) 2000/01. HSSS 102 GW v Gau (Kby) 2000/01. BBFC 3-60 GWB v EPB (PE) 1998/99. BBSS 2-78 GW v WP (Kby) 1996/97. HSLO 134 GW v NW (Kby) 2000/01. BBLO 3-37 GW v Nor (Kby) 2000/01. Rugby (GW Craven Week).

KREUSCH Justin Peter (Bdr). B 27/9/79 East London. RHB RM. Ed Selborne College, Rhodes Univ. Bdr Schools 1995-1997. FC debut Bdr v Gau (Jhb) 1999/00. HSFC 29 v KZN (EL) 1999/00. HSLO 77 Bdr v Gau (EL) 1999/00.

KRUGER Alan Kevin (GW). B 16/2/81 Kimberley. RHB RMF. Ed Floors Comprehensive. GW Schools 1997-99. FC debut GW v Ban (Kby) 2000/01. HSFC 48 GW v Ban (Kby) 2000/01. Hockey (GW 1996).

KRUGER Garnett John-Peter (EP). B 5/1/77 Port Elizabeth. RHB RMF. Ed Gelvan High, Russel Road College. EP Schools 1995. FC debut EPB v Eas (Ben) 1997/98, EP debut 1999/00. HSFC 58 SAA v Wind Isl (Arnos Vale) 2000/01. BBFC 7-64 EP v Bdr (EL) 1999/00. HSSA 22 EPB v NW (PE) 1997/98. HSSS 13* EP v Nor (PE) 2000/01. BBLO 6-23 EP v NW (PE) 1999/00. Tours: SAA to WI 2000/01.

KRUIS Gideon Jacobus (GW). B 9/5/74 Pretoria. RHB RFM. Ed St Albans College. NT Schools 1991-93, SA Schools 1993. FC debut NTB v OFSB (Bfn) 1993/94, GW debut 1997/98. NT 1995/96-1996/97, NTB 1993/94-1995/96. HSFC 59 GW v Ban (Kby) 2000/01. BBFC 7-58 GW v Nor (Cent) 1997/98. HSSS 57* GW v NW (Potch) 1999/00. HSLO 28* GW v WP (Kby) 2000/01. BBLO 4-26 GW v Bol (Kby) 1999/00.

LAING Dean Ralph (Gau). B 18/9/70 Durban. RHB RM. Ed Bedfordview, Jeppe BHS, RAU. Tvl Schools 1985-88, SA Schools 1987-88. Nephew of KR Cooper (Ntl/NtlB 1973-1985). FC debut TvlB v NTB (Jhb) 1989/90, Tvl same season.

Nottinghamshire 1990. HSFC 128 Tvl v EP (Jhb) 1996/97. BBFC 3-18 Tvl v EP (Jhb) 1993/94. HSLO 85 Tvl v Bol (Jhb) 1993/94. BBLO 4-16 Tvl v GW (Jhb) 1996/97. Soccer (SA Schools, Tvl Currie Cup), Baseball (SA Junior Springbok).

LANGEVELDT Charl Kenneth (Bol/Pres). B 17/12/74 Stellenbosch. RHB RFM. Ed Luckhoff Secondary. WP Senior Schools 1990-92. FC debut Bol v Nor (Cent) 1997/98. HSFC 56 Bol v EP (PE) 1999/00. BBFC 5-19 Bol v FS (Paarl) 2000/01. HSLO 19* Bol v EP (Paarl) 1999/00. BBLO 5-7 SA Pres v Ban (Pmb) 2000/01. BBDLO 5-35 Bol v WP (Paarl) 1999/00. Tours: SAA to WI 2000/01. Soccer (WP 1989-91).

LAVINE Mark John (NW). B 4/3/73 Black Bess, St Peter, Barbados. D 12/5/01, Coventry, England. RHB RF. FC debut Barbados v Leeward Islands (Nevis) 1992/93, NW debut 1996/97. Barbados 1992/93. HSFC 113 NW v Bdr (Potch) 2000/01. BBFC 6-53 NW v Bol (Paarl) 2000/01. HSLO 72 NW v GW (Potch) 1999/00 and 72 NW v FS (Potch) 2000/01. BBLO 2-22 Barbados v Trinidad & Tobago (Bridgetown) 1992/93. BBDLO 2-25 NW v Eas (Potch) 2000/01.

LAWSON Andrew Grant (NW). B 4/3/67 Durban. LHB SLA. Ed Parktown BHS. Tvl Schools 1985. FC debut Bdr v OFS (Bfn) 1991/92, scoring 117* and carrying his bat, NW debut 1997/98. Bdr 1991/92-1994/95, BdrB 1994/95, EP/EPB 1995/96. HSFC 117* Bdr v OFS (Bfn) 1991/92. HSLO 99* Bdr v OFS (EL) 1991/92.

LETSHELA Seate Lavious (Sonnyboy) (Gau). B 5/10/81 Krugersdorp. RHB LB. Ed Ahmed Timol. Gau Schools 1998-2000. No FC, LO debut for Gau 2000/01. HSLO 26* Gau v NW (Potch) 2000/01. Soccer (Kaizer Chiefs Youth 1996).

LEWIS Mohammad Rasheed (FS). B 24/4/75 Cape Town. RHB RMF. Ed Bridgetown HS. WP Schools 1993-94. FC debut WPB v KZNB (Dbn) 1998/99, FS debut 2000/01. WPB 1998/99. HSFC 49* FS v Eas (Ben) 2000/01. BBFC 2-44 FS v Nor (Cent) 2000/01.

LIEBENBERG Gerhardus Frederick Johannes (FS). B 7/4/72 Upington. RHB RFM WK. Ed Diamantveld HS. GW Schools 1987-90, SA Schools 1989-90. FC debut GW v WPB (Kby) 1989/90, OFS debut 1990/91. GW 1989/90-1990/91. Tests: 5 (1997/98-1998). LOIs: 4 (1995/96-1998). HSTest 45 v SL (Cent) 1997/98. HSLOI 39 v Eng (Manchester) 1998. HSFC 229 FS v Ntl (Bfn) 1995/96. HSLO 170* SA U-24 v SL U-24 (Moratuwa) 1995/96. HSDLO 114* FS v Nor (Bfn) 1998/99. Tours: SA to Eng 1994, 1998; Zim 1995/96; SAA to Zim 1994/95; Eng 1996. SA U-24 to SL 1995/96. Tennis (GW 1982-87), Athletics (GW 1989).

LIGHT Craig (NW). B 23/9/72 Randburg. RHB OB. Ed Monument HS. Tvl Schools 1989-91. FC debut OFSB v Zim Brd (Har) 1993/94, NW debut 1998/99. FS/FSB 1993/94-1995/96, GW 1996/97-1997/98. HSFC 121 OFSB v ET (Spr) 1994/95. BBFC 4-42 NW v GW (Potch) 1999/00. HSSS 108 NW v GW (Potch) 1999/00. HSLO 93* GW v Bdr (EL) 1997/98. BBLO 3-25 NW v Bol (Potch) 1999/00.

LOUW Johann (GW). B 12/4/79 Cape Town. RHB RMF. Ed Moregrove, Hoerskool Fraserburg, UPE. FC debut GW v Nor (Cent) 2000/01. HSFC 50 GW v KZN (Dbn) 2000/01. BBFC 3-25 GW v Gau (Jhb) 2000/01. HSLO 72 GW v Nor (Kby) 2000/01. BBLO 5-43 GW v NW (Kby) 2000/01.

LOVE Geoff Terry (Bdr). B 19/9/76 Port Elizabeth. RHB OB. Ed Selborne College, UPE. Bdr Schools 1994. FC debut BdrB v NtlB (Dbn) 1995/96, Bdr debut 1998/99. BdrB 1995/96, EP 1996/97-1997/98, EPB 1996/97. HSFC 85* Bdr v WP (CT) 1998/99. BBFC 7-116 Bdr v WP (CT) 2000/01. HSLO 23* Bdr v Bol (EL) 1999/00. BBLO 2-28 Bdr v Eas (Ben) 2000/01. Hockey (Bdr Schools 1994).

MABHENA Elite Funyana (Eas). B 14/5/80 Alexandra, Johannesburg. RHB. Ed Parktown BHS. Gau Schools 1997-98. Cousin of WB Masimula (Gau 1998-2000). FC debut Eas v Bdr (EL) 2000/01. HSLO 17* Eas v GW (Ben) 2000/01.

MacQUEEN Robert Bruce (KZN). B 6/9/77 Durban. RHB OB. Ed Durban HS, UNISA. NtlB Schools 1994-95. FC debut NtlB v EPB (Dbn) 1996/97, Ntl debut 1997/98. HSFC 42 NtlB v EPB (Dbn) 1996/97 and 42 KZN v GW (Kby) 2000/01. BBFC 5-125 Ntl v WP (Dbn) 1997/98. HSLO 45* KZN v Eas (Dbn) 1998/99. BBLO 3-57 Ntl v Gau (Jhb) 1997/98. SA U-19 v Pak U-19 1996/97.

MAFA Johnson Tumelo (Gau). B 5/2/78 Johannesburg. RHB RFM. Ed Sparrow School. Tvl Schools 1996. FC debut Gau v SL (Jhb) 1997/98. BBFC 6-62 Gau v GW (Jhb) 2000/01. BBLO 3-33 Gau v Bol (Jhb) 1999/00.

MAGIET Rashaad (WP). B 30/5/79 Cape Town. RHB LB. Ed SACS. WP Schools 1996-97. Son of S Magiet (WP SACB 1971- 1990), nephew of R Magiet (WP SACB 1971-1980, Convenor National Selectors). FC debut WPB v NW (CT) 1998/99, WP debut 1999/00. HSFC 122 WPB v KZNB (Dbn) 1998/99. HSSS 46 WP v KZN (CT) 1999/00.

MAKALIMA Dumisa Liko (Bdr). B 29/12/80 King William's Town. RHB OB. Ed Dale College. Bdr Schools 1996-97. FC debut Bdr v FS (EL) 1997/98. HSFC 78 Bdr/EP v SLA (PE) 1999/00. HSSS 42* Bdr v WP (CT) 2000/01. HSLO 28 Bdr v NZ (Alice) 2000/01. HSDLO 25* Bdr v WP (CT) 2000/01. Tours: SA U-19 to World Cup 2000.

MALL Ashraf (KZN). B 8/10/78 Durban. LHB. Ed Loghart Islamia. NtlB Schools 1994-95, Ntl Schools 1996. FC debut NtlB v WPB (Dbn) 1996/97, KZN debut 1998/99. HSFC 86 KZNB v Eas (Ben) 1998/99. HSSS 72 KZN v WP (CT) 1998/99. HSLO 77 KZN v Bol (Dbn) 2000/01.

MANACK Hussein Ahmed (Gau). B 10/4/68 Pretoria. RHB RM. Ed Topaz High, Wits Univ, UNISA. Tvl High Schools SACOS 1983-84. Cousin of AH Manack (Tvl/TvlB 1991-1992). FC debut Tvl v OFS (Vga) 1991/92. Gau 1991/92-1997/98 and 2000/01, TvlB 1991/92-1996/97, Eas 1998/99-1999/00. HSFC 173 TvlB v WPB (CT) 1996/97. HSSS 25 Gau v FS (Jhb) 1997/98. HSLO 28 SA Inv v Ind (Pmb) 1992/93. HSDLO 19 Eas v KZN (Dbn) 1998/99.

MASIMULA Walter Bafana (Gau). B 23/10/75 Alexandra, Johannesburg. RHB RF. Ed West Bank High. Tvl Schools 1992-93. Cousin of EF Mabhena (Eas 2000/01). FC debut Gau v Bol (Jhb) 1998/99. HSFC 22 Gau v FS (Bfn) 2000/01. BBFC 4-35 Gau v EP (Jhb) 1999/00. HSLO 14 Gau v EP (Jhb) 2000/01. Tours: SA U-19 to Eng 1995.

MATABOGE Tshepo Khotso (Nicholas) (Gau). B 18/11/78 Soweto. RHB LFM. Ed Masekheng HP, Thloohore SS, Jhb Training College. Gau Schools 1997. FC debut Gau v KZN (Jhb) 2000/01. HSLO 10 Gau v NW (Potch) 2000/01.

MATOMELA Mzuvukile (Mats) (Bdr). B 28/4/80 Mdantsane. RHB RF. Ed Cambridge HS. Bdr Schools 1998-99. FC debut Bdr v NZ (EL) 2000/01. Hockey (Bdr U-21, 2000).

McKENZIE Neil Douglas (Nor/SA). B 24/11/75 Johannesburg. RHB RM. Ed King Edward VII, RAU. Tvl Schools 1992-94, SA Schools 1993-94(C). Son of KA McKenzie (NET/Tvl/TvlB/SA 1966-1986). FC debut TvlB v EPB (PE) 1994/95, Nor debut 1999/00. Gau 1995/96-1998/99, TvlB 1995/96. Tests: 14 (2000-2000/01). LOIs: 26 (1999/00-2000/01). HSTest 120 v NZ (PE) 2000/01. HSLOI 120* v SL (EL) 2000/01. HSFC 175 Nor v Gau (Cent) 1999/00. HSLO 120* SA v SL (EL) 2000/01. BBLO 2-19 Gau v GW (Kby) 1997/98. HSDLO 118 Tvl v NW (Foch) 1996/97. Tours: SA to Aus 2000; Ind 1999/00; SL 2000; WI 2000/01; Ken 2000/01; Shar 1999/00; Sing 2000; SA U-19 to Eng 1995(C). COY 2001.

McLAREN Adrian Peter (GW). B 21/4/80 Kimberley. RHB WK. Ed Kimberley BHS. GW Schools 1996-98. Son of K McLaren (GW 1971-1984), nephew of P McLaren (GW 1977-1994). FC debut GWB v NorB (Cent) 1998/99, GW debut 1999/00. HSFC 67 GWB v EPB (PE) 1998/99. HSSS 27 GW v KZN (Kby) 2000/01. HSLO 12 GW v WP (Kby) 2000/01. Hockey (GW 1998).

MITCHELL Ian (Bdr). B 14/12/77 Johannesburg. LHB RM WK. Ed Queens College. Bdr Schools 1994-95. SA U-19 B 1995. FC debut BdrB v FSB (Bfn) 1995/96, Bdr debut 1997/98. HSFC 96 Bdr v WP (CT) 1998/99. BBFC 2-0 Bdr v EP (PE) 2000/01. HSLO 67 Bdr v NW (EL) 2000/01. SA U-19 v Pak U-19 1996/97.

MOKOENANYANA Ernest Teboho (Eas). B 15/8/76 Bloemfontein. LHB LFM. Ed Moemedi SS. Brother of TJ Mokoenanyana (FS 1999-2000). FC debut OFSB v NTB (Bfn) 1993/94, Eas debut 2000/01. OFSB 1993/94, NorB 1997/98. HSFC 28 Eas v EP (Ben) 2000/01.

MOKOENANYANA Tseko Johannes (FS). B 5/12/77 Bloemfontein. LHB SLA. Brother of ET Mokoenanyana (OFSB/NorB/Eas 1993-2000). FC debut FS v Bol (Paarl) 2000/01, LO debut 1999/00. Tennis (FS 1992), Volleyball (FS 1992).

MORKEL Johannes Albertus (Albie) (Eas/Pres). B 10/6/81 Vereeniging. LHB RMF. Ed Hoerskool Vereeniging. Gau Schools 1997-98. SA Schools 1998. FC debut Eas v Nor (Ben) 1999/00. HSFC 117 Eas v NW (Ben) 2000/01. BBFC 6-36 Eas v GW (Kby) 1999/00. HSLO 40 Eas v Bol (Paarl) 1999/00. BBLO 4-23 v FS (Bfn) 1999/00. Tours: SA U-19 to World Cup 2000.

MPITSANG Phenyo Victor (FS). B 28/3/80 Kimberley. RHB RFM. Ed Grey College (Bfn). FS Schools 1996-97, SA Schools 1997(T). FC debut FS v Bdr (EL) 1997/98. LOIs: 2 (1998/99-1999/00). BBLOI 2-49 v WI (Bfn) 1998/99. HSFC 23 FS v WP (CT) 2000/01. BBFC 5-24 FS v NW (Bfn) 2000/01. HSLO 20* FS v KZN (Dbn) 1999/00. BBLO 3-26 FS v WP (Bfn) 1999/00. Tours: SA to NZ 1998/99; Ken 1999/00; SAA to WI 2000/01. SA U-19 v Pak U-19 1996/97; v EngU-19 1997/98; World Cup 1998.

MUNNIK Renier (WP). B 7/1/78 Cape Town. RHB RFM. Ed Hoerskool Tygerberg. WP Schools 1994-1996, SA Schools 1996. FC debut WPB v NtlB (CT) 1997/98, WP debut 1998/99. HSFC 138 WPB v GWB (Kby) 1998/99. BBFC 4-58 WP v Nor (Cent) 2000/01. HSSS 64 WP v Gau (Jhb) 1998/99. HSLO 29 WP v EP (CT) 1998/99. BBLO 4-50 WP v Gau (Jhb) 2000/01. SA U-19 v Pak U-19 1996/97.

MURRAY Denys Wayne (EP). B 29/7/77 Graaff-Reinet. RHB WK. Ed St Andrews College, PE Technikon. EP Schools 1993-95. FC debut EPB v NtlB (PE) 1997/98, EP debut 1999/00. HSFC 103* EPB v WPB (Bellville) 1997/98. HSSS 58* EP v Eas (Ben) 2000/01. HSLO 57 EP v Eas (PE) 2000/01. Rugby (EP Schools 1995), Squash (EP Schools 1993).

MYBURGH Johannes Gerhardus (Nor). B 22/10/80 Pretoria. RHB OB. Ed Pretoria BHS. Nor Schools 1996-98, SA Schools 1997. FC debut NorB v WPB (Cent) 1997/98, Nor debut 1999/00. HSFC 203 NorB v Eas (Pta) 1997/98, the youngest South African to score a first-class double century at 17 years, 122 days. HSSS 68 Nor v EP (PE) 2000/01. HSLO 95 Nor v Eas (Cent) 2000/01. BBLO 2-27 Nor v KZN (Dbn) 2000/01 Tours: SA U-19 to Pak 1998/99; World Cup 2000. SA U-19 v Eng U-19 1997/98; World Cup 1998.

NDIMA Solomzi Solomon (Solly) (Gau). B 16/5/77 Johannesburg. RHB. Ed Boston City Campus. FC debut Gau v FS (Jhb) 1999/00. HSFC 38 Gau v GW (Jhb) 2000/01. HSLO 22 Gau v NZ (Soweto) 2000/01. HSDLO 12 Gau v EP (Jhb) 1999/00.

NEL Andre (Eas/Pres). B 15/7/77 Germiston. RHB RFM. Ed Dr EG Jansen (Boksburg). FC debut Eas v TvlB (Ben) 1996/97. LOIs: 1 (2000/01). BBLOI 3-20 v WI (Port-of-Spain) 2000/01. HSFC 44 Eas v FS (Ben) 2000/01. BBFC 5-43 Eas v FS (Ben) 2000/01. HSLO 17* Eas v EP (Ben) 1997/98. BBLO 6-27 Eas v GW (Ben) 2000/01. Tours: SA to WI 2000/01.

NGAM Mfuneko (EP/SA/Pres) 29/1/79 Middledrift. RHB RFM. Ed Douglas Mbopha. EP Schools 1996-97, SA Schools 1997 (R), SA U18 Colts 1997. FC debut EPB v NorB (PE) 1997/98, EP debut 1999/00. Tests: 3 (2000/01). BBTest 3-26 v SL (CT) 2000/01. HSFC 18* EP v KZN (Dbn) 2000/01. BBFC 4-25 EPB v GWB (PE) 1998/99. BBSS 4-78 EP v WP (PE) 2000/01. BBLO 4-20 SA Pres v Ban (Dbn) 2000/01. BBDLO 4-26 EP v Bol (PE) 2000/01. Tours: SAA to WI 2000/01. COY 2001.

NIEWOUDT Riaan (NW). B 8/5/76 Cradock. RHB RM. Ed Pietersburg HS. FC debut NW v Nor (Potch) 2000/01. HSFC 98 NW v EP (PE) 2000/01. HSLO 41 NW v Gau (Potch) 2000/01.

NTINI Makhaya (Bdr/SA). B 6/7/77 Mdingi. RHB RF. Ed Dale College, EL Technical College. Bdr Schools 1994-95, SA Schools 1995. FC debut Bdr v Eng (EL) 1995/96. Tests: 15 (1997/98-2000/01). LOIs: 23 (1997/98-2000/01). HSTest: 11 v WI (Georgetown) 2000/01. BBTest 6-66 v NZ (Bfn) 2000/01. BBLOI 5-37 v SL (CT) 2000/01. HSFC 34* Bdr v Gau (Jhb) 1999/00. BBFC 6-49 Bdr v WP (CT) 1996/97. BBLO 5-37 SA v SL (CT) 2000/01. BBDLO 5-38 Bdr v NW (Foch) 1997/98.

Tours: SA to Aus 1997/98, 2000; Eng 1998; SL 2000; WI 2000/01; Ken 2000/01; Shar 1999/00; Sing 2000; SA U-19 to Eng 1995; Ind 1995/96. COY 2001.

ONTONG Justin Lee (Bol/Pres). B 4/1/80 Paarl. RHB OB/LB. Ed Paarl Gymnasium. Bol Schools 1996-97. FC debut Bol v Ntl (Paarl) 1997/98. LOIs: 6 (2000/01). HSLOI 11 v WI (Kingston) 2000/01. BBLOI 2-12 v WI (St George's) 2000/01. HSFC 131* Bol v EP (Paarl) 2000/01. BBFC 4-120 Bol v Bdr (EL) 2000/01. HSLO 81 Bol v FS (Paarl) 1999/00. BBLO 2-12 SA v WI (St George's) 2000/01 and Bol v KZN (Dbn) 2000/01. Tours: SA to WI 2000/01; SAA to WI 2000/01; SA U-19 to Pak 1998/99.

OTTO Johannes Marthinus (Gau). B 4/9/80 Pretoria. RHB RM. Ed Randburg Hoerskool, RAU. Gau Schools 1996-98. FC debut Gau v KZN (Jhb) 2000/01. HSFC 88 Gau v GW (Kby) 2000/01. HSLO 70 Gau v NW (Potch) 2000/01.

OUTRAM Gary (NW). B 13/2/76 Johannesburg. RHB. Ed Potchefstroom Boys HS, Potch Univ. WT Schools 1993-94. FC debut NW v Nor (Potch) 2000/01, LO debut 1996/97. HSFC 14 NW v Nor (Potch) 2000/01. HSLO 83 NW v Bdr (Potch) 1999/00. Hockey (WT Schools 1993-96), Squash (WT Schools 1992).

PALEKER Allahudien (Nor). B 1/1/78 Cape Town. RHB OB WK. Ed Cravenby Secondary School, UWC. WP Schools 1994-1995. FC debut WPB v EPB (Bellville) 1997/98, Nor debut 2000/01. WPB 1997/98. HSFC 46 WPB v Eas (Benoni) 1997/98. HSSS 38* Nor v Eas (Cent) 2000/01. HSLO 30 Nor v Gau (Cent) 2000/01.

PALFRAMAN Steven John (Bol). B 12/5/70 East London. RHB WK. Ed Dale College, Rhodes U. Bdr Schools 1986-87. FC debut EPB v NTB (PE) 1990/91, Bol debut 1997/98. EPB 1990/91, Bdr 1991/92-1996/97. LOIs: 7 (1995/96). HSLOI 28 v Eng (Rawalpindi) 1995/96. HSFC 147 Bol v Gau (Jhb) 1998/99. HSLO 90* Bdr v GW (EL) 1994/95. Tours: SA to SL 1993/94; World Cup 1996; SAA to Zim 1994/95; Eng 1996. Hockey (EP U-21 1990).

PETERSEN Alviro Nathan (Nor). B 25/11/80 Port Elizabeth. RHB RM. Ed Gelvandale HS, Otto du Plessis HS, Eastern Cape Training College. FC debut Nor v WP (Cent) 2000/01. HSFC 30 Nor v WP (Cent) 2000/01. Soccer (EP U-15, 1993), Hockey (EP U-16, 1994).

PETERSON Robin John (EP). B 4/8/79 Port Elizabeth. LHB SLA. Ed Alexander Road HS, UPE. EP Schools 1995-97, SA Schools 1996 (T)-97. FC debut EPB v NW (Foch) 1998/99, EP same season. HSFC 96* EP v Eas (Ben) 2000/01. BBFC 6-67 EP v Bdr (EL) 1999/00. HSLO 94 EP v KZN (Dbn) 2000/01. BBLO 3-28 SAA v Jam (East Kingston) 2000/01. BBDLO 3-33 EP v GW (PE) 2000/01. Tours: SAA to WI 2000/01. SA U-19 v Pak U-19 1996/97; v Eng U-19 1997/98; World Cup 1998.

PLAYER Bradley Todd (Bol). B 18/1/67 Benoni. RHB RFM/OB. Ed Welkom HS. FC debut OFS v NtlB (Bfn) 1984/85, Bol debut 1999/00. FS/FSB 1984/85-1996/97, WP/WPB 1997/98-1998/99. HSFC 133* FS v GW (Kby) 1996/97. BBFC 6-43 OFS v Tvl (Jhb) 1991/92. HSLO 83 FS v Tvl (Jhb) 1995/96. BBLO 5-27 OFS v Ntl (Dbn) 1993/94.

POLLOCK Graeme Anthony (Eas). B 7/4/73 Port Elizabeth. LHB OB. Ed King Edward VII, RAU. TvlB Schools 1990, Tvl Schools 1991, SA Schools 1991. Son of RG Pollock (EP/Tvl/SA 1960-1986), nephew of PM Pollock (EP/SA 1958-1971), brother of AG Pollock (Tvl/TvlB/Eas 1991-1997), cousin of SM Pollock (KZN/NtlB/Warw/SA 1991-2000). FC debut TvlB v NtlB (Jhb) 1991/92, Eas debut 1999/00. Tvl/TvlB 1991/92-1996/97, NorB 1997/98-1998/99. HSFC 115 TvlB v OFSB (Bfn) 1991/92 and 115 TvlB v EPB (Jhb) 1996/97. BBFC 3-21 TvlB v BdrB (Randjesfontein) 1994/95. HSSS 74 Tvl v WP (Jhb) 1994/95. HSLO 94* Tvl v NT (Jhb) 1991/92.

POLLOCK Shaun Maclean (KZN/SA). B 16/7/73 Port Elizabeth. RHB RFM. Ed Northwood HS, Ntl Univ (Dbn). Ntl Schools 1991, SA Schools 1991. Son of PM Pollock (EP/SA 1958-1971), nephew of RG Pollock (EP/Tvl/SA 1960-1986), cousin of AG Pollock (Tvl/TvlB/Eas 1991-1997) and GA Pollock (Tvl/TvlB/NorB/Eas 1991-2000). FC debut NtlB v WPB (Pmb) 1991/92, Ntl debut 1992/93. Warwickshire 1996. Tests: 56 (1995/96-2000/01, 14 as captain) . LOIs: 132 (1995/96-2000/01, 36 as captain). HSTest 111 v SL (Cent) 2000/01. BBTest 7-87 v Aus (Adelaide) 1997/98. HSLOI 75 v Zim (Jhb) 1996/97. BBLOI 6-35 v WI (EL) 1998/99. HSFC 150* Warw v Glam (Birmingham) 1996. BBFC 7-33 Ntl v Bdr (EL) 1995/96. HSSA 111 SA v SL (Cent) 2000/01. HSSS 92 KZN v Gau (Jhb) 1998/99. HSLO 87 SA v Nott (Nottingham) 1998. BBLO 6-21 Warw v Leic (Birmingham) 1996. HSDLO 30 KZN v Bol (Paarl) 1998/99. BBDLO 3-25 Ntl v EP (PE) 1993/94. Tours: SA to Aus 1997/98, 2000 (capt); Eng 1998; Ind 1999/00; NZ 1998/99; Pak 1997/98; SL 2000 (capt); WI 2000/01 (capt); Zim 1999/00; Ken 1999/00, 2000/01 (capt); Shar 1995/96, 1999/00; Sing 2000 (capt); World Cup 1996, 1999; SA U-24 to SL 1995/96. COY 1996, 1998, 2001. Hockey (Ntl Mynahs).

POOLE Ezra Glynn (NW). B 10/2/75 Cape Town. RHB WK. Ed Kensington HS, UWC. WP Schools 1992-93. FC debut NW v Eas (Ben) 1996/97. HSFC 50 NW v Eas (Ben) 2000/01. HSLO 36* NW v WP (CT) 1997/98.

POPE Steven Charles (Bdr). B 15/11/72 East London. RHB LB WK. Ed Queens College, Dale College, St Andrew's (Gtn), UPE. Bdr Schools 1989-90, EP Schools 1991. Son of CWS Pope (Bdr 1966-1978), nephew of KS McEwan (EP/WP/Bdr/Ess/WAus/SA 1971-1991). FC debut EP v OFS (Bfn) 1992/93, Bdr debut 1995/96. EP 1992/93-1994/95, EPB 1993/94-1994/95. HSFC 125 Bdr v Bol (EL) 2000/01. BBFC 7-62 Bdr v FS (EL) 1995/96. HSLO 93 Bdr v NW (Potch) 1999/00. BBLO 4-38 Bdr v NZ (Alice) 2000/01.

POTHAS Nic (Gau/Pres). B 18/11/73 Johannesburg. RHB WK. Ed King Edward VII, RAU. Tvl Schools 1990-91, SA Schools 1990(R). FC debut Tvl v NT (Jhb) 1993/94. LOIs: 3 (2000/01). HSLOI 24 v Pak (Singapore) 2000. HSFC 165 Gau v KZN (Jhb) 1998/99. HSLO 101 Tvl v EP (Jhb) 1995/96. Tours: SA to Sing 2000; SAA to Eng 1996; SL 1998/99; WI 2000/01. Hockey (SA Schools, ST).

PRETORIUS Dewald (FS/Pres). B 6/12/77 Pretoria. RHB RF. Ed Hoerskool Dr Viljoen. FS Schools 1996-97. FC debut FS v Pak (Bfn) 1997/98. HSFC 43 FS v WP (Bfn) 1998/99. BBFC 5-50 FS v Bol (Stb) 1998/99. BBLO 4-39 FS v GW (Kby) 1999/00.

PRINCE Ashwell Gavin (WP). B 28/5/77 Port Elizabeth. LHB. Ed St Thomas Senior Secondary, UPE. EP Schools 1993-94. FC debut EPB v GW (PE) 1995/96, WP debut 1997/98. EP 1995/96-1996/97, EPB 1995/96-1997/98. HSFC 133 WP v GW (Kby) 1998/99. HSLO 76* WP v KZN (Dbn) 2000/01. Tours: SAA to SL 1998/99; WI 2000/01; SA U-19 to Eng 1995; Ind 1995/96. Soccer (EP U-16 & EP Schools 1992-93), Athletics (EP Schools 1991-93).
PRINGLE Andrew Alexander Welsh (Bol). B 7/2/78 Bedford. RHB RF. Ed St Andrews Coll (Gtn), Stell Univ. EP Schools 1994- 96. Cousin of MW Pringle (OFS/EP/EPB/WP/WPB/Sus/SA 1985-2000). FC debut Bol v FS (Paarl) 2000/01. HSFC 27 Bol v Nor (Cent) 2000/01. BBFC 4-49 Bol v Bdr (EL) 2000/01. BBLO 3-36 Bol v Bdr (Paarl) 2000/01.
PRINGLE Meyrick Wayne (EP). B 22/6/66 Adelaide, Cape Province. RHB RFM. Ed Dale College, Kingswood College. EP Schools 1983-84, SA Schools 1983-84. Cousin of MG Beamish (EP/EPB 1993-1998) and AAW Pringle (Bol 2000/01). FC debut OFS v Bdr (EL) 1985/86, EP debut 1987/88. OFS 1985/86, EP 1987/88-1988/89 and 1997/98-2000/01, EPB 1987/88-1988/89, WP 1989/90-1996/97, WPB 1990/91, Sussex 1987-1988. Tests: 4 (1991/92-1995/96). LOIs: 17 (1991/92-1994/95). HSTest 33 v Ind (Dbn) 1992/93. BBTest 2-62 v WI (Bridgetown) 1991/92. HSLOI 13* v Pak (Karachi) 1994/95. BBLOI 4-11 v WI (Christchurch) 1991/92. HSFC 105 SAA v Worc (Worc) 1996. BBFC 7-60 WP v Ntl (CT) 1989/90. HSSA 83 EP v Gau (Jhb) 1999/00. HSLO 31 WP v OFS (CT) 1993/94. BBLO 6-30 WP v Bdr (EL) 1989/90. Tours: SA to Pak 1994/95; WI 1991/92; World Cup 1992. SAA to Eng 1996. COY 1992.
PUTTICK Andrew George (WP). B 11/12/80 Cape Town. LHB. Ed Rondebosch BHS. WP Schools 1996-98, SA Schools 1998 (T). FC debut WP v EP (PE) 2000/01, LO debut 1999/00. HSFC 153* WP v Eas (CT) 2000/01. HSLO 75* WP v Nor (Cent) 2000/01. Tours: SA U-19 to Pak 1998/99; World Cup 2000. SA U-19 v Eng U-19 1997/98.
REDDY Brendon Leigh (Eas). B 6/11/83 Durban. RHB RFM. Ed Veritus College (Springs). Eas Schools 1999-2000. FC debut Eas v Nor (Cent) 2000/01. HSFC 28 Eas v NW (Ben) 2000/01. BBFC 3-39 Eas v Bol (Paarl) 2000/01. HSLO 10 Eas v EP (PE) 2000/01. BBLO 3-46 Eas v EP (PE) 2000/01.
RHODES Jonathan Neil (Jonty) (KZN/SA). B 27/7/69 Pietermaritzburg. RHB RM. Ed Maritzburg College, Ntl Univ (Pmb). Ntl Schools 1986-87, SA Schools 1986-87. Brother of CB Rhodes (EPB/NtlB 1990-1993). FC debut Ntl v WP (Dbn) 1988/89, scoring 108. Tests: 52 (1992/93-2000). LOIs: 200 (1991/92-2000/01). HSTest 117 v Eng (Lord's) 1998. HSLOI 121 v Pak (Nairobi) 1996/97. HSFC 156* Ntl v FS (Dbn) 1996/97. HSLO 121 SA v Pak (Nairobi) 1996/97. HSDLO 86* Ntl v Tvl (Dbn) 1990/91. Tours: SA to Aus 1993/94, 1997/98, 2000; Eng 1994, 1998; Ind 1993/94, 1996/97; NZ 1994/95, 1998/99; Pak 1994/95, 1997/98; SL 1993/94, 2000; WI 1991/92, 2000/01; Zim 1995/96, 1999/00; Ban 1998/99; Ken 1996/97, 1999/00, 2000/01; Shar 1995/96; World Cup 1992, 1996, 1999. COY 1992, 1999. Wisden 1999. Hockey (SA Schools 1985-87, Ntl Schools 1984-87, Ntl, NtlB, SA, SA B).
RINDEL Michael John Raymond (Eas). B 9/2/63 Durban. LHB LMF/SLA. Ed Northlands BHS, St Johns College, Wits Univ. Tvl Schools 1980-81. FC debut TvlB v GW (Jhb) 1983/84, Eas debut 2000/01. TvlB 1983/84, Nor 1986/87-1999/00, NTB 1985/86-1993/94. LOIs: 22 (1994/95-1998/99). HSLOI 106 v Pak (Jhb) 1994/95. BBLOI 2-15 v NZ (CT) 1994/95. HSFC 174 NT v FS (Bfn) 1995/96. BBFC 4-17 Nor v Bol (Cent) 1997/98. HSLO 144* Nor v GW (Kby) 1997/98. BBLO 4-28 NT v Ntl (Dbn) 1992/93. Tours: SA to Eng 1998; NZ 1994/95; Ban 1998/99. COY 1989.
ROE Garth Anthony (NW). B 9/7/73 Port Elizabeth. RHB RFM. Ed Grey HS (PE), UPE. FC debut EPB v WPB (CT-NG) 1993/94, NW debut 2000/01. EP/EPB 1993/94-1995/96, GW 1996/97-1999-00. HSFC 66 NW v GW (Kby) 2000/01. BBFC 7-47 NW v FS (Bfn) 2000/01. HSLO 16 NW v Eas (Potch) 2000/01. BBLO 5-49 GW v NW (Kby) 1996/97.
RUDOLPH Jacobus Andries (Jacques) (Nor/Pres). 4/5/81 Springs. LHB LBG. Ed Afrikaanse Hoer Seunskool. Nor Schools 1996-99, SA Schools 1997-99(C). FC debut NorB v WPB (Cent) 1997/98, Nor debut 1999/00. HSFC 144 Nor v Eas (Cent) 2000/01. BBFC 5-87 NorB v GWB (Cent) 1998/99. BBSS 2-13 Nor v EP (PE) 2000/01. HSLO 110 Nor v Bdr (Cent) 2000/01. Tours: SA U-19 to Pak 1998/99; World Cup 2000. SA U-19 v Eng U-19 1997/98; World Cup 1998.
SCHORN James Robin (FS). B 2/4/82 Pietermaritzburg. RHB WK. Ed Hilton College. KZN Schools 1998-2000, SA Schools 1999-2000. FC debut FS v WP (CT) 2000/01. HSFC 11 FS v WP (CT) 2000/01. Tours: SA U-19 to NZ 2000/01.
SCHULTZ Brett Nolan (Gau). B 26/8/70 East London. LHB LF. Ed Alexander Road HS, Kingswood College, UPE. EP Schools 1988-89, SA Schools 1989. FC debut EPB v NtlB (Dbn) 1989/90, LO debut for Gau 2000/01. EP 1989/90-1995/96, EPB 1989/90-1993/94, WP 1996/97-1997/98, WPB 1996/97. Tests: 9 (1992/93-1997/98). LOIs: 1 (1992/93). BBTest 5-48 v SL (Colombo-SSC) 1993/94. HSFC 36* EP v Bol (Worc) 1991/92. BBFC 8-36 WP v WIA (CT) 1997/98. HSSS 31 EP v WP (CT) 1992/93. BBSS 6-84 EP v NT (Cent) 1995/96. BBLO 6-22 EP v Tvl (Jhb) 1995/96. Tours: SA to Pak 1997/98; SL 1993/94; Zim 1995/96; SAA to Eng 1996. Rugby (EP U-19), Soccer (EP U-19).
SENEKAL Dewald Meyer (EP). B 12/1/81 Uitenhage. RHB RFM. Ed Daniel Pienaar Tech HS. EP Schools 1998-99, SA Schools 1999. FC debut UCB Inv v GW (Kby) 1999/00, EP debut 2000/01. HSFC 15 EP v Eas (Ben) 2000/01. BBFC 3-42 EP v Eas (Ben) 2000/01. Tours: SA U-19 to World Cup 2000. Action Cricket (SA U-19 1996-97).
SEYMORE Andre Johan (Gau/Eas). B 16/2/75 Rustenburg. RHB. Ed Hendrik Verwoerd HS, UNISA. NT Schools 1991-93, SA Schools 1992-93. FC debut NT v Barbados (Vbg) 1993/94, Eas debut 2000/01. NT 1993/94-1996/97, NTB 1994/95, Gau 1997/98-2000/01. HSFC 174 Eas v Nor (Cent) 2000/01. HSLO 101 NT v FS (Bfn) 1996/97.
SMIT Willem Johannes (Wiaan) (FS). B 1/8/74 Calvinia. RHB RM. Ed Paarl Gymnasium, Stell Univ. Bol Schools 1990-91(C)-92(C). FC debut Bol v Tvl (Jhb) 1994/95, FS debut 1997/98. Bol 1994/95, BolB 1994/95-1995/96. HSFC 94 FS v GW (Kby) 2000/01. HSLO 111 Bol v ET (Spr) 1994/95. BBLO 2-35 FS v Eas (Bfn) 1998/99. Rugby (Stell Univ).
SMITH Graeme Craig (WP/Pres). B 1/2/81 Johannesburg. LHB RM. Ed King Edward VII. Gau Schools 1998-99, SA Schools 1998-99. FC debut UCB Inv v GW (Kby) 1999/00, scoring 187, the second highest score on first-class debut by a

South African, debut for WP 2000/01. LO for Gau 1999/00. HSFC 187 UCB Inv v GW (Kby) 1999/00. HSSS 183 WP v Bdr (CT) 2000/01. HSLO 106 WP v NW (Potch) 2000/01. BBLO 3-46 WP v NW (Potch) 2000/01. Tours: SAA to WI 2000/01; SA U-19 to World Cup 2000.

SMITH Gregory James (Nor). B 30/10/71 Pretoria. RHB LFM. Ed Pretoria BHS, Pretoria Technikon. NT Schools 1989-90. FC debut NTB v TvlB (Jhb) 1993/94, NT same season. Nottinghamshire 2001. HSFC 68 NT v WP (Cent) 1995/96. BBFC 6-35 Nor v WP (Cent) 1997/98. BBLO 5-11 NT v GW (Kby) 1995/96. Tours: SAA to Eng 1996.

STEWART Errol Leslie Rae (KZN). B 30/7/69 Durban. RHB RM WK. Ed Westville BHS, Ntl Univ (Dbn). Ntl Schools 1987, SA Schools 1987. Great-nephew of PR Davidson (NET 1950/51). FC debut NtlB v Bdr (Dbn) 1988/89, Ntl debut 1990/91. LOIs: 5 (1992/93-1993/94). HSLOI 23* v WI (Bfn) 1992/93. HSFC 207* NtlB v BdrB (Dbn) 1995/96. HSSS 177 KZN v Bol (Dbn) 1998/99. HSLO 90 Ntl v WT (Potch) 1992/93. Tours: SA to Aus 1993/94. Rugby (SA Schools, Ntl U-20, Ntl), Hockey (Ntl Schools), Tennis (1st Division). His mother, Shirley, played hockey for SA (1977-79).

STEYN Philippus Jeremia Rudolf (Nor). B 30/6/67 Kimberley. RHB RM WK. Ed Diamantveld HS, UOFS. GW Schools 1983-85. FC debut GW v NtlB (Dbn) 1985/86, Nor debut 1997/98. GW 1985/86, OFS 1986/87-1994/95, Ntl 1995/96-1996/97, NtlB 1996/97. Tests: 3 (1994/95). LOIs: 1 (1995/96). HSTest 46 v NZ (Auckland) 1994/95. HSFC 188* Nor v GW (Cent) 2000/01. HSLO 127* OFS v NTCD (Pietersburg) 1991/92. Tours: SA to NZ 1994/95; Zim 1995/96; SAA to Zim 1994/95. Rugby (GW Craven Week 1985), Tennis (GW 1977-84).

STILL Quentin Raxham (Nor). B 8/8/74 Pietermaritzburg. RHB SLA. Ed Selborne College, Rhodes Univ. Bdr Schools 1989-92, SA Schools 1992. FC debut BdrB v NtlB (EL) 1993/94, NorB debut 1997/98, Nor debut 1998/99. Bdr/BdrB 1993/94-1995/96. HSFC 129* BdrB v OFSB (Qtn) 1993/94. BBFC 5-53 BdrB v NtlB (EL) 1993/94. HSSS 85 Nor v KZN (Cent) 1998/99. BBSS 3-45 Nor v Bol (Cent) 1998/99. HSLO 20 Bdr v Tvl (EL) 1992/93.

STREET Matthew Russell (Gau). B 17/12/78 Johannesburg. RHB WK. Ed St John's College, Wits Univ. TvlB Schools 1995, Tvl Schools 1996, SA Schools 1995-96. FC debut Gau v Bol (Paarl) 1999/00. HSFC 47 UCB Inv v GW (Kby) 1999/00. HSSS 33* Gau v WP (CT) 1999/00. SA U-19 v Pak U-19 1996/97; v Eng U-19 1997/98 (capt); World Cup 1998 (capt). Hockey (S Tvl U16 1994).

STRYDOM Johannes Gerhardus (Bol). B 6/9/79 Cape Town. LHB. Ed Paul Roos Gimnasium. Bol Schools 1995-97. FC debut Bol v WP (CT) 2000/01, LO debut 1999/00. HSFC 73 Bol v WP (Paarl) 2000/01. HSLO 43* Bol v Eas (Ben) 2000/01.

STRYDOM Morne (NW). B 20/2/74 Port Elizabeth. RHB OB. Ed Victoria Park HS, UPE, Vaal Technikon. EP Schools 1991. FC debut WT v NtlB (Dbn) 1995/96. GW 1997/98. NW 1995/96-1996/97 and 1998/99-2000/01. HSFC 129 NW v EPB (Potch) 1996/97. BBFC 6-23 NW v GW (Kby) 2000/01. HSSS 124 NW v WP (Potch) 2000/01. HSLO 103 SAAc v NZAc (Dbn) 1997/98. BBLO 4-16 NW v WP (Foch) 1998/99. HSDLO 93 NW v WP (Foch) 1998/99. Hockey (EP Schools 1989-91, SA Schools 1991).

STRYDOM Pieter Coenraad (Bdr). B 10/6/69 Somerset East. RHB SLA. Ed Grey HS (PE), UPE. EP Schools 1986-87(C), SA Schools 1987. FC debut EPB v Bol (Stb) 1987/88, Bdr debut 1992/93. Tests: 2 (1999/00). LOIs: 10 (1999/00). HSTest 30 v Eng (Cent) 1999/00. HSLOI 34 v Eng (Bfn) 1999/00. HSFC 127 Bdr v NT (Vbg) 1994/95. BBFC 4-12 Bdr v Nor (Cent) 1998/99. HSLO 106* Bdr v NW (EL) 1998/99. BBLO 4-8 Bdr v Bol (Paarl) 1998/99. Tours: SA to Ind 1999/00; Shar 1999/00. Rugby (EP Craven Week), Squash (EP), Table Tennis (EP).

SUGDEN Craig Brian (Bdr). B 7/3/74 Durban. RHB. Ed Michaelhouse. Ntl Schools 1992, SA Schools 1992. FC debut NtlB v BdrB (EL) 1993/94, Bdr debut 1998/99. KZN 1996/97-1997/98 and 1999/00, NtlB 1993/94-1997/98, Bdr 1998/99 and 2000/01. HSFC 106 NtlB v GW (Kby) 1994/95. BBFC 2-24 NtlB v TvlB (Dbn) 1996/97. HSSS 72 Bdr v Nor (Cent) 1998/99. HSLO 86 Bdr v Nor (EL) 1998/99.

SWANEPOEL Adriaan Johannes (GW). B 19/3/72 Kimberley. LHB LFM. Ed Kimberley Tech HS. GW Schools 1990. FC debut GW v Bol (Kby) 1991/92. HSFC 39 GW v Bdr (Kby) 1997/98. BBFC 5-29 GW v NTB (Kby) 1995/96. BBSS 3-23 GW v Bol (Kby) 1997/98. HSLO 19 GW v EP (Kby) 1996/97. BBLO 5-32 GW v Bdr (Kby) 1999/00.

TATTON Craig Ross (GW). B 29/1/75 Bulawayo, Rhodesia. RHB SLA. Ed Alexandra HS. Ntl Schools 1992. FC debut Ntl v WP (Dbn) 1997/98, GW debut 2000/01. KZN 1997/98-1998/99, KZNB 1998/99. HSFC 14* GW v Gau (Kby) 2000/01. BBFC 5-80 GW v NW (Kby) 2000/01. BBLO 2-31 GW v WP (Kby) 2000/01. Action Cricket (Ntl U23, 1997).

TELEMACHUS Roger (WP/SA). B 27/3/73 Stellenbosch. RHB RFM. Ed Cloetesville HS (Stell). WP Schools 1992-93. FC debut BolB v BdrB (EL) 1994/95, WP debut 1999/00. Bol 1994/95-1998/99, BolB 1994/95. LOIs: 25 (1997/98-2000/01). HSLOI 13 v Ind (Nairobi) 2000/01. BBLOI 4-43 v SL (Jhb) 1997/98. HSFC 59 BolB v ET (Bfel) 1994/95. BBFC 6-21 Bol v GW (Paarl) 1996/97. HSSS 46* Bol v EP (PE) 1995/96. HSLO 37 Bol v Nor (Paarl) 1997/98. BBLO 5-54 Bol v EP (PE) 1996/97. Tours: SA to Aus 2000; SL 2000; WI 2000/01; Ken 2000/01; Sing 2000; SAA to Eng 1996; SA U-24 to SL 1995/96.

TERBRUGGE David John (Gau). B 31/1/77 Ladysmith. RHB RFM. Ed St Stithian's, RAU. Tvl Schools 1992-94, SA Schools 1993-94. FC debut TvlB v EPB (PE) 1994/95, Tvl debut 1996/97. Tests: 4 (1998/99). LOIs: 4 (1999/00-2000). BBTest 3-27 v WI (PE) 1998/99. BBLOI 4-20 v Pak (Colombo-SSC) 2000. HSFC 20 TvlB v WPB (CT) 1996/97. BBFC 5-32 Gau v Bdr (EL) 1998/99. HSSS 17 Gau v Nor (Jhb) 1997/98. HSLO 16* Gau v EP (Jhb) 1999/00. BBLO 4-20 SA v Pak (Colombo-SSC) 2000. BBDLO 4-31 Gau v WP (Jhb) 2000/01. Tours: SA to Aus 2000; SL 2000; Sing 2000; SA U-19 to Eng 1995.

THOMAS Alfonso Clive (NW). B 9/2/77 Cape Town. RHB RFM. Ed Ravensmead SSS, Parow High. WP Schools 1995-96. FC debut WPB v NW (CT) 1998/99, NW debut 2000/01. WPB 1998/99. HSFC 106* NW v GW (Kby) 2000/01. BBFC 6-26 NW v Eas (Ben) 2000/01. HSLO 20* NW v Bol (Paarl) 2000/01. BBLO 2-42 NW v Bdr (EL) 2000/01.

TOWNSEND David Hume (Nor). B 22/12/77 Port Elizabeth. RHB RFM. Ed Willowridge HS. NT Schools 1995. FC debut NorPr v WIA (Cent) 1997/98, Nor debut 1998/99. HSFC 45 Nor v Eas (Cent) 2000/01. BBFC 6-36 Nor v KZN (Cent) 1998/99.
TOYANA Geoffrey (Gau). B 27/2/74 Soweto. LHB RM. Ed Orlando High School. Tvl Schools 1992-93. FC debut SA Inv v Eng (Soweto) 1995/96, TvlB same season, Gau debut 1997/98. HSFC 63 Gau v Bdr (Jhb) 1999/00. HSLO 41 Gau v WP (CT) 1999/00. Soccer (Orlando Liverpool 1990-94).
TROTT Ian Jonathan Leonard (Bol/Pres). B 22/4/81 Cape Town. RHB RM. Ed Rondebosch BHS, Stell Univ. WP Schools 1996- 99, SA Schools 1998-99. Half brother of KC Jackson (WP/WPB/Bol 1988-2000). FC debut Bol v FS (Paarl) 2000/01, LO debut 1999/00. HSFC 93 Bol v WP (CT) 2000/01. HSLO 108* Bol v NW (Paarl) 2000/01. BBLO 2-32 Bol v EP (Paarl) 1999/00. Tours: SA U-19 to Pak 1998/99; World Cup 2000. Hockey (WP Schools 1999).
TSOLEKILE Thami Lungisa (WP/Pres). B 9/10/80 Cape Town. RHB OB WK. Ed Pinelands HS. WP Schools 1998-99, SA Schools 1998(C)-99(C, but did not play). FC debut SAAc v Ire (Dublin) 1999, WP debut 1999/00. HSFC 95 WP v Eas (CT) 2000/01. HSLO 44 WP v GW (CT) 1999/00. Tours: SA U-19 to Pak 1998/99 (capt); World Cup 2000 (capt).
TUCKER Brett Hurst (GW). B 4/4/79 Johannesburg. RHB. Ed St Johns. SA Schools 1997(C). FC debut GWB v NorB (Cent) 1998/99, GW debut 2000/01. HSFC 47 GW v KZN (Dbn) 2000/01. HSLO 59 GW v FS (Bfn) 2000/01.
TWEEDIE Andrew Neil Walter (KZN). B 27/11/75 Durban. RHB RFM. Ed Kearsney College, Ntl Technikon. Ntl Schools 1993. FC debut NtlB v WPB (CT) 1997/98, KZN debut 2000/01. HSFC 29 NtlB v WPB (CT) 1997/98. BBFC 4-65 KZN v GW (Kby) 2000/01. HSSS 20* KZN v GW (Kby) 2000/01. HSLO 70* KZN v WA (Perth) 2000/01. BBLO 2-27 Herefordshire v Wiltshire (Brockhampton) 1999. Hockey (Ntl B 1994-97, Ntl U21 1994-96).
UYS Johannes (Eas). B 14/2/78 Benoni. RHB RM. Ed Hoerskool Brandwag, UNISA. Eas Schools 1995-96. FC debut Eas v NW (Foch) 1997/98. HSFC 57 Eas v WPB (CT) 1998/99. BBFC 5-87 Eas v WPB (Ben) 1997/98. HSSS 26 Eas v Bol (Paarl) 2000/01. HSLO 28 Eas v NW (Foch) 1998/99. BBLO 2-1 Eas v WP (CT) 1998/99.
VAN DEN BERG Adolf Matthys (Aldo) (Eas). B 9/3/78 Randfontein. RHB OB. Ed Jan Viljoen, Randfontein. Tvl Schools 1995-96, SA Schools 1996. FC debut SAAc v Ire (Dublin) 1999, Eas debut 1999/00. HSFC 94 SAAc v Scot (Dundee) 1999. HSSA 59 Eas v Bol (Paarl) 2000/01. BBFC 2-44 Eas v Bdr (EL) 1999/00. HSLO 32 Eas v EP (PE) 2000/01. Rugby (Tvl Afrikaans Schools 1996).
VAN DER MERWE Francois (Sweis) (NW). B 5/7/76 Kempton Park. RHB RMF. Ed HS Klerksdorp. NW Schools 1994. FC debut NW v GW (Potch) 1999/00, LO debut 1995/96. HSFC 24* NW v Bdr (Potch) 2000/01. BBFC 5-62 NW v EP (PE) 2000/01. BBLO 3-44 NW v Gau (Potch) 2000/01.
VAN DER WATH Johannes Jacobus (FS). B 10/1/78 Newcastle. RHB RF. Ed Ermelo High School. SACD Schools 1994-95, Eas Schools 1996, SA Schools 1996. FC debut Eas v TvlB (Ben) 1996/97, FS debut 1997/98. HSFC 57* FS v Bol (Bfn) 1999/00. BBFC 5-26 FS v WI (Bfn) 1998/99. BBSS 5-46 FS v Bdr (Bfn) 1998/99. HSLO 91 FS v GW (Bfn) 2000/01. BBLO 4-45 FS v Bdr (EL) 2000/01. SA U-19 v Pak U-19 1996/97. Rugby (SE Tvl Craven Week), Wrestling (SE Tvl 1986).
VAN JAARSVELD Martin (Nor/Pres). B 18/6/74 Klerksdorp. RHB RM. Ed Warmbaths, Pretoria Univ. SACD/NT Schools 1990-92. FC debut NTB v NtlB (Dbn) 1994/95, NT debut 1995/96. HSFC 238* Nor v GW (Kby) 1999/00. HSLO 123 NT v EP (Cent) 1996/97. Tours: SAA to SL 1998/99.
VAN LOGGENBERG Petrus Johannes (NW). B 25/4/76 Pretoria. RHB RFM. No FC, LO debut 2000/01.
VAN WYK Cornelius Francoius Kruger (Nor). B 7/2/80 Wolmaransstad. RHB WK. Ed Afrikaanse Hoer Seunskool, Pretoria Univ. Nor Schools 1995-98. FC debut Nor v GW (Cent) 2000/01. HSFC 59 Nor v FS (Cent) 2000/01. HSLO 50* Nor v KZN (Dbn) 2000/01. Hockey (Nor U-16, U-18, U-21, Seniors).
VAN WYK Jacques Merlin (Bol). B 27/1/78 Stellenbosch. RHB RFM. Ed Kylemore Secondary, Stellenbosch College. Bol Schools 1997-98. FC debut Bol v FS (Stb) 1998/99. HSFC 19 Bol v GW (Paarl) 1998/99. HSLO 12 Bol v WP (Paarl) 1998/99.
VAN WYK Morne Nico (FS). B 20/3/79 Bloemfontein. RHB SLA WK. Ed Grey College (Bfn). FS Schools 1995-97, SA Schools 1997. FC debut FS v Bdr (Bfn) 1996/97, as substitute. HSFC 121 FS v Bdr (EL) 1997/98. BBFC 2-25 FS v Eas (Ben) 2000/01. HSLO 102* FS v Bol (Bfn) 2000/01. BBLO 2-28 FS v Gau (Bfn) 2000/01. SA U-19 v Eng U-19 1997/98; World Cup 1998. Hockey (SA U-16 1995, FS Schools 1995-96).
VEENSTRA Ross Edward (KZN). B 22/4/72 Estcourt. RHB LFM. Ed Maritzburg College, UPE. Ntl Schools 1988-89. FC debut EPB v NTB (PE) 1990/91, Ntl debut 1994/95. EP 1990/91-1993/94, EPB 1990/91-1991/92, KZN 1994/95-1995/96 and 1999/00-2000/01, NtlB 1994/95-1995/96, Gau 1996/97-1998/99. HSFC 135* Tvl v Bdr (EL) 1996/97. BBFC 6-38 Ntl v Bol (Paarl) 1995/96. HSLO 40 Gau v WP (CT) 1998/99. BBLO 6-34 KZN v Gau (Dbn) 1999/00. Tours: SA U-24 to SL 1995/96. Rugby (Ntl Schools).
VENTER Jacobus Francois (Kosie) (FS). B 1/10/69 Bloemfontein. LHB OB. Ed Grey College (Bfn), UOFS. Brother of EJ Venter (OFS/OFSB 1983-1991). OFS Schools 1985-88, SA Schools 1988. FC debut OFS v SADF (Bfn) 1989/90. FS 1989/90 and 1991/92-2000/01, OFSB 1989/90 and 1991/92-1993/94, TvlB 1990/91. HSFC 193 OFSB v NTB (Bfn) 1993/94. BBFC 6-78 FS v Nor (Bfn) 1999/00. HSSS 142* FS v GW (Kby) 1998/99. HSLO 118* FS v Bol (Paarl) 1999/00. BBLO 5-21 OFS v Tvl (Bfn) 1993/94. Rugby (OFS).
VENTER Martin Colin (NW). B 12/12/68 East London. RHB RM. Ed Ixopo HS, UPE. Ntl Schools 1986. FC debut NTB v TvlB (Jhb) 1988/89, NW debut 1996/97. NTB 1988/89, EP 1990/91-1994/95, EPB 1988/89-1995/96. HSFC 129 EP v NT (Vbg) 1990/91. HSLO 166* NW v Ntl (Foch) 1997/98.

WATSON Douglas James (KZN/Pres). B 15/5/73 Pietermaritzburg. RHB RM. Ed Maritzburg College. Ntl Schools 1991, SA Schools 1991. FC debut NtlB v BdrB (EL) 1993/94, Ntl same season. HSFC 220 KZN v NW (Potch) 1999/00. BBFC 2-7 Ntl v Bdr (EL) 1997/98. HSLO 116 KZN v Nor (Dbn) 2000/01. BBLO 2-22 Ntl v FS (Dbn) 1997/98. Tours: SAA to WI 2000/01.

WHITE Brad Middleton (Eas). B 15/5/70 Port Elizabeth. LHB RM. Ed King Edward VII. TvlB Schools 1988, SA Schools 1988. FC debut TvlB v Bdr (EL) 1988/89, Eas debut 2000/01. Tvl 1990/91-1995/96, TvlB 1989/90-1995/96, Bdr 1996/97-1999/00. HSFC 180* TvlB v EPB (PE) 1995/96. BBFC 3-23 Bdr v GW (Kby) 1997/98. HSSS 159* Tvl v Bol (Jhb) 1995/96. HSLO 100* Bdr v Eas (EL) 1997/98. BBLO 4-31 Bdr v WP (CT) 1997/98.

WIBLIN Wayne (Bdr). B 13/2/69 Grahamstown. RHB RM. Ed Graeme College, Rhodes Univ. EP Schools 1986-87. FC debut BdrB v WT (Qtn) 1995/96, Bdr same season. HSFC 177 Bdr v WP (EL) 1997/98. HSLO 82 Bdr v GW (EL) 1997/98. Squash (EP Schools 1984).

WILKINSON Louis Johannes (FS). B 19/11/66 Vereeniging. RHB RM. Ed Grey College (Bfn), UOFS. OFS Schools 1984-86. FC debut OFS v AusXI (Bfn) 1986/87. HSFC 226* FS v Bol (Bfn) 1995/96. HSLO 102 OFS v Bdr (EL) 1991/92. BBLO 4-48 OFS v Imp (Vga) 1987/88. Tours: SAA to Zim 1994/95.

WILLIAMS Henry Smith (Bol). B 11/6/67 Pniel, near Stellenbosch. RHB RFM. Ed Luckhoff SSS. WP SASA XI 1986-87, SASA Schools 1987. Nephew of Bert Erickson, senior WP administrator. FC debut Bol v Bdr (Bredasdorp) 1992/93. LOIs: 7 (1998/99-1999/00). BBLOI 3-38 v Zim (Dbn) 1999/00. HSFC 33 Bol v Bdr (EL) 2000/01. BBFC 6-27 Bol v NW (Paarl) 1999/00. HSLO 15 Bol v Nor (Paarl) 1997/98. BBLO 4-35 Bol v Ntl (Paarl) 1996/97. Tours: SA to Ind 1999/00; SAA to Zim 1994/95; SL 1998/99.

WILLIAMS Jody Wendell (Eas). B 9/1/80 Johannesburg. RHB RFM. Ed Roosevelt College. Gau Schools 1998-99. FC debut Eas v FS (Ben) 2000/01.

WILLOUGHBY Charl Myles (WP/Pres). B 3/12/74 Cape Town. LHB LFM. Ed Wynberg BHS, Stell Univ. WP Schools 1991-92. FC debut Bol v Tvl (Jhb) 1994/95, WP debut 2000/01. Bol 1994/95-1999/00, BolB 1994/95-1995/96. LOIs: 1 (1999/00). BBLOI 2-39 v Pak (Sharjah) 1999/00. HSFC 17* Bol v NW (Paarl) 1999/00. BBFC 5-26 WP v FS (CT) 2000/01. HSLO 11 Bol v NT (Cent) 1996/97. BBLO 6-24 SAA v Bar (Bridgetown) 2000/01. BBDLO 5-39 Bol v Gau (Jhb) 1999/00. Tours: SA to Shar 1999/00; SAA to WI 2000/01.

WILSON James Godfrey Hartland (Bdr). B 3/11/78 Queenstown. RHB RFM. Ed Queens College, EL Tech. Bdr Schools 1995-97. FC debut Bdr/EP v SLA (PE) 1999/00, LO debut for Bdr 2000/01.

WINGFIELD Wade Richard (KZN). B 17/12/77 Scottburgh. RHB RM. Ed Durban HS, Ntl Technikon. Ntl Schools 1993-95, SA Schools 1995. FC debut NtlB v WPB (CT) 1997/98, KZN debut 1998/99. HSFC 89* KZN v Gau (Dbn) 2000/01. BBFC 2-18 NtlB v NW (Dbn) 1997/98. BBSS 2-36 KZN v Gau (Jhb) 2000/01. HSLO 83 KZN v Nor (Dbn) 1998/99. BBLO 4-42 KZN v FS (Dbn) 1999/00. Tours: SA U-19 to Ind 1995/96. SA U-19 v Pak U-19 1996/97. Rugby (Ntl U21, 1996-97), Baseball (SA Allstars 1992).

ZONDEKI Monde (Bdr). B 25/7/82 King William's Town. RHB RF. Ed Dale College. Bdr Schools 1997-2000. FC debut Bdr v NZ (EL) 2000/01. HSFC 12 Bdr v NZ (EL) 2000/01. Tours: SA U-19 to NZ 2000/01. Rugby (Bdr U-13).

SUPERSPORT SERIES

Western Province bounced back from a disappointing campaign in 1999/2000 to capture the SuperSport Series for the second time in three seasons. Border, for the third successive season, were the beaten finalists.

Western Province set the pace virtually from the start of the competition and were worthy winners, going through the season unbeaten and winning seven of their nine matches.

The two provinces with the best overall record in the competition, Gauteng and KwaZulu-Natal, were unable to reach the Super Eight phase, with Gauteng dropping from champions to last place in the Shield in the course of a single season.

SUPERSPORT SERIES TABLES 2000/01

First round	**P**	**W**	**L**	**D**	**Bat**	**Bowl**	**Pts**	**Super 8**
Pool A								
Northerns	5	3	0	2	13	17	60	25
Free State	5	2	1	2	16	15	51	27
Boland	5	2	1	2	8	16	44	38
North West	5	1	3	1	10	19	39	16
Griqualand West	5	0	3	2	11	18	29	DNQ
Gauteng	5	1	1	3	7	8	25	DNQ
Pool B								
Western Province	4	3	0	1	14	14	58	52
Easterns	4	2	2	0	7	14	41	25
Border	4	1	1	2	10	13	33	26
Eastern Province	4	0	2	2	12	16	28	19
KwaZulu-Natal	4	0	1	3	7	14	21	DNQ

Note: The match between Boland and Gauteng was abandoned without a ball being bowled, and is reflected as a draw in the above table.

Super Eights	**P**	**W**	**L**	**D**	**Bat**	**Bowl**	**Pts**
Western Province	7	6	0	1	30	21	111
Border	7	5	1	1	16	26	92
Easterns	7	4	3	0	14	23	77
Northerns	7	2	3	2	18	23	61
Boland	7	2	3	2	13	26	59
Free State	7	2	4	1	12	26	58
North West	7	1	5	1	16	26	52
Eastern Province	7	1	4	2	14	24	48
Shield Competition							
Griqualand West	4	1	0	3	11	15	41.8
KwaZulu-Natal	4	0	0	4	13	14	32.25
Gauteng	4	0	1	3	13	12	30

Note: Average points were carried over from the first round.

MATCH-WINNER . . . Graeme Smith plays a square cut during his man of the match performance in the SuperSport Series final at Newlands

Picture: Tertius Pickard, TOUCHLINE PHOTO

WESTERN PROVINCE v BORDER

SuperSport Series Final

Played at Newlands, Cape Town on 21,22,23,24 March 2001 Toss: Western Province
Umpires: IL Howell & BG Jerling (TV: AG O'Connor)
Debuts: WP: None. Bdr: None
Close of Play: Day 1: Bdr (1) 247-7 (Makalima 40*, Drakes 46*, 91.4 overs). Day 2: WP (1) 229-2 (Smith 120*, Ackerman 4*, 84.4 overs). Day 3: WP (1) 446-7 (Dawson 11*, Henderson 18*, 182 overs).
Result: Western Province won by an innings and 26 runs
Man of Match: Graeme Smith

Western Province seized the initiative when HD Ackerman sent Border in on a good five-day pitch, which had some early life before becoming an ideal batting surface. Roger Telemachus, whose departure to join the national team in the West Indies had been delayed so that he could remain active by playing to the end of the SuperSport Series, gave the top-order batsmen plen=ty of problems before Sugden top-edged a hook to fine leg. Fellow opener Botha was caught at short leg soon afterwards. Telemachus took two for seven in a six-over opening spell.

Wiblin skied a catch to extra cover off Henderson and Border were in deep trouble. Steven Pope played a sensible, patient innings but, despite useful stands with Strydom and Gamiet, was unable to relieve the pressure on the Border batting. Pope was finally out, dragging a ball from Dawson onto his stumps, shortly after the final drinks break on the first day but Makalima and Drakes batted positively until close of play.

Telemachus struck twice early on the second morning and it soon became obvious that Border's total was inadequate. The young left-handers, Smith and Puttick, saw the shine off the new ball before Smith and Ferreira took control in a second-wicket stand of 166 which was only ended when Drakes had Ferreira caught behind off the second new ball towards the end of the second day.

Western Province batted throughout the third day and although it was unspectacular it took the match beyond Border's reach. With the Border pace attack blunted, it was the off-spinner, Love, who carried the Border attack and he was rewarded on the fourth morning when he took the last three wickets to finish with career-best figures.

Gamiet was promoted to open for Border and played a fine innings but the visitors never seemed likely to avoid defeat after Willoughby dismissed Botha early and Dawson ended a promising second-wicket stand of 52 between Gamiet and Pope. Henderson made victory sure for Western Province with his third five-wicket haul of the season.

BORDER

FIRST INNINGS	*Runs*	*Mins*	*Balls*	*4*	*6*	*SECOND INNINGS*	*Runs*	*Mins*	*Balls*	*4*	*6*
CB Sugden c Willoughby b Telemachus	1	35	20	-	-	(6) lbw b Telemachus	11	37	34	2	-
PJ Botha c Ferreira b Telemachus	10	43	35	-	-	(1) lbw b Willoughby	1	7	4	-	-
SC Pope b Dawson	58	256	186	7	-	c Tsolekile b Dawson	26	94	74	4	-
W Wiblin c Puttick b Henderson	24	55	44	5	-	c Prince b Willoughby	0	29	16	-	-
*PC Strydom c Johnson b Dawson	28	75	60	5	-	c Tsolekile b Henderson	22	42	28	4	-
LL Gamiet c Tsolekile b Johnson	24	67	59	3	-	(2) c Puttick b Henderson	80	251	189	11	-
†I Mitchell c Johnson b Henderson	3	4	2	-	-	c Tsolekile b Henderson	12	47	33	1	-
DL Makalima not out	42	133	92	6	-	b Henderson	0	22	9	-	-
VC Drakes c Smith b Telemachus	46	82	62	6	1	c Puttick b Henderson	2	8	3	-	-
GT Love c Tsolekile b Telemachus	2	2	2	-	-	not out	7	15	6	1	-
T Henderson c Ackerman b Willoughby	1	3	4	-	-	b Dawson	12	12	12	2	-
Extras (lb 7, w 1, nb 5)	13					Extras (lb 2, nb 16)	18				
TOTAL (93.3 overs)	**252**					**TOTAL (65.2 overs)**	**191**				

WESTERN PROVINCE

GC Smith c Mitchell b Love	183	604	477	18	1
AG Puttick c Mitchell b Drakes	12	107	70	1	-
LD Ferreira c Mitchell b Drakes	81	219	163	8	3
*HD Ackerman c Sugden b Love	17	109	71	3	-
AG Prince lbw b Drakes	53	204	168	5	-
NC Johnson lbw b Love	2	2	2	-	-
†TL Tsolekile c Sugden b Love	53	85	70	6	1
AC Dawson c Sugden b Love	19	99	73	2	-
CW Henderson not out	28	93	74	4	-
R Telemachus lbw b Love	2	23	17	-	-
CM Willoughby b Love	0	21	12	-	-
Extras (b 3, lb 1, w 2, nb 13)	19				
TOTAL (197.2 overs)	**469**				

Bowling	*O*	*M*	*R*	*W*	*O*	*M*	*R*	*W*
WESTERN PROVINCE								
Telemachus	13	2	47	4	12	0	47	1
Willoughby	19.3	7	56	1	13	4	38	2
Dawson	17	5	58	2	15.2	6	29	2
Henderson	31	11	62	2	19	4	62	5
Johnson	13	6	22	1	6	1	13	0
BORDER								
Drakes	42	11	127	3				
Botha	23	6	49	0				
Henderson	32	12	60	0				
Love	56.2	21	116	7				
Strydom	32	12	75	0				
Pope	7	1	20	0				
Wiblin	5	1	18	0				

Fall of Wickets	Bdr	WP	Bdr
	1st	1st	2nd
1st	14 (1)	49 (2)	7 (1)
2nd	15 (2)	215 (3)	59 (3)
3rd	48 (4)	257 (4)	72 (4)
4th	104 (5)	357 (1)	121 (5)
5th	147 (6)	359 (6)	143 (6)
6th	150 (7)	378 (5)	165 (2)
7th	172 (3)	425 (7)	170 (7)
8th	249 (9)	454 (8)	172 (9)
9th	251 (10)	464 (10)	172 (8)
10th	252 (11)	469 (11)	191 (11)

SUPERSPORT SERIES 2000/01 LEADING BATTING AVERAGES

	Name	M	Inns	NO	Runs	HS	Avg	100	50
1	LD Ferreira (WP)	4	6	0	397	201	66.16	1	2
2	ND McKenzie (Nor)	3	6	1	305	123	61.00	1	2
3	SG Koenig (Gau)	7	13	0	789	155	60.69	3	4
4	JM Kemp (EP)	5	8	0	452	188	56.50	1	2
5	AG Prince (WP)	8	14	4	539	120*	53.90	1	2
6	JC Kent (KZN)	6	12	3	434	178*	48.22	1	2
7	HD Ackerman (WP)	9	16	3	606	128	46.61	3	2
8	DJJ de Vos (Nor)	3	6	1	233	97	46.60	0	2
9	AC Thomas (NW)	9	16	5	512	106*	46.54	1	2
10	GFJ Liebenberg (FS)	8	13	0	595	202	45.76	1	4
11	DN Crookes (Eas)	8	16	1	671	117	44.73	1	5
12	JM Arthur (GW)	3	5	0	222	165	44.40	1	0
13	LJ Wilkinson (FS)	9	15	0	642	169	42.80	1	3
14	MI Gidley (GW)	9	15	1	596	151	42.57	1	4
15	LL Bosman (GW)	6	10	2	338	115*	42.25	1	2
	GC Smith (WP)	9	16	0	676	183	42.25	2	3
17	JL Ontong (Bol)	8	14	2	490	131*	40.83	1	3
18	CC Bradfield (EP)	7	14	1	524	91	40.30	0	3
19	JM Henderson (Bol)	7	14	1	523	98	40.23	0	4
20	PC Strydom (Bdr)	9	16	0	643	86	40.18	0	7

(Qualification: 5 completed innings)

LEADING BOWLING AVERAGES

	Name	M	Overs	Mdns	Runs	Wkts	Avg	BB	5I	10M
1	GA Roe (NW)	8	291.1	92	631	40	15.77	7-47	3	0
2	CK Langeveldt (Bol)	5	125.4	33	359	21	17.09	5-19	1	0
3	PJ Botha (Bdr)	6	152.3	54	375	21	17.85	4-48	0	0
4	KCG Benjamin (Eas)	5	190.4	45	549	29	18.93	6-73	1	0
5	HS Williams (Bol)	5	214.2	63	541	28	19.32	6-40	4	0
6	DJ Callaghan (EP)	8	156	51	356	18	19.77	5-24	3	1
7	A Nel (Eas)	4	154	38	361	17	21.23	5-43	2	0
8	AC Dawson (WP)	7	238.2	74	583	27	21.59	5-51	1	0
9	CM Willoughby (WP)	8	298.5	107	683	31	22.03	5-26	1	0
10	PV Mpitsang (FS)	9	268.1	62	733	33	22.21	5-24	3	0
11	CW Henderson (WP)	7	400.3	138	801	36	22.25	5-6	3	0
12	PC Strydom (Bdr)	9	210.5	59	518	22	23.54	3-29	0	0
13	JM Kemp (EP)	5	198.4	61	426	18	23.66	6-56	2	0
14	S Elworthy (Nor)	7	243.2	65	711	30	23.70	5-41	2	0
15	VC Drakes (Bdr)	9	368	100	975	41	23.78	5-80	1	0
16	D Pretorius (FS)	8	276.3	57	881	37	23.81	4-51	0	0
17	GJ Kruis (GW)	9	391	110	962	40	24.05	5-50	1	0
18	JC Kent (KZN)	6	161	33	507	21	24.14	6-77	1	0
19	R Telemachus (WP)	6	168.5	34	552	22	25.09	6-54	1	0
20	AG Botha (Eas)	7	244.2	80	614	24	25.58	6-106	1	0

(Qualification: 15 wickets)

LEADING WICKETKEEPERS

	Name	M	Ct	St	Total
1	D Jennings (Eas)	8	37	2	39
2	CFK van Wyk (Nor)	9	35	2	37
3	W Bossenger (GW)	9	35	1	36
	EG Poole (NW)	9	36	0	36
5	DW Murray (EP)	8	35	0	35
6	I Mitchell (Bdr)	8	32	2	34
7	TL Tsolekile (WP)	9	30	1	31
8	GL Brophy (FS)	8	27	2	29
9	SJ Palframan (Bol)	6	22	3	25
	ELR Stewart (KZN)	8	24	1	25

Note: One of Mitchell's catches was taken as a fielder.

LEADING FIELDERS

	Name	M	Ct
1	NC Johnson (WP)	9	24
2	LJ Koen (Bol)	8	17
3	JL Ontong (Bol)	8	16
	GC Smith (WP)	9	16
	M van Jaarsveld (Nor)	9	16
6	GD Elliott (GW)	9	13
	W Wiblin (Bdr)	9	13
8	DN Crookes (Eas)	8	11
9	HD Ackerman (WP)	9	10
	CC Bradfield (EP)	7	10
	MJ Lavine (NW)	9	10
	GFJ Liebenberg (FS)	8	10
	BT Player (Bol)	7	10

CURRIE CUP/CASTLE CUP/SUPERSPORT SERIES WINNERS

Winners	Year	Winners	Year
CURRIE CUP			
Transvaal	1889/90	Natal	1966/67
Kimberley	1890/91	Natal	1967/68
Western Province	1892/93	Transvaal	1968/69
Western Province	1893/94	Transvaal/WP (tied)	1969/70
Transvaal	1894/95	Transvaal	1970/71
Western Province	1896/97	Transvaal	1971/72
Western Province	1897/98	Transvaal	1972/73
Transvaal	1902/03	Natal	1973/74
Transvaal	1903/04	Western Province	1974/75
Transvaal	1904/05	Natal	1975/76
Transvaal	1906/07	Natal	1976/77
Western Province	1908/09	Western Province	1977/78
Natal	1910/11	Transvaal	1978/79
Natal	1912/13	Transvaal	1979/80
Western Province	1920/21	Natal	1980/81
Transvaal/Natal/WP (tied)	1921/22	Western Province	1981/82
Transvaal	1923/24	Transvaal	1982/83
Transvaal	1925/26	Transvaal	1983/84
Transvaal	1926/27	Transvaal	1984/85
Transvaal	1929/30	Western Province	1985/86
Western Province	1931/32	Transvaal	1986/87
Natal	1933/34	Transvaal	1987/88
Transvaal	1934/35	Eastern Province	1988/89
Natal	1936/37	EP/WP (tied)	1989/90
Natal/Transvaal (tied)	1937/38	Western Province	1990/91
Natal	1946/47	**CASTLE CUP**	
Natal	1947/48	Eastern Province	1991/92
Transvaal	1950/51	Orange Free State	1992/93
Natal	1951/52	Orange Free State	1993/94
Western Province	1952/53	Natal	1994/95
Natal	1954/55	Western Province	1995/96
Western Province	1955/56	**SUPERSPORT SERIES**	
Transvaal	1958/59	Natal	1996/97
Natal	1959/60	Free State	1997/98
Natal	1960/61	Western Province	1998/99
Natal	1962/63	Gauteng	1999/00
Natal	1963/64	Western Province	2000/01
Natal/Transvaal (tied)	1965/66		

GAUTENG (previously Transvaal) have won the competition outright 25 times and, including ties, 29 times.
KWAZULU-NATAL (previously Natal) have won outright 20 times and, including ties, 23 times.
WESTERN PROVINCE have won outright 17 times and, including ties, 20 times.
EASTERN PROVINCE have won outright twice, including 1988/89 their centenary year and, including one tie, three times.
FREE STATE (previously Orange Free State) have won outright three times.
GRIQUALAND WEST (previously Kimberley) have won outright once.

SUPERSPORT SERIES

BATTING

WICKET PARTNERSHIP RECORDS

1st	424	IJ Siedle and JFW Nicolson	Natal v Orange Free State	1926/27
2nd	338	PG Amm and LJ Koen	Eastern Province v Boland	1995/96
3rd	337	PG Amm and KS McEwan	Eastern Province v Transvaal	1988/89
4th	342	EAB Rowan and PJM Gibb	Transvaal v NE Transvaal	1952/53
5th	355	AJ Lamb and JJ Strydom	Orange Free State v Eastern Province	1987/88
6th	259	SA Jones and O Henry	Boland v Border	1987/88
7th	299	B Mitchell and A Melville	Transvaal v Griqualand West	1946/47
8th	222	SSL Steyn and DPB Morkel	Western Province v Border	1929/30
9th	217	AW Nourse and BC Cooley	Natal v Western Province	1906/07
10th	174	HR Lance and D Mackay-Coghill	Transvaal v Natal	1965/66
	174	AC Thomas and GA Roe	North West v Griqualand West	2000/01

MOST RUNS IN A SEASON (INDIVIDUALS)

	M	Inns	NO	Runs	HS	Avg	100	50	Season
BA Richards (Natal)	8	15	1	1089	219	77.78	4	4	1971/72
BA Richards (Natal)	8	16	1	1064	197	70.93	4	5	1972/73
M Yachad (N Tvl)	10	20	0	994	179	49.70	4	5	1990/91
PN Kirsten (WP)	8	14	1	967	173*	74.38	5	1	1976/77
RG Pollock (Tvl)	8	11	1	961	233	96.10	5	3	1978/79
HH Dippenaar (FS)	8	16	3	938	147	72.15	4	5	1998/99
BA Richards (Natal)	8	12	1	898	186*	81.63	3	6	1973/74
AJ Lamb (OFS)	6	12	2	878	294	87.80	3	3	1987/88
BA Richards (Natal)	8	15	4	868	159	78.90	3	3	1975/76
HD Ackerman (WP)	8	14	1	866	202*	66.61	5	1	1997/98
AD Nourse (Natal)	8	11	2	864	214*	96.00	4	2	1947/48
KC Wessels (EP)	8	14	4	847	179*	84.70	4	2	1997/98
KS McEwan (EP)	8	11	1	846	191	84.60	3	4	1988/89
KR Rutherford (Gau)	10	18	2	818	195*	51.12	3	3	1999/00
LJ Koen (EP)	8	15	1	815	186	58.21	2	5	1996/97
RG Pollock (EP)	8	15	4	810	194	73.63	2	4	1975/76
KR Rutherford (Gau)	8	15	2	810	160*	62.30	3	4	1998/99

Note also the following exceptional performances:

	M	Inns	NO	Runs	HS	Avg	100	50	Season
EAB Rowan (Tvl)	6	9	2	765	277*	109.28	3	2	1950/51
A Bacher (Tvl)	6	9	1	748	189	93.50	3	3	1968/69
KG Viljoen (Tvl)	5	9	2	715	124	102.14	3	4	1936/37
AM Bacher (Tvl)	5	9	2	710	210	101.42	4	1	1996/97
MJ Procter (Rhodesia)	6	6	0	680	174	113.33	5	0	1970/71
AD Nourse (Natal)	4	4	1	666	260*	222.00	3	0	1936/37

5000 RUNS IN A CAREER

+ Denotes current player

	M	Inns	NO	Runs	HS	Avg	100	50
RG Pollock	157	261	34	12409	233	54.66	35	64
PN Kirsten	170	300	19	11835	271	42.11	29	57
SJ Cook	163	289	33	11307	201*	44.16	32	48
KC Wessels	114	195	23	8487	197	49.34	22	45

SUPERSPORT SERIES

HR Fotheringham	132	220	21	7981	184	40.10	19	44
EJ Barlow	122	217	11	7881	212	38.25	20	35
CEB Rice	164	259	43	7714	150*	35.71	11	41
BA Richards	79	140	15	7551	219	60.40	26	36
MW Rushmere	119	207	25	7074	188	38.86	17	34
RF Pienaar	131	232	17	6832	151*	31.77	9	40
AL Wilmot	124	226	23	6606	222*	32.54	10	29
AP Kuiper	129	219	27	6436	161*	33.52	7	39
+MJR Rindel	104	191	16	6388	174	36.50	12	35
KS McEwan	104	174	18	6215	191	39.83	15	31
KA McKenzie	122	188	21	6076	188	36.38	12	30
+AC Hudson	94	170	13	6029	206	38.40	13	29
CP Wilkins	114	207	8	6022	150	30.26	8	33
BL Irvine	81	145	13	5978	193	45.28	17	26
M Yachad	93	175	8	5850	200	35.02	12	30
+DJ Callaghan	111	188	19	5780	148	34.20	13	27
+DJ Cullinan	88	156	25	5762	337*	43.98	14	29
+PJR Steyn	108	198	15	5761	188*	31.48	9	25
L Seeff	102	190	18	5756	156	33.46	9	31
+JM Arthur	95	179	8	5621	165	32.87	11	27
+LJ Koen	83	144	13	5467	202*	41.73	10	32
A Bacher	76	136	7	5460	189	42.32	14	31
MJ Procter	110	180	15	5405	174	32.75	10	32
VF du Preez	102	196	15	5357	200*	29.59	9	26
PG Amm	94	168	11	5301	214	33.76	8	32
+LJ Wilkinson	95	166	8	5263	226*	33.31	8	26
HM Ackerman	107	186	20	5262	200*	31.69	8	26
DD Dyer	99	172	14	5211	196*	32.98	8	27
MJD Doherty	83	156	10	5205	130*	35.65	12	23
+G Kirsten	69	123	15	5079	244	47.02	13	26

Note also:

AJ Lamb	69	121	16	4948	294	47.12	12	29
+GFJ Liebenberg	85	155	5	4799	229	31.99	9	23
AD Nourse	52	74	6	4478	260*	65.85	19	15
EAB Rowan	55	87	5	4208	277*	51.31	12	19
TL Goddard	58	93	5	4071	222	46.26	14	14
DJ McGlew	62	92	6	3785	186	44.01	8	22
RA McLean	56	84	6	3610	182	46.28	7	25
AW Nourse	53	76	9	3482	212	51.97	13	12
HW Taylor	39	58	3	3226	250*	58.65	12	11

BOWLING

MOST WICKETS IN A SEASON (INDIVIDUALS)

	M	Runs	Wkts	Avg	5I	10M	Season
VC Drakes (Bdr)	10	979	60	16.31	3	0	1999/00
MJ Procter (Natal)	8	936	59	15.86	7	2	1976/77
ST Clarke (Tvl)	10	738	58	12.72	6	1	1984/85
VAP van der Bijl (Natal)	8	804	57	14.10	7	3	1981/82
VC Drakes (Bdr)	9	820	56	14.64	5	0	1998/99

JT Botten (NE Tvl)	6	555	55	10.09	6	2	1958/59
VAP van der Bijl (Natal)	8	513	54	9.50	3	1	1980/81
SD Jack (Tvl)	10	865	54	16.01	3	1	1990/91
JE Waddington (G West)	6	893	53	16.84	7	3	1952/53
GS le Roux (WP)	8	773	53	14.58	4	1	1977/78
AE Hall (Tvl)	6	650	52	12.50	6	2	1926/27
AJ Kourie (Tvl)	8	734	52	14.11	5	1	1980/81
EO Simons (N Tvl)	10	727	51	14.25	2	0	1984/85
MJ Procter (Rhodesia)	8	912	50	18.24	4	2	1972/73
P Anker (Bol)	7	731	50	14.62	5	1	1981/82
CJPG van Zyl (OFS)	6	676	50	13.52	5	2	1984/85
AJ Kourie (Tvl)	10	1009	50	20.18	3	0	1984/85

Note also the following exceptional performances:

JJ Kotze (WP)	5	460	43	10.69	7	3	1906/07
EP Nupen (Tvl)	5	434	43	10.09	5	3	1931/32
AEE Vogler (EP)	5	401	41	9.78	6	2	1906/07

250 WICKETS IN A CAREER

	M	Runs	Wkts	Avg	Best	5I	10M
VAP van der Bijl	109	9395	572	16.42	8-35	36	9
MJ Procter	110	9120	471	19.36	9-71	26	10
CEB Rice	164	7975	396	20.13	7-62	11	1
AJ Kourie	107	8364	378	22.12	8-113	21	3
O Henry	103	8937	375	23.83	7-82	19	2
+MW Pringle	90	8245	366	22.52	7-60	14	3
GS le Roux	83	7125	365	19.52	7-40	16	2
WK Watson	108	8373	347	24.12	7-50	12	0
+CE Eksteen	97	9855	336	29.33	7-29	15	1
TG Shaw	112	9784	331	29.55	7-79	12	2
RW Hanley	82	6321	323	19.56	7-31	17	3
DL Hobson	90	8661	319	27.15	9-64	18	5
JE Waddington	59	6896	317	21.75	9-105	32	8
EJ Barlow	122	6881	317	21.70	7-24	10	1
+S Elworthy	88	8286	304	27.25	7-65	12	3
EO Simons	108	7714	297	25.97	6-26	9	1
RC Ontong	104	8690	296	29.35	7-60	11	0
ST Jefferies	73	7103	291	24.40	10-59	13	3
CJPG van Zyl	80	6405	287	22.31	8-84	10	2
+CW Henderson	74	7671	284	27.01	7-57	9	0
JT Botten	62	5337	280	19.06	9-23	18	4
NV Radford	70	6277	280	22.41	9-102	13	2
AH McKinnon	56	5343	278	19.21	7-37	25	6
PB Clift	92	7005	270	25.94	7-38	7	0
PD Swart	106	6321	269	23.49	6-85	5	1
PS de Villiers	59	5297	260	20.37	6-47	12	0

Note also:

HJ Tayfield	49	5166	241	21.43	8-129	16	6
PM Pollock	60	4786	239	20.02	7-19	10	1
+RE Bryson	69	5790	232	24.95	7-68	14	3

+EAE Baptiste	67	4940	218	22.66	5-30	11	1
+AA Donald	63	5881	218	26.97	8-37	7	0
GB Lawrence	47	3495	209	16.72	8-42	7	1
+VC Drakes	42	3918	204	19.20	8-59	11	1
EP Nupen	27	2346	184	12.75	9-48	19	9
JH Sinclair	27	2207	164	13.45	8-40	16	5
CP Carter	33	2558	155	16.50	7-37	10	1

ALL-ROUND PLAY

THE DOUBLE (3000 runs and 150 wickets)

RLS Armitage	3583 runs	189 wickets
EJ Barlow	7881 runs	317 wickets
+PJ Botha	4485 runs	189 wickets
PD de Vaal	3457 runs	226 wickets
JH du Preez	3285 runs	224 wickets
AM Ferreira	4602 runs	232 wickets
I Foulkes	4005 runs	178 wickets
TL Goddard	4071 runs	187 wickets
O Henry	3890 runs	375 wickets
IL Howell	3528 runs	226 wickets
AJ Kourie	3962 runs	378 wickets
RA le Roux	4303 runs	170 wickets
BM McMillan	4027 runs	173 wickets
RC Ontong	4050 runs	296 wickets
MJ Procter	5405 runs	471 wickets
CEB Rice	7714 runs	396 wickets
EO Simons	3802 runs	297 wickets
PD Swart	3719 runs	269 wickets
+JF Venter	3893 runs	176 wickets

WICKETKEEPING

WICKETKEEPER'S DOUBLE (3000 runs and 150 dismissals)

NT Day	4821 runs	337 dismissals
RJ East	4653 runs	289 dismissals
BL Irvine	5978 runs	171 dismissals
RV Jennings	3622 runs	538 dismissals
DT Lindsay	3542 runs	181 dismissals
DJ Richardson	4276 runs	344 dismissals
AJS Smith	3273 runs	286 dismissals
+ELR Stewart	4463 runs	174 dismissals

MOST DISMISSALS IN A SEASON

46 (ct 45,st 1)	NT Day (N Tvl)	1984/85
46 (ct 40,st 6)	RV Jennings (Tvl)	1984/85
44 (ct 42,st 2)	RV Jennings (N Tvl)	1990/91
43 (ct 42,st 1)	P Kirsten (WP)	1995/96
42 (ct 37,st 5)	G Morgan (Nor/Nor B)	1998/99
41 (ct 39,st 2)	RJ Ryall (WP)	1990/91
40 (ct 34,st 6)	RJ Ryall (WP)	1984/85

WICKETKEEPERS WHO HAVE DISMISSED 200 BATSMEN IN A CAREER

	M	Ct	St	Total
RV Jennings	137	490	48	538
RJ Ryall	111	354	34	388
DJ Richardson	119	318	26	344
NT Day	101	308	29	337
B McBride	80	261	30	291
RJ East	92	281	8	289
AJS Smith	90	276	10	286
GP Pfuhl	82	249	30	279
+SJ Palframan	70	221	18	239
D Gamsy	59	191	22	213

Note: Some of the catches may have been taken while the player was not keeping wicket.
Note also:

	M	Ct	St	Total
+N Pothas	59	167	19	186

FIELDING

MOST CATCHES IN A SEASON

24	NC Johnson (WP)	2000/01	19	GFJ Liebenberg (FS)	1999/00
21	AJ Kourie (Tvl)	1984/85	18	DN Crookes (Gau)	1999/00
21	LJ Koen (Bol)	1999/00	17	LJ Wilkinson (FS)	1997/98
20	LJ Barnard (N Tvl)	1985/86	17	LJ Koen (Bol)	2000/01
19	EJ Barlow (WP)	1976/77			

FIELDERS WHO HAVE TAKEN 100 CATCHES IN A CAREER

	M	Ct		M	Ct
RG Pollock	157	155	HR Fotheringham	132	120
EJ Barlow	122	152	CEB Rice	164	112
+LJ Koen	83	133	O Henry	103	109
KA McKenzie	122	127	KC Wessels	114	109
AJ Kourie	107	124	D Bestall *	106	108

Note: Some of the catches may have been taken while the player occasionally kept wicket. * Has also taken one stumping.

MOST APPEARANCES

170 PN Kirsten (Western Province/Border)
164 CEB Rice (Transvaal/Transvaal B/Natal)
163 SJ Cook (Transvaal/Transvaal B)
157 RG Pollock (Eastern Province/Transvaal)
137 RV Jennings (Transvaal/Transvaal B/Northern Transvaal)
132 HR Fotheringham (Natal/Natal B/Transvaal/Transvaal B)
131 RF Pienaar (Transvaal/Transvaal B/Western Province/Western Province B/Northerns/Northerns B)
129 AP Kuiper (Western Province/Western Province B/Boland)
124 AL Wilmot (Eastern Province/Border)
122 EJ Barlow (Transvaal/Eastern Province/Western Province/Boland)
122 KA McKenzie (NE Transvaal/Transvaal/Transvaal B)

MOST APPEARANCES FOR ONE TEAM

150 CEB Rice (Transvaal)

CONSOLIDATED PLAYING RECORD 1889/90-2000/01

	First Match	Played	Won	Lost	Drawn	Tied
Boland	1980/81	140	42	59	38	1
Boland B	1993/94	15	2	9	4	0
Border	1897/98	365	120	150	95	0
Border B	1993/94	15	2	5	8	0
Eastern Province	1893/94	408	102	166	140	0
Eastern Province B	1977/78	113	24	35	52	2
Easterns	1991/92	58	15	19	24	0
Free State	1903/04	376	100	165	111	0
Free State B	1989/90	30	4	10	16	0
Gauteng	1889/90	445	223	69	153	0
Gauteng B	1959/60	194	84	44	66	0

Griqualand West	1889/90	363	61	186	116	0
Griqualand West B	1998/99	6	0	3	3	0
KwaZulu-Natal	1893/94	420	181	89	150	0
KwaZulu-Natal B	1965/66	177	53	42	81	1
Northerns	1937/38	318	88	130	100	0
Northerns B	1981/82	88	22	34	32	0
North West	1991/92	58	11	23	24	0
Rhodesia	1904/05	183	58	64	61	0
Rhodesia B/Zim Board XI	1977/78	29	4	9	16	0
South Western Districts	1904/05	1	0	1	0	0
Western Province	1892/93	433	190	111	132	0
Western Province B	1975/76	131	63	26	42	0
	Totals:	4366	1449	1449	1464	4

SUPERSPORT CHALLENGE 2000/01

KwaZulu-Natal won the inaugural SuperSport Challenge when they beat Northerns in the final of a four-team tournament in Durban on 1 October 2000. The tournament was launched as a season pipe-opener with three matches, of 25 overs a side, played in a single day. The prize for the victorious team was a holiday in Mauritius for the players and their wives or partners.

Two centuries were hit, both by Northerns players, with Johan Myburgh hitting an unbeaten 109 off 76 balls against Eastern Province, while Rudi Steyn lacked support as he made 105 not out off 77 balls in an unsuccessful attempt to overhaul KwaZulu-Natal's total of 186 for nine.

Players wore microphones to be in contact with television commentators and the occasion was used as an experiment, with umpires able to refer lbw decisions to a television umpire.

SCORES IN BRIEF

EP 164-7 in 25 overs (MR Benfield 55, MW Creed 28, G Dros 2-23, JG Myburgh 2-29). Nor 168-1 in 20.4 overs (PJR Steyn 50, JG Myburgh 109*). Northerns won by 9 wickets.

WP 178-4 in 25 overs (JH Kallis 33, HD Ackerman 53*, LD Ferreira 34*, L Klusener 2-35). KZN 179-5 in 24.1 overs (AM Amla 31, L Klusener 52*, SM Pollock 44*, JH Kallis 2-27). KwaZulu-Natal won by 5 wickets.

Final

KZN 186-9 in 25 overs (ML Bruyns 46, AM Amla 29, GJ Smith 3-38, JG Myburgh 4-28). Nor 175-6 in 25 overs (PJR Steyn 105*). KwaZulu-Natal won by 11 runs.

BOLAND CRICKET BOARD

PO Box 2969, Paarl 7620.
Tel (021) 862 4580/1/2/3/4. Fax (021) 862 1298.

Executive Chairman: Henry Paulse
Executive Vice-Chairman: Peter Cyster
Treasurer: Peter Ingwersen
Director: Professional Cricket: Andre Bruyns
Manager: Amateur Cricket: Pietie Williams
Academy Manager: Deon Muller
Youth Manager: Moos Nicholas
Financial Manager: Cassie Viljoen
2001/02 contracted players: Louis Koen, Steve Palframan, James Henderson, Brad Player, Justin Ontong, Charl Langeveldt, Andrew Pringle, Neil Carter, Jonathan Trott, Henry Williams, Con de Lange, Donovan Koch, Kenny Jackson, Henry Davids, Andrew Cyster, Gerhard Strydom, Willem du Toit.

REVIEW OF THE SEASON 2000/01

Altus Momberg

SUPERSPORT SERIES: P9 W2 L3 D4 (fifth) (includes one match abandoned without a ball bowled)
CAPTAIN: LJ Koen (8)
STANDARD BANK CUP: P10 W4 L6 (eighth)

Boland started out brilliantly in the four-day competition, beating bogey team Free State by ten wickets, and seemed set to build on the previous season's successes. But nothing is ever easy in Boland cricket and even in that first win, the signs of later struggles were there.

In the 1999/2000 season, Charl Willoughby and Henry Williams combined for 90 first-class wickets, but Boland were without both for the start of the season. Willoughby joined neighbours Western Province, while Williams was suffering from a series of injury niggles which kept him out of the side until January. Willoughby was never adequately replaced and Boland's key bowler, Charl Langeveldt, also struggled with injuries.

It meant that a large responsibility rested on the shoulders of Neil Carter - a veteran of two first-class matches before the season started - and Andrew Pringle, a rookie.

Veteran all-rounder Bradley Player was magnificent throughout the season and Boland relied too heavily on a player with a history of back problems, who turned 34 during the season.

Boland were well-served by a trio of spinners in Justin Ontong, James Henderson and Con de Lange and were still able to bowl sides out. The difference from the previous season was that the sides were then bowled out for very little and Boland's own failings with the bat were less exposed.

Pieter Barnard, the experienced Griquas player, joined Boland and added solidity to the top of the order but he retired midway through the season.

DRIVING FORWARD . . . Justin Ontong had another successful season for Boland and was rewarded with a call-up to the South African one-day international team.

Picture: Tertius Pickard, TOUCHLINE PHOTO

BOLAND CRICKET BOARD

Although Boland were second at the start of the Super Eights phase of the SuperSport Series, poor results late in the season saw them drop to fifth in the four-day competition. Things were not much better in the Standard Bank Cup, where Boland, the defending champions, finished eighth after only winning four of their matches.

On the positive side was the emergence of several young players in the first team. New coach Omar Henry had a policy of promoting from within the province and several youngsters, including Henry Davids, Gerhard Strydom and Willem du Toit, showed that they were good enough to play at first-class level.

Davids announced his arrival with a splendid attacking century against the Titans at Centurion in difficult circumstances and it will be a brave bowler who tests him with the short ball again after the pasting he dished out to the Northerns pace attack. Strydom is a steady and solid opener, with excellent ability in the slips. Du Toit burst onto the scene with seven for 82 against Easterns and is a young bowling all-rounder of rich potential.

By far the most gratifying aspect of the season was the improvement of Justin Ontong. He averaged over 40 in first-class cricket and consistently scored runs for Boland. He won the match against North West and then later saved games against Western Province and Eastern Province - scoring his maiden first-class century against the latter. He also claimed 17 wickets in the SuperSport Series and his all-round ability - he is also a fabulous fielder - saw him selected for the tour of the West Indies where he made his debut in one-day international cricket.

Ontong has also been awarded a national contract which means that it will be a lot easier for Boland to hold on to a 21-year-old who had received offers from the big provinces up-country.

If Boland are to do better in the coming season, they have to get runs from players other than Ontong and captain Louis Koen. If those two failed, Boland failed. It is time for talented players like Jonathan Trott and James Henderson to start scoring runs consistently. Henry Williams, Player and wicketkeeper Steve Palframan are all approaching retirement age and the younger players must step up to fill the void they will leave.

PROVINCIAL RECORDS

Honours:
Standard Bank Cup (1): 1999/00
UCB Bowl (4): 1981/82, 1985/86, 1987/88, 1992/93

Highest innings totals:

For:	575-5*	v Western Province (Worcester) (FC)	1993/94
	502-6*	v Border (East London) (CC)	1987/88
Against:	509-7*	by Western Province (Cape Town)	1996/97

Lowest innings totals:

For:	59	v Western Province (Cape Town)	1998/99
Against:	64	by Eastern Transvaal (Brackenfell)	1992/93

Highest individual innings:

For:	307*	TN Lazard	v Western Province (Worcester) (FC)	1993/94
	209*	SA Jones v	Border (East London) (CC)	1987/88
Against:	226*	LJ Wilkinson	for Free State (Bloemfontein)	1995/96

Most runs in a season:

SS and Bowl				All FC			
584	(Avg 53.09)	EJ Barlow	1981/82	853	(Avg 65.61)	TN Lazard	1993/94

Most runs in a career:

SS and Bowl				All FC			
2685	(Avg 30.16)	KC Jackson	1993-2000	2873	(Avg 29.02)	KC Jackson	1993-2000

BOLAND CRICKET BOARD

Most 100s in a career:

SS and Bowl			All FC		
5	A du Toit	1980-86	5	A du Toit 1980-86,WS Truter	1987-96

Best bowling in an innings:

For:	9-72	GJ Parsons	v Transvaal B (Johannesburg)	1984/85
Against:	7-16	GL Long f	or Eastern Province B (Port Elizabeth)	1980/81

Best bowling in a match:

For:	12-66	AP Igglesden	v Griqualand West (Kimberley)	1992/93
Against:	11-90	O Henry	for Western Province B (Stellenbosch)	1982/83

Most wickets in a season:

SS and Bowl			All FC		
50	(Avg 14.62) P Anker	1981/82	50	(Avg 14.62) P Anker	1981/82

Most wickets in a career:

SS and Bowl			All FC		
198	(Avg 26.60) CW Henderson	1990-97	221	(Avg 28.41) CW Henderson	1990-97

Most dismissals (wicketkeepers) in an innings:

6	(ct 6,st 0)	L-M Germishuys	v Western Province (Cape Town)	1994/95
6	(ct 6,st 0)	SJ Palframan	v Griqualand West (Paarl)	1998/99

Most dismissals (wicketkeepers) in a match:

8	(ct 7,st 1)	MS de Kock	v Easterns (Paarl)	2000/01

Most dismissals (wicketkeepers) in a season:

SS and Bowl			All FC		
36	(ct 34,st 2) SJ Palframan	1998/99	38	(ct 35,st 3) SJ Palframan	1998/99

Most dismissals (wicketkeepers) in a career:

SS and Bowl			All FC		
115	(ct 109,st 6) SJ Palframan	1997-2000	120	(ct 113,st 7) SJ Palframan	1997-2000

Most catches (fielders) in an innings:

4	P Anker	v Northern Transvaal B (Stellenbosch)	1981/82
4	KC Jackson	v Free State (Bloemfontein)	1995/96
4	E Liebenberg	v Transvaal (Johannesburg)	1996/97
4	CR Wilson	v KwaZulu-Natal (Durban)	1999/00

Most catches (fielders) in a match:

5	CR Wilson	v KwaZulu-Natal (Durban)	1999/00
5	LJ Koen	v Northerns (Centurion)	1999/00
5	JL Ontong	v Border (East London)	2000/01

Most catches (fielders) in a season:

SS and Bowl			All FC		
21	LJ Koen	1999/00	21	LJ Koen	1999/00

Most catches (fielders) in a career:

SS and Bowl			All FC		
53	KC Jackson	1993-2000	54	KC Jackson	1993-2000

Most appearances:

SS and Bowl			All FC		
56	HS Williams	1992-2000	62	HS Williams	1992-2000

Most captaincies:

SS and Bowl			All FC		
30	SA Jones	1983-87	32	SA Jones	1983-87

RECORD WICKET PARTNERSHIPS

1st	198	EJ Barlow and A du Toit v Orange Free State (Stellenbosch)	1982/83
	198	WS Truter and NM Snyman v Western Transvaal (Brackenfell)	1991/92
2nd	171	JM Henderson and PH Barnard v Free State (Paarl)	2000/01
3rd	360	TN Lazard and JB Commins v Western Province (Worcester) (FC) (The South African domestic record for this wicket)	1993/94
	151	LJ Koen and JL Ontong v Western Province (Paarl) (SS)	1999/00
4th	153	JS Roos and KJ Bridgens v Western Transvaal (Potchefstroom)	1991/92
5th	182	A du Toit and J Kennedy v Border (Stellenbosch)	1980/81
6th	259	SA Jones and O Henry v Border (East London) (The South African record for this wicket)	1987/88
7th	185	SA Jones and JD du Toit v Transvaal B (Johannesburg)	1986/87

8th	141	O Henry and EE van Rooyen v Natal B (Stellenbosch)	1985/86
9th	105	HWH Bergins and P Anker v Orange Free State (Stellenbosch)	1983/84
10th	80*	P Anker and CJ Coetzee v Eastern Province B (Port Elizabeth)	1983/84

PERFORMANCES AGAINST OTHER TEAMS

HIGHEST AND LOWEST TOTALS

Opponents	Highest Total For			Lowest Total For		
Border	502-6*		1987/88	71		1987/88
Eastern Province	360-9*		2000/01	120	(FC)	1989/90
				133	(SS)	1998/99
Easterns	404-9*		1991/92	169		2000/01
Free State	413		1999/00	158		1997/98
Gauteng	454		1993/94	95		1999/00
Griqualand West	349		1991/92	166		1997/98
KwaZulu-Natal	351		1993/94	110		1999/00
Northerns	369		2000/01	84		1997/98
North West	362-8*		1991/92	191		1999/00
Western Province	575-5*	(FC)	1993/94	59		1998/99
	398	(SS)	2000/01			

BEST INDIVIDUAL PERFORMANCES

Opponents	Highest score	Best bowling (innings)	Best bowling (match, 8+)
Border	209* SA Jones,1987/88	6-28 SJBase,1987/88	9-123 P Anker,1981/82
Eastern Province	131* JL Ontong, 2000/01	7-57 CW Henderson,1994/95	9-129 CM Willoughby, 1999/00
Easterns	155 WN van As,1991/92	7-82 CW Henderson,1992/93	9-64 AP Igglesden,1992/93
		7-82 WJ du Toit, 2000/01	
Free State	153 EJ Barlow,1982/83	6-88 P Anker,1983/84	9-130 P Anker,1983/84
Gauteng	155 AP Kuiper,1995/96	5-43 R Telemachus, 1997/98	-
Griqualand West	177* LJ Koen,1990/91	7-28 AP Igglesden,1992/93	12-66 AP Igglesden,1992/93
KwaZulu-Natal	87 AP Kuiper,1995/96	6-57 HS Williams, 1996/97	-
Northerns	124 H Davids,2000/01	6-39 HS Williams, 1999/00	9-91 HS Williams, 1999/00
North West	137 NM Snyman,1991/92	7-102 CW Henderson,1991/92	9-66 HS Williams, 1999/00
Western Province	307* (FC) TN Lazard,1993/94	6-122 NM Carter, 2000/01	9-88 R Telemachus, 1997/98
	113 (SS) LJ Koen, 1999/00		

BOLAND SUPERSPORT AVERAGES 2000/01

Batting & Fielding

Name	M	Inns	NO	Runs	HS	Avg	100	50	Ct	St
JL Ontong	8	14	2	490	131*	40.83	1	3	16	0
JM Henderson	7	14	1	523	98	40.23	0	4	1	0
LJ Koen	8	14	0	546	97	39	0	5	17	0
H Davids	5	10	1	314	124	34.88	1	1	2	0
PH Barnard	4	6	0	184	120	30.66	1	0	5	0
JG Strydom	4	8	0	216	73	27	0	1	4	0
HS Williams	5	9	7	53	33	26.5	0	0	2	0
IJL Trott	8	16	2	344	93	24.57	0	3	4	0
WJ du Toit	1	2	0	38	32	19	0	0	0	0
SJ Palframan	6	10	0	172	46	17.2	0	0	22	3
BT Player	7	12	2	172	73	17.2	0	1	10	0
AW Cyster	1	2	0	24	21	12	0	0	0	0
KC Jackson	2	3	0	34	25	11.33	0	0	2	0
CK Langeveldt	5	8	1	72	20	10.28	0	0	2	0
NM Carter	6	10	1	67	21	7.44	0	0	1	0
CdeW de Lange	4	7	0	51	25	7.28	0	0	2	0
AAW Pringle	5	8	1	47	27	6.71	0	0	3	0
MS de Kock	2	4	1	20	17*	6.66	0	0	10	1
Totals	88	157	19	3367	131*		3	18	103	4
			Extras	300				subs	0	
			Total	3667		26.57			103	

Bowling

Name	Overs	Mdns	Runs	Wkts	Avg	BB	5I	10M
CK Langeveldt	125.4	33	359	21	17.09	5-19	1	0
WJ du Toit	56	6	154	8	19.25	7-82	1	0
HS Williams	214.2	63	541	28	19.32	6-40	4	0
NM Carter	221.4	47	752	26	28.92	6-63	2	0
JL Ontong	188.1	24	610	17	35.88	4-120	0	0
BT Player	189.4	58	431	12	35.91	5-26	1	0
AAW Pringle	170.3	35	486	13	37.38	4-49	0	0
CdeW de Lange	138	39	363	7	51.85	2-44	0	0
JM Henderson	48	7	168	3	56.00	2-39	0	0
JG Strydom	1	0	1	0	-	-	0	0
LJ Koen	1	0	5	0	-	-	0	0
IJL Trott	19.1	7	65	0	-	-	0	0
Totals	1373.1	319	3935	135		7-82	9	0
		b & lb	110	5	run outs			
		Total	4045	140	28.89			

MATCH REPORTS AND SCORECARDS

BOLAND v FREE STATE

SuperSport Series Pool A

Played at Boland PKS Park, Paarl on 27,28,29 October 2000

Toss: Boland

Umpires: CJ Mitchley & AG O'Connor

Debuts: Bol: AAW Pringle & IJL Trott (both FC), PH Barnard (FC for Bol). FS: TJ Mokoenanyana (FC)

Close of Play: Day 1: Bol (1) 217-2 (Barnard 108*, Ontong 4*, 68 overs). Day 2: FS (2) 184-4 (Venter 35*, Brophy 8*, 64 overs).

Result: Boland won by 10 wickets

Man of Match: Bradley Player

Points: Bol: 18 (bat 4, bowl 4, match 10). FS: 2 (bat 0, bowl 2, match 0)

Boland, who had often struggled against the Bloemfontein side, end won this match at a canter. By the end of the first day, the hosts had a lead of 115 with eight wickets in hand, after Charl Langeveldt had destroyed the Free State top order. There was no way back into the match as new recruit Pieter Barnard - who joined the team from Griquas - was unbeaten on 108 at the end of the day.

Free State fared better in the second innings with veteran Louis Wilkinson among the runs but former Free State all-rounder, Bradley Player, was the destroyer-in-chief in the second innings.

FREE STATE

FIRST INNINGS	*Runs*	*Mins*	*Balls*	*4*	*6*	*SECOND INNINGS*	*Runs*	*Mins*	*Balls*	*4*	*6*
GFJ Liebenberg run out (Ontong)	8	11	13	-	-	c and b Pringle	25	71	49	5	-
AI Gait c Jackson b Langeveldt	5	59	29	-	-	c Palframan b Player	18	64	43	2	-
LJ Wilkinson c Jackson b Langeveldt	11	27	26	2	-	c Ontong b Pringle	89	150	119	12	-
MN van Wyk c Koen b Player	39	76	52	7	-	lbw b Player	3	13	13	-	-
JF Venter c Barnard b Pringle	19	60	43	3	-	c Langeveldt b Carter	40	260	191	4	-
*†GL Brophy c Barnard b Langeveldt	4	11	5	1	-	lbw b Pringle	27	122	96	3	-
JJ van der Wath c Palframan b Player	5	23	22	-	-	c Palframan b Langeveldt	19	40	22	4	-
HC Bakkes c Player b Langeveldt	0	2	4	-	-	c Ontong b Player	5	27	20	-	-
PV Mpitsang c Palframan b Langeveldt	0	15	5	-	-	c Palframan b Player	11	42	28	-	-
D Pretorius c Palframan b Player	4	9	6	1	-	b Player	0	4	1	-	-
TJ Mokoenanyana not out	0	6	4	-	-	not out	0	34	29	-	-
Extras (w 2, nb 5)	7					Extras (lb 4, w 2, nb 6)	12				
TOTAL (34 overs)	**102**					**TOTAL (100.5 overs)**	**249**				

BOLAND											
IJL Trott c Bakkes b van der Wath	19	54	34	2	-	(2) not out	14	24	21	3	-
JM Henderson c Wilkinson b Venter	76	254	188	10	-	(1) not out	3	24	15	-	-
PH Barnard c van Wyk b Pretorius	120	305	214	12	-						
JL Ontong c Brophy b Mpitsang	16	47	48	-	-						
KC Jackson c Mokoenanyana b Venter	25	87	61	2	-						
*LJ Koen c Pretorius b Venter	41	86	62	6	-						
†SJ Palframan c Brophy b van der Wath	6	22	18	1	-						
BT Player c van der Wath b Venter	2	4	2	-	-						
NM Carter not out	0	18	7	-	-						
CK Langeveldt c van der Wath b Venter	5	7	6	1	-						
AAW Pringle c van Wyk b Venter	0	1	3	-	-						
Extras (b 6, lb 4, w 1, nb 9)	20					Extras (b 4, lb 1, w 1)	6				
TOTAL (105.4 overs)	**330**					**TOTAL (for 0 wkts) (6 overs)**	**23**				

Bowling	*O*	*M*	*R*	*W*		*O*	*M*	*R*	*W*
BOLAND									
Carter	8	1	36	0		19	6	57	1
Langeveldt	11	4	19	5		18	4	49	1
Pringle	9	1	36	1	(4)	21	6	55	3
Player	6	2	11	3	(3)	27.5	18	26	5
Ontong						5	0	33	0
Henderson						10	1	25	0
FREE STATE									
Bakkes	19	7	42	0	(2)	3	0	14	0
Pretorius	20	2	63	1	(1)	3	2	4	0
van der Wath	17	1	68	2					
Mpitsang	12	3	33	1					
Venter	30.4	5	90	6					
Mokoenanyana	7	1	24	0					

Fall of Wickets	**FS**	**Bol**	**FS**	**Bol**
	1st	1st	2nd	2nd
1st	8 (1)	28 (1)	40 (2)	-
2nd	25 (3)	199 (2)	45 (1)	-
3rd	51 (2)	241 (4)	52 (4)	-
4th	89 (4)	259 (3)	164 (3)	-
5th	89 (5)	293 (5)	212 (6)	-
6th	96 (6)	313 (7)	213 (5)	-
7th	96 (8)	320 (8)	237 (8)	-
8th	98 (7)	325 (6)	237 (7)	-
9th	98 (9)	330 (10)	237 (10)	-
10th	102 (10)	330 (11)	249 (9)	-

BOLAND v GAUTENG — SuperSport Series Pool A

At Boland PKS Park, Paarl on 17,18,19,20 November 2000 - no play, rain

The match was abandoned without a ball bowled after torrential rain on the first day and second morning soaked the outfield. The poor drainage at Boland Park, a former stock car racing venue, did not help matters but it was strange that the cricketers were so reluctant to play.

BOLAND v NORTH WEST — SuperSport Series Pool A

Played at Boland PKS Park, Paarl on 24,25,26,27 November 2000 — Toss: North West

Umpires: DF Becker & M Gajjar

Debuts: Bol: None. NW: None

Close of Play: Day 1: Bol (1) 40-3 (Henderson 14*, 20 overs). Day 2: NW (2) 92-5 (Light 39*, Poole 3*, 29 overs). Day 3: Bol (2) 102-3 (Koen 57*, Ontong 2*, 57 overs).

Result: Boland won by 1 wicket

Man of Match: Mark Lavine & Justin Ontong

Points: Bol: 16 (bat 2, bowl 4, match 10). NW: 6 (bat 2, bowl 4, match 0)

Notes: MC Venter retired hurt with his score on 44 and the total on 92-3 in North West's 1st innings.

In easily the most exciting game of the season in Paarl, both sides were in with a chance of winning as Garth Roe bowled the last ball on the fourth day.

After four days of thrilling cricket Boland were not exactly cruising, but at 216 for seven, chasing 218, they finally seemed to have subdued the Potchefstroom side. Mark Lavine had other ideas, however, and dismissed Charl Langeveldt and Neil Carter with successive deliveries to give his side an unlikely chance of winning the game. No 11 Andrew Pringle had a few nervous deliveries before Justin Ontong scored the winning runs of Roe in the next over.

The match served as a coming of age for Ontong, who carried the team on his back throughout the final day. He survived a couple of close lbw appeals but took to the bowling of spinner Morne Strydom.

NORTH WEST

FIRST INNINGS	*Runs*	*Mins*	*Balls*	*4*	*6*	*SECOND INNINGS*	*Runs*	*Mins*	*Balls*	*4*	*6*
AG Lawson c Koen b Carter	5	37	31	-	-	(2) run out (Ontong)	3	7	3	-	-
HM de Vos b Langeveldt	0	2	1	-	-	(1) c Player b Carter	12	20	16	1	-
*MC Venter retired hurt	44	146	102	7	-	absent hurt					
GM Hewitt c Palframan b Langeveldt	34	102	78	3	-	(3) c Koen b Langeveldt	0	18	10	-	-
A Jacobs lbw b Langeveldt	2	18	10	-	-	(4) c Palframan b Player	25	52	44	2	-
MJ Lavine lbw b Carter	0	7	5	-	-	(8) c Player b Carter	11	50	21	-	-
C Light c Koen b Carter	31	80	52	6	-	(5) c Koen b Ontong	101	278	207	16	-
M Strydom b Pringle	12	44	34	1	-	(6) c Barnard b Langeveldt	16	42	22	1	-
†EG Poole b Ontong	17	60	40	2	-	(7) b Langeveldt	6	26	17	-	-
AC Thomas c Ontong b Langeveldt	33	105	92	3	-	(9) c Langeveldt b Player	43	115	104	4	-
GA Roe not out	19	76	49	2	-	(10) not out	0	6	3	-	-
Extras (b 6, lb 9, w 1, nb 3)	19					Extras (b 1, lb 3, nb 4)	8				
TOTAL (81.5 overs)	**216**					**TOTAL (73.5 overs)**	**225**				

BOLAND

	Runs	Mins	Balls	4	6		Runs	Mins	Balls	4	6
IJL Trott lbw b Lavine	5	12	12	1	-	c Poole b Roe	2	7	8	-	-
JM Henderson c Poole b Thomas	86	338	271	10	-	c Hewitt b Roe	19	134	102	1	-
*LJ Koen b Lavine	0	2	2	-	-	b Thomas	77	302	205	8	1
PH Barnard lbw b Lavine	19	74	59	2	-	c Jacobs b Light	16	74	74	1	-
JL Ontong c Poole b Roe	14	80	45	1	-	not out	68	254	176	5	1
KC Jackson c Poole b Lavine	7	29	16	1	-	c Poole b Lavine	2	15	9	-	-
†SJ Palframan lbw b Lavine	31	59	58	4	-	c Roe b Lavine	2	37	26	-	-
BT Player lbw b Lavine	31	96	77	3	1	c Poole b Roe	1	15	9	-	-
NM Carter c Jacobs b Roe	1	21	12	-	-	(10) c Roe b Lavine	0	1	1	-	-
CK Langeveldt not out	3	15	7	-	-	(9) lbw b Lavine	20	70	38	2	-
AAW Pringle lbw b Roe	7	9	7	1	-	not out	0	10	4	-	-
Extras (b 3, lb 8, nb 9)	20					Extras (lb 2, w 1, nb 8)	11				
TOTAL (92.5 overs)	**224**					**TOTAL (for 9 wkts) (107.2 overs)**	**218**				

Bowling	*O*	*M*	*R*	*W*		*O*	*M*	*R*	*W*
BOLAND									
Langeveldt	18.5	4	48	4	(2)	14	3	51	3
Carter	22	4	50	3	(1)	15	1	60	2
Player	18	6	38	0		15.5	1	44	2
Pringle	15	4	45	1		20	4	48	0
Ontong	7	2	14	1		9	1	18	1
Henderson	1	0	6	0					
NORTH WEST									
Lavine	26	10	53	6		37	12	71	4
Roe	25.5	7	57	3		26.2	12	37	3
Thomas	17	3	36	1		21	10	23	1
Strydom	14	2	41	0		14	2	59	0
Light	7	3	21	0		9	1	26	1
Jacobs	3	1	5	0					

Fall of Wickets	**NW**	**Bol**	**NW**	**Bol**
	1st	1st	2nd	2nd
1st	1 (2)	7 (1)	9 (2)	3 (1)
2nd	22 (1)	7 (3)	17 (1)	53 (2)
3rd	88 (4)	40 (4)	21 (3)	90 (4)
4th	98 (6)	76 (5)	56 (4)	148 (3)
5th	98 (5)	96 (6)	88 (6)	156 (6)
6th	128 (8)	145 (7)	95 (7)	165 (7)
7th	151 (7)	211 (2)	145 (8)	166 (8)
8th	166 (9)	213 (8)	221 (5)	216 (9)
9th	216 (10)	213 (9)	225 (9)	216 (10)
10th	-	224 (11)	-	-

Northerns v Boland, Centurion, 1-4 December 2000. Northerns won by 53 runs.
Griqualand West v Boland, Kimberley, 8-11 December 2000. Match drawn.
Western Province v Boland, Cape Town, 1-4 February 2001. Match drawn.

BOLAND v EASTERN PROVINCE — SuperSport Series Super Eight

Played at Boland PKS Park, Paarl on 1,2,3,4 March 2001 — Toss: Boland

Umpires: SB Lambson & CM Schoof

Debuts: Bol: None. EP: None

Close of Play: Day 1: EP (1) 21-0 (Bradfield 13*, U Abrahams 4*, 12 overs). Day 2: EP (1) 318-8 (S Abrahams 80*, Hayward 18*, 116 overs). Day 3: Bol (2) 278-6 (Ontong 81*, 97.5 overs).

Result: Match drawn

Man of Match: Justin Ontong

Points: Bol: 5 (bat 2, bowl 3, match 0). EP: 7 (bat 3, bowl 4, match 0)

Notes: M Hayward was banned from bowling in Boland's 1st innings for running on the pitch.

Justin Ontong continued his great form and got another monkey off his back as he scored his maiden first-class century. A player of undoubted class, one of the criticisms of the player had been that he did not turn 60s and 70s into centuries but he had visibly matured as the season progressed. Ontong's century was a match-saving performance as Boland struggled to overcome a 92-run deficit on the first innings. He received great support from Jonathan Trott who broke out of a horrible slump with his 65.

BOLAND

FIRST INNINGS	*Runs*	*Mins*	*Balls*	*4*	*6*	*SECOND INNINGS*	*Runs*	*Mins*	*Balls*	*4*	*6*
JG Strydom c S Abrahams b Kruger	0	1	1	-	-	(2) c Murray b Peterson	41	137	98	3	-
JM Henderson c Murray b Creed	4	59	28	-	-	(1) c Murray b Hayward	19	75	54	3	-
*LJ Koen lbw b Kruger	50	158	103	6	-	b Hayward	24	65	49	3	1
JL Ontong lbw b Callaghan	7	49	34	-	-	not out	131	393	275	11	1
IJL Trott c Murray b Hayward	74	234	171	8	-	lbw b Creed	65	215	170	6	-
H Davids lbw b Peterson	21	95	86	1	-	lbw b Hayward	12	34	26	2	-
†SJ Palframan c Murray b Peterson	26	60	66	5	-	(8) c Murray b Kruger	3	51	34	-	-
CdeW de Lange lbw b Hayward	11	39	35	1	-	(7) c Murray b Kruger	1	23	16	-	-
BT Player not out	8	30	12	2	-	c S Abrahams b Peterson	2	24	13	-	-
NM Carter b Kruger	7	13	10	1	-	c Bryant b Kruger	15	38	34	2	-
AAW Pringle c S Abrahams b Kruger	0	3	2	-	-						
Extras (lb 10, w 7, nb 11)	28					Extras (b 7, lb 18, w 4, nb 18)	47				
TOTAL (89.3 overs)	**236**					**TOTAL (for 9 wkts dec) (125.2 overs)**	**360**				

EASTERN PROVINCE

*CC Bradfield lbw b Ontong	35	128	90	1	-	lbw b Carter	85	187	173	14	-
U Abrahams c Trott b Ontong	13	143	101	-	-	c Koen b Player	51	116	90	5	-
JDC Bryant c Carter b de Lange	44	146	115	5	-	c Ontong b Carter	44	109	77	4	-
DJ Callaghan c Strydom b Carter	17	60	53	2	-	not out	42	108	64	3	-
MR Benfield st Palframan b Ontong	14	29	28	1	-	b Player	8	21	17	1	-
MW Creed c Koen b Pringle	47	137	108	4	-	b Carter	13	25	16	1	-
RJ Peterson c Palframan b de Lange	0	8	1	-	-	not out	11	21	9	1	-
S Abrahams lbw b Pringle	85	210	162	12	1						
†DW Murray run out (Strydom)	16	46	34	2	-						
M Hayward not out	21	82	46	2	-						
GJ-P Kruger c Ontong b Carter	0	6	7	-	-						
Extras (b 5, lb 2, w 2, nb 27)	36					Extras (b 5, lb 4, w 1, nb 2)	12				
TOTAL (119.4 overs)	**328**					**TOTAL (for 5 wkts) (74 overs)**	**266**				

Bowling	*O*	*M*	*R*	*W*		*O*	*M*	*R*	*W*
EASTERN PROVINCE									
Kruger	18.3	3	49	4		32.2	12	66	3
Hayward	11.3	1	47	2	(4)	25	6	69	3

Fall of Wickets

	Bol	**EP**	**Bol**	**EP**
	1st	1st	2nd	2nd
1st	0 (1)	65 (1)	43 (1)	102 (2)

BORDER BEARS 2000/01

Back , from left: Geoff Love, Evert Ferreira. Middle : Solomon Pango (Selector), Laden Gamiet, Steven Pope, Monde Zondeki, Jamie Wilson, Tyron Henderson, Liam Graham, Francois Klopper, Craig Sugden, Mats Matomela, Geoff Gamiet (Convenor of Selectors) Front: Wayne Wiblin, Vasbert Drakes, Piet Botha, Richard Pybus (Coach), Ray Mali (President) Reunert Bauser (CEO), Pieter Strydom (Captain), Ian Mitchell, Greg King (Fitness Trainer)

BORDER CRICKET BOARD

PO Box 803, East London 5200. Tel (043) 7437757. Fax (043) 7433293. Professional Cricket Office: (043) 7420858. Amateur Cricket Office: (043) 7438176. Fax (043) 7433293. E-mail: border@borderbears.co.za

President: Ray Mali
Vice-president: CM Wilson
Chief Executive Officer: Reunert Bauser
Personal Assistant: Diane Owen-Smith
Professional Cricket Manager: Stephen Jones
Amateur Cricket Manager: Greg Hayes
Marketing Manager: Clare-Anne Nel
Stadium Manager: Greg Dreyer
Coach: Alan Mansell
2001/02 contracted players: Pieter Strydom (captain), Piet Botha, Mark Bruyns, Burton de Wett, Vasbert Drakes, Leyden Gamiet, Liam Graham, Tyron Henderson, Justin Kreusch, Geoff Love, Dumisa Makalima, Ian Mitchell, Tap-Tap Nelani, Steven Pope, Craig Sugden, Wayne Wiblin, Monde Zondeki. **UCB contracted players:** Mark Boucher, Makhaya Ntini.

REVIEW OF THE SEASON 2000/01

Peter Martin

SUPERSPORT SERIES: P9 W5 L2 D2 (beaten finalists)
CAPTAIN: PC Strydom (9)
STANDARD BANK CUP: P13 W7 L6 (beaten semifinalists)

For the Border Bears the 2000/01 season was virtually a repeat of the previous two summers. They produced some fine play during the season to advance to the SuperSport Series final, only to come unstuck once again at the last hurdle.

In the final at Newlands, against a strong Western Province side, well led by HD Ackerman, Border batted first but were then batted out of the game as Province took a lead of 217 runs on the first innings. Border, kept in the field for more than two days, then collapsed to lose by an innings and 26 runs.

Earlier in the season Province won the round robin match by 77 runs. Those two defeats were the only SuperSport games Border lost throughout the summer. Border were the only team in the Super Eight competition to win all four Super Eight matches.

The only other first-class loss was to the visiting New Zealand team when a weakened Border were soundly beaten.

Injuries to key bowlers Piet Botha (back), Tyron Henderson (ankle) and Francois Klopper (groin), gave an opportunity to left-hand medium-pacer Liam Graham to make his debut for Border and he grabbed his chances well to head the Standard Bank bowling averages.

BORDER CRICKET BOARD

Border started their Standard Bank Cup campaign slowly, losing their first three games by narrow margins, but reached the semifinals with a great fightback. The three losses - by 15 runs, six runs and six runs again against Easterns, the Highveld Strikers and Eastern Province respectively during October - made the Bears determined to come right. They realised they had the players and the talent to win and so it proved in the next match against Western Province at Newlands. A four-wicket victory chasing a target of 221 and Border had recorded their first win of the season to set them on a phenomenal run which took them through to the semifinals.

After a two-wicket win with four balls to spare in the first leg at Centurion against Northerns, with Border scoring their highest-ever score of 278, it seemed that nothing could stop Border from advancing to yet another Standard Bank final.

But the cricket gods had other ideas. In the second leg Northerns snatched victory at Buffalo Park after being set the huge task of scoring 272, forcing a third semifinal leg played two days later. Border reached their nadir in this match, bundled out for 84 in a dismal batting performance and Northerns were through to the final.

Strydom had an excellent Standard Bank series, making plenty of runs, taking wickets and leading the side with flair, while taking the Man of the Match award in five of the last six round robin matches.

Strydom was Mr Consistency in the SuperSport Series while Steven Pope, with two centuries towards the end of the season, gave good support.

Again Border relied on their pace attack - Drakes, Botha and Henderson - for victories and Drakes, the West Indian professional, although dropping his wicket tally to 41 after taking 60 wickets in 1999/2000, was always a handful for most provincial sides.

And so it's back to the drawing board. With the Bears proving beyond a doubt that they are a power in the land, perhaps this season will see them take a major trophy for the first time.

PROVINCIAL RECORDS

Honours:

Currie Cup B Section/UCB Bowl (4): 1958/59, 1988/89, 1989/90 (shared), 1990/91 (shared)

Highest innings totals:

For:	530-6*	v Orange Free State B (East London)	1989/90
Against:	601	by Western Province (Cape Town)	1929/30

Lowest innings totals:

For:	16 and 18	v Natal (East London)	1959/60
Against:	41	by Eastern Province (East London)	1936/37

Highest individual innings:

For:	271	PN Kirsten	v Northern Transvaal (East London)	1993/94
Against:	261*	SSL Steyn	for Western Province (Cape Town)	1929/30

Most runs in a season:

SS and Bowl				All FC			
743	(Avg 57.15)	EN Trotman	1988/89	871	(Avg 54.43)	EN Trotman	1988/89

Most runs in a career:

SS and Bowl				All FC			
3987	(Avg 37.26)	PC Strydom	1992-2000	4277	(Avg 35.94)	PC Strydom	1992-2000

Most 100s in a career:

SS and Bowl			All FC	
9	PN Kirsten	1990-9610	WS Farrer	1954-69

Best bowling in an innings:

For:	9-32	AF Hagemann	v Griqualand West (Kimberley)	1960/61
Against:	9-88	VI Smith	for Natal (Pietermaritzburg)	1946/47

Best bowling in a match:

For:	14-59	AF Hagemann	v Griqualand West (Kimberley)	1960/61
Against:	13-59	JE Waddington	for Griqualand West (Kimberley)	1947/48

Most wickets in a season:

SS and Bowl				All FC			
60	(Avg 16.31)	VC Drakes	1999/00	60	(Avg 16.31)	VC Drakes	1999/00

Most wickets in a career:

SS and Bowl				All FC			
204	(Avg 19.20)	VC Drakes	1996-2000	207	(Avg 35.71)	IL Howell	1984-97

Most dismissals (wicketkeepers) in an innings:

7	(ct 6,st 1)	N Kirsten	v Rhodesia (East London)	1959/60

Most dismissals (wicketkeepers) in a match:

9	(ct 7,st 2)	N Kirsten	v Rhodesia (East London)	1959/60
9	(ct 9,st 0)	CWS Pope	v Transvaal B (East London)	1971/72
9	(ct 9,st 0)	SJ Palframan	v Natal (Durban)	1994/95

Most dismissals (wicketkeepers) in a season:

SS and Bowl				All FC			
36	(ct 30,st 6)	EN Trotman	1988/89	42	(ct 33,st 9)	EN Trotman	1988/89

Most dismissals (wicketkeepers) in a career:

SS and Bowl				All FC			
108	(ct 97,st 11)	SJ Palframan	1991-96	113	(ct 102,st 11)	SJ Palframan	1991-96

Most catches (fielders) in an innings:

5	C de L White	v Griqualand West (Queenstown)	1946/47

Most catches (fielders) in a match:

6	C de L White	v Griqualand West (Queenstown)	1946/47

Most catches (fielders) in a season:

SS and Bowl			All FC		
16	BM White	1996/97	17	NR Boonzaaier	1988/89
16	W Wiblin	1999/00			

Most catches (fielders) in a career:

SS and Bowl			All FC		
55	IL Howell	1984-97	57	IL Howell	1984-97

Most appearances:

SS and Bowl			All FC		
90	IL Howell	1984-97	100	IL Howell	1984-97

Most captaincies:

SS and Bowl			All FC		
40	PC Strydom	1996-2000	44	PC Strydom	1996-2000

RECORD WICKET PARTNERSHIPS

1st	229	GC Holmes and GL Long v Western Province B (East London)	1989/90
2nd	271	WS Farrer and PJ Muzzell v Orange Free State (Bloemfontein)	1968/69
3rd	255	OC Dawson and KN Kirton v Rhodesia (East London)	1954/55
4th	200	WS Farrer and PJ Muzzell v Eastern Province (East London) (FC)	1968/69
	188	PN Kirsten and PC Strydom v Northern Transvaal (East London) (CC)	1993/94
5th	253	W Wiblin and SC Pope v Western Province (East London)	1997/98
6th	242*	KS McEwan and DH Howell v Transvaal (East London)	1991/92
7th	208	R Watson-Smith and DFL Tricker v Orange Free State (Bloemfontein)	1969/70
8th	181	I Mitchell and GT Love v Western Province (Cape Town)	1998/99
9th	109	RD Moult and WK Watson v Eastern Province (East London) (FC)	1989/90
	108	DC McKenna and GL Hayes v Orange Free State (Bloemfontein) (CC)	1974/75
10th	86	SJ Schmidt and DS Scott v Orange Free State (East London)	1978/79

BORDER CRICKET BOARD

PERFORMANCES AGAINST OTHER TEAMS

HIGHEST AND LOWEST TOTALS

Opponents	Highest Total For		Lowest Total For	
Boland	463-7*	1990/91	67	1984/85
Eastern Province	440-5*	1925/26	34	1946/47
Easterns	453-8*	1999/00	244	2000/01
Free State	509	1969/70	75	1958/59
Gauteng	442	1952/53	43	1908/09
Griqualand West	456-8*	1978/79	65	1929/30
KwaZulu-Natal	436	1998/99	16	1959/60
Northerns	502-9*	1974/75	58	1954/55
North West	283	2000/01	274	2000/01
Western Province	428-9*	1998/99	47	1920/21

BEST INDIVIDUAL PERFORMANCES

Opponents	Highest score	Best bowling (innings)		Best bowling (match , 8 +)	
Boland	195 GL Long, 1990/91	6-32	PJ Botha, 1997/98	10-78	HC Lindenberg, 1990/91
Eastern Province	211 (FC) WS Farrer,1968/69	8-38	GV Wienand, 1946/47	12-58	GV Wienand,1946/47
	206* (CC) AJ Clarke,1925/26				
Easterns	125 PC Strydom, 1999/00	4-47	VC Drakes, 2000/01	8-95	VC Drakes, 2000/01
Free State	207 WS Farrer,1965/66	7-28	IB Gardiner,1937/38	11-108	ML Harper,1970/71
Gauteng	182 OC Dawson, 1952/53	8-64	RJ Evans, 1937/38	10-93	RJ Evans, 1937/38
Griqualand West	173* PN Kirsten, 1996/97	9-32	AF Hagemann, 1960/61	14-59	AF Hagemann, 1960/61
KwaZulu-Natal	189 C de L White,1934/35	8-59	VC Drakes, 1996/97	13-125	OD Gibson,1994/95
Northerns	271 PN Kirsten,1993/94	7-34	S Knott, 1952/53	11-103	EF Schreiber,1958/59
North West	100 SC Pope, 2000/01	4-53	T Henderson, 2000/01	-	
Western Province	177 W Wiblin 1997/98	7-33	(FC) RK Thorne, 1964/65	10-86	(FC) RKThorne, 1964/65
		7-44	(CC)GPD Hartigan,1910/11	10-151	(CC)ODGibson 1992/93

BORDER SUPERSPORT AVERAGES 2000/01

Batting & Fielding

Name	M	Inns	NO	Runs	HS	Avg	100	50	Ct	St
MV Boucher	2	4	2	86	33*	43.00	0	0	10	1
PC Strydom	9	16	0	643	86	40.18	0	7	6	0
SC Pope	9	17	0	605	125	35.58	2	3	2	0
I Mitchell	8	15	1	413	83	29.50	0	3	32	2
W Wiblin	9	17	2	411	88	27.40	0	3	13	0
VC Drakes	9	16	1	360	53	24.00	0	1	3	0
LL Gamiet	9	16	0	365	80	22.81	0	1	8	0
GT Love	9	15	7	182	30	22.75	0	0	5	0
PJ Botha	6	11	0	229	50	20.81	0	1	3	0
CB Sugden	9	17	0	351	54	20.64	0	2	9	0
DL Makalima	7	13	1	147	42*	12.25	0	0	4	0
T Henderson	7	13	2	108	22*	9.81	0	0	1	0
L Graham	3	4	1	26	19	8.66	0	0	2	0
JWF Klopper	1	1	0	0	0	0.00	0	0	0	0
M Ntini	2	2	2	9	5*	-	0	0	1	0
Totals	99	177	19	3935	125		2	21	99	3
			Extras	269				subs	1	
			Total	4204		26.60			100	

Bowling

Name	Overs	Mdns	Runs	Wkts	Avg	BB	5I	10M
I Mitchell	4.1	2	10	2	5.00	2-0	0	0
PJ Botha	152.3	54	375	21	17.85	4-48	0	0
M Ntini	93.1	28	246	13	18.92	6-59	1	0
PC Strydom	210.5	59	518	22	23.54	3-29	0	0

VC Drakes	368	100	975	41	23.78	5-80	1	0
T Henderson	196.1	56	525	18	29.16	6-56	1	0
GT Love	341	94	868	28	31.00	7-116	1	0
L Graham	84	22	213	6	35.50	3-69	0	0
SC Pope	27	8	65	1	65.00	1-18	0	0
W Wiblin	6	1	19	0	-	-	0	0
JWF Klopper	4	0	23	0	-	-	0	0
Totals	1486.5	424	3837	152		7-116	4	0
		b & lb	106	3	run outs			
		Total	3943	155	25.43			

MATCH REPORTS AND SCORECARDS

BORDER v WESTERN PROVINCE — SuperSport Series Pool B

Played at Buffalo Park, East London on 3,4,5,6 November 2000 — Toss: Border
Umpires: BG Jerling & DL Orchard (TV: CM Schoof)
Debuts: Bdr: L Graham (FC). WP: None
Close of Play: Day 1: WP (1) 286-5 (Prince 9*, Dawson 14*, 104 overs). Day 2: Bdr (1) 182-7 (Mitchell 41*, Love 7*, 77 overs). Day 3: Bdr (2) 3-1 (Sugden 3*, Love 0*, 2 overs).
Result: Western Province won by 77 runs
Man of Match: Herschelle Gibbs
Points: Bdr: 4 (bat 2, bowl 2, match 0). WP: 17 (bat 3, bowl 4, match 10)

Put in to bat by Border, Province batted solidly, with Herschelle Gibbs making an aggressive 91 after a slow start. Despite disciplined innings by Wayne Wiblin and Ian Mitchell, Border fell 98 runs short. After a Province declaration Border were set 321 to win and with nine wickets down for 191 it looked a rout, but Mitchell and Liam Graham, making his first-class debut, added 52 for the last wicket to add some respectability to the Border total.

WESTERN PROVINCE

FIRST INNINGS	*Runs*	*Mins*	*Balls*	*4*	*6*	*SECOND INNINGS*	*Runs*	*Mins*	*Balls*	*4*	*6*
HH Gibbs c Mitchell b Drakes	91	247	184	12	1	b Strydom	46	123	82	9	-
GC Smith c Gamiet b Graham	24	44	39	5	-	hit wicket b Drakes	15	41	33	2	-
AG Puttick c Makalima b Henderson	66	216	160	8	-	c Mitchell b Pope	30	95	81	5	-
*HD Ackerman c Mitchell b Strydom	42	102	78	8	-	st Mitchell b Strydom	68	109	107	11	1
NC Johnson c Wiblin b Strydom	31	94	66	3	1	not out	53	127	104	5	-
AG Prince not out	46	151	133	9	-	not out	7	30	24	-	-
AC Dawson c Wiblin b Drakes	14	38	41	1	-						
†TL Tsolekile lbw b Henderson	5	15	10	1	-						
CW Henderson c Mitchell b Graham	14	59	38	2	-						
PR Adams c Love b Graham	7	27	24	-	-						
CM Willoughby											
Extras (lb 3, w 1, nb 6)	10					Extras (b 1, lb 2)	3				
TOTAL (for 9 wkts dec) (129 overs)	**350**					**TOTAL (for 4 wkts dec) (72 overs)**	**222**				

BORDER

	Runs	*Mins*	*Balls*	*4*	*6*		*Runs*	*Mins*	*Balls*	*4*	*6*
CB Sugden c Smith b Henderson	16	53	58	1	-	c Dawson b Willoughby	11	56	48	1	-
DL Makalima c Smith b Henderson	18	82	54	1	-	lbw b Willoughby	0	3	1	-	-
SC Pope c Tsolekile b Willoughby	7	38	24	1	-	(4) c Prince b Dawson	22	75	71	4	-
W Wiblin c Tsolekile b Willoughby	51	140	124	7	-	(5) b Adams	22	50	52	2	-
*PC Strydom c Tsolekile b Adams	30	76	69	5	-	(6) run out (Smith)	26	86	71	4	-
LL Gamiet c Johnson b Adams	5	21	15	-	-	(7) c Henderson b Johnson	30	78	66	4	1
†I Mitchell c Smith b Henderson	61	152	126	8	1	(8) not out	46	155	124	7	-
VC Drakes b Adams	1	17	18	-	-	(9) c Johnson b Adams	24	62	53	2	-
GT Love b Dawson	30	117	95	2	1	(3) c Gibbs b Willoughby	24	45	37	5	-
T Henderson not out	22	26	18	3	-	c Smith b Henderson	7	15	8	-	1
L Graham c Johnson b Willoughby	5	15	15	-	-	c Ackerman b Dawson	19	59	54	2	-
Extras (b 3, lb 2, w 1)	6					Extras (b 11, w 1)	12				
TOTAL (102.4 overs)	**252**					**TOTAL (98.1 overs)**	**243**				

Bowling	*O*	*M*	*R*	*W*		*O*	*M*	*R*	*W*
BORDER									
Drakes	30	5	94	2		17	2	58	1
Graham	26	5	69	3	(3)	7	2	29	0
Henderson	25	10	56	2	(2)	14	3	42	0
Love	34	9	100	0	(6)	8	1	25	0
Strydom	14	2	28	2	(4)	17	2	47	2
Pope					(5)	9	2	18	1
WESTERN PROVINCE									
Willoughby	25.4	7	52	3		20	7	57	3
Dawson	25	6	72	1		18.1	8	29	2
Johnson	7	3	11	0	(5)	6	1	18	1
Henderson	32	6	79	3		23	10	37	1
Adams	13	2	33	3	(3)	31	9	91	2

Fall of Wickets	**WP**	**Bdr**	**WP**	**Bdr**
	1st	1st	2nd	2nd
1st	30 (2)	27 (1)	25 (2)	1 (2)
2nd	182 (1)	39 (2)	91 (1)	31 (3)
3rd	187 (3)	43 (3)	93 (3)	36 (1)
4th	258 (4)	90 (5)	191 (4)	75 (5)
5th	263 (5)	115 (6)	-	83 (4)
6th	286 (7)	135 (4)	-	136 (6)
7th	293 (8)	141 (8)	-	142 (7)
8th	332 (9)	223 (7)	-	178 (9)
9th	350 (10)	232 (9)	-	191 (10)
10th	-	252 (11)	-	243 (11)

Eastern Province v Border, Port Elizabeth, 10-13 November 2000. Match drawn.

BORDER v EASTERNS — SuperSport Series Pool B

Played at Buffalo Park, East London on 17,18 (no play),19,20 November 2000 Toss: Border
Umpires: SB Lambson & AE Williams
Debuts: Bdr: JWF Klopper (FC). Eas: EF Mabhena (FC)
Close of Play: Day 1: Eas (1) 40-4 (Flusk 14*, Rindel 0*, 20 overs). Day 2: No play. Day 3: Bdr (2) 63-2 (Sugden 35*, Wiblin 13*, 21.1 overs).
Result: Border won by 56 runs
Man of Match: Steven Pope
Points: Bdr: 16 (bat 2, bowl 4, match 10). Eas: 6 (bat 2, bowl 4, match 0)

Pope batted well and by stumps on the first day Easterns were in a position from which they were unable to recover, falling 32 runs short of Border's first innings. The second day was lost to rain with not a ball being bowled. Set 235 to win in 80 overs Easterns had no answer to Vasbert Drakes and Geoff Love and were bowled out for 178 with 13 overs to spare.

BORDER

FIRST INNINGS	*Runs*	*Mins*	*Balls*	*4*	*6*	*SECOND INNINGS*	*Runs*	*Mins*	*Balls*	*4*	*6*
CB Sugden c Jennings b Morkel	26	90	65	3	-	c Jennings b Flusk	54	174	135	6	1
DL Makalima b Benjamin	3	8	10	-	-	c Jordaan b Benjamin	1	19	12	-	-
SC Pope lbw b Benjamin	92	226	201	18	-	hit wicket b Benjamin	4	22	14	-	-
W Wiblin lbw b Benjamin	11	21	18	2	-	c White b Morkel	39	85	61	4	-
*PC Strydom c Flusk b Botha	63	127	93	9	1	c Jennings b Flusk	28	22	20	6	-
†I Mitchell c Jennings b Benjamin	0	12	9	-	-	c White b Botha	2	15	5	-	-
LL Gamiet b Benjamin	4	34	26	1	-	c Jennings b Flusk	39	57	47	6	-
VC Drakes not out	25	60	42	4	-	c Benjamin b Flusk	2	22	10	-	-
GT Love c de Bruyn b Benjamin	0	8	7	-	-	(10) not out	1	11	3	-	-
JWF Klopper c de Bruyn b Botha	0	3	2	-	-						
T Henderson c Jordaan b Botha	3	21	20	-	-	(9) c Botha b Flusk	12	16	13	2	-
Extras (b 4, lb 10, nb 3)	17					Extras (lb 6, w 1, nb 13)	20				
TOTAL (81.4 overs)	**244**					**TOTAL (for 9 wkts dec) (51.1 overs)**	**202**				

EASTERNS

	Runs	*Mins*	*Balls*	*4*	*6*		*Runs*	*Mins*	*Balls*	*4*	*6*
†D Jennings lbw b Love	17	40	36	3	-	c Makalima b Henderson	11	19	18	2	-
BM White lbw b Love	2	33	20	-	-	c Wiblin b Drakes	6	36	27	1	-
*D Jordaan c Sugden b Drakes	4	22	11	1	-	lbw b Drakes	16	52	41	3	-
GE Flusk c Mitchell b Drakes	14	45	44	1	-	(11) not out	2	6	3	-	-
EF Mabhena lbw b Strydom	2	22	14	-	-	(10) lbw b Drakes	2	13	11	-	-
MJR Rindel c Gamiet b Love	64	129	90	12	-	(4) b Love	49	92	59	8	-
DN Crookes b Drakes	0	7	5	-	-	(6) c Mitchell b Strydom	33	42	41	5	-
P de Bruyn c Wiblin b Henderson	53	220	178	4	-	(7) c Sugden b Drakes	15	117	109	3	-
AG Botha not out	34	157	125	2	-	(8) run out (Makalima)	7	45	33	1	-
JA Morkel run out (Sugden)	9	25	26	1	-	(9) c Mitchell b Love	19	70	57	2	-
KCG Benjamin c Strydom b Drakes	2	10	7	-	-	(5) c Gamiet b Love	9	4	6	2	-
Extras (b 2, lb 3, nb 6)	11					Extras (b 4, lb 3, nb 2)	9				
TOTAL (91.4 overs)	**212**					**TOTAL (67 overs)**	**178**				

Bowling	*O*	*M*	*R*	*W*		*O*	*M*	*R*	*W*
EASTERNS									
Benjamin	22	4	73	6		20	2	78	2
Morkel	15	4	52	1		12	2	42	1
de Bruyn	9	0	26	0					
Crookes	11	5	34	0					
Botha	21.4	13	23	3	(4)	4	1	21	1
Flusk	3	0	22	0	(3)	15.1	1	55	5
BORDER									
Drakes	26.4	9	48	4		18	5	47	4
Henderson	18	4	52	1	(3)	10.1	2	38	1
Love	31	7	63	3	(2)	22	8	55	3
Strydom	12	7	21	1		16.5	8	31	1
Klopper	4	0	23	0					

Fall of Wickets	Bdr 1st	Eas 1st	Bdr 2nd	Eas 2nd
1st	5 (2)	17 (2)	9 (2)	17 (1)
2nd	58 (1)	20 (1)	29 (3)	27 (2)
3rd	74 (4)	31 (3)	100 (4)	54 (3)
4th	208 (3)	40 (5)	140 (5)	63 (5)
5th	208 (5)	46 (4)	143 (1)	128 (6)
6th	208 (6)	50 (7)	166 (6)	132 (4)
7th	222 (7)	142 (6)	180 (8)	145 (8)
8th	223 (9)	193 (8)	190 (9)	174 (7)
9th	224 (10)	205 (10)	202 (7)	176 (9)
10th	244 (11)	212 (11)	-	178 (10)

KwaZulu-Natal v Border, Durban, 8-11 December 2000. Match drawn.

BORDER v NORTHERNS — SuperSport Series Super Eight

Played at Buffalo Park, East London on 1,2,3 February 2001 — Toss: Northerns
Umpires: SB Lambson & S Wadvalla
Debuts: Bdr: None. Nor: None
Close of Play: Day 1: Bdr (1) 114-5 (Strydom 33*, Gamiet 18*, 39 overs). Day 2: Bdr (2) 10-1 (Sugden 1*, 3.4 overs).
Result: Border won by 7 wickets
Man of Match: Pieter Strydom
Points: Bdr: 16 (bat 2, bowl 4, match 10). Nor: 5 (bat 1, bowl 4, match 0)

A total of 15 wickets fell on a sweltering opening day and Border took a 46-run lead early on the second morning. Northerns collapsed again in their second knock and the home team made short work of the target, cruising to a seven-wicket victory with a day to spare.

NORTHERNS

FIRST INNINGS	*Runs*	*Mins*	*Balls*	*4*	*6*	*SECOND INNINGS*	*Runs*	*Mins*	*Balls*	*4*	*6*
JG Myburgh c Love b Botha	24	74	52	4	-	lbw b Drakes	11	54	39	1	-
JA Rudolph c Gamiet b Ntini	20	54	35	2	-	c Pope b Drakes	39	143	95	6	-
M van Jaarsveld b Love	11	69	55	-	-	c Boucher b Drakes	0	1	1	-	-
ND McKenzie c Boucher b Ntini	13	55	30	2	-	b Drakes	24	98	87	2	-
*G Dros c Gamiet b Love	35	110	81	3	2	c Wiblin b Strydom	4	3	4	1	-
A Paleker c Boucher b Henderson	19	51	37	3	-	(9) not out	6	49	47	1	-
†CFK van Wyk c Boucher b Botha	30	89	40	4	-	c Boucher b Ntini	18	49	34	3	-
S Elworthy not out	22	50	23	1	2	c Ntini b Strydom	17	33	27	2	1
NG Brouwers c Boucher b Love	4	8	9	1	-	(6) c Boucher b Botha	14	76	53	2	-
DH Townsend c Love b Botha	1	3	8	-	-	c Boucher b Botha	0	5	4	-	-
GJ Smith c Strydom b Ntini	2	25	20	-	-	c Gamiet b Strydom	12	23	14	2	-
Extras (lb 7, nb 2)	9					Extras (lb 3, nb 2)	5				
TOTAL (64.4 overs)	**190**					**TOTAL (67.1 overs)**	**150**				

BORDER

	Runs	*Mins*	*Balls*	*4*	*6*		*Runs*	*Mins*	*Balls*	*4*	*6*
PJ Botha c Rudolph b Elworthy	5	10	14	1	-	c Paleker b Smith	8	15	19	-	-
CB Sugden c McKenzie b Townsend	30	109	70	5	-	c van Wyk b Elworthy	5	35	20	1	-
SC Pope c Myburgh b Townsend	14	32	25	3	-	run out (Paleker)	33	93	70	6	-
W Wiblin c van Wyk b Townsend	0	3	4	-	-	not out	23	92	45	3	-
†MV Boucher c Paleker b Elworthy	6	15	11	1	-	not out	27	19	22	6	-
*PC Strydom c van Jaarsveld b Townsend	86	172	126	14	-						
LL Gamiet c van Wyk b Smith	18	63	51	3	-						
VC Drakes lbw b Dros	35	97	65	6	-						
GT Love c van Wyk b Dros	15	26	21	3	-						
T Henderson c Myburgh b Townsend	11	10	12	2	-						
M Ntini not out	5	9	4	1	-						
Extras (b 1, lb 6, nb 4)	11					Extras (b 4, lb 5, nb 3)	12				
TOTAL (66.3 overs)	**236**					**TOTAL (for 3 wkts) (28.5 overs)**	**108**				

Bowling	*O*	*M*	*R*	*W*		*O*	*M*	*R*	*W*
BORDER									
Drakes	16	6	33	0	(2)	15	7	35	4
Ntini	16.4	4	32	3	(1)	16	6	43	1
Henderson	12	1	44	1	(4)	4	1	4	0
Botha	9	5	16	3	(5)	6	3	13	2
Love	11	1	58	3	(3)	13	5	23	0
Strydom						13.1	6	29	3
NORTHERNS									
Elworthy	20	4	67	2		8	2	19	1
Smith	16	3	52	1		8	1	30	1
Townsend	16.3	6	49	5	(4)	6.5	1	33	0
Dros	8	2	25	2	(3)	6	0	17	0
Brouwers	5	1	31	0					
Rudolph	1	0	5	0					

Fall of Wickets	Nor 1st	Bdr 1st	Nor 2nd	Bdr 2nd
1st	35 (2)	6 (1)	29 (1)	10 (1)
2nd	51 (1)	33 (3)	29 (3)	21 (2)
3rd	71 (3)	33 (4)	69 (2)	72 (3)
4th	71 (4)	47 (5)	74 (5)	-
5th	103 (6)	72 (2)	83 (4)	-
6th	160 (5)	114 (7)	104 (7)	-
7th	164 (7)	188 (6)	129 (6)	-
8th	171 (9)	219 (9)	133 (8)	-
9th	172 (10)	220 (8)	133 (10)	-
10th	190 (11)	236 (10)	150 (11)	-

Free State v Border, Bloemfontein, 1-4 March 2001. Border won by 162 runs.

BORDER v BOLAND

SuperSport Series Super Eight

Played at Buffalo Park, East London on 8,9,10,11 March 2001 — Toss: Boland
Umpires: CJ Mitchley & AG O'Connor
Debuts: Bdr: None. Bol: MS de Kock (FC)
Close of Play: Day 1: Bol (1) 87-5 (Ontong 29*, de Kock 3*, 41 overs). Day 2: Bdr (2) 235-4 (Pope 104*, Gamiet 0*, 83 overs). Day 3: Bol (2) 159-5 (Henderson 76*, 63.4 overs).
Result: Border won by 164 runs
Man of Match: Steven Pope
Points: Bdr: 15 (bat 1, bowl 4, match 10). Bol: 5 (bat 1, bowl 4, match 0)

Some excellent bowling by Geoff Love late on the first day had Boland in a spin after Border were dismissed for a disappointing 192. Boland were soon out on the second morning and thereafter it was all Steven Pope and Pieter Strydom as the two added 128 aggressive runs for the fourth wicket. Pope went to the first century of the season for Border - his third and career-highest. Others to enhance their career-best figures were Justin Ontong and Andrew Pringle with the ball. The match ended just before lunch on the last day.

BORDER

FIRST INNINGS	*Runs*	*Mins*	*Balls*	*4*	*6*	*SECOND INNINGS*	*Runs*	*Mins*	*Balls*	*4*	*6*
CB Sugden c Koen b Williams	0	1	4	-	-	(2) c Koen b Carter	43	113	76	7	1
PJ Botha c Pringle b Williams	16	61	40	1	-	(1) lbw b Williams	20	34	34	4	-
SC Pope c Player b Pringle	26	83	58	4	-	c Ontong b Williams	125	333	239	16	-
W Wiblin c Ontong b Pringle	15	84	55	2	-	c Williams b Ontong	5	25	27	-	-
*PC Strydom c Ontong b Carter	55	99	81	10	-	c Trott b Henderson	63	168	144	7	-
LL Gamiet c Ontong b Pringle	7	45	29	1	-	c and b Ontong	31	116	79	3	-
†I Mitchell c de Kock b Williams	17	35	24	4	-	lbw b Henderson	14	51	32	1	-
DL Makalima c Strydom b Pringle	23	69	42	4	-	(9) c Koen b Ontong	10	31	26	-	-
VC Drakes c de Kock b Williams	23	30	19	5	-	(10) run out (sub - CdeW de Lange)	28	46	46	1	1
GT Love lbw b Williams	0	2	3	-	-	(11) not out	8	32	30	-	-
T Henderson not out	0	3	2	-	-	(8) c de Kock b Ontong	1	10	6	-	-
Extras (lb 4, nb 6)	10					Extras (b 1, lb 3, nb 2)	6				
TOTAL (58.3 overs)	**192**					**TOTAL (122.5 overs)**	**354**				

BOLAND

	Runs	*Mins*	*Balls*	*4*	*6*		*Runs*	*Mins*	*Balls*	*4*	*6*
JM Henderson lbw b Drakes	3	22	19	-	-	(2) lbw b Botha	98	316	281	13	-
JG Strydom c Mitchell b Henderson	27	76	64	4	-	(1) c Botha b Drakes	1	10	14	-	-
*LJ Koen b Love	12	64	28	1	-	c Mitchell b Botha	62	126	88	9	-
JL Ontong c Mitchell b Botha	33	88	88	5	-	c Sugden b Love	11	36	21	-	-
IJL Trott lbw b Love	4	8	7	-	-	c Mitchell b Drakes	0	4	6	-	-
H Davids c Mitchell b Love	5	36	25	-	-	(7) c Botha b Drakes	24	71	83	3	-
†MS de Kock not out	17	112	74	2	-	(6) c Makalima b Strydom	3	46	46	-	-
BT Player c Mitchell b Botha	7	33	21	1	-	c Mitchell b Botha	0	18	12	-	-
NM Carter c Mitchell b Drakes	1	5	5	-	-	c Wiblin b Drakes	8	26	19	1	-
AAW Pringle lbw b Botha	3	5	6	-	-	b Botha	10	16	9	2	-
HS Williams c Henderson b Love	33	33	28	4	1	not out	0	2	2	-	-
Extras (b 1, nb 7)	8					Extras (b 6, lb 2, nb 4)	12				
TOTAL (59.4 overs)	**153**					**TOTAL (96.1 overs)**	**229**				

Bowling	*O*	*M*	*R*	*W*		*O*	*M*	*R*	*W*
BOLAND									
Williams	16	7	38	5		27.5	8	73	2
Carter	16	4	68	1	(4)	18	6	45	1
Pringle	16.3	4	49	4	(2)	17	4	51	0
Player	10	2	33	0	(5)	11	5	22	0
Ontong					(3)	36	4	120	4
Henderson						13	1	39	2
BORDER									
Drakes	20	5	58	2		21	8	42	4
Botha	14	5	38	3		19.1	5	48	4
Wiblin	1	0	1	0					
Love	15.4	5	26	4	(3)	33	9	77	1
Henderson	8	3	29	1	(4)	9	2	16	0
Strydom	1	1	0	0	(5)	13	3	36	1
Pope					(6)	1	0	2	0

Fall of Wickets	**Bdr**	**Bol**	**Bdr**	**Bol**
	1st	1st	2nd	2nd
1st	0 (1)	7 (1)	28 (1)	2 (1)
2nd	36 (2)	44 (2)	89 (2)	110 (3)
3rd	47 (3)	54 (3)	104 (4)	131 (4)
4th	86 (4)	58 (5)	232 (5)	131 (5)
5th	122 (5)	73 (6)	268 (3)	159 (6)
6th	126 (6)	91 (4)	307 (7)	207 (2)
7th	150 (7)	102 (8)	307 (6)	211 (7)
8th	190 (9)	103 (9)	310 (8)	219 (8)
9th	190 (10)	106 (10)	327 (9)	229 (9)
10th	192 (8)	153 (11)	354 (10)	229 (10)

North West v Border, Potchefstroom, 15-18 March 2001. Border won by 90 runs.

(A report of the SuperSport Series final between Western Province and Border appears in the section, SuperSport Series, on page 297)

EASTERN CRICKET UNION

PO Box 596, Benoni 1500. Tel (011) 421 4443/421 4454.
Fax (011) 421 4463. E-mail: easterns@icon.co.za

President: Cassim Suliman
Administration Officer: Gail Matthews
Director of Finance: Ashraf Seedat
Director of Representative Cricket: Andrew O'Connor
Director of Amateur Cricket: Dennis Timcke
Director of Development: Keke Dali
Director of Transformation: Conrad Jantjes
Director of Marketing: Mahomed Sibda
Director of Stadium: David New
Head coach: Ray Jennings
Development Manager: Mohammed Ganchi
2001/02 contracted players: Derek Crookes (captain) - other contracted players not available at time of going to print. **UCB contracted player:** Andre Nel.

REVIEW OF SEASON 2000/01

Trevor Cramer

SUPERSPORT SERIES: P8 W5 L3 D0 (third)
CAPTAIN: D Jordaan (5), DN Crookes (3)
STANDARD BANK CUP: P10 W4 L5 Tied 1 (sixth)

Trophies were not foremost on the agenda for Easterns but in only their second season of genuine top-flight cricket they positioned themselves as a potential threat to the more established sides. On that basis, the realisation of the third phase of head coach Ray Jennings' simple, goal-orientated acronym EPT - to Establish, Position and then set their sights on a Trophy - is not merely a pipedream.

Achieving the critical third phase requires a well-managed process of fine-tuning, coupled with a healthy dose of luck but at the same time Jennings knows all too well that his charges have to maintain realistic expectations without slipping back to phase two.

The progress of the team through the season can probably best be likened to a young child who needs time to figure out what to do with its new-found independence and what learning experience will be gleaned from its failures.

A highly creditable third place finish in the SuperSport Series and a satisfactory Standard Bank Cup campaign in which they were always in the hunt for honours but ended three points shy of a semifinal spot, suggests they have certainly made tangible progress.

Backed up by a compact, organised administration, the resources to succeed were lined up at the beginning of the season. Jennings had at his disposal a strong playing unit comprising a tidy blend of youth and experience. Their limitations were, however, exposed later in the season due chiefly to a lack of experience in certain quarters, coupled with some minor internal strife at the tail-end of the season involving captain Deon Jordaan's alleged spat with coach Jennings.

Their poor away form was of particular concern and had they accomplished more on their travels, then the trophy cabinet could well have displayed some silverware. They lost just one SuperSport match at home, to North West, when their prospects of reaching the final rested heavily on winning, while their limited overs form in Benoni fluctuated.

While strengthening their resources with an injection of experience in the form of players like Mike Rindel, Derek Crookes and overseas professional Kenny Benjamin, the province also showed a fervent commitment to invest in their "young guns" and mould them into formidable cricketers.

As the individual statistics clearly indicate, the contributions of their experienced campaigners was evident but placing too much of a reliance on them, more often than not, proved to be Easterns' downfall. Easterns consistently found themselves having to play around Crookes, Rindel, captain Deon Jordaan and Benjamin, finding it difficult to build an innings in both forms of the game, if one or all of the above failed. Benjamin's input was curtailed by injury and unfortunately Easterns had to make do without him during the critical latter part of the season.

Crookes, who, like Benjamin, needed little persuasion to abandon a desperately drifting Gauteng ship, proved great value, particularly as a batsman, scoring 671 runs (average 44.73) in the SuperSport Series and contributing 335 runs (average 37.22) in the Standard Bank Cup.

Northerns Titans cast-off Mike Rindel adapted comfortably to his new environment and scored 504 runs in the first-class game (average 36.00) and an equally respectable 467 runs in the limited overs version (average 46.70).

Jennings' theory is that a team like Easterns, in its formative years of development, needs what he terms recognisable "heroes" for the younger players to look up to. Starved of first class exposure for many years, Easterns hasn't exactly attracted top players into their fold, leaving the emergent crop with no genuine role-models within their own set-up. This inevitably leads to aspirations of furthering their careers elsewhere.

With these seniors to look up to, quite a number of individuals achieved new heights in their cricketing career.

Andre Seymore re-ignited what appeared to be a fading career living in the shadow of incumbent Sven Koenig at Gauteng and in just three outings for his adopted province, scored 365 runs (average 60.83). Former Northerns all-rounder Pierre de Bruyn also found his new home to his liking and showed great character to often bat his side out of some very thorny situations.

Every provincial coach is ultimately striving to produce quality players capable of playing at international level and the biggest feather in coach Jennings' cap was undoubtedly local product Andre Nel's elevation to the SA side for the season-ending West Indies tour. Nel took 17 wickets, including two five wicket hauls, in the SuperSport Series (average 21.23), impressive figures considering he missed four matches, and was effective in the shorter game with 22 victims (average 15.50). Beyond Nel and Benjamin, however, Easterns always lacked that additional strike bowler to sustain the pressure.

The attributes of Nel, 23, including enthusiasm, passion and raw talent, reminded one of the early rise to prominence of a young Allan Donald. It is no secret that Nel idolises Donald but that hero worship took an unexpected twist when Nel decked his idol with a wicked bouncer during a victorious SuperSport clash against Free State in Benoni, causing Donald to retire hurt.

Nobody could have anticipated the repercussions. Jennings was hauled before a UCB disciplinary committee after allegedly offering Nel a financial reward for bouncing Donald, while Nel was let off the hook for dangerous play. Captain Jordaan subsequently found himself out in the cold for allegedly "ratting" on his coach, but his omission from the side was based on his indifferent form. The matter was eventually put to bed following a lengthy apology to all concerned parties from Jennings.

Nel was in the headlines earlier in the season when he was suspended for a match for unsporting behaviour following a verbal altercation with KwaZulu Natal's Goolam Bodi.

The team's facelift is at an advanced stage. With the 2003 World Cup in mind, a drastic facelift has now been commissioned at Easterns' Willowmoore Park home ground over the coming two seasons. Among the changes which will be evident in the coming season are five new playing surfaces and a new administration, VIP and media block as well as a fully functional electronic scoreboard.

PROVINCIAL RECORDS

Honours:
UCB Bowl (1): 1991/92

Highest innings totals:				
For:	533	v Border B (Springs)		1994/95
Against:	453-8*	by Border (East London)		1999/00
Lowest innings totals:				
For:	64	v Boland (Brackenfell)		1992/93
Against:	109	by Eastern Province B (Springs)		1994/95
Highest individual innings:				
For:	201*	MJ Mitchley	v Western Province B (Cape Town)	1996/97
Against:	203	JG Myburgh	for Northerns B (Pretoria)	1997/98
Most runs in a season:				
679	(Avg 61.72)	Shakeel Ahmed		1998/99
Most runs in a career:				
2438	(Avg 35.85)	CR Norris		1991-98
Most 100s in a career:				
3	KA Moxham 1991-93, MJ Mitchley 1995-98, Shakeel Ahmed 1998-99			
Best bowling in an innings:				
For:	7-94	PD de Vaal	v Western Transvaal (Potchefstroom)	1991/92
Against:	8-134	AV Birrell	for Eastern Province B (Port Elizabeth)	1996/97
Best bowling in a match:				
For:	12-148	LCR Jordaan	v Boland B (Brackenfell)	1994/95
Against:	12-94	M Hayward	for Eastern Province (Port Elizabeth)	1999/00
Most wickets in a season:				
38	(Avg 15.81)	LCR Jordaan		1994/95
Most wickets in a career:				
95	(Avg 22.93)	LCR Jordaan		1991-95
Most dismissals (wicketkeepers) in an innings:				
6	(ct 4,st 2)	B Randall	v Griqualand West (Kimberley)	1991/92
6	(ct 6,st 0)	D Jennings	v KwaZulu-Natal (Benoni)	2000/01
Most dismissals (wicketkeepers) in a match:				
8	(ct 6,st 2)	B McBride	v Border B (Springs)	1994/95
8	(ct 8,st 0)	D Jennings	v KwaZulu-Natal (Benoni)	2000/01
Most dismissals (wicketkeepers) in a season:				
39	(ct 37,st 2)	D Jennings		2000/01

EASTERN CRICKET UNION

Most dismissals (wicketkeepers) in a career:
68 (ct 51,st 17) B Randall 1991-95
Most catches (fielders) in an innings:
4 D Jordaan v Griqualand West (Benoni) 1999/00
Most catches (fielders) in a match:
6 IA Hoffmann v Orange Free State B (Springs) 1994/95
Most catches (fielders) in a career:
29 TA Marsh 1991-96
Most appearances:
43 CR Norris 1991-98
Most captaincies:
12 PD de Vaal 1991-92
12 D Jordaan 1999-2000

RECORD WICKET PARTNERSHIPS

1st	234	KA Moxham and HM Human v Western Transvaal (Potchefstroom)	1992/93
2nd	160	AG Botha and D Jordaan v Griqualand West (Kimberley)	1999/00
3rd	135	D Jordaan and Shakeel Ahmed v Griqualand West (Benoni)	1999/00
4th	197	CR Norris and T Jamal v Western Transvaal (Potchefstroom)	1993/94
5th	181	KA Moxham and PA Cottey v Boland (Springs)	1991/92
	181	WR Radford and TA Marsh v Griqualand West (Springs)	1993/94
6th	165	Shakeel Ahmed and D Brand v KwaZulu-Natal B (Benoni)	1998/99
7th	146	P de Bruyn and JA Morkel v North West (Benoni)	2000/01
8th	79	SM Skeete and LD Botha v Border B (Springs)	1994/95
9th	125*	PD de Vaal and TA Marsh v Western Transvaal (Potchefstroom)	1991/92
10th	91	SM Skeete and LCR Jordaan v Border B (Springs)	1994/95

PERFORMANCES AGAINST OTHER TEAMS

HIGHEST AND LOWEST TOTALS

Opponents	Highest Total For		Lowest Total For	
Boland	340	2000/01	64	1992/93
Border	238	1999/00	178	2000/01
Eastern Province	284	1999/00	172	2000/01
Free State	309	2000/01	224	2000/01
Gauteng	150	1999/00	83	1999/00
Griqualand West	421-7*	1999/00	224	1993/94
KwaZulu-Natal	284-8*	2000/01	224	2000/01
Northerns	380	2000/01	140	1999/00
North West	440-8*	1991/92	106	2000/01
Western Province	228	2000/01	195	2000/01

BEST INDIVIDUAL PERFORMANCES

Opponents	Highest score	Best bowling (innings)	Best bowling (match, 8+)
Boland	122 KA Moxham, 1991/92	6-70 LD Botha, 1992/93	-
Border	64 MJR Rindel, 2000/01	6-73 KCG Benjamin, 2000/01	8-151 KCG Benjamin, 2000/01
Eastern Province	122 PV Simmons, 1999/00	5-61 A Nel, 1999/00	-
Free State	95 DN Crookes, 2000/01	5-43 A Nel, 2000/01	-
Gauteng	73* D Jordaan, 1999/00	4-25 A Nel, 1999/00	-
Griqualand West	157 WR Radford, 1993/94	6-36 JA Morkel, 1999/00	8-90 JA Morkel, 1999/00
KwaZulu-Natal	83 P de Bruyn, 2000/01	5-64 A Nel, 2000/01	-
Northerns	174 AJ Seymore, 2000/01	3-34 AG Botha, 2000/01	-
North West	117 KA Moxham 1992/93	7-94 PD de Vaal, 1991/92	10-126 PD de Vaal, 1991/92
	117 JA Morkel, 2000/01		
Western Province	91 MJR Rindel, 2000/01	3-59 KCG Benjamin, 2000/01	-

EASTERNS SUPERSPORT AVERAGES 2000/01

Batting & Fielding

Name	M	Inns	NO	Runs	HS	Avg	100	50	Ct	St
AJ Seymore	3	6	0	365	174	60.83	1	2	2	0
DN Crookes	8	16	1	671	117	44.73	1	5	11	0
J Uys	1	2	1	43	26	43.00	0	0	0	0
MJR Rindel	7	14	0	504	91	36.00	0	4	0	0
P de Bruyn	8	16	2	447	83	31.92	0	4	6	0
AG Botha	7	14	4	259	59	25.90	0	1	9	0
A Nel	4	6	2	84	44	21.00	0	0	1	0
D Brand	3	6	0	125	39	20.83	0	0	5	0
D Jordaan	5	10	0	206	75	20.60	0	1	5	0
JA Morkel	7	12	0	241	117	20.08	1	0	1	0
AM van den Berg	3	6	0	116	59	19.33	0	1	0	0
KCG Benjamin	5	9	3	110	48*	18.33	0	0	3	0
BL Reddy	3	5	1	69	28	17.25	0	0	1	0
BM White	3	6	0	99	33	16.50	0	0	2	0
D Jennings	8	16	2	188	53	13.42	0	1	37	2
ET Mokoenanyana	3	6	0	76	28	12.66	0	0	7	0
GE Flusk	8	13	2	126	31*	11.45	0	0	4	0
EF Mabhena	1	2	0	4	2	2.00	0	0	0	0
JW Williams	1	2	2	0	0*	-	0	0	0	0
Totals	88	167	20	3733	174		3	19	94	2
			Extras	222				subs	1	
			Total	3955		26.90			95	

Bowling

Name	Overs	Mdns	Runs	Wkts	Avg	BB	5I	10M
KCG Benjamin	190.4	45	549	29	18.93	6-73	1	0
A Nel	154	38	361	17	21.23	5-43	2	0
P de Bruyn	105.4	21	306	12	25.50	4-34	0	0
AG Botha	244.2	80	614	24	25.58	6-106	1	0
GE Flusk	195	36	618	24	25.75	5-55	1	0
D Brand	37	8	83	3	27.66	1-5	0	0
JA Morkel	199.2	49	621	19	32.68	4-36	0	0
BL Reddy	83	18	242	4	60.50	3-39	0	0
DN Crookes	86.5	25	254	3	84.66	2-49	0	0
J Uys	1	0	4	0	-	-	0	0
MJR Rindel	2	0	8	0	-	-	0	0
D Jordaan	1	0	13	0	-	-	0	0
AM van den Berg	4	1	18	0	-	-	0	0
Totals	1303.5	321	3691	135		6-73	5	0
		b & lb	156	7	run outs			
		Total	3847	142	27.09			

MATCH REPORTS AND SCORECARDS

EASTERNS v KWAZULU-NATAL — SuperSport Series Pool B

Played at Willowmoore Park, Benoni on 27,28,29,30 October 2000 — Toss: KwaZulu-Natal
Umpires: DF Becker & M Gajjar (TV: ST Jivan)
Debuts: Eas: KCG Benjamin, DN Crookes, D Jennings, ET Mokoenanyana & BM White (All FC for Eas). KZN: None
Close of Play: Day 1: Eas (1) 222-8 (Morkel 14*, Benjamin 11*, 84 overs). Day 2: Eas (2) 104-2 (Jordaan 38*, de Bruyn 14*, 43 overs). Day 3: KZN (2) 73-3 (Watson 15*, Benkenstein 4*, 28 overs).
Result: Easterns won by 108 runs
Man of Match: Kenny Benjamin
Points: Eas: 16 (bat 2, bowl 4, match 10). KZN: 4 (bat 0, bowl 4, match 0)

EASTERN CRICKET UNION

The impact of quality West Indies import Kenny Benjamin, who was snapped up following his failure to negotiate terms with neighbouring Gauteng, was immediately felt. The visitors would have been well satisfied restricting their hosts to a moderate 245 early on day two after winning the toss. Jon Kent vindicated his skipper Dale Benkenstein's decision to bowl first with a personal-best return of six for 77. Only Pierre de Bruyn's SuperSport Series career-best contribution of 83 stood out for Easterns.

Man-of-the-Match Benjamin was at the forefront and with assistance from a lively track and some atrocious KZN shot making ensured his side a 122-run first innings cushion, while skipper Deon Jordaan scored a consolidating 75 in the second knock. Not even an aggressive maiden century by tail-ender Goolam Bodi could prevent his side losing.

EASTERNS

FIRST INNINGS	*Runs*	*Mins*	*Balls*	*4*	*6*	*SECOND INNINGS*	*Runs*	*Mins*	*Balls*	*4*	*6*
BM White c Stewart b Benkenstein	33	152	118	3	-	c Kent b Bastow	12	58	40	2	-
ET Mokoenanyana c Bruyns b Veenstra	6	25	17	1	-	c Stewart b Baptiste	20	84	59	3	-
*D Jordaan c Kent b Bastow	5	29	22	-	-	c Watson b Bastow	75	297	237	7	-
P de Bruyn c Baptiste b Kent	83	177	138	15	1	c Benkenstein b Bodi	20	138	88	2	-
DN Crookes c Stewart b Kent	24	111	82	2	-	c Stewart b Kent	15	64	53	2	-
AG Botha c Kent b Baptiste	3	71	36	-	-	c Stewart b Kent	19	68	46	1	-
†D Jennings c Bastow b Kent	14	31	25	2	-	b Kent	3	45	31	-	-
JA Morkel c Baptiste b Kent	21	96	54	1	1	lbw b Bodi	9	48	28	-	1
GE Flusk c Stewart b Kent	6	10	8	1	-	not out	31	92	64	5	-
KCG Benjamin c Stewart b Kent	15	49	46	2	-	not out	48	66	58	7	1
A Nel not out	11	24	26	2	-						
Extras (lb 12, w 2, nb 10)	24					Extras (b 8, lb 14, w 7, nb 3)	32				
TOTAL (93.4 overs)	**245**					**TOTAL (for 8 wkts dec) (117 overs)**	**284**				

KWAZULU-NATAL

	Runs	*Mins*	*Balls*	*4*	*6*		*Runs*	*Mins*	*Balls*	*4*	*6*
ML Bruyns c Morkel b Flusk	32	97	70	4	-	lbw b Nel	4	13	8	1	-
DJ Watson c Jennings b Benjamin	0	19	11	-	-	c Jennings b Benjamin	25	139	85	4	-
AM Amla c Jennings b Benjamin	0	17	9	-	-	c Jordaan b Benjamin	13	16	17	2	-
AC Hudson c and b Benjamin	25	69	54	4	-	lbw b Benjamin	28	71	64	6	-
*DM Benkenstein c Jennings b Flusk	19	69	40	3	-	c Jennings b Morkel	13	67	40	2	-
†ELR Stewart c Jennings b Nel	1	11	8	-	-	c Botha b Nel	19	72	57	4	-
JC Kent c Jennings b Flusk	2	21	17	-	-	c Crookes b Nel	0	12	8	-	-
RE Veenstra c Jennings b de Bruyn	22	56	41	3	-	lbw b Nel	38	123	73	2	1
GH Bodi lbw b Morkel	0	17	9	-	-	c Crookes b Nel	104	140	94	11	6
EAE Baptiste not out	7	16	11	1	-	c Mokoenanyana b Benjamin	23	45	32	5	-
JE Bastow b Morkel	0	4	3	-	-	not out	1	26	8	-	-
Extras (lb 4, w 4, nb 7)	15					Extras (b 10, lb 6, nb 14)	30				
TOTAL (44.3 overs)	**123**					**TOTAL (78.4 overs)**	**298**				

Bowling	*O*	*M*	*R*	*W*		*O*	*M*	*R*	*W*
KWAZULU-NATAL									
Veenstra	23	7	55	1		17	2	37	0
Bastow	19	7	50	1		22.5	7	39	2
Baptiste	17	7	27	1		22	7	26	1
Kent	24.4	5	77	6		25.1	5	75	3
Benkenstein	10	4	24	1	(7)	1	0	6	0
Bodi					(5)	27	4	75	2
Bruyns					(6)	2	0	4	0
EASTERNS									
Benjamin	10	3	23	3		23.4	5	79	4
Nel	12	6	24	1		25	3	64	5
Flusk	12	4	31	3	(4)	6	1	19	0
Morkel	9.3	1	40	2	(3)	15	6	45	1
de Bruyn	1	0	1	1		3	1	7	0
Crookes						1	0	15	0
Botha						5	0	53	0

Fall of Wickets

	Eas 1st	**KZN** 1st	**Eas** 2nd	**KZN** 2nd
1st	9 (2)	5 (2)	26 (1)	9 (1)
2nd	21 (3)	11 (3)	49 (2)	25 (3)
3rd	93 (1)	62 (1)	114 (4)	65 (4)
4th	154 (4)	63 (4)	152 (5)	87 (2)
5th	167 (5)	68 (6)	181 (3)	98 (5)
6th	171 (6)	82 (7)	189 (6)	104 (7)
7th	183 (7)	97 (5)	194 (7)	117 (6)
8th	192 (9)	108 (9)	203 (8)	248 (8)
9th	228 (10)	118 (8)	-	286 (9)
10th	245 (8)	123 (11)	-	298 (10)

EASTERNS v EASTERN PROVINCE — SuperSport Series Pool B

Played at Willowmoore Park, Benoni on 3,4,5,6 November 2000 — Toss: Eastern Province
Umpires: CJ Mitchley & AE Williams
Debuts: Eas: MJR Rindel (FC for Eas). EP: DM Senekal (FC for EP)
Close of Play: Day 1: EP (1) 106-4 (Kemp 8*, Creed 3*, 40.2 overs). Day 2: Eas (1) 172 all out. Day 3: Eas (2) 40-1 (Mokoenanyana 20*, Jordaan 2*, 14.1 overs).
Result: Easterns won by 5 wickets
Man of Match: Derek Crookes
Points: Eas: 15 (bat 1, bowl 4, match 10). EP: 7 (bat 3, bowl 4, match 0)

Easterns showed tremendous character to bounce back from an 84-run first innings deficit and secure an unlikely victory in a rain-affected match. Andre Nel was given a reprieve on a one-match suspension until an appeal had been conducted. EP were bailed out by a defiant unbeaten lower order knock by Robin Peterson on a difficult batting track. Old warhorse Dave Callaghan and new boy on the block Dewald Senekal conspired to bowl the hosts out cheaply.

Benjamin took a further four second innings wickets to give his side a remote chance of salvaging matters but even the eternal optimist wouldn't have banked on Easterns chasing down 276 to win with a maximum 107 overs at their disposal. Derek Crookes and Pierre de Bruyn combined and showed scant respect for the EP attack, the former, who earned the Man of the Match award, run out when he had brought the hosts to the brink of victory.

EASTERN PROVINCE

FIRST INNINGS	*Runs*	*Mins*	*Balls*	*4*	*6*	*SECOND INNINGS*	*Runs*	*Mins*	*Balls*	*4*	*6*
MR Benfield c Jennings b Benjamin	26	70	47	4	-	(2) lbw b Benjamin	1	13	10	-	-
*CC Bradfield c Mokoenanyana b Morkel	46	150	126	9	-	(1) lbw b Morkel	25	76	60	4	-
JDC Bryant b Crookes	1	24	21	-	-	(7) b Benjamin	0	3	2	-	-
DJ Callaghan c Jordaan b Nel	6	33	25	-	-	c Mokoenanyana b Nel	12	48	41	1	-
JM Kemp c Jennings b Benjamin	10	90	53	-	-	b Benjamin	10	48	34	-	-
MW Creed c Mokoenanyana b Nel	16	41	27	2	-	run out (Nel)	23	104	77	3	-
GV Grace c Jennings b Benjamin	8	28	22	-	-	(3) b Benjamin	13	116	68	2	-
RJ Peterson not out	96	112	77	13	3	b Nel	12	93	61	1	-
†DW Murray c Jennings b Flusk	4	8	6	1	-	not out	58	139	97	6	-
DM Senekal b Morkel	10	65	54	1	-	c Jennings b de Bruyn	15	52	57	-	-
M Ngam st Jennings b Crookes	10	7	20	1	-	c Jennings b Flusk	4	49	28	-	-
Extras (b 7, lb 10, w 1, nb 5)	23					Extras (b 4, lb 11, w 1, nb 2)	18				
TOTAL (78.5 overs)	**256**					**TOTAL (88.5 overs)**	**191**				

EASTERNS

	Runs	*Mins*	*Balls*	*4*	*6*		*Runs*	*Mins*	*Balls*	*4*	*6*
BM White c Murray b Senekal	31	148	138	4	-	b Kemp	15	45	25	1	-
ET Mokoenanyana c Murray b Callaghan	18	76	46	2	-	c and b Ngam	28	108	81	4	-
*D Jordaan c Callaghan b Senekal	47	145	108	6	-	b Peterson	14	85	68	1	-
P de Bruyn c Senekal b Kemp	2	32	32	-	-	(6) not out	71	204	170	9	-
MJR Rindel b Kemp	4	6	11	1	-	(4) c Murray b Senekal	14	54	39	2	-
DN Crookes c Murray b Senekal	14	24	13	3	-	(5) run out (Grace)	117	226	184	13	1
†D Jennings lbw b Callaghan	0	6	7	-	-	not out	0	8	7	-	-
JA Morkel c Bryant b Callaghan	12	28	23	2	-						
GE Flusk b Callaghan	2	40	33	-	-						
KCG Benjamin b Callaghan	8	28	18	1	-						
A Nel not out	17	14	16	4	-						
Extras (b 4, lb 5, w 1, nb 7)	17					Extras (b 3, lb 9, w 2, nb 3)	17				
TOTAL (73.1 overs)	**172**					**TOTAL (for 5 wkts) (95.2 overs)**	**276**				

Bowling	*O*	*M*	*R*	*W*		*O*	*M*	*R*	*W*
EASTERNS									
Benjamin	19	4	66	3		23	7	35	4
Nel	18	6	37	2		25	5	57	2
Morkel	11	2	62	2	(4)	16	4	33	1
Crookes	22.5	9	49	2	(5)	7	0	20	0
Flusk	7	2	12	1	(6)	0.5	0	1	1
Jordaan	1	0	13	0					
de Bruyn					(3)	17	5	30	1
EASTERN PROVINCE									
Ngam	6	2	9	0		22	3	86	1
Senekal	16	3	42	3		21	3	54	1
Callaghan	18.1	11	24	5	(4)	23	7	55	0
Kemp	20	7	46	2	(3)	17	7	24	1
Peterson	13	3	42	0		11.2	2	39	1
Creed						1	0	6	0

Fall of Wickets

	EP 1st	**Eas** 1st	**EP** 2nd	**Eas** 2nd
1st	55 (1)	49 (2)	10 (2)	34 (1)
2nd	72 (3)	93 (1)	40 (1)	54 (2)
3rd	80 (4)	105 (4)	60 (4)	67 (3)
4th	102 (2)	110 (5)	60 (3)	93 (4)
5th	120 (6)	131 (6)	78 (5)	269 (5)
6th	129 (5)	132 (7)	78 (7)	-
7th	135 (7)	132 (3)	99 (6)	-
8th	140 (9)	146 (8)	122 (8)	-
9th	201 (10)	151 (9)	160 (10)	-
10th	256 (11)	172 (10)	191 (11)	-

Border v Easterns, East London, 17-20 November 2000. Border won by 56 runs. Western Province v Easterns, Cape Town, 24-27 November 2000. Western Province won by 194 runs.

EASTERNS v FREE STATE — SuperSport Series Super Eight

Played at Willowmoore Park, Benoni on 1,2,3,4 February 2001 Toss: Free State
Umpires: JD Cloete & DL Orchard (TV: AG O'Connor)
Debuts: Eas: JW Williams (FC). FS: None
Close of Play: Day 1: FS (1) 64-2 (Liebenberg 22*, Smit 17*, 17 overs). Day 2: Eas (2) 180-4 (Crookes 40*, Nel 10*, 41 overs). Day 3: FS (2) 116-1 (Liebenberg 59*, Wilkinson 30*, 32 overs).
Result: Easterns won by 109 runs
Man of Match: Mike Rindel
Points: Eas: 16 (bat 2, bowl 4, match 10). FS: 5 (bat 1, bowl 4, match 0)
Notes: AA Donald retired hurt with his score on 13 and the total on 201-7 in Free State's 2nd innings.

Brought down to earth by successive away defeats to Border and Western Province in the qualifying stage, Easterns had to resurrect their campaign against the erratic Free Staters. Senior campaigners Rindel and Ant Botha stood out in a mediocre first innings effort after Easterns were sent in.

Left-arm spinner Botha and Albie Morkel waded through a Free State batting line-up in which only Gerhardus Liebenberg and Wiaan Smit scored anything of consequence to ensure a slender first innings lead. Rindel scored his second consecutive half century and Crookes fell five short of another ton as Easterns surged beyond the elusive 300-barrier for the first time in the season, leaving the Free Staters with a steep task of amassing 339 to win on a deteriorating pitch. They failed to respond to the task, but their chase was overshadowed by the antagonistic duel that ensued between Nel and Allan Donald, which left Donald retired hurt.

EASTERNS

FIRST INNINGS	*Runs*	*Mins*	*Balls*	*4*	*6*	*SECOND INNINGS*	*Runs*	*Mins*	*Balls*	*4*	*6*
†D Jennings c Wilkinson b Donald	5	31	26	1	-	c Mpitsang b van Wyk	37	169	132	3	-
D Brand c Liebenberg b Mpitsang	19	62	40	3	-	c Donald b Mpitsang	4	14	7	1	-
*D Jordaan c Brophy b Pretorius	5	46	31	1	-	c Lewis b Pretorius	8	35	26	2	-
MJR Rindel c Brophy b Venter	69	125	86	8	1	c Pretorius b Venter	78	135	89	11	1
DN Crookes c Lewis b Venter	12	68	44	-	-	b van Wyk	95	148	113	12	-
P de Bruyn c Gait b Venter	9	49	39	-	-	(7) c Wilkinson b Mpitsang	21	66	57	3	-
AG Botha c Lewis b Donald	59	163	139	7	-	(8) c and b Pretorius	11	53	44	1	-
JA Morkel run out (Lewis)	25	104	79	1	1	(9) c Brophy b Mpitsang	5	18	9	1	-
GE Flusk run out (van Wyk)	0	3	1	-	-	(10) c Brophy b Pretorius	0	1	1	-	-
A Nel c Lewis b Donald	10	34	17	2	-	(6) c Smit b Venter	44	106	82	4	1
JW Williams not out	0	10	10	-	-	not out	0	4	3	-	-
Extras (b 2, lb 1, w 1, nb 7)	11					Extras (lb 2, w 1, nb 3)	6				
TOTAL (84.1 overs)	**224**					**TOTAL (93.1 overs)**	**309**				

FREE STATE

GFJ Liebenberg c Jennings b Flusk	54	178	134	6	-	c de Bruyn b Flusk	73	167	136	9	-
AI Gait lbw b Morkel	0	24	19	-	-	lbw b Brand	24	67	41	2	-
LJ Wilkinson b Flusk	17	18	11	3	-	c Jennings b Nel	36	61	45	6	-
WJ Smit b Botha	49	125	100	4	1	b Nel	0	14	5	-	-
MN van Wyk b Botha	8	27	24	1	-	c Jennings b Nel	0	3	3	-	-
JF Venter c Nel b Botha	0	11	8	-	-	c Botha b Nel	8	26	19	1	-
*†GL Brophy c Jennings b Morkel	11	54	38	2	-	c Flusk b Botha	11	43	26	2	-
MR Lewis not out	25	76	67	4	-	not out	49	115	71	8	-
D Pretorius c Crookes b Morkel	1	14	9	-	-	(10) c Jennings b Flusk	10	14	7	2	-
PV Mpitsang run out (Crookes)	4	8	4	-	-	(11) b Nel	0	11	11	-	-
AA Donald c Crookes b Morkel	0	4	2	-	-	(9) retired hurt	13	50	39	2	-
Extras (b 3, lb 7, w 1, nb 15)	26					Extras (b 1, lb 3, nb 1)	5				
TOTAL (66.5 overs)	**195**					**TOTAL (67 overs)**	**229**				

Bowling	*O*	*M*	*R*	*W*		*O*	*M*	*R*	*W*
FREE STATE									
Donald	19.1	6	46	3		10	3	31	0
Mpitsang	14	2	27	1		13.1	4	38	3
Pretorius	18	3	64	1	(5)	23	7	58	3
Lewis	8	1	30	0	(6)	7	0	27	0
Venter	25	7	54	3	(3)	32	5	128	2
van Wyk					(4)	8	2	25	2
EASTERNS									
Nel	14	5	28	0		22	5	43	5
Morkel	15.5	2	36	4		4	0	30	0
Flusk	7	1	35	2		13	0	61	2
Crookes	8	1	30	0					
Botha	17	4	50	3		17	2	55	1
Brand	5	1	6	0		9	2	31	1
de Bruyn						2	0	5	0

Fall of Wickets	Eas	FS	Eas	FS
	1st	1st	2nd	2nd
1st	17 (1)	6 (2)	7 (2)	66 (2)
2nd	31 (2)	38 (3)	16 (3)	122 (3)
3rd	37 (3)	135 (4)	122 (1)	132 (4)
4th	91 (5)	147 (1)	141 (4)	132 (5)
5th	122 (4)	148 (6)	256 (6)	144 (1)
6th	125 (6)	149 (5)	278 (5)	144 (6)
7th	194 (8)	170 (7)	303 (7)	170 (7)
8th	194 (9)	176 (9)	309 (8)	222 (10)
9th	223 (10)	194 (10)	309 (10)	229 (11)
10th	224 (7)	195 (11)	309 (9)	-

Northerns v Easterns, Centurion, 1-4 March 2001. Easterns won by 4 wickets.

EASTERNS v NORTH WEST — SuperSport Series Super Eight

Played at Willowmoore Park, Benoni on 8,9,10,11 March 2001 — Toss: North West
Umpires: ST Jivan & CM Schoof
Debuts: Eas: None. NW: None
Close of Play: Day 1: NW (1) 117-3 (Strydom 21*, Light 8*, 38 overs). Day 2: Eas (2) 3-0 (Seymore 1*, van den Berg 2*, 4 overs). Day 3: NW (2) 41-0 (Niewoudt 25*, Lawson 8*, 9 overs).
Result: North West won by 10 wickets
Man of Match: Alfonso Thomas
Points: Eas: 3 (bat 0, bowl 3, match 0). NW: 17 (bat 3, bowl 4, match 10)
Notes: AG Lawson retired hurt with his score on 25 and the total on 90-2 in North West's 1st innings and returned at the fall of the 7th wicket.

A morale-boosting four-wicket away win over Northerns Titans just four days earlier left Easterns with a chance of qualifying for the final to make it a fairytale second season as a top-flight province. The visiting team put Easterns in to bat on a lively deck and the hosts probably watched their championship dreams evaporating in just one innings. Unheralded Alfonso Thomas destroyed the Easterns batting with a personal-best six for 26 in 18.3 overs, leaving Easterns' opening gambit in ruins. The bulk of the North West batsmen chipped in as they consolidated their advantage.

Only the batting of lone ranger Albie Morkel, with a maiden first-class century, ensured that North West would have to bat again, but it was all in vain as they slumped to a big defeat.

EASTERNS

FIRST INNINGS	*Runs*	*Mins*	*Balls*	*4*	*6*	*SECOND INNINGS*	*Runs*	*Mins*	*Balls*	*4*	*6*
AJ Seymore c Poole b Thomas	32	105	78	5	-	c Poole b Roe	7	44	34	1	-
AM van den Berg c Niewoudt b Thomas	16	63	51	2	-	c Lavine b van der Merwe	20	106	83	3	-
†D Jennings c Hewitt b Thomas	0	15	11	-	-	c Poole b Lavine	0	19	14	-	-
MJR Rindel c Light b Thomas	12	17	13	3	-	b Roe	42	135	95	6	-
*DN Crookes c Poole b Thomas	8	24	17	1	-	c Poole b Roe	9	38	35	-	-
P de Bruyn c Poole b Roe	1	47	37	-	-	c Lavine b Roe	33	193	132	1	-
AG Botha not out	14	148	108	2	-	lbw b Roe	0	2	2	-	-
JA Morkel c Strydom b Roe	0	8	4	-	-	c Venter b van der Merwe	117	142	118	18	1
GE Flusk c Poole b van der Merwe	11	71	50	1	-	c Niewoudt b Roe	15	34	18	2	-
KCG Benjamin c Poole b van der Merwe	0	2	2	-	-	(11) not out	10	29	18	1	-
BL Reddy c Strydom b Thomas	4	32	26	-	-	(10) c Poole b Thomas	28	58	50	3	-
Extras (b 1, lb 2, w 1, nb 4)	8					Extras (b 3, lb 6, w 2, nb 7)	18				
TOTAL (65.3 overs)	**106**					**TOTAL (98.4 overs)**	**299**				

NORTH WEST												
R Niewoudt b Flusk	44	66	49	7	1	not out	43	90	73	4	1
AG Lawson c de Bruyn b Benjamin	64	326	246	8	-	not out	15	90	73	1	-
*MC Venter c Botha b Morkel	6	35	26	1	-						
M Strydom c Jennings b Flusk	37	90	68	4	1						
GM Hewitt c Botha b Benjamin	2	19	20	-	-						
C Light b Morkel	25	88	55	4	-						
MJ Lavine c Jennings b Morkel	26	43	27	5	-						
AC Thomas c Crookes b Botha	32	88	78	3	-						
†EG Poole st Jennings b Botha	50	163	117	5	1						
GA Roe c sub (JW Williams) b de Bruyn	24	79	65	5	-						
F van der Merwe not out	2	35	20	-	-						
Extras (b 1, lb 8, w 3, nb 12)	24					Extras (lb 5, nb 7)	12				
TOTAL (126.5 overs)	**336**					**TOTAL (for 0 wkts) (23.1 overs)**	**70**				

Bowling	*O*	*M*	*R*	*W*		*O*	*M*	*R*	*W*
NORTH WEST									
Lavine	17	9	18	0		25	6	74	1
Roe	14	8	17	2		25	11	31	6
Thomas	18.3	8	26	6		25.4	6	86	1
van der Merwe	16	5	42	2		13	1	64	2
Strydom						10	0	35	0
EASTERNS									
Benjamin	27	8	91	2					
Morkel	28	5	77	3	(1)	3	0	21	0
Flusk	22	8	54	2	(2)	4	0	12	0
Reddy	17	6	36	0	(3)	9	2	12	0
de Bruyn	16	7	32	1					
Botha	16.5	8	37	2	(4)	7.1	2	20	0

Fall of Wickets	**Eas**	**NW**	**Eas**	**NW**
	1st	1st	2nd	2nd
1st	34 (2)	62 (1)	13 (1)	-
2nd	36 (3)	81 (3)	16 (3)	-
3rd	60 (4)	98 (5)	46 (2)	-
4th	65 (1)	139 (4)	68 (5)	-
5th	72 (5)	154 (6)	92 (4)	-
6th	76 (6)	200 (7)	92 (7)	-
7th	76 (8)	239 (8)	238 (6)	-
8th	93 (9)	263 (2)	244 (8)	-
9th	93 (10)	306 (10)	269 (9)	-
10th	106 (11)	336 (9)	299 (10)	-

Boland v Easterns, Paarl, 15-18 March 2001. Easterns won by 139 runs.

EASTERN PROVINCE JUMBOS 2000/01

Back, from left: Umar Abrahams, Mark Benfield, Johan Botha, Mfuneko Ngam, Garnett Kruger, Dewald Senekal, Wayne Murray, Robin Peterson, Murray Creed, Kevin Duckworth, Graham Grace, Lulama Masikazana. Front: Justin Kemp, Mornantau Hayward, Adrian Birrell (coach), Carl Bradfield (captain), Dave Emslie (chief executive), Dave Callaghan, Meyrick Pringle, James Bryant.

EASTERN PROVINCE CRICKET

PO Box 12327, Centrahil 6006. Tel (041) 585 1646.
Fax (041) 586 4259. E-mail: epcb@iafrica.com

President: Mr Justice Ronnie Pillay
Chief Executive Officer: Dave Emslie
Director of Finance and Administration: Kevin Horn.
Development Manager: Tono Mle
Senior Coach: Adrian Birrell. **Youth coach:** Russell Domingo
2001/02 contracted players: Carl Bradfield (captain), Umar Abrahams, Mark Benfield, Johan Botha, James Bryant, Dave Callaghan, Murray Creed, Kevin Duckworth, Bruce Friderichs, Graham Hayward, Garnett Kruger, Lyall Meyer, Wayne Murray, Robin Peterson, Meyrick Pringle. **Nationally contracted players:** Mornantau Hayward, Justin Kemp, Mfuneko Ngam.

REVIEW OF THE SEASON 2000/01

Neale Emslie

SUPERSPORT SERIES: P8 W1 L4 D 3 (eighth)
CAPTAIN: CC Bradfield (7), DJ Callaghan (1)
STANDARD BANK CUP: P14 W7 L5 Tied 1 NR1 (beaten semifinalists)

Applying the theory that you're only as good as your last match would suggest that Eastern Province experienced a very poor season in 2000/01. The Jumbos' last two matches were the low points of their summer and although they were not a strictly accurate reflection of their season, they must have left the EP camp, both players and officials, with plenty to consider in the off-season.

In those games, Carl Bradfield's side lost to Northerns at home and Free State (away) in their final two four-day Super Eight games to end a disappointing last on the log. Even more disturbing was the way they were unable to put together any sort of batting form, losing both games inside three days.

There were extenuating circumstances in Bloemfontein with an untypical seaming pitch being prepared for the match, on which medium-pacer Dave Callaghan had a career-best match haul of 10 for 110. When Free State, who could manage only 110 in their first innings, came out to bat needing an improbable 258 to win, they threw caution to the winds and achieved their target with a limited overs batting approach which paid handsome dividends.

The bottom line for EP, though, at the conclusion of the four-day competition, was that they had managed to win just one of their eight first-class games during the season.

The inability of their batsmen to post the sort of totals needed consistently to put their opponents under pressure was their biggest failing. Only Justin Kemp (56.50) and Carl Bradfield (40.30) were able to average above the 40-mark, meaning that most of the time there just weren't enough runs for their bowlers to play with.

Frustratingly, when they did achieve supremacy with the bat, for example against Easterns, Natal and Boland, they were unable to finish off their opponents in the second innings. This allowed Easterns to score an excellent victory, chasing 276 at Benoni, and let Natal and Boland off the hook, denying EP points which could have been crucial in their bid to make an impact on the first-class competition.

Probably the biggest disappointment was No 3 James Bryant, who could total only 276 runs after being such a success the previous summer. He didn't simply become a bad batsman – he proved that with a string of excellent knocks in the one-day competition – but he, like a number of other colleagues, will need to learn the art of selling his wicket dearly.

The bowling also lacked the necessary penetration at times. In fairness, they suffered a spate of injuries in the first two months of the season, with Meyrick Pringle, Garnett Kruger, Mfuneko Ngam and Nantie Hayward all sidelined at one stage.

On top of it, Hayward experienced an "annus horribilis". After struggling with a sore knee, he lost his control and confidence and was sidelined after a disastrous one-day match in Gauteng. He also experienced some traumatic personal problems which clearly affected his general state of mind.

For a person of such volatile character, it is to Hayward's credit that he fought his way back in the last two months to produce bowling more closely resembling that which made him a player of the year the previous season. He played a match-winning role in the Standard Bank Cup semifinal second leg against Natal but there's a lot of hard work ahead for him to regain the form which earned him a national contract.

On the plus side, tall all-rounder Justin Kemp emerged as one of the country's players of the future. Always highly rated, he began to produce the sort of dominant play expected from a player of his talent. Against Border, carrying the attack, he returned his first-class career best of six for 56, followed that with six for 20 in a one-day game against Free State – the best performance in SA domestic limited overs cricket – and then struck North West off-spinner Morne Strydom for five sixes in one over as he blitzed an unforgettable career-best innings of 188.

Even before that, Kemp achieved his national colours against Sri Lanka in both forms of the game, due to an injury to Lance Klusener, and although failing with the bat, he took five wickets on his Test debut.

If the four-day competition was a barren one for EP, the Standard Bank Cup provided much more encouragement. They started with three tension-filled victories and were the early trail-blazers by winning their first five matches. The wheels fell off against a full-strength Western Province side and although the Jumbos' winning form faded, they did enough to again qualify for the semifinals.

Like the previous season against Gauteng, they were outplayed at home by KwaZulu-Natal in the semifinal first leg but hit back to win in Durban and were odds-on favourites for a berth in the final when they reached 253 for two in 41.2 overs in the deciding leg. Rain then intervened and when it finally cleared up on the following day, the Jumbos ran out of steam as the Natalians finished deserving winners.

Bryant, shrugging off his indifferent four-day form, slammed 578 runs in 14 matches at an average of 52.54 and Callaghan played several important innings.

At times, the Jumbos did lean towards inconsistency but if they can instil a sense of self-belief in their performances, the potential is there to develop into a combative unit.

Despite talks with KwaZulu-Natal batsman Mark Bruyns, EP contracted no new players for the 2001/02 season, preferring to rely on the home-grown talent emerging from the

Lennon EP Academy. They lost experienced spinner Shafiek Abrahams and young fast bowler Dewald Senekal to Northerns, while Carl Bradfield will again captain the side.

Off the field, EPCB president Flip Potgieter indicated he would not be available for re-election at the annual meeting after 22 years of being involved at an executive level. There appeared to be behind-the-scenes friction between Potgieter and provincial monitoring committee chairman Rajan Moodaley, with Potgieter saying he hoped his retirement would ease tensions in the boardroom.

PROVINCIAL RECORDS

Honours:
Currie/Castle Cup (3): 1988/89, 1989/90 (shared), 1991/92
B&H Series (2): 1989/90, 1991/92
Gillette/Nissan Shield (4): 1971/72, 1975/76, 1987/88, 1989/90
Currie Cup B Section (2): 1954/55, 1959/60 (shared)

Highest innings totals:

For:	594-6*	v Western Province (Cape Town)		1962/63
Against:	587-7*	by Western Province (Cape Town) (CC)		1983/84
	587	by Natal (Pietermaritzburg) (FC)		1939/40

Lowest innings totals:

For:	34	v Natal (Port Elizabeth)	1980/81
Against:	34	by Border (East London)	1946/47

Highest individual innings:

For:	284	EAB Rowan	v Griqualand West (Port Elizabeth) (FC)	1945/46
	222*	AL Wilmot	v Rhodesia (Salisbury) (CC)	1965/66
Against:	294	AJ Lamb	for Orange Free State (Bloemfontein)	1987/88

Most runs in a season:

SS				All FC			
847	(Avg 84.70)	KC Wessels	1997/98	984	(Avg 82.00)	RG Pollock	1974/75

Most runs in a career:

SS				All FC			
7740	(Avg 53.75)	RG Pollock	1960-77	8736	(Avg 53.26)	RG Pollock	1960-77

Most 100s in a career:

SS			All FC		
21	RG Pollock	1960-77	25	RG Pollock	1960-77
			25	KC Wessels	1986-97

Best bowling in an innings:

For:	10-26	AEE Vogler	v Griqualand West (Johannesburg)	1906/07
Against:	9-64	DL Hobson	for Western Province (Cape Town)	1978/79

Best bowling in a match:

For:	16-38	AEE Vogler	v Griqualand West (Johannesburg)	1906/07
Against:	15-68	GK Glover	for Griqualand West (Cape Town)	1893/94

Most wickets in a season:

SS				All FC			
48	(Avg 23.70)	JN Maguire	1990/91	60	(Avg 15.05)	JN Maguire	1989/90

Most wickets in a career:

SS				All FC			
287	(Avg 30.59)	TG Shaw	1981-96	345	(Avg 29.30)	TG Shaw	1981-96

Most dismissals (wicketkeepers) in an innings:

7 (ct 7,st 0)	DJ Richardson	v Orange Free State (Bloemfontein)	1988/89

Most dismissals (wicketkeepers) in a match:

10 (ct 10,st 0)	DJ Richardson	v Orange Free State (Bloemfontein)	1988/89
10 (ct 9,st 1)	DJ Richardson	Northern Transvaal (Verwoerdburg)	1989/90

Most dismissals (wicketkeepers) in a season:

SS				All FC			
38	(ct 34,st 4)	DJ Richardson	1990/91	42	(ct 37,st 5)	DJ Richardson	1990/91

Most dismissals (wicketkeepers) in a career:

SS			All FC		
337	(ct 311,st 26) DJ Richardson (includes 1 ct as fielder)	1978-97	386	(ct 355,st 31) DJ Richardson (includes 1 ct as fielder)	1978-97

Most catches (fielders) in an innings:

4 JM Buchanan, AL Wilmot, GM Den, SJ Bezuidenhout, LJ Koen

Most catches (fielders) in a match:

6	B Wood v Transvaal (Port Elizabeth)	1971/72
6	AL Wilmot v Western Province (Port Elizabeth)	1971/72

Most catches (fielders) in a season:

SS			All FC		
15	LJ Koen	1996/97	18	LJ Koen	1995/96
15	LJ Koen	1998/99			

Most catches (fielders) in a career:

SS			All FC		
100	RG Pollock	1960-77	110	RG Pollock	1960-77

Most appearances:

SS			All FC		
112	DJ Richardson	1978-97	125	DJ Richardson	1978-97

Most captaincies:

SS			All FC		
81	KC Wessels	1986-97	94	KC Wessels	1986-97

RECORD WICKET PARTNERSHIPS

1st	312	GF Dakin and CG Rushmere v Western Province (Cape Town)	1962/63
2nd	338	PG Amm and LJ Koen v Boland (Port Elizabeth) (The South African domestic record for this wicket)	1995/96
3rd	337	PG Amm and KS McEwan v Transvaal (Port Elizabeth) (The SuperSport Series, but not South African, record for this wicket)	1988/89
4th	289	KC Wessels and DJ Callaghan v Border (Port Elizabeth)	1997/98
5th	338	RG Pollock and AL Wilmot v Natal (Port Elizabeth) (The first four wickets had fallen for 15 runs)	1975/76
6th	194	RG Pollock and DJ Brickett v Rhodesia (Port Elizabeth)	1977/78
7th	192*	DJ Callaghan and TG Shaw v Transvaal (Port Elizabeth)	1995/96
8th	150	GS Cowley and TG Shaw v Western Province (Port Elizabeth)	1983/84
9th	151	DJ Brickett and WK Watson v Northern Transvaal (Port Elizabeth)	1982/83
10th	108	L Masikazana and M Hayward v Boland (Port Elizabeth)	1997/98

PERFORMANCES AGAINST OTHER TEAMS

HIGHEST AND LOWEST TOTALS

Opponents	Highest Total For		Lowest Total For	
Boland	452-3*	1995/96	87	1999/00
Border	514	1992/93	41	1936/37
	514-5*	1997/98		
Easterns	375	1999/00	191	2000/01
Free State	529-8*	1946/47	40	1910/11
Gauteng	561	1988/89	36	1937/38
Griqualand West	515-6* (FC)	1945/46	48	1934/35
	476-6* (SS)	1996/97		
KwaZulu-Natal	476-6*	1998/99	34	1980/81
Northerns	526	1999/00	53	1967/68
North West	448	2000/01	-	
Western Province	594-6*	1962/63	37	1933/34

BEST INDIVIDUAL PERFORMANCES

Opponents	Highest score	Best bowling (innings)	Best bowling (match, 8+)
Boland	202* LJ Koen, 1995/96	6-99 AG Huckle, 1993/94	10-54(FC) JN Maguire 1989/90
Border	207 (FC) AL Wilmot,1968/69	7-62 (FC) AL Biggs,1970/71	11-89 AH McKinnon,1954/55
	179* (SS) KC Wessels, 1997/98	7-64 (SS) GJ-P Kruger, 1999/00	
Easterns	125 JDC Bryant, 1999/00	6-31 M Hayward, 1999/00	12-94 M Hayward, 1999/00
Free State	173 KC Wessels, 1995/96	8-24 AEE Vogler, 1906/07	14-58 AEE Vogler, 1906/07
Gauteng	214 PG Amm, 1988/89	7-78 MW Pringle, 1997/98	10-131 MW Pringle 1997/98
Griqualand West	284 (FC) EAB Rowan,1945/46	10-26 AEE Vogler,1906/07	16-38 AEE Vogler,1906/07
	219 (CC) JHB Waite, 1950/51		
KwaZulu-Natal	194 RG Pollock, 1975/76	7-50 WK Watson, 1982/83	10-103 DJ Brickett, 1979/80
Northerns	197 KC Wessels, 1990/91	6-25 PA Rayment, 1991/92	10-93 EAE Baptiste, 1996/97
North West	188 JM Kemp, 2000/01	5-37 S Abrahams, 2000/01	-
Western Province	180* RG Pollock,1976/77	8-49 DJ Brickett,1973/74	10-43 AW Greig,1971/72

EASTERN PROVINCE SUPERSPORT AVERAGES 2000/01

Batting & Fielding

Name	M	Inns	NO	Runs	HS	Avg	100	50	Ct	St
JM Kemp	5	8	0	452	188	56.50	1	2	1	0
CC Bradfield	7	14	1	524	91	40.30	0	3	10	0
M Hayward	6	9	5	114	26	28.50	0	0	1	0
DJ Callaghan	8	14	1	338	129	26.00	1	0	6	0
MW Creed	7	12	0	305	47	25.41	0	0	3	0
RJ Peterson	7	13	2	265	96*	24.09	0	1	0	0
MR Benfield	7	14	1	307	93	23.61	0	2	4	0
J Botha	2	4	0	88	43	22.00	0	0	0	0
MW Pringle	3	4	1	64	25	21.33	0	0	1	0
S Abrahams	6	9	0	190	85	21.11	0	1	6	0
DW Murray	8	13	1	249	58*	20.75	0	1	35	0
JDC Bryant	8	16	2	276	70	19.71	0	1	7	0
U Abrahams	4	8	0	150	51	18.75	0	1	0	0
DM Senekal	2	4	2	31	15	15.50	0	0	1	0
M Ngam	3	5	1	34	18*	8.50	0	0	1	0
GV Grace	2	4	0	30	13	7.50	0	0	0	0
GJ-P Kruger	3	4	1	18	13*	6.00	0	0	0	0
Totals	88	155	18	3435	188		2	12	76	0
			Extras	225				subs	1	
			Total	3660		26.71			77	

Bowling

Name	Overs	Mdns	Runs	Wkts	Avg	BB	5I	10M
DJ Callaghan	156	51	356	18	19.77	5-24	3	1
J Botha	16	9	45	2	22.50	1-4	0	0
MW Pringle	109.1	32	234	10	23.40	4-32	0	0
JM Kemp	198.4	61	426	18	23.66	6-56	2	0
GJ-P Kruger	143.5	37	391	15	26.06	4-49	0	0
DM Senekal	61	8	174	5	34.80	3-42	0	0
M Ngam	124	24	363	10	36.30	4-78	0	0
RJ Peterson	322.5	78	895	24	37.29	5-87	1	0
M Hayward	203.3	24	714	18	39.66	3-69	0	0
S Abrahams	149.1	48	325	8	40.62	5-37	1	0
MW Creed	51.3	9	177	3	59.00	1-24	0	0
Totals	1535.4	381	4100	131		6-56	7	1
		b & lb	152	8	run outs			
		Total	4252	139	30.58			

MATCH REPORTS AND SCORECARDS

EASTERN PROVINCE v WESTERN PROVINCE SuperSport Series Pool B

Played at St George's Park, Port Elizabeth on 27,28,29,30 October 2000 Toss: Eastern Province
Umpires: IL Howell & S Wadvalla
Debuts: EP: None. WP: AG Puttick (FC), NC Johnson, GC Smith & CM Willoughby (all FC for WP)
Close of Play: Day 1: WP (1) 362 all out. Day 2: EP (1) 256-7 (Callaghan 124*, Hayward 8*, 104 overs). Day 3: WP (2) 117-6 (Smith 42*, Dawson 6*, 55 overs).
Result: Western Province won by 127 runs
Man of Match: Claude Henderson
Points: EP: 7 (bat 3, bowl 4, match 0). WP: 18 (bat 5, bowl 3, match 10)

Western Province captain HD Ackerman led the way with his 14th first-class century as the visitors made a healthy total. EP veteran Dave Callaghan held the Jumbos' innings together with a century but once EP had conceded a first innings lead of 80, the pressure was always on them.

Young EP paceman Mfuneko Ngam took seven wickets in the match to give an early preview of his exciting potential. He reduced WP to 97 for six in their second innings but Alan Dawson and Graeme Smith struck important half-centuries to set EP 293 to win. Left-arm spinner Claude Henderson finished off the job for WP with five wickets as EP's batting crumbled on the last day.

WESTERN PROVINCE

FIRST INNINGS	*Runs*	*Mins*	*Balls*	*4*	*6*	*SECOND INNINGS*	*Runs*	*Mins*	*Balls*	*4*	*6*
HH Gibbs c Benfield b Ngam	61	153	135	11	-	c Murray b Ngam	11	15	11	2	-
GC Smith c Kemp b Peterson	35	100	60	5	-	c sub (GV Grace) b Kemp	80	274	217	7	-
AG Puttick b Ngam	5	27	19	-	-	b Hayward	25	33	29	5	-
*HD Ackerman b Hayward	128	204	177	20	-	b Ngam	10	33	19	2	-
NC Johnson c Bryant b Ngam	30	105	72	2	1	c Callaghan b Ngam	0	16	11	-	-
AG Prince c Bradfield b Callaghan	47	124	86	6	-	c Murray b Peterson	3	30	19	-	-
†TL Tsolekile c Bryant b Ngam	1	10	13	-	-	lbw b Kemp	2	23	21	-	-
AC Dawson not out	20	70	47	1	-	not out	53	181	116	5	1
CW Henderson run out (Bryant)	3	13	10	-	-	run out (Callaghan)	1	8	4	-	-
PR Adams c Callaghan b Hayward	0	2	2	-	-	not out	5	11	11	-	-
CM Willoughby b Kemp	10	12	7	1	-						
Extras (b 1, lb 7, w 2, nb 12)	22					Extras (b 2, lb 7, w 5, nb 8)	22				
TOTAL (102.4 overs)	**362**					**TOTAL (for 8 wkts dec) (75 overs)**	**212**				

EASTERN PROVINCE

	Runs	Mins	Balls	4	6		Runs	Mins	Balls	4	6
MR Benfield c Gibbs b Willoughby	0	4	6	-	-	(2) c Gibbs b Dawson	6	13	12	-	-
*CC Bradfield c Tsolekile b Johnson	18	98	80	3	-	(1) c Tsolekile b Adams	28	78	51	5	-
JDC Bryant lbw b Johnson	21	104	73	4	-	c Smith b Henderson	40	130	123	5	1
DJ Callaghan b Dawson	129	313	270	18	2	b Henderson	16	88	74	1	-
JM Kemp c Adams b Henderson	44	115	97	7	1	c Ackerman b Willoughby	29	88	88	2	-
MW Creed b Adams	13	64	56	1	-	c Johnson b Henderson	18	71	68	1	-
RJ Peterson b Dawson	0	15	10	-	-	c Tsolekile b Henderson	11	33	22	1	1
†DW Murray run out (Smith/Tsolekile)	19	55	26	3	-	c Johnson b Adams	15	30	18	2	-
M Hayward not out	23	67	47	3	-	not out	1	7	4	-	-
M Ngam lbw b Adams	2	17	19	-	-	c Smith b Henderson	0	4	7	-	-
MW Pringle absent hurt						absent hurt					
Extras (b 3, lb 7, nb 3)	13					Extras (b 1)	1				
TOTAL (113.3 overs)	**282**					**TOTAL (77.5 overs)**	**165**				

Bowling	*O*	*M*	*R*	*W*		*O*	*M*	*R*	*W*
EASTERN PROVINCE									
Pringle	12	1	37	0					
Hayward	24	2	94	2	(1)	7	0	41	1
Ngam	23	3	78	4	(2)	24	3	59	3
Peterson	21	3	76	1		24	6	63	1
Kemp	13.4	2	43	1		13	3	32	2
Callaghan	9	2	26	1	(3)	7	3	8	0
WESTERN PROVINCE									
Willoughby	25	14	38	1		15	7	25	1
Dawson	27	9	67	2		12	3	28	1
Henderson	33	9	86	1	(5)	19.5	5	40	5
Johnson	11	3	35	2	(3)	3	0	16	0
Adams	17.3	5	46	2	(4)	28	9	55	2

Fall of Wickets

	WP	EP	WP	EP
	1st	1st	2nd	2nd
1st	84 (2)	0 (1)	12 (1)	8 (2)
2nd	101 (3)	40 (2)	45 (3)	52 (1)
3rd	132 (1)	49 (3)	67 (4)	84 (3)
4th	224 (5)	126 (5)	70 (5)	93 (4)
5th	302 (4)	177 (6)	89 (6)	137 (5)
6th	305 (7)	183 (7)	97 (7)	139 (6)
7th	343 (6)	232 (8)	190 (2)	160 (7)
8th	349 (9)	269 (4)	196 (9)	164 (8)
9th	349 (10)	282 (10)	-	165 (10)
10th	362 (11)	-	-	-

Easterns v Eastern Province, Benoni, 3-6 November 2000. Easterns won by 5 wickets.

EASTERN PROVINCE v BORDER — SuperSport Series Pool B

Played at St George's Park, Port Elizabeth on 10,11,12,13 November 2000 — Toss: Eastern Province
Umpires: KH Hurter & DL Orchard
Debuts: EP: J Botha (FC). Bdr: None
Close of Play: Day 1: Bdr (1) 103-3 (Pope 53*, Strydom 4*, 28 overs). Day 2: EP (2) 154-3 (Bradfield 69*, Kemp 61*, 49 overs). Day 3: EP (2) 276-6 (Abrahams 17*, Peterson 22*, 97 overs).
Result: Match drawn
Man of Match: Justin Kemp
Points: EP: 5 (bat 1, bowl 4, match 0). Bdr: 6 (bat 2, bowl 4, match 0)
Notes: Mitchell replaced Boucher as wicketkeeper in the 70th over of Eastern Province's 2nd innings, taking 3 catches and a stumping.

EP again conceded a first innings lead, this time of 54, as Makhaya Ntini took six wickets and when the Jumbos slumped to 34 for three in their second innings, Border looked good for a win. But Justin Kemp joined skipper Carl Bradfield in a match-saving fourth-wicket partnership of 153 and Border, set a victory target of 279 in a minimum of 78 overs, settled for a draw.

It proved to be a fine match for Kemp as he showed the form and ability which was to earn him national colours later in the season. He returned career-best figures of six for 56 in Border's first innings and contributed innings of 25 and 81.

EASTERN PROVINCE

FIRST INNINGS	*Runs*	*Mins*	*Balls*	*4*	*6*	*SECOND INNINGS*	*Runs*	*Mins*	*Balls*	*4*	*6*
*CC Bradfield c Mitchell b Ntini	35	131	95	5	-	c Drakes b Strydom	91	315	257	12	-
GV Grace c Wiblin b Ntini	6	8	6	1	-	lbw b Drakes	3	19	9	-	-
JDC Bryant c Strydom b Ntini	0	7	3	-	-	lbw b Drakes	0	1	1	-	-
DJ Callaghan lbw b Drakes	4	56	38	-	-	c Boucher b Ntini	12	28	19	2	-
JM Kemp c Strydom b Ntini	25	47	39	5	-	c Strydom b Drakes	81	184	150	11	1
MW Creed lbw b Graham	19	102	64	3	-	c Mitchell b Drakes	31	91	77	2	-
S Abrahams c Boucher b Ntini	0	8	3	-	-	c Love b Drakes	35	109	82	4	-
RJ Peterson c Drakes b Ntini	21	45	31	2	-	c Mitchell b Ntini	36	131	92	3	-
J Botha st Boucher b Mitchell	23	113	96	3	-	c Mitchell b Ntini	7	25	19	1	-
†DW Murray c Graham b Mitchell	39	67	61	5	-	st Mitchell b Strydom	9	50	39	1	-
DM Senekal not out	0	7	6	-	-	not out	6	37	35	-	-
Extras (lb 2, nb 3)	5					Extras (b 1, lb 10, nb 10)	21				
TOTAL (73.1 overs)	**177**					**TOTAL (128.2 overs)**	**332**				

BORDER

FIRST INNINGS	*Runs*	*Mins*	*Balls*	*4*	*6*	*SECOND INNINGS*	*Runs*	*Mins*	*Balls*	*4*	*6*
CB Sugden lbw b Kemp	0	3	6	-	-	c Callaghan b Peterson	23	63	52	3	-
I Mitchell c Abrahams b Kemp	14	47	37	2	-	c Murray b Peterson	37	141	127	4	-
SC Pope lbw b Kemp	55	117	94	10	-	lbw b Callaghan	2	22	24	-	-
†MV Boucher c Murray b Creed	20	35	26	3	-	(8) not out	33	50	46	3	-
*PC Strydom c Bradfield b Kemp	12	74	53	2	-	lbw b Peterson	0	6	6	-	-
W Wiblin c Bradfield b Senekal	18	51	40	2	1	(4) not out	64	197	165	9	-
LL Gamiet c Bryant b Botha	37	113	115	4	1	(6) b Peterson	25	42	52	4	-
VC Drakes c Bradfield b Peterson	39	80	72	4	1	(7) c Bradfield b Peterson	18	42	36	3	-
GT Love lbw b Kemp	15	44	41	1	-						
L Graham c Callaghan b Kemp	0	21	20	-	-						
M Ntini not out	4	7	3	1	-						
Extras (lb 5, nb 12)	17					Extras (b 1, lb 11, nb 1)	13				
TOTAL (82.3 overs)	**231**					**TOTAL (for 6 wkts) (84.3 overs)**	**215**				

Bowling	*O*	*M*	*R*	*W*		*O*	*M*	*R*	*W*
BORDER									
Drakes	20.3	4	57	1		30	8	80	5
Ntini	20.3	7	59	6		40	11	112	3
Graham	13	7	22	1		12	3	30	0
Love	11	7	17	0		18	4	34	0
Strydom	7	2	20	0		25.2	7	55	2
Mitchell	1.1	1	0	2		3	1	10	0
EASTERN PROVINCE									
Kemp	26.3	12	56	6		17.3	3	40	0
Senekal	17	2	51	1		7	0	27	0
Callaghan	5	2	12	0	(4)	17	5	22	1
Creed	5	1	24	1					
Botha	7	3	22	1					
Abrahams	10	3	44	0	(5)	8	1	27	0
Peterson	12	7	17	1	(3)	35	11	87	5

Fall of Wickets

	EP 1st	**Bdr** 1st	**EP** 2nd	**Bdr** 2nd
1st	8 (2)	0 (1)	9 (2)	51 (1)
2nd	10 (3)	46 (2)	9 (3)	57 (3)
3rd	39 (4)	95 (4)	34 (4)	81 (2)
4th	67 (5)	107 (3)	187 (5)	81 (5)
5th	74 (1)	134 (5)	228 (1)	135 (6)
6th74	(7) 137	(6) 236	(6) 179	(7)
7th	108 (8)	211 (8)	303 (7)	-
8th	117 (6)	212 (7)	313 (9)	-
9th	177 (10)	224 (10)	318 (8)	-
10th	177 (9)	231 (9)	332 (10)	-

KwaZulu-Natal v Eastern Province, Durban, 1-4 December 2000. Match drawn.

EASTERN PROVINCE v NORTH WEST SuperSport Series Super Eight

Played at St George's Park, Port Elizabeth on 1,2,3,4 February 2001 Toss: North West
Umpires: IL Howell & CJ Mitchley
Debuts: EP: U Abrahams (FC for EP). NW: None
Close of Play: Day 1: NW (1) 304-7 (Poole 15*, Thomas 6*, 104 overs). Day 2: EP (1) 230-4 (Kemp 53*, Creed 7*, 76 overs). Day 3: NW (2) 83-5 (van der Merwe 1*, 45.1 overs).
Result: Eastern Province won by 9 wickets
Man of Match: Justin Kemp
Points: EP: 16 (bat 3, bowl 3, match 10). NW: 6 (bat 3, bowl 3, match 0)
Notes: JM Kemp hit 31 runs off an over from M Strydom in Eastern Province's 1st innings, including 5 consecutive sixes.

Kemp came within one hit of equalling the world record for most runs off an over as he struck an explosive 188 to set up EP's only four-day victory of the season. Kemp made a sleepy Saturday afternoon eminently memorable by smashing five sixes off an over from off-spinner Morne Strydom – the first two from reverse sweeps – and then taking a single off the final ball as he went for the world record of six sixes in an over shared by Sir Garfield Sobers and Ravi Shastri.

Facing North West's substantial first innings of 341, EP, due mainly to Kemp, charged to 448, the 10th-wicket stand of 70 between the all-rounder and Hayward coming off just 28 deliveries.

Tall seamer Garnett Kruger led the way as North West were dismissed for 227 in their second innings, allowing EP to win with time to spare on the final day.

NORTH WEST

FIRST INNINGS	*Runs*	*Mins*	*Balls*	*4*	*6*	*SECOND INNINGS*	*Runs*	*Mins*	*Balls*	*4*	*6*
R Niewoudt lbw b S Abrahams	98	219	174	16	-	c Murray b Kruger	1	2	2	-	-
HM de Vos c Murray b Peterson	17	101	81	1	-	c Benfield b Kruger	9	63	55	1	-
*AG Lawson b S Abrahams	61	268	218	7	-	lbw b S Abrahams	29	121	96	1	-
A Jacobs c and b S Abrahams	17	30	43	2	-	c Creed b Peterson	22	97	88	4	-
C Light run out (Hayward)	10	16	19	2	-	lbw b Peterson	10	20	24	1	-
MJ Lavine lbw b S Abrahams	21	24	23	3	1	(7) b Kruger	8	13	14	-	1
M Strydom c Hayward b Kruger	24	41	24	5	-	(8) c Murray b Kruger	11	34	40	1	-
†EG Poole c Murray b Kruger	21	99	87	-	1	(9) b S Abrahams	27	50	45	4	1
AC Thomas c Murray b Hayward	14	66	61	-	-	(10) not out	41	109	94	4	-
JN Dreyer not out	12	43	30	1	-	(11) c Benfield b Peterson	40	94	96	3	2
F van der Merwe b S Abrahams	6	37	41	-	-	(6) run out (Benfield/Murray)	10	96	81	1	-
Extras (b 5, lb 7, w 7, nb 21)	40					Extras (b 2, lb 4, w 2, nb 11)	19				
TOTAL (130.1 overs)	**341**					**TOTAL (104 overs)**	**227**				

EASTERN PROVINCE

	Runs	Mins	Balls	4	6		Runs	Mins	Balls	4	6
MR Benfield c Dreyer b van der Merwe	19	45	27	3	-	not out	66	121	98	10	-
U Abrahams b Thomas	26	75	63	4	-	c Poole b Thomas	30	74	60	5	-
JDC Bryant lbw b van der Merwe	70	184	160	8	3	not out	19	46	41	3	-
*DJ Callaghan b van der Merwe	38	75	92	3	1						
JM Kemp b Thomas	188	331	259	16	9						
MW Creed c Poole b van der Merwe	33	103	79	5	-						
RJ Peterson c Jacobs b van der Merwe	4	11	11	1	-						
S Abrahams lbw b Jacobs	5	20	10	1	-						
†DW Murray lbw b Light	32	77	87	4	-						
GJ-P Kruger lbw b Lavine	4	18	10	1	-						
M Hayward not out	6	23	9	-	-						
Extras (lb 7, nb 16)	23					Extras (lb 2, w 2, nb 4)	8				
TOTAL (131.4 overs)	**448**					**TOTAL (for 1 wkt) (32.3 overs)**	**123**				

Bowling	*O*	*M*	*R*	*W*		*O*	*M*	*R*	*W*
EASTERN PROVINCE									
Kemp	28	6	60	0	(5)	12	3	30	0
Hayward	18	1	52	1		7	1	28	0
Kruger	30	9	87	2	(1)	28	6	70	4
Creed	8	2	24	0					
Peterson	24	6	69	1	(4)	30	8	74	3
S Abrahams	22.1	9	37	5	(3)	27	15	19	2
NORTH WEST									
Lavine	7	0	41	1		6	0	34	0
Dreyer	22	1	95	0	(4)	6	0	24	0
van der Merwe	33	12	62	5	(2)	9	1	30	0
Thomas	20.4	5	70	2	(3)	5	0	17	1
Strydom	6	0	74	0					
Light	30	10	57	1	(5)	4	1	7	0
Niewoudt	4	0	12	0					
Jacobs	9	2	30	1					
de Vos					(6)	1.3	0	8	0
Lawson					(7)	1	0	1	0

Fall of Wickets	NW	EP	NW	EP
	1st	1st	2nd	2nd
1st	71 (2)	38 (1)	2 (1)	81 (2)
2nd	157 (1)	59 (2)	35 (2)	-
3rd	181 (4)	140 (4)	61 (3)	-
4th	197 (5)	204 (3)	74 (5)	-
5th	226 (6)	271 (6)	83 (4)	-
6th	262 (7)	277 (7)	91 (7)	-
7th	288 (3)	293 (8)	103 (8)	-
8th	319 (8)	349 (9)	126 (6)	-
9th	321 (9)	378 (10)	141 (9)	-
10th	341 (11)	448 (5)	227 (11)	-

Boland v Eastern Province, Paarl, 1-4 March 2001. Match drawn.

EASTERN PROVINCE v NORTHERNS — SuperSport Series Super Eight

Played at St George's Park, Port Elizabeth on 8,9,10 March 2001 — Toss: Northerns
Umpires: BG Jerling & SB Lambson
Debuts: EP: None. Nor: None
Close of Play: Day 1: Nor (1) 308-3 (Steyn 46*, de Vos 40*, 104 overs). Day 2: Nor (2) 26-1 (Rudolph 15*, van Jaarsveld 8*, 11 overs).
Result: Northerns won by 368 runs
Man of Match: Pierre Joubert
Points: EP: 1 (bat 0, bowl 1, match 0). Nor: 17 (bat 3, bowl 4, match 10)

EP reached their low point of their season as they were humbled inside three days by the Titans. A superb batting performance by the visitors saw them post an imposing total and then the trio of Greg Smith, Pierre Joubert and Rudi Bryson did the major damage as the Jumbos crumbled twice.

Despite enjoying a massive first innings lead of 343, Northerns captain Martin van Jaarsveld decided not to enforce the follow-on and was rewarded with another EP batting collapse. Only opener and skipper Carl Bradfield, who carried his bat in the second innings, could hold his head high.

NORTHERNS

FIRST INNINGS	*Runs*	*Mins*	*Balls*	*4*	*6*	*SECOND INNINGS*	*Runs*	*Mins*	*Balls*	*4*	*6*
JG Myburgh c Murray b Peterson	68	224	155	9	-	c and b Pringle	2	10	9	-	-
JA Rudolph b Kruger	36	101	82	5	-	c Bryant b Kruger	35	85	57	6	-
*M van Jaarsveld b Peterson	94	175	145	13	1	c Callaghan b Hayward	10	59	36	1	-
PJR Steyn c Murray b Hayward	59	200	160	5	-	c Murray b Pringle	35	35	31	6	-
DJJ de Vos c Murray b Pringle	48	161	133	5	1	not out	60	107	83	2	2
FC Brooker lbw b Pringle	31	111	77	4	1	lbw b Pringle	2	6	5	-	-
†CFK van Wyk c Murray b Hayward	3	7	6	-	-	c Bryant b Pringle	0	2	2	-	-
P Joubert not out	72	169	167	7	1	not out	24	81	66	2	-
DH Townsend lbw b Hayward	7	30	30	-	-						
GJ Smith lbw b S Abrahams	2	18	14	-	-						
RE Bryson not out	11	27	16	-	1						
Extras (b 2, lb 4, w 1, nb 13)	20					Extras (nb 6)	6				
TOTAL (for 9 wkts dec) (162 overs)	**451**					**TOTAL (for 6 wkts dec) (47 overs)**	**174**				

EASTERN PROVINCE												
*CC Bradfield c Brooker b Smith	0	1	1	-	-	not out	64	224	151	8	-
U Abrahams b Joubert	10	64	38	2	-	c Joubert b Bryson	0	7	4	-	-
JDC Bryant b Smith	0	10	9	-	-	c Steyn b Bryson	8	23	24	1	-
DJ Callaghan lbw b Smith	0	9	10	-	-	c van Jaarsveld b Bryson	2	3	5	-	-
MR Benfield lbw b Smith	16	27	21	1	-	c de Vos b Townsend	15	52	36	1	-
RJ Peterson c Smith b Joubert	28	72	37	4	-	c van Wyk b Bryson	18	25	19	3	-
S Abrahams c van Wyk b Joubert	12	35	28	1	-	c van Wyk b Joubert	11	33	20	2	-
†DW Murray b Joubert	1	12	9	-	-	c van Wyk b Smith	0	1	1	-	-
MW Pringle c and b Joubert	0	2	1	-	-	c Steyn b Rudolph	21	62	43	2	-
M Hayward b Smith	22	31	16	5	-	b Bryson	6	5	4	1	-
GJ-P Kruger not out	13	22	17	1	1	b Rudolph	1	5	5	-	-
Extras (b 1, lb 2, nb 3)	6					Extras (lb 1, nb 2)	3				
TOTAL (30.4 overs)	**108**					**TOTAL (51.4 overs)**	**149**				

Bowling	*O*	*M*	*R*	*W*		*O*	*M*	*R*	*W*
EASTERN PROVINCE									
Pringle	35	8	68	2		14	4	32	4
Kruger	24	6	77	1		11	1	42	1
Hayward	41	3	128	3		5	0	35	1
Callaghan	8	0	30	0	(6)	1	0	1	0
Peterson	25	5	82	2	(4)	11	1	41	0
S Abrahams	29	6	60	1	(5)	5	0	23	0
NORTHERNS									
Smith	10.4	5	25	5		15	3	46	1
Bryson	7	1	30	0		12	1	33	5
Joubert	8	4	10	5	(4)	11	2	22	1
Townsend	3	0	24	0	(3)	9	2	29	1
de Vos	2	0	16	0		1	0	5	0
Rudolph						3.4	1	13	2

Fall of Wickets	Nor	EP	Nor	EP
	1st	1st	2nd	2nd
1st	54 (2)	0 (1)	4 (1)	0 (2)
2nd	166 (1)	0 (3)	43 (3)	11 (3)
3rd	225 (3)	2 (4)	69 (2)	13 (4)
4th	316 (4)	29 (5)	90 (4)	49 (5)
5th	321 (5)	33 (2)	92 (6)	69 (6)
6th	324 (7)	63 (7)	92 (7)	96 (7)
7th	391 (6)	67 (8)	-	99 (8)
8th	405 (9)	67 (9)	-	140 (9)
9th	412 (10)	72 (6)	-	148 (10)
10th	-	108 (10)	-	149 (11)

Free State v Eastern Province, Bloemfontein, 15-17 March 2001. Free State won by 4 wickets.

FREE STATE CRICKET UNION

PO Box 4357, Bloemfontein 9300. Tel (051) 447 5715.
Ticket office: (051) 430 6365. Fax (051) 447 2208.
E-mail: info@fscu.co.za

President: Charlie Robinson
Vice-President: Tim Khumalo
General Manager: Seppie Lusardi
Stadium Manager: Bob van Zyl
Financial Supervisor: Helene Pieterse
Youth Cricket Manager: Cobus van Wyk
Development Manager: Aubrey Litsheo
Academy Manager: Philip Radley
Coach: Andy Moles
Goodyear Eagles Squad 2001/02: Herman Bakkes, Jonathan Beukes, Gerard Brophy, Clifford Deacon, Andrew Gait, Rasheed Lewis, Gerhardus Liebenberg, Victor Mpitsang, Johannes Mokoenanyana, Dewald Pretorius, James Schorn, Sipho Sibande, Johan van der Wath, Morne van Wyk, Kosie Venter, Louis Wilkinson. **UCB contracted players:** Nicky Boje, Boeta Dippenaar, Allan Donald. **Fitness trainer:** Adrian le Roux.

REVIEW OF THE SEASON 2000/01

Jan Bosman

SUPERSPORT SERIES: P9 W3 L4 D2 (sixth)
CAPTAIN: GL Brophy (7), N Boje (1), LJ Wilkinson (1)
STANDARD BANK CUP: P10 W6 L4 (seventh)

Let's say it's part of the learning curve. The Free State Eagles played brilliantly at times but inconsistency, perhaps due to inexperience among the young players in the side, ensured that the trophy cabinet remained barren for another season. The Eagles would probably feel that a promising start to the season was squandered.

In the Standard Bank Cup competition, supporters of the Eagles had high hopes that their team would at least reach the semifinals after the Eagles won their first four games at Goodyear Park, beating Boland, Northerns, the Highveld Strikers and Griquas.

Three Free State limited overs records tumbled in the match against Griquas. Andrew Gait's score of 138 not out was the best by an Eagle, Gait and Johan van der Wath put on 156 for the second wicket and the total of 315/2 was the best by the side.

Unfortunately, things fell apart for the Eagles in the latter part of the season. The defeat at the hands of the Dolphins, when chasing a reachable target in their final match at home, was the final nail in the coffin for the Eagles. Free State, needing 152 in 33 overs for victory, were on 116/2 after 22 overs when Jon Bastow struck four times in the 23rd over. Not many people can boast about being on a hat-trick twice in one over. The Eagles eventually fell 13 runs short of the target.

This obviously was a huge setback, but the Eagles really only have themselves to blame. Six victories should have ensured them a place in the semifinals. Ultimately the failure of the Eagles to score a single bonus point - the only team not to do so - dashed their hopes.

In the SuperSport Series the Eagles had a terrible start when they were dismissed for a mere 102 by Boland in the first innings of their first match on their way to a heavy defeat in Paarl. They recovered from that and secured a spot in the Super Eights with two victories, against North West and Griquas, and two draws in their next four matches.

In the Super Eight series, Free State did not play well. They lost heavily to Easterns, in the match where Allan Donald was felled by an Andre Nel bouncer, Border and Western Province, before beating Eastern Province convincingly within three days in the battle for the wooden spoon.

Despite some solid individual performances, lack of consistency frequently had the Eagles in difficulty.

Kosie Venter was probably the player of the season. He performed well with the bat in both forms of cricket. In limited overs games he scored 410 runs (average 41.00) and in the SuperSport Series he scored 494 runs at 38.00. The stocky all-rounder also took 31 wickets at 27.67 in the four-day competition.

In his benefit season, Gerhardus Liebenberg was Free State's most successful batsman in the SuperSport Series. He scored 595 runs at 45.76 with a top score of 202 against Northerns at Centurion. Veteran Louis Wilkinson was also in top form, scoring 642 runs at 42.80. The young batsmen in the side disappointed, with only Wiaan Smit averaging more than 30.

Three batsmen averaged more than 40 in limited overs cricket, Morné van Wyk, Andrew Gait and Venter, with Van Wyk and Gait scoring centuries.

The Eagles' best bowlers by far were the speedsters, Victor Mpitsang and Dewald Pretorius. In the SuperSport Series Mpitsang took 33 wickets (avg 22.21) and Pretorius 37 (avg 23.81). Pretorius also topped the Free State bowling averages in the Standard Bank Cup.

There were efforts to lure Mpitsang and Pretorius to other provinces but Free State managed to retain their services. The promising James Schorn, one of the star batsmen for the SA under 19 side in New Zealand, joined the Eagles in the latter part of the season. He made his first-class debut against Western Province and also played against Eastern Province.

PROVINCIAL RECORDS

Honours:
Castle Cup/SuperSport Series (3): 1992/93, 1993/94, 1997/98
B&H Series (4): 1988/89, 1993/94, 1994/95, 1995/96
Nissan Shield/Total Power Series (2): 1991/92, 1992/93
Currie Cup B Section (2): 1951/52, 1975/76

Highest innings totals:				
For:	552	v Natal (Bloemfontein)		1926/27
Against:	609	by Transvaal (Johannesburg)		1934/35
Lowest innings totals:				
For:	37	v Transvaal (Bloemfontein)		1936/37
Against:	40	by Eastern Province (Durban)		1910/11
Highest individual innings:				
For:	294	AJ Lamb	v Eastern Province (Bloemfontein)	1987/88
Against:	279*	P Holmes	for MCC (Bloemfontein) (FC)	1927/28
	279*	RA Gripper	for Rhodesia (Bloemfontein) (CC)	1967/68

FREE STATE CRICKET UNION

Most runs in a season:

SS and Bowl				All FC			
938	(Avg 72.15)	HH Dippenaar	1998/99	1025	(Avg 68.33)	HH Dippenaar	1998/99

Most runs in a career:

SS and Bowl				All FC			
5203	(Avg 33.14)	LJ Wilkinson	1986-2000	5481	(Avg 32.24)	LJ Wilkinson	1986-2000

Most 100s in a career:

SS and Bowl				All FC			
12		WJ Cronje	1987-99	15		WJ Cronje	1987-99

Best bowling in an innings:

For:	8-32	L Tuckett	v Griqualand West (Kimberley)	1951/52
Against:	10-59	ST Jefferies	for Western Province (Cape Town)	1987/88

Best bowling in a match:

For:	13-66	L Tuckett	v Griqualand West (Kimberley)	1951/52
Against:	14-58	AEE Vogler	for Eastern Province (Johannesburg)	1906/07

Most wickets in a season:

SS and Bowl				All FC			
50	(Avg 13.52)	CJPG van Zyl	1984/85	50	(Avg 13.52)	CJPG van Zyl	1984/85

Most wickets in a career:

SS and Bowl				All FC			
287	(Avg 22.31)	CJPG van Zyl	1981-93	314	(Avg 22.08)	CJPG van Zyl	1981-93

Most dismissals (wicketkeepers) in an innings:

7	(ct 6,st 1)	RJ East	v Western Province B (Cape Town)	1984/85
7	(ct 7,st 0)	PJL Radley	v Western Province (Cape Town)	1990/91

Most dismissals (wicketkeepers) in a match:

10	(ct 10,st 0)	MN van Wyk	v Border (Bloemfontein)	2000/01

Most dismissals (wicketkeepers) in a season:

SS and Bowl				All FC			
31	(ct 30,st 1)	PJL Radley	1990/91	31	(ct 30,st 1)	PJL Radley	1990/91
31	(ct 28,st 3)	GL Brophy	1999/00	31	(ct 28,st 3)	GL Brophy	1999/00

Most dismissals (wicketkeepers) in a career:

SS and Bowl				All FC			
287	(ct 279,st 8)	RJ East	1973-88	294	(ct 286,st 8)	RJ East	1973-88
	(includes 12 ct as fielder)				(includes 12 ct as fielder)		

Most catches (fielders) in an innings:

4 KG Hill , JPG Glover, RC le Sueur, IEF Kirby, LJ Wilkinson, N Boje, AI Gait, GFJ Liebenberg

Most catches (fielders) in a match:

5 JPG Glover, KJ Funston, IEF Kirby, N Boje, GFJ Liebenberg

Most catches (fielders) in a season:

SS and Bowl			All FC		
19	GFJ Liebenberg	1999/00	19	GFJ Liebenberg	1999/00

Most catches (fielders) in a career:

SS and Bowl			All FC		
96	LJ Wilkinson	1986-2000	100	LJ Wilkinson	1986-2000

Most appearances:

SS and Bowl			All FC		
94	LJ Wilkinson	1986-2000	102	LJ Wilkinson	1986-2000

Most captaincies:

SS and Bowl			All FC		
32	RJ East	1976-83	37	WJ Cronje	1989-99

RECORD WICKET PARTNERSHIPS

1st	236*	SK Coen and JMM Commaille v Eastern Province (Port Elizabeth)	1926/27
		(They knocked off the runs required for victory in an unbroken stand)	
2nd	305	SK Coen and JMM Commaille v Natal (Bloemfontein)	1926/27
3rd	300*	HH Dippenaar and LJ Wilkinson v Western Province (Bloemfontein)	1996/97
4th	265	N Rosendorff and S Strydom v Transvaal B (Vereeniging)	1965/66
5th	355	AJ Lamb and JJ Strydom v Eastern Province (Bloemfontein)	1987/88
		(The South African domestic record for this wicket)	
6th	172	RJ East and N Rosendorff v Eastern Province B (Port Elizabeth)	1977/78
7th	161	SL Hanson and PR Carlstein v Natal (Bloemfontein)	1954/55

8th	191	MN van Wyk and HC Bakkes v Boland (Bloemfontein)	1997/98
9th	135*	WJ Cronje and JJ van der Wath v West Indians (Bloemfontein) (FC)	1998/99
	125	FD Stephenson and HC Bakkes v Eastern Province (Port Elizabeth) (CC)	1995/96
10th	129	LR Tuckett and F Caulfield v Western Province (Bloemfontein)	1925/26

(Second innings. In the first innings, Tuckett and LG Fuller made 115 for the 10th wicket, the only occasion that 100 has been made for this wicket twice in the same match anywhere in the world)

PERFORMANCES AGAINST OTHER TEAMS

HIGHEST AND LOWEST TOTALS

Opponents	Highest Total For		Lowest Total For	
Boland	471	1997/98	102	2000/01
Border	537-5*	1969/70	64	1960/61
Eastern Province	517-8*	1987/88	51	1906/07
	517-9*	1995/96		
Easterns	229	2000/01	195	2000/01
Gauteng	525-7*	2000/01	37	1936/37
Griqualand West	511-8*	1958/59	84	1951/52
KwaZulu-Natal	552	1926/27	57	1937/38
Northerns	447	1955/56	46	1937/38
North West	302	2000/01	244	1999/00
Western Province	483-2	1996/97	85	1912/13
			85	1934/35

BEST INDIVIDUAL PERFORMANCES

Opponents	Highest score		Best bowling (innings)		Best bowling (match, 8+)	
Boland	226*	LJ Wilkinson,1995/96	6-50	CJPG van Zyl,1983/84	10-205	JF Venter, 1996/97
Border	200*	DI de Villiers,1923/24	7-30	LE de Villiers,1931/32	12-85	LE de Villiers,1931/32
Eastern Province	294	AJ Lamb,1987/88	8-71	(FC) TW Fraser 1939/40	11-75	LE de Villiers,1929/30
			7-11	(CC) SF Burke 1958/59		
Easterns	73	GFJ Liebenberg, 2000/01	3-38	PV Mpitsang., 2000/01	-	
Gauteng	200*	KG Viljoen,1933/34	8-37	AA Donald,1986/87	9-50	CF Craven, 1997/98
Griqualand West	180	C Richardson,1958/59	8-32	L Tuckett,1951/52	13-66	L Tuckett,1951/52
KwaZulu-Natal	229	GFJ Liebenberg,1995/96	8-107	EA Budgen,1921/22	12-170	EA Budgen,1921/22
Northerns	202	GFJ Liebenberg, 2000/01	8-64	L Tuckett,1946/47	13-105	L Tuckett,1946/47
North West	76*	N Boje, 1999/00	5-24	PV Mpitsang, 2000/01	9-57	PV Mpitsang, 2000/01
Western Province	178	PJR Steyn, 1988/89	7-65	LE de Villiers,1929/30	11-210	JR Liddle, 1954/55

FREE STATE SUPERSPORT AVERAGES 2000/01

Batting & Fielding

Name	M	Inns	NO	Runs	HS	Avg	100	50	Ct	St
N Boje	1	2	0	182	105	91.00	1	1	0	0
GFJ Liebenberg	8	13	0	595	202	45.76	1	4	10	0
LJ Wilkinson	9	15	0	642	169	42.80	1	3	9	0
JF Venter	9	15	2	494	112*	38.00	1	3	4	0
WJ Smit	5	7	0	247	94	35.28	0	2	2	0
AI Gait	8	13	0	374	112	28.76	1	2	7	0
MR Lewis	8	11	4	176	49*	25.14	0	0	9	0
GL Brophy	8	12	2	241	40	24.10	0	0	27	2
HC Bakkes	7	9	1	154	54*	19.25	0	1	4	0
MN van Wyk	7	11	0	179	49	16.27	0	0	15	0
JA Beukes	3	6	0	86	64	14.33	0	1	4	0
HH Dippenaar	1	2	0	28	28	14.00	0	0	0	0
JJ van der Wath	4	8	1	92	49	13.14	0	0	7	0
AA Donald	1	2	1	13	13*	13.00	0	0	1	0
D Pretorius	8	11	4	50	14*	7.14	0	0	4	0
JR Schorn	2	4	0	28	11	7.00	0	0	2	0
PV Mpitsang	9	11	2	56	23	6.22	0	0	1	0
TJ Mokoenanyana	1	2	2	0	0*	-	0	0	1	0
Totals	99	154	19	3637	202		5	17	107	2
			Extras	263				subs	0	
			Total	3900		28.88			107	

Bowling

Name	Overs	Mdns	Runs	Wkts	Avg	BB	5I	10M
N Boje	63.1	24	114	7	16.28	5-67	1	0
MN van Wyk	13	4	36	2	18.00	2-25	0	0
PV Mpitsang	268.1	62	733	33	22.21	5-24	3	0
D Pretorius	276.3	57	881	37	23.81	4-51	0	0
AA Donald	29.1	9	77	3	25.66	3-46	0	0
JJ van der Wath	127.3	21	411	15	27.40	5-59	1	0
JF Venter	289.2	66	858	31	27.67	6-90	2	0
HC Bakkes	221.3	67	625	20	31.25	6-108	1	0
MR Lewis	101	23	341	8	42.62	2-44	0	0
JA Beukes	1	1	0	0	-	-	0	0
GFJ Liebenberg	2	1	5	0	-	-	0	0
TJ Mokoenanyana	7	1	24	0	-	-	0	0
Totals	1399.2	336	4105	156		6-90	8	0
		b & lb	148	3	run outs			
		Total	4253	159	26.74			

MATCH REPORTS AND SCORECARDS

Boland v Free State, Paarl, 27-29 October 2000. Boland won by 10 wickets.

FREE STATE v GAUTENG — SuperSport Series Pool A

Played at Goodyear Park, Bloemfontein on 3,4,5,6 November 2000 — Toss: Gauteng
Umpires: JD Cloete & SB Lambson
Debuts: FS: MR Lewis (FC for FS). Gau: None
Close of Play: Day 1: Gau (1) 229-1 (Koenig 109*, Seymore 50*, 73 overs). Day 2: FS (1) 177-2 (Wilkinson 44*, Smit 28*, 72 overs). Day 3: Gau (2) 23-0 (Koenig 11*, Bacher 7*, 7.3 overs).
Result: Match drawn
Man of Match: Herman Bakkes
Points: FS: 6 (bat 4, bowl 2, match 0). Gau: 4 (bat 3, bowl 1, match 0)

On the sort of strip batsmen would like to take home with them a draw was almost inevitable. Only 22 wickets were lost - one being Louis Wilkinson who was run out on 99 - before rain ended the torment of the bowlers at tea on the fourth day.

After reaching 229/1 in 73 overs on day 1, the Strikers were dismissed for 368, mainly due to fine bowling by Herman Bakkes. The Eagles scored at the healthy rate of almost 3.5 runs an over but when captain Gerard Brophy declared with a lead of 157 shortly before the close of play on day three it was clear that victory for either side was unlikely.

GAUTENG

FIRST INNINGS	*Runs*	*Mins*	*Balls*	*4*	*6*	*SECOND INNINGS*	*Runs*	*Mins*	*Balls*	*4*	*6*
AM Bacher lbw b Lewis	58	231	183	7	-	(2) b Pretorius	38	124	91	5	-
SG Koenig c Brophy b Bakkes	116	345	234	14	-	(1) b Pretorius	36	134	93	3	-
AJ Seymore lbw b Venter	50	70	60	7	-	c and b Venter	29	76	54	4	-
Z de Bruyn c Brophy b Bakkes	35	75	65	8	-	not out	59	176	154	10	-
G Toyana c Wilkinson b Bakkes	10	51	36	1	-	lbw b Pretorius	11	42	38	2	-
†N Pothas c van Wyk b Pretorius	10	96	59	-	-	(7) not out	19	61	51	1	1
OD Gibson b Bakkes	2	8	6	-	-	(6) b Venter	0	2	2	-	-
*CE Eksteen b Bakkes	8	21	13	-	-						
MF George c Lewis b Venter	29	53	37	4	1						
DJ Terbrugge not out	12	42	44	2	-						
WB Masimula c van Wyk b Bakkes	22	37	27	2	1						
Extras (lb 4, w 1, nb 11)	16					Extras (b 5, lb 4, nb 3)	12				
TOTAL (125.3 overs)	**368**					**TOTAL (for 5 wkts) (80 overs)**	**204**				

	FREE STATE				
GFJ Liebenberg c Seymore b Terbrugge	67	134	101	9	-
AI Gait lbw b Eksteen	29	100	78	4	-
LJ Wilkinson run out (Masimula)	99	254	187	9	2
WJ Smit c Pothas b Gibson	88	237	163	11	-
MN van Wyk lbw b Masimula	49	136	96	7	-
JF Venter not out	112	275	178	9	1
*†GL Brophy c Seymore b Eksteen	23	73	51	2	-
HC Bakkes lbw b de Bruyn	19	42	36	-	-
MR Lewis not out	21	36	30	1	1
PV Mpitsang					
D Pretorius					
Extras (b 2, lb 7, w 1, nb 8)	18				
TOTAL (for 7 wkts dec) (152 overs)	**525**				

Bowling	*O*	*M*	*R*	*W*		*O*	*M*	*R*	*W*
FREE STATE									
Pretorius	30	10	90	1	(4)	12	3	23	3
Bakkes	31.3	7	108	6		13	4	29	0
Mpitsang	29	8	69	0	(1)	18	5	36	0
Lewis	12	2	29	1	(3)	6	1	30	0
Venter	22	6	63	2		26	10	66	2
Liebenberg	1	0	5	0					
van Wyk					(6)	5	2	11	0
GAUTENG									
Terbrugge	24	6	67	1					
Gibson	30	3	106	1					
de Bruyn	20	4	75	1					
George	16	1	84	0					
Eksteen	44	12	123	2					
Masimula	16	4	54	1					
Bacher	2	0	7	0					

Fall of Wickets	Gau	FS	Gau
	1st	1st	2nd
1st	153 (1)	88 (2)	81 (2)
2nd	229 (3)	106 (1)	86 (1)
3rd	260 (2)	290 (3)	122 (3)
4th	277 (4)	299 (4)	152 (5)
5th	286 (5)	385 (5)	153 (6)
6th	290 (7)	433 (7)	-
7th	300 (8)	481 (8)	-
8th	327 (6)	-	-
9th	334 (9)	-	-
10th	368 (11)	-	-

Griqualand West v Free State, Kimberley, 10-13 November 2000. Free State won by 54 runs.
Northerns v Free State, Centurion, 17-20 November 2000. Match drawn.

FREE STATE v NORTH WEST — SuperSport Series Pool A

Played at Goodyear Park, Bloemfontein on 1,2,3 December 2000 — Toss: North West
Umpires: IL Howell & AE Williams
Debuts: FS: None. NW: None
Close of Play: Day 1: NW (1) 1-0 (Lawson 1*, de Vos 0*, 1.4 overs). Day 2: NW (1) 126 all out.
Result: Free State won by an innings and 53 runs
Man of Match: Victor Mpitsang
Points: FS: 18 (bat 4, bowl 4, match 10). NW: 4 (bat 0, bowl 4, match 0)

Free State scored a comfortable innings victory when the Dragons' batting crumbled twice against the Eagles' pace attack. Victor Mpitsang was especially devastating. Garth Roe bowled superbly for North West after Free State were asked to bat first but he had little support from his fellow bowlers. North West were in trouble from the time Andrew Lawson was dismissed off the first ball of the second day, with two more wickets falling almost immediately.

	FREE STATE				
FIRST INNINGS	*Runs*	*Mins*	*Balls*	*4*	*6*
GFJ Liebenberg c Jacobs b Roe	60	216	172	7	-
AI Gait b Roe	2	43	16	-	-
LJ Wilkinson c Thomas b Dreyer	32	110	74	5	-
WJ Smit c Poole b Dreyer	0	14	12	-	-
MN van Wyk c Hewitt b Strydom	38	103	64	6	1
JF Venter c Hewitt b Roe	57	149	111	10	-
*†GL Brophy lbw b Roe	33	80	64	6	-
HC Bakkes c Lavine b Roe	34	48	41	5	-
MR Lewis lbw b Roe	0	1	4	-	-
PV Mpitsang c Jacobs b Roe	8	44	18	1	-
D Pretorius not out	3	9	6	-	-
Extras (b 6, lb 5, w 6, nb 18)	35				
TOTAL (94.1 overs)	**302**				

NORTH WEST											
AG Lawson c Liebenberg b Bakkes	1	6	9	-	-	lbw b Mpitsang	0	12	12	-	-
HM de Vos c Brophy b Mpitsang	2	44	30	-	-	absent hurt					
M Strydom b Bakkes	5	21	16	1	-	(2) c Brophy b Mpitsang	0	29	16	-	-
*GM Hewitt c Brophy b Pretorius	21	75	42	3	-	(3) c Lewis b Pretorius	26	76	40	3	1
A Jacobs c Liebenberg b Pretorius	33	102	75	4	-	(4) c Liebenberg b Lewis	16	37	26	3	-
C Light c Liebenberg b Lewis	0	3	1	-	-	(5) lbw b Mpitsang	22	92	50	2	-
MJ Lavine b Pretorius	31	61	41	3	-	(6) b Pretorius	28	30	21	5	-
†EG Poole c Liebenberg b Mpitsang	13	81	54	1	-	(7) c Gait b Bakkes	2	12	12	-	-
AC Thomas c Lewis b Mpitsang	9	33	24	2	-	(8) c Gait b Mpitsang	11	34	27	2	-
GA Roe not out	2	27	16	-	-	(9) not out	3	20	14	-	-
JN Dreyer c Pretorius b Mpitsang	0	4	4	-	-	(10) c Brophy b Mpitsang	1	9	6	-	-
Extras (lb 6, w 2, nb 1)	9					Extras (b 4, lb 3, w 3, nb 4)	14				
TOTAL (51.5 overs)	**126**					**TOTAL (36.4 overs)**	**123**				

Bowling	*O*	*M*	*R*	*W*	*O*	*M*	*R*	*W*
NORTH WEST								
Lavine	24	4	92	0				
Roe	20.1	5	47	7				
Dreyer	21	5	73	2				
Thomas	21	5	51	0				
Strydom	3	0	13	1				
Light	5	1	15	0				
FREE STATE								
Mpitsang	16.5	5	33	4	12.4	4	24	5
Bakkes	12	5	32	2	11	6	29	1
Lewis	9	5	11	1	7	1	40	1
Pretorius	14	2	44	3	6	2	23	2

Fall of Wickets	**FS**	**NW**	**NW**
	1st	1st	2nd
1st	28 (2)	1 (1)	0 (1)
2nd	96 (3)	8 (3)	3 (2)
3rd	103 (4)	10 (2)	34 (4)
4th	127 (1)	55 (4)	58 (3)
5th	183 (5)	58 (6)	93 (6)
6th	251 (7)	85 (5)	99 (7)
7th	254 (6)	106 (7)	113 (5)
8th	254 (9)	117 (9)	120 (8)
9th	293 (8)	126 (8)	123 (10)
10th	302 (10)	126 (11)	-

Easterns v Free State, Benoni, 1-4 February 2001. Easterns won by 109 runs.

FREE STATE v BORDER — SuperSport Series Super Eight

Played at Goodyear Park, Bloemfontein on 1,2,3,4 March 2001 — Toss: Free State

Umpires: AG O'Connor & S Wadvalla

Debuts: FS: None. Bdr: None

Close of Play: Day 1: FS (1) 2-0 (Liebenberg 1*, Gait 1*, 1 over). Day 2: Bdr (2) 80-2 (Makalima 0*, Pope 0*, 21 overs). Day 3: FS (2) 89-2 (Beukes 46*, Wilkinson 35*, 30.2 overs).

Result: Border won by 162 runs

Man of Match: Pieter Strydom

Points: FS: 6 (bat 2, bowl 4, match 0). Bdr: 18 (bat 4, bowl 4, match 10)

The faint hopes Free State had of reaching the final were effectively dashed when they were completely outplayed by the Bears. After winning the toss, the Eagles would have hoped to dismiss Border for less than the 308 runs they scored.

Shortly after lunch on day two the Eagles suffered a blow from which they never recovered. After losing their second wicket on 109, they lost four more wickets while only 13 runs were scored. Andrew Gait did his utmost but he received little support from the middle and lower order.

BORDER											
FIRST INNINGS	*Runs*	*Mins*	*Balls*	*4*	*6*	*SECOND INNINGS*	*Runs*	*Mins*	*Balls*	*4*	*6*
CB Sugden c van Wyk b van der Wath	22	89	80	2	-	(2) c van Wyk b Lewis	50	82	69	8	-
PJ Botha c van Wyk b Mpitsang	42	183	119	4	-	(1) b van der Wath	21	66	42	3	-
SC Pope c van Wyk b Pretorius	14	43	39	2	-	(4) c van Wyk b Bakkes	2	29	20	-	-
W Wiblin c Gait b Pretorius	11	32	22	-	-	(5) c van Wyk b Pretorius	88	249	172	8	1
*PC Strydom b Lewis	42	114	60	5	-	(6) c Bakkes b Venter	50	108	81	10	-
LL Gamiet lbw b van der Wath	3	36	24	-	-	(7) c Beukes b Venter	7	10	10	-	1
†I Mitchell c van Wyk b Bakkes	58	129	104	11	1	(8) c Gait b Venter	30	45	40	6	-
DL Makalima c Beukes b Bakkes	18	55	45	2	-	(3) c van Wyk b Bakkes	0	33	20	-	-
VC Drakes c van Wyk b Pretorius	30	47	38	4	-	c van Wyk b van der Wath	5	23	18	1	-
GT Love not out	22	57	32	2	-	not out	13	61	43	1	-
T Henderson c van der Wath b Pretorius	20	23	18	3	1	c Beukes b Pretorius	4	10	11	-	-
Extras (b 3, lb 9, nb 14)	26					Extras (b 8, lb 14, nb 6)	28				
TOTAL (94.3 overs)	**308**					**TOTAL (86.4 overs)**	**298**				

FREE STATE										
GFJ Liebenberg b Botha	14	49	26	2	-	(7) lbw b Henderson	34	127	94	4	-
AI Gait c Sugden b Strydom	112	295	229	15	1	c Wiblin b Botha	0	7	4	-	-
*LJ Wilkinson lbw b Botha	43	97	69	6	1	(4) c Wiblin b Henderson	56	114	94	7	1
JA Beukes lbw b Botha	0	3	3	-	-	(3) lbw b Love	64	188	146	6	-
JF Venter c Wiblin b Drakes	0	13	4	-	-	(1) b Love	7	57	43	1	-
†MN van Wyk c Makalima b Love	2	28	27	-	-	(5) c Mitchell b Henderson	7	24	12	1	-
JJ van der Wath c Mitchell b Love	0	10	5	-	-	(6) c Strydom b Henderson	1	24	18	-	-
HC Bakkes run out (Love)	3	38	34	-	-	b Henderson	18	66	60	1	-
MR Lewis c Drakes b Strydom	26	70	52	2	-	not out	16	55	40	2	-
PV Mpitsang not out	8	30	16	1	-	b Henderson	0	1	1	-	-
D Pretorius b Strydom	1	8	10	-	-	b Drakes	1	14	9	-	-
Extras (b 3, lb 6, nb 7)	16					Extras (b 4, nb 6, pen 5)	15				
TOTAL (78 overs)	**225**					**TOTAL (85.5 overs)**	**219**				

Bowling	*O*	*M*	*R*	*W*		*O*	*M*	*R*	*W*
FREE STATE									
Mpitsang	25	6	59	1	(2)	10	3	26	0
Bakkes	16	2	61	2	(1)	17	3	46	2
van der Wath	21	3	72	2	(4)	20	4	51	2
Pretorius	20.3	3	66	4	(3)	17.4	1	71	2
Venter	4	0	16	0	(6)	16	1	60	3
Lewis	8	3	22	1	(5)	6	1	22	1
BORDER									
Strydom	7	0	37	3	(5)	4	1	9	0
Henderson	16	4	54	0	(4)	20	6	56	6
Drakes	19	6	38	1	(1)	22.5	7	44	1
Botha	16	7	35	3	(2)	12	4	30	1
Pope	2	0	10	0					
Love	18	6	42	2	(3)	27	5	71	2

Fall of Wickets	Bdr 1st	FS 1st	Bdr 2nd	FS 2nd
1st	59 (1)	29 (1)	74 (1)	0 (2)
2nd	85 (3)	109 (3)	80 (2)	34 (1)
3rd	103 (4)	109 (4)	81 (3)	120 (4)
4th	110 (2)	111 (5)	87 (4)	138 (5)
5th	136 (6)	122 (6)	175 (6)	138 (3)
6th	196 (5)	122 (7)	187 (7)	146 (6)
7th	234 (8)	146 (8)	235 (8)	187 (8)
8th	239 (7)	202 (2)	248 (9)	218 (7)
9th	275 (9)	222 (9)	294 (5)	218 (10)
10th	308 (11)	225 (11)	298 (11)	219 (11)

Western Province v Free State, Cape Town, 8-11 March 2001. Western Province won by 127 runs.

FREE STATE v EASTERN PROVINCE — SuperSport Series Super Eight

Played at Goodyear Park, Bloemfontein on 15,16,17 March 2001 — Toss: Free State
Umpires: IL Howell & KH Hurter
Debuts: FS: None. EP: None
Close of Play: Day 1: FS (1) 47-2 (Venter 19*, Beukes 4*, 20 overs). Day 2: EP (2) 129-5 (Creed 25*, Botha 27*, 43 overs).
Result: Free State won by 4 wickets
Man of Match: Dave Callaghan
Points: FS: 14 (bat 0, bowl 4, match 10). EP: 5 (bat 1, bowl 4, match 0)

On a bowler-friendly pitch, both teams were bowled out cheaply in the first innings, with the visitors taking a useful lead thanks to the best innings performance of his career by the medium-paced Callaghan. A target of 258 to win seemed a tall order for Free State but they were given an ideal start by Venter and Gait, who batted aggressively to take their side to within 96 runs of victory. Callaghan dismissed both openers, however, and went on to the first ten-wicket haul of a long career before the Eagles won.

EASTERN PROVINCE											
FIRST INNINGS	*Runs*	*Mins*	*Balls*	*4*	*6*	*SECOND INNINGS*	*Runs*	*Mins*	*Balls*	*4*	*6*
*CC Bradfield c van der Wath b Bakkes	35	122	91	4	-	c Brophy b van der Wath	38	90	65	6	-
U Abrahams lbw b Mpitsang	13	78	50	2	-	c Brophy b Bakkes	7	24	20	1	-
JDC Bryant c van der Wath b Mpitsang	0	10	8	-	-	b Bakkes	1	8	7	-	-
DJ Callaghan c Brophy b Mpitsang	0	1	1	-	-	c Brophy b van der Wath	18	61	37	2	-
MR Benfield c Wilkinson b Lewis	19	49	43	1	-	c Gait b van der Wath	3	14	8	-	-
MW Creed c Beukes b Bakkes	32	145	93	3	-	lbw b Mpitsang	28	137	95	3	-
J Botha c Brophy b van der Wath	15	36	27	1	-	lbw b van der Wath	43	149	92	6	-
S Abrahams c Brophy b Mpitsang	17	65	45	3	-	c Venter b Mpitsang	10	17	8	2	-
†DW Murray b Bakkes	0	7	5	-	-	c van der Wath b Bakkes	8	33	21	1	-
MW Pringle b Mpitsang	25	37	29	3	1	not out	18	35	18	2	-
M Hayward not out	8	20	5	1	-	c Brophy b van der Wath	1	8	4	-	-
Extras (lb 4, w 2, nb 10)	16					Extras (lb 2, nb 10)	12				
TOTAL (64.3 overs)	**180**					**TOTAL (60.5 overs)**	**187**				

FREE STATE CRICKET UNION

FREE STATE												
JF Venter run out (Creed)	28	313	208	2	-	lbw b Callaghan	79	148	99	14	-
AI Gait c Murray b Pringle	12	65	49	2	-	b Callaghan	74	138	96	10	3
MN van Wyk b Callaghan	1	21	16	-	-	c Bradfield b Callaghan	32	53	33	5	-
JA Beukes c Creed b Callaghan	5	18	9	1	-	lbw b Callaghan	2	2	3	-	-
LJ Wilkinson lbw b Callaghan	7	34	23	1	-	lbw b Pringle	26	78	53	3	-
JR Schorn lbw b Botha	10	70	45	1	-	lbw b Callaghan	0	3	4	-	-
JJ van der Wath c Bradfield b Callaghan	1	27	21	-	-	not out	17	67	23	3	-
*†GL Brophy c Murray b Pringle	3	4	5	-	-	not out	10	33	41	1	-
HC Bakkes b Callaghan	1	13	10	-	-						
MR Lewis lbw b Pringle	17	46	39	2	-						
PV Mpitsang not out	2	8	1	-	-						
Extras (b 5, lb 7, w 5, nb 6)	23					Extras (lb 2, w 2, nb 14)	18				
TOTAL (70 overs)	**110**					**TOTAL (for 6 wkts) (56.1 overs)**	**258**				

Bowling	*O*	*M*	*R*	*W*		*O*	*M*	*R*	*W*
FREE STATE									
Bakkes	19	9	31	3		20	8	45	3
Mpitsang	20.3	5	70	5		16	2	63	2
van der Wath	15	3	53	1		20.5	4	59	5
Lewis	8	3	11	1		4	1	18	0
Venter	2	0	11	0					
EASTERN PROVINCE									
Pringle	27	15	27	3		21.1	4	70	1
Hayward	16	6	22	0	(4)	6	0	49	0
Creed	3	1	14	0	(6)	1	0	12	0
Callaghan	19	9	31	5	(3)	20	4	80	5
Botha	5	4	4	1	(2)	4	2	19	0
S Abrahams					(5)	4	1	26	0

Fall of Wickets	**EP**	**FS**	**EP**	**FS**
	1st	1st	2nd	2nd
1st	48 (2)	30 (2)	14 (2)	162 (2)
2nd	48 (3)	42 (3)	18 (3)	163 (1)
3rd	48 (4)	48 (4)	69 (1)	165 (4)
4th	83 (5)	58 (5)	70 (4)	219 (3)
5th	86 (1)	77 (6)	75 (5)	219 (6)
6th	110 (7)	83 (7)	145 (6)	243 (5)
7th	139 (6)	86 (8)	160 (8)	-
8th	143 (9)	88 (9)	160 (7)	-
9th	156 (8)	108 (10)	184 (9)	-
10th	180 (10)	110 (1)	187 (11)	-

CAPTAIN EKSTEEN . . . toiled manfully during a season where the on field problems matched those in the boardroom. *Picture: Tertius Pickard, TOUCHLINE PHOTO*

GAUTENG CRICKET BOARD

PO Box 55309, Northlands 2116. Tel (011) 340 1500/788 1008. Fax (011) 880 6229. E-mail: general@cricketgauteng.co.za. Website: www.gcb.org.za.

President: Joe Pamensky
Chairman: Dr Mtutuzeli Nyoka
Chief Executive: Thabo Moseki
Cricket Director: Alan Kourie
Financial Manager: Brian Walsh
Stadium Manager: Gary Parker-Nance
2001/02 contracted players: Not available at time of going to print.

REVIEW OF THE SEASON 2000/01

Pieter Oosthuizen

SUPERSPORT SERIES: P5 W1 L1 D3 (sixth in group) (includes one match abandoned without a ball bowled)
SUPERSPORT SHIELD: P4 L1 D3 (third)
CAPTAIN: CE Eksteen (4), AM Bacher (4)
STANDARD BANK CUP: P10 W3 L7 (tenth)

New name, wrong game? This is how their most loyal supporters must have felt after the Highveld Strikers had staggered, like a punch-drunk boxer, from one corner to another in a summer that was to become "The Longest Season".

That may sound a bit melodramatic but it got so bad that it could only get better. The team did not live up to expectations because they could not fill the gap left by their batting bastion of the previous five years, Ken Rutherford, as well as West Indian fast bowler Kenny Benjamin.

Never before in the history of this province had the team gone from hero to zero in such humiliating fashion. The defending SuperSport Series champions did not even make it to the Super Eight phase and they joined KwaZulu Natal and Griqualand West in the Shield competition, where they played without captain Clive Eksteen and finished last.

Talk about adding insult to injury . . . just to get to the end of the season seemed a miracle.

Gauteng seemed in need of a major overhaul. They needed to rebuild by bringing in more youngsters, like middle order batsman Marthinus Otto, whose performances in difficult circumstances showed that there was light up ahead in the tunnel. With Stephen Cook, son of Jimmy Cook, set to join the senior ranks on a more permanent basis, plus a handful of others, surely it could only get better.

Gauteng's problems were reflected not only in the fact that they could only manage four wins in 18 matches. To many cricket lovers it must now seem that Gauteng cannot get through a season without the Wanderers hierarchy floundering. This time around, the infighting saw the resignation of general manager Ziggy Wadvalla after his brother, Shahid, as well as Mandy Yachad, had resigned from their positions on the board. But these losses seemed insignificant when compared to the talent already lost to Gauteng because of administrative sloppiness.

The Gauteng Cricket Board also had to reverse its decision to use three players of colour in a season when the United Cricket Board quota system only required two such players. It was obvious that, given this sort of recipe, the selectors struggled to find the right balance.

In retrospect one can say that the very first four-day match of the season against Griqualand West at the Wanderers was as bad an omen as there could be. Gauteng were hoping that playing at the country's most intimidating ground would be too overwhelming for some of the inexperienced players in the visiting side but it was the home side who showed a lack of application.

In the next home match, against their neighbours, Gauteng were again bowled out for 184 in their first innings. But unlike Griquas, who were perhaps too conservative, or did not expect to get into a winning position so easily, Northerns pressed home the advantage and beat Gauteng by 139 runs. One of the opposing batsman, Neil McKenzie, scored 123 runs in this match. He and Graeme Smith are two of the new generation batsmen that Gauteng should never have lost to other provinces.

It was criminal for Gauteng to get only two and three bonus points respectively in their only two SuperSport Series matches at home. By the end of the first round, they had managed to score only seven batting points and eight with the ball.

Even worse was to come after failing at home. It got so bad that Gauteng's only victory, against North West at Potchefstroom, was overshadowed by all the negatives and bad luck, like the totally washed out game at Paarl, where Gauteng needed a couple of points to stay with the other teams.

And when they eventually lost to Griquas in a low-scoring Shield match at the Wanderers, no-one seemed surprised. It came as a surprise though, when all-rounder Andrew Hall did not pitch up at net practices for this match and was accordingly dropped. He was reported to the United Cricket Board but they confirmed that Hall was struggling with a sore shoulder. By then it seemed obvious that Hall, like so many before him, was set to join Easterns.

In the Standard Bank Cup, the semifinalists of the previous season finished second from the bottom, 17 points adrift. This came as a shock to their supporters, who, responding to the promotional hoorah-hoorah that accompanied the birth of the Strikers, for the first time in many years pushed the crowd numbers past the 9000 mark at the Wanderers.

In the one-day series, opener Sven Koenig started with a great hundred at home against Border to set up victory by six runs, which certainly made things look up. They then lost by 99 runs to a star-studded KwaZulu-Natal, even though Shaun Pollock, Jonty Rhodes and Lance Klusener only managed 36 runs between them.

It was in the next home match where Otto put up his hand with a mature batting performance, which saw him scoring 47 not out to help Gauteng beat Western Province by 21 runs. Next up at home was Eastern Province, who bowled Gauteng out cheaply to win by five wickets. Gauteng finished their home run with a five-wicket win over Easterns, thanks to Nic Pothas' unbeaten 79.

The most consistent one-day batsman for Gauteng, however, was Adam Bacher, who scored the most runs (367) for his province in the league stages.

It came as no surprise when the Gauteng Cricket Board decided not to renew the contract of their overseas player, Ottis Gibson. Although he tried his best, it was obvious that the province desperately needed a classy, genuine fast bowler to join David Terbrugge.

GAUTENG CRICKET BOARD

Gauteng lost Andre Seymore halfway through the season to - yes, you guessed it - Easterns, where Derek Crookes and Benjamin were enjoying much happier times.

It was hoped that the off-season appointment of Alan Kourie, the tough former Transvaal and Springbok all-rounder, as director of cricket would herald the start of a revival at the Wanderers. His first major signing was that of the former West Indies Test fast bowler Franklyn Rose.

PROVINCIAL RECORDS

Honours:
Currie/Castle Cup/SuperSport Series (29): 1889/90, 1894/95, 1902/03, 1903/04, 1904/05, 1906/07, 1921/22 (shared), 1923/24, 1925/26, 1926/27, 1929/30, 1934/35, 1937/38 (shared), 1950/51, 1958/59, 1965/66 (shared), 1968/69, 1969/70 (shared), 1970/71, 1971/72, 1972/73, 1978/79, 1979/80, 1982/83, 1983/84, 1984/85, 1986/87, 1987/88, 1999/00
B&H Series (4): 1981/82, 1982/83, 1984/85, 1992/93
Gillette Cup/Datsun/Nissan Shield (9): 1973/74, 1978/79, 1979/80, 1980/81, 1982/83, 1983/84, 1984/85, 1985/86, 1990/91
Standard Bank Cup (1): 1997/98
Currie Cup B Section (1): 1952/53

Highest innings totals:

For:	640-5*	v Griqualand West (Kimberley)		1999/00
Against:	594-8	by MCC (Johannesburg) (FC)		1956/57
	562	by Natal (Johannesburg) (CC)		1936/37

Lowest innings totals:

For:	53	v Australians (Johannesburg) (FC)		1949/50
	58	v Natal (Durban) (CC)		1910/11
Against:	29	by Griqualand West (Johannesburg)		1950/51

Highest individual innings:

For:	337*	DJ Cullinan	v Northern Transvaal (Johannesburg)	1993/94
Against:	304*	AW Nourse	for Natal (Johannesburg) (FC)	1919/20
	260*	AD Nourse	for Natal (Johannesburg) (CC)	1936/37

Most runs in a season:

SS			All FC		
961	(Avg 96.10) RG Pollock	1978/79	961	(Avg 96.10) RG Pollock	1978/79

Most runs in a career:

SS			All FC		
10160	(Avg 43.60) SJ Cook	1972-94	10812	(Avg 43.42) SJ Cook	1972-94

Most 100s in a career:

SS			All FC		
28	SJ Cook	1972-94	29	SJ Cook	1972-94

Best bowling in an innings:

For:	9-19	AMB Rowan	v Australians (Johannesburg) (FC)	1949/50
	9-48	EP Nupen	v Griqualand West (Johannesburg) (CC)	1931/32
Against:	9-71	MJ Procter	for Rhodesia (Bulawayo)	1972/73

Best bowling in a match:

For:	16-136	EP Nupen	v Griqualand West (Johannesburg)	1931/32
Against:	12-100	J Middleton	for Western Province (Cape Town)	1897/98

Most wickets in a season:

SS			All FC		
58	(Avg 12.72) ST Clarke	1984/85	58	(Avg 12.72) ST Clarke	1984/85

Most wickets in a career:

SS			All FC		
351	(Avg 20.33) CEB Rice	1970-91	366	(Avg 20.88) CEB Rice	1970-91

Most dismissals (wicketkeepers) in an innings:
6 (on 10 occasions)WR Endean (ct 6,st 0), A Bacher (ct 5,st 1), BL Irvine (ct 6,st 0 - twice), RV Jennings (on five occasions- ct 5,st 1 once, ct 6,st 0 four times), B McBride (ct 6,st 0)

Most dismissals (wicketkeepers) in a match:

10 (ct 10,st 0)	RV Jennings	v Arosa Sri Lanka (Johannesburg) (FC)	1982/83
10 (ct 10,st 0)	RV Jennings	v Northern Transvaal (Verwoerdburg) (CC)	1986/87
10 (ct 10,st 0)	RV Jennings	v Orange Free State (Johannesburg) (CC)	1986/87

Most dismissals (wicketkeepers) in a season:

SS				All FC			
46	(ct 40,st 6)	RV Jennings	1984/85	55	(ct 49,st 6)	RV Jennings	1984/85

Most dismissals (wicketkeepers) in a career:

SS				All FC			
389	(ct 356,st 33)	RV Jennings	1975-89	419	(ct 385,st 34)	RV Jennings	1975-89

Most catches (fielders) in an innings:

4 LJ Tancred, EB Lundie, AHC Cooper, MJ Susskind, B Mitchell (twice), EJ Barlow, KA McKenzie, DD Dyer, BM McMillan, KR Rutherford, AJ Seymore, DN Crookes, AM Bacher

Most catches (fielders) in a match:

5 LJ Tancred, MJ Susskind, B Mitchell, GG Ritchie, D Mackay-Coghill, HR Lance, DS van der Knaap, KA McKenzie (twice), HR Fotheringham, BM McMillan, KR Rutherford, DN Crookes, AM Bacher

Most catches (fielders) in a season:

SS			All FC		
21	AJ Kourie	1984/85	21	AJ Kourie	1984/85

Most catches (fielders) in a career:

SS			All FC		
106	KA McKenzie	1971-86	111	AJ Kourie	1974-86
106	AJ Kourie	1974-86			

Most appearances:

SS			All FC		
150	CEB Rice	1970-91	160	CEB Rice	1970-91
			160	SJ Cook	1972-94

Most captaincies:

SS			All FC		
77	CEB Rice	1981-91	80	CEB Rice	1981-91

RECORD WICKET PARTNERSHIPS

1st	290	SJ Cook and HR Fotheringham v Orange Free State (Bloemfontein)	1988/89
2nd	265*	MS Venter and HR Fotheringham v Arosa Sri Lanka (Johannesburg) (FC)	1982/83
	225	SJ Cook and HR Fotheringham v Natal (Johannesburg) (CC)	1978/79
3rd	267	PR Carlstein and JHB Waite v Cavaliers (Johannesburg) (FC)	1962/63
	210*	BL Irvine and BF Bath v Western Province (Johannesburg) (CC)	1973/74
4th	342	EAB Rowan and PJM Gibb v North-Eastern Transvaal (Johannesburg) (The South African record for this wicket)	1952/53
5th	327	AW Briscoe and HB Cameron v Griqualand West (Johannesburg)	1934/35
6th	207	MJ Susskind and HB Cameron v Eastern Province (Johannesburg)	1926/27
7th	299	B Mitchell and A Melville v Griqualand West (Kimberley) (The South African record for this wicket)	1946/47
8th	147	AD Pinkerton and DA Clark v Griqualand West (Kimberley)	1952/53
9th	221	NV Lindsay and GR McCubbin v Rhodesia (Bulawayo) (FC) (The South African domestic record for this wicket)	1922/23
	166	RK Muzzell and GLG Watson v Eastern Province (Johannesburg) (CC)	1968/69
10th	174	HR Lance and D Mackay-Coghill v Natal (Johannesburg) (The joint South African record for this wicket)	1965/66

PERFORMANCES AGAINST OTHER TEAMS

HIGHEST AND LOWEST TOTALS

Opponents	Highest Total For		Lowest Total For	
Boland	365	1995/96	143	1999/00
Border	459-4*	1946/47	100 (FC)	1957/58
			102 (CC)	1910/11
Eastern Province	583	1926/27	110	1990/91
Easterns	311	1999/00	122	1999/00
Free State	609	1934/35	89	1997/98

GAUTENG CRICKET BOARD

Griqualand West	640-5*	1999/00	86 (FC)	1913/14
			117 (CC)	1889/90
KwaZulu-Natal	608-6* (FC)	1939/40	58	1910/11
	532-6* (CC)	1983/84		
Northerns	602-9*	1993/94	74	1997/98
North West	322	2000/01	224	2000/01
Western Province	511-8*	1954/55	68	1897/98

BEST INDIVIDUAL PERFORMANCES

Opponents	**Highest score**		**Best bowling (innings)**		**Best bowling (match, 8+)**	
Boland	159*	BM White, 1995/96	7-52	CE Eksteen, 1998/99	9-123	SD Jack, 1995/96
Border	204*	WR Endean, 1959/60	7-36	DEJ Ironside,1952/53	13-101	EP Nupen, 1923/24
Eastern Province	247	WR Endean, 1955/56	9-102	NV Radford,1988/89	13-185	JH Sinclair,1902/03
Easterns	74	DN Crookes, 1999/00	5-22	KCG Benjamin, 1999/00	8-49	KCG Benjamin, 1999/00
Free State	235	WR Endean, 1954/55	8-39 (FC)	NAT Adcock,1953/54	13-65(FC)	NATAdcock, 1953/54
			7-25 (CC)	RO Schwarz, 1906/07	11-96(CC)	GC White,1903/04
Griqualand West	277*	EAB Rowan, 1950/51	9-48	EP Nupen, 1931/32	16-136	EP Nupen, 1931/32
KwaZulu-Natal	306*(FC)	EAB Rowan,1939/40	8-80	AE Hall, 1926/27	14-115	AE Hall,1926/27
	195*(SS)	KR Rutherford, 1999/00				
Northerns	337*	DJ Cullinan, 1993/94	7-58	EW Kidwell, 1997/98	10-74	R Dumbrill, 1967/68
North West	93	N Pothas, 2000/01	5-39	DJ Terbrugge, 2000/01	8-92	DJ Terbrugge, 2000/01
Western Province	233	RG Pollock, 1978/79	8-40	JH Sinclair, 1897/98	13-124	JH Sinclair,1903/04

GAUTENG SUPERSPORT AVERAGES 2000/01

Batting & Fielding

Name	M	Inns	NO	Runs	HS	Avg	100	50	Ct	St
SG Koenig	7	13	0	789	155	60.69	3	4	4	0
F Herbst	2	3	2	45	35*	45.00	0	0	1	0
SC Cook	2	4	1	132	55	44.00	0	1	0	0
AM Bacher	8	15	1	552	190	39.42	1	3	3	0
AJ Hall	3	5	1	157	92	39.25	0	1	4	0
MF George	6	9	4	178	58	35.60	0	1	1	0
N Pothas	8	14	1	418	93	32.15	0	4	16	0
Z de Bruyn	8	14	1	404	66	31.07	0	3	5	0
JM Otto	4	6	0	149	88	24.83	0	2	2	0
AJ Seymore	4	8	0	178	58	22.25	0	2	6	0
OD Gibson	5	8	1	143	52	20.42	0	1	2	0
SS Ndima	1	2	0	38	38	19.00	0	0	0	0
DJ Terbrugge	5	7	4	47	12*	15.66	0	0	0	0
BP Horan	2	3	0	43	23	14.33	0	0	2	0
WB Masimula	3	5	2	41	22	13.66	0	0	1	0
NA Fusedale	3	4	2	26	20*	13.00	0	0	0	0
CE Eksteen	4	7	0	89	50	12.71	0	1	1	0
G Toyana	5	9	0	114	42	12.66	0	0	2	0
HA Manack	2	3	0	19	12	6.33	0	0	0	0
DJ Cullinan	1	2	0	12	12	6.00	0	0	2	0
TK Mataboge	2	1	0	2	2	2.00	0	0	1	0
JT Mafa	3	5	0	0	0	0.00	0	0	1	0
Totals	88	147	20	3576	190		4	23	54	0
			Extras	197				subs	2	
			Total	3773		29.70			56	

Bowling

Name	Overs	Mdns	Runs	Wkts	Avg	BB	5I	10M
HA Manack	5	2	16	1	16.00	1-16	0	0
WB Masimula	56.4	12	175	7	25.00	3-44	0	0
OD Gibson	162.3	41	444	16	27.75	6-53	1	0
NA Fusedale	143.1	27	438	15	29.20	5-170	1	0
JT Mafa	85.5	17	352	11	32.00	6-62	1	0
DJ Terbrugge	166.5	46	363	11	33.00	5-39	1	0
AJ Hall	94	22	277	8	34.62	5-93	1	0
CE Eksteen	183.4	61	429	9	47.66	2-62	0	0
BP Horan	44	11	109	2	54.50	2-17	0	0
MF George	119	15	420	7	60.00	2-43	0	0
Z de Bruyn	120	19	434	7	62.00	2-34	0	0
TK Mataboge	44	9	144	1	144.00	1-48	0	0
JM Otto	1	0	3	0	-	-	0	0
SG Koenig	1	0	5	0	-	-	0	0
AM Bacher	10	2	29	0	-	-	0	0
G Toyana	8	2	31	0	-	-	0	0
F Herbst	15	3	46	0	-	-	0	0
Totals	1259.4	289	3715	95		6-53	5	0
		b & lb	107	5	run outs			
		Total	3822	100	38.22			

MATCH REPORTS AND SCORECARDS

GAUTENG v GRIQUALAND WEST — SuperSport Series Pool A

Played at Wanderers Stadium, Johannesburg on 20,21,22,23 October 2000 — Toss: Griqualand West
Umpires: WA Diedricks & KH Hurter
Debuts: Gau: MF George & OD Gibson (Both FC for Gau). GW: J Brooker & CR Tatton (Both FC for GW)
Close of Play: Day 1: GW (1) 243-0 (Arthur 155*, Gidley 85*, 80 overs). Day 2: Gau (1) 75-4 (Koenig 36*, Pothas 0*, 33 overs). Day 3: Gau (2) 163-3 (Koenig 76*, Eksteen 0*, 67 overs).
Result: Match drawn
Man of Match: Mickey Arthur & Martyn Gidley
Points: Gau: 2 (bat 1, bowl 1, match 0). GW: 7 (bat 3, bowl 4, match 0)

Any thoughts of it being an easy first match of the season were dispelled as Arthur and Gidley batted through a rain-shortened first day. Gauteng's first innings then set the dismal standard for what was to become a major stumbling block for a team that was now lacking the aggressive batting of Ken Rutherford. The home side were bowled out for 184 and were in danger of being humbled. Koenig, though, after being the star batsman in the first innings, led a home team resistance in the second innings and went to a hard-earned century after falling six short in his first effort.

GRIQUALAND WEST

FIRST INNINGS	*Runs*	*Mins*	*Balls*	*4*	*6*
JM Arthur b Terbrugge	165	324	244	27	1
*MI Gidley lbw b Gibson	86	335	275	7	1
GD Elliott c Pothas b George	13	61	37	2	-
WM Dry lbw b Gibson	0	11	10	-	-
PPJ Koortzen not out	82	244	175	7	1
†W Bossenger not out	72	205	166	8	-
J Brooker					
GJ Kruis					
CR Tatton					
ZA Abrahim					
CA Copeland					
Extras (lb 7, w 1, nb 1)	9				
TOTAL (for 4 wkts dec) (151 overs)	**427**				

GAUTENG

AM Bacher c Elliott b Kruis	6	26	26	-	-	run out (Kruis/Bossenger)	35	104	114	5	-
SG Koenig c Arthur b Copeland	94	292	213	16	-	lbw b Gidley	108	378	321	12	-
AJ Seymore c Arthur b Kruis	0	15	13	-	-	b Tatton	6	40	32	1	-
Z de Bruyn c Arthur b Copeland	26	76	53	5	-	c Bossenger b Koortzen	28	73	55	4	-
G Toyana c Bossenger b Copeland	1	7	9	-	-	(6) b Copeland	42	136	126	5	-
†N Pothas c Kruis b Abrahim	13	51	38	2	-	(7) c Bossenger b Kruis	20	56	42	3	-
SS Ndima c Elliott b Kruis	0	3	1	-	-	(9) c Gidley b Tatton	38	66	43	7	-
OD Gibson c Gidley b Copeland	23	65	43	3	-	c Elliott b Copeland	29	51	45	3	1
*CE Eksteen c Bossenger b Copeland	6	25	28	-	-	(5) c Elliott b Abrahim	11	82	80	1	-
MF George not out	4	31	32	-	-	not out	33	89	87	6	-
DJ Terbrugge b Kruis	2	16	19	-	-	not out	10	71	58	1	-
Extras (lb 5, w 2, nb 2)	9					Extras (b 9, lb 7, w 1, nb 7)	24				
TOTAL (78.4 overs)	**184**					**TOTAL (for 9 wkts) (166 overs)**	**384**				

Bowling	*O*	*M*	*R*	*W*		*O*	*M*	*R*	*W*
GAUTENG									
Terbrugge	25	10	37	1					
Gibson	31	9	97	2					
George	28	3	102	1					
de Bruyn	17	1	58	0					
Eksteen	42	12	104	0					
Bacher	8	2	22	0					
GRIQUALAND WEST									
Kruis	21.4	8	43	4		33	11	71	1
Abrahim	15	4	47	1		20	6	48	1
Copeland	24	7	52	5	(4)	34	9	112	2
Elliott	10	2	23	0	(3)	15	4	38	0
Tatton	7	3	14	0		27	9	48	2
Gidley	1	1	0	0	(7)	17	6	22	1
Koortzen					(6)	20	12	29	1

Fall of Wickets	**GW**	**Gau**	**Gau**
	1st	1st	2nd
1st	254 (1)	12 (1)	62 (1)
2nd	254 (2)	20 (3)	84 (3)
3rd	254 (4)	72 (4)	157 (4)
4th	279 (3)	74 (5)	185 (5)
5th	-	96 (6)	223 (2)
6th	-	96 (7)	273 (7)
7th	-	155 (8)	273 (6)
8th	-	167 (9)	326 (8)
9th	-	178 (2)	341 (9)
10th	-	184 (11)	-

North West v Gauteng, Potchefstroom, 27-30 October 2000. Gauteng won by 121 runs.
Free State v Gauteng, Bloemfontein, 3-6 November 2000. Match drawn.

GAUTENG v NORTHERNS — SuperSport Series Pool A

Played at Wanderers Stadium, Johannesburg on 10,11,12,13 November 2000 — Toss: Northerns
Umpires: M Gajjar & RE Koertzen (TV: DF Becker)
Debuts: Gau: None. Nor: None
Close of Play: Day 1: Nor (1) 306-7 (Elworthy 36*, Brouwers 0*, 101.1 overs). Day 2: Gau (1) 170-8 (Pothas 17*, Masimula 0*, 75 overs). Day 3: Gau (2) 30-1 (Bacher 19*, Seymore 3*, 9 overs).
Result: Northerns won by 139 runs
Man of Match: Steve Elworthy
Points: Gau: 3 (bat 1, bowl 2, match 0). Nor: 18 (bat 4, bowl 4, match 10)

Gauteng's second home match followed a similar pattern to the first, with the visitors posting a big total and then skittling the home side. Northerns' fine batting effort was led by McKenzie, a batsman the hosts had let get away. Unlike Griquas, Northerns did not let the Strikers off the hook, with Elworthy working hard on a pitch which became more batsman-friendly.

NORTHERNS

FIRST INNINGS	*Runs*	*Mins*	*Balls*	*4*	*6*	*SECOND INNINGS*	*Runs*	*Mins*	*Balls*	*4*	*6*
PJR Steyn c Mafa b Hall	22	43	33	4	-	lbw b Terbrugge	3	18	15	-	-
JA Rudolph c Bacher b Hall	3	31	20	-	-	c sub (IR Kuiler) b Mafa	65	182	139	6	1
M van Jaarsveld c Pothas b de Bruyn	59	198	139	5	-	b Eksteen	58	300	216	3	-
ND McKenzie c Seymore b Masimula	123	284	215	21	-	b Eksteen	0	5	3	-	-
*G Dros c Cullinan b Masimula	49	180	123	8	1	not out	100	160	132	14	2
A Paleker c Bacher b Hall	1	27	20	-	-						
S Elworthy not out	75	148	115	10	3						
†CFK van Wyk b Eksteen	3	13	11	-	-	(6) not out	7	29	12	-	-
NG Brouwers lbw b Hall	0	21	18	-	-						
GJ Smith c Pothas b Hall	1	16	12	-	-						
DH Townsend c Cullinan b Eksteen	7	42	26	-	-						
Extras (lb 4, w 1, nb 8)	13					Extras (b 1, lb 6, nb 8)	15				
TOTAL (120.4 overs)	**356**					**TOTAL (for 4 wkts dec) (84.5 overs)**	**248**				

GAUTENG

AM Bacher c McKenzie b Townsend	61	248	186	7	-	lbw b Dros	54	166	127	11	-
SG Koenig c Smith b Elworthy	16	50	36	2	-	c Dros b Elworthy	4	26	14	-	-
AJ Seymore c van Wyk b Townsend	19	60	48	3	-	c McKenzie b Elworthy	16	46	33	3	-
DJ Cullinan b Townsend	0	2	1	-	-	c Brouwers b Townsend	12	38	26	3	-
Z de Bruyn run out (Paleker/McKenzie/van Wyk)	24	83	62	6	-	c van Wyk b Dros	66	183	138	13	-
AJ Hall c van Wyk b Elworthy	4	17	13	1	-	c van Wyk b Elworthy	30	93	76	4	-
†N Pothas b Elworthy	27	112	74	2	-	c Smith b Townsend	60	118	97	11	1
*CE Eksteen b Smith	10	30	32	1	-	c van Wyk b Dros	0	2	2	-	-
DJ Terbrugge b Smith	1	8	6	-	-	not out	11	94	62	2	-
WB Masimula not out	4	41	27	-	-	lbw b Elworthy	2	6	4	-	-
JT Mafa b Elworthy	0	2	1	-	-	c van Jaarsveld b Elworthy	0	6	1	-	-
Extras (lb 13, w 1, nb 4)	18					Extras (b 7, lb 14, w 2, nb 3)	26				
TOTAL (80.2 overs)	**184**					**TOTAL (96.1 overs)**	**281**				

Bowling	*O*	*M*	*R*	*W*		*O*	*M*	*R*	*W*
GAUTENG									
Terbrugge	23	4	66	0		17.5	6	30	1
Hall	30	10	93	5		11	2	36	0
Mafa	9	2	45	0	(6)	10	1	49	1
Eksteen	30.4	11	63	2	(5)	31	11	63	2
Masimula	17	5	32	2	(3)	8	0	28	0
de Bruyn	11	1	53	1	(4)	7	2	35	0
NORTHERNS									
Elworthy	15.2	4	34	4		27.1	7	81	5
Smith	21	8	28	2		21	9	52	0
Townsend	20	5	48	3		20	8	42	2
Dros	12	2	29	0	(5)	11	3	37	3
Brouwers	12	4	32	0	(4)	8	1	24	0
Rudolph						9	3	24	0

Fall of Wickets	Nor 1st	Gau 1st	Nor 2nd	Gau 2nd
1st	20 (2)	27 (2)	4 (1)	19 (2)
2nd	28 (1)	71 (3)	97 (2)	55 (3)
3rd	152 (3)	71 (4)	101 (4)	77 (4)
4th	251 (4)	132 (5)	194 (3)	120 (1)
5th	261 (6)	137 (6)	-	192 (6)
6th	303 (5)	147 (1)	-	209 (5)
7th	306 (8)	161 (8)	-	209 (8)
8th	314 (9)	163 (9)	-	274 (7)
9th	316 (10)	184 (7)	-	281 (10)
10th	356 (11)	184 (11)	-	281 (11)

Boland v Gauteng, Paarl, 17-20 November 2000. No play - rain.

GAUTENG v KWAZULU-NATAL — SuperSport Series Shield

Played at Wanderers Stadium, Johannesburg on 26,27,28 January 2001 — Toss: KwaZulu-Natal

Umpires: DF Becker & ST Jivan

Debuts: Gau: TK Mataboge & JM Otto (Both FC). KZN: None

Close of Play: Day 1: Gau (1) 1-0 (Bacher 0*, Koenig 1*, 2 overs). Day 2: KZN (2) 31-0 (Bruyns 12*, Watson 19*, 10 overs).

Result: Match drawn

Man of Match: Adam Bacher

Points: Gau: 8 (bat 4, bowl 4, match 0). KZN: 6 (bat 4, bowl 2, match 0)

What in most seasons would have been one of the highlights of the provincial cricket programme was a battle of the also-rans, with the Natalians also having failed to advance to the Super Eight stage and being condemned to playing three-day matches for the remainder of the season. Bacher was in top form in a match which never was likely to produce a result.

KWAZULU-NATAL

FIRST INNINGS	*Runs*	*Mins*	*Balls*	*4*	*6*	*SECOND INNINGS*	*Runs*	*Mins*	*Balls*	*4*	*6*
ML Bruyns c George b Hall	53	131	105	11	-	c Pothas b Mataboge	22	94	55	1	-
DJ Watson c Pothas b de Bruyn	33	119	90	4	-	c Gibson b George	36	144	120	4	-
AM Amla lbw b de Bruyn	50	117	86	6	-	c Pothas b George	20	59	47	3	-
JC Kent c Otto b Gibson	34	74	64	6	-	lbw b Hall	33	117	80	6	-
*DM Benkenstein c Mataboge b Gibson	14	44	24	2	-	c Hall b Gibson	19	64	46	4	-
WR Wingfield lbw b Gibson	2	10	5	-	-	c de Bruyn b Hall	1	5	8	-	-
†ELR Stewart c Otto b Gibson	30	132	96	1	-	(8) not out	38	122	74	5	-
GH Bodi c Pothas b George	0	12	10	-	-	(7) not out	70	158	127	10	-
EAE Baptiste b Gibson	57	121	96	6	-						
GM Gilder not out	7	16	6	-	1						
JE Bastow c de Bruyn b Gibson	4	10	9	-	-						
Extras (b 2, lb 8, nb 9)	19					Extras (b 4, lb 3, w 2, nb 4)	13				
TOTAL (97.1 overs)	**303**					**TOTAL (for 6 wkts) (92 overs)**	**252**				

GAUTENG					
*AM Bacher c Benkenstein b Wingfield	190	399	309	27	2
SG Koenig b Gilder	78	241	185	8	-
HA Manack c Bruyns b Bodi	6	14	17	-	-
JM Otto b Kent	0	7	4	-	-
†N Pothas c Baptiste b Bodi	1	9	6	-	-
Z de Bruyn c Stewart b Wingfield	19	82	63	3	-
AJ Hall not out	29	40	29	4	1
OD Gibson					
MF George					
TK Mataboge					
DJ Terbrugge					
Extras (b 1, lb 1, w 3, nb 5)	10				
TOTAL (for 6 wkts dec) (101.2 overs)	**333**				

Bowling	*O*	*M*	*R*	*W*		*O*	*M*	*R*	*W*	*Fall of Wickets*	KZN	Gau	KZN
GAUTENG											1st	1st	2nd
Terbrugge	15	5	34	0		17	4	37	0				
George	14	3	40	1	(3)	17	2	43	2	1st	81 (2)	165 (2)	48 (1)
Mataboge	19	3	79	0	(5)	15	3	48	1	2nd	95 (1)	177 (3)	84 (2)
Gibson	21.1	5	53	6	(2)	21	5	63	1	3rd	161 (4)	178 (4)	91 (3)
Hall	16	3	53	1	(4)	18	4	33	2	4th	187 (3)	187 (5)	123 (5)
de Bruyn	12	1	34	2		3	1	16	0	5th	194 (6)	270 (6)	124 (6)
Koenig						1	0	5	0	6th	197 (5)	333 (1)	145 (4)
KWAZULU-NATAL										7th	202 (8)	-	-
Bastow	16	6	44	0						8th	286 (7)	-	-
Gilder	20	4	69	1						9th	289 (9)	-	-
Kent	18	2	57	1						10th	303 (11)	-	-
Wingfield	13.2	3	36	2									
Bodi	27	5	94	2									
Baptiste	6	0	27	0									
Bruyns	1	0	4	0									

Griqualand West v Gauteng, Kimberley, 2-4 February 2001. Match drawn.

GAUTENG v GRIQUALAND WEST — SuperSport Series Shield

Played at Wanderers Stadium, Johannesburg on 2,3,4 March 2001 — Toss: Griqualand West

Umpires: WA Diedricks & KH Hurter

Debuts: Gau: SC Cook & F Herbst (FC), BP Horan (FC for Gau). GW: None

Close of Play: Day 1: GW (1) 126-7 (Gidley 56*, Abrahim 28*, 47 overs). Day 2: GW (2) 71-4 (Elliott 29*, Bossenger 16*, 22.1 overs).

Result: Griqualand West won by 1 wicket

Man of Match: Zahir Abrahim

Points: Gau: 5 (bat 1, bowl 4, match 0). GW: 15 (bat 1, bowl 4, match 10)

The destination of the Shield was effectively decided in a low-scoring match, with Abrahim playing a key role by making valuable lower order contributions in both innings as well as taking the best SuperSport figures of his career. He and last man Kidwell came together with 30 runs still needed but saw their side to victory.

GAUTENG

FIRST INNINGS	*Runs*	*Mins*	*Balls*	*4*	*6*	*SECOND INNINGS*	*Runs*	*Mins*	*Balls*	*4*	*6*
SC Cook b Kruis	43	166	135	3	-	(2) run out (Tatton/Abrahim)	15	41	38	1	-
*AM Bacher lbw b Kidwell	0	11	9	-	-	(1) lbw b Kruis	2	3	6	-	-
Z de Bruyn b Kruis	41	90	70	7	-	c Bossenger b Louw	14	59	36	2	-
JM Otto c Louw b Abrahim	59	105	100	11	1	c Bossenger b Louw	0	1	1	-	-
†N Pothas c Koortzen b Kruis	4	3	5	1	-	lbw b Abrahim	60	117	109	9	-
G Toyana run out (Gidley)	10	26	21	1	-	st Bossenger b Gidley	24	68	48	3	1
F Herbst not out	0	28	20	-	-	lbw b Kruis	10	68	57	-	-
MF George b Abrahim	0	6	8	-	-	lbw b Gidley	6	16	18	-	-
BP Horan b Abrahim	0	3	2	-	-	c Abrahim b Louw	20	74	57	1	1
NA Fusedale b Abrahim	0	1	1	-	-	not out	20	49	45	2	-
JT Mafa b Abrahim	0	2	3	-	-	lbw b Kruis	0	1	1	-	-
Extras (lb 1, nb 14)	15					Extras (lb 3, nb 2)	5				
TOTAL (60 overs)	**172**					**TOTAL (69.1 overs)**	**176**				

GRIQUALAND WEST											
BH Tucker b Fusedale	7	31	24	1	-	(3) lbw b Mafa	17	39	25	1	-
MI Gidley not out	73	216	162	9	-	lbw b Horan	0	7	3	-	-
GD Elliott b George	4	9	10	1	-	(4) c de Bruyn b Fusedale	52	186	144	7	-
LL Bosman c Toyana b Fusedale	12	41	31	2	-	(5) b Fusedale	1	4	3	-	-
PPJ Koortzen c Pothas b Mafa	7	11	11	1	-	(1) lbw b Mafa	4	4	6	1	-
*†W Bossenger b Mafa	2	2	2	-	-	b Horan	33	84	70	3	-
J Louw lbw b Mafa	5	29	23	1	-	b Fusedale	20	50	46	4	-
GJ Kruis b Mafa	0	4	2	-	-	c Pothas b de Bruyn	5	23	19	-	-
ZA Abrahim lbw b Mafa	42	71	70	8	-	not out	43	90	84	4	-
CR Tatton run out (Horan/Pothas)	1	3	4	-	-	b Fusedale	1	34	26	-	-
EW Kidwell c Pothas b Mafa	0	4	1	-	-	not out	2	38	19	-	-
Extras (b 1, lb 1, nb 5)	7					Extras (b 2, lb 4, w 3, nb 3)	12				
TOTAL (55.5 overs)	**160**					**TOTAL (for 9 wkts) (73.4 overs)**	**190**				

Bowling	*O*	*M*	*R*	*W*		*O*	*M*	*R*	*W*
GRIQUALAND WEST									
Kruis	19	4	64	3		19.1	5	55	3
Kidwell	6	0	15	1		3	1	6	0
Abrahim	12	4	22	5		18	2	42	1
Tatton	14	2	61	0	(7)	1	0	6	0
Gidley	9	5	9	0	(6)	15	7	22	2
Louw					(4)	6	2	25	3
Elliott					(5)	7	2	17	0
GAUTENG									
Mafa	17.5	6	62	6		18	3	49	2
Horan	10	1	27	0		10	4	17	2
Fusedale	18	5	48	2		32.4	7	83	4
George	6	2	19	1		2	0	23	0
Toyana	4	2	2	0					
de Bruyn					(5)	11	4	12	1

Fall of Wickets	**Gau**	**GW**	**Gau**	**GW**
	1st	1st	2nd	2nd
1st	4 (2)	24 (1)	2 (1)	4 (1)
2nd	76 (3)	36 (3)	20 (2)	4 (2)
3rd	141 (1)	65 (4)	20 (4)	26 (3)
4th	145 (5)	73 (5)	36 (3)	27 (5)
5th	170 (6)	75 (6)	105 (6)	101 (6)
6th	172 (4)	93 (7)	121 (5)	134 (7)
7th	172 (8)	93 (8)	128 (8)	137 (4)
8th	172 (9)	155 (9)	138 (7)	145 (8)
9th	172 (10)	157 (10)	176 (9)	159 (10)
10th	172 (11)	160 (11)	176 (11)	-

KwaZulu-Natal v Gauteng, Durban, 9-11 March 2001. Match drawn.

GRIQUALAND WEST CRICKET BOARD

PO Box 297, Kimberley 8300. Tel (053) 833 2601.
Fax (053) 832 2196. E-mail: gwcricket@intekom.co.za

Chairman: Ahmed Jinnah
Vice-chairman: Wayne Schonegevel
General Manager: Brian Kidson
Development Manager: Jeremy Fredericks
Youth Manager: Eugene Jacobs
Marketing Manager: Derick Blomerus
Stadium Manager: Ben Neethling
Cricket Manager: Mickey Arthur
2001/02 contracted players: Wendell Bossenger, Craig Tatton, Zahir Abrahim, Martyn Gidley, Deon Kruis, Pieter Koortzen, Loots Bosman, Wayne Kidwell, Jason Brooker, Johann Louw, Alan Kruger, Adrian McLaren, Brett Tucker, Charl Pietersen, Patrick Ndopu, Elton Tsamaisi.

REVIEW OF THE SEASON 2000/01

John Harrison

SUPERSPORT SERIES: P5 W0 L3 D2 (fifth in group)
SUPERSPORT SHIELD COMPETITION: P4 W1 L0 D3 (winners)
CAPTAIN: MI Gidley (5), W Bossenger (4)
STANDARD BANK CUP: P10 W4 L6 (ninth)

Short on experience, though not on keenness and enthusiasm, the Griqua Diamonds had a roller- coaster season. The Diamonds began their campaign with long-serving opening batting partners, Martyn Gidley and Mickey Arthur, respectively captain and player-coach, and former Natal Dolphins left-arm spinner, Craig Tatton, their only squad newcomer from outside the province.

With Arthur indicating from the outset that this would be the first year of a three-year rebuilding process, only six weeks into the season he opted to lay aside his bat to concentrate fully on his coaching responsibility.

Off the field, Mike Doherty's decision to call it a day after years of exceptional service to Griqua cricket, saw farmer, Ken Dugmore, as the new chairperson and another former Griqua cricketer, businessman, Ahmed Jinnah, as his deputy.

The generally young Diamonds squad made an encouraging start, which included home wins against eventual Standard Bank Cup champions, the KwaZulu-Natal Dolphins and the ICC's newest full members, Bangladesh, and at one stage were well-placed to qualify for the SuperSport Series Super Eight phase. Disappointingly, though, they again missed out in the four-day competition and also lost five successive Cup matches.

Early in January, Martyn Gidley announced that he was relinquishing the captaincy in the interests of the team and to concentrate on regaining his batting form.

MOVING ON ... Mickey Arthur retired from playing during the 2000/01 season and moved into the coaches position at Griqualand West. *Picture: Thomas Turck, TOUCHLINE PHOTO*

Wicketkeeper-batsman Wendell Bossenger, handed this responsibility, immediately set about lifting Griqua spirits and performances. His enthusiastic and positive leadership, allied to Gidley again finding his batting touch, and a number of outstanding individual and team performances firmly founded on growing confidence out in the middle, saw the young Diamonds suddenly turn their season around.

Home wins in three of their last four Standard Bank Cup fixtures and topping the three-team SuperSport Shield competition, augured well for the season ahead. The youth policy adopted at the start of the season reaped handsome dividends.

Home product Pieter Koortzen, straight from a winter at the Plascon Academy, improved beyond recognition. Giving the first hint of things to come when scoring his maiden first-class century against Bangladesh, the 21-year-old went on to score 441 runs in the SuperSport Series at an average of 31.50 and a provincial record-breaking total of 563 runs (including two centuries and two 99s) at an average of 70.37 in the Standard Bank Cup.

Fast bowler Deon Kruis performed magnificently with the ball, taking 40 SuperSport wickets at 24.05 and 20 at 19.55 in the Standard Bank Cup. Only a fortnight into the season he had match figures of 6/121 against Bangladesh. He also achieved a hat-trick when dismissing Mark Bruyns, Dale Benkenstein and Wade Wingfield during KwaZulu-Natal's first innings of the Shield fixture in Durban.

Seamer Zahir Abrahim, who played in only three SuperSport Series matches the previous season, made huge strides. Capturing 28 wickets at 28.21 and scoring 267 runs at 26.70, he developed into a genuine bowling all-rounder.

Young leg-spinner Craig Copeland, who started with an impressive 12 wickets for 213 runs match haul against Bangladesh and followed this up with seven wickets in the opening SuperSport Series match against the Highveld Strikers at The Wanderers, was unable to sustain his early form and lost his place.

Hard-hitting batsman Loots Bosman, after an injury-delayed start, was one of four century-makers in the SuperSport Series and had an average of 42.25. He played some aggressive innings at the top of the innings in the Standard Bank Cup competition.

Returning to Gauteng for the 2001/02 season is batting all-rounder Grant Elliott, who, after compiling his maiden first-class century against Bangladesh, batted well in patches during the remainder of the season.

Recommended to Griquas by former captain Kepler Wessels, another young player making huge strides was Johann Louw, who went from trialist to genuine all-rounder during the summer. Another local player, Jason Brooker, younger brother of former Griqua batsman, Finley Brooker, played mature innings of 71 and 77 in the first home four-day match of the season against Free State in Kimberley. Though unable to sustain this run-scoring consistency, his inclusion in the 2001 Plascon Academy was expected to reap dividends.

The season ended with Mickey Arthur appointed provincial coach for the next three seasons and officially announcing his retirement from first-class cricket. First representing Griquas during the 1986/87 season, Arthur climaxed his playing career by heading Diamonds' SuperSport competition batting averages. His tally included a career-best 165 against the Highveld Strikers in Johannesburg. In this match he and Martyn Gidley, whose 596 runs at 42.57 saw him finishing second to Arthur in the averages, set a provincial first wicket record of 254 runs.

Arthur played 110 first-class matches for Griquas, Free State and South Africa A, scoring 6657 runs, including 13 centuries, at an average of 33.45. He also played in 150 limited overs matches.

GRIQUALAND WEST CRICKET BOARD

After a somewhat disappointing summer with the bat, senior player, Willie Dry, who made his Griqua debut during the 1995/96 season, was not offered a contract.

A highlight for the board was their first hosting of a one-day international involving the South African team. The De Beers Diamond Oval was packed to capacity when South Africa and New Zealand met on October 28.

Griquas' rare victory against a touring team was tinged with sadness. Their dedicated scorer, Peter Hourani, collapsed and died at the ground before the start of the second morning's play against Bangladesh.

PROVINCIAL RECORDS

Honours:
Currie Cup (1): 1890/91 (as Kimberley)
Standard Bank Cup (1): 1998/99
UCB Bowl (1): 1995/96 (shared)
SuperSport Series Shield (1): 2000/01

Highest innings totals:

For:	603	v Western Province (Kimberley)	1929/30
Against:	676	by MCC (Kimberley) (FC)	1938/39
	640-5*	by Gauteng (Kimberley) (SS)	1999/00

Lowest innings totals:

For:	29	v Transvaal (Johannesburg)	1950/51
Against:	48	by Eastern Province (Kimberley)	1934/35

Highest individual innings:

For:	250	PH Barnard	v Gauteng (Kimberley)	1998/99
Against:	284	EAB Rowan	for Eastern Province (Port Elizabeth) (FC)	1945/46
	277*	EAB Rowan	for Transvaal (Johannesburg) (CC)	1950/51

Most runs in a season:

SS and Bowl				All FC			
760	(Avg 63.33)	K Sharp	1982/83	831	(Avg 59.35)	PH Barnard	1998/99

Most runs in a career:

SS and Bowl				All FC			
5205	(Avg 35.65)	MJD Doherty	1965-84	5238	(Avg 34.92)	MJD Doherty	1964-84

Most 100s in a career:

SS and Bowl			All FC		
12	MJD Doherty	1965-84	12	MJD Doherty	1964-84

Best bowling in an innings:

For:	9-54	K McLaren	v Natal B (Umzinto)	1973/74
Against:	10-26	AEE Vogler	for Eastern Province (Johannesburg)	1906/07

Best bowling in a match:

For:	15-68	GK Glover	v Eastern Province (Cape Town)	1893/94
Against:	16-38	AEE Vogler	for Eastern Province (Johannesburg)	1906/07

Most wickets in a season:

SS and Bowl				All FC			
53	(Avg 16.84)	JE Waddington	1952/53	53	(Avg 16.84)	JE Waddington	1952/53

Most wickets in a career:

SS and Bowl				All FC			
317	(Avg 21.75)	JE Waddington	1934-58	367	(Avg 23.89)	JE Waddington	1934-58

Most dismissals (wicketkeepers) in an innings:

7	(ct 7,st 0)	P Kirsten	v Western Transvaal (Potchefstroom)	1993/94

Most dismissals (wicketkeepers) in a match:

10	(ct 10,st 0)	J Burger	v Northern Transvaal B (Kimberley)	1995/96

Most dismissals (wicketkeepers) in a season:

SS and Bowl				All FC			
37	(ct 33,st 4)	W Bossenger	1998/99	39	(ct 35,st 4)	W Bossenger	1998/99
				39	(ct 38,st 1)	W Bossenger	2000/01

GRIQUALAND WEST CRICKET BOARD

Most dismissals (wicketkeepers) in a career:

SS and Bowl			All FC		
141	(ct 132,st 9) W Bossenger	1996-2000	153	(ct 144,st 9) W Bossenger	1996-2000

Most catches (fielders) in an innings:

5	PJR Steyn	v Western Province B (Kimberley)	1985/86

Most catches (fielders) in a match:

6	JE Morris	v Northern Transvaal B (Kimberley)	1988/89

Most catches (fielders) in a season:

SS and Bowl			All FC		
15	JE Morris	1988/89	16	JE Morris	1988/89

Most catches (fielders) in a career:

SS and Bowl			All FC		
52	JE Waddington	1934-58	59	JE Waddington	1934-58

Most appearances:

SS and Bowl			All FC		
83	MJD Doherty	1965-84	85	MJD Doherty	1964-84

Most captaincies:

SS and Bowl			All FC		
30	EJ Draper	1959-67	32	JE Waddington	1949-58

RECORD WICKET PARTNERSHIPS

1st	254	JM Arthur and MI Gidley v Gauteng (Johannesburg)	2000/01
2nd	173	MI Gidley and PH Barnard v Free State (Kimberley)	1998/99
3rd	256	MI Gidley and PH Barnard v Natal B (Durban)	1995/96
4th	216	KG Viljoen and XC Balaskas v Western Province (Kimberley)	1929/30
5th	243	PH Barnard and LL Bosman v Free State (Bloemfontein)	1997/98
6th	173	XC Balaskas and RH Henderson v Rhodesia (Kimberley)	1929/30
7th	141	CD Helfrich and LE McNamara v Australians (Kimberley) (FC)	1949/50
	136	PPJ Koortzen and J Brooker v Free State (Kimberley) (SS)	2000/01
8th	148	FC Brooker and W Bossenger v West Indians (Kimberley) (FC)	1998/99
	124	JE Waddington and D Lee v Transvaal (Kimberley) (CC)	1952/53
9th	115	CW Symcox and GP van Rensburg v Eastern Province B (Kimberley)	1985/86
10th	95	CE Finlason and AE Cooper v Transvaal (Johannesburg)	1890/91

PERFORMANCES AGAINST OTHER TEAMS

HIGHEST AND LOWEST TOTALS

Opponents	Highest Total For		Lowest Total For	
Boland	366	1998/99	78	1992/93
Border	497	1951/52	74	1946/47
Eastern Province	531	1950/51	51 and 51 (same match)	1906/07
Easterns	438-9*	1993/94	139	1991/92
Free State	477	1966/67	50	1976/77
Gauteng	559-6*	1998/99	29	1950/51
KwaZulu-Natal	489	1925/26	31	1906/07
Northerns	541-6*	1996/97	41	1958/59
North West	428-3*	1991/92	179	2000/01
Western Province	603	1929/30	64	1946/47

BEST INDIVIDUAL PERFORMANCES

Opponents	Highest score	Best bowling (innings)	Best bowling (match, 8+)
Boland	148 JM Arthur, 1998/99	6-58 IM Kidson, 1990/91	9-144 IM Kidson, 1990/91
Border	177 RG Draper, 1952/53	9-91 JP McNally, 1951/52	13-59 JE Waddington, 1947/48
Eastern Province	165 CD Helfrich, 1950/51	9-105 JE Waddington, 1954/55	15-68 GK Glover, 1893/94
Easterns	127 GC Abbott, 1991/92	6-50 P McLaren, 1991/92	8-83 P McLaren, 1991/92
Free State	187 WVS Ling, 1923/24	8-64 JE Waddington, 1958/59	11-107 JP McNally, 1931/32
Gauteng	250 PH Barnard, 1998/99	7-89 S Webb, 1904/05	10-122(FC) JGWhitehead, 1913/14
		9-156 (CC) JP McNally, 1933/34	
KwaZulu-Natal	137 JM Arthur, 1998/99	7-52(FC) W Brockwell, 1889/90	10-87 (FC) W Brockwell, 1889/90
		7-101(CC)HLE Promnitz,1931/32	8-78 (CC) JM Powell, 1897/98

Northerns	212	PH Barnard, 1996/97	7-42 JE Waddington, 1947/48	13-104 JE Waddington, 1952/53
North West	153*	WE Schonegevel,1991/92	5-30 MN Angel, 1991/92	8-119 MN Angel, 1992/93
Western Province	215	KG Viljoen, 1929/30	8-50(FC) JE Waddington,1939/40 7-46 (CC) JP McNally, 1934/35	12-235 XC Balaskas, 1929/30

GRIQUALAND WEST SUPERSPORT AVERAGES 2000/01

Batting & Fielding

Name	M	Inns	NO	Runs	HS	Avg	100	50	Ct	St
JM Arthur	3	5	0	222	165	44.40	1	0	5	0
MI Gidley	9	15	1	596	151	42.57	1	4	5	0
LL Bosman	6	10	2	338	115*	42.25	1	2	3	0
PPJ Koortzen	9	15	1	441	102	31.50	1	2	2	0
W Bossenger	9	15	2	402	74*	30.92	0	3	35	1
GD Elliott	9	15	0	408	83	27.20	0	3	13	0
J Brooker	5	8	0	216	77	27.00	0	2	2	0
AP McLaren	1	1	0	27	27	27.00	0	0	0	0
ZA Abrahim	9	14	4	267	57	26.70	0	1	4	0
BH Tucker	4	6	0	135	47	22.50	0	0	0	0
J Louw	5	8	0	132	50	16.50	0	1	9	0
WM Dry	5	9	0	135	80	15.00	0	1	1	0
GJ Kruis	9	14	1	153	46	11.76	0	0	4	0
EW Kidwell	6	10	4	53	11*	8.83	0	0	2	0
CA Copeland	3	4	1	15	10	5.00	0	0	2	0
CR Tatton	7	11	1	42	14*	4.20	0	0	3	0
Totals	99	160	17	3582	165		4	19	90	1
			Extras	222				subs	1	
			Total	3804		26.60			91	

Bowling

Name	Overs	Mdns	Runs	Wkts	Avg	BB	5I	10M
GJ Kruis	391	110	962	40	24.05	5-50	1	0
ZA Abrahim	273.1	58	790	28	28.21	5-22	1	0
EW Kidwell	140.3	18	486	17	28.58	4-71	0	0
CA Copeland	81	18	302	9	33.55	5-52	1	0
J Louw	121.4	24	414	12	34.50	3-25	0	0
PPJ Koortzen	54.1	16	152	4	38.00	1-12	0	0
GD Elliott	146	37	390	10	39.00	2-18	0	0
CR Tatton	236	64	651	15	43.40	5-80	1	0
MI Gidley	84.1	22	236	4	59.00	2-22	0	0
LL Bosman	15	2	36	0	-	-	0	0
J Brooker	11	2	43	0	-	-	0	0
Totals	1553.4	371	4462	139		5-22	4	0
		b & lb	97	6	run outs			
		Total	4559	145	31.44			

MATCH REPORTS AND SCORECARDS

Gauteng v Griqualand West, Johannesburg, 20-23 October 2000. Match drawn.
Northerns v Griqualand West, Centurion, 3-6 November 2000. Northerns won by 153 runs.

GRIQUALAND WEST v FREE STATE — SuperSport Series Pool A

Played at De Beers Diamond Oval, Kimberley on 10,11,12,13 November 2000 — Toss: Free State
Umpires: CJ Mitchley & S Wadvalla
Debuts: GW: None. FS: None
Close of Play: Day 1: GW (1) 11-0 (Arthur 7*, Gidley 4*, 6 overs). Day 2: FS (2) 5-0 (Dippenaar 0*, Liebenberg 1*, 3.3 overs). Day 3: GW (2) 50-2 (Tatton 5*, Elliott 13*, 20 overs).
Result: Free State won by 54 runs
Man of Match: Nicky Boje
Points: GW: 7 (bat 3, bowl 4, match 0). FS: 18 (bat 5, bowl 3, match 10)

GRIQUALAND WEST CRICKET BOARD

Having already drawn away to the Highveld Strikers and lost against Northerns Titans at Centurion, Griquas needed a good opening home match result against neighbours, Free State, but they ran into acting skipper, Nicky Boje, in superb all-round form. Louis Wilkinson, who hammered a brilliant first-day 169, and Boje put on 184 for the fourth wicket in only 123 minutes.

Despite good efforts by Dry and rookie Jason Brooker, Griquas trailed by 75 runs, with Boje taking five wickets. Boje hit an aggressive century and Wiaan Smit made a career-best 94 as a fourth wicket stand of 180 in 152 minutes enabled the visitors to set a challenging victory target of 356 off a minimum of 124 overs. Griquas collapsed before youngsters Pieter Koortzen and Brooker added 136 for the seventh wicket.

FREE STATE

FIRST INNINGS	*Runs*	*Mins*	*Balls*	*4*	*6*	*SECOND INNINGS*	*Runs*	*Mins*	*Balls*	*4*	*6*
HH Dippenaar c Bossenger b Kruis	0	10	12	-	-	c Copeland b Tatton	28	117	104	2	-
GFJ Liebenberg c Bossenger b Abrahim	4	13	7	1	-	run out (Dry/Bossenger)	31	136	109	3	-
LJ Wilkinson c Bossenger b Koortzen	169	244	202	25	4	c Bossenger b Kruis	4	10	6	1	-
WJ Smit c Arthur b Tatton	14	52	38	2	-	b Abrahim	94	183	160	11	1
*N Boje lbw b Copeland	77	125	105	10	3	c Kruis b Koortzen	105	151	126	15	1
JF Venter c and b Copeland	8	12	15	2	-	not out	4	27	15	-	-
†GL Brophy b Abrahim	40	93	93	3	-						
HC Bakkes c Brooker b Tatton	20	69	51	2	-						
MR Lewis b Abrahim	2	25	21	-	-						
PV Mpitsang c and b Abrahim	0	23	20	-	-						
D Pretorius not out	14	19	14	2	-						
Extras (w 1, nb 3)	4					Extras (b 7, lb 3, nb 4)	14				
TOTAL (95.5 overs)	**352**					**TOTAL (for 5 wkts dec) (86 overs)**	**280**				

GRIQUALAND WEST

	Runs	Mins	Balls	4	6		Runs	Mins	Balls	4	6
JM Arthur lbw b Pretorius	27	71	55	5	-	b Venter	21	46	36	3	-
*MI Gidley st Brophy b Boje	42	166	149	3	-	lbw b Boje	11	50	40	1	-
GD Elliott c Wilkinson b Pretorius	1	8	5	-	-	(4) lbw b Pretorius	15	24	26	2	-
WM Dry b Pretorius	80	185	157	12	-	(5) lbw b Venter	7	11	8	1	-
PPJ Koortzen lbw b Pretorius	11	22	19	2	-	(6) lbw b Venter	78	156	141	11	1
†W Bossenger c Bakkes b Boje	16	57	27	1	-	(7) b Pretorius	0	7	5	-	-
J Brooker b Boje	71	131	105	8	2	(8) lbw b Pretorius	77	176	158	9	-
GJ Kruis c Liebenberg b Boje	8	67	56	1	-	(9) lbw b Boje	34	96	94	4	-
ZA Abrahim lbw b Boje	4	34	35	-	-	(10) not out	19	78	80	2	-
CR Tatton c Wilkinson b Venter	0	9	4	-	-	(3) b Pretorius	8	52	48	1	-
CA Copeland not out	0	4	5	-	-	lbw b Venter	5	26	28	-	-
Extras (b 7, lb 6, nb 4)	17					Extras (b 15, lb 11)	26				
TOTAL (102.1 overs)	**277**					**TOTAL (110.4 overs)**	**301**				

Bowling	*O*	*M*	*R*	*W*		*O*	*M*	*R*	*W*
GRIQUALAND WEST									
Kruis	18	4	58	1		24	8	62	1
Abrahim	23.5	4	68	4		13.5	4	33	1
Elliott	7	0	32	0	(4)	5	2	8	0
Tatton	30	4	114	2	(5)	29	8	87	1
Gidley	2	0	28	0	(3)	1.1	0	2	0
Copeland	8	1	40	2		5	0	36	0
Koortzen	7	1	12	1	(8)	6	0	33	1
Brooker					(7)	2	0	9	0
FREE STATE									
Bakkes	17	4	35	0	(2)	10	3	39	0
Boje	27.1	6	67	5	(4)	36	18	47	2
Mpitsang	13	2	30	0	(5)	5	1	21	0
Pretorius	22	8	51	4	(1)	23	4	63	4
Venter	21	4	63	1	(3)	35.4	8	105	4
Lewis	2	0	18	0					
Liebenberg					(6)	1	1	0	0

Fall of Wickets	**FS** 1st	**GW** 1st	**FS** 2nd	**GW** 2nd
1st	4 (1)	43 (1)	63 (1)	32 (1)
2nd	4 (2)	45 (3)	68 (3)	32 (2)
3rd	52 (4)	99 (2)	71 (2)	54 (4)
4th	236 (5)	116 (5)	251 (5)	63 (5)
5th	246 (6)	180 (6)	280 (4)	67 (3)
6th	294 (3)	189 (4)	-	71 (7)
7th	322 (7)	234 (8)	-	207 (6)
8th	338 (9)	262 (9)	-	249 (8)
9th	338 (8)	273 (10)	-	288 (9)
10th	352 (10)	277 (7)	-	301 (11)

GRIQUALAND WEST v NORTH WEST — SuperSport Series Pool A

Played at De Beers Diamond Oval, Kimberley on 17,18,19,20 November 2000 — Toss: North West
Umpires: JD Cloete & CJ Mitchley
Debuts: GW: None. NW: None
Close of Play: Day 1: NW (1) 199-9 (Thomas 36*, Roe 29*, 88.1 overs). Day 2: GW (1) 155-7 (Bosman 47*, Abrahim 14*, 70 overs). Day 3: NW (2) 142-6 (Jacobs 9*, Strydom 1*, 72 overs).
Result: North West won by 65 runs
Man of Match: Morne Strydom
Points: GW: 7 (bat 3, bowl 4, match 0). NW: 16 (bat 2, bowl 4, match 10)

Coach Mickey Arthur, making way for the previously injured Loots Bosman, effectively brought the curtain down on his first-class cricket career. The contest, during which the temperature changes were as marked as the match fluctuations, was decided by Griquas' fourth afternoon batting collapse.

A North West win seemed unlikely when the visitors crashed to 72 for seven at lunch on the first day before former Western Province B player, number ten Alfonso Thomas, and last man in, former Griqua player, Garth Roe, staged a brilliant recovery, equalling the South African first-class 10th wicket record, adding 174 runs. Thomas, in only his second SuperSport Series match, made a maiden first-class century, showing great application, and Roe made his highest score.

Bosman made a fighting maiden century for Griquas and number 10, Zahir Abrahim, a spirited half-century. Tatton's five wickets restricted North West's second innings. Griquas, with a target of 245 off a minimum of 72 overs, collapsed to the off-spinners, Morne Strydom and Craig Light, bowling in tandem.

NORTH WEST

FIRST INNINGS	*Runs*	*Mins*	*Balls*	*4*	*6*	*SECOND INNINGS*	*Runs*	*Mins*	*Balls*	*4*	*6*
AG Lawson c Elliott b Abrahim	1	17	17	-	-	(2) c Kidwell b Kruis	52	230	180	4	-
HM de Vos c Bossenger b Kruis	9	47	38	2	-	(1) c and b Tatton	21	109	83	1	-
*MC Venter c Bossenger b Abrahim	0	1	1	-	-	b Tatton	5	29	31	-	-
GM Hewitt c Bossenger b Abrahim	30	97	81	2	-	c Elliott b Kruis	39	110	84	6	-
A Jacobs c Bosman b Kidwell	17	33	27	3	-	c Elliott b Tatton	17	65	44	2	-
MJ Lavine c Bossenger b Kidwell	0	7	4	-	-	lbw b Kruis	8	8	8	-	1
C Light lbw b Kidwell	0	3	5	-	-	lbw b Kruis	0	1	1	-	-
M Strydom c and b Kruis	43	153	116	6	-	c Gidley b Tatton	7	48	46	-	-
†EG Poole lbw b Tatton	22	106	80	2	1	c Koortzen b Tatton	24	88	70	5	-
AC Thomas not out	106	264	229	13	-	not out	27	78	68	4	-
GA Roe lbw b Koortzen	66	245	191	5	1	c Elliott b Abrahim	0	3	3	-	-
Extras (b 3, lb 6, w 2, nb 8)	19					Extras (b 4, lb 2, nb 9)	15				
TOTAL (130.1 overs)	**313**					**TOTAL (101.3 overs)**	**215**				

GRIQUALAND WEST

	Runs	*Mins*	*Balls*	*4*	*6*		*Runs*	*Mins*	*Balls*	*4*	*6*
WM Dry c Light b Roe	0	7	8	-	-	c Lavine b Thomas	31	83	53	5	-
*MI Gidley c Poole b Lavine	1	36	19	-	-	c Lawson b Roe	36	138	101	6	-
GD Elliott lbw b Thomas	36	146	105	5	-	c Lawson b Strydom	59	124	105	6	-
†W Bossenger c Jacobs b Lavine	21	52	38	2	-	(6) c Jacobs b Strydom	11	38	43	-	-
PPJ Koortzen c de Vos b Roe	16	31	30	2	-	(4) c and b Strydom	23	54	52	2	-
LL Bosman not out	115	297	241	10	4	(5) c Hewitt b Light	7	8	13	-	-
J Brooker c Hewitt b Lavine	5	35	22	1	-	c Lavine b Strydom	6	9	14	-	-
GJ Kruis c Venter b Lavine	4	10	9	1	-	c Jacobs b Light	4	15	14	-	-
ZA Abrahim c Poole b Lavine	57	135	126	8	-	not out	0	27	28	-	-
CR Tatton lbw b Roe	2	11	7	-	-	c de Vos b Strydom	0	11	17	-	-
EW Kidwell run out (Lavine)	10	66	42	2	-	c Hewitt b Strydom	0	7	8	-	-
Extras (b 2, lb 5, nb 10)	17					Extras (nb 2)	2				
TOTAL (106.1 overs)	**284**					**TOTAL (74.2 overs)**	**179**				

Bowling	*O*	*M*	*R*	*W*		*O*	*M*	*R*	*W*
GRIQUALAND WEST									
Kruis	32	13	60	2		28	5	53	4
Abrahim	27	8	56	3		17.3	4	31	1
Elliott	16	3	41	0	(4)	7	2	13	0
Kidwell	22	5	38	3	(3)	9	1	32	0
Koortzen	3.1	0	17	1					
Tatton	24	8	62	1	(5)	40	13	80	5
Gidley	3	0	13	0					
Brooker	3	0	17	0					
NORTH WEST									
Lavine	34	9	97	5		14	4	30	0
Roe	29	9	70	3		9	0	37	1
Thomas	22	3	79	1		14	5	30	1
Light	15.1	6	19	0	(6)	17	5	48	2
Strydom	6	3	12	0		19.2	7	23	6
Lawson					(4)	1	0	11	0

Fall of Wickets	NW 1st	GW 1st	NW 2nd	GW 2nd
1st	3 (1)	1 (1)	52 (1)	45 (1)
2nd	3 (3)	9 (2)	61 (3)	81 (2)
3rd	21 (2)	41 (4)	115 (2)	149 (4)
4th	47 (5)	68 (5)	132 (4)	158 (5)
5th	48 (6)	84 (3)	140 (6)	160 (3)
6th	49 (7)	105 (7)	140 (7)	167 (7)
7th	68 (4)	115 (8)	154 (5)	177 (8)
8th	125 (9)	206 (9)	159 (8)	179 (6)
9th	139 (8)	211 (10)	211 (9)	179 (10)
10th	313 (11)	284 (11)	215 (11)	179 (11)

GRIQUALAND WEST v BOLAND — SuperSport Series Pool A

Played at De Beers Diamond Oval, Kimberley on 8,9,10,11 (no play) December 2000 — Toss: Boland
Umpires: CM Schoof & AE Williams
Debuts: GW: None. Bol: None
Close of Play: Day 1: GW (1) 111-7 (Bosman 42*, Abrahim 13*, 35.3 overs). Day 2: Bol (1) 190-8 (Ontong 60*, Carter 0*, 75 overs). Day 3: Bol (2) 31-0 (Trott 4*, Davids 25*, 9 overs).
Result: Match drawn
Man of Match: Henry Williams
Points: GW: 4 (bat 0, bowl 4, match 0). Bol: 6 (bat 2, bowl 4, match 0)

Unseasonal heavy rain before the match and humid conditions on the first morning, made it an important toss to win. Boland skipper Louis Koen called correctly and Henry Williams bowled splendidly.

Boland's promising young newcomer, opener Henry Davids, and Justin Ontong took Boland to a useful lead and left-arm fast bowler Neil Carter had career-best figures as Boland moved towards victory, only to be denied by rain which prevented play on the final day.

GRIQUALAND WEST

FIRST INNINGS	*Runs*	*Mins*	*Balls*	*4*	*6*	*SECOND INNINGS*	*Runs*	*Mins*	*Balls*	*4*	*6*
WM Dry c Palframan b Carter	10	40	27	2	-	c Davids b Carter	6	32	27	-	-
*MI Gidley c Barnard b Williams	1	18	10	-	-	b Williams	31	150	107	3	-
GD Elliott c Player b Williams	5	38	18	1	-	c Player b Carter	1	25	17	-	-
PPJ Koortzen b Williams	4	5	4	1	-	c and b de Lange	23	74	65	4	-
†W Bossenger c Davids b Langeveldt	6	30	23	-	-	(6) c Barnard b Ontong	30	122	93	4	-
LL Bosman not out	53	172	96	7	-	(5) c Palframan b Carter	33	57	48	3	2
J Brooker c Koen b Langeveldt	5	17	12	1	-	c Palframan b Ontong	8	60	60	-	1
GJ Kruis c and b Williams	13	31	26	2	-	c de Lange b Carter	46	82	64	4	1
ZA Abrahim c Palframan b Williams	13	48	36	2	-	c Player b Carter	11	43	42	1	-
CR Tatton c Palframan b Williams	1	4	6	-	-	lbw b Carter	0	9	8	-	-
EW Kidwell c Palframan b Langeveldt	10	47	45	1	-	not out	5	11	5	1	-
Extras (lb 4, w 1, nb 11)	16					Extras (lb 3, nb 8)	11				
TOTAL (48.4 overs)	**137**					**TOTAL (88 overs)**	**205**				

BOLAND

	Runs	*Mins*	*Balls*	*4*	*6*		*Runs*	*Mins*	*Balls*	*4*	*6*
IJL Trott run out (Brooker/Bosman)	2	16	8	-	-	not out	4	39	25	-	-
H Davids b Tatton	51	190	121	5	1	not out	25	39	31	3	1
*LJ Koen b Kruis	0	2	1	-	-						
PH Barnard lbw b Abrahim	25	71	62	4	-						
JL Ontong c Tatton b Kruis	68	240	175	6	1						
†SJ Palframan c Tatton b Kruis	10	45	40	-	-						
CdeW de Lange c Gidley b Tatton	2	25	30	-	-						
BT Player c Bossenger b Tatton	4	13	13	-	-						
CK Langeveldt lbw b Abrahim	8	33	26	-	-						
NM Carter lbw b Kruis	21	40	30	2	1						
HS Williams not out	8	18	11	1	-						
Extras (b 1, lb 6, w 1, nb 23)	31					Extras (nb 2)	2				
TOTAL (82.2 overs)	**230**					**TOTAL (for 0 wkts) (9 overs)**	**31**				

Bowling	*O*	*M*	*R*	*W*	*O*	*M*	*R*	*W*
BOLAND								
Williams	14	4	40	6	16	4	35	1
Carter	20	5	56	1	25	10	63	6
Langeveldt	7.4	1	20	3	6	1	14	0
Player	7	2	17	0	3	2	5	0
de Lange					29	10	63	1
Ontong					9	2	22	2
GRIQUALAND WEST								
Kruis	23.2	3	61	4	5	2	12	0
Abrahim	20	5	65	2	4	0	19	0
Kidwell	11	1	49	0				
Elliott	5	1	13	0				
Tatton	22	9	35	3				
Koortzen	1	1	0	0				

Fall of Wickets	GW 1st	Bol 1st	GW 2nd	Bol 2nd
1st	8 (2)	8 (1)	13 (1)	-
2nd	15 (1)	8 (3)	27 (3)	-
3rd	23 (4)	65 (4)	66 (4)	-
4th	25 (3)	123 (2)	74 (2)	-
5th	32 (5)	148 (6)	107 (5)	-
6th	50 (7)	157 (7)	137 (7)	-
7th	75 (8)	161 (8)	143 (6)	-
8th	111 (9)	189 (9)	186 (9)	-
9th	116 (10)	198 (5)	188 (10)	-
10th	137 (11)	230 (10)	205 (8)	-

KwaZulu-Natal v Griqualand West, Durban, 12-14 January 2001. Match drawn.

GRIQUALAND WEST v GAUTENG — SuperSport Series Shield

Played at De Beers Diamond Oval, Kimberley on 2,3,4 February 2001 — Toss: Gauteng
Umpires: DF Becker & AE Williams
Debuts: GW: None. Gau: NA Fusedale (FC for Gau)
Close of Play: Day 1: GW (1) 50-0 (Tucker 30*, Gidley 18*, 18 overs). Day 2: GW (1) 406 all out.
Result: Match drawn
Man of Match: Martyn Gidley
Points: GW: 7 (bat 4, bowl 3, match 0). Gau: 6 (bat 5, bowl 1, match 0)

Griquas, well-placed on the final morning to press for an outright win, let the Strikers off the hook and the match fizzled out.

Strikers opener Sven Koenig's career-best 155 and a forceful innings by Nic Pothas enabled the visitors to post a big first-day total before centuries by Martyn Gidley and Pieter Koortzen earned the home team a 56-run first innings lead. Collapsing in dramatic fashion on the final morning, the Strikers had Andrew Hall and Marthinus Otto to thank for a splendid recovery.

GAUTENG

FIRST INNINGS	*Runs*	*Mins*	*Balls*	*4*	*6*	*SECOND INNINGS*	*Runs*	*Mins*	*Balls*	*4*	*6*
*AM Bacher c Bossenger b Kruis	4	34	28	-	-	(2) c Louw b Kidwell	25	68	35	4	-
SG Koenig c Bossenger b Abrahim	155	367	263	24	-	(1) c Bossenger b Kidwell	10	40	35	1	-
HA Manack c Bossenger b Kruis	1	31	15	-	-	b Elliott	12	54	40	2	-
JM Otto c Bossenger b Kidwell	1	3	3	-	-	b Kruis	88	247	192	10	-
†N Pothas c Louw b Kidwell	83	109	102	15	-	c Louw b Elliott	0	2	2	-	-
Z de Bruyn c sub (AK Kruger) b Elliott	66	141	108	8	1	c Elliott b Tatton	5	3	3	1	-
AJ Hall c Abrahim b Elliott	2	20	12	-	-	c Bosman b Kruis	92	245	195	11	-
OD Gibson not out	21	32	21	4	-	c Bossenger b Kruis	0	2	1	-	-
MF George not out	0	8	6	-	-	not out	23	57	35	3	-
						TK Mataboge c Louw b Kidwell	2	9	6	-	-
						NA Fusedale not out	5	17	12	-	-
Extras (lb 6, w 4, nb 7)	17					Extras (lb 5, w 2, nb 4)	11				
TOTAL (for 7 wkts dec) (91.5 overs)	**350**					**TOTAL (for 9 wkts) (92 overs)**	**273**				

GRIQUALAND WEST

	Runs	Mins	Balls	4	6
BH Tucker lbw b Gibson	35	91	77	4	-
MI Gidley c sub (WB Masimula) b George	151	414	320	15	4
GD Elliott c Pothas b Fusedale	34	106	86	3	-
LL Bosman c Pothas b George	11	44	35	2	-
PPJ Koortzen c Pothas b Manack	102	235	144	16	-
*†W Bossenger c Hall b Fusedale	12	33	34	-	-
J Louw b Fusedale	10	13	12	1	1
GJ Kruis run out (Gibson/Fusedale)	3	25	21	-	-
ZA Abrahim c Hall b Fusedale	8	21	27	-	1
CR Tatton not out	14	21	17	3	-
EW Kidwell c Hall b Fusedale	6	8	10	1	-
Extras (b 3, lb 10, w 4, nb 3)	20				
TOTAL (130 overs)	**406**				

Bowling	*O*	*M*	*R*	*W*		*O*	*M*	*R*	*W*
GRIQUALAND WEST									
Kruis	21	7	52	2		22	2	77	3
Kidwell	16.5	0	69	2		17	6	43	3
Abrahim	12	0	56	1	(6)	11	4	15	0
Louw	6	0	31	0	(7)	10	1	30	0
Tatton	14	3	57	0	(4)	17	2	53	1
Koortzen	3	1	14	0					
Bosman	4	0	9	0					
Elliott	12	3	40	2	(3)	6	1	18	2
Gidley	3	0	16	0	(5)	9	1	32	0
GAUTENG									
Hall	19	3	62	0					
George	17	2	44	2					
Mataboge	10	3	17	0					
Gibson	19	5	42	1					
Fusedale	48	6	170	5					
de Bruyn	11	1	39	0					
Otto	1	0	3	0					
Manack	5	2	16	1					

Fall of Wickets	Gau	GW	Gau
	1st	1st	2nd
1st	17 (1)	56 (1)	32 (1)
2nd	32 (3)	142 (3)	37 (2)
3rd	33 (4)	168 (4)	54 (3)
4th	151 (5)	331 (2)	54 (5)
5th	290 (6)	361 (6)	59 (6)
6th	312 (7)	373 (7)	229 (4)
7th	339 (2)	377 (5)	229 (8)
8th	-	380 (8)	257 (7)
9th	-	394 (9)	262 (10)
10th	-	406 (11)	-

Gauteng v Griqualand West, Johannesburg, 2-4 March 2001. Griqualand West won by 1 wicket.

GRIQUALAND WEST v KWAZULU-NATAL — SuperSport Series Shield

Played at De Beers Diamond Oval, Kimberley on 16,17,18 March 2001 — Toss: KwaZulu-Natal
Umpires: JD Cloete & S Wadvalla
Debuts: GW: None. KZN: None
Close of Play: Day 1: GW (1) 32-1 (Tucker 15*, Louw 1*, 12 overs). Day 2: KZN (2) 85-0 (Bruyns 31*, Watson 51*, 22.4 overs).
Result: Match drawn
Man of Match: Deon Kruis
Points: GW: 7 (bat 3, bowl 4, match 0). KZN: 7 (bat 3, bowl 4, match 0)

Having achieved the only win in the Shield Series, log-leaders Griquas were favourites to win the Shield unless KwaZulu-Natal defeated them. Giving as good as they got until a final afternoon storm brought the match to a premature end, Wendell Bossenger's team ended their season on an encouraging note.

Just before the match-ending storm arrived, fast bowler Wayne Kidwell dismissed Robbie MacQueen and Andrew Tweedie with successive deliveries and had Gary Gilder dropped in the slips off the hat-trick delivery.

KWAZULU-NATAL

FIRST INNINGS	*Runs*	*Mins*	*Balls*	*4*	*6*	*SECOND INNINGS*	*Runs*	*Mins*	*Balls*	*4*	*6*
ML Bruyns c Bosman b Kruis	5	20	16	1	-	c Gidley b Louw	41	129	88	5	-
DJ Watson lbw b Kruis	9	53	37	1	-	b Abrahim	58	123	100	10	-
A Mall c Bossenger b Louw	40	99	75	6	-	c Bossenger b Abrahim	0	7	2	-	-
*DM Benkenstein c Louw b Kruis	23	108	77	1	-	c Louw b Elliott	25	48	38	5	-
JN Rhodes c Bossenger b Kruis	13	58	37	1	-	c Elliott b Kruis	9	22	18	1	-
†ELR Stewart c Bossenger b Kruis	79	224	176	6	-	c Louw b Kidwell	53	174	102	4	-
WR Wingfield c Kruis b Abrahim	6	28	28	1	-	c Louw b Abrahim	15	39	43	-	-
GH Bodi c Bossenger b Elliott	7	24	19	1	-	not out	74	139	110	10	1
RB MacQueen lbw b Kidwell	42	113	109	4	-	c Bossenger b Kidwell	4	19	12	-	-
GM Gilder b Louw	1	2	4	-	-	(11) not out	2	5	2	-	-
ANW Tweedie not out	20	30	18	3	-	(10) b Kidwell	0	2	1	-	-
Extras (lb 3, w 1, nb 9)	13					Extras (lb 6, w 1, nb 4)	11				
TOTAL (97.5 overs)	**258**					**TOTAL (for 9 wkts) (85.2 overs)**	**292**				

GRIQUALAND WEST					
BH Tucker c and b Tweedie	16	59	44	1	-
MI Gidley b Gilder	15	34	30	2	-
J Louw lbw b Tweedie	13	41	30	2	-
GD Elliott run out (Bodi)	83	209	170	13	1
LL Bosman b Wingfield	19	50	49	4	-
PPJ Koortzen lbw b Wingfield	4	3	5	1	-
*†W Bossenger not out	74	213	153	10	-
AP McLaren lbw b Bodi	27	17	16	6	-
GJ Kruis c Watson b Bodi	5	10	15	1	-
ZA Abrahim c Bodi b Tweedie	1	17	11	-	-
EW Kidwell c Bruyns b Tweedie	9	28	27	-	-
Extras (b 2, lb 1, w 1, nb 10)	14				
TOTAL (90 overs)	**280**				

Bowling	*O*	*M*	*R*	*W*		*O*	*M*	*R*	*W*
GRIQUALAND WEST									
Kruis	28.5	9	50	5		9	2	27	1
Kidwell	14	0	70	1		18	0	70	3
Abrahim	10	0	35	1	(4)	18	2	56	3
Louw	22	6	43	2	(3)	20.2	5	83	1
Elliott	10	2	21	1		8	4	18	1
Gidley	8	1	19	0		1	0	5	0
Koortzen	5	1	17	0					
Bosman					(7)	11	2	27	0
KWAZULU-NATAL									
Gilder	25	9	60	1					
Wingfield	16	2	44	2					
Bodi	21	7	77	2					
Tweedie	18	3	65	4					
MacQueen	7	1	30	0					
Benkenstein	3	2	1	0					

Fall of Wickets	**KZN**	**GW**	**KZN**
	1st	1st	2nd
1st	8 (1)	27 (2)	103 (2)
2nd	37 (2)	39 (1)	103 (1)
3rd	77 (3)	48 (3)	103 (3)
4th	97 (4)	79 (5)	125 (5)
5th	102 (5)	83 (6)	143 (4)
6th	117 (7)	203 (4)	174 (7)
7th	128 (8)	244 (8)	261 (6)
8th	223 (9)	253 (9)	286 (9)
9th	224 (10)	264 (10)	286 (10)
10th	258 (6)	280 (11)	-

KWAZULU-NATAL CRICKET UNION

PO Box 47266, Greyville 4023.
Tel (031) 332 9703. Fax (031) 332 5288.

President: Dr Logan Naidoo
Vice-Presidents: Dr R Govender and Dr C van der Merwe
Chief Executive: Cassim Docrat
Manager, professional cricket: Phil Russell
Manager, amateur cricket: Jay Naidoo
Treasurer: Sathie Govender
Senior coach: Eldine Baptiste.
2001/02 contracted players: Doug Watson, Ashraf Mall, Jon Kent, Ahmed Amla, Hashim Amla, Dale Benkenstein, Errol Stewart, Goolam Bodi, Wade Wingfield, Gary Gilder, Duncan Brown, Rivash Gobind, Ross Veenstra. **UCB contracted players:** Shaun Pollock, Lance Klusener, Jonty Rhodes.

REVIEW OF THE SEASON 2000/01

Ken Borland

SUPERSPORT SERIES: P4 W0 L1 D3 (fifth in group)
SUPERSPORT SHIELD: P4 W0 L0 D4 (second)
CAPTAIN: DM Benkenstein (8)
STANDARD BANK CUP: P15 W10 L4 NR1 (champions)

Despite the embarrassment of being relegated to the plate section of the first class competition, KwaZulu-Natal still came out of the season with smiling faces thanks to their efforts in the limited overs game, where they mustered up their first day/night trophy in four seasons and performed with credit in the Champions Cup tournament in Australia.

After losing their first two Standard Bank Cup matches, to supposed minnows Griquas and Easterns, Natal embarked on a tremendous run of wins, losing only to eventual finalists Northerns in their last eight league matches.

Dale Benkenstein's team were flat and uninspiring in the SuperSport Series but the remarkable limited overs form of players like Watson, the eventual Player of the Series, Kent, Wingfield, Mall and Bodi meant they performed with zest under lights.

A prolonged semifinal tussle with Eastern Province, the UCB's rules for rain-delayed or abandoned matches being inadequate, saw Natal eventually emerge victorious at Kingsmead, although the visitors were clearly on top when the third leg was first played.

The final at Kingsmead two days later was an epic, white-knuckle affair, Natal's ever-reliable stalwart wicketkeeper, Errol Stewart, eventually seeing them home, Wingfield, Mall, Kent and Baptiste capping memorable day/night campaigns with vintage contributions.

Having already won a holiday in Mauritius for winning the SuperSport Challenge at the start of the season, Natal then went to Perth to represent South Africa in the inaugural

CELEBRATION TIME . . . the KwaZulu-Natal Dolphins players get together and show their joy after winning the Standard Bank Cup final against Northerns at Kingsmead *Picture: Duif du Toit, TOUCHLINE PHOTO*

Champions Cup. They went on to reach the final, where they fell to hosts Western Australia, who were better suited to the renowned WACA pitch.

Natal's SuperSport Series woes were due to the persistent problem of not having a genuine strike bowler to take the new ball and, more disappointingly, the batsmen's failure to live up to expectations. Despite having one of the strongest, deepest batting orders in the country, only one player, Kent, averaged over 40. By their high standards, Bruyns, Benkenstein, Watson and Stewart all had bad first-class seasons, which did not make it any easier for the bowlers, who were too often looking to defend small totals.

They began their SuperSport Series campaign in Benoni against Easterns and the surprise packages of the season had them under the whip throughout, only Bodi's stunning 81-ball century saving some face. They did not lose another first-class game but if they are honest in their appraisal of the season, they will concede that the opposition mostly had the upper hand in the other matches.

Having their internationals available against Western Province at Newlands was cold comfort for Natal as they battled to a draw and lost the bonus points race 6-4. They were then thoroughly outplayed by Eastern Province at home, with Kent playing the innings of his life to save the match.

Needing an outright win against Border at Kingsmead to have any chance of advancing to the Super Eights, Benkenstein set the pace on the first day with his best innings of the season but Natal were unable to bowl Border out cheaply enough and the weather intervened.

Natal went into the SuperSport Shield as the bottom-ranked team, so poor was their haul of bonus, points but it was a source of great relief that they avoided finishing in that position, leaving the dreadful title of the country's worst first-class team to Gauteng.

Baptiste is taking over as coach for 2001/02, although Phil Russell's influence will not be far removed, the former groundsman and Derbyshire stalwart being the manager of professional cricket.

There were several positives Natal could take from the season, the most obvious of which were the brilliant showings of the young all-rounders, Kent and Bodi, who thoroughly deserved their call-ups to the South Africa A team.

Coming into the season, Bodi was under pressure to keep his place in the side but the Indian-born wrist-spinner and dashing left-handed batsman emerged as one of the hottest properties in domestic cricket, while Kent is clearly set for greater things now that his bowling (he broke the Natal record for the most wickets in a day/night season) is catching up with his elegant batting skills.

Wingfield and Mall, both marvellously clean strikers of the ball, look top prospects and will be aiming to carry their wonderful limited-overs form into the first-class arena.

But there is no substitute for a deadly fast bowler and Natal's search for one continues. With Ross Veenstra injured for most of the season, Shaun Adam not coming through and Gary Gilder too inconsistent, Natal were left with meagre new-ball options.

Natal will be without two stalwart batsmen this season, Bruyns having left for Border, while Andrew Hudson, who had given so much pleasure over the years, sadly just drifted into retirement.

KWAZULU-NATAL CRICKET UNION

PROVINCIAL RECORDS

Honours:
Currie/Castle Cup/SuperSport Series (23): 1910/11, 1912/13, 1921/22 (shared), 1933/34, 1936/37, 1937/38 (shared), 1946/47, 1947/48, 1951/52, 1954/55, 1959/60, 1960/61, 1962/63, 1963/64, 1965/66 (shared), 1966/67, 1967/68, 1973/74, 1975/76, 1976/77, 1980/81, 1994/95, 1996/97
B&H Series (1): 1983/84
Gillette/Nissan Shield: (3) 1974/75, 1976/77, 1986/87
Standard Bank Cup (2): 1996/97, 2000/01

Highest innings totals:

For:	664-6*	v Western Province (Durban)	1936/37
Against:	608-6*	by Transvaal (Johannesburg) (FC)	1939/40
	552	by Orange Free State (Bloemfontein) (CC)	1926/27

Lowest innings totals:

For:	45	v Australian Imperial Forces (Pietermaritzburg) (FC)	1919/20
	52	v Transvaal (Johannesburg) (CC)	1955/56
Against:	16 and 18	by Border (East London)	1959/60

Highest individual innings:

For:	304*	AW Nourse	v Transvaal (Johannesburg) (FC)	1919/20
	265*	IJ Siedle	v Orange Free State (Durban) (CC)	1929/30
Against:	306*	EAB Rowan	for Transvaal (Johannesburg) (FC)	1939/40
	229	GFJ Liebenberg	for Free State (Bloemfontein) (CC)	1995/96

Most runs in a season:

SS				All FC			
1089	(Avg 77.78)	BA Richards	1971/72	1147	(Avg 67.47)	BA Richards	1972/73

Most runs in a career:

SS				All FC			
7551	(Avg 60.40)	BA Richards	1965-82	8321	(Avg 59.43)	BA Richards	1964-82

Most 100s in a career:

SS			All FC		
26	BA Richards	1965-82	27	BA Richards	1964-82

Best bowling in an innings:

For:	9-88	VI Smith	v Border (Pietermaritzburg)	1946/47
Against:	9-32	JM Gregory	for Australian Imperial Forces (Durban) (FC)	1919/20
	9-52	MH Bowditch	for Western Province (Cape Town) (CC)	1965/66

Best bowling in a match:

For:	14-111	VAP van der Bijl	v Northern Transvaal (Pretoria)	1981/82
Against:	14-86	JM Gregory	for Australian Imperial Forces (Durban) (FC)	1919/20
	14-113	DL Hobson	for Western Province (Cape Town) (CC)	1975/76

Most wickets in a season:

SS				All FC			
59	(Avg 15.86)	MJ Procter	1976/77	59	(Avg 15.86)	MJ Procter	1976/77

Most wickets in a career:

SS				All FC			
531	(Avg 16.34)	VAP van der Bijl	1968-81	569	(Avg 16.09)	VAP van der Bijl	1968-81

Most dismissals (wicketkeepers) in an innings:

7	(ct 7,st 0)	MS Smith	v Border (East London)	1959/60

Most dismissals (wicketkeepers) in a match:

9	(ct 8,st 1)	D Gamsy	v Transvaal (Johannesburg)	1959/60
9	(ct 7,st 2)	D Gamsy	v Orange Free State (Pietermaritzburg)	1960/61
9	(ct 7,st 2)	D Gamsy	v North-Eastern Transvaal (Pretoria)	1967/68
9	(ct 9,st 0)	ML Bruyns	v Boland (Paarl)	1995/96

Most dismissals (wicketkeepers) in a season:

SS				All FC			
32	(ct 30,st 2)	KA Forde	1996/97	41	(ct 39,st 2)	KA Forde	1996/97

Most dismissals (wicketkeepers) in a career:

SS				All FC			
286	(ct 276,st 10)	AJS Smith	1972-83	304	(ct 293,st 11)	AJS Smith	1972-83

KWAZULU-NATAL CRICKET UNION

Most catches (fielders) in an innings:

5	AD Nourse	v Border (Durban) (CC)	1933/34
5	DN Crookes	v Northamptonshire (Durban) (FC)	1991/92

Most catches (fielders) in a match:

6	AD Nourse	v Border (Durban)	1933/34
6	AC Hudson	v Orange Free State (Bloemfontein)	1987/88
6	SM Pollock	v Boland (Durban)	1999/00

Most catches (fielders) in a season:

SS			All FC		
14	DD Dyer	1973/74	15	DD Dyer 1973/74; NC Johnson	1996/97

Most catches (fielders) in a career:

SS			All FC		
72	D Bestall	1972-87	79	D Bestall	1972-87

Most appearances:

SS			All FC		
101	VAP van der Bijl	1968-81	109	VAP van der Bijl	1968-81

Most captaincies:

SS			All FC		
54	DJ McGlew	1951-66	75	DJ McGlew	1951-66

RECORD WICKET PARTNERSHIPS

1st	424	IJ Siedle and JFW Nicolson v Orange Free State (Bloemfontein) (The South African record for this wicket)	1926/27
2nd	316	ML Bruyns and ELR Stewart v Boland (Durban)	1998/99
3rd	235	ELR Stewart and JN Rhodes v Eastern Province (Port Elizabeth)	1996/97
4th	222*	RM Bentley and KM Curran v Orange Free State (Bloemfontein)	1988/89
5th	291	AW Nourse and JM Blanckenberg v Western Province (Johannesburg)	1923/24
6th	233	AJS Smith and PH Williams v Northern Transvaal (Pretoria)	1979/80
7th	240	AD Nourse and LW Payn v Transvaal (Johannesburg)	1936/37
8th	174	OC Dawson and LA Markham v Orange Free State (Durban)	1947/48
9th	217	AW Nourse and BC Cooley v Western Province (Johannesburg) (The SuperSport Series, but not South African, record for this wicket)	1906/07
10th	87	PL Symcox and SM Pollock v Western Province (Cape Town)	1994/95

PERFORMANCES AGAINST OTHER TEAMS

HIGHEST AND LOWEST TOTALS

Opponents	Highest Total For		Lowest Total For	
Boland	450-8*	1994/95	187	1993/94
Border	488	1936/37	90	1959/60
Eastern Province	587 (FC)	1939/40	64	1971/72
	533 (CC)	1962/63		
Easterns	298	2000/01	123	2000/01
Free State	554-5*	1998/99	106	1997/98
Gauteng	562	1936/37	52	1955/56
Griqualand West	499-2*	1934/35	106 (FC)	1889/90
			108 (CC)	1897/98
Northerns	548-6*	1982/83	76	1960/61
North West	504-3*	1999/00	-	
Western Province	664-6*	1936/37	76	1971/72
			76	1972/73

BEST INDIVIDUAL PERFORMANCES

Opponents	Highest score	Best bowling (innings)	Best bowling (match) (8+)
Boland	177 ELR Stewart, 1998/99	6-38 RE Veenstra,1995/96	10-90 L Klusener, 1998/99
Border	213* (FC) DJ McGlew,1957/58	9-88 VI Smith, 1946/47	12-194 VI Smith,1946/47
	162* (CC) MK Elgie, 1959/60		
Eastern Province	208 (FC) WW Wade,1939/40	7-35 (FC) GA Kempis, 1889/90	14-153 VI Smith,1955/56
	190 (CC) HF Wade, 1936/37	7-41 (CC) VI Smith, 1947/48	
Easterns	104 GH Bodi, 2000/01	6-77 JC Kent, 2000/01	9-152 JC Kent, 2000/01

KWAZULU-NATAL CRICKET UNION

Free State	265*	IJ Siedle, 1929/30	8-40	SV Samuelson,1910/11	13-147	SV Samuelson,1910/11
Gauteng	304*	(FC) AW Nourse,1919/20	8-20	JL Cox, 1910/11	11-99	KM Curran, 1988/89
	260*	(CC) AD Nourse,1936/37				
Griqualand West	214*	AD Nourse, 1947/48	7-10	AC King, 1906/07	13-111	SV Samuelson, 1910/11
Northerns	150*	AJS Smith,1979/80	8-47	VAP van der Bijl,1981/82	14-111	VAP van der Bijl,1981/82
North West	220	DJ Watson, 1999/00	5-95	RE Veenstra, 1999/00	-	
Western Province	240	AD Nourse, 1936/37	8-34	L Klusener, 1995/96	13-53	VAP van der Bijl,1971/72

KWAZULU-NATAL SUPERSPORT SERIES AVERAGES 2000/01

Batting & Fielding

Name	M	Inns	NO	Runs	HS	Avg	100	50	Ct	St
JC Kent	6	12	3	434	178*	48.22	1	2	9	0
GH Bodi	8	12	2	332	104	33.20	1	2	2	0
ELR Stewart	8	14	3	359	79	32.63	0	2	24	1
DJ Watson	8	16	2	451	64*	32.21	0	4	6	0
JN Rhodes	3	5	0	159	76	31.80	0	1	1	0
DM Benkenstein	8	15	2	399	86	30.69	0	2	4	0
ML Bruyns	8	16	1	459	102*	30.60	1	2	9	0
RE Veenstra	1	2	0	60	38	30.00	0	0	0	0
AM Amla	3	6	0	161	69	26.83	0	2	1	0
A Mall	5	9	0	236	64	26.22	0	1	3	0
EAE Baptiste	6	8	2	157	57	26.16	0	1	6	0
RB MacQueen	2	3	0	77	42	25.66	0	0	1	0
WR Wingfield	5	9	3	153	89*	25.50	0	1	1	0
AC Hudson	2	4	0	97	38	24.25	0	0	2	0
L Klusener	1	1	0	16	16	16.00	0	0	0	0
ANW Tweedie	2	3	1	20	20*	10.00	0	0	1	0
GM Gilder	6	7	2	39	14	7.80	0	0	2	0
JE Bastow	5	6	2	19	6	4.75	0	0	2	0
SM Pollock	1	1	0	0	0	0.00	0	0	1	0
Totals	88	149	23	3628	178*		3	20	75	1
			Extras	291				subs		
			Total	3919		31.10			75	

Bowling

Name	Overs	Mdns	Runs	Wkts	Avg	BB	5I	10M
ANW Tweedie	30	4	109	5	21.80	4-65	0	0
JC Kent	161	33	507	21	24.14	6-77	1	0
GH Bodi	225.3	45	697	27	25.81	6-63	1	0
JE Bastow	145.1	43	364	14	26.00	4-46	0	0
L Klusener	50.4	11	156	5	31.20	4-111	0	0
WR Wingfield	62.2	9	188	6	31.33	2-36	0	0
DM Benkenstein	42	15	104	3	34.66	1-19	0	0
EAE Baptiste	117	39	241	6	40.16	1-23	0	0
SM Pollock	50	20	90	2	45.00	2-65	0	0
GM Gilder	142	33	472	10	47.20	2-48	0	0
ML Bruyns	22	3	83	1	83.00	1-47	0	0
RE Veenstra	40	9	92	1	92.00	1-55	0	0
RB MacQueen	37	12	125	1	125.00	1-80	0	0
Totals	1124.4	276	3228	102		6-63	2	0
		b & lb	95	1	run outs			
		Total	3323	103	32.26			

MATCH REPORTS AND SCORECARDS

Easterns v KwaZulu-Natal, Benoni, 27-30 October 2000. Easterns won by 108 runs.
Western Province v KwaZulu-Natal, Cape Town, 10-13 November 2000. Match drawn.

KWAZULU-NATAL v EASTERN PROVINCE — SuperSport Series Pool B

Played at Kingsmead, Durban on 1,2,3,4 December 2000 — Toss: KwaZulu-Natal
Umpires: CJ Mitchley & AG O'Connor
Debuts: KZN: None. EP: None
Close of Play: Day 1: EP (1) 386-9 (Murray 24*, Ngam 7*, 104 overs). Day 2: KZN (1) 202-8 (Stewart 19*, Gilder 4*, 84.4 overs). Day 3: KZN (2) 185-5 (Kent 65*, Stewart 4*, 77 overs).
Result: Match drawn
Man of Match: Jon Kent
Points: KZN: 6 (bat 2, bowl 4, match 0). EP: 9 (bat 5, bowl 4, match 0)

KwaZulu-Natal were in all sorts of trouble for the first three days, before the 21-year-old Kent played the innings of his life to save the home team after they had been forced to follow on.

Natal's wayward bowlers took a battering on the first day, Benfield leading the way with a highly aggressive innings, while Kemp announced himself as a batsman of quality with a hard-hit half-century before falling to a brilliant reflex catch by Baptiste at mid-off. Natal's top-order batsmen all got starts in their first innings but gave their wickets away cheaply and were back in again for 77 overs before the close of the third day. Kent, who had come in with Natal in early trouble, stayed at the crease for nearly eight hours, his astonishing, career-best effort saving the match and leaving EP under some pressure as they were due to bat out 36 overs before the close.

EASTERN PROVINCE

FIRST INNINGS	*Runs*	*Mins*	*Balls*	*4*	*6*	*SECOND INNINGS*	*Runs*	*Mins*	*Balls*	*4*	*6*
MR Benfield c Watson b Benkenstein	93	169	117	16	1	(2) lbw b Bastow	21	22	15	3	1
*CC Bradfield c Stewart b Gilder	0	5	2	-	-	(1) c Benkenstein b Gilder	24	40	27	4	-
JDC Bryant c Mall b Kent	27	62	49	6	-	(4) not out	1	15	6	-	-
DJ Callaghan b Bodi	42	135	108	5	-						
JM Kemp c Baptiste b Gilder	65	110	111	8	2						
MW Creed c Watson b Bastow	32	121	87	2	1						
RJ Peterson c Kent b Baptiste	28	87	61	2	-	(3) c Stewart b Bastow	0	1	1	-	-
S Abrahams c Bodi b Kent	15	42	23	3	-						
†DW Murray c Watson b Bastow	48	89	64	7	1						
M Hayward c Watson b Bodi	26	32	29	4	-						
M Ngam not out	18	54	40	2	-						
Extras (b 8, lb 6, w 2, nb 11)	27					Extras (w 1)	1				
TOTAL (113.2 overs)	**421**					**TOTAL (for 3 wkts) (8.1 overs)**	**47**				

KWAZULU-NATAL

	Runs	Mins	Balls	4	6		Runs	Mins	Balls	4	6
ML Bruyns c Murray b Hayward	43	116	91	7	-	c Murray b Hayward	22	96	73	2	-
DJ Watson c Murray b Hayward	19	77	63	2	-	c Murray b Kemp	5	37	30	1	-
A Mall c Bradfield b Peterson	30	161	125	3	-	b Peterson	10	38	29	2	-
JC Kent c Bradfield b Peterson	17	70	55	3	-	not out	178	470	359	26	-
*DM Benkenstein c Benfield b Ngam	11	44	50	1	-	run out (Callaghan/Abrahams)	25	74	71	4	-
JN Rhodes c Creed b Kemp	19	38	32	-	1	c Murray b Kemp	42	73	75	4	-
†ELR Stewart not out	41	149	109	5	-	c Murray b Kemp	26	76	62	3	-
GH Bodi c Abrahams b Peterson	7	4	4	1	-	run out (Bradfield)	17	51	45	3	-
EAE Baptiste c Murray b Ngam	6	39	30	1	-	lbw b Kemp	22	97	65	2	-
GM Gilder c Murray b Hayward	14	32	21	3	-	b Hayward	1	2	3	-	-
JE Bastow c Bradfield b Peterson	6	36	27	1	-	lbw b Kemp	5	56	32	1	-
Extras (b 2, lb 9, w 4, nb 17)	32					Extras (b 1, lb 12, w 11, nb 5)	29				
TOTAL (98.3 overs)	**245**					**TOTAL (139.5 overs)**	**382**				

Bowling	*O*	*M*	*R*	*W*		*O*	*M*	*R*	*W*
KWAZULU-NATAL									
Bastow	20.2	5	68	2	(2)	4	0	23	2
Gilder	17	5	64	2	(1)	4.1	0	24	1
Baptiste	17	6	39	1					
Kent	20	4	84	2					
Bodi	24	0	101	2					
Benkenstein	10	3	27	1					
Bruyns	5	1	24	0					
EASTERN PROVINCE									
Hayward	23	1	70	3	(5)	20	3	79	2
Ngam	26	7	70	2	(1)	23	6	61	0
Kemp	16	5	26	1	(2)	35	13	69	5
Peterson	25.3	5	65	4		30	6	90	1
Abrahams	8	6	3	0	(6)	20	3	43	0
Creed					(3)	8	2	16	0
Callaghan						3.5	1	11	0

Fall of Wickets	**EP**	**KZN**	**KZN**	**EP**
	1st	1st	2nd	2nd
1st	2 (2)	54 (2)	14 (2)	35 (2)
2nd	62 (3)	81 (1)	33 (3)	35 (3)
3rd	165 (1)	110 (4)	50 (1)	47 (1)
4th	192 (4)	142 (5)	101 (5)	-
5th	259 (5)	144 (3)	173 (6)	-
6th	290 (6)	170 (6)	230 (7)	-
7th	327 (7)	177 (8)	266 (8)	-
8th	327 (8)	197 (9)	338 (9)	-
9th	366 (10)	225 (10)	339 (10)	-
10th	421 (9)	245 (11)	382 (11)	-

KWAZULU-NATAL v BORDER — SuperSport Series Pool B

Played at Kingsmead, Durban on 8,9,10,11 (no play) December 2000 — Toss: Border
Umpires: JD Cloete & ST Jivan
Debuts: KZN: None. Bdr: None
Close of Play: Day 1: KZN (1) 231-7 (Wingfield 25*, Baptiste 1*, 92 overs). Day 2: Bdr (1) 126-4 (Strydom 5*, Gamiet 0*, 40 overs). Day 3: KZN (2) 117-5 (Benkenstein 56*, Stewart 7*, 43.3 overs).
Result: Match drawn
Man of Match: Dale Benkenstein & Pieter Strydom
Points: KZN: 7 (bat 3, bowl 4, match 0). Bdr: 7 (bat 4, bowl 3, match 0)

With KwaZulu-Natal needing a win to qualify for the Super Eights, the weather intervened on all four days, leaving them struggling at the end with a lead of 49 runs and five second-innings wickets intact. Having been sent in to bat, captain Benkenstein played a fine innings to enable the home side to declare but their quest for an early breakthrough failed as the Border top-order of Sugden, Botha and Pope got the visitors off to a solid start, and then Strydom combined well with the lower-order to give Border a handy lead on the third day. Bodi, the wrist-spinner, was the last bowler used by Benkenstein but he was also the most effective, claiming the key wicket of the Border captain.

Kent, the hero of the previous weekend, made a pair, bowled by Drakes in both innings.

KWAZULU-NATAL

FIRST INNINGS	*Runs*	*Mins*	*Balls*	*4*	*6*	*SECOND INNINGS*	*Runs*	*Mins*	*Balls*	*4*	*6*
ML Bruyns c Mitchell b Graham	12	117	97	-	-	c Graham b Drakes	0	9	8	-	-
DJ Watson c Sugden b Graham	14	139	98	-	-	c Pope b Strydom	24	113	73	2	-
A Mall c Wiblin b Strydom	36	87	61	4	-	c Mitchell b Drakes	17	41	29	-	-
JC Kent b Drakes	0	11	5	-	-	b Drakes	0	9	5	-	-
*DM Benkenstein b Drakes	86	176	146	8	1	not out	56	109	90	3	2
†ELR Stewart c Gamiet b Love	29	96	89	4	-	(7) not out	7	34	33	1	-
WR Wingfield not out	29	84	55	2	-	(6) c Botha b Strydom	5	24	27	1	-
GH Bodi c Love b Botha	1	21	17	-	-						
EAE Baptiste not out	19	36	28	2	-						
GM Gilder											
JE Bastow											
Extras (b 3, lb 9, nb 15)	27					Extras (b 3, lb 1, nb 4)	8				
TOTAL (for 7 wkts dec) (97.2 overs)	**253**					**TOTAL (for 5 wkts) (43.3 overs)**	**117**				

BORDER

	Runs	*Mins*	*Balls*	*4*	*6*
CB Sugden c Stewart b Kent	34	138	82	3	2
PJ Botha c Stewart b Kent	39	113	76	6	-
SC Pope c Mall b Wingfield	25	73	64	4	-
W Wiblin c Stewart b Bastow	7	31	19	1	-
*PC Strydom c Kent b Bodi	80	158	127	11	-
LL Gamiet c Kent b Baptiste	1	15	16	-	-
†I Mitchell b Bastow	31	161	115	1	-
DL Makalima b Bodi	28	94	64	4	-
VC Drakes c Bastow b Bodi	27	41	32	4	-
GT Love c Bruyns b Bodi	14	28	21	3	-
L Graham not out	2	12	11	-	-
Extras (lb 14, w 1, nb 18)	33				
TOTAL (101.3 overs)	**321**				

Bowling	*O*	*M*	*R*	*W*		*O*	*M*	*R*	*W*	*Fall of Wickets*	KZN	Bdr	KZN
BORDER											1st	1st	2nd
Drakes	27	6	71	2		10	4	20	3	1st	31 (1)	80 (2)	1 (1)
Botha	21.2	8	50	1		7	1	18	0	2nd	45 (2)	97 (1)	26 (3)
Pope	3	2	8	0						3rd	52 (4)	117 (4)	29 (4)
Love	18	3	51	1		9.3	2	31	0	4th	87 (3)	126 (3)	79 (2)
Graham	20	5	41	2	(3)	6	0	22	0	5th	194 (6)	128 (6)	96 (6)
Strydom	8	1	20	1	(5)	11	2	22	2	6th	210 (5)	239 (5)	-
KWAZULU-NATAL										7th	222 (8)	257 (7)	-
Bastow	26	7	59	2						8th	-	302 (9)	-
Gilder	21	0	104	0						9th	-	304 (8)	-
Kent	19	5	55	2						10th	-	321 (10)	-
Baptiste	12	5	23	1									
Wingfield	9	2	29	1									
Bodi	14.3	3	37	4									

KWAZULU-NATAL v GRIQUALAND WEST — SuperSport Series Shield

Played at Kingsmead, Durban on 12,13,14 January 2001 — Toss: KwaZulu-Natal
Umpires: JD Cloete & KH Hurter
Debuts: KZN: None. GW: BH Tucker (FC for GW)
Close of Play: Day 1: KZN (1) 88-0 (Bruyns 33*, Watson 46*, 22 overs). Day 2: GW (2) 167-5 (Bossenger 24*, Louw 14*, 63 overs).
Result: Match drawn
Man of Match: Deon Kruis
Points: KZN: 6 (bat 2, bowl 4, match 0). GW: 7 (bat 3, bowl 4, match 0)
Note: Kruis took a hat-trick in Kwa Zulu-Natal's 1st innings. His victims were Bruyns, Benkenstein and Wingfield.

KwaZulu-Natal dominated a hot first day, although when Gidley and Bosman were together in their aggressive 112-run third-wicket partnership, the home side's bowlers were looking hard-pressed. That was until Bastow, who had picked up the first two wickets, had the in-form Bosman caught behind and spinner Bodi claimed three middle-order wickets to have the visitors all out in the hour after tea.

Watson and Bruyns gave Natal the best of starts but Watson's run-out sparked a collapse as the home side lost four wickets in four balls, Kruis taking a hat-trick as he dismissed Bruyns, Benkenstein and Wingfield after Louw had trapped Amla lbw with the last ball of the previous over. Kent got his head down and ground out an invaluable half-century with fine support from Bodi, before Griquas collapsed due to a series of injudicious strokes, leaving Natal to score 261 in 92 overs on a true pitch. Skipper Benkenstein was well on the way to taking his team to victory, after Amla had returned to form, when the rain swept in shortly after tea, with Natal requiring a further 63 runs in 36 overs.

GRIQUALAND WEST

FIRST INNINGS	*Runs*	*Mins*	*Balls*	*4*	*6*	*SECOND INNINGS*	*Runs*	*Mins*	*Balls*	*4*	*6*
BH Tucker lbw b Bastow	13	33	31	2	-	lbw b Bodi	47	148	125	6	-
MI Gidley c Stewart b Baptiste	60	202	135	7	-	c Stewart b Bastow	12	45	30	2	-
GD Elliott b Bastow	1	20	14	-	-	c Baptiste b Kent	29	118	98	4	-
LL Bosman c Stewart b Bastow	71	108	79	9	3	b Bodi	16	24	25	2	1
PPJ Koortzen c Stewart b Bodi	32	66	53	6	-	lbw b Bodi	13	25	27	3	-
*†W Bossenger c Gilder b Bodi	45	130	101	8	-	c Stewart b Gilder	24	68	46	3	-
J Louw c Kent b Bodi	0	7	5	-	-	c Baptiste b Kent	50	116	94	8	1
GJ Kruis c Stewart b Kent	2	12	12	-	-	c Bruyns b Gilder	0	13	9	-	-
ZA Abrahim c Stewart b Bastow	8	37	31	-	1	c Amla b Kent	18	44	26	3	-
CR Tatton lbw b Gilder	14	77	52	2	-	c Stewart b Bodi	1	7	7	-	-
EW Kidwell not out	11	37	26	1	-	not out	0	3	0	-	-
Extras (b 1, lb 8, w 1, nb 12)	22					Extras (b 4, lb 2, nb 6)	12				
TOTAL (87.5 overs)	**279**					**TOTAL (80.1 overs)**	**222**				

KWAZULU-NATAL											
ML Bruyns lbw b Kruis	52	135	102	9	-	c Elliott b Louw	20	42	37	3	-
DJ Watson run out (Tucker/Bossenger)	51	93	75	8	-	c Kidwell b Gidley	33	96	73	2	-
AM Amla lbw b Louw	9	37	38	1	-	lbw b Louw	69	140	115	10	-
JC Kent c Bossenger b Kidwell	58	122	95	9	-	c Bossenger b Kruis	19	42	41	-	1
*DM Benkenstein b Kruis	0	2	1	-	-	not out	42	81	53	2	3
WR Wingfield lbw b Kruis	0	1	1	-	-	not out	6	38	25	-	-
†ELR Stewart c Abrahim b Kidwell	5	24	24	-	-						
GH Bodi c Bossenger b Kidwell	26	76	47	3	-						
EAE Baptiste c Bossenger b Kidwell	14	42	24	3	-						
GM Gilder b Kruis	5	12	9	1	-						
JE Bastow not out	3	19	16	-	-						
Extras (nb 18)	18					Extras (nb 9)	9				
TOTAL (69 overs)	**241**					**TOTAL (for 4 wkts) (56 overs)**	**198**				

Bowling	*O*	*M*	*R*	*W*		*O*	*M*	*R*	*W*
KWAZULU-NATAL									
Bastow	22	6	46	4		15	5	35	1
Gilder	14.5	1	47	1		16	4	48	2
Kent	13	3	44	1	(5)	12.1	2	34	3
Wingfield	10	1	40	0					
Bodi	19	4	60	3	(3)	30	9	88	4
Benkenstein	2	0	7	0					
Baptiste	7	1	26	1	(4)	6	3	7	0
Bruyns					(6)	1	0	4	0
GRIQUALAND WEST									
Kruis	20	6	57	4		18	4	51	1
Kidwell	18	4	71	4		5.4	0	23	0
Abrahim	12	1	63	0					
Louw	11	1	32	1	(3)	12.2	1	49	2
Elliott	5	2	11	0					
Tatton	3	2	7	0	(5)	8	1	27	0
Gidley					(4)	12	1	48	1

Fall of Wickets	**GW**	**KZN**	**GW**	**KZN**
	1st	1st	2nd	2nd
1st	23 (1)	96 (2)	30 (2)	36 (1)
2nd	35 (3)	122 (3)	93 (1)	76 (2)
3rd	147 (4)	122 (1)	113 (3)	109 (4)
4th	172 (2)	122 (5)	114 (4)	164 (3)
5th	199 (5)	122 (6)	137 (5)	-
6th	199 (7)	142 (7)	167 (6)	-
7th	206 (8)	214 (8)	171 (8)	-
8th	228 (9)	215 (4)	220 (9)	-
9th	260 (6)	221 (10)	222 (10)	-
10th	279 (10)	241 (9)	222 (7)	-

Gauteng v KwaZulu-Natal, Johannesburg, 26-28 January 2001. Match drawn.

KWAZULU-NATAL v GAUTENG — SuperSport Series Shield

Played at Kingsmead, Durban on 9,10,11 March 2001 — Toss: KwaZulu-Natal
Umpires: DF Becker & AE Williams
Debuts: KZN: ANW Tweedie (FC for KZN). Gau: None
Close of Play: Day 1: KZN (1) 250-6 (Rhodes 73*, Wingfield 25*, 63.1 overs). Day 2: Gau (1) 174-3 (Cook 55*, Pothas 6*, 61 overs).
Result: Match drawn
Man of Match: Goolam Bodi
Points: KZN: 8 (bat 4, bowl 4, match 0). Gau: 6 (bat 3, bowl 3, match 0)

KwaZulu-Natal produced some top-class cricket as they outplayed a new-look Gauteng team who enjoyed precious few moments of ascendancy in the last match of their dismal season. Crucially, 170 minutes were lost on the first day, the match not starting before 1pm due to the umpires believing the field was too wet for play to be safe, although the Natalians played a game of soccer in mid-morning to show there was no danger of anyone turning an ankle.

Gauteng managed to knock over six KwaZulu-Natal batsmen on the first day, most of the damage being self-inflicted. Rhodes batted beautifully through to the second day and Wingfield struck the ball superbly. Bacher, Koenig and Cook batted solidly for Gauteng but things fell apart after Wingfield made the breakthrough early on the final day, wrist-spinner Bodi coming away with career-best figures as reward for his tight, probing spell.

Bruyns and Watson batted well to set up a declaration that left Gauteng with a "target" of 270 in 42 overs.

KWAZULU-NATAL CRICKET UNION

KWAZULU-NATAL

FIRST INNINGS	*Runs*	*Mins*	*Balls*	*4*	*6*	*SECOND INNINGS*	*Runs*	*Mins*	*Balls*	*4*	*6*
ML Bruyns run out (Bacher)	31	77	51	5	-	not out	102	143	120	16	1
DJ Watson lbw b Mafa	3	26	15	-	-	not out	64	143	110	7	2
A Mall run out (Bacher)	64	131	98	10	-						
*DM Benkenstein c Horan b Mafa	20	52	36	3	-						
JN Rhodes c Pothas b de Bruyn	76	134	101	9	-						
†ELR Stewart c Pothas b de Bruyn	10	27	18	1	-						
GH Bodi c Horan b Fusedale	12	33	20	2	-						
WR Wingfield not out	89	206	181	16	-						
RB MacQueen b Fusedale	31	116	89	6	-						
GM Gilder b Fusedale	9	12	10	1	-						
ANW Tweedie c Herbst b Fusedale	0	6	3	-	-						
Extras (b 4, lb 3, w 1, nb 7)	15					Extras (b 2, nb 2)	4				
TOTAL (102.3 overs)	**360**					**TOTAL (for 0 wkts dec) (38 overs)**	**170**				

GAUTENG

	Runs	*Mins*	*Balls*	*4*	*6*		*Runs*	*Mins*	*Balls*	*4*	*6*
*AM Bacher c Wingfield b Bodi	26	65	56	4	-	not out	27	79	78	2	1
SG Koenig c Rhodes b Bodi	76	178	145	6	4	c and b Gilder	10	39	19	1	-
SC Cook lbw b Wingfield	55	150	155	9	-	not out	19	38	36	2	-
Z de Bruyn c Bruyns b MacQueen	0	7	4	-	-						
†N Pothas c Bruyns b Bodi	27	86	75	2	-						
G Toyana c MacQueen b Gilder	2	14	8	-	-						
F Herbst not out	35	100	92	3	-						
JM Otto lbw b Tweedie	1	4	7	-	-						
BP Horan lbw b Bodi	23	44	48	5	-						
NA Fusedale b Bodi	1	12	13	-	-						
JT Mafa c Stewart b Bodi	0	1	1	-	-						
Extras (b 4, lb 1, nb 10)	15					Extras (nb 1)	1				
TOTAL (99 overs)	**261**					**TOTAL (for 1 wkt) (22 overs)**	**57**				

Bowling	*O*	*M*	*R*	*W*		*O*	*M*	*R*	*W*
GAUTENG									
Mafa	24	5	119	2		7	0	28	0
Horan	19	3	55	0		5	3	10	0
Herbst	9	2	27	0	(6)	6	1	19	0
de Bruyn	20	3	74	2		2	0	23	0
Fusedale	30.3	8	78	4	(3)	14	1	59	0
Toyana					(5)	4	0	29	0
KWAZULU-NATAL									
Gilder	16	8	35	1		8	2	21	1
Wingfield	12	1	34	1		2	0	5	0
Bodi	34	8	63	6		7	2	16	0
Tweedie	12	1	44	1					
MacQueen	25	10	80	1	(4)	5	1	15	0

Fall of Wickets	**KZN** 1st	**Gau** 1st	**KZN** 2nd	**Gau** 2nd
1st	19 (2)	49 (1)	-	21 (2)
2nd	79 (1)	152 (2)	-	-
3rd	127 (4)	161 (4)	-	-
4th	144 (3)	176 (3)	-	-
5th	177 (6)	182 (6)	-	-
6th	202 (7)	209 (5)	-	-
7th	257 (5)	211 (8)	-	-
8th	338 (9)	252 (9)	-	-
9th	352 (10)	261 (10)	-	-
10th	360 (11)	261 (11)	-	-

Griqualand West v KwaZulu-Natal, Kimberley, 16-18 March 2001. Match drawn.

Northerns Titans 2000/01

Back, from left: Finley Brooker, Johann Myburgh, Dirkie de Vos, Jacques Rudolph, Quentin Still, Victor Faul, David Townsend, Allahudien Paleker, Kruger van Wyk, Rupert Bailey, Ian Repton (Physiotherapist). Front: Chris van Noordwyk (Assistant Coach), Pierre Joubert, Greg Smith, Steve Elworthy, Dave Nosworthy (Coach), Gerald Dros (Captain), Martin van Jaarsveld, Rudi Bryson, Rob Walter (Exercise Physiologist). Inset: Neil McKenzie

NORTHERNS CRICKET UNION

PO Box 7706, Centurion 0046. Tel (012) 663 1005.
Fax (012) 663 3329. E-mail: elisel@cricket.co.za

President: Brandon Foot
Vice-president: Grant Webber
Executive Director: Elise Lombard
Manager, Academy: Grant Morgan
Manager, Clubs: Brian Frost
Manager, Youth: Johan Rudolph
Manager, Development: Wally Nel
2001/02 contracted players: Gerald Dros (captain) - other contracted players not available at time of going to print. **UCB contracted player:** Neil McKenzie. **Coach:** Dave Nosworthy.

REVIEW OF THE SEASON 2000/01

Trevor Chesterfield

SUPERSPORT SERIES: P9 W4 L3 D2 (fourth)
CAPTAIN: G Dros (6), S Elworthy (1), M van Jaarsveld (2)
STANDARD BANK CUP: P14 W9 L5 (runners-up)

For a season during which Northerns concentrated on their long-term team refurbishing programme and consolidated some of the few gains of the millennium summer, the general success might have escaped most casual observers of the Titans' progress. Those who have followed them more closely in recent summers were far from surprised, however, at how smoothly they moved forward.

Sure, there was a decided stumble at the end in the Super Eights of the SuperSport Series, the top domestic competition which was dismissed by much of the so-called "important" media (often TV coverage was available to those only with a DSTV facility). To all but the few who keenly followed the progress of their teams, the season seemed to have ended on February 28. Yet even the lack of exposure during March could not remove the entertainment and interest value.

Losing badly to an Easterns side packed with "hired hands" and then crumbling against a solid Western Province bowling performance on what was the last day of the season, were distinct lows on a barometer of mixed success. It was all a matter of the last month of the summer failing to deliver the bigger promise of the exciting side which had reached the final of the Standard Bank Cup. An injury to the captain Gerald Dros did not help either, although Martin van Jaarsveld did a more than creditable job in his place.

If you listen to coach Dave Nosworthy, who can be as jovial as Friar Tuck but with that iron fist in a velvet glove approach, the season had by that stage become one innings too long, especially after losing the cup final to KwaZulu-Natal Dolphins at Kingsmead in Durban. Winning the trophy might have lifted the side mentally and given them the drive they needed to go through the last matches of the Super Eights with a more determined thrust and a fusion of the talent which had emerged since the start of the season.

Through much of the season, Northerns went into matches with an unbalanced side because of quota system pressures. Three early off-season signings should solve this problem. Two of the three are from Eastern Province, Shafiek Abrahams and the 21-year-old Dewald Senekal, while the third is the talented Mulligan George, who was seemingly not wanted by Gauteng. Abrahams is eager to reignite a stalled international career and the national selectors cannot make up their minds who they want as a second or third spinner.

Do Northerns need two new fast bowlers? What with the career of that fine craftsman of swing and pace, Steve Elworthy, slowly winding down and Greg Smith now tied to a contract with the England county Nottinghamshire there is no harm in creating a competitiveness in the ranks. Also it is hard to say what appetite Smith would have for a full South Africa season. The big left-arm quick did not quite convince the national selectors with their pet theories; such is his progress, however, he may yet earn an England A team cap.

What did emerge from the season was the culmination of impressive growth planning: Jacques Rudolph, Johan Myburgh, Kruger van Wyk, Allahudien Palakar and at the end Alviro Petersen created the youth balance which Nosworthy and his assistant, Chris van Noordwyk, had been working towards.

From the time Rudolph, aged 10, scored a century at the St Alban's College open 11 day of 1991 it was obvious that here was a special talent. His close friend, Myburgh, at 17 years and 122 days in 1997/98, had already become the youngest batsman in South Africa to score a first-class double century. Both were in the SA under 19 teams at the 1998 and 2000 youth World Cups. The diminutive Van Wyk came through as the most exciting young wicket-keeper since Mark Boucher, often displaying character and courage in difficult conditions.

It was a hook for six and a cover-drive for four off Alan Dawson by Van Wyk which set up an incredible day/night victory over Western Province on a balmy late spring night in Centurion. It did much to set up Northerns' domestic Standard Bank Cup progress, with Dros, the captain, and Van Jaarsveld often leading the way by example and Van Wyk always helping out.

Nosworthy felt that playing in the Standard Bank Cup final was a bonus as a semifinal spot and fourth place on the Super Eights log was about as good as it was going to get. There were times when the charge for bonus points created their own risk but the desire always to be competitive could not be faulted.

PROVINCIAL RECORDS

Honours:

Currie Cup B Section/UCB Bowl (5): 1965/66, 1966/67 (as NE Transvaal), 1971/72, 1977/78, 1978/79

Standard Bank League (2): 1996/97, 1998/99

Highest innings totals:

For:	562-7*	v Griqualand West (Kimberley)		1999/00
Against:	602-9*	by Transvaal (Johannesburg)		1993/94
Lowest innings totals:				
For:	41	v Eastern Province (Benoni)		1967/68
Against:	41	by Griqualand West (Pretoria)		1958/59
Highest individual innings:				
For:	238*	M van Jaarsveld	v Griqualand West (Kimberley)	1999/00
Against:	337*	DJ Cullinan	for Transvaal (Johannesburg)	1993/94

NORTHERNS CRICKET UNION

Most runs in a season:

SS and Bowl				All FC			
994	(Avg 49.70)	M Yachad	1990/91	994	(Avg 49.70)	M Yachad	1990/91

Most runs in a career:

SS and Bowl				All FC			
5061	(Avg 36.67)	MJR Rindel	1986-98	5449	(Avg 37.32)	MJR Rindel	1986-98

Most 100s in a career:

SS and Bowl				All FC			
10		MJR Rindel	1986-98	11		MJR Rindel	1986-98

Best bowling in an innings:

For:	9-23	JT Botten	v Griqualand West (Pretoria)	1958/59
Against:	8-47	VAP van der Bijl	for Natal (Pretoria)	1981/82

Best bowling in a match:

For:	15-49	JT Botten	v Griqualand West (Pretoria)	1958/59
Against:	14-111	VAP van der Bijl	for Natal (Pretoria)	1981/82

Most wickets in a season:

SS and Bowl				All FC			
55	(Avg 10.09)	JT Botten	1958/59	55	(Avg 10.09)	JT Botten	1958/59

Most wickets in a career:

SS and Bowl				All FC			
280	(Avg 19.06)	JT Botten	1958-71	320	(Avg 20.07)	JT Botten	1957-71

Most dismissals (wicketkeepers) in an innings:

6	(ct 6,st 0)	CG Bromham	v Western Province (Cape Town) (FC)	1939/40
6	(ct 6,st 0)	CI Dey	v Natal B (Pretoria) (CC)	1974/75
6	(ct 6,st 0)	NT Day	v Western Province (Cape Town) (CC)	1987/88
6	(ct 6,st 0)	RV Jennings	v Western Province (Verwoerdburg) (CC)	1991/92
6	(ct 5,st 1)	KJ Rule	v Orange Free State (Verwoerdburg) (CC)	1994/95

Most dismissals (wicketkeepers) in a match:

9	(ct 9,st 0)	NT Day	v Natal (Pretoria)	1984/85
9	(ct 9,st 0)	RV Jennings	v Transvaal (Johannesburg)	1991/92
9	(ct 9,st 0)	RV Jennings	v Western Province (Verwoerdburg)	1991/92

Most dismissals (wicketkeepers) in a season:

SS and Bowl				All FC			
46	(ct 45,st 1)	NT Day	1984/85	46	(ct 45,st 1)	NT Day	1984/85

Most dismissals (wicketkeepers) in a career:

SS and Bowl				All FC			
191	(ct 173,st 18)	NT Day	1982-89	195	(ct 168,st 27)	DT Lindsay (includes 12 ct as fielder)	1958-73

Most catches (fielders) in an innings:

5	AH Jordaan	v Border (East London)	1972/73

Most catches (fielders) in a match:

7	SP de Vigne	v Orange Free State (Benoni)	1950/51
7	CB Lambert	v Boland (Paarl)	1994/95

Most catches (fielders) in a season

SS and Bowl			All FC		
20	LJ Barnard	1985/86	20	LJ Barnard	1985/86

Most catches (fielders) in a career:

SS and Bowl			All FC		
67	LJ Barnard	1982-91	69	LJ Barnard	1982-91

Most appearances:

SS and Bowl			All FC		
88	AM Ferreira	1974-89	93	AM Ferreira	1974-91

Most captaincies:

SS and Bowl			All FC		
57	LJ Barnard	1982-89	60	LJ Barnard	1982-89

RECORD WICKET PARTNERSHIPS

1st	268	PC Davies and FA Seyfried v Orange Free State (Bloemfontein)	1955/56
2nd	308	CB Lambert and JJ Strydom v Transvaal (Johannesburg)	1993/94
3rd	249	MD Haysman and LP Vorster v Eastern Province (Verwoerdburg)	1990/91
4th	294	TL Goddard and HM Ackerman v Western Province (Cape Town)	1966/67

5th	221	HM Ackerman and CI Dey v Border (Benoni)	1966/67
6th	152	KD Verdoorn and AM Ferreira v Natal (Durban)	1982/83
7th	189	MB Hofmeyr and JW Blewett v Border (Pretoria)	1951/52
8th	131	NV Alistoun and TA Rolfe v Natal B (Pretoria)	1968/69
9th	103	GE McMillan and PA Robinson v Transvaal (Johannesburg)	1983/84
10th	108	PS de Villiers and RE Bryson v Border (Verwoerdburg)	1994/95

PERFORMANCES AGAINST OTHER TEAMS

HIGHEST AND LOWEST TOTALS

Opponents	Highest Total For		Lowest Total For	
Boland	343-4*	2000/01	95	1995/96
Border	473-7*	1966/67	107	1951/52
Eastern Province	451-9*	2000/01	41	1967/68
Easterns	415	2000/01	192	2000/01
Free State	552-8*	1955/56	49	1950/51
Gauteng	517-8*	1993/94	61	1984/85
Griqualand West	562-7*	1999/00	108	1947/48
KwaZulu-Natal	368-9*	1990/91	58	1960/61
North West	175-7	2000/01	-	
Western Province	524-6*	1966/67	65	2000/01

BEST INDIVIDUAL PERFORMANCES

Opponents	Highest score		Best bowling (innings)		Best bowling (match, 8+)	
Boland	141	JA Rudolph, 2000/01	6-80	MJG Davis, 1996/97	9-65	PS de Villiers,1997/98
Border	200*	VF du Preez,1986/87	8-98	HE Patterson,1950/51	12-122	JT Botten,1958/59
Eastern Province	141	LP Vorster,1990/91	7-69	GR Grobler,1989/90	10-96	SF Burke,1964/65
Easterns	144	JA Rudolph, 2000/01	4-53	S Elworthy, 2000/01	-	
Free State	220	PC Davies,1955/56	7-4	WA Henderson,1937/38	11-45	AA Jones,1972/73
Gauteng	214	CB Lambert,1993/94	6-57	EO Simons,1984/85	10-143	LS Brown,1937/38
Griqualand West	238*	M van Jaarsveld, 1999/00	9-23	JT Botten,1958/59	15-49	JT Botten,1958/59
KwaZulu-Natal	179	M Yachad,1990/91	7-65	S Elworthy,1994/95	9-97	GR Grobler,1984/85
North West	45	PJR Steyn, 2000/01	4-84	GJ Smith, 2000/01	-	
Western Province	222	TL Goddard,1966/67	6-35	GJ Smith, 1997/98	11-104	T Bosch,1991/92

NORTHERNS SUPERSPORT AVERAGES 2000/01

Batting & Fielding

Name	M	Inns	NO	Runs	HS	Avg	100	50	Ct	St
P Joubert	3	5	3	137	72*	68.50	0	1	2	0
ND McKenzie	3	6	1	305	123	61.00	1	2	4	0
DJJ de Vos	3	6	1	233	97	46.60	0	2	2	0
G Dros	6	10	2	308	100*	38.50	1	0	7	0
PJR Steyn	8	15	1	527	188*	37.64	1	2	3	0
JA Rudolph	9	17	0	638	144	37.52	2	2	7	0
M van Jaarsveld	9	17	0	630	132	37.05	1	5	16	0
A Paleker	4	6	2	127	38*	31.75	0	0	3	0
S Elworthy	7	11	3	224	75*	28.00	0	1	0	0
JG Myburgh	3	6	0	138	68	23.00	0	1	2	0
NG Brouwers	6	8	2	127	59	21.16	0	1	2	0
QR Still	3	5	1	81	34	20.25	0	0	1	0
CFK van Wyk	9	15	2	256	59	19.69	0	1	35	2
AN Petersen	1	2	0	32	30	16.00	0	0	1	0
FC Brooker	6	10	1	135	31	15.00	0	0	2	0
DH Townsend	8	10	0	89	45	8.90	0	0	1	0
GJ Smith	9	11	3	45	15	5.62	0	0	3	0
RE Bryson	2	2	2	11	11*	-	0	0	0	0
Totals	99	162	24	4043	188*		6	18	91	2
			Extras	235				subs		
			Total	4278		31.00			91	

Bowling

Name	Overs	Mdns	Runs	Wkts	Avg	BB	5I	10M
RE Bryson	51	10	193	10	19.30	5-33	1	0
S Elworthy	243.2	65	711	30	23.70	5-41	2	0
G Dros	116.3	29	332	14	23.71	3-32	0	0
P Joubert	89	28	221	9	24.55	5-10	1	0
DH Townsend	239.2	63	761	29	26.24	5-49	1	0
QR Still	17	2	53	2	26.50	1-4	0	0
GJ Smith	330.4	87	869	30	28.96	5-25	1	0
NG Brouwers	86	24	247	6	41.16	3-43	0	0
JA Rudolph	67.5	14	214	5	42.80	2-13	0	0
DJJ de Vos	69	8	234	1	234.00	1-70	0	0
M van Jaarsveld	2	1	5	0	-	-	0	0
JG Myburgh	4	1	7	0	-	-	0	0
Totals	1315.4	332	3847	136		5-10	6	0
		b & lb	160	3	run outs			
		Total	4007	139	28.82			

MATCH REPORTS AND SCORECARDS

NORTHERNS v GRIQUALAND WEST — SuperSport Series Pool A

Played at SuperSport Park, Centurion on 3,4,5,6 November 2000 — Toss: Griqualand West
Umpires: DF Becker & KH Hurter
Debuts: Nor: CFK van Wyk (FC), NG Brouwers & A Palekar (both FC for Nor). GW: J Louw (FC)
Close of Play: Day 1: Nor (1) 160-3 (McKenzie 39*, Dros 2*, 56 overs). Day 2: GW (1) 109-3 (Gidley 45*, Koortzen 18*, 46 overs). Day 3: GW (2) 29-1 (Gidley 6*, Abrahim 11*, 8 overs).
Result: Northerns won by 153 runs
Man of Match: Rudi Steyn
Points: Nor: 17 (bat 3, bowl 4, match 10). GW: 4 (bat 2, bowl 2, match 0)

Dropped by the national selectors, McKenzie continued his impressive form and shared a partnership of 101 with Van Jaarsveld for the third wicket on a rain-delayed first day. The visitors did not help their cause by dropping catches and then batted badly against good bowling although Bossenger played well for his half-century. Northerns gained a first innings lead of 111 and were rarely troubled. Steyn top-scored with a solid unbeaten 188 to earn the man of the match award and the visitors were left 401 to win, a task well beyond their limited capabilities.

NORTHERNS

FIRST INNINGS	*Runs*	*Mins*	*Balls*	*4*	*6*	*SECOND INNINGS*	*Runs*	*Mins*	*Balls*	*4*	*6*
JA Rudolph c Elliott b Louw	33	92	79	6	-	(2) c Bossenger b Elliott	13	58	40	2	-
PJR Steyn c Brooker b Abrahim	2	14	10	-	-	(1) not out	188	227	203	27	4
M van Jaarsveld c Arthur b Louw	70	181	137	10	-	c Bossenger b Elliott	6	35	26	1	-
ND McKenzie c Bossenger b Kruis	70	219	183	11	1	not out	75	132	116	9	-
*G Dros b Abrahim	40	137	107	7	-						
A Paleker c Dry b Elliott	36	131	88	3	-						
S Elworthy c Bossenger b Abrahim	9	39	32	1	-						
†CFK van Wyk b Abrahim	20	40	35	1	1						
NG Brouwers c Elliott b Louw	11	29	24	2	-						
GJ Smith not out	4	16	11	1	-						
DH Townsend lbw b Elliott	5	13	11	1	-						
Extras (lb 14, w 4, nb 3)	21					Extras (b 1, lb 5, nb 1)	7				
TOTAL (119 overs)	**321**					**TOTAL (for 2 wkts dec) (64 overs)**	**289**				

GRIQUALAND WEST

	Runs	Mins	Balls	4	6		Runs	Mins	Balls	4	6
JM Arthur c Dros b Elworthy	0	17	12	-	-	b Smith	9	16	17	1	-
*MI Gidley run out (Townsend)	62	244	181	7	-	b Smith	15	64	42	2	-
GD Elliott b Brouwers	34	109	85	3	1	(4) b Elworthy	41	149	111	6	-
WM Dry lbw b Dros	1	20	18	-	-	(5) lbw b Dros	0	2	1	-	-
PPJ Koortzen c Dros b Elworthy	23	52	53	1	2	(6) c van Wyk b Townsend	19	39	41	4	-
†W Bossenger lbw b Brouwers	54	89	70	10	-	(7) c van Wyk b Townsend	2	8	6	-	-
J Brooker st van Wyk b Brouwers	1	33	28	-	-	(8) c van Jaarsveld b Dros	43	114	93	10	-
J Louw c Dros b Rudolph	15	22	19	3	-	(9) b Smith	19	111	89	1	-
GJ Kruis c Townsend b Smith	7	29	25	-	1	(10) not out	22	75	56	3	-
ZA Abrahim not out	1	20	12	-	-	(3) c van Jaarsveld b Dros	42	90	71	8	-
CA Copeland c McKenzie b Smith	0	1	1	-	-	c van Wyk b Elworthy	10	21	24	2	-
Extras (b 5, lb 6, nb 1)	12					Extras (b 10, lb 9, w 1, nb 5)	25				
TOTAL (83.5 overs)	**210**					**TOTAL (91 overs)**	**247**				

Bowling	*O*	*M*	*R*	*W*		*O*	*M*	*R*	*W*
GRIQUALAND WEST									
Kruis	36	14	70	1		13	3	39	0
Abrahim	24	6	73	4		15	4	61	0
Louw	30	8	75	3	(6)	4	0	46	0
Elliott	18	6	38	2	(3)	15	3	59	2
Copeland	5	0	34	0	(4)	5	1	28	0
Brooker	6	2	17	0					
Gidley					(5)	3	0	20	0
Koortzen					(7)	9	0	30	0
NORTHERNS									
Elworthy	19	7	42	2		23	7	56	2
Smith	18.5	7	33	2		23	7	55	3
Townsend	16	5	47	0		16	3	52	2
Brouwers	14	3	43	3	(5)	14	4	24	0
Dros	15	7	30	1	(4)	13	4	35	3
Rudolph	1	0	4	1		2	0	6	0

Fall of Wickets	**Nor**	**GW**	**Nor**	**GW**
	1st	1st	2nd	2nd
1st	7 (2)	4 (1)	37 (2)	15 (1)
2nd	57 (1)	79 (3)	83 (3)	50 (2)
3rd	158 (3)	86 (4)	-	82 (3)
4th	228 (4)	118 (5)	-	82 (5)
5th	236 (5)	150 (2)	-	111 (6)
6th	248 (7)	181 (7)	-	115 (7)
7th	284 (8)	190 (6)	-	161 (4)
8th	312 (6)	202 (8)	-	199 (8)
9th	312 (9)	210 (9)	-	228 (9)
10th	321 (11)	210 (11)	-	247 (11)

Gauteng v Northerns, Johannesburg, 10-13 November 2000. Northerns won by 139 runs.

NORTHERNS v FREE STATE — SuperSport Series Pool A

Played at SuperSport Park, Centurion on 17,18,19,20 November 2000 — Toss: Free State
Umpires: M Gajjar & IL Howell
Debuts: Nor: FC Brooker (FC for Nor). FS: None
Close of Play: Day 1: FS (1) 54-0 (Leibenberg 24*, Gait 23*, 21.5 overs). Day 2: FS (1) 63-0 (Liebenberg 29*, Gait 27*, 27 overs). Day 3: FS (1) 224-5 (Liebenberg 109*, Brophy 7*, 88.1 overs).
Result: Match drawn
Man of Match: Gerhardus Liebenberg & Victor Mpitsang
Points: Nor: 5 (bat 3, bowl 2, match 0). FS: 7 (bat 3, bowl 4, match 0)

Free State dominated a rain-affected match, taking a substantial first innings lead through Gerry Liebenberg's double century. Liebenberg was involved in a first wicket partnership of 147 with Andrew Gait as the Northerns bowlers battled. Victor Mpitsang and Dewald Pretorius had Northerns under pressure with Gerald Dros and Kruger van Wyk sharing an important seventh-wicket stand to take Northerns into a slender lead before rain thwarted Free State's efforts.

NORTHERNS

FIRST INNINGS	*Runs*	*Mins*	*Balls*	*4*	*6*	*SECOND INNINGS*	*Runs*	*Mins*	*Balls*	*4*	*6*
PJR Steyn c Bakkes b Lewis	66	146	104	11	1	lbw b Pretorius	30	73	44	6	-
JA Rudolph c Smit b Bakkes	8	40	22	1	-	b Mpitsang	6	26	22	1	-
M van Jaarsveld c Venter b Mpitsang	0	12	8	-	-	b Mpitsang	0	2	2	-	-
QR Still c Brophy b Mpitsang	14	41	39	3	-	lbw b Mpitsang	7	63	48	1	-
*G Dros c Brophy b Mpitsang	34	70	57	6	-	not out	31	122	74	4	-
FC Brooker c Brophy b Mpitsang	14	53	30	2	-	c Brophy b Mpitsang	0	2	2	-	-
S Elworthy c Brophy b Mpitsang	9	24	18	1	-	c van Wyk b Pretorius	8	17	13	2	-
†CFK van Wyk c Liebenberg b Lewis	59	104	73	9	1	c Brophy b Pretorius	36	67	47	5	1
NG Brouwers c Wilkinson b Venter	59	89	70	13	-	not out	7	13	11	1	-
P Joubert c Liebenberg b Pretorius	6	17	11	-	1						
GJ Smith not out	2	12	12	-	-						
Extras (b 1, lb 2, w 1, nb 16)	20					Extras (lb 3, nb 12)	15				
TOTAL (71.2 overs)	**291**					**TOTAL (for 7 wkts) (42 overs)**	**140**				

FREE STATE					
GFJ Liebenberg c van Wyk b Smith	202	478	375	30	3
AI Gait c van Wyk b Smith	64	208	149	10	-
LJ Wilkinson lbw b Elworthy	8	15	18	1	-
WJ Smit b Joubert	2	39	18	-	-
MN van Wyk lbw b Dros	0	10	7	-	-
JF Venter c Brouwers b Dros	4	30	26	-	-
*†GL Brophy b Dros	14	93	72	2	-
HC Bakkes not out	54	112	88	7	-
MR Lewis b Still	14	20	17	3	-
D Pretorius not out	11	13	14	-	1
PV Mpitsang					
Extras (b 11, lb 16, w 1, nb 16)	44				
TOTAL (for 8 wkts dec) (128 overs)	**417**				

Bowling	*O*	*M*	*R*	*W*		*O*	*M*	*R*	*W*
FREE STATE									
Bakkes	22	6	76	1	(2)	11	3	38	0
Pretorius	15.2	1	75	1	(3)	13	4	56	3
Mpitsang	18	4	64	5	(1)	18	6	43	4
Lewis	8	2	44	2					
Venter	8	1	29	1					
NORTHERNS									
Elworthy	29	10	100	1					
Smith	39	4	112	2					
Joubert	29	14	61	1					
Brouwers	8	2	42	0					
Dros	15	5	32	3					
Still	8	0	43	1					

Fall of Wickets	**Nor**	**FS**	**Nor**
	1st	1st	2nd
1st	34 (2)	147 (2)	15 (2)
2nd	42 (3)	158 (3)	15 (3)
3rd	68 (4)	197 (4)	48 (1)
4th	123 (1)	202 (5)	50 (4)
5th	137 (5)	210 (6)	50 (6)
6th	155 (7)	269 (7)	67 (7)
7th	161 (6)	377 (1)	127 (8)
8th	282 (9)	405 (9)	-
9th	282 (8)	-	-
10th	291 (10)	-	-

NORTHERNS v BOLAND

SuperSport Series Pool A

Played at SuperSport Park, Centurion on 1,2,3,4 December 2000

Toss: Boland

Umpires: DF Becker & ST Jivan

Debuts: Nor: None. Bol: None

Close of Play: Day 1: Bol (1) 17-1 (Henderson 8*, Koen 8*, 6 overs). Day 2: Nor (2) 160-1 (Rudolph 72*, van Jaarsveld 81*, 49 overs). Day 3: Bol (2) 95-0 (Henderson 25*, Davids 63*, 19 overs).

Result: Northerns won by 53 runs

Man of Match: Martin van Jaarsveld

Points: Nor: 16 (bat 2, bowl 4, match 10). Bol: 4 (bat 0, bowl 4, match 0)

In a match dominated by batsmen, teenager Jacques Rudolph scored his first SuperSport Series century with immaculate strokeplay, notable for hard driving in front of the wicket and placement in cutting as the Boland bowlers battled to find the right line. Rudolph and man of the match, Martin van Jaarsveld, added 261 for the second wicket, 47 runs short of the Northerns record, with some of the finest batting seen during the summer. Van Jaarsveld batted superbly but no national selector watched either innings. Steve Elworthy and David Townsend routed Boland but Northerns were forced to battle for their victory as Rookie of the Match, Henry Davids, scored a maiden century and there was steady resistance from Louis Koen and Steve Palframan on a pitch which had flattened out.

NORTHERNS

FIRST INNINGS	*Runs*	*Mins*	*Balls*	*4*	*6*	*SECOND INNINGS*	*Runs*	*Mins*	*Balls*	*4*	*6*
PJR Steyn c Koen b Langeveldt	4	23	21	1	-	c Palframan b Pringle	0	5	6	-	-
JA Rudolph b Williams	4	28	16	1	-	c Palframan b Langeveldt	141	413	294	23	1
M van Jaarsveld c Koen b Pringle	91	268	192	14	-	c Pringle b Langeveldt	132	344	238	20	-
QR Still c Ontong b Langeveldt	34	110	82	6	-	(5) not out	17	61	35	1	-
*G Dros c Henderson b Williams	8	33	25	2	-	(4) c Koen b Williams	4	23	14	1	-
FC Brooker lbw b Williams	0	2	1	-	-						
S Elworthy c and b Ontong	6	61	41	1	-	(6) not out	31	22	15	2	3
†CFK van Wyk c Ontong b Langeveldt	48	124	112	7	-						
NG Brouwers c Palframan b Williams	4	32	25	-	-						
DH Townsend c Trott b Williams	5	20	15	1	-						
GJ Smith not out	0	15	3	-	-						
Extras (lb 3, nb 4)	7					Extras (b 5, lb 3, w 9, nb 1)	18				
TOTAL (88.1 overs)	**211**					**TOTAL (for 4 wkts dec) (100 overs)**	**343**				

BOLAND

	R	M	B	4	6		R	M	B	4	6
JM Henderson b Townsend	19	118	74	3	-	c van Jaarsveld b Dros	26	105	69	5	-
H Davids c Dros b Elworthy	0	2	3	-	-	st van Wyk b Brouwers	124	241	190	20	-
*LJ Koen b Smith	26	106	84	3	-	c van Jaarsveld b Townsend	97	255	191	12	2
PH Barnard c Rudolph b Townsend	4	33	21	1	-	lbw b Smith	0	4	6	-	-
JL Ontong lbw b Elworthy	20	69	44	4	-	c van Jaarsveld b Smith	1	7	9	-	-
IJL Trott c van Wyk b Townsend	9	18	15	2	-	c van Wyk b Townsend	11	79	70	-	-
†SJ Palframan c van Jaarsveld b Townsend	0	2	1	-	-	b Smith	46	105	75	8	-
BT Player not out	37	53	36	5	1	c van Wyk b Townsend	5	37	22	-	-
CK Langeveldt c Brooker b Elworthy	2	9	7	-	-	c van Jaarsveld b Townsend	4	16	15	1	-
AAW Pringle b Elworthy	0	1	1	-	-	c van Wyk b Dros	27	45	33	6	-
HS Williams c Dros b Elworthy	7	18	10	1	-	not out	1	20	9	-	-
Extras (lb 4, w 1, nb 3)	8					Extras (b 4, lb 8, w 6, nb 9)	27				
TOTAL (48.5 overs)	**132**					**TOTAL (113.3 overs)**	**369**				

Bowling	*O*	*M*	*R*	*W*		*O*	*M*	*R*	*W*
BOLAND									
Williams	18	8	43	5	(2)	31	9	66	1
Langeveldt	20.1	7	53	3	(3)	27	9	88	2
Pringle	21	5	42	1	(1)	19	0	96	1
Player	15	2	24	0		14	3	39	0
Ontong	11	0	38	1	(6)	5	0	32	0
Henderson	3	0	8	0					
Trott					(5)	4	1	14	0
NORTHERNS									
Elworthy	16.5	4	41	5		8	1	44	0
Smith	16	5	43	1		36	9	99	3
Townsend	14	3	35	4		27	6	116	4
Dros	2	0	9	0		18.3	2	57	2
Brouwers						18	7	35	1
Still						6	2	6	0

Fall of Wickets

	Nor	**Bol**	**Nor**	**Bol**
	1st	1st	2nd	2nd
1st	9 (1)	0 (2)	2 (1)	107 (1)
2nd	13 (2)	48 (3)	263 (3)	204 (2)
3rd	71 (4)	48 (1)	270 (4)	205 (4)
4th	98 (5)	65 (4)	302 (2)	207 (5)
5th	98 (6)	77 (6)	-	267 (6)
6th	130 (7)	77 (7)	-	292 (3)
7th	171 (3)	99 (5)	-	318 (8)
8th	190 (9)	104 (9)	-	325 (9)
9th	196 (10)	104 (10)	-	347 (7)
10th	211 (8)	132 (11)	-	369 (10)

North West v Northerns, Potchefstroom, 8-11 December 2000. Match drawn.
Border v Northerns, East London, 1-3 February 2001. Border won by 7 wickets.

NORTHERNS v EASTERNS — SuperSport Series Super Eight

Played at SuperSport Park, Centurion on 1,2,3,4 March 2001 — Toss: Northerns
Umpires: BG Jerling & EA Watkin
Debuts: Nor: None. Eas: BL Reddy (FC), AJ Seymore (FC for Eas)
Close of Play: Day 1: Nor (1) 362-6 (de Vos 92*, Paleker 10*, 104 overs). Day 2: Eas (1) 238-5 (Seymore 113*, 80.3 overs). Day 3: Nor (2) 106-7 (Paleker 10*, Elworthy 14*, 52 overs).
Result: Easterns won by 4 wickets
Man of Match: Andre Seymore
Points: Nor: 7 (bat 5, bowl 2, match 0). Eas: 16 (bat 4, bowl 2, match 10)

After scoring 415 in their first innings against what was a largely makeshift Easterns bowling attack, with Rudolph scoring his second century of the season, Northerns seemed well placed to improve their log position. But the innings of former Northerns and Gauteng opener Andre Seymore was crucial, while the umpiring of visiting New Zealander Evan Watkin was not without some controversy. A second-innings batting debacle by Northerns and two of Watkin's decisions added to the discomfort of a home team that was captained by Elworthy after Dros was ruled out with a finger injury. Considering the depleted state of the visiting attack it was a poor Northerns batting effort which enabled Easterns to win by four wickets.

NORTHERNS

FIRST INNINGS	*Runs*	*Mins*	*Balls*	*4*	*6*	*SECOND INNINGS*	*Runs*	*Mins*	*Balls*	*4*	*6*
JG Myburgh c Reddy b de Bruyn	27	61	48	6	-	c Jennings b Morkel	6	43	35	-	-
JA Rudolph run out (van den Berg)	144	343	269	18	2	b Reddy	18	32	28	3	-
M van Jaarsveld c Seymore b Morkel	22	67	61	4	-	lbw b Morkel	25	79	54	4	-
PJR Steyn b Flusk	31	114	89	2	1	c Jennings b de Bruyn	6	32	23	1	-
DJJ de Vos lbw b Flusk	97	205	148	14	2	run out (van den Berg)	6	18	11	1	-
*S Elworthy c Brand b de Bruyn	20	22	19	3	-	(9) run out (de Bruyn/Jennings)	18	38	34	2	1
†CFK van Wyk c Jennings b de Bruyn	0	3	1	-	-	(8) c Brand b Botha	2	8	6	-	-
A Paleker c Crookes b Botha	27	75	65	3	-	(6) not out	38	222	174	5	-
FC Brooker not out	15	32	22	2	-	(7) c Crookes b Botha	10	53	47	-	-
DH Townsend c Seymore b Botha	9	19	18	1	-	c Botha b Brand	45	93	79	6	1
GJ Smith run out (Reddy/Jennings)	2	7	5	-	-	c Crookes b Botha	5	11	10	1	-
Extras (b 1, lb 12, w 7, nb 1)	21					Extras (lb 5, w 2, nb 6)	13				
TOTAL (124.1 overs)	**415**					**TOTAL (82.3 overs)**	**192**				

EASTERNS

	Runs	*Mins*	*Balls*	*4*	*6*		*Runs*	*Mins*	*Balls*	*4*	*6*
†D Jennings lbw b Elworthy	0	1	2	-	-	lbw b Elworthy	4	49	36	1	-
AJ Seymore c van Jaarsveld b Smith	174	490	365	23	-	c Rudolph b Elworthy	69	176	122	10	-
AM van den Berg c Paleker b de Vos	7	35	29	1	-	c van Wyk b Townsend	14	38	29	2	-
D Brand c van Jaarsveld b Smith	19	44	27	3	1	c van Jaarsveld b Elworthy	39	90	70	4	1
*DN Crookes c Steyn b Townsend	59	113	104	6	1	(6) lbw b Elworthy	5	23	11	-	-
P de Bruyn c Rudolph b Townsend	36	99	93	3	-	(7) not out	32	66	46	4	1
MJR Rindel b Elworthy	12	16	16	2	-	(5) c de Vos b Rudolph	45	68	51	8	-
AG Botha c van Jaarsveld b Rudolph	33	93	77	5	-	not out	16	24	26	3	-
JA Morkel c van Wyk b Elworthy	15	47	30	2	-						
GE Flusk c van Wyk b Smith	7	25	26	-	1						
BL Reddy not out	11	12	12	-	1						
Extras (b 6, w 1)	7					Extras (lb 5)	5				
TOTAL (130.1 overs)	**380**					**TOTAL (for 6 wkts) (65.1 overs)**	**229**				

Bowling	*O*	*M*	*R*	*W*		*O*	*M*	*R*	*W*
EASTERNS									
Morkel	25	10	61	1		22	8	50	2
Reddy	17	1	77	0		8	2	26	1
Flusk	30	5	95	2		18	4	43	0
de Bruyn	18	3	78	3		10	3	21	1
Botha	30.1	10	73	2		19.3	10	34	3
van den Berg	4	1	18	0					
Rindel					(6)	2	0	8	0
Brand					(7)	3	1	5	1
NORTHERNS									
Elworthy	27	6	70	3		17	6	53	4
Smith	26.1	6	62	3		16	2	45	0
de Vos	27	3	70	1		14	2	48	0
Townsend	19	8	81	2		7	0	31	1
Rudolph	31	4	91	1		7.1	1	40	1
Myburgh						4	1	7	0

Fall of Wickets

	Nor 1st	Eas 1st	Nor 2nd	Eas 2nd
1st	48 (1)	0 (1)	25 (2)	12 (1)
2nd	101 (3)	16 (3)	27 (1)	45 (3)
3rd	175 (4)	65 (4)	42 (4)	129 (2)
4th	292 (2)	166 (5)	60 (5)	130 (4)
5th	330 (6)	238 (6)	70 (3)	156 (6)
6th	335 (7)	255 (7)	85 (7)	202 (5)
7th	389 (8)	319 (8)	87 (8)	-
8th	389 (5)	350 (9)	111 (9)	-
9th	412 (10)	362 (10)	187 (10)	-
10th	415 (11)	380 (2)	192 (11)	-

Eastern Province v Northerns, Port Elizabeth, 8-10 March 2001. Northerns won by 368 runs.

NORTHERNS v WESTERN PROVINCE — SuperSport Series Super Eight

Played at SuperSport Park, Centurion on 15,16,17,18 March 2001 — Toss: Western Province

Umpires: BG Jerling & CJ Mitchley (TV: AG O'Connor)

Debuts: Nor: AN Petersen (FC). WP: None

Close of Play: Day 1: Nor (1) 0-0 (Rudolph 0*, Petersen 0*, 1.4 overs). Day 2: WP (2) 0-0 (Puttick 0*, Smith 0*, 1.5 overs). Day 3: WP (2) 314-3*.

Result: Western Province won by 298 runs

Man of Match: Ashwell Prince

Points: Nor: 7 (bat 3, bowl 4, match 0). WP: 18 (bat 4, bowl 4, match 10)

Western Province, already in the final of the SuperSport Series, gave a highly polished display after an initial top-order collapse against tidy, penetrative bowling. While the Titans, who were hit by injuries, held their batting together in the first innings with Rudolph top-scoring, the visitors took the game away from Northerns in the second innings despite more umpiring errors.

NORTHERNS CRICKET UNION

There were excellent centuries from HD Ackerman and Ashwell Prince as Province declared, leaving Northerns to chase a difficult target of 364 to win. Left-arm spinner Claude Henderson, no doubt wondering why he was bowling at SuperSport Park and not in the West Indies, gave an immaculate display as Northerns crumbled in the most abject manner of the season.

The total of 65 included a partnership of 52 between Brooker and De Vos. It appeared to be a world record low total for an innings including a fifty partnership, the previous lowest being 67 by Yorkshire against Northamptonshire in 1927.

WESTERN PROVINCE

FIRST INNINGS	*Runs*	*Mins*	*Balls*	*4*	*6*	*SECOND INNINGS*	*Runs*	*Mins*	*Balls*	*4*	*6*
GC Smith c van Wyk b Bryson	1	5	2	-	-	(2) c van Wyk b Bryson	29	49	38	4	-
AG Puttick c van Wyk b Smith	2	12	9	-	-	(1) c Petersen b Townsend	31	129	76	4	-
LD Ferreira b Townsend	62	182	119	11	-	c van Wyk b Joubert	11	23	17	2	-
*HD Ackerman c van Wyk b Bryson	8	22	15	1	-	not out	109	320	272	18	-
AG Prince c van Jaarsveld b Joubert	79	159	124	13	-	not out	120	263	182	18	-
NC Johnson b Bryson	84	184	130	12	1						
R Munnik c van Jaarsveld b Townsend	0	6	4	-	-						
†TL Tsolekile c van Wyk b Smith	49	136	121	7	-						
CW Henderson not out	17	65	43	3	-						
R Telemachus c van Wyk b Bryson	4	18	15	1	-						
CM Willoughby not out	0	9	1	-	-						
Extras (b 1, lb 5, w 3, nb 1)	10					Extras (lb 10, w 1, nb 3)	14				
TOTAL (for 9 wkts dec) (97 overs)	**316**					**TOTAL (for 3 wkts dec) (97 overs)**	**314**				

NORTHERNS

	Runs	Mins	Balls	4	6		Runs	Mins	Balls	4	6
JA Rudolph c Johnson b Willoughby	71	197	149	12	-	b Telemachus	0	3	5	-	-
AN Petersen c Tsolekile b Munnik	30	90	55	6	-	c Ferreira b Willoughby	2	16	6	-	-
*M van Jaarsveld c Willoughby b Henderson	23	66	52	3	1	c Smith b Willoughby	6	17	13	1	-
PJR Steyn c Tsolekile b Telemachus	35	92	79	5	-	(7) c Prince b Henderson	1	14	9	-	-
DJJ de Vos c Tsolekile b Munnik	5	13	8	1	-	c Johnson b Henderson	17	47	25	4	-
FC Brooker lbw b Henderson	11	52	46	2	-	(4) c Ackerman b Johnson	28	57	41	3	-
†CFK van Wyk c Puttick b Munnik	10	43	30	2	-	(8) c Smith b Henderson	1	16	11	-	-
P Joubert not out	35	134	116	5	1	(6) c Johnson b Henderson	0	12	10	-	-
DH Townsend b Willoughby	9	30	26	-	1	c Johnson b Henderson	1	17	9	-	-
GJ Smith c Smith b Munnik	15	71	48	1	-	c Smith b Johnson	0	6	6	-	-
						RE Bryson not out	0	2	0	-	-
Extras (lb 6, w 3, nb 14)	23					Extras (lb 1, nb 8)	9				
TOTAL (for 9 wkts dec) (99.1 overs)	**267**					**TOTAL (21.3 overs)**	**65**				

Bowling	*O*	*M*	*R*	*W*		*O*	*M*	*R*	*W*
NORTHERNS									
Smith	20	5	51	2		16	4	52	0
Bryson	16	4	65	4		16	4	65	1
Townsend	23	5	65	2	(4)	22	6	57	1
Joubert	19	3	63	1	(3)	22	5	65	1
de Vos	15	2	61	0		10	1	34	0
Rudolph	2	2	0	0		11	3	31	0
van Jaarsveld	2	1	5	0					
WESTERN PROVINCE									
Telemachus	21	6	52	1		4	0	16	1
Willoughby	20	6	64	2		5	1	20	2
Johnson	3	0	9	0	(5)	4	0	5	2
Henderson	37	12	78	2	(4)	5.3	4	6	5
Munnik	18.1	4	58	4	(3)	3	0	17	0

Fall of Wickets

	WP 1st	**Nor** 1st	**WP** 2nd	**Nor** 2nd
1st	3 (1)	71 (2)	42 (2)	0 (1)
2nd	7 (2)	117 (3)	56 (3)	8 (2)
3rd	19 (4)	148 (1)	87 (1)	8 (3)
4th	155 (3)	161 (5)	-	60 (5)
5th	155 (5)	183 (4)	-	62 (4)
6th	156 (7)	193 (6)	-	62 (6)
7th	273 (8)	218 (7)	-	63 (7)
8th	303 (6)	231 (9)	-	64 (8)
9th	313 (10)	267 (10)	-	65 (10)
10th	-	-	-	65 (9)

NORTH WEST CRICKET BOARD

PO Box 19959, Noordbrug 2520.
Tel (018) 294 6666. Fax (018) 294 5628

President: Mickey Gordon
Vice-President: Archie Pretorius
Treasurer: Fanie Gericke
Secretary: Ben Zeitsman
General manager: John Openshaw
Coach: Gordon Parsons
Cricket Co-ordinator: Bazil Clarke
2001/02 contracted players: Not available at time of going to print.

REVIEW OF SEASON 2000/01

Noel Lathleiff

SUPERSPORT SERIES: P9 W2 L6 D1 (seventh)
CAPTAIN: MC Venter (6), GM Hewitt (2), AG Lawson (1)
STANDARD BANK CUP: P10 W2 L8 (eleventh)

North West completed the 1999/2000 cricket season, their debut season in the top league, by becoming the initial winners of the SuperSport Shield competition. While this achievement was greeted with deserved applause, it was not really viewed as anything more than a consolation prize and a target was immediately set for the 2000/01 season. It was not over-ambitious - in fact somewhat cautious - and amounted simply to a firm resolution to finish among the top eight next time round. In other words, to move one rung upwards on the SuperSport ladder.

The season started with everything looking very rosy indeed in North West's cricket garden. The ground, admirably groomed by head groundsman Louis Kruger, was looking beautiful and equal in quality to any in the country. This must have played a major role in the decision of the United Cricket Board to grant North West its first international cricket match - a one-day contest between the touring New Zealand team and South Africa on October 20.

Leading up to this historic occasion, North West had recorded two Standard Bank Cup losses, one against Eastern Province and the other against Northerns, neither of which gave real cause for concern since the local team had given a good account of themselves on both occasions. The Dragons had also recorded a welcome and deserved win against Western Province, which did much to raise local public interest.

It was unfortunate that the weather ultimately determined the outcome of the international match at a time when the ground had been filled to near capacity and South Africa were in a strong position. Nicky Bojè had laid a solid foundation by scoring a crowd-pleasing century while batting at number three. The magnificently furnished Ali Bacher Lounge was filled with VIPs brimming with enthusiasm and there could be no doubting that at that stage North West cricket was on a high.

NORTH WEST 2000/01

Back, from left: Morne Strydom, Burton de Wett, Francois van der Merwe, Arno Jacobs, Craig Light, Garth Roe, Riaan Niewoudt, P van Niekerk, Gary Outram, Ezra Poole. Front: Glen Hewitt, Hennie de Vos, Mark Lavine, Jaco Peens (manager), Martin Venter (captain), John Openshaw (general manager), Gordon Parsons (coach), Andrew Lawson, Jannie Dreyer.

So much for the start of the season. Thereafter, things began to go wrong and weak, timid batting became a major problem for the remainder of the season. There were many who shook their heads at some of the team selections as the season progressed. That brittle batting, probably due to a lack of basic concentration, was the root cause of the team's woes is evidenced by the fact that in no fewer than 11 innings during the season, the top five batsmen were dismissed for less than half of the eventual total. In eight innings, the top six batsmen were out for fewer than 100 runs.

Yet, in spite of this, batsmen who did well in the Standard Bank Cup were eventually excluded from the SuperSport Series matches. Gary Outram, for example, was given a single outing in the SuperSport competition. He opened the innings against Northerns, was out after batting for 61 minutes and, in spite of consistent failures by most of the top batsmen, was never given another opportunity. Young, in-form premier league batsmen such as Wikus van Vuuren of the Potchefstroom University and Jimmy Schlebusch of the Potchefstroom Cricket Club, both of whom scored in excess of 500 runs during the season, were extremely unlucky not to have been given an opportunity to show their wares.

Two players, acquired before the start of the season, proved to be worth their weight in gold. Garth Roe was undoubtedly the best of the North West bowlers, taking 40 wickets, while young Alfonso Thomas delighted all and sundry with both bat and ball, featuring in a SA record-equalling tenth-wicket partnership of 174 with Roe against Griqualand West and scoring 95 not out in an eighth-wicket partnership of 204 with Mornè Strydom against Western Province. It was truly encouraging to note that Strydom seemed to have got through his bad patch and was again playing good cricket.

Although he learned his cricket in Barbados, Mark Lavine really developed his game in the North West. His tragic and untimely death while playing in England during the off-season came as a great shock. Coach Gordon Parsons put the loss into perspective when he stated at a memorial service held in Potchefstroom, that "here was a player who simply could not be replaced". He was a superb all-round cricketer, a gentleman and a good friend to all who had the privilege of knowing him.

One addition to the squad for the coming season is Graham Grace, a promising batsman formerly of Eastern Province.

Last year I expressed concern about club cricket in the North West Province. The situation seems to have further deteriorated. Three of the eight clubs in the province's premier league seem set to withdraw their first teams in the coming season. The clubs, Fochville, Lafarge and Klerksdorp, were barely able to complete the past season due to losses of players. All had, earlier in the season, withdrawn teams from the lower leagues for the same reason.

The Potchefstroom University, once a power of strength in North West Cricket, are once again set to win the Premier Castle League. However, this institution, which has the advantage of being able to draw most of the province's top schoolboy cricketers, is barely able to field two full teams. Their first team contains a number of non-student provincial players while the third XI consists almost entirely of schoolboys.

One gets the feeling that club cricket in the North West has degenerated into a "social cricket" scenario rather than being a competitive breeding ground from which new players of ability will emerge. The underlying reason for this might well be that club players have got the message that provincial players, when required, are sourced from other provinces rather than from the league system.

NORTH WEST CRICKET BOARD

PROVINCIAL RECORDS

Honours:
SuperSport Series Shield (1): 1999/00
UCB Bowl (2): 1997/98, 1998/99

Highest innings totals:

For:	373-8*	v Eastern Province B (Potchefstroom)	1996/97
	373-9	v Western Province B (Potchefstroom)	1997/98
Against:	504-3*	by KwaZulu-Natal (Potchefstroom)	1999/00

Lowest innings totals:

For:	59	v Natal B (Durban)	1995/96
Against:	64	by Northerns B (Fochville)	1997/98

Highest individual innings:

For:	151	GM Hewitt	v KwaZulu-Natal (Potchefstroom)	1999/00
Against:	220	DJ Watson	for KwaZulu-Natal (Potchefstroom)	1999/00

Most runs in a season:

SS and Bowl				All FC			
512	(Avg 46.54)	AC Thomas	2000/01	531	(Avg 40.84)	AC Thomas	2000/01

Most runs in a career:

SS and Bowl				All FC			
2031	(Avg 27.08)	HM de Vos	1991-2000	2051	(Avg 26.63)	HM de Vos	1991-2000

Best bowling in an innings:

For:	7-47	GA Roe	v Free State (Bloemfontein)	2000/01
Against:	8-37	MJG Davis	for Northern Transvaal B (Potchefstroom)	1994/95

Best bowling in a match:

For:	11-81	DJ Pryke	v Western Province B (Potchefstroom)	1997/98
Against:	12-84	MJG Davis	for Northern Transvaal B (Potchefstroom)	1994/95

Most wickets in a season:

SS and Bowl				All FC			
40	(Avg 15.77)	GA Roe	2000/01	40	(Avg 15.77)	GA Roe	2000/01

Most wickets in a career:

SS and Bowl				All FC			
99	(Avg 28.41)	MJ Lavine	1996-2000	99	(Avg 28.41)	MJ Lavine	1996-2000

Most dismissals (wicketkeepers) in an innings:

7	(ct 7,st 0)	HM de Vos	v Eastern Transvaal (Potchefstroom)	1993/94

Most dismissals (wicketkeepers) in a match:

10	(ct 10,st 0)	HM de Vos	v Eastern Transvaal (Potchefstroom)	1993/94

Most dismissals (wicketkeepers) in a season:

SS and Bowl				All FC			
36	(ct 36,st 0)	EG Poole	2000/01	37	(ct 37,st 0)	EG Poole	2000/01

Most dismissals (wicketkeepers) in a career:

SS and Bowl				All FC			
112	(ct 102,st 10)	EG Poole	1996-2000	113	(ct 103,st 10)	EG Poole	1996-2000

Most catches (fielders) in a career:

SS and Bowl				All FC			
31		MJ Lavine	1996-2000	31		MJ Lavine	1996-2000

Most appearances:

SS and Bowl				All FC			
45		HM de Vos	1991-2000	46		HM de Vos	1991-2000

Most captaincies:

SS and Bowl				All FC			
18		MC Venter	1997-2000	19		MC Venter	1997-2000

RECORD WICKET PARTNERSHIPS

1st	158	S Nicolson and AG Lawson v Eastern Province B (Port Elizabeth)	1997/98
2nd	176	AG Lawson and GM Hewitt v Easterns (Fochville)	1997/98
3rd	111	HM de Vos and A Jacobs v KwaZulu-Natal (Potchefstroom)	1999/00
4th	127	MC Venter and C Light v Western Province B (Cape Town)	1998/99
5th	106	LP Vorster and MJ Lavine v Natal B (Durban)	1997/98

6th 173	A Cilliers and HM de Vos v Eastern Transvaal (Potchefstroom)	1993/94
7th 137	MJ Lavine and M Strydom v Easterns (Benoni)	1996/97
8th 204	M Strydom and AC Thomas v Western Province (Potchefstroom)	2000/01
9th 87	C Light and F van der Merwe v Griqualand West (Potchefstroom)	1999/00
10th 174	AC Thomas and GA Roe v Griqualand West (Kimberley) (The joint South African record for this wicket)	2000/01

PERFORMANCES AGAINST OTHER TEAMS

HIGHEST AND LOWEST TOTALS

Opponents	Highest Total For		Lowest Total For	
Boland	354	1991/92	96	1991/92
Border	248	2000/01	219	2000/01
Eastern Province	341	2000/01	227	2000/01
Easterns	361-9	1997/98	122	1996/97
Free State	276	1999/00	123	2000/01
Gauteng	277	2000/01	148	2000/01
Griqualand West	352	1999/00	168	1991/92
KwaZulu-Natal	362	1999/00	-	
Northerns	327	2000/01	-	
Western Province	330	2000/01	126	2000/01

BEST INDIVIDUAL PERFORMANCES

Opponents	Highest score		Best bowling (innings)		Best bowling (match, 8+)
Boland	101	C Light, 2000/01	6-53	MJ Lavine, 2000/01	10-124 MJ Lavine, 2000/01
Border	113	MJ Lavine, 2000/01	5-84	F van der Merwe, 2000/01	-
Eastern Province	98	R Niewoudt, 2000/01	5-62	F van der Merwe, 2000/01	-
Easterns	117*	AJ van Deventer, 1992/93	6-26	AC Thomas, 2000/01	8-48 GA Roe, 2000/01
	117*	S Nicolson, 1995/96			
Free State	63	GM Hewitt, 1999/00	7-47	GA Roe, 2000/01	-
Gauteng	85	MJ Lavine, 2000/01	6-55	MJ Lavine, 2000/01	-
Griqualand West	119	JPB Mulder, 1991/92	6-23	M Strydom, 2000/01	-
KwaZulu-Natal	151	GM Hewitt, 1999/00	2-31	DJ Pryke, 1999/00	-
Northerns	89*	M Strydom, 2000/01	2-25	GA Roe, 2000/01	-
Western Province	124	M Strydom, 2000/01	5-79	GA Roe, 2000/01	-

NORTH WEST SUPERSPORT SERIES AVERAGES 2000/01

Batting & Fielding

Name	M	Inns	NO	Runs	HS	Avg	100	50	Ct	St
AC Thomas	9	16	5	512	106*	46.54	1	2	3	0
R Niewoudt	5	9	1	287	98	35.87	0	1	6	0
M Strydom	8	14	2	406	124	33.83	1	1	5	0
MJ Lavine	9	16	0	477	113	29.81	1	1	10	0
GM Hewitt	7	12	0	334	62	27.83	0	1	9	0
LCR Jordaan	1	2	1	25	20*	25.00	0	0	0	0
GA Roe	8	14	5	175	66	19.44	0	1	3	0
AG Lawson	8	16	1	289	64	19.26	0	3	6	0
C Light	8	14	0	268	101	19.14	1	0	2	0
BC de Wett	1	2	0	36	30	18.00	0	0	0	0
A Jacobs	6	11	0	180	33	16.36	0	0	9	0
G Outram	1	1	0	14	14	14.00	0	0	0	0
EG Poole	9	16	0	222	50	13.87	0	1	36	0
HM de Vos	5	9	0	110	35	12.22	0	0	2	0
MC Venter	6	10	1	107	44*	11.88	0	0	6	0
F van der Merwe	4	7	2	52	24*	10.40	0	0	2	0
JN Dreyer	4	7	1	58	40	9.66	0	0	1	0
Totals	99	176	19	3552	124	0	4	11	100	0
			Extras	315				subs	1	
			Total	3867		24.63			101	

Bowling

Name	Overs	Mdns	Runs	Wkts	Avg	BB	5I	10M
GA Roe	291.1	92	631	40	15.77	7-47	3	0
F van der Merwe	135.1	36	448	17	26.35	5-62	2	0
AC Thomas	275	78	740	28	26.42	6-26	1	0
MJ Lavine	323	80	995	30	33.16	6-53	3	1
A Jacobs	12	3	35	1	35.00	1-30	0	0
M Strydom	97.2	19	317	8	39.62	6-23	1	0
C Light	90.1	28	196	4	49.00	2-48	0	0
JN Dreyer	93	11	405	7	57.85	2-57	0	0
HM de Vos	1.3	0	8	0	-	-	0	0
AG Lawson	2	0	12	0	-	-	0	0
R Niewoudt	4	0	12	0	-	-	0	0
LCR Jordaan	7	1	34	0	-	-	0	0
Totals	1331.2	348	3833	135		7-47	10	1
		b & lb	91	2	run outs			
		Total	3924	137	28.64			

MATCH REPORTS AND SCORECARDS

NORTH WEST v GAUTENG

SuperSport Series Pool A

Played at North West Stadium, Potchefstroom on 27,28,29,30 October 2000

Toss: North West

Umpires: JD Cloete & KH Hurter

Debuts: NW: AC Thomas & GA Roe (Both FC for NW). Gau: None

Close of Play: Day 1: NW (1) 6-0 (Lawson 3*, de Vos 2*, 9 overs). Day 2: Gau (2) 25-1 (Koenig 9*, Seymore 5*, 8.2 overs). Day 3: NW (2) 21-1 (Lawson 2*, Jacobs 10*, 10.5 overs).

Result: Gauteng won by 121 runs

Man of Match: Mark Lavine

Points: NW: 7 (bat 3, bowl 4, match 0). Gau: 16 (bat 2, bowl 4, match 10)

Mark Lavine enabled North West to take a first innings advantage, bowling well to justify the decision to send the Strikers in, then playing an excellent innings.The visitors came back with a vengeance in the second innings with Koenig, Seymore, Eksteen and George contributing good scores. North West's batting in the second innings followed a pattern which was to become all too predictable during the rest of the season, collapsing to some fine bowling by Terbrugge.

GAUTENG

FIRST INNINGS	*Runs*	*Mins*	*Balls*	*4*	*6*	*SECOND INNINGS*	*Runs*	*Mins*	*Balls*	*4*	*6*
AM Bacher c Venter b Lavine	17	76	60	1	-	c Poole b Lavine	9	25	19	2	-
SG Koenig b Lavine	6	16	10	-	-	b Thomas	80	258	191	9	-
AJ Seymore c Poole b Lavine	0	4	1	-	-	lbw b Dreyer	58	156	116	10	-
Z de Bruyn c Poole b Lavine	5	33	30	-	-	b Roe	16	84	66	2	-
G Toyana c Poole b Roe	12	58	48	-	-	c Poole b Roe	2	20	14	-	-
†N Pothas c Lawson b Thomas	93	244	179	13	-	c Jacobs b Thomas	1	4	3	-	-
OD Gibson c Thomas b Lavine	52	79	58	9	-	c Lawson b Roe	16	23	14	3	-
*CE Eksteen c Poole b Lavine	4	39	35	-	-	c Poole b Dreyer	50	100	61	7	-
MF George c sub (BC de Wett) b Dreyer	25	60	42	5	-	c Lavine b Thomas	58	78	72	5	3
DJ Terbrugge c Poole b Thomas	3	18	10	-	-	not out	8	17	8	1	-
WB Masimula not out	0	1	0	-	-	c Venter b Thomas	13	15	17	2	-
Extras (lb 1, nb 6)	7					Extras (lb 6, w 2, nb 3)	11				
TOTAL (78 overs)	**224**					**TOTAL (96 overs)**	**322**				

NORTH WEST

AG Lawson lbw b Gibson	25	173	124	1	-	(2) lbw b Gibson	23	116	72	2	-
HM de Vos c Koenig b Masimula	35	113	85	6	-	(1) lbw b Terbrugge	5	21	23	-	-
A Jacobs c Eksteen b Masimula	0	1	1	-	-	c Seymore b Terbrugge	18	48	38	2	-
GM Hewitt c Seymore b Terbrugge	29	109	75	2	1	c de Bruyn b Terbrugge	38	126	79	5	-
*MC Venter b Eksteen	35	134	111	5	-	c Koenig b Gibson	0	8	5	-	-
MJ Lavine c Masimula b Gibson	85	142	97	10	3	c Koenig b Masimula	14	17	10	3	-
†EG Poole lbw b Eksteen	0	1	2	-	-	c Koenig b Eksteen	16	39	30	2	1
AC Thomas c de Bruyn b Terbrugge	5	27	25	-	-	not out	6	59	51	1	-
JN Dreyer c Toyana b Terbrugge	1	18	16	-	-	c Seymore b Terbrugge	4	3	3	1	-
GA Roe c Gibson b Masimula	25	70	41	4	-	lbw b Terbrugge	0	2	2	-	-
LCR Jordaan not out	20	64	60	1	1	c Bacher b Gibson	5	35	25	-	-
Extras (b 3, lb 11, w 1, nb 2)	17					Extras (b 9, lb 10)	19				
TOTAL (105.4 overs)	**277**					**TOTAL (56.2 overs)**	**148**				

Bowling	*O*	*M*	*R*	*W*		*O*	*M*	*R*	*W*
NORTH WEST									
Roe	24	7	44	1		27	10	58	3
Lavine	23	6	55	6		21	3	72	1
Thomas	16	5	36	2	(4)	25	7	84	4
Dreyer	10	2	68	1	(3)	21	3	88	2
Jordaan	5	1	20	0		2	0	14	0
GAUTENG									
Terbrugge	25	6	53	3	(2)	20	5	39	5
Gibson	23	8	47	2	(1)	17.2	6	36	3
George	14	2	50	0	(4)	5	0	15	0
Masimula	11.4	3	44	3	(3)	4	0	17	1
Eksteen	28	10	62	2	(6)	8	5	14	1
de Bruyn	4	1	7	0	(5)	2	0	8	0

Fall of Wickets	**Gau** 1st	**NW** 1st	**Gau** 2nd	**NW** 2nd
1st	13 (2)	48 (2)	18 (1)	5 (1)
2nd	15 (3)	48 (3)	132 (3)	41 (3)
3rd	30 (4)	86 (1)	172 (2)	61 (2)
4th	33 (1)	109 (4)	174 (4)	63 (5)
5th	61 (5)	187 (5)	175 (6)	82 (6)
6th	145 (7)	187 (7)	181 (5)	123 (7)
7th	169 (8)	200 (8)	200 (7)	133 (4)
8th	208 (9)	222 (9)	301 (9)	137 (9)
9th	224 (6)	228 (6)	301 (8)	137 (10)
10th	224 (10)	277 (10)	322 (11)	148 (11)

Griqualand West v North West, Kimberley, 17-20 November 2000. North West won by 65 runs.
Boland v North West, Paarl, 24-27 November 2000. Boland won by 1 wicket.
Free State v North West, Bloemfontein, 1-3 December 2000. Free State won by innings and 53 runs.

NORTH WEST v NORTHERNS — SuperSport Series Pool A

Played at North West Stadium, Potchefstroom on 8,9,10 (no play),11 December 2000 Toss: Northerns
Umpires: IL Howell & AG O'Connor
Debuts: NW: R Niewoudt & G Outram (Both FC). Nor: None
Close of Play: Day 1: NW (1) 143-4 (Light 19*, Lavine 48*, 48 overs). Day 2: Nor (1) 152-7 (van Wyk 11*, Brouwers 15*, 51 overs). Day 3: No play.
Result: Match drawn
Man of Match: Morne Strydom
Points: NW: 6 (bat 3, bowl 3, match 0). Nor: 4 (bat 1, bowl 3, match 0)

Rain on the first day delayed the start of the match until 3pm and North West built a strong position, with Strydom and the lower order batsmen making good contributions. No play was possible on the third day and there were only 19 minutes of play on the final day.

NORTH WEST

FIRST INNINGS	*Runs*	*Mins*	*Balls*	*4*	*6*
R Niewoudt c Rudolph b Smith	35	123	82	5	-
G Outram c Dros b Townsend	14	61	47	1	-
*GM Hewitt lbw b Elworthy	5	13	10	-	-
A Jacobs c van Wyk b Smith	13	43	33	3	-
C Light c Still b Brouwers	47	164	122	7	-
MJ Lavine lbw b Smith	49	83	58	5	2
M Strydom not out	89	223	177	14	-
†EG Poole c Rudolph b Brouwers	11	18	20	2	-
AC Thomas c van Wyk b Smith	31	96	74	5	-
GA Roe c van Wyk b Townsend	21	33	21	4	-
JN Dreyer c Rudolph b Still	0	3	3	-	-
Extras (b 2, lb 4, w 1, nb 5)	12				
TOTAL (107 overs)	**327**				

NORTHERNS					
PJR Steyn c Hewitt b Dreyer	45	80	67	8	-
JA Rudolph run out (Hewitt)	2	27	12	-	-
M van Jaarsveld b Thomas	23	61	36	3	-
QR Still b Dreyer	9	11	8	2	-
*G Dros c Niewoudt b Lavine	3	42	32	-	-
FC Brooker c Poole b Roe	24	67	52	4	-
S Elworthy c Strydom b Roe	9	36	23	-	-
†CFK van Wyk not out	19	72	53	-	-
NG Brouwers not out	28	66	53	2	-
DH Townsend					
GJ Smith					
Extras (b 1, lb 6, nb 6)	13				
TOTAL (for 7 wkts) (55 overs)	**175**				

Bowling	*O*	*M*	*R*	*W*	*O*	*M*	*R*	*W*
NORTHERNS								
Elworthy	33	7	104	1				
Smith	28	9	84	4				
Townsend	20	5	52	2				
Dros	16	4	61	0				
Brouwers	7	2	16	2				
Still	3	0	4	1				
NORTH WEST								
Lavine	16	1	73	1				
Roe	14	5	25	2				
Dreyer	13	0	57	2				
Thomas	7	4	7	1				
Strydom	4	1	5	0				
Light	1	0	1	0				

Fall of Wickets	NW	Nor
	1st	1st
1st	40 (2)	16 (2)
2nd	52 (3)	73 (1)
3rd	73 (4)	79 (3)
4th	76 (1)	87 (4)
5th	144 (6)	106 (5)
6th	195 (5)	123 (6)
7th	214 (8)	124 (7)
8th	280 (9)	-
9th	326 (10)	-
10th	327 (11)	-

Eastern Province v North West, Port Elizabeth, 1-4 February 2001. Eastern Province won by 9 wickets.

NORTH WEST v WESTERN PROVINCE SuperSport Series Super Eight

Played at North West Stadium, Potchefstroom on 1,2,3 March 2001 Toss: North West
Umpires: DL Orchard & AE Williams
Debuts: NW: BC de Wett (FC). WP: None
Close of Play: Day 1: NW (1) 282-7 (Strydom 121*, Thomas 58*, 104 overs). Day 2: WP (1) 268-5 (Ferreira 120*, Tsolekile 0*, 64 overs).
Result: Western Province won by an innings and 7 runs
Man of Match: Lloyd Ferreira
Points: NW: 7 (bat 3, bowl 4, match 0). WP: 20 (bat 7, bowl 3, match 10)

The fragility of the top order batting of North West was vividly and embarrassingly displayed. The home team had slumped to 87 for seven when Thomas and Strydom put on 204 runs for the eighth wicket to lift their team's total to a level of some respectability. Strydom displayed great patience and concentration in scoring 124 while Thomas was five runs short of his century when the last wicket fell. Western Province hammered the North West bowling, with Ferreira making a double century. The top order again failed and this time there was no rescue act by the tail as North West fell to an innings defeat.

NORTH WEST

FIRST INNINGS	*Runs*	*Mins*	*Balls*	*4*	*6*	*SECOND INNINGS*	*Runs*	*Mins*	*Balls*	*4*	*6*
R Niewoudt c Tsolekile b Dawson	23	102	78	4	-	b Telemachus	0	4	3	-	-
AG Lawson c Ackerman b Willoughby	2	36	22	-	-	run out (Prince)	0	13	6	-	-
BC de Wett lbw b Dawson	6	33	26	-	-	c Johnson b Dawson	30	55	46	2	-
*MC Venter lbw b Dawson	0	11	10	-	-	c Ackerman b Willoughby	4	41	18	1	-
C Light c Johnson b Dawson	0	6	2	-	-	lbw b Willoughby	4	9	6	1	-
MJ Lavine c Tsolekile b Telemachus	39	41	34	8	1	lbw b Henderson	10	19	9	1	1
M Strydom c Johnson b Willoughby	124	323	290	15	-	not out	33	120	87	5	-
†EG Poole lbw b Henderson	0	3	2	-	-	run out (Dawson)	13	54	54	1	-
AC Thomas not out	95	402	330	12	-	c Tsolekile b Willoughby	2	30	29	-	-
GA Roe c sub (PL Harris) b Henderson	0	26	16	-	-	c Ferreira b Henderson	4	9	9	1	-
F van der Merwe lbw b Willoughby	3	79	69	-	-	c Ackerman b Henderson	4	7	9	1	-
Extras (lb 7, w 4, nb 27)	38					Extras (b 1, lb 6, w 1, nb 14)	22				
TOTAL (142 overs)	**330**					**TOTAL (43.4 overs)**	**126**				

WESTERN PROVINCE					
GC Smith b Lavine	0	2	3	-	-
AG Puttick c Thomas b Lavine	6	31	20	1	-
LD Ferreira lbw b Lavine	201	402	290	26	1
*HD Ackerman lbw b Roe	3	5	2	-	-
AG Prince c and b van der Merwe	39	71	54	7	-
NC Johnson c Niewoudt b Roe	76	142	119	12	1
†TL Tsolekile c Lawson b Roe	78	145	115	12	-
CW Henderson c van der Merwe b Lavine	12	16	14	1	-
AC Dawson c Poole b Roe	1	8	4	-	-
R Telemachus c Venter b Roe	15	12	8	2	-
CM Willoughby not out	0	9	0	-	-
Extras (lb 8, nb 24)	32				
TOTAL (100.5 overs)	**463**				

Bowling	*O*	*M*	*R*	*W*	*O*	*M*	*R*	*W*	*Fall of Wickets*			
WESTERN PROVINCE										**NW**	**WP**	**NW**
Telemachus	25	6	99	1	9	0	36	1		1st	1st	2nd
Willoughby	38	14	64	3	12	4	34	3	1st	21 (2)	1 (1)	1 (1)
Dawson	8	5	11	4	8	2	24	1	2nd	28 (3)	25 (2)	6 (2)
Henderson	45	22	65	2	14.4	8	25	3	3rd	33 (4)	36 (4)	44 (4)
Johnson	24	5	72	0					4th	43 (5)	101 (5)	48 (3)
Smith	2	0	12	0					5th	52 (1)	264 (6)	52 (5)
NORTH WEST									6th	84 (6)	435 (7)	67 (6)
Lavine	24	0	144	4					7th	87 (8)	435 (3)	97 (8)
Roe	26.5	6	79	5					8th	291 (7)	442 (9)	108 (9)
van der Merwe	22	4	113	1					9th	296 (10)	448 (8)	121 (10)
Thomas	14	0	73	0					10th	330 (11)	463 (10)	126 (11)
Strydom	12	1	44	0								
Light	2	1	2	0								

Easterns v North West, Benoni, 8-11 March 2001. North West won by 10 wickets.

NORTH WEST v BORDER — SuperSport Series Super Eight

Played at North West Stadium, Potchefstroom on 15,16,17,18 March 2001 Toss: Border
Umpires: DF Becker & ST Jivan
Debuts: NW: None. Bdr: None
Close of Play: Day 1: NW (1) 16-0 (Niewoudt 10*, Lawson 4*, 5 overs). Day 2: Bdr (2) 86-3 (Pope 3*, Wiblin 2*, 33.3 overs). Day 3: NW (2) 78-5 (Hewitt 22*, Lavine 13*, 32 overs).
Result: Border won by 90 runs
Man of Match: Steven Pope
Points: NW: 6 (bat 2, bowl 4, match 0). Bdr: 17 (bat 3, bowl 4, match 10)

The final fixture of the season, sadly for the handful of local fans, followed a pattern to which they had become accustomed. North West were in trouble in their first innings before Hewitt and Lavine mounted a spectacular recovery to enable the teams to be evenly matched. Pope made a fine century in the second innings before Border skittled the North West batsmen to secure an easy win for the visitors, with the tail unable to come to the rescue, although Lavine and Thomas saved the side from humiliation.

BORDER

FIRST INNINGS	*Runs*	*Mins*	*Balls*	*4*	*6*	*SECOND INNINGS*	*Runs*	*Mins*	*Balls*	*4*	*6*
CB Sugden c Poole b Roe	0	7	5	-	-	(2) c Niewoudt b van der Merwe	25	84	65	5	-
PJ Botha b Roe	17	18	17	2	-	(1) c Lavine b van der Merwe	50	110	94	9	-
SC Pope c Poole b Lavine	0	11	3	-	-	c Hewitt b Thomas	100	313	215	13	-
W Wiblin c Niewoudt b Thomas	13	70	50	1	-	(5) c Poole b van der Merwe	20	117	89	3	-
*PC Strydom c Poole b Thomas	54	142	111	11	-	(6) c Poole b van der Merwe	4	8	9	1	-
LL Gamiet c and b Roe	15	52	38	2	-	(7) c Lavine b Roe	39	105	66	8	-
†I Mitchell c Lawson b van der Merwe	83	242	182	14	-	(8) c Lavine b Thomas	5	15	14	1	-
DL Makalima c Lavine b Thomas	4	22	20	1	-	(4) c Poole b van der Merwe	0	3	3	-	-
VC Drakes c and b Strydom	53	131	103	9	-	lbw b Thomas	2	15	12	-	-
GT Love not out	21	70	48	3	-	(11) not out	10	29	22	2	-
T Henderson c Venter b van der Merwe	2	6	2	-	-	(10) b Thomas	13	37	32	2	-
Extras (lb 4, nb 8)	12					Extras (b 6, lb 7, nb 2)	15				
TOTAL (95.1 overs)	**274**					**TOTAL (103.1 overs)**	**283**				

NORTH WEST CRICKET BOARD

NORTH WEST

R Niewoudt b Drakes	15	29	20	-	1	lbw b Henderson	28	33	27	4	-
AG Lawson c Mitchell b Botha	4	35	25	-	-	c Mitchell b Henderson	4	42	23	1	-
*MC Venter b Botha	12	50	34	1	-	c Mitchell b Drakes	1	12	9	-	-
M Strydom lbw b Botha	0	7	4	-	-	c Wiblin b Botha	5	44	24	-	-
GM Hewitt lbw b Love	62	200	154	10	-	lbw b Strydom	48	131	118	8	-
C Light lbw b Henderson	16	38	35	2	-	c Wiblin b Strydom	2	23	18	-	-
MJ Lavine c Gamiet b Henderson	113	144	108	16	3	c Mitchell b Drakes	34	49	39	5	-
AC Thomas c Sugden b Henderson	0	2	1	-	-	c Mitchell b Love	57	88	90	7	-
†EG Poole lbw b Henderson	0	3	2	-	-	c sub (L Graham) b Strydom	0	1	5	-	-
GA Roe not out	4	28	16	-	-	c Mitchell b Drakes	7	32	28	1	-
F van der Merwe lbw b Strydom	3	17	12	-	-	not out	24	33	34	3	1
Extras (lb 13, nb 6)	19					Extras (b 3, lb 2, nb 4)	9				
TOTAL (67.3 overs)	**248**					**TOTAL (68.3 overs)**	**219**				

Bowling	*O*	*M*	*R*	*W*		*O*	*M*	*R*	*W*
NORTH WEST									
Lavine	28	8	95	1	(4)	21	8	46	0
Roe	26	8	70	3	(1)	24	4	59	1
Thomas	21	10	46	3	(2)	27.1	7	76	4
van der Merwe	14.1	3	53	2	(3)	28	10	84	5
Strydom	6	3	6	1		3	0	5	0
BORDER									
Drakes	18	2	67	1		15	5	56	3
Henderson	18	5	53	4	(3)	10	3	21	2
Botha	13	5	54	3	(2)	12	5	24	1
Pope	5	3	7	0					
Strydom	7.3	0	33	1	(4)	22	5	55	3
Love	6	0	21	1	(5)	9.3	1	58	1

Fall of Wickets	**Bdr**	**NW**	**Bdr**	**NW**
	1st	1st	2nd	2nd
1st	3 (1)	21 (1)	57 (2)	30 (1)
2nd	18 (2)	21 (2)	84 (1)	31 (2)
3rd	18 (3)	23 (4)	84 (4)	31 (3)
4th	61 (4)	48 (3)	130 (5)	50 (4)
5th	95 (6)	68 (6)	138 (6)	65 (6)
6th	118 (5)	233 (5)	240 (7)	118 (7)
7th	138 (8)	234 (8)	247 (8)	133 (5)
8th	217 (9)	234 (9)	255 (9)	133 (9)
9th	266 (7)	239 (7)	264 (3)	162 (10)
10th	274 (11)	248 (11)	283 (10)	219 (8)

WESTERN PROVINCE CRICKET ASSOCIATION

PO Box 23401, Claremont 7735. Tel (021) 683 6420.
Fax (021) 683 4934. E-mail: info@wpca.co.za.

President: Arnold Bloch
Vice-President: Sadick Emeran
Treasurer: Haroon Lorgat
Chief Executive: Arthur Turner
General Manager: Peter Heeger
Cricket Manager: Vincent Barnes
Youth Cricket Manager: Nabeal Dien
Executive Secretary: Carol van Vuuren
2001//02 contracted players: Hylton Ackerman (captain), Alan Dawson (vice-captain), Jean Paul Duminy, Lloyd Ferreira, Paul Harris, Claude Henderson, Neil Johnson, Rashaad Magiet, Jonathan Maclean, Antonio Mullins, Renier Munnik, Ashwell Prince, Andrew Puttick, Graeme Smith, Thami Tsolekile, Charl Willoughby. **UCB contracted players:** Paul Adams, Herschelle Gibbs, Jacques Kallis, Gary Kirsten, Roger Telemachus. **Coaching staff:** Western Province A team: Vincent Barnes, Eric Simons. Western Province B team/Academy team: Peter Kirsten, Faiek Davids.

REVIEW OF THE SEASON 2000/01

Michael Owen-Smith

SUPERSPORT SERIES: P9 W7 L0 D2 (champions)
CAPTAINS: HD Ackerman (9)
STANDARD BANK CUP: P10 W5 L5 (fifth)

Western Province put the nightmare of 2000 firmly behind them to win the SuperSport Series for the third time since unity in the most emphatic manner. They finished 19 points clear of all their rivals in the Super Eight round and then won their home final against Border by more than an innings with plenty of time to spare.

They also improved their Standard Bank standings by five places to finish just out of qualification for the knockout phase. In truth, they must have been disappointed not to get through to the semifinals in view of some of the narrow defeats they suffered.

In the limited overs competition they were unable to overcome two major weaknesses.

One was the sudden decision of long-serving all-rounder Brian McMillan to retire on the eve of the season. The experienced international might not have held down a regular place in the four-day side following the recruitment of Neil Johnson as overseas player but he was desperately missed as the fifth bowler in the one-day combination. It was a problem that Western Province were not able to overcome all season, particularly after Johnson suffered a long-term finger injury that turned him into a part-time off-spinner rather than a front-line seamer.

VICTORY . . . the Western Province players celebrate winning the SuperSport Series for the second time in three seasons.
Picture: Tertius Pickard, TOUCHLINE PHOTO

The other problem was the general inexperience of a youthful side. This was best summed up by the fact that vice-captain Alan Dawson was the old man of the team at the age of 31 while there were three virtual debutants among the seven batsmen in Graeme Smith, Andrew Puttick and Thami Tsolekile. All three progressed magnificently during the course of the season and there is every evidence that this trio will pay Western Province a magnificent dividend in the years ahead. That is until they take the inevitable step up to international level.

The SuperSport Series was a success story from start to finish. Under the new leadership team of captain HD Ackerman, Dawson and joint coaches Eric Simons and Vincent Barnes, they swept everything before them, winning three of their four pool matches outright and achieving the same result in the Super Eight phase.

They may have been luckier than some of their major opponents in taking their three victories from the pool phase through to the Super Eight. This had the effect of almost putting them into the final at the halfway stage. But there was no doubting their calibre and this was demonstrated by the way they continued on their winning path throughout the Super Eight.

If there was one lesson they had for all the other provinces, it was the traditional value of producing good four-day pitches that enabled their batsmen, their seamers and their spinners all to have their share of the limelight. Western Province's total of 30 batting points was substantially more than any of their opponents. This may have prevented them from collecting as many bowling points as their opponents but it did lay the groundwork for the seven outright victories out of nine matches.

There were not many changes to the playing staff with Smith and Charl Willoughby being the notable recruits in addition to Johnson. The big change was the inquiry into the state of the Western Province professional arm that took place during the off-season. It was something that was overdue and allowed some straight talking both from management and players.

The result was that just about every member of the squad played to his potential. The availability of Herschelle Gibbs on a regular basis for the first half of the season was an unexpected bonus although he did not do quite as well as one might have anticipated. Western Province also found an able replacement for him in Lloyd Ferreira with the result that the middle order of Ferrreira, Ackerman, Ashwell Prince, Johnson and Tsolekile became the most stable and consistent in the competition.

Ackerman seemed to thrive on the leadership responsibility and scored three of Western Province's eight centuries. The others were fairly evenly spread with both Smith and Puttick scoring their maiden centuries at SuperSport level. There were five batsmen who had averages in excess of 40 with Prince exceeding 50 and Ferreira topping the national domestic averages at an imposing 66.16.

The secret of Western Province's success was, in fact, their strength in depth because the bowling depended on a well-balanced attack rather than a couple of individuals. Pride of place nevertheless had to go to Claude Henderson, who claimed 36 wickets at 22.25 with three fifers, including a remarkable Western Province career-best of five for six against the Northerns Titans. He was the official reserve for the South African Test squad in the West Indies and he has certainly left Paul Adams with work to do to stay ahead of him in the national rankings.

Willoughby made a slow start as he adapted to the different length required at Newlands compared to his previous home ground at Paarl but finished the season strongly in partnership with Dawson and Roger Telemachus.

Trophies apart, one of the main pluses for Western Province's season was the restoration of their reputation as a developer of national talent. There were five Western Province players in the South African A side chosen for the aborted tour of India in addition to the five who travelled to the West Indies. To that can be added the exciting young talent represented by the likes of Puttick and Tsolekile as well as the new contracted players Paul Harris, JP Duminy and Jonno McLean. The message is clear that Western Province cricket is moving forward again after a period in the doldrums.

PROVINCIAL RECORDS

Honours:
Currie/Castle Cup/SuperSport Series (20): 1892/93, 1893/94, 1896/97, 1897/98, 1908/09, 1920/21, 1921/22 (shared), 1931/32, 1952/53, 1955/56, 1969/70 (shared), 1974/75, 1977/78, 1981/82, 1985/86, 1989/90 (shared), 1990/91, 1995/96, 1998/99, 2000/01
B&H Series (4): 1985/86, 1986/87, 1987/88, 1990/91
Gillette/Datsun/Nissan Shield (5): 1969/70, 1970/71, 1972/73, 1981/82, 1988/89
Standard Bank League (1): 1997/98
Currie Cup B Section (1): 1968/69

Highest innings totals:

For:	601	v Border (Cape Town)	1929/30
Against:	664-6*	by Natal (Durban)	1936/37

Lowest innings totals:

For:	44	v Orange Free State (Cape Town)	1926/27
Against:	37	by Eastern Province (Port Elizabeth)	1933/34

Highest individual innings:

For:	271*	JE Cheetham	v Orange Free State (Bloemfontein)	1950/51
Against:	307*	TN Lazard	for Boland (Worcester) (FC)	1993/94
	240	AD Nourse	for Natal (Durban) (CC)	1936/37

Most runs in a season:

SS				All FC			
967	(Avg 74.38)	PN Kirsten	1976/77	985	(Avg 65.66)	HD Ackerman	1997/98

Most runs in a career:

SS				All FC			
8587	(Avg 40.50)	PN Kirsten	1973-89	9087	(Avg 41.87)	PN Kirsten	1973-89

Most 100s in a career:

SS			All FC		
20	PN Kirsten	1973-89	21	PN Kirsten	1973-89

Best bowling in an innings:

For:	10-59	ST Jefferies	v Orange Free State (Cape Town)	1987/88
Against:	9-23	WP Howell	for Australians (Cape Town) (FC)	1902/03
	8-34	L Klusener	for Natal (Durban) (CC)	1995/96

Best bowling in a match:

For:	14-113	DL Hobson	v Natal (Cape Town)	1975/76
Against:	17-54	WP Howell	for Australians (Cape Town) (FC)	1902/03
	13-53	VAP van der Bijl	for Natal (Pietermaritzburg) (CC)	1971/72

Most wickets in a season:

SS				All FC			
53	(Avg 14.58)	GS le Roux	1977/78	54	(Avg 10.83)	JJ Kotze	1906/07

Most wickets in a career:

SS				All FC			
358	(Avg 19.27)	GS le Roux	1975-88	372	(Avg 18.98)	GS le Roux	1975-88

Most dismissals (wicketkeepers) in an innings:

6	(ct 6,st 0)	GP Pfuhl	v Rhodesia (Salisbury) (FC)	1970/71
6	(ct 6,st 0)	RA Drummond	v Eastern Province (Port Elizabeth) (CC)	1978/79
6	(ct 6,st 0)	GP Pfuhl	v Eastern Province (Cape Town) (CC)	1979/80
6	(ct 6,st 0)	RJ Ryall	v Boland (Worcester) (FC)	1990/91
6	(ct 5,st 1)	RJ Ryall	v Eastern Province (Port Elizabeth) (CC)	1991/92

Most dismissals (wicketkeepers) in a match:

10	(ct 8,st 2)	RJ Ryall	v Transvaal (Cape Town)	1984/85

WESTERN PROVINCE CRICKET ASSOCIATION

Most dismissals (wicketkeepers) in a season:

SS				All FC			
43	(ct42,st 1)	P Kirsten	1995/96	47	(ct 45,st 2)	RJ Ryall	1990/91

Most dismissals (wicketkeepers) in a career:

SS				All FC			
356	(ct 329,st 27)	RJ Ryall	1980-94	388	(ct 357,st 31)	RJ Ryall	1980-94

Most catches (fielders) in an innings:

4 JH Anderson , JE White, EJ Barlow (twice), SFAF Bacchus, ST Jefferies, DB Rundle

Most catches (fielders) in a match:

6 JE White, KS McEwan (twice)

Most catches (fielders) in a season:

SS			All FC		
24	NC Johnson	2000/01	24	NC Johnson	2000/01

Most catches (fielders) in a career:

SS			All FC		
101	EJ Barlow	1968-80	111	EJ Barlow	1968-80

Most appearances:

SS			All FC		
128	PN Kirsten	1973-89	133	PN Kirsten	1973-89

Most captaincies:

SS			All FC		
72	EJ Barlow	1968-80	79	EJ Barlow	1968-80

RECORD WICKET PARTNERSHIPS

1st	293	GA Gooch and L Seeff v Eastern Province (Cape Town)	1983/84
2nd	252	G Kirsten and PN Kirsten v Eastern Province (Port Elizabeth)	1989/90
3rd	257	JH Kallis and HH Gibbs v Natal (Cape Town)	1996/97
4th	247	A Bruyns and HM Ackerman v Transvaal (Cape Town)	1975/76
5th	267	AJ Lamb and AP Kuiper v Northern Transvaal (Cape Town)	1992/93
6th	244*	JMM Commaille and AW Palm v Griqualand West (Johannesburg)	1923/24
		(The first five wickets fell for 27)	
7th	262*	DPB Morkel and AW Palm v Natal (Cape Town)	1929/30
8th	222	SSL Steyn and DPB Morkel v Border (Cape Town)	1929/30
		(The South African record for this wicket)	
9th	157	EO Simons and CR Matthews v Northern Transvaal (Verwoerdburg)	1990/91
10th	89	AC Dawson and R Joffe v Border (East London)	1998/99

PERFORMANCES AGAINST OTHER TEAMS

HIGHEST AND LOWEST TOTALS

Opponents	Highest Total For		Lowest Total For	
Boland	509-7*	1996/97	121	1997/98
Border	601	1929/30	96 (FC)	1964/65
			105 (CC)	1910/11
Eastern Province	587-7*	1983/84	68-9*	1971/72
Easterns	332-8*	2000/01	-	
Free State	506-8*	1936/37	44	1926/27
Gauteng	503-9*	1998/99	57 (FC)	1961/62
			74 (CC)	1926/27
Griqualand West	509	1906/07	111 (FC)	1890/91
			113 (CC)	1934/35
KwaZulu-Natal	538-6*	1929/30	55	1926/27
Northerns	581-7*	1997/98	75	1998/99
North West	463	2000/01	284	1999/00

BEST INDIVIDUAL PERFORMANCES

Opponents	Highest score	Best bowling (innings)	Best bowling (match) (8+)
Boland	189 (FC) G Kirsten, 1990/91	6-41 MW Pringle, 1995/96	11-108 MW Pringle, 1995/96
	148* (SS) JB Commins, 1996/97		
Border	261* SSL Steyn, 1929/30	8-28 FTM Drummer,1966/67	11-45 S de laC Snooke,1910/11
Eastern Province	217* JD Nel, 1952/53	9-64 DL Hobson, 1978/79	13-61 AJ Bell, 1929/30

Easterns	153*	AG Puttick, 2000/01	5-51	AC Dawson, 2000/01	8-83	AC Dawson, 2000/01
Free State	271*	JE Cheetham, 1950/51	10-59	ST Jefferies, 1987/88	13-90	JJ Kotze, 1906/07
Gauteng	173	SK Coen, 1931/32	9-78	JM Blanckenberg,1920/21	12-100	J Middleton,1897/98
Griqualand West	220	AI Paine, 1896/97	8-31	RJ Crisp, 1931/32	11-56	EA Budgen, 1910/11
KwaZulu-Natal	219*	(FC) AW Nourse,1932/33	9-52	MH Bowditch, 1965/66	14-113	DL Hobson, 1975/76
	208*	(CC) DPB Morkel, 1929/30				
Northerns	206*	AJ Lamb, 1992/93	7-42	(FC) JB Plimsoll,1945/46	12-124	MA Hanley,1946/47
			7-45	(CC) MA Hanley,1946/47		
North West	201	LD Ferreira, 2000/01	6-78	PR Adams, 1999/00	-	

WESTERN PROVINCE SUPERSPORT AVERAGES 2000/01

Batting & Fielding

Name	M	Inns	NO	Runs	HS	Avg	100	50	Ct	St
JH Kallis	2	4	0	292	99	73.00	0	3	2	0
LD Ferreira	4	6	0	397	201	66.16	1	2	4	0
AG Prince	8	14	4	539	120*	53.90	1	2	7	0
PR Adams	5	7	4	159	61*	53.00	0	1	4	0
HD Ackerman	9	16	3	606	128	46.61	3	2	10	0
G Kirsten	1	2	0	92	54	46.00	0	1	1	0
GC Smith	9	16	0	676	183	42.25	2	3	16	0
AG Puttick	7	12	1	441	153*	40.09	1	2	5	0
NC Johnson	9	15	2	490	84	37.69	0	5	24	0
TL Tsolekile	9	12	0	382	95	31.83	0	3	30	1
HH Gibbs	5	10	0	315	91	31.50	0	2	8	0
R Munnik	2	3	0	80	45	26.66	0	0	1	0
AC Dawson	7	9	4	111	53*	22.20	0	1	1	0
CW Henderson	7	9	2	113	28*	16.14	0	0	4	0
R Telemachus	6	7	1	65	24	10.83	0	0	1	0
PL Harris	1	2	1	10	8	10.00	0	0	0	0
CM Willoughby	8	6	3	29	17	9.66	0	0	2	0
Totals	99	150	25	4797	201		8	27	120	1
			Extras	264				subs	1	
			Total	5061		40.48			121	

Bowling

Name	Overs	Mdns	Runs	Wkts	Avg	BB	5I	10M
AC Dawson	238.2	74	583	27	21.59	5-51	1	0
R Munnik	37.1	8	109	5	21.80	4-58	0	0
CM Willoughby	298.5	107	683	31	22.03	5-26	1	0
CW Henderson	400.3	138	801	36	22.25	5-6	3	0
JH Kallis	74	25	190	8	23.75	3-77	0	0
R Telemachus	168.5	34	552	22	25.09	6-54	1	0
NC Johnson	115	25	322	12	26.83	2-5	0	0
PR Adams	203.3	53	582	18	32.33	3-33	0	0
PL Harris	55.2	15	145	4	36.25	3-56	0	0
GC Smith	4	0	17	0	-	-	0	0
Totals	1595.3	479	3984	163		6-54	6	0
		b & lb	129	9	run outs			
		Total	4113	172	23.91			

REPORTS AND SCORECARDS

Eastern Province v Western Province, Port Elizabeth, 27-30 October 2000. Western Province won by 127 runs.

Border v Western Province, East London, 3-6 November 2000. Western Province won by 77 runs.

WESTERN PROVINCE v KWAZULU-NATAL — SuperSport Series Pool B

Played at Newlands, Cape Town on 10,11,12,13 November 2000 — Toss: Western Province
Umpires: BG Jerling & CM Schoof
Debuts: WP: None. KZN: None
Close of Play: Day 1: WP (1) 238-6 (Kallis 86*, Tsolekile 19*, 93 overs). Day 2: KZN (1) 118-4 (Benkenstein 6*, Stewart 0*, 55 overs). Day 3: WP (2) 45-1 (Kirsten 26*, Kallis 14*, 22 overs).
Result: Match drawn
Man of Match: Jacques Kallis
Points: WP: 6 (bat 3, bowl 3, match 0). KZN: 4 (bat 2, bowl 2, match 0)

With two away victories already under their belt, Western Province were as intent on shutting their opponents out of further progress in the competition as anything else. It was one of the rare occasions when the national players were available and Jacques Kallis made a notable contribution in both innings without going on to the centuries expected of him.

Paul Adams made what was then his highest first-class score, while Lance Klusener, given a rare opportunity to take the new ball, claimed his 250th wicket.

WESTERN PROVINCE

FIRST INNINGS	*Runs*	*Mins*	*Balls*	*4*	*6*	*SECOND INNINGS*	*Runs*	*Mins*	*Balls*	*4*	*6*
HH Gibbs c Benkenstein b Kent	43	189	132	6	-	c Stewart b Klusener	5	31	26	1	-
G Kirsten c Bruyns b Klusener	38	121	90	6	-	c Mall b Baptiste	54	159	111	9	-
JH Kallis c Pollock b Kent	99	338	259	12	-	st Stewart b Bruyns	84	263	204	12	-
*HD Ackerman b Klusener	10	56	35	2	-	b Benkenstein	33	103	88	5	-
NC Johnson b Klusener	0	18	14	-	-	not out	36	47	37	6	1
GC Smith c Hudson b Pollock	27	83	58	3	-	c Kent b Bodi	1	5	8	-	-
AC Dawson c Kent b Pollock	0	1	2	-	-	not out	0	10	8	-	-
†TL Tsolekile c Stewart b Kent	29	128	82	4	-						
R Telemachus c Hudson b Bodi	24	74	60	3	-						
PR Adams not out	42	80	50	4	1						
CM Willoughby c Bruyns b Klusener	17	24	18	2	-						
Extras (b 1, lb 2, w 4, nb 16)	23					Extras (b 5, w 1, nb 2)	8				
TOTAL (130.4 overs)	**352**					**TOTAL (for 5 wkts dec) (80 overs)**	**221**				

KWAZULU-NATAL

	Runs	*Mins*	*Balls*	*4*	*6*		*Runs*	*Mins*	*Balls*	*4*	*6*
ML Bruyns c Ackerman b Dawson	18	72	57	3	-	c Tsolekile b Willoughby	2	40	30	-	-
DJ Watson c Tsolekile b Dawson	17	81	61	2	-	not out	60	179	121	7	-
A Mall lbw b Dawson	25	127	89	4	-	c and b Kallis	14	23	15	3	-
AC Hudson c Tsolekile b Dawson	38	139	113	6	-	c Kirsten b Johnson	6	36	27	1	-
*DM Benkenstein lbw b Telemachus	37	135	91	7	-	run out (Adams)	9	12	8	2	-
†ELR Stewart c Adams b Johnson	16	97	80	2	-	c Gibbs b Johnson	5	25	21	-	-
JC Kent not out	74	157	98	11	-	not out	19	38	42	3	-
L Klusener c Adams b Kallis	16	61	47	2	-						
SM Pollock c Tsolekile b Kallis	0	7	8	-	-						
GH Bodi c Smith b Telemachus	14	55	41	1	1						
EAE Baptiste c Johnson b Adams	9	13	14	1	-						
Extras (b 9, lb 5, nb 15)	29					Extras (b 4, lb 6, w 3, nb 6)	19				
TOTAL (114 overs)	**293**					**TOTAL (for 5 wkts) (43 overs)**	**134**				

Bowling	*O*	*M*	*R*	*W*		*O*	*M*	*R*	*W*
KWAZULU-NATAL									
Pollock	35	13	65	2		15	7	25	0
Klusener	38.4	9	111	4		12	2	45	1
Kent	22	5	70	3	(5)	7	2	11	0
Baptiste	20	6	42	0	(3)	10	4	24	1
Benkenstein	7	3	20	0	(6)	9	3	19	1
Bodi	8	0	41	1	(4)	14	3	45	1
Bruyns						13	2	47	1
WESTERN PROVINCE									
Telemachus	24	4	79	2		2	1	2	0
Willoughby	23	9	42	0		11	2	32	1
Kallis	26	10	46	2	(4)	5	0	22	1
Dawson	26	9	69	4	(3)	11	3	25	0
Adams	13	7	34	1	(6)	5	1	18	0
Johnson	2	1	9	1	(5)	7	3	20	2
Smith						2	0	5	0

Fall of Wickets	**WP** 1st	**KZN** 1st	**WP** 2nd	**KZN** 2nd
1st	58 (2)	35 (1)	17 (1)	13 (1)
2nd	115 (1)	36 (2)	92 (2)	44 (3)
3rd	136 (4)	108 (3)	170 (4)	68 (4)
4th	139 (5)	117 (4)	208 (3)	86 (5)
5th	206 (6)	167 (6)	209 (6)	96 (6)
6th	206 (7)	179 (5)	-	-
7th	263 (3)	234 (8)	-	-
8th	266 (8)	235 (9)	-	-
9th	306 (9)	275 (10)	-	-
10th	352 (11)	293 (11)	-	-

WESTERN PROVINCE v EASTERNS

SuperSport Series Pool B

Played at Newlands, Cape Town on 24,25,26,27 November 2000

Toss: Western Province

Umpires: WA Diedricks & ST Jivan

Debuts: WP: None. Eas: None

Close of Play: Day 1: WP (1) 273-6 (Puttick 120*, 103.4 overs). Day 2: WP (2) 14-1 (Gibbs 10*, Tsolekile 0*, 5 overs). Day 3: Eas (2) 36-2 (Jennings 26*, Flusk 4*, 22 overs).

Result: Western Province won by 194 runs

Man of Match: Andrew Puttick

Points: WP: 17 (bat 3, bowl 4, match 10). Eas: 4 (bat 2, bowl 2, match 0)

Andrew Puttick made his maiden first-class century to provide almost half of Western Province's first innings total. In all, he was at the crease for 476 minutes, faced 386 balls and hit 21 fours and one six. It was a remarkable indication of his potential that he should turn his first century into an unbeaten 153.

Two older hands, Mike Rindel and Derek Crookes, shared a partnership of 140 in 39.3 overs before Western Province youth took over again with a career-best 95 from Thami Tsolekile. Kenny Benjamin took his 400th wicket when he dismissed Herschelle Gibbs.

WESTERN PROVINCE

FIRST INNINGS	*Runs*	*Mins*	*Balls*	*4*	*6*	*SECOND INNINGS*	*Runs*	*Mins*	*Balls*	*4*	*6*
GC Smith c Mokoenanyana b Botha	57	189	146	8	-	c Mokoenanyana b Nel	0	1	2	-	-
HH Gibbs c Jennings b Nel	1	16	11	-	-	c Jordaan b Benjamin	20	41	19	2	-
AG Puttick not out	153	476	386	21	1	(4) c Benjamin b Flusk	39	172	112	3	-
*HD Ackerman c Botha b Benjamin	50	118	92	8	-	(5) c Jennings b Flusk	0	12	8	-	-
NC Johnson c de Bruyn b Benjamin	0	17	12	-	-	(6) c Jennings b Benjamin	50	102	82	7	1
AG Prince b Botha	22	59	30	4	-	(7) not out	40	85	70	4	-
†TL Tsolekile lbw b Crookes	7	16	17	1	-	(3) b Botha	95	262	209	9	-
R Telemachus c Mokoenanyana b Benjamin	0	11	10	-	-	not out	20	17	18	3	1
PR Adams c Botha b Morkel	24	74	41	4	-						
AC Dawson not out	0	3	4	-	-						
CM Willoughby											
Extras (b 2, lb 10, w 1, nb 5)	18					Extras (b 3, lb 7, w 1, nb 10)	21				
TOTAL (for 8 wkts dec) (124 overs)	**332**					**TOTAL (for 6 wkts dec) (85 overs)**	**285**				

EASTERNS

	Runs	*Mins*	*Balls*	*4*	*6*		*Runs*	*Mins*	*Balls*	*4*	*6*
†D Jennings c Gibbs b Telemachus	2	10	9	-	-	c and b Telemachus	53	190	149	8	-
ET Mokoenanyana c Tsolekile b Willoughby	4	41	34	-	-	c Tsolekile b Telemachus	0	5	1	-	-
*D Jordaan b Adams	26	76	47	6	-	c Puttick b Dawson	6	65	36	1	-
MJR Rindel lbw b Dawson	91	194	132	15	-	(5) c Ackerman b Willoughby	6	18	14	1	-
DN Crookes c Smith b Dawson	79	203	186	12	-	(6) not out	87	175	127	11	-
P de Bruyn c Tsolekile b Adams	0	8	4	-	-	(7) c Johnson b Adams	4	23	13	1	-
AG Botha c Johnson b Dawson	0	7	6	-	-	(8) c Tsolekile b Dawson	1	23	24	-	-
JA Morkel c Prince b Dawson	0	6	2	-	-	(9) c Gibbs b Dawson	9	16	14	1	-
GE Flusk c Johnson b Adams	13	23	18	2	-	(4) c Tsolekile b Willoughby	4	30	20	1	-
KCG Benjamin not out	5	13	8	-	-	c Prince b Adams	13	16	15	1	1
A Nel b Dawson	0	6	7	-	-	b Telemachus	2	24	17	-	-
Extras (lb 4, nb 4)	8					Extras (lb 6, nb 4)	10				
TOTAL (74.5 overs)	**228**					**TOTAL (71 overs)**	**195**				

Bowling	*O*	*M*	*R*	*W*		*O*	*M*	*R*	*W*
EASTERNS									
Benjamin	27	6	59	3	(2)	19	6	45	2
Nel	24	6	53	1	(1)	14	2	55	1
Crookes	23	8	65	1	(5)	14	2	41	0
Morkel	19	5	55	1		4	0	17	0
Botha	19	7	44	2	(3)	23	4	72	1
Flusk	8	0	31	0		8	1	30	2
de Bruyn	4	0	13	0		3	0	15	0
WESTERN PROVINCE									
Telemachus	11	3	40	1		12	4	20	3
Willoughby	16	5	50	1		14	5	35	2
Dawson	19.5	3	51	5		17	6	32	3
Adams	20	4	61	3		28	5	102	2
Johnson	8	0	22	0					

Fall of Wickets

	WP 1st	**Eas** 1st	**WP** 2nd	**Eas** 2nd
1st	12 (2)	2 (1)	0 (1)	3 (2)
2nd	131 (1)	18 (2)	30 (2)	25 (3)
3rd	207 (4)	57 (3)	156 (4)	37 (4)
4th	212 (5)	197 (4)	158 (5)	53 (5)
5th	258 (6)	200 (6)	184 (3)	106 (1)
6th	273 (7)	201 (7)	263 (6)	127 (7)
7th	274 (8)	207 (8)	-	146 (8)
8th	329 (9)	222 (9)	-	156 (9)
9th	-	224 (5)	-	175 (10)
10th	-	228 (11)	-	195 (11)

WESTERN PROVINCE v BOLAND — SuperSport Series Super Eight

Played at Newlands, Cape Town on 1,2,3,4 February 2001 — Toss: Boland
Umpires: BG Jerling & RE Koertzen
Debuts: WP: None. Bol: JG Strydom (FC)
Close of Play: Day 1: Bol (1) 274-4 (Trott 66*, Davids 15*, 104 overs). Day 2: WP (1) 206-3 (Smith 79*, Ackerman 9*, 56 overs). Day 3: Bol (2) 133-2 (Strydom 60*, Ontong 19*, 48 overs).
Result: Match drawn
Man of Match: Graeme Smith
Points: WP: 6 (bat 5, bowl 1, match 0). Bol: 7 (bat 3, bowl 4, match 0)

Newlands continued to be the scene of young batsmen coming to the fore, Jonathan Trott and Justin Ontong both falling narrowly short of what would have been maiden first-class centuries for Boland. Graeme Smith was more successful for Western Province.

With both sides scoring heavily and being well matched on the first innings, an outright result was never on the cards but there was an unusual opportunity for Paul Adams to score his maiden half-century from a top order batting position.

BOLAND

FIRST INNINGS	*Runs*	*Mins*	*Balls*	*4*	*6*	*SECOND INNINGS*	*Runs*	*Mins*	*Balls*	*4*	*6*
JM Henderson c Kallis b Telemachus	42	163	134	7	1	b Telemachus	4	35	27	1	-
JG Strydom c Smith b Adams	34	170	119	4	-	c Prince b Adams	73	237	173	13	-
*LJ Koen c Johnson b Henderson	14	43	31	3	-	c Gibbs b Adams	46	113	93	4	2
JL Ontong b Kallis	84	183	139	11	-	b Kallis	20	49	51	2	-
IJL Trott run out (Tsolekile)	93	314	245	10	-	c Tsolekile b Telemachus	12	46	35	3	-
H Davids c Henderson b Johnson	42	133	105	7	-	c Tsolekile b Telemachus	10	83	65	1	-
†SJ Palframan c Prince b Kallis	18	30	32	2	-	c Adams b Telemachus	30	94	66	3	-
CdeW de Lange run out (Ackerman)	25	65	48	4	-	c Ackerman b Kallis	4	34	19	1	-
NM Carter c Gibbs b Kallis	0	17	16	-	-	c Henderson b Telemachus	14	37	22	2	-
CK Langeveldt c Johnson b Henderson	13	31	31	2	-	c Johnson b Telemachus	17	16	11	2	1
HS Williams not out	4	12	14	1	-	not out	0	5	0	-	-
Extras (b 1, lb 8, w 3, nb 17)	29					Extras (b 9, lb 5, nb 11)	25				
TOTAL (149.3 overs)	**398**					**TOTAL (91.5 overs)**	**255**				

WESTERN PROVINCE

	Runs	*Mins*	*Balls*	*4*	*6*		*Runs*	*Mins*	*Balls*	*4*	*6*
HH Gibbs c Palframan b Carter	20	25	23	5	-	c Palframan b Williams	17	38	44	2	-
GC Smith lbw b Williams	126	331	268	16	-	c Koen b de Lange	52	124	75	7	-
AG Prince b Carter	24	37	22	5	-	(6) st Palframan b Ontong	7	9	8	1	-
JH Kallis st Palframan b de Lange	69	117	107	9	1	(3) c Koen b Ontong	40	93	87	1	2
*HD Ackerman c Ontong b Carter	11	32	28	1	-	(7) not out	7	44	43	1	-
NC Johnson c Palframan b Carter	75	109	86	7	1	(5) run out (Davids/Palframan)	8	35	18	1	-
†TL Tsolekile b Carter	12	54	39	2	-						
AC Dawson b Williams	4	9	7	1	-						
CW Henderson c Koen b Ontong	21	93	57	4	-						
R Telemachus c Palframan b Carter	0	3	1	-	-						
PR Adams not out	20	51	36	2	-	(4) not out	61	98	76	3	3
Extras (b 1, lb 3, w 2, nb 6)	12					Extras (b 7, lb 3, nb 3)	13				
TOTAL (111.1 overs)	**394**					**TOTAL (for 5 wkts) (58 overs)**	**205**				

Bowling	*O*	*M*	*R*	*W*		*O*	*M*	*R*	*W*
WESTERN PROVINCE									
Telemachus	19	5	60	1		16.5	3	54	6
Dawson	26	8	71	0		8	1	17	0
Kallis	27	9	77	3	(4)	16	6	45	2
Henderson	49.3	20	87	2	(3)	23	6	46	0
Adams	21	3	66	1		27	8	76	2
Johnson	7	2	28	1		1	0	3	0
BOLAND									
Langeveldt	3	0	17	0					
Carter	27	3	122	6	(3)	7	0	35	0
Williams	28	7	82	2	(1)	11	2	39	1
Henderson	7	2	22	0	(5)	1	0	5	0
Ontong	21.1	1	73	1	(4)	14	1	57	2
de Lange	25	6	74	1	(2)	25	8	59	1

Fall of Wickets	**Bol** 1st	**WP** 1st	**Bol** 2nd	**WP** 2nd
1st	82 (1)	28 (1)	18 (1)	24 (1)
2nd	83 (2)	66 (3)	106 (3)	120 (2)
3rd	106 (3)	190 (4)	138 (4)	126 (3)
4th	242 (4)	209 (5)	166 (2)	166 (5)
5th	332 (6)	332 (6)	166 (5)	175 (6)
6th	355 (7)	334 (2)	211 (6)	-
7th	355 (5)	338 (8)	215 (7)	-
8th	360 (9)	359 (7)	221 (8)	-
9th	389 (10)	359 (10)	249 (10)	-
10th	398 (8)	394 (9)	255 (9)	-

North West v Western Province, Potchefstroom, 1-3 March 2001. Western Province won by an innings and 7 runs.

WESTERN PROVINCE v FREE STATE — SuperSport Series Super Eight

Played at Newlands, Cape Town on 8,9,10,11 March 2001 — Toss: Western Province
Umpires: IL Howell & EA Watkin (TV: WA Diedricks)
Debuts: WP: PL Harris (FC for WP). FS: JR Schorn (FC)
Close of Play: Day 1: FS (1) 55-1 (Gait 20*, Venter 12*, 25 overs). Day 2: WP (2) 18-1 (Puttick 10*, Ferreira 2*, 8 overs). Day 3: FS (2) 13-3 (Venter 1*, Beukes 2*, 5 overs).
Result: Western Province won by 127 runs
Man of Match: Kosie Venter
Points: WP: 15 (bat 3, bowl 2, match 10). FS: 6 (bat 2, bowl 4, match 0)

Western Province surprisingly trailed on the first innings but an attacking century from HD Ackerman still put them in position to come from behind after setting Free State a target of 274. Charl Willoughby's second innings return of five for 26 represented his first-class best.

WESTERN PROVINCE

FIRST INNINGS	*Runs*	*Mins*	*Balls*	*4*	*6*	*SECOND INNINGS*	*Runs*	*Mins*	*Balls*	*4*	*6*
GC Smith lbw b Venter	41	114	86	6	-	(2) c Brophy b Pretorius	5	21	18	-	-
AG Puttick c Lewis b van der Wath	12	23	18	2	-	(1) c Schorn b Venter	60	213	183	7	-
LD Ferreira lbw b Pretorius	8	41	21	1	-	st Brophy b Venter	34	100	54	4	-
AG Prince c Venter b Pretorius	43	106	87	7	-	(5) c Brophy b Venter	9	22	16	2	-
NC Johnson c Gait b Mpitsang	38	74	56	4	-	(6) c Liebenberg b Venter	7	25	15	-	-
*HD Ackerman b Pretorius	10	42	27	1	-	(4) not out	100	295	219	9	1
R Munnik c Schorn b Venter	45	109	79	6	-	run out (Mpitsang)	35	96	72	4	1
†TL Tsolekile b Pretorius	31	58	50	5	1	c van der Wath b Mpitsang	20	38	26	2	-
CW Henderson c Wilkinson b van der Wath	12	47	29	2	-	c Lewis b Venter	5	29	17	-	-
PL Harris b van der Wath	8	31	29	1	-	not out	2	14	13	-	-
CM Willoughby not out	2	8	6	-	-						
Extras (lb 2, w 1, nb 12)	15					Extras (b 5, lb 10, w 1, nb 6)	22				
TOTAL (79.2 overs)	**265**					**TOTAL (for 8 wkts dec) (104.2 overs)**	**299**				

FREE STATE

	Runs	*Mins*	*Balls*	*4*	*6*		*Runs*	*Mins*	*Balls*	*4*	*6*
GFJ Liebenberg c Johnson b Henderson	19	47	32	2	-	c Smith b Willoughby	4	12	6	-	-
AI Gait c Tsolekile b Henderson	34	120	120	4	-	lbw b Willoughby	0	1	1	-	-
JF Venter c Johnson b Munnik	86	259	213	11	-	(4) b Willoughby	42	217	172	2	1
JA Beukes c Munnik b Henderson	9	16	15	1	-	(5) c Tsolekile b Willoughby	6	21	21	1	-
LJ Wilkinson b Willoughby	26	83	70	3	-	(6) c Henderson b Harris	19	78	58	3	-
JR Schorn c Smith b Henderson	7	31	28	-	-	(7) c Johnson b Harris	11	47	43	1	-
JJ van der Wath run out (sub - EO Moleon)	49	101	137	4	-	(8) lbw b Harris	0	2	3	-	-
*†GL Brophy st Tsolekile b Harris	36	91	89	6	-	(9) not out	29	113	95	2	-
MR Lewis lbw b Johnson	0	7	5	-	-	(3) lbw b Henderson	6	12	12	1	-
PV Mpitsang b Johnson	0	5	1	-	-	c Ferreira b Willoughby	23	44	44	3	-
D Pretorius not out	5	10	7	1	-	run out (Ferreira)	0	4	3	-	-
Extras (b 4, lb 9, w 2, nb 5)	20					Extras (lb 2, nb 4)	6				
TOTAL (118.2 overs)	**291**					**TOTAL (75.4 overs)**	**146**				

Bowling	*O*	*M*	*R*	*W*		*O*	*M*	*R*	*W*
FREE STATE									
Mpitsang	12	1	50	1	(3)	15	1	47	1
van der Wath	15.2	4	46	3	(4)	18.2	2	62	0
Pretorius	20	1	78	4	(1)	19	4	52	1
Venter	25	8	70	2	(2)	42	11	103	5
Lewis	7	2	19	0	(6)	9	1	20	0
Beukes					(5)	1	1	0	0
WESTERN PROVINCE									
Willoughby	23	9	50	1		18.4	6	26	5
Johnson	13	0	39	2					
Henderson	40	12	71	4	(2)	28	9	57	1
Harris	32.2	5	89	1		23	10	56	3
Munnik	10	1	29	1	(3)	6	3	5	0

Fall of Wickets

	WP 1st	**FS** 1st	**WP** 2nd	**FS** 2nd
1st	23 (2)	33 (1)	15 (2)	1 (2)
2nd	53 (3)	76 (2)	87 (3)	10 (1)
3rd	87 (1)	90 (4)	130 (1)	10 (3)
4th	143 (4)	163 (5)	140 (5)	18 (5)
5th	158 (5)	180 (6)	158 (6)	64 (6)
6th	168 (6)	205 (3)	223 (7)	81 (7)
7th	223 (8)	275 (8)	262 (8)	81 (8)
8th	251 (7)	278 (9)	283 (9)	110 (4)
9th	260 (9)	282 (10)	-	146 (10)
10th	265 (10)	291 (7)	-	146 (11)

Northerns v Western Province, Centurion, 15-18 March 2001. Western Province won by 298 runs.

(A report on the SuperSport Series final between Western Province and Border appears in the section, SuperSport Series, on Page 297)

STANDARD BANK CUP

The KwaZulu-Natal Dolphins won the Standard Bank Cup at the end of a competition in which fortunes fluctuated wildly. The Dolphins had a disappointing season at first-class level, failing to win a game, and they lost their first two matches in the Standard Bank Cup.

Thereafter, however, they lost only once more in the round robin stage as they climbed to the top of the log. They gained a comfortable win in the first leg of the semifinals against Eastern Province in Port Elizabeth but lost the return game at home. Two days later they seemed on their way out of the competition as Eastern Province piled up 253 for two in 41.2 overs before rain came to their rescue and the game had to start again on the Monday. Rain interfered once more and KwaZulu-Natal went through under the Duckworth-Lewis method.

Lack of penetration by their bowlers was a season-long problem in the first-class game but it was not a major handicap in the limited overs competition, where three KwaZulu-Natal bowlers featured among the top nine in the Standard Bank Cup averages. The Dolphins also had the leading run-scorer in Doug Watson, while Wade Wingfield and Ashraf Mall were first and fourth respectively in the batting averages.

Northerns did well to reach the final, considering their problems in finding the right balance under the quota system. It was a remarkable fact that neither of their two players of colour batted nor bowled in any of the three legs of the semifinal or the final.

In the second half of the season, Northerns fielded arguably the most exciting opening batting combination in the country in the form of the youthful Johan Myburgh and Jacques Rudolph, who gave the side some thrilling starts, while Steve Elworthy and Greg Smith were effective strike bowlers. Gerald Dros had a fine all-round season and his injury while bowling in the final was a critical blow which exposed the side's lack of depth.

STANDARD BANK CUP TABLE 2000/01

	P	W	L	NR	Bonus	Pts	Net RR	
KwaZulu-Natal	10	7	3	0	0	5	33	0.52
Border	10	6	4	0	0	6	30	0.47
Northerns		10	7	3	0	0	1	29
-0.07								
Eastern Province	10	6	3	1	0	2	28	0.10
Western Province	10	5	5	0	0	6	26	0.48
Easterns	10	4	5	1	0	7	25	0.28
Free State	10	6	4	0	0	0	24	-0.20
Boland	10	4	6	0	0	4	20	0.07
Griqualand West	10	4	6	0	0	4	20	-0.12
Gauteng	10	3	7	0	0	4	16	-0.44
North West	10	2	8	0	0	2	10	-1.14

STANDARD BANK CUP 2000/01: LEADING BATTING AVERAGES

	Name	M	Inns	NO	Runs	HS	Avg	100	50	BF	SR
1	WR Wingfield (KZN)	11	10	6	304	73*	76.00	0	2	407	74.69
2	PPJ Koortzen (GW)	10	10	2	563	134	70.37	2	3	553	101.80
3	AG Prince (WP)	8	7	3	272	76*	68.00	0	3	346	78.61
4	A Mall (KZN)	7	6	0	333	77	55.50	0	3	458	72.70
5	NC Johnson (WP)	10	9	0	489	111	54.33	1	3	600	81.50
6	JDC Bryant (EP)	14	14	3	578	105*	52.54	1	5	855	67.60
7	M van Jaarsveld (Nor)	14	14	3	542	88*	49.27	0	4	664	81.62
8	CFK van Wyk (Nor)	14	11	6	239	50*	47.80	0	1	253	94.46
9	G Dros (Nor)	14	13	4	421	86	46.77	0	2	513	82.06
10	MJR Rindel (Eas)	10	10	0	467	128	46.70	1	4	513	91.03
11	N Pothas (Gau)	10	10	4	280	79*	46.66	0	3	336	83.33
12	MN van Wyk (FS)	9	9	2	325	102*	46.42	1	2	345	94.20
13	JA Rudolph (Nor)	10	10	1	416	110	46.22	1	2	571	72.85
14	J Louw (GW)	7	5	1	184	72	46.00	0	2	162	113.58
15	SJ Palframan (Bol)	10	9	4	226	76*	45.20	0	2	253	89.32
16	DJ Watson (KZN)	15	14	1	581	116	44.69	1	5	873	66.55
17	PC Strydom (Bdr)	13	13	3	444	89*	44.40	0	4	483	91.92
18	AI Gait (FS)	8	8	1	310	138*	44.28	1	0	376	82.44
19	DJ Callaghan (EP)	14	13	1	494	75	41.16	0	5	663	74.50
20	JF Venter (FS)	10	10	0	410	89	41.00	0	5	595	68.90

(Qualification: 4 completed innings)

LEADING BOWLING AVERAGES

	Name	M	Overs	Mdns	Runs	Wkts	Avg	RpO	BB	4I
1	L Graham (Bdr)	6	44.3	3	174	12	14.50	3.91	3-18	0
2	A Nel (Eas)	10	86.2	7	341	22	15.50	3.94	6-27	2
3	AC Dawson (WP)	10	90	16	339	21	16.14	3.76	5-13	2
4	M Ngam (EP)	6	46	5	176	10	17.60	3.82	4-26	1
5	JC Kent (KZN)	14	110.2	4	500	26	19.23	4.53	4-29	1
6	GJ Kruis (GW)	10	84	5	391	20	19.55	4.65	4-55	1
7	GH Bodi (KZN)	15	78	2	378	18	21.00	4.84	5-46	1
8	GJ Smith (Nor)	10	86.2	8	377	17	22.17	4.36	5-44	1
9	EAE Baptiste (KZN)	15	112	7	406	18	22.55	3.62	3-17	0
10	HS Williams (Bol)	8	69.4	4	249	11	22.63	3.57	3-21	0
11	GA Roe (NW)	10	80	6	431	18	23.94	5.38	3-44	0
12	D Pretorius (FS)	9	76	2	411	17	24.17	5.40	3-34	0
13	DJ Terbrugge (Gau)	8	66.3	6	316	13	24.30	4.75	4-31	2
14	S Elworthy (Nor)	14	122	12	540	22	24.54	4.42	3-29	0
15	T Henderson (Bdr)	12	91.5	6	395	16	24.68	4.30	3-10	0
16	CK Langeveldt (Bol)	9	75.4	5	298	12	24.83	3.93	3-42	0
17	KCG Benjamin (Eas)	9	75.1	6	283	11	25.72	3.76	3-25	0
18	NM Carter (Bol)	10	80.5	6	361	14	25.78	4.46	3-41	0
19	M Hayward (EP)	8	43	0	268	10	26.80	6.23	4-42	1
20	PC Strydom (Bdr)	13	94.3	1	433	15	28.86	4.58	3-19	0

(Qualification: 10 wickets)

LEADING WICKETKEEPERS

Name		M	Ct	St	Total
1	ELR Stewart (KZN)	15	29	2	31
2	SJ Palframan (Bol)	10	14	2	16
3	D Jennings (Eas)	10	12	2	14
	I Mitchell (Bdr)	12	11	3	14
	CFK van Wyk (Nor)	14	12	2	14
6	W Bossenger (GW)	10	12	1	13
	GL Brophy (FS)	10	12	1	13
	DW Murray (EP)	14	10	3	13

Note: One of Mitchell's catches was taken as a fielder.

LEADING FIELDERS

Name		M	Ct
1	MJ Lavine (NW)	10	7
	MN van Wyk (FS)	9	7
3	HC Bakkes (FS)	9	6
	WM Dry (GW)	7	6
	HH Gibbs (WP)	9	6
	JM Otto (Gau)	8	6
7	AC Dawson (WP)	10	5
	P de Bruyn (Eas)	10	5
	G Dros (Nor)	14	5
	JC Kent (KZN)	14	5
	LJ Koen (Bol)	10	5
	GFJ Liebenberg (FS)	8	5
	C Light (NW)	8	5
	JG Myburgh (Nor)	13	5
	PC Strydom (Bdr)	13	5
	CB Sugden (Bdr)	13	5
	M van Jaarsveld (Nor)	14	5

BOLAND

Free State v Boland, Bloemfontein, 6 October 2000. Free State won by 6 wickets.
Eastern Province v Boland, Port Elizabeth, 13 October 2000. Eastern Province won by 1 run.

BOLAND v NORTH WEST — Standard Bank Cup

Played at Boland PKS Park, Paarl on 3 November 2000 — Toss: Boland
Umpires: ST Jivan & S Wadvalla
Debuts: Bol: None. NW: None
Result: Boland won by 28 runs
Man of Match: Jonathan Trott
Points: Bol 4, NW 0.

BOLAND	Runs	Mins	Balls	4	6
JM Henderson c Jacobs b Roe	5	18	18	-	-
IJL Trott not out	108	172	146	8	2
*LJ Koen run out (Venter/Poole)	27	65	45	4	-
JL Ontong b Jordaan	25	35	25	3	-
PH Barnard b Thomas	25	39	33	2	-
†SJ Palframan not out	14	11	6	1	-
BT Player					
CdeW de Lange					
NM Carter					
CK Langeveldt					
AAW Pringle					
Extras (lb 2, w 1, nb 3)	6				
TOTAL (for 4 wkts) (45 overs)	**210**				

NORTH WEST	Runs	Mins	Balls	4	6
GM Hewitt run out (Carter/Palframan)	1	7	6	-	-
HM de Vos c Henderson b Pringle	11	57	42	-	-
A Jacobs c and b Pringle	79	145	115	5	1
*MC Venter c Palframan b Player	18	44	29	2	-
C Light c Pringle b Player	9	16	11	1	-
MJ Lavine run out (Ontong)	6	3	3	-	1
CT Enslin c Palframan b Henderson	5	8	8	-	-
†EG Poole c Palframan b Langeveldt	22	49	29	1	-
AC Thomas not out	20	31	27	1	-
GA Roe not out	0	2	2	-	-
LCR Jordaan					
Extras (b 6, lb 1, w 2, nb 2)	11				
TOTAL (for 8 wkts) (45 overs)	**182**				

NW	O	M	R	W
Roe	9	2	40	1
Lavine	9	1	31	0
Thomas	9	0	37	1
Jordaan	9	1	34	1
Enslin	5	0	45	0
Light	4	0	21	0

Bol	O	M	R	W
Langeveldt	9	0	29	1
de Lange	9	2	20	0
Pringle	9	2	33	2
Carter	9	0	42	0
Player	5	0	27	2
Henderson	4	0	24	1

Fall of Wickets	Bol	NW
1st	8 (1)	3 (1)
2nd	66 (3)	38 (2)
3rd	111 (4)	91 (4)
4th	175 (5)	107 (5)
5th	-	114 (6)
6th	-	121 (7)
7th	-	148 (3)
8th	-	182 (8)

KwaZulu-Natal v Boland, Durban, 15 December 2000. KwaZulu-Natal won by 5 wickets.

BOLAND v GRIQUALAND WEST

Standard Bank Cup

Played at Boland PKS Park, Paarl on 22 December 2000

Toss: Boland

Umpires: DF Becker & SB Lambson

Debuts: Bol: None. GW: None

Result: Boland won by 58 runs

Man of Match: Louis Koen

Points: Bol 5, GW 0.

BOLAND	Runs	Mins	Balls	4	6
*LJ Koen c and b Elliott	106	174	131	9	1
H Davids c Elliott b Kruis	23	54	34	2	-
JL Ontong st Bossenger b Elliott	60	84	70	3	-
IJL Trott run out (Elliott/Gidley)	11	23	21	1	-
†SJ Palframan b Elliott	6	6	7	1	-
JG Strydom not out	4	9	6	-	-
BT Player c Tatton b Kruis	1	5	3	-	-
CdeW de Lange					
CK Langeveldt					
NM Carter					
HS Williams					
Extras (b 5, lb 6, w 9, nb 2)	22				
TOTAL (for 6 wkts) (45 overs)	**233**				

GRIQUALAND WEST	Runs	Mins	Balls	4	6
PPJ Koortzen b Langeveldt	24	32	26	2	1
*MI Gidley c Langeveldt b de Lange	24	61	45	2	-
LL Bosman c Strydom b de Lange	6	11	8	-	-
GD Elliott st Palframan b Ontong	21	72	43	-	-
BH Tucker c Palframan b Carter	42	61	53	4	-
†W Bossenger c Langeveldt b Carter	14	40	25	1	-
J Louw b Carter	6	16	12	-	-
GJ Kruis c Palframan b Ontong	9	11	11	1	-
ZA Abrahim not out	10	30	23	-	-
CR Tatton run out (Langeveldt/Palframan)	0	6	0	-	-
AJ Swanepoel b Williams	6	17	15	-	1
Extras (b 1, lb 1, w 4, nb 7)	13				
TOTAL (42.2 overs)	**175**				

GW	O	M	R	W
Abrahim	4	0	22	0
Swanepoel	7	0	30	0
Kruis	8	0	38	2
Louw	6	0	31	0
Tatton	9	0	41	0
Gidley	4	0	28	0
Elliott	7	0	32	3

Bol	O	M	R	W
Williams	8.2	0	31	1
Langeveldt	7	0	27	1
de Lange	9	0	34	2
Carter	9	0	43	3
Player	2	0	17	0
Ontong	7	1	21	2

Fall of Wickets	Bol	GW
1st	64 (2)	38 (1)
2nd	193 (3)	51 (3)
3rd	214 (4)	62 (2)
4th	223 (5)	128 (4)
5th	224 (1)	128 (5)
6th	233 (7)	142 (7)
7th	-	155 (8)
8th	-	158 (6)
9th	-	158 (10)
10th	-	175 (11)

BOLAND v GAUTENG

Standard Bank Cup

Played at Boland PKS Park, Paarl on 3 January 2001

Toss: Gauteng

Umpires: DF Becker & JD Cloete (TV: BG Jerling)

Debuts: Bol: None. Gau: None

Result: Boland won by 3 wickets

Man of Match: Steve Palframan

Points: Bol 4, Gau 1.

GAUTENG	Runs	Mins	Balls	4	6	BOLAND	Runs	Mins	Balls	4	6
SG Koenig c Palframan b Carter	10	50	38	1	-	*LJ Koen c Pothas b Gibson	12	37	23	-	-
AJ Hall c and b Carter	12	43	35	-	-	H Davids lbw b Hall	20	60	45	2	-
AM Bacher c and b Player	27	73	47	2	-	JL Ontong c Otto b Eksteen	9	50	34	1	-
JM Otto b Williams	40	79	56	2	2	IJL Trott lbw b Hall	0	1	1	-	-
†N Pothas not out	53	76	49	3	-	†SJ Palframan not out	76	129	91	5	2
Z de Bruyn c and b Player	1	5	4	-	-	JG Strydom run out (Terbrugge)	23	48	38	1	-
OD Gibson c Davids b Langeveldt	6	16	12	-	-	NM Carter b Gibson	3	10	7	-	-
*CE Eksteen c Palframan b Carter	10	22	17	-	-	BT Player c Pothas b Terbrugge	19	31	25	1	-
TK Mataboge run out (de Lange)	5	5	5	1	-	CdeW de Lange not out	6	11	6	-	-
DJ Terbrugge not out	6	11	8	-	-	CK Langeveldt					
JT Mafa						HS Williams					
Extras (lb 2, w 3, nb 1)	6					Extras (b 1, lb 5, w 2, nb 2)	10				
TOTAL (for 8 wkts) (45 overs)	**176**					**TOTAL (for 7 wkts) (44.4 overs)**	**178**				

Bol	O	M	R	W	Gau	O	M	R	W	Fall of Wickets	Gau	Bol
Langeveldt	9	2	21	1	Terbrugge	8.4	1	45	1	1st	24 (2)	23 (1)
de Lange	9	1	29	0	Gibson	9	0	26	2	2nd	25 (1)	46 (2)
Carter	9	1	41	3	Hall	9	1	33	2	3rd	93 (3)	46 (4)
Williams	9	0	36	1	Eksteen	9	1	21	1	4th	105 (4)	59 (3)
Player	9	0	47	2	Mafa	2	0	14	0	5th	106 (6)	105 (6)
					Mataboge	7	0	33	0	6th	119 (7)	112 (7)
										7th	144 (8)	147 (8)
										8th	151 (9)	-

Easterns v Boland, Benoni, 5 January 2001. Boland won by 7 wickets.

BOLAND v NORTHERNS — Standard Bank Cup

Played at Boland PKS Park, Paarl on 17 January 2001 — Toss: Boland
Umpires: BG Jerling & RE Koertzen (TV: M Gajjar)
Debuts: Bol: None. Nor: R Bailey
Result: Northerns won by 6 wickets
Man of Match: Martin van Jaarsveld
Points: Nor 4, Bol 0.

BOLAND	Runs	Mins	Balls	4	6	NORTHERNS	Runs	Mins	Balls	4	6
JM Henderson c and b Joubert	40	85	65	4	-	PJR Steyn c Koen b Carter	9	35	23	-	-
H Davids c and b Joubert	16	54	40	1	-	JA Rudolph b Williams	28	55	46	1	1
*LJ Koen c Dros b Joubert	5	15	15	1	-	M van Jaarsveld not out	76	143	89	6	-
JL Ontong c van Wyk b Dros	33	61	44	3	-	DJJ de Vos c Koen b Carter	9	32	19	-	-
JG Strydom c and b van Jaarsveld	29	59	49	2	-	*G Dros c Palframan b Langeveldt	28	40	39	2	-
†SJ Palframan not out	32	46	33	3	-	†CFK van Wyk not out	26	51	32	1	-
CdeW de Lange b Smith	13	28	19	-	-	R Bailey					
BT Player not out	7	7	5	-	-	S Elworthy					
NM Carter						A Paleker					
CK Langeveldt						P Joubert					
HS Williams						GJ Smith					
Extras (lb 5, w 4, nb 1)	10					Extras (lb 2, w 6, nb 3)	11				
TOTAL (for 6 wkts) (45 overs)	**185**					**TOTAL (for 4 wkts) (40.5 overs)**	**187**				

Nor	O	M	R	W	Bol	O	M	R	W	Fall of Wickets	Bol	Nor
Elworthy	9	0	51	0	Langeveldt	9	2	42	1	1st	48 (2)	36 (1)
Smith	8	1	28	1	de Lange	4	0	27	0	2nd	58 (3)	46 (2)
Joubert	9	2	28	3	Williams	8	1	32	1	3rd	75 (1)	74 (4)
de Vos	9	0	39	0	Carter	7.5	1	37	2	4th	124 (4)	121 (5)
Rudolph	2	0	8	0	Ontong	5	0	21	0	5th	133 (5)	-
Dros	5	1	15	1	Player	7	0	26	0	6th	173 (7)	-
van Jaarsveld	3	0	11	1								

Western Province v Boland, Cape Town, 19 January 2001. Western Province won by 5 runs.

BOLAND v BORDER — Standard Bank Cup

Played at Boland PKS Park, Paarl on 24 January 2001 — Toss: Boland
Umpires: WA Diedricks & S Wadvalla
Debuts: Bol: WJ du Toit. Bdr: None
Result: Border won by 4 wickets
Man of Match: Pieter Strydom
Points: Bdr 4, Bol 1.

BOLAND	Runs	Mins	Balls	4	6
*LJ Koen c Strydom b Drakes	69	124	85	7	1
H Davids c Mitchell b Ntini	1	13	10	-	-
JL Ontong c Pope b Henderson	17	49	37	-	-
KC Jackson c Boucher b Botha	6	12	14	1	-
IJL Trott run out (Strydom)	51	93	72	3	-
†SJ Palframan c Ntini b Pope	8	19	12	-	-
WJ du Toit b Ntini	6	12	12	-	-
NM Carter c Boucher b Drakes	13	28	16	1	-
CdeW de Lange lbw b Drakes	4	6	5	-	-
AAW Pringle c Ntini b Henderson	2	5	3	-	-
HS Williams not out	0	3	0	-	-
Extras (lb 1)	1				
TOTAL (44.2 overs)	**178**				

BORDER	Runs	Mins	Balls	4	6
LL Gamiet lbw b Pringle	1	13	8	-	-
†I Mitchell c Palframan b Pringle	10	30	19	2	-
SC Pope c Palframan b Pringle	9	21	17	1	-
MV Boucher b Williams	9	16	17	2	-
*PC Strydom not out	70	150	100	6	-
CB Sugden c Trott b Carter	16	40	31	2	-
W Wiblin c Jackson b Carter	46	87	66	3	-
PJ Botha not out	3	10	9	-	-
VC Drakes					
T Henderson					
M Ntini					
Extras (b 3, lb 5, w 4, nb 3)	15				
TOTAL (for 6 wkts) (44 overs)	**179**				

Bdr	O	M	R	W
Drakes	8.2	0	25	3
Ntini	9	0	25	2
Botha	5	0	27	1
Henderson	9	0	37	2
Strydom	5	0	30	0
Pope	8	0	33	1

Bol	O	M	R	W
Williams	9	1	26	1
Pringle	8	0	36	3
Carter	9	0	47	2
du Toit	9	1	27	0
Ontong	9	0	35	0

Fall of Wickets	Bol	Bdr
1st	6 (2)	7 (1)
2nd	60 (3)	26 (2)
3rd	69 (4)	31 (3)
4th	116 (1)	37 (4)
5th	137 (6)	78 (6)
6th	149 (7)	171 (7)
7th	166 (5)	-
8th	172 (9)	-
9th	177 (10)	-
10th	178 (8)	-

BORDER

Easterns v Border, Benoni, 6 October 2000. Easterns won by 15 runs.
Gauteng v Border, Johannesburg, 13 October 2000. Gauteng won by 6 runs.

BORDER v EASTERN PROVINCE

Standard Bank Cup

Toss: Border

Played at Buffalo Park, East London on 18 October 2000
Umpires: BG Jerling & IL Howell (TV: CM Schoof)
Debuts: Bdr: None. EP: None
Result: Eastern Province won by 6 runs
Man of Match: Carl Bradfield
Points: EP 4, Bdr 1.

EASTERN PROVINCE	Runs	Mins	Balls	4	6
*CC Bradfield st Boucher b Strydom	91	170	114	7	-
MR Benfield c Sugden b Strydom	50	84	68	7	-
JDC Bryant c Strydom b Ntini	62	80	64	7	1
DJ Callaghan not out	37	19	17	5	1
JM Kemp not out	5	13	7	-	-
MW Creed					
†DW Murray					
S Abrahams					
MW Pringle					
M Hayward					
M Ngam					
Extras (b 4, lb 6, w 5)	15				
TOTAL (for 3 wkts) (45 overs)	**260**				

BORDER	Runs	Mins	Balls	4	6
LL Gamiet c Bradfield b Callaghan	57	66	61	8	-
I Mitchell c Murray b Pringle	53	119	79	3	-
CB Sugden c Murray b Ngam	84	117	77	8	1
†MV Boucher c Murray b Pringle	0	8	2	-	-
*PC Strydom c and b Hayward	7	13	11	1	-
SC Pope b Abrahams	23	18	22	3	-
JWF Klopper c Abrahams b Kemp	0	2	2	-	-
VC Drakes run out (Ngam)	5	15	6	-	-
GT Love c and b Hayward	0	4	1	-	-
T Henderson not out	0	5	0	-	-
M Ntini c Ngam b Hayward	4	4	4	1	-
Extras (lb 8, w 11, nb 2)	21				
TOTAL (43.5 overs)	**254**				

Bdr	O	M	R	W
Drakes	9	1	36	0
Ntini	9	0	56	1
Klopper	8	0	44	0
Henderson	7	0	42	0
Love	4	0	25	0
Strydom	8	0	47	2

EP	O	M	R	W
Ngam	8	0	38	1
Pringle	9	0	39	2
Kemp	4	0	33	1
Hayward	8.5	0	56	3
Callaghan	5	0	33	1
Abrahams	9	0	47	1

Fall of Wickets	EP	Bdr
1st	88 (2)	85 (1)
2nd	210 (3)	173 (2)
3rd	217 (1)	185 (4)
4th	-	196 (5)
5th	-	228 (6)
6th	-	229 (7)
7th	-	249 (8)
8th	-	250 (3)
9th	-	250 (9)
10th	-	254 (11)

Western Province v Border, Cape Town, 1 December 2000. Border won by 4 wickets.
Northerns v Border, Centurion, 17 December 2000. Border won by 4 wickets.

BORDER v NORTH WEST

Standard Bank Cup

Played at Buffalo Park, East London on 22 December 2000
Toss: Border
Umpires: IL Howell & S Wadvalla
Debuts: Bdr: None. NW: None
Result: Border won by 125 runs
Man of Match: Pieter Strydom
Points: Bdr 5, NW 0.

BORDER	*Runs*	*Mins*	*Balls*	*4*	*6*
LL Gamiet c Niewoudt b Roe	6	46	30	-	-
I Mitchell b Thomas	67	143	107	9	-
SC Pope b van der Merwe	8	25	17	2	-
†MV Boucher c and b van der Merwe	15	32	24	1	-
*PC Strydom c Strydom b Light	79	78	58	7	2
CB Sugden not out	53	45	32	5	2
VC Drakes c Roe b Thomas	2	4	3	-	-
W Wiblin not out	0	2	1	-	-
PJ Botha					
T Henderson					
M Ntini					
Extras (lb 7, w 10, nb 2)	19				
TOTAL (for 6 wkts) (45 overs)	**249**				

NORTH WEST	*Runs*	*Mins*	*Balls*	*4*	*6*
R Niewoudt c Boucher b Drakes	7	27	16	1	-
G Outram b Henderson	29	60	58	3	-
*GM Hewitt b Henderson	14	57	33	-	-
A Jacobs c Wiblin b Drakes	16	53	22	-	-
C Light c Boucher b Henderson	0	2	4	-	-
MJ Lavine c Pope b Botha	17	42	32	1	-
M Strydom c Mitchell b Botha	13	27	33	1	-
†EG Poole c Henderson b Strydom	6	13	7	-	-
AC Thomas not out	1	15	6	-	-
GA Roe c Sugden b Strydom	13	9	9	1	1
F van der Merwe c Drakes b Strydom	0	1	1	-	-
Extras (lb 1, w 5, nb 2)	8				
TOTAL (36.3 overs)	**124**				

NW	*O*	*M*	*R*	*W*
Lavine	9	1	50	0
Roe	9	0	36	1
Thomas	9	0	42	2
van der Merwe	9	0	35	2
Light	4	0	30	1
Niewoudt	3	0	21	0
Strydom	2	0	28	0

Bdr	*O*	*M*	*R*	*W*
Drakes	7	0	26	2
Ntini	7	1	23	0
Henderson	6	0	10	3
Botha	9	0	45	2
Strydom	7.3	0	19	3

Fall of Wickets	*Bdr*	*NW*
1st	37 (1)	16 (1)
2nd	63 (3)	46 (2)
3rd	90 (4)	66 (3)
4th	142 (2)	66 (5)
5th	239 (5)	87 (4)
6th	247 (7)	98 (6)
7th	-	106 (7)
8th	-	109 (8)
9th	-	124 (10)
10th	-	124 (11)

BORDER v KWAZULU-NATAL

Standard Bank Cup

Played at Buffalo Park, East London on 29 December 2000
Toss: KwaZulu-Natal
Umpires: SB Lambson & CJ Mitchley (TV: AE Williams)
Debuts: Bdr: None. KZN: None
Result: KwaZulu-Natal won by 58 runs (D/L method), target revised to 207 in 40 overs
Man of Match: Ashraf Mall
Points: KZN 5, Bdr 0.

KWAZULU-NATAL	*Runs*	*Mins*	*Balls*	*4*	*6*
DJ Watson lbw b Botha	14	17	14	3	-
A Mall b Botha	65	132	104	7	-
WR Wingfield c Botha b Graham	24	71	49	1	-
JN Rhodes c Gamiet b Graham	6	9	7	-	-
*DM Benkenstein c Drakes b Strydom	32	44	43	1	-
JC Kent c Botha b Strydom	8	17	11	-	-
†ELR Stewart not out	15	36	16	-	-
GH Bodi c Pope b Henderson	29	21	21	5	-
EAE Baptiste b Henderson	9	11	9	-	-
GM Gilder					
JE Bastow					
Extras (lb 8, w 4, nb 4)	16				
TOTAL (for 8 wkts) (45 overs)	**218**				

BORDER	*Runs*	*Mins*	*Balls*	*4*	*6*
LL Gamiet c Kent b Baptiste	36	124	79	4	-
†I Mitchell b Gilder	10	27	14	2	-
SC Pope c Stewart b Gilder	13	26	17	2	-
*PC Strydom lbw b Kent	9	5	6	2	-
CB Sugden c Watson b Kent	11	18	12	2	-
W Wiblin b Kent	9	18	15	1	-
DL Makalima b Baptiste	1	15	4	-	-
PJ Botha b Wingfield	15	27	20	1	-
VC Drakes c Baptiste b Bastow	14	36	22	-	-
T Henderson b Benkenstein	9	5	6	-	1
L Graham not out	3	11	11	-	-
Extras (lb 4, w 13, nb 1)	18				
TOTAL (34.1 overs)	**148**				

Bdr	*O*	*M*	*R*	*W*
Botha	9	0	53	2
Drakes	9	1	52	0
Henderson	9	1	36	2
Graham	9	1	32	2
Strydom	9	0	37	2

KZN	*O*	*M*	*R*	*W*
Bastow	6.1	1	19	1
Gilder	7	1	25	2
Kent	7	0	42	3
Baptiste	6	0	20	2
Benkenstein	4	0	23	1
Wingfield	4	0	15	1

Fall of Wickets	*KZN*	*Bdr*
1st	32 (1)	19 (2)
2nd	92 (3)	42 (3)
3rd	106 (4)	51 (4)
4th	144 (2)	74 (5)
5th	163 (5)	93 (6)
6th	163 (6)	102 (7)
7th	203 (8)	107 (1)
8th	218 (9)	129 (8)
9th	-	140 (10)
10th	-	148 (9)

BORDER v FREE STATE

Standard Bank Cup

Played at Buffalo Park, East London on 3 January 2001
Toss: Border
Umpires: KH Hurter & SB Lambson
Debuts: Bdr: None. FS: None
Result: Border won by 55 runs
Man of Match: Pieter Strydom
Points: Bdr 5, FS 0.

BORDER	Runs	Mins	Balls	4	6
LL Gamiet b Mokoenanyana	23	60	34	1	1
†I Mitchell c van der Wath b Mpitsang	2	12	13	-	-
SC Pope c van Wyk b van der Wath	48	101	65	6	-
*PC Strydom c Gait b Mpitsang	25	40	36	2	-
CB Sugden c Brophy b van der Wath	32	61	43	1	-
W Wiblin b van der Wath	36	58	43	2	1
DL Makalima not out	17	34	20	1	-
VC Drakes b van der Wath	12	18	13	-	-
PJ Botha not out	1	5	3	-	-
T Henderson					
L Graham					
Extras (b 1, lb 6, w 6)	13				
TOTAL (for 7 wkts) (45 overs)	**209**				

FREE STATE	Runs	Mins	Balls	4	6
JF Venter b Henderson	23	54	49	3	-
AI Gait c Mitchell b Strydom	34	76	47	6	-
JJ van der Wath b Graham	17	40	34	1	-
HH Dippenaar c Makalima b Strydom	9	25	18	-	-
MN van Wyk run out (Gamiet)	11	30	21	-	-
WJ Smit lbw b Drakes	2	7	5	-	-
*†GL Brophy st Mitchell b Strydom	37	56	41	4	-
HC Bakkes c Henderson b Graham	0	3	2	-	-
D Pretorius c Wiblin b Botha	1	5	3	-	-
PV Mpitsang b Botha	3	8	6	-	-
TJ Mokoenanyana not out	3	158	12	-	-
Extras (lb 8, w 2, nb 4)	14				
TOTAL (39 overs)	**154**				

FS	O	M	R	W
Mpitsang	9	2	24	2
Bakkes	9	1	39	0
Pretorius	9	0	44	0
van der Wath	9	0	45	4
Mokoenanyana	5	0	25	1
Venter	4	0	25	0

Bdr	O	M	R	W
Drakes	7	0	38	1
Henderson	9	2	20	1
Botha	8	0	31	2
Graham	7	0	27	2
Strydom	8	0	30	3

Fall of Wickets	Bdr	FS
1st	5 (2)	51 (1)
2nd	54 (1)	73 (2)
3rd	98 (4)	91 (3)
4th	107 (3)	93 (4)
5th	161 (5)	96 (6)
6th	178 (6)	118 (5)
7th	201 (8)	119 (8)
8th	-	123 (9)
9th	-	134 (10)
10th	-	154 (7)

BORDER v GRIQUALAND WEST

Standard Bank Cup

Played at Buffalo Park, East London on 19 January 2001
Toss: Griqualand West
Umpires: CM Schoof & S Wadvalla
Debuts: Bdr: None. GW: None
Result: Border won by 8 wickets
Man of Match: Pieter Strydom
Points: Bdr 5, GW 0.

GRIQUALAND WEST	Runs	Mins	Balls	4	6
PPJ Koortzen c Sugden b Graham	23	45	39	4	-
LL Bosman c and b Botha	17	50	31	2	-
ZA Abrahim c Botha b Graham	0	1	1	-	-
WM Dry c Wiblin b Graham	32	81	62	2	1
MI Gidley b Strydom	28	67	57	3	-
GD Elliott not out	40	61	48	1	-
BH Tucker not out	29	47	41	-	-
*†W Bossenger					
J Louw					
GJ Kruis					
AJ Swanepoel					
Extras (b 1, lb 5, w 7, nb 9)	22				
TOTAL (for 5 wkts) (45 overs)	**191**				

BORDER	Runs	Mins	Balls	4	6
LL Gamiet not out	71	149	105	9	-
†I Mitchell b Kruis	0	10	7	-	-
SC Pope c Bossenger b Abrahim	29	35	28	5	-
*PC Strydom not out	84	103	74	11	1
CB Sugden					
W Wiblin					
DL Makalima					
VC Drakes					
PJ Botha					
T Henderson					
L Graham					
Extras (b 1, lb 1, w 6, nb 2)	10				
TOTAL (for 2 wkts) (35.2 overs)	**194**				

Bdr	O	M	R	W
Henderson	7	0	32	0
Drakes	9	2	34	0
Graham	7	0	37	3
Botha	7	0	28	1
Strydom	9	0	32	1
Pope	6	0	22	0

GW	O	M	R	W
Kruis	8	1	37	1
Abrahim	7	2	19	1
Swanepoel	7	0	42	0
Elliott	3	0	21	0
Louw	5.2	0	40	0
Gidley	5	0	33	0

Fall of Wickets	GW	Bdr
1st	46 (1)	2 (2)
2nd	46 (3)	48 (3)
3rd	46 (2)	-
4th	105 (5)	-
5th	120 (4)	-

Boland v Border, Paarl, 24 January 2001. Border won by 4 wickets.

EASTERNS

EASTERNS v BORDER

Standard Bank Cup

Played at Willowmoore Park, Benoni on 6 October 2000

Toss: Easterns

Umpires: M Gajjar & CJ Mitchley

Debuts: Eas: ET Mokoenanyana. Bdr: None

Result: Easterns won by 15 runs

Man of Match: Derek Crookes

Points: Eas 4, Bdr 0.

EASTERNS	Runs	Mins	Balls	4	6
D Brand c Mitchell b Drakes	12	10	12	3	-
GE Flusk c Mitchell b Botha	14	31	20	2	-
ET Mokoenanyana b Love	4	32	16	-	-
*D Jordaan b Henderson	72	128	118	3	-
MJR Rindel st Mitchell b Love	18	27	20	3	-
DN Crookes not out	58	97	81	3	-
†D Jennings run out (Botha/Mitchell)	1	4	1	-	-
P de Bruyn not out	3	3	2	-	-
JA Morkel					
KCG Benjamin					
A Nel					
Extras (b 1, lb 5, w 1)	7				
TOTAL (for 6 wkts) (45 overs)	**189**				

BORDER	Runs	Mins	Balls	4	6
†I Mitchell c Jennings b Benjamin	12	49	24	2	-
LL Gamiet c Rindel b Nel	1	9	9	-	-
T Henderson c Jennings b Nel	19	24	20	3	-
EJ Ferreira c Jennings b Morkel	11	29	22	1	-
*PC Strydom c Jennings b Morkel	6	21	19	1	-
CB Sugden c Brand b Morkel	10	30	24	1	-
SC Pope run out (Brand/de Bruyn)	27	79	55	3	-
VC Drakes lbw b Crookes	0	22	8	-	-
PJ Botha lbw b Crookes	21	27	34	1	1
DL Makalima b Nel	21	29	29	2	-
GT Love not out	14	24	20	1	-
Extras (b 8, lb 5, w 14, nb 5)	32				
TOTAL (43.1 overs)	**174**				

Bdr	O	M	R	W
Drakes	6	0	27	1
Botha	7	1	30	1
Love	9	1	28	2
Henderson	6	0	19	1
Strydom	9	0	40	0
Pope	8	0	39	0

Eas	O	M	R	W
Benjamin	9	0	31	1
Nel	7.1	1	35	3
Morkel	9	1	27	3
de Bruyn	9	0	34	0
Crookes	8	0	30	2
Rindel	1	0	4	0

Fall of Wickets	Eas	Bdr
1st	14 (1)	2 (2)
2nd	30 (2)	32 (3)
3rd	36 (3)	42 (1)
4th	65 (5)	51 (4)
5th	177 (4)	56 (5)
6th	180 (7)	72 (6)
7th	-	99 (8)
8th	-	131 (9)
9th	-	132 (7)
10th	-	174 (10)

EASTERNS v KWAZULU-NATAL

Standard Bank Cup

Played at Willowmoore Park, Benoni on 11 October 2000

Toss: Easterns

Umpires: JD Cloete & SB Lambson (TV: KH Hurter)

Debuts: Eas: None. KZN: None

Result: Easterns won by 79 runs

Man of Match: Mike Rindel

Points: Eas 5, KZN 0.

EASTERNS	Runs	Mins	Balls	4	6
D Brand c Hudson b Baptiste	15	46	29	1	-
MJR Rindel c Stewart b Veenstra	128	167	139	18	-
KCG Benjamin b Benkenstein	12	28	16	2	-
GE Flusk c and b Benkenstein	0	8	6	-	-
DN Crookes c Bruyns b Bodi	37	62	52	3	-
P de Bruyn c Stewart b Veenstra	26	30	20	3	-
JA Morkel run out (Watson/Stewart)	1	5	2	-	-
†D Jennings not out	3	9	3	-	-
*D Jordaan lbw b Veenstra	0	2	3	-	-
ET Mokoenanyana run out (Bruyns/Veenstra)	0	1	1	-	-
A Nel					
Extras (b 1, lb 3, w 5, nb 1)	10				
TOTAL (for 9 wkts) (45 overs)	**232**				

KWAZULU-NATAL	Runs	Mins	Balls	4	6
ML Bruyns c Jennings b Benjamin	12	29	19	2	-
DJ Watson b Nel	8	23	17	1	-
AM Amla lbw b Benjamin	5	14	7	1	-
GH Bodi c and b Nel	0	6	6	-	-
*DM Benkenstein b Benjamin	2	16	12	-	-
AC Hudson c Brand b Morkel	16	40	35	1	-
†ELR Stewart b Nel	32	69	58	2	-
RE Veenstra b de Bruyn	3	17	12	-	-
EAE Baptiste b de Bruyn	6	9	7	-	-
KS Bender not out	14	55	42	-	-
GM Gilder c Morkel b Flusk	36	37	28	1	4
Extras (lb 4, w 15)	19				
TOTAL (40.3 overs)	**153**				

KZN	O	M	R	W
Veenstra	9	0	47	3
Gilder	7	0	35	0
Baptiste	8	0	42	1
Benkenstein	9	0	42	2
Bender	6	0	30	0
Bodi	6	0	32	1

Eas	O	M	R	W
Benjamin	9	1	25	3
Nel	9	1	25	3
Crookes	6	0	42	0
Jordaan	3	0	7	0
Morkel	6	0	20	1
de Bruyn	5	0	19	2
Flusk	2.3	0	11	1

Fall of Wickets	Eas	KZN
1st	50 (1)	21 (2)
2nd	82 (3)	29 (1)
3rd	92 (4)	31 (4)
4th	182 (5)	31 (3)
5th	214 (2)	39 (5)
6th	225 (7)	64 (6)
7th	231 (6)	79 (8)
8th	232 (9)	89 (9)
9th	232 (10)	103 (7)
10th	-	153 (11)

EASTERNS v GRIQUALAND WEST

Standard Bank Cup

Played at Willowmoore Park, Benoni on 1 December 2000
Toss: Griqualand West
Umpires: SB Lambson & CM Schoof
Debuts: Eas: EF Mabhena. GW: None
Result: Easterns won by 1 wicket
Man of Match: Andre Nel
Points: Eas 4, GW 1.

GRIQUALAND WEST	Runs	Mins	Balls	4	6
WM Dry c Jennings b Nel	3	34	24	-	-
*MI Gidley c Jennings b Nel	3	24	18	-	-
GD Elliott c Jennings b Nel	0	1	1	-	-
PPJ Koortzen c Jennings b Nel	8	17	18	-	-
LL Bosman c Pollock b Flusk	40	73	60	5	1
†W Bossenger not out	48	134	101	4	-
J Brooker c Jennings b Nel	23	30	40	3	-
GJ Kruis b Nel	1	7	7	-	-
ZA Abrahim c Flusk b Benjamin	3	12	6	-	-
CR Tatton not out	2	3	2	-	-
AJ Swanepoel					
Extras (lb 8, w 11, nb 7)	26				
TOTAL (for 8 wkts) (45 overs)	**157**				

EASTERNS	Runs	Mins	Balls	4	6
†D Jennings c Bossenger b Swanepoel	12	64	46	1	-
MJR Rindel b Swanepoel	53	77	58	9	-
KCG Benjamin b Elliott	3	10	8	-	-
*D Jordaan lbw b Kruis	6	16	14	1	-
DN Crookes lbw b Abrahim	14	63	41	1	-
GA Pollock lbw b Kruis	0	1	2	-	-
P de Bruyn b Tatton	16	63	41	2	-
JA Morkel run out (Bosman/Tatton)	1	16	12	-	-
EF Mabhena not out	17	38	28	1	-
GE Flusk run out (Bosman/Bossenger)	7	17	12	-	-
A Nel not out	3	16	10	-	-
Extras (lb 7, w 17, nb 2)	26				
TOTAL (for 9 wkts) (45 overs)	**158**				

Eas	O	M	R	W
Benjamin	9	1	25	1
Nel	9	2	27	6
de Bruyn	2	1	2	0
Morkel	9	1	29	0
Rindel	3	0	11	0
Flusk	9	0	37	1
Crookes	4	1	18	0

GW	O	M	R	W
Kruis	9	1	27	2
Abrahim	9	2	32	1
Swanepoel	9	1	27	2
Elliott	8	1	29	1
Tatton	7	1	30	1
Gidley	3	0	6	0

Fall of Wickets	GW	Eas
1st	11 (2)	71 (1)
2nd	11 (3)	74 (3)
3rd	15 (1)	76 (2)
4th	23 (4)	84 (4)
5th	91 (5)	84 (6)
6th	126 (7)	119 (5)
7th	130 (8)	127 (7)
8th	152 (9)	128 (8)
9th	-	139 (10)

Western Province v Easterns, Cape Town, 8 December 2000. Western Province won by 7 runs.
North West v Easterns, Potchefstroom, 15 December 2000. Easterns won by 59 runs.

EASTERNS v BOLAND

Standard Bank Cup

Played at Willowmoore Park, Benoni on 5 January 2001
Toss: Easterns
Umpires: BG Jerling & AG O'Connor
Debuts: Eas: None. Bol: None
Result: Boland won by 7 wickets
Man of Match: Louis Koen
Points: Bol 4, Eas 1.

EASTERNS	Runs	Mins	Balls	4	6
MJR Rindel b Langeveldt	0	1	1	-	-
GE Flusk run out (Trott/Langeveldt)	9	29	18	2	-
AJ Seymore c Palframan b de Lange	30	63	49	4	-
*D Jordaan st Palframan b de Lange	12	21	13	3	-
DN Crookes c Strydom b Williams	7	21	16	-	-
P de Bruyn c Trott b Williams	53	116	74	4	-
GA Pollock c Strydom b Williams	0	7	7	-	-
†D Jennings c and b Player	27	69	61	2	-
EF Mabhena b Langeveldt	5	7	8	-	-
KCG Benjamin run out (Ontong)	17	25	18	1	-
A Nel not out	9	6	5	-	1
Extras (lb 9, w 3, nb 2)	14				
TOTAL (44.4 overs)	**183**				

BOLAND	Runs	Mins	Balls	4	6
IJL Trott c Jennings b Benjamin	2	14	5	-	-
H Davids b Nel	0	11	10	-	-
*LJ Koen not out	68	200	120	6	-
JL Ontong lbw b Crookes	41	114	71	3	-
JG Strydom not out	43	82	55	3	-
†SJ Palframan					
BT Player					
CdeW de Lange					
NM Carter					
CK Langeveldt					
HS Williams					
Extras (b 1, lb 3, w 24, nb 2)	30				
TOTAL (for 3 wkts) (43.1 overs)	**184**				

Bol	O	M	R	W
Langeveldt	8.4	0	39	2
Carter	6	0	37	0
de Lange	7	1	26	2
Williams	9	0	21	3
Player	7	1	23	1
Ontong	7	0	28	0

Eas	O	M	R	W
Benjamin	9	1	33	1
Nel	9	0	32	1
Flusk	4	0	22	0
de Bruyn	8	0	42	0
Crookes	9	1	28	1
Rindel	4	0	22	0
Jordaan	0.1	0	1	0

Fall of Wickets	Eas	Bol
1st	0 (1)	6 (2)
2nd	26 (2)	6 (1)
3rd	55 (4)	102 (4)
4th	58 (3)	-
5th	66 (5)	-
6th	70 (7)	-
7th	139 (8)	-
8th	147 (9)	-
9th	171 (6)	-
10th	183 (10)	-

Northerns v Easterns, Centurion, 7 January 2001. Northerns won by 11 runs.
Gauteng v Easterns, Johannesburg, 10 January 2001. Gauteng won by 5 wickets.
Eastern Province v Easterns, Port Elizabeth, 19 January 2001. Match tied.

EASTERNS v FREE STATE — Standard Bank Cup

Played at Willowmoore Park, Benoni on 24 January 2001 — Toss: Free State
Umpires: CJ Mitchley & AG O'Connor (TV: KH Hurter)
Debuts: Eas: None. FS: WA Deacon & MR Lewis
Result: Free State won by 1 run (D/L method), target revised to 206 in 39 overs
Man of Match: Derek Brand
Points: FS 4, Eas 1.

FREE STATE	Runs	Mins	Balls	4	6
JF Venter b Reddy	69	135	104	4	-
AI Gait c Flusk b Crookes	8	13	12	1	-
MN van Wyk b de Bruyn	24	50	37	3	-
LJ Wilkinson not out	52	100	58	2	-
*†GL Brophy lbw b Nel	10	24	21	-	-
JJ van der Wath not out	10	4	4	-	-
GFJ Liebenberg					
WA Deacon					
MR Lewis					
D Pretorius					
PV Mpitsang					
Extras (lb 7, w 8, nb 2)	17				
TOTAL (for 4 wkts) (39 overs)	**190**				

EASTERNS	Runs	Mins	Balls	4	6
D Brand c Lewis b van Wyk	75	114	87	10	-
MJR Rindel c and b van der Wath	37	77	40	6	-
AJ Seymore run out (Liebenberg)	21	60	43	1	-
*D Jordaan b van Wyk	0	3	4	-	-
DN Crookes lbw b Mpitsang	22	29	22	3	-
P de Bruyn c Wilkinson b Pretorius	0	12	3	-	-
AM van den Berg not out	12	33	17	-	-
†D Jennings c Liebenberg b Pretorius	5	7	8	-	-
GE Flusk run out (Venter)	5	10	7	-	-
BL Reddy run out (Pretorius)	3	4	3	-	-
A Nel not out	1	4	1	-	-
Extras (b 4, lb 8, w 10, nb 1)	23				
TOTAL (for 9 wkts) (39 overs)	**204**				

Eas	O	M	R	W
Nel	8	0	27	1
Crookes	6	1	16	1
Rindel	3	0	16	0
Reddy	7	0	41	1
de Bruyn	8	0	44	1
Flusk	5	0	25	0
van den Berg	2	0	14	0

FS	O	M	R	W
Mpitsang	7	0	36	1
Pretorius	8	0	40	2
Venter	5	0	23	0
Deacon	2	0	18	0
Lewis	5	0	21	0
van der Wath	7	0	26	1
van Wyk	5	0	28	2

Fall of Wickets	FS	Eas
1st	12 (2)	98 (2)
2nd	62 (3)	142 (1)
3rd	154 (1)	142 (4)
4th	177 (5)	173 (3)
5th	-	176 (5)
6th	-	178 (6)
7th	-	186 (8)
8th	-	194 (9)
9th	-	199 (10)

EASTERN PROVINCE

North West v Eastern Province, Potchefstroom, 4 October 2000. Eastern Province won by 8 runs.

EASTERN PROVINCE v BOLAND — Standard Bank Cup

Played at St George's Park, Port Elizabeth on 13 October 2000 — Toss: Eastern Province
Umpires: WA Diedricks & CM Schoof
Debuts: EP: None. Bol: None
Result: Eastern Province won by 1 run
Man of Match: Justin Kemp
Points: EP 4, Bol 1.

EASTERN PROVINCE	Runs	Mins	Balls	4	6
MR Benfield c Palframan b Williams	2	13	7	-	-
*CC Bradfield c and b Carter	0	5	3	-	-
JDC Bryant c Koen b Langeveldt	4	28	16	-	-
DJ Callaghan c Henderson b Langeveldt	13	38	33	1	-
JM Kemp not out	95	139	126	8	2
MW Creed lbw b Player	1	19	19	-	-
RJ Peterson c Ontong b Player	1	18	11	-	-
†DW Murray c and b de Lange	25	57	37	2	-
MW Pringle not out	25	32	21	-	2
M Hayward					
M Ngam					
Extras (lb 9, w 5, nb 3)	17				
TOTAL (for 7 wkts) (45 overs)	**183**				

BOLAND	Runs	Mins	Balls	4	6
JM Henderson c Benfield b Ngam	13	41	35	1	-
*LJ Koen b Ngam	9	34	22	1	-
IJL Trott run out (Creed/Murray)	18	53	40	2	-
PH Barnard c and b Hayward	59	145	98	4	-
JL Ontong lbw b Peterson	4	13	6	-	-
†SJ Palframan lbw b Pringle	1	6	7	-	-
CdeW de Lange run out (Bryant/Kemp)	0	2	0	-	-
BT Player b Ngam	36	62	53	3	1
NM Carter c Bradfield b Ngam	0	1	2	-	-
CK Langeveldt not out	5	16	10	-	-
HS Williams run out (Bryant)	3	9	4	-	-
Extras (lb 8, w 18, nb 8)	34				
TOTAL (44.5 overs)	**182**				

Bol	O	M	R	W
Williams	9	0	42	1
Carter	9	1	30	1
Langeveldt	9	0	30	2
Player	9	1	28	2
de Lange	9	1	44	1

EP	O	M	R	W
Pringle	9	0	27	1
Ngam	9	2	26	4
Kemp	9	0	41	0
Hayward	8.5	0	44	1
Peterson	9	1	36	1

Fall of Wickets	EP	Bol
1st	2 (2)	28 (2)
2nd	5 (1)	33 (1)
3rd	20 (3)	75 (3)
4th	30 (4)	87 (5)
5th	36 (6)	91 (6)
6th	45 (7)	92 (7)
7th	121 (8)	163 (8)
8th	-	163 (9)
9th	-	173 (4)
10th	-	182 (11)

Border v Eastern Province, East London, 18 October 2000. Eastern Province won by 6 runs.

EASTERN PROVINCE v FREE STATE — Standard Bank Cup

Played at St George's Park, Port Elizabeth on 22 November 2000 — Toss: Eastern Province
Umpires: DF Becker & BG Jerling (TV: M Gajjar)
Debuts: EP: GS Hayward. FS: None
Result: Eastern Province won by 50 runs
Man of Match: Justin Kemp
Points: EP 5, FS 0.

EASTERN PROVINCE	Runs	Mins	Balls	4	6
*CC Bradfield c Smit b Boje	40	86	74	5	-
MR Benfield c Bakkes b Boje	11	25	22	1	-
RJ Peterson c Liebenberg b Boje	61	78	49	5	2
JDC Bryant not out	56	92	70	3	1
DJ Callaghan c Donald b Mokoenanyana	6	11	7	1	-
JM Kemp c Mokoenanyana b Mpitsang	17	30	27	1	-
MW Creed c Boje b Donald	5	12	10	-	-
GS Hayward run out (Dippenaar/Bakkes)	10	15	10	-	-
†DW Murray run out (Boje)	0	1	1	-	-
S Abrahams not out	1	4	1	-	-
M Ngam					
Extras (lb 5, w 4, nb 1)	10				
TOTAL (for 8 wkts) (45 overs)	**217**				

FREE STATE	Runs	Mins	Balls	4	6
JF Venter b Ngam	2	39	32	-	-
HH Dippenaar lbw b Ngam	3	11	3	-	-
GFJ Liebenberg c Abrahams b Kemp	0	13	13	-	-
*N Boje c Hayward b Kemp	0	9	3	-	-
WJ Smit b Hayward	45	75	69	5	-
LJ Wilkinson c Ngam b Kemp	51	90	75	4	-
†GL Brophy run out (Creed/Abrahams)	23	23	23	2	-
HC Bakkes c Abrahams b Kemp	14	30	21	1	-
AA Donald c Bradfield b Kemp	8	18	16	-	-
PV Mpitsang c Murray b Kemp	2	8	6	-	-
TJ Mokoenanyana not out	0	1	0	-	-
Extras (lb 8, w 10, nb 1)	19				
TOTAL (43.2 overs)	**167**				

FS	O	M	R	W
Mpitsang	9	1	27	1
Bakkes	9	0	41	0
Boje	9	1	39	3
Donald	9	0	51	1
Venter	5	0	33	0
Mokoenanyana	4	0	21	1

EP	O	M	R	W
Ngam	8	2	14	2
Kemp	8.2	0	20	6
Callaghan	9	1	26	0
Peterson	5	0	29	0
Abrahams	9	0	48	0
Hayward	4	0	22	1

Fall of Wickets	EP	FS
1st	23 (2)	4 (2)
2nd	101 (1)	7 (3)
3rd	127 (3)	10 (4)
4th	141 (5)	11 (1)
5th	171 (6)	101 (5)
6th	181 (7)	138 (6)
7th	207 (8)	143 (7)
8th	207 (9)	159 (9)
9th	-	167 (8)
10th	-	167 (10)

Gauteng v Eastern Province, Johannesburg, 20 December 2000. Eastern Province won by 5 wickets.

Western Province v Eastern Province, Cape Town, 22 December 2000. Western Province won by 9 wickets.

EASTERN PROVINCE v NORTHERNS

Standard Bank Cup

Played at St George's Park, Port Elizabeth on 27 December 2000
Toss: Eastern Province
Umpires: SB Lambson & CM Schoof (TV: M Gajjar)
Debuts: EP: None. Nor: None
Result: Northerns won by 6 wickets
Man of Match: Gerald Dros
Points: Nor 4, EP 0.

EASTERN PROVINCE	*Runs*	*Mins*	*Balls*	*4*	*6*
*CC Bradfield c de Vos b Elworthy	12	33	24	3	-
JM Kemp c and b Brouwers	27	71	56	3	-
RJ Peterson b Elworthy	0	3	3	-	-
JDC Bryant b Joubert	7	11	15	1	-
DJ Callaghan b Brouwers	12	39	36	1	-
MR Benfield run out (Bryson/van Wyk)	72	95	78	2	4
MW Creed run out (Dros)	43	56	49	4	-
†DW Murray c sub (JA Rudolph) b Elworthy	4	16	11	-	-
MW Pringle not out	1	5	1	-	-
S Abrahams not out	4	1	1	1	-
GJ-P Kruger					
Extras (b 5, lb 2, w 2, nb 4)	13				
TOTAL (for 8 wkts) (45 overs)	**195**				

NORTHERNS	*Runs*	*Mins*	*Balls*	*4*	*6*
PJR Steyn c Creed b Kruger	0	13	11	-	-
JG Myburgh c Kemp b Kruger	21	42	29	4	-
M van Jaarsveld lbw b Creed	36	96	70	6	-
DJJ de Vos b Kemp	4	19	12	-	-
*G Dros not out	71	113	93	6	3
†CFK van Wyk not out	44	65	52	4	-
A Paleker					
S Elworthy					
P Joubert					
NG Brouwers					
RE Bryson					
Extras (b 1, w 7, nb 12)	20				
TOTAL (for 4 wkts) (42.3 overs)	**196**				

Nor	*O*	*M*	*R*	*W*
Elworthy	9	1	29	3
Bryson	9	0	54	0
Joubert	9	1	18	1
Brouwers	9	0	38	2
de Vos	5	0	29	0
Dros	3	0	11	0
Myburgh	1	0	9	0

EP	*O*	*M*	*R*	*W*
Kruger	7.3	1	58	2
Pringle	6	0	22	0
Callaghan	7	0	29	0
Kemp	9	4	22	1
Abrahams	6	0	20	0
Creed	6	1	33	1
Peterson	1	0	11	0

Fall of Wickets	*EP*	*Nor*
1st	33 (1)	7 (1)
2nd	33 (3)	42 (2)
3rd	42 (4)	53 (4)
4th	56 (2)	89 (3)
5th	70 (5)	-
6th	162 (7)	-
7th	188 (8)	-
8th	191 (6)	-

EASTERN PROVINCE v GRIQUALAND WEST

Standard Bank Cup

Played at St George's Park, Port Elizabeth on 5 January 2001
Toss: Eastern Province
Umpires: KH Hurter & SB Lambson
Debuts: EP: None. GW: None
Result: Eastern Province won by 67 runs
Man of Match: Dave Callaghan
Points: EP 5, GW 0.

EASTERN PROVINCE	*Runs*	*Mins*	*Balls*	*4*	*6*
*CC Bradfield c Elliott b Swanepoel	1	4	2	-	-
JM Kemp b Kruis	26	25	19	4	1
JDC Bryant c Tatton b Elliott	69	86	91	11	-
DJ Callaghan b Kruis	75	135	86	4	2
MR Benfield c Bosman b Gidley	23	32	29	2	-
MW Creed c Elliott b Kruis	17	19	17	2	-
RJ Peterson not out	25	25	20	3	-
†DW Murray c Swanepoel b Kruis	0	1	1	-	-
S Abrahams not out	8	6	6	1	-
MW Pringle					
GJ-P Kruger					
Extras (lb 3, w 1, nb 1)	5				
TOTAL (for 7 wkts) (45 overs)	**249**				

GRIQUALAND WEST	*Runs*	*Mins*	*Balls*	*4*	*6*
PPJ Koortzen b Pringle	0	1	1	-	-
*MI Gidley b Peterson	27	69	46	4	-
GD Elliott c Bryant b Kemp	31	54	48	3	-
LL Bosman c Callaghan b Peterson	32	58	52	3	-
BH Tucker st Murray b Peterson	3	7	7	-	-
†W Bossenger b Abrahams	17	28	25	2	-
J Brooker st Murray b Abrahams	9	20	21	-	-
J Louw not out	37	43	27	1	3
GJ Kruis b Pringle	13	19	21	-	-
CR Tatton lbw b Pringle	0	1	1	-	-
AJ Swanepoel run out (Bryant/Pringle)	5	9	6	1	-
Extras (lb 3, w 4, nb 1)	8				
TOTAL (42.2 overs)	**182**				

GW	O	M	R	W
Kruis	9	0	55	4
Swanepoel	9	1	65	1
Louw	9	0	35	0
Elliott	9	0	34	1
Tatton	5	0	35	0
Gidley	4	0	22	1

EP	O	M	R	W
Pringle	6.2	0	25	3
Kruger	7	1	29	0
Kemp	8	0	35	1
Callaghan	3	0	25	0
Peterson	9	0	33	3
Abrahams	9	1	32	2

Fall of Wickets	EP	GW
1st	1 (1)	0 (1)
2nd	38 (2)	54 (3)
3rd	124 (3)	68 (2)
4th	176 (5)	74 (5)
5th	208 (6)	113 (6)
6th	236 (4)	121 (4)
7th	236 (8)	131 (7)
8th	-	166 (9)
9th	-	166 (10)
10th	-	182 (11)

KwaZulu-Natal v Eastern Province, Durban, 10 January 2001. KwaZulu-Natal won by 9 wickets.

EASTERN PROVINCE v EASTERNS

Standard Bank Cup

Played at St George's Park, Port Elizabeth on 19 January 2001

Toss: Eastern Province

Umpires: IL Howell & KH Hurter (TV: DF Becker)

Debuts: EP: DM Senekal. Eas: BL Reddy

Result: Match tied

Man of Match: Derek Crookes

Points: EP 2, Eas 2.

EASTERN PROVINCE	Runs	Mins	Balls	4	6
*CC Bradfield b Nel	4	5	9	1	-
†DW Murray c de Bruyn b Reddy	57	73	51	7	2
JDC Bryant run out (Benjamin/Jennings)	18	48	40	2	-
DJ Callaghan run out (Crookes)	52	87	75	5	-
MR Benfield st Jennings b van den Berg	41	64	51	1	2
MW Creed run out (Flusk/Jennings)	0	3	1	-	-
RJ Peterson not out	27	44	27	3	-
S Abrahams b Reddy	3	8	6	-	-
MW Pringle c de Bruyn b Reddy	8	19	12	-	-
DM Senekal not out	2	5	1	-	-
GJ-P Kruger					
Extras (lb 2, w 7, nb 3)	12				
TOTAL (for 8 wkts) (45 overs)	**224**				

EASTERNS	Runs	Mins	Balls	4	6
AJ Seymore c Murray b Creed	31	58	53	6	-
MJR Rindel b Abrahams	27	75	36	5	-
*D Jordaan c Bryant b Creed	2	7	4	-	-
DN Crookes c Benfield b Peterson	56	116	83	3	-
AM van den Berg run out (Callaghan/Peterson)	32	87	53	1	-
P de Bruyn run out (Bradfield/Murray)	24	57	22	1	-
†D Jennings c Bryant b Peterson	5	15	10	-	-
GE Flusk st Murray b Peterson	6	10	8	-	-
BL Reddy run out (Murray)	10	15	6	-	1
A Nel not out	1	3	1	-	-
KCG Benjamin					
Extras (lb 11, w 13, nb 6)	30				
TOTAL (for 9 wkts) (45 overs)	**224**				

Eas	O	M	R	W
Benjamin	5.1	0	22	0
Nel	9	1	34	1
de Bruyn	3	0	31	0
Crookes	9	0	32	0
Reddy	7	0	46	3
van den Berg	9	0	41	1
Flusk	2.5	0	16	0

EP	O	M	R	W
Pringle	9	0	44	0
Senekal	4	1	22	0
Kruger	7	0	48	0
Creed	7	0	25	2
Abrahams	9	0	33	1
Peterson	9	0	41	3

Fall of Wickets	EP	Eas
1st	5 (1)	60 (1)
2nd	83 (3)	67 (3)
3rd	88 (2)	70 (2)
4th	178 (5)	155 (5)
5th	179 (6)	174 (4)
6th	185 (4)	190 (7)
7th	192 (8)	201 (8)
8th	216 (9)	222 (9)
9th	-	224 (6)

FREE STATE

FREE STATE v BOLAND

Standard Bank Cup

Played at Goodyear Park, Bloemfontein on 6 October 2000

Toss: Free State

Umpires: DF Becker & KH Hurter

Debuts: FS: None. Bol: AAW Pringle

Result: Free State won by 6 wickets

Man of Match: Morne van Wyk

Points: FS 4, Bol 0.

BOLAND	Runs	Mins	Balls	4	6
*LJ Koen c Bakkes b Pretorius	29	73	53	5	-
JM Henderson c Brophy b Bakkes	6	20	15	-	-
IJL Trott c van Wyk b Liebenberg	65	106	90	7	-
PH Barnard c Liebenberg b Venter	31	50	42	3	-
JL Ontong not out	55	46	41	4	1
†SJ Palframan c Bakkes b Pretorius	27	32	23	3	-
BT Player not out	5	11	6	-	-
CK Langeveldt					
NM Carter					
CdeW de Lange					
AAW Pringle					
Extras (b 1, lb 2, w 4)	7				
TOTAL (for 5 wkts) (45 overs)	**225**				

FREE STATE	Runs	Mins	Balls	4	6
JF Venter b Pringle	23	64	54	2	-
JJ van der Wath c Palframan b Langeveldt	5	18	14	1	-
WJ Smit c Langeveldt b Ontong	47	97	57	2	1
MN van Wyk not out	102	119	86	6	1
LJ Wilkinson b Carter	21	32	22	1	-
GFJ Liebenberg not out	14	36	16	-	-
*†GL Brophy					
HC Bakkes					
D Pretorius					
PV Mpitsang					
TJ Mokoenanyana					
Extras (b 1, lb 3, w 9, nb 1)	14				
TOTAL (for 4 wkts) (41.2 overs)	**226**				

FS	O	M	R	W
Bakkes	7	1	40	1
Mpitsang	5	2	17	0
Pretorius	9	0	48	2
van der Wath	2	0	14	0
Mokoenanyana	9	0	35	0
Venter	9	0	42	1
Liebenberg	4	0	26	1

Bol	O	M	R	W
Langeveldt	8	0	40	1
Carter	7	0	20	1
Player	6	0	38	0
Pringle	6.2	0	35	1
de Lange	3	0	27	0
Henderson	5	0	27	0
Ontong	6	0	35	1

Fall of Wickets	Bol	FS
1st	17 (2)	16 (2)
2nd	74 (1)	46 (1)
3rd	137 (4)	116 (3)
4th	138 (3)	165 (5)
5th	207 (6)	-

FREE STATE v NORTHERNS — Standard Bank Cup

Played at Goodyear Park, Bloemfontein on 11 October 2000 — Toss: Free State
Umpires: DF Becker & S Wadvalla (TV: AG O'Connor)
Debuts: FS: None. Nor: None
Result: Free State won by 3 wickets
Man of Match: Gerard Brophy
Points: FS 4, Nor 1.

NORTHERNS	Runs	Mins	Balls	4	6
PJR Steyn c Brophy b Pretorius	30	53	40	4	1
JG Myburgh c Brophy b Mpitsang	0	7	6	-	-
JA Rudolph c Brophy b Bakkes	1	11	6	-	-
M van Jaarsveld not out	88	160	111	5	-
*G Dros st Brophy b Venter	1	25	19	-	-
S Elworthy c Bakkes b Venter	0	5	6	-	-
FC Brooker c Bakkes b Mokoenanyana	39	66	59	3	-
P Joubert b Pretorius	0	2	3	-	-
†CFK van Wyk c Brophy b Pretorius	18	19	16	2	-
NG Brouwers not out	2	5	4	-	-
GJ Smith					
Extras (lb 7, w 5)	12				
TOTAL (for 8 wkts) (45 overs)	**191**				

FREE STATE	Runs	Mins	Balls	4	6
JF Venter b Elworthy	16	23	17	2	-
AI Gait run out (Myburgh)	18	37	29	3	-
WJ Smit st van Wyk b Myburgh	32	89	64	3	-
MN van Wyk c sub (QR Still) b Elworthy	8	7	10	1	-
LJ Wilkinson b Joubert	8	11	10	1	-
GFJ Liebenberg c van Wyk b Joubert	5	15	17	-	-
*†GL Brophy c van Wyk b Joubert	47	76	67	3	-
HC Bakkes not out	32	51	44	2	-
PV Mpitsang not out	3	14	10	-	-
D Pretorius					
TJ Mokoenanyana					
Extras (lb 7, w 8, nb 10)	25				
TOTAL (for 7 wkts) (43.1 overs)	**194**				

FS	O	M	R	W
Bakkes	9	1	30	1
Mpitsang	9	2	36	1
Pretorius	9	1	46	3
Venter	9	0	29	2
Mokoenanyana	8	0	35	1
Liebenberg	1	0	8	0

Nor	O	M	R	W
Elworthy	9	1	32	2
Smith	9	0	44	0
Joubert	8.1	0	48	3
Myburgh	9	0	31	1
Brouwers	8	0	32	0

Fall of Wickets	Nor	FS
1st	0 (2)	34 (1)
2nd	8 (3)	43 (2)
3rd	40 (1)	53 (4)
4th	56 (5)	68 (5)
5th	58 (6)	82 (6)
6th	157 (7)	130 (3)
7th	157 (8)	176 (7)
8th	185 (9)	-

Eastern Province v Free State, Port Elizabeth, 22 November 2000. Eastern Province won by 50 runs.

FREE STATE v GAUTENG — Standard Bank Cup

Played at Goodyear Park, Bloemfontein on 6 December 2000 — Toss: Free State
Umpires: JD Cloete & CM Schoof (TV: AG O'Connor)
Debuts: FS: None. Gau: JM Otto
Result: Free State won by 6 runs
Man of Match: Morne van Wyk
Points: FS 4, Gau 1.

FREE STATE	Runs	Mins	Balls	4	6
JF Venter lbw b Laing	89	144	111	6	-
AI Gait b Hall	41	68	54	4	1
WJ Smit c Laing b Masimula	1	12	11	-	-
MN van Wyk c Eksteen b Hall	62	71	64	5	1
*†GL Brophy not out	9	19	11	-	-
JA Beukes run out (Fusedale)	1	1	1	-	-
GFJ Liebenberg not out	4	8	4	-	-
HC Bakkes					
PV Mpitsang					
D Pretorius					
TJ Mokoenanyana					
Extras (lb 4, w 6, nb 5)	15				
TOTAL (for 5 wkts) (42 overs)	**222**				

GAUTENG	Runs	Mins	Balls	4	6
SG Koenig c Brophy b Pretorius	38	66	64	4	-
AJ Hall c Brophy b Pretorius	20	49	24	3	-
AM Bacher c Smit b van Wyk	40	74	48	3	-
JM Otto c Liebenberg b van Wyk	25	59	46	1	-
†N Pothas not out	39	59	33	3	-
DR Laing c Beukes b Venter	12	60	18	-	-
OD Gibson c Bakkes b Mpitsang	20	19	14	3	-
G Toyana c sub (AP Abrahams) b Mpitsang	4	12	6	-	-
*CE Eksteen lbw b Mpitsang	0	2	1	-	-
NA Fusedale c van Wyk b Pretorius	0	3	2	-	-
WB Masimula not out	0	3	0	-	-
Extras (b 2, lb 7, w 5, nb 4)	18				
TOTAL (for 9 wkts) (42 overs)	**216**				

Gau	O	M	R	W
Gibson	9	0	46	0
Fusedale	7	0	43	0
Hall	9	0	37	2
Masimula	6	0	21	1
Eksteen	7	0	44	0
Laing	4	0	27	1

FS	O	M	R	W
Mpitsang	9	0	51	3
Bakkes	8	0	34	0
Pretorius	9	0	34	3
Venter	8	0	40	1
Mokoenanyana	3.3	0	20	0
van Wyk	4.3	0	28	2

Fall of Wickets	FS	Gau
1st	90 (2)	53 (2)
2nd	94 (3)	73 (1)
3rd	195 (1)	139 (3)
4th	206 (4)	139 (4)
5th	209 (6)	162 (6)
6th	-	199 (7)
7th	-	209 (8)
8th	-	209 (9)
9th	-	210 (10)

FREE STATE v GRIQUALAND WEST

Standard Bank Cup

Played at Goodyear Park, Bloemfontein on 15 December 2000

Toss: Free State

Umpires: JD Cloete & CJ Mitchley

Debuts: FS: None. GW: J Louw & BH Tucker

Result: Free State won by 33 runs

Man of Match: Andrew Gait

Points: FS 4, GW 0.

FREE STATE	Runs	Mins	Balls	4	6
JF Venter c and b Kruis	50	77	52	7	1
AI Gait not out	138	180	137	12	2
JJ van der Wath c Abrahim b Kruis	91	75	65	13	2
MN van Wyk not out	24	26	18	2	-
WJ Smit					
GFJ Liebenberg					
*†GL Brophy					
HC Bakkes					
PV Mpitsang					
D Pretorius					
TJ Mokoenanyana					
Extras (lb 1, w 9, nb 2)	12				
TOTAL (for 2 wkts) (45 overs)	**315**				

GRIQUALAND WEST	Runs	Mins	Balls	4	6
PPJ Koortzen b van Wyk	99	123	98	14	-
*MI Gidley c Smit b Pretorius	16	31	15	2	-
GJ Kruis b Bakkes	2	5	4	-	-
GD Elliott c Liebenberg b Pretorius	3	20	16	-	-
BH Tucker run out (Venter)	59	113	81	4	-
LL Bosman c van Wyk b Mokoenanyana	3	8	7	-	-
†W Bossenger c and b van Wyk	14	17	12	1	-
J Louw c van Wyk b Bakkes	59	41	32	6	2
ZA Abrahim not out	9	23	9	1	-
CR Tatton not out	0	2	1	-	-
AJ Swanepoel					
Extras (lb 6, w 7, nb 5)	18				
TOTAL (for 8 wkts) (45 overs)	**282**				

GW	O	M	R	W
Abrahim	9	0	59	0
Swanepoel	8	1	47	0
Kruis	9	0	57	2
Tatton	7	0	50	0
Koortzen	2	0	20	0
Louw	4	0	32	0
Elliott	3	0	25	0
Gidley	3	0	24	0

FS	O	M	R	W
Mpitsang	7	0	59	0
Bakkes	9	0	58	2
Pretorius	9	1	64	2
Mokoenanyana	9	1	26	1
Venter	3	0	23	0
van Wyk	8	0	46	2

Fall of Wickets	FS	GW
1st	107 (1)	50 (2)
2nd	263 (3)	54 (3)
3rd	-	71 (4)
4th	-	162 (1)
5th	-	171 (6)
6th	-	192 (7)
7th	-	241 (5)
8th	-	281 (8)

Western Province v Free State, Cape Town, 27 December 2000. Western Province won by 50 runs.

Border v Free State, East London, 3 January 2001. Border won by 55 runs.

North West v Free State, Potchefstroom, 5 January 2001. Free State won by 5 wickets.

FREE STATE v KWAZULU-NATAL

Standard Bank Cup

Played at Goodyear Park, Bloemfontein on 19 January 2001

Toss: Free State

Umpires: JD Cloete & AE Williams

Debuts: FS: None. KZN: None

Result: KwaZulu-Natal won by 12 runs (D/L method), target revised to 152 in 33 overs

Man of Match: Jonathan Bastow

Points: KZN 4, FS 0.

KWAZULU-NATAL	Runs	Mins	Balls	4	6
DJ Watson c Brophy b Pretorius	22	88	58	-	1
GH Bodi c Brophy b Mpitsang	3	8	3	-	-
AM Amla b Bakkes	3	22	15	-	-
ML Bruyns b Bakkes	0	7	4	-	-
WR Wingfield not out	46	84	67	5	-
*DM Benkenstein c van der Wath b Venter	18	32	25	2	-
JC Kent c Mokoenanyana b van der Wath	24	27	30	2	-
†ELR Stewart not out	1	2	1	-	-
EAE Baptiste					
KS Bender					
JE Bastow					
Extras (lb 1, w 5, nb 1)	7				
TOTAL (for 6 wkts) (33.4 overs)	**124**				

FREE STATE	Runs	Mins	Balls	4	6
WJ Smit c Stewart b Bastow	0	3	4	-	-
AJ Gait lbw b Bodi	33	85	48	2	-
MN van Wyk c Kent b Bastow	65	95	76	9	-
JJ van der Wath c Stewart b Bastow	7	15	7	-	-
JF Venter c Stewart b Bastow	0	5	2	-	-
GFJ Liebenberg c Stewart b Bastow	9	23	17	1	-
*†GL Brophy b Bastow	0	1	1	-	-
HC Bakkes b Bodi	3	19	9	-	-
D Pretorius b Wingfield	2	15	3	-	-
PV Mpitsang not out	4	16	20	-	-
TJ Mokoenanyana run out (Bender)	0	2	1	-	-
Extras (lb 5, w 8, nb 3)	16				
TOTAL (30.5 overs)	**139**				

FS	O	M	R	W
Bakkes	7	3	14	2
Mpitsang	9	2	33	1
Pretorius	5	0	14	1
van der Wath	2.4	0	13	1
Venter	8	0	36	1
Mokoenanyana	2	0	13	0

KZN	O	M	R	W
Bastow	7	0	26	6
Wingfield	3.5	0	18	1
Bender	3	0	15	0
Kent	7	0	24	0
Baptiste	5	0	27	0
Bodi	5	0	24	2

Fall of Wickets	KZN	FS
1st	5 (2)	0 (1)
2nd	22 (3)	102 (2)
3rd	22 (4)	116 (3)
4th	43 (1)	116 (4)
5th	81 (6)	117 (5)
6th	123 (7)	117 (7)
7th	-	128 (6)
8th	-	129 (8)
9th	-	139 (9)
10th	-	139 (11)

Easterns v Free State, Benoni, 24 January 2001. Free State won by 1 run (D/L method).

GAUTENG

GAUTENG v BORDER — Standard Bank Cup

Played at Wanderers Stadium, Johannesburg on 13 October 2000 — Toss: Gauteng
Umpires: JD Cloete & RE Koertzen
Debuts: Gau: None. Bdr: None
Result: Gauteng won by 6 runs
Man of Match: Sven Koenig
Points: Gau 4, Bdr 1.

GAUTENG	Runs	Mins	Balls	4	6
AM Bacher c Mitchell b Klopper	10	52	37	2	-
SG Koenig lbw b Drakes	109	185	131	10	1
Z de Bruyn c Strydom b Klopper	6	11	9	1	-
DJ Cullinan b Pope	39	46	36	3	2
OD Gibson st Mitchell b Strydom	30	31	31	4	-
G Toyana c Makalima b Botha	9	61	12	1	-
†N Pothas c and b Henderson	0	6	4	-	-
*CE Eksteen c Mitchell b Drakes	1	3	2	-	-
MF George run out (Strydom)	0	1	1	-	-
DJ Terbrugge not out	8	11	9	-	-
WB Masimula					
Extras (lb 5, w 6, nb 6)	17				
TOTAL (for 9 wkts) (45 overs)	**229**				

BORDER	Runs	Mins	Balls	4	6
†I Mitchell c Pothas b Gibson	15	51	40	2	-
LL Gamiet c Cullinan b Gibson	5	32	16	1	-
EJ Ferreira c George b Gibson	2	9	8	-	-
*PC Strydom not out	89	165	93	7	2
CB Sugden c Masimula b Eksteen	4	18	14	1	-
SC Pope c Cullinan b de Bruyn	63	103	80	5	1
JWF Klopper run out (Cullinan)	9	16	12	-	-
T Henderson run out (Pothas/Terbrugge)	5	12	7	-	-
VC Drakes not out	1	4	1	-	-
PJ Botha					
DL Makalima					
Extras (b 1, lb 10, w 18, nb 1)	30				
TOTAL (for 7 wkts) (45 overs)	**223**				

Bdr	O	M	R	W
Drakes	9	1	31	2
Botha	9	0	48	1
Henderson	9	2	33	1
Klopper	6	0	39	2
Strydom	9	0	45	1
Pope	3	0	28	1

Gau	O	M	R	W
Terbrugge	9	1	29	0
Gibson	9	0	44	3
George	6	0	38	0
Eksteen	9	2	41	1
Masimula	5	0	21	0
de Bruyn	7	1	39	1

Fall of Wickets	Gau	Bdr
1st	42 (1)	27 (2)
2nd	51 (3)	32 (3)
3rd	124 (4)	36 (1)
4th	171 (5)	53 (5)
5th	205 (6)	186 (6)
6th	212 (7)	206 (7)
7th	213 (8)	218 (8)
8th	213 (9)	-
9th	229 (2)	-

GAUTENG v KWAZULU-NATAL — Standard Bank Cup

Played at Wanderers Stadium, Johannesburg on 24 November 2000 — Toss: Gauteng
Umpires: JD Cloete & KH Hurter (TV: AG O'Connor)
Debuts: Gau: None. KZN: None
Result: KwaZulu-Natal won by 99 runs (D/L method), target revised to 244 in 39 overs
Man of Match: Doug Watson
Points: KZN 5, Gau 0.

KWAZULU-NATAL	Runs	Mins	Balls	4	6
DJ Watson run out (de Bruyn)	99	175	117	10	1
A Mall b Gibson	71	121	95	8	1
SM Pollock c sub (TN Savage) b Masimula	10	28	16	1	-
L Klusener c Gibson b Eksteen	17	12	12	1	1
JN Rhodes c Hall b de Bruyn	9	12	7	1	-
*DM Benkenstein c Bacher b Gibson	9	8	7	1	-
†ELR Stewart not out	9	18	9	-	-
GH Bodi run out (Ndima/Pothas)	4	6	6	-	-
JC Kent not out	2	3	4	-	-
EAE Baptiste					
JE Bastow					
Extras (lb 8, w 17, nb 3)	28				
TOTAL (for 7 wkts) (45 overs)	**258**				

GAUTENG	Runs	Mins	Balls	4	6
SG Koenig lbw b Pollock	13	29	18	2	-
AJ Hall lbw b Bastow	80	156	104	9	-
AM Bacher b Bastow	0	5	4	-	-
Z de Bruyn b Pollock	0	6	6	-	-
†N Pothas b Baptiste	8	34	22	2	-
G Toyana c Bodi b Baptiste	2	16	13	-	-
OD Gibson b Kent	9	22	11	-	-
SS Ndima run out (Bodi/Stewart)	8	9	8	-	-
*CE Eksteen c Stewart b Kent	0	2	2	-	-
WB Masimula c sub (ML Bruyns) b Kent	1	3	2	-	-
BN Schultz not out	2	21	9	-	-
Extras (b 1, lb 7, w 12, nb 1)	21				
TOTAL (33 overs)	**144**				

Gau	O	M	R	W
Gibson	9	2	24	2
Schultz	3	0	31	0
Hall	9	0	43	0
Masimula	9	0	40	1
Eksteen	8	0	56	1
de Bruyn	6	0	41	1
Bacher	1	0	15	0

KZN	O	M	R	W
Pollock	8	2	16	2
Bastow	6	0	42	2
Klusener	6	1	29	0
Baptiste	8	0	26	2
Kent	5	0	23	3

Fall of Wickets	KZN	Gau
1st	162 (2)	33 (1)
2nd	188 (3)	35 (3)
3rd	209 (4)	37 (4)
4th	231 (1)	62 (5)
5th	231 (5)	77 (6)
6th	244 (6)	111 (7)
7th	254 (8)	122 (8)
8th	-	123 (9)
9th	-	125 (10)
10th	-	144 (2)

Free State v Gauteng, Bloemfontein, 6 December 2000. Free State won by 6 runs.

GAUTENG v WESTERN PROVINCE

Standard Bank Cup

Played at Wanderers Stadium, Johannesburg on 16 December 2000
Toss: Gauteng
Umpires: KH Hurter & CJ Mitchley (TV: SB Lambson)
Debuts: Gau: None. WP: M de Stadler
Result: Gauteng won by 21 runs
Man of Match: Herschelle Gibbs
Points: Gau 4, WP 0.

GAUTENG	Runs	Mins	Balls	4	6
AM Bacher c Puttick b Munnik	73	124	95	8	-
OD Gibson c Gibbs b Munnik	18	42	30	3	-
†N Pothas c Gibbs b Henderson	16	58	51	-	-
DJ Cullinan c Johnson b Dawson	22	14	14	3	1
JM Otto not out	47	64	41	4	2
DR Laing c Puttick b Munnik	4	9	7	-	-
Z de Bruyn c Puttick b Munnik	24	33	23	3	-
G Toyana c and b Dawson	1	2	2	-	-
*CE Eksteen not out	8	9	8	1	-
DJ Terbrugge					
WB Masimula					
Extras (lb 1, w 11, nb 1)	13				
TOTAL (for 7 wkts) (45 overs)	**226**				

WESTERN PROVINCE	Runs	Mins	Balls	4	6
NC Johnson c Otto b Terbrugge	0	8	7	-	-
HH Gibbs c Pothas b Terbrugge	105	139	94	13	2
GC Smith run out (Cullinan/Eksteen)	17	73	41	1	-
*HD Ackerman lbw b Eksteen	3	13	10	-	-
AG Prince b Laing	19	73	49	-	-
†AG Puttick lbw b de Bruyn	7	13	13	-	-
R Munnik run out (Bacher/Otto)	1	9	9	-	-
AC Dawson c Masimula b Terbrugge	6	23	10	-	-
CW Henderson not out	27	27	22	3	1
M de Stadler run out (de Bruyn)	1	8	3	-	-
CM Willoughby b Terbrugge	0	1	2	-	-
Extras (lb 8, w 8, nb 3)	19				
TOTAL (42.5 overs)	**205**				

WP	O	M	R	W
Dawson	9	0	46	2
Willoughby	9	2	39	0
Munnik	8	0	50	4
Henderson	9	0	39	1
de Stadler	3	0	20	0
Johnson	7	0	31	0

Gau	O	M	R	W
Terbrugge	8.5	1	31	4
Gibson	8	1	40	0
Masimula	2	0	21	0
Laing	8	0	37	1
Eksteen	9	0	38	1
de Bruyn	7	0	30	1

Fall of Wickets	Gau	WP
1st	34 (2)	3 (1)
2nd	105 (3)	80 (3)
3rd	137 (4)	97 (4)
4th	140 (1)	152 (2)
5th	150 (6)	164 (6)
6th	214 (7)	169 (7)
7th	215 (8)	171 (5)
8th	-	192 (8)
9th	-	205 (10)
10th	-	205 (11)

GAUTENG v EASTERN PROVINCE

Standard Bank Cup

Played at Wanderers Stadium, Johannesburg on 20 December 2000
Toss: Eastern Province
Umpires: KH Hurter & CJ Mitchley (TV: S Wadvalla)
Debuts: Gau: None. EP: None
Result: Eastern Province won by 5 wickets
Man of Match: Garnett Kruger
Points: EP 4, Gau 0.
Notes: Match reduced to 42 overs per side

GAUTENG	Runs	Mins	Balls	4	6
SG Koenig c Murray b Kemp	0	7	8	-	-
AJ Hall c Callaghan b Kruger	16	50	26	2	-
AM Bacher c Murray b Ngam	38	86	66	6	-
DJ Cullinan b Kruger	0	8	7	-	-
†N Pothas c Murray b Kruger	1	10	8	-	-
JM Otto b Kruger	0	6	6	-	-
G Toyana lbw b Kemp	3	32	18	-	-
OD Gibson b Callaghan	17	27	23	1	1
*CE Eksteen c Bradfield b Callaghan	12	25	19	1	-
DJ Terbrugge not out	6	36	31	-	-
WB Masimula b Kruger	14	17	14	2	-
Extras (b 1, lb 1, w 17, nb 2)	21				
TOTAL (37.2 overs)	**128**				

EASTERN PROVINCE	Runs	Mins	Balls	4	6
*CC Bradfield lbw b Gibson	39	134	85	5	-
MR Benfield b Hall	10	42	16	1	-
JDC Bryant lbw b Eksteen	9	67	63	1	-
†DW Murray not out	23	67	30	2	-
JM Kemp lbw b Gibson	0	2	2	-	-
DJ Callaghan run out (Gibson/Pothas)	4	4	5	1	-
RJ Peterson not out	24	36	22	4	-
S Abrahams					
M Hayward					
GJ-P Kruger					
M Ngam					
Extras (lb 6, w 13, nb 1)	20				
TOTAL (for 5 wkts) (37 overs)	**129**				

EP	O	M	R	W
Ngam	8	0	24	1
Kemp	9	2	32	2
Hayward	1	0	16	0
Kruger	7.2	0	28	5
Callaghan	6	2	11	2
Abrahams	6	0	15	0

Gau	O	M	R	W
Terbrugge	7	3	20	0
Gibson	9	0	33	2
Hall	9	3	20	1
Masimula	5	1	16	0
Eksteen	5	0	20	1
Otto	2	0	14	0

Fall of Wickets	Gau	EP
1st	2 (1)	21 (2)
2nd	47 (2)	54 (3)
3rd	56 (4)	82 (1)
4th	64 (5)	82 (5)
5th	66 (6)	87 (6)
6th	73 (3)	-
7th	88 (7)	-
8th	93 (8)	-
9th	110 (9)	-
10th	128 (11)	-

Northerns v Gauteng, Centurion, 22 December 2000. Northerns won by 3 wickets.
Boland v Gauteng, Paarl, 3 January 2001. Boland won by 3 wickets.

GAUTENG v EASTERNS — Standard Bank Cup

Played at Wanderers Stadium, Johannesburg on 10 January 2001 — Toss: Easterns
Umpires: IL Howell & CM Schoof (TV: JD Cloete)
Debuts: Gau: SL Letshela. Eas: None
Result: Gauteng won by 5 wickets
Man of Match: Nic Pothas
Points: Gau 4, Eas 1.

EASTERNS	Runs	Mins	Balls	4	6
AJ Seymore b Eksteen	46	96	82	6	-
MJR Rindel run out (Otto/Pothas)	60	103	63	7	2
KCG Benjamin c de Bruyn b Eksteen	22	39	27	3	-
DN Crookes lbw b Eksteen	25	46	46	2	-
*D Jordaan not out	23	49	28	2	-
P de Bruyn c Otto b Terbrugge	15	20	20	1	-
AM van den Berg run out (Otto/Terbrugge/Pothas)	10	10	6	1	-
†D Jennings run out (Terbrugge)	1	1	1	-	-
GE Flusk					
EF Mabhena					
A Nel					
Extras (lb 7, w 13, nb 3)	23				
TOTAL (for 7 wkts) (45 overs)	**225**				

GAUTENG	Runs	Mins	Balls	4	6
AM Bacher c Crookes b de Bruyn	13	47	30	1	-
AJ Hall b Benjamin	5	17	12	1	-
SG Koenig c Seymore b de Bruyn	56	118	91	5	-
JM Otto c Seymore b Crookes	37	42	34	6	-
†N Pothas not out	79	94	77	7	-
Z de Bruyn c van den Berg b de Bruyn	17	36	21	2	-
OD Gibson not out	1	12	4	-	-
*CE Eksteen					
SL Letshela					
TK Mataboge					
DJ Terbrugge					
Extras (lb 6, w 11, nb 1)	18				
TOTAL (for 5 wkts) (44.4 overs)	**226**				

Gau	O	M	R	W
Terbrugge	9	0	26	1
Gibson	9	0	51	0
Eksteen	9	0	57	3
Hall	9	1	32	0
de Bruyn	5	0	31	0
Mataboge	4	0	21	0

Eas	O	M	R	W
Benjamin	9	1	41	1
Nel	8.4	0	46	0
Flusk	4	0	23	0
de Bruyn	9	1	48	3
Rindel	3	0	22	0
Crookes	9	0	31	1
van den Berg	2	0	9	0

Fall of Wickets	Eas	Gau
1st	120 (1)	16 (2)
2nd	132 (2)	41 (1)
3rd	156 (3)	95 (4)
4th	177 (4)	146 (3)
5th	207 (6)	206 (6)
6th	224 (7)	-
7th	225 (8)	-

Griqualand West v Gauteng, Kimberley, 17 January 2001. Griqualand West won by 66 runs.
North West v Gauteng, Potchefstroom, 19 January 2001. North West won by 2 runs (D/L method).

GRIQUALAND WEST

GRIQUALAND WEST v KWAZULU-NATAL — Standard Bank Cup

Played at De Beers Diamond Oval, Kimberley on 4 October 2000 — Toss: Griqualand West
Umpires: BG Jerling & RE Koertzen (TV: M Gajjar)
Debuts: GW: J Brooker & CR Tatton. KZN: DL Brown
Result: Griqualand West won by 6 wickets
Man of Match: Pieter Koortzen
Points: GW 4, KZN 1.

KWAZULU-NATAL	Runs	Mins	Balls	4	6
ML Bruyns c Bossenger b Kruis	19	51	32	3	-
DJ Watson run out (Abrahim)	78	137	105	7	2
AM Amla run out (Elliott/Bossenger)	18	22	22	3	-
*DM Benkenstein b Abrahim	38	45	48	4	-
JC Kent b Kruis	62	52	44	8	1
†ELR Stewart not out	26	30	21	2	-
DL Brown not out	1	1	1	-	-
EAE Baptiste					
GH Bodi					
RE Veenstra					
GM Gilder					
Extras (lb 10, w 10, nb 3)	23				
TOTAL (for 5 wkts) (45 overs)	**265**				

GRIQUALAND WEST	Runs	Mins	Balls	4	6
WM Dry c Amla b Kent	35	67	45	4	1
*MI Gidley c Baptiste b Veenstra	10	46	29	-	-
GD Elliott lbw b Kent	94	132	93	10	1
LL Bosman c Gilder b Baptiste	11	24	19	-	1
PPJ Koortzen not out	99	92	81	6	2
GJ Kruis not out	2	5	4	-	-
†W Bossenger					
J Brooker					
CR Tatton					
ZA Abrahim					
AJ Swanepoel					
Extras (lb 4, w 12, nb 2)	18				
TOTAL (for 4 wkts) (44.5 overs)	**269**				

GW	O	M	R	W
Abrahim	8	0	55	1
Swanepoel	8	1	31	0
Kruis	9	0	34	2
Tatton	6	0	44	0
Gidley	7	0	39	0
Elliott	3	0	25	0
Brooker	4	0	27	0

KZN	O	M	R	W
Veenstra	8.5	0	39	1
Gilder	9	0	56	0
Kent	9	0	52	2
Baptiste	5	0	24	1
Bodi	5	0	29	0
Benkenstein	6	0	42	0
Bruyns	2	0	23	0

Fall of Wickets	KZN	GW
1st	64 (1)	48 (2)
2nd	90 (3)	65 (1)
3rd	156 (4)	89 (4)
4th	195 (2)	259 (3)
5th	264 (5)	-

GRIQUALAND WEST v WESTERN PROVINCE — Standard Bank Cup

Played at De Beers Diamond Oval, Kimberley on 18 October 2000 — Toss: Griqualand West
Umpires: M Gajjar & CJ Mitchley
Debuts: GW: AP McLaren. WP: None
Result: Western Province won by 144 runs
Man of Match: Alan Dawson
Points: WP 5, GW 0.

WESTERN PROVINCE	Runs	Mins	Balls	4	6
HH Gibbs c Dry b Tatton	71	100	77	8	1
G Kirsten c McLaren b Gidley	51	90	79	5	-
NC Johnson c Dry b Gidley	26	46	32	1	-
LD Ferreira run out (Brooker/Bossenger)	3	4	8	-	-
AG Puttick b Tatton	12	13	12	-	1
GC Smith lbw b Kruis	18	30	27	-	-
†TL Tsolekile not out	19	34	21	-	-
*AC Dawson run out (Tatton/Bossenger)	18	19	13	2	-
CW Henderson not out	2	1	2	-	-
R Telemachus					
CM Willoughby					
Extras (lb 3, w 5, nb 1)	9				
TOTAL (for 7 wkts) (45 overs)	**229**				

GRIQUALAND WEST	Runs	Mins	Balls	4	6
WM Dry c Johnson b Dawson	4	10	16	-	-
*MI Gidley c Smith b Willoughby	3	37	18	-	-
GD Elliott c Gibbs b Dawson	0	7	4	-	-
PPJ Koortzen c Tsolekile b Dawson	0	1	1	-	-
†W Bossenger c Tsolekile b Henderson	12	53	37	2	-
J Brooker c Johnson b Telemachus	1	5	4	-	-
AP McLaren b Dawson	12	48	36	2	-
GJ Kruis not out	28	70	61	4	-
CR Tatton c Johnson b Dawson	1	12	9	-	-
ZA Abrahim c Dawson b Johnson	1	8	10	-	-
AJ Swanepoel c Dawson b Johnson	16	32	27	1	1
Extras (lb 1, w 3, nb 3)	7				
TOTAL (36.4 overs)	**85**				

GW	O	M	R	W
Abrahim	8	0	45	0
Swanepoel	7	1	40	0
Kruis	8	0	44	1
Tatton	9	0	31	2
Gidley	9	0	45	2
Koortzen	4	0	21	0

WP	O	M	R	W
Dawson	9	4	13	5
Willoughby	7	2	10	1
Telemachus	7	2	11	1
Henderson	9	2	21	1
Johnson	4.4	0	29	2

Fall of Wickets	WP	GW
1st	119 (2)	4 (1)
2nd	131 (1)	6 (3)
3rd	134 (4)	6 (4)
4th	158 (5)	16 (2)
5th	180 (3)	17 (6)
6th	195 (6)	33 (5)
7th	227 (8)	37 (7)
8th	-	41 (9)
9th	-	43 (10)
10th	-	85 (11)

Easterns v Griqualand West, Benoni, 1 December 2000. Easterns won by 1 wicket.
Free State v Griqualand West, Bloemfontein, 15 December 2000. Free State won by 33 runs.
Boland v Griqualand West, Paarl, 22 December 2000. Boland won by 58 runs.
Eastern Province v Griqualand West, Port Elizabeth, 5 January 2001. Eastern Province won by 67 runs.

GRIQUALAND WEST v NORTH WEST — Standard Bank Cup

Played at De Beers Diamond Oval, Kimberley on 10 January 2001
Toss: Griqualand West
Umpires: DF Becker & S Wadvalla
Debuts: GW: None. NW: None
Result: Griqualand West won by 167 runs
Man of Match: Pieter Koortzen
Points: GW 5, NW 0.

GRIQUALAND WEST	Runs	Mins	Balls	4	6
PPJ Koortzen b Roe	134	140	103	15	4
LL Bosman c Niewoudt b Enslin	86	87	48	11	5
BH Tucker run out (van der Merwe/Enslin)	1	2	2	-	-
GD Elliott c Lavine b Enslin	10	20	18	1	-
MI Gidley c Lavine b Roe	32	56	45	-	1
J Louw b Roe	10	24	17	-	-
WM Dry b van der Merwe	10	20	17	-	-
*†W Bossenger c Jacobs b Strydom	0	4	1	-	-
GJ Kruis c Outram b Enslin	10	18	18	1	-
ZA Abrahim not out	3	7	3	-	-
EW Kidwell not out	1	1	1	-	-
Extras (b 4, lb 2, w 12, nb 3)	21				
TOTAL (for 9 wkts) (45 overs)	**318**				

NORTH WEST	Runs	Mins	Balls	4	6
R Niewoudt c Koortzen b Kidwell	0	17	13	-	-
G Outram c Bossenger b Kruis	0	9	6	-	-
BC de Wett b Louw	34	88	60	4	-
†A Jacobs run out (Bosman)	6	16	8	1	-
MJ Lavine c Gidley b Abrahim	46	37	35	6	1
CT Enslin b Kruis	38	47	35	3	1
*AG Lawson not out	10	39	24	-	-
M Strydom c Bossenger b Louw	1	3	2	-	-
AC Thomas c Bossenger b Louw	0	1	1	-	-
GA Roe c Bossenger b Louw	0	1	2	-	-
F van der Merwe c Koortzen b Louw	1	7	6	-	-
Extras (lb 8, w 5, nb 2)	15				
TOTAL (31.4 overs)	**151**				

NW	O	M	R	W
Lavine	9	1	58	0
Roe	9	0	55	3
Thomas	2	0	35	0
Strydom	9	0	72	1
van der Merwe	8	0	45	1
Enslin	8	0	47	3

GW	O	M	R	W
Kruis	9	1	26	2
Kidwell	5	1	16	1
Elliott	2	0	22	0
Abrahim	7	0	36	1
Louw	8.4	1	43	5

Fall of Wickets	GW	NW
1st	173 (2)	1 (2)
2nd	175 (3)	4 (1)
3rd	204 (4)	15 (4)
4th	251 (1)	69 (5)
5th	287 (6)	109 (3)
6th	288 (5)	146 (6)
7th	292 (8)	147 (8)
8th	306 (7)	147 (9)
9th	316 (9)	147 (10)
10th	-	151 (11)

GRIQUALAND WEST v GAUTENG — Standard Bank Cup

Played at De Beers Diamond Oval, Kimberley on 17 January 2001
Toss: Griqualand West
Umpires: JD Cloete & AG O'Connor
Debuts: GW: None. Gau: None
Result: Griqualand West won by 66 runs
Man of Match: Pieter Koortzen
Points: GW 5, Gau 0.

GRIQUALAND WEST	Runs	Mins	Balls	4	6
PPJ Koortzen not out	107	193	113	12	-
LL Bosman b Eksteen	89	102	78	10	2
GD Elliott c Pothas b Mataboge	1	5	6	-	-
BH Tucker c and b Eksteen	4	6	9	1	-
MI Gidley b Terbrugge	69	68	59	6	2
WM Dry not out	11	8	6	1	-
*†W Bossenger					
J Louw					
GJ Kruis					
ZA Abrahim					
AJ Swanepoel					
Extras (lb 16, w 8, nb 1)	25				
TOTAL (for 4 wkts) (45 overs)	**306**				

GAUTENG	Runs	Mins	Balls	4	6
AM Bacher c Bossenger b Abrahim	22	34	32	3	-
AJ Hall c Dry b Abrahim	4	4	4	1	-
JM Otto c Dry b Swanepoel	25	52	34	3	-
SG Koenig c Bossenger b Kruis	1	4	2	0	-
†N Pothas c Gidley b Louw	71	96	69	7	-
Z de Bruyn c and b Swanepoel	72	115	82	4	1
OD Gibson c Swanepoel b Louw	7	14	14	-	-
SL Letshela not out	22	41	25	2	-
*CE Eksteen c Bossenger b Kruis	0	3	1	-	-
TK Mataboge b Kruis	0	2	3	-	-
DJ Terbrugge not out	5	10	6	-	-
Extras (lb 2, w 7, nb 2)	11				
TOTAL (for 9 wkts) (45 overs)	**240**				

Gau	O	M	R	W	GW	O	M	R	W	Fall of Wickets	GW	Gau
Terbrugge	9	0	70	1	Kruis	9	1	47	3	1st	169 (2)	13 (2)
Gibson	9	0	60	0	Abrahim	9	0	46	2	2nd	172 (3)	45 (1)
Hall	7	1	51	0	Swanepoel	9	0	51	2	3rd	177 (4)	50 (4)
de Bruyn	2	0	23	0	Louw	9	1	44	2	4th	288 (5)	85 (3)
Eksteen	9	1	33	2	Gidley	9	0	50	0	5th	-	173 (5)
Mataboge	9	0	53	1						6th	-	191 (7)
										7th	-	226 (6)
										8th	-	228 (9)
										9th	-	228 (10)

Border v Griqualand West, East London, 19 January 2001. Border won by 8 wickets.

GRIQUALAND WEST v NORTHERNS

Standard Bank Cup

Played at De Beers Diamond Oval, Kimberley on 24 January 2001

Toss: Griqualand West

Umpires: BG Jerling & CM Schoof

Debuts: GW: None. Nor: None

Result: Griqualand West won by 63 runs

Man of Match: Pieter Koortzen

Points: GW 5, Nor 0.

GRIQUALAND WEST	Runs	Mins	Balls	4	6
PPJ Koortzen c Smith b Joubert	69	92	73	8	-
LL Bosman c Paleker b Elworthy	3	34	18	-	-
J Louw b Smith	72	94	74	4	2
MI Gidley run out (de Vos)	20	42	27	2	-
GD Elliott b Dros	12	28	25	-	-
BH Tucker lbw b de Vos	22	27	21	-	-
WM Dry c van Jaarsveld b Elworthy	11	18	10	1	-
*†W Bossenger not out	11	26	15	-	-
GJ Kruis b Elworthy	8	8	6	1	-
ZA Abrahim not out	6	3	4	-	-
AJ Swanepoel					
Extras (lb 6, w 10, nb 3)	19				
TOTAL (for 8 wkts) (45 overs)	**253**				

NORTHERNS	Runs	Mins	Balls	4	6
JG Myburgh c Bossenger b Abrahim	24	24	23	4	-
JA Rudolph c Dry b Kruis	0	2	1	-	-
M van Jaarsveld c Dry b Swanepoel	18	57	41	2	-
DJJ de Vos run out (Dry/Louw)	41	83	52	2	1
*G Dros c Bossenger b Koortzen	11	32	25	1	-
A Paleker b Koortzen	8	17	10	-	-
†CFK van Wyk b Abrahim	48	70	50	5	-
S Elworthy b Koortzen	8	7	4	-	1
R Bailey run out (Swanepoel/Bossenger)	14	43	28	-	-
P Joubert run out (Elliott)	1	3	2	-	-
GJ Smith not out	4	8	6	-	-
Extras (b 2, lb 6, w 2, nb 3)	13				
TOTAL (39.5 overs)	**190**				

Nor	O	M	R	W	GW	O	M	R	W	Fall of Wickets	GW	Nor
Elworthy	9	0	54	3	Kruis	6	1	26	1	1st	30 (2)	3 (2)
Smith	9	0	35	1	Abrahim	7.5	0	44	2	2nd	130 (1)	31 (1)
Joubert	9	0	49	1	Swanepoel	7	2	24	1	3rd	174 (3)	67 (3)
de Vos	9	0	62	1	Louw	9	0	45	0	4th	175 (4)	94 (5)
Rudolph	3	0	20	0	Gidley	1.5	0	6	0	5th	209 (5)	104 (4)
Dros	6	0	27	1	Koortzen	8.1	0	37	3	6th	215 (6)	109 (6)
										7th	233 (7)	119 (8)
										8th	246 (9)	172 (9)
										9th	-	175 (10)
										10th	-	190 (7)

KWAZULU-NATAL

Griqualand West v KwaZulu-Natal, Kimberley, 4 October 2000. Griqualand West won by 6 wickets.
Easterns v KwaZulu-Natal, Benoni, 11 October 2000. Easterns won by 79 runs.

KWAZULU-NATAL v WESTERN PROVINCE

Standard Bank Cup

Played at Kingsmead, Durban on 17 November 2000

Toss: KwaZulu-Natal

Umpires: DF Becker & CM Schoof

Debuts: KZN: A Mall. WP: None

Result: KwaZulu-Natal won by 28 runs

Man of Match: Eldine Baptiste

Points: KZN 4, WP 0.

KWAZULU-NATAL	Runs	Mins	Balls	4	6
ML Bruyns c Smith b Willoughby	15	50	41	2	-
DJ Watson b Willoughby	10	41	30	-	-
A Mall c Gibbs b Smith	40	64	43	4	-
JC Kent b Telemachus	4	7	7	-	-
*DM Benkenstein c Henderson b Telemachus	1	14	7	-	-
JN Rhodes c and b Henderson	42	58	45	4	-
†ELR Stewart not out	45	81	57	3	-
GH Bodi run out (Smith)	22	34	25	2	-
EAE Baptiste b Dawson	11	16	13	1	-
GM Gilder b Dawson	0	2	1	-	-
JE Bastow not out	4	4	3	-	-
Extras (lb 6, w 13, nb 3)	22				
TOTAL (for 9 wkts) (45 overs)	**216**				

WESTERN PROVINCE	Runs	Mins	Balls	4	6
NC Johnson c Rhodes b Bodi	48	106	80	7	-
HH Gibbs c Stewart b Kent	13	48	30	-	1
GC Smith c Stewart b Baptiste	1	5	5	-	-
*HD Ackerman lbw b Baptiste	0	1	1	-	-
AG Prince not out	76	136	96	4	1
AG Puttick c Rhodes b Baptiste	4	10	10	-	-
AC Dawson b Benkenstein	18	29	26	1	-
†TL Tsolekile c Watson b Kent	1	5	5	-	-
R Telemachus c Mall b Benkenstein	0	3	1	-	-
CW Henderson b Gilder	13	11	7	1	1
CM Willoughby not out	6	21	10	-	-
Extras (b 4, lb 2, w 1, nb 1)	8				
TOTAL (for 9 wkts) (45 overs)	**188**				

WP	O	M	R	W
Dawson	9	1	35	2
Willoughby	9	2	39	2
Telemachus	9	1	36	2
Henderson	9	0	42	1
Johnson	6	0	36	0
Smith	3	0	22	1

KZN	O	M	R	W
Bastow	9	1	39	0
Gilder	8	1	34	1
Kent	9	0	35	2
Baptiste	9	3	17	3
Bodi	7	1	30	1
Benkenstein	3	0	27	2

Fall of Wickets	KZN	WP
1st	26 (2)	51 (2)
2nd	33 (1)	52 (3)
3rd	44 (4)	52 (4)
4th	55 (5)	89 (1)
5th	108 (3)	96 (6)
6th	141 (6)	129 (7)
7th	184 (8)	134 (8)
8th	209 (9)	136 (9)
9th	209 (10)	159 (10)

Gauteng v KwaZulu-Natal, Johannesburg, 24 November 2000. KwaZulu-Natal won by 99 runs (D/L method).

KWAZULU-NATAL v BOLAND — Standard Bank Cup

Played at Kingsmead, Durban on 15 December 2000 — Toss: Boland
Umpires: AG O'Connor & RB Shah
Debuts: KZN: None. Bol: H Davids
Result: KwaZulu-Natal won by 5 wickets
Man of Match: Ashraf Mall
Points: KZN 4, Bol 0.

BOLAND	Runs	Mins	Balls	4	6
IJL Trott c Watson b Baptiste	18	68	45	2	-
H Davids c Bodi b Kent	26	60	48	5	-
*LJ Koen c Stewart b Kent	6	12	11	-	-
JL Ontong c Stewart b Kent	9	26	24	-	-
PH Barnard c Stewart b Baptiste	2	26	17	-	-
†SJ Palframan not out	56	85	68	7	-
BT Player c Adam b Bodi	9	24	18	-	-
CdeW de Lange not out	30	53	39	2	-
CK Langeveldt					
NM Carter					
HS Williams					
Extras (lb 3, w 8)	11				
TOTAL (for 6 wkts) (45 overs)	**167**				

KWAZULU-NATAL	Runs	Mins	Balls	4	6
DJ Watson c Player b Williams	2	24	22	-	-
A Mall c Barnard b Ontong	77	142	102	11	-
AC Hudson c Koen b Player	22	47	28	4	-
JC Kent c Ontong b de Lange	27	54	42	2	-
*DM Benkenstein not out	28	41	37	2	-
†ELR Stewart c Williams b Ontong	7	15	8	-	-
WR Wingfield not out	4	1	9	1	-
GH Bodi					
EAE Baptiste					
JE Bastow					
SM Adam					
Extras (w 4)	4				
TOTAL (for 5 wkts) (41.2 overs)	**171**				

KZN	O	M	R	W
Bastow	9	3	26	0
Adam	9	0	46	0
Kent	9	1	27	3
Baptiste	9	0	16	2
Bodi	6	0	28	1
Wingfield	3	0	21	0

Bol	O	M	R	W
Williams	8.2	1	30	1
Carter	7	1	22	0
Langeveldt	7	1	28	0
Player	9	0	47	1
de Lange	6	0	32	1
Ontong	4	0	12	2

Fall of Wickets	Bol	KZN
1st	49 (2)	13 (1)
2nd	49 (1)	63 (3)
3rd	57 (3)	127 (4)
4th	67 (4)	148 (2)
5th	71 (5)	162 (6)
6th	88 (7)	-

Border v KwaZulu-Natal, East London, 29 December 2000. KwaZulu-Natal won by 58 runs (D/L method).

KWAZULU-NATAL v NORTHERNS

Standard Bank Cup

Played at Kingsmead, Durban on 5 January 2001
Toss: KwaZulu-Natal
Umpires: ST Jivan & DL Orchard (TV: JD Cloete)
Debuts: KZN: None. Nor: None
Result: Northerns won by 4 wickets
Man of Match: Doug Watson
Points: Nor 4, KZN 1.

KWAZULU-NATAL	Runs	Mins	Balls	4	6
DJ Watson c Dros b Elworthy	116	162	144	8	1
GH Bodi c Joubert b Elworthy	11	34	22	1	-
WR Wingfield c Bryson b Joubert	31	53	41	4	-
JC Kent st van Wyk b de Vos	20	26	23	1	-
*DM Benkenstein c Rudolph b Dros	3	3	5	-	-
JN Rhodes run out (van Jaarsveld/van Wyk)	8	10	9	1	-
†ELR Stewart not out	31	32	23	1	1
AM Amla not out	2	3	3	-	-
EAE Baptiste					
GM Gilder					
JE Bastow					
Extras (lb 4, w 3, nb 1)	8				
TOTAL (for 6 wkts) (45 overs)	**230**				

NORTHERNS	Runs	Mins	Balls	4	6
JG Myburgh c Wingfield b Bodi	46	126	82	5	-
JA Rudolph c Rhodes b Baptiste	38	64	45	7	-
M van Jaarsveld b Wingfield	43	76	54	3	1
DJJ de Vos not out	36	76	44	3	-
*G Dros c Stewart b Bastow	8	7	7	2	-
†CFK van Wyk c sub (ML Bruyns) b Wingfield	19	28	21	3	-
A Paleker lbw b Wingfield	0	1	1	-	-
S Elworthy not out	27	19	15	1	3
P Joubert					
NG Brouwers					
RE Bryson					
Extras (lb 2, w 4, nb 8)	14				
TOTAL (for 6 wkts) (43.2 overs)	**231**				

Nor	O	M	R	W
Elworthy	9	0	37	2
Bryson	7	0	42	0
Joubert	9	0	35	1
Brouwers	8	0	45	0
de Vos	6	0	21	1
Dros	6	0	46	1

KZN	O	M	R	W
Gilder	7	0	50	0
Bastow	9	0	46	1
Kent	8.2	0	59	0
Baptiste	9	0	31	1
Bodi	3	0	14	1
Wingfield	7	0	29	3

Fall of Wickets	KZN	Nor
1st	38 (2)	71 (2)
2nd	102 (3)	123 (1)
3rd	151 (4)	145 (3)
4th	156 (5)	156 (5)
5th	170 (6)	192 (6)
6th	225 (1)	192 (7)

KWAZULU-NATAL v EASTERN PROVINCE

Standard Bank Cup

Played at Kingsmead, Durban on 10 January 2001
Toss: Eastern Province
Umpires: CJ Mitchley & ST Jivan (TV: AG O'Connor)
Debuts: KZN: None. EP: None
Result: KwaZulu-Natal won by 9 wickets
Man of Match: Goolam Bodi
Points: KZN 4, EP 0.

EASTERN PROVINCE	Runs	Mins	Balls	4	6
*CC Bradfield c Bruyns b Bender	6	21	17	1	-
†DW Murray c Stewart b Bastow	31	25	20	5	-
JDC Bryant c Stewart b Kent	21	50	33	2	-
DJ Callaghan c Kent b Bodi	73	141	106	7	2
MR Benfield c Stewart b Kent	10	13	14	1	-
MW Creed b Kent	13	21	22	1	1
RJ Peterson c Stewart b Kent	0	3	4	-	-
S Abrahams c Baptiste b Bodi	33	41	34	3	1
MW Pringle not out	15	20	19	1	1
M Hayward not out	5	6	3	1	-
GJ-P Kruger					
Extras (b 1, lb 6, w 1, nb 2)	10				
TOTAL (for 8 wkts) (45 overs)	**217**				

KWAZULU-NATAL	Runs	Mins	Balls	4	6
DJ Watson c and b Peterson	72	140	104	5	1
GH Bodi not out	106	162	118	11	3
WR Wingfield not out	21	20	19	2	1
*DM Benkenstein					
ML Bruyns					
JC Kent					
†ELR Stewart					
AM Amla					
EAE Baptiste					
KS Bender					
JE Bastow					
Extras (lb 7, w 6, nb 7)	20				
TOTAL (for 1 wkt) (39 overs)	**219**				

KZN	O	M	R	W
Bastow	7	0	48	1
Bender	9	0	40	1
Kent	9	1	29	4
Baptiste	9	2	35	0
Wingfield	4	0	28	0
Bodi	7	0	30	2

EP	O	M	R	W
Pringle	9	0	43	0
Kruger	9	0	23	0
Hayward	3	0	34	0
Abrahams	4	0	27	0
Callaghan	4	0	22	0
Peterson	8	0	50	1
Creed	2	0	13	0

Fall of Wickets	EP	KZN
1st	34 (1)	178 (1)
2nd	38 (2)	-
3rd	95 (3)	-
4th	113 (5)	-
5th	129 (6)	-
6th	129 (7)	-
7th	180 (8)	-
8th	200 (4)	-

Free State v KwaZulu-Natal, Bloemfontein, 19 January 2001. KwaZulu-Natal won by 12 runs (D/L method).

KWAZULU-NATAL v NORTH WEST

Standard Bank Cup

Played at Kingsmead, Durban on 24 January 2001
Toss: North West
Umpires: M Gajjar & SB Lambson
Debuts: KZN: None. NW: None
Result: KwaZulu-Natal won by 7 wickets
Man of Match: Wade Wingfield
Points: KZN 5, NW 0.

NORTH WEST	Runs	Mins	Balls	4	6
R Niewoudt lbw b Bastow	0	6	8	-	-
C Light c Stewart b Pollock	1	10	5	-	-
BC de Wett run out (Wingfield)	35	95	59	6	-
†A Jacobs c Wingfield b Kent	26	42	38	5	-
MJ Lavine c Amla b Kent	0	7	4	-	-
G Outram c and b Bodi	33	90	71	2	-
*AG Lawson b Bodi	6	31	23	-	-
CT Enslin c Stewart b Baptiste	1	4	5	-	-
AC Thomas c Stewart b Wingfield	12	22	24	1	-
GA Roe not out	8	26	12	-	-
F van der Merwe b Pollock	8	15	20	1	-
Extras (w 8, nb 3)	11				
TOTAL (44.2 overs)	**141**				

KWAZULU-NATAL	Runs	Mins	Balls	4	6
DJ Watson c Roe b Lavine	15	41	30	3	-
GH Bodi c Jacobs b Roe	12	46	28	2	-
WR Wingfield not out	73	91	78	10	3
*DM Benkenstein b Light	20	61	45	4	-
ML Bruyns not out	8	24	15	-	-
JC Kent					
†ELR Stewart					
SM Pollock					
AM Amla					
EAE Baptiste					
JE Bastow					
Extras (lb 1, w 10, nb 3)	14				
TOTAL (for 3 wkts) (32.1 overs)	**142**				

KZN	O	M	R	W
Pollock	8.2	4	10	2
Bastow	7	1	36	1
Kent	9	2	27	2
Baptiste	8	0	33	1
Bodi	9	1	26	2
Wingfield	3	0	9	1

NW	O	M	R	W
Lavine	9	0	28	1
Roe	6	1	25	1
Thomas	7	0	28	0
van der Merwe	5	1	21	0
Light	5	0	38	1
de Wett	0.1	0	1	0

Fall of Wickets	NW	KZN
1st	1 (1)	34 (1)
2nd	1 (2)	34 (2)
3rd	46 (4)	114 (4)
4th	48 (5)	-
5th	85 (3)	-
6th	105 (7)	-
7th	106 (8)	-
8th	119 (6)	-
9th	130 (9)	-
10th	141 (11)	-

NORTHERNS

NORTHERNS v WESTERN PROVINCE

Standard Bank Cup

Played at SuperSport Park, Centurion on 6 October 2000
Toss: Northerns
Umpires: BG Jerling & RE Koertzen
Debuts: Nor: NG Brouwers, JA Rudolph & CFK van Wyk. WP: None
Result: Northerns won by 3 wickets
Man of Match: Rudi Steyn
Points: Nor 4, WP 1.

WESTERN PROVINCE	Runs	Mins	Balls	4	6
HH Gibbs c Brouwers b Elworthy	2	16	14	-	-
GC Smith c Smith b Joubert	17	75	45	1	-
NC Johnson c van Wyk b Elworthy	18	25	19	3	-
*HD Ackerman c Myburgh b Elworthy	92	120	87	9	2
LD Ferreira b Joubert	0	2	3	-	-
AG Puttick not out	75	101	92	3	2
R Munnik lbw b Joubert	13	17	12	-	1
†TL Tsolekile					
AC Dawson					
CW Henderson					
CM Willoughby					
Extras (lb 8, w 2, nb 2)	12				
TOTAL (for 6 wkts) (45 overs)	**229**				

NORTHERNS	Runs	Mins	Balls	4	6
PJR Steyn not out	111	182	122	12	1
JG Myburgh c Tsolekile b Dawson	1	8	10	-	-
JA Rudolph c sub (AG Prince) b Dawson	8	32	24	1	-
M van Jaarsveld c and b Henderson	19	23	21	3	-
*G Dros c Willoughby b Smith	36	57	44	3	1
FC Brooker c Dawson b Smith	1	9	8	-	-
S Elworthy b Ferreira	5	11	5	1	-
P Joubert b Dawson	22	25	24	2	-
†CFK van Wyk not out	15	12	11	1	1
NG Brouwers					
GJ Smith					
Extras (w 8, nb 6)	14				
TOTAL (for 7 wkts) (44 overs)	**232**				

Nor	O	M	R	W
Elworthy	9	2	34	3
Smith	9	1	36	0
Joubert	9	1	51	3
Myburgh	9	0	43	0
Brouwers	6	0	34	0
Dros	3	0	23	0

WP	O	M	R	W
Willoughby	9	0	40	0
Dawson	9	2	38	3
Johnson	7	0	41	0
Munnik	4	0	35	0
Henderson	9	1	40	1
Smith	5	0	30	2
Ferreira	1	0	8	1

Fall of Wickets	WP	Nor
1st	2 (1)	2 (2)
2nd	28 (3)	41 (3)
3rd	62 (2)	74 (4)
4th	62 (5)	154 (5)
5th	196 (4)	166 (6)
6th	229 (7)	178 (7)
7th	-	212 (8)

Free State v Northerns, Bloemfontein, 11 October 2000. Free State won by 3 wickets.

NORTHERNS v NORTH WEST — Standard Bank Cup

Played at SuperSport Park, Centurion on 18 October 2000 — Toss: North West
Umpires: RE Koertzen & DL Orchard
Debuts: Nor: A Paleker. NW: None
Result: Northerns won by 29 runs
Man of Match: Gerald Dros
Points: Nor 4, NW 0.

NORTHERNS	Runs	Mins	Balls	4	6
PJR Steyn c Jacobs b Thomas	22	62	35	1	-
JG Myburgh c de Vos b Lavine	11	21	18	1	-
M van Jaarsveld lbw b Roe	4	7	6	-	-
ND McKenzie c Light b Roe	103	138	109	12	-
*G Dros c Lavine b Roe	86	101	99	6	3
S Elworthy not out	6	5	3	-	-
†CFK van Wyk not out	0	2	0	-	-
A Paleker					
P Joubert					
NG Brouwers					
GJ Smith					
Extras (b 1, lb 3, w 3)	7				
TOTAL (for 5 wkts) (45 overs)	**239**				

NORTH WEST	Runs	Mins	Balls	4	6
HM de Vos c van Wyk b Smith	1	5	5	-	-
GM Hewitt c Steyn b Dros	20	59	48	3	-
A Jacobs c and b Smith	0	11	10	-	-
*MC Venter c van Wyk b Smith	1	20	14	-	-
C Light b Dros	20	50	35	3	-
MJ Lavine c and b Brouwers	63	72	56	3	6
CT Enslin b Dros	52	63	57	2	3
†EG Poole not out	34	38	33	2	1
AC Thomas not out	9	19	15	-	-
GA Roe					
LCR Jordaan					
Extras (lb 2, w 5, nb 3)	10				
TOTAL (for 7 wkts) (45 overs)	**210**				

NW	O	M	R	W
Roe	9	0	44	3
Lavine	9	0	35	1
Thomas	9	0	50	1
Jordaan	9	1	40	0
Light	4	1	23	0
Enslin	5	0	43	0

Nor	O	M	R	W
Elworthy	9	1	34	0
Smith	9	2	24	3
Joubert	9	2	28	0
Dros	9	1	52	3
Myburgh	5	0	39	0
Brouwers	4	0	31	1

Fall of Wickets	Nor	NW
1st	20 (2)	1 (1)
2nd	28 (3)	3 (3)
3rd	51 (1)	23 (4)
4th	232 (5)	37 (2)
5th	238 (4)	65 (5)
6th	-	151 (6)
7th	-	186 (7)

NORTHERNS v BORDER — Standard Bank Cup

Played at SuperSport Park, Centurion on 17 December 2000 — Toss: Northerns
Umpires: KH Hurter & SB Lambson
Debuts: Nor: None. Bdr: None
Result: Border won by 4 wickets
Man of Match: Pieter Strydom
Points: Bdr 5, Nor 0.

NORTHERNS	Runs	Mins	Balls	4	6
PJR Steyn c Makalima b Graham	26	53	32	3	1
JG Myburgh c Mitchell b Drakes	6	20	14	1	-
M van Jaarsveld b Botha	1	5	5	-	-
DJJ de Vos c Mitchell b Drakes	36	69	54	5	-
*G Dros c Mitchell b Graham	14	43	27	2	-
FC Brooker lbw b Graham	0	5	1	-	-
S Elworthy c Pope b Henderson	16	50	47	1	1
†CFK van Wyk c and b Strydom	5	15	12	1	-
NG Brouwers run out (Drakes/Strydom)	4	21	12	-	-
P Joubert c Strydom b Henderson	13	22	23	1	-
RE Bryson not out	4	12	11	-	-
Extras (lb 3, w 4, nb 5)	12				
TOTAL (38.5 overs)	**137**				

BORDER	Runs	Mins	Balls	4	6
LL Gamiet c Steyn b Bryson	3	6	8	-	-
†I Mitchell c van Wyk b Bryson	16	68	54	3	-
SC Pope c van Wyk b Joubert	28	45	30	5	-
*PC Strydom b Elworthy	41	56	39	5	1
CB Sugden c van Jaarsveld b de Vos	9	21	17	2	-
W Wiblin not out	28	40	37	6	-
DL Makalima c Steyn b Bryson	3	14	11	-	-
PJ Botha not out	2	6	3	-	-
VC Drakes					
T Henderson					
L Graham					
Extras (lb 5, w 2, nb 1)	8				
TOTAL (for 6 wkts) (33 overs)	**138**				

Bdr	O	M	R	W
Drakes	9	0	41	2
Botha	7	1	27	1
Henderson	8.5	1	28	2
Graham	6	0	18	3
Strydom	8	1	20	1

Nor	O	M	R	W
Elworthy	9	1	34	1
Bryson	9	1	37	3
Joubert	9	0	28	1
de Vos	4	0	21	1
Brouwers	1	0	11	0
Myburgh	1	0	2	0

Fall of Wickets	Nor	Bdr
1st	23 (2)	4 (1)
2nd	24 (3)	53 (3)
3rd	52 (1)	59 (2)
4th	89 (4)	85 (5)
5th	89 (5)	122 (4)
6th	91 (6)	134 (7)
7th	99 (8)	-
8th	113 (9)	-
9th	124 (7)	-
10th	137 (10)	-

NORTHERNS v GAUTENG

Standard Bank Cup

Played at SuperSport Park, Centurion on 22 December 2000 — Toss: Gauteng
Umpires: KH Hurter & CJ Mitchley
Debuts: Nor: None. Gau: TK Mataboge
Result: Northerns won by 3 wickets
Man of Match: Adam Bacher
Points: Nor 4, Gau 1.

GAUTENG	Runs	Mins	Balls	4	6
SG Koenig c Joubert b Bryson	8	30	29	1	-
AJ Hall c Steyn b Elworthy	17	49	30	1	-
AM Bacher not out	134	139	113	13	5
DJ Cullinan run out (Joubert/van Wyk)	93	102	91	7	3
OD Gibson lbw b Elworthy	2	4	3	-	-
JM Otto c Dros b Elworthy	2	10	4	-	-
†N Pothas not out	1	3	1	-	-
*CE Eksteen					
DJ Terbrugge					
TK Mataboge					
WB Masimula					
Extras (b 1, lb 3, w 7, nb 1)	12				
TOTAL (for 5 wkts) (45 overs)	**269**				

NORTHERNS	Runs	Mins	Balls	4	6
PJR Steyn c Otto b Terbrugge	17	22	11	-	2
JG Myburgh c Pothas b Hall	43	44	40	7	-
M van Jaarsveld run out (Otto/Terbrugge)	8	29	13	-	-
ND McKenzie not out	83	161	87	9	-
*G Dros c Eksteen b Terbrugge	33	59	50	4	-
†CFK van Wyk run out (Eksteen)	9	19	12	1	-
A Paleker c Otto b Hall	30	51	28	4	1
S Elworthy b Mataboge	15	13	12	-	2
P Joubert not out	7	9	8	1	-
NG Brouwers					
RE Bryson					
Extras (lb 13, w 9, nb 3)	25				
TOTAL (for 7 wkts) (43 overs)	**270**				

Nor	O	M	R	W
Elworthy	9	2	32	3
Bryson	9	0	49	1
Joubert	9	0	66	0
Dros	7	0	35	0
Myburgh	9	0	66	0
Brouwers	2	0	17	0

Gau	O	M	R	W
Terbrugge	7	0	47	2
Gibson	8	0	62	0
Hall	9	0	35	2
Eksteen	9	0	42	0
Masimula	5	0	46	0
Mataboge	5	0	25	1

Fall of Wickets	Gau	Nor
1st	24 (1)	48 (1)
2nd	29 (2)	64 (2)
3rd	229 (4)	71 (3)
4th	232 (5)	144 (5)
5th	261 (6)	166 (6)
6th	-	243 (7)
7th	-	261 (8)

Eastern Province v Northerns, Port Elizabeth, 27 December 2000. Northerns won by 6 wickets.
KwaZulu-Natal v Northerns, Durban, 5 January 2001. Northerns won by 4 wickets.

NORTHERNS v EASTERNS

Standard Bank Cup

Played at SuperSport Park, Centurion on 7 January 2001 — Toss: Easterns
Umpires: JD Cloete & BG Jerling (TV: AE Williams)
Debuts: Nor: None. Eas: None
Result: Northerns won by 11 runs
Man of Match: Johan Myburgh
Points: Nor 4, Eas 1.

NORTHERNS	Runs	Mins	Balls	4	6
JG Myburgh c and b Flusk	95	121	100	12	2
JA Rudolph c Rindel b de Bruyn	76	163	110	6	-
*G Dros b Nel	20	18	18	3	-
M van Jaarsveld c de Bruyn b Benjamin	39	32	22	2	2
S Elworthy c Flusk b Benjamin	14	19	10	-	1
†CFK van Wyk not out	5	12	10	-	-
DJJ de Vos not out	1	2	1	-	-
A Paleker					
P Joubert					
NG Brouwers					
GJ Smith					
Extras (lb 1, w 12, nb 1)	14				
TOTAL (for 5 wkts) (45 overs)	**264**				

EASTERNS	Runs	Mins	Balls	4	6
AJ Seymore c Myburgh b Elworthy	9	27	19	2	-
MJR Rindel c and b de Vos	62	68	54	10	1
*D Jordaan run out (de Vos/Joubert)	77	143	98	7	-
DN Crookes b Smith	41	57	50	4	-
P de Bruyn b Joubert	5	19	13	-	-
JA Morkel b Smith	19	26	14	1	1
†D Jennings not out	13	20	12	-	-
GE Flusk not out	12	17	11	-	-
EF Mabhena					
KCG Benjamin					
A Nel					
Extras (lb 8, w 6, nb 1)	15				
TOTAL (for 6 wkts) (45 overs)	**253**				

Eas	O	M	R	W
Benjamin	9	1	33	2
Nel	9	0	48	1
de Bruyn	4	0	41	1
Morkel	5	0	44	0
Crookes	9	0	41	0
Flusk	9	0	56	1

Nor	O	M	R	W
Elworthy	9	1	48	1
Smith	9	1	41	2
Joubert	8	0	51	1
de Vos	9	0	41	1
Brouwers	2	0	17	0
Dros	8	0	47	0

Fall of Wickets	Nor	Eas
1st	156 (1)	31 (1)
2nd	187 (3)	79 (2)
3rd	231 (2)	153 (4)
4th	248 (4)	175 (5)
5th	261 (5)	223 (3)
6th	-	224 (6)

Boland v Northerns, Paarl, 17 January 2001. Northerns won by 6 wickets.
Griqualand West v Northerns, 24 January 2001. Griqualand West won by 63 runs.

NORTH WEST

NORTH WEST v EASTERN PROVINCE — Standard Bank Cup

Played at North West Stadium, Potchefstroom on 4 October 2000 — Toss: North West
Umpires: WA Diedricks & IL Howell (TV: AG O'Connor)
Debuts: NW: AC Thomas & PJ van Loggenberg. EP: None
Result: Eastern Province won by 8 runs
Man of Match: Murray Creed
Points: EP 4, NW 1.

EASTERN PROVINCE	Runs	Mins	Balls	4	6
*CC Bradfield c Poole b van Loggenberg	43	60	47	5	1
MR Benfield c Hewitt b Lavine	3	14	9	-	-
JDC Bryant c Light b Enslin	54	111	79	5	3
DJ Callaghan run out (Jacobs)	38	7	46	4	-
JM Kemp b Light	17	21	24	1	1
MW Creed run out (Thomas/Poole)	43	46	37	5	-
RJ Peterson c Thomas b Roe	9	13	16	-	-
†DW Murray not out	16	13	9	2	-
MW Pringle not out	6	15	4	-	-
M Hayward					
M Ngam					
Extras (lb 3, w 13, nb 1)	17				
TOTAL (for 7 wkts) (45 overs)	**246**				

NORTH WEST	Runs	Mins	Balls	4	6
HM de Vos c Bryant b Pringle	22	57	42	2	-
GM Hewitt c Creed b Ngam	12	28	21	2	-
A Jacobs c Pringle b Peterson	38	85	63	3	1
*MC Venter c Pringle b Callaghan	25	71	48	2	-
MJ Lavine c Murray b Ngam	4	4	5	1	-
C Light c Kemp b Callaghan	34	24	24	5	-
CT Enslin not out	39	64	41	3	1
†EG Poole c and b Peterson	30	24	18	4	1
AC Thomas run out (Benfield/Ngam)	3	12	5	-	-
PJ van Loggenberg b Hayward	0	4	2	-	-
GA Roe not out	7	6	8	-	-
Extras (b 2, lb 6, w 9, nb 7)	24				
TOTAL (for 9 wkts) (45 overs)	**238**				

NW	O	M	R	W
Roe	9	1	51	1
Lavine	9	2	48	1
van Loggenberg	5	0	40	1
Thomas	6	1	27	0
Light	9	0	33	1
Enslin	7	0	44	1

EP	O	M	R	W
Pringle	7	0	31	1
Ngam	9	1	34	2
Hayward	9	0	36	1
Kemp	9	0	39	0
Peterson	8	0	61	2
Callaghan	3	0	29	2

Fall of Wickets	EP	NW
1st	8 (2)	27 (2)
2nd	73 (1)	56 (1)
3rd	149 (4)	110 (3)
4th	160 (3)	115 (5)
5th	181 (5)	124 (4)
6th	220 (7)	161 (6)
7th	228 (6)	215 (8)
8th	-	226 (9)
9th	-	230 (10)

NORTH WEST v WESTERN PROVINCE — Standard Bank Cup

Played at North West Stadium, Potchefstroom on 13 October 2000 — Toss: Western Province
Umpires: CJ Mitchley & AG O'Connor
Debuts: NW: None. WP: None
Result: North West won by 4 wickets
Man of Match: Graeme Smith
Points: NW 4, WP 1.

WESTERN PROVINCE	Runs	Mins	Balls	4	6
HH Gibbs c de Vos b Roe	22	36	26	5	-
GC Smith run out (Light)	106	180	135	7	-
NC Johnson c Light b Jordaan	58	76	54	4	1
LD Ferreira c Lavine b Roe	38	57	43	3	1
AG Prince not out	15	38	10	1	-
AG Puttick c Lavine b Roe	7	3	4	1	-
R Munnik not out	1	5	2	-	-
†TL Tsolekile					
*AC Dawson					
CW Henderson					
CM Willoughby					
Extras (lb 2, w 5, nb 4)	11				
TOTAL (for 5 wkts) (45 overs)	**258**				

NORTH WEST	Runs	Mins	Balls	4	6
GM Hewitt c sub (R Magiet) b Smith	42	65	44	8	-
HM de Vos not out	82	212	118	4	-
A Jacobs c Tsolekile b Smith	18	46	34	-	-
*MC Venter b Smith	3	8	7	-	-
C Light c Tsolekile b Dawson	33	40	35	5	-
MJ Lavine c Gibbs b Dawson	44	31	21	2	4
CT Enslin c Prince b Willoughby	11	16	11	1	-
†EG Poole not out	0	2	1	-	-
AC Thomas					
GA Roe					
LCR Jordaan					
Extras (lb 3, w 23, nb 2)	28				
TOTAL (for 6 wkts) (44.5 overs)	**261**				

NW	O	M	R	W
Roe	9	0	55	3
Lavine	9	1	37	0
Enslin	5	0	50	0
Light	4	0	33	0
Thomas	9	0	46	0
Jordaan	9	1	35	1

WP	O	M	R	W
Willoughby	8.5	1	52	1
Dawson	9	1	36	2
Munnik	1.4	0	15	0
Henderson	9	1	44	0
Smith	8.2	0	46	3
Johnson	8	0	65	0

Fall of Wickets	WP	NW
1st	40 (1)	61 (1)
2nd	143 (3)	103 (3)
3rd	220 (4)	116 (4)
4th	239 (2)	166 (5)
5th	247 (6)	237 (6)
6th	-	255 (7)

Northerns v North West, Centurion, 18 October 2000. Northerns won by 29 runs.
Boland v North West, Paarl, 3 November 2000. Boland won by 28 runs.

NORTH WEST v EASTERNS — Standard Bank Cup

Played at North West Stadium, Potchefstroom on 15 December 2000 — Toss: Easterns
Umpires: KH Hurter & ST Jivan
Debuts: NW: R Niewoudt. Eas: None
Result: Easterns won by 59 runs
Man of Match: Andre Nel
Points: Eas 5, NW 0.

EASTERNS	Runs	Mins	Balls	4	6
D Brand c Lavine b Roe	0	7	7	-	-
MJR Rindel c Poole b Lavine	0	2	1	-	-
*D Jordaan c Jacobs b Lavine	49	118	83	4	-
DN Crookes c Strydom b Roe	2	17	13	-	-
P de Bruyn c Strydom b van der Merwe	68	126	92	6	1
KCG Benjamin c Light b van der Merwe	21	23	23	2	-
GA Pollock c Lavine b Light	34	29	28	3	-
†D Jennings run out (Lavine)	2	7	3	-	-
GE Flusk c Strydom b Thomas	12	17	13	-	-
EF Mabhena not out	2	7	3	-	-
A Nel not out	7	4	6	-	-
Extras (lb 3, w 9, nb 1)	13				
TOTAL (for 9 wkts) (45 overs)	**210**				

NORTH WEST	Runs	Mins	Balls	4	6
R Niewoudt c Jennings b Nel	8	15	14	1	-
*GM Hewitt c Jordaan b Nel	0	5	2	-	-
A Jacobs c Jordaan b Nel	0	18	11	-	-
C Light c Brand b Nel	9	21	15	2	-
MJ Lavine c de Bruyn b Benjamin	6	17	8	1	-
M Strydom c and b de Bruyn	39	97	82	3	-
CT Enslin lbw b de Bruyn	14	24	15	1	-
†EG Poole run out (Pollock/Jennings)	23	46	42	-	-
AC Thomas not out	14	52	45	-	-
GA Roe c Brand b Flusk	16	17	18	1	-
F van der Merwe c Crookes b Nel	4	1	9	-	-
Extras (lb 4, w 14)	18				
TOTAL (43.3 overs)	**151**				

NW	O	M	R	W
Lavine	9	2	25	2
Roe	7	1	21	2
van der Merwe	9	1	45	2
Thomas	8	0	37	1
Light	8	0	48	1
Strydom	2	0	15	0
Enslin	2	0	16	0

Eas	O	M	R	W
Benjamin	7	0	19	1
Nel	8.3	0	27	5
Crookes	9	1	32	0
Jordaan	2	0	14	0
de Bruyn	9	0	29	2
Flusk	8	0	26	1

Fall of Wickets	Eas	NW
1st	1 (2)	4 (2)
2nd	1 (1)	9 (1)
3rd	7 (4)	16 (3)
4th	103 (3)	26 (4)
5th	139 (6)	30 (5)
6th	155 (5)	59 (7)
7th	166 (8)	102 (8)
8th	197 (7)	120 (6)
9th	201 (9)	143 (10)
10th	-	151 (11)

Border v North West, East London, 22 December 2000. Border won by 125 runs.

NORTH WEST v FREE STATE — Standard Bank Cup

Played at North West Stadium, Potchefstroom on 5 January 2001 — Toss: North West
Umpires: CJ Mitchley & AE Williams
Debuts: NW: BC de Wett. FS: None
Result: Free State won by 5 wickets
Man of Match: Arno Jacobs
Points: FS 4, NW 1.

NORTH WEST	Runs	Mins	Balls	4	6
R Niewoudt b Pretorius	34	71	57	6	-
G Outram b Bakkes	2	19	9	-	-
BC de Wett b Mpitsang	4	23	13	1	-
†A Jacobs c van Wyk b van der Wath	106	137	102	11	-
MJ Lavine lbw b Venter	72	70	62	6	4
CT Enslin c Venter b Pretorius	20	24	20	2	-
*AG Lawson not out	4	16	8	-	-
M Strydom not out	2	4	2	-	-
AC Thomas					
GA Roe					
F van der Merwe					
Extras (lb 4, w 14, nb 3)	21				
TOTAL (for 6 wkts) (45 overs)	**265**				

FREE STATE	Runs	Mins	Balls	4	6
HH Dippenaar c Jacobs b Lavine	1	3	2	-	-
AI Gait c van der Merwe b Strydom	35	69	38	3	-
MN van Wyk c Thomas b Roe	8	14	10	1	-
JF Venter c Lawson b van der Merwe	58	93	65	5	-
GFJ Liebenberg not out	75	134	89	5	-
*†GL Brophy b Enslin	35	46	34	3	-
JJ van der Wath not out	35	40	24	2	1
HC Bakkes					
D Pretorius					
PV Mpitsang					
TJ Mokoenanyana					
Extras (lb 5, w 12, nb 3)	20				
TOTAL (for 5 wkts) (43.1 overs)	**267**				

FS	O	M	R	W
Bakkes	7	1	31	1
Mpitsang	9	1	48	1
Pretorius	9	0	60	2
Mokoenanyana	6	0	41	0
Venter	9	0	45	1
van der Wath	5	0	36	1

NW	O	M	R	W
Lavine	5	0	21	1
Roe	7	0	53	1
Thomas	8.1	0	58	0
Strydom	9	0	44	1
van der Merwe	9	0	58	1
Enslin	5	0	28	1

Fall of Wickets	NW	FS
1st	15 (2)	2 (1)
2nd	36 (3)	18 (3)
3rd	55 (1)	81 (2)
4th	201 (5)	132 (4)
5th	246 (6)	196 (6)
6th	261 (4)	-

Griqualand West v North West, Kimberley, 10 January 2001. Griqualand West won by 167 runs.

NORTH WEST v GAUTENG — Standard Bank Cup

Played at North West Stadium, Potchefstroom on 19 January 2001 — Toss: North West
Umpires: ST Jivan & CJ Mitchley
Debuts: NW: None. Gau: None
Result: North West won by 2 runs (D/L method), target revised to 220 in 31 overs
Man of Match: Marthinus Otto
Points: NW 4, Gau 1.

NORTH WEST	Runs	Mins	Balls	4	6
R Niewoudt c Mataboge b Hall	41	58	39	5	1
C Light c Bacher b Terbrugge	7	13	11	1	-
BC de Wett b Eksteen	26	57	45	2	-
†A Jacobs c Mataboge b Otto	38	77	50	3	-
MJ Lavine c Otto b Eksteen	41	56	41	3	2
G Outram not out	46	53	32	4	1
CT Enslin b Eksteen	10	15	13	1	-
*AG Lawson c Hall b Terbrugge	6	8	11	1	-
AC Thomas b Terbrugge	3	10	5	-	-
GA Roe b Terbrugge	6	7	4	1	-
F van der Merwe not out	1	1	1	-	-
Extras (lb 5, w 13, nb 6)	24				
TOTAL (for 9 wkts) (41 overs)	**249**				

GAUTENG	Runs	Mins	Balls	4	6
AM Bacher c Jacobs b Roe	10	16	16	1	-
AJ Hall lbw b Roe	23	27	13	4	-
OD Gibson b Light	23	39	21	3	1
JM Otto c Light b van der Merwe	70	95	59	7	1
†N Pothas b van der Merwe	12	20	22	-	-
Z de Bruyn c Jacobs b van der Merwe	6	12	10	1	-
SG Koenig run out (Lawson)	2	5	5	-	-
SL Letshela not out	26	37	27	3	-
*CE Eksteen c Outram b Lavine	6	13	11	-	-
TK Mataboge run out (Outram/Roe)	10	9	6	-	-
DJ Terbrugge not out	0	2	1	-	-
Extras (lb 12, w 12, nb 5)	29				
TOTAL (for 9 wkts) (31 overs)	**217**				

Gau	O	M	R	W
Terbrugge	8	0	48	4
Gibson	7	0	67	0
Hall	8	1	41	1
Mataboge	5	0	28	0
Eksteen	9	1	24	3
de Bruyn	2.4	0	28	0
Otto	1.2	0	8	1

NW	O	M	R	W
Lavine	6	0	37	1
Roe	6	1	51	2
Thomas	3	0	27	0
Light	7	0	24	1
van der Merwe	6	0	44	3
Enslin	3	0	22	0

Fall of Wickets	NW	Gau
1st	12 (2)	26 (1)
2nd	74 (1)	39 (2)
3rd	87 (3)	95 (3)
4th	159 (5)	127 (5)
5th	168 (4)	147 (6)
6th	195 (7)	150 (7)
7th	204 (8)	183 (4)
8th	224 (9)	198 (9)
9th	248 (10)	216 (10)

KwaZulu-Natal v North West, Durban, 24 January 2001. KwaZulu-Natal won by 7 wickets.

WESTERN PROVINCE

Northerns v Western Province, Centurion, 6 October 2000. Northerns won by 3 wickets.
North West v Western Province, Potchefstroom, 13 October 2000. North West won by 4 wickets.
Griqualand West v Western Province, Kimberley, 18 October 2000. Western Province won by 144 runs.
KwaZulu-Natal v Western Province, Durban, 17 November 2000. KwaZulu-Natal won by 28 runs.

WESTERN PROVINCE v BORDER

Standard Bank Cup

Played at Newlands, Cape Town on 1 December 2000
Toss: Western Province
Umpires: M Gajjar & KH Hurter
Debuts: WP: None. Bdr: L Graham & JGH Wilson
Result: Border won by 4 wickets
Man of Match: Neil Johnson
Points: Bdr 4, WP 1.

WESTERN PROVINCE	Runs	Mins	Balls	4	6
NC Johnson c Sugden b Wilson	94	147	116	9	-
HH Gibbs run out (Wilson)	18	35	33	3	-
GC Smith c Mitchell b Strydom	25	60	37	4	-
*HD Ackerman c Drakes b Graham	15	29	31	-	-
AG Prince c Drakes b Graham	6	14	13	-	-
AG Puttick b Strydom	12	23	13	1	-
AC Dawson not out	19	31	18	2	-
†TL Tsolekile b Drakes	12	8	8	-	1
R Telemachus not out	4	4	3	-	-
CW Henderson					
CM Willoughby					
Extras (lb 6, w 7, nb 2)	15				
TOTAL (for 7 wkts) (45 overs)	**220**				

BORDER	Runs	Mins	Balls	4	6
LL Gamiet c Tsolekile b Henderson	45	95	76	3	1
†I Mitchell c Tsolekile b Dawson	4	16	11	1	-
SC Pope b Johnson	55	89	71	7	-
*PC Strydom c Henderson b Johnson	1	8	7	-	-
CB Sugden b Willoughby	33	45	39	1	1
W Wiblin b Henderson	9	15	16	-	-
DL Makalima not out	25	54	32	1	1
VC Drakes not out	29	26	19	2	-
GT Love					
L Graham					
JGH Wilson					
Extras (b 5, lb 7, w 5, nb 4)	21				
TOTAL (for 6 wkts) (44.3 overs)	**222**				

Bdr	O	M	R	W
Drakes	9	1	41	1
Wilson	9	1	50	1
Graham	9	0	42	2
Love	9	0	37	0
Strydom	9	0	44	2

WP	O	M	R	W
Dawson	9	1	45	1
Willoughby	9	3	38	1
Telemachus	8.3	0	46	0
Henderson	9	0	41	2
Johnson	9	0	40	2

Fall of Wickets	WP	Bdr
1st	38 (2)	14 (2)
2nd	104 (3)	111 (1)
3rd	144 (4)	111 (4)
4th	162 (5)	119 (3)
5th	167 (1)	145 (6)
6th	195 (6)	172 (5)
7th	214 (8)	-

WESTERN PROVINCE v EASTERNS

Standard Bank Cup

Played at Newlands, Cape Town on 8 December 2000
Toss: Western Province
Umpires: SB Lambson & S Wadvalla (TV: CJ Mitchley)
Debuts: WP: None. Eas: None
Result: Western Province won by 7 runs
Man of Match: Neil Johnson
Points: WP 4, Eas 1.

WESTERN PROVINCE	Runs	Mins	Balls	4	6
NC Johnson st Jennings b Crookes	111	146	128	16	1
HH Gibbs run out (de Bruyn)	3	25	10	-	-
GC Smith c Jordaan b Benjamin	47	107	63	6	-
*HD Ackerman not out	41	59	38	3	-
AG Prince b Nel	28	39	27	1	1
AG Puttick not out	7	6	6	1	-
AC Dawson					
†TL Tsolekile					
R Telemachus					
CW Henderson					
CM Willoughby					
Extras (lb 5, w 4, nb 2)	11				
TOTAL (for 4 wkts) (45 overs)	**248**				

EASTERNS	Runs	Mins	Balls	4	6
†D Jennings c Tsolekile b Willoughby	0	7	7	-	-
MJR Rindel c Tsolekile b Johnson	82	154	101	7	1
*D Jordaan run out (Smith)	22	64	53	2	-
DN Crookes lbw b Johnson	73	101	72	7	1
GA Pollock not out	34	38	27	2	1
JA Morkel not out	14	18	13	-	-
EF Mabhena					
P de Bruyn					
GE Flusk					
KCG Benjamin					
A Nel					
Extras (lb 7, w 6, nb 3)	16				
TOTAL (for 4 wkts) (45 overs)	**241**				

Eas	O	M	R	W
Benjamin	9	1	54	1
Nel	9	2	40	1
Morkel	8	0	51	0
de Bruyn	6	0	47	0
Crookes	9	1	32	1
Flusk	4	0	19	0

WP	O	M	R	W
Dawson	9	3	26	0
Willoughby	9	0	53	1
Telemachus	9	0	49	0
Henderson	9	0	47	0
Johnson	9	0	59	2

Fall of Wickets	WP	Eas
1st	19 (2)	2 (1)
2nd	161 (3)	61 (3)
3rd	172 (1)	175 (2)
4th	237 (5)	207 (4)

Gauteng v Western Province, Johannesburg, 16 December 2000. Gauteng won by 21 runs.

WESTERN PROVINCE v EASTERN PROVINCE

Standard Bank Cup

Played at Newlands, Cape Town on 22 December 2000
Toss: Eastern Province
Umpires: RE Koertzen & AG O'Connor (TV: ST Jivan)
Debuts: WP: None. EP: None
Result: Western Province won by 9 wickets
Man of Match: James Bryant
Points: WP 5, EP 0.

EASTERN PROVINCE	Runs	Mins	Balls	4	6
MR Benfield lbw b Dawson	0	2	3	-	-
*CC Bradfield c Tsolekile b Kallis	34	79	59	3	-
JDC Bryant not out	105	177	139	8	2
DJ Callaghan b Kallis	35	75	53	3	-
JM Kemp b Kallis	2	7	4	-	-
MW Creed b Kallis	0	2	1	-	-
RJ Peterson c Tsolekile b Kallis	6	9	10	-	-
†DW Murray not out	5	3	2	1	-
S Abrahams					
GJ-P Kruger					
M Ngam					
Extras (lb 5, w 5, nb 1)	11				
TOTAL (for 6 wkts) (45 overs)	**198**				

WESTERN PROVINCE	Runs	Mins	Balls	4	6
G Kirsten not out	85	123	95	13	-
HH Gibbs c Peterson b Creed	90	108	74	9	2
JH Kallis not out	15	14	16	3	-
*HD Ackerman					
NC Johnson					
AG Prince					
AC Dawson					
†TL Tsolekile					
CW Henderson					
R Telemachus					
CM Willoughby					
Extras (lb 2, w 6, nb 2)	10				
TOTAL (for 1 wkt) (30.3 overs)	**200**				

WP	O	M	R	W
Dawson	9	2	39	1
Willoughby	8	0	41	0
Telemachus	7	0	23	0
Henderson	9	0	30	0
Kallis	9	0	47	5
Johnson	3	1	13	0

EP	O	M	R	W
Ngam	4	0	40	0
Kruger	5	0	27	0
Kemp	4	0	28	0
Peterson	3	0	22	0
Abrahams	8	0	35	0
Callaghan	4	0	21	0
Creed	2.3	0	25	1

Fall of Wickets	EP	WP
1st	1 (1)	175 (2)
2nd	76 (2)	-
3rd	171 (4)	-
4th	183 (5)	-
5th	183 (6)	-
6th	193 (7)	-

WESTERN PROVINCE v FREE STATE

Standard Bank Cup

Played at Newlands, Cape Town on 27 December 2000
Toss: Western Province
Umpires: DF Becker & ST Jivan
Debuts: WP: None. FS: None
Result: Western Province won by 50 runs
Man of Match: Neil Johnson
Points: WP 5, FS 0.

WESTERN PROVINCE	Runs	Mins	Balls	4	6
NC Johnson b van Wyk	91	144	117	10	-
HH Gibbs c Brophy b Bakkes	0	7	3	-	-
GC Smith b Venter	18	47	31	2	-
*HD Ackerman c Brophy b Pretorius	5	13	13	-	-
AG Prince not out	67	117	75	4	1
†AG Puttick c Venter b Pretorius	22	33	25	-	-
LD Ferreira not out	18	8	6	3	1
AC Dawson					
R Telemachus					
CW Henderson					
CM Willoughby					
Extras (lb 6, w 17)	23				
TOTAL (for 5 wkts) (45 overs)	**244**				

FREE STATE	Runs	Mins	Balls	4	6
JF Venter b Dawson	80	133	109	9	-
AI Gait c Ferreira b Dawson	3	17	11	-	-
WJ Smit st Puttick b Henderson	35	64	52	5	1
MN van Wyk c Smith b Telemachus	21	33	23	2	-
LJ Wilkinson c Puttick b Henderson	3	27	14	-	-
JJ van der Wath st Puttick b Henderson	2	7	5	-	-
*†GL Brophy b Dawson	13	23	17	-	-
HC Bakkes c Gibbs b Telemachus	26	26	25	2	-
D Pretorius b Dawson	2	7	4	-	-
PV Mpitsang b Telemachus	0	10	1	-	-
TJ Mokoenanyana not out	2	8	8	-	-
Extras (lb 4, w 2, nb 1)	7				
TOTAL (44.4 overs)	**194**				

FS	O	M	R	W
Mpitsang	9	0	62	0
Bakkes	9	3	29	1
Pretorius	9	0	61	2
Venter	9	1	25	1
Mokoenanyana	4	0	31	0
van der Wath	2	0	17	0
van Wyk	3	0	13	1

WP	O	M	R	W
Dawson	9	2	29	4
Willoughby	9	0	30	0
Telemachus	8.4	0	33	3
Henderson	9	0	46	3
Johnson	9	0	52	0

Fall of Wickets	WP	FS
1st	4 (2)	11 (2)
2nd	56 (3)	86 (3)
3rd	68 (4)	133 (4)
4th	165 (1)	144 (1)
5th	214 (6)	148 (6)
6th	-	149 (5)
7th	-	188 (7)
8th	-	192 (8)
9th	-	192 (9)
10th	-	194 (10)

WESTERN PROVINCE v BOLAND

Standard Bank Cup

Played at Newlands, Cape Town on 19 January 2001

Toss: Western Province

Umpires: WA Diedricks & BG Jerling

Debuts: WP: None. Bol: None

Result: Western Province won by 5 runs

Man of Match: Ashwell Prince

Points: WP 4, Bol 1.

WESTERN PROVINCE	Runs	Mins	Balls	4	6
NC Johnson c Ontong b Carter	43	63	47	7	-
GC Smith c Koen b Pringle	1	9	5	-	-
†AG Puttick c Henderson b Williams	10	42	32	1	-
*HD Ackerman c Palframan b Carter	2	19	13	-	-
AG Prince c Jackson b Williams	61	119	76	4	1
LD Ferreira b Langeveldt	20	52	49	1	-
AC Dawson run out (Williams)	14	32	22	-	-
CW Henderson b Langeveldt	19	16	13	1	-
R Telemachus b Langeveldt	1	2	2	-	-
PR Adams not out	5	10	6	-	-
CM Willoughby not out	6	5	5	1	-
Extras (lb 7, w 2)	9				
TOTAL (for 9 wkts) (45 overs)	**191**				

BOLAND	Runs	Mins	Balls	4	6
JM Henderson c Prince b Willoughby	5	7	11	1	-
*LJ Koen c Puttick b Telemachus	13	34	18	2	-
JL Ontong c Smith b Telemachus	66	138	100	7	-
KC Jackson lbw b Henderson	22	63	48	2	-
BT Player c Puttick b Adams	4	4	7	1	-
JG Strydom c Puttick b Henderson	7	12	12	1	-
†SJ Palframan c and b Adams	6	9	6	1	-
NM Carter c Dawson b Telemachus	27	54	43	-	1
CK Langeveldt run out (Smith)	17	45	20	1	-
AAW Pringle c Ferreira b Dawson	2	5	4	-	-
HS Williams not out	2	4	2	-	-
Extras (lb 4, w 7, nb 4)	15				
TOTAL (44.3 overs)	**186**				

Bol	O	M	R	W
Langeveldt	9	0	42	3
Pringle	7	1	27	1
Williams	9	1	31	2
Carter	8	2	42	2
Ontong	4	0	16	0
Player	8	0	26	0

WP	O	M	R	W
Dawson	9	0	32	1
Willoughby	9	0	33	1
Telemachus	8.3	0	37	3
Henderson	9	0	42	2
Adams	9	0	38	2

Fall of Wickets	WP	Bol
1st	7 (2)	5 (1)
2nd	49 (3)	27 (2)
3rd	57 (1)	86 (4)
4th	58 (4)	91 (5)
5th	101 (6)	103 (6)
6th	136 (7)	122 (7)
7th	172 (8)	133 (3)
8th	174 (9)	175 (8)
9th	180 (5)	178 (10)
10th	-	186 (9)

SEMIFINALS

NORTHERNS v BORDER

Standard Bank Cup Semifinal 1st leg

Played at SuperSport Park, Centurion on 7 February 2001

Toss: Border

Umpires: KH Hurter & CJ Mitchley (TV: S Wadvalla)

Debuts: Nor: None. Bdr: None

Result: Border won by 2 wickets

Man of Match: Jacques Rudolph

A splendid century by Rudolph, and a 134-run second-wicket stand between Rudolph and Van Jaarsveld, seemed to have given the home team the edge but Border replied in kind on a good pitch, with Gamiet playing an outstanding innings and sharing a century opening stand with Sugden.

NORTHERNS	Runs	Mins	Balls	4	6
JG Myburgh c Boucher b Henderson	12	45	36	1	-
JA Rudolph c Henderson b Drakes	110	176	116	11	1
M van Jaarsveld b Henderson	77	82	64	6	1
ND McKenzie c and b Ntini	12	18	14	-	-
*G Dros not out	47	39	31	3	2
S Elworthy not out	10	11	10	-	-
†CFK van Wyk					
FC Brooker					
A Paleker					
P Joubert					
GJ Smith					
Extras (lb 4, w 4, nb 1)	9				
TOTAL (for 4 wkts) (45 overs)	**277**				

BORDER	Runs	Mins	Balls	4	6
LL Gamiet run out (Joubert/Dros)	87	119	81	8	1
CB Sugden lbw b Myburgh	53	66	54	6	1
SC Pope c Myburgh b Joubert	6	7	9	-	-
†MV Boucher c Rudolph b Dros	28	64	45	1	-
*PC Strydom b Dros	2	7	5	-	-
W Wiblin b Elworthy	52	64	43	5	1
I Mitchell b Smith	17	29	13	2	-
VC Drakes b Elworthy	5	22	11	-	-
PJ Botha not out	2	10	2	-	-
T Henderson not out	10	7	5	1	-
M Ntini					
Extras (lb 6, w 8, nb 2)	16				
TOTAL (for 8 wkts) (44.2 overs)	**278**				

Bdr	O	M	R	W
Drakes	9	1	45	1
Ntini	9	0	47	1
Henderson	9	0	67	2
Botha	6	1	34	0
Pope	3	0	21	0
Strydom	9	0	59	0

Nor	O	M	R	W
Elworthy	9	0	46	2
Smith	8.2	0	68	1
Joubert	7	0	51	1
Myburgh	9	0	44	1
Dros	9	0	52	2
McKenzie	2	0	11	0

Fall of Wickets	Nor	Bdr
1st	41 (1)	106 (2)
2nd	175 (3)	113 (3)
3rd	195 (4)	172 (1)
4th	255 (2)	179 (5)
5th	-	186 (4)
6th	-	236 (7)
7th	-	265 (8)
8th	-	266 (6)

BORDER v NORTHERNS — Standard Bank Cup Semifinal 2nd leg

Played at Buffalo Park, East London on 9 February 2001 — Toss: Border
Umpires: WA Diedricks & RE Koertzen (TV: SB Lambson)
Debuts: Bdr: None. Nor: None
Result: Northerns won by 7 wickets
Man of Match: Johan Myburgh
Notes: GJ Smith took a hat-trick in Border's innings. His victims were Mitchell, Drakes and Henderson.

For the second time in three days, a total above 270 proved not to be enough. Sugden and Pope laid the foundation and Boucher played a thrilling innings before a flurry of wickets by Smith, including a hat-trick off the last three balls of the innings, meant that Border lost their momentum at the end. Myburgh hammered the bowling and Rudolph was again in fine form as Northerns gained a surprisingly comfortable win.

BORDER	Runs	Mins	Balls	4	6
LL Gamiet c van Wyk b Smith	6	23	15	1	-
CB Sugden c Elworthy b Myburgh	71	105	102	7	-
SC Pope lbw b McKenzie	71	80	70	9	-
†MV Boucher c Dros b Elworthy	70	55	48	7	2
*PC Strydom c Rudolph b Smith	28	33	23	2	1
W Wiblin not out	10	14	6	1	-
I Mitchell lbw b Smith	6	3	4	1	-
VC Drakes lbw b Smith	0	1	1	-	-
T Henderson c van Jaarsveld b Smith	0	1	1	-	-
PJ Botha					
M Ntini					
Extras (lb 6, w 3)	9				
TOTAL (for 8 wkts) (45 overs)	**271**				

NORTHERNS	Runs	Mins	Balls	4	6
JG Myburgh c Sugden b Henderson	44	30	34	8	1
JA Rudolph c Boucher b Ntini	89	146	97	8	-
M van Jaarsveld lbw b Henderson	76	110	78	11	-
ND McKenzie not out	21	38	22	1	-
*G Dros not out	32	33	24	3	-
FC Brooker					
A Paleker					
S Elworthy					
†CFK van Wyk					
P Joubert					
GJ Smith					
Extras (lb 5, w 4, nb 1)	10				
TOTAL (for 3 wkts) (42.2 overs)	**272**				

Nor	O	M	R	W
Elworthy	9	1	58	1
Smith	9	1	44	5
Joubert	9	0	49	0
Myburgh	9	0	36	1
Dros	5	0	41	0
McKenzie	2	0	17	1
van Jaarsveld	2	0	20	0

Bdr	O	M	R	W
Drakes	8.2	1	46	0
Henderson	8	0	57	2
Botha	9	0	51	0
Ntini	9	0	54	1
Strydom	4	0	30	0
Pope	4	0	29	0

Fall of Wickets	Bdr	Nor
1st	18 (1)	50 (1)
2nd	148 (3)	217 (3)
3rd	168 (2)	218 (2)
4th	252 (5)	-
5th	263 (4)	-
6th	271 (7)	-
7th	271 (8)	-
8th	271 (9)	-

BORDER v NORTHERNS — Standard Bank Cup Semifinal 3rd leg

Played at Buffalo Park, East London on 11 February 2001 — Toss: Northerns
Umpires: WA Diedricks & RE Koertzen (TV: SB Lambson)
Debuts: Bdr: None. Nor: None
Result: Northerns won by 9 wickets
Man of Match: Greg Smith

After the batting heroics of the first two legs, Border collapsed after being sent in, with Smith ripping out the first three batsmen. Border were unable to recover and their campaign ended in anti-climax.

BORDER	Runs	Mins	Balls	4	6
LL Gamiet c Paleker b Smith	4	18	17	-	-
CB Sugden c van Wyk b Smith	17	50	31	1	-
SC Pope c Myburgh b Smith	1	5	5	-	-
†MV Boucher b Joubert	18	44	39	1	-
*PC Strydom c McKenzie b Dros	3	25	12	-	-
W Wiblin b Dros	10	46	37	-	-
PJ Botha run out (van Wyk)	3	9	9	-	-
VC Drakes c van Jaarsveld b Dros	10	24	15	1	-
T Henderson run out (Rudolph)	0	17	9	-	-
L Graham not out	10	14	14	2	-
M Ntini lbw b Myburgh	0	2	1	-	-
Extras (lb 5, w 3)	8				
TOTAL (31.3 overs)	**84**				

NORTHERNS	Runs	Mins	Balls	4	6
JG Myburgh b Drakes	25	57	41	2	-
JA Rudolph not out	33	101	76	3	-
M van Jaarsveld not out	21	43	33	3	-
ND McKenzie					
*G Dros					
FC Brooker					
A Paleker					
S Elworthy					
†CFK van Wyk					
P Joubert					
GJ Smith					
Extras (w 3, nb 3)	6				
TOTAL (for 1 wkt) (24.3 overs)	**85**				

Nor	O	M	R	W
Smith	7	1	15	3
Elworthy	6	0	18	0
Joubert	9	0	19	1
Dros	8	0	21	3
Myburgh	1.3	0	6	1

Bdr	O	M	R	W
Drakes	7	0	32	1
Henderson	4	0	14	0
Ntini	5	0	18	0
Graham	6.3	2	18	0
Wiblin	2	0	3	0

Fall of Wickets	Bdr	Nor
1st	16 (1)	50 (1)
2nd	19 (3)	-
3rd	36 (2)	-
4th	48 (4)	-
5th	50 (5)	-
6th	57 (7)	-
7th	72 (8)	-
8th	73 (6)	-
9th	83 (9)	-
10th	84 (11)	-

EASTERN PROVINCE v KWAZULU-NATAL Standard Bank Cup Semifinal 1st leg

Played at St George's Park, Port Elizabeth on 14 February 2001 Toss: KwaZulu-Natal
Umpires: IL Howell & AG O'Connor (TV: BG Jerling)
Debuts: EP: None. KZN: None
Result: KwaZulu-Natal won by 9 wickets
Man of Match: Doug Watson

Bastow and Pollock put Eastern Province under pressure from the start and the back-up seamers kept a clamp on the home team batsmen. Watson's solidity and Bodi's aggression enabled the Dolphins to hurry to victory.

EASTERN PROVINCE	Runs	Mins	Balls	4	6
*CC Bradfield b Bastow	1	5	3	-	-
†DW Murray c Stewart b Pollock	0	13	10	-	-
JDC Bryant c Stewart b Kent	31	58	46	5	-
JM Kemp c and b Baptiste	16	45	31	1	1
DJ Callaghan b Kent	30	78	63	-	-
MR Benfield c Watson b Baptiste	21	38	34	1	-
MW Creed c and b Bastow	20	42	34	1	-
RJ Peterson run out (Kent/Stewart)	14	18	11	-	1
S Abrahams c Benkenstein b Pollock	7	33	18	-	-
MW Pringle not out	24	25	20	1	1
GJ-P Kruger not out	1	2	1	-	-
Extras (b 1, lb 3, w 2, nb 1)	7				
TOTAL (for 9 wkts) (45 overs)	**172**				

KWAZULU-NATAL	Runs	Mins	Balls	4	6
DJ Watson not out	72	125	92	6	2
GH Bodi c Callaghan b Abrahams	56	77	50	8	-
WR Wingfield not out	40	47	51	3	1
L Klusener					
*DM Benkenstein					
JC Kent					
†ELR Stewart					
AM Amla					
SM Pollock					
EAE Baptiste					
JE Bastow					
Extras (b 1, lb 3, w 2, nb 2)	8				
TOTAL (for 1 wkt) (31.5 overs)	**176**				

KZN	O	M	R	W
Pollock	9	0	23	2
Bastow	9	0	36	2
Baptiste	9	1	29	2
Kent	9	0	40	2
Bodi	6	0	27	0
Klusener	2	0	9	0
Wingfield	1	0	4	0

EP	O	M	R	W
Pringle	9	1	31	0
Kruger	5	0	29	0
Kemp	4	0	30	0
Abrahams	5	0	37	1
Creed	5	0	21	0
Peterson	3.5	0	24	0

Fall of Wickets	EP	KZN
1st	1 (1)	111 (2)
2nd	6 (2)	-
3rd	50 (4)	-
4th	52 (3)	-
5th	87 (6)	-
6th	120 (5)	-
7th	126 (7)	-
8th	139 (8)	-
9th	170 (9)	-

KWAZULU-NATAL v EASTERN PROVINCE Standard Bank Cup Semifinal 2nd leg

Played at Kingsmead, Durban on 16 February 2001 Toss: KwaZulu-Natal
Umpires: JD Cloete & DL Orchard (TV: DF Becker)
Debuts: KZN: None. EP: None
Result: Eastern Province won by 28 runs
Man of Match: Meyrick Pringle

Pringle's superb opening spell plunged the Dolphins into trouble and Hayward showed a return to form after a miserable season, bowling at high pace to put the home side in a position from which not even a fine innings by Klusener could rescue them.

EASTERN PROVINCE	Runs	Mins	Balls	4	6
*CC Bradfield c Stewart b Pollock	9	18	16	2	-
RJ Peterson c Stewart b Kent	38	55	29	4	1
JDC Bryant c Stewart b Bodi	44	109	79	6	-
JM Kemp c Pollock b Kent	7	30	20	1	-
DJ Callaghan st Stewart b Bodi	56	68	61	5	1
MR Benfield st Stewart b Bodi	28	36	31	3	-
†DW Murray c and b Bodi	0	1	1	-	-
S Abrahams not out	20	29	16	2	-
MW Pringle c Benkenstein b Bodi	11	17	17	-	1
GJ-P Kruger not out	0	1	0	-	-
M Hayward					
Extras (b 2, lb 2, w 8)	12				
TOTAL (for 8 wkts) (45 overs)	**225**				

KWAZULU-NATAL	Runs	Mins	Balls	4	6
DJ Watson lbw b Hayward	15	62	37	2	-
GH Bodi lbw b Pringle	1	11	6	-	-
AM Amla c Murray b Pringle	17	23	26	3	-
WR Wingfield c Kemp b Pringle	0	1	1	-	-
*DM Benkenstein b Hayward	4	37	26	-	-
JC Kent lbw b Callaghan	16	72	37	2	-
†ELR Stewart b Hayward	2	6	3	-	-
L Klusener b Callaghan	51	47	32	7	2
SM Pollock c Pringle b Kruger	25	51	30	-	1
EAE Baptiste not out	33	52	39	1	-
JE Bastow b Hayward	10	7	8	-	1
Extras (lb 13, w 10)	23				
TOTAL (40.5 overs)	**197**				

KZN	O	M	R	W
Pollock	9	0	43	1
Bastow	9	0	61	0
Kent	7	0	31	2
Baptiste	9	1	27	0
Bodi	9	0	46	5
Wingfield	2	0	13	0

EP	O	M	R	W
Pringle	8	3	29	3
Kemp	9	1	26	0
Kruger	8	0	39	1
Hayward	6.5	0	42	4
Abrahams	6	0	26	0
Callaghan	3	0	22	2

Fall of Wickets	EP	KZN
1st	19 (1)	5 (2)
2nd	65 (2)	29 (3)
3rd	92 (4)	29 (4)
4th	151 (3)	45 (1)
5th	185 (5)	50 (5)
6th	185 (7)	52 (7)
7th	200 (6)	122 (8)
8th	224 (9)	125 (6)
9th	-	186 (9)
10th	-	197 (11)

KWAZULU-NATAL v EASTERN PROVINCE Standard Bank Cup Semifinal 3rd leg

Played at Kingsmead, Durban on 18 February 2001 Toss: KwaZulu-Natal
Umpires: JD Cloete & DL Orchard (TV: DF Becker)
Debuts: KZN: None. EP: None
Result: No Result

Seldom has rain made a more cruel intervention. Peterson hammered the bowling and Bryant and Kemp were well-set, going into the last four overs, when all their efforts were undone. A fresh start was ordered for the following day.

EASTERN PROVINCE	Runs	Mins	Balls	4	6
*CC Bradfield c Stewart b Baptiste	15	42	38	1	-
RJ Peterson c Kent b Pollock	94	105	73	5	5
JDC Bryant not out	77	125	89	6	-
JM Kemp not out	57	62	47	3	3
DJ Callaghan					
MR Benfield					
†DW Murray					
S Abrahams					
MW Pringle					
GJ-P Kruger					
M Hayward					
Extras (b 4, lb 4, w 2)	10				
TOTAL (for 2 wkts) (41.2 overs)	**253**				

KWAZULU-NATAL
DJ Watson
GH Bodi
WR Wingfield
*DM Benkenstein
A Mall
JC Kent
†ELR Stewart
L Klusener
SM Pollock
EAE Baptiste
JE Bastow

KZN	O	M	R	W
Bastow	9	0	51	0
Pollock	7	0	21	1
Baptiste	7	0	41	1
Kent	5.2	0	29	0
Bodi	7	0	52	0
Klusener	3	0	28	0
Wingfield	3	0	23	0

Fall of Wickets	EP
1st	43 (1)
2nd	155 (2)

KWAZULU-NATAL v EASTERN PROVINCE Standard Bank Cup Semifinal 3rd leg replay

Played at Kingsmead, Durban on 19 February 2001 Toss: KwaZulu-Natal
Umpires: JD Cloete & DL Orchard (TV: DF Becker)
Debuts: KZN: None. EP: None
Result: KwaZulu-Natal won by 7 wickets (D/L method), target revised to 165 in 33 overs
Man of Match: Doug Watson

Gilder returned to the KwaZulu-Natal team and did his job by dismissing both openers. Despite a fine innings by Callaghan and good hitting by Benfield, Eastern Province were unable to mount a big enough total. When rain stopped play with KwaZulu-Natal on 59 for no wicket, the rain rules again hurt the visitors, with the Dolphins' target revised to 165 in 33 overs.

EASTERN PROVINCE	*Runs*	*Mins*	*Balls*	*4*	*6*	KWAZULU-NATAL	*Runs*	*Mins*	*Balls*	*4*	*6*
*CC Bradfield c Kent b Gilder	6	34	30	1	-	DJ Watson lbw b Kruger	56	148	84	6	-
RJ Peterson b Gilder	7	22	12	1	-	A Mall c Kruger b Hayward	40	85	63	7	-
JDC Bryant c Klusener b Kent	21	48	31	2	-	GH Bodi c Kemp b Abrahams	32	47	31	4	-
JM Kemp c Stewart b Wingfield	27	42	34	3	-	L Klusener not out	15	19	13	2	-
DJ Callaghan run out (Pollock)	63	87	75	5	-	WR Wingfield not out	4	6	3	-	-
MR Benfield c Mall b Bodi	51	53	45	3	3	*DM Benkenstein					
†DW Murray c Stewart b Pollock	22	38	23	2	-	JC Kent					
MW Pringle c Benkenstein b Kent	0	7	8	-	-	†ELR Stewart					
S Abrahams b Kent	3	8	5	-	-	SM Pollock					
M Hayward not out	1	4	1	-	-	EAE Baptiste					
GJ-P Kruger run out (Stewart)	0	2	1	-	-	GM Gilder					
Extras (b 3, lb 1, w 2, nb 3)	9					Extras (lb 1, w 12, nb 5)	18				
TOTAL (43.4 overs)	**210**					**TOTAL (for 3 wkts) (31.3 overs)**	**165**				

KZN	*O*	*M*	*R*	*W*	EP	*O*	*M*	*R*	*W*	Fall of Wickets	*EP*	*KZN*
Pollock	8	3	23	1	Pringle	7	0	36	0	1st	10 (2)	85 (2)
Gilder	7	0	33	2	Kemp	7	1	28	0	2nd	21 (1)	141 (3)
Wingfield	9	0	46	1	Kruger	6	1	30	1	3rd	64 (3)	155 (1)
Kent	8.4	0	42	3	Hayward	5.3	0	40	1	4th	66 (4)	-
Klusener	4	0	28	0	Callaghan	3	0	13	0	5th	150 (6)	-
Baptiste	2	0	11	0	Abrahams	3	0	17	1	6th	202 (5)	-
Bodi	5	0	23	1						7th	204 (8)	-
										8th	208 (7)	-
										9th	210 (9)	-
										10th	210 (11)	-

KWAZULU-NATAL v NORTHERNS Standard Bank Cup Final

Played at Kingsmead, Durban on 21 February 2001 Toss: KwaZulu-Natal
Umpires: IL Howell & RE Koertzen (TV: DL Orchard)
Debuts: KZN: None. Nor: None
Result: KwaZulu-Natal won by 3 wickets
Man of Match: Wade Wingfield

Myburgh and Rudolph gave Northerns a solid start but the KwaZulu-Natal seam bowlers stuck to their task, with Baptiste bowling impeccably in his last match. The diminutive Van Wyk played audaciously as he and Dros put on 85 off the last 74 balls of the innings. Van Wyk hit four boundaries off the last over of the innings, bowled by Pollock.

Watson's early dismissal gave Northerns hope but Mall and Wingfield steadied the innings. Myburgh and Joubert struck crucial blows and were well supported by McKenzie, who held a sensational left-handed diving catch at extra cover and pulled off a smart run-out. Northerns were handicapped by an injury to Dros, who hurt his right hand stopping a drive by Wingfield, and an under-strength bowling line-up could not stop Stewart and Kent turning the match back in KwaZulu-Natal's favour as the match reached a tense conclusion.

NEW TALENT . . . Jacques Rudolph in action in the Standard Bank Cup final as he completes a successful season for Northerns *Picture: Duif du Toit, TOUCHLINE PHOTO*

STANDARD BANK CUP

NORTHERNS	*Runs*	*Mins*	*Balls*	*4*	*6*
JG Myburgh c Mall b Baptiste	29	59	49	4	-
JA Rudolph c Pollock b Baptiste	33	84	50	2	1
M van Jaarsveld c Klusener b Bodi	36	80	57	1	-
ND McKenzie c Pollock b Bodi	25	55	43	1	-
*G Dros not out	34	51	37	3	-
†CFK van Wyk not out	50	49	37	7	-
A Paleker					
FC Brooker					
S Elworthy					
P Joubert					
GJ Smith					
Extras (b 1, lb 2, w 1, nb 3)	7				
TOTAL (for 4 wkts) (45 overs)	**214**				

KWAZULU-NATAL	*Runs*	*Mins*	*Balls*	*4*	*6*
DJ Watson c van Wyk b Smith	2	19	19	-	-
A Mall c McKenzie b Myburgh	40	83	51	6	-
WR Wingfield run out (McKenzie/van Wyk)	61	108	89	5	-
GH Bodi c Dros b Myburgh	7	15	13	1	-
*DM Benkenstein c van Wyk b Joubert	22	43	31	-	-
L Klusener b Joubert	5	6	4	1	-
†ELR Stewart not out	25	47	27	3	-
JC Kent c Myburgh b Elworthy	29	34	27	2	-
SM Pollock not out	5	4	3	1	-
EAE Baptiste					
GM Gilder					
Extras (lb 12, w 9)	21				
TOTAL (for 7 wkts) (44 overs)	**217**				

KZN	*O*	*M*	*R*	*W*
Pollock	9	1	41	0
Gilder	5	0	30	0
Kent	8	0	40	0
Baptiste	9	0	27	2
Klusener	7	0	38	0
Bodi	3	0	17	2
Wingfield	4	0	18	0

Nor	*O*	*M*	*R*	*W*
Elworthy	8	2	33	1
Smith	9	1	42	1
Joubert	9	0	50	2
Dros	4.3	0	29	0
Myburgh	9	0	27	2
Rudolph	3	0	14	0
McKenzie	1.3	0	10	0

Fall of Wickets	*Nor*	*KZN*
1st	57 (1)	13 (1)
2nd	79 (2)	88 (2)
3rd	129 (3)	100 (4)
4th	129 (4)	138 (3)
5th	-	147 (6)
6th	-	154 (5)
7th	-	204 (8)

DOMESTIC LIMITED OVERS RECORDS

COMPETITION WINNERS

Benson & Hedges Series

Season	Winners	Runners-up	Margin of victory
1981/82	Transvaal	Natal	3 wickets
1982/83	Transvaal	Western Province	6 wickets
1983/84	Natal	Eastern Province	7 wickets
1984/85	Transvaal	Northern Transvaal	7 wickets
1985/86	Western Province	Northern Transvaal	12 runs
1986/87	Western Province	Transvaal	41 runs
1987/88	Western Province	Transvaal	5 wickets
1988/89	Orange Free State	Western Province	61 runs
1989/90	Eastern Province	Natal	1 wicket
1990/91	Western Province	Natal	6 wickets
1991/92	Eastern Province	Western Province	6 wickets
1992/93	Transvaal	Natal	1 run
1993/94	Orange Free State	Natal	7 wickets
1994/95	Orange Free State	Eastern Province	113 runs
1995/96	Free State	Transvaal	142 runs

In 1981/82, 1993/94 and 1994/95 matches were contested over 50 overs per side.
In all other seasons matches were contested over 45 overs per side.

Standard Bank League

Season	Winners	Runners-up
1996/97	Northern Transvaal	Western Province
1997/98	Western Province	Northerns
1998/99	Northerns	Gauteng

From 1999/2000, the Standard Bank competition was played as a single tournament (see Standard Bank Cup below)

Standard Bank Cup

Season	Winners	Runners-up	Margin of victory
1996/97	Natal	Western Province	2-1 (best of three)
1997/98	Gauteng	Northerns	3 wickets
1998/99	Griqualand West	Border	6 wickets
1999/2000	Boland	Eastern Province	36 runs
2000/01	KwaZulu-Natal	Northerns	3 wickets

Gillette Cup

Season	Winners	Runners-up	Margin of victory
1969/70	Western Province	Natal	2 runs
1970/71	Western Province	Transvaal	3 wickets
1971/72	Eastern Province	Natal	31 runs
1972/73	Western Province	Eastern Province	7 wickets
1973/74	Transvaal	Natal	10 runs
1974/75	Natal	Western Province	31 runs
1975/76	Eastern Province	Western Province	128 runs
1976/77	Natal	Eastern Province	7 wickets

Datsun Shield

Season	Winners	Runners-up	Margin of victory
1977/78	Rhodesia	Eastern Province	runs/wkts ratio
1978/79	Transvaal	Natal	76 runs
1979/80	Transvaal	Western Province	7 wickets
1980/81	Transvaal	Eastern Province	7 wickets
1981/82	Western Province	Natal	2 runs
1982/83	Transvaal	Western Province	109 runs

Nissan Shield

1983/84	Transvaal	Western Province	89 runs
1984/85	Transvaal	Western Province	9 wickets
1985/86	Transvaal	Western Province	7 wickets
1986/87	Natal	Transvaal	faster scoring rate
1987/88	Eastern Province	Northern Transvaal	7 wickets
1988/89	Western Province	Transvaal	2-0 (best of three)
1989/90	Eastern Province	Northern Transvaal	2-0 (best of three)
1990/91	Transvaal	Eastern Province	7 wickets
1991/92	Orange Free State	Eastern Province	6 wickets

Total Power Series

1992/93	Orange Free State	Eastern Province	6 wickets

Matches were contested over 60 overs per side from 1969/70 to 1980/81 and 55 overs per side from 1981/82 to 1992/93, except for 1986/87 when matches were contested over 50 overs per side.

SUMMARY OF WINNERS

Team	Nissan Shield*	Benson & Hedges	Std Bank League	Std Bank Cup	Total
Gauteng	9	4	0	1	14
Western Province	5	4	1	0	10
Eastern Province	4	2	0	0	6
Free State	2	4	0	0	6
KwaZulu-Natal	3	1	0	2	6
Northerns	0	0	2	0	2
Rhodesia	1	0	0	0	1
Griqualand West	0	0	0	1	1
Boland	0	0	0	1	1

* Includes Gillette Cup, Datsun Shield and Total Power Series

TABLE OF RESULTS
(current teams)

Team	P	W	L	Tie	NR	%Won
Western Province	266	170	91	0	5	65.13
Gauteng	264	162	89	1	12	64.28
Eastern Province	260	148	100	1	11	59.43
KwaZulu-Natal	250	136	98	1	15	57.87
Free State	184	91	80	1	12	52.90
Northerns	219	101	106	1	11	48.55
Boland	112	43	66	1	2	39.09
Border	154	53	90	0	11	37.06
Griqualand West	103	29	71	0	3	29.00
Easterns	73	19	46	1	7	28.78
North West	73	12	56	1	4	17.39

Includes abandoned match Rho v Tvl 1977/78, reflected as "no result" although Rhodesia won on drawing of lots. Includes results in all Domestic Limited Overs matches. The % Won calculation does not include "no result" matches. Prior to 1995/96, Easterns were known as Eastern Transvaal and Free State were known as Orange Free State. Prior to 1996/97, North West were known as Western Transvaal. Prior to 1997/98, Northerns were known as Northern Transvaal and Gauteng were known as Transvaal. Prior to 1998/99, KwaZulu-Natal were known as Natal.

STANDARD BANK CUP RECORDS

The following records include the Benson & Hedges Series and the Standard Bank League and Cup. Performances in the Gillette Cup/Datsun Shield/Nissan Shield/Total Power Series are also noted when they are better than those in the Standard Bank/Benson & Hedges competitions.

TEAM RECORDS

HIGHEST INNINGS TOTALS

341-3	Transvaal	v	Western Transvaal	Potchefstroom	1994/95
319-6	Natal	v	Western Transvaal	Fochville	1995/96
318-9	Griqualand West	v	North West	Kimberley	2000/01
316-4	Transvaal	v	North West	Fochville	1996/97
315-2	Free State	v	Griqualand West	Bloemfontein	2000/01
311	Free State	v	Easterns	Springs	1995/96
309-8	Natal	v	Mashonaland	Durban	1996/97
307-3	Natal	v	Impalas	Durban	1984/85
306-4	Griqualand West	v	Gauteng	Kimberley	2000/01
303-5	Transvaal	v	Free State	Johannesburg	1996/97
302-6	Free State	v	Transvaal	Johannesburg	1996/97
302-3	Northerns	v	Easterns	Centurion	1997/98
300-7	Western Province	v	Eastern Province	Cape Town	1982/83
300-8	Western Transvaal	v	Transvaal	Potchefstroom	1994/95

The highest total in the Nissan Shield was 378-5 by Transvaal v Griqualand West at Kimberley, 1977/78.

HIGHEST TOTAL BY A SIDE BATTING SECOND

303-5 (Won)	Transvaal	v	Free State	Johannesburg	1996/97
300-7 (Won)	Western Province	v	Eastern Province	Cape Town	1982/83
300-8 (Lost by 41 runs)	Western Transvaal	v	Transvaal	Potchefstroom	1994/95

The highest total in the Nissan Shield by a side batting second was 342 by Eastern Province v Western Province at Johannesburg, 1969/70. They lost by 13 runs.

LOWEST TOTALS

47	Border	v	Western Province	East London	1991/92
56	Western Province	v	Border	East London	1998/99
58	Griqualand West	v	Northern Transvaal	Kimberley	1995/96
61	Transvaal	v	Eastern Transvaal	Johannesburg	1994/95
64	Boland	v	Western Province	Paarl	1998/99
69	Boland	v	Gauteng	Paarl	1998/99
70	Easterns	v	Western Province	Benoni	1997/98
76	North West	v	Gauteng	Johannesburg	1999/00
79	Impalas	v	Transvaal	Johannesburg	1984/85
81	Impalas	v	Western Province	Cape Town	1988/89

The lowest total in the Nissan Shield was 46 by Natal Country Districts v Eastern Province at Empangeni 1990/91

LOWEST TOTAL BY A SIDE BATTING FIRST AND WINNING

107	Western Province	bt	Orange Free State	Cape Town	1992/93

LARGEST MARGINS OF VICTORY

By runs

219	Natal	bt	Western Transvaal	Fochville	1995/96
171	Eastern Province	bt	Impalas	Port Elizabeth	1991/92
171	Transvaal	bt	North West	Fochville	1996/97
167	Griqualand West	bt	North West	Kimberley	2000/01
151	Western Province	bt	Natal	Durban	1984/85

The largest margin of victory in the Nissan Shield was 283 runs by Natal v SA African XI at Durban, 1975/76.

By wickets

9 Achieved on 23 occasions by Gauteng (5 occasions), Free State (4), Northerns (4), Western Province(4), Eastern Province (2), KwaZulu-Natal (2), Border and North West

Note: Natal beat Northern Transvaal by 10 wickets in a match reduced to 43 overs per side, Verwoerdburg 1991/92

There were 3 matches won by 10 wickets in the Nissan Shield.

DOMESTIC LIMITED OVERS RECORDS

TIED MATCHES

Transvaal (230-8)	v	Natal (230-8)	Johannesburg	1995/96
Northern Transvaal (214-8)	v	Free State (214)	Centurion	1995/96

(Under previous rules this would have been a win for Northern Transvaal on fewer wickets lost)

Boland (235-7)	v	North West (235-7)	Paarl	1998/99
Eastern Province (224-8)	v	Easterns (224-9)	Port Elizabeth	2000/01

SMALLEST MARGINS OF VICTORY

Losing fewer wickets in a tie

	Impalas	bt	Northern Transvaal	Verwoerdburg	1987/88
	Eastern Province	bt	Western Province	Cape Town	1989/90
	Transvaal	bt	Natal	Johannesburg	1994/95
	Eastern Province	bt	Transvaal	Port Elizabeth	1994/95

This occurred 3 times in the Nissan Shield

By runs

1	Transvaal	bt	Natal	Durban	1992/93
1	Griqualand West	bt	Free State	Bloemfontein	1996/97
1	Border	bt	Western Province	Cape Town	1997/98
1	Eastern Province	bt	Boland	Port Elizabeth	2000/01

There was 1 match won by 1 run in the Nissan Shield

By wickets

1	Transvaal	bt	Western Province	Cape Town	1983/84
1	Northern Transvaal	bt	Eastern Province	Pretoria	1984/85
1	Transvaal	bt	Natal	Johannesburg	1987/88
1	Eastern Province	bt	Natal	Durban	1989/90
1	Transvaal	bt	Northern Transvaal	Johannesburg	1991/92
1	Natal	bt	Orange Free State	Bloemfontein	1992/93
1	Eastern Province	bt	Transvaal	Johannesburg	1994/95
1	Eastern Province	bt	Western Province	Port Elizabeth	1994/95
1	Northern Transvaal	bt	Western Province	Centurion	1996/97
1	Natal	bt	North West	Durban	1996/97
1	Border	bt	Free State	East London	1998/99
1	Easterns	bt	Griqualand West	Benoni	2000/01

There were 4 matches won by 1 wicket in the Nissan Shield

MOST RUNS IN A MATCH

641	Western Transvaal	v	Transvaal	Potchefstroom	1994/95
605	Transvaal	v	Free State	Johannesburg	1996/97
599	Western Province	v	Eastern Province	Cape Town	1982/83
597	Free State	v	Griqualand West	Bloemfontein	2000/01
565	Griqualand West	v	Eastern Province	Kimberley	1998/99
561	Transvaal	v	Boland	Johannesburg	1995/96
555	Northerns	v	Border	Centurion	2000/01
552	Transvaal	v	Western Province	Johannesburg	1982/83

The most runs in a Nissan Shield match was 697, Western Province v Eastern Province, Johannesburg, 1969/70.

FEWEST RUNS IN A COMPLETED MATCH

98	Border	v	Western Province	East London	1991/92
113	Border	v	Western Province	East London	1998/99
117	Griqualand West	v	Northern Transvaal	Kimberley	1995/96

SHORTEST MATCH

25.3 overs	Transvaal (15.4)	v	Eastern Transvaal (9.5)	Johannesburg	1994/95

BATTING

HIGHEST INDIVIDUAL SCORES

166*	MC Venter	North West	v	Natal	Fochville	1997/98
151	LJ Koen	Eastern Province	v	Griqualand West	Kimberley	1998/99
150*	WM Dry	Griqualand West	v	Border	Kimberley	1999/00
146*	NC Johnson	Natal	v	Griqualand West	Kimberley	1996/97
146	RP Snell	Transvaal	v	Western Transvaal	Potchefstroom	1994/95

DOMESTIC LIMITED OVERS RECORDS

144*	MJR Rindel	Northerns	v	Griqualand West	Kimberley	1997/98
140	AM Bacher	Transvaal	v	North West	Fochville	1996/97
139*	AM Bacher	Transvaal	v	Western Transvaal	Potchefstroom	1994/95
138*	AI Gait	Free State	v	Griqualand West	Bloemfontein	2000/01
137	AM Bacher	Transvaal	v	Free State	Johannesburg	1996/97

The highest individual score in the Nissan Shield was 222* by RG Pollock (EP v Bdr, East London, 1974/75).

MOST CENTURIES

9 MJR Rindel
6 AM Bacher, KC Wessels
5 LJ Koen
4 SJ Cook, WJ Cronje, NC Johnson, PJR Steyn
3 HR Fotheringham, HH Gibbs, DL Haynes, ND McKenzie, RF Pienaar, M Yachad

The most centuries in all Domestic Limited Overs matches are:
13 SJ Cook
11 RG Pollock, KC Wessels (RG Pollock made 10 centuries in the Nissan Shield)

MOST RUNS IN A SEASON

785	(Avg 71.36)	MJR Rindel (Nor)	1997/98
766	(Avg 58.92)	MJR Rindel (NT)	1996/97
667	(Avg 74.11)	KR Rutherford (Gau)	1997/98
624	(Avg 52.00)	DJ Watson (Ntl)	1996/97
617	(Avg 56.09)	DJ Callaghan (EP)	1999/00
614	(Avg 61.40)	KC Jackson (Bol)	1995/96
612	(Avg 51.00)	AJ Hall (Gau)	1999/00
605	(Avg 60.50)	AM Bacher (Tvl)	1996/97
595	(Avg 42.50)	PG Amm (EP)	1994/95
581	(Avg 44.69)	DJ Watson (KZN)	2000/01

The most runs in all Domestic Limited Overs matches in a season is 889 (avg 55.56) by KC Wessels (EP) in 1990/91.

MOST RUNS IN A CAREER

Name	M	Inns	NO	Runs	HS	Avg	100	50
KC Wessels	109	107	15	4651	124	50.55	6	38
RF Pienaar	138	134	12	3950	124*	32.37	3	32
MJR Rindel	118	112	16	3907	144*	40.69	9	24
DJ Callaghan	130	123	25	3639	107*	37.13	1	28
PN Kirsten	107	104	9	3555	134*	37.42	2	29
MW Rushmere	130	120	23	3543	121	36.52	2	25
AP Kuiper	128	121	18	3348	118	32.50	2	24
LJ Koen	104	101	8	3101	151	33.34	5	13
SJ Cook	98	97	10	2975	116	34.19	4	21
JM Arthur	118	115	4	2966	126*	26.72	1	17

The leading run-scorers in all Domestic Limited Overs matches are:

Name	M	Inns	NO	Runs	HS	Avg	100	50
KC Wessels	157	155	19	6575	146	48.34	11	45
PN Kirsten	179	176	14	5962	134*	36.80	7	44
SJ Cook	168	164	17	5928	164*	40.32	13	38
RF Pienaar	190	183	16	5669	135	33.94	6	42

The leading run-scorer in the Nissan Shield was SJ Cook (2953 runs, avg 49.21).

RECORD WICKET PARTNERSHIPS

1st	240	RF Pienaar and MJR Rindel	Northerns v Free State (Bloemfontein)	1998/99
2nd	211*	HR Fotheringham and RF Pienaar	Transvaal v Orange Free State (Johannesburg)	1988/89
3rd	243	AM Bacher and ND McKenzie	Transvaal v North West (Fochville)	1996/97
4th	181	ND McKenzie and G Dros	Northerns v North West (Centurion)	2000/01
5th	144	PC Strydom and SC Pope	Border v North West (East London)	1998/99
6th	158	DR Laing and N Pothas	Transvaal v Eastern Province (Johannesburg)	1995/96
7th	126	DR Laing and AJ Hall	Transvaal v Eastern Province (Port Elizabeth)	1996/97
8th	88	FJC Cronje and IL Howell	Border v Boland (Stellenbosch)	1993/94
9th	76	AP Kuiper and CR Matthews	Western Province v Impalas (Cape Town)	1987/88
10th	78*	CE Eksteen and EW Kidwell	Gauteng v Griqualand West (Johannesburg)	1998/99

The following higher partnerships were recorded in the Nissan Shield:

1st	274	KC Wessels and PG Amm	Eastern Province v Natal CD (Empageni)	1990/91
2nd	240*	KD Robinson and KJ Hughes	Natal v Border CD (King William's Town)	1990/91
3rd	303*	A Barrow and HR Fotheringham	Natal v SA African XI (Durban)	1975/76
4th	187*	SJ Cook and SB Smith	Transvaal v Orange Free State (Bloemfontein)	1990/91
	187	MS Venter and KA McKenzie	Transvaal v Eastern Province (Johannesburg)	1983/84
5th	159	NE Wright and ELR Stewart	Natal v Western Transvaal (Potchefstroom)	1992/93
6th	173	PH Williams and D Bestall	Natal v Transvaal (Durban)	1979/80
8th	91	RC Ontong and PD de Vaal	Northern Transvaal v Border (East London)	1979/80

BOWLING

BEST BOWLING

6-20	JM Kemp	Eastern Province	v	Free State	Port Elizabeth	2000/01
6-22	BN Schultz	Eastern Province	v	Transvaal	Johannesburg	1995/96
6-23	GJ-P Kruger	Eastern Province	v	North West	Port Elizabeth	1999/00
6-25	GM Gilder	Natal	v	North West	Fochville	1997/98
6-26	DJJ de Vos	Northerns	v	Easterns	Benoni	1998/99
6-26	JE Bastow	KwaZulu-Natal	v	Free State	Bloemfontein	2000/01
6-27	A Nel	Easterns	v	Griqualand West	Benoni	2000/01
6-29	CW Henderson	Boland	v	Easterns	Paarl	1997/98
6-30	MW Pringle	Western Province	v	Border	East London	1989/90
6-34	RE Veenstra	KwaZulu-Natal	v	Gauteng	Durban	1999/00

The best bowling in the Nissan Shield was 7-21 by PP Henwood (Ntl v Bdr, East London, 1972/73).

HAT-TRICKS

GS le Roux	Western Province	v	Transvaal	Cape Town	1982/83
BC Fourie	Impalas	v	Natal	Durban	1988/89
PA Rayment	Western Province	v	Orange Free State	Cape Town	1990/91
EO Simons	Western Province	v	Border	East London	1991/92
BN Schultz	Eastern Province	v	Transvaal	Johannesburg	1995/96
M Hayward	Eastern Province	v	Western Province	Cape Town	1996/97
DJJ de Vos	Northerns	v	Easterns	Benoni	1998/99
M Hayward	Eastern Province	v	KwaZulu-Natal	Durban	1998/99
RE Veenstra	KwaZulu-Natal	v	Gauteng	Durban	1999/00
GJ Smith	Northerns	v	Border	East London	2000/01

There were 3 hat-tricks taken in the Nissan Shield

MOST WICKETS IN A SEASON

30	(Avg 13.50)	EO Simons (WP)	1996/97
26	(Avg 19.23)	JC Kent (KZN)	2000/01
25	(Avg 11.48)	FD Stephenson (OFS)	1994/95
24	(Avg 12.83)	BT Player (OFS)	1993/94
24	(Avg 16.04)	M Hayward (EP)	1996/97
24	(Avg 17.45)	RE Bryson (NT)	1996/97
24	(Avg 16.58)	CK Langeveldt (Bol)	1999/00
23	(Avg 23.39)	GJ-P Kruger (EP)	1999/00
23	(Avg 19.43)	MW Pringle (EP)	1999/00
22	(Avg 12.72)	FD Stephenson (OFS)	1993/94
22	(Avg 13.18)	AC Dawson (WP)	1997/98
22	(Avg 12.81)	T Henderson (Bdr)	1998/99
22	(Avg 21.22)	DJ Callaghan (EP)	1999/00
22	(Avg 15.50)	A Nel (Eas)	2000/01
22	(Avg 24.54)	S Elworthy (Nor)	2000/01

The most wickets in all Domestic Limited Overs matches in a season is 33 (avg 14.30) by AP Kuiper (WP) in 1988/89.

MOST WICKETS IN A CAREER

Name	M	Balls	Runs	Wkts	Ave	RpO	BB	4I
EO Simons	125	5585	3609	182	19.82	3.87	4-3	12
MW Pringle	121	5785	3931	163	24.11	4.07	6-30	7
RE Bryson	107	5047	3741	144	25.97	4.44	4-17	7
EAE Baptiste	106	5073	3207	139	23.07	3.79	4-22	1

S Elworthy	106	4970	3336	135	24.71	4.02	4-23	4
BT Player	114	5000	3442	125	27.53	4.13	5-27	5
CR Matthews	95	4296	2754	120	22.95	3.84	4-24	4
CE Eksteen	111	5196	3317	118	28.11	3.83	5-13	2
TG Shaw	100	4800	2727	113	24.13	3.40	4-31	2
AC Dawson	72	3445	2186	112	19.51	3.80	5-13	5
DN Crookes	92	3572	2509	112	22.40	4.21	4-29	5

The leading wicket-takers in all Domestic Limited Overs matches are:

Name	M	Balls	Runs	Wkts	Ave	RpO	BB	4I
EO Simons	166	7905	5105	249	20.50	3.87	6-8	19
MW Pringle	141	6878	4548	188	24.19	3.96	6-30	7
CEB Rice	157	6157	3888	179	21.72	3.78	5-43	4
RE Bryson	131	6346	4663	177	26.34	4.40	4-17	8
CR Matthews	119	5675	3528	163	21.64	3.73	5-11	5
AP Kuiper	182	5107	3573	162	22.05	4.19	5-47	6
EAE Baptiste	117	5751	3556	160	22.22	3.70	6-13	2
TG Shaw	145	7440	4153	155	26.79	3.34	4-31	2
S Elworthy	122	5876	3956	151	26.19	4.03	4-23	4

ECONOMICAL BOWLING (Qualification: 6 overs)

RpO							
0.16	6-5-1-0	PA Rayment	Eastern Province	v	Transvaal	Johannesburg	1987/88
0.44	9-5-4-1	GR Dilley	Natal	v	Impalas	Pietermaritzburg	1985/86
0.66	9-5-6-1	DB Rundle	Western Province	v	Border	East London	1991/92
0.66	9-5-6-2	LCR Jordaan	North West	v	Western Province	Cape Town	1999/00
0.70	10-7-7-4	BT Player	Orange Free State	v	Impalas	Bloemfontein	1993/94

EXPENSIVE BOWLING (Qualification: 5 overs)

RpO							
11.20	5-0-56-0	CJ van Heerden	Impalas	v	Natal	Durban	1984/85
10.80	5-0-54-0	S Jacobs	Transvaal	v	Natal	Johannesburg	1990/91
10.20	5-0-51-0	RP Snell	Transvaal	v	North West	Fochville	1996/97
Most expensive off 9 overs:							
9.33	9-0-84-3	LB Taylor	Natal	v	Western Province	Cape Town	1983/84

WICKETKEEPING

MOST DISMISSALS IN A MATCH

8 (ct 5,st 3)	SJ Palframan	Boland	v	Easterns	Paarl	1997/98
7 (all ct)	I Mitchell	Border	v	Western Province	East London	1998/99
6 (all ct)	W Bossenger	Griqualand West	v	Northern Transvaal	Centurion	1996/97
5 (all ct)	DH Howell	Eastern Province	v	Northern Transvaal	Pretoria	1983/84
5 (ct 4,st 1)	RV Jennings	Transvaal	v	Orange Free State	Virginia	1987/88
5 (all ct)	RV Jennings	Transvaal	v	Impalas	Johannesburg	1988/89
5 (all ct)	RA Brown	Orange Free State	v	Border	Virginia	1989/90
5 (ct 4,st1)	RJ Ryall	Western Province	v	Natal	Durban	1990/91
5 (all ct)	UH Goedeke	Natal	v	Eastern Province	Port Elizabeth	1993/94
5 (ct 4,st 1)	G Morgan	Eastern Province	v	Eastern Transvaal	Port Elizabeth	1994/95
5 (all ct)	KA Forde	Natal	v	Transvaal	Durban	1996/97
5 (all ct)	P Kirsten	Western Province	v	Border	East London	1996/97
5 (all ct)	I Mitchell	Border	v	Northerns	Centurion	1997/98
5 (ct 3,st 2)	KA Forde	KwaZulu-Natal	v	Easterns	Benoni	1998/99
5 (all ct)	MV Boucher	Border	v	North West	East London	1998/99
5 (ct 3,st 2)	G Morgan	Northerns	v	Boland	Centurion	1998/99
5 (all ct)	EG Poole	North West	v	Western Province	Cape Town	1999/00
5 (ct 4,st 1)	GL Brophy	Free State	v	Northerns	Bloemfontein	2000/01
5 (all ct)	D Jennings	Easterns	v	Griqualand West	Benoni	2000/01
5 (ct 3,st 2)	ELR Stewart	KwaZulu-Natal	v	Eastern Province	Durban	2000/01

The most dismissals in a match in the Nissan Shield was 6 (ct 3,st3) by AJS Smith (Ntl v Bdr, East London, 1972/73).

DOMESTIC LIMITED OVERS RECORDS

MOST DISMISSALS IN A SEASON

31 (ct 29,st 2)	ELR Stewart (KZN)	2000/01
28 (ct 24,st 4)	SJ Palframan (Bol)	1997/98
27 (all ct)	P Kirsten (WP)	1996/97
24 (ct 19,st 5)	KA Forde (Ntl)	1996/97
23 (ct 16,st 7)	DW Murray (EP)	1999/00
21 (ct 20,st 1)	UH Goedeke (Ntl)	1993/94
20 (all ct)	RJ Ryall (WP)	1987/88

MOST DISMISSALS IN A CAREER

Name	M	Ct	St	Total
SJ Palframan	92	116	21	137
RJ Ryall	98	123	5	128
DJ Richardson	86	81	6	87
N Pothas	81	67	17	84
ELR Stewart	98	79	4	83
RV Jennings	68	73	8	81

The most dismissals in all Domestic Limited Overs matches is 194 (ct 184,st 10) by RJ Ryall.
The most dismissals in the Nissan Shield was 92 (ct 84,st 8) by RV Jennings.

FIELDING

MOST CATCHES IN A MATCH

5	KC Jackson	Boland	v	Natal	Durban	1995/96
4	EO Simons	Western Province	v	Transvaal	Johannesburg	1995/96
4	ML Bruyns	Natal	v	Boland	Durban	1997/98
4	ND McKenzie	Northerns	v	Gauteng	Johannesburg	1999/00

The most catches in a match in the Nissan Shield was 5 by AJ Kourie (Tvl v WP, Johannesburg, 1979/80).

MOST CATCHES IN A SEASON

13	DB Rundle (WP)	1995/96
12	LJ Koen (Bol)	1999/00
11	KC Jackson (Bol)	1995/96

The most catches in all Domestic Limited Overs matches in a season is 17 by DJ Cullinan (WP) in 1987/88.

MOST CATCHES IN A CAREER

Name	M	Ct
LJ Koen	104	56
DJ Cullinan	87	52
DB Rundle	95	46
KC Wessels	109	46
PN Kirsten	107	43
AP Kuiper	128	43

The most catches in all Domestic Limited Overs matches is 70 by DJ Cullinan and KC Wessels. The most catches in the Nissan Shield was 27 by RG Pollock.

RECORDS FOR THE PROVINCES

HIGHEST AND LOWEST TOTALS

Team	Highest Total				Lowest Total			
Boland	293-3	v	GW, Kimberley	1995/96	64	v	WP, Paarl	1998/99
Border	278-8	v	Nor, Centurion	2000/01	47	v	WP, East London	1991/92
Eastern Province	299-9	v	WP, Cape Town	1982/83	98	v	Bdr, Port Elizabeth	1998/99
Easterns	285-4	v	NW, Benoni	1999/00	70	v	WP, Benoni	1997/98
Free State	315-2	v	GW, Bloemfontein	2000/01	87	v	WP, Cape Town	1992/93
					87	v	Gau, Johannesburg	1997/98
Gauteng	341-3	v	WTvl,Potchefstroom	1994/95	61	v	ETvl, Johannesburg	1994/95
Griqualand West	318-9	v	NW, Kimberley	2000/01	58	v	N Tvl, Kimberley	1995/96
Impalas	262-4	v	Bol, Springs	1993/94	79	v	Tvl, Johannesburg	1984/85
KwaZulu-Natal	319-6	v	W Tvl, Fochville	1995/96	92	v	EP,Pietermaritzburg	1982/83
Northerns	302-3	v	Eas, Centurion	1997/98	91	v	WP, Cape Town	1990/91

DOMESTIC LIMITED OVERS RECORDS

North West	300-8	v	Tvl, Potchefstroom	1994/95	76	v	Gau, Johannesburg	1999/00
Western Province	300-7	v	EP, Cape Town	1982/83	56	v	Bdr, East London	1998/99

The following teams have made higher or lower totals in the Nissan Shield:

Boland					63	v	WP, Stellenbosch	1990/91
Border	329-4	v	GW, East London	1988/89				
Eastern Province	372-5	v	Bdr, East London	1974/75	93	v	Ntl, Port Elizabeth	1985/86
Free State	322-7	v	GW, Bloemfontein	1971/72	64	v	Ntl, Bloemfontein	1982/83
Gauteng	378-5	v	GW, Kimberley	1977/78				
KwaZulu-Natal	364-2	v	ETCD, Witbank	1991/92				
Northerns					78	v	Bdr, East London	1980/81
Western Province	360-4	v	Bdr, East London	1970/71				

HIGHEST INDIVIDUAL SCORE FOR EACH PROVINCE

Boland	125*	LD Ferreira	v	Border	Paarl	1996/97
Border	134*	PN Kirsten	v	Northern Transvaal	Verwoerdburg	1993/94
Eastern Province	151	LJ Koen	v	Griqualand West	Kimberley	1998/99
Easterns	131	D Brand	v	North West	Benoni	1999/00
Free State	138*	AI Gait	v	Griqualand West	Bloemfontein	2000/01
Gauteng	146	RP Snell	v	Western Transvaal	Potchefstroom	1994/95
Griqualand West	150*	WM Dry	v	Border	Kimberley	1999/00
KwaZulu-Natal	146*	NC Johnson	v	Griqualand West	Kimberley	1996/97
Northerns	144*	MJR Rindel	v	Griqualand West	Kimberley	1997/98
North West	166*	MC Venter	v	Natal	Fochville	1997/98
Western Province	132	SFAF Bacchus	v	Natal	Durban	1984/85

The highest scores for each province in all Domestic Limited Overs matches (where better than above) are:

Border	153*	LM Phillips	v	Griqualand West	East London	1988/89
Eastern Province	222*	RG Pollock	v	Border	East London	1974/75
Gauteng	169	CEB Rice	v	Griqualand West	Kimberley	1977/78
KwaZulu-Natal	202*	A Barrow	v	SA African XI	Durban	1975/76
Northerns	145	M Yachad	v	Border	Verwoerdburg	1989/90
Western Province	186	EJ Barlow	v	Eastern Province	Johannesburg	1969/70

BEST BOWLING FOR EACH PROVINCE

Boland	6-29	CW Henderson	v	Easterns	Paarl	1997/98
Border	5-5	T Henderson	v	Western Province	East London	1998/99
Eastern Province	6-20	JM Kemp	v	Free State	Port Elizabeth	2000/01
Easterns	6-27	A Nel	v	Griqualand West	Benoni	2000/01
Free State	5-7	HC Bakkes	v	Western Province	Cape Town	1997/98
Gauteng	5-13	CE Eksteen	v	Boland	Paarl	1995/96
Griqualand West	5-32	AJ Swanepoel	v	Border	Kimberley	1999/00
KwaZulu-Natal	6-25	GM Gilder	v	North West	Fochville	1997/98
Northerns	6-26	DJJ de Vos	v	Easterns	Benoni	1998/99
North West	4-16	M Strydom	v	Western Province	Fochville	1998/99
	4-16	DJ Pryke	v	Western Province	Cape Town	1999/00
Western Province	6-30	MW Pringle	v	Border	East London	1989/90

The best bowling figures for each province in all Domestic Limited Overs matches (where better than above) are:

Eastern Province	6-13	EAE Baptiste	v	NTCD	Pietersburg	1992/93
Free State	6-31	ST Clarke	v	Northern Transvaal	Verwoerdburg	1987/88
Gauteng	5-10	ST Clarke	v	Western Province B	Cape Town	1983/84
Griqualand West	5-30	P McLaren	v	Western Transvaal	Potchefstroom	1989/90
KwaZulu-Natal	7-21	PP Henwood	v	Border	East London	1972/73
Western Province	7-27	DL Hobson	v	Northern Transvaal	Pretoria	1974/75

LIMITED OVERS CAREER RECORDS

Note: These career records are based on List A Limited Overs matches as per the Association of Cricket Statisticians and Historians. Matches included in List A are: limited overs internationals, other international matches (eg. Commonwealth Games and 'A' team internationals), domestic limited overs tournaments and matches involving major first-class teams against international touring teams.

Name	M	Inns	NO	Runs	HS	Avg	100	50	Ct	St	Balls	Runs	Wkts	Avg	RpO	BB	4I
S Abrahams	83	43	26	378	40	22.23	0	0	17	0	3581	2446	61	40.09	4.09	4-15	1
U Abrahams	1	1	0	5	5	5.00	0	0	0	0	0	0	0	-	-	-	0
ZA Abrahim	10	7	4	32	10*	10.66	0	0	1	0	437	381	10	38.10	5.23	2-23	0
HD Ackerman	86	81	11	2076	92	29.65	0	14	34	0	48	52	0	-	6.50	-	0
SM Adam	6	2	0	9	5	4.50	0	0	1	0	252	191	7	27.28	4.54	3-29	0
PR Adams	41	14	7	44	15*	6.28	0	0	11	0	1730	1208	54	22.37	4.18	3-12	0
AM Amla	20	15	2	161	68	12.38	0	1	8	0	0	0	0	-	-	-	0
JM Arthur	150	146	5	3774	126*	26.76	2	19	41	0	6	2	0	-	2.00	-	0
AM Bacher	79	77	4	2739	140	37.52	6	14	25	0	120	134	1	134.00	6.70	1-19	0
R Bailey	2	1	0	14	14	14.00	0	0	0	0	0	0	0	-	-	-	0
HC Bakkes	78	50	16	630	82	18.52	0	1	24	0	3537	2428	85	28.56	4.11	5-7	2
EAE Baptiste	309	210	43	2732	65	16.35	0	9	98	0	14735	9744	365	26.69	3.96	6-13	12
PH Barnard	56	52	5	1393	85	29.63	0	10	11	0	0	0	0	-	-	-	0
JE Bastow	14	4	1	15	10	5.00	0	0	2	0	631	516	16	32.25	4.90	6-26	1
KS Bender	7	5	1	33	19	8.25	0	0	2	0	300	223	4	55.75	4.46	2-34	0
MR Benfield	30	29	0	682	72	23.51	0	5	8	0	0	0	0	-	-	-	0
KCG Benjamin	93	46	17	281	22	9.68	0	0	9	0	4563	2972	124	23.96	3.90	4-33	1
DM Benkenstein	131	116	28	2705	107*	30.73	1	10	43	0	928	742	29	25.58	4.79	4-23	1
JA Beukes	17	10	2	103	35	12.87	0	0	4	0	0	0	0	-	-	-	0
GH Bodi	22	17	1	348	106*	21.75	1	2	5	0	678	575	20	28.75	5.08	5-46	1
N Boje	139	93	27	1775	129	26.89	2	5	39	0	5892	4068	128	31.78	4.14	4-16	5
LL Bosman	25	23	2	522	89	24.85	0	2	2	0	73	65	1	65.00	5.34	1-36	0
W Bossenger	56	39	20	516	48*	27.15	0	0	64	8	0	0	0	-	-	-	0
AG Botha	35	23	6	262	36	15.41	0	0	16	0	1113	832	25	33.28	4.48	3-16	0
PJ Botha	110	92	16	1967	105	25.88	1	12	26	0	3948	2793	99	28.21	4.24	4-37	2
MV Boucher	129	99	26	1537	70	21.05	0	10	171	9	0	0	0	-	-	-	0
CC Bradfield	37	37	2	849	96*	24.25	0	5	8	0	0	0	0	-	-	-	0
D Brand	19	18	0	597	131	33.16	1	4	8	0	18	13	2	6.50	4.33	2-8	0
FC Brooker	51	40	3	508	40	13.72	0	0	13	0	0	0	0	-	-	-	0

LIMITED OVERS CAREER RECORDS

Name	M	Inns	NO	Runs	HS	Avg	100	50	Ct	St	Balls	Runs	Wkts	Avg	RpO	BB	4I
J Brooker	4	3	0	33	23	11.00	0	0	0	0	24	27	0	-	6.75	-	0
GL Brophy	22	16	3	276	50*	21.23	0	1	23	4	0	0	0	-	-	-	0
NG Brouwers	8	2	1	6	4	6.00	0	0	3	0	240	225	3	75.00	5.62	2-38	0
DL Brown	2	2	1	15	14	15.00	0	0	1	0	0	0	0	-	-	-	0
ML Bruyns	93	87	16	2202	111	31.01	1	13	48	5	378	326	9	36.22	5.17	1-6	0
JDC Bryant	31	31	6	923	105*	36.92	1	7	10	0	0	0	0	-	-	-	0
RE Bryson	150	60	22	459	44*	12.07	0	0	21	0	7307	5485	202	27.15	4.50	4-17	10
DJ Callaghan	198	183	38	4935	169*	34.03	2	31	42	0	5045	3858	134	28.79	4.58	4-31	2
NM Carter	17	10	3	54	27	7.71	0	0	2	0	839	592	23	25.73	4.23	4-31	1
MW Creed	30	26	4	383	47	17.40	0	0	6	0	387	354	9	39.33	5.48	2-22	0
DN Crookes	147	124	15	2470	114	22.66	1	11	54	0	5793	4168	159	26.21	4.31	4-29	6
DJ Cullinan	290	281	39	7841	124	32.40	7	46	141	0	306	259	6	43.16	5.07	2-30	0
H Davids	6	6	0	86	26	14.33	0	0	1	0	0	0	0	-	-	-	0
AC Dawson	85	48	12	608	44*	16.88	0	0	22	0	4112	2665	129	20.65	3.88	5-13	5
P de Bruyn	21	17	5	293	68	24.41	0	2	9	0	864	672	24	28.00	4.66	4-28	1
Z de Bruyn	44	41	10	976	104*	31.48	1	5	5	0	825	760	26	29.23	5.52	3-24	0
CdeW de Lange	17	10	6	108	30*	27.00	0	0	3	0	768	483	16	30.18	3.77	3-17	0
M de Stadler	1	1	0	1	1	1.00	0	0	0	0	18	20	0	-	6.66	-	0
DJJ de Vos	52	39	8	692	84	22.32	0	2	25	0	1387	1105	32	34.53	4.78	6-26	1
HM de Vos	38	37	2	801	91	22.88	0	4	14	2	0	0	0	-	-	-	0
BC de Wett	4	4	0	99	35	24.75	0	0	0	0	1	1	0	-	6.00	-	0
WA Deacon	1	0	0	0	0	-	0	0	0	0	12	18	0	-	9.00	-	0
HH Dippenaar	64	55	7	1395	77	29.06	0	10	16	0	6	2	0	-	2.00	-	0
AA Donald	407	126	65	504	23*	8.26	0	0	62	0	20546	13260	623	21.28	3.87	6-15	37
VC Drakes	141	104	19	1356	104	15.95	1	1	27	0	6631	4692	185	25.36	4.24	5-19	7
JN Dreyer	30	18	4	175	45*	12.50	0	0	3	0	1132	1046	28	37.35	5.54	3-38	0
G Dros	51	46	10	1607	105*	44.63	3	10	17	0	533	483	14	34.50	5.43	3-21	0
WM Dry	60	57	6	1415	150*	27.74	1	6	19	0	72	101	1	101.00	8.41	1-17	0
WJ du Toit	1	1	0	6	6	6.00	0	0	0	0	54	27	0	-	3.00	-	0
CE Eksteen	137	61	23	448	55*	11.78	0	1	41	0	6498	4139	145	28.54	3.82	5-13	3
GD Elliott	21	18	4	419	94	29.92	0	3	7	0	312	290	8	36.25	5.57	3-32	0
S Elworthy	193	127	43	1885	116*	22.44	1	6	38	0	9063	6267	234	26.78	4.14	4-14	6
CT Enslin	41	37	8	590	52	20.34	0	1	5	0	1288	1236	39	31.69	5.75	4-39	1
EJ Ferreira	27	27	0	544	123	20.14	1	3	5	0	0	0	0	-	-	-	0
LD Ferreira	66	65	3	1677	125*	27.04	2	10	21	0	24	34	1	34.00	8.50	1-8	0
GE Flusk	18	13	2	109	20	9.90	0	0	5	0	378	310	8	38.75	4.92	2-14	0

LIMITED OVERS CAREER RECORDS

Name	M	Inns	NO	Runs	HS	Avg	100	50	Ct	St	Balls	Runs	Wkts	Avg	RpO	BB	4I
NA Fusedale	42	28	7	120	32*	5.71	0	0	14	0	1849	1230	41	30.00	3.99	3-26	0
AI Gait	11	11	1	415	138*	41.50	1	1	1	0	0	0	0	-	-	-	0
LL Gamiet	21	20	3	484	87	28.47	0	4	2	0	0	0	0	-	-	-	0
MF George	5	2	1	10	10*	10.00	0	0	1	0	234	210	7	30.00	5.38	2-34	0
HH Gibbs	151	142	12	4116	125	31.66	8	23	68	0	66	57	2	28.50	5.18	1-16	0
OD Gibson	144	115	25	1886	76	20.95	0	4	39	0	6920	4964	206	24.09	4.30	5-19	13
MI Gidley	93	89	10	2240	108*	28.35	2	14	13	0	3149	2396	46	52.08	4.56	4-11	1
GM Gilder	49	22	8	113	36	8.07	0	0	11	0	2015	1462	57	25.64	4.35	6-25	4
R Gobind	1	1	0	14	14	14.00	0	0	0	0	0	0	0	-	-	-	0
GV Grace	4	3	0	64	62	21.33	0	1	1	0	0	0	0	-	-	-	0
L Graham	7	3	3	37	24*	-	0	0	1	0	297	193	13	14.84	3.89	3-18	0
AJ Hall	83	70	13	1906	129*	33.43	1	11	21	0	2903	2211	69	32.04	4.56	4-58	1
GS Hayward	1	1	0	10	10	10.00	0	0	1	0	24	22	1	22.00	5.50	1-22	0
M Hayward	68	21	10	99	19*	9.00	0	0	14	0	3112	2625	105	25.00	5.06	5-37	6
CW Henderson	93	53	32	376	32	17.90	0	0	27	0	4409	3018	103	29.30	4.10	6-29	2
JM Henderson	24	24	0	610	83	25.41	0	4	8	0	222	172	4	43.00	4.64	2-40	0
T Henderson	32	20	7	198	59*	15.23	0	1	6	0	1393	953	44	21.65	4.10	5-5	1
GM Hewitt	36	36	1	950	108	27.14	1	6	14	0	84	110	1	110.00	7.85	1-21	0
BBN Hlongwane	1	1	1	0	0*	-	0	0	0	0	30	30	0	-	6.00	-	0
BP Horan	12	4	1	25	10	8.33	0	0	2	0	366	297	6	49.50	4.86	3-40	0
AC Hudson	206	204	7	5884	161	29.86	4	41	50	0	24	16	1	16.00	4.00	1-10	0
KC Jackson	113	111	7	3089	105*	29.70	1	19	44	0	387	347	10	34.70	5.37	3-24	0
A Jacobs	38	36	1	962	116*	27.48	2	3	26	2	12	21	1	21.00	10.50	1-21	0
D Jennings	13	11	3	73	27	9.12	0	0	15	3	0	0	0	-	-	-	0
NC Johnson	160	152	19	4935	146*	37.10	10	29	71	0	4725	4017	123	32.65	5.10	4-19	3
D Jordaan	73	69	5	1661	116	25.95	1	13	22	0	381	330	7	47.14	5.19	1-5	0
LCR Jordaan	48	21	12	39	7	4.33	0	0	6	0	2200	1422	35	40.62	3.87	3-25	0
P Joubert	34	15	5	156	50*	15.60	0	1	6	0	1663	1152	39	29.53	4.15	3-23	0
JH Kallis	204	198	29	6949	155*	41.11	12	47	73	0	6699	4979	179	27.81	4.45	5-30	4
JM Kemp	54	46	12	853	95*	25.08	0	5	25	0	2050	1514	59	25.66	4.43	6-20	2
JC Kent	31	23	4	493	81*	25.94	0	4	11	0	1427	1104	36	30.66	4.64	4-29	1
EW Kidwell	19	8	7	47	37*	47.00	0	0	1	0	740	578	25	23.12	4.68	5-36	2
G Kirsten	247	243	20	8189	188*	36.72	14	50	80	1	138	112	3	37.33	4.86	1-25	0
JWF Klopper	9	7	1	24	9	4.00	0	0	2	0	234	218	4	54.50	5.58	2-39	0
L Klusener	161	135	43	3714	142*	40.36	3	20	37	0	6876	5356	187	28.64	4.67	6-49	8
DM Koch	20	17	9	172	26*	21.50	0	0	7	0	726	525	17	30.88	4.33	3-25	0

LIMITED OVERS CAREER RECORDS

Name	M	Inns	NO	Runs	HS	Avg	100	50	Ct	St	Balls	Runs	Wkts	Avg	RpO	BB	4I
LJ Koen	124	121	9	3743	151	33.41	6	17	68	0	0	0	0	-	-	-	0
SG Koenig	32	32	0	609	109	19.03	1	1	4	0	0	0	0	-	-	-	0
PPJ Koortzen	15	15	4	619	134	56.27	2	3	2	0	163	149	5	29.80	5.48	3-37	0
GJ-P Kruger	27	4	2	3	2	1.50	0	0	4	0	1203	931	38	24.50	4.64	6-23	2
GJ Kruis	38	20	6	174	28*	12.42	0	0	11	0	1768	1438	57	25.22	4.88	4-26	2
DR Laing	110	87	10	1504	85	19.53	0	6	21	0	3775	2674	76	35.18	4.25	4-16	1
CK Langeveldt	39	16	5	78	19*	7.09	0	0	6	0	1860	1256	68	18.47	4.05	5-7	5
MJ Lavine	56	49	2	984	72	20.93	0	9	18	0	2448	2120	42	50.47	5.19	2-22	0
AG Lawson	37	35	5	879	99*	29.30	0	6	9	0	0	0	0	-	-	-	0
SL Letshela	3	2	2	48	26*	-	0	0	0	0	0	0	0	-	-	-	0
MR Lewis	1	0	0	0	0	-	0	0	1	0	30	21	0	-	4.20	-	0
GFJ Liebenberg	139	121	22	3062	170*	30.92	3	16	73	4	36	42	1	42.00	7.00	1-26	0
C Light	46	44	5	789	93*	20.23	0	2	12	0	846	709	14	50.64	5.02	3-25	0
J Louw	7	5	1	184	72	46.00	0	2	0	0	306	270	7	38.57	5.29	5-43	1
GT Love	17	10	4	56	23*	9.33	0	0	1	0	594	478	7	68.28	4.82	2-28	0
EF Mabhena	6	3	2	24	17*	24.00	0	0	0	0	0	0	0	-	-	-	0
RB MacQueen	17	9	5	86	45*	21.50	0	0	6	0	636	462	13	35.53	4.35	3-57	0
JT Mafa	8	1	1	1	1*	-	0	0	1	0	264	236	6	39.33	5.36	3-33	0
DL Makalima	9	7	2	95	28	19.00	0	0	3	0	0	0	0	-	-	-	0
A Mall	12	11	0	447	77	40.63	0	3	4	0	0	0	0	-	-	-	0
HA Manack	7	7	0	109	28	15.57	0	0	2	0	0	0	0	-	-	-	0
WB Masimula	8	3	1	15	14	7.50	0	0	2	0	258	209	3	69.66	4.86	1-21	0
TK Mataboge	6	3	0	15	10	5.00	0	0	2	0	240	214	3	71.33	5.35	1-25	0
M Matomela	1	0	0	0	0	-	0	0	0	0	42	22	0	-	3.14	-	0
ND McKenzie	87	78	9	2193	120*	31.78	4	10	25	0	184	175	4	43.75	5.70	2-19	0
AP McLaren	1	1	0	12	12	12.00	0	0	1	0	0	0	0	-	-	-	0
I Mitchell	34	28	6	382	67	17.36	0	2	44	8	6	12	0	-	12.00	-	0
ET Mokoenanyana	2	2	0	4	4	2.00	0	0	0	0	0	0	0	-	-	-	0
TJ Mokoenanyana	10	4	3	5	3*	5.00	0	0	2	0	345	278	4	69.50	4.83	1-21	0
JA Morkel	15	11	5	127	40	21.16	0	0	3	0	738	516	23	22.43	4.19	4-23	1
PV Mpitsang	27	12	6	43	20*	7.16	0	0	1	0	1194	894	18	49.66	4.49	3-26	0
R Munnik	15	11	1	91	29	9.10	0	0	5	0	507	411	20	20.55	4.86	4-50	1
DW Murray	30	24	6	339	57	18.83	0	1	26	11	0	0	0	-	-	-	0
JG Myburgh	14	14	1	416	95	32.00	0	2	5	0	375	303	6	50.50	4.84	2-27	0
SS Ndima	11	7	2	55	22	11.00	0	0	2	0	0	0	0	-	-	-	0
A Nel	37	17	12	68	17*	13.60	0	0	8	0	1786	1153	58	19.87	3.87	6-27	3

LIMITED OVERS CAREER RECORDS

Name	M	Inns	NO	Runs	HS	Avg	100	50	Ct	St	Balls	Runs	Wkts	Avg	RpO	BB	4I
M Ngam	14	1	1	0	0*	-	0	0	4	0	602	404	24	16.83	4.02	4-20	2
R Niewoudt	6	6	0	90	41	15.00	0	0	2	0	18	21	0	-	7.00	-	0
M Ntini	64	17	6	32	8	2.90	0	0	15	0	2754	1998	80	24.97	4.35	5-37	3
JL Ontong	44	39	5	815	81	23.97	0	6	18	0	934	691	15	46.06	4.43	2-12	0
JM Otto	8	8	1	246	70	35.14	0	1	6	0	20	22	1	22.00	6.60	1-8	0
G Outram	20	19	4	331	83	22.06	0	1	5	0	6	10	0	-	10.00	-	0
A Paleker	11	3	0	38	30	12.66	0	0	2	0	0	0	0	-	-	-	0
SJ Palframan	113	94	16	1970	90*	25.25	0	12	146	25	0	0	0	-	-	-	0
RJ Peterson	21	16	3	313	94	24.07	0	2	5	0	626	501	19	26.36	4.80	3-28	0
BT Player	148	104	25	1281	83	16.21	0	2	21	0	6738	4538	150	30.25	4.04	5-27	5
GA Pollock	32	28	6	555	94*	25.22	0	3	7	0	30	41	0	-	8.20	-	0
SM Pollock	228	149	44	2391	87	22.77	0	10	76	0	11212	7039	319	22.06	3.76	6-21	13
EG Poole	37	25	8	336	36*	19.76	0	0	33	2	0	0	0	-	-	-	0
SC Pope	71	61	5	1545	93	27.58	0	10	30	3	360	312	7	44.57	5.20	4-38	1
N Pothas	100	78	32	1574	101	34.21	1	6	91	21	0	0	0	-	-	-	0
D Pretorius	22	9	3	17	7*	2.83	0	0	2	0	1043	814	35	23.25	4.68	4-39	1
AG Prince	48	42	7	738	76*	21.08	0	4	19	0	0	0	0	-	-	-	0
AAW Pringle	4	2	0	4	2	2.00	0	0	2	0	182	131	7	18.71	4.31	3-36	0
MW Pringle	165	85	30	617	31	11.21	0	0	34	0	8088	5393	220	24.51	4.00	6-30	9
AG Puttick	13	13	2	222	75*	20.18	0	1	9	2	0	0	0	-	-	-	0
BL Reddy	2	2	0	13	10	6.50	0	0	0	0	84	87	4	21.75	6.21	3-46	0
JN Rhodes	295	272	53	6857	121	31.31	1	34	132	0	74	44	2	22.00	3.56	1-2	0
MJR Rindel	183	173	18	5468	144*	35.27	11	31	55	0	2483	1912	57	33.54	4.62	4-28	1
GA Roe	72	28	14	143	16	10.21	0	0	12	0	3439	2502	72	34.75	4.36	5-49	4
JA Rudolph	11	11	1	464	110	46.40	1	2	4	0	48	42	0	-	5.25	-	0
BN Schultz	80	13	9	17	5	4.25	0	0	12	0	4022	2508	136	18.44	3.74	6-22	8
DM Senekal	1	1	1	2	2*	-	0	0	0	0	24	22	0	-	5.50	-	0
AJ Seymore	31	29	5	842	101	35.08	1	4	16	0	0	0	0	-	-	-	0
WJ Smit	37	31	5	899	111	34.57	2	2	12	0	444	397	13	30.53	5.36	2-35	0
GC Smith	16	16	2	429	106	30.64	1	2	4	0	98	98	6	16.33	6.00	3-46	0
GJ Smith	39	10	5	23	9	4.60	0	0	7	0	1944	1426	58	24.58	4.40	5-11	4
ELR Stewart	122	101	24	2148	90	27.89	0	9	100	4	6	6	0	-	6.00	-	0
PJR Steyn	150	140	17	3848	127*	31.28	5	22	31	0	0	0	0	-	-	-	0
QR Still	2	2	1	24	20	24.00	0	0	2	0	12	14	0	-	7.00	-	0
MR Street	3	3	3	13	8*	-	0	0	5	0	0	0	0	-	-	-	0

Name	M	Inns	NO	Runs	HS	Avg	100	50	Ct	St	Balls	Runs	Wkts	Avg	RpO	BB	4I
JG Strydom	7	7	2	140	43*	28.00	0	0	4	0	0	0	0	-	-	-	0
M Strydom	39	38	3	1162	103	33.20	1	8	11	0	1331	1127	29	38.86	5.08	4-16	1
PC Strydom	106	91	17	2212	106*	29.89	1	16	29	0	1829	1322	39	33.89	4.33	4-8	1
CB Sugden	37	31	7	755	86	31.45	0	6	18	0	0	2	0	-	-	-	0
AJ Swanepoel	57	22	6	107	19	6.68	0	0	15	0	2557	1957	65	30.10	4.59	5-32	1
CR Tatton	6	5	2	3	2*	1.00	0	0	2	0	258	231	3	77.00	5.37	2-31	0
R Telemachus	81	41	14	270	37	10.00	0	0	17	0	4082	2818	121	23.28	4.14	5-54	2
DJ Terbrugge	36	14	12	53	16*	26.50	0	0	5	0	1573	1067	44	24.25	4.06	4-20	3
AC Thomas	10	8	4	62	20*	15.50	0	0	2	0	421	387	5	77.40	5.51	2-42	0
DH Townsend	2	2	2	4	4*	-	0	0	1	0	96	78	2	39.00	4.87	1-37	0
G Toyana	21	21	4	240	41	14.11	0	0	4	0	72	43	0	-	3.58	-	0
IJL Trott	17	17	1	515	108*	32.18	1	3	5	0	18	32	2	16.00	10.66	2-32	0
TL Tsolekile	18	11	2	188	44	20.88	0	0	25	1	0	0	0	-	-	-	0
BH Tucker	7	7	1	160	59	26.66	0	1	0	0	0	0	0	-	-	-	0
ANW Tweedie	6	3	2	70	70*	70.00	0	1	0	0	270	240	6	40.00	5.33	2-27	0
J Uys	15	12	4	149	28	18.62	0	0	0	0	244	233	4	58.25	5.72	2-1	0
AM van den Berg	9	6	1	85	32	17.00	0	0	1	0	150	125	1	125.00	5.00	1-41	0
F van der Merwe	10	8	3	31	8*	6.20	0	0	2	0	390	354	11	32.18	5.44	3-44	0
JJ van der Wath	29	25	5	428	91	21.40	0	2	4	0	918	787	26	30.26	5.14	4-45	1
M van Jaarsveld	67	63	9	2117	123	39.20	3	12	41	0	30	31	1	31.00	6.20	1-11	0
PJ van Loggenberg	1	1	0	0	0	0.00	0	0	0	0	30	40	1	40.00	8.00	1-40	0
CFK van Wyk	14	11	6	239	50*	47.80	0	1	12	2	0	0	0	-	-	-	0
JM van Wyk	1	1	0	12	12	12.00	0	0	0	0	54	43	0	-	4.77	-	0
MN van Wyk	41	37	5	1038	102*	32.43	1	5	23	3	123	115	7	16.42	5.60	2-28	0
RE Veenstra	71	35	8	371	40	13.74	0	0	17	0	3045	2063	76	27.14	4.06	6-34	2
JF Venter	95	88	9	2312	118*	29.26	1	12	36	0	2680	2057	69	29.81	4.60	5-21	2
MC Venter	93	86	9	1846	166*	23.97	1	8	27	0	0	0	0	-	-	-	0
DJ Watson	73	72	6	2555	116	38.71	2	21	23	0	48	50	2	25.00	6.25	2-22	0
BM White	55	51	4	1103	100*	23.46	1	6	16	0	914	671	32	20.96	4.40	4-31	2
W Wiblin	43	39	3	871	82	24.19	0	10	10	0	20	14	0	-	4.20	-	0
LJ Wilkinson	129	118	15	2799	102	27.17	1	16	44	0	450	374	10	37.40	4.98	4-48	1
HS Williams	89	38	13	113	15	4.52	0	0	11	0	4354	2880	106	27.16	3.96	4-35	2
CM Willoughby	75	27	15	57	11	4.75	0	0	9	0	3821	2586	102	25.35	4.06	6-24	4
JGH Wilson	1	0	0	0	0	-	0	0	0	0	54	50	1	50.00	5.55	1-50	0
WR Wingfield	35	29	11	865	83	48.05	0	6	9	0	1134	910	29	31.37	4.81	4-42	1

UCB BOWL 2000/01

Western Province won the UCB Bowl three-day competition, beating the Zimbabwe Board XI in the final. The Zimbabweans turned the tables, however, when the same two teams met in the final of the one-day competition.

UCB BOWL TABLES 2000/01

POOL A

Three-day	P	W	L	D	Bat	Bowl	Pts
Western Province B	5	3	0	2	18	18	66
Free State B	5	2	2	1	17	17	54
Eastern Province B	5	2	1	2	18	15	53
Boland B	5	1	0	4	17	17	44
Griqualand West B	5	1	3	1	13	18	41
Namibia	5	1	4	0	9	19	38

Points deducted for slow over-rates: None

One-day	P	W	L	T	NR	Bonus	Pts	NRR
Western Province B	5	5	0	0	0	2	22	1.29
Namibia	5	3	2	0	0	1	13	0.08
Boland B	5	3	2	0	0	0	12	-0.02
Free State B	5	2	3	0	0	2	10	0.07
Eastern Province B	5	2	3	0	0	0	8	-0.69
Griqualand West B	5	0	5	0	0	2	2	-0.65

POOL B

Three-day	P	W	L	D	Bat	Bowl	Pts
Zimbabwe Board XI	6	3	2	1	19	20	69
Border B	6	3	2	1	15	21	66
Easterns B	6	1	2	3	23	19	51
Northerns B	6	1	0	5	18	20	47
KwaZulu-Natal B	6	1	1	4	19	19	46
Gauteng B	6	1	1	4	16	17	41
North West B	6	0	2	4	16	22	38

Points deducted for slow over-rates: Easterns B 1, Gauteng B 2, KwaZulu-Natal B 2, Northerns B 1.

One-day	P	W	L	Tied	NR	Bonus	Pts	NRR
Zimbabwe Board XI	6	5	0	1	0	2	22	0.48
Border B	6	4	0	1	1	2	20	0.53
Northerns B	6	3	2	0	1	2	16	0.28
Easterns B	6	3	3	0	0	2	14	0.18
Gauteng B	6	1	2	0	3	1	11	0.08
KwaZulu-Natal B	6	1	5	0	0	2	6	-0.47
North West B	6	0	5	0	1	1	3	-1.03

UCB BOWL 2000/01

RESULTS

THREE-DAY COMPETITION

Pool A

Cape Town, 26-28 October 2000: WPB 269 (LD Ferreira 80, H Pangarker 43, M de Stadler 34, CE Feris 3-26) and 233-9* (R Magiet 71, J McLean 44, LD Ferreira 42, MR Lewis 3-45, CE Feris 4-26). **FSB** 224 (G Fourie 64, WJ Smit 40, JW Shutte 3-54, M de Stadler 5-53) and 161 (WJ Smit 30, JA Beukes 43, D Mokopanele 31, PL Harris 6-72). Western Province B won by 117 runs. WPB 17 pts, FSB 7.

Kimberley, 2-4 November 2000: GWB 138 (A Mabuya 41, M de Stadler 4-19) and 154 (JL Aspeling 43, BH Tucker 53, PL Harris 6-55, M de Stadler 3-22). **WPB** 213 (S Ahmed 54, S Ackermann 46, R Munnik 43, EW Kidwell 6-58) and 83-1 (R Magiet 35*, LD Ferreira 40*). Western Province B won by 9 wickets. WPB 17 pts, GWB 5.

Windhoek, 2-4 November 2000: Nam 337-8 (S Swanepoel 50, D Keulder 40, D Kotze 39, M van Schoor 34, L Louw 43, JB Burger 58, GS Hayward 3-62) and 232-5* (G Murgatroyd 102*, M van Schoor 40*). **EPB** 280 (GI Loon 42, C Esau 100, M Nienaber 35, R Scholtz 3-29, D Kotze 3-69, L Louw 3-56) and 224 (R Domingo 43, B Friedrichs 60, GS Hayward 44, D Kotze 3-46). Namibia won by 65 runs. Nam 16 pts, EPB 7.

Cape Town, 16-18 November 2000: BolB 257 (AW Cyster 42, MS de Kock 34, JG Strydom 39, H Davids 38, B Hector 33, R Munnik 3-43). **WPB** 354-7 (R Magiet 87, S Ahmed 64, LD Ferreira 111). Match drawn. WPB 7 pts, BolB 5.

Port Elizabeth, 23-25 November 2000: GWB 215 (J Brooker 69, J Louw 79, D Bergins 3-44, M Hayward 3- 42,) and 184 (J Brooker 34, BW Lemmetjies 31, DM Senekal 3-42, D Bergins 3-37, J Botha 3-55). **EPB** 392 (KD Duckworth 46, MR Benfield 113, U Abrahams 72, J Louw 3-83, AK Kruger 3-87) and 8-0. Eastern Province B won by 10 wickets. EPB 19 pts, GWB 6.

Bloemfontein, 23-25 November 2000: Nam 142 (G Murgatroyd 70, MR Lewis 6-35) and 185 (G Murgatroyd 54, JB Burger 38, B Kotze 33, WA Deacon 3-20, JJ van der Wath 3-34). **FSB** 348 (JA Beukes 99, WA Deacon 88, AP Abrahams 48*, C Bothma 34). Free State B won by an innings and 21 runs. FSB 19 pts, Nam 5.

Kraaifontein, 11-13 January 2001: Nam 118 (D Keulder 45, WJ du Toit 4-32, G Goetham 4-47) and 81 (JM van Wyk 3-23). **BolB** 253 (JM Henderson 68, B Kotze 3-62, D Kotze 3-48). Boland B won by an innings and 54 runs. BolB 17 pts, Nam 5.

Port Elizabeth, 25-27 January 2001: EPB 228 (U Abrahams 46, KD Duckworth 62, B Friedrichs 30, PR Adams 4-49) and 244 (KD Duckworth 44, GI Loon 32, GV Grace 44, MW Creed 52, PL Harris 6-97). **WPB** 241 (R Magiet 42, GC Smith 103, TL Tsolekile 62, GS Hayward 6-72, D Willemse 3-58) and 169-7 (AG Puttick 39, LD Ferreira 47, D Willemse 3-39). Match drawn. WPB 7 pts, EPB 6.

Kimberley, 26-28 January 2001: BolB 265-9* (B Hector 48, CdeW de Lange 64*, CR Tatton 3-53) and 150 (B Hector 38, MS de Kock 42, AK Kruger 4-27). **GWB** 162 (AP McLaren 53, WJ du Toit 4-37, G Goetham 4-61) and 249-9 (DK Dobson 61, MC Arthur 36, AP McLaren 93, CdeW de Lange 6-101). Match drawn. BolB 7 pts, GWB 5.

Paarl, 1-3 February 2001: FSB 222 (S Sibande 57, WA Deacon 39, G Botha 34, DS Combrink 3-18, S McConnachie 5-49). **BolB** 221-3 (AW Cyster 78, KC Jackson 92). Match drawn. BolB 7 pts, FSB 4.

Bloemfontein, 8-10 February 2001: EPB 258 (U Abrahams 60, KD Duckworth 39, L Dipha 37*, JJ van der Wath 4-72, SA Cilliers 4-68) and 131 (KD Duckworth 37, JJ van der Wath 3-20, WA Deacon 4-37). **FSB** 206 (JA Beukes 43, H Moreeng 34, DM Senekal 5-64, GS Hayward 3-30) and 162 (JA Beukes 31, L Meyer 4-47). Eastern Province B won by 21 runs. EPB 17 pts, FSB 7.

Windhoek, 8-10 February 2001: GWB 348 (DK Dobson 85, WM Dry 163, J Brooker 32, D Kotze 4-57, L Louw 3-45) and 18-2. **Nam** 179 (M van Schoor 35, AJ Swanepoel 3-50) and 185 (G Murgatroyd 91, MP Ndopu 4-22). Griqualand West B won by 8 wickets. GWB 19 pts, Nam 6.

Cape Town, 15-17 February 2001: WPB 271 (AG Puttick 31, J McLean 51, W Euley 38, M de Stadler 42, PL Harris 31, B Kotze 5-67) and 223-3* (AG Puttick 75, LD Ferreira 100*). **Nam** 162 (G Murgatroyd 51, PL Harris 8-57) and 331 (D Seager 57, G Murgatroyd 121, PL Harris 4-96). Western Province B won by 1 run. WPB 18 pts, Nam 6.

Port Elizabeth, 22-24 February 2001: BolB 378-7* (KC Jackson 191*, B Hector 41, GN Myers 61, L Meyer 4-92, D Willemse 3-90) and 163-8* (B Layman 38, KC Jackson 54, D Willemse 3-40). **EPB** 266 (U Abrahams 35, R Domingo 50, B Friedrichs 30, DM Senekal 35, CdeW de Lange 5-89) and 163-7 (U Abrahams 40, KD Duckworth 37, GI Loon 32, CdeW de Lange 3-62). Match drawn. BolB 8 pts, EPB 4.
Kimberley, 1-3 March 2001: FSB 232 (WA Deacon 32, J Vorster 39, CE Feris 47, C Pieterson 3-36) and 216 (JR Schorn 80, C Pieterson 3-44). **GWB** 191 (DK Dobson 41, AK Kruger 41*, WA Deacon 5-63, C Bothma 3-43) and 191 (DK Dobson 32, WM Dry 57, WA Deacon 3-35, SA Cilliers 3-38). Free State B won by 66 runs. FSB 17 pts, GWB 6.

Pool B
East London, 26-28 October 2000: GauB 259-9* (WA Dugmore 59, JM Otto 75, TMS Savage 43) and 265-5* (WA Dugmore 66, JM Otto 89, DR Laing 56, JWF Klopper 3-40). **BdrB** 214 (W Wiblin 56, S Nelani 42, NA Fusedale 4-66) and 240-5 (GM Hammond 33, W Wiblin 48, JWF Klopper 58, BC Fourie 44*). Match drawn. GauB 8 pts, BdrB 7.
Kwekwe, 26-28 October 2000: Zim Brd 332 (TR Gripper 84, GJ Rennie 33, DD Ebrahim 122*, T Taibu 39, RA de Vry 3-50, RB MacQueen 3-118) and 223-8* (GJ Rennie 92, GB Brent 32, RB MacQueen 3-73, S Power 3-65). **KZNB** 282 (MD Sanders 38, A Mall 70, R Gobind 49, WR Wingfield 30, DL Brown 36, GA Lamb 3-59, RW Price 3-73) and 159 (G Rowley 103*, RW Price 5-59). Zimbabwe Board XI won by 114 runs. Zim Brd 18 pts, KZNB 6.
Boksburg, 2-4 November 2000: EasB 291-8* (D Brand 51, J Uys 100, AM van den Berg 61, GA Pollock 31, S Power 3-55). **KZNB** 224-9 (A Mall 59, R Gobind 35, WR Wingfield 47, D Brand 4-66). Match drawn. EasB 8 pts, KZNB 4.
Fochville, 2-4 November 2000: NWB 210 (M Strydom 70*, RE Bryson 3-35) and 192 (BC de Wett 58, Q Ferreira 3-59, P Joubert 3-31). **NorB** 157-7* (R Bailey 37, AN Smith 44, JN Dreyer 3-49, F van der Merwe 3-62) and 139-5 (AN Smith 51*, MLG Pedi 39, G Marais 3-19). Match drawn. NorB 6 pts, NWB 5.
Pretoria, 9-11 November 2000: NorB 361 (FC Brooker 104, DJJ de Vos 89, JG Myburgh 61, DP Viljoen 6-70) and 244-6* (QR Still 104, FC Brooker 33, DJJ de Vos 43, M Mbangwa 3-33). **Zim Brd** 322-7* (MA Vermeulen 38, CB Wishart 129, GA Lamb 70, RE Bryson 3-52) and 104-7 (P Joubert 5-12). Match drawn. NorB 8 pts, Zim Brd 6.
Durban, 9-11 November 2000: BdrB 229 (JWF Klopper 89, B Esterhuizen 32, GM Gilder 3-44) and 121 (DL Makalima 32, GM Gilder 5-40). **KZNB** 212 (R Gobind 88, AM Amla 40, GM Gilder 34, JWF Klopper 3-30) and 142-8 (G Rowley 67*, BC Fourie 3-23). KwaZulu-Natal B won by 2 wickets. KZNB 16 pts, BdrB 6.
Boksburg, 16-18 November 2000: EasB 309-9* (D Brand 34, J Uys 36, SP O'Connor 93, G Mbangeni 67*, JN Dreyer 6-66) and 141-2 (AM van den Berg 47*, GA Pollock 50*). **NWB** 429-6 (G Outram 36, C de Swardt 91, BC de Wett 113, R Niewoudt 104, PM van Niekerk 55, T Lange 3-68). Match drawn. NWB 8 pts, EasB 6.
Johannesburg, 16-17 November 2000: Zim Brd 120 (CN Evans 43, JT Mafa 3-37, F Herbst 4-48) and 133 (GA Lamb 37*, TK Mataboge 4-28, F Herbst 4-30). **GauB** 108 (DT Hondo 4-48, M Mbangwa 3-34, CN Evans 3-1) and 146-4 (DR Laing 72*). Gauteng B won by 6 wickets. GauB 15 pts, Zim Brd 5.
Potchefstroom, 23-24 November 2000: BdrB 299 (BC Fourie 38, EJ Ferreira 31, W Hinkel 52, M Maketa 36, B Esterhuizen 37*, J Malao 3-55) and 26-2. **NWB** 79 (PM van Niekerk 40*, BC Fourie 5-33, JGH Wilson 5-34) and 245 (G Outram 91, R Niewoudt 37, JGH Wilson 3-25, GM Hammond 3-12). Border B won by 8 wickets. BdrB 18 pts, NWB 4.
Mutare, 23-24 November 2000: EasB 249 (D Brand 41, AM van den Berg 80, P Dharman 53*, RW Price 6-89) and 63 (AJ MacKay 3-17, RW Price 4-18). **Zim Brd** 275 (MA Vermeulen 30, DD Ebrahim 101, CN Evans 50, T Taibu 34, JW Williams 5-50) and 41-1. Zimbabwe Board XI won by 9 wickets. Zim Brd 18 pts, EasB 7.
Johannesburg, 11-13 January 2001: EasB 378-9* (D Brand 79, AG Botha 38, GA Pollock 45, JA Morkel 130, S Conrad 4-89) and 248-5* (D Brand 40, AM van den Berg 124*). **GauB** 294 (SC Cook 81, MR Street 34, HA Manack 58, J Buxton-Foreman 43, AG Botha 4-66) and 221 (SC Cook 37, MR Street 61, J Buxton-Foreman 40, AG Botha 3-32). Easterns B won by 111 runs. EasB 18 pts, GauB 8.

Pietermaritzburg, 11-13 January 2001: NWB 261-9* (C Light 105, I Mohammed 39, RB MacQueen 4-82) and 275-5* (HM de Vos 140, I Mohammed 42, C Light 56). **KZNB** 256-7* (HM Amla 47, G Rowley 104, RP Symcox 69*, M Holmes 3-29) and 212-8 (HM Amla 111, G Rowley 35, JN Dreyer 3-62, J Kgamadi 4-72). Match drawn. KZNB 8 pts, NWB 7.

Pretoria, 25-27 January 2001: NorB 180 (AN Petersen 32, J Mokonyama 36, BL Reddy 3-41, AG Botha 3-26) and 285-2 (QR Still 84, AN Smith 61, AN Petersen 52*, FC Brooker 60*). **EasB** 311 (D Brand 62, AG Botha 85, GA Pollock 76, DH Townsend 5-52). Match drawn. EasB 8 pts, NorB 4.

East London, 1-3 February 2001: NorB 362-6* (QR Still 150*, DJJ de Vos 114, BC Fourie 3-88) and 35-1. **BdrB** 159 (DL Makalima 51, BC Fourie 43, RE Bryson 3-42, DJJ de Vos 3-23) and 237 (GM Hammond 75, W Hinkel 35, Q Ferreira 3-51, PG van Rooyen 4-32). Northerns B won by 9 wickets. NorB 18 pts, BdrB 3.

Durban, 1-3 February 2001: GauB 269 (CDT Vorster 31, M van Zijl 58, J Buxton-Foreman 66, SM Adam 3- 32, ANW Tweedie 5-79) and 256-7* (CDT Vorster 57, G Toyana 55, MR Street 49). **KZNB** 303 (MD Sanders 46, LE Zondi 59, G Rowley 41, RP Symcox 56, T Essack 49, GW Jansen 4-66, S Conrad 4-68) and 99-2 (DL Brown 38*). Match drawn. KZNB 7 pts, GauB 5.

Harare South, 1-3 February 2001: Zim Brd 290-9* (MA Vermeulen 137, DD Ebrahim 47, GM Hewitt 4-41) and 99-4* (CB Wishart 36*). **NWB** 153 (GM Hewitt 39, CT Enslin 48, RW Price 5-12) and 158 (GM Hewitt 50, RW Price 7-46). Zimbabwe Board XI won by 78 runs. Zim Brd 18 pts, NWB 6.

Centurion, 9-11 February 2001: NorB 188 (R Bailey 45, G Morgan 35*, ANW Tweedie 5-50) and 317-6* (DH Townsend 60, AN Petersen 88, T Henning 42, R Bailey 56, ANW Tweedie 3-81). **KZN B** 279 (KS Bender 41, DL Brown 137, DH Townsend 3-70, QR Still 4-52) and 39 for 2. Match drawn. KZNB 7 pts, NorB 5.

Springs, 15-16 February 2001: EasB 122 (L Graham 5-32, BC Fourie 3-33) and 168 (AM van den Berg 54, M Matomela 3-13, W Hinkel 4-41). **BdrB** 125 (GM Hammond 30, JW Williams 3-22, AG Botha 3-11) and 169-4 (GM Hammond 40, BC Fourie 56*, JP Kreusch 30*). Border B won by 6 wickets. BdrB 15 pts, EasB 5.

Potchefstroom, 15-17 February 2001: GauB 184 (GW Jansen 30, CT Enslin 4-47) and 117-3 (WA Dugmore 44, G Toyana 42). **NWB** 332 (D Jacobs 46, MC Venter 89, BC de Wett 81, CT Enslin 50, F Herbst 3-42, S Conrad 3-78). Match drawn. NWB 8 pts, GauB 4.

Johannesburg, 22-24 February 2001: NorB 315-5* (QR Still 128, AN Smith 41, R Bailey 35, PG van Rooyen 30*) and 46-3. **GauB** 199 (CDT Vorster 47, G Toyana 31, J Buxton-Foreman 41). Match drawn. NorB 7 pts, GauB 3.

East London, 22-24 February 2001: Zim Brd 136 (MA Vermeulen 47, L Graham 3-19, BC Fourie 3-42, JWF Klopper 3-31) and 218 (TN Madondo 98*, BC Fourie 3-64, JWF Klopper 3-29). **BdrB** 320 (W Hinkel 62, BC Fourie 98, JWF Klopper 63, L Graham 40, BT Watambwa 3-81, DT Mutendera 3-45) and 36-1. Border B won by 9 wickets. BdrB 17 pts, Zim Brd 4.

Final

Cape Town, 15-17 March 2001: Zim Brd 194 (AM Blignaut 72, T Taibu 35, Q Friend 3-59, PL Harris 4-42) and 214 (GJ Rennie 37, H Masakadza 42, DD Ebrahim 64, R Joffe 3-44, PL Harris 4-77). **WPB** 323 (JP Duminy 39, J McLean 72, H Pangarker 50, W Euley 60) and 90-4 (JP Duminy 31*, W Euley 36). Western Province B won by 6 wickets.

UCB BOWL 2000/01

UCB BOWL THREE-DAY COMPETITION WINNERS

Winners	Year	Winners	Year
Orange Free State	1951/52	Northern Transvaal	1978/79
Transvaal	1952/53	Natal B	1979/80
Eastern Province	1954/55	Western Province B	1980/81
Rhodesia	1955/56	Boland	1981/82
Border	1958/59	Western Province B	1982/83
Eastern Province/Transvaal B	1959/60	Western Province B	1983/84
Transvaal B	1962/63	Transvaal B	1984/85
Rhodesia	1963/64	Boland	1985/86
NE Transvaal	1965/66	Transvaal B	1986/87
NE Transvaal	1966/67	Boland	1987/88
Rhodesia	1967/68	Border	1988/89
Western Province	1968/69	Border/Western Province B	1989/90
Transvaal B	1969/70	Border/Western Province B	1990/91
Rhodesia	1970/71	Eastern Transvaal	1991/92
Northern Transvaal	1971/72	Boland	1992/93
Transvaal B	1972/73	Transvaal B/W Province B	1993/94
Natal B	1973/74	Natal B	1994/95
Transvaal B	1974/75	Griqualand West/Natal B	1995/96
Orange Free State	1975/76	Eastern Province B	1996/97
Transvaal B	1976/77	North West	1997/98
Northern Transvaal	1977/78	North West	1998/99

Note: The Bowl was known as the B Section until 1976/77 and renamed the UCB Bowl in 1991/92.
(all the above comnpetitions were classified as first-class. From 1999/2000 the UCB Bowl competition did not have first-class status)

Western Province	1999/00	Western Province	2000/01

PRESIDENT'S COMPETITION/CUP WINNERS

(Instituted 1978/79 for 2nd XIs of major provinces, re-instituted in 1991/92 as President's Cup)

Transvaal B	1978/79	Western Province B	1991/92

LIMITED OVERS COMPETITION

Pool A

Cape Town, 29 October 2000: FSB 156 in 42.2 overs (WJ Smit 54, M de Stadler 4-37, PL Harris 3-33). **WPB** 157-2 in 26.4 overs (R Magiet 49*, LD Ferreira 79). Western Province B won by 8 wickets.

Kimberley, 5 November 2000: WPB 230-8 in 45 overs (LD Ferreira 43, H Pangarker 44, R Munnik 43, GA de Kock 52*, E Tsamaisi 3-39). **GWB** 228-4 in 44 overs (DK Dobson 100*, AK Kruger 69). Western Province B won by 2 runs.

Windhoek, 5 November 2000: Nam 238 in 44.5 overs (JB Burger 48, D Kotze 73, M van Schoor 40, GS Hayward 4-58, C Esau 3-27). **EPB** 194 in 41.5 overs (GI Loon 50, B Friedrichs 53,R Scholtz 3-47). Namibia won by 44 runs.

Cape Town, 19 November 2000: WPB 223-8 in 45 overs (R Magiet 48, AG Puttick 34, R Munnik 45, JM van Wyk 3-57). **BolB** 210-8 in 45 overs (AW Cyster 74, CdeW de Lange 33*). Western Province B won by 13 runs.

Port Elizabeth, 26 November 2000: EPB 216-7 in 45 overs (GI Loon 93*, J Brooker 3-33). **GWB** 201-8 in 45 overs (DK Dobson 30, BH Tucker 31, J Louw 32, C Esau 4-40). Eastern Province B won by 15 runs.

Bloemfontein, 26 November 2000: FSB 193-7 in 45 overs (G Fourie 36, AK Volsteedt 41*, B van Rooi 3-36). **Nam** 194-4 in 42.5 overs (D Keulder 87). Namibia won by 6 wickets.

Kraaifontein, 14 January 2001: BolB 174-5 in 45 overs (IJL Trott 68*, B Hector 33). **Nam** 170-9 in 45 overs (S Swanepoel 36, D Kotze 43, WJ du Toit 4-22). Boland B won by 4 runs.

Port Elizabeth, 28 January 2001: WPB 239-9 in 45 overs (R Magiet 56, GC Smith 46, J McLean 62, GS Hayward 4-47). **EPB** 109-9 in 45 overs (GV Grace 32, R Domingo 40*, PL Harris 3-26). Western Province B won by 130 runs.
Kimberley, 29 January 2001: BolB 214-9 in 45 overs (IJL Trott 66, B Hector 64, CdeW de Lange 31*, AJ Swanepoel 5-24). **GWB** 208-4 in 45 overs (DK Dobson 51, JL Aspeling 89*). Boland B won by 6 runs.
Paarl, 4 February 2001: FSB 193-8 in 45 overs (JA Beukes 67, WA Deacon 44). **BolB** 176-9 in 45 overs (JJ van der Wath 4-35). Free State B won by 17 runs.
Bloemfontein, 11 February 2001: EPB 187-8 in 45 overs (KD Duckworth 33, GV Grace 50*). **FSB** 167 in 42.3 overs. Eastern Province B won by 20 runs.
Windhoek, 11 February 2001: GWB 145 in 42 overs (DK Dobson 36, RJ Kirtley 3-13). **Nam** 146-7 in 42 overs (JB Burger 45, M van Schoor 38*, WM Dry 3-26). Namibia won by 3 wickets.
Cape Town, 18 February 2001: WPB 240-6 in 45 overs (AG Puttick 97, S Ackermann 79). **Nam** 194-9 in 45 overs (S Swanepoel 30, W Rademeyer 30, M de Stadler 3-24, PL Harris 4-45). Western Province B won by 46 runs.
Port Elizabeth, 25 February 2001: EPB 204 in 45 overs (GV Grace 30, GS Hayward 67, W Albertyn 4-25, WJ du Toit 3-24). **BolB** 208-6 in 42.2 overs (B Hector 52, GN Myers 49, CdeW de Lange 39*). Boland B won by 4 wickets.
Kimberley, 4 March 2001: FSB 246-9 in 45 overs (JR Schorn 69, WA Deacon 55, E Tsamaisi 6-27). **GWB** 139 in 29.3 overs (WM Dry 42, WA Deacon 3-38, J Vorster 4-31). Free State B won by 107 runs.

Pool B
East London, 29 October 2000: GauB 144 in 39 overs (JM Otto 80, JWF Klopper 3-22, M Matomela 3-38). **BdrB** did not bat. No Result.
Kwekwe, 29 October 2000: KZNB 195-6 in 40 overs (A Mall 66, DL Brown 35*, GA Lamb 3-51). **Zim Brd** 199-6 in 36.2 overs (CB Wishart 30, CN Evans 85*, ANW Tweedie 3-30). Zimbabwe Board XI won by 4 wickets.
Boksburg, 5 November 2000: KZNB 204-5 in 45 overs (MD Sanders 85, WR Wingfield 47*). **EasB** 208-3 in 34.2 overs (D Brand 58, AG Botha 73, AM van den Berg 39). Easterns B won by 7 wickets.
Fochville, 5 November 2000: NorB 249-9 in 45 overs (JG Myburgh 53, DJJ de Vos 37, Q Ferreira 54, JN Dreyer 3-42). **NWB** 230-4 in 45 overs (R Niewoudt 53, BC de Wett 54, M Strydom 79*). Northerns B won by 19 runs.
Durban, 12 November 2000: BdrB 158 in 43 overs (BC Fourie 33). **KZNB** 98 in 26.4 overs (DL Brown 44, M Matomela 3-12, BC Fourie 4-35). Border B won by 60 runs.
Pretoria, 12 November 2000: NorB 221-6 in 45 overs (QR Still 55, JG Myburgh 57, FC Brooker 33, Q Ferreira 30). **Zim Brd** 222-6 in 45 overs (GA Lamb 58, CB Wishart 45, CN Evans 37). Zimbabwe Board XI won by 4 wickets.
Johannesburg, 18 November 2000: GauB 206-7 in 35 overs (WA Dugmore 88, MR Street 42, DR Laing 37, RW Price 3-34). **Zim Brd** 130-4 in 23 overs (MA Vermeulen 59, DJR Campbell 40). Zimbabwe Board XI won by 7 runs (D/L method).
Boksburg, 19 November 2000: NWB 138 in 41.4 overs (PM van Niekerk 31, C de Swardt 44, J Uys 4-30). **EasB** 140-2 in 27 overs (J Uys 76*, AM van den Berg 44). Easterns B won by 8 wickets.
Potchefstroom, 25 November 2000: NWB 211-6 in 45 overs (G Outram 31, BC de Wett 40, CT Enslin 39, C de Swardt 55*). **BdrB** 212-4 in 44.1 overs (GM Hammond 76*, JP Kreusch 50*). Border B won by 6 wickets.
Mutare, 26 November 2000: EasB 142 in 41 overs (GA Pollock 30, RW Price 3-25). **Zim Brd** 143-8 in 35.1 overs (AJ Mackay 73, GA Pollock 3-26). Zimbabwe Board XI won by 2 wickets.
Johannesburg, 14 January 2001: GauB 160 in 44.2 overs (G Toyana 56). **EasB** 161-5 in 39.1 overs (D Brand 37, JA Morkel 54*). Easterns B won by 5 wickets.
Pietermaritzburg, 14 January 2001: KZNB 254-7 in 45 overs (R Gobind 47, G Rowley 66, K Smit 42*). **NWB** 184 in 40.2 overs (I Mohammed 73*, L Pillay 3-40). KwaZulu-Natal B won by 70 runs.
Pretoria, 28 January 2001: NorB 209-7 in 45 overs (T Henning 59, QR Still 48, Q Ferreira 43). **EasB** 184 in 41.2 overs (D Brand 43, AG Botha 35, QR Still 5-36). Northerns B won by 25 runs.

UCB BOWL 2000/01

East London, 4 February 2001: BdrB 195-7 in 45 overs (B Bennett 69*, DL Makalima 40, Q Ferreira 3-43). **NorB** 189 in 44 overs (QR Still 63, T Henning 31, BC Fourie 4-34). Border B won by 6 runs.
Durban, 4 February 2001: GauB 177-9 in 45 overs (WA Dugmore 59, MR Street 38, RB MacQueen 3-36). **KZNB** 137 in 40.5 overs (DL Brown 34). Gauteng B won by 40 runs.
Harare South, 4 February 2001: Zim Brd 185 in 43 overs (H Masakadza 66, C de Swardt 3-38). **NWB** 145 in 44.4 overs (CT Enslin 33, DT Mutendera 3-32, PA Strang 3-28). Zimbabwe Board XI won by 40 runs.
Pretoria, 8 February 2001: KZNB 119 in 40.4 overs (ANW Tweedie 30*, Q Ferreira 3-29). **NorB** 120-9 in 39.3 overs (T Henning 37). Northerns B won by 1 wicket.
Springs, 17 February 2001: EasB 179 in 42.3 overs (J Uys 32, AM van den Berg 40, L Graham 3-26, W Hinkel 3-32). **BdrB** 183-2 in 35.1 overs (GM Hammond 67*, DL Makalima 39, BC Fourie 44*). Border B won by 8 wickets.
Potchefstroom, 18 February 2001: NWB 185-2 in 34.4 overs (G Outram 88*, MC Venter 33, GM Hewitt 43*). **GauB** did not bat. No result.
Johannesburg, 25 February 2001: GauB v NorB abandoned without a ball being bowled.
East London, 26 February 2001: Zim Brd 192 in 43.5 overs (MA Vermeulen 57, DD Ebrahim 70*, M Maketa 5-44). **BdrB** 192 in 44.4 overs (JP Kreusch 49, BC Fourie 41, A Stander 31, DT Mutendera 3-32). Match tied.

Final
Cape Town, 13 March 2001: WPB 215-5 in 45 overs (R Magiet 49, H Pangarker 106). **Zim Brd** 216-7 in 44.2 overs (AM Blignaut 90, CB Wishart 49). Zimbabwe Board XI won by 3 wickets.

UCB BOWL LIMITED OVERS COMPETITION WINNERS

Winners	Year	Winners	Year
Western Province B	1995/96	Western Province B	1998/99
Eastern Province B	1996/97	Free State B	1999/00
Northerns B	1997/98	Zimbabwe Board XI	2000/01

SACBOC/SACB CRICKET

Compiled by Krish Reddy

SOUTH AFRICAN COLOURED CRICKET BOARD and SOUTH AFRICAN MALAY CRICKET BOARD

BARNATO TROPHY

1904	Western Province	1933-44	No tournaments held
1908	Western Province	1945/46	Western Province
1910	Griqualand West	1947/48	Transvaal
1912/13	Western Province	1949/50	Transvaal
1922/23	Western Province	1951/52	Western Province
1924/25	Western Province	1953/54	Western Province
1927/28	Western Province	1954/55	Western Province
1929/30	Western Province	1957/58	Eastern Province
1932	Western Province		

The above tournament was administered initially by the SA Coloured Cricket Board and eventually by the SA Malay Cricket Board. This was an open tournament not restricted by race but latterly played for predominantly by Malays. No tournaments were held between 1933 and 1944 because this pioneering cricket organisation lay dormant, mainly because of the emergence of racial splinter groups - SA Coloureds (1926), SA Bantus (1932) and SA Indians (1940).

SA COLOURED CRICKET ASSOCIATION

SIR DAVID HARRIS TROPHY

1926/27	Natal	1948/49	Western Province
1928/29	Western Province	1950/51 (shared)	Western Province/Transvaal
1930/31	Eastern Province	1952/53	Eastern Province
1933/34	Griqualand West	1954/55	Western Province
1937/38	Western Province	1956/57	Western Province
1946/47	WP/EP/GW (triple tie)	1957/58	Western Province

The SA Coloured Cricket Association was formed by cricketers who broke away from the Barnato group in 1926. Until 1948 it was known as the SA Independent Coloured Cricket Board.

SOUTH AFRICAN BANTU CRICKET BOARD

NRC TROPHY

1933	Transvaal	1947	Western Province
1934	Transvaal	1950	Transvaal
1935	Border	1952/53	Western Province
1936	Border	1954	Western Province
1938/39	Transvaal	1956	Eastern Province
1940	Transvaal	1958	Eastern Province
1946	Transvaal		

SOUTH AFRICAN INDIAN CRICKET UNION

CHRISTOPHER TROPHY

1940/41	Natal	1950/51	Natal
1941/42	Natal	1952/53	Transvaal
1944/45	Natal	1954/55	Transvaal
1946/47	Transvaal	1957/58	Transvaal/Natal (shared)
1948/49	Transvaal		

After 1958 the racial/ethnic nature of tournaments ceased and tournaments were organised on a non-racial basis.

SOUTH AFRICAN CRICKET BOARD OF CONTROL (SACBOC)

DADABHAY TROPHY

Year	Venue	Winners
1950/51	Johannesburg	SA Indian Cricket Union
1952/53	Johannesburg	SA Coloured Cricket Association
1954/55	Johannesburg	SA Indian Cricket Union
1957/58	Cape Town	SA Coloured Cricket Association

The above tournaments were centralised with two-day matches being played and organised by SACBOC on an ethnic basis.

Season	Venue	Winners
1961/62	Johannesburg	Transvaal
1963/64	Port Elizabeth	Western Province
1965/66	Durban	Western Province
1967/68	Cape Town	Western Province
1969/70	Kimberley	Western Province/Transvaal (shared)

The above tournaments were centralised with two-day matches being played on an inter-provincial nonracial basis. Thereafter matches were decentralised.

Season	Winners
1970/71	Western Province and Transvaal shared (single round of two-day matches)
1971/72-1972/73	Western Province and Natal shared (three-day matches, home-and-away round robin played over two seasons)
1973/74	Western Province (three-day matches, home-and-away round robin played in one season)
1974/75	Transvaal

SFW TROPHY

(replaced Dadabhay Trophy)

Season	Winners	Season	Winners
1975/76	Western Province	1976/77	No competition

SFW TROPHY

(limited overs knockout)

1973/74	Western Province	1974/75	Natal

SOUTH AFRICAN CRICKET BOARD (SACB)

(succeeded SACBOC)

HOWA BOWL

(replaced SFW Trophy three-day competition, contested until unity between SACB and SA Cricket Union in 1991)

Season	Winners	Season	Winners
1977/78	Western Province	1984/85	Eastern Province
1978/79	Eastern Province	1985/86	Eastern Province
1979/80	Western Province	1986/87	Western Province
1980/81	Western Province	1987/88	Western Province
1981/82	Western Province	1988/89	Western Province
1982/83	Western Province	1989/90	Western Province
1983/84	Western Province	1990/91	Western Province

BENSON & HEDGES TROPHY

(limited overs knockout)

1982/83	Western Province
1983/84	Western Province/Eastern Province (final abandoned because of rain)
1984/85	Western Province

RECORDS

STATISTICAL HIGHLIGHTS 1950/51-1957/58

(two-day national inter-race tournaments, not first-class)

HIGHEST INNINGS TOTAL

386-7*	SA Coloureds v SA Malays at Johannesburg	1954/55

LOWEST INNINGS TOTAL

56	SA Bantus v SA Coloureds at Johannesburg	1954/55

CENTURIES

153	BL D'Oliveira, SA Col v SA Mal at Johannesburg	1954/55
134	J Barnes, SA Mal v SA Col at Johannesburg	1952/53
118	SN Solomon, SA Col v SA Ind at Cape Town	1957/58
117	CA Meyer, SA Col v SA Ind at Johannesburg	1954/55
116	F Roro, SA Ban v SA Ind at Johannesburg	1950/51
102	BL D'Oliveira, SA Col v SA Ban at Cape Town	1957/58
102	GH Abed, SA Mal v SA Ban at Cape Town	1957/58
100*	AI Deedat, SA Inds v SA Ban at Cape Town	1957/58

MOST RUNS

572 (Avg 57.20) BL D'Oliveira

WICKET PARTNERSHIP RECORDS

1st	158	L Herman and CA Meyer, SA Col v SA Ind at Johannesburg	1954/55
2nd	138	SN Solomon and B Witten, SA Col v SA Ind at Cape Town	1957/58
3rd	167	L Herman and BL D'Oliveira, SA Col v SA Mal at Johannesburg	1954/55
4th	111	BL D'Oliveira and S Raziet, SA Col v SA Mal at Cape Town	1957/58
5th	140	A Dinath and S van Haaght, SA Ind v SA Ban at Johannesburg	1954/55

6th	108	A Dinath and A Kazi, SA Ind v SA Col at Johannesburg	1954/55
7th	128	G Abed and S Nackerdien, SA Mal v SA Col at Johannesburg	1954/55
8th	159	G Abed and S Nackerdien, SA Mal v SA Ind at Johannesburg	1954/55
9th	58	AFW Stephens and M Anthony, SA Ind v SA Mal at Johannesburg	1954/55
10th	46	J Kumalo and M Ledimo, SA Ban v SA Ind at Johannesburg	1954/55

SEVEN WICKETS OR MORE IN AN INNINGS

10-57	AFW Stephens, SA Ind v SA Ban at Johannesburg	1954/55
8-32	B Waterwich, SA Col v SA Ban at Johannesburg	1950/51
7-42	B Waterwich, SA Col v SA Ind at Johannesburg	1950/51
7-47	M Garda, SA Ind v SA Col at Johannesburg	1952/53
7-50	R Simon, SA Col v SA Ban at Johannesburg	1952/53
7-51	G Langa, SA Ban v SA Mal at Johannesburg	1952/53
7-54	E Petersen, SA Mal v SA Col at Cape Town	1957/58
7-68	E Petersen, SA Mal v SA Ind at Cape Town	1957/58

Note: AFW Stephens' performance is the only instance of taking all 10 wickets in an innings in the history of SACBOC/SACB official competitions.

TEN WICKETS OR MORE IN A MATCH

14-98 (4-41 & 10-57)	AFW Stephens, SA Ind v SA Ban at Johannesburg	1954/55
12-76 (8-32 & 4-44)	B Waterwich, SA Col v SA Ban at Johannesburg	1950/51
10-65 (6-41 & 4-24)	E Petersen, SA Mal v SA Ban at Johannesburg	1952/53
10-86 (3-18 & 7-68)	E Petersen, SA Mal v SA Ind at Cape Town	1957/58
10-104 (7-54 & 3-50)	E Petersen, SA Mal v SA Col at Cape Town	1957/58

MOST WICKETS

58 (Avg 12.74) E Petersen

PLAYERS WHO REPRESENTED TWO NATIONAL TEAMS

G Abed	SA Indians (1950/51) and SA Malays (1952/53-1957/58)
GH Abed	SA Indians (1954/55) and SA Malays (1957/58)

PLAYERS APPEARING IN ALL FOUR TOURNAMENTS

G Abed (SA Indians 1950/51, SA Malays 1952/53-1957/58), EI Jeewa (SA Indians), G Langa (SA Bantus), Julius Mahanjana (SA Bantus)

NATIONAL CAPTAINS

SA Bantus: F Roro (1950/51), S Voss (1952/53), Julius Mahanjana (1954/55-1957/58)
SA Coloureds: D Hurling (1951), B Waterwich (1953), BL D'Oliveira (1955-1958)
SA Indians: AI Timol (1950/51), GHM Docrat (1952/53), S van Haaght (1954/55), A Variawa (1957/58)
SA Malays: AJ Freeman (1952/53), S Nackerdien (1954/55), G Abed (1957/58)

STATISTICAL HIGHLIGHTS 1961/62-1970/71

(two-day inter-provincial matches, not first-class)

HIGHEST INNINGS TOTAL

481	Ntl v SWD at Port Elizabeth	1963/64

LOWEST INNINGS TOTAL

22	Bdr v SWD at Port Elizabeth	1963/64
22	SWD v WP at Port Elizabeth	1963/64

SACBOC/SACB CRICKET

INDIVIDUAL SCORES OF 120 OR MORE

230	A Coericius, SWD v Bdr at Port Elizabeth	1963/64
194*	S Conrad, WP v GW at Durban	1965/66
174	Y Garda, Tvl v Bdr at Port Elizabeth	1963/64
155*	EI Laher, Ntl v Bdr at Port Elizabeth	1963/64
145*	S Abed, WP v Tvl at Kimberley	1969/70
145	I D'Oliveira, WP v GW at Johannesburg	1961/62
132	G Jardine, WP v GW at Johannesburg	1961/62
126	YI Laher, Ntl v EP at Johannesburg	1961/62
126	J Govender, Ntl v WP at Kimberley	1969/70
124	I Garda, Tvl v Ntl at Johannesburg	1970/71

WICKET PARTNERSHIP RECORDS

1st	283	I D'Oliveira and G Jardine, WP v GW at Johannesburg	1961/62
2nd	210	S Conrad and N Lakay, WP v GW at Durban	1965/66
3rd	159	S Saloojee and C Jacobs, GW v Ntl at Johannesburg	1961/62
4th	120	S Conrad and MB Maclons, WP v Ntl at Kimberley	1969/70
5th	144	O Vawda and O Rambaran, Ntl v GW at Cape Town	1967/68
6th	194	R Cader and A Moola, GW v EP at Johannesburg	1961/62
7th	163	AL Barnes and H Rasdien, Tvl v EP at Johannesburg	1961/62
8th	81	MS Dollie and G Williams, WP v SWD at Cape Town	1967/68
9th	133	DA Asmal and H Samuel, Ntl v Tvl at Durban	1965/66
10th	103*	S Patel and H Ayob, Tvl v Ntl at Port Elizabeth	1963/64

BEST BOWLING IN AN INNINGS

8-11	G Williams, WP v Bdr at Port Elizabeth	1963/64

TEN WICKETS OR MORE IN A MATCH

12-41	(6-17 & 6-24)	T Parsuramen, Ntl v SWD at Port Elizabeth	1963/64
12-67	(5-40 & 7-27)	AL Adams, WP v SWD at Kimberley	1969/70
12-70	(6-47 & 6-23)	H Ayob, Tvl v GW at Durban	1965/66
11-28	(7-6 & 4-22)	OL Williams, WP v SWD at Port Elizabeth	1963/64
11-122	(6-46 & 5-76)	D Malgas, SWD v EP at Kimberley	1969/70
10-35	(4-10 & 6-25)	AL Adams, WP v GW at Cape Town	1967/68
10-42	(4-25 & 6-17)	M Patrick, Ntl v GW at Cape Town	1967/68
10-48	(3-10 & 7-38)	I Ebrahim, Ntl v SWD at Kimberley	1969/70
10-62	(5-25 & 5-37)	T Parsuramen, Ntl v EP at Port Elizabeth	1963/64
10-62	(5-29 & 5-33)	AH Jinnah, GW v SWD at Cape Town	1967/68
10-62	(6-22 & 4-40)	OL Williams, WP v Tvl at Kimberley	1969/70
10-65	(4-24 & 6-41)	M Wilson, EP v Ntl at Port Elizabeth	1963/64
10-70	(5-40 & 5-30)	H Jairam, Tvl v Ntl at Johannesburg	1970/71
10-86	(7-55 & 3-31)	A Rubidge, Tvl v EP at Johannesburg	1961/62
10-115	(3-57 & 7-58)	JJ Neethling, WP v Tvl at Durban	1965/66
10-134	(7-44 & 3-90)	M Wilson, EP v GW at Johannesburg	1961/62

100 WICKETS

AL Adams (GW & WP, 1963/64 to 1969/70) and H Ayob (Tvl, 1961/62 to 1969/70)

PLAYERS APPEARING IN ALL FIVE TOURNAMENTS

H Ayob (Tvl), AL Barnes (Tvl), S Chotia (Tvl), N Lakay (WP), JJ Neethling (WP), Y Bhayat (GW).

SACBOC/SACB CRICKET

STATISTICAL HIGHLIGHTS 1971/72-1990/91

(three-day inter-provincial matches, first-class)

During the period 1971 to 1991, three-day matches were played between the provincial teams of the South African Cricket Board of Control (SACBOC) and its successor, the South African Cricket Board. The United Cricket Board has granted these three-day matches first-class status in retrospect.

TEAM RECORDS

HIGHEST INNINGS TOTAL

436-6*	Western Province v Natal at Cape Town	1986/87

LOWEST INNINGS TOTAL

38	Transvaal v Western Province at Cape Town	1981/82

HIGHEST AND LOWEST INNINGS TOTAL FOR EACH PROVINCE

	Highest		Lowest	
Eastern Province	372-9* v Tvl at Port Elizabeth	1972/73	42 v WP at Cape Town	1979/80
Natal	356-4* v EP at Port Elizabeth	1975/76	39 v WP at Cape Town	1981/82
Transvaal	406-9* v Ntl at Johannesburg	1972/73	38 v WP at Cape Town	1981/82
Western Province	436-6* v Ntl at Cape Town	1986/87	41 v EP at Port Elizabeth	1982/83

BATTING

HIGHEST INDIVIDUAL INNINGS

188*	RB Kanhai, Tvl v EP at Johannesburg	1974/75

CENTURIES

188*	RB Kanhai, Tvl v EP at Johannesburg	1974/75
182	BL D'Oliveira, EP v Tvl at Port Elizabeth	1972/73
174*	Y Omar, Ntl v EP at Port Elizabeth	1975/76
166	S Conrad, WP v Tvl at Cape Town	1972/73
149	Y Omar, Ntl v WP at Durban	1978/79
148*	D Kemp, WP v Ntl at Cape Town	1988/89
146	F Davids, WP v EP at Cape Town	1987/88
143	N Fortune, WP v Ntl at Cape Town	1981/82
142	Y Randeree, NTL v Tvl at Johannesburg	1972/73
142	I Behardien, WP v Ntl at Cape Town	1990/91
140	I Garda, Tvl v Ntl at Johannesburg	1972/73
139	S Conrad, WP v Tvl at Johannesburg	1971/72
137	J Lambert, WP v EP at Cape Town	1973/74
137	S Hendricks, WP v Tvl at Johannesburg	1986/87
134	RB Kanhai, Tvl v Ntl at Johannesburg	1974/75
132*	N Dindar, Tvl v WP at Johannesburg	1988/89
131	Y Omar, Ntl v Tvl at Johannesburg	1974/75
127	A Gabru, Tvl v Ntl at Johannesburg	1972/73
125	M Saley, Tvl v Ntl at Johannesburg	1986/87
125*	N White, WP v Ntl at Cape Town	1990/91
123	Y Omar, Ntl v EP at Port Elizabeth	1977/78
121	H Lorgat, EP v WP at Cape Town	1985/86
119	Y Omar, Ntl v Tvl at Newcastle	1977/78
119	A Dinath, Tvl v EP at Johannesburg	1985/86
118	Y Omar, Ntl v EP at Durban	1972/73

118*	N Francis, EP v Tvl at Port Elizabeth	1975/76
118	E Mall, Ntl v Tvl at Durban	1989/90
117	MG Majola, EP v Tvl at Johannesburg	1986/87
116	Y Thomas, WP v Tvl at Johannesburg	1985/86
114*	H Lorgat, Tvl v EP at Johannesburg	1987/88
111	AL Barnes, Tvl v Ntl at Durban	1975/76
110	N Francis, EP v Tvl at Johannesburg	1975/76
109	G Francois, Ntl v Tvl at Johannesburg	1975/76
109	M Abdullah, WP v Ntl at Cape Town	1986/87
109	N White, WP v Tvl at Cape Town	1990/91
108	R Musson, WP v Tvl at Cape Town	1980/81
108	I Behardien, WP v Ntl at Durban	1989/90
107	N Francis, EP v Tvl at Port Elizabeth	1975/76
107	AL Barnes, Tvl v EP at Johannesburg	1975/76
107	M Abdullah, WP v Tvl at Johannesburg	1983/84
107	Y Omar, Ntl v WP at Cape Town	1986/87
107*	F Davids, WP v Tvl at Johannesburg	1987/88
106	N Francis, EP v Tvl at Johannesburg	1973/74
106	S Kruger, EP v Ntl at Port Elizabeth	1983/84
106	G Cuddumbey, EP v Tvl at Port Elizabeth	1984/85
106	F Davids, WP v Tvl at Johannesburg	1989/90
106*	H Lorgat, Tvl v Ntl at Durban	1990/91
104	AL Barnes, Tvl v WP at Johannesburg	1973/74
104	RB Kanhai, Tvl v WP at Cape Town	1974/75
104	AL Barnes, Tvl v WP at Johannesburg	1974/75
104*	RL Naidoo, Ntl v Tvl at Ladysmith	1986/87
103	E Isaacs, WP v Ntl at Durban	1979/80
102*	A Manack, Tvl v WP at Cape Town	1981/82
102	M Abdullah, WP v EP at Cape Town	1983/84
102*	F Kimmie, Tvl v Ntl at Johannesburg	1984/85
101*	M Khan, Ntl v EP at Pietermaritzburg	1981/82
101*	S Gabriels, WP v Ntl at Tongaat	1984/85
100	V Moodie, WP v Tvl at Cape Town	1972/73
100	E Mall, Ntl v EP at Durban	1982/83
100*	G Cuddumbey, EP v Ntl at Port Elizabeth	1983/84
100*	Y Thomas, WP v Tvl at Cape Town	1983/84
100*	S Magiet, WP v Ntl at Cape Town	1986/87
100*	S Magiet, WP v Ntl at Pietermaritzburg	1986/87
100*	G Piedt, EP v Ntl at Estcourt	1988/89

A CENTURY IN EACH INNINGS

107	118*	N Francis, EP v Tvl at Port Elizabeth	1975/76

MOST CENTURIES IN A SEASON

3	RB Kanhai (Tvl)	1974/75
3	N Francis (EP)	1975/76

MOST CENTURIES IN THE COMPETITION

7	Y Omar (Ntl)	1971-86

CARRYING BAT THROUGH A COMPLETED INNINGS

R Musson	90*	(209)	WP v Ntl at Cape Town	1980/81
A Douglas	69*	(180)	EP v WP at Cape Town	1972/73

S Mohammed	42*	(86)	Tvl v EP at Port Elizabeth	1983/84
J Sandan	39*	(109)	EP v WP at Cape Town	1984/85
E Mall	39*	(127)	Ntl v Tvl at Johannesburg	1985/86
E Mall	11*	(39)	Ntl v WP at Cape Town	1981/82

MOST RUNS IN A SEASON

498	(Avg 45.27)	Y Omar (Ntl)	1977/78

BEST BATTING AVERAGE IN A SEASON

460 runs	(Avg 115.00)	RB Kanhai (Tvl)	1974/75

WICKET PARTNERSHIP RECORDS

1st	178	Y Omar (149) and G Francois (85) Ntl v WP at Durban	1978/79
2nd	273	I Garda (140) and A Gabru (127) Tvl v Ntl at Johannesburg	1972/73
3rd	183	A Viljoen (81) and N White (109) WP v Tvl at Cape Town	1990/91
4th	135	N Francis (106) and D Carter (50) EP v Tvl at Johannesburg	1973/74
5th	231	I Behardien (142) and N White (125*) WP v Ntl at Cape Town	1990/91
6th	191	RB Kanhai (188*) and A Bhabha (70) Tvl v EP at Johannesburg	1974/75
7th	136	N White (36) and S Magiet (97) WP v EP at Port Elizabeth	1990/91
8th	185	Y Begg (78) and F Kimmie (102*) Tvl v Ntl at Johannesburg	1984/85
9th	108	AH Manack (83) and Y Begg (59) Tvl v EP at Johannesburg	1990/91
10th	82	VA Barnes (41*) and AL Adams (39) WP v Ntl at Cape Town	1979/80

CENTURY PARTNERSHIPS

1st		
178	Y Omar (149) and G Francois (85) Ntl v WP at Durban	1978/79
172	S Kruger (106) and G Cuddumbey (100*) EP v Ntl at Port Elizabeth	1983/84
165	Y Omar (81) and G Francois (81) Ntl v Tvl at Johannesburg	1978/79
146	I Garda (68) and A Bhamjee (75) Tvl v WP at Johannesburg	1971/72
129	Y Omar (119) and G Francois (67) Ntl v Tvl at Newcastle	1977/78
123	Y Omar (87) and E Mall (46) Ntl v Tvl at Johannesburg	1983/84
111	S Conrad (99) and E Isaacs (54) WP v Ntl at Durban	1972/73
111	Y Omar (49) and G Francois (109) Ntl v Tvl at Johannesburg	1975/76
111	I Garda (71) and E Amod (32) Tvl v EP at Johannesburg	1975/76
110	R Yearwood (34) and G Barry (69) EP v Ntl at Durban	1989/90
110	R Yearwood (58) and E van Heerden (64) EP v Tvl at Johannesburg	1990/91
107	E Gafieldien (48) and S Gabriels (52) WP v Ntl at Cape Town	1989/90
106	E Isaacs (73) and R Musson (28) WP v Ntl at Cape Town	1980/81
105	J Sandan (64) and G Cuddumbey (42) EP v Ntl at Port Elizabeth	1980/81
103	S Hendricks (55) and S Gabriels (101*) WP v Ntl at Tongaat	1984/85
103*	S Hendricks (51*) and S Gabriels (42*) WP v EP at Cape Town	1986/87
102	J Sandan (70) and G Cuddumbey (50) EP v Ntl at Durban	1979/80
100	S Hendricks (70) and S Gabriels (40) WP v EP at Cape Town	1987/88
2nd		
273	I Garda (140) and A Gabru (127) Tvl v Ntl at Johannesburg	1972/73
232	S Conrad (166) and V Moodie (100) WP v Tvl at Cape Town	1972/73
144	E Isaacs (103) and N Fortune (71) WP v Ntl at Durban	1979/80
119	AL Barnes (111) and I Garda (47) Tvl v Ntl at Durban	1975/76
114	G Cuddumbey (59) and MG Majola (65) EP v Ntl at Port Elizabeth	1985/86
109	I Munshi (75) and I Khan (77) Tvl v Ntl at Durban	1989/90
107	Y Omar (131) and G Francois (69) Ntl v Tvl at Johannesburg	1974/75
101	S Conrad (139) and E Isaacs (50) WP v Tvl at Johannesburg	1971/72

3rd		
183	A Viljoen (81) and N White (109) WP v Tvl at Cape Town	1990/91
164	I Behardien (108) and N White (76) WP v Ntl at Durban	1989/90
149	A Bhamjee (89) and M Mangera (98) Tvl v EP at Johannesburg	1973/74
146	F Abrahams (86) and W Fischer (60) EP v Tvl at Johannesburg	1977/78
141	I Behardien (72) and M Abdullah (109) WP v Ntl at Cape Town	1986/87
138	G Cuddumbey (106) and MG Majola (70) EP v Tvl at Port Elizabeth	1984/85
123	N Francis (118*) and K Majola (42) EP v Tvl at Port Elizabeth	1975/76
115	N Fortune (65) and M Abdullah (58) WP v Tvl at Cape Town	1981/82
114	Y Omar (131) and Y Randeree (49) Ntl v Tvl at Johannesburg	1974/75
110	G Cuddumbey (91) and K Miller (50) EP v Tvl at Johannesburg	1985/86
108	I Garda (65) and S Chothia (42) Tvl v EP at Port Elizabeth	1975/76
102	A Rajah (63) and A Dinath (45) Tvl v WP at Johannesburg	1985/86
4th		
135	N Francis (106) and D Carter (50) EP v Tvl at Johannesburg	1973/74
132	MG Majola (89) and H Lorgat (74) EP v Tvl at Johannesburg	1985/86
114	S Hendricks (137) and M Abdullah (61) WP v Tvl at Johannesburg	1986/87
107	E Amod (74) and S Nana (55) Tvl v Ntl at Durban	1978/79
106	N Fortune (59) and N Antulay (64) WP v Ntl at Cape Town	1982/83
5th		
231	I Behardien (142) and N White (125*) WP v Ntl at Cape Town	1990/91
216	M Abdullah (76*) and F Davids (146) WP v EP at Cape Town	1987/88
175	F Davids (106) and B Dammert (57) WP v Tvl at Johannesburg	1989/90
168	Y Randeree (142) and M Patrick (90) Ntl v Tvl at Johannesburg	1972/73
158*	Y Omar (174*) and J Govender (72*) Ntl v EP at Port Elizabeth	1975/76
145	Y Omar (118) and I Timol (52) Ntl v EP at Durban	1972/73
125	M Abdullah (79) and Y Thomas (59) WP v Tvl at Johannesburg	1982/83
114	F Davids (81) and S Magiet (61) WP v EP at Cape Town	1985/86
113	Y Omar (123) and A Bawa (39) Ntl v EP at Port Elizabeth	1977/78
112	M Abdullah (107) and Y Thomas (85) WP v Tvl at Johannesburg	1983/84
111	E Mall (118) and Y Moorad (52) Ntl v Tvl at Durban	1989/90
102	H Lorgat (61) and N Dindar (54) Tvl v WP at Cape Town	1988/89
100	M Patrick (51) and I Timol (44) Ntl v WP at Cape Town	1971/72
6th		
191	RB Kanhai (188*) and A Bhabha (70) Tvl v EP at Johannesburg	1974/75
145	MG Majola (117) and K Majola (70) EP v Tvl at Johannesburg	1986/87
140	A Dinath (119) and N Edwards (48) Tvl v EP at Johannesburg	1985/86
135	M Khan (99*) and R L Naidoo (58) Ntl v WP at Pietermaritzburg	1987/88
134	H Lorgat (121) and A Frans (83) EP v WP at Cape Town	1985/86
122*	N White (64*) and Y Thomas (75*) WP v Tvl at Johannesburg	1990/91
114	N Fortune (143) and S Magiet (37) WP v Ntl at Cape Town	1981/82
108	S Magiet (100*) and Y Thomas (43) WP v Ntl at Cape Town	1986/87
107	A Jabaar (48) and S Magiet (54) WP v Ntl at Cape Town	1977/78
102	HA Manack (65*) and AH Manack (39) Tvl v Ntl at Durban	1990/91
7th		
136	N White (36) and S Magiet (97) WP v EP at Port Elizabeth	1990/91
124	AH Manack (57) and N Dindar (81) Tvl v Ntl at Johannesburg	1988/89
121	E Amod (37) and F Kimmie (75) Tvl v Ntl at Tongaat	1984/85
118	R Dolley (80) and K Majola (68) EP v Ntl at Estcourt	1988/89
112	R Dolley (97*) and A Coetzee (51) EP v Ntl at Port Elizabeth	1987/88
110	F Davids (58) and Y Thomas (116) WP v Tvl at Johannesburg	1985/86
110	H Lorgat (114*) and N Dindar (42) Tvl v EP at Johannesburg	1987/88
103	M Jajbhay (61*) and N Dindar (61) Tvl v WP at Johannesburg	1987/88

102	BL D'Oliveira (99) and I Hendricks (51) EP v WP at Cape Town	1973/74
102	H Lorgat (63) and K Majola (38) EP v WP at Port Elizabeth	1984/85
8th		
185	Y Begg (78) and F Kimmie (102*) Tvl v Ntl at Johannesburg	1984/85
139	K Majola (68) and G Piedt (100*) EP v Ntl at Estcourt	1988/89
135	BL D'Oliveira (182) and D Govindjee (34) EP v Tvl at Port Elizabeth	1972/73
133	G Williams (80) and S Magiet (89) WP v EP at Port Elizabeth	1971/72
131	Y Thomas (100*) and A Jabaar (61) WP v Tvl at Cape Town	1983/84
119	B O'Connell (79) and W Carelse (61*) WP v EP at Cape Town	1975/76
111	C Kisten (84) and R Dolley (52*) EP v Ntl at Durban	1985/86
106*	W Fischer (64*) and I Hendricks (50*) EP v Ntl at Port Elizabeth	1979/80
9th		
108	AH Manack (83) and Y Begg (59) Tvl v EP at Johannesburg	1990/91

LEADING RUN SCORERS

	Career	M	I	NO	Runs	HS	Avg	100	50
Y Omar (Ntl)	1971-86	51	92	6	3052	174*	35.48	7	11
K Majola (EP)	1973-90	85	143	12	2735	80	20.87	-	11
H Lorgat (EP/Tvl)	1977-90	74	119	11	2717	121	25.15	3	11
S Magiet (WP)	1971-90	63	97	11	2296	100*	26.69	2	13
M Khan (Ntl)	1971-88	74	130	12	2269	101*	19.22	1	6
G Cuddumbey (EP)	1974-88	66	117	9	2247	106*	20.80	2	8
M Abdullah (WP/Tvl)	1980-90	52	79	3	2198	109	28.92	3	12
S Gabriels (Tvl/WP)	1977-90	65	105	9	2040	101*	21.25	1	14
G Francois (Ntl)	1972-81	46	83	3	2039	109	25.48	1	12
A Peters (EP)	1982-90	43	82	4	1831	78	23.47	-	10
A Jabaar (WP/Tvl)	1974-90	55	84	12	1611	71	22.37	-	4
F Davids (WP)	1983-90	33	50	6	1610	146	36.59	3	11
N Edwards (Tvl)	1977-86	48	87	2	1582	82	18.61	-	6
D Govender (Ntl)	1978-90	52	94	5	1564	97	17.57	-	6
E Mall (Ntl)	1980-90	45	85	2	1479	118	17.81	2	5
E Isaacs (WP)	1971-83	50	83	6	1450	103	18.83	1	5
F Abrahams (EP)	1973-86	58	91	13	1417	86	18.16	-	4
Y Thomas (WP)	1982-90	38	51	6	1320	116	29.33	2	7
S Hendricks (WP)	1980-88	35	59	5	1268	137	23.48	1	5
J Govender (Ntl)	1971-80	41	68	6	1261	74	20.33	-	4
N Francis (EP)	1971-75	20	38	2	1215	118*	33.75	4	4
J Sandan (EP)	1974-82	28	49	1	1151	77	23.97	-	7
MG Majola (EP)	1977-90	30	52	5	1132	117	24.08	1	5
D Jacobs (EP)	1971-80	34	59	3	1105	84*	19.73	-	3
D Govindjee (EP)	1971-82	39	57	8	1101	57*	22.46	-	2
AL Barnes (Tvl)	1971-75	20	32	2	1062	111	35.40	4	2
A Rajah (Tvl)	1981-87	32	61	0	1045	83	17.13	-	2
N Fortune (WP)	1978-83	25	45	3	1023	143	24.35	1	6
I Behardien (WP)	1985-90	25	37	1	1013	142	28.13	2	3

BOWLING

SEVEN WICKETS OR MORE IN AN INNINGS

9-46	VA Barnes, WP v Ntl at Ladysmith	1983/84
9-57	N Edwards, Tvl v Ntl at Tongaat	1984/85
8-29	VA Barnes, WP v Ntl at Durban	1982/83
8-29	VA Barnes, Tvl v WP at Johannesburg	1985/86

8-35	M Rampersad, Ntl v Tvl at Johannesburg	1984/85
8-53	S Gabriels, WP v Ntl at Durban	1985/86
8-64	S Gabriels, WP v Ntl at Cape Town	1985/86
8-96	K Majola, EP v WP at Port Elizabeth	1984/85
7-17	AH Manack, WP v EP at Port Elizabeth	1989/90
7-19	VA Barnes, WP v EP at Cape Town	1982/83
7-29	S Chothia, Tvl v EP at Johannesburg	1971/72
7-31	D Jacobs, EP v Tvl at Port Elizabeth	1978/79
7-32	H Lorgat, Tvl v Ntl at Johannesburg	1988/89
7-35	R Magiet, WP v Tvl at Cape Town	1978/79
7-37	E Frans, EP v WP at Port Elizabeth	1980/81
7-38	A Jabaar, WP v Ntl at Cape Town	1981/82
7-40	A Jabaar, WP v EP at Cape Town	1983/84
7-41	JH Frans, EP v Ntl at Port Elizabeth	1978/79
7-41	E Frans, EP v Ntl at Durban	1980/81
7-41	VA Barnes, WP v EP at Cape Town	1986/87
7-44	G Johannesie, Tvl v EP at Port Elizabeth	1973/74
7-46	A Manack, Tvl v EP at Benoni	1981/82
7-47	A Snyman, EP v WP at Cape Town	1972/73
7-49	D Reid, EP v Ntl at Estcourt	1988/89
7-56	S Gabriels, Tvl v EP at Johannesburg	1979/80
7-56	S Gabriels, WP v Ntl at Cape Town	1983/84
7-57	T le Roux, Ntl v Tvl at Newcastle	1985/86
7-61	AH Manack, Tvl v WP at Johannesburg	1984/85
7-76	S Gabriels, Tvl v Ntl at Durban	1979/80
7-85	G Paul, EP v Tvl at Johannesburg	1990/91
7-92	M Rampersad, Ntl v Tvl at Johannesburg	1988/89
7-106	M Khan, Ntl v EP at Port Elizabeth	1980/81

TEN WICKETS OR MORE IN A MATCH

12-82	(3-36 and 9-46)	VA Barnes, WP v Ntl at Ladysmith	1983/84
12-83	(5-27 and 7-56)	S Gabriels, WP v Ntl at Cape Town	1983/84
12-99	(8-29 and 4-70)	VA Barnes, Tvl v WP at Johannesburg	1985/86
11-45	(6-9 and 5-36)	A Jabaar, WP v Ntl at Cape Town	1977/78
11-51	(6-27 and 5-24)	HWH Bergins, WP v Tvl at Johannesburg	1975/76
11-52	(8-29 and 3-23)	VA Barnes, WP v Ntl at Durban	1982/83
11-58	(4-18 and 7-40)	A Jabaar, WP v EP at Cape Town	1983/84
11-89	(4-48 and 7-41)	VA Barnes, WP v EP at Cape Town	1986/87
11-107	(6-46 and 5-61)	A Jabaar, Tvl v Ntl at Johannesburg	1990/91
11-112	(8-53 and 3-59)	S Gabriels, WP v Ntl at Durban	1985/86
11-115	(4-58 and 7-57)	T le Roux, Ntl v Tvl at Newcastle	1985/86
11-124	(6-70 and 5-54)	I Ebrahim, Ntl v WP at Cape Town	1974/75
11-137	(6-54 and 5-83)	AL Adams, WP v Ntl at Durban	1972/73
10-15	(4-8 and 6-7)	AL Adams, WP v EP at Cape Town	1979/80
10-33	(5-11 and 5-22)	VA Barnes, WP v Ntl at Cape Town	1988/89
10-34	(6-10 and 4-24)	D Govindjee, EP v Tvl at Port Elizabeth	1981/82
10-35	(6-22 and 4-13)	S Draai, EP v Tvl at Johannesburg	1979/80
10-41	(5-23 and 5-18)	S Draai, EP v Ntl at Tongaat	1983/84
10-56	(5-23 and 5-33)	R Magiet, WP v Tvl at Cape Town	1977/78
10-58	(1-1 and 9-57)	N Edwards, Tvl v Ntl at Tongaat	1984/85
10-64	(6-27 and 4-37)	S Gabriels, WP v Tvl at Johannesburg	1986/87
10-67	(4-8 and 6-59)	S Draai, EP v WP at Port Elizabeth	1982/83

10-68	(4-9 and 6-59)	S Gabriels, WP v Tvl at Cape Town	1981/82
10-78	(7-49 and 3-29)	D Reid, EP v Ntl at Estcourt	1988/89
10-80	(8-64 and 2-16)	S Gabriels, WP v Ntl at Cape Town	1985/86
10-89	(5-26 and 5-63)	N Ramnarain, Ntl v EP at Port Elizabeth	1986/87
10-93	(6-62 and 4-31)	M Khan, Ntl v Tvl at Durban	1981/82
10-97	(6-50 and 4-47)	AL Barnes, Tvl v EP at Johannesburg	1975/76
10-99	(6-44 and 4-55)	AL Barnes, Tvl v EP at Johannesburg	1974/75
10-105	(6-45 and 4-60)	R Galant, Tvl v EP at Port Elizabeth	1982/83
10-115	(4-50 and 6-65)	AH Manack, Tvl v Ntl at Johannesburg	1985/86

MOST WICKETS IN A SEASON

42 (Avg 10.14) VA Barnes (WP) 1986/87

BEST BOWLING AVERAGE IN A SEASON

17 wkts (Avg 5.06) D Govindjee (EP) 1981/82

LEADING WICKET TAKERS

	Career	M	Runs	Wkts	Avg	Best	5I	10M
VA Barnes (WP/Tvl)	1980-90	55	3099	277	11.18	9-46	21	5
S Gabriels (Tvl/WP)	1977-90	65	3661	245	14.94	8-53	17	5
M Khan (Ntl)	1971-88	74	4681	242	19.34	7-106	12	1
A Jabaar (WP/Tvl)	1974-90	55	3117	234	13.32	7-38	15	3
K Majola (EP)	1973-90	85	3517	214	16.43	8-96	11	-
S Draai (EP)	1973-86	48	2461	209	11.77	6-21	14	3
AH Manack (Tvl/WP)	1983-90	40	2875	197	14.59	7-17	12	1
H Lorgat (EP/Tvl)	1977-90	74	3201	186	17.20	7-32	10	-
S Magiet (WP)	1971-90	63	2115	175	12.08	6-24	7	-
JH Frans (EP)	1973-87	50	2084	133	15.66	7-41	3	-
AL Adams (WP)	1971-79	23	1579	115	13.73	6-7	8	2
D Govindjee (EP)	1971-82	39	2017	102	19.77	6-10	4	1

ALL-ROUND PLAY

CENTURY AND TEN WICKETS IN A MATCH

AL Barnes	107	6-50/4-47	Tvl v EP at Johannesburg	1975/76

CENTURY AND FIVE WICKETS IN AN INNINGS

AL Barnes (see above)				
A Manack	102*	5-29	Tvl v WP at Cape Town	1981/82
H Lorgat	121	5-57	EP v WP at Cape Town	1985/86

1000 RUNS AND 100 WICKETS IN A CAREER

	Runs	Avg	Wickets	Avg
K Majola (EP)	2735	(20.87)	214	(16.43)
M Khan (Ntl)	2269	(19.22)	242	(19.34)
S Gabriels (Tvl/WP)	2040	(21.25)	245	(14.94)
H Lorgat (EP/Tvl)	2717	(25.15)	186	(17.20)
S Magiet (WP)	2296	(26.69)	175	(12.08)
A Jabaar (WP/Tvl)	1611	(22.37)	234	(13.32)
D Govindjee (EP)	1101	(22.46)	102	(19.77)

WICKETKEEPING

MOST DISMISSALS IN AN INNINGS

7 (ct 4,st 3)	F Abrahams EP v Ntl at Durban	1986/87
7 (ct 6,st 1)	A Coetzee EP v Tvl at Port Elizabeth	1987/88
7 (ct 5,st 2)	N White WP v Ntl at Cape Town	1989/90

MOST DISMISSALS IN A MATCH

9 (ct 9)	F Abrahams EP v Ntl at Ladysmith	1975/76
9 (ct 8,st 1)	E Isaacs WP v Ntl at Ladysmith	1983/84
9 (ct 9)	F Abrahams EP v Tvl at Port Elizabeth	1986/87
9 (ct 7,st 2)	N White WP v Ntl at Cape Town	1986/87
9 (ct 6,st 3)	F Abrahams EP v Ntl at Durban	1986/87
9 (ct 6,st 3)	N White WP v Ntl at Cape Town	1989/90
9 (ct 9)	A Coetzee EP v Ntl at Port Elizabeth	1989/90

MOST DISMISSALS IN A SEASON

31 (ct 28,st 3)	F Abrahams (EP)	1986/87

MOST DISMISSALS IN THE COMPETITION

174 (ct 146,st 28)	F Abrahams (EP) in 58 matches	1973-86
156 (ct 117,st 39)	E Isaacs (WP) in 50 matches	1971-83
143 (ct 122,st 21)	Y Begg (Tvl) in 48 matches	1981-90

FIELDING

MOST CATCHES IN AN INNINGS

4	B Patel Tvl v Ntl at Johannesburg	1972/73
4	AL Barnes Tvl v WP at Cape Town	1975/76
4	R Musson Tvl v WP at Cape Town	1978/79
4	I Behardien WP v Tvl at Johannesburg	1989/90

MOST CATCHES IN A MATCH

6	J Govender Ntl v EP at Durban	1973/74
6	I Behardien WP v Tvl at Johannesburg	1989/90

MOST CATCHES IN A SEASON

12	S Magiet (WP)	1974/75
12	I Behardien (WP)	1987/88

MOST CATCHES IN THE COMPETITION

63	K Majola (EP) in 85 matches	1973-90
57	S Magiet (WP) in 63 matches	1971-90
50	J Govender (Ntl) in 41 matches	1971-80

MISCELLANEOUS

MOST APPEARANCES IN THE COMPETITION

85	K Majola (EP)	1973-90

MOST APPEARANCES FOR EACH PROVINCE IN THE COMPETITION

Eastern Province	85	K Majola	1973-90
Natal	74	M Khan	1971-88
Transvaal	48	N Edwards	1977-86
	48	Y Begg	1981-90
Western Province	63	S Magiet	1971-90

Note:

K Majola (EP) represented his province for 17 consecutive seasons.

S Magiet (WP) is the only player to have appeared in the first season (1971/1972) and in the last (1990/1991).

SACBOC/SACB CRICKET

TEAM PERFORMANCES

On the 18 occasions that the championship was contested, Western Province were winners 14 times, sharing the trophy once with Natal. Eastern Province won on 3 occasions while Transvaal and Natal were winners once each, Natal sharing the trophy with Western Province in their only success.

SUMMARY OF RESULTS FOR EACH PROVINCE

A total of 216 matches was played in the competition, each province playing 108 matches. A result was not achieved only on 3 occasions because of rain. There was 1 tie on the single innings and 1 on the double, both involving Western Province and Eastern Province.

	P	W	W1	T	T1	L	L1	NR
Western Province	108	65	11	1	1	18	12	-
Eastern Province	108	46	12	1	1	28	18	2
Transvaal	108	22	25	-	-	49	11	1
Natal	108	17	13	-	-	56	19	3

STATISTICAL HIGHLIGHTS 1971/72-1990/91

(other three-day matches, first-class)

CENTURIES

128	S Magiet, Rest of SACBOC v EP at Lenasia	1985/86
112	I Garda, Rest of SACBOC v WP at Stellenbosch	1975/76
106	I Garda, Rest of SACBOC v WP at Cape Town	1972/73
104	Y Omar, Rest of SACBOC v EP at Lenasia	1985/86
103*	Y Snyders, North v South at Lenasia	1972/73
101*	M Saleh, Rest of SACBOC v EP at Lenasia	1985/86
100*	BL D'Oliveira, Rest of SACBOC v WP at Cape Town	1972/73

CENTURY PARTNERSHIPS

6th	159	Y Thomas and S Magiet, Rest of SACBOC v EP at Lenasia	1985/86
2nd	104	I Garda and Y Omar, Rest of SACBOC v WP at Cape Town	1972/73

TEN WICKETS IN A MATCH

13-56 (6-33 and 7-23)	VA Barnes, SACB XI v President's XI at Cape Town	1987/88
10-67 (4-23 and 6-44)	AL Barnes, Rest of SACBOC v WP at Stellenbosch	1975/76

A NOTE ON THE COMPILATION OF THESE RECORDS

As far as career statistics for players are concerned, in certain cases complete accuracy could not be achieved, as full details of a few innings could not be traced. However, the variability factor is only between one and two per cent.

Editor's Note: Krish Reddy has completed the massive task of compiling individual career records of all those cricketers who played in SACBOC/SACB first-class matches between 1971/72 and 1990/91. These records will be thoroughly cross-checked and will be published in the 2002 Mutual & Federal SA Cricket Annual.

Section D: Other cricket

MTN NATIONAL CLUB CHAMPIONSHIP

John Young

The rise and rise of Easterns cricket continued at the 2000 MTN Club championships hosted by Northern Titans in September 2000. Coming off a fine performance by the Easterns senior team in reaching the semifinals of the Standard Bank Cup in 1999/2000, Boksburg CC emerged as the country's champion club by defeating the University of Cape Town in the final played at SuperSport Park.

Rain affected play in the early stages of the week but the tournament was well organised and produced some fine cricket. Boksburg's four-wicket victory was a typical team effort and extended their record of wins at the club champs to ten out of eleven games played over two seasons.

Andre Nel's three wickets helped restrict UCT to 179/9. Openers Derek Brand and Mark Conyers then swung the game Boksburg's way in dramatic fashion by smashing 43 runs off the first three overs. Captain Aldo van den Berg nailed down the advantage with a half-century from number three.

Brand had a great tournament with a century and three fifties, an average of 88 and a strike rate of 139.00. Andre Nel confirmed his status as a rising star to watch with consistently economical bowling.

For the losing finalists, John McClean performed well with the bat during the week with support from Bradley van Beuge and Neil Kruger. Neil Crawford and Alastair Murray took important wickets for UCT.

UCT lost one game during the week when Morne van Wyk led Free State University's successful run chase. Stellenbosch University came closest to beating the eventual winners. The students reduced Boksburg to 80/4 in reply to 207 but Van den Berg combined with Eita Mabhena to steer the East Rand team home.

RAU produced the batting performance of the week when they raced to 309/1 against Peshawars from the Free State. Andre Seymore led the way with 154 not out and Warren Dugmore scored 101.

The biggest match aggregate came in the university clash between Free State and Potchefstroom. Potch went past Free State's 45-over total of 261/7 in just 38.5 overs, with Arno Jacobs hitting an undefeated 112.

Yorkshire CC from Galashewe became the first township team to attend the championships as winners of the Griqualand West league. Although they didn't win a game, their appearance was significant for South African cricket. The achievement of former Board club United CC from East London in reaching the national finals was also noteworthy.

RESULTS

Sunday 20 September 2000

Section One:

Old Grey v Stellenbosch University - no game due to wet table.

RAU 178/5 in 20 overs (G Flint 71*, E Tsamaisi 2-18) beat Yorkshire 75/5 in 19 overs (Gehle 2-15).

Peshawars 112/7 in 24 overs (M Conyers 3-21) lost to Boksburg 115/0 in 15.1 overs (D Brand 79*).

Section Two:

UFS 261/6 in 40 overs (M van Wyk 80, H Wessels 81, C Deacon 41, L Gamiet 2-21) beat United 150/8 in 40 overs (F Plaatjes 52*, G Fourie 2-15).

Potchefstroom University 137/9 in 24 overs lost to UCT 138/5 in 22.4 overs (B van Beuge 34, J McClean 30, G Marais 3-25).
Berea Rovers 140/5 in 23 overs (A van Vuuren 53*, G Rowley 39, S Elworthy 2-17) beat CBCOB 130/8 in 23 overs (C Coetzee 30, G Scott 4-24).
Monday 21 September
Section One:
UFS 259/7 in 45 overs (A Volsteedt 113*, S Meyer 68, S Greyvenstein 3-40) beat Berea Rovers 168 in 41.1 overs (W Scott 86, H Botha 4-25).
CBCOB 137 in 41.3 overs (S Elworthy 59, A Murray 4-20) lost to UCT 138/4 in 35.3 overs (A Murray 47*, D. Townsend 3-39).
Potchefstroom University 223/6 in 45 overs (A Jacobs 78, G Outram 57, A Lawson 35*, K Bennett 2-32) beat United 76/9 in 29 overs (B Esterhuizen 14, T Enslin 3-20).
Section Two:
Yorkshire 113 in 35.2 overs (A Masuya 50, T Kruger 4-13) lost to Peshawars 114/3 in 26.3 overs (K Claassen 50*, T Blair 36*, B Sekonyane 2-13).
Old Grey 209/9 in 45 overs (W Field 45, C Giaconi 41, C Kruger 3-33) lost to Boksburg 210/3 in 30.5 overs (D Brand 122, W Field 2-52).
Stellenbosch University 196/6 in 45 overs (A Cyster 55, M Otto 2-21) beat RAU 169 in 45 overs (A Seymore 70, J Henderson 2-17).
Tuesday 22 September
Section One:
UCT 164 in 44.2 overs (N Kruger 57, HE Austen 5-25) lost to UFS 168/4 in 34.3 overs (M van Wyk 83*).
CBC 182 in 41.4 overs (D Smit 54, A Thomas 3-30) lost to Potchefstroom University 184/8 in 43 overs (A Lawson 58, D Townsend 4-50).
Berea Rovers 227 in 44.5 (G Rowley 114, T Ngxoweni 3-35) beat United 172/9 in 45 overs (D Brown 32, G Scott 2-20).
Section Two:
RAU 135 in 45 overs (T Vorster 47, D Brand 2-21) lost to Boksburg 136/5 in 22 overs (D Brand 50, I Kuiler 2-44).
Peshawars 217 in 44.2 overs (S Pargeter 94, G Puttergill 3-46) lost to Old Grey 218/4 in 35 overs (G Loan 84*, W Field 72, H Jordaan 2-41).
Yorkshire 93 in 40 overs (E Tsamaisi 33, A Pringle 3-10, G Myers 4-8) lost to Stellenbosch University 94/5 in 30 overs (G Myers 40, E Tsamaisi 4-18).
Wednesday 23 September
Section One:
FSU 261/7 in 45 overs (G Fourie 130, A Volsteedt 46, J Dreyer 3-26) lost to Potchefstroom University 262/3 in 38.5 overs (A Jacobs 112*, G Outram 73).
United 184/9 in 45 overs (L Gamiet 86, S Elworthy 4-17) lost to CBCOB 187/6 in 44 overs (A Smith 43).
Berea Rovers 153 in 42.3 overs (W Scott 49*, R Herd 4-20) lost to UCT 154/6 in 35 overs (J McClean 44, L Murray 2-26).
Section Two:
RAU 309/1 in 45 overs (A Seymore 154*, W Dugmore 101) beat Peshawars 190 in 36.2 overs (S Pargeter 51, W Dugmore 4-39).
Yorkshire 153/3 in 45 overs (M Bosman 63*) lost to Old Grey 154/1 in 21 overs (K Duckworth 83).
Stellenbosch University 188/9 in 45 overs (J Henderson 56, L Grayson 40*, M Conyers 3-38) lost to Boksburg 189/4 in 41.5 overs (A van den Berg 65*, T Blake 43, A Pringle 2-33).
Thursday 24 September
Section One:
FSU 219 in 44.2 overs (M van Wyk 45, H Wessels 42, A Volsteedt 41, C Coetzee 2-37) lost to CBCOB 221/6 in 30 overs (D Townsend 64, N Martin 60).
Berea Rovers 178/8 in 45 overs (W Scott 54, A Thomas 3-30) lost to Potchefstroom University 181/5 in 35 overs (A Lawson 33*, T Enslin 31*, R de Vry 3-32).
United 113 in 42.5 overs (A Crawford 5-21) lost to UCT 117/3 in 10.5 overs (B van Beuge 58, N Kruger 48, B Bennett 2-7).
Section Two:
RAU 176/6 in 45 overs (A Seymore 95, W Field 2-19) lost to Old Grey 177/2 in 26.4 overs (K Duckworth 104*).
Peshawars 227/5 in 45 overs (T Blair 49, T Kruger 40*, R van Wyk 39) lost to Stellenbosch 231/3 in 35.1 overs (A Cyster 120, J Henderson 72, Jordaan 2-63).
Boksburg 197/8 in 45 overs (D Brand 71) beat Yorkshire 101 in 40 overs (M Billy 32, T Blake 4-17).
Friday 25 September
Final:
UCT 179/9 in 45 overs (J McClean 65, A Nel 3-41, S Schaper 3-20) lost to Boksburg 180/6 in 36.1 overs (A van den Berg 52, J Lerm 45, J Schutte 3-33, R Herd 3-32).
Statistics supplied by Dalecia Ferreira.

S.A. COUNTRY CRICKET ASSOCIATION

PO Box 1281, Howick 3290. Tel (0332) 304968. Fax (0332) 305650.
President: Dennis Carlstein. Secretary: Terry Chadwick.

The 48th South African Country Cricket Association tournament was held in Pietersburg from 26 January to 2 February 2001. Fourteen teams, including one from Zimbabwe, participated.

The SA Country team selected at the end of the week to play against a Northern Titans Colts XI was: C Handley (EP Grahamstown, captain), K Forde (KZN, vice-captain), P Puren (KZN Mynahs), P van Vuuren (FS), A Pool (Boland), JP Michau (EP Midlands), JP Holder (EP Grahamstown), S Bosch (North West), B Ess (Boland), M Howarth (EP Grahamstown), K Storey (KZN). 12th man, R van Rooyen (Northerns).

SACD made 224-9 in their 50 overs, with Howarth scoring 70 not out, but the Northerns Colts team overtook this total with three wickets to spare. Van Vuuren took 3-36.

The final of the SACCA Competition was played between EP Midlands and EP Grahamstown.

Scores: **EP Midlands** 230 (JP Michau 69, G Flexanzec 39, C Handley 3-42). **EP Grahamstown** 210 (JP Holder 58, G Dixon 77). EP Midlands won by 20 runs.

PLASCON CRICKET ACADEMY

The following players were invited to attend the 2001 Plascon Cricket Academy in Johannesburg:

Jonathan Trott (Boland), Henry Davids (Boland), Justin Kreusch (Border), Dumisa Makalima (Border), Albie Morkel (Easterns), Umar Abrahams (EP), Johan Botha (EP), Dewald Senekal (EP), Johannes Mokoenanyane (Free State), Christoff Bothma (Free State), Jason Brooker (Griqualand West), Nicholas Mataboge (Gauteng), Rivash Gobind (KZN), Duncan Brown (KZN), Bongwa Hlongwane (KZN), Hashim Amla (KZN), Kruger van Wyk (Northerns), Johan Myburgh (Northerns), Burton de Wett (North West), Paul Harris (WP).
Director: Anton Ferreira
Coaches: Hylton Ackerman (head coach), Shukri Conrad, Raymond Booi.

WOMEN'S WORLD CUP 2000

Shan Cade

The Women's World Cup tournament was held in New Zealand in December 2000. The previous tournament was in India in 1997. Generally it is held once every four years but New Zealand and the International Women's Cricket Council wanted to use the millennium year as a selling point.

The next World Cup will be held in South Africa in February / March 2005 in the Western Province and Boland. Sponsorship is still to be found for the event.

The late Sir Conrad Hunte would have been proud of our ladies in the 2000 World Cup. As a tribute to him the players wore black armbands during their semifinal match against Australia.

Preparations for the tour started in earnest some 20 months earlier. A national squad was selected and getting the players to a suitable fitness level became a priority. Diets and strict fitness programmes were put in place.

A tour of England showed the need for even greater fitness and it was a tribute to the dedication of the players that they achieved the revised targets. The UCB organised two four-day camps. In total the squad had 14 training days together and a three-week tour to England before the World Cup. This was not sufficient to produce a World Cup winning team but showed the potential of the team should the correct support and sponsorship be obtained in the future.

The South African squad was: Kim Price (WP, captain), Cindy Eksteen (FS, vice-captain), Alison Hodgkinson (Nor), Kerri-Ann Laing (Gau), Linda Olivier (Gau), Sunnette Viljoen (NW), Levonia Lewis (WP), Nolubabalo Ndzundzu (Bor), Helen Davies (WP), Yulandi van der Merwe (Nor), Magdaleen Terblanche (Gau), Ally Kuylaars (WP), Denise Reid (WP), Anina Burger (Nor), Sune van Zyl (WP). Manager, Shan Cade; coach, Rodney Willemburg; physio: Marie van der Merwe.

Despite a spread of ages from 17 to 38, a good team spirit was established. The arrival in New Zealand was a refreshing change - the press and television people were there in abundance, to interview, to film and promote the tournament. We have had great difficulty in South Africa getting the media to take note of the women's game. The coverage by the New Zealand media was outstanding in all aspects during the tournament.

The team had eight days of preparation in Christchurch and beat a Canterbury XI in two warm-up matches at the Hagley Oval before moving to Lincoln University, where each team had a block of 24 individual rooms. As manager, I would go so far as to say that all the teams living in close proximity made it difficult for the ladies to stay focused - friendships had been formed on other tours and familiarity became a problem in keeping their eyes on the goal set ahead.

SOUTH AFRICA v INDIA

The first match South Africa played was against India at the Hagley Oval. The players were nervous and there was an awareness that South Africa lost to India in the quarterfinals in the previous World Cup. The same "pensive" mood that was on the bus seemed to carry over onto the field and the ladies never were able to rid themselves of it. We lost to India not due to our skills but due to the mind aspect.

SOUTH AFRICAN TEAM, WOMEN'S WORLD CUP 2000

Back, from left: Noor Rhode (assistant coach), Shan Cade (manager), Helen Davies, Linda Olivier, Levona Lewis, Hanri Strydom, Daleen Terblanche, Denise Reid, Anina Burger, Aluis Kuylaars, Marie van der Merwe (physiotherapist), Rodney Willemberg (coach). Front: Alison Hodgkinson, Yulandi van der Merwe, Cindy Eksteen (vice-captain), Kim Price (captain), Nolubabald Ndzundzu, Sune van Zyl, Sunette Viljoen

Hagley Oval, Christchurch, 30 November 2000. South Africa 128-9 in 50 overs (Y van der Merwe 42*, R Purnima 3-12). **India** 129-2 in 39.4 overs (R Mithali 69*). India won by 8 wickets.

SOUTH AFRICA v ENGLAND

The second match was also going to be a psychological battle. We had lost the series to England 3-2 in June but with this in mind the ladies were prepared to sink their teeth into the game and beat England once and for all. It was almost as if this was the most important match of the tournament. This match was played at the attractive BIL Oval at Lincoln University, a new ground prepared by the New Zealand Cricket Board, with the clubhouse only finished the night before the first game there.

It was a perfect setting for a game of cricket. South Africa beat England and much celebrating was done that evening by our ladies. Sunnette Viljoen, 17, won the player of the match award for a superb innings of 54 not out off 64 balls.

BIL Oval, Lincoln, 2 December 2000. England 143 in 47.5 overs (KM Leng 46, Y van der Merwe 3-25). **South Africa** 144-5 in 46.5 overs (M Terblanche 41, S Viljoen 54*). South Africa won by 5 wickets.

SOUTH AFRICA v HOLLAND

The third round robin match was against the Netherlands, again at Hagley Oval. Player of the match was Daleen Terblanche.

Hagley Oval, Christchurch, 4 December 2000. Holland 92 in 37.1 overs (LP Lewis 4-20). **South Africa** 93-6 in 26.2 overs (C Oudolf 3-31). South Africa won by 4 wickets.

SOUTH AFRICA v SRI LANKA

South Africa won for the third successive time, with Daleen Terblanche collecting her second player of the match award against the Sri Lankans at Lincoln Green at Lincoln University, a ground with not much room for spectators but again in a beautiful setting.

Lincoln Green, Lincoln, 8 December 2000. Sri Lanka 134-9 in 50 overs. **South Africa** 135-4 in 45.3 overs (M Terblanche 53*). South Africa won by 6 wickets.

SOUTH AFRICA v NEW ZEALAND

The fifth match was against New Zealand, played at Lincoln Green. The ladies awoke feeling quite tense - this was to be a very big game for them and a test of their skills and team spirit. We were beaten by a team with strong batsmen disciplined bowlers.

Lincoln Green, Lincoln, 11 December 2000. New Zealand 265-5 in 50 overs (RJ Rolls 44, EC Drumm 108*). **South Africa** 107 in 35.4 overs (CE Eksteen 47*, HM Watson 3-14). New Zealand won by 158 runs.

SOUTH AFRICA v AUSTRALIA

The South Africans were anxious about facing Cathryn Fitzpatrick, the fastest bowler in the tournament, but went on to make the highest total recorded against the tournament favourites up to that point. Australia raced to victory, however, with Karen Rolton making a rapid century.

sixth match was the nightmare the ladies had endured for days and months prior to the world cup - South Africa versus Australia, on the 13 December 2000 at the BIL Oval, the reigning champions. The fear of "the fast bowler Fitzpatrick" was very real to them and again the coach came back with the catch phrase - "we play the ball not the person". As it turned out we batted tremendously well against their "fast" bowling and up until the final match South Africa had scored the highest runs against Australia throughout the tournament. Australia won by 9 wickets.

BIL Oval, Lincoln, 13 December 2000. South Africa 169-8 in 50 overs (AA Burger 44, CE Eksteen 46, CL Mason 3-29. **Australia** 171-1 in 25 overs (BJ Clark 49*, KL Rolton 107*). Australia won by 9 wickets.

SOUTH AFRICA v IRELAND

South Africa needed a win in their seventh and final round robin match to make sure of a place in the semifinals. The players were confident in the bus, which is usually a good sign. They had never lost to Ireland and some of the players might have been guilty of thinking "it's in the bag". South Africa awoke with a bang. Ireland batted first and made 176 runs, the highest total yet against South Africa in the tournament. Fortunately for South Africa, Linda Olivier made a century and we scored the required runs with only one wicket down.

Hagley Oval, Christchurch, 16 December 2000. Ireland 176-9 in 50 overs (A Linehan 40, H Strydom 3-33, S Viljoen 3-27). **South Africa** 177-1 in 26.2 overs (L Olivier 101*, H Strydom 46). South Africa won by 9 wickets.

SOUTH AFRICA v AUSTRALIA (Semifinal)

Sponsors CricInfo put on a Christmas party for all the teams on 16 December, with the date chosen because teams that did not reach the semifinals were going home afterwards. It was a successful party and some players did not return until 2.30am, causing more stress for the management with the semifinal only one day's break away.

After losing horribly to them in the round robin the girls battled a little to get a grip on their "minds" but went in with a strong team spirit and a mindset of " let's take the game to them".

South Africa lost to Australia. Again our batting was good but the bowling was not tight enough to restrict Australia's strong batters. South Africa needs to develop bowlers with consistency in line and length.

First semifinal, BIL Oval, Lincoln, 18 December 2000. South Africa 180-8 in 50 overs (L Olivier 41, CL Mason 3-39). **Australia** 181-1 in 31.2 overs (BJ Clark 75, LM Keightley 91*). Australia won by 9 wickets.
Second semifinal, BIL Oval, Lincoln, 20 December 2000. India 117 in 45.2 overs (R Purnima 67*). **New Zealand** 121-1 in 26.5 overs (AM O'Leary 50*, EC Drumm 47*). New Zealand won by 9 wickets.
Final, BIL Oval, Lincoln, 23 December 2000. New Zealand 184-4 in 48.4 overs (KA Ramel 41, C Fitzpatrick 3-52). **Australia** 180 in 49.1 overs (BJ Clark 91). New Zealand won by 4 runs.

The World Cup 2000 tournament in New Zealand was a great success, well organised by New Zealand Cricket and CricInfo and well communicated to all role-players from staff, to players, to sponsors, to internet, to the media and the community. It was encouraging to the South African team to get e-mails of encouragement from people not known to any of the team.

The South African team reaching the semifinals must have a positive impact on the promotion and development of women's cricket in South Africa.

The official website run by CricInfo recorded 3.6 million page impressions with people logging on from more than 100 different countries to follow the action.

The way forward is to analyse the tour in detail, prepare the players for the next World Cup, selecting players who are team players, not only players with specific skills, structuring a comprehensive player profile sheet covering all Human Resource issues as well as skills and potential. We need to develop young players and nurture them to their full potential in readiness for national squad selection. We need to find sponsors and promote women's cricket by participation in a provincial league and by arranging incoming tours that will bring credit to the women's game.

SOUTH AFRICA: WOMEN'S WORLD CUP 2000 AVERAGES

Batting and Fielding

Name	Mat	I	NO	Runs	HS	Avg	SR	100	50	Ct	St
M Terblanche	8	8	3	200	53*	40.00	47.16	-	1	5	3
L Olivier	7	7	1	229	101*	38.16	49.03	1	-	-	-
Y van der Merwe	7	4	2	62	42*	31.00	70.45	-	-	1	-
CE Eksteen	7	6	1	117	47*	23.40	53.66	-	-	1	-
S Viljoen	8	7	1	128	54*	21.33	77.57	-	1	1	-
K Price	8	3	2	20	19*	20.00	44.44	-	-	-	-
AA Burger	6	4	0	75	44	18.75	55.97	-	-	2	-
H Strydom	5	5	0	92	46	18.40	47.91	-	-	2	-
DJ Reid	6	5	3	19	14*	9.50	65.51	-	-	1	-
HA Davies	5	4	0	36	24	9.00	30.76	-	-	2	-
SD van Zyl	6	1	0	9	9	9.00	45.00	-	-	-	-
A Hodgkinson	5	5	0	43	22	8.60	32.33	-	-	-	-
A Kuylaars	5	3	1	3	3*	1.50	18.75	-	-	-	-
N Ndzundzu	3	1	0	0	0	0.00	0.00	-	-	1	-
LP Lewis	2	0	-	-	-	-	-	-	-	-	-

Bowling

Name	Mat	O	M	Runs	Wkts	Avg	Best	4w	SR	Econ
N Ndzundzu	3	26	8	52	3	17.33	2-16	-	52.0	2.00
A Hodgkinson	5	17	1	45	1	45.00	1-18	-	102.0	2.64
LP Lewis	2	16.1	1	49	5	9.80	4-20	1	19.4	3.03
K Price	8	62	13	189	5	37.80	2-20	-	74.4	3.04
HA Davies	5	30.4	4	109	6	18.16	2-0	-	30.6	3.55
CE Eksteen	7	53	8	229	5	45.80	2-28	-	63.6	4.32
SD van Zyl	6	38.5	7	168	2	84.00	1-13	-	116.5	4.32
H Strydom	5	16.2	1	71	3	23.66	3-33	-	32.6	4.34
S Viljoen	8	15	2	66	3	22.00	3-27	-	30.0	4.40
Y van der Merwe	7	50	7	228	6	38.00	3-25	-	50.0	4.56
DJ Reid	6	6	0	41	0	-	-	-	-	6.83

WOMEN'S INTERPROVINCIAL

Northerns won the interprovincial tournament, hosted by Boland in the Paarl region during April 2001. Twelve teams competed in two sections, with Northerns and Gauteng the only two unbeaten teams before they met on the last day. Gauteng could score only 105-9 in their 50 overs and Northerns won on better run rate when rain stopped play with their total on 92-3 in 31 overs.

In a breakthrough for women's cricket, the same two teams had met at the Wanderers Stadium on February 11, with Northerns emerging as winners in that match as well. Carli Venter hit 81 in a Northerns total of 221-6, which was good enough for a 65-run win.

S.A. STUDENTS CRICKET

STANDARD BANK S.A. STUDENTS CRICKET WEEK

Stellenbosch University won the A Section by the narrowest of margins, edging Potchefstroom University by 0.57 in a run-rate countdown as no play was possible on the final day due to rain. Potchefstroom won the B Section in 1999. The tournament was hosted by the University of Pretoria from 4 to 8 December 2000.

The ten teams (nine universities and one technikon) were evenly matched, with five teams finishing with three wins and 12 points. Everything had to go right for Stellenbosch on the fourth and final pool day. Front-runners Potchefstroom and Pretoria had to lose and Stellenbosch had to win in double quick time even to have a chance of playing in the final. PE Tech beat Potchefstroom, UCT beat Pretoria and Stellenbosch chased down the 149-run target set by Maritzburg in just 22 overs, with Boland player Andrew Cyster to the fore.

Another provincial player to shine at the tournament was Eastern Province's Graham Grace, playing for PE Tech while his provincial teammate, Murray Creed, of UPE, was one of only two century-makers, the other being Gary Myers of Stellenbosch. All matches were played to a 50-overs format.

The best batsman award went to Pieter van Niekerk (Potchefstroom), who scored 211 runs, while Ryan Ten Doeschate (UCT) was best bowler with 12 wickets.

Log positions: 1 Stellenbosch, 2 Potchefstroom, 3 Cape Town, 4 Pretoria, 5 Free State, 6 Port Elizabeth, 7 Rand Afrikaans, 8 PE Technikon, 9 Rhodes, 10 Natal (Pietermaritzburg).

The following squad was selected from the A Section, although a representative match did not take place: A Cyster, M Holmes, G Myers (Stellenbosch), W Dugmore, T Vorster (RAU), T Essack (Natal, Pmb), B Friderichs, M Wilson (UPE),G Fourie (Free State), G Grace (PE Tech), F Lambrecht, P van Niekerk, E Wyma (Potchefstroom), C Parker, P van Rooyen (Pretoria), R Ten Doeschate (UCT).

SECTION A RESULTS

4 December

UPE 233-9 (Collett 55, Deacon 3-43). **Free State** 234-7 (Fourie 74, Kruger 82*). Free State won by 3 wickets.

Pretoria 139 (McDavid 3-18). **Rhodes** 110 (Van Zyl 3-13, Van Rooyen 3-20). Pretoria won by 29 runs.

RAU 218-7 (Vorster 54, Osman 3-46). **PE Tech** 160 (Grace 68, Oosthuizen 3-26). RAU won by 58 runs.

Stellenbosch 220-4 (Myers 101*). **UCT** 162. Stellenbosch won by 58 runs.

Potchefstroom 204-6 (Lambrecht 63). **Maritzburg** 157 (Essack 53, Wyma 6-21). Potchefstroom won by 47 runs.

5 December

Rhodes 27 (Schutte 4-7, Ten Doeschate 6-16). **UCT** 28-1. UCT won by 9 wickets.

Maritzburg 192-9. **Pretoria** 195-7 (Parker 72, Essack 4-23). Pretoria won by 3 wickets.

Free State 153 (Du Plessis 3-53). **Potchefstroom** 154-3 (Van Vuuren 62). Potchefstroom won by 7 wick ets.

RAU 232-4 (Dugmore 82, Williams 3-29). **UPE** 233-4 (Biggs 72, Roberts 57). UPE won by 6 wickets.

PE Tech 154 (Holmes 6-27). **Stellenbosch** 157-4. Stellenbosch won by 6 wickets.

6 December

Potchefstroom 254-6 (Van Niekerk 85, De Swardt 73). **UPE** 149 (Wyma 3-16). Potchefstroom won by 104 runs.

S.A. STUDENTS CRICKET

Free State 241-9 (Myer 53, Van Deventer 3-34). **PE Tech** 173-7 (Grace 51). Free State won by 68 runs.
Pretoria 207-6 (Parker 81). **Stellenbosch** 177 (Hector 57, Van Zyl 3/37). Pretoria won by 30 runs.
Rhodes 190-8 (Southey 54). **Maritzburg** 129 (McDavid 3-18). Rhodes won by 61 runs.
RAU 184-8 (Ten Doeschate 3-28). **UCT** 185-5 (Burger 78). UCT won by 5 wickets.
7 December
Maritzburg 148 (Manning 3-29). **Stellenbosch** 149-2 (Cyster 84*). Stellenbosch won by 8 wickets.
Pretoria 184-7 (Van Rooyen 92, Ten Doeschate 3-35). **UCT** 185-5 (McLean 71). UCT won by 2 wickets.
Potchefstroom 225-8 (Van Niekerk 79). **PE Tech** 226-5 (Funde 92, Grace 64). PE Tech won by 5 wickets.
RAU 210-5 (Horsten 57*). **Free State** 211-8 (Pargeter 51). Free State won by 2 wickets.
UPE 245-6 (Creed 100*). **Rhodes** 154 (Pienaar 3-31, Smith 3-22, Wilson 3-32). UPE won by 91 runs.

STANDARD BANK SASSU B CRICKET WEEK

Cape Technikon hosted a tournament from 4 to 8 December for the B and C Sections.
Final Placings:
B Section: 1 University of the Western Cape, 2 Cape Technikon,3 Free State Technikon, 4 Technikon Pretoria, 5 Wits University, 6 Vaal Technikon, 7 University of Fort Hare, 8 Peninsula Technikon.
C Section: 1 Wits Technikon, 2 Border Technikon, 3 ML Sultan Technikon, 4 Technikon Northern Gauteng, 5 Vista Port Elizabeth, 6 University Durban-Westville, 7 Medunsa.

A tournament team played against a WP invitation team at Newlands: S Hulley (capt), F de Wet (Pretoria Tech), D Makopanela, H van der Linde (FS Tech), D Lees, G Holmes (Cape Tech), S Sejamoholo (Wits Tech), F Jardine, E Solomons, J Albanie, L Flanigan (UWC). 12th man, H van der Bergh (Vaal Tech).

D SECTION

The D section was played concurrently with the A Section at the University of Pretoria. Only four teams contested this section after UNITRA withdrew the week before the tournament and East Cape Technikon failed to arrive, citing transport problems. Matches were played over 40 overs. Coaching was provided and the teams made full use of the extra net practice opportunities.

Final placings: 1 University of the North, 2 Mangosuthu Technikon, 3 University of Zululand, 4 Vista University (Bloemfontein). Best batsman: Wayne Louw (348 runs). Best bowler: M Mtshali (10 wickets).

The following tournament team was named: S Buthelezi, S Zondi, J Tidimane (Mangosuthu Technikon), W Louw, T Mxinyathi, G Trefz (University of Zululand), T Chuene, D Maboya, X Masomi, T Sello, K Semadi (University of the North).

STANDARD BANK SASSU COLLEGES' CRICKET WEEK

The Colleges tournament was played at Potchefstroom Teachers College from 4 to 8 December 2000. Rain washed out the final day when Normaal College Pretoria were due to play East London College in the final. The team selected from the tournament was: A Stander (capt), D Randall, J Collins (ELC), K van Zyl (DOK), R Krynauw, F van der Berg, R Oosthuisen (NKP), G Stander (POK), T Nqolo, O Gqamane (Bor), R George (WCC), C Lilford (JCE). Manager, Dr Carl Kirsten; Coach; David Gray.

SOUTH AFRICAN SCHOOLS 2000/01

Back, from left: J Vorster (scorer), C Barry (umpire), Craig Thysen, Lazola Dipha, Hashim Amla, Christo Karemaker, Stephen Cook, Ian Postman, I Logan (umpire), AD Dende (umpire), D Saunders (scorer). Front: Chad Baxter, James Schorn, Saait Magiet (manager), Johan Botha (captain), Morgan Pillay (organising secretary), Zwelibanzi Homani, Gerhard de Bruin, Jean-Paul Duminy.

COCA-COLA CRICKET WEEK

Gauteng won the 2000 Coca-Cola under 19 cricket week in Bloemfontein, beating the 1999 champions, Eastern Province, in the final. Of the 16 teams which participated, Gauteng were the only side to remain unbeaten through the week.

A fine innings of 84 off 131 balls by Stephen Cook, son of former Test player Jimmy, enabled Gauteng to make 220 for six. Eastern Province's batsmen, who had shone at the start of the week, struggled against tight bowling and the contest was effectively over when they slumped to 107 for seven. Gauteng won by 57 runs.

Hashim Amla was the leading batsman at the tournament, scoring 278 runs at an average of 92.66, while Johannes Wolmarans of North West, playing in the Gold division, was the leading wicket-taker with 12 at 11.17.

The tournament was hosted by Grey College, with the players accommodated at the college's hostels. Eight top-quality fields were available at the school and the nearby Free State University.

Test umpire Rudi Koertzen was the convenor of umpires and spent many hours, often working late into the night, with the young umpires who handled the matches. For the first time, the Duckworth-Lewis method was used to decide rain interrupted matches - and was needed in four of the eight matches on the first day.

A "unity audit" revealed that of the 188 players, 107 were white, 38 black African, 30 coloured and 13 of Asian descent.

Former national player Hugh Page was again convenor of selectors.

The South African Schools XI selected to play against the senior Free State team was: Johan Botha (Grey High, EP, captain), Hashim Amla (Durban High, KZN), Chad Baxter (St Andrew's, EP), Stephen Cook (King Edward VII, Gauteng), Gerhard de Bruin (Marais Viljoen, Gauteng), Lazola Dipha (Grey High, EP), Zwelabanzi Homani (Grey High, EP), Christo Karemaker (Centurion High, Gauteng North), Ian Postman (Selborne College, Border), James Schorn (Hilton College, KZN), Craig Thysen (Grey High, EP). 12th man, Jean-Paul Duminy (Plumstead High, USSASA U-17). Manager: Saait Magiet (WP).

The SA Colts XI which played against Zimbabwe was: Graeme Marais (St John's, Gauteng), AB de Villiers (Afrikaans Hoer, Gauteng North), Pieter Ferreira (Dr Malan Hoer, USSASA Country), William Hantam (Sarepta High, USSASA Country), Davey Jacobs (Klerksdorp High, NW), Imraan Khan (Durban High, KZN), Brent Kopps (St Thomas, EP), Donovan Lentz (Dale College, Border), Abner Letsie (Pretoria BHS, Gauteng North), Dominic Ridley (Bishops, WP), Sipho Sibande (Welkom High, FS), Johannes Wolmarans (Klerksdorp High, NW). Manager: Fabien Gregory (Border).

A South African under 19 team was selected to tour New Zealand. This team and a full report on the tour are published in a separate section.

RESULTS

Saturday 16 December

Platinum Group:

Easterns 195 (C Pretorius 47, A McFarlane 41, R Hugo 40, P Harold 3-31, C Karemaker 2-37). **Gauteng North** 197-6 (A Letsie 61*, A McFarlane 4-45, B Reddy 2-55). Gauteng North won by 4 wickets.

Free State 136 (S Sibande 48, C Birch 3-14, M Dipha 2-25, L Dipha 2-34). **Eastern Province** 137-5 (J Botha 36, D du Preez 2-22). Eastern Province won by 5 wickets.

KwaZulu-Natal 174 (H Amla 51, J Vorster 30, S Ervine 3-18, J Nicolle 2-27, B Rogers 2-31, S Masakadza 2-23). **Zimbabwe** 175- 7 (T Taibu 41, G Goosen 39, R Symcox 2-44, U Govender 2-20). Zimbabwe won by 3 wickets.

SOUTH AFRICAN COLTS 2000/01

Back, from left: J Kemp (umpire), Abner Letsie, Dominic Ridley, Brent Kopps, Pieter Ferreira, Johannes Wolmarans, Davey Jacobs, S Ndaba (umpire), J Grobbelaar (scorer), C Selesho (umpire), A Kock (scorer). Front: Sipho Sibande, AB de Villiers, Fabian Gregory (coach), Graeme Marais (captain), Morgan Pillay (organising secretary), Donovan Lentz (vice-captain), William Hantam, Imraan Khan

Gauteng 263-5 (S Cook 59, W Swan 48, J Geoghegan 46, A Nel 2-54). **Boland** 150 (J Kotze 57, G Grobbelaar 3-24, W Swan 2- 47). Gauteng won by 113 runs.
Border 206 (A Sodumo 62, R Kleinveld 6-35). **Western Province** 164-5 (D Ridley 89, D Lentz 3-50, R Schutte 2-33). Western Province won on faster scoring rate (D/L method).
Gold Group:
USSASA U-17 225-6 (J-P Duminy 78, R de Kock 55, J Wolmarans 3-22). **North West** 138-2 (D van Niekerk 53*, D Jacobs 31*). North West won by 8 wickets (D/L method).
USSASA Country 199 (P Ferreira 62, W Lamprecht 47, B Sekonyane 4-32, S Burger 2-23, C Pietersen 2-24). **Griqualand West** 107-4 (S Hayes 50, G Bhayat 2-15, R Steenkamp 2-23). USSASA Country won by 13 runs (D/L method).
KZN Mynahs 282-8 (D Perry 103, M Rosenberg 37, J Smith 2-52). **Northern Province** 202-8 (J Thomson 59, L Bischoff 33, B Reddy 2-11, B Hulley 2-28, K Nagan 2-54). KZN Mynahs won by 19 runs (D/L method).
Sunday 17 December
Platinum Group:
Eastern Province 304-6 (C Baxter 108, J Botha 81, C Thysen 39, A Gray 2-52). **Western Province** 135 (A Gray 35, J Botha 2-6, S McGillewie 2-19). Eastern Province won by 169 runs.
Easterns 200-9 (L Cronje 34, A McFarlane 34, L Makere 34*, R McLaren 2-38, D du Preez 2-21, B Joubert 2-21, A Motsamai 2-41). **Free State** 179 (B Joubert 46, A Strauss 30, L Cronje 4-26). Easterns won by 21 runs.
Gauteng 259-8 (S Cook 47, V van Jaarsveld 45, G Marais 36, G Daniels 3-43, F du Plessis 2-43). **Gauteng North** 234 (F du Plessis 63, A de Villiers 46, C Karemaker 32, G de Bruin 3-50, V van Jaarsveld 2-36). Gauteng won by 25 runs.
Boland 194 (J Kotze 63, H Gericke 34, R Symcox 2-28, J Anderson 2-33, T Harvey 2-14). **KwaZulu-Natal** 195/7 (H Amla 94*, T. Harvey 36, J Schorn 35). KwaZulu-Natal won by 3 wickets.
Zimbabwe 113 (A Durham 29, I Postman 3-21, M Zondeki 3-22). **Border** 114-4 (S Friedrichs 51, F Vermaak 25). Border won by 6 wickets.
Gold Group:
Northern Province 189 (F van den Bergh 58, J Smith 26*, J van der Linde 3-22, L Ndlovu 3-47, S Burger 2-25). **Griqualand West** 193-5 (G McLaren 63, S Burger 56*, D Steyn 3-32). Griqualand West won by 5 wickets.
USSASA Country 217-7 (W Lambrecht 57, DeW du Buson 27, W Hantam 26, J Wolmarans 2-27). **North West** 159 (D Jacobs 75, F van der Merwe 3-16, G Bhayat 2-43). USSASA Country won by 58 runs.
KZN Mynahs 284-4 (D Perry 60, B Martin 78, M Rosenberg 42, G Spilsbury 38*, W van Vuuren 36). **USSASA U-17** 244 (R de Kock 68, N Winspear 49, L Xhonga 37*, B Pietersen 3-56). KZN Mynahs won by 40 runs.
Monday 18 December
Platinum Group:
Gauteng 217 (G Marais 63, W Swan 27, R Breesies 3-49, B Joubert 2-36). **Free State** 189 (S Sibande 47, E Lekhanya 34, J Geoghegan 4-29). Gauteng won by 28 runs.
Boland 198-6 (S van der Merwe 49, J Koopman 47*, T van Wyk 37*, I Postman 3-29, G Young 2-29). **Border** 202-7 (F Vermaak 59, A Dyili 34, D Lentz 23*, T van Vuuren 2-31, J Mong 2-45). Border won by 3 wickets.
Easterns 218-9 (L Cronje 48, S Kola 38, B Reddy 37, C Thysen 4-34, S McGillewie 2-40). **Eastern Province** 219-1 (L Dipha 98*, C Baxter 52, H Keaton 44*). **Eastern Province** won by 9 wickets.
Western Province 252-9 (D Ridley 67, R Bailey 40, R Kleinveld 26, P Nel 26, A Durham 3-3, C McMillan 2-51, B Rogers 2-31, S Matsikenyire 2-38). **Zimbabwe** 253-6 (H Masakadza 113, S Ervine 39, T Duffin 29). Zimbabwe won by 4 wickets.
Gauteng North 310-7 (F Geldenhuys 100, A Letsie 41, J Coetzer 41*, AB de Villiers 37, J Anderson 3-59, M van Vuuren 2-49). **KwaZulu-Natal** 273-6 (H Amla 88, T Harvey 63, J Mokanyana 3-33, J Coetzer 3-51). Gauteng North won by 37 runs.
Gold Group:
KZN Mynahs 264-9 (R Reeves 80, B Martin 70, W van Vuuren 27, M Rosenberg 23, C Pietersen 4-41, S Burger 2-40). **Griqualand West** 202 (J van der Linde 63*, L Strydom 26, L Mokasana 3-34, J Mbili 3-45). KZN Mynahs won by 62 runs.
North West 167 (J Kgamadi 33, J Grobler 32, D Steyn 3-19, F van den Bergh 2-38, E Mbalaki 2-21). **Northern Province** 135 (F van den Bergh 32, W Viljoen 31, J Wolmarans 4-20, J Kgamadi 2-11). North West won by 32 runs.
USSASA Country 317-6 (W Hantam 102, P Ferreira 100, R Cilliers 51, L Xhongo 2-61). **USSASA U-17** 223 (D van Byleveldt 73, J-P Duminy 70, F van der Merwe 2-27, R Steenkamp 2-42). USSASA Country won by 94 runs.
Tuesday 19 December
Platinum Group:
Boland 87 (S Ervine 4-7, C McMillan 3-18). **Zimbabwe** 91-2 (H Masakadza 42*, T Taibu 24). Zimbabwe won by 8 wickets.
Western Province 191-7 (A Gray 58*, M Abbas 42, P Nel 27, R Symcox 3-41). **KwaZulu-Natal** 194-6 (J Schorn 49, J Vorster 24, T Harvey 24, R Bailey 3-30). KwaZulu-Natal won by 4 wickets.
Border 246 (A Sodumo 76, R Schutte 59, S Friedrichs 30, G Botha 2-22, S Motsamai 2-24, R McLaren 2-39). **Free State** 225 (G. Botha 63, R McLaren 57, S Sibande 47, D Lentz 4-42, I Postman 3-44). Border won by 21 runs.
Eastern Province 231 (C Thysen 57, Z Homani 39, C Birch 35*, C Karemaker 4-54, A Roodtman 2-33). **Gauteng North** 232-5 (AB de Villiers 105, A Letsie 50, F Geldenhuys 32, B Kopps 3-47). Gauteng North won by 5 wickets.
Gauteng 263 (J Geoghegan 74, S Letshela 70, S Cook 29, A McFarlane 2-34). **Easterns** 203 (R Hugo 44, B Smith 35, C Pretorius 24, E Nkwe 2-30, W Swan 2-31, G de Bruin 2-39). Gauteng won by 60 runs.

Gold Group:
Griqualand West 147 (G McLaren 51, J Van der Linde 30, J Wolmarans 2-23, G Rautenbach 2-23). **North West** 151-5 (D Jacobs 66*, D Steyn 34, J van der Linde 2-26). North West won by 5 wickets.
KZN Mynahs 206 (B Hulley 42, D Perry 33, R Reddy 30, B Moses 28, W Hantam 3-20, G Bhayat 2-33). **USSASA Country** 210-9 (P Ferreira 82, S Arries 27, M Rosenberg 3-45, B Hulley 3-31). USSASA Country won by 1 wicket.
Northern Province 159 (G Helm 33, D Steyn 28, F van den Bergh 23, R de Kock 4-52, L Xhongo 2-29) .**USSASA U-17** 160-3 (J-P Duminy 69, R de Kock 22). USSASA U-17 won by 7 wickets.
Wednesday 20 December
Platinum Group:
First place match: Gauteng 220-6 (S Cook 84, W Swan 39, G Marais 22, S McGillewie 3-44, J Botha 2-37). **Eastern Province** 163 (S McGillewie 30, G Anderson 27, C Birch 23, V van Jaarsveld 3-18, G de Bruin 2-14). Gauteng won by 57 runs.
Third place match: Gauteng North 258 (J Mokanyana 45, C Karemaker 40*, AB de Villiers 42, F du Plessis 39, G Lotriet 30, G Young 2-24). **Border** 233 (F Vermaak 46*, R Schutte 40, S Friedrichs 35, A Dyili 33, J Coetzer 2-32). Gauteng North won by 25 runs.
Fifth place match: Zimbabwe 194 (B Rogers 70, A Stone 27, H Masakadza 21, G Goosen 20, C McMillan 20, F Lazarus 3-42, I Khan 3-25). **KwaZulu-Natal** 197-1 (J Schorn 79*, I Khan 48, H Amla 32*). KwaZulu-Natal won by 9 wickets.
Seventh place match: Western Province 247 (D Frew 120, M Abbas 39, P Nel 28, N Grobler 3-35, A Swart 2-47). **Easterns** 157 (B Smith 51, A Swart 35, A Gray 3-32, R Bailey 3-32, G Magoda 2-44). Western Province won by 90 runs.
Ninth place match: Boland 212 (S van der Merwe 67, I Cornelissen 63, R. McLaren 3-39, G Motsamai 3-36, D du Preez 2-34). **Free State** 213-8 (E Lekhanya 62, D du Preez 61, G Miltiadgu 30, H Gericke 3-26). Free State won by 2 wickets.
Gold Group:
KZN Mynahs 232-7 (M Rosenberg 46, D Perry 43, B Martin 32, B Hulley 30*, D Jacobs 3-52, J Grobler 2-38). **North West** 227 (D Jacobs 88, M Osman 38, D Steyn 32, R Reeves 3-46, J Mbili 3-47). KZN Mynahs won by 6 runs.
USSASA U-17 266 (J-P Duminy 85, E Springer 59, D van Byleveldt 52, G McLaren 4-57). **Griqualand West** 206 (G McLaren 55, M Bosman 49, A Doherty 20, L Xhongo 2-29, J Rossouw 2-29). USSASA U-17 won by 60 runs.
USSASA Country 258 (J Rheeder 68, S Arries 57, P Ferreira 31, D Steyn 3-58, J Smith 3-56, F van den Bergh 2-34). **Northern Province** 174 (J Smith 41, D Steyn 38, W Viljoen 29, C Neuhoff 24, G Bhayat 3-43, C Crotz 2-11, P van der Merwe 2-37). USSASA Country won by 84 runs.
Final placings: 1 USSASA Country, 2 KZN Mynahs, 3 North West, 4 USSASA U-17, 5 Griqualand West, 6 Northern Province.

FREE STATE v SOUTH AFRICAN SCHOOLS — Limited Overs Match

Played at Goodyear Park, Bloemfontein on 21 December 2000 — Toss: SA Schools
Umpires: C Barry & I Logan
Result: Free State won by 36 runs

Botha's decision to send Free State in seemed set to pay off until Pretorius played a remarkable attacking innings. Schorn batted impressively for the schoolboys but the rest of the batting was disappointing.

FREE STATE	*Runs*	*Mins*	*Balls*	*4*	*6*
MD Mokopanele c Homani b de Bruin	5	12	14	1	-
AI Gait c Dipha b Botha	24	71	39	4	-
WJ Smit c Baxter b Karemaker	6	26	16	1	-
MN van Wyk c Homani b Karemaker	3	10	5	-	-
JA Beukes b Thyssen	41	108	80	3	-
JJ van der Wath lbw b Postman	27	57	50	4	-
C Deacon b Thyssen	12	24	24	-	-
*†GL Brophy c Dipha b Karemaker	31	55	32	2	-
MR Lewis c Homani b Botha	6	8	8	1	-
D Pretorius run out (Karemaker)	50	35	29	5	1
AP Abrahams not out	1	9	6	-	-
Extras (lb 4, w 10, nb 3)	17				
TOTAL (50 overs)	**223**				

SOUTH AFRICAN SCHOOLS	*Runs*	*Mins*	*Balls*	*4*	*6*
SC Cook b Pretorius	3	14	10	-	-
JR Schorn c van Wyk b Deacon	45	68	44	10	-
HM Amla c van der Wath b Deacon	9	17	9	2	-
C Baxter lbw b Lewis	14	27	18	1	1
*J Botha b Pretorius	11	34	24	2	-
L Dipha lbw b Deacon	19	74	53	1	-
C Thysen c Brophy b Abrahams	4	19	16	-	-
†Z Homani run out (Brophy)	0	1	0	-	-
I Postman not out	27	67	56	1	-
G de Bruin st Brophy b Abrahams	3	5	7	-	-
C Karemaker lbw b van Wyk	34	30	26	3	2
Extras (lb 6, w 10, nb 2)	18				
TOTAL (43.3 overs)	**187**				

SAS	*O*	*M*	*R*	*W*
de Bruin	5	0	23	1
Karemaker	10	0	31	3
Botha	9	2	40	2
Thyssen	9	0	44	2
Postman	10	0	39	1
Dipha	7	0	42	0

FS	*O*	*M*	*R*	*W*
van der Wath	6	1	21	0
Pretorius	10	0	38	2
Deacon	10	0	51	3
Lewis	6	0	28	1
Abrahams	8	0	36	2
van Wyk	3.3	0	7	1

Fall of Wickets	*FS*	*SAS*
1st	8 (1)	12 (1)
2nd	21 (3)	43 (3)
3rd	34 (4)	63 (4)
4th	48 (2)	78 (2)
5th	107 (6)	99 (5)
6th	133 (7)	106 (7)
7th	134 (5)	106 (8)
8th	145 (9)	131 (6)
9th	214 (10)	135 (10)
10th	223 (8)	187 (11)

S.A. SCHOOLS XI AND SOUTH AFRICA UNDER-19 CAPS

Note: The names of those who obtained caps before the formation of the United Cricket Board in 1991 are omitted unless they are of special interest. The full list of all players capped until 1976 appeared in the 1977 Annual and all those capped between 1977 and 1998 appeared in the 1999 Annual.

+ International honours * Other first-class cricket

(E) Overseas tour, (C) Captain, (T) Twelfth man, (S) Capped, but did not play, (R) Capped, not in original 12, but played on tour or against England U-19 in 1997. Two Nuffield Weeks were held in 1970 and 1976, in January and December. They are differentiated by the suffixes (J) and (D).

The team selected at the end of the 1994 and 1995 Coca-Cola Weeks was open to all players under 19. The team selected at the end of the 1995 Week was a South African Schools team with eligibility restricted to those boys still at school. From 1996 onwards, selection was again restricted to boys under 18 on 1 January of that year. Players selected for subsequent Under-19 representative tours and matches have been listed separately.

*Abrahams U (Grey PE)	Eastern Province	1998-99
*Ackerman HM (Dale)	Border	1962-63-63(E)-64- 65(C)-66(C)
*Amla HM (Durban)	KwaZulu-Natal	2000
+*Armitage RLS (St Andrew's G'tn)	Eastern Province	1974
+*Arnott KJ (Prince Edward)	Rhodesia	1977-78(T)
+*Bacher A (King Edward)	Transvaal	1959-60
+*Barlow EJ (Pretoria)	NE Transvaal	1958
+*Barnard LJ (King Edward)	Transvaal	1974(C)-75(C)
Baxter C (St Andrew's G'tn)	Eastern Province	2000
* Benfield MR (St Stithian's)	Transvaal	1993-94(T)
+*Benkenstein DM (Michaelhouse)	Natal	1992(C)
*Biggs AL (Union HS Graaff-Reinet)	Eastern Province	1963-63(E)-64-65
+*Bland KC (Milton)	Rhodesia	1956-57
*Bodi GH (Lenasia)	Gauteng	1997
+*Boje N (Grey Bfn)	Orange Free State	1989(T)-90-91(C)
*Botha AG (Maritzburg)	Natal	1995
*Botha J (Grey PE)	Eastern Province	1999-00(C)
Bothma C (Grey Bfn)	Free State	1999
+*Botten JT (Pretoria)	NE Transvaal	1956-57
+*Boucher MV (Selborne)	Border	1994
*Bradfield CC (Kingswood)	Eastern Province	1993
*Brink MM (Brackenfell)	Boland	1993
+*Burger CG de V (Michaelhouse)	Natal	1953-54
+*Callaghan DJ (Grey PE)	Eastern Province	1983-83(E)
+*Carlstein PR (St Andrew's Bfn)	Orange Free State	1956-57-58(C)
Chree K (Grey PE)	Eastern Province	1992
+*Commins JB (Rondebosch)	Western Province	1982
*Conrad S (Groenvlei)	Western Province	1983(E)-84
*Cook SC (King Edward)	Gauteng	2000
*Creed MW (Grey PE)	Eastern Province	1997
*Cronje FJC (Grey Bfn)	Orange Free State	1985
+*Cronje WJ (Grey Bfn)	Orange Free State	1986-87(C)
+*Crookes DN (Hilton)	Natal	1988(C)
+*Cullinan DJ (Queens)	Border	1983-83(E)-84(C)
*Cullinan RE (Queens)	Border	1983-83(E)
*Dakin GF (Grey PE)	Eastern Province	1954
De Bruin G (Marais Viljoen)	Gauteng	2000
*De Bruin QE (Durban)	Natal	1993
*De Bruyn Z (Randburg)	Transvaal	1994

*De Lange CdeW (Worcester Gym)	Boland	1999
*De Nobrega JJ (Bishops)	Western Province	1996
*De Vos DJJ (Potchefstroom Gym)	W Transvaal	1992-93
Dipha L (Grey PE)	Eastern Province	2000
+*Dippenaar HH (Grey Bfn)	Orange Free State	1995(T)
+*Donald AA (Hoer Tegniese)	Orange Free State	1984(T)-85
*Dros G (St Alban's)	N Transvaal	1992
+*Dumbrill R (Durban)	Natal	1957
Duminy J-P (Plumstead)	USSASA U-17	2000(T)
*Du Plessis M (Grey Bfn)	Orange Free State	1967
*Du Toit JD (Paul Roos)	Western Province	1976(J)-76(D)-77
*Du Toit WJ (Paul Roos)	Boland	1998
*Ehrke JA (St John's)	Transvaal	1991
+*Eksteen CE (Northcliff)	Transvaal	1984
*Elliott GD (St Stithian's)	Gauteng	1997
*Emslie PAN (Graeme)	Eastern Province	1986(C)
*English CV (Kimberley)	Griqualand West	1992
*Featherstone NG (King Edward)	Transvaal	1966-67-67(E)-68
+*Fotheringham HR (Michaelhouse)	Natal	1970(J)(T)-70(D)
*Gain DR (Hilton)	Natal	1995(C)
+*Gamsy D (Durban)	Natal	1958(T)
+*Gibbs HH (Bishops)	Western Province	1991-92
*Gilder GM (Northwood)	Natal	1992
Gobind R (Effingham)	KwaZulu-Natal	1999
+*Goddard TL (Durban)	Natal	1949
+*Greig AW (Queens)	Border	1965-66
+*Greig IA (Queens)	Border	1975
+*Griffin GM (Durban)	Natal	1958
Groom R (Kearsney)	Natal	1995
+*Halse CG (Maritzburg)	Natal	1953
Hauptfleisch W (Glenwood)	KwaZulu-Natal	1998
+*Hayward M (Daniel Pienaar)	Eastern Province	1995
*Hearle PK (St Stithian's)	Transvaal	1996(C)
*Henderson CW (Worcester)	Boland	1990
+*Hobson DL (Kingswood)	Eastern Province	1970(D)
Homani Z (Grey PE)	Eastern Province	1999-00
*Horan BP (Grey PE)	Eastern Province	1992
*Hughes BK (Durban)	Natal	1994
+*Innes GAS (Bishops)	Western Province	1949(T)-50(C)-51(C)
+*Ironside DEJ (Parktown)	Transvaal	1942
+*Irvine BL (Durban)	Natal	1963(C)
Jantjes C (CBC Boksburg)	Easterns	1996
+*Jefferies ST (Plumstead)	Western Province	1978
+*Jennings RV (King Edward)	Transvaal	1970(D)-72-73
+*Johnson NC (Kingswood)	Eastern Province	1988
*Johnston MO (Jeppe)	Transvaal	1988-89
Jones GD (Hilton)	Natal	1994
*Joubert P (Eldoraigne)	N Transvaal	1995-96
+*Kallis JH (Wynberg)	Western Province	1993
Karemaker C (Centurion)	Gauteng North	2000
*Kent JC (Durban)	KwaZulu-Natal	1997
*Kerr KJ (Sandown)	Transvaal	1977-78-79
+*Kirsten G (Rondebosch)	Western Province	1985(C)

S.A. SCHOOLS XI AND SOUTH AFRICA UNDER-19 CAPS

+*Kirsten PN (SACS)	Western Province	1973(T)-74
+*Koen LJ (Paarl Gym)	Boland	1985
*Koenig SG (Hilton)	Natal	1991
+*Kourie AJ (Jeppe)	Transvaal	1970(J)
*Kruis GJ (St Alban's)	N Transvaal	1993
+*Kuiper AP (Bishops)	Western Province	1977(C)
*Laing DR (Jeppe)	Transvaal	1987-88
+*Lamb AJ (Wynberg)	Western Province	1973
+*Lance HR (CBC Pretoria)	NE Transvaal	1958
+*Liebenberg GFJ (Diamantveld)	Griqualand West	1989-90
*Lindsay-Smith DR (King Edward)	Transvaal	1963(E)-64-66
*Lumb MJ (St Stithian's)	Gauteng	1997
*Macdonald RH (Rondebosch)	Western Province	1983(E)
MacKay DD (Maritzburg)	Natal	1993
*Madsen MB (Glenwood)	Natal	1967(E)-69(C)
+*Madsen TR (Glenwood)	Natal	1975
Maier RJ (Kloof)	Natal	1991
+*Markham LA (Glenwood)	Natal	1942
*Masikazana L (Chapman)	Eastern Province	1991-92
+*McEwan KS (Queens)	Border	1970(J)-70(D)(C)
+*McGlew DJ (Maritzburg)	Natal	1948(C)
+*McKenzie KA (King Edward)	Transvaal	1967
+*McKenzie ND (King Edward)	Transvaal	1993-94(C)
*McLoughlin PR (Hamilton)	Rhodesia	1967-67(E)-68
Mfobo M (SACS)	Western Province	1991
*Michau JP (Cradock)	SA Country	1995
*Miller GK (Grey PE)	Eastern Province	1991
*Morgan G (Grey PE)	Eastern Province	1989
*Morkel JA (Vereeniging)	Gauteng	1998
Morkel M (Vereeniging)	Transvaal	1995-96
*Morris RET (Rondebosch)	Western Province	1963(E)-64(T)-65
+*Mpitsang PV (Grey Bfn)	Free State	1997(T)
*Mullins AK (Crestway)	Western Province	1998
*Munnik R (Tygerberg)	Western Province	1996
*Muzzell PJ (Queens)	Border	1956-57(C)
*Muzzell RK (Queens)	Border	1963
*Myburgh JG (Pretoria)	Northerns	1997
*Nackerdien MS (Paulus Joubert)	Boland	1983-83(E)
+*Ngam M (Douglas)	Eastern Province	1997(R)
Ngxoweni T (Selborne)	Border	1994-95-96
Nkomo AN (Wynberg)	Western Province	1997-98
+*Ntini M (Dale)	Border	1995
*Omar AM (Topaz)	Transvaal	1994
*Orchard DL (Maritzburg)	Natal	1967-67(E)-68
+*Ovenstone DM (Bishops)	Western Province	1940(C)
*Peterson RJ (Alexander Road)	Eastern Province	1996(T)-97
+*Pienaar RF (St Stithian's)	Transvaal	1978(C)
+*Pithey AJ (Plumtree)	Rhodesia	1951-52-53
+*Pithey DB (Plumtree)	Rhodesia	1954
*Pollock GA (King Edward)	Transvaal	1991
+*Pollock PM (Grey PE)	Eastern Province	1959
+*Pollock RG (Grey PE)	Eastern Province	1960-61(C)
+*Pollock SM (Northwood)	Natal	1991

S.A. SCHOOLS XI AND SOUTH AFRICA UNDER-19 CAPS

Postman I (Selborne)	Border	2000
*Pothas N (King Edward)	Transvaal	1990(R)
*Pretorius NW (Wessel Maree)	Orange Free State	1986-87-88
+*Pringle MW (Kingswood)	Eastern Province	1983-84
+*Procter MJ (Hilton)	Natal	1963-63(E)-64
*Procter WC (St Andrew's G'tn)	Eastern Province	1940
*Puttick AG (Rondebosch)	Western Province	1998(T)
+*Radford NV (Athlone)	Transvaal	1976(J)
*Reece-Edwards HM (Northlands)	Natal	1978-79
*Rhodes CB (Maritzburg)	Natal	1989
+*Rhodes JN (Maritzburg)	Natal	1986-87
+*Richards BA (Durban)	Natal	1962-63-63(EC)-64(C)
*Rosendorff N (CBC Bloemfontein)	Orange Free State	1962(T)-63(T)-63(E)-64
*Rudolph JA (Afrikaans Seuns)	Northerns	1997-98-99(C)
+*Rundle DB (St Stithian's)	Transvaal	1982-83-83(E)
+*Rushmere MW (Woodridge)	Eastern Province	1982(C)-83(C)-83(EC)
*Schorn JR (Hilton)	KwaZulu-Natal	1999-00
+*Schultz BN (Kingswood)	Eastern Province	1989
+*Seeff L (Herzlia)	Western Province	1976(D)
*Senekal DM (Daniel Pienaar)	Eastern Province	1999
*September J (Kingswood)	Eastern Province	1994
*Seymore AJ (HF Verwoerd)	N Transvaal	1992-93
*Shaw GB (Kingswood)	Eastern Province	1992
Sierra R (St John's)	Transvaal	1996
+*Smith CL (Northlands)	Natal	1976(J)
*Smith GC (King Edward)	Gauteng	1998-99
+*Smith RA (Northlands)	Natal	1979-80
+*Snell RP (Durban)	Natal	1986(S)-87
+*Stewart ELR (Westville)	Natal	1987
*Stigant BG (Grey PE)	Eastern Province	1993
*Still QR (Selborne)	Border	1992
*Street MR (St John's)	Transvaal	1995-96
+*Strydom PC (Grey PE)	Eastern Province	1987
*Sugden CB (Michaelhouse)	Natal	1992
*Tayfield A (Durban)	Natal	1947-48-49
*Tayfield C (Durban)	Natal	1949-50-51
*Tayfield IR (Durban)	Natal	1967(E)-68
+*Terbrugge DJ (St Stithian's)	Transvaal	1993-94
Thysen C (Grey PE)	Eastern Province	2000
*Trott IJL (Rondebosch)	Western Province	1998-99
*Tsolekile TL (Pinelands)	Western Province	1998(C)
(Abbot's College)	Western Province	1999(C)(S)
*Tucker BH (St John's)	Gauteng	1997 (C)
*Van Aswegen IG (Hentie Cilliers)	Orange Free State	1994
*Van den Berg AM (Jan Viljoen)	Transvaal	1996
*Van der Wath JJ (Ermelo)	Easterns	1996
*Van Heerden CJ (Hentie Cilliers)	Orange Free State	1980
*Van Noordwyk C (Kearsney)	Natal	1989
+*Van Ryneveld CB (Bishops)	Western Province	1946(C)
*Van Wyk MN (Grey Bfn)	Free State	1997
Van Wyk R (Afrikaans Seuns)	Northerns	1997(R)
*Venter JF (Grey Bfn)	Orange Free State	1988

S.A. SCHOOLS XI AND SOUTH AFRICA UNDER-19 CAPS

*Vermeulen VBN (St Stithian's)	Transvaal	1989
(Jeppe)	Transvaal	1990-91
*Volsteedt AK (Grey Bfn)	Orange Free State	1993(C)
*Vorster CJ (Paarl Gym)	Boland	1994
+*Waite JHB (Hilton)	Natal	1948
+*Watkins JC (Glenwood)	Natal	1940-41-42(C)
*Watson DJ (Maritzburg)	Natal	1991
*Watson GLG (Potchefstroom)	Transvaal	1963(E)
+*Watson WK (Dale)	Border	1975
+*Wesley C (Durban)	Natal	1956
+*Wessels KC (Grey Bfn)	Orange Free State	1973-75-76(J)(C)
*White BM (King Edward)	Transvaal	1988
+*Whitfield BJ (Beachwood)	Natal	1976(D)
*Whyte RJD (St Andrew's G'tn)	Eastern Province	1975-76(J)-76(D)
Williams M (Grey PE)	Eastern Province	1998
*Wilmot AL (Graeme)	Eastern Province	1959-60-61
*Wingfield WR (Durban)	Natal	1995
+*Winslow PL (King Edward)	Transvaal	1947-48

SOUTH AFRICA UNDER-19 CAPS

South African Under-19 teams toured England in 1995, India in 1995/96, Pakistan in 1998/99, played in the 1999/2000 Under 19 World Cup in Sri Lanka and toured New Zealand in 2000/01. Schools of the selected players are listed although in several cases the players had left school when they represented South Africa Under-19.

*Abrahams AP (Highlands North)	Free State	1999(WC)
*Abrahams U (Grey PE)	Eastern Province	1998(P)-99(WC)
*Adam SM (Durban)	KwaZulu-Natal	1998(P)
*Amla AM (Tongaat)	KwaZulu-Natal	1998(P)
*Amla, HM (Durban)	KwaZulu-Natal	2000(NZ)
Baxter C (St Andrew's G'tn)	Eastern Province	2000(NZ)
*Benfield MR (St Stithian's)	Transvaal	1995(I)
*Bodi GH (Lenasia)	Gauteng	1997
*Botha AG (Maritzburg)	Natal	1995(I)
*Botha J (Grey PE)	Eastern Province	1999(WC)-2000(NZ)
+*Boucher MV (Selborne)	Border	1995(E)-95(I)
Clark BW (Wynberg)	Western Province	1995(E)
*Cook SC (King Edward)	Gauteng	2000(NZ)
Cowley DJ (Maritzburg)	Natal	1995(I)
*Creed MW (Grey PE)	Eastern Province	1997
De Bruin G (Marais Viljoen)	Gauteng	2000(NZ)
*De Lange CdeW (Worcester Gym)	Boland	1998(P)
*De Nobrega JJ (Bishops)	Western Province	1997
+*Dippenaar HH (Grey Bfn)	Orange Free State	1995(E)-95(I)
*Du Toit WJ (Paul Roos)	Boland	1998(P)
*Elliott GD (St Stithian's)	Transvaal	1996-97
*Gain DR (Hilton)	Natal	1995(I) (C)
*Gait AI (Kearsney)	KwaZulu-Natal	1997
*Gamiet LL (Selborne)	Border	1996
Gobind R (Effingham)	KwaZulu-Natal	1999(WC)-2000(NZ)(C)
Hauptfleisch W (Glenwood)	KwaZulu-Natal	2000(NZ)
+*Hayward M (Daniel Pienaar)	Eastern Province	1995(I)
*Hearle PK (St Stithian's)	Transvaal	1996(C)

S.A. SCHOOLS XI AND SOUTH AFRICA UNDER-19 CAPS

*Henry D (Wynberg)	Western Province	1997
*Hofmeyr S (Wynberg)	Western Province	1996
Homani Z (Grey PE)	Eastern Province	1999(WC)-2000(NZ)
*Hughes BK (Durban)	Natal	1995(E)
Jantjes C (CBC Boksburg)	Easterns	1996
*Joubert P (Eldoraigne)	N Transvaal	1995(E)-95(I)-96
Karemaker C (Centurion)	Gauteng North	2000(NZ)
+*Kemp JM (Queens)	Border	1995(I)
*Kent JC (Durban)	KwaZulu-Natal	1997
Khan I (Durban)	KwaZulu-Natal	2000(NZ)
*Lumb MJ (St Stithian's)	Gauteng	1997
*MacQueen RB (Durban)	KwaZulu-Natal	1996
*Makalima DL (Dale)	Border	1999(WC)
*Masimula WB (Eastbank)	Transvaal	1995(E)
+*McKenzie ND (King Edward)	Transvaal	1995(E) (C)
*Mitchell I (Queens)	Border	1996
*Moleon EO (Garlandale)	Western Province	1995(I)
*Morkel JA (Vereeniging)	Gauteng	1999(WC)
Morkel M (Vereeniging)	Transvaal	1995(E)
+*Mpitsang PV (Grey Bfn)	Free State	1996-97
*Munnik R (Tygerberg)	Western Province	1996
*Myburgh JG (Pretoria)	Northerns	1997-98(P)-99(WC)
Ngxoweni T (Selborne)	Border	1995(E)-95 (I)
Nkomo AN (Wynberg)	Western Province	1997-98(P)
+*Ntini M (Dale)	Border	1995(E)-95 (I)
*Omar AM (Topaz)	Transvaal	1995(E)
+*Ontong JL (Paarl Gym)	Boland	1998(P)
*Peterson RJ (Alexander Road)	Eastern Province	1996-97
Postman I (Selborne)	Border	2000(NZ)
Price M (St Andrew's G'tn)	Eastern Province	2000(NZ)
*Prince AG (St Thomas)	Eastern Province	1995(E)-95 (I)
*Puttick AG (Rondebosch)	Western Province	1997-98(P)-99(WC)
*Rudolph JA (Afrikaans Seuns)	Northerns	1997-98(P)-99(WC)
Samsodien W (Montrose CC)	Western Province	1997
*Schorn JR (Hilton)	KwaZulu-Natal	2000(NZ)
*Senekal DM (Daniel Pienaar)	Eastern Province	1999(WC)
*September J (Kingswood)	Eastern Province	1995(E)
*Smith GC (King Edward)	Gauteng	1998(P)-99(WC)
*Stigant BG (Grey PE)	Eastern Province	1995(E)
*Street MR (St John's)	Transvaal	1996-97(C)
+*Terbrugge DJ (St Stithian's)	Transvaal	1995(E)
Thysen C (Grey PE)	Eastern Province	2000(NZ)
*Trott IJL (Rondebosch)	Western Province	1998(P)-99(WC)
Tsamaisi E (St Boniface)	Griqualand West	1998(P)
*Tsolekile TL (Pinelands, Abbot's College)	Western Province	1998(P)(C)-99(WC)(C)
*Van der Wath JJ (Ermelo)	Easterns	1996
*Van Olst M (Grey PE)	Eastern Province	1995(I)
*Van Wyk MN (Grey Bfn)	Free State	1997
*Vorster CJ (Paarl Gym)	Boland	1995(E)
Williams M (Grey PE)	Eastern Province	1998(P)
*Wingfield WR (Durban)	Natal	1995(I)-96
*Zondeki M (Dale)	Border	2000(NZ)
*Zondi LE (Glenwood)	Natal	1995(E)

PG BISON UNDER 15 CRICKET WEEK

The PG Bison Under 15 Week was held in Port Elizabeth from 11 to 15 December 2000. Teams that played cricket of a high standard throughout the tournament included Boland, Border, Eastern Province, North Gauteng and Western Province.

Most of the matches in a well-organised Week were played on good pitches, while the behaviour of the players was generally good, although there were a number of instances of appeals for lbw from square leg and fine leg, and of showing unhappiness with umpires' decisions.

The transformation target of players of colour making up 45 percent of the participants was not quite met. Of the 176 players, 62 percent were white, 22.8 percent black African, 10.2 percent coloured and 4.5 percent Asian.

RESULTS

Monday 11 December

SA Country 146 (J O'Kelly 42, D Smit 44, R Jephtha 4-17). **Boland** 151-6 (W Mouton 57, M Hugo 43).
Border 137 (S Makongola 30, Z Mtyupu 43, Z Abdullah 3-23). **Western Province** 143-7 (W Murray 31*).
Free State 119 (D Munro 34, S Oosthuizen 3-23). **North West** 95 (D van Wyk 4-17, D Munro 3-11).
KwaZulu-Natal 121 (E Randal 4-12). **Griqualand West** 123-3 (L Crowie 48).
North Gauteng 146-7 (J Kotze 53). **Eastern Province** 138-6 (C Ingram 46, B Nelson 42*).
Easterns 208-6 (J Booysen 47, C Pinker 71). **Zimbabwe** N/A (B Grootboom 3-9, L Moolman 3-27).
Gauteng 109 (C van Williegh 3-11). **Northern Province** 85 (B Pelser 3-21).

Tuesday 12 December

Free State 169 (D van Wyk 54). **Boland** 170-7 (P Bergh 45, W Mouton 37*, D van Wyk 4-33).
Zimbabwe N/A (S de Kock 3-10). **Border** 154-8 (B Kennedy 42).
Western Province 150 (M Holmes 41, S Nkosana 4-21, M Klopper 3-22). **Eastern Province** 152-9 (R Esau 55*)
KwaZulu-Natal 131 (R Diack 37*, L Brink 3-27, C Ponela 3-18). **North Gauteng** 132-2 (I Naidoo 67*, J Kotze 46*).
Griqualand West 109-5 (F Holtzhausen 56*). **North West** 104-9.
Easterns 196-8 (J Booysen 62, J Coetzer 41, B Pelser 3-32, D Joubert 3-36). **Gauteng** 112 (M van der Berg 42, B Grootboom 4-19, J Booysen 3-20).
Northern Province 40 (D Smit 5-18). **SA Country** 41-5.

Wednesday 13 December

Gauteng 155 (M van der Berg 39, B Snijman 41). **Boland** 154 (M Mouton 37*, J Carstens 52, W Bezuidenhout 3-18).
Griqualand West 145-9 (M Walters 3-26). **Border** 146-0 (S Makongola 78*, Z Mtyupu 64*).
Free State 171-8 (W van der Sckyff 57*, M Maritz 3-22). **North Gauteng** 174-6 (I Naidoo 56, J Kotze 51, H Klopper 5-37).
Western Province 186-8 (R Jappie 53). **Easterns** 142 (C Pinker 36, A Mouton 4-26, Z Abdullah 3-13).
North West 156-9 (A Huisamen 39, J Lobley 34*). **KwaZulu-Natal** 133 (R Hillerman 32, D Joubert 4-28).
SA Country 174 (J O'Kelly 34, S Nkosana 4-44). **Eastern Province** 145 (C Ingram 38).
Zimbabwe N/A (S du Toit 4-36). **Northern Province** 162-5 (S du Toit 52*).

Thursday 14 December

Griqualand West 170-7 (F Holtzhausen 41, L Crowie 36, W Bruintjies 3-36). **Boland** 171-7 (W Mouton 34, A Botha 50, C Solomons 31).
Border 186-8 (M Walters 82*). **North Gauteng** 172-9 (W van Wyk 37, J du Toit 4-25).
Zimbabwe N/A (H Klopper 3-22). **Free State** 148-5 (D van Wyk 59, D Schabort 37).
Western Province 172-7 (Z Abdullah 51, V Philander 30, R Jappie 46*). **Gauteng** 173-6 (B Snijman 75, R da Camara 50).
KwaZulu-Natal 124 (R Diack 34, S du Toit 4-36). **Northern Province** 128-4 (D Enslin 54).
Eastern Province 219-5 (C Ingram 76, M Siwana 55, S Fensham 32*). **Easterns** 176-8 (J Booysen 36, M Klopper 3-24, W Bell 3-26).
North West 149 (Q Kruger 48, J O'Kelly 4-15). **SA Country** 105.

Friday 15 December

Eastern Province 138-8 (M Siwana 37, M Hugo 3-10). **Boland** 139-6 (P Bergh 33, J Carstens 40, B Nelson 3-33).
Border 173-9 (Z Mtyupu 31, W Bezuidenhout 3-28). **Gauteng** 86.
Western Province N/A (S Stevens 4-18). **Free State** N/A
KwaZulu-Natal 167 (T Stedman 34). **Zimbabwe** N/A (D Cameron 3-40).
North Gauteng 232-6 (I Naidoo 86, J Kotze 42, L Brink 41*). **Griqualand West** 161-9 (F Holtzhausen 31, S Keet 48).
SA Country 142 (A Snyman 3-22). **Easterns** 145-3 (J Booysen 51*, A Snyman 31).
North West 146-4 (Q Kruger 34, J Mostert 34*). **Northern Province** 51 (J Campher 4-16, J Mostert 3-5).

STANDARD BANK UNDER 13 WEEK

The USSASA Standard Bank Under 13 Week was held in East London from 8 to 12 December 2000.

RESULTS

Friday 8 December

Gauteng 172-5 (L Suping 46, M Jurgenson 30). **North West** 106 (N Bredenkamp 53, R van den Berg 3-15).
Easterns 110 (F le Clus 45, M Tile 3-17). **Border** 111-3 (M Tile 36*).
KwaZulu-Natal 214-5 (K Abbott 116*). **Zimbabwe** 93 (P Mommsen 5-23).
Eastern Province 107 (P Furstenburg 33, E Olivier 4-11, T Rankolo 4-30). **Free State** 108-2 (M Matseo 38).
Northerns 126-8 (G Abrahams 4-13, P Daneel 3-25). **Boland** 130-8 (P Daneel 39, W Kotze 3-19).
Western Province 226-6 (J Hodges 74, R Leni 50, C Kieswetter 39, L de Jager 30, C van Wyk 3-45). **Griqualand West** 196-8 (A Boonzaaier 55, J de Kock 34).
South Western Districts 143 (I Prinsloo 62, H Snyman 5-44). **Northern Province** 132 (A Jones 34, I Prinsloo 7-20).

Saturday 9 December

Easterns 170-8 (F le Clus 46, S Venter 33). **Boland** 171-9 (P Daneel 55, K Pritchard 31, T Bronkhorst 4-31, L Arendse 3-30).
Gauteng 72 (O Mkuto 4-8, T Main 3-16). **Western Province** 76-6 (A Tsatsi 3-15).
Eastern Province 168-6 (P Furstenburg 39, A Majola 38, V Wheeler 3-38). **KwaZulu-Natal** 168 (K Abbott 61).
Northern Province 122 (M Botha 34, M Tile 3-17). **Border** 123-3 (C Alers 41*).
Northerns 114 (T Rankholo 3-23, G Niewoudt 3-21). **Free State** 115-8 (E Zorgman 4-35).
North West 176 (E Hack 63, N Mwayenga 3-21). **Zimbabwe** 177-8 (M Marabini 49, K Samunderu 34, N Bredenkamp 3-34, K van Rensburg 3-41).
South Western Districts 141. **Griqualand West** 143-7 (J de Kock 43).

Sunday 10 December

Griqualand West 158-9. **Easterns** 154 (F Cilliers 3-41).
Eastern Province 198-9 (J Heathcote 41, A Majola 31, R Dullabh 6-27). **Gauteng** 113 (P van Tonder 3-29, J Heathcote 4-23).
Boland 165 (I Carstens 37*, E Linder 30, K Abbott 3-16). KwaZulu-Natal 142 (K Abbott 47, W Jacobs 4-22, P Daneel 4-19).
Western Province 201 (S van Zyl 63, J Bijl 41, H Bezuidenhout 3-19). **Northern Province** 198-9 (T Sekola 64).
Free State 158-7 (D Elgar 33, M Odendaal 31). **Border** 160-8 (R Cramp 36, M Tile 32, C Alers 31, F Matroos 3-11).
Zimbabwe 113 (T Thema 7-27). **Northerns** 114-4 (C Bruwer 37).
South Western Districts 126-8 (M Serame 3-24). **North West** 110 (W Erasmus 37, A Carelse 3-21, M Botha 3-18).

Monday 11 December

Free State 227-9 (J Greyling 102, J van Wyk 3-40). **Easterns** 97 (E Olivier 3-11).
Gauteng 166-9 (R van der Berg 49, S Masondo 37, N Mahonga 3-27, R Ramoo 3-25). **Border** 169-2 (C Raffan 55*, R Cramp 41).
KwaZulu-Natal 232-4 (K Nelson-Esch 58*, S Mabuya 51*, K Abbott 33, C Nhlapo 32). **South Western Districts** 92 (G Randles 3-20).
Northerns 169-9 (K Bruwer 62, T Thema 30, J Bijl 5-40). **Western Province** 81 (R Levi 45, E Zorgman 5-24, G Rudolf 3-17).
Griqualand West 201-7 (A Boonzaaier 62, J de Kock 51*, R Kamberami 3-18). **Zimbabwe** 113 (I Gous 3-18).
North West 164-8 (W Erasmus 72, E Hack 43, W Daniels 3-25). **Eastern Province** 165-6.
Northern Province 86 (H Snyman 34, W Jacobs 3-15). **Boland** 87-1 (P Daneel 33, D Malan 30).

Tuesday 12 December

Eastern Province 214-6 (P van Tonder 53*, K Bennet 44). **Easterns** 204-7 (F le Clus 81, Z Makima 52).
Boland 96 (P du Plessis 39, R Ramoo 3-29, N Mahonga 3-16). **Border** 100-3.
South Western Districts 165-9 (M Botha 43*, L Mosena 3-26). **Free State** 168-3 (D Elgar 77*).
Western Province 233-4 (R Levi 114*, C Kieswetter 50). **KwaZulu-Natal** 236-5 (P Mommsen 45, M Mbatha 40, S Mabuya 39, K Abbott 38).
Zimbabwe 208-7 (R Kamberami 52, R Benade 49, M Marabini 43*, S le Roux 3-46). **Gauteng** 210-3 (W Liebenberg 82, X van der Westhuizen 51*).
North West 153 (N Bredenkamp 60, E Zorgman 4-16). **Northerns** 154-4 (K Bruwer 39*, T Thema 30).
Griqualand West 138-8 (A Boonzaaier 40, T Sebola 3-23). **Northern Province** 139-9 (M Botha 50).

SOUTH AFRICAN UMPIRES 2000/01

UMPIRES WHO STOOD IN FIRST-CLASS MATCHES (59), LIMITED OVERS INTERNATIONALS (12) AND STANDARD BANK CUP MATCHES (63) IN 2000/01

	Test	SS	Other FC	Total FC	LOI	SB
BORDER						
IL Howell	1	8	2	11	2	7
CM Schoof	-	4	1	5	-	8
EASTERN PROVINCE						
M Gajjar	-	5	1	6	-	4
BG Jerling	-	7	-	7	2	9
RE Koertzen	2	2	-	4	7	9
EASTERNS						
KH Hurter	-	7	1	8	-	12
GAUTENG						
DF Becker	-	8	-	8	2	8
ST Jivan	-	6	1	7	-	6
SB Lambson	-	5	1	6	2	10
CJ Mitchley	-	8	-	8	-	13
S Wadvalla	-	5	-	5	-	7
GRIQUALAND WEST						
AE Williams	-	7	1	8	-	2
KWAZULU-NATAL						
DL Orchard	3	4	1	8	6	5
RB Shah	-	-	-	-	-	1
NORTHERNS						
JD Cloete	-	7	-	7	-	12
NORTH WEST						
AG O'Connor	-	5	1	6	-	7
WESTERN PROVINCE						
WA Diedricks	-	4	2	6	3	6
INTERNATIONAL						
AV Jayaprakash (Ind)	1	-	-	1	-	-
EA Nicholls	1	-	-	1	-	-
Riazuddin (Pak)	1	-	-	1	-	-
ID Robinson (Zim)	1	-	-	1	-	-
G Sharp (Eng)	1	-	-	1	-	-
EA Watkin (NZ)	-	2	-	2	-	-
P Willey (Eng)	1	-	-	1	-	-
Totals	12	94	12	118	24	126

UMPIRES WHO'S WHO 2000/01

All details as at 31 May 2001.

BECKER Danzel Frank (Danny) (Gau). B 21/1/48 Pretoria. Ed Robert Hicks, Clapham HS (Pta). FC debut TvlB v Zim Brd (Jhb) 1993/94. LOIs: 15 (1996/97-2000/01). 65 FC matches. 72 DLO matches. Played for NE Tvl (1968-1970), Tvl/TvlB (1971-1974). 35 FC matches, 770 runs (avg 18. 78), HS 57 TvlB v Bdr (EL) 1972/73, 18 cts, 112 wkts (avg 23.10), BB 6-23 NET v SAU (Pta) 1970/71. Also played for Defence, Iscor, Pirates, Zoo Lake. RHB RM. Held world badminton endurance record of 77 hours.

CLOETE Johannes Daniel (Nor) B 21/7/71 Klerksdorp. Ed Stilfontein High, Potch Univ. FC debut WT v GW (Potch) 1993/94. 21 FC matches. 28 DLO matches. Rugby (Craven Week U-13 1984), Athletics (WT 1988), Indoor Hockey (Potch Univ 1991-1993).

DIEDRICKS Wilfred Andrew (WP). B 6/3/45 Cape Town. Ed Harold Cressy HS. FC debut EPB v NtlB (PE) 1991/92. Tests: 1 (1992/93). LOIs: 30 (1992/93-2000/01). 81 FC matches. 72 DLO matches. Played for Parow CC, Universals CC, Bharat CC. Umpired Howa Bowl matches for 15 years from 1974/75.

GAJJAR Mookesh (Mike) (EP). B 16/8/58 Uitenhage. Ed Uitenhage High School. FC debut EPB v WT (PE) 1993/94. 21 FC matches. 10 DLO matches. Played for Walmer CC, EP Senior Schools 1976 (SACOS).

HOWELL Ian Lester (Bdr). B 20/5/58 Port Elizabeth. Ed Grey HS (PE), UPE. Son of EJ Howell (Hon Sec SACUA 1962-1969), Nephew of HC Howell (WP 1949-1954), twin brother of DH Howell (EP/EPB/WPB/Tvl/TvlB/Bdr 1976-1991). FC debut Eas v KZNB (Ben) 1998/99. Tests: 1 (2000/01). LOIs: 4 (1999/00-2000/01). 23 FC matches. Umpired in 2 FC matches in NZ 1999/00. 20 DLO matches. Played for EPB (1981-1983), EP (1982/83), Bdr (1984-1997). 119 FC matches, 3767 runs (avg 26.90), HS 115* Bdr v EP (PE) 1991/92, 69 cts, 243 wkts (avg 35.74), BB 6-38 Bdr v Ntl (EL) 1991/92. LHB LM. Hockey (EP 1979-1981, SAU 1980-1981).

HURTER Karl Heinrich (Eas). B 12/2/64 Port Elizabeth. Ed Pearson. FC debut Eas v WPB (Ben) 1997/98. 19 FC matches. 21 DLO matches.

JERLING Brian George (EP). B 13/8/58 Port Elizabeth. Ed PE Tech HS. FC debut Bol v SADF (Wdk) 1988/89. LOIs: 2 (2000/01). 72 FC matches. Umpired in 1 FC match in NZ 2000/01. 76 DLO matches. Played for SADF EP Command (1978-1981), SADF Rundu Sector (1982-1986).

JIVAN Satish Thakor (Gau). B 21/6/54 Johannesburg. Ed Roodepoort HS. FC debut NorB v NW (Cent) 1998/99. 13 FC matches. 10 DLO matches. Played for Bharats, Hinds, Aryans, Oxfords and Spurs (1965-1991), SA Country Districts (1996). Soccer (Real Madrid, Mohawks, Bharats, Ipswich Town 1964-1990, Remains of Africa 1991-1999).

KOERTZEN Rudolf Eric (Rudi) (EP). B 26/3/49 Knysna. Ed Despatch HS, PE Technical College. FC debut GW v WPB (Kby) 1981/82. Tests: 25 (1992/93-2000/01). LOIs: 69 (1992/93-2000/01). 124 FC matches. 143 DLO matches. Played for Despatch CC (1970-1975), De Beers CC (1976-1981). Soccer (NFL for Drostdy Park 1967-1970), Golf (7 handicap, Uitenhage Golf Club). On international umpires panel.

LAMBSON Simon Barry (Gau). B 28/8/58 Johannesburg. Ed St Albans College, Wits Univ. FC debut TvlB v GW (Jhb) 1985/86. Tests: 5 (1992/93-1994/95). LOIs: 34 (1992/93-2000/01). 107 FC matches. 151 DLO matches. Played for Kroonstad Defence.

MITCHLEY Cyril John (Gau). B 4/7/38 Johannesburg. Ed Troyeville HS. Father of CD Mitchley (Tvl/TvlB/NT/ET 1982-1991), MJ Mitchley (Tvl/TvlB/NT/Eas 1986-1998) and SE Mitchley (ET 1991/92). FC debut TvlB v NTB (Jhb) 1981/82. Tests: 26 (1992/93-1999/00). LOIs: 61 (1992/93-1999/00). 127 FC matches. 145 DLO matches. Played for TvlB (1967-1968). 8 FC matches, 224 runs (avg 20.36), HS 66 TvlB v Rhod (Sby) 1967/68, 20 ct and 9 st. Also played for Kensington Poly CC, Southern Suburbs CC. RHB WK.

O'CONNOR Andrew George (NW). B 20/9/47 Johannesburg. Ed The Hill HS. Father of SP O'Connor (Eas 1997-1998). FC debut NW v EPB (Potch) 1996/97. 10 FC matches. 7 DLO matches. Played for Southern Suburbs (1962-1970). Soccer (STvl U18 1967).

ORCHARD David Lynton (KZN). B 24/6/48 Pietermaritzburg. Ed Maritzburg College. Son of KR Orchard (Ntl 1946-1948), father of J Orchard (FSB 1995/96), nephew of EA Orchard (Ntl 1947/48). FC debut NtlB v WPB (Pmb) 1991/92. Tests: 23 (1995/96-2000/01). LOIs: 70 (1994/95-2000/01). 87 FC matches. 69 DLO matches. Played for Ntl/NtlB (1967-1978). 43 FC matches, 1634 runs (avg 24.38), HS 110* NtlB v TvlB (Dbn) 1978/79, 21 cts, 47 wkts (avg 29.02), BB 7-90 Ntl v EP (PE) 1970/71. Ntl Schools 1966-68, SA Schools 1967-67(E)-68. Also played for Old Collegians CC and Rawtenstall CC (Lancs League). LHB RM. On International umpires panel.

SCHOOF Craig Michael (Bdr). B 13/8/65 East London. Ed Selborne College, PE Tech. Son of DD Schoof (first-class umpire), nephew of OR Schoof (first-class umpire). FC debut GauXI v Eng A (Jhb) 1998/99. 13 FC matches. 15 DLO matches. Played for Bohemian CC (1989-1994). Golf (10 Handicap), Go-karting (1992-1997).

SOUTH AFRICAN UMPIRES 2000/01

SHAH Ramesh Buddree (KZN). B 3/6/46 Durban. Ed Sastri College, Springfield College, ML Sultan Technikon, Dbn/Westville Univ. FC debut NTB v TvlB (Vbg) 1991/92. 18 FC matches. 21 DLO matches. Played for David Landu, Overport Youth, Crimson CC. SACB Umpire from 1975/76.

WADVALLA Shahid (Gau). B 25/7/49 Zeerust. FC debut NT v Tvl (Pta) 1992/93. 44 FC matches. Umpired in 2 FC matches in NZ 1998/99. 40 DLO matches. 6 Howa Bowl games. Played for Ntl, Tvl (SACB), Jhb Protea, Crescents.

WILLIAMS Abraham Edward (Abe) (GW). B 8/3/45 Kimberley. Ed William Pescod HS. FC debut GWB v WPB (Kby) 1998/99. 17 FC matches. 6 DLO matches. Played for Universals CC (1958-1978), Pirates CC (1979-1980), Diamond Park CC (1981-1992), GWCU (1970-1985), SACCA (1967). Rugby (Universal & GW Rugby Union 1960-1980).

TEST UMPIRES IN SOUTH AFRICA 1888/89-2000/01

	Period	Series	Tests		Period	Series	Tests
Adams HV (WP)	1921-27	2	2	*Leaney J (England)	1891	1	1
Allsop G (Tvl)	1895	1	1	Liebenberg KE (Ntl) (b)	1992-95	4	5
Anderson WP (Tvl)	1961	1	2	+Mahboob Shah (Pakistan)	1993	1	1
Ashman RGA (Tvl)	1935-49	4	14	Malan BV (Ntl)	1949-56	3	6
Atfield AJ (Tvl)	1909-13	2	8	Marais W (Ntl)	1956-57	2	5
Baxter LM (Tvl)	1964-66	2	4	McCabe AN (Ntl)	1953	1	1
Beves G (Tvl)	1895	1	1	McMenamin JH (Tvl)	1956-57	2	4
Birkett A (Tvl)	1957	1	2	*Miller AM (England)	1895	1	2
+Bucknor SA (West Indies)	1992-99	3	5	Mitchley CJ (Gau) (b)	1992-99	10	13
Coetzee CMP (EP)	1969	1	3	+Nicholls EA (West Indies)	2000	1	1
Collings JC (WP)	1930-35	2	9	Orchard DL (KZN) (b)	1995-00	9	13
Collins DV (WP)	1948-61	6	10	Page ES (EP)	1927	1	1
Collins S (WP)	1953	1	1	Parry G (Tvl)	1961	1	2
+Cooray BC (Sri Lanka)	1999	1	1	Payne FRW (EP)	1953	1	1
Coote CD (N Tvl)	1953	1	1	*Phillips J (England)	1905	1	5
Costello VJ (WP)	1956-64	3	6	+Randell SG (Australia)	1995	1	1
+Cowie DB (New Zealand)	1999	1	1	Reid J (Tvl)	1922	1	1
Creese WH (Tvl)	1902	1	1	+Riazuddin (Pakistan)	2000	1	1
Deare CR (EP)	1888	1	1	+Robinson ID (Zimbabwe)	1994-00	2	2
Diedricks WA (Ntl)	1992	1	1	Routledge WG (Tvl)	1935	1	2
Draper JG (Ntl)	1964-69	3	5	Ryan WT	1930	1	2
Drew DT (Ntl)	1949-53	2	3	Saunders C	1927	1	1
+Dunne RS (New Zealand)	1996-99	4	4	+Sharp G (England)	2000	1	1
Fell DR (Ntl)	1961	1	1	+Shepherd DR (England)	1992-98	3	6
+Francis KT (Sri Lanka)	1994	1	1	Sickler GL (WP)	1938-48	2	7
Gibbon GD (EP)	1961	1	1	Smith D (EP)	1913	1	1
Goldman G (WP)	1966-69	2	2	Smith FE (Tvl)	1902-09	3	5
Grey FW (Tvl)	1909-22	4	10	Soames A (Tvl)	1898-02	2	2
+Hair DB (Australia)	1995-99	3	3	Thomas CN (WP)	1891	1	1
Harris SL (Tvl)	1909-22	3	4	*Thompson GJ (England)	1922	1	2
Hart-Davis JV (Ntl)	1948-49	2	4	+Tiffin RB (Zimbabwe)	1998	1	1
Hearne F (WP)	1898-05	3	6	Treadwell GB (Tvl)	1927-30	2	4
Hickson JAE (GW)	1888	1	1	+Venkataraghavan S (India)	1995-99	4	6
Howell IL (Bdr)	2000	1	1	Verheyen GA (GW)	1927	1	1
+Javed Akhtar (Pakistan)	1997	1	1	Wade WW (Ntl)	1969	1	1
+Jayaprakash AV (India)	2000	1	1	Wainwright W	1922	1	1
+Khizer Hayat (Pakistan)	1994	1	1	Warner AJ (Tvl)	1969	1	2
Kidson HC (Tvl)	1961-66	3	11	Warner JE (WP)	1961-64	2	2
King AC (Ntl)	1930	1	3	*Warton RG (England)	1888	1	2

SOUTH AFRICAN UMPIRES 2000/01

+Kitchen MJ (England)	1996-97	2	2	Webster HH (EP)	1888	1	1
Koertzen RE (EP) (b)	1992-00	9	11	*White A (England)	1898	1	2
Lambson SB (Tvl) (b)	1992-94	3	4	+Willey P (England)	1996-00	3	3
Laver AG (Tvl)	1921-27	3	10	Unidentified	1896	1	2

* Touring umpire from England accompanying the team. + Neutral umpire provided by the ICC.
(a) Three umpires (two South African and one ICC) stood in all four Tests v India 1992/93.
(b) South African umpires have also stood, as the ICC umpire, in the following Tests:

RE Koertzen 14 (1 in Aus, 1 in Eng, 2 in Ind, 1 in NZ, 1 in Pak, 4 in SL, 2 in WI, 2 in Zim), 1997/98-2000/01.

SB Lambson: 1 (1 in Eng), 1994

KE Liebenberg: 4 (2 in Aus, 1 in Pak, 1 in WI), 1994/95-1995/96.

CJ Mitchley: 13 (2 in Aus, 4 in Eng, 1 in Ind, 2 in Pak, 1 in SL, 3 in WI), 1994/95-1997/98.

DL Orchard 10 (2 in Eng, 1 in Ind, 3 in Pak, 2 in SL, 2 in WI) 1996/97-2000/01.

OBITUARIES

ROBERT LAWRENCE SUGDEN ARMITAGE. Born Grahamstown, Cape Province 9.7.1955. Died Grahamstown, Eastern Cape 9.12.2000 aged 45. A left-hand batsman and off-break bowler, with a high-action, who was known as "Mr Dependable" by virtue of his all-round performances for Eastern Province. He was a sturdy batsman. Although his driving could be lusty and free, he was often called upon to defend grimly with a straight bat.

He grew up in a cricket-mad family, with his father serving on the executive of the SA Country Cricket Association from 1956 until 1973, and secretary from 1965 until 1973. His career started on the front lawn of the family home with a loquat tree as the wicket. His companions were his elder brother, Christopher, and a friend, Bruce Morton. From St Andrew's Prep School in Grahamstown he moved to St Andrew's College and then Rhodes University. His cricket was developed by such men as Ashley Brooker, the Under 14A coach, "Geoff" Arnold, Paul Marsh, Harry Birrell and Eric Norton - all masters. There was professional coaching from David Steele and Tony Greig at St Andrew's College and later Lorrie Wilmot, Don Wilson and Tom Dean aided his development. He was selected for the Eastern Province Nuffield XI from 1972 to 1974 (being captain in 1974) and the SA Schools XI in 1974.

He made his first-class debut for Eastern Province against Transvaal, at Johannesburg, in 1973/74 and for the next four seasons, two of which were spent on military service, usually batted lower down the order. In 1974/75, as well as making three first-class appearances for Eastern Province, he appeared for SA Universities against Transvaal, at Johannesburg, scoring the first half-century of his career with 63 in the second innings.

In 1975/76 he appeared in six out of eight Currie Cup matches for Eastern Province and for the next twelve seasons was more likely than not to be an ever-present in the side. He took a career-best 7-97 (off 40 overs) in the first innings against Transvaal, at St George's Park.

The following season he played in Eastern Province's first four Currie Cup matches but was then called into the services halfway through the season. Whilst doing his military service he was given special dispensation to play for Northern Transvaal, unique at the time, and he played in three Currie Cup Section B matches for them. The following season he played in Northern Transvaal's opening three Castle Bowl fixtures before returning to Eastern Province.

He switched to the number three batting position in 1978/79 but only scored one half-century, against Natal at Kingsmead. In the following season he took ten wickets in a match (5-71 and 5-25) for the only time in his career in a seven-wicket win at Bulawayo against Zimbabwe-Rhodesia.

In 1980/81 his batting showed marked improvement and, shrugging off his image of being a defensive batsman, scored a match-winning, maiden, first-class century, 148 against Transvaal at St George's Park.

He had an excellent season with the bat in 1981/82, scoring 465 runs (avg 35.76) and scored two hundreds, 118 against Natal at St George's Park and a career-best 171 not out against Northern Transvaal, at Berea Park, in Pretoria. His performances earned him selection as a Cricketer of the Year in the 1982 Annual.

His finest season was in 1982/83 when he was extremely consistent, with 515 runs (avg 36.78) which included four half-centuries and a highest score of 97 not out against Northern Transvaal at Pretoria. He achieved "my ultimate - to play for South Africa" by playing in three unofficial one-day internationals against the West Indies XI in 1982/83. He played in two matches at the Wanderers and then one at Kingsmead. In the second Wanderers game he scored 46 as an opening batsman. In Durban he took 3-33 in nine overs.

He lived in Walmer with his wife of 17 years Carolynne and two sons, Greg and Craig. He went to visit his parents so he could be present for their golden jubilee wedding anniversary and died at their Grahamstown home, on the day of their anniversary, after a long battle with cancer. His wife had gone with their two sons to Johannesburg to support Craig, who was playing for the Eastern Province Under-13 B side, in an inter-provincial tournament. His firm, Key Entermark, sold six months previously to Primedia, ran the marketing portfolio for Eastern Province cricket from 1994.

In 109 first-class matches between 1973/74 and 1987/88 he scored 3923 runs (avg 23.21) with four centuries and 15 half-centuries. He took 205 wickets at 31.65, taking five wickets in an innings on seven occasions.

BRIAN BASSANO. Born East London, South Africa 21.3.1936. Died Launceston, Tasmania, Australia 10.7.2001 aged 65. Arguably the most knowledgeable of authorities on South African Test cricket until his death, he researched more than 235 South African Test cricketers and provided invaluable biographical information for the *South African Cricket Annual* over the last 30 years.

Educated in East London, he captained his school first XI and played first league cricket.

He moved to the United Kingdom in 1961 and played club cricket in Sussex and for Sussex Martlets, representing Sussex Clubs against the Club Cricket Conference in 1966. A prolific wicket-taker in English club cricket, he was offered a trial by Sussex CCC but was prevented from accepting by a serious arm injury which effectively ended his bowling career.

He returned to South Africa in 1966 to see the touring Australians and stayed there before emigrating to Tasmania in late 1988. He was the co-founder, in defiance of the apartheid laws, and captain of Rainbow CC, the first multiracial team in the Border Premier League in 1976/77. He was Honorary Secretary of the Border Cricket Union from 1971/72 to 1976/77. He worked on the SACU Development committee to promote cricket in the black townships.

He became a full-time journalist with the Daily Dispatch (East London) and broadcast commentaries, on SABC radio, on first-class matches in East London for more than 12 years before moving to Port Elizabeth at the end of 1980 where he worked for the now-defunct Evening Post. He was also the first editor of the now-defunct monthly cricket magazine *SA Cricket.*

He published numerous cricket books including *MCC in South Africa 1938-39; South Africa in International Cricket 1888-1970* (made into a 30-part TV series by SABC)*; South Africa v England - 106 Years of Test Match Glory* and, undoubtedly, his most important contribution to South African cricket, *The History of South African Cricket Volume IV 1947-1960.* He also co- authored two books with Tasmanian writer Rick Smith entitled *A Springbok Down Under - South Africa On Tour 1931-32* and *Vic's Boys - Australian's In South Africa 1935-36.* His final book was on *Aubrey Faulkner* in the *Association of Cricket Statisticians Famous Cricketer* series which, sadly, he did not live to see published.

His son, Chris, played for Tasmania second XI before moving to England. Shortly before his father's death he scored 186 not out and 106 for Derbyshire against Gloucestershire, the first player to score a century in each innings on County Championship debut.

He died in Launceston General Hospital of complications following a stroke. He was survived by his second wife Annabel and two sons and two daughters by a previous marriage.

DALKEITH VALENTINE COLLINS. Born Cape Town 31.7.1907. Died Cape Town 7.1.2001 aged 93. One of South Africa's most experienced umpires after the Second World War who, according to the limited records available for that period, stood in at least 25 first-class matches.

He made his debut as an umpire in 1938 and in 1939/40 and stood in his first provincial match after only 12 months experience. Due to the Second World War his next first-class appearance was at Newlands, for Western Province's match against Natal, in 1947/48. He stood in ten Test matches between 1948/49 and 1961/62.

He was the brother of Stanley Collins (1909-1993) and they stood together in the Western Province v Transvaal match in 1950/51 and the third Test against New Zealand, Stanley's only Test, at Newlands in 1953/54.

An electrical contractor, he served as an executive member, later being elected Vice-President and then President, of the Western Province Cricket Umpires Association and was Vice-Chairman and subsequently President of the South African Cricket Umpires Association.

FRANK DAVIDSON. Born Vryburg, Cape Province 30.12.1912. Died Marondera, Zimbabwe 28.12.1999 aged 86. A right-hand, aggressive, stroke-making batsman and wicketkeeper who made three first-class appearances. His debut was for Rhodesia against Wally Hammond's MCC touring team on a matting pitch at Queens Ground, Bulawayo, in 1938/39. Batting at number five he scored 23, his highest first-class score.

He was the younger brother of DA [Don] Davidson (Griqualand West/Eastern Province/Border 1924/25-1936/37) and TM [Tom] Davidson (Border/Western Province/Rhodesia 1926/27-1938/39). Tom played alongside him in the match against MCC, at Bulawayo, in 1938/39.

PETER ROBIN DAVIDSON. Born Kearsney, Natal 19.8.1924. Died Umkomaas, KwaZulu-Natal 4.5.2001 aged 76. A right-hand, middle-order, batsman and right-arm medium bowler who appeared in all six of North-Eastern Transvaal's Currie Cup fixtures in 1950/51. In his fourth match he scored a career-best 103 against Griqualand West, at Olympia Park, Springs.

A star all-round sportsman at Kearsney College, he went on to see active service in Italy as a pilot in the SA Air Force during the war. In 1955, he and his wife Sheila, who were married for 55 years, moved to Umzinto and began an association with the district that lasted some 46 years.

He was especially proud of his twin sister Wendy's grandson, Errol Stewart, who played for both Natal and South Africa at cricket.

He died of cancer from a melanoma at the Lighthouse Hospice, Umkomaas.

In his six first-class matches he scored 363 runs (avg 33.00) with a century and three fifties.

PERCIVAL CHARLES DAVIS. Born Brackley, Northamptonshire, England 24.5.1915. Died Leicester, Leicestershire, England 4.7.2001 aged 86. (Northamptonshire 1935-1952). A professional cricket coach at Dale College from October 1952 to December 1980, one of his star pupils was Hylton Ackerman, whose record of five SA Schools caps between 1962 and 1966 seems unlikely to be broken.

ABDULHAY "GARY" GARDA. Born Johannesburg 27.1.1931. Died Johannesburg 29.4.2001 aged 70. One of the leading umpires in the SACBOC era, he stood in the second "Test" between South Africa and the Kenyan Asians in Johannesburg in 1956/57. He also umpired in the Dadabhay Trophy three-day inter-provincial matches in the early 1970s, as well as Transvaal B against Natal B at Lenasia in 1977/78.

JUNE GLEASON. Born Lusaka, Northern Rhodesia, 12.9.1940. Died Johannesburg 10.7.2001 aged 60. June Gleason organised travel for South African cricketers and administrators for almost 20 years. Born to a farming family, she was head girl of Lusaka's convent and played hockey for the then Northern Rhodesia and Zambia.

She was a travel agent for most of her adult life. She opened an in-house branch of Rennies at the United Cricket Board in the early 1990s. She fought uncomplainingly against cancer for six-and-a-half years. Typically, she was at work on the day before her death, where, unusually, she told friend and colleague Trish Lewis she felt "so sore". In the early hours of the next morning she died in the arms of David Gleason, her ex-husband, with whom she had again become close friends.

ROBERT LYON "BOB" HARVEY. Born Swinburne, Orange Free State 14.9.1911. Died Kloof, KwaZulu-Natal 20.7.2000 aged 88. A right-hand attacking batsman, a useful right-arm medium opening bowler and a positive captain, he was one of Natal's key players between 1933 and 1940.

His made his first-class debut for Natal in 1933/34. His third first-class match was for Natal against the Australians, at Kingsmead, in November 1935. In only his fourth first-class innings he scored 104, out of 254, in the second innings as the tourists won by an innings and 26 runs. Dudley Nourse, with two centuries, was the only other South African batsman to score hundreds against the Australians that season.

His next first-class appearance was his Test debut in the fourth Test at The Wanderers - a match over in two days as Australia won by an innings and 184 runs. In the second innings he and Bruce Mitchell (48 not out) were the only batsmen to reach double figures in the home side's total of 98. His 17 included hitting Grimmett for six. Between the fourth and fifth Tests, Natal played their second match against the Australians and he scored a magnificent career-best 138 in 240 minutes, out of 272, in the first innings with one six and 16 fours. His final Test appearance, at Kingsmead, saw him achieve his highest Test score of 28 in the first innings.

Natal won the Currie Cup in 1936/37 and he appeared in all six matches. He captained Natal in all six of their Currie Cup matches the following season as they tied with Transvaal at the top of the log. He captained Natal in both matches against the touring MCC team in 1938/39 but, despite scoring an attractive 92 in the first match, he was overlooked for further Test honours.

He failed to reach top form in his final season of first-class cricket, 1939/40, but achieved a career-best 5-21 against Border, at Kingsmead, and in his final innings scored 80 against Western Province at the same venue.

He represented Natal at rugby as a midfield back between 1933 and 1937.

During the Second World War he was a Regimental Survey Officer in the South African Artillery and was awarded the MBE for "unusual zeal and outstanding devotion to duty in North Italy".

Educated at Michaelhouse, he was the father of MM Harvey (Border/Natal/Natal B 1968/69 to 1972/73) and RD Harvey (Natal B 1967/68). Until his death he was South Africa's second oldest living Test player with only Norman (Mobil) Gordon, 6.8.1911, born before him.

In 25 first-class matches he scored 1298 runs (avg 38.17) with two centuries and 11 half-centuries and took 37 wickets at 26.10, taking five wickets in an innings twice.

DEMITRI "DUP" HAYIDAKIS. Born East London 6.9.1916. Died King William's Town, EC 25.8.2000 aged 83. Educated at Selborne College, a right-hand batsman and right-arm bowler who appeared in ten Currie Cup games for Border. He made his first-class debut against Eastern Province, at East London, in the final match of the 1936/37 season. In the following season, against Western Province, at Newlands, he scored a career-best 77. Border went on to win the game by seven wickets, the first time in their history they had beaten Western Province in a first-class match.

He returned after the Second World War, playing two Currie Cup matches in 1946/47 and another two in 1947/48.

In ten first-class matches, he scored 202 runs (avg 11.88) with one half-century.

PETER LEE HOLMES. Born Kaffir River, Orange Free State 14.8.1917. Died Margate, KwaZulu- Natal 12.11.2000 aged 83. Born on a farm in the Orange Free State, he attended Kingswood College in Grahamstown where he played first-team cricket for four years. He made his first-class debut for Eastern Province in 1937/38. His highest score was 52 against Western Province at Newlands.

The grandson of an 1820 Settler, he served as a captain in the Second World War.

In seven first-class matches he scored 136 runs (avg 13.60) with one half-century.

PIET HOURANI. Died Kimberley 13.10.2000 aged 67. Administrators, players and management from both Griqualand West and North West expressed shock and dismay at the sudden collapse and death, at the start of the second day in the match between the Bangladeshis and Griqualand West, of dependable scorer Piet Hourani.

From Klerksdorp, he had been a senior scorer for Griqualand West since 1995 but had been involved in scoring matches in the area for the previous 35 years. He collapsed in the scorer's box, soon after arriving at the ground, with a suspected heart attack. Players, spectators and administrators from both teams lined the pitch before the start of the match in a show of respect for the humble, loveable and loyal "Piet Pencil".

CECIL VICTOR "VIO" IRVINE. Born Cape Town 16.8.1916. Died Harare, Zimbabwe 11.3.2001 aged 84. A right-hand, middle-order, batsman and leg-break bowler who played one first-class match for Rhodesia in 1936/37. In a first-class friendly against Transvaal, at Johannesburg, he had an analysis of 7-1-52-0 in the Transvaal innings of 262 and then scored nought and two in the Rhodesia innings of 83 and 106 respectively. He did not take a catch.

One of Rhodesia's greatest all-round sportsmen, he was the only person to represent his country in four different sports. He was an excellent tennis player who played in the men's singles at Wimbledon in 1952. A hockey centre-forward, he captained South Africa in 1948, with Russell Endean in the same team. He was Rhodesia's squash champion in 1948 (amateurs only) and also played soccer as a centre-half.

A Commissioned Officer in the Army during the Second World War, he returned to Salisbury in 1945, giving up cricket for tennis. He was a tennis coach until 1995.

MOHAMED NASEER "NAZ" KHOTA. Born Breyten, Eastern Transvaal 21.9.1953. Died Lenasia 8.5.2001 aged 47. A capable wicketkeeper-batsman, Naz Khota, was a regular member of the Transvaal B side which played in SACB's Booley Bowl competition. He captained the side with a fair degree of success. He made one first-class appearance for Transvaal against Eastern Province in a Howa Bowl match in December 1985, taking five catches behind the stumps. He died in a car crash.

MARK JOHN LAVINE. Born Black Bess, St Peter, Barbados, West Indies 4.3.1973. Died Walsgrave Hospital, Walsgrave, Coventry, Warwickshire, England 12.5.2001 aged 28. A cousin of the former West Indies batsman Gordon Greenidge, he was a right-hand batsman and right-arm fast bowler who contributed enormously to North West's improving performances in South African domestic cricket over the last few years.

He played in two first-class matches for Barbados in 1992/93 and in the following season was a member of the Barbados party that toured South Africa but did not play in the only first-class match, against Northern Transvaal. He appeared in four limited-overs matches, was offered a three-month club contract at the end of the tour and eventually settled in South Africa.

It wasn't until 1996/97 that he made his first-class debut, for North West, in South African domestic cricket. He scored a then career-best 107 in his first innings for his new province against Easterns, at Benoni, having earlier in the game taken a then career-best 4-58 off 23 overs.

The following season, he was named North West Cricketer of the Year as North West won the UCB Bowl Division One log by ten points over Northerns B. He had another consistent season when North West retained their UCB Bowl title the following season.

He had a successful 1999/00 season as North West appeared in the SuperSport Series for the first time. In six matches he scored 213 runs (avg 21.30) and took 21 wickets (avg 27.52) with an improved career-best 5-44, against Free State, at Potchefstroom.

In his final season, 2000/01, he achieved his highest first-class aggregate with 477 runs (avg 29.81) - the third highest aggregate in a season by any North West player. He took 30 wickets (avg 33.16) in nine SuperSport Series matches. He again improved his career-best bowling with 6-55 off 23 overs against Gauteng at Potchefstroom, followed this with 5-97 against Griqualand West at Kimberley and achieved a final career-best 6-53 of 26 overs (match 10-124) against Boland at Paarl. In what turned out to be his final first-class match he scored a career-best 113 off 108 balls against Border, at Potchefstroom.

He had recently acquired South African citizenship and his goal was to play cricket for his adopted country.

In his first season with Coventry & North Warwickshire Cricket Club, he died during a Birmingham and District Premier League home match against Barnt Green Cricket Club, at Binley Road, Coventry after collapsing around 5.40pm. He had just scored 127 runs and had bowled a few overs when he complained of chest pains. Within minutes he was unconscious. The Paramedics arrived within five minutes but could not revive him and he was pronounced dead on arrival at Walsgrave Hospital. He died of complications caused by a thrombosis in a leg.

A minute's silence was observed the following Saturday at every Birmingham League ground in his memory. He is survived by his wife Patricia, whom he married in Johannesburg in 2000, and their young daughter Nikita.

In 33 first-class matches, he scored 1522 runs (avg 29.26) with two centuries and six half-centuries and took 100 wickets (avg 28.61), taking five wickets in an innings four time.

He played in 46 Standard Bank League and Cup matches for North West, with career-best scores of 72 against Griqualand West, at Potchefstroom, in 1999/00 and 72 against Free State, at Potchefstroom, in 2000/01. His career-best bowling analysis was 9-2-25-2 against Easterns, at Potchefstroom, in 2000/01.

WILLIAM CHARLES "BILL" LAWLER. Born Durban 10.10.1923. Died Durban 20.1.2001 aged 77. Bill Lawler, who died in Durban's Parklands hospital after a short illness while on holiday from Australia, where he settled in 1996, was a highly-respected sports administrator in Natal. He was a founder member of the Pirates cricket club (now Pirates Kismet) in 1939 and served them as secretary for 25 years and chairman for a further 32 years. He was a member of the executive of both the Durban and District Cricket Union and Natal Cricket Association from 1978 to 1991, being honoured with a plaque by the NCA for dedicated service to the game. At the time of his death, he was a patron of both these cricket bodies.

TREVOR NYASHA MADONDO. Born Mount Darwin, Rhodesia 22.11.1976. Died 11.6.2001 Harare, Zimbabwe aged 24. One of Zimbabwe's most promising black cricketers, he suffered a severe bout of malaria at the end of May 2001. He was admitted to Mutare General Hospital and was later transferred to Parirenyatwa Hospital, Harare, on 7 June. He died of cerebral malaria and was buried at Yeoville Cemetery in Mutare on 12 June.

He was the first black cricketer to be selected for Zimbabwe as a batsman. In the few matches he played for Zimbabwe, he looked talented but inexperienced. His stint with the national team was interrupted by injuries, a slump in form and, on some occasions, an undisciplined lifestyle which landed him in trouble with the authorities.

He attended Falcon College, Bulawayo, which has produced many Zimbabwe Test players. He represented Zimbabwe Schools in South Africa for two years and while still at school made his first-class debut, as wicketkeeper, for Matabeleland against Glamorgan in April 1995.

After leaving school in 1995 he won a place at Rhodes University in Grahamstown, South Africa, to study for a Bachelor of Commerce degree. He played in the first team at Rhodes and was a regular selection for the Zimbabwe Board XI in the UCB Bowl competition (not first-class).

As a right-handed batsman, he played three Tests for Zimbabwe, scoring 90 runs (avg 30.00) with a highest score of 74 not out against New Zealand in Wellington in 2000/01.

He played in 13 one-day internationals, scoring 191 runs (avg 15.91) with a highest score of 71 against India, at Rajkot, in December 2000.

KHAYA MAJOLA. Born Port Elizabeth 17.5.1953. Died Johannesburg 28.8.2000 aged 47. One of South Africa's leading cricketers in the 1970s and 1980s, and one of the country's top crick et administrators during the 1990s, he died after a brave fight against cancer.

He was Director of Amateur Cricket at the United Cricket Board at the time of his death and had held the position since cricket unity in 1991, when he and Ali Bacher were given the task of setting up a national development programme for the new UCB. The programme became cricket's flagship in the 1990s, introducing some 20 000 children to the game annually. Majola headed a team of 40 administrators nationally and oversaw an annual budget of R21-million.

From New Brighton in Port Elizabeth, Majola was born into a sporting family and showed special talent at an early age. His father and mentor, Eric Majola, was a double black Springbok in rugby and cricket during the 1950s and 1960s. During the early 1970s he followed in his father's footsteps, making his way via the Passmore Schools Week and senior provincial cricket into the national African team. In 1973, aged 20, he was selected to play against the Derrick Robins touring team and Robins invited him to play in England in 1974 under the captaincy of Clive Rice.

However, on his return to South Africa he turned his back on the SA African Board and its growing involvement with the establishment's multinational sports policy to join the non-racial South African Cricket Board of Control (SACBOC). Majola never wavered from the commitment to the struggle for freedom in South Africa, even if it meant jeopardising a promising career and returning to the matting wickets and poor facilities in the townships.

In 17 consecutive seasons, playing for Eastern Province in the non-racial competi tions, he played in no fewer than 85 of the 216 three-day inter-provincial matches organised by SACBOC and its successor, SACB, between 1971 and cricket unity in 1991, more than any other player. Although he was selected captain of the SACB national team in the 1980s he hoped, until the end of his career, to fulfil his childhood dream of playing in official Tests for his country but it was not to be.

Cricket unity in 1991, and the attainment of democracy in 1994, opened up unexpected new avenues for him. He gained satisfaction from creating opportunities for young cricketers and was particularly pleased when 39 black cricketers participated in provincial fixtures in the

1999/2000 season, finally broaching the glass ceiling that had kept the elite level all-white for so long.

He played a major role behind the scenes in recent transformation initiatives, which have led to significant changes in the balance of power in South African cricket, and seen black administrators come to the fore in significant numbers. In helping maintain a threatened tradition of African cricket and to carry the banner of nonracial sport in the difficult apartheid years, as well as helping to develop and guide the game in the decade since unity, he left cricket with a huge legacy.

For more than two years he fought illness, working right to the end. He is survived by his wife Cynthia, two children, mother Milase, three brothers and a sister. His brother, Gerald, is a former provincial cricketer and national selector, who succeeded Dr Ali Bacher as chief executive of the UCB.

(With acknowledgements to Andre Odendaal)

HASSEN EBRAHIM MALL. Born Ghala, India 19.6.1922. Died Durban 18.8.2000 aged 78. The first captain of the Western Province Indian team to play in the Christopher Trophy interprovincial competition, Mall was a useful leg-spin and googly bowler. He returned match figures of 9-56 (3-16 and 6-40) against Eastern Province in the fourth Christopher Trophy tournament in Johannesburg in 1947. He played a significant role in raising the standard of play among Indian cricketers in Cape Town while a student at the University of Cape Town in the late 1940s and early 1950s.

He made an important decision when the regular wicketkeeper failed to turn up for a league match in Cape Town in the mid 1940s and he asked a young Salie "Lobo" Abed to put on the gloves. Abed became the greatest black wicketkeeper in the country.

Mall became a judge and gained fame as an eminent jurist and humanitarian. He died in St Augustine's hospital from kidney and heart failure.

LAWRENCE ANDERSON "FISH" MARKHAM. Born Mbabane, Swaziland 12.9.1924. Died Pietermaritzburg 5.8.2000 aged 75. A right-hand, lower-order, batsman and leg-break/googly bowler who, although not always as accurate as other bowlers of his type, gained effective pace off the pitch. He made his first-class debut for Natal in their opening Currie Cup fixture against Griqualand West, at Kimberley, in 1946/47.

He was an ever-present the following season, appearing in all eight Currie Cup matches for Natal, and established himself as one of the leading bowlers of his type, taking 32 wickets (avg 12.87) and finishing second in the Currie Cup bowling averages. With fellow spinners Ian Smith and Les Payn he helped Natal retain the Currie Cup. He took a career-best 7-106, off 28.2 overs, in the drawn game against Western Province at Newlands. In the penultimate game of the season, against Orange Free State at Kingsmead, he scored a career-best 134 batting at number nine, adding 174 for the eighth wicket with Ossie Dawson, which remains the provincial record for this wicket.

He was strongly expected to obtain a Test place against the MCC in 1948/49 but contracted jaundice and was out of action for the first half of the season. However the selectors, gambling on his sharp spin, selected him for the fourth Test on the plumb Ellis Park pitch although he hadn't appeared in a single first-class match since the previous summer. His length suffered, in an effort to produce big leg-spin, before he had settled down to the Test match atmosphere and he conceded 38 runs off five overs in the first innings. In the second innings he bowled Denis Compton (25) with a well-disguised googly to finish with 1-34 off eight overs. In the South African first innings he came in at 161-7 and hit an invaluable 20 which helped avoid the follow-on. He was not selected for the final Test.

In 1949/50 he played for Natal against the touring Australians, at Kingsmead, taking the wickets of skipper Lindsay Hassett and Ken Archer. His final first-class appearances for Natal were four Currie Cup matches in 1950/51.

Educated at Glenwood High School, in 1941 he took 9-15 against Maritzburg College who were dismissed for 43. His nickname "Fish" was derived from the Swazi word for "young boy". He was the elder brother of NE Markham (Natal 1951/52 to 1956/57). He died of lung cancer.

In 17 first-class matches he scored 268 runs (avg 15.76), with one century, and took 53 wickets (avg 16.84), taking five wickets in an innings on three occasions.

NEVILLE EVELYN MARKHAM. Born Mbabane, Swaziland 1.2.1926. Died Pietermaritzburg 26.4.2000 aged 74. A right-hand, lower-order, batsman and right-arm fast bowler who made an impressive first-class debut in Currie Cup cricket for Natal against Western Province, at Pietermaritzburg, in 1951/52. Opening the bowling he took a career-best 6-77 off 20 overs in a match Natal won on the first innings. He took 15 wickets (avg 24.80) in his six Currie Cup appearances as Natal won the competition in convincing fashion.

He played in just two first-class matches for Natal the following season and none in 1953/54. He re-appeared for Natal in all six Currie Cup matches in 1954/55 and took 12 wickets (avg 27.58) as they won the competition outright for the eighth time in their history.

Five Currie Cup appearances in 1955/56 saw him take 15 wickets (avg 16.53) to finish third in the national bowling averages. He scored a career-best 78 in the innings victory over Western Province, at Pietermaritzburg, in the final match of the season. His final two first-class appearances for Natal were against the touring MCC in 1956/57.

A former President of the Maritzburg Cricket Union, he was the younger brother of LA Markham (Natal/South Africa 1946/47 to 1950/51) and died of lymph cancer.

In 23 first-class matches he scored 365 runs (avg 14.60), with two half-centuries, and took 62 wickets (avg 25.90), twice taking five wickets in an innings.

CUAN NEIL McCARTHY. Born Pietermaritzburg 24.3.1929. Died Johannesburg 14.8.2000 aged 71. Educated at Pietermaritzburg College, he was brought up on the game by his father on his poultry farm near Pietermaritzburg, who built him two wickets, one of concrete and the other of grass.

A right-hand, lower-order, batsman and right-arm fast bowler, he made his debut, aged 18, for Natal against Border at East London in 1947/48. He was tall (6 ft 2 in) and long-legged, with a double-jointed wrist action, which inclined critics to the view he threw the ball. In seven Currie Cup appearances he took 29 wickets (avg 16.10). In the final match of the season against North-Eastern Transvaal, at Pietermaritzburg, he took 6-43 off 20 overs and 4-45 off 19 overs (10-88 his career-best match analysis) as Natal won by an innings and 64 runs to win the Currie Cup.

He played in eight first-class matches the following season, all against the touring MCC. Two were for Natal and in the first, at Kingsmead, he took 5-110 in the first innings - his pace being the main reason for the early uneasiness of the MCC batting. One of just 12 South Africans to represent his country as a teenager, he was aged 19 on his sensational Test debut at Kingsmead. He took a Test career-best 6-43 from 12 overs in the second innings. He maintained pace, length and hostility in a spell which took South Africa near to victory (they lost by two wickets off the last possible ball of the match bowled by Lindsey Tuckett). He took 5-114 off 35.7 overs in the first innings of the drawn fourth Test at Johannesburg. He played in all five Tests taking 21 wickets (avg 26.71).

The visit of the Australians in 1949/50 saw him find wickets much harder to come by. He took three wickets against them in the first Natal game, at Durban, and only five wickets (avg 107.20) off 144 overs in the five Tests – though he had at least eleven catches dropped off his bowling.

The following season, his final first-class appearances in South Africa, he had injury problems and played in only three Currie Cup matches for Natal taking two wickets (avg 33.50).

The 1951 tour to England was a disappointment in terms of Test results (a 3-1 defeat) but the results at Manchester and The Oval may have gone the other way with a bit of luck. He took 59 wickets (avg 23.96) on tour, including 10 wickets (avg 41.30) in the Test matches but he was too erratic and his persistence in bowling the short-pitched bumper, on a treacherous pitch, was reckoned by the critics to have cost South Africa the Old Trafford Test. He took a career-best 8-36, against Sussex, at Hove including the hat-trick. After the tour, he and Eric Rowan received notification from the SACA that their services would no longer be required for the national side.

He played in 12 matches for Cambridge University in 1952 (being awarded his Blue) and headed their bowling averages with 44 wickets (avg 17.20). He was no-balled for throwing once, by Paddy Corrall, against Worcestershire at Worcester and didn't appear again in first-class cricket after the season ended.

Educated at Maritzburg College, he played cricket for Dorset (1958-59). He was awarded his boxing Blue at Cambridge University. He was an agriculturist writer and died of renal failure.

In 60 first-class matches he scored 141 runs (avg 4.27) and took 176 wickets (avg 25.85), taking five wickets in an innings on eight occasions. In 15 Test matches he scored 28 runs (avg 3.11) and took 36 wickets (avg 41.94), taking five wickets in an innings on two occasions.

KRISHNASAMY SOOBIAH "SADHA" NAIDOO. Born Pietermaritzburg 2.11.1934. Died Durban 21.2.2001 aged 66. Professor KS Naidoo, who died in Wentworth hospital after undergoing surgery for a second heart bypass, was a cautious top-order batsman with a fine technique and a superb fielder, particularly at mid-off.

When he was at Patna University in India in the late 1950s he regularly represented the university team and was selected for the state of Baroda, playing in the Ranji Trophy. He was only the second Indian from Natal to play in the prestige competition, the first being Dr EI Bhorat, from Stanger. On his return to Pietermaritzburg, he toured the then Rhodesias with a Northern Natal team in Easter 1964, under the captaincy of AI Deedat.

He spent most of his working life at King Edward VII hospital in Durban and the University of Natal's medical school. He gained international renown as an orthopaedic surgeon and a teacher.

JOHN PETER SIERRA. Born Mossel Bay, Cape Province 26.3.1922. Died East London 17.5.2000 aged 78. A right-hand opening batsman, with a sound defence, who made his first-class debut for Western Province, at Bloemfontein, in his team's final Currie Cup fixture of the 1947/48 season. He scored 60, in the first innings total of 207, in a match the home side won by 165 runs.

His other five first-class appearances were for Rhodesia in the 1950/51 Currie Cup tournament. He scored a career-best 62 against Eastern Province, at St George's Park.

In six first-class matches he scored 216 runs (avg 19.63) with two half-centuries.

IZAK FRANCOIS NEL WEIDEMAN. Born Johannesburg 19.9.1960. Died Maraisburg, Gauteng 4.6.2001 aged 40. A right-hand batsman and right-arm fast-medium bowler who made his first-class debut for SA Universities against Northern Transvaal, at Berea Park, Pretoria in 1980/81. He scored 38 in the first innings. He appeared in four Bowl games for Transvaal B taking 16 wickets (avg 18.43). He also played in Transvaal's final Currie Cup game of the season, against Eastern Province, at Johannesburg.

The following season he took 21 wickets (avg 12.42) in four Bowl games and headed the bowling averages for Transvaal B. In 1982/83 he scored a career-best 47 not out for Transvaal B against Griqualand West, at Johannesburg, in their opening fixture of the season and improved on his career-best bowling with 4-29 (off 17 overs) for Transvaal in their 111-run victory over Northern Transvaal at Johannesburg.

From 1983/84 onwards he played for Northern Transvaal. In 1984/85 he took 22 wickets (avg 31.27) in nine Currie Cup matches, including a career-best bowling 6-43 against Eastern Province, at Port Elizabeth. Three Bowl appearances for Northern Transvaal B in 1986/87 brought an end to his first-class career.

His highest score in the Benson and Hedges Series was an unbeaten 60 for Northern Transvaal, at Technikon Oval, Pretoria, against Transvaal in 1984/85 with a best bowling analysis of 3-46 for Transvaal, in the competition's first final, against Natal at Johannesburg, in 1981/82.

He was educated at Auckland Park Primary, Vorentoe HS and RAU. He played for the Transvaal Nuffield XI in 1978. His career came to an end when his right foot was run over by a motor-driven roller. With Hoosain Ayob he co-authored a coaching manual in Afrikaans.

He was shot dead in a robbery shortly after he arrived at the CMR [Consolidated Main Reef] Golf Course where he was the greenkeeper, being hit in the neck, stomach and leg, around 7am. His wallet and car keys were taken but his vehicle was not stolen.

Ali Bacher described his death as "a great loss" and said: "He regularly coached individuals in the townships and was an outstanding South African".

In 40 first-class matches he scored 662 runs (avg 15.39) and took 135 wickets (avg 22.34), twice taking five wickets in an innings.

ATHOLL GENE WOOD. Born Pietermaritzburg 22.2.1941. Died Pietermaritzburg 18.2.2001 aged 59. A right-hand, tail-end, batsman and opening right-arm medium bowler who played in 14 Currie Cup B Section matches for Natal B between 1969/70 and 1972/73. His career-best bowling was 6-26 in 23 overs against Orange Free State at Settlers Park, Ladysmith in 1970/71. He made his highest score of 34 against Border at Jan Smuts Ground, East London, in the same season.

With blond hair and being relatively short in height for a provincial fast bowler, he bowled at a brisk pace and was respected for his whole-hearted approach and accuracy.

Educated at Merchiston Prep and Technical HS (Pietermaritzburg), he first showed his skills captaining the Tech side in rugby and cricket. After leaving school he added prowess in soccer to his range of sporting talents. Later he turned to bowls and was selected for the Natal Inland Bowling Association's A team three years before his death from heart illness.

In 14 first-class matches he scored 173 runs (avg 19.22) and took 31 wickets (avg 36.51), taking five wickets in an innings on two occasions.

Any assistance in keeping track of the deaths of first-class cricketers and any details, even if incomplete, are always most valuable. Corrections or additions to the current Who's Who, or previously published biographical details of any first class cricketer, would also be gratefully received as would information on the deaths of any umpires, administrators etc. Please contact Andrew Samson, c/o United Cricket Board, PO Box 55009, Northlands, 2116. Fax: (011) 880 6229.

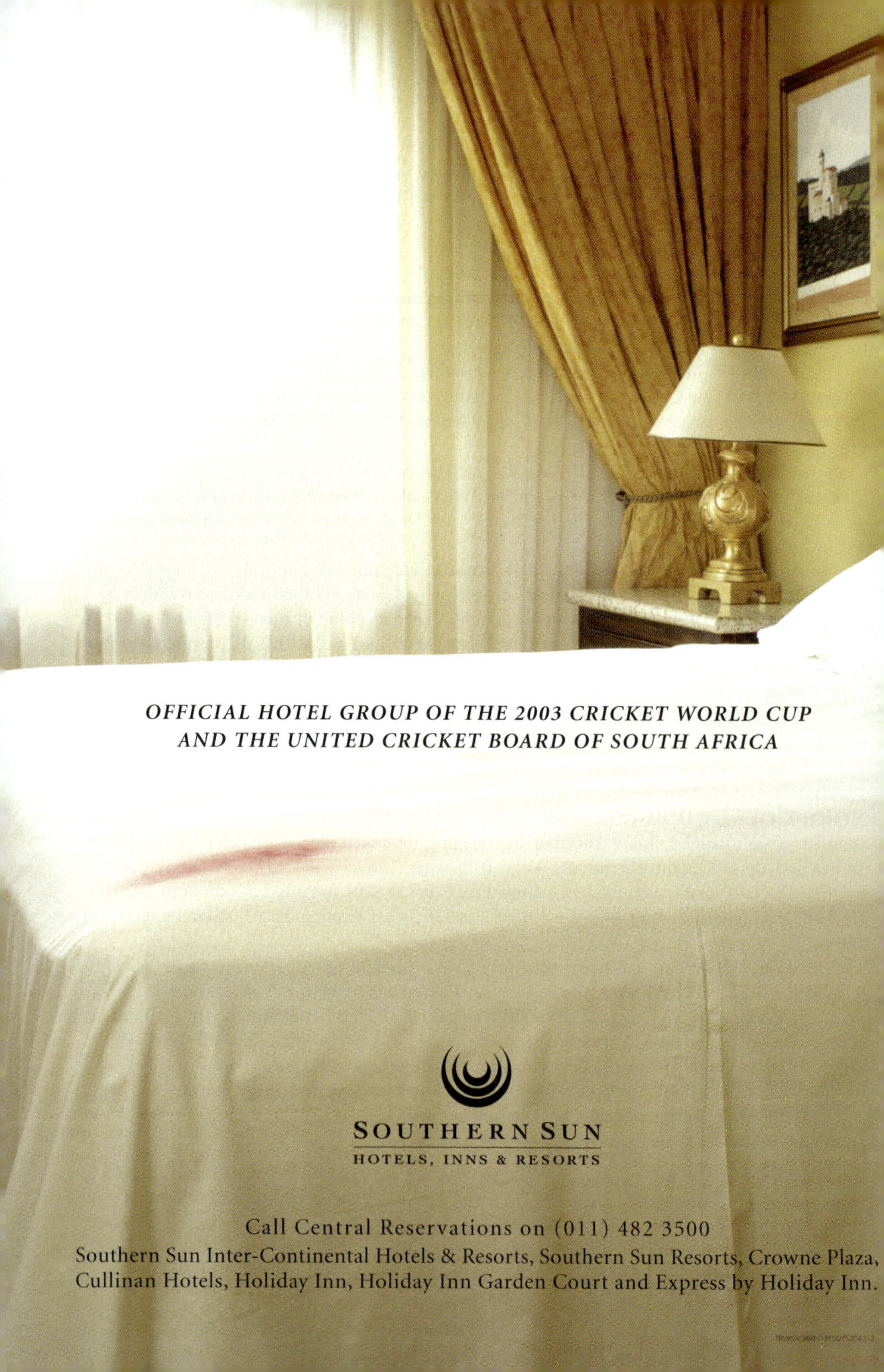
OFFICIAL HOTEL GROUP OF THE 2003 CRICKET WORLD CUP
AND THE UNITED CRICKET BOARD OF SOUTH AFRICA
SOUTHERN SUN
HOTELS, INNS & RESORTS
Call Central Reservations on (011) 482 3500
Southern Sun Inter-Continental Hotels & Resorts, Southern Sun Resorts, Crowne Plaza, Cullinan Hotels, Holiday Inn, Holiday Inn Garden Court and Express by Holiday Inn.

FIXTURES 2001/2002

INTERNATIONAL MATCHES

SOUTH AFRICA IN ZIMBABWE

September			
Fri. 7-Tue 11	Zimbabwe	1st Test	Harare
Fri 14-Tue 18	Zimbabwe	2nd Test	Bulawayo
Fri. 21 Day	Zimbabwe A	1-day tour	Bulawayo
Sun 23 Day	Zimbabwe	1st ODI	Bulawayo
Sat 29 Day	Zimbabwe	2nd ODI	Harare
Sun 30 Day	Zimbabwe	3rd ODI	Harare

INDIA AND KENYA IN SOUTH AFRICA

September			
Sun 30 Day	SA Country Districts v Kenya	1-day tour	Pietersburg
October			
Mon 1 Day	N Oppenheimer XI v India	1-day tour	Randjesfontein
Tue 2 Day	Gauteng XI v Kenya	1-day tour	Soweto
Wed 3 D/N	South Africa A v India	1-day tour	Benoni
Fri 5 D/N	South Africa v India	1st ODI	Johannesburg
Sun 7 Day	South Africa v Kenya	2nd ODI	Benoni
Tue 9 Day	South Africa A v Kenya	1-day tour	Laudium
Wed 10 D/N	South Africa v India	3rd ODI	Centurion
Fri 12 D/N	India v Kenya	4th ODI	Bloemfontein
Sun 14 Day	South Africa v Kenya	5th ODI	Kimberley
Wed 17 D/N	India v Kenya	6th ODI	Port Elizabeth
Fri 19 D/N	South Africa v India	7th ODI	East London
Sat 20 Day	SA Students XI v Kenya	1-day tour	UWC Bellville
Mon 22 D/N	South Africa v Kenya	8th ODI	Cape Town
Wed 24 D/N	India v Kenya	9th ODI	Paarl
Fri 26 D/N	FINAL	10th ODI	Durban
Sat 27 Day	Reserve Day		
Mon 29-Wed 31	President's XI v India	3-day tour	Chatsworth
November 2001			
Sat 3-Mon 7	South Africa v India	1st Test	Bloemfontein
Sat 10-Tue 13	South Africa A v India	4-day tour	East London
Fri 16-Tue 20	South Africa v India	2nd Test	Port Elizabeth
Fri 23-Tue 27	South Africa v India	3rd Test	Centurion

SOUTH AFRICA IN AUSTRALIA

Date		Match	Type	Venue
December				
Wed 5	Day	ACB Chairman's XI	1-day tour	Lilac Hill, Perth
Fri 7-Mon 10		Western Warriors	4-day tour	WACA, Perth
Fri 14-Tue 18		Australia v South Africa	1st Test	Adelaide
Thu 20-Sun 23		New South Wales Blues	4-day tour	Sydney
Wed 26-Sun 30		Australia v South Africa	2nd Test	Melbourne
January				
Wed 2-Sun 6		Australia v South Africa	3rd Test	Sydney
Thu 10	D/N	Australia A v South Africa	1-day tour	Adelaide
Fri. 11	D/N	Australia v New Zealand	ODI	Melbourne
Sun 13	D/N	Australia v South Africa	ODI	Melbourne
Tue 15	Day	New Zealand v South Africa	ODI	Hobart
Thu 17	D/N	Australia v New Zealand	ODI	Sydney
Sat 19	D/N	New Zealand v South Africa	ODI	Brisbane
Sun 20	D/N	Australia v South Africa	ODI	Brisbane
Tue 22	D/N	Australia v South Africa	ODI	Sydney
Sat 26	D/N	Australia v New Zealand	ODI	Adelaide
Sun 27	D/N	New Zealand v South Africa	ODI	Adelaide
Tue 29	D/N	Australia v New Zealand	ODI	Melbourne
February				
Fri 1	D/N	New Zealand v South Africa	ODI	Perth
Sun 3	Day	Australia v South Africa	ODI	Perth
Wed 6	D/N	FIRST FINAL	ODI	Melbourne
Fri 8	D/N	SECOND FINAL	ODI	Sydney
Sun 10	D/N	THIRD FINAL (if necessary)	ODI	Sydney

AUSTRALIA IN SOUTH AFRICA

Date		Match	Type	Venue
February				
Sun 17-Tue 19		South Africa A v Australia	3-day tour	Potchefstroom
Fri. 22-Tue 26		South Africa v Australia	1st Test	Johannesburg
March				
Fri 1-Mon 4		South Africa A v Australia	4-day tour	Port Elizabeth
Fri 8-Tue 12		South Africa v Australia	2nd Test	Cape Town
Fri. 15-Tue 19		South Africa v Australia	3rd Test	Durban
Fri 22	Day	South Africa v Australia	1st ODI	Johannesburg
Sun 24	Day	South Africa v Australia	2nd ODI	Centurion
Wed 27	Day	South Africa v Australia	3rd ODI	Potchefstroom
Sat 30	Day	South Africa v Australia	4th ODI	Bloemfontein
April				
Wed 3	D/N	South Africa v Australia	5th ODI	Durban
Sat 6	Day	South Africa v Australia	6th ODI	Port Elizabeth
Tue 9	D/N	South Africa v Australia	7th ODI	Cape Town

DOMESTIC MATCHES

SUPERSPORT SERIES

Date	Match	Venue	Pool
October			
Fri 5-Mon 8	Griqualand West v Gauteng	Kimberley	Pool A
	North West v Boland	Potchefstroom	Pool A
	Western Province v Easterns	Cape Town	Pool A
	Eastern Province v Border	Port Elizabeth	Pool B
	Free State v Northerns	Bloemfontein	Pool B
Fri 12-Mon 15	Boland v Griqualand West	Paarl	Pool A
	Easterns v North West	Benoni	Pool A
	Gauteng v Western Province	Johannesburg	Pool A
	Border v Free State	East London	Pool B
	KwaZulu-Natal v Northerns	Durban	Pool B
Fri 19-Mon 22	Easterns v Griqualand West	Benoni	Pool A
	Gauteng v Boland	Johannesburg	Pool A
	North West v Western Province	Potchefstroom	Pool A
	Free State v KwaZulu-Natal	Bloemfontein	Pool B
	Northerns v Eastern Province	Centurion	Pool B
Thu 25-Tue 28	Easterns v Boland	Benoni	Pool A
	North West v Gauteng	Potchefstroom	Pool A
	Western Province v Griqualand West	Cape Town	Pool A
	Border v KwaZulu-Natal	East London	Pool B
	Eastern Province v Free State	Port Elizabeth	Pool B
November			
Fri 2-Mon 5	Boland v Western Province	Paarl	Pool A
	Gauteng v Easterns	Johannesburg	Pool A
	Griqualand West v North West	Kimberley	Pool A
	KwaZulu-Natal v Eastern Province	Durban	Pool B
	Northerns v Border	Centurion	Pool B
February			
Fri 15-Mon 18	Shield Series, 1st Round		TBA
Fri 22-Mon 25	Super Six and Shield Series, 1st/ 2nd Round		TBA
Fri 1-Mon 4	Shield Series, 3rd Round		TBA
Fri 8-Mon 11	Super Six and Shield Series, 2nd/4th Round		TBA
Fri 15-Mon 18	Super Six and Shield Series, 3rd/5th Round		TBA
Thu 11-Mon 15	SuperSport Series Final		TBA

STANDARD BANK CUP

November			
Fri 16	D/N	KwaZulu-Natal v Gauteng	Durban
	D/N	Northerns v Griqualand West	Centurion
	D/N	North West v Boland	Potchefstroom
Sun 18	Day	Easterns v Western Province	Benoni
	Day	Free State v Border	Bloemfontein
Fri 23	D/N	Border v Easterns	East London
	D/N	Griqualand West v Eastern Province	Kimberley
	D/N	Western Province v Gauteng	Cape Town
Sun 25	Day	Boland v Free State	Paarl
	Day	North West v Northerns	Potchefstroom
Fri 30	D/N	Free State v North West	Bloemfontein
	D/N	Gauteng v Boland	Johannesburg
	D/N	KwaZulu-Natal v Griqualand West	Durban
December			
Sun 2	Day	Easterns v Northerns	Benoni
	Day	Eastern Province v Border	Port Elizabeth
Wed 5	D/N	Northerns v KwaZulu-Natal	Centurion
Fri 7	D/N	Border v Gauteng	East London
	D/N	Griqualand West v Easterns	Kimberley
	D/N	Western Province v North West	Cape Town
Sun 9	Day	Free State v Eastern Province	Bloemfontein
Wed 12	D/N	Eastern Province v KwaZulu-Natal	Port Elizabeth
	D/N	Northerns v Free State	Centurion
Fri 14	D/N	Boland v KwaZulu-Natal	Paarl
	D/N	Gauteng v Northerns	Johannesburg
	D/N	North West v Griqualand West	Potchefstroom
Wed 19	D/N	Easterns v Eastern Province	Benoni
	D/N	Free State v Western Province	Bloemfontein
Fri 21	D/N	Eastern Province v Gauteng	Port Elizabeth
	D/N	Griqualand West v Free State	Kimberley
	D/N	KwaZulu-Natal v Easterns	Durban
Sun 23	Day	Border v Boland	East London
Wed 26	D/N	Western Province v Northerns	Cape Town
Fri 28	D/N	Boland v Western Province	Paarl
	D/N	Gauteng v Griqualand West	Johannesburg
Sun 30	Day	North West v Border	Potchefstroom
January			
Wed 2	D/N	SuperSport Challenge	Cape Town
Fri 4	D/N	Easterns v Gauteng	Benoni
	D/N	Eastern Province v North West	Port Elizabeth
Wed 9	D/N	Border v Western Province	East London
	D/N	Griqualand West v Boland	Kimberley
	D/N	KwaZulu-Natal v Free State	Durban

Fri 11	D/N	Boland v Easterns	Paarl
	D/N	Northerns v Eastern Province	Centurion
	D/N	Western Province v KwaZulu-Natal	Cape Town
Wed 16	D/N	Gauteng v North West	Johannesburg
	D/N	Griqualand West v Border	Kimberley
Fri 18	D/N	Free State v Easterns	Bloemfontein
	D/N	North West v KwaZulu-Natal	Potchefstroom
	D/N	Western Province v Griqualand West	Cape Town
Sun 20	Day	Boland v Eastern Province	Paarl
	Day	Border v Northerns	East London
Fri 25	D/N	Easterns v North West	Benoni
	D/N	Eastern Province v Western Province	Port Elizabeth
	D/N	Northerns v Boland	Centurion
Sun 27	Day	Gauteng v Free State	Johannesburg
	Day	KwaZulu-Natal v Border	Durban
Wed 30	D/N	Semifinals 1 and 2, 1st Legs	TBA
Thu 31	Day	Reserve Day	As above
February			
Fri 1	D/N	Semifinals 1 and 2, 2nd. Legs	TBA
Sat 2	Day	Reserve Day	As above
Sun 3	Day	Semifinals 1 and 2, 3rd. Legs	As above
Mon 4	Day	Reserve Day	As above
Sat 9	Day	FINAL	TBA
Sun 10	Day	Reserve Day	As above

UNITED CRICKET BOARD BOWL

(Three-day matches followed by one-day matches)

October			
Fri 12-Mon 15	Boland v Eastern Province	Paarl	Pool A
	Free State v Griqualand West	Bloemfontein	Pool A
	Namibia v Western Province	Windhoek	Pool A
Fri 19-Mon 22	Border v Easterns	East London	Pool B
	Gauteng v North West	Johannesburg	Pool B
	KwaZulu-Natal v Northerns	Durban	Pool B
Fri 26-Mon 29	Eastern Province v Free State	Port Elizabeth	Pool A
	Griqualand West v Namibia	Kimberley	Pool A
	KZ-Natal Inland v Boland	Pietermaritzburg	Pool A
November			
Fri 2-Mon 5	Easterns v Gauteng	Benoni	Pool B
	Northerns v Border	Centurion	Pool B
	North West v Zimbabwe	Potchefstroom	Pool B
Fri 9-Mon 12	Free State v Boland	Bloemfontein	Pool A
	Griqualand West v Eastern Province	Kimberley	Pool A
	Western Province v KZ-Natal Inland	Cape Town	Pool A

FIXTURES 2001/2002

Fri 16-Mon 19	Border v North West	East London	Pool B
	KwaZulu-Natal v Easterns	Durban	Pool B
	Zimbabwe v Northerns	Harare	Pool B
Fri 23-Mon 26	Boland v Griqualand West	Paarl	Pool A
	Free State v Western Province	Bloemfontein	Pool A
	KZ-Natal Inland v Namibia	Pietermaritzburg	Pool A
January			
Fri 11-Mon 14	Border v KwaZulu-Natal	East London	Pool B
	Northerns v North West	Centurion	Pool B
	Zimbabwe v Gauteng	Bulawayo	Pool B
Fri 18-Mon 21	Griqualand West v KZ-Natal Inland	Kimberley	Pool A
	Namibia v Boland	Windhoek	Pool A
	Western Province v Eastern Province	Cape Town	Pool A
Fri 25-Mon 28	Easterns v Zimbabwe	Benoni	Pool B
	Gauteng v Border	Johannesburg	Pool B
	North West v KwaZulu-Natal	Potchefstroom	Pool B
February			
Fri 1-Mon 4	Boland v Western Province	Paarl	Pool A
	Eastern Province v Namibia	Port Elizabeth	Pool A
	KZ-Natal Inland v Free State	Pietermaritzburg	Pool A
Fri 8-Mon 11	Easterns v Northerns	Benoni	Pool B
	Gauteng v KwaZulu-Natal	Johannesburg	Pool B
	Zimbabwe v Border	Harare	Pool B
Fri 15-Mon 18	Eastern Province v KZ-Natal Inland	Port Elizabeth	Pool A
	Namibia v Free State	Windhoek	Pool A
	Western Province v Griqualand West	Cape Town	Pool A
Fri 22-Mon 25	KwaZulu-Natal v Zimbabwe	Durban	Pool B
	Northerns v Gauteng	Centurion	Pool B
	North West v Easterns	Potchefstroom	Pool B
March			
Fri 8-Mon 11	Four-day final	TBA	
Sat 16	One-day final	TBA	
Sun 17	Reserve day	As above	

UNDER 19 COMPETITION

November			
Fri 30-Sun 2 Dec	Eastern Province v Boland	Port Elizabeth	Pool A
	Griqualand West v Free State	Kimberley	Pool A
	Western Province v Border	Cape Town	Pool A
	Easterns v Zimbabwe	Benoni	Pool B
	Gauteng v Northerns	Johannesburg	Pool B
	KwaZulu-Natal v North West	Durban	Pool B

FIXTURES 2001/2002

December			
Fri 7-Mon 9	Border v Free State	East London	Pool A
	Eastern Province v Griqualand West	Port Elizabeth	Pool A
	Western Province v Boland	Cape Town	Pool A
	Gauteng v Easterns	Johannesburg	Pool B
	North West v Northerns	Potchefstroom	Pool B
	Zimbabwe v KwaZulu-Natal	Bulawayo	Pool B
January			
Fri 4-Mon 6	Boland v Border	Paarl	Pool A
	Free State v Eastern Province	Bloemfontein	Pool A
	Griqualand West v Western Province	Kimberley	Pool A
	KwaZulu-Natal v Easterns	Durban	Pool B
	Northerns v Zimbabwe	Centurion	Pool B
	North West v Gauteng	Potchefstroom	Pool B
March			
Fri 1-Mon 3	Final	TBA	

NATIONAL WEEKS AND TOURNAMENTS

September		
Wed 19-Sun 23	MTN National Club Championship	Pretoria
Mon 24	MTN National Club Championship Final	SuperSport Park
Fri 28-Sun 30	Satellite Under 16 Dundee, Pietersburg, Kimberley, Port Alfred	
December		
Mon 3-Fri 7	Tertiary Week 'A' and 'B'	Grahamstown
	Tertiary Week Colleges, 'C' and 'D'	Worcester
Tue 4-Fri 7	USSASA Country Under 15	Secunda
Fri 7-Tue 11	USSASA Under 13	Cape Town
Sun 9-Wed 12	USSASA Country Under 19	Potchefstroom
Mon 10-Fri 14	Standard Bank Under 13	Durban
	PG Bison Under 15	East London
	Girls Under 19	Kimberley
Tue 11-Sat 15	USSASA Under 17	Cape Town
Mon 17-Thu 20	Under 19 'B' Tournament	Vereeniging
Mon 17-Fri 21	Coca-Cola Under 19	Vereeniging
January		
Sat 12-Sun 10 Feb	Under 19 Youth World Cup	New Zealand
Sat 26-Wed 30	South African Country Cricket Association	Potchefstroom
TBA	Girls Under 15 Festival	Regional
TBA	Girls Under 19 Tournament	Regional
April		
TBA	SA Women's Cricket	Cape Town

FUTURE INTERNATIONAL TOURS

		Tests
2002/03		
September	Zimbabwe in South Africa	2
October	Sri Lanka in South Africa	2
November	Triangular ODI - South Africa, Sri Lanka, Pakistan	-
December	Pakistan in South Africa	2
February/March	2003 World Cup in South Africa	-
April	South Africa in Bangladesh	2
2003		
July	South Africa in England	3
2003/04		
October	South Africa in Pakistan	3
December/January	West Indies in South Africa	5
February	South Africa in New Zealand	3
2004		
August	South Africa in Sri Lanka	3
2004/05		
November	South Africa in India	3
December/January	England in South Africa	5
February	Zimbabwe in South Africa	2
March	South Africa in West Indies	5
2005/06		
October	New Zealand in South Africa	3
December	South Africa in Australia	3
February	Australia in South Africa	3